Collins
French
Dictionary

HarperCollins Publishers
Westerhill Road
Bishopbriggs
Glasgow
G64 2QT
Great Britain

First Edition 2006

© HarperCollins Publishers 2006

ISBN-13 978-0-00-723145-4
ISBN-10 0-00-723145-8

Collins® is a registered trademark of
HarperCollins Publishers Limited

www.collins.co.uk

A catalogue record for this book is
available from the British Library

Typeset by Thomas Callan

Printed and bound in Italy by
Legoprint S.P.A.

Acknowledgements
We would like to thank those
authors and publishers who kindly
gave permission for copyright
material to be used in the Collins
Word Web. We would also like to
thank Times Newspapers Ltd for
providing valuable data.

EDITORIAL DIRECTOR
Michela Clari

CONTRIBUTORS
Jean-François Allain
Gaëlle Amiot-Cadey
Cécile Aubinière-Robb
Sabine Citron
Wendy Lee
Catherine Love
Rose Rociola

EDITORIAL COORDINATION
Joyce Littlejohn

SERIES EDITOR
Lorna Knight

BASED ON THE COLLINS FRENCH GEM
Pierre-Henri Cousin
Renée Birks
Elizabath Campbell
Hélène Lewis
Claude Nimmo
Philippe Patry
Lorna Knight

TABLE DES MATIÈRES   CONTENTS

William Collins' dream of knowledge for all began with the publication of his first book in 1819. A self-educated mill worker, he not only enriched millions of lives, but also founded a flourishing publishing house. Today, staying true to this spirit, Collins books are packed with inspiration, innovation, and practical expertise. They place you at the centre of a world of possibility and give you exactly what you need to explore it.

Language is the key to this exploration, and at the heart of Collins Dictionaries is language as it is really used. New words, phrases, and meanings spring up every day, and all of them are captured and analysed by the Collins Word Web. Constantly updated, and with over 2.5 billion entries, this living language resource is unique to our dictionaries.

Words are tools for life. And a Collins Dictionary makes them work for you.

Collins. Do more.

INTRODUCTION

Nous sommes très heureux que vous ayez choisi ce dictionnaire et espérons que vous aimerez l'utiliser et que vous en tirerez profit au lycée, à la maison, en vacances ou au travail.

INTRODUCTION

We are delighted that you have decided to buy this dictionary and hope you will enjoy and benefit from using it at school, at home, on holiday or at work.

ABRÉVIATIONS

ABBREVIATIONS

abréviation	*ab(b)r*	abbreviation
adjectif, locution adjectivale	*adj*	adjective, adjectival phrase
administration	*Admin*	administration
adverbe, locution adverbiale	*adv*	adverb, adverbial phrase
agriculture	*Agr*	agriculture
anatomie	*Anat*	anatomy
architecture	*Archit*	architecture
article défini	*art déf*	definite article
article indéfini	*art indéf*	indefinite article
automobile	*Aut(o)*	the motor car and motoring
aviation, voyages aériens	*Aviat*	flying, air travel
biologie	*Bio(l)*	biology
botanique	*Bot*	botany
anglais britannique	*BRIT*	British English
chimie	*Chem*	chemistry
commerce, finance, banque	*Comm*	commerce, finance, banking
informatique	*Comput*	computing
conjonction	*conj*	conjunction
construction	*Constr*	building
nom utilisé comme adjectif	*cpd*	compound element
cuisine	*Culin*	cookery
article défini	*def art*	definite article
déterminant: article; adjectif démonstratif ou indéfini *etc*	*dét*	determiner: article, demonstrative *etc*
économie	*Écon, Econ*	economics
électricité, électronique	*Élec, Elec*	electricity, electronics
en particulier	*esp*	especially
exclamation, interjection	*excl*	exclamation, interjection
féminin	*f*	feminine
langue familière (! emploi vulgaire)	*fam(!)*	colloquial usage (! particularly offensive)
emploi figuré	*fig*	figurative use
(verbe anglais) dont la particule est inséparable	*fus*	(phrasal verb) where the particle is inseparable
généralement	*gén, gen*	generally
géographie, géologie	*Géo, Geo*	geography, geology
géométrie	*Géom, Geom*	geometry
langue familière (! emploi vulgaire)	*inf(!)*	colloquial usage (! particularly offensive)
infinitif	*infin*	infinitive
informatique	*Inform*	computing
invariable	*inv*	invariable
irrégulier	*irreg*	irregular
domaine juridique	*Jur*	law

ABRÉVIATIONS

grammaire, linguistique	*Ling*	grammar, linguistics
masculin	*m*	masculine
mathématiques, algèbre	*Math*	mathematics, calculus
médecine	*Méd, Med*	medical term, medicine
masculin ou féminin	*m/f*	masculine or feminine
domaine militaire, armée	*Mil*	military matters
musique	*Mus*	music
nom	*n*	noun
navigation, nautisme	*Navig, Naut*	sailing, navigation
nom ou adjectif numéral	*num*	numeral noun or adjective
	o.s.	oneself
péjoratif	*péj, pej*	derogatory, pejorative
photographie	*Phot(o)*	photography
physiologie	*Physiol*	physiology
pluriel	*pl*	plural
politique	*Pol*	politics
participe passé	*pp*	past participle
préposition	*prép, prep*	preposition
pronom	*pron*	pronoun
psychologie, psychiatrie	*Psych*	psychology, psychiatry
temps du passé	*pt*	past tense
quelque chose	*qch*	
quelqu'un	*qn*	
religion, domaine ecclésiastique	*Rel*	religion
	sb	somebody
enseignement, système scolaire et universitaire	*Scol*	schooling, schools and universities
singulier	*sg*	singular
	sth	something
subjonctif	*sub*	subjunctive
sujet (grammatical)	*su(b)j*	(grammatical) subject
superlatif	*superl*	superlative
techniques, technologie	*Tech*	technical term, technology
télécommunications	*Tél, Tel*	telecommunications
télévision	*TV*	television
typographie	*Typ(o)*	typography, printing
anglais des USA	*US*	American English
verbe (auxiliare)	*vb (aux)*	(auxiliary) verb
verbe intransitif	*vi*	intransitive verb
verbe transitif	*vt*	transitive verb
zoologie	*Zool*	zoology
marque déposée	®	registered trademark
indique une équivalence culturelle	≈	introduces a cultural equivalent

ABBREVIATIONS

TRANCRIPTION PHONÉTIQUE

CONSONNES		CONSONANTS
NB. **p, b, t, d, k, g** sont suivis d'une aspiration en anglais.		NB. **p, b, t, d, k, g** are not aspirated in French.
poupée	p	puppy
bombe	b	baby
tente thermal	t	tent
dinde	d	daddy
coq qui képi	k	cork kiss chord
gage bague	g	gag guess
sale ce nation	s	so rice kiss
zéro rose	z	cousin buzz
tache chat	ʃ	sheep sugar
gilet juge	ʒ	pleasure beige
	tʃ	church
	dʒ	judge general
fer phare	f	farm raffle
verveine	v	very revel
	θ	thin maths
	ð	that other
lent salle	l	little ball
rare rentrer	ʀ	
	r	rat rare
maman femme	m	mummy comb
non bonne	n	no ran
agneau vigne	ɲ	
	ŋ	singing bank
	h	hat rehearse
yeux paille pied	j	yet
nouer oui	w	wall wail
huile lui	ɥ	
	x	loch

DIVERS		MISCELLANEOUS
pour l'anglais: le r final se prononce en liaison devant une voyelle	ʳ	in English transcription: final r can be pronounced before a vowel
pour l'anglais: précède la syllabe accentuée	'	in French wordlist: no liaison before aspirate h

En règle générale, la prononciation est donnée entre crochets après chaque entrée. Toutefois, du côté anglais-français et dans le cas des expressions composées de deux ou plusieurs mots non réunis par un trait d'union et faisant l'objet d'une entrée séparée, la prononciation doit être cherchée sous chacun des mots constitutifs de l'expression en question.

PHONETIC TRANCRIPTION

VOYELLES		VOWELS

NB. La mise en équivalence de certains sons n'indique qu'une ressemblance approximative.

NB. The pairing of some vowel sounds only indicates approximate equivalence.

ici vie lyrique	i i:	heel bead
	ɪ	hit pity
jouer été	e	
lait jouet merci	ɛ	set tent
plat amour	a æ	bat apple
bas pâte	ɑ ɑ:	after car calm
	ʌ	fun cousin
le premier	ə	over above
beurre peur	œ	
peu deux	ø əː	urgent fern work
or homme	ɔ	wash pot
mot eau gauche	o ɔː	born cork
genou roue	u	full hook
	u:	boom shoe
rue urne	y	

DIPHTONGUES		DIPHTHONGS
	ɪə	beer tier
	ɛə	tear fair there
	eɪ	date plaice day
	aɪ	life buy cry
	au	owl foul now
	əu	low no
	ɔɪ	boil boy oily
	uə	poor tour

NASALES		NASAL VOWELS
matin plein	ɛ̃	
brun	œ̃	
sang an dans	ɑ̃	
non pont	ɔ̃	

In general, we give the pronunciation of each entry in square brackets after the word in question. However, on the English-French side, where the entry is composed of two or more unhyphenated words, each of which is given elsewhere in this dictionary, you will find the pronunciation of each word in its alphabetical position.

FRENCH VERB TABLES

1 Present participle 2 Past participle 3 Present 4 Imperfect 5 Future
6 Conditional 7 Present subjunctive

acquérir 1 acquérant 2 acquis
   3 acquiers, acquérons,
   acquièrent 4 acquérais
   5 acquerrai 7 acquière
ALLER 1 allant 2 allé 3 vais, vas, va,
   allons, allez, vont 4 allais 5 irai
   6 irais 7 aille
asseoir 1 asseyant 2 assis 3 assieds,
   asseyons, asseyez, asseyent
   4 asseyais 5 assiérai 7 asseye
atteindre 1 atteignant 2 atteint
   3 atteins, atteignons
   4 atteignais 7 atteigne
AVOIR 1 ayant 2 eu 3 ai, as, a,
   avons, avez, ont 4 avais 5 aurai
   6 aurais 7 aie, aies, ait, ayons,
   ayez, aient
battre 1 battant 2 battu 3 bats, bat,
   battons 4 battais 7 batte
boire 1 buvant 2 bu 3 bois, buvons,
   boivent 4 buvais 7 boive
bouillir 1 bouillant 2 bouilli 3 bous,
   bouillons 4 bouillais 7 bouille
conclure 1 concluant 2 conclu
   3 conclus, concluons
   4 concluais 7 conclue
conduire 1 conduisant 2 conduit
   3 conduis, conduisons
   4 conduisais 7 conduise
connaître 1 connaissant 2 connu
   3 connais, connaît, connaissons
   4 connaissais 7 connaisse
coudre 1 cousant 2 cousu 3 couds,
   cousons, cousez, cousent
   4 cousais 7 couse
courir 1 courant 2 couru 3 cours,
   courons 4 courais 5 courrai
   7 coure
couvrir 1 couvrant 2 couvert
   3 couvre, couvrons 4 couvrais
   7 couvre

craindre 1 craignant 2 craint
   3 crains, craignons 4 craignais
   7 craigne
croire 1 croyant 2 cru 3 crois,
   croyons, croient 4 croyais
   7 croie
croître 1 croissant 2 crû, crue, crus,
   crues 3 croîs, croissons
   4 croissais 7 croisse
cueillir 1 cueillant 2 cueilli
   3 cueille, cueillons 4 cueillais
   5 cueillerai 7 cueille
devoir 1 devant 2 dû, due, dus,
   dues 3 dois, devons, doivent
   4 devais 5 devrai 7 doive
dire 1 disant 2 dit 3 dis, disons,
   dites, disent 4 disais 7 dise
dormir 1 dormant 2 dormi 3 dors,
   dormons 4 dormais 7 dorme
écrire 1 écrivant 2 écrit 3 écris,
   écrivons 4 écrivais 7 écrive
ÊTRE 1 étant 2 été 3 suis, es, est,
   sommes, êtes, sont 4 étais
   5 serai 6 serais 7 sois, sois, soit,
   soyons, soyez, soient
FAIRE 1 faisant 2 fait 3 fais, fais,
   fait, faisons, faites, font
   4 faisais 5 ferai 6 ferais 7 fasse
falloir 2 fallu 3 faut 4 fallait
   5 faudra 7 faille
FINIR 1 finissant 2 fini 3 finis,
   finis, finit, finissons, finissez,
   finissent 4 finissais 5 finirai
   6 finirais 7 finisse
fuir 1 fuyant 2 fui 3 fuis, fuyons,
   fuient 4 fuyais 7 fuie
joindre 1 joignant 2 joint 3 joins,
   joignons 4 joignais 7 joigne
lire 1 lisant 2 lu 3 lis, lisons 4 lisais
   7 lise
luire 1 luisant 2 lui 3 luis, luisons

4 luisais **7** luise

maudire 1 maudissant **2** maudit
3 maudis, maudissons
4 maudissait **7** maudisse

mentir 1 mentant **2** menti **3** mens,
mentons **4** mentais **7** mente

mettre 1 mettant **2** mis **3** mets,
mettons **4** mettais **7** mette

mourir 1 mourant **2** mort **3** meurs,
mourons, meurent **4** mourais
5 mourrai **7** meure

naître 1 naissant **2** né **3** nais, naît,
naissons **4** naissais **7** naisse

offrir 1 offrant **2** offert **3** offre,
offrons **4** offrais **7** offre

PARLER 1 parlant **2** parlé **3** parle,
parles, parle, parlons, parlez,
parlent **4** parlais, parlais,
parlait, parlions, parliez,
parlaient **5** parlerai, parleras,
parlera, parlerons, parlerez,
parleront **6** parlerais, parlerais,
parlerait, parlerions, parleriez,
parleraient **7** parle, parles,
parle, parlions, parliez, parlent
impératif parle! parlons! parlez!

partir 1 partant **2** parti **3** pars,
partons **4** partais **7** parte

plaire 1 plaisant **2** plu **3** plais, plaît,
plaisons **4** plaisais **7** plaise

pleuvoir 1 pleuvant **2** plu **3** pleut,
pleuvent **4** pleuvait **5** pleuvra
7 pleuve

pourvoir 1 pourvoyant **2** pourvu
3 pourvois, pourvoyons,
pourvoient **4** pourvoyais
7 pourvoie

pouvoir 1 pouvant **2** pu **3** peux,
peut, pouvons, peuvent **4**
pouvais **5** pourrai **7** puisse

prendre 1 prenant **2** pris **3** prends,
prenons, prennent **4** prenais
7 prenne

prévoir like voir **5** prévoirai

RECEVOIR 1 recevant **2** reçu
3 reçois, reçois, reçoit, recevons,
recevez, rerçoivent **4** recevais

5 recevrai **6** recevrais **7** reçoive

RENDRE 1 rendant **2** rendu
3 rends, rends, rend, rendons,
rendez, rendent **4** rendais
5 rendrai **6** rendrais **7** rende

résoudre 1 résolvant **2** résolu
3 résous, résout, résolvons
4 résolvais **7** résolve

rire 1 riant **2** ri **3** ris, rions **4** riais
7 rie

savoir 1 sachant **2** su **3** sais,
savons, savent **4** savais **5** saurai
7 sache *impératif* sache! sachons!
sachez!

servir 1 servant **2** servi **3** sers,
servons **4** servais **7** serve

sortir 1 sortant **2** sorti **3** sors,
sortons **4** sortais **7** sorte

souffrir 1 souffrant **2** souffert
3 souffre, souffrons **4** souffrais
7 souffre

suffire 1 suffisant **2** suffi **3** suffis,
suffisons **4** suffisais **7** suffise

suivre 1 suivant **2** suivi **3** suis,
suivons **4** suivais **7** suive

taire 1 taisant **2** tu **3** tais, taisons
4 taisais **7** taise

tenir 1 tenant **2** tenu **3** tiens,
tenons, tiennent **4** tenais
5 tiendrai **7** tienne

vaincre 1 vainquant **2** vaincu
3 vaincs, vainc, vainquons
4 vainquais **7** vainque

valoir 1 valant **2** valu **3** vaux, vaut,
valons **4** valais **5** vaudrai **7** vaille

venir 1 venant **2** venu **3** viens,
venons, viennent **4** venais
5 viendrai **7** vienne

vivre 1 vivant **2** vécu **3** vis, vivons
4 vivais **7** vive

voir 1 voyant **2** vu **3** vois, voyons,
voient **4** voyais **5** verrai **7** voie

vouloir 1 voulant **2** voulu **3** veux,
veut, voulons, veulent **4** voulais
5 voudrai **7** veuille; *impératif*
veuillez!

VERBES IRRÉGULIERS ANGLAIS

PRÉSENT	PASSÉ	PARTICIPE	PRÉSENT	PASSÉ	PARTICIPE
arise	arose	arisen	fight	fought	fought
awake	awoke	awoken	find	found	found
be	was, were	been	flee	fled	fled
(am, is,			fling	flung	flung
are; being)			fly	flew	flown
bear	bore	born(e)	forbid	forbad(e)	forbidden
beat	beat	beaten	forecast	forecast	forecast
become	became	become	forget	forgot	forgotten
begin	began	begun	forgive	forgave	forgiven
bend	bent	bent	forsake	forsook	forsaken
bet	bet,	bet,	freeze	froze	frozen
	betted	betted	get	got	got,
bid (at auction,	bid	bid			(us) gotten
cards)			give	gave	given
bid (say)	bade	bidden	go (goes)	went	gone
bind	bound	bound	grind	ground	ground
bite	bit	bitten	grow	grew	grown
bleed	bled	bled	hang	hung	hung
blow	blew	blown	hang (execute)	hanged	hanged
break	broke	broken	have	had	had
breed	bred	bred	hear	heard	heard
bring	brought	brought	hide	hid	hidden
build	built	built	hit	hit	hit
burn	burnt,	burnt,	hold	held	held
	burned	burned	hurt	hurt	hurt
burst	burst	burst	keep	kept	kept
buy	bought	bought	kneel	knelt,	knelt,
can	could	(been able)		kneeled	kneeled
cast	cast	cast	know	knew	known
catch	caught	caught	lay	laid	laid
choose	chose	chosen	lead	led	led
cling	clung	clung	lean	leant,	leant,
come	came	come		leaned	leaned
cost	cost	cost	leap	leapt,	leapt,
cost (work	costed	costed		leaped	leaped
out price of)			learn	learnt,	learnt,
creep	crept	crept		learned	learned
cut	cut	cut	leave	left	left
deal	dealt	dealt	lend	lent	lent
dig	dug	dug	let	let	let
do (does)	did	done	lie (lying)	lay	lain
draw	drew	drawn	light	lit,	lit,
dream	dreamed,	dreamed,		lighted	lighted
	dreamt	dreamt	lose	lost	lost
drink	drank	drunk	make	made	made
drive	drove	driven	may	might	–
dwell	dwelt	dwelt	mean	meant	meant
eat	ate	eaten	meet	met	met
fall	fell	fallen	mistake	mistook	mistaken
feed	fed	fed	mow	mowed	mown,
feel	felt	felt			mowed

xii

PRÉSENT	PASSÉ	PARTICIPE	PRÉSENT	PASSÉ	PARTICIPE
must	(had to)	(had to)	spend	spent	spent
pay	paid	paid	spill	spilt,	spilt,
put	put	put		spilled	spilled
quit	quit,	quit,	spin	spun	spun
	quitted	quitted	spit	spat	spat
read	read	read	spoil	spoiled,	spoiled,
rid	rid	rid		spoilt	spoilt
ride	rode	ridden	spread	spread	spread
ring	rang	rung	spring	sprang	sprung
rise	rose	risen	stand	stood	stood
run	ran	run	steal	stole	stolen
saw	sawed	sawed,	stick	stuck	stuck
		sawn	sting	stung	stung
say	said	said	stink	stank	stunk
see	saw	seen	stride	strode	stridden
seek	sought	sought	strike	struck	struck
sell	sold	sold	strive	strove	striven
send	sent	sent	swear	swore	sworn
set	set	set	sweep	swept	swept
sew	sewed	sewn	swell	swelled	swollen,
shake	shook	shaken			swelled
shear	sheared	shorn,	swim	swam	swum
		sheared	swing	swung	swung
shed	shed	shed	take	took	taken
shine	shone	shone	teach	taught	taught
shoot	shot	shot	tear	tore	torn
show	showed	shown	tell	told	told
shrink	shrank	shrunk	think	thought	thought
shut	shut	shut	throw	threw	thrown
sing	sang	sung	thrust	thrust	thrust
sink	sank	sunk	tread	trod	trodden
sit	sat	sat	wake	woke,	woken,
slay	slew	slain		waked	waked
sleep	slept	slept	wear	wore	worn
slide	slid	slid	weave	wove	woven
sling	slung	slung	weave (wind)	weaved	weaved
slit	slit	slit	wed	wedded,	wedded,
smell	smelt,	smelt,		wed	wed
	smelled	smelled	weep	wept	wept
sow	sowed	sown,	win	won	won
		sowed	wind	wound	wound
speak	spoke	spoken	wring	wrung	wrung
speed	sped,	sped,	write	wrote	written
	speeded	speeded			
spell	spelt,	spelt,			
	spelled	spelled			

LES NOMBRES

		NUMBERS
un (une)	1	one
deux	2	two
trois	3	three
quatre	4	four
cinq	5	five
six	6	six
sept	7	seven
huit	8	eight
neuf	9	nine
dix	10	ten
onze	11	eleven
douze	12	twelve
treize	13	thirteen
quatorze	14	fourteen
quinze	15	fifteen
seize	16	sixteen
dix-sept	17	seventeen
dix-huit	18	eighteen
dix-neuf	19	nineteen
vingt	20	twenty
vingt et un (une)	21	twenty-one
vingt-deux	22	twenty-two
trente	30	thirty
quarante	40	forty
cinquante	50	fifty
soixante	60	sixty
soixante-dix	70	seventy
soixante-et-onze	71	seventy-one
soixante-douze	72	seventy
quatre-vingts	80	eighty
quatre-vingt-un (-une)	81	eighty-one
quatre-vingt-dix	90	ninety
cent	100	a hundred, one hundred
cent un (une)	101	a hundred and one
deux cents	200	two hundred
deux cent un (une)	201	two hundred and one
quatre cents	400	four hundred
mille	1000	a thousand
cinq mille	5000	five thousand
un million	1000000	a million

LES NOMBRES

premier (première), 1er (1ère)
deuxième, 2e or 2ème
troisième, 3e or 3ème
quatrième, 4e or 4ème
cinquième, 5e or 5ème
sixième, 6e or 6ème
septième
huitième
neuvième
dixième
onzième
douzième
treizième
quartorzième
quinzième
seizième
dix-septième
dix-huitième
dix-neuvième
vingtième
vingt-et-unième
vingt-deuxième
trentième
centième
cent-unième
millième

NUMBERS

first, 1st
second, 2nd
third, 3rd
fourth, 4th
fifth, 5th
sixth, 6th
seventh
eighth
ninth
tenth
eleventh
twelfth
thirteenth
fourteenth
fifteenth
sixteenth
seventeenth
eighteenth
nineteenth
twentieth
twenty-first
twenty-second
thirtieth
hundredth
hundred-and-first
thousandth

LES FRACTIONS ETC

un demi
un tiers
un quart
un cinquième
zéro virgule cinq, 0,5
trois virgule quatre, 3,4
dix pour cent
cent pour cent

FRACTIONS ETC

a half
a third
a quarter
a fifth
(nought) point five, 0.5
three point four, 3.4
ten per cent
a hundred per cent

EXEMPLES

elle habite au septième (étage)
il habite au sept
au chapitre/à la page sept
il est arrivé (le) septième

EXAMPLES

she lives on the 7th floor
he lives at number 7
chapter/page 7
he came in 7th

L'HEURE

quelle heure est-il?

il est ...

minuit
une heure (du matin)

une heure cinq
une heure dix
une heure et quart

une heure vingt-cinq

une heure et demie, une heure trente
deux heures moins vingt-cinq, une
    heure trente-cinq
deux heures moins vingt, une heure
    quarante
deux heures moins le quart, une heure
    quarante-cinq
deux heures moins dix, une heure
    cinquante
midi

deux heures (de l'après-midi),
    quatorze heures
sept heures (du soir), dix-sept heures

à quelle heure?

à minuit
à sept heures

dans vingt minutes
il y a un quart d'heure

THE TIME

what time is it?

it's ou it is ...

midnight, twelve p.m.
one o'clock (in the
    morning), one (a.m.)

five past one
ten past one
a quarter past one,
    one fifteen
twenty-five past one,
    one twenty-five
half-past one, one thirty
twenty-five to two,
    one thirty-five
twenty to two, one forty

a quarter to two,
    one forty-five
ten to two, one fifty

twelve o'clock, midday,
    noon
two o'clock (in the
    afternoon), two (p.m.)
seven o'clock (in the
    evening), seven (p.m.)

(at) what time?

at midnight
at seven o'clock

in twenty minutes
fifteen minutes ago

FRANÇAIS | ANGLAIS
FRENCH | ENGLISH

7 (*caractérisation, manière*): **l'homme aux yeux bleus** the man with the blue eyes; **à leur grande surprise** much to their surprise; **à ce qu'il prétend** according to him, from what he says; **à la russe** the Russian way; **à nous deux nous n'avons pas su le faire** we couldn't do it, even between the two of us

8 (*but, destination*): **tasse à café** coffee cup; **maison à vendre** house for sale; **je n'ai rien à lire** I don't have anything to read; **à bien réfléchir ...** thinking about it ..., on reflection ...

9 (*rapport, évaluation, distribution*): **100 km/unités à l'heure** 100 km/units per *ou* an hour; **payé au mois/à l'heure** paid monthly/by the hour; **cinq à six** five to six; **ils sont arrivés à quatre** four of them arrived

a [a] *vb voir* **avoir**

 MOT-CLÉ

à [a] (*à + le* = **au**, *à + les* = **aux**) *prép* **1** (*endroit, situation*) at, in; **être à Paris/au Portugal** to be in Paris/Portugal; **être à la maison/à l'école** to be at home/at school; **à la campagne** in the country; **c'est à 10 km/à 20 minutes (d'ici)** it's 10 km/20 minutes away

2 (*direction*) to; **aller à Paris/au Portugal** to go to Paris/Portugal; **aller à la maison/à l'école** to go home/to school; **à la campagne** to the country

3 (*temps*): **à 3 heures/minuit** at 3 o'clock/midnight; **au printemps/mois de juin** in the spring/the month of June; **à Noël/Pâques** at Christmas/Easter; **à demain/lundi!** see you tomorrow/on Monday!

4 (*attribution, appartenance*) to; **le livre est à Paul/à lui/à nous** this book is Paul's/his/ours; **un ami à moi** a friend of mine; **donner qch à qn** to give sth to sb

5 (*moyen*) with; **se chauffer au gaz** to have gas heating; **à bicyclette** on a *ou* by bicycle; **à pied** on foot; **à la main/machine** by hand/machine

6 (*provenance*) from; **boire à la bouteille** to drink from the bottle

abaisser [abese] *vt* to lower, bring down; (*manette*) to pull down; **s'abaisser** *vi* to go down; (*fig*) to demean o.s.

abandon [abɑ̃dɔ̃] *nm* abandoning; giving up; withdrawal; **être à l'~** to be in a state of neglect; **laisser à l'~** to abandon

abandonner [abɑ̃dɔne] *vt* (*personne*) to abandon; (*projet, activité*) to abandon, give up; (*Sport*) to retire *ou* withdraw from; (*céder*) to surrender; **s'~ à** (*paresse, plaisirs*) to give o.s. up to

abat-jour [abaʒuʀ] *nm inv* lampshade

abats [aba] *nmpl* (*de bœuf, porc*) offal *sg*; (*de volaille*) giblets

abattement [abatmɑ̃] *nm*: **abattement fiscal** ≈ tax allowance

abattoir [abatwaʀ] *nm* slaughterhouse

abattre [abatʀ] *vt* (*arbre*) to cut down, fell; (*mur, maison*) to pull down; (*avion, personne*) to shoot down; (*animal*) to shoot, kill; (*fig*) to wear out, tire out; to demoralize; **s'abattre** *vi* to crash down; **ne pas se laisser ~** to keep one's spirits up, not to let things get one down; **s'~ sur** to beat down on; (*fig*) to rain down on; **~ du travail** *ou* **de la besogne** to get through a lot of work

abbaye [abei] *nf* abbey

abbé [abe] *nm* priest; (*d'une abbaye*) abbot

abcès [apsɛ] *nm* abscess

abdiquer [abdike] *vi* to abdicate

abdominaux [abdɔmino] *nmpl*: **faire des ~** to do sit-ups

abeille [abej] *nf* bee

aberrant, e [abeʀɑ̃, ɑ̃t] *adj* absurd

aberration [abeʀasjɔ̃] *nf* aberration

abîme [abim] *nm* abyss, gulf

abîmer [abime] *vt* to spoil, damage; **s'abîmer** *vi* to get spoilt *ou* damaged

aboiement [abwamɑ̃] *nm* bark, barking

abolir [abɔliʀ] *vt* to abolish

abominable [abɔminabl] *adj* abominable

abondance [abɔ̃dɑ̃s] nf abundance

abondant, e [abɔ̃dɑ̃, ɑ̃t] adj plentiful, abundant, copious; **abonder** vi to abound, be plentiful; **abonder dans le sens de qn** to concur with sb

abonné, e [abɔne] nm/f subscriber; season ticket holder

abonnement [abɔnmɑ̃] nm subscription; (transports, concerts) season ticket

abonner [abɔne] vt: **s'~ à** to subscribe to, take out a subscription to

abord [abɔʀ] nm: **au premier ~** at first sight, initially; **abords** nmpl (environs) surroundings; **d'~** first

abordable [abɔʀdabl] adj (prix) reasonable; (personne) approachable

aborder [abɔʀde] vi to land ▷ vt (sujet, difficulté) to tackle; (personne) to approach; (rivage etc) to reach

aboutir [abutiʀ] vi (négociations etc) to succeed; **~ à** to end up at; **n'~ à rien** to come to nothing

aboyer [abwaje] vi to bark

abréger [abʀeʒe] vt to shorten

abreuver [abʀœve] vt: **s'abreuver** vi to drink; **abreuvoir** nm watering place

abréviation [abʀevjasjɔ̃] nf abbreviation

abri [abʀi] nm shelter; **être à l'~** to be under cover; **se mettre à l'~** to shelter; **à l'~ de** (vent, soleil) sheltered from; (danger) safe from

abricot [abʀiko] nm apricot

abriter [abʀite] vt to shelter; **s'abriter** vt to shelter, take cover

abrupt, e [abʀypt] adj sheer, steep; (ton) abrupt

abruti, e [abʀyti] adj stunned, dazed ▷ nm/f (fam) idiot, moron; **~ de travail** overworked

absence [apsɑ̃s] nf absence; (Méd) blackout; **avoir des ~s** to have mental blanks

absent, e [apsɑ̃, ɑ̃t] adj absent ▷ nm/f absentee; **absenter: s'absenter** vi to take time off work; (sortir) to leave, go out

absolu, e [apsɔly] adj absolute; **absolument** adv absolutely

absorbant, e [apsɔʀbɑ̃, ɑ̃t] adj absorbent

absorber [apsɔʀbe] vt to absorb; (gén Méd: manger, boire) to take

abstenir [apstəniʀ] vb: **s'~ de qch/de faire** to refrain from sth/from doing

abstrait, e [apstʀɛ, ɛt] adj abstract

absurde [apsyʀd] adj absurd

abus [aby] nm abuse; **~ de confiance** breach of trust; **il y a de l'~!** (fam) that's a bit much!; **abuser** vi to go too far, overstep the mark; **abuser de** (duper) to take advantage of; **s'abuser** vi (se méprendre) to be mistaken; **abusif, -ive** adj exorbitant; (punition) excessive

académie [akademi] nf academy; (Scol: circonscription) ≈ regional education authority

● **ACADÉMIE FRANÇAISE**
●
● The **Académie française** was founded by
● Cardinal Richelieu in 1635, during the reign
● of Louis XIII. It is made up of forty elected
● scholars and writers who are known as 'les
● Quarante' or 'les Immortels'. One of the
● **Académie**'s functions is to keep an eye on
● the development of the French language,
● and its recommendations are frequently
● the subject of lively public debate. It has
● produced several editions of its famous
● dictionary and also awards various literary
● prizes.

acajou [akaʒu] nm mahogany

acariâtre [akaʀjɑtʀ] adj cantankerous

accablant, e [akablɑ̃, ɑ̃t] adj (chaleur) oppressive; (témoignage, preuve) overwhelming

accabler [akable] vt to overwhelm, overcome; **~ qn d'injures** to heap ou shower abuse on sb; **~ qn de travail** to overwork sb

accalmie [akalmi] nf lull

accaparer [akapaʀe] vt to monopolize; (suj: travail etc) to take up (all) the time ou attention of

accéder [aksede]: **~ à** vt (lieu) to reach; (accorder: requête) to grant, accede to

accélérateur [akseleʀatœʀ] nm accelerator

accélérer [akseleʀe] vt to speed up ▷ vi to accelerate

accent [aksɑ̃] nm accent; (Phonétique, fig) stress; **mettre l'~ sur** (fig) to stress; **~ aigu/grave/circonflexe** acute/grave/circumflex accent; **accentuer** vt (Ling) to accent; (fig) to accentuate, emphasize; **s'accentuer** vi to become more marked ou pronounced

acceptation [akseptasjɔ̃] nf acceptance

accepter [aksepte] vt to accept; **~ de faire** to agree to do; **acceptez-vous les cartes de crédit?** do you take credit cards?

accès [aksɛ] nm (à un lieu) access; (Méd: de toux) fit; (: de fièvre) bout; **d'~ facile** easily accessible; **facile d'~** easy to get to; **accès de colère** fit of anger; **accessible** adj accessible; (livre, sujet): **accessible à qn** within the reach of sb

accessoire [akseswaʀ] adj secondary; incidental ▷ nm accessory; (Théâtre) prop

accident [aksidɑ̃] nm accident; **par ~** by chance; **j'ai eu un ~** I've had an accident; **accident de la route** road accident; **accidenté, e** adj damaged; injured; (relief, terrain) uneven; hilly; **accidentel, le** adj accidental

acclamer [aklame] vt to cheer, acclaim

acclimater [aklimate]: **s'acclimater** vi (personne) to adapt (o.s.)

accolade [akɔlad] nf (amicale) embrace; (signe) brace

accommoder [akɔmɔde] vt (Culin) to prepare; **s'accommoder de** vt to put up with; (se contenter de) to make do with

accompagnateur, -trice [akɔ̃paɲatœr, tris] nm/f (Mus) accompanist; (de voyage: guide) guide; (de voyage organisé) courier

accompagner [akɔ̃paɲe] vt to accompany, be ou go ou come with; (Mus) to accompany

accompli, e [akɔ̃pli] adj accomplished; voir aussi **fait**

accomplir [akɔ̃plir] vt (tâche, projet) to carry out; (souhait) to fulfil; **s'accomplir** vi to be fulfilled

accord [akɔr] nm agreement; (entre des styles, tons etc) harmony; (Mus) chord; **d'~!** OK!; **se mettre d'~** to come to an agreement; **être d'~ (pour faire qch)** to agree (to do sth)

accordéon [akɔrdeɔ̃] nm (Mus) accordion

accorder [akɔrde] vt (faveur, délai) to grant; (harmoniser) to match; (Mus) to tune; (valeur, importance) attach

accoster [akɔste] vt (Navig) to draw alongside ▷ vi to berth

accouchement [akuʃmɑ̃] nm delivery, (child)birth; labour

accoucher [akuʃe] vi to give birth, have a baby; **~ d'un garçon** to give birth to a boy

accouder [akude]: **s'accouder** vt: **s'~ à/contre/sur** to rest one's elbows on/against/on; **accoudoir** nm armrest

accoupler [akuple] vt to couple; (pour la reproduction) to mate; **s'accoupler** vt to mate

accourir [akurir] vi to rush ou run up

accoutumance [akutymɑ̃s] nf (gén) adaptation; (Méd) addiction

accoutumé, e [akutyme] adj (habituel) customary, usual

accoutumer [akutyme] vt: **s'~ à** to get accustomed ou used to

accroc [akro] nm (déchirure) tear; (fig) hitch, snag

accrochage [akrɔʃaʒ] nm (Auto) collision; (dispute) clash, brush

accrocher [akrɔʃe] vt (fig) to catch, attract; **s'accrocher** (se disputer) to have a clash ou brush; **~ qch à** (suspendre) to hang sth (up) on; (attacher: remorque) to hitch sth (up) to; **~ qch (à)** (déchirer) to catch sth (on); **il a accroché ma voiture** he bumped into my car; **s'~ à** (rester pris à) to catch on; (agripper, fig) to hang on ou cling to

accroissement [akrwasmɑ̃] nm increase

accroître [akrwatr]: **s'accroître** vi to increase

accroupir [akrupir]: **s'accroupir** vi to squat, crouch (down)

accru, e [akry] pp de **accroître**

accueil [akœj] nm welcome; **comité d'~** reception committee; **accueillir** vt to welcome; (aller chercher) to meet, collect

accumuler [akymyle] vt to accumulate, amass; **s'accumuler** vi to accumulate; to pile up

accusation [akyzasjɔ̃] nf (gén) accusation; (Jur) charge; (partie): **l'~** the prosecution

accusé, e [akyze] nm/f accused; defendant; **accusé de réception** acknowledgement of receipt

accuser [akyze] vt to accuse; (fig) to emphasize, bring out; to show; **~ qn de** to accuse sb of; (Jur) to charge sb with; **~ réception de** to acknowledge receipt of

acéré, e [asere] adj sharp

acharné, e [aʃarne] adj (efforts) relentless; (lutte, adversaire) fierce, bitter

acharner [aʃarne] vb: **s'~ contre** to set o.s. against; (suj: malchance) to dog; **s'~ à faire** to try doggedly to do; (persister) to persist in doing; **s'~ sur qn** to hound sb

achat [aʃa] nm purchase; **faire des ~s** to do some shopping; **faire l'~ de qch** to purchase sth

acheter [aʃ(ə)te] vt to buy, purchase; (soudoyer) to buy; **~ qch à** (marchand) to buy ou purchase sth from; (ami etc: offrir) to buy sth for; **où est-ce que je peux ~ des cartes postales?** where can I buy (some) postcards?; **acheteur, -euse** nm/f buyer; shopper; (Comm) buyer

achever [aʃ(ə)ve] vt to complete, finish; (blessé) to finish off; **s'achever** vi to end

acide [asid] adj sour, sharp; (Chimie) acid(ic) ▷ nm (Chimie) acid; **acidulé, e** adj slightly acid; **bonbons acidulés** acid drops

acier [asje] nm steel; **aciérie** nf steelworks sg

acné [akne] nf acne

acompte [akɔ̃t] nm deposit

à-côté [akote] nm side-issue; (argent) extra

à-coup [aku] nm: **par ~s** by fits and starts

acoustique [akustik] nf (d'une salle) acoustics pl

acquéreur [akerœr] nm buyer, purchaser

acquérir [akerir] vt to acquire

acquis, e [aki, iz] pp de **acquérir** ▷ nm (accumulated) experience; **son aide nous est ~e** we can count on her help

acquitter [akite] vt (Jur) to acquit; (facture) to pay, settle; **s'acquitter de** vt (devoir) to discharge; (promesse) to fulfil

âcre [akr] adj acrid, pungent

acrobate [akrɔbat] nm/f acrobat; **acrobatie** nf acrobatics sg

acte [akt] nm act, action; (Théâtre) act; **prendre ~ de** to note, take note of; **faire ~ de candidature** to apply; **faire ~ de présence** to put in an appearance; **acte de naissance**

birth certificate

acteur [aktœʀ] nm actor

actif, -ive [aktif, iv] adj active ▷ nm (Comm) assets pl; (fig): **avoir à son ~** to have to one's credit; **population active** working population

action [aksjɔ̃] nf (gén) action; (Comm) share; **une bonne ~** a good deed; **actionnaire** nm/f shareholder; **actionner** vt (mécanisme) to activate; (machine) to operate

activer [aktive] vt to speed up; **s'activer** vi to bustle about; to hurry up

activité [aktivite] nf activity; **en ~** (volcan) active; (fonctionnaire) in active life

actrice [aktʀis] nf actress

actualité [aktyalite] nf (d'un problème) topicality; (événements): **l'~** current events; **actualités** nfpl (Cinéma, TV) the news; **d'~** topical

actuel, le [aktyɛl] adj (présent) present; (d'actualité) topical; **à l'heure ~le** at the present time; **actuellement** adv at present, at the present time

> Attention à ne pas traduire **actuellement** par **actually**.

acuponcture [akypɔ̃ktyʀ] nf acupuncture

adaptateur [adaptatœʀ] nm (Élec) adapter

adapter [adapte] vt to adapt; **s'adapter (à)** (suj: personne) to adapt (to); **~ qch à** (approprier) to adapt sth to (fit); **~ qch sur/dans/à** (fixer) to fit sth on/into/to

addition [adisjɔ̃] nf addition; (au café) bill; **l'~, s'il vous plaît** could I have the bill, please?; **additionner** vt to add (up)

adepte [adɛpt] nm/f follower

adéquat, e [adekwa(t), at] adj appropriate, suitable

adhérent, e [adeʀɑ̃, ɑ̃t] nm/f member

adhérer [adeʀe] **~ à** vt (coller) to adhere ou stick to; (se rallier à) to join; **adhésif, -ive** adj adhesive, sticky; **ruban adhésif** sticky ou adhesive tape

adieu, x [adjø] excl goodbye ▷ nm farewell

adjectif [adʒɛktif] nm adjective

adjoint, e [adʒwɛ̃, wɛ̃t] nm/f assistant; **adjoint au maire** deputy mayor; **directeur adjoint** assistant manager

admettre [admɛtʀ] vt (laisser entrer) to admit; (candidat: Scol) to pass; (tolérer) to allow, accept; (reconnaître) to admit, acknowledge

administrateur, -trice [administʀatœʀ, tʀis] nm/f (Comm) director; (Admin) administrator

administration [administʀasjɔ̃] nf administration; **l'A~** ≈ the Civil Service

administrer [administʀe] vt (firme) to manage, run; (biens, remède, sacrement etc) to administer

admirable [admiʀabl] adj admirable, wonderful

admirateur, -trice [admiʀatœʀ, tʀis] nm/f admirer

admiration [admiʀasjɔ̃] nf admiration

admirer [admiʀe] vt to admire

admis, e [admi, iz] pp de **admettre**

admissible [admisibl] adj (candidat) eligible; (comportement) admissible, acceptable

ADN sigle m (= acide désoxyribonucléique) DNA

adolescence [adɔlesɑ̃s] nf adolescence

adolescent, e [adɔlesɑ̃, ɑ̃t] nm/f adolescent, teenager

adopter [adɔpte] vt to adopt; **adoptif, -ive** adj (parents) adoptive; (fils, patrie) adopted

adorable [adɔʀabl] adj delightful, adorable

adorer [adɔʀe] vt to adore; (Rel) to worship

adosser [adose] vt: **~ qch à ou contre** to stand sth against; **s'adosser à/contre** to lean with one's back against

adoucir [adusiʀ] vt (goût, température) to make milder; (avec du sucre) to sweeten; (peau, voix) to soften; (caractère) to mellow

adresse [adʀɛs] nf (domicile) address; (dextérité) skill, dexterity; **~ électronique** email address

adresser [adʀese] vt (lettre: expédier) to send; (: écrire l'adresse sur) to address; (injure, compliments) to address; **s'adresser à** (parler à) to speak to, address; (s'informer auprès de) to go and see; (: bureau) to inquire at; (suj: livre, conseil) to be aimed at; **~ la parole à** to speak to, address

adroit, e [adʀwa, wat] adj skilful, skilled

ADSL sigle m (= asymmetrical digital subscriber line) ADSL, broadband

adulte [adylt] nm/f adult, grown-up ▷ adj (chien, arbre) fully-grown, mature; (attitude) adult, grown-up

adverbe [advɛʀb] nm adverb

adversaire [advɛʀsɛʀ] nm/f (Sport, gén) opponent, adversary

aération [aeʀasjɔ̃] nf airing; (circulation de l'air) ventilation

aérer [aeʀe] vt to air; (fig) to lighten

aérien, ne [aeʀjɛ̃, jɛn] adj (Aviat) air cpd, aerial; (câble, métro) overhead; (fig) light; **compagnie ~ne** airline

aéro... [aeʀɔ] préfixe: **aérobic** nm aerobics sg; **aérogare** nf airport (buildings); (en ville) air terminal; **aéroglisseur** nm hovercraft; **aérophagie** nf (Méd) wind, aerophagia (Méd); **aéroport** nm airport; **aérosol** nm aerosol

affaiblir [afebliʀ] **s'affaiblir** vi to weaken

affaire [afɛʀ] nf (problème, question) matter; (criminelle, judiciaire) case; (scandaleuse etc) affair; (entreprise) business; (marché, transaction) deal; business no pl; (occasion intéressante) bargain; **affaires** nfpl (intérêts publics et privés) affairs; (activité commerciale) business *sg*; (*effets personnels*) things, belongings; **ce sont mes ~s** (*cela me concerne*) that's my business; **occupe-toi de tes ~s!** mind your own business!; **ça fera l'~** that will do (nicely); **se tirer d'~** to sort it *ou* things out for o.s.; **avoir ~ à** (*être en contact*) to be dealing with; **les A~s étrangères** Foreign Affairs; **affairer: s'affairer** *vi* to busy o.s., bustle about

affamé, e [afame] *adj* starving

affecter [afɛkte] *vt* to affect; **~ qch à** to allocate *ou* allot sth to; **~ qn à** to appoint sb to; (*diplomate*) to post sb to

affectif, -ive [afɛktif, iv] *adj* emotional

affection [afɛksjɔ̃] *nf* affection; (*mal*) ailment; **affectionner** *vt* to be fond of; **affectueux, -euse** *adj* affectionate

affichage [afiʃaʒ] *nm* billposting; (*électronique*) display; **"~ interdit"** "stick no bills"; **affichage à cristaux liquides** liquid crystal display, LCD

affiche [afiʃ] *nf* poster; (*officielle*) notice; (*Théâtre*) bill; **être à l'~** to be on

afficher [afiʃe] *vt* (*affiche*) to put up; (*réunion*) to put up a notice about; (*électroniquement*) to display; (*fig*) to exhibit, display; **"défense d'~"** "no bill posters"; **s'afficher** *vr* (*péj*) to flaunt o.s.; (*électroniquement*) to be displayed

affilée [afile] : **d'~** *adv* at a stretch

affirmatif, -ive [afiʀmatif, iv] *adj* affirmative

affirmer [afiʀme] *vt* to assert

affligé, e [afliʒe] *adj* distressed, grieved; **~ de** (*maladie, tare*) afflicted with

affliger [afliʒe] *vt* (*peiner*) to distress, grieve

affluence [aflyɑ̃s] *nf* crowds *pl*; **heures d'~** rush hours; **jours d'~** busiest days

affluent [aflyɑ̃] *nm* tributary

affolement [afɔlmɑ̃] *nm* panic

affoler [afɔle] *vt* to throw into a panic; **s'affoler** *vi* to panic

affranchir [afʀɑ̃ʃiʀ] *vt* to put a stamp *ou* stamps on; (*à la machine*) to frank (BRIT), meter (US); (*fig*) to free, liberate; **affranchissement** *nm* postage

affreux, -euse [afʀø, øz] *adj* dreadful, awful

affront [afʀɔ̃] *nm* affront; **affrontement** *nm* clash, confrontation

affronter [afʀɔ̃te] *vt* to confront, face

affût [afy] *nm*: **à l'~ (de)** (*gibier*) lying in wait (for); (*fig*) on the look-out (for)

Afghanistan [afganistɑ̃] *nm*: **l'~** Afghanistan

afin [afɛ̃]: **~ que** *conj* so that, in order that; **~ de faire** in order to do, so as to do

africain, e [afʀikɛ̃, ɛn] *adj* African ▷ *nm/f*: **A~, e** African

Afrique [afʀik] *nf*: **l'~** Africa; **l'Afrique du Nord/Sud** North/South Africa

agacer [agase] *vt* to irritate

âge [aʒ] *nm* age; **quel ~ as-tu?** how old are you?; **prendre de l'~** to be getting on (in years); **le troisième ~** (*période*) retirement; (*personnes âgées*) senior citizens; **âgé, e** *adj* old, elderly; **âgé de 10 ans** 10 years old

agence [aʒɑ̃s] *nf* agency, office; (*succursale*) branch; **agence de voyages** travel agency; **agence immobilière** estate (BRIT) *ou* real estate (US) agent's (office)

agenda [aʒɛ̃da] *nm* diary; **~ électronique** PDA

▐ Attention à ne pas traduire *agenda* par le mot anglais *agenda*.

agenouiller [aʒ(ə)nuje]: **s'agenouiller** *vi* to kneel (down)

agent, e [aʒɑ̃, ɑ̃t] *nm/f* (*aussi*: **~(e) de police**) policeman(policewoman); (*Admin*) official, officer; **agent immobilier** estate agent (BRIT), realtor (US)

agglomération [aglɔmeʀasjɔ̃] *nf* town; built-up area; **l'~ parisienne** the urban area of Paris

aggraver [agʀave]: **s'aggraver** *vi* to worsen

agile [aʒil] *adj* agile, nimble

agir [aʒiʀ] *vi* to act; **il s'agit de** (*ça traite de*) it is about; (*il est important de*) it's a matter *ou* question of; **il s'agit de faire** we (*ou* you *etc*) must do; **de quoi s'agit-il?** what is it about?

agitation [aʒitasjɔ̃] *nf* (hustle and) bustle; (*trouble*) agitation, excitement; (*politique*) unrest, agitation

agité, e [aʒite] *adj* fidgety, restless; (*troublé*) agitated, perturbed; (*mer*) rough

agiter [aʒite] *vt* (*bouteille, chiffon*) to shake; (*bras, mains*) to wave; (*préoccuper, exciter*) to perturb

agneau, x [aɲo] *nm* lamb

agonie [agɔni] *nf* mortal agony, death pangs *pl*; (*fig*) death throes *pl*

agrafe [agʀaf] *nf* (*de vêtement*) hook, fastener; (*de bureau*) staple; **agrafer** *vt* to fasten; to staple; **agrafeuse** *nf* stapler

agrandir [agʀɑ̃diʀ] *vt* to enlarge; **s'agrandir** *vi* (*ville, famille*) to grow, expand; (*trou, écart*) to get bigger; **agrandissement** *nm* (*Photo*) enlargement

agréable [agʀeabl] *adj* pleasant, nice

agréé, e [agʀee] *adj*: **concessionnaire ~** registered dealer

agréer [agʀee] *vt* (*requête*) to accept; **~ à** to please, suit; **veuillez ~, Monsieur/Madame, mes salutations distinguées** (*personne nommée*) yours sincerely; (*personne non nommée*) yours faithfully

agrégation [agʀegasjɔ̃] *nf* highest teaching diploma in France; **agrégé, e** *nm/f* holder of the agrégation

agrément [agʀemɑ̃] *nm* (*accord*) consent, approval; (*attraits*) charm, attractiveness; (*plaisir*) pleasure

agresser[agʀese] vt to attack; **agresseur** nm aggressor, attacker; (Pol, Mil) aggressor; **agressif, -ive** adj aggressive

agricole[agʀikɔl] adj agricultural; **agriculteur** nm farmer; **agriculture** nf agriculture, farming

agripper[agʀipe] vt to grab, clutch; **s'agripper à** to cling (on) to, clutch, grip

agro-alimentaire[agʀoalimɑ̃tɛʀ] nm farm-produce industry

agrumes[agʀym] nmpl citrus fruit(s)

aguets[agɛ] nmpl: **être aux ~** to be on the look out

ai[ɛ] vb voir **avoir**

aide[ɛd] nm/f assistant; carer ▷ nf assistance, help; (secours financier) aid; **à l'~ de** (avec) with the help ou aid of; **appeler (qn) à l'~** to call for help (from sb); **à l'~!** help!; **aide judiciaire** legal aid; **aide ménagère** = home help (BRIT) ou helper (US); **aide-mémoire** nm inv memoranda pages pl; (key facts) handbook; **aide-soignant, e** nm/f auxiliary nurse

aider[ede] vt to help; **~ à qch** to help (towards) sth; **~ qn à faire qch** to help sb to do sth; **pouvez-vous m'~?** can you help me?; **s'aider de** (se servir de) to use, make use of

aïe[aj] excl ouch!

aie etc [ɛ] vb voir **avoir**

aigle[ɛgl] nm eagle

aigre[ɛgʀ] adj sour, sharp; (fig) sharp, cutting; **aigre-doux, -ce** adj (sauce) sweet and sour; **aigreur** nf sourness; sharpness; **aigreurs d'estomac** heartburn sg

aigu, ë[egy] adj (objet, douleur) sharp; (son, voix) high-pitched, shrill; (note) high(-pitched)

aiguille[eguij] nf needle; (de montre) hand; **aiguille à tricoter** knitting needle

aiguiser[egize] vt to sharpen; (fig) to stimulate; (: sens) to excite

ail[aj] nm garlic

aile[ɛl] nf wing; **aileron** nm (de requin) fin; **ailier** nm winger

aille etc [aj] vb voir **aller**

ailleurs[ajœʀ] adv elsewhere, somewhere else; **partout/nulle part ~** everywhere/ nowhere else; **d'~** (du reste) moreover, besides; **par ~** (d'autre part) moreover, furthermore

aimable[ɛmabl] adj kind, nice

aimant[ɛmɑ̃] nm magnet

aimer[eme] vt to love; (d'amitié, affection, par goût) to like; (souhait): **j'aimerais ...** I would like ...; **j'aime faire du ski** I like skiing; **je t'aime** I love you; **bien ~ qn/qch** to like sb/sth; **j'aime mieux Paul (que Pierre)** I prefer Paul (to Pierre); **j'aimerais mieux faire** I'd much rather do

aine[ɛn] nf groin

aîné, e[ene] adj elder, older; (le plus âgé) eldest, oldest ▷ nm/f oldest child ou one, oldest boy

ou son/girl ou daughter

ainsi[ɛ̃si] adv (de cette façon) like this, in this way, thus; (ce faisant) thus ▷ conj thus, so; **~ que** (comme) (just) as; (et aussi) as well as; **pour ~ dire** so to speak; **et ~ de suite** and so on

air[ɛʀ] nm air; (mélodie) tune; (expression) look, air; **prendre l'~** to get some (fresh) air; **avoir l'~** (sembler) to look, appear; **il a l'~ triste/malade** he looks sad/ill; **avoir l'~ de** to look like; **il a l'~ de dormir** he looks as if he's sleeping; **en l'~** (promesses) empty

airbag[ɛʀbag] nm airbag

aisance[ɛzɑ̃s] nf ease; (richesse) affluence

aise[ɛz] nf comfort; **être à l'~** ou **à son ~** to be comfortable; (pas embarrassé) to be at ease; (financièrement) to be comfortably off; **se mettre à l'~** to make o.s. comfortable; **être mal à l'~** to be uncomfortable; (gêné) to be ill at ease; **en faire à son ~** to do as one likes; **aisé, e** adj easy; (assez riche) well-to-do, well-off

aisselle[ɛsɛl] nf armpit

ait[ɛ] vb voir **avoir**

ajonc[aʒɔ̃] nm gorse no pl

ajourner[aʒuʀne] vt (réunion) to adjourn; (décision) to defer, postpone

ajouter[aʒute] vt to add

alarme[alaʀm] nf alarm; **donner l'~** to give ou raise the alarm; **alarmer** vt to alarm; **s'alarmer** vi to become alarmed

Albanie[albani] nf: **l'~** Albania

album[albɔm] nm album

alcool[alkɔl] nm: **l'~** alcohol; **un ~** a spirit, a brandy; **bière sans ~** non-alcoholic ou alcohol-free beer; **alcool à brûler** methylated spirits (BRIT), wood alcohol (US); **alcool à 90°** surgical spirit; **alcoolique** adj, nm/f alcoholic; **alcoolisé, e** adj alcoholic; **une boisson non alcoolisée** a soft drink; **alcoolisme** nm alcoholism; **alco(o)test®** nm Breathalyser®; (test) breath-test

aléatoire[aleatwaʀ] adj uncertain; (Inform) random

alentour[alɑ̃tuʀ] adv around, round about; **alentours** nmpl (environs) surroundings; **aux ~s de** in the vicinity ou neighbourhood of, round about; (temps) round about

alerte[alɛʀt] adj agile, nimble; brisk, lively ▷ nf alert; warning; **alerte à la bombe** bomb scare; **alerter** vt to alert

algèbre[alʒɛbʀ] nf algebra

Alger[alʒe] n Algiers

Algérie[alʒeʀi] nf: **l'~** Algeria; **algérien, ne** adj Algerian ▷ nm/f: **Algérien, ne** Algerian

algue[alg] nf (gén) seaweed no pl; (Bot) alga

alibi[alibi] nm alibi

aligner[aliɲe] vt to align, line up; (idées, chiffres) to string together; (adapter): **~ qch sur** to bring sth into alignment with; **s'aligner**

(soldats etc) to line up; **s'~ sur** (Pol) to align o.s. on

aliment[alimɑ̃] nm food; **alimentation** nf (commerce) food trade; (magasin) grocery store; (régime) diet; (en eau etc, de moteur) supplying; (Inform) feed; **alimenter** vt to feed; (Tech): **alimenter (en)** to supply (with); to feed (with); (fig) to sustain, keep going

allaiter[alete] vt to (breast-)feed, nurse; (suj: animal) to suckle

allécher[aleʃe] vt: **~ qn** to make sb's mouth water; to tempt ou entice sb

allée[ale] nf (de jardin) path; (en ville) avenue, drive; **~s et venues** comings and goings

allégé, e[aleʒe] adj (yaourt etc) low-fat

alléger[aleʒe] vt (voiture) to make lighter; (chargement) to lighten; (souffrance) to alleviate, soothe

Allemagne[alman] nf: **l'~** Germany; **allemand, e** adj German ▷ nm/f: **Allemand, e** German ▷ nm (Ling) German

aller[ale] nm (trajet) outward journey; (billet: aussi: **~ simple**) single (BRIT) ou one-way (US) ticket; **~ (et) retour** return (ticket) (BRIT), round-trip ticket (US) ▷ vi (gén) to go; **~ à** (convenir) to suit; (suj: forme, pointure etc) to fit; **~ (bien) avec** (couleurs, style etc) to go (well) with; **je vais y**/**me fâcher** I'm going to go/to get angry; **~ chercher qn** to go and get ou fetch (BRIT) sb; **~ voir** to go and see, to go to see; **allez!** come on!; **allons!** come now!; **comment allez-vous?** how are you?; **comment ça va?** how are you?; (affaires etc) how are things?; **il va bien/mal** he's well/not well, he's fine/ill; **ça va bien/mal** (affaires etc) it's going well/not going well; **~ mieux** to be better; **s'en ~** (partir) to be off, go, leave; (disparaître) to go away

allergie[alɛrʒi] nf allergy

allergique[alɛrʒik] adj: **~ à** allergic to; **je suis ~ à la pénicilline** I'm allergic to penicillin

alliance[aljɑ̃s] nf (Mil, Pol) alliance; (bague) wedding ring

allier[alje] vt (Pol, gén) to ally; (fig) to combine; **s'allier** to become allies; to combine

allô[alo] excl hullo, hallo

allocation[alɔkasjɔ̃] nf allowance; **allocation (de) chômage** unemployment benefit; **allocations familiales** ≈ child benefit

allonger[alɔ̃ʒe] vt to lengthen, make longer; (étendre: bras, jambe) to stretch (out); **s'allonger** vi to get longer; (se coucher) to lie down, stretch out; **~ le pas** to hasten one's step(s)

allumage[alymaʒ] nm (Auto) ignition

allume-cigare[alymsigar] nm inv cigar lighter

allumer[alyme] vt (lampe, phare, radio) to put ou switch on; (pièce) to put ou switch

the light(s) on in; (feu) to light; **s'allumer** vi (lumière, lampe) to come up ou go on; **je n'arrive pas à ~ le chauffage** I can't turn the heating on

allumette[alymɛt] nf match

allure[alyr] nf (vitesse) speed, pace; (démarche) walk; (aspect, air) look; **avoir de l'~** to have style; **à toute ~** at top speed

allusion[a(l)lyzjɔ̃] nf allusion; (sous-entendu) hint; **faire ~ à** to allude ou refer to; to hint at

MOT-CLÉ

alors[alɔr] adv **1** (à ce moment-là) then, at that time; **il habitait alors à Paris** he lived in Paris at that time

2 (par conséquent) then; **tu as fini? alors je m'en vais** have you finished? I'm going then; **et alors?** so what?

▷ conj: **alors que 1** (au moment où) when, as; **il est arrivé alors que je partais** he arrived as I was leaving

2 (tandis que) whereas, while; **alors que son frère travaillait dur, lui se reposait** while his brother was working hard, HE would rest

3 (bien que) even though; **il a été puni alors qu'il n'a rien fait** he was punished, even though he had done nothing

alourdir[alurdir] vt to weigh down, make heavy

Alpes[alp] nfpl: **les ~** the Alps

alphabet[alfabɛ] nm alphabet; (livre) ABC (book)

alpinisme[alpinism] nm mountaineering, climbing

Alsace[alzas] nf Alsace; **alsacien, ne** adj Alsatian ▷ nm/f: **Alsacien, ne** Alsatian

altermondialisme[altɛrmɔ̃djalism] nm anti-globalism; **altermondialiste** adj, nm/f anti-globalist

alternatif, -ive[altɛrnatif, iv] adj alternating; **alternative** nf (choix) alternative; **alterner** vi to alternate

altitude[altityd] nf altitude, height

alto[alto] nm (instrument) viola

aluminium[alyminjɔm] nm aluminium (BRIT), aluminum (US)

amabilité[amabilite] nf kindness

amaigrissant, e[amegrisɑ̃, ɑ̃t] adj (régime) slimming

amande[amɑ̃d] nf (de l'amandier) almond; **amandier** nm almond (tree)

amant[amɑ̃] nm lover

amas[ama] nm heap, pile; **amasser** vt to amass

amateur[amatœr] nm amateur; **en ~** (péj) amateurishly; **amateur de musique/sport** music/sport lover

ambassade [ɑ̄basad] nf embassy; **l'~ de France** the French Embassy; **ambassadeur, -drice** nm/f ambassador(-dress)

ambiance [ɑ̄bjɑ̄s] nf atmosphere; **il y a de l'~** there's a great atmosphere

ambigu, ë [ɑ̄bigy] adj ambiguous

ambitieux, -euse [ɑ̄bisjø, jøz] adj ambitious

ambition [ɑ̄bisjɔ̄] nf ambition

ambulance [ɑ̄bylɑ̄s] nf ambulance; **appelez une ~!** call an ambulance!; **ambulancier, -ière** nm/f ambulance man(-woman) (BRIT), paramedic (US)

âme [ɑm] nf soul; **âme sœur** kindred spirit

amélioration [ameljɔrasjɔ̄] nf improvement

améliorer [ameljɔre] vt to improve; **s'améliorer** vi to improve, get better

aménager [amenaʒe] vt (agencer, transformer) to fit out; to lay out; (: quartier, territoire) to develop; (installer) to fix up, put in; **ferme aménagée** converted farmhouse

amende [amɑ̄d] nf fine; **faire ~ honorable** to make amends

amener [am(ə)ne] vt to bring; (causer) to bring about; **s'amener** vi to show up (fam), turn up; **~ qn à faire qch** to lead sb to do sth

amer, amère [amɛr] adj bitter

américain, e [amerikɛ̄, ɛn] adj American ▷ nm/f: **A~, e** American

Amérique [amerik] nf: **l'~** America; **Amérique centrale/latine** Central/Latin America; **l'Amérique du Nord/Sud** North/ South America

amertume [amɛrtym] nf bitterness

ameublement [amœbləmɑ̄] nm furnishing; (meubles) furniture

ami, e [ami] nm/f friend; (amant/maîtresse) boyfriend/girlfriend ▷ adj: **pays/groupe ~** friendly country/group; **petit ~/petite ~e** boyfriend/girlfriend

amiable [amjabl]: **à l'~** adv (Jur) out of court; (gén) amicably

amiante [amjɑ̄t] nm asbestos

amical, e, -aux [amikal, o] adj friendly; **amicalement** adv in a friendly way; (dans une lettre) (with) best wishes

amincir [amɛ̄sir] vt: **~ qn** to make sb thinner ou slimmer; (suj: vêtement) to make sb look slimmer

amincissant, e [amɛ̄sisɑ̄, ɑ̄t] adj: **régime ~** (slimming) diet; **crème ~e** slimming cream

amiral, -aux [amiral, o] nm admiral

amitié [amitje] nf friendship; **prendre en ~ to** befriend; **faire ou présenter ses ~s à qn** to send sb one's best wishes; **"~s"** (dans une lettre) "(with) best wishes"

amonceler [amɔ̄s(ə)le] vt to pile ou heap up; **s'amonceler** vi to pile ou heap up; (fig) to accumulate

amont [amɔ̄]: **en ~** adv upstream

amorce [amɔrs] nf (sur un hameçon) bait; (explosif) cap; primer; priming; (fig: début) beginning(s), start

amortir [amɔrtir] vt (atténuer: choc) to absorb, cushion; (bruit, douleur) to deaden; (Comm: dette) to pay off; **~ un achat** to make a purchase pay for itself; **amortisseur** nm shock absorber

amour [amur] nm love; **faire l'~** to make love; **amoureux, -euse** adj (regard, tempérament) amorous; (vie, problèmes) love cpd; (personne) **être amoureux (de qn)** to be in love (with sb); **tomber amoureux (de qn)** to fall in love (with sb) ▷ nmpl courting couple(s); **amour-propre** nm self-esteem, pride

ampère [ɑ̄pɛr] nm amp(ere)

amphithéâtre [ɑ̄fiteatr] nm amphitheatre; (d'université) lecture hall ou theatre

ample [ɑ̄pl] adj (vêtement) roomy, ample; (gestes, mouvement) broad; (ressources) ample; **amplement** adv: **c'est amplement suffisant** that's more than enough; **ampleur** nf (de dégâts, problème) extent

amplificateur [ɑ̄plifikatœr] nm amplifier

amplifier [ɑ̄plifje] vt (fig) to expand, increase

ampoule [ɑ̄pul] nf (électrique) bulb; (de médicament) phial; (aux mains, pieds) blister

amusant, e [amyzɑ̄, ɑ̄t] adj (divertissant, spirituel) entertaining, amusing; (comique) funny, amusing

amuse-gueule [amyzgœl] nm inv appetizer, snack

amusement [amyzmɑ̄] nm (divertissement) amusement; (jeu etc) pastime, diversion

amuser [amyze] vt (divertir) to entertain, amuse; (égayer, faire rire) to amuse; **s'amuser** vi (jouer) to play; (se divertir) to enjoy o.s., have fun; (fig) to mess around

amygdale [amidal] nf tonsil

an [ɑ̄] nm year; **avoir quinze ans** to be fifteen (years old); **le jour de l'an, le premier de l'an, le nouvel an** New Year's Day

analphabète [analfabɛt] nm/f illiterate

analyse [analiz] nf analysis; (Méd) test; **analyser** vt to analyse; to test

ananas [anana(s)] nm pineapple

anatomie [anatɔmi] nf anatomy

ancêtre [ɑ̄sɛtr] nm/f ancestor

anchois [ɑ̄ʃwa] nm anchovy

ancien, ne [ɑ̄sjɛ̄, jɛn] adj old; (de jadis, de l'antiquité) ancient; (précédent, ex-) former, old; (par l'expérience) senior ▷ nm/f (dans une tribu) elder; **ancienneté** nf (Admin) (length of) service; (privilèges obtenus) seniority

ancre [ɑ̄kr] nf anchor; **jeter/lever l'~** to cast/ weigh anchor; **ancrer** vt (Constr: câble etc) to anchor; (fig) to fix firmly

Andorre [ɑ̄dɔr] nf Andorra

andouille [ɑ̄duj] nf (Culin) sausage made of

chitterlings; (fam) clot, nit

âne [ɑn] nm donkey, ass; (péj) dunce

anéantir [aneɑ̃tiʀ] vt to annihilate, wipe out; (fig) to obliterate, destroy

anémie [anemi] nf anaemia; **anémique** adj anaemic

anesthésie [anɛstezi] nf anaesthesia; **faire une ~ locale/générale à qn** to give sb a local/general anaesthetic

ange [ɑ̃ʒ] nm angel; **être aux ~s** to be over the moon

angine [ɑ̃ʒin] nf throat infection; **angine de poitrine** angina

anglais, e [ɑ̃glɛ, ɛz] adj English ▷ nm/f: **A~, e** Englishman(-woman) ▷ nm (Ling) English; **les A~** the English; **filer à l'~e** to take French leave

angle [ɑ̃gl] nm angle; (coin) corner; **angle droit** right angle

Angleterre [ɑ̃glətɛʀ] nf: **l'~** England

anglo... [ɑ̃glɔ] préfixe Anglo-, anglo(-); **anglophone** adj English-speaking

angoisse [ɑ̃gwas] nf anguish, distress; **angoissé, e** adj (personne) distressed

anguille [ɑ̃gij] nf eel

animal, e, -aux [animal, o] adj, nm animal

animateur, -trice [animatœʀ, tʀis] nm/f (de télévision) host; (de groupe) leader, organizer

animation [animasjɔ̃] nf (voir animé) busyness; liveliness; (Cinéma: technique) animation

animé, e [anime] adj (lieu) busy, lively; (conversation, réunion) lively, animated

animer [anime] vt (ville, soirée) to liven up; (mener) to lead

anis [ani(s)] nm (Culin) aniseed; (Bot) anise

ankyloser [ɑ̃kiloze]: **s'ankyloser** vi to get stiff

anneau, x [ano] nm (de rideau, bague) ring; (de chaîne) link

année [ane] nf year

annexe [anɛks] adj (problème) related; (document) appended; (salle) adjoining ▷ nf (bâtiment) annex(e); (jointe à une lettre) enclosure

anniversaire [anivɛʀsɛʀ] nm birthday; (d'un événement, bâtiment) anniversary

annonce [anɔ̃s] nf announcement; (signe, indice) sign; (aussi: **~ publicitaire**) advertisement; **les petites ~s** the classified advertisements, the small ads

annoncer [anɔ̃se] vt to announce; (être le signe de) to herald; **s'~ bien/difficile** to look promising/difficult

annuaire [anɥɛʀ] nm yearbook, annual; **annuaire téléphonique** (telephone) directory, phone book

annuel, le [anɥɛl] adj annual, yearly

annulation [anylasjɔ̃] nf cancellation

annuler [anyle] vt (rendez-vous, voyage) to cancel, call off; (jugement) to quash (BRIT), repeal (US); (Math, Physique) to cancel out; **je voudrais ~ ma réservation** I'd like to cancel my reservation

anonymat [anɔnima] nm anonymity; **garder l'~** to remain anonymous

anonyme [anɔnim] adj anonymous; (fig) impersonal

anorak [anɔʀak] nm anorak

anorexie [anɔʀɛksi] nf anorexia

anormal, e, -aux [anɔʀmal, o] adj abnormal

ANPE sigle f (= Agence nationale pour l'emploi) national employment agency

antarctique [ɑ̃taʀktik] adj Antarctic ▷ nm: **l'A~** the Antarctic

antenne [ɑ̃tɛn] nf (de radio) aerial; (d'insecte) antenna, feeler; (poste avancé) outpost; (petite succursale) sub-branch; **passer à l'~** to go on the air; **antenne parabolique** satellite dish

antérieur, e [ɑ̃teʀjœʀ] adj (d'avant) previous, earlier; (de devant) front

anti... [ɑ̃ti] préfixe anti...; **antialcoolique** adj anti-alcohol; **antibiotique** nm antibiotic; **antibrouillard** adj: **phare antibrouillard** fog lamp (BRIT) ou light (US)

anticipation [ɑ̃tisipasjɔ̃] nf: **livre/film d'~** science fiction book/film

anticipé, e [ɑ̃tisipe] adj: **avec mes remerciements ~s** thanking you in advance ou anticipation

anticiper [ɑ̃tisipe] vt (événement, coup) to anticipate, foresee

anti...: **anticorps** nm antibody; **antidote** nm antidote; **antigel** nm antifreeze; **antihistaminique** nm antihistamine

antillais, e [ɑ̃tijɛ, ɛz] adj West Indian, Caribbean ▷ nm/f: **A~, e** West Indian, Caribbean

Antilles [ɑ̃tij] nfpl: **les ~** the West Indies; **les Grandes/Petites ~** the Greater/Lesser Antilles

antilope [ɑ̃tilɔp] nf antelope

anti...: **antimite(s)** adj, nm: **(produit) antimite(s)** mothproofer; moth repellent; **antimondialisation** nf anti-globalization; **antipathique** adj unpleasant, disagreeable; **antipelliculaire** adj anti-dandruff

antiquaire [ɑ̃tikɛʀ] nm/f antique dealer

antique [ɑ̃tik] adj antique; (très vieux) ancient, antiquated; **antiquité** nf (objet) antique; **l'Antiquité** Antiquity; **magasin d'antiquités** antique shop

anti...: **antirabique** adj rabies cpd; **antirouille** adj inv anti-rust cpd; **antisémite** adj anti-Semitic; **antiseptique** adj, nm antiseptic

antivirus [ɑ̃ti'virys] nm (Inform) antivirus; **antivol** adj, nm: **(dispositif) antivol** anti-theft device

anxieux, -euse [ɑ̃ksjø, jøz] adj anxious

worried

AOC sigle f (= appellation d'origine contrôlée) label guaranteeing the quality of wine

août [u(t)] nm August

apaiser [apeze] vt (colère, douleur) to soothe; (personne) to calm (down), pacify; **s'apaiser** vi (tempête, bruit) to die down, subside; (personne) to calm down

apercevoir [apɛRsəvwaR] vt to see; **s'apercevoir de** vt to notice; **s'~ que** to notice that

aperçu [apɛRsy] nm (vue d'ensemble) general survey

apéritif [apeRitif] nm (boisson) aperitif; (réunion) drinks pl

à-peu-près [apøpRɛ] (péj) nm inv vague approximation

apeuré, e [apœRe] adj frightened, scared

aphte [aft] nm mouth ulcer

apitoyer [apitwaje] vt to move to pity; **s'apitoyer (sur)** to feel pity (for)

aplatir [aplatiR] vt to flatten; **s'aplatir** vi to become flatter; (écrasé) to be flattened

aplomb [aplɔ̃] nm (équilibre) balance, equilibrium; (fig) self-assurance; nerve; **d'~** steady

apostrophe [apɔstRɔf] nf (signe) apostrophe

apparaître [apaRɛtR] vi to appear

appareil [apaRɛj] nm (outil, machine) piece of apparatus, device; (électrique, ménager) appliance; (avion) (aero)plane, aircraft inv; (téléphonique) phone; (dentier) brace (BRIT), braces (US); **"qui est à l'~?"** "who's speaking?"; **dans le plus simple ~** in one's birthday suit; **appareil(-photo)** camera; **appareiller** vi (Navig) to cast off, get under way ▷ vt (assortir) to match up

apparemment [apaRamɑ̃] adv apparently

apparence [apaRɑ̃s] nf appearance; **en ~** apparently

apparent, e [apaRɑ̃, ɑ̃t] adj visible; (évident) obvious; (superficiel) apparent

apparenté, e [apaRɑ̃te] adj: **~ à** related to; (fig) similar to

apparition [apaRisjɔ̃] nf appearance; (surnaturelle) apparition

appartement [apaRtəmɑ̃] nm flat (BRIT), apartment (US)

appartenir [apaRtəniR]: **~ à** vt to belong to; **il lui appartient de** it is his duty to

apparu, e [apaRy] pp de **apparaître**

appât [apɑ] nm (Pêche) bait; (fig) lure, bait

appel [apɛl] nm (nominal) roll call; (Mil: recrutement) call-up; **faire ~ à** (invoquer) to appeal to; (avoir recours à) to call on; (nécessiter) to call for, require; **faire** ou **interjeter ~** (Jur) to appeal; **faire l'~** to call the roll; (Scol) to call the register; **sans ~** (fig) final, irrevocable; **faire un ~ de phares** to

flash one's headlights; **appel d'offres** (Comm) invitation to tender; **appel (téléphonique)** (tele)phone call

appelé [ap(ə)le] nm (Mil) conscript

appeler [ap(ə)le] vt to call; (faire venir: médecin etc) to call, send for; **s'appeler** vi: **elle s'appelle Gabrielle** her name is Gabrielle, she's called Gabrielle; **comment vous appelez-vous?** what's your name?; **comment ça s'appelle?** what is it called?; **être appelé à** (fig) to be destined to

appendicite [apɑ̃disit] nf appendicitis

appesantir [apəzɑ̃tiR]: **s'appesantir** vi to grow heavier; **s'~ sur** (fig) to dwell on

appétissant, e [apetisɑ̃, ɑ̃t] adj appetizing, mouth-watering

appétit [apeti] nm appetite; **bon ~!** enjoy your meal!

applaudir [aplodiR] vt to applaud ▷ vi to applaud, clap; **applaudissements** nmpl applause sg, clapping sg

application [aplikasjɔ̃] nf application

appliquer [aplike] vt to apply; (loi) to enforce; **s'appliquer** vi (élève etc) to apply o.s.; **s'~ à** to apply to

appoint [apwɛ̃] nm (extra) contribution ou help; **avoir/faire l'~** to have/give the right change ou money; **chauffage d'~** extra heating

apporter [apɔRte] vt to bring

appréciable [apResjabl] adj appreciable

apprécier [apResje] vt to appreciate; (évaluer) to estimate, assess

appréhender [apReɑ̃de] vt (craindre) to dread; (arrêter) to apprehend

apprendre [apRɑ̃dR] vt to learn; (événement, résultats) to learn of, hear of; **~ qch à qn** (informer) to tell sb (of) sth; (enseigner) to teach sb sth; **~ à faire qch** to learn to do sth; **~ à qn à faire qch** to teach sb to do sth; **apprenti, e** nm/f apprentice; **apprentissage** nm learning; (Comm, Scol: période) apprenticeship

apprêter [apRɛte] vt: **s'~ à faire qch** to get ready to do sth

appris, e [apRi, iz] pp de **apprendre**

apprivoiser [apRivwaze] vt to tame

approbation [apRɔbasjɔ̃] nf approval

approcher [apRɔʃe] vi to approach, come near ▷ vt to approach; (rapprocher): **~ qch (de qch)** to bring ou put sth near (to sth); **s'approcher de** to approach, go ou come near to; **~ de** (lieu, but) to draw near to; (quantité, moment) to approach

approfondir [apRɔfɔ̃diR] vt to deepen; (question) to go further into

approprié, e [apRɔpRije] adj: **~ (à)** appropriate (to), suited to

approprier [apRɔpRije]: **s'approprier** vt to appropriate, take over; **s'~ en** to stock up with

approuver [apʀuve] vt to agree with; (trouver louable) to approve of

approvisionner [apʀovizjɔne] vt to supply; (compte bancaire) to pay funds into; **s'approvisionner en** to stock up with

approximatif, -ive [apʀɔksimatif, iv] adj approximate, rough; (termes) vague

appt abr = **appartement**

appui [apɥi] nm support; **prendre ~ sur** to lean on; (objet) to rest on; **l'~ de la fenêtre** the windowsill, the window ledge

appuyer [apɥije] vt (poser): **~ qch sur/contre** to lean ou rest sth on/against; (soutenir: personne, demande) to support, back (up) ▷ vi: **~ sur** (bouton) to press, push; (mot, détail) to stress, emphasize; **~ sur le frein** to brake, to apply the brakes; **s'appuyer sur** to lean on; (fig: compter sur) to rely on

après [apʀɛ] prép after ▷ adv afterwards; **2 heures ~** 2 hours later; **~ qu'il est** ou **soit parti** after he left; **~ avoir fait** after having done; **d'~** (selon) according to; **~ coup** after the event, afterwards; **~ tout** (au fond) after all; **et (puis) ~?** so what?; **après-demain** adv the day after tomorrow; **après-midi** nm ou nf inv afternoon; **après-rasage** nm inv aftershave; **après-shampooing** nm inv conditioner; **après-ski** nm inv snow boot

après-soleil [apʀɛsɔlɛj] adj inv after-sun cpd ▷ nm after-sun cream ou lotion

apte [apt] adj capable; **~ à qch/faire qch** capable of sth/doing sth; **~ (au service)** (Mil) fit (for service)

aquarelle [akwaʀɛl] nf watercolour

aquarium [akwaʀjɔm] nm aquarium

arabe [aʀab] adj Arabic; (désert, cheval) Arabian; (nation, peuple) Arab ▷ nm/f: **A~** Arab ▷ nm (Ling) Arabic

Arabie [aʀabi] nf: **l'~ (Saoudite)** Saudi Arabia

arachide [aʀaʃid] nf (plante) groundnut (plant); (graine) peanut, groundnut

araignée [aʀeɲe] nf spider

arbitraire [aʀbitʀɛʀ] adj arbitrary

arbitre [aʀbitʀ] nm (Sport) referee; (: Tennis, Cricket) umpire; (fig) arbiter, judge; (Jur) arbitrator; **arbitrer** vt to referee; to umpire; to arbitrate

arbre [aʀbʀ] nm tree; (Tech) shaft

arbuste [aʀbyst] nm small shrub

arc [aʀk] nm (arme) bow; (Géom) arc; (Archit) arch; **en ~ de cercle** semi-circular

arcade [aʀkad] nf arch(way); **arcades** nfpl (série) arcade sg, arches

arc-en-ciel [aʀkɑ̃sjɛl] nm rainbow

arche [aʀʃ] nf arch; **arche de Noé** Noah's Ark

archéologie [aʀkeɔlɔʒi] nf arch(a)eology; **archéologue** nm/f arch(a)eologist

archet [aʀʃɛ] nm bow

archipel [aʀʃipɛl] nm archipelago

architecte [aʀʃitɛkt] nm architect

architecture [aʀʃitɛktyʀ] nf architecture

archives [aʀʃiv] nfpl (collection) archives

arctique [aʀktik] adj Arctic ▷ nm: **l'A~** the Arctic

ardent, e [aʀdɑ̃, ɑ̃t] adj (soleil) blazing; (amour) ardent, passionate; (prière) fervent

ardoise [aʀdwaz] nf slate

ardu, e [aʀdy] adj (travail) arduous; (problème) difficult

arène [aʀɛn] nf arena; **arènes** nfpl (amphithéâtre) bull-ring sg

arête [aʀɛt] nf (de poisson) bone; (d'une montagne) ridge

argent [aʀʒɑ̃] nm (métal) silver; (monnaie) money; **argent de poche** pocket money; **argent liquide** ready money, (ready) cash; **argenterie** nf silverware

argentin, e [aʀʒɑ̃tɛ̃, in] adj Argentinian ▷ nm/f: **A~, e** Argentinian

Argentine [aʀʒɑ̃tin] nf: **l'~** Argentina

argentique [aʀʒɑ̃tik] adj (appareil-photo) film cpd

argile [aʀʒil] nf clay

argot [aʀgo] nm slang; **argotique** adj slang cpd; (très familier) slangy

argument [aʀgymɑ̃] nm argument

argumenter [aʀgymɑ̃te] vi to argue

aride [aʀid] adj arid

aristocratie [aʀistɔkʀasi] nf aristocracy; **aristocratique** adj aristocratic

arithmétique [aʀitmetik] adj arithmetic(al) ▷ nf arithmetic

arme [aʀm] nf weapon; **armes** nfpl (armement) weapons, arms; (blason) (coat of) arms; **~s de destruction massive** weapons of mass destruction; **arme à feu** firearm

armée [aʀme] nf army; **armée de l'air** Air Force; **armée de terre** Army

armer [aʀme] vt to arm; (arme à feu) to cock; (appareil-photo) to wind on; **~ qch de** to reinforce sth with; **s'armer de** to arm o.s. with

armistice [aʀmistis] nm armistice; **l'A~** ≈ Remembrance (BRIT) ou Veterans (US) Day

armoire [aʀmwaʀ] nf (tall) cupboard; (penderie) wardrobe (BRIT), closet (US)

armure [aʀmyʀ] nf armour no pl, suit of armour; **armurier** nm gunsmith

arnaque [aʀnak] (fam) nf swindling; **c'est de l'~** it's a swindle; **arnaquer** (fam) vt to swindle

arobase [aʀobaz] nf (symbole) at symbol; **"paul ~ société point fr"** "paul at société dot fr"

aromates [aʀɔmat] nmpl seasoning sg, herbs (and spices)

aromathérapie [aʀomateʀapi] nf aromatherapy

aromatisé, e [aʀomatize] adj flavoured

arôme [aʀom] nm aroma

arracher [aʀaʃe] vt to pull out; (page etc) to tear off, tear out; (légumes, herbe) to pull up; (bras etc) to tear off; **s'arracher** vt (article recherché) to fight over; **~ qch à qn** to snatch sth from sb; (fig) to wring sth out of sb

arrangement [aʀɑ̃ʒmɑ̃] nm agreement, arrangement

arranger [aʀɑ̃ʒe] vt (gén) to arrange; (réparer) to fix, put right; (régler: différend) to settle, sort out; (convenir à) to suit, be convenient for; **cela m'arrange** that suits me (fine); **s'arranger** vi (se mettre d'accord) to come to an agreement; **je vais m'~** I'll manage; **ça va s'~** it'll sort itself out

arrestation [aʀɛstasjɔ̃] nf arrest

arrêt [aʀɛ] nm stopping; (de bus etc) stop; (Jur) judgment, decision; **à l'~** stationary; **tomber en ~ devant** to stop short in front of; **sans ~** (sans interruption) non-stop; (très fréquemment) continually; **arrêt de travail** stoppage (of work)

arrêter [aʀete] vt to stop; (chauffage etc) to turn off, switch off; (fixer: date etc) to appoint, decide on; (criminel, suspect) to arrest; **s'arrêter** vi to stop; **~ de faire** to stop doing; **arrêtez-vous ici/au coin, s'il vous plaît** could you stop here/at the corner, please?

arrhes [aʀ] nfpl deposit sg

arrière [aʀjɛʀ] nm back; (Sport) fullback ▷ adj inv **siège/roue ~** back ou rear seat/wheel; **à l'~** behind, at the back; **en ~** behind; (regarder) back, behind; (tomber, aller) backwards; **arrière-goût** nm aftertaste; **arrière-grand-mère** nf great-grandmother; **arrière-grand-père** nm great-grandfather; **arrière-pays** nm inv hinterland; **arrière-pensée** nf ulterior motive; mental reservation; **arrière-plan** nm background; **à l'arrière-plan** in the background; **arrière-saison** nf late autumn

arrimer [aʀime] vt to secure; (cargaison) to stow

arrivage [aʀivaʒ] nm consignment

arrivée [aʀive] nf arrival; (ligne d'arrivée) finish

arriver [aʀive] vi to arrive; (survenir) to happen, occur; **il arrive à Paris à 8h** he gets to ou arrives in Paris at 8; **à quelle heure arrive le train de Lyon?** what time does the train from Lyons get in?; **~ à** (atteindre) to reach; **~ à faire qch** to succeed in doing sth; **en ~ à** (finir par) to come to; **il arrive que** it happens that; **il lui arrive de faire** he sometimes does

arrobase [aʀɔbaz] nf (Inform) @, 'at' sign

arrogance [aʀɔgɑ̃s] nf arrogance

arrogant, e [aʀɔgɑ̃, ɑ̃t] adj arrogant

arrondissement [aʀɔ̃dismɑ̃] nm (Admin) ≈ district

arroser [aʀoze] vt to water; (victoire) to celebrate (over a drink); (Culin) to baste; **arrosoir** nm watering can

arsenal, -aux [aʀsənal, o] nm (Navig) naval dockyard; (Mil) arsenal; (fig) gear, paraphernalia

art [aʀ] nm art

artère [aʀtɛʀ] nf (Anat) artery; (rue) main road

arthrite [aʀtʀit] nf arthritis

artichaut [aʀtiʃo] nm artichoke

article [aʀtikl] nm article; (Comm) item, article; **à l'~ de la mort** at the point of death

articulation [aʀtikylasjɔ̃] nf articulation; (Anat) joint

articuler [aʀtikyle] vt to articulate

artificiel, le [aʀtifisjɛl] adj artificial

artisan [aʀtizɑ̃] nm artisan, (self-employed) craftsman; **artisanal, e, -aux** adj of ou made by craftsmen; (péj) cottage industry cpd; **de fabrication artisanale** home-made; **artisanat** nm arts and crafts pl

artiste [aʀtist] nm/f artist; (de variétés) entertainer; (musicien etc) performer; **artistique** adj artistic

as¹ [a] vb voir **avoir**

as² [ɑs] nm ace

ascenseur [asɑ̃sœʀ] nm lift (BRIT), elevator (US)

ascension [asɑ̃sjɔ̃] nf ascent; (de montagne) climb; **l'A~** (Rel) the Ascension

● **ASCENSION**
●
● The **fête de l'Ascension** is a public holiday
● in France. It always falls on a Thursday,
● usually in May. Many French people take
● the following Friday off work too and enjoy
● a long weekend.

asiatique [azjatik] adj Asiatic, Asian ▷ nm/f: **A~** Asian

Asie [azi] nf: **l'~** Asia

asile [azil] nm (refuge) refuge, sanctuary; (Pol): **droit d'~** (political) asylum

aspect [aspɛ] nm appearance, look; (fig) aspect, side; **à l'~ de** at the sight of

asperge [aspɛʀʒ] nf asparagus no pl

asperger [aspɛʀʒe] vt to spray, sprinkle

asphalte [asfalt] nm asphalt

asphyxier [asfiksje] vt to suffocate, asphyxiate; (fig) to stifle

aspirateur [aspiʀatœʀ] nm vacuum cleaner; **passer l'~** to vacuum

aspirer [aspiʀe] vt (air) to inhale; (liquide) to suck (up); (suj: appareil) to suck up; **~ à** to aspire to

aspirine [aspiʀin] nf aspirin

assagir [asaʒiʀ]: **s'assagir** vi to quieten down, settle down

assaisonnement [asɛzɔnmɑ̃] nm seasoning

assaisonner [asɛzɔne] vt to season

assassin [asasɛ̃] nm murderer; assassin;

assassiner vt to murder; (*esp Pol*) to assassinate

assaut [aso] nm assault, attack; **prendre d'~** to storm, assault; **donner l'~ à** to attack

assécher [asefe] vt to drain

assemblage [asɑ̃blaʒ] nm (*action*) assembling; (*de couleurs, choses*) collection

assemblée [asɑ̃ble] nf (*réunion*) meeting; (*assistance*) gathering; (*Pol*) assembly; **l'A~ nationale** the National Assembly (*the lower house of the French Parliament*)

assembler [asɑ̃ble] vt (*joindre, monter*) to assemble, put together; (*amasser*) to gather (together), collect (together); **s'assembler** vi to gather

asseoir [aswar] vt (*malade, bébé*) to sit up; (*personne debout*) to sit down; (*autorité, réputation*) to establish; **s'asseoir** vi to sit (o.s.) down

assez [ase] adv (*suffisamment*) enough, sufficiently; (*passablement*) rather, quite, fairly; **~ de pain/livres** enough ou sufficient bread/ books; **vous en avez ~?** have you got enough?; **j'en ai ~!** I've had enough!

assidu, e [asidy] adj (*appliqué*) assiduous, painstaking; (*ponctuel*) regular

assied *etc* [asje] vb voir **asseoir**

assiérai *etc* [asjere] vb voir **asseoir**

assiette [asjɛt] nf plate; (*contenu*) plate(ful); **il n'est pas dans son ~** he's not feeling quite himself; **assiette à dessert** dessert plate; **assiette anglaise** assorted cold meats; **assiette creuse** (soup) dish, soup plate; **assiette plate** (dinner) plate

assimiler [asimile] vt to assimilate, absorb; (*comparer*): **~ qch/qn à** to liken ou compare sth/sb to; **s'assimiler** vr (*s'intégrer*) to be assimilated, assimilate

assis, e [asi, iz] pp de **asseoir** ▷ adj sitting (down), seated

assistance [asistɑ̃s] nf (*public*) audience; (*aide*) assistance; **enfant de l'A~ publique** child in care

assistant, e [asistɑ̃, ɑ̃t] nm/f assistant; (*d'université*) probationary lecturer; **assistant(e) social(e)** social worker

assisté, e [asiste] adj (*Auto*) power assisted; **~ par ordinateur** computer-assisted; **direction ~e** power steering

assister [asiste] vt (*aider*) to assist; **~ à** (*scène, événement*) to witness; (*conférence, séminaire*) to attend, be at; (*spectacle, match*) to be at, see

association [asɔsjasjɔ̃] nf association

associé, e [asɔsje] nm/f associate; (*Comm*) partner

associer [asɔsje] vt to associate; **s'associer** vi to join together; **s'~ à qn pour faire** to join (forces) with sb to do; **s'~ à** (*couleurs, qualités*) to be combined with; (*opinions, joie de qn*) to

share in; **~ qn à** (*profits*) to give sb a share of; (*affaire*) to make sb a partner in; (*joie, triomphe*) to include sb in; **~ qch à** (*allier à*) to combine sth with

assoiffé, e [aswafe] adj thirsty

assommer [asɔme] vt (*étourdir, abrutir*) to knock out, stun

Assomption [asɔ̃psjɔ̃] nf: **l'~** the Assumption

● **ASSOMPTION**
●
● The **fête de l'Assomption**, more
● commonly known as 'le 15 août' is a national
● holiday in France. Traditionally, large
● numbers of holidaymakers leave home
● on 15 August, frequently causing chaos on
● the roads.

assorti, e [asɔrti] adj matched, matching; (*varié*) assorted; **~ à** matching; **assortiment** nm assortment, selection

assortir [asɔrtir] vt to match; **~ qch à** to match sth with; **~ qch de** to accompany sth with

assouplir [asuplir] vt to make supple; (*fig*) to relax; **assouplissant** nm (*fabric*) softener

assumer [asyme] vt (*fonction, emploi*) to assume, take on

assurance [asyrɑ̃s] nf (*certitude*) assurance; (*confiance en soi*) (self-)confidence; (*contrat*) insurance (policy); (*secteur commercial*) insurance; **assurance au tiers** third-party insurance; **assurance maladie** health insurance; **assurance tous risques** (*Auto*) comprehensive insurance; **assurances sociales** ≈ National Insurance (BRIT), ≈ Social Security (US); **assurance-vie** nf life assurance ou insurance

assuré, e [asyre] adj (*certain: réussite, échec*) certain, sure; (*air*) assured; (*pas*) steady ▷ nm/f insured (person); **assurément** adv assuredly, most certainly

assurer [asyre] vt (*Finance*) to insure; (*victoire etc*) to ensure; (*frontières, pouvoir*) to make secure; (*service*) to provide, operate; **s'assurer** (*contre*) (*Comm*) to insure o.s. (against); **s'~ de/que** (*vérifier*) to make sure of/that; **s'~ (de)** (*aide de qn*) to secure; **~ à qn que** to assure sb that; **~ qn de** to assure sb of

asthmatique [asmatik] adj, nm/f asthmatic

asthme [asm] nm asthma

asticot [astiko] nm maggot

astre [astr] nm star

astrologie [astrɔlɔʒi] nf astrology

astronaute [astronot] nm/f astronaut

astronomie [astronomi] nf astronomy

astuce [astys] nf shrewdness, astuteness; (*truc*) trick, clever way; **astucieux, -euse** adj clever

atelier [atəlje] nm workshop; (de peintre) studio

athée [ate] adj atheistic ▷ nm/f atheist

Athènes [atɛn] n Athens

athlète [atlɛt] nm/f (Sport) athlete; **athlétisme** nm athletics sg

atlantique [atlãtik] adj Atlantic ▷ nm: **l'(océan) A~** the Atlantic (Ocean)

atlas [atlɑs] nm atlas

atmosphère [atmɔsfɛʀ] nf atmosphere

atome [atom] nm atom; **atomique** adj atomic, nuclear

atomiseur [atɔmizœʀ] nm atomizer

atout [atu] nm trump; (fig) asset

atroce [atʀɔs] adj atrocious

attachant, e [ataʃã, ãt] adj engaging, lovable, likeable

attache [ataʃ] nf clip, fastener; (fig) tie

attacher [ataʃe] vt to tie up; (étiquette) to attach, tie on; (ceinture) to fasten ▷ vi (poêle, riz) to stick; **s'attacher à** (par affection) to become attached to; **~ qch à** to tie ou attach sth to

attaque [atak] nf attack; (cérébrale) stroke; (d'épilepsie) fit

attaquer [atake] vt to attack ▷ vi to attack; **s'attaquer à** vt (personne) to attack; (problème) to tackle; **~ qn en justice** to bring an action against sb, sue sb

attarder [ataʀde]: **s'attarder** vi to linger

atteindre [atɛ̃dʀ] vt to reach; (blesser) to hit; (émouvoir) to affect; **atteint, e** adj (Méd): **être atteint de** to be suffering from; **atteinte** nf: **hors d'atteinte** out of reach; **porter atteinte à** to strike a blow at

attendant [atãdã] adv: **en ~** meanwhile, in the meantime

attendre [atãdʀ] vt (gén) to wait for; (être destiné ou réservé à) to await, be in store for ▷ vi to wait; **s'attendre à (ce que)** to expect (that); **attendez-moi, s'il vous plaît** wait for me, please; **~ un enfant** to be expecting a baby; **~ de faire/d'être** to wait until one does/is; **attendez qu'il vienne** wait until he comes; **~ qch de** to expect sth of

> Attention à ne pas traduire **attendre** par **to attend**.

attendrir [atãdʀiʀ] vt to move (to pity); (viande) to tenderize

attendu, e [atãdy] adj (visiteur) expected; (événement) long-awaited; **~ que** considering that, since

attentat [atãta] nm assassination attempt; **attentat à la pudeur** indecent assault no pl; **attentat suicide** suicide bombing

attente [atãt] nf wait; (espérance) expectation

attenter [atãte]: **~ à** vt (liberté) to violate; **~ à la vie de qn** to make an attempt on sb's life

attentif, -ive [atãtif, iv] adj (auditeur) attentive; (examen) careful; **~ à** careful to

attention [atãsjɔ̃] nf attention; (prévenance) attention, thoughtfulness no pl; **à l'~ de** for the attention of; **faire ~ (à)** to be careful (of); **faire ~ (à ce) que** to be ou make sure that; **~!** careful!, watch out!; **~ à la voiture!** watch out for that car!; **attentionné, e** adj thoughtful, considerate

atténuer [atenɥe] vt (douleur) to alleviate, ease; (couleurs) to soften; **s'atténuer** vi to ease; (violence etc) to abate

atterrir [ateʀiʀ] vi to land; **atterrissage** nm landing

attestation [atɛstasjɔ̃] nf certificate

attirant, e [atiʀã, ãt] adj attractive, appealing

attirer [atiʀe] vt to attract; (appâter) to lure, entice; **~ qn dans un coin/vers soi** to draw sb into a corner/towards one; **~ l'attention de qn** to attract sb's attention; **~ l'attention de qn sur** to draw sb's attention to; **s'~ des ennuis** to bring trouble upon o.s., get into trouble

attitude [atityd] nf attitude; (position du corps) bearing

attraction [atʀaksjɔ̃] nf (gén) attraction; (de cabaret, cirque) number

attrait [atʀɛ] nm appeal, attraction

attraper [atʀape] vt (gén) to catch; (habitude, amende) to get, pick up; (fam: duper) to con; **se faire ~** (fam) to be told off

attrayant, e [atʀɛjã, ãt] adj attractive

attribuer [atʀibɥe] vt (prix) to award; (rôle, tâche) to allocate, assign; (imputer): **~ qch à** to attribute sth to; **s'attribuer** vt (s'approprier) to claim for o.s.

attrister [atʀiste] vt to sadden

attroupement [atʀupmã] nm crowd

attrouper [atʀupe]: **s'attrouper** vi to gather

au [o] prép +dét = **à +le**

aubaine [obɛn] nf godsend

aube [ob] nf dawn, daybreak; **à l'~** at dawn ou daybreak

aubépine [obepin] nf hawthorn

auberge [obɛʀʒ] nf inn; **auberge de jeunesse** youth hostel

aubergine [obɛʀʒin] nf aubergine

aucun, e [okœ̃, yn] dét no, tournure négative +any; (positif) any ▷ pron none, tournure négative +any; any(one); **sans ~ doute** without any doubt; **plus qu'~ autre** more than any other; **il le fera mieux qu'~ de nous** he'll do it better than any of us; **~ des deux** neither of the two; **~ d'entre eux** none of them

audace [odas] nf daring, boldness; (péj) audacity; **audacieux, -euse** adj daring, bold

au-delà [od(ə)la] adv beyond ▷ nm: **l'~** the hereafter; **~ de** beyond

au-dessous [odsu] adv underneath; below;

~ de under(neath), below; (*limite, somme etc*) below, under; (*dignité, condition*) below

au-dessus[odsy] *adv* above; **~ de** above

au-devant[od(ə)vã]: **~ de** *prép*: **aller ~ de** (*personne, danger*) to go (out) and meet; (*souhaits de qn*) to anticipate

audience[odjãs] *nf* audience; (*Jur: séance*) hearing

audiovisuel, le[odjovizɥɛl] *adj* audiovisual

audition[odisjɔ̃] *nf* (*ouïe, écoute*) hearing; (*Jur: de témoins*) examination; (*Mus, Théâtre: épreuve*) audition

auditoire[oditwaʀ] *nm* audience

augmentation[ogmãtasjɔ̃] *nf* increase; **augmentation (de salaire)** rise (in salary) (*BRIT*), (pay) raise (*US*)

augmenter[ogmãte] *vt* (*gén*) to increase; (*salaire, prix*) to increase, raise, put up; (*employé*) to increase the salary of ▷ *vi* to increase

augure[ogyʀ] *nm*: **de bon/mauvais ~** of good/ill omen

aujourd'hui[oʒuʀdɥi] *adv* today

aumône[omon] *nf inv* alms *sg*; **aumônier** *nm* chaplain

auparavant[opaʀavã] *adv* before(hand)

auprès[opʀɛ]: **~ de** *prép* next to, close to; (*recourir, s'adresser*) to; (*en comparaison de*) compared with

auquel[okɛl] *prép* +*pron* = **à** +**lequel**

aurai *etc* [ɔʀe] *vb voir* **avoir**

aurons *etc* [oʀɔ̃] *vb voir* **avoir**

aurore[ˋʀ] *nf* dawn, daybreak

ausculter[ɔskylte] *vt* to sound (the chest of)

aussi[osi] *adv* (*également*) also, too; (*de comparaison*) as ▷ *conj* therefore, consequently; **~ fort que** as strong as; **moi ~** me too

aussitôt[osito] *adv* straight away, immediately; **~ que** as soon as

austère[ostɛʀ] *adj* austere

austral, e[ɔstʀal] *adj* southern

Australie[ɔstʀali] *nf*: **l'~** Australia; **australien, ne** *adj* Australian ▷ *nm/f*: **Australien, ne** Australian

autant[otã] *adv* (*intensité*) so much; **je ne savais pas que tu la détestais ~** I didn't know you hated her so much; (*comparatif*): **~ (que)** as much (as); (*nombre*) as many (as); **~ (de)** so much (*ou* many); as much (*ou* many); **~ partir** we (*ou* you *etc*) may as well leave; **~ dire que ...** one might as well say that ...; **pour ~** for all that; **d'~ plus/mieux (que)** all the more/the better (since)

autel[otɛl] *nm* altar

auteur[otœʀ] *nm* author

authentique[otãtik] *adj* authentic, genuine

auto[oto] *nf* car

auto...: **autobiographie** *nf* autobiography;

autobronzant *nm* self-tanning cream (*or* lotion *etc*); **autobus** *nm* bus; **autocar** *nm* coach

autochtone[ɔtɔktɔn] *nm/f* native

auto...: **autocollant, e** *adj* self-adhesive; (*enveloppe*) self-seal ▷ *nm* sticker; **autocuiseur** *nm* pressure cooker; **autodéfense** *nf* self-defence; **autodidacte** *nm/f* self-taught person; **auto-école** *nf* driving school; **autographe** *nm* autograph

automate[ɔtɔmat] *nm* (*machine*) (automatic) machine

automatique[ɔtɔmatik] *adj* automatic ▷ *nm*: **l'~** direct dialling

automne[ɔtɔn] *nm* autumn (*BRIT*), fall (*US*)

automobile[ɔtɔmɔbil] *adj* motor *cpd*, car *cpd* ▷ *nf* (motor) car; **automobiliste** *nm/f* motorist

autonome[ɔtɔnɔm] *adj* autonomous; **autonomie** *nf* autonomy; (*Pol*) self-government, autonomy

autopsie[ɔtɔpsi] *nf* post-mortem (examination), autopsy

autoradio[otoʀadjo] *nm* car radio

autorisation[ɔtɔʀizasjɔ̃] *nf* permission, authorization; (*papiers*) permit

autorisé, e[ɔtɔʀize] *adj* (*opinion, sources*) authoritative

autoriser[ɔtɔʀize] *vt* to give permission for, authorize; (*fig*) to allow (of)

autoritaire[ɔtɔʀitɛʀ] *adj* authoritarian

autorité[ɔtɔʀite] *nf* authority; **faire ~** to be authoritative; **les ~s** the authorities

autoroute[otoʀut] *nf* motorway (*BRIT*), highway (*US*); **~ de l'information** (*Inform*) information superhighway

⬤ **AUTOROUTE**

⬤
⬤
⬤ Motorways in France, indicated by blue
⬤ road signs with the letter A followed by a
⬤ number, are toll roads. The speed limit is
⬤ 130 km/h (110 km/h when it is raining). At
⬤ the tollgate, the lanes marked 'réservé' and
⬤ with an orange 't' are reserved for people
⬤ who subscribe to 'télépéage', an electronic
⬤ payment system.

auto-stop[otostɔp] *nm*: **faire de l'~** to hitch-hike; **prendre qn en ~** to give sb a lift; **auto-stoppeur, -euse** *nm/f* hitch-hiker

autour[otuʀ] *adv* around; **~ de** around; **tout ~** all around

MOT-CLÉ

autre[otʀ] *adj* **1** (*différent*) other, different; **je préférerais un autre verre** I'd prefer another *ou* a different glass

2 (*supplémentaire*) other; **je voudrais un autre verre d'eau** I'd like another glass of water **3** : **autre chose** something else; **autre part** somewhere else; **d'autre part** on the other hand ▷ *pron* : **un autre** another (one); **nous/vous autres** us/you; **d'autres** others; **l'autre** the other (one); **les autres** the others; (*autrui*) others; **l'un et l'autre** both of them; **se détester l'un l'autre/les uns les autres** to hate each other *ou* one another; **d'une semaine à l'autre** from one week to the next; (*incessamment*) any week now; **entre autres** (*personnes*) among others; (*choses*) among other things

autrefois [otʀəfwa] *adv* in the past
autrement [otʀəmã] *adv* differently; (*d'une manière différente*) in another way; (*sinon*) otherwise; **~ dit** in other words
Autriche [otʀiʃ] *nf* : **l'~** Austria; **autrichien, ne** *adj* Austrian ▷ *nm/f* : **Autrichien, ne** Austrian
autruche [otʀyʃ] *nf* ostrich
aux [o] *prép* +*dét* = **à +les**
auxiliaire [ɔksiljɛʀ] *adj, nm/f* auxiliary
auxquelles [okɛl] *prép* +*pron* = **à +lesquelles**
auxquels [okɛl] *prép* +*pron* = **à +lesquels**
avalanche [avalɑ̃ʃ] *nf* avalanche
avaler [avale] *vt* to swallow
avance [avɑ̃s] *nf* (*de troupes etc*) advance; progress; (*d'argent*) advance; (*sur un concurrent*) lead; **avances** *nfpl* (*amoureuses*) advances; **(être) en ~** (to be) early; (*sur un programme*) (to be) ahead of schedule; **à l'~, d'~** in advance
avancé, e [avɑ̃se] *adj* advanced; (*travail*) well on, well under way
avancement [avɑ̃smɑ̃] *nm* (*professionnel*) promotion
avancer [avɑ̃se] *vi* to move forward, advance; (*projet, travail*) to make progress; (*montre, réveil*) to be fast; to gain ▷ *vt* to move forward, advance; (*argent*) to advance; (*montre, pendule*) to put forward; **s'avancer** *vi* to move forward, advance; (*fig*) to commit o.s.
avant [avɑ̃] *prép, adv* before ▷ *adj inv* : **siège/ roue ~** front seat/wheel ▷ *nm* (*d'un véhicule, bâtiment*) front; (*Sport: joueur*) forward; **~ qu'il (ne) parte** before he goes *ou* leaves; **~ de partir** before leaving; **~ tout** (*surtout*) above all; **à l'~** (*dans un véhicule*) in (the) front; **en ~** (*se pencher, tomber*) forward(s); **partir en ~** to go on ahead; **en ~ de** in front of
avantage [avɑ̃taʒ] *nm* advantage; **avantages sociaux** fringe benefits; **avantager** *vt* (*favoriser*) to favour; (*embellir*) to flatter; **avantageux, -euse** *adj* (*prix*) attractive
avant... : **avant-bras** *nm inv* forearm; **avant-coureur** *adj inv* : **signe avant-coureur** advance indication *ou* sign; **avant-dernier, -ière** *adj, nm/f* next to last, last but one; **avant- goût** *nm* foretaste; **avant-hier** *adv* the day before yesterday; **avant-première** *nf* (*de film*) preview; **avant-veille** *nf* : **l'avant-veille** two days before

avare [avaʀ] *adj* miserly, avaricious ▷ *nm/f* miser; **~ de** (*compliments etc*) sparing of
avec [avɛk] *prép* with; (*à l'égard de*) to(wards), with; **et ~ ça?** (*dans magasin*) anything else?
avenir [avniʀ] *nm* future; **à l'~** in future; **politicien/métier d'~** politician/job with prospects *ou* a future
aventure [avɑ̃tyʀ] *nf* adventure; (*amoureuse*) affair; **aventureux, -euse** *adj* adventurous, venturesome; (*projet*) risky, chancy
avenue [avny] *nf* avenue
avérer [aveʀe] : **s'avérer** *vb* +*attrib* to prove (to be)
averse [avɛʀs] *nf* shower
averti, e [avɛʀti] *adj* (well-)informed
avertir [avɛʀtiʀ] *vt* : **~ qn (de qch/que)** to warn sb (of sth/that); (*renseigner*) to inform sb (of sth/that); **avertissement** *nm* warning; **avertisseur** *nm* horn, siren
aveu, x [avø] *nm* confession
aveugle [avœgl] *adj* blind ▷ *nm/f* blind man/woman
aviation [avjasjɔ̃] *nf* aviation; (*sport*) flying; (*Mil*) air force
avide [avid] *adj* eager; (*péj*) greedy, grasping
avion [avjɔ̃] *nm* (*aero*)plane (BRIT), (air)plane (US); **aller (quelque part) en ~** to go (somewhere) by plane, fly (somewhere); **par ~** by airmail; **avion à réaction** jet (plane)
aviron [aviʀɔ̃] *nm* oar; (*sport*) : **l'~** rowing
avis [avi] *nm* opinion; (*notification*) notice; **à mon ~** in my opinion; **changer d'~** to change one's mind; **jusqu'à nouvel ~** until further notice
aviser [avize] *vt* (*informer*) : **~ qn de/que** to advise *ou* inform sb of/that ▷ *vi* to think about things, assess the situation; **nous ~ons sur place** we'll work something out once we're there; **s'~ de qch/que** to become suddenly aware of sth/that; **s'~ de faire** to take it into one's head to do
avocat, e [avɔka, at] *nm/f* (*Jur*) barrister (BRIT), lawyer ▷ *nm* (*Culin*) avocado (pear); **~ de la défense** counsel for the defence; **avocat général** assistant public prosecutor
avoine [avwan] *nf* oats *pl*

 MOT-CLÉ

avoir [avwaʀ] *nm* assets *pl*, resources *pl*; (*Comm*) credit
▷ *vt* **1** (*posséder*) to have; **elle a 2 enfants/une belle maison** she has (got) 2 children/a lovely

house; **il a les yeux bleus** he has (got) blue eyes; **vous avez du sel?** do you have any salt?; **avoir du courage/de la patience** to be brave/patient
2 (*âge, dimensions*) to be; **il a 3 ans** he is 3 (years old); **le mur a 3 mètres de haut** the wall is 3 metres high; *voir aussi* **faim**; **peur** *etc*
3 (*fam: duper*) to do, have; **on vous a eu!** (*dupé*) you've been done *ou* had!; (*fait une plaisanterie*) we *ou* they had you there
4: **en avoir après** *ou* **contre qn** to have a grudge against sb; **en avoir assez** to be fed up; **j'en ai pour une demi-heure** it'll take me half an hour
5 (*obtenir, attraper*) to get; **j'ai réussi à avoir mon train** I managed to get *ou* catch my train; **j'ai réussi à avoir le renseignement qu'il me fallait** I managed to get (hold of) the information I needed
6 (*éprouver*): **avoir de la peine** to be *ou* feel sad
▷ *vb aux* **1** to have; **avoir mangé/dormi** to have eaten/slept
2 (*avoir + à + infinitif*): **avoir à faire qch** to have to do sth; **vous n'avez qu'à lui demander** you only have to ask him
▷ *vb impers* **1**: **il y a** (+ *singulier*) there is; (+ *pluriel*) there are; **il y avait du café/des gâteaux** there was coffee/there were cakes; **qu'y-a-t-il?, qu'est-ce qu'il y a?** what's the matter?, what is it?; **il doit y avoir une explication** there must be an explanation; **il n'y a qu'à ...** we (*ou* you *etc*) will just have to ...; **il ne peut y en avoir qu'un** there can only be one
2 (*temporel*): **il y a 10 ans** 10 years ago; **il y a 10 ans/longtemps que je le sais** I've known it for 10 years/a long time; **il y a 10 ans qu'il est arrivé** it's 10 years since he arrived

avortement [avɔʀtəmɑ̃] *nm* abortion
avouer [avwe] *vt* (*crime, défaut*) to confess (to); **~ avoir fait/que** to admit *ou* confess to having done/that
avril [avʀil] *nm* April
axe [aks] *nm* axis; (*de roue etc*) axle; (*fig*) main line; **axe routier** main road, trunk road (*BRIT*), highway (*US*)
ayons *etc* [ɛjɔ̃] *vb voir* **avoir**

bâbord [babɔʀ] *nm*: **à ~** to port, on the port side
baby-foot [babifut] *nm* table football
bac [bak] *abr m* = **baccalauréat** ▷ *nm* (*récipient*) tub
baccalauréat [bakalɔʀea] *nm* high school diploma
bâcler [bakle] *vt* to botch (up)
baffe [baf] (*fam*) *nf* slap, clout
bafouiller [bafuje] *vi, vt* to stammer
bagage [baɡaʒ] *nm* piece of luggage; (*connaissances*) background, knowledge; **nos ~s ne sont pas arrivés** our luggage hasn't arrived; **bagage à main** piece of hand-luggage
bagarre [baɡaʀ] *nf* fight, brawl; **bagarrer: se bagarrer** *vi* to have a fight *ou* scuffle, fight
bagnole [baɲɔl] (*fam*) *nf* car
bague [baɡ] *nf* ring; **bague de fiançailles** engagement ring
baguette [baɡɛt] *nf* stick; (*cuisine chinoise*) chopstick; (*de chef d'orchestre*) baton; (*pain*) stick of (French) bread; **baguette magique** magic wand
baie [bɛ] *nf* (*Géo*) bay; (*fruit*) berry; **baie (vitrée)** picture window
baignade [bɛɲad] *nf* bathing; **"~ interdite"** "no bathing"
baigner [bɛɲe] *vt* (*bébé*) to bath; **se baigner** *vi* to have a swim, go swimming *ou* bathing;

baignoire nf bath(tub)

bail [baj, bo] (pl **baux**) nm lease

bâiller [baje] vi to yawn; (être ouvert) to gape

bain [bɛ̃] nm bath; **prendre un ~** to have a bath; **se mettre dans le ~** (fig) to get into it ou things; **bain de bouche** mouthwash; **bain moussant** bubble bath; **bain de soleil**: **prendre un bain de soleil** to sunbathe; **bain-marie** nm: **faire chauffer au bain-marie** (boîte etc) to immerse in boiling water

baiser [beze] nm kiss ▷ vt (main, front) to kiss; (fam!) to screw (!)

baisse [bɛs] nf fall, drop; **être en ~** to be falling, be declining

baisser [bese] vt to lower; (radio, chauffage) to turn down ▷ vi to fall, drop, go down; (vue, santé) to fail, dwindle; **se baisser** vi to bend down

bal [bal] nm dance; (grande soirée) ball; **bal costumé** fancy-dress ball

balade [balad] (fam) nf (à pied) walk, stroll; (en voiture) drive; **balader** (fam): **se balader** vi to go for a walk ou stroll; to go for a drive; **baladeur** nm personal stereo, Walkman®

balai [balɛ] nm broom, brush

balance [balɑ̃s] nf scales pl; (signe): **la B~** Libra; **balance commerciale** balance of trade

balancer [balɑ̃se] vt to swing; (fam: lancer) to fling, chuck; (: jeter) to chuck out; **se balancer** vi to swing, rock; **se ~ de** (fam) not to care about; **balançoire** nf swing; (sur pivot) seesaw

balayer [baleje] vt (feuilles etc) to sweep up, brush up; (pièce) to sweep; (objections) to sweep aside; (suj: radar) to scan; **balayeur, -euse** nm/f roadsweeper

balbutier [balbysje] vi, vt to stammer

balcon [balkɔ̃] nm balcony; (Théâtre) dress circle; **avez-vous une chambre avec ~?** do you have a room with a balcony?

Bâle [bal] n Basle, Basel

Baléares [baleaʀ] nfpl: **les ~** the Balearic Islands, the Balearics

baleine [balɛn] nf whale

balise [baliz] nf (Navig) beacon; (marker) buoy; (Aviat) runway light, beacon; (Auto, Ski) sign, marker; **baliser** vt to mark out (with lights etc)

balle [bal] nf (de fusil) bullet; (de sport) ball; (fam: franc) franc

ballerine [bal(ə)ʀin] nf (danseuse) ballet dancer; (chaussure) ballet shoe

ballet [balɛ] nm ballet

ballon [balɔ̃] nm (de sport) ball; (jouet, Aviat) balloon; **ballon de football** football

balnéaire [balneɛʀ] adj seaside cpd; **station ~** seaside resort

balustrade [balystʀad] nf railings pl, handrail

bambin [bɑ̃bɛ̃] nm little child

bambou [bɑ̃bu] nm bamboo

banal, e [banal] adj banal, commonplace; (péj) trite; **banalité** nf banality

banane [banan] nf banana; (sac) waist-bag, bum-bag

banc [bɑ̃] nm seat, bench; (de poissons) shoal; **banc d'essai** (fig) testing ground

bancaire [bɑ̃kɛʀ] adj banking; (chèque, carte) bank cpd

bancal, e [bɑ̃kal] adj wobbly

bandage [bɑ̃daʒ] nm bandage

bande [bɑ̃d] nf (de tissu etc) strip; (Méd) bandage; (motif) stripe; (magnétique etc) tape; (groupe) band; (: péj) bunch; **faire ~ à part** to keep to o.s.; **bande dessinée** comic strip; **bande sonore** sound track

bande-annonce [bɑ̃danɔ̃s] nf trailer

bandeau, x [bɑ̃do] nm headband; (sur les yeux) blindfold

bander [bɑ̃de] vt (blessure) to bandage; **~ les yeux à qn** to blindfold sb

bandit [bɑ̃di] nm bandit

bandoulière [bɑ̃duljɛʀ] nf: **en ~** (slung ou worn) across the shoulder

Bangladesh [bɑ̃ɡladɛʃ] nm: **le ~** Bangladesh

banlieue [bɑ̃ljø] nf suburbs pl; **lignes/ quartiers de ~** suburban lines/areas; **trains de ~** commuter trains

bannir [baniʀ] vt to banish

banque [bɑ̃k] nf bank; (activités) banking; **banque de données** data bank

banquet [bɑ̃kɛ] nm dinner; (d'apparat) banquet

banquette [bɑ̃kɛt] nf seat

banquier [bɑ̃kje] nm banker

banquise [bɑ̃kiz] nf ice field

baptême [batɛm] nm christening; baptism; **baptême de l'air** first flight

baptiser [batize] vt to baptize, christen

bar [baʀ] nm bar

baraque [baʀak] nf shed; (fam) house; (d'une fête foraine) stall, booth; **baraqué, e** (fam) adj well-built, hefty

barbare [baʀbaʀ] adj barbaric

barbe [baʀb] nf beard; **la ~!** (fam) damn it!; **quelle ~!** (fam) what a drag ou bore!; **à la ~ de qn** under sb's nose; **barbe à papa** candy-floss (BRIT), cotton candy (US)

barbelé [baʀbəle] adj, nm: **(fil de fer) ~** barbed wire no pl

barbiturique [baʀbityʀik] nm barbiturate

barbouiller [baʀbuje] vt to daub; **avoir l'estomac barbouillé** to feel queasy

barbu, e [baʀby] adj bearded

barder [baʀde] (fam) vi: **ça va ~** sparks will fly, things are going to get hot

barème [baʀɛm] nm (Scol) scale; (table de référence) table

baril [baʀi(l)] nm barrel; (poudre) keg

bariolé, e [baʀjɔle] adj gaudily-coloured

baromètre [baʀɔmɛtʀ] nm barometer

baron, ne [baʀɔ̃] nm/f baron(ess)

baroque [baʀɔk] adj (Art) baroque; (fig) weird

barque [baʀk] nf small boat

barquette [baʀkɛt] nf (pour repas) tray; (pour fruits) punnet

barrage [baʀaʒ] nm dam; (sur route) roadblock, barricade

barre [baʀ] nf bar; (Navig) helm; (écrite) line, stroke

barreau, x [baʀo] nm bar; (Jur): **le ~** the Bar

barrer [baʀe] vt (route etc) to block; (mot) to cross out; (chèque) to cross (BRIT); (Navig) to steer; **se barrer** (fam) to clear off

barrette [baʀɛt] nf (pour cheveux) (hair) slide (BRIT) ou clip (US)

barricader [baʀikade]: **se barricader** vi to barricade o.s.

barrière [baʀjɛʀ] nf fence; (obstacle) barrier; (porte) gate

barrique [baʀik] nf barrel, cask

bar-tabac [baʀtaba] nm bar (which sells tobacco and stamps)

bas, basse [ba, bas] adj low ▷ nm bottom, lower part; (vêtement) stocking ▷ adv low; (parler) softly; **au ~ mot** at the lowest estimate; **en ~** down below; (d'une liste, d'un mur etc) at/to the bottom; (dans une maison) downstairs; **en ~ de** at the bottom of; **un enfant en ~ âge** a young child; **à ~ ...!** down with ...!

bas-côté [bakote] nm (de route) verge (BRIT), shoulder (US)

basculer [baskyle] vi to fall over, topple (over); (benne) to tip up ▷ vt (contenu) to tip out; (benne) to tip up

base [baz] nf base; (Pol) rank and file; (fondement, principe) basis; **de ~** basic; **à ~ de café** etc coffee etc -based; **base de données** database; **baser** vt to base; **se baser sur** vt (preuves) to base one's argument on

bas-fond [bafɔ̃] nm (Navig) shallow; **bas-fonds** nmpl (fig) dregs

basilic [bazilik] nm (Culin) basil

basket [baskɛt] nm trainer (BRIT), sneaker (US); (aussi: **~-ball**) basketball

basque [bask] adj Basque ▷ nm/f: **B~** Basque; **le Pays Basque** the Basque Country

basse [bas] adj voir **bas** ▷ nf (Mus) bass; **basse-cour** nf farmyard

bassin [basɛ̃] nm (pièce d'eau) pond, pool; (de fontaine;: Géo) basin; (Anat) pelvis; (portuaire) dock

bassine [basin] nf (ustensile) basin; (contenu) bowl(ful)

basson [basɔ̃] nm bassoon

bat [ba] vb voir **battre**

bataille [bataj] nf (Mil) battle; (rixe) fight; **elle avait les cheveux en ~** her hair was a mess

bateau, x [bato] nm boat, ship; **bateau-mouche** nm passenger pleasure boat (on the Seine)

bâti, e [bɑti] adj: **bien ~** well-built; **terrain ~** piece of land that has been built on

bâtiment [bɑtimɑ̃] nm building; (Navig) ship, vessel; (industrie) building trade

bâtir [bɑtiʀ] vt to build

bâtisse [bɑtis] nf building

bâton [bɑtɔ̃] nm stick; **parler à ~s rompus** to chat about this and that

bats [ba] vb voir **battre**

battement [batmɑ̃] nm (de cœur) beat; (intervalle) interval; **10 minutes de ~** 10 minutes to spare

batterie [batʀi] nf (Mil, Élec) battery; (Mus) drums pl, drum kit; **batterie de cuisine** pots and pans pl, kitchen utensils pl

batteur [batœʀ] nm (Mus) drummer; (appareil) whisk

battre [batʀ] vt to beat; (blé) to thresh; (passer au peigne fin) to scour; (cartes) to shuffle ▷ vi (cœur) to beat; (volets etc) to bang, rattle; **se battre** vi to fight; **~ la mesure** to beat time; **~ son plein** to be at its height, be going full swing; **~ des mains** to clap one's hands

baume [bom] nm balm

bavard, e [bavaʀ, aʀd] adj (very) talkative; gossipy; **bavarder** vi to chatter; (commérer) to gossip; (divulguer un secret) to blab

baver [bave] vi to dribble; (chien) to slobber; **en ~** (fam) to have a hard time (of it)

bavoir [bavwaʀ] nm bib

bavure [bavyʀ] nf smudge; (fig) hitch; (policière etc) blunder

bazar [bazaʀ] nm general store; (fam) jumble; **bazarder** (fam) vt to chuck out

BCBG sigle adj (= bon chic bon genre) preppy, smart and trendy

BD sigle f = **bande dessinée**

bd abr = **boulevard**

béant, e [beɑ̃, ɑ̃t] adj gaping

beau, bel, belle [bo, bɛl] (mpl **~x**) adj beautiful, lovely; (homme) handsome; (femme) beautiful ▷ adv: **il fait ~** the weather's fine ▷ nm: **faire le ~** (chien) to sit up and beg; **un ~ jour** one (fine) day; **de plus belle** more than ever, even more; **on a ~ essayer** however hard we try; **bel et bien** well and truly; **le plus ~ c'est que ...** the best of it is that ...

 MOT-CLÉ

beaucoup [boku] adv **1** a lot; **il boit beaucoup** he drinks a lot; **il ne boit pas beaucoup** he doesn't drink much ou a lot **2** (suivi de plus, trop etc) much, a lot; **il est beaucoup plus grand** he is much ou a lot taller; **c'est beaucoup plus cher** it's a lot ou much more expensive; **il a beaucoup plus de temps que moi** he has much *ou* a lot more time than me; **il y a beaucoup plus de touristes ici** there are a lot *ou* many more tourists here; **beaucoup trop vite** much too fast; **il fume beaucoup trop** he smokes far too much

3: **beaucoup de** (*nombre*) many, a lot of; (*quantité*) a lot of; **beaucoup d'étudiants/de touristes** a lot of *ou* many students/tourists; **beaucoup de courage** a lot of courage; **il n'a pas beaucoup d'argent** he hasn't got much *ou* at lot of money

4: **de beaucoup** by far

beau...: **beau-fils** nm son-in-law; (*remariage*) stepson; **beau-frère** nm brother-in-law; **beau-père** nm father-in-law; (*remariage*) stepfather

beauté [bote] nf beauty; **de toute ~** beautiful; **finir qch en ~** to complete sth brilliantly

beaux-arts [bozar] nmpl fine arts

beaux-parents [boparã] nmpl wife's/husband's family, in-laws

bébé [bebe] nm baby

bec [bɛk] nm beak, bill; (*de théière*) spout; (*de casserole*) lip; (*fam*) mouth; **bec de gaz** (street) gaslamp

bêche [bɛʃ] nf spade; **bêcher** vt to dig

bedaine [bədɛn] nf paunch

bedonnant, e [bədɔnã, ãt] adj potbellied

bée [be] adj: **bouche ~** gaping

bégayer [begeje] vt, vi to stammer

beige [bɛʒ] adj beige

beignet [bɛɲɛ] nm fritter

bel [bɛl] adj voir **beau**

bêler [bele] vi to bleat

belette [bəlɛt] nf weasel

belge [bɛlʒ] adj Belgian ▷ nm/f: **B~** Belgian

Belgique [bɛlʒik] nf: **la ~** Belgium

bélier [belje] nm ram; (*signe*): **le B~** Aries

belle [bɛl] adj voir **beau** ▷ nf (*Sport*): **la ~** the decider; **belle-fille** nf daughter-in-law; (*remariage*) stepdaughter; **belle-mère** nf mother-in-law; stepmother; **belle-sœur** nf sister-in-law

belvédère [bɛlvedɛr] nm panoramic viewpoint (*or small building there*)

bémol [bemɔl] nm (*Mus*) flat

bénédiction [benediksjɔ̃] nf blessing

bénéfice [benefis] nm (*Comm*) profit; (*avantage*) benefit; **bénéficier**: **bénéficier de** vt to enjoy; (*situation*) to benefit by *ou* from; **bénéfique** adj beneficial

Benelux [benelyks] nm: **le ~** Benelux, the Benelux countries

bénévole [benevɔl] adj voluntary, unpaid

bénin, -igne [benɛ̃, iɲ] adj minor, mild; (*tumeur*) benign

bénir [benir] vt to bless; **bénit, e** adj

consecrated; **eau bénite** holy water

benne [bɛn] nf skip; (*de téléphérique*) (cable) car; **benne à ordures** (*amovible*) skip

béquille [bekij] nf crutch; (*de bicyclette*) stand

berceau, x [bɛrso] nm cradle, crib

bercer [bɛrse] vt to rock, cradle; (*suj: musique etc*) to lull; **~ qn de** (*promesses etc*) to delude sb with; **berceuse** nf lullaby

béret [bere] nm (*aussi*: **~ basque**) beret

berge [bɛrʒ] nf bank

berger, -ère [bɛrʒe, ɛr] nm/f shepherd(-ess); **berger allemand** alsatian (*BRIT*), German shepherd

Berlin [bɛrlɛ̃] n Berlin

Bermudes [bɛrmyd] nfpl: **les (îles) ~** Bermuda

Berne [bɛrn(ə)] n Bern

berner [bɛrne] vt to fool

besogne [bəzɔɲ] nf work no pl, job

besoin [bəzwɛ̃] nm need; **avoir ~ de qch/faire qch** to need sth/to do sth; **au ~** if need be; **le ~** (*pauvreté*) need, want; **être dans le ~** to be in need *ou* want; **faire ses ~s** to relieve o.s.

bestiole [bɛstjɔl] nf (tiny) creature

bétail [betaj] nm livestock, cattle pl

bête [bɛt] nf animal; (*bestiole*) insect, creature ▷ adj stupid, silly; **il cherche la petite ~** he's being pernickety *ou* over fussy; **bête noire** pet hate; **bête sauvage** wild beast *ou* animal

bêtise [betiz] nf stupidity; (*action*) stupid thing (to say *ou* do)

béton [betɔ̃] nm concrete; **(en) ~** (*alibi, argument*) cast iron; **béton armé** reinforced concrete

betterave [bɛtrav] nf beetroot (*BRIT*), beet (*US*); **betterave sucrière** sugar beet

Beur [bœr] nm/f person of North African origin living in France

beurre [bœr] nm butter; **beurrer** vt to butter; **beurrier** nm butter dish

biais [bjɛ] nm (*moyen*) device, expedient; (*aspect*) angle; **en ~, de ~** (*obliquement*) at an angle; **par le ~ de** by means of

bibelot [biblo] nm trinket, curio

biberon [bibrɔ̃] nm (feeding) bottle; **nourrir au ~** to bottle-feed

bible [bibl] nf bible

biblio... [bibl] *préfixe*: **bibliobus** nm mobile library van; **bibliothécaire** nm/f librarian; **bibliothèque** nf library; (*meuble*) bookcase

bic® [bik] nm Biro®

bicarbonate [bikarbɔnat] nm: **~ (de soude)** bicarbonate of soda

biceps [bisɛps] nm biceps

biche [biʃ] nf doe

bicolore [bikɔlɔr] adj two-coloured

bicoque [bikɔk] (*péj*) nf shack

bicyclette [bisiklɛt] nf bicycle

bidet [bidɛ] nm bidet
bidon [bidɔ̃] nm can ▷ adj inv (fam) phoney
bidonville [bidɔ̃vil] nm shanty town
bidule [bidyl] (fam) nm thingumajig

 MOT-CLÉ

bien [bjɛ̃] nm **1** (avantage, profit): **faire du
bien à qn** to do sb good; **dire du bien de** to
speak well of; **c'est pour son bien** it's for his
own good
2 (possession, patrimoine) possession, property;
son bien le plus précieux his most treasured
possession; **avoir du bien** to have property;
biens (de consommation etc) (consumer
etc) goods
3 (moral): **le bien** good; **distinguer le bien du
mal** to tell good from evil
▷ adv **1** (de façon satisfaisante) well; **elle
travaille/mange bien** she works/eats well;
croyant bien faire, je/il ... thinking I/he
was doing the right thing, I/he ...; **tiens-toi
bien!** (assieds-toi correctement) sit up straight!;
(debout) stand up straight!; (sois sage) behave
yourself!; (prépare-toi) wait for it!; **c'est bien
fait!** it serves him (ou her etc) right!
2 (valeur intensive) quite; **bien jeune** quite
young; **bien assez** quite enough; **bien mieux**
(very) much better; **j'espère bien y aller** I do
hope to go; **je veux bien le faire** (concession)
I'm quite willing to do it; **il faut bien le faire** it
has to be done; **Paul est bien venu, n'est-ce
pas?** Paul did come, didn't he?; **où peut-il bien
être passé?** where can he have got to?
3 (beaucoup): **bien du temps/des gens** quite a
time/a number of people
4 (au moins) at least; **cela fait bien deux ans
que je ne l'ai pas vu** I haven't seen him for at
least ou a good two years
▷ adj inv **1** (en bonne forme, à l'aise): **je me sens
bien** I feel fine; **je ne me sens pas bien** I don't
feel well; **on est bien dans ce fauteuil** this
chair is very comfortable
2 (joli, beau) good-looking; **tu es bien dans
cette robe** you look good in that dress
3 (satisfaisant) good; **elle est bien, cette
maison/secrétaire** it's a good house/she's a
good secretary; **c'est bien?** is that ou it O.K.?;
c'est très bien (comme ça) it's fine (like that)
4 (moralement) right; (: personne) good, nice;
(respectable) respectable; **ce n'est pas bien
de ...** it's not right to ...; **elle est bien, cette
femme** she's a nice woman, she's a good sort;
des gens bien respectable people
5 (en bons termes): **être bien avec qn** to be on
good terms with sb
▷ préfixe: **bien-aimé, e** adj, nm/f beloved; **bien-
être** nm well-being; **bienfaisance** nf charity;
bienfait nm act of generosity, benefaction;

(de la science etc) benefit; **bienfaiteur, -trice**
nm/f benefactor/benefactress; **bien-fondé**
nm soundness; **bien que** conj (al)though;
bien sûr adv certainly

bientôt [bjɛ̃to] adv soon; **à ~** see you soon
bienveillant, e [bjɛ̃vɛjɑ̃, ɑ̃t] adj kindly
bienvenu, e [bjɛ̃vny] adj welcome;
bienvenue nf: **souhaiter la bienvenue à** to
welcome; **bienvenue à** welcome to
bière [bjɛʀ] nf (boisson) beer; (cercueil) bier;
bière blonde lager; **bière brune** brown ale
(BRIT), dark beer (US); **bière (à la) pression**
draught beer
bifteck [biftɛk] nm steak
bigorneau, x [bigɔʀno] nm winkle
bigoudi [bigudi] nm curler
bijou, x [biʒu] nm jewel; **bijouterie** nf
jeweller's (shop); **bijoutier, -ière** nm/f jeweller
bikini [bikini] nm bikini
bilan [bilɑ̃] nm (fig) (net) outcome; (: de
victimes) toll; (Comm) balance sheet(s); **un ~
de santé** a (medical) checkup; **faire le ~ de**
to assess, review; **déposer son ~** to file a
bankruptcy statement
bile [bil] nf bile; **se faire de la ~** (fam) to worry
o.s. sick
bilieux, -euse [biljø, øz] adj bilious; (fig:
colérique) testy
bilingue [bilɛ̃g] adj bilingual
billard [bijaʀ] nm (jeu) billiards sg; (table)
billiard table
bille [bij] nf (gén) ball; (du jeu de billes) marble
billet [bijɛ] nm (aussi: **~ de banque**)
(bank)note; (de cinéma, de bus etc) ticket;
(courte lettre) note; **billet électronique** e-
ticket; **billetterie** nf ticket office; (distributeur)
ticket machine; (Banque) cash dispenser
billion [biljɔ̃] nm billion (BRIT), trillion (US)
bimensuel, le [bimɑ̃sɥɛl] adj bimonthly
bio [bjo] adj inv organic
bio... [bjo] préfixe bio...; **biochimie** nf
biochemistry; **biographie** nf biography;
biologie nf biology; **biologique** adj
biological; (produits, aliments) organic;
biométrie nf biometrics; **biotechnologie**
nf biotechnology; **bioterrorisme** nm
bioterrorism
Birmanie [biʀmani] nf Burma
bis [bis] adv: **12 ~** 12a ou A ▷ excl, nm encore
biscotte [biskɔt] nf toasted bread (sold in
packets)
biscuit [biskɥi] nm biscuit (BRIT), cookie (US)
bise [biz] nf (fam: baiser) kiss; (vent) North
wind; **grosses ~s (de)** (sur lettre) love and
kisses (from)
bisexuel, le [bisɛksɥɛl] adj bisexual
bisou [bizu] (fam) nm kiss
bissextile [bisɛkstil] adj: **année ~** leap year

bistro(t) [bistʁo] nm bistro, café

bitume [bitym] nm asphalt

bizarre [bizaʁ] adj strange, odd

blague [blag] nf (propos) joke; (farce) trick; **sans ~!** no kidding!; **blaguer** vi to joke

blaireau, x [blɛʁo] nm (Zool) badger; (brosse) shaving brush

blâme [blɑm] nm blame; (sanction) reprimand; **blâmer** vt to blame

blanc, blanche [blɑ̃, blɑ̃ʃ] adj white; (non imprimé) blank ▷ nm/f white, white man(-woman) ▷ nm (couleur) white; (espace non écrit) blank; (aussi: **~ d'œuf**) (egg-)white; (aussi: **~ de poulet**) breast, white meat; (aussi: **vin ~**) white wine; **~ cassé** off-white; **chèque en ~** blank cheque; **à ~** (chauffer) white-hot; (tirer, charger) with blanks; **blanche** nf (Mus) minim (BRIT), half-note (US); **blancheur** nf whiteness

blanchir [blɑ̃ʃiʁ] vt (gén) to whiten; (linge) to launder; (Culin) to blanch; (fig: disculper) to clear ▷ vi (cheveux) to go white; **blanchisserie** nf laundry

blason [blazɔ̃] nm coat of arms

blasphème [blasfɛm] nm blasphemy

blazer [blazɛʁ] nm blazer

blé [ble] nm wheat; **blé noir** buckwheat

bled [blɛd] nm (péj) hole

blême [blɛm] adj pale

blessé, e [blese] adj injured ▷ nm/f injured person, casualty

blesser [blese] vt to injure; (délibérément) to wound; (offenser) to hurt; **se blesser** to injure o.s.; **se ~ au pied** to injure one's foot; **blessure** nf (accidentelle) injury; (intentionnelle) wound

bleu, e [blø] adj blue; (bifteck) very rare ▷ nm (couleur) blue; (contusion) bruise; (vêtement: aussi: **~s**) overalls pl; (fromage) blue cheese; **bleu marine** navy blue; **bleuet** nm cornflower

bloc [blɔk] nm (de pierre etc) block; (de papier à lettres) pad; (ensemble) group, block; **serré à ~** tightened right down; **en ~** as a whole; **bloc opératoire** operating ou theatre block; **blocage** nm (des prix) freezing; (Psych) hang-up; **bloc-notes** nm note pad

blog, blogue [blɔg] nm blog; **bloguer** vi to blog

blond, e [blɔ̃, blɔ̃d] adj fair, blond; (sable, blés) golden

bloquer [blɔke] vt (passage) to block; (pièce mobile) to jam; (crédits, compte) to freeze

blottir [blɔtiʁ]: **se blottir** vi to huddle up

blouse [bluz] nf overall

blouson [bluzɔ̃] nm blouson jacket; **blouson noir** (fig) ≈ rocker

bluff [blœf] nm bluff

bobine [bɔbin] nf reel; (Élec) coil

bobo [bobo] abr m/f = bourgeois bohème (fam) boho

bocal, -aux [bɔkal, o] nm jar

bock [bɔk] nm glass of beer

bœuf [bœf] nm ox; (Culin) beef

bof [bɔf] (fam) excl don't care!; (pas terrible) nothing special

bohémien, ne [bɔemjɛ̃, -ɛn] nm/f gipsy

boire [bwaʁ] vt to drink; (s'imprégner de) to soak up; **~ un coup** (fam) to have a drink

bois [bwa] nm wood; **de ~, en ~** wooden; **boisé, e** adj woody, wooded

boisson [bwasɔ̃] nf drink

boîte [bwat] nf box; (fam: entreprise) firm; **aliments en ~** canned ou tinned (BRIT) foods; **boîte à gants** glove compartment; **boîte à ordures** dustbin (BRIT), trashcan (US); **boîte aux lettres** letter box; **boîte d'allumettes** box of matches; (vide) matchbox; **boîte de conserves** can ou tin (BRIT) of food; **boîte (de nuit)** night club; **boîte de vitesses** gear box; **boîte postale** PO Box; **boîte vocale** (Tél) voice mail

boiter [bwate] vi to limp; (fig: raisonnement) to be shaky

boîtier [bwatje] nm case

boive etc [bwav] vb voir **boire**

bol [bɔl] nm bowl; **un ~ d'air** a breath of fresh air; **j'en ai ras le ~** (fam) I'm fed up with this; **avoir du ~** (fam) to be lucky

bombarder [bɔ̃baʁde] vt to bomb; **~ qn de** (cailloux, lettres) to bombard sb with

bombe [bɔ̃b] nf bomb; (atomiseur) (aerosol) spray

⬤ **MOT-CLÉ**

bon, bonne [bɔ̃, bɔn] adj **1** (agréable, satisfaisant) good; **un bon repas/restaurant** a good meal/restaurant; **être bon en maths** to be good at maths (BRIT) ou math (US)

2 (charitable): **être bon (envers)** to be good (to)

3 (correct) right; **le bon numéro/moment** the right number/moment

4 (souhaits): **bon anniversaire!** happy birthday!; **bon voyage!** have a good trip!; **bonne chance!** good luck!; **bonne année!** happy New Year!; **bonne nuit!** good night!

5 (approprié, apte): **bon à/pour** fit to/for; **à quoi bon?** what's the use?

6: **bon enfant** adj inv accommodating, easy-going; **bonne femme** (péj) woman; **de bonne heure** early; **bon marché** adj inv, adv cheap; **bon mot** witticism; **bon sens** common sense; **bon vivant** jovial chap; **bonnes œuvres** charitable works, charities

▷ nm **1** (billet) voucher; (aussi: **bon cadeau**) gift voucher; **bon d'essence** petrol coupon; **bon du Trésor** Treasury bond

2: **avoir du bon** to have its good points; **pour**

de bon for good
▷ *adv*: **il fait bon** it's *ou* the weather is fine;
sentir bon to smell good; **tenir bon** to stand
firm
▷ *excl* good!; **ah bon?** really?; **bon, je reste**
right then, I'll stay; *voir aussi* **bonne**

bonbon[bɔ̃bɔ̃] *nm* (boiled) sweet
bond[bɔ̃] *nm* leap; **faire un ~** to leap in the air
bondé, e[bɔ̃de] *adj* packed (full)
bondir[bɔ̃diʀ] *vi* to leap
bonheur[bɔnœʀ] *nm* happiness; **porter ~ (à
qn)** to bring (sb) luck; **au petit ~** haphazardly;
par ~ fortunately
bonhomme[bɔnɔm] (*pl* **bonshommes**) *nm*
fellow; **bonhomme de neige** snowman
bonjour[bɔ̃ʒuʀ] *excl, nm* hello; (*selon l'heure*)
good morning/afternoon; **c'est simple
comme ~!** it's easy as pie!
bonne[bɔn] *adj voir* **bon** ▷ *nf* (*domestique*)
maid
bonnet[bɔnɛ] *nm* hat; (*de soutien-gorge*) cup;
bonnet de bain bathing cap
bonsoir[bɔ̃swaʀ] *excl* good evening
bonté[bɔ̃te] *nf* kindness *no pl*
bonus[bɔnys] *nm* no-claims bonus; (*de DVD*)
extras *pl*
bord[bɔʀ] *nm* (*de table, verre, falaise*) edge;
(*de rivière, lac*) bank; (*de route*) side; **(monter)
à ~** (to go) on board; **le commandant de/les
hommes du ~** the ship's master/crew; **au ~ de
la mer** at the seaside; **au ~ de la route** at the
roadside; **être au ~ des larmes** to be on the
verge of tears
bordeaux[bɔʀdo] *nm* Bordeaux (wine) ▷ *adj
inv* maroon
bordel[bɔʀdɛl] *nm* brothel; (*fam!*) bloody
mess (!)
border[bɔʀde] *vt* (*être le long de*) to line; (*qn
dans son lit*) to tuck up; (*garnir*): **~ qch de** to
edge sth with
bordure[bɔʀdyʀ] *nf* border; **en ~ de** on the
edge of
borne[bɔʀn] *nf* boundary stone; (*aussi:
~ kilométrique*) kilometre-marker,
≈ milestone; **bornes** *nfpl* (*fig*) limits; **dépasser
les ~s** to go too far
borné, e[bɔʀne] *adj* (*personne*) narrow-
minded
borner[bɔʀne] *vt*: **se ~ à faire** (*se contenter de*)
to content o.s. with doing; (*se limiter à*) to limit
o.s. to doing
bosniaque[bɔsnjak] *adj* Bosnian ▷ *nm/f*:
B~ Bosnian
Bosnie-Herzégovine[bɔsniɛʀzegɔvin] *nf*
Bosnia-Herzegovina
bosquet[bɔskɛ] *nm* grove
bosse[bɔs] *nf* (*de terrain etc*) bump; (*enflure*)

lump; (*du bossu, du chameau*) hump; **avoir la
~ des maths** *etc* (*fam*) to have a gift for maths
etc; **il a roulé sa ~** (*fam*) he's been around
bosser[bɔse] (*fam*) *vi* (*travailler*) to work;
(*travailler dur*) to slave (away)
bossu, e[bɔsy] *nm/f* hunchback
botanique[bɔtanik] *nf* botany ▷ *adj*
botanic(al)
botte[bɔt] *nf* (*soulier*) (high) boot; (*gerbe*): **~ de
paille** bundle of straw; **botte de radis/
d'asperges** bunch of radishes/asparagus;
bottes de caoutchouc wellington boots
bottin[bɔtɛ̃] *nm* directory
bottine[bɔtin] *nf* ankle boot
bouc[buk] *nm* goat; (*barbe*) goatee; **bouc
émissaire** scapegoat
boucan[bukɑ̃] (*fam*) *nm* din, racket
bouche[buʃ] *nf* mouth; **faire du ~ à ~ à qn**
to give sb the kiss of life *ou* mouth-to-mouth
resuscitation (*BRIT*); **rester ~ bée** to stand
open-mouthed; **bouche d'égout** manhole;
bouche d'incendie fire hydrant; **bouche de
métro** métro entrance
bouché, e[buʃe] *adj* (*flacon etc*) stoppered;
(*temps, ciel*) overcast; (*péj fam: personne*) thick
(*fam*); **c'est un secteur ~** there's no future in
that area; **avoir le nez ~** to have a blocked(-
up) nose; **l'évier est ~** the sink's blocked
bouchée[buʃe] *nf* mouthful; **bouchées à la
reine** chicken vol-au-vents
boucher, -ère[buʃe] *nm/f* butcher ▷ *vt* (*trou*)
to fill up; (*obstruer*) to block (up); **se boucher**
vi (*tuyau etc*) to block up, get blocked up; **j'ai
le nez bouché** my nose is blocked; **se ~ le nez**
to hold one's nose; **boucherie** *nf* butcher's
(shop); (*fig*) slaughter
bouchon[buʃɔ̃] *nm* stopper; (*de tube*) top; (*en
liège*) cork; (*fig: embouteillage*) holdup; (*Pêche*)
float
boucle[bukl] *nf* (*forme, figure*) loop; (*objet*)
buckle; **boucle (de cheveux)** curl; **boucle
d'oreille** earring
bouclé, e[bukle] *adj* (*cheveux*) curly
boucler[bukle] *vt* (*fermer: ceinture etc*) to
fasten; (*terminer*) to finish off; (*fam: enfermer*) to
shut away; (*quartier*) to seal off ▷ *vi* to curl
bouder[bude] *vi* to sulk ▷ *vt* to stay away
from
boudin[budɛ̃] *nm*: **~ (noir)** black pudding;
boudin blanc white pudding
boue[bu] *nf* mud
bouée[bwe] *nf* buoy; **bouée (de sauvetage)**
lifebuoy
boueux, -euse[bwø, øz] *adj* muddy
bouffe[buf] (*fam*) *nf* grub (*fam*), food
bouffée[bufe] *nf* (*de cigarette*) puff; **une ~
d'air pur** a breath of fresh air; **bouffée de
chaleur** hot flush (*BRIT*) *ou* flash (*US*)
bouffer[bufe] (*fam*) *vi* to eat

bouffi, e [bufi] *adj* swollen
bouger [buʒe] *vi* to move; *(dent etc)* to be loose; *(s'activer)* to get moving ▷ *vt* to move; **les prix/les couleurs n'ont pas bougé** prices/colours haven't changed
bougie [buʒi] *nf* candle; *(Auto)* spark(ing) plug
bouillabaisse [bujabɛs] *nf type of fish soup*
bouillant, e [bujɑ̃, ɑ̃t] *adj (qui bout)* boiling; *(très chaud)* boiling (hot)
bouillie [buji] *nf (de bébé)* cereal; **en ~** *(fig)* crushed
bouillir [bujiʀ] *vi, vt* to boil; **~ d'impatience** to seethe with impatience
bouilloire [bujwaʀ] *nf* kettle
bouillon [bujɔ̃] *nm (Culin)* stock *no pl*; **bouillonner** *vi* to bubble; *(fig: idées)* to bubble up
bouillotte [bujɔt] *nf* hot-water bottle
boulanger, -ère [bulɑ̃ʒe, ɛʀ] *nm/f* baker; **boulangerie** *nf* bakery
boule [bul] *nf (gén)* ball; *(de pétanque)* bowl; **boule de neige** snowball
boulette [bulɛt] *nf (de viande)* meatball
boulevard [bulvaʀ] *nm* boulevard
bouleversement [bulvɛʀsəmɑ̃] *nm* upheaval
bouleverser [bulvɛʀse] *vt (émouvoir)* to overwhelm; *(causer du chagrin)* to distress; *(pays, vie)* to disrupt; *(papiers, objets)* to turn upside down
boulimie [bulimi] *nf* bulimia
boulimique [bulimik] *adj* bulimic
boulon [bulɔ̃] *nm* bolt
boulot, te [bulo, ɔt] *adj* plump, tubby ▷ *nm (fam: travail)* work
boum [bum] *nm* bang ▷ *nf (fam)* party
bouquet [bukɛ] *nm (de fleurs)* bunch (of flowers), bouquet; *(de persil etc)* bunch; **c'est le ~!** *(fam)* that takes the biscuit!
bouquin [bukɛ̃] *(fam) nm* book; **bouquiner** *(fam) vi* to read
bourdon [buʀdɔ̃] *nm* bumblebee
bourg [buʀ] *nm* small market town
bourgeois, e [buʀʒwa, waz] *(péj) adj* ≈ (upper) middle class; **bourgeoisie** *nf* ≈ upper middle classes *pl*
bourgeon [buʀʒɔ̃] *nm* bud
Bourgogne [buʀgɔɲ] *nf*: **la ~** Burgundy ▷ *nm*: **bourgogne** burgundy (wine)
bourguignon, ne [buʀgiɲɔ̃, ɔn] *adj* of *ou* from Burgundy, Burgundian
bourrasque [buʀask] *nf* squall
bourratif, -ive [buʀatif, iv] *(fam) adj* filling, stodgy *(pej)*
bourré, e [buʀe] *adj (fam: ivre)* plastered, tanked up *(BRIT)*; *(rempli)*: **~ de** crammed full of
bourrer [buʀe] *vt (pipe)* to fill; *(poêle)* to pack; *(valise)* to cram (full)
bourru, e [buʀy] *adj* surly, gruff

bourse [buʀs] *nf (subvention)* grant; *(porte-monnaie)* purse; **la B~** the Stock Exchange
bous [bu] *vb voir* **bouillir**
bousculade [buskylad] *nf (hâte)* rush; *(cohue)* crush; **bousculer** *vt (heurter)* to knock into; *(fig)* to push, rush
boussole [busɔl] *nf* compass
bout [bu] *vb voir* **bouillir** ▷ *nm* bit; *(d'un bâton etc)* tip; *(d'une ficelle, table, rue, période)* end; **au ~ de** at the end of, after; **pousser qn à ~** to push sb to the limit; **venir à ~ de** to manage to finish; **à ~ portant** (at) point-blank (range)
bouteille [butɛj] *nf* bottle; *(de gaz butane)* cylinder
boutique [butik] *nf* shop
bouton [butɔ̃] *nm* button; *(sur la peau)* spot; *(Bot)* bud; **boutonner** *vt* to button up; **boutonnière** *nf* buttonhole; **bouton-pression** *nm* press stud
bovin, e [bɔvɛ̃, in] *adj* bovine; **bovins** *nmpl* cattle *pl*
bowling [bulin] *nm* (tenpin) bowling; *(salle)* bowling alley
boxe [bɔks] *nf* boxing
BP *abr* = **boîte postale**
bracelet [bʀaslɛ] *nm* bracelet
braconnier [bʀakɔnje] *nm* poacher
brader [bʀade] *vt* to sell off; **braderie** *nf* cut-price shop/stall
braguette [bʀagɛt] *nf* fly *ou* flies *pl* (BRIT), zipper (US)
braise [bʀɛz] *nf* embers *pl*
brancard [bʀɑ̃kaʀ] *nm (civière)* stretcher; **brancardier** *nm* stretcher-bearer
branche [bʀɑ̃ʃ] *nf* branch
branché, e [bʀɑ̃ʃe] *(fam) adj* trendy
brancher [bʀɑ̃ʃe] *vt* to connect (up); *(en mettant la prise)* to plug in
brandir [bʀɑ̃diʀ] *vt* to brandish
braquer [bʀake] *vi (Auto)* to turn (the wheel) ▷ *vt (revolver etc)*: **~ qch sur** to aim sth at, point sth at; *(mettre en colère)*: **~ qn** to put sb's back up
bras [bʀa] *nm* arm; **~ dessus, ~ dessous** arm in arm; **se retrouver avec qch sur les ~** *(fam)* to be landed with sth; **bras droit** *(fig)* right hand man
brassard [bʀasaʀ] *nm* armband
brasse [bʀas] *nf (nage)* breast-stroke; **brasse papillon** butterfly (stroke)
brassée [bʀase] *nf* armful
brasser [bʀase] *vt* to mix; **~ l'argent/les affaires** to handle a lot of money/business
brasserie [bʀasʀi] *nf (restaurant)* café-restaurant; *(usine)* brewery
brave [bʀav] *adj (courageux)* brave; *(bon, gentil)* good, kind
braver [bʀave] *vt* to defy
bravo [bʀavo] *excl* bravo ▷ *nm* cheer

bravoure [bravur] nf bravery
break [brɛk] nm (Auto) estate car
brebis [brəbi] nf ewe; **brebis galeuse** black sheep
bredouiller [brəduje] vi, vt to mumble, stammer
bref, brève [brɛf, ɛv] adj short, brief ▷ adv in short; **d'un ton ~** sharply, curtly; **en ~** in short, in brief
Brésil [brezil] nm Brazil
Bretagne [brətaɲ] nf Brittany
bretelle [brətɛl] nf (de vêtement, de sac) strap; (d'autoroute) slip road (BRIT), entrance/exit ramp (US); **bretelles** nfpl (pour pantalon) braces (BRIT), suspenders (US)
breton, ne [brətɔ̃, ɔn] adj Breton ▷ nm/f: **B~, ne** Breton
brève [brɛv] adj voir **bref**
brevet [brəvɛ] nm diploma, certificate; **brevet des collèges** exam taken at the age of 15; **brevet (d'invention)** patent; **breveté, e** adj patented
bricolage [brikɔlaʒ] nm: **le ~** do-it-yourself
bricoler [brikɔle] vi (petits travaux) to do DIY jobs; (passe-temps) to potter about ▷ vt (réparer) to fix up; **bricoleur, -euse** nm/f handyman(-woman), DIY enthusiast
bridge [bridʒ] nm (Cartes) bridge
brièvement [brijɛvmɑ̃] adv briefly
brigade [brigad] nf (Police) squad; (Mil) brigade; **brigadier** nm sergeant
brillamment [brijamɑ̃] adv brilliantly
brillant, e [brijɑ̃, ɑ̃t] adj (remarquable) bright; (luisant) shiny, shining
briller [brije] vi to shine
brin [brɛ̃] nm (de laine, ficelle etc) strand; (fig): **un ~ de** a bit of
brindille [brɛ̃dij] nf twig
brioche [brijɔʃ] nf brioche (bun); (fam: ventre) paunch
brique [brik] nf brick; (de lait) carton
briquet [brikɛ] nm (cigarette) lighter
brise [briz] nf breeze
briser [brize] vt to break; **se briser** vi to break
britannique [britanik] adj British ▷ nm/f: **B~** British person, Briton; **les B~s** the British
brocante [brɔkɑ̃t] nf junk, second-hand goods pl; **brocanteur, -euse** nm/f junkshop owner; junk dealer
broche [brɔʃ] nf brooch; (Culin) spit; (Méd) pin; **à la ~** spit-roasted
broché, e [brɔʃe] adj (livre) paper-backed
brochet [brɔʃe] nm pike inv
brochette [brɔʃɛt] nf (ustensile) skewer; (plat) kebab
brochure [brɔʃyr] nf pamphlet, brochure, booklet
broder [brɔde] vt to embroider ▷ vi: **~ (sur les faits ou une histoire)** to embroider the facts;

broderie nf embroidery
bronches [brɔ̃ʃ] nfpl bronchial tubes; **bronchite** nf bronchitis
bronze [brɔ̃z] nm bronze
bronzer [brɔ̃ze] vi to get a tan; **se bronzer** to sunbathe
brosse [brɔs] nf brush; **coiffé en ~** with a crewcut; **brosse à cheveux** hairbrush; **brosse à dents** toothbrush; **brosse à habits** clothesbrush; **brosser** vt (nettoyer) to brush; (fig: tableau etc) to paint; **se brosser les dents** to brush one's teeth
brouette [bruɛt] nf wheelbarrow
brouillard [brujar] nm fog
brouiller [bruje] vt (œufs, message) to scramble; (idées) to mix up; (rendre trouble) to cloud; (désunir: amis) to set at odds; **se brouiller** vi (vue) to cloud over; (gens): **se ~ (avec)** to fall out (with)
brouillon, ne [brujɔ̃, ɔn] adj (sans soin) untidy; (qui manque d'organisation) disorganized ▷ nm draft; **(papier) ~** rough paper
broussailles [brusaj] nfpl undergrowth sg; **broussailleux, -euse** adj bushy
brousse [brus] nf: **la ~** the bush
brouter [brute] vi to graze
brugnon [bryɲɔ̃] nm (Bot) nectarine
bruiner [bryine] vb impers: **il bruine** it's drizzling, there's a drizzle
bruit [brɥi] nm: **un ~** a noise, a sound; (fig: rumeur) a rumour; **le ~** noise; **sans ~** without a sound, noiselessly; **bruit de fond** background noise
brûlant, e [brylɑ̃, ɑ̃t] adj burning; (liquide) boiling (hot)
brûlé, e [bryle] adj (fig: démasqué) blown ▷ nm: **odeur de ~** smell of burning
brûler [bryle] vt to burn; (suj: eau bouillante) to scald; (consommer: électricité, essence) to use; (feu rouge, signal) to go through ▷ vi to burn; (jeu): **tu brûles!** you're getting hot!; **se brûler** to burn o.s.; (s'ébouillanter) to scald o.s.
brûlure [brylyr] nf (lésion) burn; **brûlures d'estomac** heartburn sg
brume [brym] nf mist
brun, e [brœ̃, bryn] adj (gén, bière) brown; (cheveux, tabac) dark; **elle est ~e** she's got dark hair
brunch [brœntʃ] nm brunch
brushing [brœʃiŋ] nm blow-dry
brusque [brysk] adj abrupt
brut, e [bryt] adj (minerai, soie) raw; (diamant) rough; (Comm) gross; **(pétrole) ~** crude (oil)
brutal, e, -aux [brytal, o] adj brutal
Bruxelles [brysɛl] n Brussels
bruyamment [brɥijamɑ̃] adv noisily
bruyant, e [brɥijɑ̃, ɑ̃t] adj noisy
bruyère [bryjɛr] nf heather

BTS sigle m (= brevet de technicien supérieur) vocational training certificate taken at the end of a higher education course

bu, e [by] pp de **boire**

buccal, e, -aux [bykal, o] adj: **par voie ~e** orally

bûche [byʃ] nf log; **prendre une ~** (fig) to come a cropper; **bûche de Noël** Yule log

bûcher [byʃe] nm (funéraire) pyre; (supplice) stake ▷ vi (fam) to swot (BRIT), slave (away) ▷ vt (fam) to swot up (BRIT), slave away at

budget [bydʒɛ] nm budget

buée [bɥe] nf (sur vitre) mist

buffet [byfɛ] nm (meuble) sideboard; (de réception) buffet; **buffet (de gare)** (station) buffet, snack bar

buis [bɥi] nm box tree; (bois) box(wood)

buisson [bɥisɔ̃] nm bush

bulbe [bylb] nm (Bot, Anat) bulb

Bulgarie [bylgaʀi] nf Bulgaria

bulle [byl] nf bubble

bulletin [byltɛ̃] nm (communiqué, journal) bulletin; (Scol) report; **bulletin d'informations** news bulletin; **bulletin (de vote)** ballot paper; **bulletin météorologique** weather report

bureau, x [byʀo] nm (meuble) desk; (pièce, service) office; **bureau de change** (foreign) exchange office ou bureau; **bureau de poste** post office; **bureau de tabac** tobacconist's (shop); **bureaucratie** [byʀokʀasi] nf bureaucracy

bus[1] [by] vb voir **boire**

bus[2] [bys] nm bus; **à quelle heure part le ~?** what time does the bus leave?

buste [byst] nm (torse) chest; (seins) bust

but[1] [by] vb voir **boire**

but[2] [by(t)] nm (cible) target; (fig) goal, aim; (Football etc) goal; **de ~ en blanc** point-blank; **avoir pour ~ de faire** to aim to do; **dans le ~ de** with the intention of

butane [bytan] nm (camping) butane; (usage domestique) Calor gas®

butiner [bytine] vi (abeilles) to gather nectar

buvais etc [byvɛ] vb voir **boire**

buvard [byvaʀ] nm blotter

buvette [byvɛt] nf bar

c' [s] dét voir **ce**

ça [sa] pron (pour désigner) this; (: plus loin) that; (comme sujet indéfini) it; **ça m'étonne que ...** it surprises me that ...; **comment ça va?** how are you?; **ça va?** (d'accord?) O.K.?, all right?; **où ça?** where's that?; **pourquoi ça?** why's that?; **qui ça?** who's that?; **ça alors!** well really!; **ça fait 10 ans (que)** it's 10 years (since); **c'est ça** that's right; **ça y est** that's it

cabane [kaban] nf hut, cabin

cabaret [kabaʀɛ] nm night club

cabillaud [kabijo] nm cod inv

cabine [kabin] nf (de bateau) cabin; (de piscine etc) cubicle; (de camion, train) cab; (d'avion) cockpit; **cabine d'essayage** fitting room; **cabine (téléphonique)** call ou (tele)phone box

cabinet [kabinɛ] nm (petite pièce) closet; (de médecin) surgery (BRIT), office (US); (de notaire etc) office; (: clientèle) practice; (Pol) Cabinet; **cabinets** nmpl (w.-c.) toilet sg; **cabinet de toilette** toilet

câble [kɑbl] nm cable; **le ~** (TV) cable television, cablevision (US)

cacahuète [kakaɥɛt] nf peanut

cacao [kakao] nm cocoa

cache [kaʃ] nm mask, card (for masking)

cache-cache [kaʃkaʃ] nm: **jouer à ~** to play hide-and-seek

cachemire [kaʃmiʀ] nm cashmere

cacher [kaʃe] vt to hide, conceal; **se cacher** vi (volontairement) to hide; (être caché) to be hidden ou concealed; **~ qch à qn** to hide ou conceal sth from sb

cachet [kaʃɛ] nm (comprimé) tablet; (de la poste) postmark; (rétribution) fee; (fig) style, character

cachette [kaʃɛt] nf hiding place; **en ~** on the sly, secretly

cactus [kaktys] nm cactus

cadavre [kadɑvʀ] nm corpse, (dead) body

caddie® [kadi] nm (supermarket) trolley (BRIT), (grocery) cart (US)

cadeau, x [kado] nm present, gift; **faire un ~ à qn** to give sb a present ou gift; **faire ~ de qch à qn** to make a present of sth to sb, give sb sth as a present

cadenas [kadnɑ] nm padlock

cadet, te [kadɛ, ɛt] adj younger; (le plus jeune) youngest ▷ nm/f youngest child ou one

cadran [kadʀɑ̃] nm dial; **cadran solaire** sundial

cadre [kɑdʀ] nm frame; (environnement) surroundings pl ▷ nm/f (Admin) managerial employee, executive; **dans le ~ de** (fig) within the framework ou context of

cafard [kafaʀ] nm cockroach; **avoir le ~** (fam) to be down in the dumps

café [kafe] nm coffee; (bistro) café ▷ adj inv coffee(-coloured); **café au lait** white coffee; **café noir** black coffee; **café tabac** tobacconist's or newsagent's serving coffee and spirits; **cafetière** nf (pot) coffee-pot

cage [kaʒ] nf cage; **cage (d'escalier)** stairwell; **cage thoracique** rib cage

cageot [kaʒo] nm crate

cagoule [kagul] nf (passe-montagne) balaclava

cahier [kaje] nm notebook; **cahier de brouillon** jotter (BRIT), rough notebook; **cahier d'exercices** exercise book

caille [kaj] nf quail

caillou, x [kaju] nm (little) stone; **caillouteux, -euse** adj (route) stony

Caire [kɛʀ] nm: **le ~** Cairo

caisse [kɛs] nf box; (tiroir où l'on met la recette) till; (où l'on paye) cash desk (BRIT), check-out; (de banque) cashier's desk; **caisse d'épargne** savings bank; **caisse de retraite** pension fund; **caisse enregistreuse** cash register; **caissier, -ière** nm/f cashier

cake [kɛk] nm fruit cake

calandre [kalɑ̃dʀ] nf radiator grill

calcaire [kalkɛʀ] nm limestone ▷ adj (eau) hard; (Géo) limestone cpd

calcul [kalkyl] nm calculation; **le ~** (Scol) arithmetic; **calcul (biliaire)** (gall)stone; **calculatrice** nf calculator; **calculer** vt to calculate, work out; **calculette** nf pocket calculator

cale [kal] nf (de bateau) hold; (en bois) wedge

calé, e [kale] (fam) adj clever, bright

caleçon [kalsɔ̃] nm (d'homme) boxer shorts; (de femme) leggings

calendrier [kalɑ̃dʀije] nm calendar; (fig) timetable

calepin [kalpɛ̃] nm notebook

caler [kale] vt to wedge ▷ vi (moteur, véhicule) to stall

calibre [kalibʀ] nm calibre

câlin, e [kɑlɛ̃, in] adj cuddly, cuddlesome; (regard, voix) tender

calmant [kalmɑ̃] nm tranquillizer, sedative; (pour la douleur) painkiller

calme [kalm] adj calm, quiet ▷ nm calm(ness), quietness; **sans perdre son ~** without losing one's cool (inf) ou composure; **calmer** vt to calm (down); (douleur, inquiétude) to ease, soothe; **se calmer** vi to calm down

calorie [kalɔʀi] nf calorie

camarade [kamaʀad] nm/f friend, pal; (Pol) comrade

Cambodge [kɑ̃bɔdʒ] nm: **le ~** Cambodia

cambriolage [kɑ̃bʀijɔlaʒ] nm burglary; **cambrioler** vt to burgle (BRIT), burglarize (US); **cambrioleur, -euse** nm/f burglar

camelote [kamlɔt] (fam) nf rubbish, trash, junk

caméra [kameʀa] nf (Cinéma, TV) camera; (d'amateur) cine-camera

Cameroun [kamʀun] nm: **le ~** Cameroon

caméscope® [kameskɔp] nm camcorder®

camion [kamjɔ̃] nm lorry (BRIT), truck; **camion de dépannage** breakdown (BRIT) ou tow (US) truck; **camionnette** nf (small) van; **camionneur** nm (chauffeur) lorry (BRIT) ou truck driver; (entrepreneur) haulage contractor (BRIT), trucker (US)

camomille [kamɔmij] nf camomile; (boisson) camomile tea

camp [kɑ̃] nm camp; (fig) side

campagnard, e [kɑ̃paɲaʀ, aʀd] adj country cpd

campagne [kɑ̃paɲ] nf country, countryside; (Mil, Pol, Comm) campaign; **à la ~** in the country

camper [kɑ̃pe] vi to camp ▷ vt to sketch; **se ~ devant** to plant o.s. in front of; **campeur, -euse** nm/f camper

camping [kɑ̃piŋ] nm camping; **faire du ~** to go camping; **(terrain de) camping** campsite, camping site; **camping-car** nm camper, motorhome (US); **camping-gaz®** nm inv camp(ing) stove

Canada [kanada] nm: **le ~** Canada; **canadien, ne** adj Canadian ▷ nm/f: **Canadien, ne** Canadian; **canadienne** nf (veste) fur-lined jacket

canal, -aux [kanal, o] nm canal; (naturel, TV) channel; **canalisation** nf (tuyau) pipe

canapé [kanape] nm settee, sofa
canard [kanar] nm duck; (fam: journal) rag
cancer [kãsɛr] nm cancer; (signe): **le C~** Cancer
cancre [kãkr] nm dunce
candidat, e [kãdida, at] nm/f candidate; (à un poste) applicant, candidate; **candidature** nf (Pol) candidature; (à poste) application; **poser sa candidature à un poste** to apply for a job
cane [kan] nf (female) duck
canette [kanɛt] nf (de bière) (flip-top) bottle
canevas [kanva] nm (Couture) canvas
caniche [kaniʃ] nm poodle
canicule [kanikyl] nf scorching heat
canif [kanif] nm penknife, pocket knife
canne [kan] nf (walking) stick; **canne à pêche** fishing rod; **canne à sucre** sugar cane
cannelle [kanɛl] nf cinnamon
canoë [kanɔe] nm canoe; (sport) canoeing; **canoë (kayak)** kayak
canot [kano] nm ding(h)y; **canot de sauvetage** lifeboat; **canot pneumatique** inflatable ding(h)y
cantatrice [kãtatris] nf (opera) singer
cantine [kãtin] nf canteen
canton [kãtɔ̃] nm district consisting of several communes; (en Suisse) canton
caoutchouc [kautʃu] nm rubber; **caoutchouc mousse** foam rubber
cap [kap] nm (Géo) cape; (promontoire) headland; (fig: tournant) watershed; (Navig): **changer de ~** to change course; **mettre le ~ sur** to head ou steer for
CAP sigle m (= Certificat d'aptitude professionnelle) vocational training certificate taken at secondary school
capable [kapabl] adj able, capable; **~ de qch/faire** capable of sth/doing
capacité [kapasite] nf (compétence) ability; (Jur, contenance) capacity
cape [kap] nf cape, cloak; **rire sous ~** to laugh up one's sleeve
CAPES [kapɛs] sigle m (= Certificat d'aptitude pédagogique à l'enseignement secondaire) teaching diploma
capitaine [kapitɛn] nm captain
capital, e, -aux [kapital, o] adj (œuvre) major; (question, rôle) fundamental ▷ nm capital; (fig) stock; **d'une importance ~e** of capital importance; **capitaux** nmpl (fonds) capital sg; **capital (social)** authorized capital; **capitale** nf (ville) capital; (lettre) capital (letter); **capitalisme** nm capitalism; **capitaliste** adj, nm/f capitalist
caporal, -aux [kapɔral, o] nm lance corporal
capot [kapo] nm (Auto) bonnet (BRIT), hood (US)
câpre [kɑpr] nf caper
caprice [kapris] nm whim, caprice; **faire des ~s** to make a fuss; **capricieux, -euse** adj (fantasque) capricious, whimsical; (enfant) awkward
Capricorne [kaprikɔrn] nm: **le ~** Capricorn
capsule [kapsyl] nf (de bouteille) cap; (Bot etc, spatiale) capsule
capter [kapte] vt (ondes radio) to pick up; (fig) to win, capture
captivant, e [kaptivã, ãt] adj captivating
capturer [kaptyre] vt to capture
capuche [kapyʃ] nf hood
capuchon [kapyʃɔ̃] nm hood; (de stylo) cap, top
car [kar] nm coach ▷ conj because, for
carabine [karabin] nf rifle
caractère [karaktɛr] nm (gén) character; **avoir bon/mauvais ~** to be good-/ill-natured; **en ~s gras** in bold type; **en petits ~s** in small print; **~s d'imprimerie** (block) capitals
caractériser [karakterize] vt to be characteristic of; **se ~ par** to be characterized ou distinguished by
caractéristique [karakteristik] adj, nf characteristic
carafe [karaf] nf (pour eau, vin ordinaire) carafe
caraïbe [karaib] adj Caribbean ▷ n: **les C~s** the Caribbean (Islands)
carambolage [karãbɔlaʒ] nm multiple crash, pileup
caramel [karamɛl] nm (bonbon) caramel, toffee; (substance) caramel
caravane [karavan] nf caravan; **caravaning** nm caravanning
carbone [karbɔn] nm carbon; (double) carbon (copy)
carbonique [karbɔnik] adj: **gaz ~** carbon dioxide; **neige ~** dry ice
carbonisé, e [karbɔnize] adj charred
carburant [karbyrã] nm (motor) fuel
carburateur [karbyratœr] nm carburettor
cardiaque [kardjak] adj cardiac, heart cpd ▷ nm/f heart patient; **être ~** to have heart trouble
cardigan [kardigã] nm cardigan
cardiologue [kardjɔlɔg] nm/f cardiologist, heart specialist
carême [karɛm] nm: **le C~** Lent
carence [karãs] nf (manque) deficiency
caresse [karɛs] nf caress
caresser [karese] vt to caress; (animal) to stroke
cargaison [kargezɔ̃] nf cargo, freight
cargo [kargo] nm cargo boat, freighter
caricature [karikatyr] nf caricature
carie [kari] nf: **la ~ (dentaire)** tooth decay; **une ~** a bad tooth
carnaval [karnaval] nm carnival
carnet [karnɛ] nm (calepin) notebook; (de

tickets, timbres etc) book; **carnet de chèques** cheque book

carotte [kaʁɔt] nf carrot

carré, e [kaʁe] adj square; (fig: franc) straightforward ▷ nm (Math) square; **mètre/ kilomètre ~** square metre/kilometre

carreau, x [kaʁo] nm (par terre) (floor) tile; (au mur) (wall) tile; (de fenêtre) (window) pane; (motif) check, square; (Cartes: couleur) diamonds pl; **tissu à ~x** checked fabric

carrefour [kaʁfuʁ] nm crossroads sg

carrelage [kaʁlaʒ] nm (sol) (tiled) floor

carrelet [kaʁlɛ] nm (poisson) plaice

carrément [kaʁemã] adv (franchement) straight out, bluntly; (sans hésiter) straight; (intensif) completely; **c'est ~ impossible** it's completely impossible

carrière [kaʁjɛʁ] nf (métier) career; (de roches) quarry; **militaire de ~** professional soldier

carrosserie [kaʁɔsʁi] nf body, coachwork no pl

carrure [kaʁyʁ] nf build; (fig) stature, calibre

cartable [kaʁtabl] nm satchel, (school)bag

carte [kaʁt] nf (de géographie) map; (marine, du ciel) chart; (d'abonnement, à jouer) card; (au restaurant) menu; **~ de visite** (visiting) card; **pouvez-vous me l'indiquer sur la ~?** can you show me (it) on the map?; **à la ~** (au restaurant) à la carte; **est-ce qu'on peut voir la ~?** can we see the menu?; **donner ~ blanche à qn** to give sb a free rein; **carte bancaire** cash card; **Carte Bleue®** debit card; **carte à puce** smart card; **carte de crédit** credit card; **carte de fidélité** loyalty card; **carte d'identité** identity card; **carte de séjour** residence permit; **carte grise** (Auto) ≈ (car) registration book, logbook; **carte memoire** (d'appareil-photo numérique) memory card; **carte postale** postcard; **carte routière** road map

carter [kaʁtɛʁ] nm sump

carton [kaʁtɔ̃] nm (matériau) cardboard; (boîte) (cardboard) box; **faire un ~** (fam) to score a hit; **carton (à dessin)** portfolio

cartouche [kaʁtuʃ] nf cartridge; (de cigarettes) carton

cas [kɑ] nm case; **ne faire aucun ~ de** to take no notice of; **en aucun ~** on no account; **au ~ où** in case; **en ~ de** in case of, in the event of; **en ~ de besoin** if need be; **en tout ~** in any case, at any rate

cascade [kaskad] nf waterfall, cascade

case [kɑz] nf (hutte) hut; (compartiment) compartment; (sur un formulaire, de mots croisés etc) box

caser [kaze] (fam) vt (placer) to put (away); (loger) to put up; **se caser** vi (se marier) to settle down; (trouver un emploi) to find a (steady) job

caserne [kazɛʁn] nf barracks pl

casier [kazje] nm (pour courrier) pigeonhole; (compartiment) compartment; (à clef) locker; **casier judiciaire** police record

casino [kazino] nm casino

casque [kask] nm helmet; (chez le coiffeur) (hair-)drier; (pour audition) (head-)phones pl, headset

casquette [kaskɛt] nf cap

casse...: **casse-croûte** nm inv snack; **casse-noix** nm inv nutcrackers pl; **casse-pieds** (fam) adj inv: **il est casse-pieds** he's a pain in the neck

casser [kɑse] vt to break; (Jur) to quash; **se casser** vi to break; **~ les pieds à qn** (fam: irriter) to get on sb's nerves; **se ~ la tête** (fam) to go to a lot of trouble

casserole [kasʁɔl] nf saucepan

casse-tête [kɑstɛt] nm inv (difficultés) headache (fig)

cassette [kasɛt] nf (bande magnétique) cassette; (coffret) casket

cassis [kasis] nm blackcurrant

cassoulet [kasulɛ] nm bean and sausage hot-pot

catalogue [katalɔɡ] nm catalogue

catalytique [katalitik] adj: **pot ~** catalytic convertor

catastrophe [katastʁɔf] nf catastrophe, disaster

catéchisme [kateʃism] nm catechism

catégorie [kateɡɔʁi] nf category; **catégorique** adj categorical

cathédrale [katedʁal] nf cathedral

catholique [katɔlik] adj, nm/f (Roman) Catholic; **pas très ~** a bit shady ou fishy

cauchemar [koʃmaʁ] nm nightmare

cause [koz] nf cause; (Jur) lawsuit, case; **à ~ de** because of, owing to; **pour ~ de** on account of; **(et) pour ~** and for (a very) good reason; **être en ~** (intérêts) to be at stake; **remettre en ~** to challenge; **causer** vt to cause ▷ vi to chat, talk

caution [kosjɔ̃] nf guarantee, security; (Jur) bail (bond); (fig) backing, support; **libéré sous ~** released on bail

cavalier, -ière [kavalje, jɛʁ] adj (désinvolte) offhand ▷ nm/f rider; (au bal) partner ▷ nm (Échecs) knight

cave [kav] nf cellar

CD sigle m (= compact disc) CD

CD-ROM [sedeʁɔm] sigle m CD-ROM

 MOT-CLÉ

ce, cette [sə, sɛt] (devant nm **cet** + voyelle ou h aspiré; pl **ces**) dét (proximité) this; these pl; (non-proximité) that; those pl; **cette maison(-ci/là)** this/that house; **cette nuit** (qui vient) tonight; (passée) last night

▷ pron 1: **c'est** it's ou it is; **c'est un peintre** he's ou he is a painter; **ce sont des peintres** they're ou they are painters; **c'est le facteur** etc (à la porte) it's the postman; **c'est toi qui lui a parlé** it was you who spoke to him; **qui est-ce?** who is it?; (en désignant) who is he/she?; **qu'est-ce?** what is it?
2: **ce qui, ce que**: **ce qui me plaît, c'est sa franchise** what I like about him ou her is his ou her frankness; **il est bête, ce qui me chagrine** he's stupid, which saddens me; **tout ce qui bouge** everything that ou which moves; **tout ce que je sais** all I know; **ce dont j'ai parlé** what I talked about; **ce que c'est grand!** it's so big!; voir aussi -**ci**; **est-ce que**; **n'est-ce pas**; **c'est-à-dire**

ceci [səsi] pron this

céder [sede] vt (donner) to give up ▷ vi (chaise, barrage) to give way; (personne) to give in; ~ **à** to yield to, give in to

CEDEX [sedɛks] sigle m (= courrier d'entreprise à distribution exceptionnelle) postal service for bulk users

cédille [sedij] nf cedilla

ceinture [sɛ̃tyʀ] nf belt; (taille) waist; **ceinture de sécurité** safety ou seat belt

cela [s(ə)la] pron that; (comme sujet indéfini) it; **m'étonne que ...** it surprises me that ...; **quand/où ~?** when/where (was that?)

célèbre [selɛbʀ] adj famous; **célébrer** vt to celebrate

céleri [sɛlʀi] nm: ~**(-rave)** celeriac; **céleri en branche** celery

célibataire [selibatɛʀ] adj single, unmarried ▷ nm bachelor ▷ nf unmarried woman

celle, celles [sɛl] pron voir **celui**

cellule [selyl] nf (gén) cell; ~ **souche** stem cell

cellulite [selylit] nf cellulite

 MOT-CLÉ

celui, celle [səlɥi, sɛl] (mpl **ceux**, fpl **celles**) pron 1: **celui-ci/là, celle-ci/là** this one/that one; **ceux-ci, celles-ci** these (ones); **ceux-là, celles-là** those (ones)
2: **celui qui bouge** the one which ou that moves; (personne) the one who moves; **celui que je vois** the one (which ou that) I see; (personne) the one (whom) I see; **celui dont je parle** the one I'm talking about; **celui de mon frère** my brother's; **celui du salon/du dessous** the one (ou from) the lounge/below
3 (valeur indéfinie): **celui qui veut** whoever wants

cendre [sɑ̃dʀ] nf ash; **cendres** nfpl (d'un défunt) ashes; **sous la ~** (Culin) in (the) embers;

cendrier nm ashtray

censé, e [sɑ̃se] adj: **être ~ faire** to be supposed to do

censeur [sɑ̃sœʀ] nm (Scol) deputy-head (BRIT), vice-principal (US)

censure [sɑ̃syʀ] nf censorship; **censurer** vt (Cinéma, Presse) to censor; (Pol) to censure

cent [sɑ̃] num a hundred, one hundred ▷ nm (US, Canada etc) cent; (partie de l'euro) cent; **centaine** nf: **une centaine (de)** about a hundred, a hundred or so; **des centaines (de)** hundreds (of); **centenaire** adj hundred-year-old ▷ nm (anniversaire) centenary; (monnaie) cent; **centième** num hundredth; **centigrade** nm centigrade; **centilitre** nm centilitre; **centime** nm centime; **centime d'euro** nm euro cent; **centimètre** nm centimetre; (ruban) tape measure, measuring tape

central, e, -aux [sɑ̃tʀal, o] adj central ▷ nm: ~ **(téléphonique)** (telephone) exchange; **centrale** nf power station; **centrale électrique/nucléaire** power/nuclear power station

centre [sɑ̃tʀ] nm centre; **centre commercial/ sportif/culturel** shopping/sports/arts centre; **centre d'appels** call centre; **centre-ville** nm town centre, downtown (area) (US)

cèpe [sɛp] nm (edible) boletus

cependant [s(ə)pɑ̃dɑ̃] adv however

céramique [seʀamik] nf ceramics sg

cercle [sɛʀkl] nm circle; **cercle vicieux** vicious circle

cercueil [sɛʀkœj] nm coffin

céréale [seʀeal] nf cereal

cérémonie [seʀemɔni] nf ceremony; **sans ~** (inviter, manger) informally

cerf [sɛʀ] nm stag

cerf-volant [sɛʀvɔlɑ̃] nm kite

cerise [s(ə)ʀiz] nf cherry; **cerisier** nm cherry (tree)

cerner [sɛʀne] vt (Mil etc) to surround; (fig: problème) to delimit, define

certain, e [sɛʀtɛ̃, ɛn] adj certain ▷ dét certain; **d'un ~ âge** past one's prime, not so young; **un ~ temps** (quite) some time; **un ~ Georges** someone called Georges; ~**s** pron some; **certainement** adv (probablement) most probably ou likely; (bien sûr) certainly, of course

certes [sɛʀt] adv (sans doute) admittedly; (bien sûr) of course

certificat [sɛʀtifika] nm certificate

certifier [sɛʀtifje] vt: ~ **qch à qn** to assure sb of sth; **copie certifiée conforme** certified copy of the original

certitude [sɛʀtityd] nf certainty

cerveau, x [sɛʀvo] nm brain

cervelas [sɛʀvəla] nm saveloy

cervelle [sɛʀvɛl] nf (Anat) brain; (Culin) brains

ces [se] *dét voir* **ce**

CES *sigle m* (= *collège d'enseignement secondaire*) ≈ (junior) secondary school (*BRIT*)

cesse [sɛs]: **sans ~** *adv* (*tout le temps*) continually, constantly; (*sans interruption*) continuously; **il n'a eu de ~ que** he did not rest until; **cesser** *vt* to stop ▷ *vi* to stop, cease; **cesser de faire** to stop doing; **cessez-le-feu** *nm inv* ceasefire

c'est-à-dire [sɛtadiʀ] *adv* that is (to say)

cet, cette [sɛt] *dét voir* **ce**

ceux [sø] *pron voir* **celui**

chacun, e [ʃakœ̃, yn] *pron* each; (*indéfini*) everyone, everybody

chagrin [ʃagʀɛ̃] *nm* grief, sorrow; **avoir du ~** to be grieved

chahut [ʃay] *nm* uproar; **chahuter** *vt* to rag, bait ▷ *vi* to make an uproar

chaîne [ʃɛn] *nf* chain; (*Radio, TV: stations*) channel; **travail à la ~** production line work; **réactions en ~** chain reaction *sg*; **chaîne de montagnes** mountain range; **chaîne (hi-fi)** hi-fi system

chair [ʃɛʀ] *nf* flesh; **avoir la ~ de poule** to have goosepimples *ou* gooseflesh; **bien en ~** plump, well-padded; **en ~ et en os** in the flesh; **~ à saucisse** sausage meat

chaise [ʃɛz] *nf* chair; **chaise longue** deckchair

châle [ʃɑl] *nm* shawl

chaleur [ʃalœʀ] *nf* heat; (*fig: accueil*) warmth; **chaleureux, -euse** *adj* warm

chamailler [ʃamaje]: **se chamailler** *vi* to squabble, bicker

chambre [ʃɑ̃bʀ] *nf* bedroom; (*Pol, Comm*) chamber; **faire ~ à part** to sleep in separate rooms; **je voudrais une ~ pour deux personnes** I'd like a double room; **chambre à air** (*de pneu*) (inner) tube; **chambre à coucher** bedroom; **chambre à un lit/à deux lits** (*à l'hôtel*) single-/two-bedded room; **chambre d'amis** spare *ou* guest room; **chambre d'hôte** ≈ bed and breakfast; **chambre meublée** bedsit(ter) (*BRIT*), furnished room; **chambre noire** (*Photo*) darkroom

chameau, x [ʃamo] *nm* camel

chamois [ʃamwa] *nm* chamois

champ [ʃɑ̃] *nm* field; **champ de bataille** battlefield; **champ de courses** racecourse

champagne [ʃɑ̃paɲ] *nm* champagne

champignon [ʃɑ̃piɲɔ̃] *nm* mushroom; (*terme générique*) fungus; **champignon de Paris** *ou* **de couche** button mushroom

champion, ne [ʃɑ̃pjɔ̃, jɔn] *adj, nm/f* champion; **championnat** *nm* championship

chance [ʃɑ̃s] *nf*: **la ~** luck; **chances** *nfpl* (*probabilités*) chances; **avoir de la ~** to be lucky; **il a des ~s de réussir** he's got a good chance of passing; **bonne ~!** good luck!

change [ʃɑ̃ʒ] *nm* (*devises*) exchange

changement [ʃɑ̃ʒmɑ̃] *nm* change; **changement de vitesses** gears *pl*

changer [ʃɑ̃ʒe] *vt* (*modifier*) to change, alter; (*remplacer, Comm*) to change ▷ *vi* to change, alter; **se changer** *vi* to change (o.s.); **~ de** (*remplacer: adresse, nom, voiture etc*) to change one's; (*échanger: place, train etc*) to change; **~ d'avis** to change one's mind; **~ de vitesse** to change gear; **il faut ~ à Lyon** you *ou* we *etc* have to change in Lyons; **où est-ce que je peux ~ de l'argent?** where can I change some money?

chanson [ʃɑ̃sɔ̃] *nf* song

chant [ʃɑ̃] *nm* song; (*art vocal*) singing; (*d'église*) hymn

chantage [ʃɑ̃taʒ] *nm* blackmail; **faire du ~** to use blackmail

chanter [ʃɑ̃te] *vt, vi* to sing; **si cela lui chante** (*fam*) if he feels like it; **chanteur, -euse** *nm/f* singer

chantier [ʃɑ̃tje] *nm* (building) site; (*sur une route*) roadworks *pl*; **mettre en ~** to put in hand; **chantier naval** shipyard

chantilly [ʃɑ̃tiji] *nf voir* **crème**

chantonner [ʃɑ̃tɔne] *vi, vt* to sing to oneself, hum

chapeau, x [ʃapo] *nm* hat; **~!** well done!

chapelle [ʃapɛl] *nf* chapel

chapitre [ʃapitʀ] *nm* chapter

chaque [ʃak] *dét* each, every; (*indéfini*) every

char [ʃaʀ] *nm* (*Mil*): **~ (d'assaut)** tank; **~ à voile** sand yacht

charbon [ʃaʀbɔ̃] *nm* coal; **charbon de bois** charcoal

charcuterie [ʃaʀkytʀi] *nf* (*magasin*) pork butcher's shop and delicatessen; (*produits*) cooked pork meats *pl*; **charcutier, -ière** *nm/f* pork butcher

chardon [ʃaʀdɔ̃] *nm* thistle

charge [ʃaʀʒ] *nf* (*fardeau*) load, burden; (*Élec, Mil, Jur*) charge; (*rôle, mission*) responsibility; **charges** *nfpl* (*du loyer*) service charges; **à la ~ de** (*dépendant de*) dependent upon; (*aux frais de*) chargeable to; **prendre en ~** to take charge of; (*suj: véhicule*) to take on; (*dépenses*) to take care of; **charges sociales** social security contributions

chargement [ʃaʀʒəmɑ̃] *nm* (*objets*) load

charger [ʃaʀʒe] *vt* (*voiture, fusil, caméra*) to load; (*batterie*) to charge ▷ *vi* (*Mil etc*) to charge; **se ~ de** to see to, take care of

chariot [ʃaʀjo] *nm* trolley; (*charrette*) waggon

charité [ʃaʀite] *nf* charity; **faire la ~ à** to give (something) to

charmant, e [ʃaʀmɑ̃, ɑ̃t] *adj* charming

charme [ʃaʀm] *nm* charm; **charmer** *vt* to charm

charpente [ʃaʀpɑ̃t] *nf* frame(work); **charpentier** *nm* carpenter

charrette [ʃaʀɛt] nf cart

charter [ʃaʀtɛʀ] nm (vol) charter flight

chasse [ʃas] nf hunting; (au fusil) shooting; (poursuite) chase; (aussi: **~ d'eau**) flush; **prendre en ~** to give chase to; **tirer la ~ (d'eau)** to flush the toilet, pull the chain; **~ à courre** hunting; **chasse-neige** nm inv snowplough (BRIT), snowplow (US); **chasser** vt to hunt; (expulser) to chase away ou out, drive away ou out; **chasseur, -euse** nm/f hunter ▷ nm (avion) fighter

chat¹ [ʃa] nm cat

chat² [tʃat] nm (Internet) chat room

châtaigne [ʃatɛɲ] nf chestnut

châtain [ʃatɛ̃] adj inv (cheveux) chestnut (brown); (personne) chestnut-haired

château, x [ʃato] nm (forteresse) castle; (résidence royale) palace; (manoir) mansion; **château d'eau** water tower; **château fort** stronghold, fortified castle

châtiment [ʃatimɑ̃] nm punishment

chaton [ʃatɔ̃] nm (Zool) kitten

chatouiller [ʃatuje] vt to tickle; **chatouilleux, -euse** adj ticklish

chatte [ʃat] nf (she-)cat

chatter [tʃate] vi (Internet) to chat

chaud, e [ʃo, ʃod] adj (gén) warm; (très chaud) hot; **il fait ~** it's warm; it's hot; **avoir ~** to be warm; to be hot; **ça me tient ~** it keeps me warm; **rester au ~** to stay in the warm

chaudière [ʃodjɛʀ] nf boiler

chauffage [ʃofaʒ] nm heating; **chauffage central** central heating

chauffe-eau [ʃofo] nm inv water-heater

chauffer [ʃofe] vt to heat ▷ vi to heat up, warm up; (trop chauffer: moteur) to overheat; **se chauffer** vi (au soleil) to warm o.s.

chauffeur [ʃofœʀ] nm driver; (privé) chauffeur

chaumière [ʃomjɛʀ] nf (thatched) cottage

chaussée [ʃose] nf road(way)

chausser [ʃose] vt (bottes, skis) to put on; (enfant) to put shoes on; **~ du 38/42** to take size 38/42

chaussette [ʃosɛt] nf sock

chausson [ʃosɔ̃] nm slipper; (de bébé) bootee; **chausson (aux pommes)** (apple) turnover

chaussure [ʃosyʀ] nf shoe; **chaussures basses** flat shoes; **chaussures montantes** ankle boots; **chaussures de ski** ski boots

chauve [ʃov] adj bald; **chauve-souris** nf bat

chauvin, e [ʃovɛ̃, in] adj chauvinistic

chaux [ʃo] nf lime; **blanchi à la ~** whitewashed

chef [ʃɛf] nm head, leader; (de cuisine) chef; **commandant en ~** commander-in-chief; **chef d'accusation** charge; **chef d'entreprise** company head; **chef d'État** head of state; **chef de famille** head of the family; **chef de file** (de parti etc) leader; **chef de gare** station master; **chef d'orchestre** conductor; **chef-d'œuvre** nm masterpiece; **chef-lieu** nm county town

chemin [ʃ(ə)mɛ̃] nm path; (itinéraire, direction, trajet) way; **en ~** on the way; **chemin de fer** railway (BRIT), railroad (US)

cheminée [ʃ(ə)mine] nf chimney; (à l'intérieur) chimney piece, fireplace; (de bateau) funnel

chemise [ʃ(ə)miz] nf shirt; (dossier) folder; **chemise de nuit** nightdress

chemisier [ʃ(ə)mizje] nm blouse

chêne [ʃɛn] nm oak (tree); (bois) oak

chenil [ʃ(ə)nil] nm kennels pl

chenille [ʃ(ə)nij] nf (Zool) caterpillar

chèque [ʃɛk] nm cheque (BRIT), check (US); **est-ce que je peux payer par ~?** can I pay by cheque?; **chèque sans provision** bad cheque; **chèque de voyage** traveller's cheque; **chéquier** [ʃekje] nm cheque book

cher, -ère [ʃɛʀ] adj (aimé) dear; (coûteux) expensive, dear ▷ adv: **ça coûte ~** it's expensive

chercher [ʃɛʀʃe] vt to look for; (gloire etc) to seek; **aller ~** to go for, go and fetch; **~ à faire** to try to do; **chercheur, -euse** nm/f researcher, research worker

chéri, e [ʃeʀi] adj beloved, dear; **(mon) ~** darling

cheval, -aux [ʃ(ə)val, o] nm horse; (Auto): **~ (vapeur)** horsepower no pl; **faire du ~** to ride; **à ~** on horseback; **à ~ sur** astride; (fig) overlapping; **cheval de course** racehorse

chevalier [ʃ(ə)valje] nm knight

chevalière [ʃ(ə)valjɛʀ] nf signet ring

chevaux [ʃəvo] nmpl de **cheval**

chevet [ʃ(ə)vɛ] nm: **au ~ de qn** at sb's bedside; **lampe de chevet** bedside lamp

cheveu, x [ʃ(ə)vø] nm hair; **cheveux** nmpl (chevelure) hair sg; **avoir les ~x courts** to have short hair

cheville [ʃ(ə)vij] nf (Anat) ankle; (de bois) peg; (pour une vis) plug

chèvre [ʃɛvʀ] nf (she-)goat

chèvrefeuille [ʃɛvʀəfœj] nm honeysuckle

chevreuil [ʃəvʀœj] nm roe deer inv; (Culin) venison

 MOT-CLÉ

chez [ʃe] prép **1** (à la demeure de) at; (: direction) to; **chez qn** at/to sb's house ou place; **je suis chez moi** I'm at home; **je rentre chez moi** I'm going home; **allons chez Nathalie** let's go to Nathalie's

2 (+profession) at; (: direction) to; **chez le boulanger/dentiste** at ou to the baker's/dentist's

3 (*dans le caractère, l'œuvre de*) in; **chez ce poète** in this poet's work; **c'est ce que je préfère chez lui** that's what I like best about him

chic [ʃik] *adj inv* chic, smart; (*fam: généreux*) nice, decent ▷ *nm* stylishness; **~ (alors)!** (*fam*) great!; **avoir le ~ de** to have the knack of
chicorée [ʃikɔʀe] *nf* (*café*) chicory; (*salade*) endive
chien [ʃjɛ̃] *nm* dog; **chien d'aveugle** guide dog; **chien de garde** guard dog
chienne [ʃjɛn] *nf* dog, bitch
chiffon [ʃifɔ̃] *nm* (*piece of*) rag; **chiffonner** *vt* to crumple; (*fam: tracasser*) to concern
chiffre [ʃifʀ] *nm* (*représentant un nombre*) figure, numeral; (*montant, total*) total, sum; **en ~s ronds** in round figures; **chiffre d'affaires** turnover; **chiffrer** *vt* (*dépense*) to put a figure to, assess; (*message*) to (en)code, cipher; **se chiffrer à** to add up to, amount to
chignon [ʃiɲɔ̃] *nm* chignon, bun
Chili [ʃili] *nm*: **le ~** Chile; **chilien, ne** *adj* Chilean ▷ *nm/f*: **Chilien, ne** Chilean
chimie [ʃimi] *nf* chemistry; **chimiothérapie** [ʃimjɔteʀapi] *nf* chemotherapy; **chimique** *adj* chemical; **produits chimiques** chemicals
chimpanzé [ʃɛ̃pɑ̃ze] *nm* chimpanzee
Chine [ʃin] *nf*: **la ~** China; **chinois, e** *adj* Chinese ▷ *nm/f*: **Chinois, e** Chinese ▷ *nm* (*Ling*) Chinese
chiot [ʃjo] *nm* pup(py)
chips [ʃips] *nfpl* crisps (BRIT), (potato) chips (US)
chirurgie [ʃiʀyʀʒi] *nf* surgery; **chirurgie esthétique** plastic surgery; **chirurgien, ne** *nm/f* surgeon
chlore [klɔʀ] *nm* chlorine
choc [ʃɔk] *nm* (*heurt*) impact, shock; (*collision*) crash; (*moral*) shock; (*affrontement*) clash
chocolat [ʃɔkɔla] *nm* chocolate; **chocolat au lait** milk chocolate
chœur [kœʀ] *nm* (*chorale*) choir; (*Opéra, Théâtre*) chorus; **en ~** in chorus
choisir [ʃwaziʀ] *vt* to choose, select
choix [ʃwa] *nm* choice, selection; **avoir le ~** to have the choice; **premier ~** (*Comm*) class one; **de ~** choice, selected; **au ~** as you wish
chômage [ʃomaʒ] *nm* unemployment; **mettre au ~** to make redundant, put out of work; **être au ~** to be unemployed *ou* out of work; **chômeur, -euse** *nm/f* unemployed person
choquer [ʃɔke] *vt* (*offenser*) to shock; (*deuil*) to shake
chorale [kɔʀal] *nf* choir
chose [ʃoz] *nf* thing; **c'est peu de ~** it's nothing (really)
chou, x [ʃu] *nm* cabbage; **mon petit ~** (my) sweetheart; **chou à la crème** choux

bun; **chou de Bruxelles** Brussels sprout; **choucroute** *nf* sauerkraut
chou-fleur [ʃuflœʀ] *nm* cauliflower
chrétien, ne [kʀetjɛ̃, jɛn] *adj, nm/f* Christian
Christ [kʀist] *nm*: **le ~** Christ; **christianisme** *nm* Christianity
chronique [kʀɔnik] *adj* chronic ▷ *nf* (*de journal*) column, page; (*historique*) chronicle; (*Radio, TV*): **la ~ sportive** the sports review
chronologique [kʀɔnɔlɔʒik] *adj* chronological
chronomètre [kʀɔnɔmɛtʀ] *nm* stopwatch; **chronométrer** *vt* to time
chrysanthème [kʀizɑ̃tɛm] *nm* chrysanthemum

chuchotement [ʃyʃɔtmɑ̃] *nm* whisper
chuchoter [ʃyʃɔte] *vt, vi* to whisper
chut [ʃyt] *excl* sh!
chute [ʃyt] *nf* fall; (*déchet*) scrap; **faire une ~ (de 10 m)** to fall (10 m); **chute (d'eau)** waterfall; **chute libre** free fall; **chutes de pluie/neige** rainfall/snowfall
Chypre [ʃipʀ] *nm/f* Cyprus
-ci [si] *adv voir* **par** ▷ *dét*: **ce garçon~** this boy; **ces femmes~** these women
cible [sibl] *nf* target
ciboulette [sibulɛt] *nf* (small) chive
cicatrice [sikatʀis] *nf* scar; **cicatriser** *vt* to heal
ci-contre [sikɔ̃tʀ] *adv* opposite
ci-dessous [sidəsu] *adv* below
ci-dessus [sidəsy] *adv* above
cidre [sidʀ] *nm* cider
Cie *abr* (= *compagnie*) Co.
ciel [sjɛl] *nm* sky; (*Rel*) heaven
cieux [sjø] *nmpl de* **ciel**
cigale [sigal] *nf* cicada
cigare [sigaʀ] *nm* cigar
cigarette [sigaʀɛt] *nf* cigarette
ci-inclus, e [siɛ̃kly, yz] *adj, adv* enclosed
ci-joint, e [siʒwɛ̃, ɛ̃t] *adj, adv* enclosed
cil [sil] *nm* (eye)lash
cime [sim] *nf* top; (*montagne*) peak
ciment [simɑ̃] *nm* cement
cimetière [simtjɛʀ] *nm* cemetery; (*d'église*) churchyard
cinéaste [sineast] *nm/f* film-maker
cinéma [sinema] *nm* cinema
cinq [sɛ̃k] *num* five; **cinquantaine** *nf*: **une cinquantaine (de)** about fifty; **avoir la**

cinquantaine (*âge*) to be around fifty;
cinquante *num* fifty; **cinquantenaire** *adj,
nm/f* fifty-year-old; **cinquième** *num* fifth ▷ *nf*
(*Scol*) year 8 (*BRIT*), seventh grade (*US*)
cintre [sɛ̃tʀ] *nm* coat-hanger
cintré, e [sɛ̃tʀe] *adj* (*chemise*) fitted
cirage [siʀaʒ] *nm* (*shoe*) polish
circonflexe [siʀkɔ̃flɛks] *adj*: **accent ~**
circumflex accent
circonstance [siʀkɔ̃stɑ̃s] *nf* circumstance;
(*occasion*) occasion; **circonstances
atténuantes** mitigating circumstances
circuit [siʀkɥi] *nm* (*Élec, Tech*) circuit; (*trajet*)
tour, (round) trip
circulaire [siʀkylɛʀ] *adj, nf* circular
circulation [siʀkylasjɔ̃] *nf* circulation; (*Auto*):
la ~ (the) traffic
circuler [siʀkyle] *vi* (*sang, devises*) to circulate;
(*véhicules*) to drive (along); (*passants*) to walk
along; (*train, bus*) to run; **faire ~** (*nouvelle*) to
spread (about), circulate; (*badauds*) to move on
cire [siʀ] *nf* wax; **ciré** *nm* oilskin; **cirer** *vt* to
wax, polish
cirque [siʀk] *nm* circus; (*fig*) chaos, bedlam;
quel ~! what a carry-on!
ciseau, x [sizo] *nm*: **~ (à bois)** chisel; **ciseaux**
nmpl (*paire de ciseaux*) (pair of) scissors
citadin, e [sitadɛ̃, in] *nm/f* city dweller
citation [sitasjɔ̃] *nf* (*d'auteur*) quotation; (*Jur*)
summons *sg*
cité [site] *nf* town; (*plus grande*) city; **cité
universitaire** students' residences *pl*
citer [site] *vt* (*un auteur*) to quote (from);
(*nommer*) to name; (*Jur*) to summon
citoyen, ne [sitwajɛ̃, jɛn] *nm/f* citizen
citron [sitʀɔ̃] *nm* lemon; **citron pressé** (fresh)
lemon juice; **citron vert** lime; **citronnade** *nf*
still lemonade
citrouille [sitʀuj] *nf* pumpkin
civet [sivɛ] *nm*: **~ de lapin** rabbit stew
civière [sivjɛʀ] *nf* stretcher
civil, e [sivil] *adj* (*mariage, poli*) civil; (*non
militaire*) civilian; **en ~** in civilian clothes; **dans
le ~** in civilian life
civilisation [sivilizasjɔ̃] *nf* civilization
clair, e [klɛʀ] *adj* light; (*pièce*) bright; (*eau,
son, fig*) clear ▷ *adv*: **voir ~** to see clearly; **tirer
qch au ~** to clear sth up, clarify sth; **mettre
au ~** (*notes etc*) to tidy up ▷ *nm*: **~ de lune**
moonlight; **clairement** *adv* clearly
clairière [klɛʀjɛʀ] *nf* clearing
clandestin, e [klɑ̃dɛstɛ̃, in] *adj* clandestine,
secret; (*mouvement*) underground; (*travailleur,
immigration*) illegal; **passager ~** stowaway
claque [klak] *nf* (*gifle*) slap; **claquer** *vi* (*porte*)
to bang, slam; (*fam: mourir*) to snuff it ▷ *vt*
(*porte*) to slam, bang; (*doigts*) to snap; (*fam:
dépenser*) to blow; **il claquait des dents** his
teeth were chattering; **être claqué** (*fam*) to

be dead tired; **se claquer un muscle** to pull *ou*
strain a muscle; **claquettes** *nfpl* tap-dancing
sg; (*chaussures*) flip-flops
clarinette [klaʀinɛt] *nf* clarinet
classe [klɑs] *nf* class; (*Scol: local*) class(room);
(*: leçon, élèves*) class; **aller en ~** to go to school;
classement *nm* (*rang: Scol*) place; (*: Sport*)
placing; (*liste: Scol*) class list (in order of merit);
(*: Sport*) placings *pl*
classer [klɑse] *vt* (*idées, livres*) to classify;
(*papiers*) to file; (*candidat, concurrent*) to grade;
(*Jur: affaire*) to close; **se ~ premier/dernier**
to come first/last; (*Sport*) to finish first/last;
classeur *nm* (*cahier*) file
classique [klasik] *adj* classical; (*sobre: coupe
etc*) classic(al); (*habituel*) standard, classic
clavecin [klav(ə)sɛ̃] *nm* harpsichord
clavicule [klavikyl] *nf* collarbone
clavier [klavje] *nm* keyboard
clé [kle] *nf* key; (*Mus*) clef; (*de mécanicien*)
spanner (*BRIT*), wrench (*US*); **prix ~s en
main** (*d'une voiture*) on-the-road price; **clé de
contact** ignition key; **clé USB** USB key
clef [kle] *nf* = **clé**
clergé [klɛʀʒe] *nm* clergy
cliché [kliʃe] *nm* (*fig*) cliché; (*négatif*) negative;
(*photo*) print
client, e [klijɑ̃, klijɑ̃t] *nm/f* (*acheteur*)
customer, client; (*d'hôtel*) guest, patron; (*du
docteur*) patient; (*de l'avocat*) client; **clientèle**
nf (*du magasin*) customers *pl*, clientèle; (*du
docteur, de l'avocat*) practice
cligner [kliɲe] *vi*: **~ des yeux** to blink (one's
eyes); **~ de l'œil** to wink; **clignotant** *nm*
(*Auto*) indicator; **clignoter** *vi* (*étoiles etc*) to
twinkle; (*lumière*) to flicker
climat [klima] *nm* climate
climatisation [klimatizasjɔ̃] *nf* air
conditioning; **climatisé, e** *adj* air-conditioned
clin d'œil [klɛ̃dœj] *nm* wink; **en un clin d'œil**
in a flash
clinique [klinik] *nf* private hospital
clip [klip] *nm* (*boucle d'oreille*) clip-on; **(vidéo)
~** (pop) video
cliquer [klike] *vt* to click; **~ sur** to click on
clochard, e [klɔʃaʀ, aʀd] *nm/f* tramp
cloche [klɔʃ] *nf* (*d'église*) bell; (*fam*) clot;
clocher *nm* church tower; (*en pointe*) steeple
▷ *vi* (*fam*) to be *ou* go wrong; **de clocher** (*péj*)
parochial
cloison [klwazɔ̃] *nf* partition (wall)
clonage [klɔnaʒ] *nm* cloning
cloner [klɔne] *vt* to clone
cloque [klɔk] *nf* blister
clore [klɔʀ] *vt* to close
clôture [klotyʀ] *nf* closure; (*barrière*) enclosure
clou [klu] *nm* nail; **clous** *nmpl* (*passage clouté*)
pedestrian crossing; **pneus à ~s** studded tyres;
le ~ du spectacle the highlight of the show;

clou de girofle clove

clown [klun] *nm* clown

club [klœb] *nm* club

CNRS *sigle m* (= *Centre nationale de la recherche scientifique*) ≈ SERC (*BRIT*), ≈ NSF (*US*)

coaguler [kɔagyle] *vt, vi* (*aussi:* **se ~**: *sang*) to coagulate

cobaye [kɔbaj] *nm* guinea-pig

coca [kɔka] *nm* Coke®

cocaïne [kɔkain] *nf* cocaine

coccinelle [kɔksinɛl] *nf* ladybird (*BRIT*), ladybug (*US*)

cocher [kɔʃe] *vt* to tick off

cochon, ne [kɔʃɔ̃, ɔn] *nm* pig ▷ *adj* (*fam*) dirty, smutty; **cochon d'Inde** guinea pig; **cochonnerie** (*fam*) *nf* (*saleté*) filth; (*marchandise*) rubbish, trash

cocktail [kɔktɛl] *nm* cocktail; (*réception*) cocktail party

cocorico [kɔkɔriko] *excl, nm* cock-a-doodle-do

cocotte [kɔkɔt] *nf* (*en fonte*) casserole; **ma ~** (*fam*) sweetie (pie); **cocotte (minute)®** pressure cooker

code [kɔd] *nm* code ▷ *adj*: **phares ~s** dipped lights; **se mettre en ~(s)** to dip one's (head)lights; **code à barres** bar code; **code civil** Common Law; **code de la route** highway code; **code pénal** penal code; **code postal** (*numéro*) post (*BRIT*) ou zip (*US*) code

cœur [kœr] *nm* heart; (*Cartes: couleur*) hearts *pl*; (: *carte*) heart; **avoir bon ~** to be kind-hearted; **avoir mal au ~** to feel sick; **par ~** by heart; **de bon ~** willingly; **cela lui tient à ~** that's (very) close to his heart

coffre [kɔfr] *nm* (*meuble*) chest; (*d'auto*) boot (*BRIT*), trunk (*US*); **coffre-fort** *nm* safe; **coffret** *nm* casket

cognac [kɔɲak] *nm* brandy, cognac

cogner [kɔɲe] *vi* to knock; **se ~ contre** to knock ou bump into; **se ~ la tête** to bang one's head

cohérent, e [kɔerã, ãt] *adj* coherent, consistent

coiffé, e [kwafe] *adj*: **bien/mal ~** with tidy/untidy hair; **~ d'un chapeau** wearing a hat

coiffer [kwafe] *vt* (*fig: surmonter*) to cover, top; **se coiffer** *vi* to do one's hair; **~ qn** to do sb's hair; **coiffeur, -euse** *nm/f* hairdresser; **coiffeuse** *nf* (*table*) dressing table; **coiffure** *nf* (*cheveux*) hairstyle, hairdo; (*art*): **la coiffure** hairdressing

coin [kwɛ̃] *nm* corner; (*pour coincer*) wedge; **l'épicerie du ~** the local grocer; **dans le ~** (*aux alentours*) in the area, around about; (*habiter*) locally; **je ne suis pas du ~** I'm not from here; **au ~ du feu** by the fireside; **regard en ~** sideways glance

coincé, e [kwɛ̃se] *adj* stuck, jammed; (*fig:*

**inhibé*) inhibited, hung up (*fam*)

coïncidence [kɔɛ̃sidɑ̃s] *nf* coincidence

coing [kwɛ̃] *nm* quince

col [kɔl] *nm* (*de chemise*) collar; (*encolure, cou*) neck; (*de montagne*) pass; **col de l'utérus** cervix; **col roulé** polo-neck

colère [kɔlɛr] *nf* anger; **une ~** a fit of anger; **(se mettre) en ~ (contre qn)** (to get) angry (with sb); **coléreux, -euse, colérique** *adj* quick-tempered, irascible

colin [kɔlɛ̃] *nm* hake

colique [kɔlik] *nf* diarrhoea

colis [kɔli] *nm* parcel

collaborer [kɔ(l)labɔre] *vi* to collaborate; **~ à** to collaborate on; (*revue*) to contribute to

collant, e [kɔlã, ãt] *adj* sticky; (*robe etc*) clinging, skintight; (*péj*) clinging ▷ *nm* (*bas*) tights *pl*; (*de danseur*) leotard

colle [kɔl] *nf* glue; (*à papiers peints*) (wallpaper) paste; (*fam: devinette*) teaser, riddle; (*Scol: fam*) detention

collecte [kɔlɛkt] *nf* collection; **collectif, -ive** *adj* collective; (*visite, billet*) group *cpd*

collection [kɔlɛksjɔ̃] *nf* collection; (*Édition*) series; **collectionner** *vt* to collect; **collectionneur, -euse** *nm/f* collector

collectivité [kɔlɛktivite] *nf* group; **collectivités locales** (*Admin*) local authorities

collège [kɔlɛʒ] *nm* (*école*) (secondary) school; (*assemblée*) body; **collégien** *nm* schoolboy

collègue [kɔ(l)lɛg] *nm/f* colleague

coller [kɔle] *vt* (*papier, timbre*) to stick (on); (*affiche*) to stick up; (*enveloppe*) to stick down; (*morceaux*) to stick ou glue together; (*Comput*) to paste; (*fam: mettre, fourrer*) to stick, shove; (*Scol: fam*) to keep in ▷ *vi* (*être collant*) to be sticky; (*adhérer*) to stick; **~ à** to stick to; **être collé à un examen** (*fam*) to fail an exam

collier [kɔlje] *nm* (*bijou*) necklace; (*de chien, Tech*) collar

colline [kɔlin] *nf* hill

collision [kɔlizjɔ̃] *nf* collision, crash; **entrer en ~ (avec)** to collide (with)

collyre [kɔlir] *nm* eye drops

colombe [kɔlɔ̃b] *nf* dove

Colombie [kɔlɔ̃bi] *nf*: **la ~** Colombia

colonie [kɔlɔni] *nf* colony; **colonie (de vacances)** holiday camp (*for children*)

colonne [kɔlɔn] *nf* column; **se mettre en ~ par deux** to get into twos; **colonne (vertébrale)** spine, spinal column

colorant [kɔlɔrã] *nm* colouring

colorer [kɔlɔre] *vt* to colour

colorier [kɔlɔrje] *vt* to colour (in)

coloris [kɔlɔri] *nm* colour, shade

colza [kɔlza] *nm* rape(seed)

coma [kɔma] *nm* coma; **être dans le ~** to be in a coma

combat [kɔ̃ba] *nm* fight, fighting *no pl*;

combat de boxe boxing match; **combattant** nm: **ancien combattant** war veteran; **combattre** vt to fight; (épidémie, ignorance) to combat, fight against

combien [kɔ̃bjɛ̃] adv (quantité) how much; (nombre) how many; **~ de** (quantité) how much; (nombre) how many; **~ de temps** how long; **~ ça coûte/pèse?** how much does it cost/weigh?; **on est le ~ aujourd'hui?** (fam) what's the date today?

combinaison [kɔ̃binɛzɔ̃] nf combination; (astuce) scheme; (de femme) slip; (de plongée) wetsuit; (bleu de travail) boiler suit (BRIT), coveralls pl (US)

combiné [kɔ̃bine] nm (aussi: **~ téléphonique**) receiver

comble [kɔ̃bl] adj (salle) packed (full) ▷ nm (du bonheur, plaisir) height; **combles** nmpl (Constr) attic sg, loft sg; **c'est le ~!** that beats everything!

combler [kɔ̃ble] vt (trou) to fill in; (besoin, lacune) to fill; (déficit) to make good; (satisfaire) to fulfil

comédie [kɔmedi] nf comedy; (fig) playacting no pl; **faire la ~** (fam) to make a fuss; **comédie musicale** musical; **comédien, ne** nm/f actor(-tress)

comestible [kɔmɛstibl] adj edible

comique [kɔmik] adj (drôle) comical; (Théâtre) comic ▷ nm (artiste) comic, comedian

commandant [kɔmɑ̃dɑ̃] nm (gén) commander, commandant; (Navig, Aviat) captain

commande [kɔmɑ̃d] nf (Comm) order; **commandes** nfpl (Aviat etc) controls; **sur ~** to order; **commander** vt (Comm) to order; (diriger, ordonner) to command; **commander à qn de faire** to command ou order sb to do; **je peux commander, s'il vous plaît?** can I order, please?

MOT-CLÉ

comme [kɔm] prép **1** (comparaison) like; **tout comme son père** just like his father; **fort comme un bœuf** as strong as an ox; **joli comme tout** ever so pretty
2 (manière) like; **faites-le comme ça** do it like this, do it this way; **comme ci, comme ça** so-so, middling; **comme il faut** (correctement) properly
3 (en tant que) as a; **donner comme prix** to give as a prize; **travailler comme secrétaire** to work as a secretary
▷ conj **1** (ainsi que) as; **elle écrit comme elle parle** she writes as she talks; **comme si** as if
2 (au moment où, alors que) as; **il est parti comme j'arrivais** he left as I arrived
3 (parce que, puisque) as; **comme il était en retard, il ...** as he was late, he ...
▷ adv: **comme il est fort/c'est bon!** he's so strong/it's so good!

commencement [kɔmɑ̃smɑ̃] nm beginning, start

commencer [kɔmɑ̃se] vt, vi to begin, start; **~ à** ou **de faire** to begin ou start doing

comment [kɔmɑ̃] adv how; **~?** (que dites-vous) pardon?; **et ~!** and how!

commentaire [kɔmɑ̃tɛr] nm (remarque) comment, remark; (exposé) commentary

commerçant, e [kɔmɛrsɑ̃, ɑ̃t] nm/f shopkeeper, trader

commerce [kɔmɛrs] nm (activité) trade, commerce; (boutique) business; **~ électronique** e-commerce; **~ équitable** fair trade; **commercial, e, -aux** adj commercial, trading; (péj) commercial; **les commerciaux** the sales people; **commercialiser** vt to market

commissaire [kɔmisɛr] nm (de police) ≈ (police) superintendent; **commissaire aux comptes** (Admin) auditor; **commissariat** nm police station

commission [kɔmisjɔ̃] nf (comité, pourcentage) commission; (message) message; (course) errand; **commissions** nfpl (achats) shopping sg

commode [kɔmɔd] adj (pratique) convenient, handy; (facile) easy; (personne): **pas ~** awkward (to deal with) ▷ nf chest of drawers

commun, e [kɔmœ̃, yn] adj common; (pièce) communal, shared; (effort) joint; **ça sort du ~** it's out of the ordinary; **le ~ des mortels** the common run of people; **en ~** (faire) jointly; **mettre en ~** to pool, share; **communs** nmpl (bâtiments) outbuildings; **d'un ~ accord** by mutual agreement

communauté [kɔmynote] nf community

commune [kɔmyn] nf (Admin) commune, ≈ district; (: urbaine) ≈ borough

communication [kɔmynikasjɔ̃] nf communication

communier [kɔmynje] vi (Rel) to receive communion

communion [kɔmynjɔ̃] nf communion

communiquer [kɔmynike] vt (nouvelle, dossier) to pass on, convey; (peur etc) to communicate ▷ vi to communicate; **se communiquer à** (se propager) to spread to

communisme [kɔmynism] nm communism; **communiste** adj, nm/f communist

commutateur [kɔmytatœr] nm (Élec) (change-over) switch, commutator

compact, e [kɔ̃pakt] adj (dense) dense; (appareil) compact

compagne [kɔ̃paɲ] nf companion

compagnie [kɔ̃paɲi] nf (firme, Mil) company;

tenir ~ à qn to keep sb company; **fausser ~ à qn** to give sb the slip, slip ou sneak away from sb; **compagnie aérienne** airline (company)

compagnon [kɔ̃paɲɔ̃] nm companion

comparable [kɔ̃paʀabl] adj: **~ (à)** comparable (to)

comparaison [kɔ̃paʀɛzɔ̃] nf comparison

comparer [kɔ̃paʀe] vt to compare; **~ qch/qn à ou et** (pour choisir) to compare sth/sb with ou and; (pour établir une similitude) to compare sth/sb to

compartiment [kɔ̃paʀtimɑ̃] nm compartment; **un ~ non-fumeurs** a non-smoking compartment

compas [kɔ̃pɑ] nm (Géom) (pair of) compasses pl; (Navig) compass

compatible [kɔ̃patibl] adj compatible

compatriote [kɔ̃patʀijɔt] nm/f compatriot

compensation [kɔ̃pɑ̃sasjɔ̃] nf compensation

compenser [kɔ̃pɑ̃se] vt to compensate for, make up for

compétence [kɔ̃petɑ̃s] nf competence

compétent, e [kɔ̃petɑ̃, ɑ̃t] adj (apte) competent, capable

compétition [kɔ̃petisjɔ̃] nf (gén) competition; (Sport: épreuve) event; **la ~ automobile** motor racing

complément [kɔ̃plemɑ̃] nm complement; (reste) remainder; **complément d'information** (Admin) supplementary ou further information; **complémentaire** adj complementary; (additionnel) supplementary

complet, -ète [kɔ̃plɛ, ɛt] adj complete; (plein: hôtel etc) full ▷ nm (aussi: **~-veston**) suit; **pain complet** wholemeal bread; **complètement** adv completely; **compléter** vt (porter à la quantité voulue) to complete; (augmenter: connaissances, études) to complement, supplement; (: garde-robe) to add to

complexe [kɔ̃plɛks] adj, nm complex; **complexe hospitalier/industriel** hospital/industrial complex; **complexé, e** adj mixed-up, hung-up

complication [kɔ̃plikasjɔ̃] nf complexity, intricacy; (difficulté, ennui) complication; **complications** nfpl (Méd) complications

complice [kɔ̃plis] nm accomplice

compliment [kɔ̃plimɑ̃] nm (louange) compliment; **compliments** nmpl (félicitations) congratulations

compliqué, e [kɔ̃plike] adj complicated, complex; (personne) complicated

comportement [kɔ̃pɔʀtəmɑ̃] nm behaviour

comporter [kɔ̃pɔʀte] vt (consister en) to consist of, comprise; (inclure) to have; **se comporter** vi to behave

composer [kɔ̃poze] vt (musique, texte) to compose; (mélange, équipe) to make up; (numéro) to dial; (constituer) to make up, form ▷ vi (transiger) to come to terms; **se composer de** to be composed of, be made up of; **compositeur, -trice** nm/f (Mus) composer; **composition** nf composition; (Scol) test

composter [kɔ̃pɔste] vt (billet) to punch

● **COMPOSTER**
●
● In France you have to punch your ticket on
● the platform to validate it before getting
● onto the train.

compote [kɔ̃pɔt] nf stewed fruit no pl; **compote de pommes** stewed apples

compréhensible [kɔ̃pʀeɑ̃sibl] adj comprehensible; (attitude) understandable

compréhensif, -ive [kɔ̃pʀeɑ̃sif, iv] adj understanding

> Attention à ne pas traduire **compréhensif** par **comprehensive**.

comprendre [kɔ̃pʀɑ̃dʀ] vt to understand; (se composer de) to comprise, consist of

compresse [kɔ̃pʀɛs] nf compress

comprimé [kɔ̃pʀime] nm tablet

compris, e [kɔ̃pʀi, iz] pp de **comprendre** ▷ adj (inclus) included; **l'entre** (situé) contained between; **l'électricité ~e/non ~e, y/non ~ l'électricité** including/excluding electricity; **100 euros tout ~** 100 euros all inclusive ou all-in

comptabilité [kɔ̃tabilite] nf (activité) accounting, accountancy; (comptes) accounts pl, books pl; (service) accounts office

comptable [kɔ̃tabl] nm/f accountant

comptant [kɔ̃tɑ̃] adv: **payer ~** to pay cash; **acheter ~** to buy for cash

compte [kɔ̃t] nm count; (total, montant) count, (right) number; (bancaire, facture) account; **comptes** nmpl (Finance) accounts, books; (fig) explanation sg; **en fin de ~** all things considered; **s'en tirer à bon ~** to get off lightly; **pour le ~ de** on behalf of; **pour son propre ~** for one's own benefit; **régler un ~** (s'acquitter de qch) to settle an account; (se venger) to get one's own back; **rendre des ~s à qn** to be answerable to sb; **tenir ~ de** to take account of; **travailler à son ~** to work for oneself; **rendre ~ (à qn) de qch** to give (sb) an account of sth; voir aussi **rendre**; **compte à rebours** countdown; **compte courant** current account; **compte rendu** account, report; (de film, livre) review; **compte-gouttes** nm inv dropper

compter [kɔ̃te] vt to count; (facturer) to charge for; (avoir à son actif, comporter) to have; (prévoir) to allow, reckon; (penser, espérer): **~ réussir** to expect to succeed ▷ vi to count; (être économe) to economize; (figurer): **~ parmi** to be ou rank among; **~ sur** to count (up)on; **~**

avec qch/qn to reckon with ou take account of sth/sb; **sans ~ que** besides which

compteur [kɔ̃tœʀ] nm meter; **compteur de vitesse** speedometer

comptine [kɔ̃tin] nf nursery rhyme

comptoir [kɔ̃twaʀ] nm (de magasin) counter; (bar) bar

con, ne [kɔ̃, kɔn] (fam!) adj damned ou bloody (BRIT) stupid (!)

concentrer [kɔ̃sɑ̃tʀe] vt to concentrate; **se concentrer** vi to concentrate

concerner [kɔ̃sɛʀne] vt to concern; **en ce qui me concerne** as far as I am concerned

concert [kɔ̃sɛʀ] nm concert; **de ~** (décider) unanimously

concessionnaire [kɔ̃sesjɔnɛʀ] nm/f agent, dealer

concevoir [kɔ̃s(ə)vwaʀ] vt (idée, projet) to conceive (of); (comprendre) to understand; (enfant) to conceive; **bien/mal conçu** well-/badly-designed

concierge [kɔ̃sjɛʀʒ] nm/f caretaker

concis, e [kɔ̃si, iz] adj concise

conclure [kɔ̃klyʀ] vt to conclude; **conclusion** nf conclusion

conçois etc [kɔ̃swa] vb voir **concevoir**

concombre [kɔ̃kɔ̃bʀ] nm cucumber

concours [kɔ̃kuʀ] nm competition; (Scol) competitive examination; (assistance) aid, help; **concours de circonstances** combination of circumstances; **concours hippique** horse show

concret, -ète [kɔ̃kʀɛ, ɛt] adj concrete

conçu, e [kɔ̃sy] pp de **concevoir**

concubinage [kɔ̃kybinaʒ] nm (Jur) cohabitation

concurrence [kɔ̃kyʀɑ̃s] nf competition; **faire ~ à** to be in competition with; **jusqu'à ~ de** up to

concurrent, e [kɔ̃kyʀɑ̃, ɑ̃t] nm/f (Sport, Écon etc) competitor; (Scol) candidate

condamner [kɔ̃dane] vt (blâmer) to condemn; (Jur) to sentence; (porte, ouverture) to fill in, block up; **~ qn à 2 ans de prison** to sentence sb to 2 years' imprisonment

condensation [kɔ̃dɑ̃sasjɔ̃] nf condensation

condition [kɔ̃disjɔ̃] nf condition; **conditions** nfpl (tarif, prix) terms; (circonstances) conditions; **sans ~s** unconditionally; **à ~ de** ou **que** provided that; **conditionnel, le** nm conditional (tense)

conditionnement [kɔ̃disjɔnmɑ̃] nm (emballage) packaging

condoléances [kɔ̃dɔleɑ̃s] nfpl condolences

conducteur, -trice [kɔ̃dyktœʀ, tʀis] nm/f driver ▷ nm (Élec etc) conductor

conduire [kɔ̃dɥiʀ] vt to drive; (délégation, troupeau) to lead; **se conduire** vi to behave; **~ à** to lead to; **~ qn quelque part** to take sb

somewhere; to drive sb somewhere

conduite [kɔ̃dɥit] nf (comportement) behaviour; (d'eau, de gaz) pipe; **sous la ~ de** led by

confection [kɔ̃fɛksjɔ̃] nf (fabrication) making; (Couture): **la ~** the clothing industry

conférence [kɔ̃feʀɑ̃s] nf conference; (exposé) lecture; **conférence de presse** press conference

confesser [kɔ̃fese] vt to confess; **confession** nf confession; (culte: catholique etc) denomination

confetti [kɔ̃feti] nm confetti no pl

confiance [kɔ̃fjɑ̃s] nf (en l'honnêteté de qn) confidence, trust; (en la valeur de qch) faith; **avoir ~ en** to have confidence ou faith in, trust; **faire ~ à qn** to trust sb; **mettre qn en ~** to win sb's trust; **confiance en soi** self-confidence

confiant, e [kɔ̃fjɑ̃, jɑ̃t] adj confident; trusting

confidence [kɔ̃fidɑ̃s] nf confidence; **confidentiel, le** adj confidential

confier [kɔ̃fje] vt: **~ à qn** (objet, travail) to entrust to sb; (secret, pensée) to confide to sb; **se ~ à qn** to confide in sb

confirmation [kɔ̃fiʀmasjɔ̃] nf confirmation

confirmer [kɔ̃fiʀme] vt to confirm

confiserie [kɔ̃fizʀi] nf (magasin) confectioner's ou sweet shop; **confiseries** nfpl (bonbons) confectionery sg

confisquer [kɔ̃fiske] vt to confiscate

confit, e [kɔ̃fi, it] adj: **fruits ~s** crystallized fruits; **confit d'oie** nm conserve of goose

confiture [kɔ̃fityʀ] nf jam

conflit [kɔ̃fli] nm conflict

confondre [kɔ̃fɔ̃dʀ] vt (jumeaux, faits) to confuse, mix up; (témoin, menteur) to confound; **se confondre** vi to merge; **se ~ en excuses** to apologize profusely

conforme [kɔ̃fɔʀm] adj: **~ à** (loi, règle) in accordance with; **conformément** adv: **conformément à** in accordance with; **conformer** vt: **se conformer à** to conform to

confort [kɔ̃fɔʀ] nm comfort; **tout ~** (Comm) with all modern conveniences; **confortable** adj comfortable

confronter [kɔ̃fʀɔ̃te] vt to confront

confus, e [kɔ̃fy, yz] adj (vague) confused; (embarrassé) embarrassed; **confusion** nf (voir confus) confusion; embarrassment; (voir confondre) confusion, mixing up

congé [kɔ̃ʒe] nm (vacances) holiday; **en ~** on holiday; **semaine/jour de ~** week/day off; **prendre ~ de qn** to take one's leave of sb; **donner son ~ à** to give in one's notice to; **congé de maladie** sick leave; **congé de maternité** maternity leave; **congés payés** paid holiday

congédier [kɔ̃ʒedje] vt to dismiss

congélateur [kɔ̃ʒelatœʀ] nm freezer

congeler [kɔ̃ʒ(ə)le] vt to freeze; **les produits congelés** frozen foods

congestion [kɔ̃ʒɛstjɔ̃] nf congestion

Congo [kɔ̃go] nm: **le ~** Congo, the Democratic Republic of the Congo

congrès [kɔ̃gʀɛ] nm congress

conifère [kɔnifɛʀ] nm conifer

conjoint, e [kɔ̃ʒwɛ̃, wɛ̃t] adj joint ▷ nm/f spouse

conjonctivite [kɔ̃ʒɔ̃ktivit] nf conjunctivitis

conjoncture [kɔ̃ʒɔ̃ktyʀ] nf circumstances pl; **la ~ actuelle** the present (economic) situation

conjugaison [kɔ̃ʒygɛzɔ̃] nf (Ling) conjugation

connaissance [kɔnɛsɑ̃s] nf (savoir) knowledge no pl; (personne connue) acquaintance; **être sans ~** to be unconscious; **perdre/reprendre ~** to lose/regain consciousness; **à ma/sa ~** to (the best of) my/his knowledge; **faire la ~ de qn** to meet sb

connaisseur, -euse [kɔnɛsœʀ, øz] nm/f connoisseur

connaître [kɔnɛtʀ] vt to know; (éprouver) to experience; (avoir: succès) to have, enjoy; **~ de nom/vue** to know by name/sight; **ils se sont connus à Genève** they (first) met in Geneva; **s'y ~ en qch** to know a lot about sth

connecter [kɔnɛkte] vt to connect; **se ~ à Internet** to log onto the Internet

connerie [kɔnʀi] (fam!) nf stupid thing (to do/say)

connexion [kɔnɛksjɔ̃] nf connection

connu, e [kɔny] adj (célèbre) well-known

conquérir [kɔ̃keʀiʀ] vt to conquer; **conquête** nf conquest

consacrer [kɔ̃sakʀe] vt (employer) to devote, dedicate; (Rel) to consecrate; **se ~ à qch** to dedicate ou devote o.s. to sth

conscience [kɔ̃sjɑ̃s] nf conscience; **avoir/prendre ~ de** to be/become aware of; **perdre ~** to lose consciousness; **avoir bonne/mauvaise ~** to have a clear/guilty conscience; **consciencieux, -euse** adj conscientious; **conscient, e** adj conscious

consécutif, -ive [kɔ̃sekytif, iv] adj consecutive; **~ à** following upon

conseil [kɔ̃sɛj] nm (avis) piece of advice; (assemblée) council; **des ~s** advice; **prendre ~ (auprès de qn)** to take advice (from sb); **conseil d'administration** board (of directors); **conseil des ministres** ≈ the Cabinet; **conseil municipal** town council

conseiller, -ère [kɔ̃seje, ɛʀ] nm/f adviser ▷ vt (personne) to advise; (méthode, action) to recommend, advise; **~ à qn de** to advise sb to; **pouvez-vous me ~ un bon restaurant?** can you suggest a good restaurant?

consentement [kɔ̃sɑ̃tmɑ̃] nm consent

consentir [kɔ̃sɑ̃tiʀ] vt to agree, consent

conséquence [kɔ̃sekɑ̃s] nf consequence; **en ~ (donc)** consequently; (de façon appropriée) accordingly; **conséquent, e** adj logical, rational; (fam: important) substantial; **par conséquent** consequently

conservateur, -trice [kɔ̃sɛʀvatœʀ, tʀis] nm/f (Pol) conservative; (de musée) curator ▷ nm (pour aliments) preservative

conservatoire [kɔ̃sɛʀvatwaʀ] nm academy

conserve [kɔ̃sɛʀv] nf (gén pl) canned ou tinned (BRIT) food; **en ~** canned, tinned (BRIT)

conserver [kɔ̃sɛʀve] vt (faculté) to retain, keep; (amis, livres) to keep; (préserver, Culin) to preserve

considérable [kɔ̃sideʀabl] adj considerable, significant, extensive

considération [kɔ̃sideʀasjɔ̃] nf consideration; (estime) esteem

considérer [kɔ̃sideʀe] vt to consider; **~ qch comme** to regard sth as

consigne [kɔ̃siɲ] nf (de gare) left luggage (office) (BRIT), checkroom (US); (ordre, instruction) instructions pl; **consigne automatique** left-luggage locker

consister [kɔ̃siste] vi: **~ en/à faire** to consist of/in doing

consoler [kɔ̃sɔle] vt to console

consommateur, -trice [kɔ̃sɔmatœʀ, tʀis] nm/f (Écon) consumer; (dans un café) customer

consommation [kɔ̃sɔmasjɔ̃] nf (boisson) drink; (Écon) consumption; **de ~** (biens, sociétés) consumer cpd

consommer [kɔ̃sɔme] vt (suj: personne) to eat ou drink, consume; (: voiture, machine) to use, consume; (mariage) to consummate ▷ vi (dans un café) to (have a) drink

consonne [kɔ̃sɔn] nf consonant

constamment [kɔ̃stamɑ̃] adv constantly

constant, e [kɔ̃stɑ̃, ɑ̃t] adj constant; (personne) steadfast

constat [kɔ̃sta] nm (de police, d'accident) report; **~ (à l')amiable** jointly-agreed statement for insurance purposes; **~ d'échec** acknowledgement of failure

constatation [kɔ̃statasjɔ̃] nf (observation) (observed) fact, observation

constater [kɔ̃state] vt (remarquer) to note; (Admin, Jur: attester) to certify

consterner [kɔ̃stɛʀne] vt to dismay

constipé, e [kɔ̃stipe] adj constipated

constitué, e [kɔ̃stitɥe] adj: **~ de** made up ou composed of

constituer [kɔ̃stitɥe] vt (équipe) to set up; (dossier, collection) to put together; (suj: éléments: composer) to make up, constitute; (représenter, être) to constitute; **se ~ prisonnier** to give o.s. up

constructeur, -trice [kɔ̃stʀyktœʀ, tʀis] nm/f manufacturer, builder

constructif, -ive [kɔ̃stʀyktif, iv] adj

constructive

construction [kɔ̃stʀyksjɔ̃] nf construction, building

construire [kɔ̃stʀɥiʀ] vt to build, construct

consul [kɔ̃syl] nm consul; **consulat** nm consulate

consultant [kɔ̃syltɑ̃] adj, nm consultant

consultation [kɔ̃syltasjɔ̃] nf consultation; **heures de ~** (Méd) surgery (BRIT) ou office (US) hours

consulter [kɔ̃sylte] vt to consult ▷ vi (médecin) to hold surgery (BRIT), be in (the office) (US)

contact [kɔ̃takt] nm contact; **au ~ de** (air, peau) on contact with; (gens) through contact with; **mettre/couper le ~** (Auto) to switch on/off the ignition; **entrer en** ou **prendre ~ avec** to get in touch ou contact with; **contacter** vt to contact, get in touch with

contagieux, -euse [kɔ̃taʒjø, jøz] adj infectious; (par le contact) contagious

contaminer [kɔ̃tamine] vt to contaminate

conte [kɔ̃t] nm tale; **conte de fées** fairy tale

contempler [kɔ̃tɑ̃ple] vt to contemplate, gaze at

contemporain, e [kɔ̃tɑ̃pɔʀɛ̃, ɛn] adj, nm/f contemporary

contenir [kɔ̃t(ə)niʀ] vt to contain; (avoir une capacité de) to hold

content, e [kɔ̃tɑ̃, ɑ̃t] adj pleased, glad; **~ de** pleased with; **contenter** vt to satisfy, please; **se contenter de** to content o.s. with

contenu [kɔ̃t(ə)ny] nm (d'un récipient) contents pl; (d'un texte) content

conter [kɔ̃te] vt to recount, relate

conteste [kɔ̃tɛst]: **sans ~** adv unquestionably, indisputably; **contester** vt to question ▷ vi (Pol, gén) rebel (against established authority)

contexte [kɔ̃tɛkst] nm context

continent [kɔ̃tinɑ̃] nm continent

continu, e [kɔ̃tiny] adj continuous; **faire la journée ~** to work without taking a full lunch break; **(courant) continu** direct current, DC

continuel, le [kɔ̃tinɥɛl] adj (qui se répète) constant, continual; (continu) continuous

continuer [kɔ̃tinɥe] vt (travail, voyage etc) to continue (with), carry on (with), go on (with); (prolonger: alignement, rue) to continue ▷ vi (vie, bruit) to continue, go on; **~ à** ou **de faire** to go on ou continue doing

contourner [kɔ̃tuʀne] vt to go round; (difficulté) to get round

contraceptif, -ive [kɔ̃tʀasɛptif, iv] adj, nm contraceptive; **contraception** nf contraception

contracté, e [kɔ̃tʀakte] adj tense

contracter [kɔ̃tʀakte] vt (muscle etc) to tense, contract; (maladie, dette) to contract; (assurance) to take out; **se contracter** vi

(muscles) to contract

contractuel, le [kɔ̃tʀaktɥɛl] nm/f (agent) traffic warden

contradiction [kɔ̃tʀadiksjɔ̃] nf contradiction; **contradictoire** adj contradictory, conflicting

contraignant, e [kɔ̃tʀɛɲɑ̃, ɑ̃t] adj restricting

contraindre [kɔ̃tʀɛ̃dʀ] vt: **~ qn à faire** to compel sb to do; **contrainte** nf constraint

contraire [kɔ̃tʀɛʀ] adj, nm opposite; **~ à** contrary to; **au ~** on the contrary

contrarier [kɔ̃tʀaʀje] vt (personne: irriter) to annoy; (fig: projets) to thwart, frustrate; **contrariété** nf annoyance

contraste [kɔ̃tʀast] nm contrast

contrat [kɔ̃tʀa] nm contract

contravention [kɔ̃tʀavɑ̃sjɔ̃] nf parking ticket

contre [kɔ̃tʀ] prép against; (en échange) (in exchange) for; **par ~** on the other hand

contrebande [kɔ̃tʀəbɑ̃d] nf (trafic) contraband, smuggling; (marchandise) contraband, smuggled goods pl; **faire la ~ de** to smuggle

contrebas [kɔ̃tʀəba]: **en ~** adv (down) below

contrebasse [kɔ̃tʀəbas] nf (double) bass

contre...: **contrecoup** nm repercussions pl; **contredire** vt (personne) to contradict; (faits) to refute

contrefaçon [kɔ̃tʀəfasɔ̃] nf forgery

contre...: **contre-indication** (pl **contre-indications**) nf (Méd) contra-indication; **"contre-indication en cas d'eczéma"** "should not be used by people with eczema"; **contre-indiqué, e** adj (Méd) contraindicated; (déconseillé) unadvisable, ill-advised

contremaître [kɔ̃tʀəmɛtʀ] nm foreman

contre-plaqué [kɔ̃tʀəplake] nm plywood

contresens [kɔ̃tʀəsɑ̃s] nm (erreur) misinterpretation; (de traduction) mistranslation; **à ~** the wrong way

contretemps [kɔ̃tʀətɑ̃] nm hitch; **à ~** (fig) at an inopportune moment

contribuer [kɔ̃tʀibɥe]: **~ à** vt to contribute towards; **contribution** nf contribution; **mettre à contribution** to call upon; **contributions directes/indirectes** direct/indirect taxation

contrôle [kɔ̃tʀol] nm checking no pl, check; (des prix) monitoring, control; (test) test, examination; **perdre le ~ de** (véhicule) to lose control of; **contrôle continu** (Scol) continuous assessment; **contrôle d'identité** identity check

contrôler [kɔ̃tʀole] vt (vérifier) to check; (surveiller: opérations) to supervise; (: prix) to monitor, control; (maîtriser, Comm: firme) to control; **contrôleur, -euse** nm/f (de train) (ticket) inspector; (de bus) (bus) conductor(-tress)

controversé, e [kɔ̃tʀɔvɛʀse] adj (personnage, question) controversial

contusion [kɔ̃tyzjɔ̃] nf bruise, contusion

convaincre [kɔ̃vɛ̃kʀ] vt: **~ qn (de qch)** to convince sb (of sth); **~ qn (de faire)** to persuade sb (to do)

convalescence [kɔ̃valesɑ̃s] nf convalescence

convenable [kɔ̃vnabl] adj suitable; (assez bon, respectable) decent

convenir [kɔ̃vniʀ] vi to be suitable; **~ à** to suit; **~ de** (bien-fondé de qch) to admit (to), acknowledge; (date, somme etc) to agree upon; **~ que** (admettre) to admit that; **~ de faire** to agree to do

convention [kɔ̃vɑ̃sjɔ̃] nf convention; **conventions** nfpl (convenances) convention sg; **convention collective** (Écon) collective agreement; **conventionné, e** adj (Admin) applying charges laid down by the state

convenu, e [kɔ̃vny] pp de **convenir** ▷ adj agreed

conversation [kɔ̃vɛʀsasjɔ̃] nf conversation

convertir [kɔ̃vɛʀtiʀ] vt: **~ qn (à)** to convert sb (to); **se convertir (à)** to be converted (to); **~ qch en** to convert sth into

conviction [kɔ̃viksjɔ̃] nf conviction

convienne etc [kɔ̃vjɛn] vb voir **convenir**

convivial, e, -aux [kɔ̃vivjal, jo] adj (Inform) user-friendly

convocation [kɔ̃vɔkasjɔ̃] nf (document) notification to attend; (: Jur) summons sg

convoquer [kɔ̃vɔke] vt (assemblée) to convene; (subordonné) to summon; (candidat) to ask to attend

coopération [kɔɔpeʀasjɔ̃] nf co-operation; (Admin): **la C~** ≈ Voluntary Service Overseas (BRIT), ≈ Peace Corps (US)

coopérer [kɔɔpeʀe] vi: **~ (à)** to co-operate (in)

coordonné, e [kɔɔʀdɔne] adj coordinated; **coordonnées** nfpl (adresse etc) address and telephone number

coordonner [kɔɔʀdɔne] vt to coordinate

copain [kɔpɛ̃] (fam) nm mate, pal; (petit ami) boyfriend

copie [kɔpi] nf copy; (Scol) script, paper; **copier** vt, vi to copy; **copier coller** (Comput) copy and paste; **copier sur** to copy from; **copieur** nm (photo)copier

copieux, -euse [kɔpjø, jøz] adj copious

copine [kɔpin] (fam) nf mate, pal; (petite amie) girlfriend

coq [kɔk] nm cock, rooster

coque [kɔk] nf (de noix, mollusque) shell; (de bateau) hull; **à la ~** (Culin) (soft-)boiled

coquelicot [kɔkliko] nm poppy

coqueluche [kɔklyʃ] nf whooping-cough

coquet, te [kɔkɛ, ɛt] adj appearance-conscious; (logement) smart, charming

coquetier [kɔk(ə)tje] nm egg-cup

coquillage [kɔkijaʒ] nm (mollusque) shellfish inv; (coquille) shell

coquille [kɔkij] nf shell; (Typo) misprint; **coquille St Jacques** scallop

coquin, e [kɔkɛ̃, in] adj mischievous, roguish; (polisson) naughty

cor [kɔʀ] nm (Mus) horn; (Méd): **~ (au pied)** corn

corail, -aux [kɔʀaj, o] nm coral no pl

Coran [kɔʀɑ̃] nm: **le ~** the Koran

corbeau, x [kɔʀbo] nm crow

corbeille [kɔʀbɛj] nf basket; **corbeille à papier** waste paper basket ou bin

corde [kɔʀd] nf rope; (de violon, raquette) string; **usé jusqu'à la ~** threadbare; **corde à linge** washing ou clothes line; **corde à sauter** skipping rope; **cordes vocales** vocal cords; **cordée** nf (d'alpinistes) rope, roped party

cordialement [kɔʀdjalmɑ̃] adv (formule épistolaire) (kind) regards

cordon [kɔʀdɔ̃] nm cord, string; **cordon de police** police cordon; **cordon ombilical** umbilical cord

cordonnerie [kɔʀdɔnʀi] nf shoe repairer's (shop); **cordonnier** nm shoe repairer

Corée [kɔʀe] nf: **la ~ du Sud/du Nord** South/North Korea

coriace [kɔʀjas] adj tough

corne [kɔʀn] nf horn; (de cerf) antler

cornée [kɔʀne] nf cornea

corneille [kɔʀnɛj] nf crow

cornemuse [kɔʀnəmyz] nf bagpipes pl

cornet [kɔʀnɛ] nm (paper) cone; (de glace) cornet, cone

corniche [kɔʀniʃ] nf (route) coast road

cornichon [kɔʀniʃɔ̃] nm gherkin

Cornouailles [kɔʀnwaj] nf Cornwall

corporel, le [kɔʀpɔʀɛl] adj bodily; (punition) corporal

corps [kɔʀ] nm body; **à ~ perdu** headlong; **prendre ~** to take shape; **corps électoral** the electorate; **corps enseignant** the teaching profession

correct, e [kɔʀɛkt] adj correct; (fam: acceptable: salaire, hôtel) reasonable, decent; **correcteur, -trice** nm/f (Scol) examiner; **correction** nf (voir corriger) correction; (voir correct) correctness; (coups) thrashing

correspondance [kɔʀɛspɔ̃dɑ̃s] nf correspondence; (de train, d'avion) connection; **cours par ~** correspondence course; **vente par ~** mail-order business

correspondant, e [kɔʀɛspɔ̃dɑ̃, ɑ̃t] nm/f correspondent; (Tél) person phoning (ou being phoned)

correspondre [kɔʀɛspɔ̃dʀ] vi to correspond, tally; **~ à** to correspond to; **~ avec qn** to correspond with sb

corrida [kɔrida] nf bullfight

corridor [kɔridɔr] nm corridor

corrigé [kɔriʒe] nm (Scol: d'exercice) correct version

corriger [kɔriʒe] vt (devoir) to correct; (punir) to thrash; **~ qn de** (défaut) to cure sb of

corrompre [kɔrɔ̃pr] vt to corrupt; (acheter: témoin etc) to bribe

corruption [kɔrypsjɔ̃] nf corruption; (de témoins) bribery

corse [kɔrs] adj, nm/f Corsican ▷ nf: **la C~** Corsica

corsé, e [kɔrse] adj (café) full-flavoured; (sauce) spicy; (problème) tough

cortège [kɔrtɛʒ] nm procession

cortisone [kɔrtizɔn] nf cortisone

corvée [kɔrve] nf chore, drudgery no pl

cosmétique [kɔsmetik] nm beauty care product

cosmopolite [kɔsmɔpɔlit] adj cosmopolitan

costaud, e [kɔsto, od] (fam) adj strong, sturdy

costume [kɔstym] nm (d'homme) suit; (de théâtre) costume; **costumé, e** adj dressed up; **bal costumé** fancy dress ball

cote [kɔt] nf (en Bourse) quotation; **cote d'alerte** danger ou flood level; **cote de popularité** (popularity) rating

côte [kot] nf (rivage) coast(line); (pente) hill; (Anat) rib; (d'un tricot, tissu) rib, ribbing no pl; **~ à ~** side by side; **la Côte (d'Azur)** the (French) Riviera

côté [kote] nm (gén) side; (direction) way, direction; **de chaque ~ (de)** on each side (of); **de tous les ~s** from all directions; **de quel ~ est-il parti?** which way did he go?; **de ce/de l'autre ~** this/the other way; **du ~ de** (provenance) from; (direction) towards; (proximité) near; **de ~** (regarder) sideways; **mettre qch de ~** to put sth aside; **mettre de l'argent de ~** to save some money; **à ~** (right) nearby; (voisins) next door; **à ~ de** beside, next to; (en comparaison) compared to; **être aux ~s de** to be by the side of

Côte d'Ivoire [kotdivwar] nf: **la Côte d'Ivoire** Côte d'Ivoire, the Ivory Coast

côtelette [kotlɛt] nf chop

côtier, -ière [kotje, jɛr] adj coastal

cotisation [kɔtizasjɔ̃] nf subscription, dues pl; (pour une pension) contributions pl

cotiser [kɔtize] vi: **~ (à)** to pay contributions (to); **se cotiser** vi to club together

coton [kɔtɔ̃] nm cotton; **coton hydrophile** cotton wool (BRIT), absorbent cotton (US); **Coton-tige®** nm cotton bud

cou [ku] nm neck

couchant [kuʃɑ̃] adj: **soleil ~** setting sun

couche [kuʃ] nf layer; (de peinture, vernis) coat; (de bébé) nappy (BRIT), diaper (US); **couches** sociales social levels ou strata

couché, e [kuʃe] adj lying down; (au lit) in bed

coucher [kuʃe] vt (personne) to put to bed; (: loger) to put up; (objet) to lay on its side ▷ vi to sleep; **~ avec qn** to sleep with sb; **se coucher** vi (pour dormir) to go to bed; (pour se reposer) to lie down; (soleil) to set; **coucher de soleil** sunset

couchette [kuʃɛt] nf couchette; (pour voyageur, sur bateau) berth

coucou [kuku] nm cuckoo

coude [kud] nm (Anat) elbow; (de tuyau, de la route) bend; **~ à ~** shoulder to shoulder, side by side

coudre [kudr] vt (bouton) to sew on ▷ vi to sew

couette [kwɛt] nf duvet, quilt; **couettes** nfpl (cheveux) bunches

couffin [kufɛ̃] nm Moses basket

couler [kule] vi to flow, run; (fuir: stylo, récipient) to leak; (nez) to run; (sombrer: bateau) to sink ▷ vt (cloche, sculpture) to cast; (bateau) to sink; (faire échouer: personne) to bring down

couleur [kulœr] nf colour (BRIT), color (US); (Cartes) suit; **film/télévision en ~s** colo(u)r film/television; **de ~** (homme, femme: vieilli) colo(u)red

couleuvre [kulœvr] nf grass snake

coulisses [kulis] nfpl (Théâtre) wings; (fig): **dans les ~** behind the scenes

couloir [kulwar] nm corridor, passage; (d'avion) aisle; (de bus) gangway; **~ aérien/de navigation** air/shipping lane

coup [ku] nm (heurt, choc) knock; (affectif) blow, shock; (agressif) blow; (avec arme à feu) shot; (de l'horloge) stroke; (tennis, golf) stroke; (boxe) blow; (fam: fois) time; **donner un ~ de balai** to give the floor a sweep; **boire un ~** (fam) to have a drink; **être dans le ~** (impliqué) to be in on it; (à la page) to be hip ou trendy; **du ~ ...** as a result; **d'un seul ~** (subitement) suddenly; (à la fois) at one go; **du premier ~** first time; **du même ~** at the same time; **à tous les ~s** (fam) every time; **tenir le ~** to hold out; **après ~** afterwards; **à ~ sûr** definitely, without fail; **~ sur ~** in quick succession; **sur le ~** outright; **sous le ~ de** (surprise etc) under the influence of; **coup de chance** stroke of luck; **coup de coude** nudge (with the elbow); **coup de couteau** stab (of a knife); **coup d'envoi** kick-off; **coup d'essai** first attempt; **coup d'État** coup; **coup de feu** shot; **coup de filet** (Police) haul; **coup de foudre** (fig) love at first sight; **coup de frein** (sharp) braking no pl; **coup de grâce** coup de grâce, death blow; **coup de main**: **donner un coup de main à qn** to give sb a (helping) hand; **coup d'œil** glance; **coup de pied** kick; **coup de poing** punch; **coup de soleil** sunburn no pl; **coup de sonnette** ring of the bell; **coup de téléphone** phone call; **coup de tête** (fig) (sudden) impulse; **coup de théâtre** (fig) dramatic turn of events; **coup de tonnerre** clap of thunder; **coup de vent** gust of wind; **en coup de vent** (rapidement) in a tearing hurry; **coup franc** free kick

coupable [kupabl] adj guilty ▷ nm/f (gén) culprit; (Jur) guilty party

coupe [kup] nf (verre) goblet; (à fruits) dish; (Sport) cup; (de cheveux, de vêtement) cut; (graphique, plan) (cross) section

couper [kupe] vt to cut; (retrancher) to cut (out); (route, courant) to cut off; (appétit) to take away; (vin à table) to dilute ▷ vi to cut; (prendre un raccourci) to take a short-cut; **se couper** vi (se blesser) to cut o.s.; **~ la parole à qn** to cut sb short; **nous avons été coupés** we've been cut off

couple [kupl] nm couple

couplet [kuplɛ] nm verse

coupole [kupɔl] nf dome

coupon [kupɔ̃] nm (ticket) coupon; (reste de tissu) remnant

coupure [kupyʀ] nf cut; (billet de banque) note; (de journal) cutting; **coupure de courant** power cut

cour [kuʀ] nf (de ferme, jardin) (court)yard; (d'immeuble) back yard; (Jur, royale) court; **faire la ~ à qn** to court sb; **cour d'assises** court of assizes; **cour de récréation** playground

courage [kuʀaʒ] nm courage, bravery; **courageux, -euse** adj brave, courageous

couramment [kuʀamɑ̃] adv commonly; (parler) fluently

courant, e [kuʀɑ̃, ɑ̃t] adj (fréquent) common; (Comm, gén: normal) standard; (en cours) current ▷ nm current; (fig) movement; (: d'opinion) trend; **être au ~ (de)** (fait, nouvelle) to know (about); **mettre qn au ~ (de)** to tell sb (about); (nouveau travail etc) to teach sb the basics (of); **se tenir au ~ (de)** (techniques etc) to keep o.s. up-to-date (on); **dans le ~ de** (pendant) in the course of; **le 10 ~ (Comm)** the 10th inst.; **courant d'air** draught; **courant électrique** (electric) current, power

courbature [kuʀbatyʀ] nf ache

courbe [kuʀb] adj curved ▷ nf curve

coureur, -euse [kuʀœʀ, øz] nm/f (Sport) runner (ou driver); (péj) womanizer; manhunter

courge [kuʀʒ] nf (Culin) marrow; **courgette** nf courgette (BRIT), zucchini (US)

courir [kuʀiʀ] vi to run ▷ vt (Sport: épreuve) to compete in; (risque) to run; (danger) to face; **~ les magasins** to go round the shops; **le bruit court que** the rumour is going round that

couronne [kuʀɔn] nf crown; (de fleurs) wreath, circlet

courons etc [kuʀɔ̃] vb voir **courir**

courriel [kuʀjɛl] nm e-mail

courrier [kuʀje] nm mail, post; (lettres à écrire) letters pl; **est-ce que j'ai du ~?** are there any letters for me?; **courrier électronique** e-mail

Attention à ne pas traduire **courrier** par le mot anglais **courier**.

courroie [kuʀwa] nf strap; (Tech) belt

courrons etc [kuʀɔ̃] vb voir **courir**

cours [kuʀ] nm (leçon) class; (: particulier) lesson; (série de leçons, cheminement) course; (écoulement) flow; (Comm: de devises) rate; (: de denrées) price; **donner libre ~ à** to give free expression to; **avoir ~** (Scol) to have a class ou lecture; **en ~** (année) current; (travaux) in progress; **en ~ de route** on the way; **au ~ de** in the course of, during; **le ~ de change** the exchange rate; **cours d'eau** waterway; **cours du soir** night school

course [kuʀs] nf running; (Sport: épreuve) race; (d'un taxi) journey, trip; (commission) errand; **courses** nfpl (achats) shopping sg; **faire des ~s** to do some shopping

court, e [kuʀ, kuʀt(ə)] adj short ▷ adv short ▷ nm: **~ (de tennis)** (tennis) court; **à ~ de** short of; **prendre qn de ~** to catch sb unawares; **court-circuit** nm short-circuit

courtoisie [kuʀtwazi] nf courtesy

couru, e [kuʀy] pp de **courir**

cousais etc [kuzɛ] vb voir **coudre**

couscous [kuskus] nm couscous

cousin, e [kuzɛ̃, in] nm/f cousin

coussin [kusɛ̃] nm cushion

cousu, e [kuzy] pp de **coudre**

coût [ku] nm cost; **le ~ de la vie** the cost of living

couteau, x [kuto] nm knife

coûter [kute] vt, vi to cost; **combien ça coûte?** how much is it?, what does it cost?; **ça coûte trop cher** it's too expensive; **coûte que coûte** at all costs; **coûteux, -euse** adj costly, expensive

coutume [kutym] nf custom

couture [kutyʀ] nf sewing; (profession) dressmaking; (points) seam; **couturier** nm fashion designer; **couturière** nf dressmaker

couvent [kuvɑ̃] nm (de sœurs) convent; (de frères) monastery

couver [kuve] vt to hatch; (maladie) to be coming down with ▷ vi (feu) to smoulder; (révolte) to be brewing

couvercle [kuvɛʀkl] nm lid; (de bombe aérosol etc, qui se visse) cap, top

couvert, e [kuvɛʀ, ɛʀt] pp de **couvrir** ▷ adj (ciel) overcast ▷ nm place setting; (place à table) place; **couverts** nmpl (ustensiles) cutlery sg; **~ de** covered with ou in; **mettre le ~** to lay the table

couverture [kuvɛʀtyʀ] nf blanket; (de livre, assurance, fig) cover; (presse) coverage

couvre-lit [kuvrəli] nm bedspread

couvrir [kuvrir] vt to cover; **se couvrir** vi (s'habiller) to cover up; (se coiffer) to put on one's hat; (ciel) to cloud over

cow-boy [koboj] nm cowboy

crabe [krab] nm crab

cracher [kraʃe] vi, vt to spit

crachin [kraʃɛ̃] nm drizzle

craie [krɛ] nf chalk

craindre [krɛ̃dr] vt to fear, be afraid of; (être sensible à: chaleur, froid) to be easily damaged by

crainte [krɛ̃t] nf fear; **de ~ de/que** for fear of/that; **craintif, -ive** adj timid

crampe [krɑ̃p] nf cramp; **j'ai une ~ à la jambe** I've got cramp in my leg

cramponner [krɑ̃pɔne] vb: **se ~ (à)** to hang ou cling on (to)

cran [krɑ̃] nm (entaille) notch; (de courroie) hole; (fam: courage) guts pl

crâne [krɑn] nm skull

crapaud [krapo] nm toad

craquement [krakmɑ̃] nm crack, snap; (du plancher) creak, creaking no pl

craquer [krake] vi (bois, plancher) to creak; (fil, branche) to snap; (couture) to come apart; (fig: accusé) to break down; (: fam) to crack up ▷ vt (allumette) to strike; **j'ai craqué** (fam) I couldn't resist it

crasse [kras] nf grime, filth; **crasseux, -euse** adj grimy, filthy

cravache [kravaʃ] nf (riding) crop

cravate [kravat] nf tie

crawl [krol] nm crawl; **dos ~é** backstroke

crayon [krɛjɔ̃] nm pencil; **crayon à bille** ball-point pen; **crayon de couleur** crayon, colouring pencil; **crayon-feutre** (pl crayons-feutres) nm felt(-tip) pen

création [kreasjɔ̃] nf creation

crèche [krɛʃ] nf (de Noël) crib; (garderie) crèche, day nursery

crédit [kredi] nm (gén) credit; **crédits** nmpl (fonds) funds; **payer/acheter à ~** to pay/buy on credit ou on easy terms; **faire ~ à qn** to give sb credit; **créditer** vt: **créditer un compte (de)** to credit an account (with)

créer [kree] vt to create

crémaillère [kremajer] nf: **pendre la ~** to have a house-warming party

crème [krɛm] nf cream; (entremets) cream dessert ▷ adj inv cream(-coloured); **un (café) ~** = a white coffee; **crème anglaise** (egg) custard; **crème Chantilly** whipped cream; **crème à raser** shaving cream; **crème solaire** suntan lotion

créneau, x [kreno] nm (de fortification) crenel(lation); (dans marché) gap, niche; (Auto): **faire un ~** to reverse into a parking space (between two cars alongside the kerb)

crêpe [krɛp] nf (galette) pancake ▷ nm (tissu) crêpe; **crêperie** nf pancake shop ou restaurant

crépuscule [krepyskyl] nm twilight, dusk

cresson [kresɔ̃] nm watercress

creuser [krøze] vt (trou, tunnel) to dig; (sol) to dig a hole in; (fig) to go (deeply) into; **ça creuse** that gives you a real appetite; **se ~ la cervelle** (fam) to rack one's brains

creux, -euse [krø, krøz] adj hollow ▷ nm hollow; **heures creuses** slack periods; (électricité, téléphone) off-peak periods; **avoir un ~** (fam) to be hungry

crevaison [krəvezɔ̃] nf puncture

crevé, e [krəve] (fam) adj (fatigué) shattered (BRIT), exhausted

crever [krəve] vt (ballon) to burst ▷ vi (pneu) to burst; (automobiliste) to have a puncture (BRIT) ou a flat (tire) (US); (fam) to die

crevette [krəvɛt] nf: **~ (rose)** prawn; **crevette grise** shrimp

cri [kri] nm cry, shout; **c'est le dernier ~** (fig) it's the latest fashion

criard, e [krijar, krijard] adj (couleur) garish, loud; (voix) yelling

cric [krik] nm (Auto) jack

crier [krije] vi (pour appeler) to shout, cry (out); (de douleur etc) to scream, yell ▷ vt (injure) to shout (out), yell (out)

crime [krim] nm crime; (meurtre) murder; **criminel, le** nm/f criminal; (assassin) murderer

crin [krɛ̃] nm (de cheval) hair no pl

crinière [krinjer] nf mane

crique [krik] nf creek, inlet

criquet [krike] nm grasshopper

crise [kriz] nf crisis; (Méd) attack; (: d'épilepsie) fit; **piquer une ~ de nerfs** to go hysterical; **crise cardiaque** heart attack; **crise de foie**: **avoir une crise de foie** to have really bad indigestion

cristal, -aux [kristal, o] nm crystal

critère [kriter] nm criterion

critiquable [kritikabl] adj open to criticism

critique [kritik] adj critical ▷ nm/f (de théâtre, musique) critic ▷ nf criticism; (Théâtre etc) article) review

critiquer [kritike] vt (dénigrer) to criticize; (évaluer) to assess, examine (critically)

croate [krɔat] adj Croatian ▷ nm/f: **C~** Croat, Croatian

Croatie [krɔasi] nf: **la ~** Croatia

crochet [krɔʃe] nm hook; (détour) detour; (Tricot: aiguille) crochet hook; (: technique) crochet; **vivre aux ~s de qn** to live ou sponge off sb

crocodile [krɔkɔdil] nm crocodile

croire [krwar] vt to believe; **se ~ fort** to think one is strong; **~ que** to believe ou think that; **~ à, ~ en** to believe in

croisade [krwazad] nf crusade

croisement [kʀwazmɑ̃] nm (*carrefour*) crossroads sg; (*Bio*) crossing; (: *résultat*) crossbreed

croiser [kʀwaze] vt (*personne, voiture*) to pass; (*route*) to cross, cut across; (*Bio*) to cross; **se croiser** vi (*personnes, véhicules*) to pass each other; (*routes, lettres*) to cross; (*regards*) to meet; **~ les jambes/bras** to cross one's legs/fold one's arms

croisière [kʀwazjɛʀ] nf cruise

croissance [kʀwasɑ̃s] nf growth

croissant [kʀwasɑ̃] nm (*à manger*) croissant; (*motif*) crescent

croître [kʀwatʀ] vi to grow

croix [kʀwa] nf cross; **la Croix Rouge** the Red Cross

croque-monsieur [kʀɔkməsjø] nm inv toasted ham and cheese sandwich

croquer [kʀɔke] vt (*manger*) to crunch; (: *fruit*) to munch; (*dessiner*) to sketch; **chocolat à croquer** plain dessert chocolate

croquis [kʀɔki] nm sketch

crotte [kʀɔt] nf droppings pl; **crottin** nm dung, manure; (*fromage*) (small round) cheese (*made of goat's milk*)

croustillant, e [kʀustijɑ̃, ɑ̃t] adj crisp

croûte [kʀut] nf crust; (*du fromage*) rind; (*Méd*) scab; **en ~** (*Culin*) in pastry

croûton [kʀutɔ̃] nm (*Culin*) crouton; (*bout du pain*) crust, heel

croyant, e [kʀwajɑ̃, ɑ̃t] nm/f believer

CRS sigle fpl (= *Compagnies républicaines de sécurité*) state security police force ▷ sigle m member of the CRS

cru, e [kʀy] pp de **croire** ▷ adj (*non cuit*) raw; (*lumière, couleur*) harsh; (*paroles*) crude ▷ nm (*vignoble*) vineyard; (*vin*) wine; **un grand ~** a great vintage; **jambon ~** Parma ham

crû [kʀy] pp de **croître**

cruauté [kʀyote] nf cruelty

cruche [kʀyʃ] nf pitcher, jug

crucifix [kʀysifi] nm crucifix

crudités [kʀydite] nfpl (*Culin*) selection of raw vegetables

crue [kʀy] nf (*inondation*) flood

cruel, le [kʀyɛl] adj cruel

crus etc [kʀy] vb voir **croire**; **croître**

crûs etc [kʀy] vb voir **croître**

crustacés [kʀystase] nmpl shellfish

Cuba [kyba] nf Cuba; **cubain, e** adj Cuban ▷ nm/f: **Cubain, e** Cuban

cube [kyb] nm cube; (*jouet*) brick; **mètre ~** cubic metre; **2 au ~** 2 cubed

cueillette [kœjɛt] nf picking; (*quantité*) crop, harvest

cueillir [kœjiʀ] vt (*fruits, fleurs*) to pick, gather; (*fig*) to catch

cuiller [kɥijɛʀ], **cuillère** [kɥijɛʀ] nf spoon; **cuiller à café** coffee spoon; (*Culin*)

≈ teaspoonful; **cuiller à soupe** soup-spoon; (*Culin*) ≈ tablespoonful; **cuillerée** nf spoonful

cuir [kɥiʀ] nm leather; **cuir chevelu** scalp

cuire [kɥiʀ] vt (*aliments*) to cook; (*au four*) to bake ▷ vi to cook; **bien cuit** (*viande*) well done; **trop cuit** overdone

cuisine [kɥizin] nf (*pièce*) kitchen; (*art culinaire*) cookery, cooking; (*nourriture*) cooking, food; **faire la ~** to cook; **cuisiné, e** adj: **plat cuisiné** ready-made meal ou dish; **cuisiner** vt to cook; (*fam*) to grill ▷ vi to cook; **cuisinier, -ière** nm/f cook; **cuisinière** nf (*poêle*) cooker

cuisse [kɥis] nf thigh; (*Culin*) leg

cuisson [kɥisɔ̃] nf cooking

cuit, e [kɥi, kɥit] pp de **cuire**

cuivre [kɥivʀ] nm copper; **les cuivres** (*Mus*) the brass

cul [ky] (*fam!*) nm arse (!)

culminant, e [kylminɑ̃, ɑ̃t] adj: **point ~** highest point

culot [kylo] (*fam*) nm (*effronterie*) cheek

culotte [kylɔt] nf (*de femme*) knickers pl (BRIT), panties pl

culte [kylt] nm (*religion*) religion; (*hommage, vénération*) worship; (*protestant*) service

cultivateur, -trice [kyltivatœʀ, tʀis] nm/f farmer

cultivé, e [kyltive] adj (*personne*) cultured, cultivated

cultiver [kyltive] vt to cultivate; (*légumes*) to grow, cultivate

culture [kyltyʀ] nf cultivation; (*connaissances etc*) culture; **les ~s intensives** intensive farming; **culture physique** physical training; **culturel, le** adj cultural

cumin [kymɛ̃] nm cumin

cure [kyʀ] nf (*Méd*) course of treatment; **cure d'amaigrissement** slimming (BRIT) ou weight-loss (US) course; **cure de repos** rest cure

curé [kyʀe] nm parish priest

cure-dent [kyʀdɑ̃] nm toothpick

curieux, -euse [kyʀjø, jøz] adj (*indiscret*) curious, inquisitive; (*étrange*) strange, curious ▷ nmpl (*badauds*) onlookers; **curiosité** nf curiosity; (*site*) unusual feature

curriculum vitae [kyʀikylɔmvite] nm inv curriculum vitae

cutané, e [kytane] adj skin

cuve [kyv] nf vat; (*à mazout etc*) tank

cuvée [kyve] nf vintage

cuvette [kyvɛt] nf (*récipient*) bowl, basin; (*Géo*) basin

CV sigle m (*Auto*) = **cheval vapeur**; (*Comm*) = **curriculum vitae**

cybercafé [sibɛʀkafe] nm Internet café

cyberespace [sibɛʀɛspas] nm cyberspace

cybernaute [sibɛʀnot] nm/f Internet user

cyclable [siklabl] adj: **piste ~** cycle track

cycle [sikl] nm cycle; **cyclisme** nm cycling; **cycliste** nm/f cyclist ▷ adj cycle cpd; **coureur cycliste** racing cyclist
cyclomoteur [siklomotœʀ] nm moped
cyclone [siklon] nm hurricane
cygne [siɲ] nm swan
cylindre [silɛ̃dʀ] nm cylinder; **cylindrée** nf (Auto) (cubic) capacity; **une (voiture de) grosse cylindrée** a big-engined car
cymbale [sɛ̃bal] nf cymbal
cynique [sinik] adj cynical
cystite [sistit] nf cystitis

d' [d] prép voir de
dactylo [daktilo] nf (aussi: **~graphe**) typist; (aussi: **~graphie**) typing
dada [dada] nm hobby-horse
daim [dɛ̃] nm (fallow) deer inv; (cuir suédé) suede
daltonien, ne [daltɔnjɛ̃, jɛn] adj colour-blind
dame [dam] nf lady; (Cartes, Échecs) queen; **dames** nfpl (jeu) draughts sg (BRIT), checkers sg (US)
Danemark [danmaʀk] nm Denmark
danger [dɑ̃ʒe] nm danger; **être en ~** (personne) to be in danger; **mettre en ~** (personne) to put in danger; (projet, carrière) to jeopardize; **dangereux, -euse** adj dangerous
danois, e [danwa, waz] adj Danish ▷ nm/f: **D~, e** Dane ▷ nm (Ling) Danish

 MOT-CLÉ

dans [dɑ̃] prép **1** (position) in; (à l'intérieur de) inside; **c'est dans le tiroir/le salon** it's in the drawer/lounge; **dans la boîte** in ou inside the box; **je l'ai lu dans le journal** I read it in the newspaper; **marcher dans la ville** to walk about the town
2 (direction) into; **elle a couru dans le salon** she ran into the lounge; **monter dans une voiture/le bus** to get into a car/on to the bus
3 (provenance) out of, from; **je l'ai pris dans**

le tiroir/salon I took it out of *ou* from the drawer/lounge; **boire dans un verre** to drink out of *ou* from a glass
4 (*temps*) in; **dans 2 mois** in 2 months, in 2 months' time
5 (*approximation*) about; **dans les 20 euros** about 20 euros

danse [dɑ̃s] *nf*: **la ~** dancing; **une ~** a dance; **la ~ classique** ballet; **danser** *vi, vt* to dance; **danseur, -euse** *nm/f* ballet dancer; (*au bal etc*) dancer; (: *cavalier*) partner
date [dat] *nf* date; **de longue ~** longstanding; **date de naissance** date of birth; **date limite** deadline; **dater** *vt, vi* to date; **dater de** to date from; **à dater de** (as) from
datte [dat] *nf* date
dauphin [dofɛ̃] *nm* (*Zool*) dolphin
davantage [davɑ̃taʒ] *adv* more; (*plus longtemps*) longer; **~ de** more

⊙ **MOT-CLÉ**

de, d' [də] (*de +le* = **du**, *de +les* = **des**) *prép*
1 (*appartenance*) of; **le toit de la maison** the roof of the house; **la voiture d'Ann/de mes parents** Ann's/my parents' car
2 (*provenance*) from; **il vient de Londres** he comes from London; **elle est sortie du cinéma** she came out of the cinema
3 (*caractérisation, mesure*): **un mur de brique/bureau d'acajou** a brick wall/mahogany desk; **un billet de 50 euros** a 50 euro note; **une pièce de 2 m de large** *ou* **large de 2 m** a room 2m wide, a 2m-wide room; **un bébé de 10 mois** a 10-month-old baby; **12 mois de crédit/travail** 12 months' credit/work; **être payé 20 euros de l'heure** to be paid 20 euros an *ou* per hour; **augmenter de 10 euros** to increase by 10 euros; **de 14 à 18** from 14 to 18
4 (*moyen*) with; **je l'ai fait de mes propres mains** I did it with my own two hands
5 (*cause*): **mourir de faim** to die of hunger; **rouge de colère** red with fury
6 (*devant infinitif*) to; **il m'a dit de rester** he told me to stay
▷ *dét* **1** (*phrases affirmatives*) some (*souvent omis*); **du vin, de l'eau, des pommes** (some) wine, (some) water, (some) apples; **des enfants sont venus** some children came; **pendant des mois** for months
2 (*phrases interrogatives et négatives*) any; **a-t-il du vin?** has he got any wine?; **il n'a pas de pommes/d'enfants** he hasn't (got) any apples/children, he has no apples/children

dé [de] *nm* (*à jouer*) die *ou* dice; (*aussi*: **dé à coudre**) thimble
déballer [debale] *vt* to unpack

débarcadère [debaʀkadɛʀ] *nm* wharf
débardeur [debaʀdœʀ] *nm* (*maillot*) tank top
débarquer [debaʀke] *vt* to unload, land ▷ *vi* to disembark; (*fig: fam*) to turn up
débarras [debaʀa] *nm* (*pièce*) lumber room; (*placard*) junk cupboard; **bon ~!** good riddance!; **débarrasser** *vt* to clear; **se débarrasser de** *vt* to get rid of; **débarrasser qn de** (*vêtements, paquets*) to relieve sb of; **débarrasser (la table)** to clear the table
débat [deba] *nm* discussion, debate; **débattre** *vt* to discuss, debate; **se débattre** *vi* to struggle
débit [debi] *nm* (*d'un liquide, fleuve*) flow; (*d'un magasin*) turnover (of goods); (*élocution*) delivery; (*bancaire*) debit; **débit de boissons** drinking establishment; **débit de tabac** tobacconist's
déblayer [debleje] *vt* to clear
débloquer [deblɔke] *vt* (*prix, crédits*) to free
déboîter [debwate] *vt* (*Auto*) to pull out; **se ~ le genou** *etc* to dislocate one's knee *etc*
débordé, e [debɔʀde] *adj*: **être ~ (de)** (*travail, demandes*) to be snowed under (with)
déborder [debɔʀde] *vi* to overflow; (*lait etc*) to boil over; **~ (de) qch** (*dépasser*) to extend beyond sth; **~ de** (*joie, zèle*) to be brimming over with *ou* bursting with
débouché [debuʃe] *nm* (*pour vendre*) outlet; (*perspective d'emploi*) opening
déboucher [debuʃe] *vt* (*évier, tuyau etc*) to unblock; (*bouteille*) to uncork ▷ *vi*: **~ de** to emerge from; **~ sur** (*études*) to lead on to
debout [d(ə)bu] *adv*: **être ~** (*personne*) to be standing, stand; (: *levé, éveillé*) to be up; **se mettre ~** to stand up; **se tenir ~** to stand; **~!** stand up!; (*du lit*) get up!; **cette histoire ne tient pas ~** this story doesn't hold water
déboutonner [debutɔne] *vt* to undo, unbutton
débraillé, e [debʀɑje] *adj* slovenly, untidy
débrancher [debʀɑ̃ʃe] *vt* to disconnect; (*appareil électrique*) to unplug
débrayage [debʀɛjaʒ] *nm* (*Auto*) clutch; **débrayer** *vi* (*Auto*) to declutch; (*cesser le travail*) to stop work
débris [debʀi] *nmpl* fragments; **des ~ de verre** bits of glass
débrouillard, e [debʀujaʀ, aʀd] (*fam*) *adj* smart, resourceful
débrouiller [debʀuje] *vt* to disentangle, untangle; **se débrouiller** *vi* to manage; **débrouillez-vous** you'll have to sort things out yourself
début [deby] *nm* beginning, start; **débuts** *nmpl* (*de carrière*) début *sg*; **~ juin** in early June; **débutant, e** *nm/f* beginner, novice; **débuter** *vi* to begin, start; (*faire ses débuts*) to start out
décaféiné, e [dekafeine] *adj* decaffeinated

décalage [dekalaʒ] nm gap; **décalage horaire** time difference

décaler [dekale] vt to shift

décapotable [dekapɔtabl] adj convertible

décapsuleur [dekapsylœʀ] nm bottle-opener

décédé, e [desede] adj deceased

décéder [desede] vi to die

décembre [desɑ̃bʀ] nm December

décennie [deseni] nf decade

décent, e [desɑ̃, ɑ̃t] adj decent

déception [desɛpsjɔ̃] nf disappointment

décès [desɛ] nm death

décevoir [des(ə)vwaʀ] vt to disappoint

décharge [deʃaʀʒ] nf (dépôt d'ordures) rubbish tip ou dump; (électrique) electrical discharge; **décharger** vt (marchandise, véhicule) to unload; (tirer) to discharge; **décharger qn de** (responsabilité) to relieve sb of, release sb from

déchausser [deʃose] vt (skis) to take off; **se déchausser** vi to take off one's shoes; (dent) to come ou work loose

déchet [deʃɛ] nm (reste) scrap; **déchets** nmpl (ordures) refuse sg, rubbish sg; **~s nucléaires** nuclear waste

déchiffrer [deʃifʀe] vt to decipher

déchirant, e [deʃiʀɑ̃, ɑ̃t] adj heart-rending

déchirement [deʃiʀmɑ̃] nm (chagrin) wrench, heartbreak; (gén pl: conflit) rift, split

déchirer [deʃiʀe] vt to tear; (en morceaux) to tear up; (arracher) to tear out; (fig: conflit) to tear (apart); **se déchirer** vi to tear, rip; **se ~ un muscle** to tear a muscle

déchirure [deʃiʀyʀ] nf (accroc) tear, rip; **déchirure musculaire** torn muscle

décidé, e [deside] adj (personne, air) determined; **c'est ~** it's decided; **décidément** adv really

décider [deside] vt: **~ qch** to decide on sth; **~ de faire/que** to decide to do/that; **~ qn (à faire qch)** to persuade sb (to do sth); **se décider (à faire)** to decide (to do), make up one's mind (to do); **se ~ pour** to decide on ou in favour of

décimal, e, -aux [desimal, o] adj decimal

décimètre [desimɛtʀ] nm decimetre

décisif, -ive [desizif, iv] adj decisive

décision [desizjɔ̃] nf decision

déclaration [deklaʀasjɔ̃] nf declaration; (discours: Pol etc) statement; **déclaration d'impôts** ou **de revenus** ≈ tax return; **déclaration de vol: faire une déclaration de vol** to report a theft

déclarer [deklaʀe] vt to declare; (décès, naissance) to register; **se déclarer** vi (feu) to break out

déclencher [deklɑ̃ʃe] vt (mécanisme etc) to release; (sonnerie) to set off; (attaque, grève) to launch; (provoquer) to trigger off; **se**

déclencher vi (sonnerie) to go off

décliner [dekline] vi to decline ▷ vt (invitation) to decline; (nom, adresse) to state

décoiffer [dekwafe] vt: **~ qn** to mess up sb's hair; **je suis toute décoiffée** my hair is in a real mess

déçois etc [deswa] vb voir **décevoir**

décollage [dekɔlaʒ] nm (Aviat) takeoff

décoller [dekɔle] vt to unstick ▷ vi (avion) to take off; **se décoller** vi to come unstuck

décolleté, e [dekɔlte] adj low-cut ▷ nm neck(line); (plongeant) cleavage

décolorer [dekɔlɔʀe]: **se décolorer** vi to fade; **se faire ~ les cheveux** to have one's hair bleached

décommander [dekɔmɑ̃de] vt to cancel; **se décommander** vi to cry off

déconcerter [dekɔ̃sɛʀte] vt to disconcert, confound

décongeler [dekɔ̃ʒ(ə)le] vt to thaw

déconner [dekɔne] (fam) vi to talk rubbish

déconseiller [dekɔ̃seje] vt: **~ qch (à qn)** to advise (sb) against sth; **c'est déconseillé** it's not recommended

décontracté, e [dekɔ̃tʀakte] adj relaxed, laid-back (fam)

décontracter [dekɔ̃tʀakte]: **se décontracter** vi to relax

décor [dekɔʀ] nm décor; (paysage) scenery; **décorateur** nm (interior) decorator; **décoration** nf decoration; **décorer** vt to decorate

décortiquer [dekɔʀtike] vt to shell; (fig: texte) to dissect

découdre [dekudʀ]: **se découdre** vi to come unstitched

découper [dekupe] vt (papier, tissu etc) to cut up; (viande) to carve; (article) to cut out

décourager [dekuʀaʒe] vt to discourage; **se décourager** vi to lose heart, become discouraged

décousu, e [dekuzy] adj unstitched; (fig) disjointed, disconnected

découvert, e [dekuvɛʀ, ɛʀt] adj (tête) bare, uncovered; (lieu) open, exposed ▷ nm (bancaire) overdraft; **découverte** nf discovery; **faire la découverte de** to discover

découvrir [dekuvʀiʀ] vt to discover; (enlever ce qui couvre) to uncover; (dévoiler) to reveal; **se découvrir** vi (chapeau) to take off one's hat; (vêtement) to take something off; (ciel) to clear

décrire [dekʀiʀ] vt to describe

décrocher [dekʀɔʃe] vt (détacher) to take down; (téléphone) to take off the hook; (: pour répondre) to lift the receiver; (fam: contrat etc) to get; (fam: abandonner) to drop out; **se ~ un muscle** land ▷ vi (fam) to switch off

déçu, e [desy] pp de **décevoir**

dédaigner [dedeɲe] vt to despise, scorn;

(*négliger*) to disregard, spurn; **dédaigneux, -euse** adj scornful, disdainful; **dédain** nm scorn, disdain

dedans [dədɑ̃] adv inside; (*pas en plein air*) indoors, inside ▷ nm inside; **au ~** inside

dédicacer [dedikase] vt: **~ (à qn)** to sign (for sb), autograph (for sb)

dédier [dedje] vt: **~ à** to dedicate to

dédommagement [dedɔmaʒmɑ̃] nm compensation

dédommager [dedɔmaʒe] vt: **~ qn (de)** to compensate sb (for)

dédouaner [dedwane] vt to clear through customs

déduire [dedɥiʀ] vt: **~ qch (de)** (*ôter*) to deduct sth (from); (*conclure*) to deduce ou infer sth (from)

défaillance [defajɑ̃s] nf (*syncope*) blackout; (*fatigue*) (sudden) weakness no pl; (*technique*) fault, failure; **défaillance cardiaque** heart failure

défaire [defɛʀ] vt to undo; (*installation*) to take down, dismantle; **se défaire** vi to come undone; **se ~ de** to get rid of

défait, e [defɛ, ɛt] adj (*visage*) haggard, ravaged; **défaite** nf defeat

défaut [defo] nm (*moral*) fault, failing, defect; (*tissus*) fault, flaw; (*manque, carence*): **~ de** shortage of; **prendre qn en ~** to catch sb out; **faire ~** (*manquer*) to be lacking; **à ~ de** for lack ou want of

défavorable [defavɔʀabl] adj unfavourable (BRIT), unfavorable (US)

défavoriser [defavɔʀize] vt to put at a disadvantage

défectueux, -euse [defɛktɥø, øz] adj faulty, defective

défendre [defɑ̃dʀ] vt to defend; (*interdire*) to forbid; **se défendre** vi to defend o.s.; **~ à qn qch/de faire** to forbid sb sth/to do; **il se défend** (*fam: se débrouille*) he can hold his own; **se ~ de/contre** (*se protéger*) to protect o.s. from/against; **se ~ de** (*se garder de*) to refrain from

défense [defɑ̃s] nf defence; (*d'éléphant etc*) tusk; **ministre de la ~** Minister of Defence (BRIT), Defence Secretary (US); **"~ de fumer"** "no smoking"

défi [defi] nm challenge; **lancer un ~ à qn** to challenge sb; **sur un ton de ~** defiantly

déficit [defisit] nm (Comm) deficit

défier [defje] vt (*provoquer*) to challenge; (*mort, autorité*) to defy; **~ qn de faire qch** to challenge ou defy sb to do sth

défigurer [defigyʀe] vt to disfigure

défilé [defile] nm (Géo) (narrow) gorge ou pass; (*soldats*) parade; (*manifestants*) procession, march

défiler [defile] vi (*troupes*) to march past;

(*sportifs*) to parade; (*manifestants*) to march; (*visiteurs*) to pour, stream; **faire ~ un document** (Comput) to scroll a document; **se défiler** vi: **il s'est défilé** (*fam*) he wriggled out of it

définir [definiʀ] vt to define

définitif, -ive [definitif, iv] adj (*final*) final, definitive; (*pour longtemps*) permanent, definitive; (*refus*) definite; **définitive** nf: **en définitive** eventually; (*somme toute*) in fact; **définitivement** adv (*partir, s'installer*) for good

déformer [defɔʀme] vt to put out of shape; (*pensée, fait*) to distort; **se déformer** vi to lose its shape

défouler [defule]: **se défouler** vi to unwind, let off steam

défunt, e [defœ̃, œ̃t] adj (*mort*) late before n ▷ nm/f deceased

dégagé, e [degaʒe] adj (*route, ciel*) clear; **sur un ton ~** casually

dégager [degaʒe] vt (*exhaler*) to give off; (*délivrer*) to free, extricate; (*désencombrer*) to clear; (*isoler: idée, aspect*) to bring out; **~ qn de** (*engagement, parole etc*) to release ou free sb from; **se dégager** vi (*passage, ciel*) to clear

dégâts [dega] nmpl damage sg; **faire des ~** to cause damage

dégel [deʒɛl] nm thaw; **dégeler** vt to thaw (out)

dégivrer [deʒivʀe] vt (*frigo*) to defrost; (*vitres*) to de-ice

dégonflé, e [degɔ̃fle] adj (*pneu*) flat

dégonfler [degɔ̃fle] vt (*pneu, ballon*) to let down, deflate; **se dégonfler** vi (*fam*) to chicken out

dégouliner [deguline] vi to trickle, drip

dégourdi, e [deguʀdi] adj smart, resourceful

dégourdir [deguʀdiʀ] vt: **se ~ les jambes** to stretch one's legs (*fig*)

dégoût [degu] nm disgust, distaste; **dégoûtant, e** adj disgusting; **dégoûté, e** adj disgusted; **dégoûté de** sick of; **dégoûter** vt to disgust; **dégoûter qn de qch** to put sb off sth

dégrader [degʀade] vt (Mil: officier) to degrade; (*abîmer*) to damage, deface; **se dégrader** vi (*relations, situation*) to deteriorate

degré [dəgʀe] nm degree

dégressif, -ive [degʀesif, iv] adj on a decreasing scale

dégringoler [degʀɛ̃gɔle] vi to tumble (down)

déguisement [degizmɑ̃] nm (*pour s'amuser*) fancy dress

déguiser [degize]: **se déguiser (en)** vi (*se costumer*) to dress up (as); (*pour tromper*) to disguise o.s.

dégustation [degystasjɔ̃] nf (*de fromages etc*) sampling; **~ de vins** wine-tasting session

déguster [degyste] vt (vins) to taste; (fromages etc) to sample; (savourer) to enjoy, savour

dehors [dəɔʀ] adv outside; (en plein air) outdoors ▷ nm outside ▷ nmpl (apparences) appearances; **mettre** ou **jeter ~** (expulser) to throw out; **au ~** outside; **au ~ de** outside; **en ~ de** (hormis) apart from

déjà [deʒa] adv already; (auparavant) before, already

déjeuner [deʒœne] vi to (have) lunch; (le matin) to have breakfast ▷ nm lunch

delà [dəla] adv: **en ~ (de), au ~ (de)** beyond

délacer [delase] vt (chaussures) to undo

délai [delɛ] nm (attente) waiting period; (sursis) extension (of time); (temps accordé) time limit; **sans ~** without delay; **dans les ~s** within the time limit

délaisser [delese] vt to abandon, desert

délasser [delase] vt to relax; **se délasser** vi to relax

délavé, e [delave] adj faded

délayer [deleje] vt (Culin) to mix (with water etc); (peinture) to thin down

delco(r) [dɛlko] nm (Auto) distributor

délégué, e [delege] nm/f representative

déléguer [delege] vt to delegate

délibéré, e [delibeʀe] adj (conscient) deliberate

délicat, e [delika, at] adj delicate; (plein de tact) tactful; (attention) thoughtful; **délicatement** adv delicately; (avec douceur) gently

délice [delis] nm delight

délicieux, -euse [delisjø, jøz] adj (au goût) delicious; (sensation) delightful

délimiter [delimite] vt (terrain) to delimit, demarcate

délinquant, e [delɛ̃kɑ̃, -ɑ̃t] adj, nm/f delinquent

délirer [deliʀe] vi to be delirious; **tu délires!** (fam) you're crazy!

délit [deli] nm (criminal) offence

délivrer [delivʀe] vt (prisonnier) to (set) free, release; (passeport) to issue

deltaplane(r) [dɛltaplan] nm hang-glider

déluge [delyʒ] nm (pluie) downpour; (biblique) Flood

demain [d(ə)mɛ̃] adv tomorrow; **~ matin/soir** tomorrow morning/evening

demande [d(ə)mɑ̃d] nf (requête) request; (revendication) demand; (d'emploi) application; (Écon): **la ~** demand; **"~s d'emploi"** (annonces) "situations wanted"

demandé, e [d(ə)mɑ̃de] adj (article etc): **très ~** (very) much in demand

demander [d(ə)mɑ̃de] vt to ask for; (chemin, heure etc) to ask; (nécessiter) to require, demand; **~ qch à qn** to ask sb for sth; **~ un service à qn** to ask sb a favour; **~ à qn de faire**

qch to ask sb to do sth; **je ne demande pas mieux que de ...** I'll be only too pleased to ...; **se ~ si/pourquoi** etc to wonder whether/why etc; **demandeur, -euse** nm/f: **demandeur d'emploi** job-seeker; **demandeur d'asile** asylum-seeker

démangeaison [demɑ̃ʒɛzɔ̃] nf itching; **avoir des ~s** to be itching

démanger [demɑ̃ʒe] vi to itch

démaquillant [demakijɑ̃] nm make-up remover

démaquiller [demakije] vt: **se démaquiller** to remove one's make-up

démarche [demaʀʃ] nf (allure) gait, walk; (intervention) step; (fig: intellectuelle) thought processes pl; **faire les ~s nécessaires (pour obtenir qch)** to take the necessary steps (to obtain sth)

démarrage [demaʀaʒ] nm start

démarrer [demaʀe] vi (conducteur) to start (up); (véhicule) to move off; (travaux) to get moving; **démarreur** nm (Auto) starter

démêlant [demɛlɑ̃] nm conditioner

démêler [demele] vt to untangle; **démêlés** nmpl problems

déménagement [demenaʒmɑ̃] nm move; **camion de déménagement** removal van

déménager [demenaʒe] vt (meubles) to (re)move ▷ vi to move (house); **déménageur** nm removal man

démerder [demɛʀde] (fam): **se démerder** vi to sort things out for o.s.

démettre [demɛtʀ] vt: **~ qn de** (fonction, poste) to dismiss sb from; **se ~ l'épaule** etc to dislocate one's shoulder etc

demeurer [d(ə)mœʀe] vi (habiter) to live; (rester) to remain

demi, e [dəmi] adj half ▷ nm (bière) ≈ half-pint (0,25 litres) ▷ préfixe: **~...** half-, semi..., demi-; **trois heures/bouteilles et ~es** three and a half hours/bottles, three hours/bottles and a half; **il est 2 heures et ~e/midi et ~** it's half past 2/half past 12; **à ~-** half-; **à la ~e** (heure) on the half-hour; **demi-douzaine** nf half-dozen, half a dozen; **demi-finale** nf semifinal; **demi-frère** nm half-brother; **demi-heure** nf half-hour, half an hour; **demi-journée** nf half-day, half a day; **demi-litre** nm half-litre, half a litre; **demi-livre** nf half-pound, half a pound; **demi-pension** nf (à l'hôtel) half-board; **demi-pensionnaire** nm/f: **être demi-pensionnaire** to take school lunches

démis, e [demi, iz] adj (épaule etc) dislocated

demi-sœur [dəmisœʀ] nf half-sister

démission [demisjɔ̃] nf resignation; **donner sa ~** to give ou hand in one's notice; **démissionner** vi to resign

demi-tarif [dəmitaʀif] nm half-price;

voyager à ~ to travel half-fare
demi-tour [dəmituʀ] *nm* about-turn; **faire ~** to turn (and go) back
démocratie [demɔkʀasi] *nf* democracy; **démocratique** *adj* democratic
démodé, e [demɔde] *adj* old-fashioned
demoiselle [d(ə)mwazɛl] *nf* (*jeune fille*) young lady; (*célibataire*) single lady, maiden lady; **demoiselle d'honneur** bridesmaid
démolir [demɔliʀ] *vt* to demolish
démon [demɔ̃] *nm* (*enfant turbulent*) devil, demon; **le D~** the Devil
démonstration [demɔ̃stʀasjɔ̃] *nf* demonstration
démonter [demɔ̃te] *vt* (*machine etc*) to take down, dismantle; **se démonter** (*meuble*) to be dismantled, be taken to pieces; (*personne*) to lose countenance
démontrer [demɔ̃tʀe] *vt* to demonstrate
démouler [demule] *vt* to turn out
démuni, e [demyni] *adj* (*sans argent*) impoverished; **~ de** without
dénicher [deniʃe] (*fam*) *vt* (*objet*) to unearth; (*restaurant etc*) to discover
dénier [denje] *vt* to deny
dénivellation [denivelasjɔ̃] *nf* (*pente*) slope
dénombrer [denɔ̃bʀe] *vt* to count
dénomination [denɔminasjɔ̃] *nf* designation, appellation
dénoncer [denɔ̃se] *vt* to denounce; **se dénoncer** to give o.s. up, come forward
dénouement [denumɑ̃] *nm* outcome
dénouer [denwe] *vt* to unknot, undo
denrée [dɑ̃ʀe] *nf*: **denrées alimentaires** foodstuffs
dense [dɑ̃s] *adj* dense; **densité** *nf* density
dent [dɑ̃] *nf* tooth; **dent de lait/de sagesse** milk/wisdom tooth; **dentaire** *adj* dental; **cabinet dentaire** dental surgery (BRIT), dentist's office (US)
dentelle [dɑ̃tɛl] *nf* lace *no pl*
dentier [dɑ̃tje] *nm* denture
dentifrice [dɑ̃tifʀis] *nm* toothpaste
dentiste [dɑ̃tist] *nm/f* dentist
dentition [dɑ̃tisjɔ̃] *nf* teeth
dénué, e [denɥe] *adj*: **~ de** devoid of
déodorant [deɔdɔʀɑ̃] *nm* deodorant
déontologie [deɔ̃tɔlɔʒi] *nf* code of practice
dépannage [depanaʒ] *nm*: **service de ~** (*Auto*) breakdown service
dépanner [depane] *vt* (*voiture, télévision*) to fix, repair; (*fig*) to bail out, help out; **dépanneuse** *nf* breakdown lorry (BRIT), tow truck (US)
dépareillé, e [depaʀeje] *adj* (*collection, service*) incomplete; (*objet*) odd
départ [depaʀ] *nm* departure; (*Sport*) start; **au ~** at the start; **la veille de son ~** the day before he leaves/left

département [depaʀtəmɑ̃] *nm* department

dépassé, e [depase] *adj* superseded, outmoded; **il est complètement ~** he's completely out of his depth, he can't cope
dépasser [depase] *vt* (*véhicule, concurrent*) to overtake; (*endroit*) to pass, go past; (*somme, limite*) to exceed; (*fig: en beauté etc*) to surpass, outshine ▷ *vi* (*jupon etc*) to show; **se dépasser** to excel o.s.
dépaysé, e [depeize] *adj* disoriented
dépaysement [depeizmɑ̃] *nm* (*changement*) change of scenery
dépêcher [depeʃe]: **se dépêcher** *vi* to hurry
dépendance [depɑ̃dɑ̃s] *nf* dependence; (*bâtiment*) outbuilding
dépendre [depɑ̃dʀ]: **~ de** *vt* to depend on; (*financièrement etc*) to be dependent on; **ça dépend** it depends
dépens [depɑ̃] *nmpl*: **aux ~ de** at the expense of
dépense [depɑ̃s] *nf* spending *no pl*, expense, expenditure *no pl*; **dépenser** *vt* to spend; (*énergie*) to expend, use up; **se dépenser** *vi* to exert o.s.
dépeupler [depœple]: **se dépeupler** *vi* to become depopulated
dépilatoire [depilatwaʀ] *adj*: **crème ~** hair-removing *ou* depilatory cream
dépister [depiste] *vt* to detect; (*voleur*) to track down
dépit [depi] *nm* vexation, frustration; **en ~ de** in spite of; **en ~ du bon sens** contrary to all good sense; **dépité, e** *adj* vexed, frustrated
déplacé, e [deplase] *adj* (*propos*) out of place, uncalled-for
déplacement [deplasmɑ̃] *nm* (*voyage*) trip, travelling *no pl*; **en ~** away
déplacer [deplase] *vt* (*table, voiture*) to move, shift; **se déplacer** *vi* to move; (*voyager*) to travel; **se ~ une vertèbre** to slip a disc
déplaire [deplɛʀ] *vt*: **ça me déplaît** I don't like this, I dislike this; **se déplaire** *vi* to be unhappy; **déplaisant, e** *adj* disagreeable
dépliant [deplijɑ̃] *nm* leaflet
déplier [deplije] *vt* to unfold
déposer [depoze] *vt* (*gén: mettre, poser*) to lay *ou* put down; (*à la banque, à la consigne*) to

deposit; (*passager*) to drop (off), set down; (*roi*) to depose; (*plainte*) to lodge; (*marque*) to register; **se déposer** vi to settle; **dépositaire** nm/f (*Comm*) agent; **déposition** nf statement

dépôt [depo] nm (*à la banque, sédiment*) deposit; (*entrepôt*) warehouse, store

dépourvu, e [depuRvy] adj: **~ de** lacking in, without; **prendre qn au ~** to catch sb unprepared

dépression [depresjɔ̃] nf depression; **dépression (nerveuse)** (nervous) breakdown

déprimant, e [deprimɑ̃, ɑ̃t] adj depressing

déprimer [deprime] vi to be/get depressed

 MOT-CLÉ

depuis [dəpɥi] prép 1 (*point de départ dans le temps*) since; **il habite Paris depuis 1983/l'an dernier** he has been living in Paris since 1983/last year; **depuis quand?** since when?; **depuis quand le connaissez-vous?** how long have you known him?

2 (*temps écoulé*) for; **il habite Paris depuis 5 ans** he has been living in Paris for 5 years; **je le connais depuis 3 ans** I've known him for 3 years

3 (*lieu*): **il a plu depuis Metz** it's been raining since Metz; **elle a téléphoné depuis Valence** she rang from Valence

4 (*quantité, rang*) from; **depuis les plus petits jusqu'aux plus grands** from the youngest to the oldest

▷ adv (*temps*) since (then); **je ne lui ai pas parlé depuis** I haven't spoken to him since (then); **depuis que** conj (ever) since; **depuis qu'il m'a dit ça** (ever) since he said that to me

député, e [depyte] nm/f (*Pol*) ≈ Member of Parliament (*BRIT*), ≈ Member of Congress (*US*)

dérangement [derɑ̃ʒmɑ̃] nm (*gêne*) trouble; (*gastrique etc*) disorder; **en ~** (*téléphone, machine*) out of order

déranger [derɑ̃ʒe] vt (*personne*) to trouble, bother; (*projets*) to disrupt, upset; (*objets, vêtements*) to disarrange; **se déranger** vi: **surtout ne vous dérangez pas pour moi** please don't put yourself out on my account; **est-ce que cela vous dérange si ...?** do you mind if ...?

déraper [derape] vi (*voiture*) to skid; (*personne, semelles*) to slip

dérégler [deregle] vt (*mécanisme*) to put out of order; (*estomac*) to upset

dérisoire [derizwar] adj derisory

dérive [deriv] nf: **aller à la ~** (*Navig, fig*) to drift

dérivé, e [derive] nm (*Tech*) by-product

dermatologue [dermatolɔg] nm/f dermatologist

dernier, -ière [dernje, jer] adj last; (*le plus récent*) latest, last; **lundi/le mois ~** last Monday/month; **c'est le ~ cri** it's the very latest thing; **en ~** last; **ce ~** the latter; **dernièrement** adv recently

dérogation [derɔgasjɔ̃] nf (special) dispensation

dérouiller [deruje] vt: **se ~ les jambes** to stretch one's legs (*fig*)

déroulement [derulmɑ̃] nm (*d'une opération etc*) progress

dérouler [derule] vt (*ficelle*) to unwind; **se dérouler** vi (*avoir lieu*) to take place; (*se passer*) to go (off); **tout s'est déroulé comme prévu** everything went as planned

dérouter [derute] vt (*avion, train*) to reroute, divert; (*étonner*) to disconcert, throw (out)

derrière [derjer] adv, prép behind ▷ nm (*d'une maison*) back; (*postérieur*) behind, bottom; **les pattes de ~** the back ou hind legs; **par ~** from behind; (*fig*) behind one's back

des [de] dét voir **de** ▷ prép +dét = **de +les**

dès [de] prép from; **~ que** as soon as; **~ son retour** as soon as he was (ou is) back

désaccord [dezakɔr] nm disagreement

désagréable [dezagreabl] adj unpleasant

désagrément [dezagremɑ̃] nm annoyance, trouble *no pl*

désaltérer [dezaltere] vt: **se désaltérer** to quench one's thirst

désapprobateur, -trice [dezaprɔbatœr, tris] adj disapproving

désapprouver [dezapruve] vt to disapprove of

désarmant, e [dezarmɑ̃, ɑ̃t] adj disarming

désastre [dezastr] nm disaster; **désastreux, -euse** adj disastrous

désavantage [dezavɑ̃taʒ] nm disadvantage; **désavantager** vt to put at a disadvantage

descendre [desɑ̃dr] vt (*escalier, montagne*) to go (ou come) down; (*valise, paquet*) to take ou get down; (*étagère etc*) to lower; (*fam: abattre*) to shoot down ▷ vi to go (ou come) down; (*passager: s'arrêter*) to get out, alight; **~ à pied/ en voiture** to walk/drive down; **~ de** (*famille*) to be descended from; **~ du train** to get out of ou get off the train; **~ de cheval** to dismount; **~ d'un arbre** to climb down from a tree; **~ à l'hôtel** to stay at a hotel

descente [desɑ̃t] nf descent, going down; (*chemin*) way down; (*Ski*) downhill (race); **au milieu de la ~** halfway down; **descente de lit** bedside rug; **descente (de police)** (police) raid

description [deskripsjɔ̃] nf description

déséquilibre [dezekilibr] nm (*position*): **en ~** unsteady; (*fig: des forces, du budget*) imbalance

désert, e [dezer, ert] adj deserted ▷ nm desert; **désertique** adj desert *cpd*

désespéré, e [dezɛspere] adj desperate

désespérer [dezɛspeʀe] vi: ~ **(de)** to despair (of); **désespoir** nm despair; **en désespoir de cause** in desperation

déshabiller [dezabije] vt to undress; **se déshabiller** vi to undress (o.s.)

déshydraté, e [dezidʀate] adj dehydrated

désigner [deziɲe] vt (montrer) to point out, indicate; (dénommer) to denote; (candidat etc) to name

désinfectant, e [dezɛ̃fɛktɑ̃, ɑ̃t] adj, nm disinfectant

désinfecter [dezɛ̃fɛkte] vt to disinfect

désintéressé, e [dezɛ̃teʀese] adj disinterested, unselfish

désintéresser [dezɛ̃teʀese] vt: **se ~ (de)** to lose interest (in)

désintoxication [dezɛ̃tɔksikasjɔ̃] nf: **faire une cure de ~** to undergo treatment for alcoholism (ou drug addiction)

désinvolte [dezɛ̃vɔlt] adj casual, off-hand

désir [deziʀ] nm wish; (sensuel) desire; **désirer** vt to want, wish for; (sexuellement) to desire; **je désire ...** (formule de politesse) I would like ...

désister [deziste]: **se désister** vi to stand down, withdraw

désobéir [dezɔbeiʀ] vi: **~ (à qn/qch)** to disobey (sb/sth); **désobéissant, e** adj disobedient

désodorisant [dezɔdɔʀizɑ̃] nm air freshener, deodorizer

désolé, e [dezɔle] adj (paysage) desolate; **je suis ~** I'm sorry

désordonné, e [dezɔʀdɔne] adj untidy

désordre [dezɔʀdʀ] nm disorder(liness), untidiness; (anarchie) disorder; **en ~** in a mess, untidy

désormais [dezɔʀmɛ] adv from now on

desquelles [dekɛl] prép +pron = **de +lesquelles**

desquels [dekɛl] prép +pron = **de +lesquels**

dessécher [deseʃe]: **se dessécher** vi to dry out

desserrer [deseʀe] vt to loosen; (frein) to release

dessert [desɛʀ] nm dessert, pudding

desservir [desɛʀviʀ] vt (ville, quartier) to serve; (débarrasser): **~ (la table)** to clear the table

dessin [desɛ̃] nm (œuvre, art) drawing; (motif) pattern, design; **dessin animé** cartoon (film); **dessin humoristique** cartoon; **dessinateur, -trice** nm/f drawer; (de bandes dessinées) cartoonist; (industriel) draughtsman(-woman) (BRIT), draftsman(-woman) (US); **dessiner** vt to draw; (concevoir) to design; **se dessiner** vi (forme) to be outlined; (fig: solution) to emerge

dessous [d(ə)su] adv underneath, beneath ▷ nm underside ▷ nmpl (sous-vêtements) underwear sg; **en ~, par ~** underneath; **au-~**

(de) below; (peu digne de) beneath; **avoir le ~** to get the worst of it; **les voisins du ~** the downstairs neighbours; **dessous-de-plat** nm inv tablemat

dessus [d(ə)sy] adv on top; (collé, écrit) on it ▷ nm top; **en ~** above; **par ~** adv over it ▷ prép over; **au-~ (de)** above; **les voisins du ~** the upstairs neighbours; **avoir le ~** to get the upper hand; **sens ~ dessous** upside down; **dessus-de-lit** nm inv bedspread

destin [dɛstɛ̃] nm fate; (avenir) destiny

destinataire [dɛstinatɛʀ] nm/f (Postes) addressee; (d'un colis) consignee

destination [dɛstinasjɔ̃] nf (lieu) destination; (usage) purpose; **à ~ de** bound for, travelling to

destiner [dɛstine] vt: **~ qch à qn** (envisager de donner) to intend sb to have sth; (adresser) to intend sth for sb; **être destiné à** (usage) to be meant for; **se ~ à l'enseignement** to intend to become a teacher

détachant [detaʃɑ̃] nm stain remover

détacher [detaʃe] vt (enlever) to detach, remove; (délier) to untie; (Admin): **~ qn (auprès de** ou **à)** to post sb (to); **se détacher** vi (se séparer) to come off; (: page) to come out; (se défaire) to come undone; **se ~ sur** to stand out against; **se ~ de** (se désintéresser) to grow away from

détail [detaj] nm detail; (Comm): **le ~** retail; **en ~** in detail; **au ~** (Comm) retail; **détaillant** nm retailer; **détaillé, e** adj (plan, explications) detailed; (facture) itemized; **détailler** vt (expliquer) to explain in detail

détecter [detɛkte] vt to detect

détective [detɛktiv] nm: **détective (privé)** private detective

déteindre [detɛ̃dʀ] vi (au lavage) to run, lose its colour; **~ sur** (vêtement) to run into; (fig) to rub off on

détendre [detɑ̃dʀ] vt (corps, esprit) to relax; **se détendre** vi (ressort) to lose its tension; (personne) to relax

détenir [det(ə)niʀ] vt (record, pouvoir, secret) to hold; (prisonnier) to detain, hold

détente [detɑ̃t] nf relaxation

détention [detɑ̃sjɔ̃] nf (d'armes) possession; (captivité) detention; **détention préventive** custody

détenu, e [det(ə)ny] nm/f prisoner

détergent [detɛʀʒɑ̃] nm detergent

détériorer [deteʀjɔʀe] vt to damage; **se détériorer** vi to deteriorate

déterminé, e [detɛʀmine] adj (résolu) determined; (précis) specific, definite

déterminer [detɛʀmine] vt (fixer) to determine; **~ qn à faire qch** to decide sb to do sth; **se ~ à faire qch** to make up one's mind to do sth

détester [detɛste] vt to hate, detest

détour [detuʀ] nm detour; (*tournant*) bend, curve; **ça vaut le ~** it's worth the trip; **sans ~** (*fig*) plainly

détourné, e [detuʀne] adj (*moyen*) roundabout

détourner [detuʀne] vt to divert; (*par la force*) to hijack; (*yeux, tête*) to turn away; (*de l'argent*) to embezzle; **se détourner** vi to turn away

détraquer [detʀake] vt to put out of order; (*estomac*) to upset; **se détraquer** vi (*machine*) to go wrong

détriment [detʀimɑ̃] nm: **au ~ de** to the detriment of

détroit [detʀwa] nm strait

détruire [detʀɥiʀ] vt to destroy

dette [dɛt] nf debt

DEUG sigle m (= *diplôme d'études universitaires générales*) diploma taken after 2 years at university

deuil [dœj] nm (*perte*) bereavement; (*période*) mourning; **être en ~** to be in mourning

deux [dø] num two; **tous les ~** both; **ses ~ mains** both his hands, his two hands; **~ fois** twice; **deuxième** num second; **deuxièmement** adv secondly; **deux-pièces** nm inv (*tailleur*) two-piece suit; (*de bain*) two-piece (swimsuit); (*appartement*) two-roomed flat (BRIT) ou apartment (US); **deux-points** nm inv colon sg; **deux-roues** nm inv two-wheeled vehicle

devais [dəvɛ] vb voir **devoir**

dévaluation [devalɥasjɔ̃] nf devaluation

devancer [d(ə)vɑ̃se] vt (*coureur, rival*) to get ahead of; (*arriver*) to arrive before; (*prévenir: questions, désirs*) to anticipate

devant [d(ə)vɑ̃] adv in front; (*à distance: en avant*) ahead ▷ prép in front of; (*en avant*) ahead of; (*avec mouvement: passer*) past; (*en présence de*) before, in front of; (*étant donné*) in view of ▷ nm front; **prendre les ~s** to make the first move; **les pattes de ~** the front legs, the forelegs; **par ~** (*boutonner*) at the front; (*entrer*) the front way; **aller au-~ de qn** to go out to meet sb; **aller au-~ de** (*désirs de qn*) to anticipate

devanture [d(ə)vɑ̃tyʀ] nf (*étalage*) display; (*vitrine*) (shop) window

développement [dev(ə)lɔpmɑ̃] nm development; **pays en voie de ~** developing countries

développer [dev(ə)lɔpe] vt to develop; **se développer** vi to develop

devenir [dəv(ə)niʀ] vb +attrib to become; **que sont-ils devenus?** what has become of them?

devez [dəve] vb voir **devoir**

déviation [devjasjɔ̃] nf (*Auto*) diversion (BRIT), detour (US)

devienne etc [dəvjɛn] vb voir **devenir**

deviner [d(ə)vine] vt to guess; (*apercevoir*) to distinguish; **devinette** nf riddle

devis [d(ə)vi] nm estimate, quotation

devise [dəviz] nf (*formule*) motto, watchword; **devises** nfpl (*argent*) currency sg

dévisser [devise] vt to unscrew, undo; **se dévisser** vi to come unscrewed

devoir [d(ə)vwaʀ] nm duty; (*Scol*) homework no pl; (: *en classe*) exercise ▷ vt (*argent, respect*): **~ qch (à qn)** to owe (sb) sth; (+infin: *obligation*): **il doit le faire** he has to do it, he must do it; (: *intention*): **le nouveau centre commercial doit ouvrir en mai** the new shopping centre is due to open in May; (: *probabilité*): **il doit être tard** it must be late; (: *fatalité*): **cela devait arriver** it was bound to happen; **combien est-ce que je vous dois?** how much do I owe you?

dévorer [devɔʀe] vt to devour

dévoué, e [devwe] adj devoted

dévouer [devwe]: **se dévouer** vi (*se sacrifier*): **se ~ (pour)** to sacrifice o.s. (for); (*se consacrer*): **se ~ à** to devote ou dedicate o.s. to

devrai [dəvʀe] vb voir **devoir**

dézipper [dezipe] vt to unzip

diabète [djabɛt] nm diabetes sg; **diabétique** nm/f diabetic

diable [djɑbl] nm devil

diabolo [djabɔlo] nm (*boisson*) lemonade with fruit cordial

diagnostic [djagnɔstik] nm diagnosis sg; **diagnostiquer** vt to diagnose

diagonal, e, -aux [djagɔnal, o] adj diagonal; **diagonale** nf diagonal; **en diagonale** diagonally

diagramme [djagʀam] nm chart, graph

dialecte [djalɛkt] nm dialect

dialogue [djalɔg] nm dialogue

diamant [djamɑ̃] nm diamond

diamètre [djamɛtʀ] nm diameter

diapositive [djapozitiv] nf transparency, slide

diarrhée [djaʀe] nf diarrhoea

dictateur [diktatœʀ] nm dictator; **dictature** nf dictatorship

dictée [dikte] nf dictation

dicter [dikte] vt to dictate

dictionnaire [diksjɔnɛʀ] nm dictionary

dièse [djɛz] nm sharp

diesel [djezɛl] nm diesel ▷ adj inv diesel

diète [djɛt] nf (*jeûne*) starvation diet; (*régime*) diet; **diététique** adj: **magasin diététique** health food shop (BRIT) ou store (US)

dieu, x [djø] nm god; **D~** God; **mon D~!** good heavens!

différemment [difeʀamɑ̃] adv differently

différence [difeʀɑ̃s] nf difference; **à la ~ de** unlike; **différencier** vt to differentiate

différent, e [difeʀɑ̃, ɑ̃t] adj (*dissemblable*) different; **~ de** different from; (*divers*) different, various

différer[difere] vt to postpone, put off ▷ vi: ~ **(de)** to differ (from)

difficile[difisil] adj difficult; (exigeant) hard to please; **difficilement** adv with difficulty

difficulté[difikylte] nf difficulty; **en ~** (bateau, alpiniste) in difficulties

diffuser[difyze] vt (chaleur) to diffuse; (émission, musique) to broadcast; (nouvelle) to circulate; (Comm) to distribute

digérer[diʒere] vt to digest; (fam: accepter) to stomach, put up with; **digestif** nm (after-dinner) liqueur; **digestion** nf digestion

digne[diɲ] adj dignified; **~ de** worthy of; **~ de foi** trustworthy; **dignité** nf dignity

digue[dig] nf dike, dyke

dilemme[dilem] nm dilemma

diligence[diliʒɑ̃s] nf stagecoach

diluer[dilɥe] vt to dilute

dimanche[dimɑ̃ʃ] nm Sunday

dimension[dimɑ̃sjɔ̃] nf (grandeur) size; (dimensions) dimensions

diminuer[diminɥe] vt to reduce, decrease; (ardeur etc) to lessen; (dénigrer) to belittle ▷ vi to decrease, diminish; **diminutif** nm (surnom) pet name

dinde[dɛ̃d] nf turkey

dindon[dɛ̃dɔ̃] nm turkey

dîner[dine] nm dinner ▷ vi to have dinner

dingue[dɛ̃g] (fam) adj crazy

dinosaure[dinɔzɔr] nm dinosaur

diplomate[diplɔmat] adj diplomatic ▷ nm diplomat; (fig) diplomatist; **diplomatie** nf diplomacy

diplôme[diplom] nm diploma; **avoir des ~s** to have qualifications; **diplômé, e** adj qualified

dire[dir] nm: **au ~ de** according to ▷ vt to say; (secret, mensonge, heure) to tell; **~ qch à qn** to tell sb sth; **~ à qn qu'il fasse** ou **de faire** to tell sb to do; **on dit que** they say that; **ceci** ou **cela dit** that being said; **si cela lui dit** (plaire) if he fancies it; **que dites-vous de** (penser) what do you think of; **on dirait que** it looks (ou sounds etc) as if; **dis/dites (donc)!** I say!; **se ~ (à soi-même)** to say to o.s.; **se ~ malade** (se prétendre) to claim one is ill; **ça ne se dit pas** (impoli) you shouldn't say that; (pas en usage) you don't say that

direct, e[dirɛkt] adj direct ▷ nm (TV): **en ~** live; **directement** adv directly

directeur, -trice[dirɛktœr, tris] nm/f (d'entreprise) director; (de service) manager (-eress); (d'école) head(teacher) (BRIT), principal (US)

direction[dirɛksjɔ̃] nf (sens) direction; (d'entreprise) management; (Auto) steering; **"toutes ~s"** "all routes"

dirent[dir] vb voir **dire**

dirigeant, e[diriʒɑ̃, ɑ̃t] adj (classe) ruling

▷ nm/f (d'un parti etc) leader

diriger[diriʒe] vt (entreprise) to manage, run; (véhicule) to steer; (orchestre) to conduct; (recherches, travaux) to supervise; **~ sur** (arme) to point ou level ou aim at; **~ son regard sur** to look in the direction of; **se diriger** vi (s'orienter) to find one's way; **se ~ vers** ou **sur** to make ou head for

dis[di] vb voir **dire**

discerner[diserne] vt to discern, make out

discipline[disiplin] nf discipline; **discipliner** vt to discipline

discontinu, e[diskɔ̃tiny] adj intermittent

discontinuer[diskɔ̃tinɥe] vi: **sans ~** without stopping, without a break

discothèque[diskɔtek] nf (boîte de nuit) disco(thèque)

discours[diskur] nm speech

discret, -ète[diskre, et] adj discreet; (parfum, maquillage) unobtrusive; **discrétion** nf discretion; **à discrétion** as much as one wants

discrimination[diskriminasjɔ̃] nf discrimination; **sans ~** indiscriminately

discussion[diskysjɔ̃] nf discussion

discutable[diskytabl] adj debatable

discuter[diskyte] vt (débattre) to discuss; (contester) to question, dispute ▷ vi to talk; (protester) to argue; **~ de** to discuss

dise[diz] vb voir **dire**

disjoncteur[disʒɔ̃ktœr] nm (Élec) circuit breaker

disloquer[dislɔke]: **se disloquer** vi (parti, empire) to break up; (meuble) to come apart; (épaule) to be dislocated

disons[dizɔ̃] vb voir **dire**

disparaître[disparetr] vi to disappear; (se perdre: traditions etc) to die out; **faire ~** (tache) to remove; (douleur) to get rid of

disparition[disparisjɔ̃] nf disappearance; **espèce en voie de ~** endangered species

disparu, e[dispary] nm/f missing person ▷ adj: **être porté ~** to be reported missing

dispensaire[dispɑ̃ser] nm community clinic

dispenser[dispɑ̃se] vt: **~ qn de** to exempt sb from

disperser[disperse] vt to scatter; **se disperser** vi to break up

disponible[dispɔnibl(ə)] adj available

disposé, e[dispoze] adj: **bien/mal ~** (humeur) in a good/bad mood; **~ à** (prêt à) willing ou prepared to

disposer[dispoze] vt to arrange ▷ vi: **vous pouvez ~** you may leave; **~ de** to have (at one's disposal); **se ~ à faire** to prepare to do, to be about to do

dispositif[dispozitif] nm device; (fig) system, plan of action

disposition[dispozisjɔ̃] nf (arrangement) arrangement, layout; (humeur) mood;

prendre ses ~s to make arrangements; **avoir des ~s pour la musique** etc to have a special aptitude for music etc; **à la ~ de qn** at sb's disposal; **je suis à votre ~** I am at your service

disproportionné, e [dispropɔrsjɔne] adj disproportionate, out of all proportion

dispute [dispyt] nf quarrel, argument; **disputer** vt (match) to play; (combat) to fight; **se disputer** vi to quarrel

disqualifier [diskalifje] vt to disqualify

disque [disk] nm (Mus) record; (forme, pièce) disc; (Sport) discus; **disque compact** compact disc; **disque dur** hard disk; **disquette** nf floppy disk, diskette

dissertation [disɛrtasjɔ̃] nf (Scol) essay

dissimuler [disimyle] vt to conceal

dissipé, e [disipe] adj (élève) undisciplined, unruly

dissolvant [disɔlvɑ̃] nm nail polish remover

dissuader [disɥade] vt: **~ qn de faire** to dissuade sb from doing

distance [distɑ̃s] nf distance; (fig: écart) gap; **à ~** at ou from a distance; **distancer** vt to outdistance

distant, e [distɑ̃, ɑ̃t] adj (réservé) distant; **~ de** (lieu) far away from

distillerie [distilri] nf distillery

distinct, e [distɛ̃(kt), ɛ̃kt] adj distinct; **distinctement** adv distinctly, clearly; **distinctif, -ive** adj distinctive

distingué, e [distɛ̃ge] adj distinguished

distinguer [distɛ̃ge] vt to distinguish; **se ~ de** to be distinguished by

distraction [distraksjɔ̃] nf (inattention) absent-mindedness; (passe-temps) distraction, entertainment

distraire [distrɛr] vt (divertir) to entertain, divert; (déranger) to distract; **se distraire** vi to amuse ou enjoy o.s.; **distrait, e** adj absent-minded

distrayant, e [distrɛjɑ̃, ɑ̃t] adj entertaining

distribuer [distribɥe] vt to distribute, hand out; (Cartes) to deal (out); (courrier) to deliver; **distributeur** nm (Comm) distributor; **distributeur (automatique)** (vending) machine; **distributeur de billets** (cash) dispenser

dit, e [di, dit] pp de **dire** ▷ adj (fixé): **le jour ~** the arranged day; (surnommé): **X, ~ Pierrot** X, known as Pierrot

dites [dit] vb voir **dire**

divan [divɑ̃] nm divan

divers, e [divɛr, ɛrs] adj (varié) diverse, varied; (différent) different, various; **~es personnes** various ou several people

diversité [divɛrsite] nf (variété) diversity

divertir [divɛrtir]: **se divertir** vi to amuse ou enjoy o.s.; **divertissement** nm distraction, entertainment

diviser [divize] vt to divide; **division** nf division

divorce [divɔrs] nm divorce; **divorcé, e** nm/f divorcee; **divorcer** vi to get a divorce, get divorced; **divorcer de** ou **d'avec qn** to divorce sb

divulguer [divylge] vt to disclose

dix [dis] num ten; **dix-huit** num eighteen; **dix-huitième** num eighteenth; **dixième** num tenth; **dix-neuf** num nineteen; **dix-neuvième** num nineteenth; **dix-sept** num seventeen; **dix-septième** num seventeenth

dizaine [dizɛn] nf: **une ~ (de)** about ten, ten or so

do [do] nm (note) C; (en chantant la gamme) do(h)

docile [dɔsil] adj docile

dock [dɔk] nm dock; **docker** nm docker

docteur [dɔktœr] nm doctor; **doctorat** nm doctorate

doctrine [dɔktrin] nf doctrine

document [dɔkymɑ̃] nm document; **documentaire** adj, nm documentary; **documentation** nf documentation, literature; **documenter** vt: **se documenter (sur)** to gather information (on)

dodo [dodo] nm (langage enfantin): **aller faire ~** to go to beddy-byes

dogue [dɔg] nm mastiff

doigt [dwa] nm finger; **à deux ~s de** within an inch of; **un ~ de lait/whisky** a drop of milk/whisky; **doigt de pied** toe

doit etc [dwa] vb voir **devoir**

dollar [dɔlar] nm dollar

domaine [dɔmɛn] nm estate, property; (fig) domain, field

domestique [dɔmɛstik] adj domestic ▷ nm/f servant, domestic

domicile [dɔmisil] nm home, place of residence; **à ~** at home; **livrer à ~** to deliver; **domicilié, e** adj: **"domicilié à ..."** "address ..."

dominant, e [dɔminɑ̃, ɑ̃t] adj (opinion) predominant

dominer [dɔmine] vt to dominate; (sujet) to master; (surpasser) to outclass, surpass; (surplomber) to tower above, dominate ▷ vi to be in the dominant position; **se dominer** vi to control o.s.

domino [dɔmino] nm domino; **dominos** nmpl (jeu) dominoes sg

dommage [dɔmaʒ] nm: **~s** (dégâts) damage no pl; **c'est ~!** what a shame!; **c'est ~ que** it's a shame ou pity that

dompter [dɔ̃(p)te] vt to tame; **dompteur, -euse** nm/f trainer

DOM-ROM [dɔmrɔm] sigle m (= départements et régions d'outre-mer) French overseas departments and regions

don [dɔ̃] nm gift; (charité) donation; **avoir des ~s pour** to have a gift ou talent for; **elle a le ~**

de m'énerver she's got a knack of getting on my nerves

donc [dɔ̃k] *conj* therefore, so; (*après une digression*) so, then

donné, e [dɔne] *adj* (*convenu: lieu, heure*) given; (*pas cher: fam*): **c'est ~** it's a gift; **étant ~ que ...** given that ...; **données** *nfpl* data

donner [dɔne] *vt* to give; (*vieux habits etc*) to give away; (*spectacle*) to put on; **~ qch à qn** to give sb sth, give sth to sb; **~ sur** (*suj: fenêtre, chambre*) to look (out) onto; **ça donne soif/faim** it makes you (feel) thirsty/hungry; **se ~ à fond** to give one's all; **se ~ du mal** to take (great) trouble; **s'en ~ à cœur joie** (*fam*) to have a great time

○ **MOT-CLÉ**

dont [dɔ̃] *pron relatif* **1** (*appartenance: objets*) whose, of which; (*appartenance: êtres animés*) whose; **la maison dont le toit est rouge** the house the roof of which is red, the house whose roof is red; **l'homme dont je connais la sœur** the man whose sister I know
2 (*parmi lesquel(le)s*): **2 livres, dont l'un est ...** 2 books, one of which is ...; **il y avait plusieurs personnes, dont Gabrielle** there were several people, among them Gabrielle; **10 blessés, dont 2 grièvement** 10 injured, 2 of them seriously
3 (*complément d'adjectif, de verbe*): **le fils dont il est si fier** the son he's so proud of; **le pays dont il est originaire** the country he's from; **la façon dont il l'a fait** the way he did it; **ce dont je parle** what I'm talking about

dopage [dɔpaʒ] *nm* (*Sport*) drug use; (*de cheval*) doping

doré, e [dɔre] *adj* golden; (*avec dorure*) gilt, gilded

dorénavant [dɔrenavɑ̃] *adv* henceforth

dorer [dɔre] *vt* to gild; **(faire) ~** (*Culin*) to brown

dorloter [dɔrlɔte] *vt* to pamper

dormir [dɔrmir] *vi* to sleep; (*être endormi*) to be asleep

dortoir [dɔrtwar] *nm* dormitory

dos [do] *nm* back; (*de livre*) spine; **"voir au ~"** "see over"; **de ~** from the back

dosage [dozaʒ] *nm* mixture

dose [doz] *nf* dose; **doser** *vt* to measure out; **il faut savoir doser ses efforts** you have to be able to pace yourself

dossier [dosje] *nm* (*documents*) file; (*de chaise*) back; (*Presse*) feature; (*Comput*) folder; **un ~ scolaire** a school report

douane [dwan] *nf* customs *pl*; **douanier, -ière** *adj* customs *cpd* ▷ *nm* customs officer

double [dublə] *adj, adv* double ▷ *nm* (*2 fois plus*):

le ~ (de) twice as much (*ou* many) (as); (*autre exemplaire*) duplicate, copy; (*sosie*) double; (*Tennis*) doubles *sg*; **en ~ (exemplaire)** in duplicate; **faire ~ emploi** to be redundant; **double-cliquer** *vi* (*Inform*) to double-click

doubler [duble] *vt* (*multiplier par 2*) to double; (*vêtement*) to line; (*dépasser*) to overtake, pass; (*film*) to dub; (*acteur*) to stand in for ▷ *vi* to double

doublure [dublyr] *nf* lining; (*Cinéma*) stand-in

douce [dus] *adj voir* **doux**; **douceâtre** *adj* sickly sweet; **doucement** *adv* gently; (*lentement*) slowly; **douceur** *nf* softness; (*de quelqu'un*) gentleness; (*de climat*) mildness

douche [duʃ] *nf* shower; **prendre une ~** to have *ou* take a shower; **doucher: se doucher** *vi* to have *ou* take a shower

doué, e [dwe] *adj* gifted, talented; **être ~ pour** to have a gift for

douille [duj] *nf* (*Élec*) socket

douillet, te [dujɛ, ɛt] *adj* cosy; (*péj: à la douleur*) soft

douleur [dulœr] *nf* pain; (*chagrin*) grief, distress; **douloureux, -euse** *adj* painful

doute [dut] *nm* doubt; **sans ~** no doubt; (*probablement*) probably; **sans aucun ~** without a doubt; **douter** *vt* to doubt; **douter de** (*sincérité de qn*) to have (one's) doubts about; (*réussite*) to be doubtful of; **douter que** to doubt if *ou* whether; **se douter de qch/que** to suspect sth/that; **je m'en doutais** I suspected as much; **douteux, -euse** *adj* (*incertain*) doubtful; (*péj*) dubious-looking

Douvres [duvr] *n* Dover

doux, douce [du, dus] *adj* soft; (*sucré*) sweet; (*peu fort: moutarde, clément: climat*) mild; (*pas brusque*) gentle

douzaine [duzɛn] *nf* (*12*) dozen; (*environ 12*): **une ~ (de)** a dozen *ou* so

douze [duz] *num* twelve; **douzième** *num* twelfth

dragée [draʒe] *nf* sugared almond

draguer [drage] *vt* (*rivière*) to dredge; (*fam*) to try to pick up

dramatique [dramatik] *adj* dramatic; (*tragique*) tragic ▷ *nf* (*TV*) (television) drama

drame [dram] *nm* drama

drap [dra] *nm* (*de lit*) sheet; (*tissu*) woollen fabric

drapeau, x [drapo] *nm* flag

drap-housse [draus] *nm* fitted sheet

dresser [drese] *vt* (*mettre vertical, monter*) to put up, erect; (*liste*) to draw up; (*animal*) to train; **se dresser** *vi* (*obstacle*) to stand; (*personne*) to draw o.s. up; **~ qn contre qn** to set sb against sb; **~ l'oreille** to prick up one's ears

drogue [drɔg] *nf* drug; **la ~** drugs *pl*; **drogué, e** *nm/f* drug addict; **droguer** *vt* (*victime*) to drug; **se droguer** vi (aux stupéfiants) to take drugs; (péj: de médicaments) to dose o.s. up; **droguerie** nf hardware shop; **droguiste** nm keeper/owner of a hardware shop

droit, e [dʀwa, dʀwat] adj (non courbe) straight; (vertical) upright, straight; (fig: loyal) upright, straight(forward); (opposé à gauche) right, right-hand ▷ adv straight ▷ nm (prérogative) right; (taxe) duty, tax; (: d'inscription) fee; (Jur): **le ~** law; **avoir le ~ de** to be allowed to; **avoir ~ à** to be entitled to; **être dans son ~** to be within one's rights; **à ~e** on the right; (direction) (to the) right; **droits d'auteur** royalties; **droits d'inscription** enrolment fee; **droite** nf (Pol): **la droite** the right (wing); **droitier, -ière** adj right-handed

drôle [dʀol] adj funny; **une ~ d'idée** a funny idea

dromadaire [dʀɔmadɛʀ] nm dromedary

du [dy] dét voir **de** ▷ prép +dét = **de + le**

dû, due [dy] vb voir **devoir** ▷ adj (somme) owing, owed; (causé par): **dû à** due to ▷ nm due

dune [dyn] nf dune

duplex [dyplɛks] nm (appartement) split-level apartment, duplex

duquel [dykɛl] prép +pron = **de +lequel**

dur, e [dyʀ] adj (pierre, siège, travail, problème) hard; (voix, climat) harsh; (sévère) hard, harsh; (cruel) hard(-hearted); (porte, col) stiff; (viande) tough ▷ adv hard ▷ nm (fam: meneur) tough nut; **~ d'oreille** hard of hearing

durant [dyʀɑ̃] prép (au cours de) during; (pendant) for; **des mois ~** for months

durcir [dyʀsiʀ] vt, vi to harden; **se durcir** vi to harden

durée [dyʀe] nf length; (d'une pile etc) life; **de courte ~** (séjour) short

durement [dyʀmɑ̃] adv harshly

durer [dyʀe] vi to last

dureté [dyʀte] nf hardness; harshness; stiffness; toughness

durit(r) [dyʀit] nf (car radiator) hose

duvet [dyvɛ] nm down; (sac de couchage) down-filled sleeping bag

DVD sigle m (= digital versatile disc) DVD

dynamique [dinamik] adj dynamic; **dynamisme** nm dynamism

dynamo [dinamo] nf dynamo

dyslexie [dislɛksi] nf dyslexia, word-blindness

eau, x [o] nf water; **eaux** nfpl (Méd) waters; **prendre l'~** to leak, let in water; **tomber à l'~** (fig) to fall through; **eau de Cologne** eau de Cologne; **eau courante** running water; **eau de javel** bleach; **eau de toilette** toilet water; **eau douce** fresh water; **eau gazeuse** sparkling (mineral) water; **eau minérale** mineral water; **eau plate** still water; **eau salée** salt water; **eau-de-vie** nf brandy

ébène [ebɛn] nf ebony; **ébéniste** nm cabinetmaker

éblouir [ebluiʀ] vt to dazzle

éboueur [ebwœʀ] nm dustman (BRIT), garbageman (US)

ébouillanter [ebujɑ̃te] vt to scald; (Culin) to blanch

éboulement [ebulmɑ̃] nm rock fall

ébranler [ebʀɑ̃le] vt to shake; (affaiblir) to weaken; **s'ébranler** vi (partir) to move off

ébullition [ebylisjɔ̃] nf boiling point; **en ~** boiling

écaille [ekɑj] nf (de poisson) scale; (matière) tortoiseshell; **écailler** vt (poisson) to scale; **s'écailler** vi to flake ou peel (off)

écart [ekaʀ] nm gap; **à l'~** out of the way; **à l'~ de** away from; **faire un ~** (voiture) to swerve

écarté, e [ekaʀte] adj (lieu) out-of-the-way, remote; (ouvert): **les jambes ~es** legs apart; **les bras ~s** arms outstretched

écarter [ekaʀte] vt (séparer) to move apart,

separate; (*éloigner*) to push back, move away; (*ouvrir: bras, jambes*) to spread, open; (: *rideau*) to draw (back); (*éliminer: candidat, possibilité*) to dismiss; **s'écarter** vi to part; (*s'éloigner*) to move away; **s'~ de** to wander from

échafaudage [eʃafodaʒ] nm scaffolding

échalote [eʃalɔt] nf shallot

échange [eʃɑ̃ʒ] nm exchange; **en ~ de** in exchange ou return for; **échanger** vt: **échanger qch (contre)** to exchange sth (for)

échantillon [eʃɑ̃tijɔ̃] nm sample

échapper [eʃape]: **~ à** vt (*gardien*) to escape (from); (*punition, péril*) to escape; **s'échapper** vi to escape; **~ à qn** (*détail, sens*) to escape sb; (*objet qu'on tient*) to slip out of sb's hands; **laisser ~** (*cri etc*) to let out; **l'~ belle** to have a narrow escape

écharde [eʃaʀd] nf splinter (of wood)

écharpe [eʃaʀp] nf scarf; **avoir le bras en ~** to have one's arm in a sling

échauffer [eʃofe] vt (*moteur*) to overheat; **s'échauffer** vi (*Sport*) to warm up; (*dans la discussion*) to become heated

échéance [eʃeɑ̃s] nf (*d'un paiement: date*) settlement date; (*fig*) deadline; **à brève ~** in the short term; **à longue ~** in the long run

échéant [eʃeɑ̃]: **le cas ~** adv if the case arises

échec [eʃɛk] nm failure; (*Échecs*): **~ et mat/au roi** checkmate/check; **échecs** nmpl (*jeu*) chess sg; **tenir en ~** to hold in check

échelle [eʃɛl] nf ladder; (*fig, d'une carte*) scale

échelon [eʃ(ə)lɔ̃] nm (*d'échelle*) rung; (*Admin*) grade; **échelonner** vt to space out

échiquier [eʃikje] nm chessboard

écho [eko] nm echo; **échographie** nf: **passer une échographie** to have a scan

échouer [eʃwe] vi to fail; **s'échouer** vi to run aground

éclabousser [eklabuse] vt to splash

éclair [eklɛʀ] nm (*d'orage*) flash of lightning, lightning no pl; (*gâteau*) éclair

éclairage [eklɛʀaʒ] nm lighting

éclaircie [eklɛʀsi] nf bright interval

éclaircir [eklɛʀsiʀ] vt to lighten; (*fig: mystère*) to clear up; (: *point*) to clarify; **s'éclaircir** vi (*ciel*) to clear; **s'~ la voix** to clear one's throat; **éclaircissement** nm (*sur un point*) clarification

éclairer [eklɛʀe] vt (*lieu*) to light (up); (*personne: avec une lampe etc*) to light the way for; (*fig: problème*) to shed light on ▷ vi: **~ mal/bien** to give a poor/good light; **s'~ à la bougie** to use candlelight

éclat [ekla] nm (*de bombe, de verre*) fragment; (*du soleil, d'une couleur etc*) brightness, brilliance; (*d'une cérémonie*) splendour; (*scandale*): **faire un ~** to cause a commotion; **éclats de voix** shouts; **éclat de rire** roar of laughter

éclatant, e [eklatɑ̃, ɑ̃t] adj brilliant

éclater [eklate] vi (*pneu*) to burst; (*bombe*) to explode; (*guerre*) to break out; (*groupe, parti*) to break up; **~ en sanglots/de rire** to burst out sobbing/laughing

écluse [eklyz] nf lock

écœurant, e [ekœʀɑ̃, ɑ̃t] adj (*gâteau etc*) sickly; (*fig*) sickening

écœurer [ekœʀe] vt: **~ qn** (*nourriture*) to make sb feel sick; (*conduite, personne*) to disgust sb

école [ekɔl] nf school; **aller à l'~** to go to school; **école maternelle** nursery school; **école primaire** primary (BRIT) ou grade (US) school; **école secondaire** secondary (BRIT) ou high (US) school; **écolier, -ière** nm/f schoolboy(-girl)

écologie [ekɔlɔʒi] nf ecology; **écologique** adj environment-friendly; **écologiste** nm/f ecologist

économe [ekɔnɔm] adj thrifty ▷ nm/f (*de lycée etc*) bursar (BRIT), treasurer (US)

économie [ekɔnɔmi] nf economy; (*gain: d'argent, de temps etc*) saving; (*science*) economics sg; **économies** nfpl (*pécule*) savings; **économique** adj (*avantageux*) economical; (*Écon*) economic; **économiser** vt, vi to save

écorce [ekɔʀs] nf bark; (*de fruit*) peel

écorcher [ekɔʀʃe] vt: **s'~ le genou/la main** to graze one's knee/one's hand; **écorchure** nf graze

écossais, e [ekɔsɛ, ɛz] adj Scottish ▷ nm/f: **É~, e** Scot

Écosse [ekɔs] nf: **l'~** Scotland

écouter [ekute] vt to listen to; **s'écouter** (*malade*) to be a bit of a hypochondriac; **si je m'écoutais** if I followed my instincts; **écouteur** nm (*Tél*) receiver; **écouteurs** nmpl (*casque*) headphones pl, headset

écran [ekʀɑ̃] nm screen; **petit ~** television; **~ total** sunblock

écrasant, e [ekʀazɑ̃, ɑ̃t] adj overwhelming

écraser [ekʀaze] vt to crush; (*piéton*) to run over; **s'écraser** vi to crash; **s'~ contre** to crash into

écrémé, e [ekʀeme] adj (*lait*) skimmed

écrevisse [ekʀəvis] nf crayfish inv

écrire [ekʀiʀ] vt to write; **s'écrire** to write to each other; **ça s'écrit comment?** how is it spelt?; **écrit** nm (*examen*) written paper; **par écrit** in writing

écriteau, x [ekʀito] nm notice, sign

écriture [ekʀityʀ] nf writing; **écritures** nfpl (*Comm*) accounts, books; **l'É~ (sainte), les É~s** the Scriptures

écrivain [ekʀivɛ̃] nm writer

écrou [ekʀu] nm nut

écrouler [ekʀule]: **s'écrouler** vi to collapse

écru, e [ekʀy] adj (*couleur*) off-white, écru

écume [ekym] nf foam

écureuil [ekyrœj] nm squirrel

écurie [ekyri] nf stable

eczéma [ɛgzema] nm eczema

EDF sigle f (= Électricité de France) national electricity company

Édimbourg [edɛ̃bur] n Edinburgh

éditer [edite] vt (publier) to publish; (annoter) to edit; **éditeur, -trice** nm/f publisher; **édition** nf edition; (industrie du livre) publishing

édredon [edrədɔ̃] nm eiderdown

éducateur, -trice [edykatœr, tris] nm/f teacher; (en école spécialisée) instructor

éducatif, -ive [edykatif, iv] adj educational

éducation [edykasjɔ̃] nf education; (familiale) upbringing; (manières) (good) manners pl; **éducation physique** physical education

éduquer [edyke] vt to educate; (élever) to bring up

effacer [efase] vt to erase, rub out; **s'effacer** vi (inscription etc) to wear off; (pour laisser passer) to step aside

effarant, e [efarɑ̃, ɑ̃t] adj alarming

effectif, -ive [efɛktif, iv] adj real ▷ nm (Scol) (pupil) numbers pl; (entreprise) staff, workforce; **effectivement** adv (réellement) actually, really; (en effet) indeed

effectuer [efɛktɥe] vt (opération) to carry out; (trajet) to make

effervescent, e [efɛrvesɑ̃, ɑ̃t] adj effervescent

effet [efɛ] nm effect; (impression) impression; **effets** nmpl (vêtements etc) things; **faire ~** (médicament) to take effect; **faire de l'~** (impressionner) to make an impression; **faire bon/mauvais ~ sur qn** to make a good/bad impression on sb; **en ~** indeed; **effet de serre** greenhouse effect

efficace [efikas] adj (personne) efficient; (action, médicament) effective; **efficacité** nf efficiency; effectiveness

effondrer [efɔ̃dre]: **s'effondrer** vi to collapse

efforcer [efɔrse]: **s'efforcer de** vt: **s'~ de faire** to try hard to do

effort [efɔr] nm effort

effrayant, e [efrejɑ̃, ɑ̃t] adj frightening

effrayer [efreje] vt to frighten, scare; **s'~ (de)** to be frightened ou scared (by)

effréné, e [efrene] adj wild

effronté, e [efrɔ̃te] adj cheeky

effroyable [efrwajabl] adj horrifying, appalling

égal, e, -aux [egal, o] adj equal; (constant: vitesse) steady ▷ nm/f equal; **être ~ à** (prix, nombre) to be equal to; **ça lui est ~** it's all the same to him, he doesn't mind; **sans ~** matchless, unequalled; **d'~ à ~** as equals; **également** adv equally; (aussi) too, as well;

égaler vt to equal; **égaliser** vt (sol, salaires) to level (out); (chances) to equalize ▷ vi (Sport) to equalize; **égalité** nf equality; **être à égalité** to be level

égard [egar] nm: **~s** mpl consideration sg; **à cet ~** in this respect; **par ~ pour** out of consideration for; **à l'~ de** towards

égarer [egare] vt to mislay; **s'égarer** vi to get lost, lose one's way; (objet) to go astray

églefin [egləfɛ̃] nm haddock

église [egliz] nf church; **aller à l'~** to go to church

égoïsme [egɔism] nm selfishness; **égoïste** adj selfish

égout [egu] nm sewer

égoutter [egute] vi to drip; **s'égoutter** vi to drip; **égouttoir** nm draining board; (mobile) draining rack

égratignure [egratiɲyr] nf scratch

Égypte [eʒipt] nf: **l'~** Egypt; **égyptien, ne** adj Egyptian ▷ nm/f: **Égyptien, ne** Egyptian

eh [e] excl hey!; **eh bien!** well!

élaborer [elabɔre] vt to elaborate; (projet, stratégie) to work out; (rapport) to draft

élan [elɑ̃] nm (Zool) elk, moose; (Sport) run up; (fig: de tendresse etc) surge; **prendre de l'~** to gather speed

élancer [elɑ̃se]: **s'élancer** vi to dash, hurl o.s.

élargir [elarʒir] vt to widen; **s'élargir** vi to widen; (vêtement) to stretch

élastique [elastik] adj elastic ▷ nm (de bureau) rubber band; (pour la couture) elastic no pl

élection [elɛksjɔ̃] nf election

électricien, ne [elɛktrisjɛ̃, jɛn] nm/f electrician

électricité [elɛktrisite] nf electricity; **allumer/éteindre l'~** to put on/off the light

électrique [elɛktrik] adj electric(al)

électrocuter [elɛktrɔkyte] vt to electrocute

électroménager [elɛktromenaʒe] adj, nm: **appareils ~s, l'~** domestic (electrical) appliances

électronique [elɛktrɔnik] adj electronic ▷ nf electronics sg

élégance [elegɑ̃s] nf elegance

élégant, e [elegɑ̃, ɑ̃t] adj elegant

élément [elemɑ̃] nm element; (pièce) component, part; **élémentaire** adj elementary

éléphant [elefɑ̃] nm elephant

élevage [el(ə)vaʒ] nm breeding; (de bovins) cattle rearing; **truite d'~** farmed trout

élevé, e [el(ə)ve] adj high; **bien/mal ~** well-/ill-mannered

élève [elɛv] nm/f pupil

élever [el(ə)ve] vt (enfant) to bring up, raise; (animaux) to breed; (hausser: taux, niveau) to raise; (édifier: monument) to put up, erect; **s'élever** vi (avion) to go up; (niveau, *température*) to rise; **s'~ à** (*suj: frais, dégâts*) to amount to, add up to; **~ contre qch** to rise up against sth; **~ la voix** to raise one's voice; **éleveur, -euse** *nm/f* breeder

éliminatoire [eliminatwaʀ] *nf* (*Sport*) heat

éliminer [elimine] *vt* to eliminate

élire [eliʀ] *vt* to elect

elle [ɛl] *pron* (*sujet*) she; (*: chose*) it; (*complément*) her; **~s** (*sujet*) they; (*complément*) them; **~-même** herself; itself; **~s-mêmes** themselves; *voir aussi* **il**

éloigné, e [elwaɲe] *adj* distant, far-off; (*parent*) distant

éloigner [elwaɲe] *vt* (*échéance*) to put off, postpone; (*soupçons, danger*) to ward off; (*objet*) **~ qch (de)** to move ou take away (from); (*personne*) **~ qn (de)** to take sb away ou remove sb (from); **s'éloigner (de)** (*personne*) to go away (from); (*véhicule*) to move away (from); (*affectivement*) to grow away (from)

élu, e [ely] *pp de* **élire** ▷ *nm/f* (*Pol*) elected representative

Élysée [elize] *nm:* **(le palais de) l'~** the Élysee Palace (*the French president's residence*)

émail, -aux [emaj, o] *nm* enamel

e-mail [imɛl] *nm* e-mail; **envoyer qch par ~** to e-mail sth

émanciper [emãsipe]: **s'émanciper** *vi* (*fig*) to become emancipated ou liberated

emballage [ãbalaʒ] *nm* (*papier*) wrapping; (*boîte*) packaging

emballer [ãbale] *vt* to wrap (up); (*dans un carton*) to pack (up); (*fig: fam*) to thrill (to bits); **s'emballer** *vi* (*moteur*) to race; (*cheval*) to bolt; (*fig: personne*) to get carried away

embarcadère [ãbaʀkadɛʀ] *nm* wharf, pier

embarquement [ãbaʀkəmã] *nm* (*de passagers*) boarding; (*de marchandises*) loading

embarquer [ãbaʀke] *vt* (*personne*) to embark; (*marchandise*) to load; (*fam*) to cart off ▷ *vi* (*passager*) to board; **s'embarquer** *vi* to board; **s'~ dans** (*affaire, aventure*) to embark upon

embarras [ãbaʀa] *nm* (*gêne*) embarrassment; **mettre qn dans l'~** to put sb in an awkward position; **vous n'avez que l'~ du choix** the only problem is choosing

embarrassant, e [ãbaʀasã, ãt] *adj* embarrassing

embarrasser [ãbaʀase] *vt* (*encombrer*) to clutter (up); (*gêner*) to hinder, hamper; **~ qn** to put sb in an awkward position; **s'~ de** to burden o.s. with

embaucher [ãboʃe] *vt* to take on, hire

embêter [ãbete] *vt* to bother; **s'embêter** *vi* (*s'ennuyer*) to be bored

emblée [ãble]: **d'~** *adv* straightaway

embouchure [ãbuʃyʀ] *nf* (*Géo*) mouth

embourber [ãbuʀbe]: **s'embourber** *vi* to get stuck in the mud

embouteillage [ãbutɛjaʒ] *nm* traffic jam

embranchement [ãbʀãʃmã] *nm* (*routier*) junction

embrasser [ãbʀase] *vt* to kiss; (*sujet, période*) to embrace, encompass

embrayage [ãbʀejaʒ] *nm* clutch

embrouiller [ãbʀuje] *vt* to muddle up; (*fils*) to tangle (up); **s'embrouiller** *vi* (*personne*) to get in a muddle

embruns [ãbʀœ̃] *nmpl* sea spray *sg*

embué, e [ãbɥe] *adj* misted up

émeraude [em(ə)ʀod] *nf* emerald

émerger [emɛʀʒe] *vi* to emerge; (*faire saillie, aussi fig*) to stand out

émeri [em(ə)ʀi] *nm:* **toile** *ou* **papier ~** emery paper

émerveiller [emɛʀveje] *vt* to fill with wonder; **s'émerveiller de** to marvel at

émettre [emɛtʀ] *vt* (*son, lumière*) to give out, emit; (*message etc: Radio*) to transmit; (*billet, timbre, emprunt*) to issue; (*hypothèse, avis*) to voice, put forward ▷ *vi* to broadcast

émeus *etc* [emø] *vb voir* **émouvoir**

émeute [emøt] *nf* riot

émigrer [emigʀe] *vi* to emigrate

émincer [emɛ̃se] *vt* to cut into thin slices

émission [emisjõ] *nf* (*Radio, TV*) programme, broadcast; (*d'un message*) transmission; (*de timbre*) issue

emmêler [ãmele] *vt* to tangle (up); (*fig*) to muddle up; **s'emmêler** *vi* to get in a tangle

emménager [ãmenaʒe] *vi* to move in; **~ dans** to move into

emmener [ãm(ə)ne] *vt* to take (with one); (*comme otage, capture*) to take away; **~ qn au cinéma** to take sb to the cinema

emmerder [ãmɛʀde] (*fam!*) *vt* to bug, bother; **s'emmerder** *vi* to be bored stiff

émoticone [emɔtikɔn] *nm* smiley

émotif, -ive [emɔtif, iv] *adj* emotional

émotion [emosjõ] *nf* emotion

émouvoir [emuvwaʀ] *vt* to move; **s'émouvoir** *vi* to be moved; (*s'indigner*) to be roused

empaqueter [ãpakte] *vt* to parcel up

emparer [ãpaʀe]: **s'emparer de** *vt* (*objet*) to seize, grab; (*comme otage, MIL*) to seize; (*suj: peur etc*) to take hold of

empêchement [ãpɛʃmã] *nm* (*unexpected*) obstacle, hitch

empêcher [ãpeʃe] *vt* to prevent; **~ qn de faire** to prevent ou stop sb (from) doing; **il n'empêche que** nevertheless; **il n'a pas pu s'~ de rire** he couldn't help laughing

empereur [ãpʀœʀ] *nm* emperor

empiffrer [ãpifʀe]: **s'~** (*fam*) *vi* to stuff o.s.

empiler [ãpile] *vt* to pile (up)

empire [ãpiʀ] *nm* empire; (*fig*) influence

empirer [ãpiʀe] *vi* to worsen, deteriorate

emplacement [ɑ̃plasmɑ̃] nm site

emploi [ɑ̃plwa] nm (utilisation) use; (Comm, Écon) employment; (poste) job, situation; **mode d'~** directions for use; **emploi du temps** timetable, schedule

employé, e [ɑ̃plwaje] nm/f employee; **employé de bureau** office employee ou clerk

employer [ɑ̃plwaje] vt to use; (ouvrier, main-d'œuvre) to employ; **s'~ à faire** to apply ou devote o.s. to doing; **employeur, -euse** nm/f employer

empoigner [ɑ̃pwaɲe] vt to grab

empoisonner [ɑ̃pwazɔne] vt to poison; (empester: air, pièce) to stink out; (fam): **~ qn** to drive sb mad

emporter [ɑ̃pɔrte] vt to take (with one); (en dérobant ou enlevant, emmener: blessés, voyageurs) to take away; (entraîner) to carry away; **s'emporter** vi (de colère) to lose one's temper; **l'~ (sur)** to get the upper hand (of); **plats à ~** take-away meals

empreinte [ɑ̃prɛ̃t] nf: **~ (de pas)** footprint; **empreintes (digitales)** fingerprints

empressé, e [ɑ̃prese] adj attentive

empresser [ɑ̃prese]: **s'empresser** vi: **s'~ auprès de qn** to surround sb with attentions; **s'~ de faire** (se hâter) to hasten to do

emprisonner [ɑ̃prizɔne] vt to imprison

emprunt [ɑ̃prœ̃] nm loan

emprunter [ɑ̃prœ̃te] vt to borrow; (itinéraire) to take, follow

ému, e [emy] pp de **émouvoir** ▷ adj (gratitude) touched; (compassion) moved

MOT-CLÉ

en [ɑ̃] prép 1 (endroit, pays) in; (direction) to; **habiter en France/ville** to live in France/town; **aller en France/ville** to go to France/town
2 (moment, temps) in; **en été/juin** in summer/June; **en 3 jours** in 3 days
3 (moyen) by; **en avion/taxi** by plane/taxi
4 (composition) made of; **c'est en verre** it's (made of) glass; **un collier en argent** a silver necklace
5 (description, état): **une femme (habillée) en rouge** a woman (dressed) in red; **peindre qch en rouge** to paint sth red; **en T/étoile** T/star-shaped; **en chemise/chaussettes** in one's shirt-sleeves/socks; **en soldat** as a soldier; **cassé en plusieurs morceaux** broken into several pieces; **en réparation** being repaired, under repair; **en vacances** on holiday; **en deuil** in mourning; **le même en plus grand** the same but ou only bigger
6 (avec gérondif) while, on, by; **en dormant** while sleeping, as one sleeps; **en sortant** on going out, as he etc went out; **sortir en courant** to run out
7 (comme) as; **je te parle en ami** I'm talking to you as a friend
▷ pron 1 (indéfini): **j'en ai/veux** I have/want some; **en as-tu?** have you got any?; **je n'en veux pas** I don't want any; **j'en ai 2** I've got 2; **combien y en a-t-il?** how many (of them) are there?; **j'en ai assez** I've got enough (of it ou them); (j'en ai marre) I've had enough
2 (provenance) from there; **j'en viens** I've come from there
3 (cause): **il en est malade/perd le sommeil** he is ill/can't sleep because of it
4 (complément de nom, d'adjectif, de verbe): **j'en connais les dangers** I know its ou the dangers; **j'en suis fier** I am proud of it ou him ou her ou them; **j'en ai besoin** I need it ou them

encadrer [ɑ̃kadre] vt (tableau, image) to frame; (fig: entourer) to surround; (personnel, soldats etc) to train

encaisser [ɑ̃kese] vt (chèque) to cash; (argent) to collect; (fam: coup, défaite) to take

en-cas [ɑ̃ka] nm snack

enceinte [ɑ̃sɛ̃t] adj f: **~ (de 6 mois)** (6 months) pregnant ▷ nf (mur) wall; (espace) enclosure; **enceinte (acoustique)** (loud)speaker

encens [ɑ̃sɑ̃] nm incense

enchaîner [ɑ̃ʃene] vt to chain up; (mouvements, séquences) to link (together) ▷ vi to carry on

enchanté, e [ɑ̃ʃɑ̃te] adj (ravi) delighted; (magique) enchanted; **~ (de faire votre connaissance)** pleased to meet you

enchère [ɑ̃ʃɛr] nf bid; **mettre/vendre aux ~s** to put up for (sale by)/sell by auction

enclencher [ɑ̃klɑ̃ʃe] vt (mécanisme) to engage; **s'enclencher** vi to engage

encombrant, e [ɑ̃kɔ̃brɑ̃, ɑ̃t] adj cumbersome, bulky

encombrement [ɑ̃kɔ̃brəmɑ̃] nm: **être pris dans un ~** to be stuck in a traffic jam

encombrer [ɑ̃kɔ̃bre] vt to clutter (up); (gêner) to hamper; **s'~ de** (bagages etc) to load ou burden o.s. with

MOT-CLÉ

encore [ɑ̃kɔr] adv 1 (continuation) still; **il y travaille encore** he's still working on it; **pas encore** not yet
2 (de nouveau) again; **j'irai encore demain** I'll go again tomorrow; **encore une fois** (once) again; **(et puis) quoi encore?** what next?
3 (en plus) more; **encore un peu de viande?** a little more meat?; **encore deux jours** two more days
4 (intensif) even, still; **encore plus fort/mieux** even louder/better, louder/better still

5 (*restriction*) even so *ou* then, only; **encore pourrais-je le faire si ...** even so, I might be able to do it if ...; **si encore** if only

encourager [ãkuraʒe] *vt* to encourage; **~ qn à faire qch** to encourage sb to do sth

encourir [ãkurir] *vt* to incur

encre [ãkr] *nf* ink; **encre de Chine** Indian ink

encyclopédie [ãsiklɔpedi] *nf* encyclopaedia

endetter [ãdete]: **s'endetter** *vi* to get into debt

endive [ãdiv] *nf* chicory *no pl*

endormi, e [ãdɔrmi] *adj* asleep

endormir [ãdɔrmir] *vt* to put to sleep; (*suj: chaleur etc*) to send to sleep; (*Méd: dent, nerf*) to anaesthetize; (*fig: soupçons*) to allay; **s'endormir** *vi* to fall asleep, go to sleep

endroit [ãdrwa] *nm* place; (*opposé à l'envers*) right side; **à l'~** (*vêtement*) the right way out; (*objet posé*) the right way round

endurance [ãdyrãs] *nf* endurance

endurant, e [ãdyrã, ãt] *adj* tough, hardy

endurcir [ãdyrsir]: **s'endurcir** *vi* (*physiquement*) to become tougher; (*moralement*) to become hardened

endurer [ãdyre] *vt* to endure, bear

énergétique [enɛrʒetik] *adj* (*aliment*) energy-giving

énergie [enɛrʒi] *nf* (*Physique*) energy; (*Tech*) power; (*morale*) vigour, spirit; **énergique** *adj* energetic, vigorous; (*mesures*) drastic, stringent

énervant, e [enɛrvã, ãt] *adj* irritating, annoying

énerver [enɛrve] *vt* to irritate, annoy; **s'énerver** *vi* to get excited, get worked up

enfance [ãfãs] *nf* childhood

enfant [ãfã] *nm/f* child; **enfantin, e** *adj* (*puéril*) childlike; (*langage, jeu etc*) children's *cpd*

enfer [ãfɛr] *nm* hell

enfermer [ãfɛrme] *vt* to shut up; (*à clef, interner*) to lock up; **s'enfermer** to shut o.s. away

enfiler [ãfile] *vt* (*vêtement*) to slip on, slip into; (*perles*) to string; (*aiguille*) to thread

enfin [ãfɛ̃] *adv* at last; (*en énumérant*) lastly; (*toutefois*) still; (*pour conclure*) in a word; (*somme toute*) after all

enflammer [ãflame]: **s'enflammer** *vi* to catch fire; (*Méd*) to become inflamed

enflé, e [ãfle] *adj* swollen

enfler [ãfle] *vi* to swell (up)

enfoncer [ãfɔ̃se] *vt* (*clou*) to drive in; (*faire pénétrer*): **~ qch dans** to push (*ou* drive) sth into; (*forcer: porte*) to break open; **s'enfoncer** *vi* to sink; **s'~ dans** to sink into; (*forêt, ville*) to disappear into

enfouir [ãfwir] *vt* (*dans le sol*) to bury; (*dans un tiroir etc*) to tuck away

enfuir [ãfɥir]: **s'enfuir** *vi* to run away *ou* off

engagement [ãgaʒmã] *nm* commitment; **sans ~** without obligation

engager [ãgaʒe] *vt* (*embaucher*) to take on; (: *artiste*) to engage; (*commencer*) to start; (*lier*) to bind, commit; (*impliquer*) to involve; (*investir*) to invest, lay out; (*inciter*) to encourage; (*introduire: clé*) to insert; **s'engager** *vi* (*promettre*) to commit o.s.; (*Mil*) to enlist; (*débuter: conversation etc*) to start (up); **s'~ à faire** to undertake to do; **s'~ dans** (*rue, passage*) to turn into; (*fig: affaire, discussion*) to enter into, embark on

engelures [ãʒlyr] *nfpl* chilblains

engin [ãʒɛ̃] *nm* machine; (*outil*) instrument; (*Auto*) vehicle; (*Aviat*) aircraft *inv*

> Attention à ne pas traduire **engin** par le mot anglais **engine**.

engloutir [ãglutir] *vt* to swallow up

engouement [ãgumã] *nm* (sudden) passion

engouffrer [ãgufre] *vt* to swallow up, devour; **s'engouffrer dans** to rush into

engourdir [ãgurdir] *vt* to numb; (*fig*) to dull, blunt; **s'engourdir** *vi* to go numb

engrais [ãgrɛ] *nm* manure; **engrais chimique** chemical fertilizer

engraisser [ãgrese] *vt* to fatten (up)

engrenage [ãgrənaʒ] *nm* gears *pl*, gearing; (*fig*) chain

engueuler [ãgœle] (*fam*) *vt* to bawl at

enhardir [ãardir]: **s'enhardir** *vi* to grow bolder

énigme [enigm] *nf* riddle

enivrer [ãnivre] *vt*: **s'~** to get drunk

enjamber [ãʒãbe] *vt* to stride over

enjeu, x [ãʒø] *nm* stakes *pl*

enjoué, e [ãʒwe] *adj* playful

enlaidir [ãledir] *vt* to make ugly ▷ *vi* to become ugly

enlèvement [ãlɛvmã] *nm* (*rapt*) abduction, kidnapping

enlever [ãl(ə)ve] *vt* (*ôter: gén*) to remove; (: *vêtement, lunettes*) to take off; (*emporter: ordures etc*) to take away; (*kidnapper*) to abduct, kidnap; (*obtenir: prix, contrat*) to win; (*prendre*): **~ qch à qn** to take sth (away) from sb

enliser [ãlize]: **s'enliser** *vi* to sink, get stuck

enneigé, e [ãneʒe] *adj* (*route, maison*) snowed-up; (*paysage*) snowy

ennemi, e [ɛnmi] *adj* hostile; (*Mil*) enemy *cpd* ▷ *nm/f* enemy

ennui [ãnɥi] *nm* (*lassitude*) boredom; (*difficulté*) trouble *no pl*; **avoir des ~s** to have problems; **ennuyer** *vt* to bother; (*lasser*) to bore; **s'ennuyer** *vi* to be bored; **si cela ne vous ennuie pas** if it's no trouble (to you); **ennuyeux, -euse** *adj* boring, tedious; (*embêtant*) annoying

énorme [enɔrm] *adj* enormous, huge;

énormément adv enormously;
énormément de neige/gens an enormous
amount of snow/number of people
enquête [ɑ̃kɛt] nf (de journaliste, de police)
investigation; (judiciaire, administrative)
inquiry; (sondage d'opinion) survey; **enquêter**
vi: **enquêter (sur)** to investigate
enragé, e [ɑ̃ʀaʒe] adj (Méd) rabid, with rabies;
(fig) fanatical
enrageant, e [ɑ̃ʀaʒɑ̃, ɑ̃t] adj infuriating
enrager [ɑ̃ʀaʒe] vi to be in a rage
enregistrement [ɑ̃ʀ(ə)ʒistʀəmɑ̃] nm
recording; **enregistrement des bagages**
baggage check-in
enregistrer [ɑ̃ʀ(ə)ʒistʀe] vt (Mus etc) to
record; (fig: mémoriser) to make a mental note
of; (bagages: à l'aéroport) to check in
enrhumer [ɑ̃ʀyme] vt: **s'~, être enrhumé** to
catch a cold
enrichir [ɑ̃ʀiʃiʀ] vt to make rich(er); (fig) to
enrich; **s'enrichir** vi to get rich(er)
enrouer [ɑ̃ʀwe]: **s'enrouer** vi to go hoarse
enrouler [ɑ̃ʀule] vt (fil, corde) to wind (up); **s'~
(autour de qch)** to wind (around sth)
enseignant, e [ɑ̃sɛɲɑ̃, ɑ̃t] nm/f teacher
enseignement [ɑ̃sɛɲ(ə)mɑ̃] nm teaching;
(Admin) education
enseigner [ɑ̃sɛɲe] vt, vi to teach; **~ qch à qn**
to teach sb sth
ensemble [ɑ̃sɑ̃bl] adv together ▷ nm
(groupement) set; (vêtements) outfit; (totalité):
l'~ du/de la the whole ou entire; (unité,
harmonie) unity; **impression/idée d'~** overall
ou general impression/idea; **dans l'~** (en gros)
on the whole
ensoleillé, e [ɑ̃sɔleje] adj sunny
ensuite [ɑ̃sɥit] adv then, next; (plus tard)
afterwards, later
entamer [ɑ̃tame] vt (pain, bouteille) to start;
(hostilités, pourparlers) to open
entasser [ɑ̃tase] vt (empiler) to pile up, heap
up; **s'entasser** vi (s'amonceler) to pile up; **s'~
dans** (personnes) to cram into
entendre [ɑ̃tɑ̃dʀ] vt to hear; (comprendre) to
understand; (vouloir dire) to mean; **s'entendre**
vi (sympathiser) to get on; (se mettre d'accord)
to agree; **j'ai entendu dire que** I've heard (it
said) that; **~ parler de** to hear of
entendu, e [ɑ̃tɑ̃dy] adj (réglé) agreed; (au
courant: air) knowing; **(c'est) ~** all right,
agreed; **bien ~** of course
entente [ɑ̃tɑ̃t] nf understanding; (accord,
traité) agreement; **à double ~** (sens) with a
double meaning
enterrement [ɑ̃tɛʀmɑ̃] nm (cérémonie)
funeral, burial
enterrer [ɑ̃tɛʀe] vt to bury
entêtant, e [ɑ̃tɛtɑ̃, ɑ̃t] adj heady
en-tête [ɑ̃tɛt] nm heading; **papier à ~** headed

notepaper
entêté, e [ɑ̃tete] adj stubborn
entêter [ɑ̃tete]: **s'entêter** vi: **s'~ (à faire)** to
persist (in doing)
enthousiasme [ɑ̃tuzjasm] nm enthusiasm;
enthousiasmer vt to fill with enthusiasm;
s'enthousiasmer (pour qch) to get
enthusiastic (about sth); **enthousiaste** adj
enthusiastic
entier, -ère [ɑ̃tje, jɛʀ] adj whole; (total:
satisfaction etc) complete; (fig: caractère)
unbending ▷ nm (Math) whole; **en ~** totally;
lait ~ full-cream milk; **entièrement** adv
entirely, wholly
entonnoir [ɑ̃tɔnwaʀ] nm funnel
entorse [ɑ̃tɔʀs] nf (Méd) sprain; (fig): **~ au
règlement** infringement of the rule
entourage [ɑ̃tuʀaʒ] nm circle; (famille) circle
of family/friends; (ce qui enclôt) surround
entourer [ɑ̃tuʀe] vt to surround; (apporter son
soutien à) to rally round; **~ de** to surround with;
s'~ de to surround o.s. with
entracte [ɑ̃tʀakt] nm interval
entraide [ɑ̃tʀɛd] nf mutual aid
entrain [ɑ̃tʀɛ̃] nm spirit; **avec/sans ~**
spiritedly/half-heartedly
entraînement [ɑ̃tʀɛnmɑ̃] nm training
entraîner [ɑ̃tʀene] vt (charrier) to carry ou
drag along; (Tech) to drive; (emmener: personne)
to take (off); (influencer) to lead; (Sport) to train;
(impliquer) to entail; **s'entraîner** vi (Sport)
to train; **s'~ à qch/à faire** to train o.s. for
sth/to do; **~ qn à faire** (inciter) to lead sb to do;
entraîneur, -euse nm/f (Sport) coach, trainer
▷ nm (Hippisme) trainer
entre [ɑ̃tʀ] prép between; (parmi) among(st);
l'un d'~ eux/nous one of them/us; **ils se
battent ~ eux** they are fighting among(st)
themselves; **~ autres (choses)** among other
things; **entrecôte** nf entrecôte ou rib steak
entrée [ɑ̃tʀe] nf entrance; (accès: au cinéma etc)
admission; (billet) (admission) ticket; (Culin)
first course
entre...: **entrefilet** nm paragraph (short
article); **entremets** nm (cream) dessert
entrepôt [ɑ̃tʀəpo] nm warehouse
entreprendre [ɑ̃tʀəpʀɑ̃dʀ] vt (se lancer dans)
to undertake; (commencer) to begin ou start
(upon)
entrepreneur, -euse [ɑ̃tʀəpʀənœʀ, øz]
nm/f: **entrepreneur (en bâtiment)** (building)
contractor
entreprise [ɑ̃tʀəpʀiz] nf (société) firm,
concern; (action) undertaking, venture
entrer [ɑ̃tʀe] vi to go (ou come) in, enter ▷ vt
(Inform) to enter, input; (faire) **~ qch dans** to
get sth into; **~ dans** (gén) to enter; (pièce) to go
(ou come) into, enter; (club) to join; (heurter) to
run into; **~ à l'hôpital** to go into hospital; **faire**

~ *(visiteur)* to show in

entre-temps [ɑ̃trətɑ̃] *adv* meanwhile

entretenir [ɑ̃trət(ə)niːr] *vt* to maintain; *(famille, maîtresse)* to support, keep; **~ qn (de)** to speak to sb (about)

entretien [ɑ̃trətjɛ̃] *nm* maintenance; *(discussion)* discussion, talk; *(pour un emploi)* interview

entrevoir [ɑ̃trəvwaːr] *vt (à peine)* to make out; *(brièvement)* to catch a glimpse of

entrevue [ɑ̃trəvy] *nf (audience)* interview

entrouvert, e [ɑ̃truvɛːr, ɛrt] *adj* half-open

énumérer [enymere] *vt* to list

envahir [ɑ̃vaiːr] *vt* to invade; *(suj: inquiétude, peur)* to come over; **envahissant, e** *(péj) (personne)* intrusive

enveloppe [ɑ̃v(ə)lɔp] *nf (de lettre)* envelope; *(crédits)* budget; **envelopper** *vt* to wrap; *(fig)* to envelop, shroud

enverrai *etc* [ɑ̃vere] *vb voir* **envoyer**

envers [ɑ̃vɛːr] *prép* towards, to ▷ *nm* other side; *(d'une étoffe)* wrong side; **à l'~** *(verticalement)* upside down; *(pull)* back to front; *(chaussettes)* inside out

envie [ɑ̃vi] *nf (sentiment)* envy; *(souhait)* desire, wish; **avoir ~ de (faire)** to feel like (doing); *(plus fort)* to want (to do); **avoir ~ que** to wish that; **cette glace me fait ~** I fancy some of that ice cream; **envier** *vt* to envy; **envieux, -euse** *adj* envious

environ [ɑ̃virɔ̃] *adv*: **~ 3 h/2 km** (around) about 3 o'clock/2 km; *voir aussi* **environs**

environnant, e [ɑ̃virɔnɑ̃, ɑ̃t] *adj* surrounding

environnement [ɑ̃virɔnmɑ̃] *nm* environment

environs [ɑ̃virɔ̃] *nmpl* surroundings; **aux ~ de** (round) about

envisager [ɑ̃vizaʒe] *vt* to contemplate, envisage; **~ de faire** to consider doing

envoler [ɑ̃vɔle]: **s'envoler** *vi (oiseau)* to fly away *ou* off; *(avion)* to take off; *(papier, feuille)* to blow away; *(fig)* to vanish (into thin air)

envoyé, e [ɑ̃vwaje] *nm/f (Pol)* envoy; *(Presse)* correspondent; **envoyé spécial** special correspondent

envoyer [ɑ̃vwaje] *vt* to send; *(lancer)* to hurl, throw; **~ chercher** to send for; **~ promener qn** *(fam)* to send sb packing

épagneul, e [epaɲœl] *nm/f* spaniel

épais, se [epɛ, ɛs] *adj* thick; **épaisseur** *nf* thickness

épanouir [epanwiːr]: **s'épanouir** *vi (fleur)* to bloom, open out; *(visage)* to light up; *(personne)* to blossom

épargne [eparɲ] *nf* saving

épargner [eparɲe] *vt* to save; *(ne pas tuer ou endommager)* to spare ▷ *vi* to save; **~ qch à qn** to spare sb sth

éparpiller [eparpije] *vt* to scatter; **s'éparpiller** *vi* to scatter; *(fig)* to dissipate one's efforts

épatant, e [epatɑ̃, ɑ̃t] *(fam) adj* super

épater [epate] *(fam) vt (étonner)* to amaze; *(impressionner)* to impress

épaule [epol] *nf* shoulder

épave [epav] *nf* wreck

épée [epe] *nf* sword

épeler [ep(ə)le] *vt* to spell

éperon [eprɔ̃] *nm* spur

épervier [epɛrvje] *nm* sparrowhawk

épi [epi] *nm (de blé, d'orge)* ear; *(de maïs)* cob

épice [epis] *nf* spice

épicé, e [epise] *adj* spicy

épicer [epise] *vt* to spice

épicerie [episri] *nf* grocer's shop; *(denrées)* groceries *pl*; **épicerie fine** delicatessen; **épicier, -ière** *nm/f* grocer

épidémie [epidemi] *nf* epidemic

épiderme [epidɛrm] *nm* skin

épier [epje] *vt* to spy on, watch closely

épilepsie [epilɛpsi] *nf* epilepsy

épiler [epile] *vt (jambes)* to remove the hair from; *(sourcils)* to pluck

épinards [epinar] *nmpl* spinach *sg*

épine [epin] *nf* thorn, prickle; *(d'oursin etc)* spine

épingle [epɛ̃gl] *nf* pin; **épingle de nourrice** *ou* **de sûreté** safety pin

épisode [epizɔd] *nm* episode; **film/roman à ~s** serial; **épisodique** *adj* occasional

épluche-légumes [eplyʃlegym] *nm inv* (potato) peeler

éplucher [eplyʃe] *vt (fruit, légumes)* to peel; *(fig)* to go over with a fine-tooth comb; **épluchures** *nfpl* peelings

éponge [epɔ̃ʒ] *nf* sponge; **éponger** *vt (liquide)* to mop up; *(surface)* to sponge; *(fig: déficit)* to soak up

époque [epɔk] *nf (de l'histoire)* age, era; *(de l'année, la vie)* time; **d'~** *(meuble)* period *cpd*

épouse [epuz] *nf* wife; **épouser** *vt* to marry

épousseter [epuste] *vt* to dust

épouvantable [epuvɑ̃tabl] *adj* appalling, dreadful

épouvantail [epuvɑ̃taj] *nm* scarecrow

épouvante [epuvɑ̃t] *nf* terror; **film d'~** horror film; **épouvanter** *vt* to terrify

époux [epu] *nm* husband ▷ *nmpl* (married) couple

épreuve [eprœv] *nf (d'examen)* test; *(malheur, difficulté)* trial, ordeal; *(Photo)* print; *(Typo)* proof; *(Sport)* event; **à toute ~** unfailing; **mettre à l'~** to put to the test

éprouver [epruve] *vt (tester)* to test; *(marquer, faire souffrir)* to afflict, distress; *(ressentir)* to experience

épuisé, e [epɥize] *adj* exhausted; *(livre)* out of

print; **épuisement** nm exhaustion

épuiser [epɥize] vt (fatiguer) to exhaust, wear ou tire out; (stock, sujet) to exhaust; **s'épuiser** vi to wear ou tire o.s. out, exhaust o.s.

épuisette [epɥizɛt] nf shrimping net

équateur [ekwatœʀ] nm equator; **(la république de) l'É~** Ecuador

équation [ekwasjɔ̃] nf equation

équerre [ekɛʀ] nf (à dessin) (set) square

équilibre [ekilibʀ] nm balance; **garder/ perdre l'~** to keep/lose one's balance; **être en ~** to be balanced; **équilibré, e** adj well-balanced; **équilibrer** vt to balance

équipage [ekipaʒ] nm crew

équipe [ekip] nf team; **travailler en ~** to work as a team

équipé, e [ekipe] adj: **bien/mal ~** well-/poorly-equipped

équipement [ekipmɑ̃] nm equipment

équiper [ekipe] vt to equip; **~ qn/qch de** to equip sb/sth with

équipier, -ière [ekipje, jɛʀ] nm/f team member

équitation [ekitasjɔ̃] nf (horse-)riding; **faire de l'~** to go riding

équivalent, e [ekivalɑ̃, ɑ̃t] adj, nm equivalent

équivaloir [ekivalwaʀ]: **~ à** vt to be equivalent to

érable [eʀabl] nm maple

érafler [eʀafle] vt to scratch; **éraflure** nf scratch

ère [ɛʀ] nf era; **en l'an 1050 de notre ~** in the year 1050 A.D.

érection [eʀɛksjɔ̃] nf erection

éroder [eʀɔde] vt to erode

érotique [eʀɔtik] adj erotic

errer [eʀe] vi to wander

erreur [eʀœʀ] nf mistake, error; **faire ~** to be mistaken; **par ~** by mistake

éruption [eʀypsjɔ̃] nf eruption; (Méd) rash

es [ɛ] vb voir **être**

ès [ɛs] prép: **licencié ès lettres/sciences** = Bachelor of Arts/Science

ESB sigle f (= encéphalopathie spongiforme bovine) BSE

escabeau, x [ɛskabo] nm (tabouret) stool; (échelle) stepladder

escalade [ɛskalad] nf climbing no pl; (Pol etc) escalation; **escalader** vt to climb

escale [ɛskal] nf (Navig: durée) call; (endroit) port of call; (Aviat) stop(over); **faire ~ à** (Navig) to put in at; (Aviat) to stop over at; **vol sans ~** nonstop flight

escalier [ɛskalje] nm stairs pl; **dans l'~** ou **les ~s** on the stairs; **escalier mécanique** ou **roulant** escalator

escapade [ɛskapad] nf: **faire une ~** to go on a jaunt; (s'enfuir) to run away ou off

escargot [ɛskaʀgo] nm snail

escarpé, e [ɛskaʀpe] adj steep

esclavage [ɛsklavaʒ] nm slavery

esclave [ɛsklav] nm/f slave

escompte [ɛskɔ̃t] nm discount

escrime [ɛskʀim] nf fencing

escroc [ɛskʀo] nm swindler, conman; **escroquer** vt: **escroquer qch (à qn)** to swindle sth (out of sb); **escroquerie** nf swindle

espace [ɛspas] nm space; **espacer** vt to space out; **s'espacer** vi (visites etc) to become less frequent

espadon [ɛspadɔ̃] nm swordfish inv

espadrille [ɛspadʀij] nf rope-soled sandal

Espagne [ɛspaɲ] nf: **l'~** Spain; **espagnol, e** adj Spanish ▷ nm/f: **Espagnol, e** Spaniard ▷ nm (Ling) Spanish

espèce [ɛspɛs] nf (Bio, Bot, Zool) species inv; (gén: sorte) sort, kind, type; (péj): **~ de maladroit/de brute!** you clumsy oaf/you brute!; **espèces** nfpl (Comm) cash sg; **payer en ~** to pay (in) cash

espérance [ɛspeʀɑ̃s] nf hope; **espérance de vie** life expectancy

espérer [ɛspeʀe] vt to hope for; **j'espère (bien)** I hope so; **~ que/faire** to hope that/to do

espiègle [ɛspjɛgl] adj mischievous

espion, ne [ɛspjɔ̃, jɔn] nm/f spy; **espionnage** nm espionage, spying; **espionner** vt to spy (up)on

espoir [ɛspwaʀ] nm hope; **dans l'~ de/que** in the hope of/that; **reprendre ~** not to lose hope

esprit [ɛspʀi] nm (intellect) mind; (humour) wit; (mentalité, d'une loi etc, fantôme etc) spirit; **faire de l'~** to try to be witty; **reprendre ses ~s** to come to; **perdre l'~** to lose one's mind

esquimau, de, -x [ɛskimo, od] adj Eskimo ▷ nm/f: **E~, de** Eskimo ▷ nm: **E~®** ice lolly (BRIT), popsicle (US)

essai [esɛ] nm (tentative) attempt, try; (de produit) testing; (Rugby) try; (Littérature) essay; **à l'~** on a trial basis; **mettre à l'~** to put to the test

essaim [esɛ̃] nm swarm

essayer [eseje] vt to try; (vêtement, chaussures) to try (on); (méthode, voiture) to try (out) ▷ vi to try; **~ de faire** to try ou attempt to do

essence [esɑ̃s] nf (de voiture) petrol (BRIT), gas(oline) (US); (extrait de plante) essence; (espèce: d'arbre) species inv

essentiel, le [esɑ̃sjɛl] adj essential; **c'est l'~** (ce qui importe) that's the main thing; **l'~ de** the main part of

essieu, x [esjø] nm axle

essor [esɔʀ] nm (de l'économie etc) rapid expansion

essorer [esɔʀe] vt (en tordant) to wring (out);

(par la force centrifuge) to spin-dry; **essoreuse** nf spin-dryer

essouffler [esufle]: **s'essouffler** vi to get out of breath

essuie-glace [esɥiglas] nm inv windscreen (BRIT) ou windshield (US) wiper

essuyer [esɥije] vt to wipe; *(fig: échec)* to suffer; **s'essuyer** vi *(après le bain)* to dry o.s.; **~ la vaisselle** to dry up

est¹ [ε] vb voir **être**

est² [ɛst] nm east ▷ adj inv east; *(région)* east(ern); **à l'~** in the east; *(direction)* to the east, east(wards); **à l'~ de** (to the) east of

est-ce que [ɛskə] adv: **~ c'est cher/c'était bon?** is it expensive/was it good?; **quand est-ce qu'il part?** when does he leave?, when is he leaving?; *voir aussi* **que**

esthéticienne [ɛstetisjɛn] nf beautician

esthétique [ɛstetik] adj attractive

estimation [ɛstimasjɔ̃] nf valuation; *(chiffre)* estimate

estime [ɛstim] nf esteem, regard; **estimer** vt *(respecter)* to esteem; *(expertiser: bijou etc)* to value; *(évaluer: coût etc)* to assess, estimate; *(penser)*: **estimer que/être** to consider that/o.s. to be

estival, e, -aux [ɛstival, o] adj summer cpd

estivant, e [ɛstivɑ̃, ɑ̃t] nm/f (summer) holiday-maker

estomac [ɛstɔma] nm stomach

estragon [ɛstʀagɔ̃] nm tarragon

estuaire [ɛstɥɛʀ] nm estuary

et [e] conj and; **et lui?** what about him?; **et alors!** so what!

étable [etabl] nf cowshed

établi [etabli] nm (work)bench

établir [etabliʀ] vt *(papiers d'identité, facture)* to make out; *(liste, programme)* to draw up; *(entreprise)* to set up; *(réputation, usage, fait, culpabilité)* to establish; **s'établir** vi to be established; **s'~ (à son compte)** to set up in business; **s'~ à/près de** to settle in/near

établissement [etablismɑ̃] nm *(entreprise, institution)* establishment; **établissement scolaire** school, educational establishment

étage [etaʒ] nm *(d'immeuble)* storey, floor; **à l'~** upstairs; **au 2ème ~** on the 2nd (BRIT) ou 3rd (US) floor; **c'est à quel ~?** what floor is it on?

étagère [etaʒɛʀ] nf *(rayon)* shelf; *(meuble)* shelves pl

étai [etɛ] nm stay, prop

étain [etɛ̃] nm pewter no pl

étais etc [etɛ] vb voir **être**

étaler [etale] vt *(carte, nappe)* to spread (out); *(peinture)* to spread; *(échelonner: paiements, vacances)* to spread, stagger; *(marchandises)* to display; *(connaissances)* to parade; **s'étaler** vi *(liquide)* to spread out; *(fam)* to fall flat on one's face; **s'~ sur** *(suj: paiements etc)* to be spread

out over

étalon [etalɔ̃] nm *(cheval)* stallion

étanche [etɑ̃ʃ] adj *(récipient)* watertight; *(montre, vêtement)* waterproof

étang [etɑ̃] nm pond

étant [etɑ̃] vb voir **être; donné**

étape [etap] nf stage; *(lieu d'arrivée)* stopping place; *(: Cyclisme)* staging point

état [eta] nm *(Pol, condition)* state; **en mauvais ~** in poor condition; **en ~ (de marche)** in (working) order; **remettre en ~** to repair; **hors d'~** out of order; **être en ~/hors d'~ de faire** to be in a/in no fit state to do; **être dans tous ses ~s** to be in a state; **faire ~ de** *(alléguer)* to put forward; **l'É~** the State; **état civil** civil status; **état des lieux** inventory of fixtures; **États-Unis** nmpl: **les États-Unis** the United States

etc. [ɛtsetera] adv etc

et c(a)etera [ɛtsetera] adv et cetera, and so on

été [ete] pp de **être** ▷ nm summer

éteindre [etɛ̃dʀ] vt *(lampe, lumière, radio)* to turn ou switch off; *(cigarette, feu)* to put out, extinguish; **s'éteindre** vi *(feu, lumière)* to go out; *(mourir)* to pass away; **éteint, e** adj *(fig)* lacklustre, dull; *(volcan)* extinct

étendre [etɑ̃dʀ] vt *(pâte, liquide)* to spread; *(carte etc)* to spread out; *(linge)* to hang up; *(bras, jambes)* to stretch out; *(fig: agrandir)* to extend; **s'étendre** vi *(augmenter, se propager)* to spread; *(terrain, forêt etc)* to stretch; *(s'allonger)* to stretch out; *(se coucher)* to lie down; *(fig: expliquer)* to elaborate

étendu, e [etɑ̃dy] adj extensive

éternel, le [etɛʀnɛl] adj eternal

éternité [etɛʀnite] nf eternity; **ça a duré une ~** it lasted for ages

éternuement [etɛʀnymɑ̃] nm sneeze

éternuer [etɛʀnɥe] vi to sneeze

êtes [ɛt(z)] vb voir **être**

Éthiopie [etjɔpi] nf: **l'~** Ethiopia

étiez [etje] vb voir **être**

étinceler [etɛ̃s(ə)le] vi to sparkle

étincelle [etɛ̃sɛl] nf spark

étiquette [etikɛt] nf label; *(protocole)*: **l'~** etiquette

étirer [etiʀe]: **s'étirer** vi *(personne)* to stretch; *(convoi, route)*: **s'~ sur** to stretch out over

étoile [etwal] nf star; **à la belle ~** in the open; **étoile de mer** starfish; **étoile filante** shooting star; **étoilé, e** adj starry

étonnant, e [etɔnɑ̃, ɑ̃t] adj amazing

étonnement [etɔnmɑ̃] nm surprise, amazement

étonner [etɔne] vt to surprise, amaze; **s'étonner que/de** to be amazed that/at; **cela m'~ait (que)** *(j'en doute)* I'd be very surprised (if)

étouffer [etufe] vt to suffocate; (bruit) to muffle; (scandale) to hush up ▷ vi to suffocate; **s'étouffer** vi (en mangeant etc) to choke; **on étouffe** it's stifling

étourderie [etuʀdəʀi] nf (caractère) absent-mindedness no pl; (faute) thoughtless blunder

étourdi, e [etuʀdi] adj (distrait) scatterbrained, heedless

étourdir [etuʀdiʀ] vt (assommer) to stun, daze; (griser) to make dizzy ou giddy; **étourdissement** nm dizzy spell

étrange [etʀɑ̃ʒ] adj strange

étranger, -ère [etʀɑ̃ʒe, ɛʀ] adj foreign; (pas de la famille, non familier) strange ▷ nm/f foreigner; stranger ▷ nm: **à l'~** abroad

étrangler [etʀɑ̃gle] vt to strangle; **s'étrangler** vi (en mangeant etc) to choke

 MOT-CLÉ

être [ɛtʀ] nm being; **être humain** human being

▷ vb +attrib 1 (état, description) to be; **il est instituteur** he is ou he's a teacher; **vous êtes grand/intelligent/fatigué** you are ou you're tall/clever/tired

2 (+à: appartenir) to be; **le livre est à Paul** the book is Paul's ou belongs to Paul; **c'est à moi/eux** it is ou it's mine/theirs

3 (+de: provenance): **il est de Paris** he is from Paris; (: appartenance): **il est des nôtres** he is one of us

4 (date): **nous sommes le 10 janvier** it's the 10th of January (today)

▷ vi to be; **je ne serai pas ici demain** I won't be here tomorrow

▷ vb aux 1 to have; to be; **être arrivé/allé** to have arrived/gone; **il est parti** he has left, he has gone

2 (forme passive) to be; **être fait par** to be made by; **il a été promu** he has been promoted

3 (+à: obligation): **c'est à réparer** it needs repairing; **c'est à essayer** it should be tried; **il est à espérer que ...** it is ou it's to be hoped that ...

▷ vb impers 1: **il est** +adjectif it is +adjective; **il est impossible de le faire** it's impossible to do it

2 (heure, date): **il est 10 heures** it is ou it's 10 o'clock

3 (emphatique): **c'est moi** it's me; **c'est à lui de le faire** it's up to him to do it

étrennes [etʀɛn] nfpl Christmas box sg

étrier [etʀije] nm stirrup

étroit, e [etʀwa, wat] adj narrow; (vêtement) tight; (fig: liens, collaboration) close; **à l'~** cramped; **~ d'esprit** narrow-minded

étude [etyd] nf studying; (ouvrage, rapport) study; (Scol: salle de travail) study room; **études** nfpl (Scol) studies; **être à l'~** (projet etc) to be under consideration; **faire des ~s (de droit/médecine)** to study (law/medicine)

étudiant, e [etydjɑ̃, jɑ̃t] nm/f student

étudier [etydje] vt, vi to study

étui [etɥi] nm case

eu, eue [y] pp de avoir

euh [ø] excl er

euro [øʀo] nm euro

Europe [øʀɔp] nf: **l'~** Europe; **européen, ne** adj European ▷ nm/f: **Européen, ne** European

eus etc [y] vb voir avoir

eux [ø] pron (sujet) they; (objet) them

évacuer [evakɥe] vt to evacuate

évader [evade]: **s'évader** vi to escape

évaluer [evalɥe] vt (expertiser) to appraise, evaluate; (juger approximativement) to estimate

évangile [evɑ̃ʒil] nm gospel; **É~** Gospel

évanouir [evanwiʀ]: **s'évanouir** vi to faint; (disparaître) to vanish, disappear; **évanouissement** nm (syncope) fainting fit

évaporer [evapɔʀe]: **s'évaporer** vi to evaporate

évasion [evazjɔ̃] nf escape

éveillé, e [eveje] adj awake; (vif) alert, sharp; **éveiller** vt to (a)waken; (soupçons etc) to arouse; **s'éveiller** vi to (a)waken; (fig) to be aroused

événement [evɛnmɑ̃] nm event

éventail [evɑ̃taj] nm fan; (choix) range

éventualité [evɑ̃tɥalite] nf eventuality; possibility; **dans l'~ de** in the event of

éventuel, le [evɑ̃tɥɛl] adj possible

> Attention à ne pas traduire **éventuel** par **eventual**.

éventuellement adv possibly

> Attention à ne pas traduire **éventuellement** par **eventually**.

évêque [evɛk] nm bishop

évidemment [evidamɑ̃] adv (bien sûr) of course; (certainement) obviously

évidence [evidɑ̃s] nf obviousness; (fait) obvious fact; **de toute ~** quite obviously ou evidently; **être en ~** to be clearly visible; **mettre en ~** (fait) to highlight; **évident, e** adj obvious, evident; **ce n'est pas évident!** (fam) it's not that easy!

évier [evje] nm (kitchen) sink

éviter [evite] vt to avoid; **~ de faire** to avoid doing; **~ qch à qn** to spare sb sth

évoluer [evɔlɥe] vi (enfant, maladie) to develop; (situation, moralement) to evolve, develop; (aller et venir) to move about; **évolution** nf development, evolution

évoquer [evɔke] vt to call to mind, evoke; (mentionner) to mention

ex- [ɛks] préfixe ex-; **son ~mari** her ex-husband;

son **~femme** his ex-wife

exact, e [ɛgza(kt), ɛgzakt] *adj* exact; (*correct*) correct; (*ponctuel*) punctual; **l'heure ~e** the right *ou* exact time; **exactement** *adv* exactly

ex aequo [ɛgzeko] *adj* equally placed; **arriver ~** to finish neck and neck

exagéré, e [ɛgzaʒeʀe] *adj* (*prix etc*) excessive

exagérer [ɛgzaʒeʀe] *vt* to exaggerate ▷ *vi* to exaggerate; (*abuser*) to go too far

examen [ɛgzamɛ̃] *nm* examination; (*Scol*) exam, examination; **à l'~** under consideration; **examen médical** (medical) examination; (*analyse*) test

examinateur, -trice [ɛgzaminatœʀ, tʀis] *nm/f* examiner

examiner [ɛgzamine] *vt* to examine

exaspérant, e [ɛgzaspeʀɑ̃, ɑ̃t] *adj* exasperating

exaspérer [ɛgzaspeʀe] *vt* to exasperate

exaucer [ɛgzose] *vt* (*vœu*) to grant

excéder [ɛksede] *vt* (*dépasser*) to exceed; (*agacer*) to exasperate

excellent, e [ɛkselɑ̃, ɑ̃t] *adj* excellent

excentrique [ɛksɑ̃tʀik] *adj* eccentric

excepté, e [ɛksɛpte] *adj, prép*: **les élèves ~s, ~ les élèves** except for the pupils

exception [ɛksɛpsjɔ̃] *nf* exception; **à l'~ de** except for, with the exception of; **d'~** (*mesure, loi*) special, exceptional; **exceptionnel, le** *adj* exceptional; **exceptionnellement** *adv* exceptionally

excès [ɛksɛ] *nm* surplus ▷ *nmpl* excesses; **faire des ~** to overindulge; **excès de vitesse** speeding *no pl*; **excessif, -ive** *adj* excessive

excitant, e [ɛksitɑ̃, ɑ̃t] *adj* exciting ▷ *nm* stimulant; **excitation** *nf* (*état*) excitement

exciter [ɛksite] *vt* to excite; (*suj: café etc*) to stimulate; **s'exciter** *vi* to get excited

exclamer [ɛksklame]: **s'exclamer** *vi* to exclaim

exclure [ɛksklyʀ] *vt* (*faire sortir*) to expel; (*ne pas compter*) to exclude, leave out; (*rendre impossible*) to exclude, rule out; **il est exclu que** it's out of the question that ...; **il n'est pas exclu que** it's not impossible that ...; **exclusif, -ive** *adj* exclusive; **exclusion** *nf* exclusion; **à l'exclusion de** with the exclusion *ou* exception of; **exclusivité** *nf* (*Comm*) exclusive rights *pl*; **film passant en exclusivité à** film showing only at

excursion [ɛkskyʀsjɔ̃] *nf* (*en autocar*) excursion, trip; (*à pied*) walk, hike

excuse [ɛkskyz] *nf* excuse; **excuses** *nfpl* (*regret*) apology *sg*, apologies; **excuser** *vt* to excuse; **s'excuser (de)** to apologize (for); **excusez-moi** I'm sorry; (*pour attirer l'attention*) excuse me

exécuter [ɛgzekyte] *vt* (*tuer*) to execute; (*tâche etc*) to execute, carry out; (*Mus: jouer*) to perform, execute; **s'exécuter** *vi* to comply

exemplaire [ɛgzɑ̃plɛʀ] *nm* copy

exemple [ɛgzɑ̃pl] *nm* example; **par ~** for instance, for example; **donner l'~** to set an example

exercer [ɛgzɛʀse] *vt* (*pratiquer*) to exercise, practise; (*influence, contrôle*) to exert; (*former*) to exercise, train; **s'exercer** *vi* (*sportif, musicien*) to practise

exercice [ɛgzɛʀsis] *nm* exercise

exhiber [ɛgzibe] *vt* (*montrer: papiers, certificat*) to present, produce; (*péj*) to display, flaunt; **s'exhiber** *vi* to parade; (*suj: exhibitionniste*) to expose o.s.; **exhibitionniste** *nm/f* flasher

exigeant, e [ɛgziʒɑ̃, ɑ̃t] *adj* demanding; (*péj*) hard to please

exiger [ɛgziʒe] *vt* to demand, require

exil [ɛgzil] *nm* exile; **exiler** *vt* to exile; **s'exiler** *vi* to go into exile

existence [ɛgzistɑ̃s] *nf* existence

exister [ɛgziste] *vi* to exist; **il existe un/des** there is a/are (some)

exorbitant, e [ɛgzɔʀbitɑ̃, ɑ̃t] *adj* exorbitant

exotique [ɛgzɔtik] *adj* exotic; **yaourt aux fruits ~s** tropical fruit yoghurt

expédier [ɛkspedje] *vt* (*lettre, paquet*) to send; (*troupes*) to dispatch; (*fam: travail etc*) to dispose of, dispatch; **expéditeur, -trice** *nm/f* sender; **expédition** *nf* sending; (*scientifique, sportive, Mil*) expedition

expérience [ɛkspeʀjɑ̃s] *nf* (*de la vie*) experience; (*scientifique*) experiment

expérimenté, e [ɛkspeʀimɑ̃te] *adj* experienced

expérimenter [ɛkspeʀimɑ̃te] *vt* to test out, experiment with

expert, e [ɛkspɛʀ, ɛʀt] *adj, nm* expert; **~ en objets d'art** art appraiser; **expert-comptable** *nm* ≈ chartered accountant (BRIT), ≈ certified public accountant (US)

expirer [ɛkspiʀe] *vi* (*prendre fin, mourir*) to expire; (*respirer*) to breathe out

explication [ɛksplikasjɔ̃] *nf* explanation; (*discussion*) discussion; (*dispute*) argument

explicite [ɛksplisit] *adj* explicit

expliquer [ɛksplike] *vt* to explain; **s'expliquer** to explain (o.s.); **s'~ avec qn** (*discuter*) to explain o.s. to sb; **son erreur s'explique** one can understand his mistake

exploit [ɛksplwa] *nm* exploit, feat; **exploitant, e** *nm/f*: **exploitant (agricole)** farmer; **exploitation** *nf* exploitation; (*d'une entreprise*) running; **exploitation agricole** farming concern; **exploiter** *vt* (*personne, don*) to exploit; (*entreprise, ferme*) to run, operate; (*mine*) to exploit, work

explorer [ɛksplɔʀe] *vt* to explore

exploser [ɛksploze] *vi* to explode, blow up; (*engin explosif*) to go off; (*personne: de colère*) to flare up; **explosif, -ive** adj, nm explosive; **explosion** nf explosion; (de joie, colère) outburst

exportateur, -trice [ɛkspɔʀtatœʀ, tʀis] adj export cpd, exporting ▷ nm exporter

exportation [ɛkspɔʀtasjɔ̃] nf (action) exportation; (produit) export

exporter [ɛkspɔʀte] vt to export

exposant [ɛkspozɑ̃] nm exhibitor

exposé, e [ɛkspoze] nm talk ▷ adj: **~ au sud** facing south

exposer [ɛkspoze] vt (marchandise) to display; (peinture) to exhibit, show; (parler de) to explain, set out; (mettre en danger, orienter, Photo) to expose; **s'~ à** (soleil, danger) to expose o.s. to; **exposition** nf (manifestation) exhibition; (Photo) exposure

exprès¹ [ɛkspʀɛ] adv (délibérément) on purpose; (spécialement) specially; **faire ~ de faire qch** to do sth on purpose

exprès², -esse [ɛkspʀɛs] adj inv (lettre, colis) express

express [ɛkspʀɛs] adj, nm: **(café) ~** espresso (coffee); **(train) ~** fast train

expressif, -ive [ɛkspʀesif, iv] adj expressive

expression [ɛkspʀesjɔ̃] nf expression

exprimer [ɛkspʀime] vt (sentiment, idée) to express; (jus, liquide) to press out; **s'exprimer** vi (personne) to express o.s

expulser [ɛkspylse] vt to expel; (locataire) to evict; (Sport) to send off

exquis, e [ɛkski, iz] adj exquisite

extasier [ɛkstazje]: **s'extasier sur** vt to go into raptures over

exténuer [ɛkstenɥe] vt to exhaust

extérieur, e [ɛksteʀjœʀ] adj (porte, mur etc) outer, outside; (au dehors: escalier, w.-c.) outside; (commerce) foreign; (influences) external; (apparent: calme, gaieté etc) surface cpd ▷ nm (d'une maison, d'un récipient etc) outside, exterior; (apparence) exterior; **à l'~** outside; (à l'étranger) abroad

externat [ɛkstɛʀna] nm day school

externe [ɛkstɛʀn] adj external, outer ▷ nm/f (Méd) non-resident medical student (BRIT), extern (US); (Scol) day pupil

extincteur [ɛkstɛ̃ktœʀ] nm (fire) extinguisher

extinction [ɛkstɛ̃ksjɔ̃] nf: **extinction de voix** loss of voice

extra [ɛkstʀa] adj inv first-rate; (fam) fantastic ▷ nm inv extra help

extraire [ɛkstʀɛʀ] vt to extract; **~ qch de** to extract sth from; **extrait** nm extract; **extrait de naissance** birth certificate

extraordinaire [ɛkstʀaɔʀdinɛʀ] adj extraordinary; (Pol: mesures etc) special

extravagant, e [ɛkstʀavagɑ̃, ɑ̃t] adj extravagant

extraverti, e [ɛkstʀavɛʀti] adj extrovert

extrême [ɛkstʀɛm] adj, nm extreme; **d'un ~ à l'autre** from one extreme to another; **extrêmement** adv extremely; **Extrême-Orient** nm Far East

extrémité [ɛkstʀemite] nf end; (situation) straits pl, plight; (geste désespéré) extreme action; **extrémités** nfpl (pieds et mains) extremities

exubérant, e [ɛgzybeʀɑ̃, ɑ̃t] adj exuberant

F abr = **franc**; (appartement): **un F2/F3** a one-/two-bedroom flat (BRIT) ou apartment (US)

fa [fa] nm inv (Mus) F; (en chantant la gamme) fa

fabricant, e [fabʀikɑ̃, ɑ̃t] nm/f manufacturer

fabrication [fabʀikasjɔ̃] nf manufacture

fabrique [fabʀik] nf factory; **fabriquer** vt to make; (industriellement) to manufacture; (fig): **qu'est-ce qu'il fabrique?** (fam) what is he doing?

fac [fak] (fam) abr f (Scol) = **faculté**

façade [fasad] nf front, façade

face [fas] nf face; (fig: aspect) side ▷ adj: **le côté ~** heads; **en ~ de** opposite; (fig) in front of; **de ~** (voir) face on; **~ à** facing; (fig) faced with, in the face of; **faire ~ à** to face; **~ à ~** adv facing each other ▷ nm inv encounter

fâché, e [faʃe] adj angry; (désolé) sorry

fâcher [faʃe] vt to anger; **se fâcher (contre qn)** vi to get angry (with sb); **se ~ avec** (se brouiller) to fall out with

facile [fasil] adj easy; (caractère) easygoing; **facilement** adv easily; **facilité** nf easiness; (disposition, don) aptitude; **facilités** (possibilités) facilities; (Comm) terms; **faciliter** vt to make easier

façon [fasɔ̃] nf (manière) way; (d'une robe etc) making-up, cut; **façons** nfpl (péj) fuss sg; **de ~ à/à ce que** so as to/that; **de toute ~** anyway, in any case; **sans ~** (accepter) without fuss; **non merci, sans ~** no thanks, honestly

facteur, -trice [faktœʀ] nm/f postman(-woman) (BRIT), mailman(-woman) (US) ▷ nm (Math, fig: élément) factor

facture [faktyʀ] nf (à payer: gén) bill; (Comm) invoice

facultatif, -ive [fakyltatif, iv] adj optional

faculté [fakylte] nf (intellectuelle, d'université) faculty; (pouvoir, possibilité) power

fade [fad] adj insipid

faible [fɛbl] adj weak; (voix, lumière, vent) faint; (rendement, revenu) low ▷ nm (pour quelqu'un) weakness, soft spot; **faiblesse** nf weakness; **faiblir** vi to weaken; (lumière) to dim; (vent) to drop

faïence [fajɑ̃s] nf earthenware no pl

faillir [fajiʀ] vi: **j'ai failli tomber** I almost ou very nearly fell

faillite [fajit] nf bankruptcy; **faire ~** to go bankrupt

faim [fɛ̃] nf hunger; **avoir ~** to be hungry; **rester sur sa ~** (aussi fig) to be left wanting more

fainéant, e [feneɑ̃, ɑ̃t] nm/f idler, loafer

 MOT-CLÉ

faire [fɛʀ] vt **1** (fabriquer, être l'auteur de) to make; **faire du vin/une offre/un film** to make wine/an offer/a film; **faire du bruit** to make a noise

2 (effectuer: travail, opération) to do; **que faites-vous?** (quel métier etc) what do you do?; (quelle activité: au moment de la question) what are you doing?; **faire la lessive** to do the washing

3 (études) to do; (sport, musique) to play; **faire du droit/du français** to do law/French; **faire du rugby/piano** to play rugby/the piano

4 (simuler): **faire le malade/l'innocent** to act the invalid/the innocent

5 (transformer, avoir un effet sur): **faire de qn un frustré/avocat** to make sb frustrated/a lawyer; **ça ne me fait rien** (m'est égal) I don't care ou mind; (me laisse froid) it has no effect on me; **ça ne fait rien** it doesn't matter; **faire que** (impliquer) to mean that

6 (calculs, prix, mesures): **2 et 2 font 4** 2 and 2 are ou make 4; **ça fait 10 m/15 euros** it's 10 m/15 euros; **je vous le fais 10 euros** I'll let you have it for 10 euros; **je fais du 40** I take a size 40

7 (distance): **faire du 50 (à l'heure)** to do 50 (km an hour); **nous avons fait 1000 km en 2 jours** we did ou covered 1000 km in 2 days; **faire l'Europe** to tour ou do Europe; **faire les magasins** to go shopping

8 qu'a-t-il fait de sa valise? what has he done with his case?

9 ne faire que: il ne fait que critiquer (sans cesse) all he (ever) does is criticize; (seulement)

he's only criticizing
10 (*dire*) to say; **"vraiment?" fit-il** "really?"
he said
11 (*maladie*) to have; **faire du diabète** to have
diabetes *sg*
▷ *vi* **1** (*agir, s'y prendre*) to act, do; **il faut
faire vite** we (*ou* you *etc*) must act quickly;
comment a-t-il fait pour? how did he
manage to?; **faites
comme chez vous** make yourself at home
2 (*paraître*) to look; **faire vieux/démodé** to
look old/old-fashioned; **ça fait bien** it looks
good
▷ *vb substitut* to do; **ne le casse pas comme je
l'ai fait** don't break it as I did; **je peux le voir?
— faites!** can I see it? — please do!
▷ *vb impers* **1**: **il fait beau** *etc* the weather is
fine *etc*; *voir aussi* **jour**; **froid** *etc*
2 (*temps écoulé, durée*): **ça fait 2 ans qu'il est
parti** it's 2 years since he left; **ça fait 2 ans
qu'il y est** he's been there for 2 years
▷ *vb semi-aux* **1**: **faire** (+*infinitif: action directe*)
to make; **faire tomber/bouger qch** to make
sth fall/move; **faire démarrer un moteur/
chauffer de l'eau** to start up an engine/heat
some water; **cela fait dormir** it makes you
sleep; **faire travailler les enfants** to make
the children work *ou* get the children to work;
il m'a fait traverser la rue he helped me to
cross the street
2 (*indirectement, par un intermédiaire*): **faire
réparer qch** to get *ou* have sth repaired;
faire punir les enfants to have the children
punished
se faire *vi* **1** (*être convenable*): **cela se fait
beaucoup/ne se fait pas** it's done a lot/not
done
2: **se faire** +*nom ou pron*: **se faire une jupe** to
make o.s. a skirt; **se faire des amis** to make
friends; **se faire du souci** to worry; **il ne s'en
fait pas** he doesn't worry
3: **se faire** +*adj* (*devenir*): **se faire vieux** to be
getting old; **se faire beau** to do o.s. up
4: **se faire à** (*s'habituer*) to get used to; **je
n'arrive pas à me faire à la nourriture/au
climat** I can't get used to the food/climate
5: **se faire** +*infinitif*: **se faire examiner la
vue/opérer** to have one's eyes tested/have an
operation; **se faire couper les cheveux** to get
one's hair cut; **il va se faire tuer/punir** he's
going to get himself killed/get punished; **il
s'est fait aider** he got somebody to help him;
il s'est fait aider par Simon he got Simon to
help him; **se faire faire un vêtement** to get a
garment made for o.s.
6 (*impersonnel*): **comment se fait-il/faisait-il
que?** how is it/was it that?

faire-part [fɛʀpaʀ] *nm inv* announcement (*of
birth, marriage etc*)
faisan, e [fəzã, an] *nm/f* pheasant
faisons [fəzɔ̃] *vb voir* **faire**
fait, e [fɛ, fɛt] *adj* (*mûr: fromage, melon*) ripe
▷ *nm* (*événement*) event, occurrence; (*réalité,
donnée*) fact; **être au ~ (de)** to be informed
(of); **au ~** (*à propos*) by the way; **en venir au
~** to get to the point; **du ~ de ceci/qu'il a
menti** because of *ou* on account of this/his
having lied; **de ce ~** for this reason; **en ~** in
fact; **prendre qn sur le ~** to catch sb in the act;
c'est bien ~ pour lui (*ou* **eux** *etc*) it serves him
(*ou* them *etc*) right; **fait divers** news item
faites [fɛt] *vb voir* **faire**
falaise [falɛz] *nf* cliff
falloir [falwaʀ] *vb impers*: **il faut qu'il parte/a
fallu qu'il parte** (*obligation*) he has to *ou*
must leave/had to leave; **il a fallu le faire**
it had to be done; **il faudrait qu'elle rentre**
she should come *ou* go back, she ought to
come *ou* go back; **il faut faire attention** you
have to be careful; **il me faudrait 100 euros**
I would need 100 euros; **il vous faut tourner
à gauche après l'église** you have to turn left
past the church; **nous avons ce qu'il (nous)
faut** we have what we need; **il ne fallait pas**
you shouldn't have (done); **comme il faut**
(*personne*) proper; (*agir*) properly; **s'en falloir**
vr: **il s'en est fallu de 100 euros/5 minutes**
we/they *etc* were 100 euros short/5 minutes
late (*ou* early); **il s'en faut de beaucoup qu'il
soit** he is far from being; **il s'en est fallu de
peu que cela n'arrive** it very nearly happened
famé, e [fame] *adj*: **mal ~** disreputable, of ill
repute
fameux, -euse [famø, øz] *adj* (*illustre*)
famous; (*bon: repas, plat etc*) first-rate, first-
class; (*valeur intensive*) real, downright
familial, e, -aux [familjal, jo] *adj* family *cpd*
familiarité [familjaʀite] *nf* familiarity
familier, -ère [familje, jɛʀ] *adj* (*connu*)
familiar; (*atmosphère*) informal, friendly; (*Ling*)
informal, colloquial ▷ *nm* regular (*visitor*)
famille [famij] *nf* family; **il a de la ~ à Paris** he
has relatives in Paris
famine [famin] *nf* famine
fanatique [fanatik] *adj* fanatical ▷ *nm/f*
fanatic
faner [fane]: **se faner** *vi* to fade
fanfare [fɑ̃faʀ] *nf* (*orchestre*) brass band;
(*musique*) fanfare
fantaisie [fɑ̃tezi] *nf* (*spontanéité*) fancy,
imagination; (*caprice*) whim ▷ *adj*: **bijou ~**
costume jewellery
fantasme [fɑ̃tasm] *nm* fantasy
fantastique [fɑ̃tastik] *adj* fantastic
fantôme [fɑ̃tom] *nm* ghost, phantom
faon [fɑ̃] *nm* fawn
FAQ *sigle f* (= *foire aux questions*) FAQ

farce [faʀs] nf (viande) stuffing; (blague) (practical) joke; (Théâtre) farce; **farcir** vt (viande) to stuff

farder [faʀde]: **se farder** vi to make (o.s.) up

farine [faʀin] nf flour

farouche [faʀuʃ] adj (timide) shy, timid

fart [faʀt] nm (ski) wax

fascination [fasinasjɔ̃] nf fascination

fasciner [fasine] vt to fascinate

fascisme [faʃism] nm fascism

fasse etc [fas] vb voir **faire**

fastidieux, -euse [fastidjø, jøz] adj tedious, tiresome

fatal, e [fatal] adj fatal; (inévitable) inevitable; **fatalité** nf (destin) fate; (coïncidence) fateful coincidence

fatidique [fatidik] adj fateful

fatigant, e [fatigɑ̃, ɑ̃t] adj tiring; (agaçant) tiresome

fatigue [fatig] nf tiredness, fatigue; **fatigué, e** adj tired; **fatiguer** vt to tire, make tired; (fig: agacer) to annoy ▷ vi (moteur) to labour, strain; **se fatiguer** to get tired

fauché, e [foʃe] (fam) adj broke

faucher [foʃe] vt (herbe) to cut; (champs, blés) to reap; (fig: véhicule) to mow down; (fam: voler) to pinch

faucon [fokɔ̃] nm falcon, hawk

faudra [fodʀa] vb voir **falloir**

faufiler [fofile]: **se faufiler** vi: **se ~ dans** to edge one's way into; **se ~ parmi/entre** to thread one's way among/between

faune [fon] nf (Zool) wildlife, fauna

fausse [fos] adj voir **faux**; **faussement** adv (accuser) wrongly, wrongfully; (croire) falsely

fausser [fose] vt (objet) to bend, buckle; (fig) to distort; **~ compagnie à qn** to give sb the slip

faut [fo] vb voir **falloir**

faute [fot] nf (erreur) mistake, error; (mauvaise action) misdemeanour; (Football etc) offence; (Tennis) fault; **c'est de sa/ma ~** it's his ou her/my fault; **être en ~** to be in the wrong; **~ de** (temps, argent) for ou through lack of; **sans ~** without fail; **faute de frappe** typing error; **faute professionnelle** professional misconduct no pl

fauteuil [fotœj] nm armchair; (au théâtre) seat; **fauteuil roulant** wheelchair

fautif, -ive [fotif, iv] adj (responsable) at fault, in the wrong; (incorrect) incorrect, inaccurate; **il se sentait ~** he felt guilty

fauve [fov] nm wildcat ▷ adj (couleur) fawn

faux¹ [fo] nf scythe

faux², fausse [fo, fos] adj (inexact) wrong; (voix) out of tune; (billet) fake, forged; (sournois, postiche) false ▷ adv (Mus) out of tune ▷ nm (copie) fake, forgery; **faire ~ bond à qn** to let sb down; **faire un ~ pas** to trip; (fig) to make a faux pas; **fausse alerte** false alarm; **fausse couche** miscarriage; **faux frais** nmpl extras, incidental expenses; **faux mouvement** awkward movement; **fausse note** wrong note; **faux témoignage** (délit) perjury; **faux-filet** nm sirloin

faveur [favœʀ] nf favour; **traitement de ~** preferential treatment; **en ~ de** in favour of

favorable [favoʀabl] adj favourable

favori, te [favoʀi, it] adj, nm/f favourite

favoriser [favoʀize] vt to favour

fax [faks] nm fax

fécond, e [fekɔ̃, ɔ̃d] adj fertile; **féconder** vt to fertilize

féculent [fekylɑ̃] nm starchy food

fédéral, e, -aux [fedeʀal, o] adj federal

fée [fe] nf fairy

feignant, e [fɛɲɑ̃, ɑ̃t] nm/f = **fainéant, e**

feindre [fɛ̃dʀ] vt to feign; **~ de faire** to pretend to do

fêler [fele] vt to crack; **se fêler** to crack

félicitations [felisitasjɔ̃] nfpl congratulations

féliciter [felisite] vt: **~ qn (de)** to congratulate sb (on)

félin, e [felɛ̃, in] nm (big) cat

femelle [fəmɛl] adj, nf female

féminin, e [feminɛ̃, in] adj feminine; (sexe) female; (équipe, vêtements etc) women's ▷ nm (Ling) feminine; **féministe** adj feminist

femme [fam] nf woman; (épouse) wife; **femme au foyer** housewife; **femme de chambre** chambermaid; **femme de ménage** cleaning lady

fémur [femyʀ] nm femur, thighbone

fendre [fɑ̃dʀ] vt (couper en deux) to split; (fissurer) to crack; (traverser: foule, air) to cleave through; **se fendre** vi to crack

fenêtre [f(ə)nɛtʀ] nf window

fenouil [fənuj] nm fennel

fente [fɑ̃t] nf (fissure) crack; (de boîte à lettres etc) slit

fer [fɛʀ] nm iron; **fer à cheval** horseshoe; **fer à friser** curling tongs pl; **fer (à repasser)** iron; **fer forgé** wrought iron

ferai etc [fəʀe] vb voir **faire**

fer-blanc [fɛʀblɑ̃] nm tin(plate)

férié, e [feʀje] adj: **jour ~** public holiday

ferions etc [fəʀjɔ̃] vb voir **faire**

ferme [fɛʀm] adj firm ▷ adv (travailler etc) hard ▷ nf (exploitation) farm; (maison) farmhouse

fermé, e [fɛʀme] adj closed, shut; (gaz, eau etc) off; (fig: milieu) exclusive

fermenter [fɛʀmɑ̃te] vi to ferment

fermer [fɛʀme] vt to close, shut; (cesser l'exploitation de) to close down, shut down; (eau, électricité, robinet) to turn off; (aéroport, route) to close ▷ vi to close, shut; (magasin: definitivement) to close down, shut down; **~ à clef** to lock; **se fermer** vi to close, shut

fermeté [fɛʀməte] *nf* firmness

fermeture [fɛʀmətyʀ] *nf* closing; (*dispositif*) catch; **heures de ~** closing times; **fermeture éclair®** *ou* **à glissière** zip (fastener) (*BRIT*), zipper (*US*)

fermier [fɛʀmje] *nm* farmer

féroce [feʀɔs] *adj* ferocious, fierce

ferons [fəʀɔ̃] *vb voir* **faire**

ferrer [feʀe] *vt* (*cheval*) to shoe

ferroviaire [feʀɔvjɛʀ] *adj* rail(way) *cpd* (*BRIT*), rail(road) *cpd* (*US*)

ferry(-boat) [fɛʀe(-bot)] *nm* ferry

fertile [fɛʀtil] *adj* fertile; **~ en incidents** eventful, packed with incidents

fervent, e [fɛʀvɑ̃, ɑ̃t] *adj* fervent

fesse [fɛs] *nf* buttock; **fessée** *nf* spanking

festin [fɛstɛ̃] *nm* feast

festival [fɛstival] *nm* festival

festivités [fɛstivite] *nfpl* festivities

fêtard, e [fɛtaʀ, aʀd] (*fam*) *nm/f* high liver, merry-maker

fête [fɛt] *nf* (*religieuse*) feast; (*publique*) holiday; (*réception*) party; (*kermesse*) fête, fair; (*du nom*) feast day, name day; **faire la ~** to live it up; **faire ~ à qn** to give sb a warm welcome; **les ~s (de fin d'année)** the festive season; **la salle des ~s** the village hall; **la ~ des Mères/Pères** Mother's/Father's Day; **fête foraine** (fun) fair; **fêter** *vt* to celebrate; (*personne*) to have a celebration for

feu, x [fø] *nm* (*gén*) fire; (*signal lumineux*) light; (*de cuisinière*) ring; **feux** *nmpl* (*Auto*) (traffic) lights; **au ~!** (*incendie*) fire!; **à ~ doux/vif** over a slow/brisk heat; **à petit ~** (*Culin*) over a gentle heat; (*fig*) slowly; **faire ~** to fire; **ne pas faire long ~** not to last long; **prendre ~** to catch fire; **mettre le ~ à** to set fire to; **faire du ~** to make a fire; **avez-vous du ~?** (*pour cigarette*) have you (got) a light?; **feu arrière** rear light; **feu d'artifice** (*spectacle*) fireworks *pl*; **feu de joie** bonfire; **feu orange/rouge/vert** amber (*BRIT*) *ou* yellow (*US*)/red/green light; **feux de brouillard** fog lights *ou* lamps; **feux de croisement** dipped (*BRIT*) *ou* dimmed (*US*) headlights; **feux de position** sidelights; **feux de route** headlights

feuillage [fœjaʒ] *nm* foliage, leaves *pl*

feuille [fœj] *nf* (*d'arbre*) leaf; (*de papier*) sheet; **feuille de calcul** spreadsheet; **feuille d'impôts** tax form; **feuille de maladie** *medical expenses claim form*; **feuille de paie** pay slip

feuillet [fœjɛ] *nm* leaf

feuilleté, e [fœjte] *adj:* **pâte ~** flaky pastry

feuilleter [fœjte] *vt* (*livre*) to leaf through

feuilleton [fœjtɔ̃] *nm* serial

feutre [føtʀ] *nm* felt; (*chapeau*) felt hat; (*aussi:* **stylo-~**) felt-tip pen; **feutré, e** *adj* (*atmosphère*) muffled

fève [fɛv] *nf* broad bean

février [fevʀije] *nm* February

fiable [fjabl] *adj* reliable

fiançailles [fjɑ̃sɑj] *nfpl* engagement *sg*

fiancé, e [fjɑ̃se] *nm/f* fiancé(e) ▷ *adj:* **être ~ (à)** to be engaged (to)

fiancer [fjɑ̃se]: **se fiancer (avec)** *vi* to become engaged (to)

fibre [fibʀ] *nf* fibre; **fibre de verre** fibreglass, glass fibre

ficeler [fis(ə)le] *vt* to tie up

ficelle [fisɛl] *nf* string *no pl*; (*morceau*) piece *ou* length of string

fiche [fiʃ] *nf* (*pour fichier*) (index) card; (*formulaire*) form; (*Élec*) plug; **fiche de paye** pay slip

ficher [fiʃe] *vt* (*dans un fichier*) to file; (*Police*) to put on file; (*fam: faire*) to do; (: *donner*) to give; (: *mettre*) to stick *ou* shove; **fiche-(moi) le camp!** (*fam*) clear off!; **fiche-moi la paix!** (*fam*) leave me alone!; **se ficher de** (*fam: rire de*) to make fun of; (*être indifférent à*) not to care about

fichier [fiʃje] *nm* file; **~ joint** (*Comput*) attachment

fichu, e [fiʃy] *pp de* **ficher** (*fam*) ▷ *adj* (*fam: fini, inutilisable*) bust, done for; (: *intensif*) wretched, darned ▷ *nm* (*foulard*) (head)scarf; **mal ~** (*fam*) feeling lousy

fictif, -ive [fiktif, iv] *adj* fictitious

fiction [fiksjɔ̃] *nf* fiction; (*fait imaginé*) invention

fidèle [fidɛl] *adj* faithful ▷ *nm/f* (*Rel*): **les ~s** (*à l'église*) the congregation *sg*; **fidélité** *nf* (*d'un conjoint*) fidelity, faithfulness; (*d'un ami, client*) loyalty

fier¹ [fje]: **se fier à** *vt* to trust

fier², fière [fjɛʀ] *adj* proud; **~ de** proud of; **fierté** *nf* pride

fièvre [fjɛvʀ] *nf* fever; **avoir de la ~/39 de ~** to have a high temperature/a temperature of 39°C; **fiévreux, -euse** *adj* feverish

figer [fiʒe]: **se figer** *vi* (*huile*) to congeal; (*personne*) to freeze

fignoler [fiɲɔle] (*fam*) *vt* to polish up

figue [fig] *nf* fig; **figuier** *nm* fig tree

figurant, e [figyʀɑ̃, ɑ̃t] *nm/f* (*Théâtre*) walk-on; (*Cinéma*) extra

figure [figyʀ] *nf* (*visage*) face; (*forme, personnage*) figure; (*illustration*) picture, diagram

figuré, e [figyʀe] *adj* (*sens*) figurative

figurer [figyʀe] *vi* to appear ▷ *vt* to represent; **se figurer que** to imagine that

fil [fil] *nm* (*brin, fig: d'une histoire*) thread; (*électrique*) wire; (*d'un couteau*) edge; **au ~ des années** with the passing of the years; **au ~ de l'eau** with the stream *ou* current; **coup de ~** (*fam*) phone call; **donner/recevoir un coup de ~** to make/get *ou* receive a phone call; **fil de fer** wire; **fil de fer barbelé** barbed wire

file [fil] *nf* line; (*Auto*) lane; **en ~ indienne** in single file; **à la ~** (*d'affilée*) in succession; **file (d'attente)** queue (BRIT), line (US)

filer [file] *vt* (*tissu, toile*) to spin; (*prendre en filature*) to shadow, tail; (*fam: donner*): **~ qch à qn** to slip sb sth ▷ *vi* (*bas*) to run; (*aller vite*) to fly past; (*fam: partir*) to make *ou* be off; **~ doux** to toe the line

filet [file] *nm* net; (*Culin*) fillet; (*d'eau, de sang*) trickle; **filet (à provisions)** string bag

filiale [filjal] *nf* (*Comm*) subsidiary

filière [filjɛʀ] *nf* (*carrière*) path; **suivre la ~** (*dans sa carrière*) to work one's way up (through the hierarchy)

fille [fij] *nf* girl; (*opposé à fils*) daughter; **vieille ~** old maid; **fillette** *nf* (little) girl

filleul, e [fijœl] *nm/f* godchild, godson/daughter

film [film] *nm* (*pour photo*) (roll of) film; (*œuvre*) film, picture, movie

fils [fis] *nm* son; **fils à papa** daddy's boy

filtre [filtʀ] *nm* filter; **filtrer** *vt* to filter; (*fig: candidats, visiteurs*) to screen

fin¹ [fɛ̃] *nf* end; **fins** *nfpl* (*but*) ends; **prendre ~** to come to an end; **mettre ~ à** to put an end to; **à la ~** in the end, eventually; **en ~ de compte** in the end; **sans ~** endless; **~ juin** at the end of June; **fin prêt** quite ready

fin², e [fɛ̃, fin] *adj* (*papier, couche, fil*) thin; (*cheveux, visage*) fine; (*taille*) neat, slim; (*esprit, remarque*) subtle ▷ *adv* (*couper*) finely; **fines herbes** mixed herbs; **avoir la vue/l'ouïe fine** to have keen eyesight/hearing; **repas/vin fin** gourmet meal/fine wine

final, e [final, o] *adj* final ▷ *nm* (*Mus*) finale; **finale** *nf* final; **quarts de finale** quarter finals; **finalement** *adv* finally, in the end; (*après tout*) after all

finance [finɑ̃s] *nf* finance; **finances** *nfpl* (*situation*) finances; (*activités*) finance *sg*; **moyennant ~** for a fee; **financer** *vt* to finance; **financier, -ière** *adj* financial

finesse [fines] *nf* thinness; (*raffinement*) fineness; (*subtilité*) subtlety

fini, e [fini] *adj* finished; (*Math*) finite ▷ *nm* (*d'un objet manufacturé*) finish

finir [finiʀ] *vt* to finish ▷ *vi* to finish, end; **~ par faire** to end up *ou* finish up doing; **~ de faire** to finish doing; (*cesser*) to stop doing; **il finit par m'agacer** he's beginning to get on my nerves; **en ~ avec** to be *ou* have done with; **il va mal ~** he will come to a bad end

finition [finisjɔ̃] *nf* (*résultat*) finish

finlandais, e [fɛ̃lɑ̃dɛ, ɛz] *adj* Finnish ▷ *nm/f*: **F~, e** Finn

Finlande [fɛ̃lɑ̃d] *nf*: **la ~** Finland

finnois, e [finwa, waz] *adj* Finnish ▷ *nm* (*Ling*) Finnish

fioul [fjul] *nm* fuel oil

firme [fiʀm] *nf* firm

fis [fi] *vb voir* **faire**

fisc [fisk] *nm* tax authorities *pl*; **fiscal, e, -aux** *adj* tax *cpd*, fiscal; **fiscalité** *nf* tax system

fissure [fisyʀ] *nf* crack; **fissurer** *vt* to crack; **se fissurer** *vi* to crack

fit [fi] *vb voir* **faire**

fixation [fiksasjɔ̃] *nf* (*attache*) fastening; (*Psych*) fixation

fixe [fiks] *adj* fixed; (*emploi*) steady, regular ▷ *nm* (*salaire*) basic salary; (*téléphone*) landline; **à heure ~** at a set time; **menu à prix ~** set menu

fixé, e [fikse] *adj*: **être ~ (sur)** (*savoir à quoi s'en tenir*) to have made up one's mind (about)

fixer [fikse] *vt* (*attacher*): **~ qch (à/sur)** to fix *ou* fasten sth (to/onto); (*déterminer*) to fix, set; (*regarder*) to stare at; **se fixer** *vi* (*s'établir*) to settle down; **se ~ sur** (*suj: attention*) to focus on

flacon [flakɔ̃] *nm* bottle

flageolet [flaʒɔlɛ] *nm* (*Culin*) dwarf kidney bean

flagrant, e [flagrɑ̃, ɑ̃t] *adj* flagrant, blatant; **en ~ délit** in the act

flair [flɛʀ] *nm* sense of smell; (*fig*) intuition; **flairer** *vt* (*humer*) to sniff (at); (*détecter*) to scent

flamand, e [flamɑ̃, ɑ̃d] *adj* Flemish ▷ *nm* (*Ling*) Flemish ▷ *nm/f*: **F~, e** Fleming

flamant [flamɑ̃] *nm* flamingo

flambant, e [flɑ̃bɑ̃, ɑ̃t] *adv*: **~ neuf** brand new

flambé, e [flɑ̃be] *adj* (*Culin*) flambé

flambée [flɑ̃be] *nf* blaze; (*fig: des prix*) explosion

flamber [flɑ̃be] *vi* to blaze (up)

flamboyer [flɑ̃bwaje] *vi* to blaze (up)

flamme [flam] *nf* flame; (*fig*) fire, fervour; **en ~s** on fire, ablaze

flan [flɑ̃] *nm* (*Culin*) custard tart *ou* pie

flanc [flɑ̃] *nm* side; (*Mil*) flank

flancher [flɑ̃ʃe] (*fam*) *vi* to fail, pack up

flanelle [flanɛl] *nf* flannel

flâner [flane] *vi* to stroll

flanquer [flɑ̃ke] *vt* to flank; (*fam: mettre*) to chuck, shove; (: *jeter*): **~ par terre/à la porte** to fling to the ground/chuck out

flaque [flak] *nf* (*d'eau*) puddle; (*d'huile, de sang etc*) pool

flash [flaʃ] (*pl* **~es**) *nm* (*Photo*) flash; **flash d'information** newsflash

flatter [flate] *vt* to flatter; **se ~ de qch** to pride o.s. on sth; **flatteur, -euse** *adj* flattering

flèche [flɛʃ] *nf* arrow; (*de clocher*) spire; **monter en ~** (*fig*) to soar, rocket; **partir en ~** to be off like a shot; **fléchette** *nf* dart

flétrir [fletʀiʀ] : **se flétrir** *vi* to wither

fleur [flœʀ] *nf* flower; (*d'un arbre*) blossom; **en ~** (*arbre*) in blossom; **à ~s** flowery

fleuri, e [flœʀi] *adj* (*jardin*) in flower *ou* bloom; (*tissu, papier*) flowery

fleurir [flœʀiʀ] *vi* (*rose*) to flower; (*arbre*) to blossom; (*fig*) to flourish ▷ *vt* (*tombe*) to put flowers on; (*chambre*) to decorate with flowers

fleuriste [flœʀist] *nm/f* florist

fleuve [flœv] *nm* river

flexible [flɛksibl] *adj* flexible

flic [flik] (*fam: péj*) *nm* cop

flipper [flipœʀ] *nm* pinball (machine)

flirter [flœʀte] *vi* to flirt

flocon [flɔkɔ̃] *nm* flake

flore [flɔʀ] *nf* flora

florissant, e [flɔʀisɑ̃, ɑ̃t] *adj* (*économie*) flourishing

flot [flo] *nm* flood, stream; **flots** *nmpl* (*de la mer*) waves; **être à ~** (*Navig*) to be afloat; **entrer à ~s** to stream *ou* pour in

flottant, e [flɔtɑ̃, ɑ̃t] *adj* (*vêtement*) loose

flotte [flɔt] *nf* (*Navig*) fleet; (*fam: eau*) water; (: *pluie*) rain

flotter [flɔte] *vi* to float; (*nuage, odeur*) to drift; (*drapeau*) to fly; (*vêtements*) to hang loose; (*fam: pleuvoir*) to rain; **faire ~** to float; **flotteur** *nm* float

flou, e [flu] *adj* fuzzy, blurred; (*fig*) woolly, vague

fluide [flɥid] *adj* fluid; (*circulation etc*) flowing freely ▷ *nm* fluid

fluor [flyɔʀ] *nm*: **dentifrice au ~** fluoride toothpaste

fluorescent, e [flyɔʀesɑ̃, ɑ̃t] *adj* fluorescent

flûte [flyt] *nf* flute; (*verre*) flute (glass); (*pain*) (thin) French stick; **~!** drat it!; **flûte traversière/à bec** flute/recorder

flux [fly] *nm* incoming tide; (*écoulement*) flow; **le ~ et le reflux** the ebb and flow

foc [fɔk] *nm* jib

foi [fwa] *nf* faith; **digne de ~** reliable; **être de bonne/mauvaise ~** to be sincere/insincere; **ma ~ ...** well ...

foie [fwa] *nm* liver; **crise de ~** stomach upset

foin [fwɛ̃] *nm* hay; **faire du ~** (*fig: fam*) to kick up a row

foire [fwaʀ] *nf* fair; (*fête foraine*) (fun) fair; **faire la ~** (*fig: fam*) to whoop it up; **~ aux questions** (*Internet*) FAQs; **foire (exposition)** trade fair

fois [fwa] *nf* time; **une/deux ~** once/twice; **2 ~ 2** 2 times 2; **une ~** (*passé*) once; (*futur*) sometime; **une ~ pour toutes** once and for all; **une ~ que** once; **des ~** (*parfois*) sometimes; **à la ~** (*ensemble*) at once

fol [fɔl] *adj voir* **fou**

folie [fɔli] *nf* (*d'une décision, d'un acte*) madness, folly; (*état*) madness, insanity; **la ~ des grandeurs** delusions of grandeur; **faire des ~s** (*en dépenses*) to be extravagant

folklorique [fɔlklɔʀik] *adj* folk *cpd*; (*fam*) weird

folle [fɔl] *adj, nf voir* **fou**; **follement** *adv* (*très*) madly, wildly

foncé, e [fɔ̃se] *adj* dark

foncer [fɔ̃se] *vi* to go darker; (*fam: aller vite*) to tear *ou* belt along; **~ sur** to charge at

fonction [fɔ̃ksjɔ̃] *nf* function; (*emploi, poste*) post, position; **fonctions** *nfpl* (*professionnelles*) duties; **voiture de ~** company car; **en ~ de** (*par rapport à*) according to; **faire ~ de** to serve as; **la ~ publique** the state *ou* civil (BRIT) service; **fonctionnaire** *nm/f* state employee, local authority employee; (*dans l'administration*) ≈ civil servant; **fonctionner** *vi* to work, function

fond [fɔ̃] *nm* (*d'un récipient, trou*) bottom; (*d'une salle, scène*) back; (*d'un tableau, décor*) background; (*opposé à la forme*) content; (*Sport*): **le ~** long distance (running); **au ~ de** at the bottom of; at the back of; **à ~** (*connaître, soutenir*) thoroughly; (*appuyer, visser*) right down *ou* home; **à ~ (de train)** (*fam*) full tilt; **dans le ~, au ~** (*en somme*) basically, really; **de ~ en comble** from top to bottom; **fond de teint** foundation (cream); *voir aussi* **fonds**

fondamental, e, -aux [fɔ̃damɑ̃tal, o] *adj* fundamental

fondant, e [fɔ̃dɑ̃, ɑ̃t] *adj* (*neige*) melting; (*poire*) that melts in the mouth

fondation [fɔ̃dasjɔ̃] *nf* founding; (*établissement*) foundation; **fondations** *nfpl* (*d'une maison*) foundations

fondé, e [fɔ̃de] *adj* (*accusation etc*) well-founded; **être ~ à** to have grounds for *ou* good reason to

fondement [fɔ̃dmɑ̃] *nm*: **sans ~** (*rumeur etc*) groundless, unfounded

fonder [fɔ̃de] *vt* to found; (*fig*) to base; **se fonder sur** (*suj: personne*) to base o.s. on

fonderie [fɔ̃dʀi] *nf* smelting works *sg*

fondre [fɔ̃dʀ] *vt* (*aussi:* **faire ~**) to melt; (*dans l'eau*) to dissolve; (*fig: mélanger*) to merge, blend ▷ *vi* (*à la chaleur*) to melt; (*dans l'eau*) to dissolve; (*fig*) to melt away; (*se précipiter*): **~ sur** to swoop down on; **~ en larmes** to burst into tears

fonds [fɔ̃] *nm* (*Comm*): **~ (de commerce)** business ▷ *nmpl* (*argent*) funds

fondu, e [fɔ̃dy] *adj* (*beurre, neige*) melted; (*métal*) molten; **fondue** *nf* (*Culin*) fondue

font [fɔ̃] *vb voir* **faire**

fontaine [fɔ̃tɛn] *nf* fountain; (*source*) spring

fonte [fɔ̃t] *nf* melting; (*métal*) cast iron; **la ~ des neiges** the (spring) thaw

foot [fut] (*fam*) *nm* football

football [futbol] *nm* football, soccer; **footballeur** *nm* footballer

footing [futiŋ] *nm* jogging; **faire du ~** to go jogging

forain, e [fɔʀɛ̃, ɛn] *adj* fairground *cpd* ▷ *nm*

(*marchand*) stallholder; (*acteur*) fairground entertainer

forçat [fɔʀsa] *nm* convict

force [fɔʀs] *nf* strength; (*Physique, Mécanique*) force; **forces** *nfpl* (*physiques*) strength *sg*; (*Mil*) forces; **à ~ d'insister** by dint of insisting; **as** he (*ou* I *etc*) kept on insisting; **de ~** forcibly, by force; **dans la ~ de l'âge** in the prime of life; **les forces de l'ordre** the police *no pl*

forcé, e [fɔʀse] *adj* forced; **c'est ~** (*fam*) it's inevitable; **forcément** *adv* inevitably; **pas forcément** not necessarily

forcer [fɔʀse] *vt* to force; (*voix*) to strain ▷ *vi* (*Sport*) to overtax o.s.; **~ la dose** (*fam*) to overdo it; **se ~ (à faire)** to force o.s. (to do)

forestier, -ère [fɔʀɛstje, jɛʀ] *adj* forest *cpd*

forêt [fɔʀɛ] *nf* forest

forfait [fɔʀfɛ] *nm* (*Comm*) all-in deal *ou* price; **déclarer ~** to withdraw; **forfaitaire** *adj* inclusive

forge [fɔʀʒ] *nf* forge, smithy; **forgeron** *nm* (black)smith

formaliser [fɔʀmalize]: **se formaliser** *vi*: **se ~ (de)** to take offence (at)

formalité [fɔʀmalite] *nf* formality; **simple ~** mere formality

format [fɔʀma] *nm* size; **formater** *vt* (*disque*) to format

formation [fɔʀmasjɔ̃] *nf* (*développement*) forming; (*apprentissage*) training; **formation permanente** *ou* **continue** continuing education

forme [fɔʀm] *nf* (*gén*) form; (*d'un objet*) shape, form; **formes** *nfpl* (*bonnes manières*) proprieties; (*d'une femme*) figure *sg*; **en ~ de poire** pear-shaped, in the shape of a pear; **être en ~** (*Sport etc*) to be on form; **en bonne et due ~** in due form

formel, le [fɔʀmɛl] *adj* (*catégorique*) definite, positive; **formellement** *adv* (*absolument*) positively; **formellement interdit** strictly forbidden

former [fɔʀme] *vt* to form; (*éduquer*) to train; **se former** *vi* to form

formidable [fɔʀmidabl] *adj* tremendous

formulaire [fɔʀmylɛʀ] *nm* form

formule [fɔʀmyl] *nf* (*gén*) formula; (*expression*) phrase; **formule de politesse** polite phrase; (*en fin de lettre*) letter ending

fort, e [fɔʀ, fɔʀt] *adj* strong; (*intensité, rendement*) high, great; (*corpulent*) stout; (*doué*) good, able ▷ *adv* (*serrer, frapper*) hard; (*parler*) loud(ly); (*beaucoup*) greatly, very much; (*très*) very ▷ *nm* (*édifice*) fort; (*point fort*) strong point, forte; **forte tête** rebel; **forteresse** *nf* stronghold

fortifiant [fɔʀtifjɑ̃] *nm* tonic

fortune [fɔʀtyn] *nf* fortune; **faire ~** to make one's fortune; **de ~** makeshift; **fortuné, e** *adj* wealthy

forum [fɔʀɔm] *nm* forum; **~ de discussion** (*Internet*) message board

fosse [fos] *nf* (*grand trou*) pit; (*tombe*) grave

fossé [fose] *nm* ditch; (*fig*) gulf, gap

fossette [fosɛt] *nf* dimple

fossile [fosil] *nm* fossil

fou (fol), folle [fu, fɔl] *adj* mad; (*déréglé etc*) wild, erratic; (*fam: extrême, très grand*) terrific, tremendous ▷ *nm/f* madman(-woman) ▷ *nm* (*du roi*) jester; **être fou de** to be mad *ou* crazy about; **avoir le fou rire** to have the giggles

foudre [fudʀ] *nf*: **la ~** lightning

foudroyant, e [fudʀwajɑ̃, ɑ̃t] *adj* (*progrès*) lightning *cpd*; (*succès*) stunning; (*maladie, poison*) violent

fouet [fwɛ] *nm* whip; (*Culin*) whisk; **de plein ~** (*se heurter*) head on; **fouetter** *vt* to whip; (*crème*) to whisk

fougère [fuʒɛʀ] *nf* fern

fougue [fug] *nf* ardour, spirit; **fougueux, -euse** *adj* fiery

fouille [fuj] *nf* search; **fouilles** *nfpl* (*archéologiques*) excavations; **fouiller** *vt* to search; (*creuser*) to dig ▷ *vi* to rummage; **fouillis** *nm* jumble, muddle

foulard [fulaʀ] *nm* scarf

foule [ful] *nf* crowd; **la ~** crowds *pl*; **une ~ de** masses of

foulée [fule] *nf* stride

fouler [fule] *vt* to press; (*sol*) to tread upon; **se ~ la cheville** to sprain one's ankle; **ne pas se ~** not to overexert o.s.; **il ne se foule pas** he doesn't put himself out; **foulure** *nf* sprain

four [fuʀ] *nm* oven; (*de potier*) kiln; (*Théâtre: échec*) flop

fourche [fuʀʃ] *nf* pitchfork

fourchette [fuʀʃɛt] *nf* fork; (*Statistique*) bracket, margin

fourgon [fuʀgɔ̃] *nm* van; (*Rail*) wag(g)on; **fourgonnette** *nf* (small) van

fourmi [fuʀmi] *nf* ant; **avoir des ~s dans les jambes/mains** to have pins and needles in one's legs/hands; **fourmilière** *nf* ant-hill; **fourmiller** *vi* to swarm

fourneau, x [fuʀno] *nm* stove

fourni, e [fuʀni] *adj* (*barbe, cheveux*) thick; (*magasin*): **bien ~ (en)** well stocked (with)

fournir [fuʀniʀ] *vt* to supply; (*preuve, exemple*) to provide, supply; (*effort*) to put in; **~ qch à qn** to supply sth to sb, supply *ou* provide sb with sth; **fournisseur, -euse** *nm/f* supplier; **fournisseur d'accès à Internet** (*Internet*) service provider, ISP; **fourniture** *nf* supply(ing); **fournitures scolaires** school stationery

fourrage [fuʀaʒ] *nm* fodder

fourré, e [fuʀe] *adj* (*bonbon etc*) filled; (*manteau etc*) fur-lined ▷ *nm* thicket

fourrer [fuʀe] (*fam*) *vt* to stick, shove; **se
fourrer dans/sous** to get into/under
fourrière [fuʀjeʀ] *nf* pound
fourrure [fuʀyʀ] *nf* fur; (*sur l'animal*) coat
foutre [futʀ] (*fam!*) *vt* = **ficher; foutu, e** (*fam!*)
adj = **fichu, e**
foyer [fwaje] *nm* (*maison*) home; (*famille*)
family; (*de cheminée*) hearth; (*de jeunes etc*)
(social) club; (*résidence*) hostel; (*salon*) foyer;
lunettes à double ~ bi-focals
fracassant, e [fʀakasɑ̃, ɑ̃t] *adj* (*succès*)
thundering
fraction [fʀaksjɔ̃] *nf* fraction
fracture [fʀaktyʀ] *nf* fracture; **fracture du
crâne** fractured skull; **fracturer** *vt* (*coffre,
serrure*) to break open; (*os, membre*) to fracture;
se fracturer le crâne to fracture one's skull
fragile [fʀaʒil] *adj* fragile, delicate; (*fig*) frail;
fragilité *nf* fragility
fragment [fʀagmɑ̃] *nm* (*d'un objet*) fragment,
piece
fraîche [fʀɛʃ] *adj voir* **frais; fraîcheur** *nf*
coolness; (*d'un aliment*) freshness; **fraîchir** *vi*
to get cooler; (*vent*) to freshen
frais, fraîche [fʀɛ, fʀɛʃ] *adj* fresh; (*froid*)
cool ▷ *adv* (*récemment*) newly, fresh(ly) ▷ *nm*:
mettre au ~ to put in a cool place ▷ *nmpl*
(*gén*) expenses; (*Comm*) costs; **il fait ~** it's cool;
servir ~ serve chilled; **prendre le ~** to take a
breath of cool air; **faire des ~** to go to a lot of
expense; **frais de scolarité** school fees (BRIT),
tuition (US); **frais généraux** overheads
fraise [fʀɛz] *nf* strawberry; **fraise des bois**
wild strawberry
framboise [fʀɑ̃bwaz] *nf* raspberry
franc, franche [fʀɑ̃, fʀɑ̃ʃ] *adj* (*personne*) frank,
straightforward; (*visage*) open; (*net: refus*)
clear; (*: coupure*) clean; (*intensif*) downright
▷ *nm* franc
français, e [fʀɑ̃sɛ, ɛz] *adj* French ▷ *nm/f*: **F~,
F~** Frenchman(-woman) ▷ *nm* (*Ling*) French
France [fʀɑ̃s] *nf*: **la ~** France; **~ 2, ~ 3** public-
sector television channels

● **FRANCE TÉLÉVISION**
●
● **France 2** and **France 3** are public-sector
● television channels. France 2 is a national
● general interest and entertainment
● channel; France 3 provides regional news
● and information as well as programmes for
● the national network.

franche [fʀɑ̃ʃ] *adj voir* **franc; franchement**
adv frankly; (*nettement*) definitely; (*tout à fait:
mauvais etc*) downright
franchir [fʀɑ̃ʃiʀ] *vt* (*obstacle*) to clear, get over;
(*seuil, ligne, rivière*) to cross; (*distance*) to cover
franchise [fʀɑ̃ʃiz] *nf* frankness; (*douanière*)

exemption; (*Assurances*) excess
franc-maçon [fʀɑ̃masɔ̃] *nm* freemason
franco [fʀɑ̃ko] *adv* (*Comm*): **~ (de port)**
postage paid
francophone [fʀɑ̃kɔfɔn] *adj* French-
speaking
franc-parler [fʀɑ̃paʀle] *nm inv*
outspokenness; **avoir son ~** to speak one's
mind
frange [fʀɑ̃ʒ] *nf* fringe
frangipane [fʀɑ̃ʒipan] *nf* almond paste
frappant, e [fʀapɑ̃, ɑ̃t] *adj* striking
frappé, e [fʀape] *adj* iced
frapper [fʀape] *vt* to hit, strike; (*étonner*) to
strike; **~ dans ses mains** to clap one's hands;
frappé de stupeur dumbfounded
fraternel, le [fʀatɛʀnɛl] *adj* brotherly,
fraternal; **fraternité** *nf* brotherhood
fraude [fʀod] *nf* fraud; (*Scol*) cheating; **passer
qch en ~** to smuggle sth in (*ou* out); **fraude
fiscale** tax evasion
frayeur [fʀejœʀ] *nf* fright
fredonner [fʀədɔne] *vt* to hum
freezer [fʀizœʀ] *nm* freezing compartment
frein [fʀɛ̃] *nm* brake; **mettre un ~ à** (*fig*) to
curb, check; **frein à main** handbrake; **freiner**
vi to brake ▷ *vt* (*progrès etc*) to check
frêle [fʀɛl] *adj* frail, fragile
frelon [fʀəlɔ̃] *nm* hornet
frémir [fʀemiʀ] *vi* (*de peur, d'horreur*) to
shudder; (*de colère*) to shake; (*feuillage*) to
quiver
frêne [fʀɛn] *nm* ash
fréquemment [fʀekamɑ̃] *adv* frequently
fréquent, e [fʀekɑ̃, ɑ̃t] *adj* frequent
fréquentation [fʀekɑ̃tasjɔ̃] *nf* frequenting;
fréquentations *nfpl* (*relations*) company
sg; **avoir de mauvaises ~s** to be in with the
wrong crowd, keep bad company
fréquenté, e [fʀekɑ̃te] *adj*: **très ~** (very) busy;
mal ~ patronized by disreputable elements
fréquenter [fʀekɑ̃te] *vt* (*lieu*) to frequent;
(*personne*) to see; **se fréquenter** to see each
other
frère [fʀɛʀ] *nm* brother
fresque [fʀɛsk] *nf* (*Art*) fresco
fret [fʀɛ(t)] *nm* freight
friand, e [fʀijɑ̃, fʀijɑ̃d] *adj*: **~ de** very fond of
▷ *nm*: **~ au fromage** cheese puff
friandise [fʀijɑ̃diz] *nf* sweet
fric [fʀik] (*fam*) *nm* cash, bread
friche [fʀiʃ]: **en ~** *adj, adv* (lying) fallow
friction [fʀiksjɔ̃] *nf* (*massage*) rub, rub-down;
(*Tech, fig*) friction
frigidaire® [fʀiʒidɛʀ] *nm* refrigerator
frigo [fʀigo] (*fam*) *nm* fridge
frigorifique [fʀigɔʀifik] *adj* refrigerating
frileux, -euse [fʀilø, øz] *adj* sensitive to
(the) cold

frimer [fʀime] (*fam*) *vi* to show off

fringale [fʀɛgal] (*fam*) *nf*: **avoir la ~** to be ravenous

fringues [fʀɛg] (*fam*) *nfpl* clothes

fripé, e [fʀipe] *adj* crumpled

frire [fʀiʀ] *vt*, *vi*: **faire ~** to fry

frisé, e [fʀize] *adj* (*cheveux*) curly; (*personne*) curly-haired

frisson [fʀisɔ̃] *nm* (*de froid*) shiver; (*de peur*) shudder; **frissonner** *vi* (*de fièvre, froid*) to shiver; (*d'horreur*) to shudder

frit, e [fʀi, fʀit] *pp* de **frire**; **frite** *nf*: **(pommes) frites** chips (*BRIT*), French fries; **friteuse** *nf* chip pan; **friteuse électrique** deep fat fryer; **friture** *nf* (*huile*) (deep) fat; (*plat*): **friture (de poissons)** fried fish

froid, e [fʀwa, fʀwad] *adj*, *nm* cold; **il fait ~** it's cold; **avoir/prendre ~** to be/catch cold; **être en ~ avec** to be on bad terms with; **froidement** *adv* (*accueillir*) coldly; (*décider*) coolly

froisser [fʀwase] *vt* to crumple (up), crease; (*fig*) to hurt, offend; **se froisser** *vi* to crumple, crease; (*personne*) to take offence; **se ~ un muscle** to strain a muscle

frôler [fʀole] *vt* to brush against; (*suj: projectile*) to skim past; (*fig*) to come very close to

fromage [fʀɔmaʒ] *nm* cheese; **fromage blanc** soft white cheese

froment [fʀɔmɑ̃] *nm* wheat

froncer [fʀɔ̃se] *vt* to gather; **~ les sourcils** to frown

front [fʀɔ̃] *nm* forehead, brow; (*Mil*) front; **de ~** (*se heurter*) head-on; (*rouler*) together (*i.e. 2 or 3 abreast*); (*simultanément*) at once; **faire ~ à** to face up to

frontalier, -ère [fʀɔ̃talje, jɛʀ] *adj* border *cpd*, frontier *cpd*; **(travailleurs) ~s** people who commute across the border

frontière [fʀɔ̃tjɛʀ] *nf* frontier, border

frotter [fʀɔte] *vi* to rub, scrape ▷ *vt* to rub; (*pommes de terre, plancher*) to scrub; **~ une allumette** to strike a match

fruit [fʀɥi] *nm* fruit *gen no pl*; **fruits de mer** seafood(s); **fruits secs** dried fruit *sg*; **fruité, e** *adj* fruity; **fruitier, -ère** *adj*: **arbre fruitier** fruit tree

frustrer [fʀystʀe] *vt* to frustrate

fuel(-oil) [fjul(ɔjl)] *nm* fuel oil; (*domestique*) heating oil

fugace [fygas] *adj* fleeting

fugitif, -ive [fyʒitif, iv] *adj* (*fugace*) fleeting ▷ *nm/f* fugitive

fugue [fyg] *nf*: **faire une ~** to run away, abscond

fuir [fɥiʀ] *vt* to flee from; (*éviter*) to shun ▷ *vi* to run away; (*gaz, robinet*) to leak

fuite [fɥit] *nf* flight; (*écoulement, divulgation*)

leak; **être en ~** to be on the run; **mettre en ~** to put to flight

fulgurant, e [fylgyʀɑ̃, ɑ̃t] *adj* lightning *cpd*, dazzling

fumé, e [fyme] *adj* (*Culin*) smoked; (*verre*) tinted; **fumée** *nf* smoke

fumer [fyme] *vi* to smoke; (*soupe*) to steam ▷ *vt* to smoke

fûmes [fym] *vb voir* **être**

fumeur, -euse [fymœʀ, øz] *nm/f* smoker

fumier [fymje] *nm* manure

funérailles [fyneʀaj] *nfpl* funeral *sg*

fur [fyʀ]: **au ~ et à mesure** *adv* as one goes along; **au ~ et à mesure que** as

furet [fyʀɛ] *nm* ferret

fureter [fyʀ(ə)te] (*péj*) *vi* to nose about

fureur [fyʀœʀ] *nf* fury; **être en ~** to be infuriated; **faire ~** to be all the rage

furie [fyʀi] *nf* fury; (*femme*) shrew, vixen; **en ~** (*mer*) raging; **furieux, -euse** *adj* furious

furoncle [fyʀɔ̃kl] *nm* boil

furtif, -ive [fyʀtif, iv] *adj* furtive

fus [fy] *vb voir* **être**

fusain [fyzɛ̃] *nm* (*Art*) charcoal

fuseau, x [fyzo] *nm* (*pour filer*) spindle; (*pantalon*) (ski) pants; **fuseau horaire** time zone

fusée [fyze] *nf* rocket

fusible [fyzibl] *nm* (*Élec: fil*) fuse wire; (: *fiche*) fuse

fusil [fyzi] *nm* (*de guerre, à canon rayé*) rifle, gun; (*de chasse, à canon lisse*) shotgun, gun; **fusillade** *nf* gunfire *no pl*, shooting *no pl*; **fusiller** *vt* to shoot; **fusiller qn du regard** to look daggers at sb

fusionner [fyzjɔne] *vi* to merge

fût [fy] *vb voir* **être** ▷ *nm* (*tonneau*) barrel, cask

futé, e [fyte] *adj* crafty; **Bison ~®** TV and radio traffic monitoring service

futile [fytil] *adj* futile; frivolous

futur, e [fytyʀ] *adj*, *nm* future

fuyard, e [fɥijaʀ, aʀd] *nm/f* runaway

g

galerie de peinture (private) art gallery; **galerie marchande** shopping arcade
galet [galɛ] nm pebble
galette [galɛt] nf flat cake; **galette des Rois** cake eaten on Twelfth Night

● **GALETTE DES ROIS**
●
● A **galette des Rois** is a cake eaten on
● Twelfth Night containing a figurine. The
● person who finds it is the king (or queen)
● and gets a paper crown. They then choose
● someone else to be their queen (or king).

galipette [galipɛt] nf somersault
Galles [gal] nfpl: **le pays de ~** Wales; **gallois, e** adj Welsh ▷ nm/f: **Gallois, e** Welshman(-woman) ▷ nm (Ling) Welsh
galon [galɔ̃] nm (Mil) stripe; (décoratif) piece of braid
galop [galo] nm gallop; **galoper** vi to gallop
gambader [gɑ̃bade] vi (animal, enfant) to leap about
gamin, e [gamɛ̃, in] nm/f kid ▷ adj childish
gamme [gam] nf (Mus) scale; (fig) range
gang [gɑ̃g] nm (de criminels) gang
gant [gɑ̃] nm glove; **gant de toilette** face flannel (BRIT), face cloth
garage [gaʀaʒ] nm garage; **garagiste** nm/f garage owner; (employé) garage mechanic
garantie [gaʀɑ̃ti] nf guarantee; **(bon de) ~** guarantee ou warranty slip
garantir [gaʀɑ̃tiʀ] vt to guarantee; **~ à qn que** to assure sb that
garçon [gaʀsɔ̃] nm boy; (célibataire): **vieux ~** bachelor; **garçon (de café)** (serveur) waiter; **garçon de courses** messenger
garde [gaʀd(ə)] nm (de prisonnier) guard; (de domaine etc) warden; (soldat, sentinelle) guardsman ▷ nf (soldats) guard; **de ~** on duty; **monter la ~** to stand guard; **mettre en ~** to warn; **prendre ~ (à)** to be careful (of); **garde champêtre** nm rural policeman; **garde du corps** nm bodyguard; **garde à vue** nf (Jur) ≈ police custody; **garde-boue** nm inv mudguard; **garde-chasse** nm gamekeeper
garder [gaʀde] vt (conserver) to keep; (surveiller: enfants) to look after; (: immeuble, lieu, prisonnier) to guard; **se garder** vi (aliment: se conserver) to keep; **se ~ de faire** to be careful not to do; **~ le lit/la chambre** to stay in bed/indoors; **pêche/chasse gardée** private fishing/hunting (ground)
garderie [gaʀdəʀi] nf day nursery, crèche
garde-robe [gaʀdəʀɔb] nf wardrobe
gardien, ne [gaʀdjɛ̃, jɛn] nm/f (garde) guard; (de prison) warder; (de domaine, réserve) warden; (de musée etc) attendant; (de phare, cimetière) keeper; (d'immeuble) caretaker; (fig) guardian;

Gabon [gabɔ̃] nm: **le ~** Gabon
gâcher [gɑʃe] vt (gâter) to spoil; (gaspiller) to waste; **gâchis** nm waste no pl
gaffe [gaf] nf blunder; **faire ~** (fam) to be careful
gage [gaʒ] nm (dans un jeu) forfeit; (fig: de fidélité, d'amour) token; **gages** nmpl (salaire) wages; **mettre en ~** to pawn
gagnant, e [gaɲɑ̃, ɑ̃t] adj: **billet/numéro ~** winning ticket/number ▷ nm/f winner
gagne-pain [gaɲpɛ̃] nm inv job
gagner [gaɲe] vt to win; (somme d'argent, revenu) to earn; (aller vers, atteindre) to reach; (envahir: sommeil, peur) to overcome; (: mal) to spread to ▷ vi to win; (fig) to gain; **~ du temps/de la place** to gain time/save space; **~ sa vie** to earn one's living
gai, e [ge] adj cheerful; (un peu ivre) merry; **gaiement** adv cheerfully; **gaieté** nf cheerfulness; **de gaieté de cœur** with a light heart
gain [gɛ̃] nm (revenu) earnings pl; (bénéfice: gén pl) profits pl
gala [gala] nm official reception; **de ~** (soirée etc) gala
galant, e [galɑ̃, ɑ̃t] adj (courtois) courteous, gentlemanly; (entreprenant) flirtatious, gallant; (scène, rendez-vous) romantic
galerie [galʀi] nf gallery; (Théâtre) circle; (de voiture) roof rack; (fig: spectateurs) audience;

gardien de but goalkeeper; **gardien de la paix** policeman; **gardien de nuit** night watchman

gare[gaʀ] nf station; **gare routière** bus station

gare²[gaʀ] excl: **~ à ...!** mind ...!; **~ à toi!** watch out!

garer[gaʀe] vt to park; **se garer** vi to park

garni, e[gaʀni] adj (plat) served with vegetables (and chips or rice etc)

garniture[gaʀnityʀ] nf (Culin) vegetables pl; **garniture de frein** brake lining

gars[ga] (fam) nm guy

Gascogne[gaskɔɲ] nf Gascony; **le golfe de ~** the Bay of Biscay

gas-oil[gazɔjl] nm diesel (oil)

gaspiller[gaspije] vt to waste

gastronome[gastʀɔnɔm] nm/f gourmet; **gastronomique** adj gastronomic

gâteau, x[gato] nm cake; **gâteau sec** biscuit

gâter[gate] vt to spoil; **se gâter** vi (dent, fruit) to go bad; (temps, situation) to change for the worse

gâteux, -euse[gatø, øz] adj senile

gauche[goʃ] adj left, left-hand; (maladroit) awkward, clumsy ▷ nf (Pol) left (wing); **le bras ~** the left arm; **le côté ~** the left-hand side; **à ~** on the left; (direction) (to the) left; **gaucher, -ère** adj left-handed; **gauchiste** nm/f leftist

gaufre[gofʀ] nf waffle

gaufrette[gofʀɛt] nf wafer

gaulois, e[golwa, waz] adj Gallic ▷ nm/f: **G~, e** Gaul

gaz[gaz] nm inv gas; **ça sent le ~** I can smell gas, there's a smell of gas

gaze[gaz] nf gauze

gazette[gazɛt] nf news sheet

gazeux, -euse[gazø, øz] adj (boisson) fizzy; (eau) sparkling

gazoduc[gazɔdyk] nm gas pipeline

gazon[gazɔ̃] nm (herbe) grass; (pelouse) lawn

geai[ʒɛ] nm jay

géant, e[ʒeɑ̃, ɑ̃t] adj gigantic; (Comm) giant-size ▷ nm/f giant

geindre[ʒɛ̃dʀ] vi to groan, moan

gel[ʒɛl] nm frost

gélatine[ʒelatin] nf gelatine

gelée[ʒ(ə)le] nf jelly; (gel) frost

geler[ʒ(ə)le] vt, vi to freeze; **il gèle** it's freezing

gélule[ʒelyl] nf (Méd) capsule

Gémeaux[ʒemo] nmpl: **les ~** Gemini

gémir[ʒemiʀ] vi to groan, moan

gênant, e[ʒɛnɑ̃, ɑ̃t] adj (irritant) annoying; (embarrassant) embarrassing

gencive[ʒɑ̃siv] nf gum

gendarme[ʒɑ̃daʀm] nm gendarme; **gendarmerie** nf military police force in countryside and small towns; their police station or barracks

gendre[ʒɑ̃dʀ] nm son-in-law

gêné, e[ʒene] adj embarrassed

gêner[ʒene] vt (incommoder) to bother; (encombrer) to be in the way; (embarrasser): **~ qn** to make sb feel ill-at-ease; **se gêner** to put o.s. out; **ne vous gênez pas!** don't mind me!

général, e, -aux[ʒeneʀal, o] adj, nm general; **en ~** usually, in general; **généralement** adv generally; **généraliser** vt, vi to generalize; **se généraliser** vi to become widespread; **généraliste** nm/f general practitioner, G.P.

génération[ʒeneʀasjɔ̃] nf generation

généreux, -euse[ʒeneʀø, øz] adj generous

générique[ʒeneʀik] nm (Cinéma) credits pl

générosité[ʒeneʀozite] nf generosity

genêt[ʒ(ə)nɛ] nm broom no pl (shrub)

génétique[ʒenetik] adj genetic

Genève[ʒ(ə)nɛv] n Geneva

génial, e, -aux[ʒenjal, jo] adj of genius; (fam: formidable) fantastic, brilliant

génie[ʒeni] nm genius; (Mil): **le ~** the Engineers pl; **génie civil** civil engineering

genièvre[ʒənjɛvʀ] nm juniper

génisse[ʒenis] nf heifer

génital, e, -aux[ʒenital, o] adj genital; **les parties ~es** the genitals

génoise[ʒenwaz] nf sponge cake

genou, x[ʒ(ə)nu] nm knee; **à ~x** on one's knees; **se mettre à ~x** to kneel down

genre[ʒɑ̃ʀ] nm kind, type, sort; (Ling) gender; **avoir bon ~** to look a nice sort; **avoir mauvais ~** to be coarse-looking; **ce n'est pas son ~** it's not like him

gens[ʒɑ̃] nmpl (f in some phrases) people pl

gentil, le[ʒɑ̃ti, ij] adj kind; (enfant: sage) good; (endroit etc) nice; **gentillesse** nf kindness; **gentiment** adv kindly

géographie[ʒeɔgʀafi] nf geography

géologie[ʒeɔlɔʒi] nf geology

géomètre[ʒeɔmɛtʀ] nm/f (arpenteur) (land) surveyor

géométrie[ʒeɔmetʀi] nf geometry; **géométrique** adj geometric

géranium[ʒeʀanjɔm] nm geranium

gérant, e[ʒeʀɑ̃, ɑ̃t] nm/f manager(-eress); **gérant d'immeuble** (managing) agent

gerbe[ʒɛʀb] nf (de fleurs) spray; (de blé) sheaf

gercé, e[ʒɛʀse] adj chapped

gerçure[ʒɛʀsyʀ] nf crack

gérer[ʒeʀe] vt to manage

germain, e[ʒɛʀmɛ̃, ɛn] adj: **cousin ~** first cousin

germe[ʒɛʀm] nm germ; **germer** vi to sprout; (semence) to germinate

geste[ʒɛst] nm gesture

gestion[ʒɛstjɔ̃] nf management

Ghana[gana] nm: **le ~** Ghana

gibier[ʒibje] nm (animaux) game

gicler[ʒikle] vi to spurt, squirt

gifle [ʒifl] nf slap (in the face); **gifler** vt to slap (in the face)

gigantesque [ʒigãtɛsk] adj gigantic

gigot [ʒigo] nm leg (of mutton ou lamb)

gigoter [ʒigɔte] vi to wriggle (about)

gilet [ʒilɛ] nm waistcoat; (pull) cardigan; **gilet de sauvetage** life jacket

gin [dʒin] nm gin; **~-tonic** gin and tonic

gingembre [ʒɛ̃ʒɑ̃bʀ] nm ginger

girafe [ʒiʀaf] nf giraffe

giratoire [ʒiʀatwaʀ] adj: **sens ~** roundabout

girofle [ʒiʀɔfl] nf: **clou de ~** clove

girouette [ʒiʀwɛt] nf weather vane ou cock

gitan, e [ʒitɑ̃, an] nm/f gipsy

gîte [ʒit] nm (maison) home; (abri) shelter; **gîte (rural)** (country) holiday cottage (BRIT), gîte (self-catering accommodation in the country)

givre [ʒivʀ] nm (hoar) frost; **givré, e** adj covered in frost; (fam: fou) nuts; **orange givrée** orange sorbet (served in peel)

glace [glas] nf ice; (crème glacée) ice cream; (miroir) mirror; (de voiture) window

glacé, e [glase] adj (mains, vent, pluie) freezing; (lac) frozen; (boisson) iced

glacer [glase] vt to freeze; (gâteau) to ice; (fig): **~ qn** (intimider) to chill sb; (paralyser) to make sb's blood run cold

glacial, e, -aux [glasjal, jo] adj icy

glacier [glasje] nm (Géo) glacier; (marchand) ice-cream maker

glacière [glasjɛʀ] nf icebox

glaçon [glasɔ̃] nm icicle; (pour boisson) ice cube

glaïeul [glajœl] nm gladiolus

glaise [glɛz] nf clay

gland [glɑ̃] nm acorn; (décoration) tassel

glande [glɑ̃d] nf gland

glissade [glisad] nf (par jeu) slide; (chute) slip; **faire des ~s sur la glace** to slide on the ice

glissant, e [glisɑ̃, ɑ̃t] adj slippery

glissement [glismɑ̃] nm: **glissement de terrain** landslide

glisser [glise] vi (avancer) to glide ou slide along; (coulisser, tomber) to slide; (déraper) to slip; (être glissant) to be slippery ▷ vt to slip; **se glisser dans/entre** to slip into/between

global, e, -aux [glɔbal, o] adj overall

globe [glɔb] nm globe

globule [glɔbyl] nm (du sang): **~ blanc/rouge** white/red corpuscle

gloire [glwaʀ] nf glory

glousser [gluse] vi to cluck; (rire) to chuckle

glouton, ne [glutɔ̃, ɔn] adj gluttonous

gluant, e [glyɑ̃, ɑ̃t] adj sticky, gummy

glucose [glykoz] nm glucose

glycine [glisin] nf wisteria

GO sigle (= grandes ondes) LW

goal [gol] nm goalkeeper

gobelet [gɔblɛ] nm (en étain, verre, argent) tumbler; (d'enfant, de pique-nique) beaker; (à dés) cup

goéland [gɔelɑ̃] nm (sea)gull

goélette [gɔelɛt] nf schooner

goinfre [gwɛ̃fʀ] nm glutton

golf [gɔlf] nm golf; (terrain) golf course; **golf miniature** crazy (BRIT) ou miniature golf

golfe [gɔlf] nm gulf; (petit) bay

gomme [gɔm] nf (à effacer) rubber (BRIT), eraser; **gommer** vt to rub out (BRIT), erase

gonflé, e [gɔ̃fle] adj swollen; **il est ~** (fam: courageux) he's got some nerve; (impertinent) he's got a nerve

gonfler [gɔ̃fle] vt (pneu, ballon: en soufflant) to blow up; (: avec une pompe) to pump up; (nombre, importance) to inflate ▷ vi to swell (up); (Culin: pâte) to rise

gonzesse [gɔ̃zɛs] (fam) nf chick, bird (BRIT)

gorge [gɔʀʒ] nf (Anat) throat; (vallée) gorge; **gorgée** nf (petite) sip; (grande) gulp

gorille [gɔʀij] nm gorilla; (fam) bodyguard

gosse [gɔs] (fam) nm/f kid

goudron [gudʀɔ̃] nm tar; **goudronner** vt to tar(mac) (BRIT), asphalt (US)

gouffre [gufʀ] nm abyss, gulf

goulot [gulo] nm neck; **boire au ~** to drink from the bottle

goulu, e [guly] adj greedy

gourde [guʀd] nf (récipient) flask; (fam) (clumsy) clot ou oaf ▷ adj oafish

gourdin [guʀdɛ̃] nm club, bludgeon

gourmand, e [guʀmɑ̃, ɑ̃d] adj greedy; **gourmandise** nf greed; (bonbon) sweet

gousse [gus] nf: **gousse d'ail** clove of garlic

goût [gu] nm taste; **avoir bon ~** to taste good; **de bon ~** tasteful; **de mauvais ~** tasteless; **prendre ~ à** to develop a taste ou a liking for

goûter [gute] vt (essayer) to taste; (apprécier) to enjoy ▷ vi to have (afternoon) tea ▷ nm (afternoon) tea; **je peux ~?** can I have a taste?

goutte [gut] nf drop; (Méd) gout; (alcool) brandy; **tomber ~ à ~** to drip; **une ~ de whisky** a drop of whisky; **goutte-à-goutte** nm (Méd) drip

gouttière [gutjɛʀ] nf gutter

gouvernail [guvɛʀnaj] nm rudder; (barre) helm, tiller

gouvernement [guvɛʀnəmɑ̃] nm government

gouverner [guvɛʀne] vt to govern

grâce [gʀas] nf (charme, Rel) grace; (faveur) favour; (Jur) pardon; **faire ~ à qn de qch** to spare sb sth; **demander ~** to beg for mercy; **~ à** thanks to; **gracieux, -euse** adj graceful

grade [gʀad] nm rank; **monter en ~** to be promoted

gradin [gʀadɛ̃] nm tier; step; **gradins** nmpl (de stade) terracing sg

gradué, e [gʀadɥe] adj: **verre ~** measuring jug

graduel, le [gʀadɥɛl] adj gradual

graduer [gradɥe] vt (effort etc) to increase gradually; (règle, verre) to graduate

graffiti [grafiti] nmpl graffiti

grain [grɛ̃] nm (gén) grain; (Navig) squall; **grain de beauté** beauty spot; **grain de café** coffee bean; **grain de poivre** peppercorn

graine [grɛn] nf seed

graissage [gresaʒ] nm lubrication, greasing

graisse [gres] nf fat; (lubrifiant) grease; **graisser** vt to lubricate, grease; (tacher) to make greasy; **graisseux, -euse** adj greasy

grammaire [gra(m)mer] nf grammar

gramme [gram] nm gramme

grand, e [grɑ̃, grɑ̃d] adj (haut) tall; (gros, vaste, large) big, large; (long) long; (plus âgé) big; (adulte) grown-up; (important, brillant) great ▷ adv: **~ ouvert** wide open; **au ~ air** in the open (air); **les grands blessés** the severely injured; **grand ensemble** housing scheme; **grand magasin** department store; **grande personne** grown-up; **grande surface** hypermarket; **grandes écoles** prestigious schools at university level; **grandes lignes** (Rail) main lines; **grandes vacances** summer holidays (BRIT) ou vacation (US); **grand-chose** n/inv: **pas grand-chose** not much; **Grande-Bretagne** nf (Great) Britain; **grandeur** nf (dimension) size; **grandeur nature** life-size; **grandiose** adj imposing; **grandir** vi to grow ▷ vt: **grandir qn** (suj: vêtement, chaussure) to make sb look taller; **grand-mère** [grate] nf grandmother; **grand-peine**: **à grand-peine** adv with difficulty; **grandpère** nm grandfather; **grands-parents** nmpl grandparents

grange [grɑ̃ʒ] nf barn

granit [granit] nm granite

graphique [grafik] adj graphic ▷ nm graph

grappe [grap] nf cluster; **grappe de raisin** bunch of grapes

gras, se [grɑ, grɑs] adj (viande, soupe) fatty; (personne) fat; (surface, main) greasy; (plaisanterie) coarse; (Typo) bold ▷ nm (Culin) fat; **faire la ~se matinée** to have a lie-in (BRIT), sleep late (US); **grassement** adv: **grassement payé** handsomely paid

gratifiant, e [gratifjɑ̃, jɑ̃t] adj gratifying, rewarding

gratin [gratɛ̃] nm (plat) cheese-topped dish; (croûte) cheese topping; (fam: élite) upper crust; **gratiné, e** adj (Culin) au gratin

gratis [gratis] adv free

gratitude [gratityd] nf gratitude

gratte-ciel [gratsjɛl] nm inv skyscraper

gratter [grate] vt (avec un outil) to scrape; (enlever: avec un outil) to scrape off; (: avec un ongle) to scratch; (enlever avec un ongle) to scratch off ▷ vi (irriter) to be scratchy; (démanger) to itch; **se gratter** to scratch (o.s.)

gratuit, e [gratɥi, ɥit] adj (entrée, billet) free; (fig) gratuitous

grave [grav] adj (maladie, accident) serious, bad; (sujet, problème) serious, grave; (air) grave, solemn; (voix, son) deep, low-pitched; **gravement** adv seriously; (parler, regarder) gravely

graver [grave] vt (plaque, nom) to engrave; (CD, DVD) to burn

graveur [gravœr] nm engraver; **graveur de CD/DVD** CD/DVD writer

gravier [gravje] nm gravel no pl; **gravillons** nmpl loose chippings ou gravel sg

gravir [gravir] vt to climb (up)

gravité [gravite] nf (de maladie, d'accident) seriousness; (de sujet, problème) gravity

graviter [gravite] vi to revolve

gravure [gravyr] nf engraving; (reproduction) print

gré [gre] nm: **à son ~** to one's liking; **de bon ~** willingly; **contre le ~ de qn** against sb's will; **de son (plein) ~** of one's own free will; **bon ~ mal ~** like it or not; **de ~ ou de force** whether one likes it or not; **savoir ~ à qn de qch** to be grateful to sb for sth

grec, grecque [grɛk] adj Greek; (classique: vase etc) Grecian ▷ nm/f: **G~, Grecque** Greek ▷ nm (Ling) Greek

Grèce [gres] nf: **la ~** Greece

greffe [gref] nf (Bot, Méd: de tissu) graft; (Méd: d'organe) transplant; **greffer** vt (Bot, Méd: tissu) to graft; (Méd: organe) to transplant

grêle [grel] adj (very) thin ▷ nf hail; **grêler** vb impers: **il grêle** it's hailing; **grêlon** nm hailstone

grelot [grəlo] nm little bell

grelotter [grəlote] vi to shiver

grenade [grənad] nf (explosive) grenade; (Bot) pomegranate; **grenadine** nf grenadine

grenier [grənje] nm attic; (de ferme) loft

grenouille [grənuj] nf frog

grès [gre] nm sandstone; (poterie) stoneware

grève [grev] nf (d'ouvriers) strike; (plage) shore; **se mettre en/faire ~** to go on/be on strike; **grève de la faim** hunger strike; **grève sauvage** wildcat strike

gréviste [grevist] nm/f striker

grièvement [grijevmɑ̃] adv seriously

griffe [grif] nf claw; (de couturier) label; **griffer** vt to scratch

grignoter [griɲote] vt (personne) to nibble at; (souris) to gnaw at ▷ vi to nibble

gril [gril] nm steak ou grill pan; **faire cuire au ~** to grill; **grillade** nf (viande etc) grill

grillage [grijaʒ] nm (treillis) wire netting; (clôture) wire fencing

grille [grij] nf (clôture) wire fence; (portail) (metal) gate; (d'égout) (metal) grate; (fig) grid

grille-pain [grijpɛ̃] nm inv toaster

griller [gʀije] vt (pain) to toast; (viande) to grill; (fig: ampoule etc) to blow; **faire ~** to toast; to grill; (châtaignes) to roast; **~ un feu rouge** to jump the lights

grillon [gʀijɔ̃] nm cricket

grimace [gʀimas] nf grimace; (pour faire rire): **faire des ~s** to make faces

grimper [gʀɛ̃pe] vi, vt to climb

grincer [gʀɛ̃se] vi (objet métallique) to grate; (plancher, porte) to creak; **~ des dents** to grind one's teeth

grincheux, -euse [gʀɛ̃ʃø, øz] adj grumpy

grippe [gʀip] nf flu, influenza; **grippe aviaire** bird flu; **grippé, e** adj: **être grippé** to have flu

gris, e [gʀi, gʀiz] adj grey; (ivre) tipsy

grisaille [gʀizaj] nf greyness, dullness

griser [gʀize] vt to intoxicate

grive [gʀiv] nf thrush

Groenland [gʀɔɛnlɑ̃d] nm Greenland

grogner [gʀɔɲe] vi to growl; (fig) to grumble; **grognon, ne** adj grumpy

grommeler [gʀɔm(ə)le] vi to mutter to o.s.

gronder [gʀɔ̃de] vi to rumble; (fig: révolte) to be brewing ▷ vt to scold; **se faire ~** to get a telling-off

gros, se [gʀo, gʀos] adj big, large; (obèse) fat; (travaux, dégâts) extensive; (épais) thick; (rhume, averse) heavy ▷ adv: **risquer/gagner ~** to risk/win a lot ▷ nm/f fat man/woman ▷ nm (Comm): **le ~** the wholesale business; **le ~ de** the bulk of; **prix de gros** wholesale price; **par ~ temps/grosse mer** in rough weather/heavy seas; **en ~** roughly; (Comm) wholesale; **gros lot** jackpot; **gros mot** swearword; **gros plan** (Photo) close-up; **gros sel** cooking salt; **gros titre** headline; **grosse caisse** big drum

groseille [gʀozɛj] nf: **~ (rouge/blanche)** red/white currant; **groseille à maquereau** gooseberry

grosse [gʀos] adj voir **gros**; **grossesse** nf pregnancy; **grosseur** nf size; (tumeur) lump

grossier, -ière [gʀosje, jɛʀ] adj coarse; (insolent) rude; (dessin) rough; (travail) roughly done; (imitation, instrument) crude; (évident: erreur) gross; **grossièrement** adv (sommairement) roughly; (vulgairement) coarsely; **grossièreté** nf rudeness; (mot): **dire des grossièretés** to use coarse language

grossir [gʀosiʀ] vi (personne) to put on weight ▷ vt (exagérer) to exaggerate; (au microscope) to magnify; (suj: vêtement): **~ qn** to make sb look bigger

grossiste [gʀosist] nm/f wholesaler

grotesque [gʀotɛsk] adj (extravagant) grotesque; (ridicule) ludicrous

grotte [gʀot] nf cave

groupe [gʀup] nm group; **groupe de parole** support group; **groupe sanguin** blood group; **groupe scolaire** school complex; **grouper** vt to group; **se grouper** vi to gather

grue [gʀy] nf crane

GSM [ʒeɛsɛm] nm, adj GSM

guenon [gənɔ̃] nf female monkey

guépard [gepaʀ] nm cheetah

guêpe [gɛp] nf wasp

guère [gɛʀ] adv (avec adjectif, adverbe): **ne ... ~** hardly; (avec verbe: pas beaucoup): **ne ... ~** tournure négative +much; (pas souvent) hardly ever; (pas longtemps) tournure négative +(very) long; **il n'y a ~ que/de** there's hardly anybody (ou anything) but/hardly any; **ce n'est ~ difficile** it's hardly difficult; **nous n'avons ~ de temps** we have hardly any time

guérilla [geʀija] nf guerrilla warfare

guérillero [geʀijeʀo] nm guerrilla

guérir [geʀiʀ] vt (personne, maladie) to cure; (membre, plaie) to heal ▷ vi (malade, maladie) to be cured; (blessure) to heal; **guérison** nf (de maladie) curing; (de membre, plaie) healing; (de malade) recovery; **guérisseur, -euse** nm/f healer

guerre [gɛʀ] nf war; **en ~** at war; **faire la ~ à** to wage war against; **guerre civile/mondiale** civil/world war; **guerrier, -ière** adj warlike ▷ nm/f warrior

guet [gɛ] nm: **faire le ~** to be on the watch ou look-out; **guet-apens** [gɛtapɑ̃] nm ambush; **guetter** vt (épier) to watch (intently); (attendre) to watch (out) for; (hostilement) to be lying in wait for

gueule [gœl] nf (d'animal) mouth; (fam: figure) face; (: bouche) mouth; **ta ~!** (fam) shut up!; **avoir la ~ de bois** (fam) to have a hangover, be hung over; **gueuler** (fam) vi to bawl

gui [gi] nm mistletoe

guichet [giʃɛ] nm (de bureau, banque) counter; **les ~s** (à la gare, au théâtre) the ticket office sg

guide [gid] nm (personne) guide; (livre) guide (book) ▷ nf (éclaireuse) girl guide; **guider** vt to guide

guidon [gidɔ̃] nm handlebars pl

guignol [giɲɔl] nm ≈ Punch and Judy show; (fig) clown

guillemets [gijmɛ] nmpl: **entre ~** in inverted commas

guindé, e [gɛ̃de] adj (personne, air) stiff, starchy; (style) stilted

Guinée [gine] nf Guinea

guirlande [giʀlɑ̃d] nf (fleurs) garland; **guirlande de Noël** tinsel garland

guise [giz] nf: **à votre ~** as you wish ou please; **en ~ de** by way of

guitare [gitaʀ] nf guitar

Guyane [gɥijan] nf: **la ~ (française)** French Guiana

gym [ʒim] nf (exercices) gym; **gymnase** nm gym(nasium); **gymnaste** nm/f gymnast; **gymnastique** nf gymnastics sg; (au réveil etc)

keep-fit exercises *pl*
gynécologie [ʒinekɔlɔʒi] *nf* gynaecology;
gynécologique *adj* gynaecological;
gynécologue *nm/f* gynaecologist

habile [abil] *adj* skilful; (*malin*) clever; **habileté**
[abilte] *nf* skill, skilfulness; cleverness
habillé, e [abije] *adj* dressed; (*chic*) dressy
habiller [abije] *vt* to dress; (*fournir en
vêtements*) to clothe; (*couvrir*) to cover;
s'habiller *vi* to dress (o.s.); (*se déguiser, mettre
des vêtements chic*) to dress up
habit [abi] *nm* outfit; **habits** *nmpl* (*vêtements*)
clothes; **habit (de soirée)** evening dress; (*pour
homme*) tails *pl*
habitant, e [abitɑ̃, ɑ̃t] *nm/f* inhabitant; (*d'une
maison*) occupant; **loger chez l'~** to stay with
the locals
habitation [abitasjɔ̃] *nf* house; **habitations
à loyer modéré** (block of) council flats
habiter [abite] *vt* to live in ▷ *vi*: **~ à/dans** to
live in; **où habitez-vous?** where do you live?
habitude [abityd] *nf* habit; **avoir l'~ de qch**
to be used to sth; **avoir l'~ de faire** to be in the
habit of doing; (*expérience*) to be used to doing;
d'~ usually; **comme d'~** as usual
habitué, e [abitɥe] *nm/f* (*de maison*) regular
visitor; (*de café*) regular (customer)
habituel, le [abitɥɛl] *adj* usual
habituer [abitɥe] *vt*: **~ qn à** to get sb used to;
s'habituer à to get used to
'hache ['aʃ] *nf* axe
'hacher ['aʃe] *vt* (*viande*) to mince; (*persil*)
to chop; **'hachis** *nm* mince *no pl*; **hachis
Parmentier** ≈ shepherd's pie

'haie['ɛ] nf hedge; (Sport) hurdle
'haillons['ɑjɔ̃] nmpl rags
'haine['ɛn] nf hatred
'haïr['aiʀ] vt to detest, hate
'hâlé, e['ɑle] adj (sun)tanned, sunburnt
haleine[alɛn] nf breath; **hors d'~** out of breath; **tenir en ~** (attention) to hold spellbound; (incertitude) to keep in suspense; **de longue ~** long-term
'haleter['alte] vt to pant
'hall['ol] nm hall
'halle['al] nf (covered) market; **halles** nfpl (d'une grande ville) central food market sg
hallucination[alysinasjɔ̃] nf hallucination
'halte['alt] nf stop, break; (endroit) stopping place ▷ excl stop!; **faire halte** to stop
haltère[altɛʀ] nm dumbbell, barbell; **haltères** nmpl: **(poids et) ~s** (activité) weightlifting sg; **haltérophilie** nf weightlifting
'hamac['amak] nm hammock
'hameau, x['amo] nm hamlet
hameçon[amsɔ̃] nm (fish) hook
'hanche['ɑ̃ʃ] nf hip
'handball['ɑdbal] nm handball
'handicapé, e['ɑ̃dikape] adj disabled, handicapped ▷ nm/f handicapped person; **handicapé mental/physique** mentally/ physically handicapped person; **'handicapé moteur** person with a movement disorder
'hangar['ɑ̃gaʀ] nm shed; (Aviat) hangar
'hanneton['ɑ̃tɔ̃] nm cockchafer
'hanter['ɑ̃te] vt to haunt
'hantise['ɑ̃tiz] nf obsessive fear
'harceler['aʀsəle] vt to harass; **harceler qn de questions** to plague sb with questions
'hardi, e['aʀdi] adj bold, daring
'hareng['aʀɑ̃] nm herring; **hareng saur** kipper, smoked herring
'hargne['aʀɲ] nf aggressiveness; **'hargneux, -euse** adj aggressive
'haricot['aʀiko] nm bean; **'haricot blanc** haricot bean; **'haricot vert** green bean; **'haricot rouge** kidney bean
harmonica[aʀmɔnika] nm mouth organ
harmonie[aʀmɔni] nf harmony; **harmonieux, -euse** adj harmonious; (couleurs, couple) well-matched
'harpe['aʀp] nf harp
'hasard['azaʀ] nm: **le hasard** chance, fate; **un hasard** a coincidence; **au hasard** (aller) aimlessly; (choisir) at random; **par hasard** by chance; **à tout hasard** (en cas de besoin) just in case; (en espérant trouver ce qu'on cherche) on the off chance (BRIT)
'hâte['ɑt] nf haste; **à la hâte** hurriedly, hastily; **en hâte** posthaste, with all possible speed; **avoir hâte de** to be eager ou anxious to; **'hâter** vt to hasten; **se hâter** vi to hurry;

'hâtif, -ive adj (travail) hurried; (décision, jugement) hasty
'hausse['os] nf rise, increase; **être en hausse** to be going up; **'hausser** vt to raise; **hausser les épaules** to shrug (one's shoulders)
'haut, e['o, 'ot] adj high; (grand) tall ▷ adv high ▷ nm top (part); **de 3 m de haut** 3 m high, 3 m in height; **des hauts et des bas** ups and downs; **en haut lieu** in high places; **à haute voix, (tout) haut** aloud, out loud; **du haut de** from the top of; **de haut en bas** from top to bottom; **plus haut** higher up, further up; (dans un texte) above; (parler) louder; **en haut** (être/aller) at/to the top; (dans une maison) upstairs; **en haut de** at the top of; **'haut débit** broadband
'hautain, e['otɛ̃, ɛn] adj haughty
'hautbois['obwɑ] nm oboe
'hauteur['otœʀ] nf height; **à la hauteur de** (accident) near; (fig: tâche, situation) equal to; **à la hauteur** (fig) up to it
'haut-parleur nm (loud)speaker
Hawaï[awai] n: **les îles ~** Hawaii
'Haye['ɛ] n: **la Haye** the Hague
hebdomadaire[ɛbdɔmadɛʀ] adj, nm weekly
hébergement[ebɛʀʒəmɑ̃] nm accommodation
héberger[ebɛʀʒe] vt (touristes) to accommodate, lodge; (amis) to put up; (réfugiés) to take in
hébergeur[ebɛʀʒœʀ] nm (Internet) host
hébreu, x[ebʀø] adj m, nm Hebrew
Hébrides[ebʀid] nf: **les ~** the Hebrides
hectare[ɛktaʀ] nm hectare
'hein['ɛ̃] excl eh?
'hélas['elɑs] excl alas! ▷ adv unfortunately
'héler['ele] vt to hail
hélice[elis] nf propeller
hélicoptère[elikɔptɛʀ] nm helicopter
helvétique[ɛlvetik] adj Swiss
hématome[ematɔm] nm nasty bruise
hémisphère[emisfɛʀ] nm: **l'~ nord/sud** the northern/southern hemisphere
hémorragie[emɔʀaʒi] nf bleeding no pl, haemorrhage
hémorroïdes[emˈid] nfpl piles, haemorrhoids
'hennir['eniʀ] vi to neigh, whinny
hépatite[epatit] nf hepatitis
herbe[ɛʀb] nf grass; (Culin, Méd) herb; **~s de Provence** mixed herbs; **en ~** unripe; (fig) budding; **herbicide** nm weed-killer; **herboriste** nm/f herbalist
héréditaire[eʀeditɛʀ] adj hereditary
'hérisson['eʀisɔ̃] nm hedgehog
héritage[eʀitaʒ] nm inheritance; (coutumes, système) heritage, legacy
hériter[eʀite] vi: **~ de qch (de qn)** to inherit sth (from sb); **héritier, -ière** nm/f heir(-ess)

hermétique [ɛʀmetik] *adj* airtight; watertight; (*fig: obscur*) abstruse; (: *impénétrable*) impenetrable

hermine [ɛʀmin] *nf* ermine

'hernie ['ɛʀni] *nf* hernia

héroïne [eʀɔin] *nf* heroine; (*drogue*) heroin

héroïque [eʀɔik] *adj* heroic

'héron ['eʀɔ̃] *nm* heron

'héros ['eʀo] *nm* hero

hésitant, e [ezitɑ̃, ɑ̃t] *adj* hesitant

hésitation [ezitasjɔ̃] *nf* hesitation

hésiter [ezite] *vi*: **~ (à faire)** to hesitate (to do)

hétérosexuel, le [eteʀɔsɛkɥɛl] *adj* heterosexual

'hêtre ['ɛtʀ] *nm* beech

heure [œʀ] *nf* hour; (*Scol*) period; (*moment*) time; **c'est l'~** it's time; **quelle ~ est-il?** what time is it?; **2 ~s (du matin)** 2 o'clock (in the morning); **être à l'~** to be on time; (*montre*) to be right; **mettre à l'~** to set right; **à une ~ avancée (de la nuit)** at a late hour (of the night); **de bonne ~** early; **à toute ~** at any time; **24 ~s sur 24** round the clock, 24 hours a day; **à l'~ qu'il est** at this time (of day); by now; **sur l'~** at once; **à quelle ~ ouvre le musée/magasin?** what time does the museum/shop open?; **heures de bureau** office hours; **heure de pointe** rush hour; (*téléphone*) peak period; **heures supplémentaires** overtime *sg*

heureusement [œʀøzmɑ̃] *adv* (*par bonheur*) fortunately, luckily

heureux, -euse [œʀø, øz] *adj* happy; (*chanceux*) lucky, fortunate

'heurt ['œʀ] *nm* (*choc*) collision; (*conflit*) clash

'heurter ['œʀte] *vt* (*mur*) to strike, hit; (*personne*) to collide with

hexagone [ɛgzagɔn] *nm* hexagon; **l'H~** (*la France*) France (*because of its shape*)

hiberner [ibɛʀne] *vi* to hibernate

'hibou, x ['ibu] *nm* owl

'hideux, -euse ['idø, øz] *adj* hideous

hier [jɛʀ] *adv* yesterday; **~ matin/midi** yesterday morning/lunchtime; **~ soir** last night, yesterday evening; **toute la journée d'~** all day yesterday; **toute la matinée d'~** all yesterday morning

'hiérarchie ['jeʀaʀʃi] *nf* hierarchy

hindou, e [ɛ̃du] *adj* Hindu ▷ *nm/f*: **H~, e** Hindu

hippique [ipik] *adj* equestrian, horse *cpd*; **un club ~** a riding centre; **un concours ~** a horse show; **hippisme** *nm* (*horse*)riding

hippodrome [ipɔdʀom] *nm* racecourse

hippopotame [ipɔpɔtam] *nm* hippopotamus

hirondelle [iʀɔ̃dɛl] *nf* swallow

'hisser ['ise] *vt* to hoist, haul up

histoire [istwaʀ] *nf* (*science, événements*) history; (*anecdote, récit, mensonge*) story; (*affaire*) business *no pl*; **histoires** *nfpl* (*chichis*)

fuss *no pl*; (*ennuis*) trouble *sg*; **historique** *adj* historical; (*important*) historic ▷ *nm*: **faire l'historique de** to give the background to

'hit-parade ['itpaʀad] *nm*: **le hit-parade** the charts

hiver [ivɛʀ] *nm* winter; **hivernal, e, -aux** *adj* winter *cpd*; (*glacial*) wintry; **hiverner** *vi* to winter

HLM *nm ou f* (= *habitation à loyer modéré*) council flat; **des ~** = council housing

'hobby ['ɔbi] *nm* hobby

'hocher ['ɔʃe] *vt*: **hocher la tête** to nod; (*signe négatif ou dubitatif*) to shake one's head

'hockey ['ɔkɛ] *nm*: **hockey (sur glace/gazon)** (ice/field) hockey

'hold-up ['ɔldœp] *nm inv* hold-up

'hollandais, e ['ɔlɑ̃dɛ, ɛz] *adj* Dutch ▷ *nm* (*Ling*) Dutch ▷ *nm/f*: **Hollandais, e** Dutchman(-woman)

'Hollande ['ɔlɑ̃d] *nf*: **la Hollande** Holland

'homard ['ɔmaʀ] *nm* lobster

homéopathique [ɔmeɔpatik] *adj* homoeopathic

homicide [ɔmisid] *nm* murder; **homicide involontaire** manslaughter

hommage [ɔmaʒ] *nm* tribute; **rendre ~ à** to pay tribute to

homme [ɔm] *nm* man; **homme d'affaires** businessman; **homme d'État** statesman; **homme de main** hired man; **homme de paille** stooge; **l'homme de la rue** the man on the street

homo...: **homogène** *adj* homogeneous; **homologue** *nm/f* counterpart; **homologué, e** *adj* (*Sport*) ratified; (*tarif*) authorized; **homonyme** *nm* (*Ling*) homonym; (*d'une personne*) namesake; **homosexuel, le** *adj* homosexual

'Hong Kong ['ɔ̃gkɔ̃g] *n* Hong Kong

'Hongrie ['ɔ̃gʀi] *nf*: **la Hongrie** Hungary; **'hongrois, e** *adj* Hungarian ▷ *nm/f*: **Hongrois, e** Hungarian ▷ *nm* (*Ling*) Hungarian

honnête [ɔnɛt] *adj* (*intègre*) honest; (*juste, satisfaisant*) fair; **honnêtement** *adv* honestly; **honnêteté** *nf* honesty

honneur [ɔnœʀ] *nm* honour; (*mérite*) credit; **en l'~ de** in honour of; (*événement*) on the occasion of; **faire ~ à** (*engagements*) to honour; (*famille*) to be a credit to; (*fig: repas etc*) to do justice to

honorable [ɔnɔʀabl] *adj* worthy, honourable; (*suffisant*) decent

honoraire [ɔnɔʀɛʀ] *adj* honorary; **professeur ~** professor emeritus; **honoraires** *nmpl* fees

honorer [ɔnɔʀe] *vt* to honour; (*estimer*) to hold in high regard; (*faire honneur à*) to do credit to

'honte ['ɔ̃t] *nf* shame; **avoir honte de** to be ashamed of; **faire honte à qn** to make sb (feel)

ashamed; **'honteux, -euse** adj ashamed;
(conduite, acte) shameful, disgraceful
hôpital, -aux [ɔpital, o] nm hospital; **où
est l'~ le plus proche?** where is the nearest
hospital?
'hoquet ['ɔkɛ] nm: **avoir le hoquet** to have
(the) hiccoughs
horaire [ɔRɛR] adj hourly ▷ nm timetable,
schedule; **horaires** nmpl (d'employé) hours;
horaire souple flexitime
horizon [ɔRizɔ̃] nm horizon
horizontal, e, -aux [ɔRizɔ̃tal, o] adj
horizontal
horloge [ɔRlɔʒ] nf clock; **l'~ parlante**
the speaking clock; **horloger, -ère** nm/f
watchmaker; clockmaker
'hormis ['ɔRmi] prép save
horoscope [`skɔp] nm horoscope
horreur [ɔRœR] nf horror; **quelle ~!** how
awful!; **avoir ~ de** to loathe ou detest;
horrible adj horrible; **horrifier** vt to horrify
'hors ['ɔR] prép: **hors de** out of; **hors pair**
outstanding; **hors de propos** inopportune;
être hors de soi to be beside o.s.; **'hors
d'usage** out of service; **'hors-bord** nm inv
speedboat (with outboard motor); **'hors-
d'œuvre** nm inv hors d'œuvre; **'hors-la-loi**
inv outlaw; **'hors-service** adj inv out of order;
'hors-taxe adj (boutique, articles) duty-free
hortensia [ɔRtɑ̃sja] nm hydrangea
hospice [ɔspis] nm (de vieillards) home
hospitalier, -ière [ɔspitalje, jɛR] adj
(accueillant) hospitable; (Méd: service, centre)
hospital cpd
hospitaliser [ɔspitalize] vt to take/send to
hospital, hospitalize
hospitalité [ɔspitalite] nf hospitality
hostie [ɔsti] nf host (Rel)
hostile [ɔstil] adj hostile; **hostilité** nf hostility
hôte [ot] nm (maître de maison) host; (invité)
guest
hôtel [otɛl] nm hotel; **aller à l'~** to stay in
a hotel; **hôtel de ville** town hall; **hôtel
(particulier)** (private) mansion; **hôtellerie** nf
hotel business

● HÔTELS
●
● There are six categories of hotel in France,
● from zero ('non classé') to four stars and
● luxury four stars ('quatre étoiles luxe').
● Prices include VAT but not breakfast. In
● some towns, guests pay a small additional
● tourist tax, the 'taxe de séjour'.

hôtesse [otɛs] nf hostess; **hôtesse (de l'air)**
stewardess, air hostess (BRIT)
'houblon ['ublɔ̃] nm (Bot) hop; (pour la bière)
hops pl

houille ['uj] nf coal; **'houille blanche**
hydroelectric power
'houle ['ul] nf swell; **'houleux, -euse** adj
stormy
'hourra ['uRa] excl hurrah!
'housse ['us] nf cover
'houx ['u] nm holly
'hublot ['yblo] nm porthole
'huche ['yʃ] nf: **huche à pain** bread bin
'huer ['ɥe] vt to boo
huile [ɥil] nf oil
huissier [ɥisje] nm usher; (Jur) ≈ bailiff
'huit ['ɥi(t)] num eight; **samedi en huit** a
week on Saturday; **dans huit jours** in a week;
'huitaine nf: **une huitaine (de jours)** a week
or so; **'huitième** num eighth
huître [ɥitR] nf oyster
humain, e [ymɛ̃, ɛn] adj human;
(compatissant) humane ▷ nm human (being);
humanitaire adj humanitarian; **humanité**
nf humanity
humble [œ̃bl] adj humble
'humer ['yme] vt (plat) to smell; (parfum) to
inhale
humeur [ymœR] nf mood; **de bonne/
mauvaise ~** in a good/bad mood
humide [ymid] adj damp; (main, yeux) moist;
(climat, chaleur) humid; (saison, route) wet
humilier [ymilje] vt to humiliate
humilité [ymilite] nf humility, humbleness
humoristique [ymɔRistik] adj humorous
humour [ymuR] nm humour; **avoir de l'~** to
have a sense of humour; **humour noir** black
humour
'huppé, e ['ype] (fam) adj posh
'hurlement ['yRləmɑ̃] nm howling no pl, howl,
yelling no pl, yell
'hurler ['yRle] vi to howl, yell
'hutte ['yt] nf hut
hydratant, e [idRatɑ̃, ɑ̃t] adj (crème)
moisturizing
hydraulique [idRolik] adj hydraulic
hydravion [idRavjɔ̃] nm seaplane
hydrogène [idRɔʒɛn] nm hydrogen
hydroglisseur [idRɔglisœR] nm hydroplane
hyène [jɛn] nf hyena
hygiène [iʒjɛn] nf hygiene
hygiénique [iʒenik] adj hygienic
hymne [imn] nm hymn
hyperlien [ipɛRljɛ̃] nm hyperlink
hypermarché [ipɛRmaRʃe] nm hypermarket
hypermétrope [ipɛRmetRɔp] adj long-
sighted
hypertension [ipɛRtɑ̃sjɔ̃] nf high blood
pressure
hypnose [ipnoz] nf hypnosis; **hypnotiser** vt
to hypnotize
hypocrisie [ipɔkRizi] nf hypocrisy; **hypocrite**
adj hypocritical

hypothèque [ipɔtɛk] *nf* mortgage
hypothèse [ipɔtɛz] *nf* hypothesis
hystérique [isterik] *adj* hysterical

iceberg [ajsbɛʀg] *nm* iceberg
ici [isi] *adv* here; **jusqu'~** as far as this; (*temps*) so far; **d'~ demain** by tomorrow; **d'~ là** by then, in the meantime; **d'~ peu** before long
icône [ikon] *nf* icon
idéal, e, -aux [ideal, o] *adj* ideal ▷ *nm* ideal; **idéaliste** *adj* idealistic ▷ *nm/f* idealist
idée [ide] *nf* idea; **avoir dans l'~ que** to have an idea that; **se faire des ~s** to imagine things, get ideas into one's head; **avoir des ~s noires** to have black *ou* dark thoughts; **idées reçues** received wisdom *sg*
identifier [idɑ̃tifje] *vt* to identify; **s'identifier** *vi*: **s'~ avec** *ou* **à qn/qch** (*héros etc*) to identify with sb/sth
identique [idɑ̃tik] *adj*: **~ (à)** identical (to)
identité [idɑ̃tite] *nf* identity
idiot, e [idjo, idjɔt] *adj* idiotic ▷ *nm/f* idiot
idole [idɔl] *nf* idol
if [if] *nm* yew
ignoble [iɲɔbl] *adj* vile
ignorant, e [iɲɔʀɑ̃, ɑ̃t] *adj* ignorant; **~ de** ignorant of, not aware of
ignorer [iɲɔʀe] *vt* not to know; (*personne*) to ignore
il [il] *pron* he; (*animal, chose, en tournure impersonnelle*) it; **il fait froid** it's cold; **Pierre est-il arrivé?** has Pierre arrived?; **il a gagné** he won; *voir* **avoir**
île [il] *nf* island; **l'île Maurice** Mauritius; **les**

îles anglo-normandes the Channel Islands; **les îles britanniques** the British Isles

illégal, e, -aux [i(l)legal, o] *adj* illegal

illimité, e [i(l)limite] *adj* unlimited

illisible [i(l)lizibl] *adj* illegible; *(roman)* unreadable

illogique [i(l)lɔʒik] *adj* illogical

illuminer [i(l)lymine] *vt* to light up; *(monument, rue: pour une fête)* to illuminate; (: *au moyen de projecteurs)* to floodlight

illusion [i(l)lyzjɔ̃] *nf* illusion; **se faire des ~s** to delude o.s.; **faire ~** to delude *ou* fool people

illustration [i(l)lystrasjɔ̃] *nf* illustration

illustré, e [i(l)lystre] *adj* illustrated ▷ *nm* comic

illustrer [i(l)lystre] *vt* to illustrate; **s'illustrer** to become famous, win fame

ils [il] *pron* they

image [imaʒ] *nf (gén)* picture; *(métaphore)* image; **image de marque** brand image; *(fig)* public image; **imagé, e** *adj (texte)* full of imagery; *(langage)* colourful

imaginaire [imaʒinɛʁ] *adj* imaginary

imagination [imaʒinasjɔ̃] *nf* imagination; **avoir de l'~** to be imaginative

imaginer [imaʒine] *vt* to imagine; *(inventer: expédient)* to devise, think up; **s'imaginer** *vt (se figurer: scène etc)* to imagine, picture; **s'~ que** to imagine that

imbécile [ɛ̃besil] *adj* idiotic ▷ *nm/f* idiot

imbu, e [ɛ̃by] *adj*: **~ de** full of

imitateur, -trice [imitatœʁ, tʁis] *nm/f (gén)* imitator; *(Music-Hall)* impersonator

imitation [imitasjɔ̃] *nf* imitation; *(de personnalité)* impersonation

imiter [imite] *vt* to imitate; *(contrefaire)* to forge; *(ressembler à)* to look like

immangeable [ɛ̃mɑ̃ʒabl] *adj* inedible

immatriculation [imatʁikylasjɔ̃] *nf* registration

● **IMMATRICULATION**
●
●
● The last two numbers on vehicle licence
● plates show which 'département' of France
● the vehicle is registered in. For example, a
● car registered in Paris has the number 75 on
● its licence plates.

immatriculer [imatʁikyle] *vt* to register; **faire/se faire ~** to register

immédiat, e [imedja, jat] *adj* immediate ▷ *nm*: **dans l'~** for the time being; **immédiatement** *adv* immediately

immense [i(m)mɑ̃s] *adj* immense

immerger [imɛʁʒe] *vt* to immerse, submerge

immeuble [imœbl] *nm* building; *(à usage d'habitation)* block of flats

immigration [imigʁasjɔ̃] *nf* immigration

immigré, e [imigʁe] *nm/f* immigrant

imminent, e [iminɑ̃, ɑ̃t] *adj* imminent

immobile [i(m)mɔbil] *adj* still, motionless

immobilier, -ière [imɔbilje, jɛʁ] *adj* property *cpd* ▷ *nm*: **l'~** the property business

immobiliser [imɔbilize] *vt (gén)* to immobilize; *(circulation, véhicule, affaires)* to bring to a standstill; **s'immobiliser** *(personne)* to stand still; *(machine, véhicule)* to come to a halt

immoral, e, -aux [i(m)mɔʁal, o] *adj* immoral

immortel, le [imɔʁtɛl] *adj* immortal

immunisé, e [im(m)ynize] *adj*: **~ contre** immune to

immunité [imynite] *nf* immunity

impact [ɛ̃pakt] *nm* impact

impair, e [ɛ̃pɛʁ] *adj* odd ▷ *nm* faux pas, blunder

impardonnable [ɛ̃paʁdɔnabl] *adj* unpardonable, unforgivable

imparfait, e [ɛ̃paʁfɛ, ɛt] *adj* imperfect

impartial, e, -aux [ɛ̃paʁsjal, jo] *adj* impartial, unbiased

impasse [ɛ̃pɑs] *nf* dead end, cul-de-sac; *(fig)* deadlock

impassible [ɛ̃pasibl] *adj* impassive

impatience [ɛ̃pasjɑ̃s] *nf* impatience

impatient, e [ɛ̃pasjɑ̃, jɑ̃t] *adj* impatient; **impatienter: s'impatienter** *vi* to get impatient

impeccable [ɛ̃pekabl] *adj (parfait)* perfect; *(propre)* impeccable; *(fam)* smashing

impensable [ɛ̃pɑ̃sabl] *adj (événement hypothétique)* unthinkable; *(événement qui a eu lieu)* unbelievable

impératif, -ive [ɛ̃peʁatif, iv] *adj* imperative ▷ *nm (Ling)* imperative; **impératifs** *nmpl (exigences: d'une fonction, d'une charge)* requirements; (: *de la mode)* demands

impératrice [ɛ̃peʁatʁis] *nf* empress

imperceptible [ɛ̃pɛʁsɛptibl] *adj* imperceptible

impérial, e, -aux [ɛ̃peʁjal, jo] *adj* imperial

impérieux, -euse [ɛ̃peʁjø, jøz] *adj (caractère, ton)* imperious; *(obligation, besoin)* pressing, urgent

impérissable [ɛ̃peʁisabl] *adj* undying

imperméable [ɛ̃pɛʁmeabl] *adj* waterproof; *(fig)*: **~ à** impervious to ▷ *nm* raincoat

impertinent, e [ɛ̃pɛʁtinɑ̃, ɑ̃t] *adj* impertinent

impitoyable [ɛ̃pitwajabl] *adj* pitiless, merciless

implanter [ɛ̃plɑ̃te]: **s'implanter** *vi* to be set up

impliquer [ɛ̃plike] *vt* to imply; **~ qn (dans)** to implicate sb (in)

impoli, e [ɛ̃pɔli] *adj* impolite, rude

impopulaire [ɛ̃pɔpylɛʀ] adj unpopular

importance [ɛ̃pɔʀtɑ̃s] nf importance; (de somme) size; (de retard, dégâts) extent; **sans ~** unimportant

important, e [ɛ̃pɔʀtɑ̃, ɑ̃t] adj important; (en quantité: somme, retard) considerable, sizeable; (: dégâts) extensive; (péj: airs, ton) self-important ▷ nm: **l'~** the important thing

importateur, -trice [ɛ̃pɔʀtatœʀ, tʀis] nm/f importer

importation [ɛ̃pɔʀtasjɔ̃] nf importation; (produit) import

importer [ɛ̃pɔʀte] vt (Comm) to import; (maladies, plantes) to introduce ▷ vi (être important) to matter; **il importe qu'il fasse** it is important that he should do; **peu m'importe** (je n'ai pas de préférence) I don't mind; (je m'en moque) I don't care; **peu importe (que)** it doesn't matter (if); voir aussi **n'importe**

importun, e [ɛ̃pɔʀtœ̃, yn] adj irksome, importunate; (arrivée, visite) inopportune, ill-timed ▷ nm intruder; **importuner** vt to bother

imposant, e [ɛ̃pozɑ̃, ɑ̃t] adj imposing

imposer [ɛ̃poze] vt (taxer) to tax; **s'imposer** (être nécessaire) to be imperative; **~ qch à qn** to impose sth on sb; **en ~ à** to impress; **s'~ comme** to emerge as; **s'~ par** to win recognition through

impossible [ɛ̃pɔsibl] adj impossible; **il m'est ~ de le faire** it is impossible for me to do it, I can't possibly do it; **faire l'~** to do one's utmost

imposteur [ɛ̃pɔstœʀ] nm impostor

impôt [ɛ̃po] nm tax; **impôt foncier** land tax; **impôt sur le chiffre d'affaires** corporation (BRIT) ou corporate (US) tax; **impôt sur le revenu** income tax; **impôts locaux** rates, local taxes (US), ≈ council tax (BRIT)

impotent, e [ɛ̃pɔtɑ̃, ɑ̃t] adj disabled

impraticable [ɛ̃pʀatikabl] adj (projet) impracticable, unworkable; (piste) impassable

imprécis, e [ɛ̃pʀesi, iz] adj imprecise

imprégner [ɛ̃pʀeɲe] vt (tissu) to impregnate; (lieu, air) to fill; **s'imprégner de** (fig) to absorb

imprenable [ɛ̃pʀənabl] adj (forteresse) impregnable; **vue ~** unimpeded outlook

impression [ɛ̃pʀesjɔ̃] nf impression; (d'un ouvrage, tissu) printing; **faire bonne/mauvaise ~** to make a good/bad impression; **impressionnant, e** adj (imposant) impressive; (bouleversant) upsetting; **impressionner** vt (frapper) to impress; (bouleverser) to upset

imprévisible [ɛ̃pʀevizibl] adj unforeseeable

imprévu, e [ɛ̃pʀevy] adj unforeseen, unexpected ▷ nm (incident) unexpected incident; **des vacances pleines d'~** holidays full of surprises; **en cas d'~** if anything unexpected happens; **sauf ~** unless anything

unexpected crops up

imprimante [ɛ̃pʀimɑ̃t] nf printer; **imprimante à laser** laser printer

imprimé [ɛ̃pʀime] nm (formulaire) printed form; (Postes) printed matter no pl; (tissu) printed fabric; **~ à fleur** floral print

imprimer [ɛ̃pʀime] vt to print; (publier) to publish; **imprimerie** nf printing; (établissement) printing works sg; **imprimeur** nm printer

impropre [ɛ̃pʀɔpʀ] adj inappropriate; **~ à** unfit for

improviser [ɛ̃pʀɔvize] vt, vi to improvise

improviste [ɛ̃pʀɔvist]: **à l'~** adv unexpectedly, without warning

imprudence [ɛ̃pʀydɑ̃s] nf (d'une personne, d'une action) carelessness no pl; (d'une remarque) imprudence no pl; **commettre une ~** to do something foolish

imprudent, e [ɛ̃pʀydɑ̃, ɑ̃t] adj (conducteur, geste, action) careless; (remarque) unwise, imprudent; (projet) foolhardy

impuissant, e [ɛ̃pɥisɑ̃, ɑ̃t] adj helpless; (sans effet) ineffectual; (sexuellement) impotent

impulsif, -ive [ɛ̃pylsif, iv] adj impulsive

impulsion [ɛ̃pylsjɔ̃] nf (Élec, instinct) impulse; (élan, influence) impetus

inabordable [inabɔʀdabl] adj (cher) prohibitive

inacceptable [inaksɛptabl] adj unacceptable

inaccessible [inaksesibl] adj inaccessible; **~ à** impervious to

inachevé, e [inaʃ(ə)ve] adj unfinished

inactif, -ive [inaktif, iv] adj inactive; (remède) ineffective; (Bourse: marché) slack

inadapté, e [inadapte] adj (gén): **~ à** not adapted to, unsuited to; (Psych) maladjusted

inadéquat, e [inadekwa(t), kwat] adj inadequate

inadmissible [inadmisibl] adj inadmissible

inadvertance [inadvɛʀtɑ̃s]: **par ~** adv inadvertently

inanimé, e [inanime] adj (matière) inanimate; (évanoui) unconscious; (sans vie) lifeless

inanition [inanisjɔ̃] nf: **tomber d'~** to faint with hunger (and exhaustion)

inaperçu, e [inapɛʀsy] adj: **passer ~** to go unnoticed

inapte [inapt] adj: **~ à** incapable of; (Mil) unfit for

inattendu, e [inatɑ̃dy] adj unexpected

inattentif, -ive [inatɑ̃tif, iv] adj inattentive; **~ à** (dangers, détails) heedless of; **inattention** nf lack of attention; **une faute** ou **une erreur d'inattention** a careless mistake

inaugurer [inogyʀe] vt (monument) to unveil; (exposition, usine) to open; (fig) to inaugurate

inavouable [inavwabl] adj shameful;

(*bénéfices*) undisclosable
incalculable [ɛ̃kalkylabl] *adj* incalculable
incapable [ɛ̃kapabl] *adj* incapable; **~ de faire** incapable of doing; (*empêché*) unable to do
incapacité [ɛ̃kapasite] *nf* (*incompétence*) incapability; (*impossibilité*) incapacity; **dans l'~ de faire** unable to do
incarcérer [ɛ̃karsere] *vt* to incarcerate, imprison
incassable [ɛ̃kasabl] *adj* unbreakable
incendie [ɛ̃sɑ̃di] *nm* fire; **incendie criminel** arson *no pl*; **incendie de forêt** forest fire; **incendier** *vt* (*mettre le feu à*) to set fire to, set alight; (*brûler complètement*) to burn down
incertain, e [ɛ̃sɛrtɛ̃, ɛn] *adj* uncertain; (*temps*) unsettled; (*imprécis: contours*) indistinct, blurred; **incertitude** *nf* uncertainty
incessamment [ɛ̃sesamɑ̃] *adv* very shortly
incident [ɛ̃sidɑ̃] *nm* incident; **incident de parcours** minor hitch *ou* setback; **incident technique** technical difficulties *pl*
incinérer [ɛ̃sinere] *vt* (*ordures*) to incinerate; (*mort*) to cremate
incisive [ɛ̃siziv] *nf* incisor
inciter [ɛ̃site] *vt*: **~ qn à (faire) qch** to encourage sb to do sth; (*à la révolte etc*) to incite sb to do sth
incivilité [ɛ̃sivilite] *nf* (*grossièreté*) incivility; **incivilités** *nfpl* antisocial behaviour *sg*
inclinable [ɛ̃klinabl] *adj*: **siège à dossier ~** reclining seat
inclinaison [ɛ̃klinɛzɔ̃] *nf* (*penchant*) inclination
incliner [ɛ̃kline] *vt* (*pencher*) to tilt ▷ *vi*: **~ à qch/à faire** to incline towards sth/doing; **s'incliner** *vr* (*se pencher*) to bow; **s'~ devant** (*par respect*) to pay one's respects
inclure [ɛ̃klyr] *vt* to include; (*joindre à un envoi*) to enclose
inclus, e [ɛ̃kly, -yz] *pp de* **inclure** ▷ *adj* included; (*joint à un envoi*) enclosed ▷ *adv*: **est-ce que le service est ~?** is service included?; **jusqu'au 10 mars ~** until 10th March inclusive
incognito [ɛ̃kɔɲito] *adv* incognito ▷ *nm*: **garder l'~** to remain incognito
incohérent, e [ɛ̃kɔerɑ̃, ɑ̃t] *adj* (*comportement*) inconsistent; (*geste, langage, texte*) incoherent
incollable [ɛ̃kɔlabl] *adj* (*riz*) non-stick; **il est ~** (*fam*) he's got all the answers
incolore [ɛ̃kɔlɔr] *adj* colourless
incommoder [ɛ̃kɔmɔde] *vt* (*chaleur, odeur*): **~ qn** to bother sb
incomparable [ɛ̃kɔ̃parabl] *adj* incomparable
incompatible [ɛ̃kɔ̃patibl] *adj* incompatible
incompétent, e [ɛ̃kɔ̃petɑ̃, ɑ̃t] *adj* incompetent
incomplet, -ète [ɛ̃kɔ̃plɛ, ɛt] *adj* incomplete

incompréhensible [ɛ̃kɔ̃preɑ̃sibl] *adj* incomprehensible
incompris, e [ɛ̃kɔ̃pri, iz] *adj* misunderstood
inconcevable [ɛ̃kɔ̃s(ə)vabl] *adj* inconceivable
inconfortable [ɛ̃kɔ̃fɔrtabl(ə)] *adj* uncomfortable
incongru, e [ɛ̃kɔ̃gry] *adj* unseemly
inconnu, e [ɛ̃kɔny] *adj* unknown ▷ *nm/f* stranger ▷ *nm*: **l'~** the unknown; **inconnue** *nf* unknown factor
inconsciemment [ɛ̃kɔ̃sjamɑ̃] *adv* unconsciously
inconscient, e [ɛ̃kɔ̃sjɑ̃, jɑ̃t] *adj* unconscious; (*irréfléchi*) thoughtless, reckless; (*sentiment*) subconscious ▷ *nm* (*Psych*): **l'~** the unconscious; **~ de** unaware of
inconsidéré, e [ɛ̃kɔ̃sidere] *adj* ill-considered
inconsistant, e [ɛ̃kɔ̃sistɑ̃, ɑ̃t] *adj* (*fig*) flimsy, weak
inconsolable [ɛ̃kɔ̃sɔlabl] *adj* inconsolable
incontestable [ɛ̃kɔ̃testabl] *adj* indisputable
incontinent, e [ɛ̃kɔ̃tinɑ̃, ɑ̃t] *adj* incontinent
incontournable [ɛ̃kɔ̃turnabl] *adj* unavoidable
incontrôlable [ɛ̃kɔ̃trolabl] *adj* unverifiable; (*irrépressible*) uncontrollable
inconvénient [ɛ̃kɔ̃venjɑ̃] *nm* disadvantage, drawback; **si vous n'y voyez pas d'~** if you have no objections
incorporer [ɛ̃kɔrpɔre] *vt*: **~ (à)** to mix in (with); **~ (dans)** (*paragraphe etc*) to incorporate (in); (*Mil: appeler*) to recruit (into); **il a très bien su s'~ à notre groupe** he was very easily incorporated into our group
incorrect, e [ɛ̃kɔrɛkt] *adj* (*impropre, inconvenant*) improper; (*défectueux*) faulty; (*inexact*) incorrect; (*impoli*) impolite; (*déloyal*) underhand
incorrigible [ɛ̃kɔriʒibl] *adj* incorrigible
incrédule [ɛ̃kredyl] *adj* incredulous; (*Rel*) unbelieving
incroyable [ɛ̃krwajabl] *adj* incredible
incruster [ɛ̃kryste] *vt* (*Art*) to inlay; **s'incruster** *vi* (*invité*) to take root
inculpé, e [ɛ̃kylpe] *nm/f* accused
inculper [ɛ̃kylpe] *vt*: **~ (de)** to charge (with)
inculquer [ɛ̃kylke] *vt*: **~ qch à** to inculcate sth in *ou* instil sth into
Inde [ɛ̃d] *nf*: **l'~** India
indécent, e [ɛ̃desɑ̃, ɑ̃t] *adj* indecent
indécis, e [ɛ̃desi, iz] *adj* (*par nature*) indecisive; (*temporairement*) undecided
indéfendable [ɛ̃defɑ̃dabl] *adj* indefensible
indéfini, e [ɛ̃defini] *adj* (*imprécis, incertain*) undefined; (*illimité, Ling*) indefinite; **indéfiniment** *adv* indefinitely; **indéfinissable** *adj* indefinable
indélébile [ɛ̃delebil] *adj* indelible

indélicat, e [ɛ̃delika, at] *adj* tactless
indemne [ɛ̃dɛmn] *adj* unharmed;
  indemniser *vt*: **indemniser qn (de)** to
  compensate sb (for)
indemnité [ɛ̃dɛmnite] *nf* (*dédommagement*)
  compensation *no pl*; (*allocation*) allowance;
  indemnité de licenciement redundancy
  payment
indépendamment [ɛ̃depɑ̃damɑ̃] *adv*
  independently; **~ de** (*abstraction faite de*)
  irrespective of; (*en plus de*) over and above
indépendance [ɛ̃depɑ̃dɑ̃s] *nf* independence
indépendant, e [ɛ̃depɑ̃dɑ̃, ɑ̃t] *adj*
  independent; **~ de** independent of;
  travailleur ~ self-employed worker
indescriptible [ɛ̃dɛskriptibl] *adj*
  indescribable
indésirable [ɛ̃dezirabl] *adj* undesirable
indestructible [ɛ̃dɛstryktibl] *adj*
  indestructible
indéterminé, e [ɛ̃detɛrmine] *adj* (*date, cause,
  nature*) unspecified; (*forme, longueur, quantité*)
  indeterminate
index [ɛ̃dɛks] *nm* (*doigt*) index finger; (*d'un livre
  etc*) index; **mettre à l'~** to blacklist
indicateur [ɛ̃dikatœr] *nm* (*Police*) informer;
  (*Tech*) gauge, indicator ▷ *adj*: **panneau ~**
  signpost; **indicateur des chemins de fer**
  railway timetable; **indicateur de rues** street
  directory
indicatif, -ive [ɛ̃dikatif, iv] *adj*: **à titre ~** for
  (your) information ▷ *nm* (*Ling*) indicative;
  (*Radio*) theme *ou* signature tune; (*Tél*) dialling
  code (BRIT), area code (US); **quel est l'~ de ...**
  what's the code for ...?
indication [ɛ̃dikasjɔ̃] *nf* indication;
  (*renseignement*) information *no pl*; **indications**
  nfpl (*directives*) instructions
indice [ɛ̃dis] *nm* (*marque, signe*) indication,
  sign; (*Police: lors d'une enquête*) clue; (*Jur:
  présomption*) piece of evidence; (*Science, Écon,
  Tech*) index; **~ de protection** (sun protection)
  factor
indicible [ɛ̃disibl] *adj* inexpressible
indien, ne [ɛ̃djɛ̃, jɛn] *adj* Indian ▷ *nm/f*: **I~,
  ne** Indian
indifféremment [ɛ̃diferamɑ̃] *adv* (*sans
  distinction*) equally (well)
indifférence [ɛ̃diferɑ̃s] *nf* indifference
indifférent, e [ɛ̃diferɑ̃, ɑ̃t] *adj* (*peu intéressé*)
  indifferent; **ça m'est ~** it doesn't matter to me;
  elle m'est ~e I am indifferent to her
indigène [ɛ̃diʒɛn] *adj* native, indigenous; (*des
  gens du pays*) local ▷ *nm/f* native
indigeste [ɛ̃diʒɛst] *adj* indigestible
indigestion [ɛ̃diʒɛstjɔ̃] *nf* indigestion *no pl*;
  avoir une ~ to have indigestion
indigne [ɛ̃diɲ] *adj* unworthy
indigner [ɛ̃diɲe] *vt*: **s'~ de qch** to get annoyed

about sth; **s'~ contre qn** to get annoyed
  with sb
indiqué, e [ɛ̃dike] *adj* (*date, lieu*) agreed;
  (*traitement*) appropriate; (*conseillé*) advisable
indiquer [ɛ̃dike] *vt* (*suj: pendule, aiguille*) to
  show; (: *étiquette, panneau*) to show, indicate;
  (*renseigner sur*) to point out, tell; (*déterminer:
  date, lieu*) to give, state; (*signaler, dénoter*) to
  indicate, point to; **~ qch/qn à qn** (*montrer du
  doigt*) to point sth/sb out to sb; (*faire connaître:
  médecin, restaurant*) to tell sb of sth/sb;
  pourriez-vous m'~ les toilettes/l'heure?
  could you direct me to the toilets/tell me the
  time?
indiscipliné, e [ɛ̃disipline] *adj* undisciplined
indiscret, -ète [ɛ̃diskrɛ, ɛt] *adj* indiscreet
indiscutable [ɛ̃diskytabl] *adj* indisputable
indispensable [ɛ̃dispɑ̃sabl] *adj*
  indispensable, essential
indisposé, e [ɛ̃dispoze] *adj* indisposed
indistinct, e [ɛ̃distɛ̃(kt), ɛ̃kt] *adj* indistinct;
  indistinctement *adv* (*voir, prononcer*)
  indistinctly; (*sans distinction*) indiscriminately
individu [ɛ̃dividy] *nm* individual; **individuel,
  le** *adj* (*gén*) individual; (*responsabilité, propriété,
  liberté*) personal; **chambre individuelle** single
  room; **maison individuelle** detached house
indolore [ɛ̃dɔlɔr] *adj* painless
Indonésie [ɛ̃dɔnezi] *nf* Indonesia
indu, e [ɛ̃dy] *adj*: **à une heure ~e** at some
  ungodly hour
indulgent, e [ɛ̃dylʒɑ̃, ɑ̃t] *adj* (*parent, regard*)
  indulgent; (*juge, examinateur*) lenient
industrialisé, e [ɛ̃dystrijalize] *adj*
  industrialized
industrie [ɛ̃dystri] *nf* industry; **industriel, le**
  adj industrial ▷ *nm* industrialist
inébranlable [inebrɑ̃labl] *adj* (*masse,
  colonne*) solid; (*personne, certitude, foi*)
  unshakeable
inédit, e [inedi, it] *adj* (*correspondance, livre*)
  hitherto unpublished; (*spectacle, moyen*) novel,
  original; (*film*) unreleased
inefficace [inefikas] *adj* (*remède, moyen*)
  ineffective; (*machine, employé*) inefficient
inégal, e, -aux [inegal, o] *adj* unequal;
  (*irrégulier*) uneven; **inégalable** *adj* matchless;
  inégalé, e *adj* (*record*) unequalled; (*beauté*)
  unrivalled; **inégalité** *nf* inequality
inépuisable [inepɥizabl] *adj* inexhaustible
inerte [inɛrt] *adj* (*immobile*) lifeless; (*sans
  réaction*) passive
inespéré, e [inɛspere] *adj* unexpected,
  unhoped-for
inestimable [inɛstimabl] *adj* priceless; (*fig:
  bienfait*) invaluable
inévitable [inevitabl] *adj* unavoidable; (*fatal,
  habituel*) inevitable
inexact, e [inɛgza(kt), akt] *adj* inaccurate

inexcusable[inɛkskyzabl] *adj* unforgivable
inexplicable[inɛksplikabl] *adj* inexplicable
in extremis[inɛkstremis] *adv* at the last
minute ▷ *adj* last-minute
infaillible[ɛ̃fajibl] *adj* infallible
infarctus[ɛ̃faʀktys] *nm:* **~ (du myocarde)**
coronary (thrombosis)
infatigable[ɛ̃fatigabl] *adj* tireless
infect, e[ɛ̃fɛkt] *adj* revolting; (*personne*)
obnoxious; (*temps*) foul
infecter[ɛ̃fɛkte] *vt* (*atmosphère, eau*) to
contaminate; (*Méd*) to infect; **s'infecter**
to become infected *ou* septic; **infection** *nf*
infection; (*puanteur*) stench
inférieur, e[ɛ̃feʀjœʀ] *adj* lower; (*en qualité,
intelligence*) inferior; **~ à** (*somme, quantité*) less
ou smaller than; (*moins bon que*) inferior to
infernal, e, -aux[ɛ̃fɛʀnal, o] *adj*
(*insupportable: chaleur, rythme*) infernal; (:
enfant) horrid; (*satanique, effrayant*) diabolical
infidèle[ɛ̃fidɛl] *adj* unfaithful
infiltrer[ɛ̃filtʀe]: **s'infiltrer** *vr:* **s'~ dans** to
get into; (*liquide*) to seep through; (*fig: groupe,
ennemi*) to infiltrate
infime[ɛ̃fim] *adj* minute, tiny
infini, e[ɛ̃fini] *adj* infinite ▷ *nm* infinity; **à l'~**
endlessly; **infiniment** *adv* infinitely; **infinité**
nf: **une infinité de** an infinite number of
infinitif[ɛ̃finitif] *nm* infinitive
infirme[ɛ̃fiʀm] *adj* disabled ▷ *nm/f* disabled
person
infirmerie[ɛ̃fiʀməʀi] *nf* medical room
infirmier, -ière[ɛ̃fiʀmje] *nm/f* nurse;
infirmière chef sister
infirmité[ɛ̃fiʀmite] *nf* disability
inflammable[ɛ̃flamabl] *adj* (in)flammable
inflation[ɛ̃flasjɔ̃] *nf* inflation
influençable[ɛ̃flyɑ̃sabl] *adj* easily influenced
influence[ɛ̃flyɑ̃s] *nf* influence; **influencer** *vt*
to influence; **influent, e** *adj* influential
informaticien, ne[ɛ̃fɔʀmatisjɛ̃, jɛn] *nm/f*
computer scientist
information[ɛ̃fɔʀmasjɔ̃] *nf* (*renseignement*)
piece of information; (*Presse, TV: nouvelle*) item
of news; (*diffusion de renseignements, Inform*)
information; (*Jur*) inquiry, investigation;
informations *nfpl* (*TV*) news *sg*
informatique[ɛ̃fɔʀmatik] *nf* (*technique*)
data processing; (*science*) computer science
▷ *adj* computer *cpd*; **informatiser** *vt* to
computerize
informer[ɛ̃fɔʀme] *vt:* **~ qn (de)** to inform sb
(of); **s'informer** *vr:* **s'~ (de/si)** to inquire *ou*
find out (about/whether); **s'~ sur** to inform
o.s. about
infos[ɛ̃fo] *nfpl:* **les ~** the news *sg*
infraction[ɛ̃fʀaksjɔ̃] *nf* offence; **~ à** violation
ou breach of; **être en ~** to be in breach of the
law

infranchissable[ɛ̃fʀɑ̃ʃisabl] *adj* impassable;
(*fig*) insuperable
infrarouge[ɛ̃fʀaʀuʒ] *adj* infrared
infrastructure[ɛ̃fʀastʀyktyʀ] *nf* (*Aviat, Mil*)
ground installations *pl*; (*Écon: touristique etc*)
infrastructure
infuser[ɛ̃fyze] *vt, vi* (*thé*) to brew; (*tisane*) to
infuse; **infusion** *nf* (*tisane*) herb tea
ingénier[ɛ̃ʒenje]: **s'ingénier** *vi:* **s'~ à faire** to
strive to do
ingénierie[ɛ̃ʒeniʀi] *nf* engineering
ingénieur[ɛ̃ʒenjœʀ] *nm* engineer; **ingénieur
du son** sound engineer
ingénieux, -euse[ɛ̃ʒenjø, jøz] *adj* ingenious,
clever
ingrat, e[ɛ̃gʀa, at] *adj* (*personne*)
ungrateful; (*travail, sujet*) thankless; (*visage*)
unprepossessing
ingrédient[ɛ̃gʀedjɑ̃] *nm* ingredient
inhabité, e[inabite] *adj* uninhabited
inhabituel, le[inabituɛl] *adj* unusual
inhibition[inibisjɔ̃] *nf* inhibition
inhumain, e[inymɛ̃, ɛn] *adj* inhuman
inimaginable[inimaʒinabl] *adj*
unimaginable
ininterrompu, e[inɛ̃teʀɔ̃py] *adj* (*file, série*)
unbroken; (*flot, vacarme*) uninterrupted, non-
stop; (*effort*) unremitting, continuous; (*suite,
ligne*) unbroken
initial, e, -aux[inisjal, jo] *adj* initial;
initiales *nfpl* (*d'un nom, sigle etc*) initials
initiation[inisjasjɔ̃] *nf:* **~ à** introduction to
initiative[inisjativ] *nf* initiative
initier[inisje] *vt:* **~ qn à** to initiate sb into;
(*faire découvrir: art, jeu*) to introduce sb to
injecter[ɛ̃ʒɛkte] *vt* to inject; **injection** *nf*
injection; **à injection** (*Auto*) fuel injection *cpd*
injure[ɛ̃ʒyʀ] *nf* insult, abuse *no pl*; **injurier** *vt*
to insult, abuse; **injurieux, -euse** *adj* abusive,
insulting
injuste[ɛ̃ʒyst] *adj* unjust, unfair; **injustice**
nf injustice
inlassable[ɛ̃lasabl] *adj* tireless
inné, e[i(n)ne] *adj* innate, inborn
innocent, e[inɔsɑ̃, ɑ̃t] *adj* innocent;
innocenter *vt* to clear, prove innocent
innombrable[i(n)nɔ̃bʀabl] *adj* innumerable
innover[inɔve] *vi* to break new ground
inoccupé, e[inɔkype] *adj* unoccupied
inodore[inɔdɔʀ] *adj* (*gaz*) odourless; (*fleur*)
scentless
inoffensif, -ive[inɔfɑ̃sif, iv] *adj* harmless,
innocuous
inondation[inɔ̃dasjɔ̃] *nf* flood
inonder[inɔ̃de] *vt* to flood; **~ de** to flood with
inopportun, e[inɔpɔʀtœ̃, yn] *adj* ill-timed,
untimely
inoubliable[inublijabl] *adj* unforgettable
inouï, e[inwi] *adj* unheard-of, extraordinary

inox [inɔks] nm stainless steel
inquiet, -ète [ɛ̃kjɛ, ɛ̃kjɛt] adj anxious;
inquiétant, e adj worrying, disturbing;
inquiéter vt to worry; **s'inquiéter** to worry;
s'inquiéter de to worry about; (s'enquérir de)
to inquire about; **inquiétude** nf anxiety
insaisissable [ɛ̃sezisabl] adj (fugitif, ennemi)
elusive; (différence, nuance) imperceptible
insalubre [ɛ̃salybʀ] adj insalubrious
insatisfait, e [ɛ̃satisfɛ, ɛt] adj (non comblé)
unsatisfied; (mécontent) dissatisfied
inscription [ɛ̃skʀipsjɔ̃] nf inscription;
(immatriculation) enrolment
inscrire [ɛ̃skʀiʀ] vt (marquer: sur son calepin
etc) to note ou write down; (: sur un mur, une
affiche etc) to write; (: dans la pierre, le métal) to
inscribe; (mettre: sur une liste, un budget etc) to
put down; **s'inscrire** (pour une excursion etc)
to put one's name down; **s'~ (à)** (club, parti)
to join; (université) to register ou enrol (at);
(examen, concours) to register (for); **~ qn à** (club,
parti) to enrol sb at
insecte [ɛ̃sɛkt] nm insect; **insecticide** nm
insecticide
insensé, e [ɛ̃sɑ̃se] adj mad
insensible [ɛ̃sɑ̃sibl] adj (nerf, membre) numb;
(dur, indifférent) insensitive
inséparable [ɛ̃sepaʀabl] adj inseparable
▷ nm: **~s** (oiseaux) lovebirds
insigne [ɛ̃siɲ] nm (d'un parti, club) badge;
(d'une fonction) insignia ▷ adj distinguished
insignifiant, e [ɛ̃siɲifjɑ̃, jɑ̃t] adj
insignificant; trivial
insinuer [ɛ̃sinɥe] vt to insinuate; **s'insinuer
dans** (fig) to worm one's way into
insipide [ɛ̃sipid] adj insipid
insister [ɛ̃siste] vi to insist; (continuer à sonner)
to keep on trying; **~ sur** (détail, sujet) to lay
stress on
insolation [ɛ̃sɔlasjɔ̃] nf (Méd) sunstroke no pl
insolent, e [ɛ̃sɔlɑ̃, ɑ̃t] adj insolent
insolite [ɛ̃sɔlit] adj strange, unusual
insomnie [ɛ̃sɔmni] nf insomnia no pl; **avoir
des ~s** to sleep badly, not be able to sleep
insouciant, e [ɛ̃susjɑ̃, jɑ̃t] adj carefree; **~ du
danger** heedless of (the) danger
insoupçonnable [ɛ̃supsɔnabl] adj
unsuspected; (personne) above suspicion
insoupçonné, e [ɛ̃supsɔne] adj unsuspected
insoutenable [ɛ̃sut(ə)nabl] adj (argument)
untenable; (chaleur) unbearable
inspecter [ɛ̃spɛkte] vt to inspect; **inspecteur,
-trice** nm/f inspector; **inspecteur
d'Académie** (regional) director of education;
inspecteur des finances ≈ tax inspector
(BRIT), ≈ Internal Revenue Service agent (US);
inspecteur (de police) (police) inspector;
inspection nf inspection
inspirer [ɛ̃spiʀe] vt (gén) to inspire ▷ vi

(aspirer) to breathe in; **s'inspirer** vr: **s'~ de** to
be inspired by
instable [ɛ̃stabl] adj unstable; (meuble,
équilibre) unsteady; (temps) unsettled
installation [ɛ̃stalasjɔ̃] nf (mise en place)
installation; **installations** nfpl (de sport,
dans un camping) facilities; **l'installation
électrique** wiring
installer [ɛ̃stale] vt (loger, placer) to put;
(meuble, gaz, électricité) to put in; (rideau,
étagère, tente) to put up; (appartement) to fit
out; **s'installer** (s'établir: artisan, dentiste etc)
to set o.s. up; (se loger) to settle; (emménager)
to settle in; (sur un siège, à un emplacement) to
settle (down); (fig: maladie, grève) to take a
firm hold
instance [ɛ̃stɑ̃s] nf (Admin: autorité) authority;
affaire en ~ matter pending; **être en ~ de
divorce** to be awaiting a divorce
instant [ɛ̃stɑ̃] nm moment, instant; **dans un
~** in a moment; **à l'~** this instant; **je l'ai vu à
l'~** I've just this minute seen him, I saw him a
moment ago; **pour l'~** for the moment, for the
time being
instantané, e [ɛ̃stɑ̃tane] adj (lait, café)
instant; (explosion, mort) instantaneous ▷ nm
snapshot
instar [ɛ̃staʀ]: **à l'~ de** prép following the
example of, like
instaurer [ɛ̃stɔʀe] vt to institute; (couvre-
feu) to impose; **s'instaurer** vr (paix) to be
established; (doute) to set in
instinct [ɛ̃stɛ̃] nm instinct; **instinctivement**
adv instinctively
instituer [ɛ̃stitɥe] vt to establish
institut [ɛ̃stity] nm institute; **institut de
beauté** beauty salon; **Institut universitaire
de technologie** ≈ polytechnic
instituteur, -trice [ɛ̃stitytœʀ, tʀis] nm/f
(primary school) teacher
institution [ɛ̃stitysjɔ̃] nf institution; (collège)
private school; **institutions** nfpl (structures
politiques et sociales) institutions
instructif, -ive [ɛ̃stʀyktif, iv] adj instructive
instruction [ɛ̃stʀyksjɔ̃] nf (enseignement,
savoir) education; (Jur) (preliminary)
investigation and hearing; **instructions**
nfpl (ordres, mode d'emploi) instructions;
instruction civique civics sg
instruire [ɛ̃stʀɥiʀ] vt (élèves) to teach;
(recrues) to train; (Jur: affaire) to conduct the
investigation for; **s'instruire** to educate o.s.;
instruit, e adj educated
instrument [ɛ̃stʀymɑ̃] nm instrument;
instrument à cordes/à vent stringed/
wind instrument; **instrument de mesure**
measuring instrument; **instrument de
musique** musical instrument; **instrument de
travail** (working) tool

insu [ɛ̃sy] *nm*: **à l'~ de qn** without sb knowing (it)

insuffisant, e [ɛ̃syfizɑ̃, ɑ̃t] *adj* (*en quantité*) insufficient; (*en qualité*) inadequate; (*sur une copie*) poor

insulaire [ɛ̃sylɛʀ] *adj* island *cpd*; (*attitude*) insular

insuline [ɛ̃sylin] *nf* insulin

insulte [ɛ̃sylt] *nf* insult; **insulter** *vt* to insult

insupportable [ɛ̃sypɔʀtabl] *adj* unbearable

insurmontable [ɛ̃syʀmɔ̃tabl] *adj* (*difficulté*) insuperable; (*aversion*) unconquerable

intact, e [ɛ̃takt] *adj* intact

intarissable [ɛ̃taʀisabl] *adj* inexhaustible

intégral, e, -aux [ɛ̃tegʀal, o] *adj* complete; **texte ~** unabridged version; **bronzage ~** all-over suntan; **intégralement** *adv* in full; **intégralité** *nf* whole; **dans son intégralité** in full; **intégrant, e** *adj*: **faire partie intégrante de** to be an integral part of

intègre [ɛ̃tegʀ] *adj* upright

intégrer [ɛ̃tegʀe] : **s'intégrer** *vr*: **s'~ à** *ou* **dans qch** to become integrated into sth; **bien s'~** to fit in

intégrisme [ɛ̃tegʀism] *nm* fundamentalism

intellectuel, le [ɛ̃telɛktɥɛl] *adj* intellectual ▷ *nm/f* intellectual; (*péj*) highbrow

intelligence [ɛ̃teliʒɑ̃s] *nf* intelligence; (*compréhension*): **l'~ de** the understanding of; (*complicité*): **regard d'~** glance of complicity; (*accord*): **vivre en bonne ~ avec qn** to be on good terms with sb

intelligent, e [ɛ̃teliʒɑ̃, ɑ̃t] *adj* intelligent

intelligible [ɛ̃teliʒibl] *adj* intelligible

intempéries [ɛ̃tɑ̃peʀi] *nfpl* bad weather *sg*

intenable [ɛ̃t(ə)nabl] *adj* (*chaleur*) unbearable

intendant, e [ɛ̃tɑ̃dɑ̃] *nm/f* (*Mil*) quartermaster; (*Scol*) bursar

intense [ɛ̃tɑ̃s] *adj* intense; **intensif, -ive** *adj* intensive; **un cours intensif** a crash course

intenter [ɛ̃tɑ̃te] *vt*: **~ un procès contre** *ou* **à** to start proceedings against

intention [ɛ̃tɑ̃sjɔ̃] *nf* intention; (*Jur*) intent; **avoir l'~ de faire** to intend to do; **à l'~ de** for; (*renseignement*) for the benefit of; (*film, ouvrage*) aimed at; **à cette ~** with this aim in view; **intentionné, e** *adj*: **bien intentionné** well-meaning *ou* -intentioned; **mal intentionné** ill-intentioned

interactif, -ive [ɛ̃teʀaktif, iv] *adj* (*Comput*) interactive

intercepter [ɛ̃teʀsɛpte] *vt* to intercept; (*lumière, chaleur*) to cut off

interchangeable [ɛ̃teʀʃɑ̃ʒabl] *adj* interchangeable

interdiction [ɛ̃teʀdiksjɔ̃] *nf* ban; **interdiction de fumer** no smoking

interdire [ɛ̃teʀdiʀ] *vt* to forbid; (*Admin*) to ban, prohibit; (: *journal, livre*) to ban; **~ à qn de faire** to forbid sb to do; (: *suj: empêchement*) to prevent sb from doing

interdit, e [ɛ̃teʀdi, it] *pp de* **interdire** ▷ *adj* (*stupéfait*) taken aback; **film ~ aux moins de 18/12 ans** ≈ 18-/12A-rated film; **"stationnement ~"** "no parking"

intéressant, e [ɛ̃teʀesɑ̃, ɑ̃t] *adj* interesting; (*avantageux*) attractive

intéressé, e [ɛ̃teʀese] *adj* (*parties*) involved, concerned; (*amitié, motifs*) self-interested

intéresser [ɛ̃teʀese] *vt* (*captiver*) to interest; (*toucher*) to be of interest to; (*Admin: concerner*) to affect, concern; **s'intéresser** *vr*: **s'~ à** to be interested in

intérêt [ɛ̃teʀɛ] *nm* interest; (*égoïsme*) self-interest; **tu as ~ à accepter** it's in your interest to accept; **tu as ~ à te dépêcher** you'd better hurry

intérieur, e [ɛ̃teʀjœʀ] *adj* (*mur, escalier, poche*) inside; (*commerce, politique*) domestic; (*cour, calme, vie*) inner; (*navigation*) inland ▷ *nm*: **l'~** (*d'une maison, d'un récipient etc*) the inside; (*d'un pays, aussi: décor, mobilier*) the interior; **à l'~ (de)** inside; **ministère de l'I'-** ≈ Home Office (*BRIT*), ≈ Department of the Interior (*US*); **intérieurement** *adv* inwardly

intérim [ɛ̃teʀim] *nm* interim period; **faire de l'~** to temp; **assurer l'~ (de)** to deputize (for); **par ~** interim

intérimaire [ɛ̃teʀimɛʀ] *adj* (*directeur, ministre*) acting; (*secrétaire, personnel*) temporary ▷ *nm/f* (*secrétaire*) temporary secretary, temp (*BRIT*)

interlocuteur, -trice [ɛ̃teʀlɔkytœʀ, tʀis] *nm/f* speaker; **son ~** the person he was speaking to

intermédiaire [ɛ̃teʀmedjɛʀ] *adj* intermediate; (*solution*) temporary ▷ *nm/f* intermediary; (*Comm*) middleman; **sans ~** directly; **par l'~ de** through

interminable [ɛ̃teʀminabl] *adj* endless

intermittence [ɛ̃teʀmitɑ̃s] *nf*: **par ~** sporadically, intermittently

internat [ɛ̃teʀna] *nm* boarding school

international, e, -aux [ɛ̃teʀnasjɔnal, o] *adj*, *nm/f* international

internaute [ɛ̃teʀnot] *nm/f* Internet user

interne [ɛ̃teʀn] *adj* internal ▷ *nm/f* (*Scol*) boarder; (*Méd*) houseman

Internet [ɛ̃teʀnɛt] *nm*: **l'~** the Internet

interpeller [ɛ̃teʀpəle] *vt* (*appeler*) to call out to; (*apostropher*) to shout at; (*Police, Pol*) to question; (*concerner*) to concern

interphone [ɛ̃teʀfɔn] *nm* intercom; (*d'immeuble*) entry phone

interposer [ɛ̃teʀpoze] *vt*: **s'interposer** to intervene; **par personnes interposées** through a third party

interprète [ɛ̃teʀpʀɛt] *nm/f* interpreter; (*porte-*

parole) spokesperson; **pourriez-vous nous servir d' ~?** could you act as our interpreter?

interpréter [ɛ̃tɛʀpʀete] *vt* to interpret; (*jouer*) to play; (*chanter*) to sing

interrogatif, -ive [ɛ̃tɛʀɔgatif, iv] *adj* (*Ling*) interrogative

interrogation [ɛ̃tɛʀɔgasjɔ̃] *nf* question; (*action*) questioning; **~ écrite/orale** (*Scol*) written/oral test

interrogatoire [ɛ̃tɛʀɔgatwaʀ] *nm* (*Police*) questioning *no pl*; (*Jur, aussi fig*) cross-examination

interroger [ɛ̃tɛʀɔʒe] *vt* to question; (*Inform*) to consult; (*Scol*) to test

interrompre [ɛ̃tɛʀɔ̃pʀ] *vt* (*gén*) to interrupt; (*négociations*) to break off; (*match*) to stop; **s'interrompre** to break off; **interrupteur** *nm* switch; **interruption** *nf* interruption; (*pause*) break; **sans interruption** without stopping; **interruption (volontaire) de grossesse** termination (of pregnancy)

intersection [ɛ̃tɛʀsɛksjɔ̃] *nf* intersection

intervalle [ɛ̃tɛʀval] *nm* (*espace*) space; (*de temps*) interval; **dans l'~** in the meantime; **à deux jours d'~** two days apart

intervenir [ɛ̃tɛʀvəniʀ] *vi* (*gén*) to intervene; **~ auprès de qn** to intervene with sb; **intervention** *nf* intervention; (*discours*) speech; **intervention chirurgicale** (*Méd*) (surgical) operation

interview [ɛ̃tɛʀvju] *nf* interview

intestin [ɛ̃tɛstɛ̃] *nm* intestine

intime [ɛ̃tim] *adj* intimate; (*vie*) private; (*conviction*) inmost; (*dîner, cérémonie*) quiet ▷ *nm/f* close friend; **un journal ~** a diary

intimider [ɛ̃timide] *vt* to intimidate

intimité [ɛ̃timite] *nf*: **dans l'~** in private; (*sans formalités*) with only a few friends, quietly

intolérable [ɛ̃tɔleʀabl] *adj* intolerable

intox [ɛ̃tɔks] (*fam*) *nf* brainwashing

intoxication [ɛ̃tɔksikasjɔ̃] *nf*: **intoxication alimentaire** food poisoning

intoxiquer [ɛ̃tɔksike] *vt* to poison; (*fig*) to brainwash

intraitable [ɛ̃tʀɛtabl] *adj* inflexible, uncompromising

intransigeant, e [ɛ̃tʀɑ̃ziʒɑ̃, ɑ̃t] *adj* intransigent

intrépide [ɛ̃tʀepid] *adj* dauntless

intrigue [ɛ̃tʀig] *nf* (*scénario*) plot; **intriguer** *vt* to puzzle, intrigue

introduction [ɛ̃tʀɔdyksjɔ̃] *nf* introduction

introduire [ɛ̃tʀɔdɥiʀ] *vt* to introduce; (*visiteur*) to show in; (*aiguille, clef*): **~ qch dans** to insert *ou* introduce sth into; **s'introduire** *vr* (*techniques, usages*) to be introduced; **s'~ (dans)** to get in(to); (*dans un groupe*) to get o.s. accepted (into)

introuvable [ɛ̃tʀuvabl] *adj* which cannot be found; (*Comm*) unobtainable

intrus, e [ɛ̃tʀy, yz] *nm/f* intruder

intuition [ɛ̃tɥisjɔ̃] *nf* intuition

inusable [inyzabl] *adj* hard-wearing

inutile [inytil] *adj* useless; (*superflu*) unnecessary; **inutilement** *adv* unnecessarily; **inutilisable** *adj* unusable

invalide [ɛ̃valid] *adj* disabled ▷ *nm*: **~ de guerre** disabled ex-serviceman

invariable [ɛ̃vaʀjabl] *adj* invariable

invasion [ɛ̃vazjɔ̃] *nf* invasion

inventaire [ɛ̃vɑ̃tɛʀ] *nm* inventory; (*Comm: liste*) stocklist; (: *opération*) stocktaking *no pl*

inventer [ɛ̃vɑ̃te] *vt* to invent; (*subterfuge*) to devise, invent; (*histoire, excuse*) to make up, invent; **inventeur** *nm* inventor; **inventif, -ive** *adj* inventive; **invention** *nf* invention

inverse [ɛ̃vɛʀs] *adj* opposite ▷ *nm*: **l'~** the opposite; **dans l'ordre ~** in the reverse order; **en sens ~** in (*ou* from) the opposite direction; **dans le sens ~ des aiguilles d'une montre** anticlockwise; **tu t'es trompé, c'est l'~** you've got it wrong, it's the other way round; **inversement** *adv* conversely; **inverser** *vt* to invert, reverse; (*Élec*) to reverse

investir [ɛ̃vɛstiʀ] *vt* to invest; **~ qn de** (*d'une fonction, d'un pouvoir*) to vest *ou* invest sb with; **s'investir** *vr*: **s'~ dans** (*Psych*) to put a lot into; **investissement** *nm* investment

invisible [ɛ̃vizibl] *adj* invisible

invitation [ɛ̃vitasjɔ̃] *nf* invitation

invité, e [ɛ̃vite] *nm/f* guest

inviter [ɛ̃vite] *vt* to invite; **~ qn à faire qch** to invite sb to do sth

invivable [ɛ̃vivabl] *adj* unbearable

involontaire [ɛ̃vɔlɔ̃tɛʀ] *adj* (*mouvement*) involuntary; (*insulte*) unintentional; (*complice*) unwitting

invoquer [ɛ̃vɔke] *vt* (*Dieu, muse*) to call upon, invoke; (*prétexte*) to put forward (as an excuse); (*loi, texte*) to refer to

invraisemblable [ɛ̃vʀɛsɑ̃blabl] *adj* (*fait, nouvelle*) unlikely, improbable; (*insolence, habit*) incredible

iode [jɔd] *nm* iodine

irai *etc* [iʀe] *vb voir* **aller**

Irak [iʀak] *nm* Iraq; **irakien, ne** *adj* Iraqi ▷ *nm/f*: **Irakien, ne** Iraqi

Iran [iʀɑ̃] *nm* Iran; **iranien, ne** *adj* Iranian ▷ *nm/f*: **Iranien, ne** Iranian

irions *etc* [iʀjɔ̃] *vb voir* **aller**

iris [iʀis] *nm* iris

irlandais, e [iʀlɑ̃dɛ, ɛz] *adj* Irish ▷ *nm/f*: **I~, e** Irishman(-woman)

Irlande [iʀlɑ̃d] *nf* Ireland; **la République d'~** the Irish Republic; **la mer d'~** the Irish Sea; **Irlande du Nord** Northern Ireland

ironie [iʀɔni] *nf* irony; **ironique** *adj* ironical; **ironiser** *vi* to be ironical

irons etc [iʀ5] vb voir **aller**
irradier [iʀadje] vt to irradiate
irraisonné, e [iʀɛzɔne] adj irrational
irrationnel, le [iʀasjɔnɛl] adj irrational
irréalisable [iʀealizabl] adj unrealizable;
(projet) impracticable
irrécupérable [iʀekypeʀabl] adj beyond
repair; (personne) beyond redemption
irréel, le [iʀeɛl] adj unreal
irréfléchi, e [iʀefleʃi] adj thoughtless
irrégularité [iʀegylaʀite] nf irregularity; (de
travail, d'effort, de qualité) unevenness no pl
irrégulier, -ière [iʀegylje, jɛʀ] adj irregular;
(travail, effort, qualité) uneven; (élève, athlète)
erratic
irrémédiable [iʀemedjabl] adj irreparable
irremplaçable [iʀɑ̃plasabl] adj irreplaceable
irréparable [iʀepaʀabl] adj (objet) beyond
repair; (dommage etc) irreparable
irréprochable [iʀepʀɔʃabl] adj
irreproachable, beyond reproach; (tenue)
impeccable
irrésistible [iʀezistibl] adj irresistible; (besoin,
désir, preuve, logique) compelling; (amusant)
hilarious
irrésolu, e [iʀezɔly] adj (personne) irresolute;
(problème) unresolved
irrespectueux, -euse [iʀɛspɛktɥø, øz] adj
disrespectful
irresponsable [iʀɛspɔ̃sabl] adj irresponsible
irriguer [iʀige] vt to irrigate
irritable [iʀitabl] adj irritable
irriter [iʀite] vt to irritate
irruption [iʀypsjɔ̃] nf: **faire ~ (chez qn)** to
burst in (on sb)
Islam [islam] nm: **l'~** Islam; **islamique** adj
Islamic; **islamophobie** nf Islamophobia
Islande [islɑ̃d] nf Iceland
isolant, e [izɔlɑ̃, ɑ̃t] adj insulating;
(insonorisant) soundproofing
isolation [izɔlasjɔ̃] nf insulation; **~
acoustique** soundproofing
isolé, e [izɔle] adj isolated; (contre le froid)
insulated
isoler [izɔle] vt to isolate; (prisonnier) to put in
solitary confinement; (ville) to cut off, isolate;
(contre le froid) to insulate; **s'isoler** vi to isolate
o.s.
Israël [isʀaɛl] nm Israel; **israélien, ne** adj
Israeli ▷ nm/f: **Israélien, ne** Israeli; **israélite**
adj Jewish ▷ nm/f: **Israélite** Jew (Jewess)
issu, e [isy] adj: **~ de** (né de) descended
from; (résultant de) stemming from; **issue**
nf (ouverture, sortie) exit; (solution) way out,
solution; (dénouement) outcome; **à l'issue de**
at the conclusion ou close of; **voie sans issue**
dead end; **issue de secours** emergency exit
Italie [itali] nf Italy; **italien, ne** adj Italian
▷ nm/f: **Italien, ne** Italian ▷ nm (Ling) Italian

italique [italik] nm: **en ~** in italics
itinéraire [itineʀeʀ] nm itinerary, route;
itinéraire bis alternative route
IUT sigle m = **Institut universitaire de
technologie**
IVG sigle f (= interruption volontaire de grossesse)
abortion
ivoire [ivwaʀ] nm ivory
ivre [ivʀ] adj drunk; **~ de** (colère, bonheur) wild
with; **ivrogne** nm/f drunkard

J

j' [ʒ] *pron voir* **je**

jacinthe [ʒasɛ̃t] *nf* hyacinth

jadis [ʒadis] *adv* long ago

jaillir [ʒajiʀ] *vi* (*liquide*) to spurt out; (*cris, réponses*) to burst forth

jais [ʒɛ] *nm* jet; **(d'un noir) de ~** jet-black

jalousie [ʒaluzi] *nf* jealousy; (*store*) slatted blind

jaloux, -ouse [ʒalu, uz] *adj* jealous; **être ~ de** to be jealous of

jamaïquain, e [ʒamaikɛ̃, -ɛn] *adj* Jamaican ⊳ *nm/f*: **J~, e** Jamaican

Jamaïque [ʒamaik] *nf*: **la ~** Jamaica

jamais [ʒamɛ] *adv* never; (*sans négation*) ever; **ne ... ~** never; **je ne suis ~ allé en Espagne** I've never been to Spain; **si ~ vous passez dans la région, venez nous voir** if you happen to be/if you're ever in this area, come and see us; **à ~** for ever

jambe [ʒɑ̃b] *nf* leg

jambon [ʒɑ̃bɔ̃] *nm* ham

jante [ʒɑ̃t] *nf* (wheel) rim

janvier [ʒɑ̃vje] *nm* January

Japon [ʒapɔ̃] *nm* Japan; **japonais, e** *adj* Japanese ⊳ *nm/f*: **Japonais, e** Japanese ⊳ *nm* (*Ling*) Japanese

jardin [ʒaʀdɛ̃] *nm* garden; **jardin d'enfants** nursery school; **jardinage** *nm* gardening; **jardiner** *vi* to do some gardening; **jardinier, -ière** *nm/f* gardener; **jardinière** *nf* planter; (*de fenêtre*) window box; **jardinière de légumes** (*Culin*) mixed vegetables

jargon [ʒaʀgɔ̃] *nm* (*baragouin*) gibberish; (*langue professionnelle*) jargon

jarret [ʒaʀɛ] *nm* back of knee; (*Culin*) knuckle, shin

jauge [ʒoʒ] *nf* (*instrument*) gauge; **jauge (de niveau) d'huile** (*Auto*) dipstick

jaune [ʒon] *adj, nm* yellow ⊳ *adv* (*fam*): **rire ~** to laugh on the other side of one's face; **jaune d'œuf** (*egg*) yolk; **jaunir** *vi, vt* to turn yellow; **jaunisse** *nf* jaundice

Javel [ʒavɛl] *nf voir* **eau**

javelot [ʒavlo] *nm* javelin

je, j' [ʒə] *pron* I

jean [dʒin] *nm* jeans *pl*

Jésus-Christ [ʒezykʀi(st)] *n* Jesus Christ; **600 avant/après ~** *ou* **J.-C.** 600 B.C./A.D.

jet [ʒɛ] *nm* (*lancer: action*) throwing *no pl*; (*: résultat*) throw; (*jaillissement: d'eaux*) jet; (*: de sang*) spurt; **jet d'eau** spray

jetable [ʒ(ə)tabl] *adj* disposable

jetée [ʒ(ə)te] *nf* jetty; (*grande*) pier

jeter [ʒ(ə)te] *vt* (*gén*) to throw; (*se défaire de*) to throw away *ou* out; **~ qch à qn** to throw sth to sb; (*de façon agressive*) to throw sth at sb; **~ un coup d'œil (à)** to take a look (at); **~ un sort à qn** to cast a spell on sb; **se ~ sur qn** to rush at sb; **se ~ dans** (*suj: fleuve*) to flow into

jeton [ʒ(ə)tɔ̃] *nm* (*au jeu*) counter

jette *etc* [ʒɛt] *vb voir* **jeter**

jeu, x [ʒø] *nm* (*divertissement, Tech: d'une pièce*) play; (*Tennis: partie, Football etc: façon de jouer*) game; (*Théâtre etc*) acting; (*série d'objets, jouet*) set; (*Cartes*) hand; (*au casino*): **le ~** gambling; **remettre en ~** (*Football*) to throw in; **être en ~** (*fig*) to be at stake; **entrer/mettre en ~** (*fig*) to come/bring into play; **jeu de cartes** pack of cards; **jeu d'échecs** chess set; **jeu de hasard** game of chance; **jeu de mots** pun; **jeu de société** board game; **jeu télévisé** television quiz; **jeu vidéo** video game

jeudi [ʒødi] *nm* Thursday

jeun [ʒœ̃]: **à ~** *adv* on an empty stomach; **être à ~** to have eaten nothing; **rester à ~** not to eat anything

jeune [ʒœn] *adj* young; **jeunes** *nmpl*: **les ~s** young people; **jeune fille** girl; **jeune homme** young man; **jeunes gens** young people

jeûne [ʒøn] *nm* fast

jeunesse [ʒœnɛs] *nf* youth; (*aspect*) youthfulness

joaillier, -ière [ʒɔaje, -jɛʀ] *nm/f* jeweller

jogging [dʒɔgiŋ] *nm* jogging; (*survêtement*) tracksuit; **faire du ~** to go jogging

joie [ʒwa] *nf* joy

joindre [ʒwɛ̃dʀ] *vt* to join; (*à une lettre*): **~ qch à** to enclose sth with; (*contacter*) to contact, get in touch with; **se ~ à qn** to join sb; **se ~ à**

qch to join in sth

joint, e [ʒwɛ̃, ɛ̃t] adj: **pièce ~e** (de lettre) enclosure; (de mail) attachment ▷ nm joint; (ligne) join; **joint de culasse** cylinder head gasket

joli, e [ʒɔli] adj pretty, attractive; **une ~e somme/situation** a tidy sum/a nice little job; **c'est du ~!** (ironique) that's very nice!; **c'est bien ~, mais ...** that's all very well but ...

jonc [ʒɔ̃] nm (bul)rush

jonction [ʒɔ̃ksjɔ̃] nf junction

jongleur, -euse [ʒɔ̃glœr, øz] nm/f juggler

jonquille [ʒɔ̃kij] nf daffodil

Jordanie [ʒɔrdani] nf: **la ~** Jordan

joue [ʒu] nf cheek

jouer [ʒwe] vt to play; (somme d'argent, réputation) to stake, wager; (simuler: sentiment) to affect, feign ▷ vi to play; (Théâtre, Cinéma) to act; (au casino) to gamble; (bois, porte: se voiler) to warp; (clef, pièce: avoir du jeu) to be loose; **~ sur** (miser) to gamble on; **~ de** (Mus) to play; **~ à** (jeu, sport, roulette) to play; **~ un tour à qn** to play a trick on sb; **~ la comédie** to put on an act; **à toi/nous de ~** it's your/our go ou turn; **bien joué!** well done!; **on joue Hamlet au théâtre X** Hamlet is on at the X theatre

jouet [ʒwɛ] nm toy; **être le ~ de** (illusion etc) to be the victim of

joueur, -euse [ʒwœr, øz] nm/f player; **être beau/mauvais ~** to be a good/bad loser

jouir [ʒwir] vi (sexe: fam) to come ▷ vt: **~ de** to enjoy

jour [ʒur] nm day; (opposé à la nuit) day, daytime; (clarté) daylight; (fig: aspect) light; (ouverture) gap; **de ~** (crème, service) cpd; **travailler de ~** to work during the day; **voyager de ~** to travel by day; **au ~ le ~** from day to day; **de nos ~s** these days; **du ~ au lendemain** overnight; **il fait ~** it's daylight; **au grand ~** (fig) in the open; **mettre au ~** to disclose; **mettre à ~** to update; **donner le ~ à** to give birth to; **voir le ~** to be born; **le ~ J** D-day; **jour férié** public holiday; **jour ouvrable** working day

journal, -aux [ʒurnal, o] nm (news)paper; (spécialisé) journal; (intime) diary; **journal de bord** log; **journal parlé/télévisé** radio/ television news sg

journalier, -ière [ʒurnalje, jɛr] adj daily; (banal) everyday

journalisme [ʒurnalism] nm journalism; **journaliste** nm/f journalist

journée [ʒurne] nf day; **faire la ~ continue** to work over lunch

joyau, x [ʒwajo] nm gem, jewel

joyeux, -euse [ʒwajø, øz] adj joyful, merry; **~ Noël!** merry Christmas!; **~ anniversaire!** happy birthday!

jubiler [ʒybile] vi to be jubilant, exult

judas [ʒyda] nm (trou) spy-hole

judiciaire [ʒydisjɛr] adj judicial

judicieux, -euse [ʒydisjø, øz] adj judicious

judo [ʒydo] nm judo

juge [ʒyʒ] nm judge; **juge d'instruction** examining (BRIT) ou (US) magistrate; **juge de paix** justice of the peace

jugé [ʒyʒe] nm: **au ~** adv by guesswork

jugement [ʒyʒmɑ̃] nm judgment; (Jur: pénal) sentence; (: au civil) decision

juger [ʒyʒe] vt to judge; (estimer) to consider; **~ qn/qch satisfaisant** to consider sb/sth (to be) satisfactory; **~ bon de faire** to see fit to do

juif, -ive [ʒɥif, ʒɥiv] adj Jewish ▷ nm/f: **J~, ive** Jew (Jewess)

juillet [ʒɥijɛ] nm July

● **14 JUILLET**
●
● **Le 14 juillet** is a national holiday in France
● and commemorates the storming of the
● Bastille during the French Revolution.
● Throughout the country there are
● celebrations, which feature parades, music,
● dancing and firework displays. In Paris a
● military parade along the Champs-Élysées
● is attended by the President.

---

juin [ʒɥɛ̃] nm June

jumeau, -elle, x [ʒymo, ɛl] adj, nm/f twin

jumeler [ʒym(ə)le] vt to twin

jumelle [ʒymɛl] adj, nf voir **jumeau**; **jumelles** nfpl (appareil) binoculars

jument [ʒymɑ̃] nf mare

jungle [ʒœ̃gl] nf jungle

jupe [ʒyp] nf skirt

jupon [ʒypɔ̃] nm waist slip

juré, e [ʒyre] nm/f juror ▷ adj: **ennemi ~** sworn enemy

jurer [ʒyre] vt (obéissance etc) to swear, vow ▷ vi (dire des jurons) to swear, curse; (dissoner): **~ (avec)** to clash (with); **~ de faire/que** to swear to do/that; **~ de qch** (s'en porter garant) to swear to sth

juridique [ʒyridik] adj legal

juron [ʒyrɔ̃] nm curse, swearword

jury [ʒyri] nm jury; (Art, Sport) panel of judges; (Scol) board of examiners

jus [ʒy] nm juice; (de viande) gravy, (meat) juice; **jus de fruit** fruit juice

jusque [ʒysk]: **jusqu'à** prép (endroit) as far as, (up) to; (moment) until, till; (limite) up to; **~ sur/ dans** up to, onto/in; (y compris) even on/in; **jusqu'à ce que** until; **jusqu'à présent** ou **maintenant** so far; **jusqu'où?** how far?

justaucorps [ʒystokɔr] nm leotard

juste [ʒyst] adj (équitable) just, fair; (légitime) just; (exact) right; (pertinent) apt; (étroit) tight;

(*insuffisant*) on the short side ▷ *adv* rightly, correctly; (*chanter*) in tune; (*exactement, seulement*) just; **~ assez/au-dessus** just enough/above; **au ~** exactly; **le ~ milieu** the happy medium; **c'était ~** it was a close thing; **pouvoir tout ~ faire** to be only just able to do; **justement** *adv* justly; (*précisément*) just, precisely; **justesse** *nf* (*précision*) accuracy; (*d'une remarque*) aptness; (*d'une opinion*) soundness; **de justesse** only just

justice [ʒystis] *nf* (*équité*) fairness, justice; (*Admin*) justice; **rendre ~ à qn** to do sb justice

justificatif, -ive [ʒystifikatif, iv] *adj* (*document*) supporting; **pièce justificative** written proof

justifier [ʒystifje] *vt* to justify; **~ de** to prove

juteux, -euse [ʒytø, øz] *adj* juicy

juvénile [ʒyvenil] *adj* youthful

K [kɑ] *nm* (*Inform*) K

kaki [kaki] *adj inv* khaki

kangourou [kɑ̃guʁu] *nm* kangaroo

karaté [kaʁate] *nm* karate

kascher [kaʃɛʁ] *adj* kosher

kayak [kajak] *nm* canoe, kayak; **faire du ~** to go canoeing

képi [kepi] *nm* kepi

kermesse [kɛʁmɛs] *nf* fair; (*fête de charité*) bazaar, (charity) fête

kidnapper [kidnape] *vt* to kidnap

kilo [kilo] *nm* = **kilogramme**

kilo...: **kilogramme** *nm* kilogramme; **kilométrage** *nm* number of kilometres travelled, ≈ mileage; **kilomètre** *nm* kilometre; **kilométrique** *adj* (*distance*) in kilometres

kinésithérapeute [kineziteʁapøt] *nm/f* physiotherapist

kiosque [kjɔsk] *nm* kiosk, stall

kir [kiʁ] *nm* kir (*white wine with blackcurrant liqueur*)

kit [kit] *nm* kit; **~ piéton** *ou* **mains libres** hands-free kit; **en ~** in kit form

kiwi [kiwi] *nm* kiwi

klaxon [klaksɔn] *nm* horn; **klaxonner** *vi, vt* to hoot (*BRIT*), honk (*US*)

km *abr* = **kilomètre**

km/h *abr* (= *kilomètres/heure*) ≈ mph

K.-O. (*fam*) *adj inv* shattered, knackered

Kosovo [kɔsɔvo] *nm* Kosovo

Koweit, Kuweit [kɔwɛt] *nm*: **le ~** Kuwait
k-way® [kawɛ] *nm* (lightweight nylon)
cagoule
kyste [kist] *nm* cyst

l' [l] *art déf voir* **le**
la [la] *art déf voir* **le** ▷ *nm* (*Mus*) A; (*en chantant la gamme*) la
là [la] *adv* there; (*ici*) here; (*dans le temps*) then; **elle n'est pas là** she isn't here; **c'est là que** this is where; **là où** where; **de là** (*fig*) hence; **par là** (*fig*) by that; *voir aussi* **-ci**; **ce**; **celui**; **là-bas** *adv* there
laboratoire [labɔʀatwaʀ] *nm* laboratory; **laboratoire de langues** language laboratory
laborieux, -euse [labɔʀjø, jøz] *adj* (*tâche*) laborious
labourer *vt* to plough
labyrinthe [labiʀɛ̃t] *nm* labyrinth, maze
lac [lak] *nm* lake
lacet [lasɛ] *nm* (*de chaussure*) lace; (*de route*) sharp bend; (*piège*) snare
lâche [lɑʃ] *adj* (*poltron*) cowardly; (*desserré*) loose, slack ▷ *nm/f* coward
lâcher [lɑʃe] *vt* to let go of; (*ce qui tombe, abandonner*) to drop; (*oiseau, animal: libérer*) to release, set free; (*fig: mot, remarque*) to let slip, come out with ▷ *vi* (*freins*) to fail; **~ les amarres** (*Navig*) to cast off (the moorings); **~ prise** to let go
lacrymogène [lakʀimɔʒɛn] *adj*: **gaz ~** teargas
lacune [lakyn] *nf* gap
là-dedans [ladədɑ̃] *adv* inside (there), in it; (*fig*) in that

là-dessous[ladsu] adv underneath, under there; (fig) behind that

là-dessus[ladsy] adv on there; (fig: sur ces mots) at that point; (: à ce sujet) about that

lagune[lagyn] nf lagoon

là-haut[lao] adv up there

laid, e[lɛ, lɛd] adj ugly; **laideur** nf ugliness no pl

lainage[lenaʒ] nm (vêtement) woollen garment; (étoffe) woollen material

laine[lɛn] nf wool

laïque[laik] adj lay, civil; (Scol) state cpd ▷ nm/f layman(-woman)

laisse[lɛs] nf (de chien) lead, leash; **tenir en ~** to keep on a lead ou leash

laisser[lese] vt to leave ▷ vb aux: **~ qn faire** to let sb do; **se ~ aller** to let o.s. go; **laisse-toi faire** let me (ou him etc) do it; **laisser-aller** nm carelessness, slovenliness; **laissez-passer** nm inv pass

lait[lɛ] nm milk; **frère/sœur de ~** foster brother/sister; **lait concentré/condensé** condensed/evaporated milk; **lait écrémé/entier**skimmed/full-cream (BRIT) ou whole milk; **laitage** nm dairy product; **laiterie** nf dairy; **laitier, -ière** adj dairy cpd ▷ nm/f milkman (dairywoman)

laiton[lɛtɔ̃] nm brass

laitue[lety] nf lettuce

lambeau, x[lãbo] nm scrap; **en ~x** in tatters, tattered

lame[lam] nf blade; (vague) wave; (lamelle) strip; **lame de fond**ground swell no pl; **lame de rasoir**razor blade; **lamelle** nf thin strip ou blade

lamentable[lamãtabl] adj appalling

lamenter[lamãte] vb: **se ~ (sur)** to moan (over)

lampadaire[lãpadɛR] nm (de salon) standard lamp; (dans la rue) street lamp

lampe[lãp] nf lamp; (Tech) valve; **lampe à bronzer**sun lamp; **lampe à pétrole**oil lamp; **lampe de poche**torch (BRIT), flashlight (US); **lampe halogène**halogen lamp

lance[lãs] nf spear; **lance d'incendie**fire hose

lancée[lãse] nf: **être/continuer sur sa ~** to be under way/keep going

lancement[lãsmã] nm launching

lance-pierres[lãspjɛR] nm inv catapult

lancer[lãse] nm (Sport) throwing no pl, throw ▷ vt to throw; (émettre, projeter) to throw out, send out; (produit, fusée, bateau, artiste) to launch; (injure) to hurl, fling; **se lancer** vi (prendre de l'élan) to build up speed; (se précipiter): **se ~ sur** ou **contre** to rush at; **se ~ dans** (discussion) to launch into; (aventure) to embark on; **~ qch à qn** to throw sth to sb; (de façon agressive) to throw sth at sb; **~ un cri** ou **un appel** to shout ou call out; **lancer du poids** putting the shot

landau[lãdo] nm pram (BRIT), baby carriage (US)

lande[lãd] nf moor

langage[lãgaʒ] nm language

langouste[lãgust] nf crayfish inv; **langoustine** nf Dublin Bay prawn

langue[lãg] nf (Anat, Culin) tongue; (Ling) language; **tirer la ~ (à)** to stick out one's tongue (at); **de ~ française** French-speaking; **quelles ~s parlez-vous?** what languages do you speak?; **langue maternelle**native language, mother tongue; **langues vivantes** modern languages

langueur[lãgœR] nf languidness

languir[lãgiR] vi to languish; (conversation) to flag; **faire ~ qn** to keep sb waiting

lanière[lanjɛR] nf (de fouet) lash; (de sac, bretelle) strap

lanterne[lãtɛRn] nf (portable) lantern; (électrique) light, lamp; (de voiture) (side)light

laper[lape] vt to lap up

lapidaire[lapidɛR] adj (fig) terse

lapin[lapɛ̃] nm rabbit; (peau) rabbitskin; (fourrure) cony; **poser un ~ à qn** (fam) to stand sb up

Laponie[laponi] nf Lapland

laps[laps] nm: **~ de temps** space of time, time no pl

laque[lak] nf (vernis) lacquer; (pour cheveux) hair spray

laquelle[lakɛl] pron voir **lequel**

larcin[laRsɛ̃] nm theft

lard[laR] nm (bacon) (streaky) bacon; (graisse) fat

lardon[laRdɔ̃] nm: **~s** chopped bacon

large[laRʒ] adj wide, broad; (fig) generous ▷ adv: **calculer/voir ~** to allow extra/think big ▷ nm (largeur): **5 m de ~** 5 m wide ou in width; (mer): **le ~** the open sea; **au ~ de** off; **large d'esprit**broad-minded; **largement** adv widely; (de loin) greatly; (au moins) easily; (généreusement) generously; **c'est largement suffisant**that's ample; **largesse** nf generosity; **largesses** nfpl (dons) liberalities; **largeur** nf (qu'on mesure) width; (impression visuelle) wideness, width; (d'esprit) broadness

larguer[laRge] vt to drop; **~ les amarres** to cast off (the moorings)

larme[laRm] nf tear; (fam: goutte) drop; **en ~s** in tears; **larmoyer** vi (yeux) to water; (se plaindre) to whimper

larvé, e[laRve] adj (fig) latent

laryngite[laRɛ̃ʒit] nf laryngitis

las, lasse[lɑ, lɑs] adj weary

laser[lazɛR] nm: **(rayon) ~** laser (beam); **chaîne** ou **platine ~** laser disc (player); **disque ~** laser disc

lasse[lɑs] adj voir **las**

lasser[lɑse] vt to weary, tire; **se lasser de** vt

to grow weary ou tired of
latéral, e, -aux [lateʀal, o] *adj* side *cpd*,
lateral
latin, e [latɛ̃, in] *adj* Latin ▷ *nm/f*: **L~, e** Latin
▷ *nm* (*Ling*) Latin
latitude [latityd] *nf* latitude
lauréat, e [lɔʀea, at] *nm/f* winner
laurier [lɔʀje] *nm* (*Bot*) laurel; **feuille de ~**
(*Culin*) bay leaf
lavable [lavabl] *adj* washable
lavabo [lavabo] *nm* washbasin; **lavabos** *nmpl*
(*toilettes*) toilet *sg*
lavage [lavaʒ] *nm* washing *no pl*, wash;
lavage de cerveau brainwashing *no pl*
lavande [lavɑ̃d] *nf* lavender
lave [lav] *nf* lava *no pl*
lave-linge [lavlɛ̃ʒ] *nm inv* washing machine
laver [lave] *vt* to wash; (*tache*) to wash off;
se laver *vi* to have a wash, wash; **se ~ les
mains/dents** to wash one's hands/clean
one's teeth; **~ la vaisselle/le linge** to wash
the dishes/clothes; **~ qn de** (*accusation*) to
clear sb of; **laverie** *nf*: **laverie (automatique)**
launderette; **lavette** *nf* dish cloth; (*fam*) drip;
laveur, -euse *nm/f* cleaner; **lave-vaisselle**
nm inv dishwasher; **lavoir** *nm* wash house;
(*évier*) sink
laxatif, -ive [laksatif, iv] *adj*, *nm* laxative
layette [lɛjɛt] *nf* baby clothes

 MOT-CLÉ

le [lə], **la**, **l'** (*pl* **les**) *art déf* **1** the; **le livre/la
pomme/l'arbre** the book/the apple/the tree;
les étudiants the students
2 (*noms abstraits*): **le courage/l'amour/la
jeunesse** courage/love/youth
3 (*indiquant la possession*): **se casser la jambe**
etc to break one's leg *etc*; **levez la main** put
your hand up; **avoir les yeux gris/le nez
rouge** to have grey eyes/a red nose
4 (*temps*): **le matin/soir** in the morning/
evening; mornings/evenings; **le jeudi** *etc*
(*d'habitude*) on Thursdays *etc*; (*ce jeudi-là etc*) on
(the) Thursday
5 (*distribution, évaluation*) a, an; **10 euros le
mètre/kilo** 10 euros a ou per metre/kilo; **le
tiers/quart de** a third/quarter of
▷ *pron* **1** (*personne: mâle*) him; (*: femelle*) her;
(*: pluriel*) them; **je le/la/les vois**
I can see him/her/them
2 (*animal, chose: singulier*) it; (*: pluriel*) them;
je le (*ou* **la**) **vois** I can see it; **je les vois** I can
see them
3 (*remplaçant une phrase*): **je ne le savais pas**
I didn't know (about it); **il était riche et ne
l'est plus** he was once rich but no longer is

lécher [leʃe] *vt* to lick; (*laper: lait, eau*) to lick

ou lap up; **se ~ les doigts/lèvres** to lick one's
fingers/lips; **lèche-vitrines** *nm*: **faire du
lèche-vitrines** to go window-shopping
leçon [l(ə)sɔ̃] *nf* lesson; **faire la ~ à** (*fig*) to
give a lecture to; **leçons de conduite** driving
lessons; **leçons particulières** private lessons
ou tuition *sg* (BRIT)
lecteur, -trice [lɛktœʀ, tʀis] *nm/f* reader;
(*d'université*) foreign language assistant
▷ *nm* (*Tech*): **~ de cassettes/CD/DVD**
cassette/CD/DVD player; **lecteur de
disquette(s)** disk drive; **lecteur MP3** MP3
player
lecture [lɛktyʀ] *nf* reading

    Attention à ne pas traduire *lecture* par le
    mot anglais *lecture*.

ledit [lədi], **ladite** (*mpl* **lesdits**, *fpl* **lesdites**)
dét the aforesaid
légal, e, -aux [legal, o] *adj* legal; **légaliser** *vt*
to legalize; **légalité** *nf* law
légendaire [leʒɑ̃dɛʀ] *adj* legendary
légende [leʒɑ̃d] *nf* (*mythe*) legend; (*de carte,
plan*) key; (*de dessin*) caption
léger, -ère [leʒe, ɛʀ] *adj* light; (*bruit, retard*)
slight; (*personne: superficiel*) thoughtless;
(*: volage*) free and easy; **à la légère** (*parler,
agir*) rashly, thoughtlessly; **légèrement** *adv*
(*s'habiller, bouger*) lightly; (*un peu*) slightly;
manger légèrement to eat a light meal;
légèreté *nf* lightness; (*d'une remarque*)
flippancy
législatif, -ive [leʒislatif, iv] *adj* legislative;
législatives *nfpl* general election *sg*
légitime [leʒitim] *adj* (*Jur*) lawful, legitimate;
(*fig*) rightful, legitimate; **en état de ~ défense**
in self-defence
legs [lɛg] *nm* legacy
léguer [lege] *vt*: **~ qch à qn** (*Jur*) to bequeath
sth to sb
légume [legym] *nm* vegetable; **légumes
secs** pulses; **légumes verts** green vegetables,
greens
lendemain [lɑ̃dmɛ̃] *nm*: **le ~** the next ou
following day; **le ~ matin/soir** the next ou
following morning/evening; **le ~ de** the day
after
lent, e [lɑ̃, lɑ̃t] *adj* slow; **lentement** *adv*
slowly; **lenteur** *nf* slowness *no pl*
lentille [lɑ̃tij] *nf* (*Optique*) lens *sg*; (*Culin*) lentil;
lentilles de contact contact lenses
léopard [leɔpaʀ] *nm* leopard
lèpre [lɛpʀ] *nf* leprosy

 MOT-CLÉ

lequel, laquelle [ləkɛl, lakɛl] (*mpl* **lesquels**,
fpl **lesquelles**) (*à + lequel =* **auquel**, *de + lequel =*
duquel *etc*) *pron* **1** (*interrogatif*) which, which
one; **lequel des deux?** which one?

2 (relatif: personne: sujet) who; (: objet, après préposition) whom; (: chose) which ▷ adj: **auquel cas** in which case

les [le] dét voir **le**
lesbienne [lɛsbjɛn] nf lesbian
léser [leze] vt to wrong
lésiner [lezine] vi: **ne pas ~ sur les moyens** (pour mariage etc) to push the boat out
lésion [lezjɔ̃] nf lesion, damage no pl
lessive [lesiv] nf (poudre) washing powder; (linge) washing no pl, wash; **lessiver** vt to wash; (fam: fatiguer) to tire out, exhaust
lest [lɛst] nm ballast
leste [lɛst] adj sprightly, nimble
lettre [lɛtR] nf letter; **lettres** nfpl (littérature) literature sg; (Scol) arts (subjects); **à la ~** literally; **en toutes ~s** in full; **lettre piégée** letter bomb
leucémie [løsemi] nf leukaemia

 MOT-CLÉ

leur [lœR] adj possessif their; **leur maison** their house; **leurs amis** their friends
▷ pron **1** (objet indirect) (to) them; **je leur ai dit la vérité** I told them the truth; **je le leur ai donné** I gave it to them, I gave them it
2 (possessif): **le(la) leur, les leurs** theirs

levain [ləvɛ̃] nm leaven
levé, e [ləve] adj: **être ~** to be up; **levée** nf (Postes) collection
lever [l(ə)ve] vt (vitre, bras etc) to raise; (soulever de terre, supprimer: interdiction, siège) to lift; (impôts, armée) to levy ▷ vi to rise ▷ nm: **au ~** on getting up; **se lever** vi to get up; (soleil) to rise; (jour) to break; (brouillard) to lift; **ça va se ~** (temps) it's going to clear up; **lever de soleil** sunrise; **lever du jour** daybreak
levier [ləvje] nm lever
lèvre [lɛvR] nf lip
lévrier [levRije] nm greyhound
levure [l(ə)vyR] nf yeast; **levure chimique** baking powder
lexique [lɛksik] nm vocabulary; (glossaire) lexicon
lézard [lezaR] nm lizard
lézarde [lezaRd] nf crack
liaison [ljezɔ̃] nf (rapport) connection; (transport) link; (amoureuse) affair; (Phonétique) liaison; **entrer/être en ~ avec** to get/be in contact with
liane [ljan] nf creeper
liasse [ljas] nf wad, bundle
Liban [libã] nm: **le ~** (the) Lebanon
libeller [libele] vt (chèque, mandat): **~ (au nom de)** to make out (to); (lettre) to word
libellule [libelyl] nf dragonfly

libéral, e, -aux [liberal, o] adj, nm/f liberal; **profession ~e** (liberal) profession
libérer [libere] vt (délivrer) to free, liberate; (relâcher: prisonnier) to discharge, release; (: d'inhibitions) to liberate; (gaz) to release; **se libérer** vi (de rendez-vous) to get out of previous engagements
liberté [libɛRte] nf freedom; (loisir) free time; **libertés** nfpl (privautés) liberties; **mettre/être en ~** to set/be free; **en ~ provisoire/surveillée/conditionnelle** on bail/probation/parole
libraire [libRɛR] nm/f bookseller
librairie [libRɛRi] nf bookshop

> Attention à ne pas traduire **librairie** par **library**.

libre [libR] adj free; (route, voie) clear; (place, salle) free; (ligne) not engaged; (Scol) non-state; **~ de qch/de faire** free from sth/to do; **la place est ~?** is this seat free?; **libre arbitre** free will; **libre-échange** nm free trade; **libre-service** nm self-service store
Libye [libi] nf: **la ~** Libya
licence [lisãs] nf (permis) permit; (diplôme) degree; (liberté) liberty; **licencié, e** nm/f (Scol): **licencié ès lettres/en droit** ≈ Bachelor of Arts/Law
licenciement [lisãsimã] nm redundancy
licencier [lisãsje] vt (débaucher) to make redundant, lay off; (renvoyer) to dismiss
licite [lisit] adj lawful
lie [li] nf dregs pl, sediment
lié, e [lje] adj: **très ~ avec** very friendly with ou close to
Liechtenstein [liʃtɛnʃtain] nm: **le ~** Liechtenstein
liège [ljɛʒ] nm cork
lien [ljɛ̃] nm (corde, fig: affectif) bond; (rapport) link, connection; **lien de parenté** family tie; **lien hypertexte** hyperlink
lier [lje] vt (attacher) to tie up; (joindre) to link up; (fig: unir, engager) to bind; **~ conversation (avec)** to strike up a conversation (with); **~ connaissance avec** to get to know
lierre [ljɛR] nm ivy
lieu, x [ljø] nm place; **lieux** nmpl (locaux) premises; (endroit: d'un accident etc) scene sg; **en ~ sûr** in a safe place; **en premier ~** in the first place; **en dernier ~** lastly; **avoir ~** to take place; **tenir ~ de** to serve as; **donner ~ à** to give rise to; **au ~ de** instead of; **arriver/être sur les ~x** to arrive at/be on the scene; **lieu commun** cliché; **lieu-dit** (pl **lieux-dits**) nm locality
lieutenant [ljøt(ə)nã] nm lieutenant
lièvre [ljɛvR] nm hare
ligament [ligamã] nm ligament
ligne [liɲ] nf (gén) line; (Transports: liaison) service; (: trajet) route; (silhouette) figure;

garder la ~ to keep one's figure; **entrer en ~ de compte** to come into it; **en ~** (*Inform*) online; **~ fixe** (*Tél*) land line (phone)

lignée [liɲe] *nf* line, lineage

ligoter [ligɔte] *vt* to tie up

ligue [lig] *nf* league

lilas [lila] *nm* lilac

limace [limas] *nf* slug

limande [limɑ̃d] *nf* dab

lime [lim] *nf* file; **lime à ongles** nail file; **limer** *vt* to file

limitation [limitasjɔ̃] *nf*: **limitation de vitesse** speed limit

limite [limit] *nf* (*de terrain*) boundary; (*partie ou point extrême*) limit; **à la ~** (*au pire*) if the worst comes (*ou* came) to the worst; **vitesse/charge ~** maximum speed/load; **cas ~** borderline case; **date ~** deadline; **date ~ de vente/consommation** sell-by/best-before date; **limiter** *vt* (*restreindre*) to limit, restrict; (*délimiter*) to border; **limitrophe** *adj* border *cpd*

limoger [limɔʒe] *vt* to dismiss

limon [limɔ̃] *nm* silt

limonade [limɔnad] *nf* lemonade

lin [lɛ̃] *nm* (*tissu*) linen

linceul [lɛ̃sœl] *nm* shroud

linge [lɛ̃ʒ] *nm* (*serviettes etc*) linen; (*lessive*) washing; (*aussi*: **~ de corps**) underwear; **lingerie** *nf* lingerie, underwear

lingot [lɛ̃go] *nm* ingot

linguistique [lɛ̃gɥistik] *adj* linguistic ▷ *nf* linguistics *sg*

lion, ne [ljɔ̃, ljɔn] *nm/f* lion (lioness); (*signe*): **le L~** Leo; **lionceau, x** *nm* lion cub

liqueur [likœr] *nf* liqueur

liquidation [likidasjɔ̃] *nf* (*vente*) sale

liquide [likid] *adj* liquid ▷ *nm* liquid; (*Comm*): **en ~** in ready money *ou* cash; **je n'ai pas de ~** I haven't got any cash; **liquider** *vt* to liquidate; (*Comm*: *articles*) to clear, sell off

lire [lir] *nf* (*monnaie*) lira ▷ *vt*, *vi* to read

lis [lis] *nm* = **lys**

Lisbonne [lizbɔn] *n* Lisbon

lisible [lizibl] *adj* legible

lisière [lizjɛʀ] *nf* (*de forêt*) edge

lisons [lizɔ̃] *vb voir* **lire**

lisse [lis] *adj* smooth

liste [list] *nf* list; **faire la ~ de** to list; **liste de mariage** wedding (present) list; **liste électorale** electoral roll; **listing** *nm* (*Inform*) printout

lit [li] *nm* bed; **petit ~, ~ à une place** single bed; **grand ~, ~ à deux places** double bed; **faire son ~** to make one's bed; **aller/se mettre au ~** to go to/get into bed; **lit de camp** campbed; **lit d'enfant** cot (*BRIT*), crib (*US*)

literie [litri] *nf* bedding, bedclothes *pl*

litige [litiʒ] *nm* dispute

litre [litr] *nm* litre

littéraire [literɛr] *adj* literary ▷ *nm/f* arts student; **elle est très ~** she's very literary

littéral, e, -aux [literal, o] *adj* literal

littérature [literatyr] *nf* literature

littoral, -aux [litɔral, o] *nm* coast

livide [livid] *adj* livid, pallid

livraison [livrɛzɔ̃] *nf* delivery

livre [livr] *nm* book ▷ *nf* (*monnaie*) pound; (*poids*) half a kilo, ≈ pound; **livre de poche** paperback

livré, e [livre] *adj*: **~ à soi-même** left to o.s. *ou* one's own devices

livrer [livre] *vt* (*Comm*) to deliver; (*otage, coupable*) to hand over; (*secret, information*) to give away; **se livrer à** (*se confier*) to confide in; (*se rendre, s'abandonner*) to give o.s. up to; (*faire: pratiques, actes*) to indulge in; (*enquête*) to carry out

livret [livrɛ] *nm* booklet; (*d'opéra*) libretto; **livret de caisse d'épargne** (savings) bankbook; **livret de famille** (official) family record book; **livret scolaire** (school) report book

livreur, -euse [livrœr, øz] *nm/f* delivery boy *ou* man/girl *ou* woman

local, e, -aux [lɔkal] *adj* local ▷ *nm* (*salle*) premises *pl*; *voir aussi* **locaux**; **localité** *nf* locality

locataire [lɔkatɛr] *nm/f* tenant; (*de chambre*) lodger

location [lɔkasjɔ̃] *nf* (*par le locataire, le loueur*) renting; (*par le propriétaire*) renting out, letting; (*Théâtre*) booking office; **"~ de voitures"** "car rental"; **habiter en ~** to live in rented accommodation; **prendre une ~ (pour les vacances)** to rent a house *etc* (for the holidays)

> Attention à ne pas traduire *location* par le mot anglais *location*.

locomotive [lɔkɔmɔtiv] *nf* locomotive, engine

locution [lɔkysjɔ̃] *nf* phrase

loge [lɔʒ] *nf* (*Théâtre: d'artiste*) dressing room; (*: de spectateurs*) box; (*de concierge, franc-maçon*) lodge

logement [lɔʒmɑ̃] *nm* accommodation *no pl* (*BRIT*), accommodations *pl* (*US*); (*appartement*) flat (*BRIT*), apartment (*US*); (*Pol, Admin*): **le ~** housing *no pl*

loger [lɔʒe] *vt* to accommodate ▷ *vi* to live; **être logé, nourri** to have board and lodging; **se loger** *vr*: **trouver à se ~** to find somewhere to live; **se ~ dans** (*suj: balle, flèche*) to lodge itself in; **logeur, -euse** *nm/f* landlord (-lady)

logiciel [lɔʒisjɛl] *nm* software

logique [lɔʒik] *adj* logical ▷ *nf* logic

logo [lɔgo] *nm* logo

loi [lwa] *nf* law; **faire la ~** to lay down the law

loin [lwɛ̃] *adv* far; (*dans le temps: futur*) a long way off; (: *passé*) a long time ago; **plus ~** further; **~ de** far from; **c'est ~ d'ici?** is it far from here?; **au ~** far off; **de ~** from a distance; (*fig: de beaucoup*) by far

lointain, e [lwɛ̃tɛ̃, ɛn] *adj* faraway, distant; (*dans le futur, passé*) distant; (*cause, parent*) remote, distant ▷ *nm*: **dans le ~** in the distance

loir [lwaR] *nm* dormouse

Loire [lwaR] *nf*: **la ~** the (River) Loire

loisir [lwaziR] *nm*: **heures de ~** spare time; **loisirs** *nmpl* (*temps libre*) leisure *sg*; (*activités*) leisure activities; **avoir le ~ de faire** to have the time *ou* opportunity to do; **à ~** at leisure

londonien, ne [lɔ̃dɔnjɛ̃, jɛn] *adj* London *cpd*, of London ▷ *nm/f*: **L~, ne** Londoner

Londres [lɔ̃dR] *n* London

long, longue [lɔ̃, lɔ̃g] *adj* long ▷ *adv*: **en savoir ~** to know a great deal ▷ *nm*: **de 3 m de ~** 3 m long, 3 m in length; **ne pas faire ~ feu** not to last long; **(tout) le ~ de** (all) along; **tout au ~ de** (*année, vie*) throughout; **de ~ en large** (*marcher*) to and fro, up and down; *voir aussi* **longue**

longer [lɔ̃ʒe] *vt* to go (*ou* walk *ou* drive) along(side); (*suj: mur, route*) to border

longiligne [lɔ̃ʒiliɲ] *adj* long-limbed

longitude [lɔ̃ʒityd] *nf* longitude

longtemps [lɔ̃tɑ̃] *adv* (for) a long time, (for) long; **avant ~** before long; **pour** *ou* **pendant ~** for a long time; **mettre ~ à faire** to take a long time to do; **il en a pour ~?** will he be long?

longue [lɔ̃g] *adj voir* **long** ▷ *nf*: **à la ~** in the end; **longuement** *adv* (*longtemps*) for a long time; (*en détail*) at length

longueur [lɔ̃gœR] *nf* length; **longueurs** *nfpl* (*fig: d'un film etc*) tedious parts; **en ~** lengthwise; **tirer en ~** to drag on; **à ~ de journée** all day long

loquet [lɔkɛ] *nm* latch

lorgner [lɔRɲe] *vt* to eye; (*fig*) to have one's eye on

lors [lɔR] *prép*: **~ de** at the time of; during

lorsque [lɔRsk] *conj* when, as

losange [lɔzɑ̃ʒ] *nm* diamond

lot [lo] *nm* (*part*) share; (*de loterie*) prize; (*fig: destin*) fate, lot; (*Comm, Inform*) batch; **le gros ~** the jackpot

loterie [lɔtRi] *nf* lottery

lotion [losjɔ̃] *nf* lotion; **lotion après rasage** aftershave (lotion)

lotissement [lɔtismɑ̃] *nm* housing development; (*parcelle*) plot, lot

loto [lɔto] *nm* lotto

lotte [lɔt] *nf* monkfish

louanges [lwɑ̃ʒ] *nfpl* praise *sg*

loubard [lubaR] (*fam*) *nm* lout

louche [luʃ] *adj* shady, fishy, dubious ▷ *nf* ladle; **loucher** *vi* to squint

louer [lwe] *vt* (*maison: suj: propriétaire*) to let, rent (out); (: *locataire*) to rent; (*voiture etc: entreprise*) to hire out (BRIT), rent (out); (: *locataire*) to hire, rent; (*réserver*) to book; (*faire l'éloge de*) to praise; **"à ~"** "to let" (BRIT), "for rent" (US); **je voudrais ~ une voiture** I'd like to hire (BRIT) *ou* rent (US) a car

loup [lu] *nm* wolf; **jeune ~** young go-getter

loupe [lup] *nf* magnifying glass; **à la ~** in minute detail

louper [lupe] (*fam*) *vt* (*manquer*) to miss; (*examen*) to flunk

lourd, e [luR, luRd] *adj, adv* heavy; **c'est trop ~** it's too heavy; **~ de** (*conséquences, menaces*) charged with; **il fait ~** the weather's close, it's sultry; **lourdaud, e** (*péj*) *adj* clumsy; **lourdement** *adv* heavily

loutre [lutR] *nf* otter

louveteau, x [luv(ə)to] *nm* wolf-cub; (*scout*) cub (scout)

louvoyer [luvwaje] *vi* (*fig*) to hedge, evade the issue

loyal, e, -aux [lwajal, o] *adj* (*fidèle*) loyal, faithful; (*fair-play*) fair; **loyauté** *nf* loyalty, faithfulness; fairness

loyer [lwaje] *nm* rent

lu, e [ly] *pp de* **lire**

lubie [lybi] *nf* whim, craze

lubrifiant [lybRifjɑ̃] *nm* lubricant

lubrifier [lybRifje] *vt* to lubricate

lubrique [lybRik] *adj* lecherous

lucarne [lykaRn] *nf* skylight

lucide [lysid] *adj* lucid; (*accidenté*) conscious

lucratif, -ive [lykRatif, iv] *adj* lucrative, profitable; **à but non ~** non profit-making

lueur [lɥœR] *nf* (*pâle*) (faint) light; (*chatoyante*) glimmer *no pl*; (*fig*) glimmer; gleam

luge [lyʒ] *nf* sledge (BRIT), sled (US)

lugubre [lygybR] *adj* gloomy, dismal

 MOT-CLÉ

lui [lɥi] *pron* **1** (*objet indirect: mâle*) (to) him; (: *femelle*) (to) her; (: *chose, animal*) (to) it; **je lui ai parlé** I have spoken to him (*ou* to her); **il lui a offert un cadeau** he gave him (*ou* her) a present

2 (*après préposition, comparatif: personne*) him; (: *chose, animal*) it; **elle est contente de lui** she is pleased with him; **je la connais mieux que lui** I know her better than he does; I know her better than him; **ce livre est à lui** this book is his, this is his book; **c'est à lui de jouer** it's his turn *ou* go

3 (*sujet, forme emphatique*) he; **lui, il est à Paris** HE is in Paris; **c'est lui qui l'a fait** HE did it

4 (objet, forme emphatique) him; **c'est lui que j'attends** I'm waiting for HIM
5: **lui-même** himself; itself

luire [lɥiʀ] vi to shine; (en rougeoyant) to glow
lumière [lymjɛʀ] nf light; **mettre en ~** (fig) to highlight; **lumière du jour** daylight
luminaire [lyminɛʀ] nm lamp, light
lumineux, -euse [lyminø, øz] adj luminous; (éclairé) illuminated; (ciel, couleur) bright; (rayon) of light, light cpd; (fig: regard) radiant
lunatique [lynatik] adj whimsical, temperamental
lundi [lœ̃di] nm Monday; **on est ~** it's Monday; **le(s) ~(s)** on Mondays; **"à ~"** "see you on Monday"; **lundi de Pâques** Easter Monday
lune [lyn] nf moon; **lune de miel** honeymoon
lunette [lynɛt] nf: **~s** nfpl glasses, spectacles; (protectrices) goggles; **lunette arrière** (Auto) rear window; **lunettes de soleil** sunglasses; **lunettes noires** dark glasses
lustre [lystʀ] nm (de plafond) chandelier; (fig: éclat) lustre; **lustrer** vt to shine
luth [lyt] nm lute
lutin [lytɛ̃] nm imp, goblin
lutte [lyt] nf (conflit) struggle; (sport) wrestling; **lutter** vi to fight, struggle
luxe [lyks] nm luxury; **de ~** luxury cpd
Luxembourg [lyksɑ̃buʀ] nm: **le ~** Luxembourg
luxer [lykse] vt: **se ~ l'épaule** to dislocate one's shoulder
luxueux, -euse [lyksɥø, øz] adj luxurious
lycée [lise] nm ≈ secondary school; **lycéen, ne** nm/f secondary school pupil
Lyon [ljɔ̃] n Lyons
lyophilisé, e [ljɔfilize] adj (café) freeze-dried
lyrique [liʀik] adj lyrical; (Opéra) lyric; **artiste ~** opera singer
lys [lis] nm lily

M abr = **Monsieur**
m' [m] pron voir **me**
ma [ma] adj voir **mon**
macaron [makaʀɔ̃] nm (gâteau) macaroon; (insigne) (round) badge
macaronis [makaʀɔni] nmpl macaroni sg; **~ au fromage** ou **en gratin** macaroni cheese (BRIT), macaroni and cheese (US)
macédoine [masedwan] nf: **~ de fruits** fruit salad; **~ de légumes** mixed vegetables; **la M~** Macedonia
macérer [maseʀe] vi, vt to macerate; (dans du vinaigre) to pickle
mâcher [maʃe] vt to chew; **ne pas ~ ses mots** not to mince one's words
machin [maʃɛ̃] (fam) nm thing(umajig); (personne): **M~(e)** nm(f) what's-his(ou her)-name
machinal, e, -aux [maʃinal, o] adj mechanical, automatic
machination [maʃinasjɔ̃] nf frame-up
machine [maʃin] nf machine; (locomotive) engine; **machine à laver/coudre** washing/sewing machine; **machine à sous** fruit machine
mâchoire [maʃwaʀ] nf jaw
mâchonner [maʃɔne] vt to chew (at)
maçon [masɔ̃] nm builder; (poseur de briques) bricklayer; **maçonnerie** nf (murs) brickwork; (pierres) masonry, stonework

Madagascar[madagaskaʀ] nf
Madagascar

Madame[madam] (pl **Mesdames**) nf:
~ **Dupont** Mrs Dupont; **occupez-vous
de ~/Monsieur/Mademoiselle** please
serve this lady/gentleman/(young) lady;
bonjour ~/Monsieur/Mademoiselle
good morning/(ton déférent) good morning
Madam/Sir/Madam; (le nom est connu) good
morning Mrs/Mr/Miss X; **~/Monsieur/
Mademoiselle!** (pour appeler) Madam/Sir/
Miss!; **~/Monsieur/Mademoiselle** (sur lettre)
Dear Madam/Sir/Madam; **chère ~/cher
Monsieur/chère Mademoiselle** Dear Mrs/
Mr/Miss X; **Mesdames** Ladies; **mesdames,
mesdemoiselles, messieurs** ladies and
gentlemen

madeleine[madlɛn] nf madeleine, small
sponge cake

Mademoiselle[madmwazɛl] (pl
Mesdemoiselles) nf Miss; voir aussi
Madame

madère[madɛʀ] nm Madeira (wine)
Madrid[madʀid] n Madrid
magasin[magazɛ̃] nm (boutique) shop;
(entrepôt) warehouse; **en ~** (Comm) in
stock

magazine[magazin] nm magazine
Maghreb[magʀɛb] nm: **le ~** North Africa;
maghrébin, e adj North African ▷ nm/f:
Maghrébin, e North African

magicien, ne[maʒisjɛ̃, jɛn] nm/f
magician

magie[maʒi] nf magic; **magique** adj magic;
(enchanteur) magical

magistral, e, -aux[maʒistʀal, o] adj (œuvre,
adresse) masterly; (ton) authoritative; **cours
~** lecture

magistrat[maʒistʀa] nm magistrate
magnétique[maɲetik] adj magnetic
magnétophone[maɲetɔfɔn] nm tape
recorder; **magnétophone à cassettes**
cassette recorder

magnétoscope[maɲetɔskɔp] nm video-
tape recorder

magnifique[maɲifik] adj
magnificent

magret[magʀɛ] nm: **~ de canard** duck
steaklet

mai[mɛ] nm May

maigre[mɛgʀ] adj (very) thin, skinny; (viande)
lean; (fromage) low-fat; (végétation) thin,
sparse; (fig) poor, meagre, skimpy; **jours ~s**
days of abstinence, fish days; **maigreur** nf
thinness; **maigrir** vi to get thinner, lose
weight; **maigrir de 2 kilos** to lose 2 kilos

mail[mɛl] nm e-mail
maille[maj] nf stitch; **maille à l'endroit/
l'envers** plain/purl stitch

maillet[majɛ] nm mallet
maillon[majɔ̃] nm link
maillot[majo] nm (aussi: ~ **de corps**) vest; (de
sportif) jersey; **maillot de bain** swimming ou
bathing (BRIT) costume, swimsuit; (d'homme)
(swimming ou bathing (BRIT)) trunks pl

main[mɛ̃] nf hand; **à la ~** (tenir, avoir) in one's
hand; (faire, tricoter etc) by hand; **se donner la
~** to hold hands; **donner** ou **tendre la ~ à qn**
to hold out one's hand to sb; **se serrer la ~** to
shake hands; **serrer la ~ à qn** to shake hands
with sb; **sous la ~** ou at hand; **haut les ~s!**
hands up!; **attaque à ~ armée** armed attack;
à remettre en ~s propres to be delivered
personally; **mettre la dernière ~ à** to put the
finishing touches to; **se faire/perdre la ~** to
get one's hand in/lose one's touch; **avoir qch
bien en ~** to have (got) the hang of sth; **main-
d'œuvre** nf manpower, labour; **mainmise** nf
(fig): **mainmise sur** complete hold on; **mains
libres** adj inv (téléphone, kit) hands-free

maint, e[mɛ̃, mɛ̃t] adj many a; **~s** many; **à
~es reprises** time and (time) again

maintenant[mɛ̃t(ə)nɑ̃] adv now;
(actuellement) nowadays

maintenir[mɛ̃t(ə)niʀ] vt (retenir, soutenir)
to support; (contenir: foule etc) to hold back;
(conserver, affirmer) to maintain; **se maintenir**
vi (prix) to keep steady; (amélioration) to persist

maintien[mɛ̃tjɛ̃] nm (sauvegarde)
maintenance; (attitude) bearing

maire[mɛʀ] nm mayor; **mairie** nf (bâtiment)
town hall; (administration) town council

mais[mɛ] conj but; **~ non!** of course not!; **~**

enfin but after all; (*indignation*) look here!
maïs [mais] *nm* maize (BRIT), corn (US)
maison [mɛzɔ̃] *nf* house; (*chez-soi*) home;
(*Comm*) firm ▷ *adj inv* (*Culin*) home-made;
(*fig*) in-house, own; **à la ~** at home; (*direction*)
home; **maison de repos** convalescent home;
maison de retraite old people's home;
maison close *ou* **de passe** brothel; **maison
de santé** mental home; **maison des jeunes**
≈ youth club; **maison mère** parent company
maître, -esse [mɛtʁ, mɛtʁɛs] *nm/f*
master (mistress); (*Scol*) teacher,
schoolmaster(-mistress) ▷ *nm* (*peintre etc*)
master; (*titre*): **M~** Maître, *term of address gen
for a barrister* ▷ *adj* (*principal, essentiel*) main;
être ~ de (*soi, situation*) to be in control of; **une
~sse femme** a managing woman; **maître
chanteur** blackmailer; **maître d'école**
schoolmaster; **maître d'hôtel** (*domestique*)
butler; (*d'hôtel*) head waiter; **maître
nageur** lifeguard; **maîtresse** *nf* (*amante*)
mistress; **maîtresse (d'école)** teacher,
(school)mistress; **maîtresse de maison**
hostess; (*ménagère*) housewife
maîtrise [mɛtʁiz] *nf* (*aussi*: **~ de soi**)
self-control, self-possession; (*habileté*) skill,
mastery; (*suprématie*) command;
(*diplôme*) ≈ master's degree; **maîtriser** *vt*
(*cheval, incendie*) to (bring under) control;
(*sujet*) to master; (*émotion*) to control, master;
se maîtriser to control o.s.
majestueux, -euse [maʒɛstɥø, øz] *adj*
majestic
majeur, e [maʒœʁ] *adj* (*important*) major; (*Jur*)
of age ▷ *nm* (*doigt*) middle finger; **en ~e partie**
for the most part; **la ~e partie de** most of
majorer [maʒɔʁe] *vt* to increase
majoritaire [maʒɔʁitɛʁ] *adj* majority *cpd*
majorité [maʒɔʁite] *nf* (*gén*) majority; (*parti*)
party in power; **en ~** mainly; **avoir la ~** to have
the majority
majuscule [maʒyskyl] *adj, nf*: **(lettre) ~**
capital (letter)
mal [mal, mo] (*pl* **maux**) *nm* (*opposé au bien*)
evil; (*tort, dommage*) harm; (*douleur physique*)
pain, ache; (*maladie*) illness, sickness *no
pl* ▷ *adv* badly ▷ *adj* bad, wrong; **être ~ à
l'aise** to be uncomfortable; **être ~ avec qn**
to be on bad terms with sb; **il a ~ compris**
he misunderstood; **se sentir** *ou* **se trouver ~**
to feel ill *ou* unwell; **dire/penser du ~ de** to
speak/think ill of sb; **ne voir aucun ~ à** to see
no harm in, see nothing wrong in; **faire ~ à
qn** to hurt sb; **se faire ~** to hurt o.s.; **avoir
du ~ à faire qch** to have trouble doing sth; **se
donner du ~ pour faire qch** to go to a lot of
trouble to do sth; **ça fait ~** it hurts; **j'ai ~ au
dos** my back hurts; **avoir ~ à la tête/à la
gorge/aux dents** to have a headache/a sore

throat/toothache; **avoir le ~ du pays** to be
homesick; *voir aussi* **cœur**; **maux**; **mal de mer**
seasickness; **mal en point** in a bad state
malade [malad] *adj* ill, sick; (*poitrine, jambe*)
bad; (*plante*) diseased ▷ *nm/f* invalid, sick
person; (*à l'hôpital etc*) patient; **tomber ~** to
fall ill; **être ~ du cœur** to have heart trouble
ou a bad heart; **malade mental** mentally ill
person; **maladie** *nf* (*spécifique*) disease, illness;
(*mauvaise santé*) illness, sickness; **maladif, -ive**
adj sickly; (*curiosité, besoin*) pathological
maladresse [maladʁɛs] *nf* clumsiness *no pl*;
(*gaffe*) blunder
maladroit, e [maladʁwa, wat] *adj* clumsy
malaise [malɛz] *nm* (*Méd*) feeling of faintness;
(*fig*) uneasiness, malaise; **avoir un ~** to feel
faint
Malaisie [malɛzi] *nf*: **la ~** Malaysia
malaria [malaʁja] *nf* malaria
malaxer [malakse] *vt* (*pétrir*) to knead;
(*mélanger*) to mix
malbouffe [malbuf] (*fam*) *nf*: **la ~** junk food
malchance [malʃɑ̃s] *nf* misfortune, ill luck *no
pl*; **par ~** unfortunately; **malchanceux, -euse**
adj unlucky
mâle [mal] *adj* (*aussi Élec, Tech*) male; (*viril: voix,
traits*) manly ▷ *nm* male
malédiction [malediksjɔ̃] *nf* curse
mal...: **malentendant, e** *nm/f*: **les
malentendants** the hard of hearing;
malentendu *nm* misunderstanding; **il
y a eu un malentendu** there's been a
misunderstanding; **malfaçon** *nf* fault;
malfaisant, e *adj* evil, harmful; **malfaiteur**
nm lawbreaker, criminal; (*voleur*) burglar, thief;
malfamé, e *adj* disreputable
malgache [malgaʃ] *adj* Madagascan,
Malagasy ▷ *nm/f*: **M~** Madagascan, Malagasy
▷ *nm* (*Ling*) Malagasy
malgré [malgʁe] *prép* in spite of, despite; **~
tout** all the same
malheur [malœʁ] *nm* (*situation*) adversity,
misfortune; (*événement*) misfortune; (:
très grave) disaster, tragedy; **faire un ~** to
be a smash hit; **malheureusement** *adv*
unfortunately; **malheureux, -euse** *adj* (*triste*)
unhappy, miserable; (*infortuné, regrettable*)
unfortunate; (*malchanceux*) unlucky;
(*insignifiant*) wretched ▷ *nm/f* poor soul
malhonnête [malɔnɛt] *adj* dishonest;
malhonnêteté *nf* dishonesty
malice [malis] *nf* mischievousness;
(*méchanceté*): **par ~** out of malice *ou* spite; **sans
~** guileless; **malicieux, -euse** *adj* mischievous

> Attention à ne pas traduire *malicieux*
> par *malicious*.

malin, -igne [malɛ̃, maliɲ] *adj* (*futé: f gén:
aussi*: **maline**) smart, shrewd; (*Méd*) malignant
malingre [malɛ̃gʁ] *adj* puny

malle[mal] nf trunk; **mallette** nf (small) suitcase; (porte-documents) attaché case

malmener[malmǝne] vt to manhandle; (fig) to give a rough handling to

malodorant, e[malɔdɔrɑ̃, ɑ̃t] adj foul- ou ill-smelling

malpoli, e[malpɔli] adj impolite

malsain, e[malsɛ̃, ɛn] adj unhealthy

malt[malt] nm malt

Malte[malt] nf Malta

maltraiter[maltrete] vt to manhandle, ill-treat

malveillance[malvɛjɑ̃s] nf (animosité) ill will; (intention de nuire) malevolence

malversation[malvɛrsasjɔ̃] nf embezzlement

maman[mamɑ̃] nf mum(my), mother

mamelle[mamɛl] nf teat

mamelon[mam(ǝ)lɔ̃] nm (Anat) nipple

mamie[mami] (fam) nf granny

mammifère[mamifɛr] nm mammal

mammouth[mamut] nm mammoth

manche[mɑ̃ʃ] nf (de vêtement) sleeve; (d'un jeu, tournoi) round; (Géo): **la M~** the Channel ▷ nm (d'outil, casserole) handle; (de pelle, pioche etc) shaft; **à ~s courtes/longues** short-/long-sleeved; **manche à balai** broomstick; (Inform, Aviat) joystick m inv

manchette[mɑ̃ʃɛt] nf (de chemise) cuff; (coup) forearm blow; (titre) headline

manchot[mɑ̃ʃo] nm one-armed man; armless man; (Zool) penguin

mandarine[mɑ̃darin] nf mandarin (orange), tangerine

mandat[mɑ̃da] nm (postal) postal ou money order; (d'un député etc) mandate; (procuration) power of attorney, proxy; (Police) warrant; **mandat d'arrêt** warrant for arrest; **mandat de perquisition** search warrant; **mandataire** nm/f (représentant) representative; (Jur) proxy

manège[manɛʒ] nm riding school; (à la foire) roundabout, merry-go-round; (fig) game, ploy

manette[manɛt] nf lever, tap; **manette de jeu** joystick

mangeable[mɑ̃ʒabl] adj edible, eatable

mangeoire[mɑ̃ʒwar] nf trough, manger

manger[mɑ̃ʒe] vt to eat; (ronger: suj: rouille etc) to eat into ou away ▷ vi to eat; **donner à ~ à** (enfant) to feed; **est-ce qu'on peut ~ quelque chose?** can we have something to eat?

mangue[mɑ̃g] nf mango

maniable[manjabl] adj (outil) handy; (voiture, voilier) easy to handle

maniaque[manjak] adj finicky, fussy ▷ nm/f (méticuleux) fusspot; (fou) maniac

manie[mani] nf (tic) odd habit; (obsession) mania; **avoir la ~ de** to be obsessive about

manier[manje] vt to handle

manière[manjɛr] nf (façon) way, manner; **manières** nfpl (attitude) manners; (chichis) fuss sg; **de ~ à** so as to; **de cette ~** in this way ou manner; **d'une certaine ~** in a way; **de toute ~** in any case; **d'une ~ générale** generally speaking, as a general rule

maniéré, e[manjere] adj affected

manifestant, e[manifɛstɑ̃, ɑ̃t] nm/f demonstrator

manifestation[manifɛstasjɔ̃] nf (de joie, mécontentement) expression, demonstration; (symptôme) outward sign; (culturelle etc) event; (Pol) demonstration

manifeste[manifɛst] adj obvious, evident ▷ nm manifesto; **manifester** vt (volonté, intentions) to show, indicate; (joie, peur) to express, show ▷ vi to demonstrate; **se manifester** vi (émotion) to show ou express itself; (difficultés) to arise; (symptômes) to appear

manigancer[manigɑ̃se] vt to plot

manipulation[manipylasjɔ̃] nf handling; (Pol, génétique) manipulation

manipuler[manipyle] vt to handle; (fig) to manipulate

manivelle[manivɛl] nf crank

mannequin[manke] nm (Couture) dummy; (Mode) model

manœuvre[manœvr] nf (gén) manoeuvre (BRIT), maneuver (US) ▷ nm labourer; **manœuvrer** vt to manoeuvre (BRIT), maneuver (US); (levier, machine) to operate ▷ vi to manoeuvre

manoir[manwar] nm manor ou country house

manque[mɑ̃k] nm (insuffisance): **~ de** lack of; (vide) emptiness, gap; (Méd) withdrawal: **être en état de ~** to suffer withdrawal symptoms

manqué, e[mɑ̃ke] adj failed; **garçon ~** tomboy

manquer[mɑ̃ke] vi (faire défaut) to be lacking; (être absent) to be missing; (échouer) to fail ▷ vt to miss ▷ vb impers: **il (nous) manque encore 10 euros** we are still 10 euros short; **il manque des pages (au livre)** there are some pages missing (from the book); **il/cela me manque** I miss him/this; **~ à** (règles etc) to be in breach of, fail to observe; **~ de** to lack; **je ne ~ai pas de le lui dire** I'll be sure to tell him; **il a manqué (de) se tuer** he very nearly got killed

mansarde[mɑ̃sard] nf attic; **mansardé, e** adj: **chambre mansardée** attic room

manteau, x[mɑ̃to] nm coat

manucure[manykyr] nf manicurist

manuel, le[manɥɛl] adj manual ▷ nm (ouvrage) manual, handbook

manufacture[manyfaktyr] nf factory; **manufacturé, e** adj manufactured

manuscrit, e[manyskri, it] adj handwritten

▷ nm manuscript

manutention [manytɑ̃sjɔ̃] nf (Comm) handling

mappemonde [mapmɔ̃d] nf (plane) map of the world; (sphère) globe

maquereau, x [makʀo] nm (Zool) mackerel inv; (fam) pimp

maquette [maket] nf (à échelle réduite) (scale) model; (d'une page illustrée) paste-up

maquillage [makijaʒ] nm making up; (crème etc) make-up

maquiller [makije] vt (personne, visage) to make up; (truquer: passeport, statistique) to fake; (: voiture volée) to do over (respray etc); **se maquiller** vi to make up (one's face)

maquis [maki] nm (Géo) scrub; (Mil) maquis, underground fighting no pl

maraîcher, -ère [maʀeʃe, ɛʀ] adj: **cultures maraîchères** market gardening sg ▷ nm/f market gardener

marais [maʀe] nm marsh, swamp

marasme [maʀasm] nm stagnation, slump

marathon [maʀatɔ̃] nm marathon

marbre [maʀbʀ] nm marble

marc [maʀ] nm (de raisin, pommes) marc

marchand, e [maʀʃɑ̃, ɑ̃d] nm/f shopkeeper, tradesman(-woman); (au marché) stallholder; (de vins, charbon) merchant ▷ adj: **prix/valeur ~(e)** market price/value; **marchand de fruits** fruiterer (BRIT), fruit seller (US); **marchand de journaux** newsagent; **marchand de légumes** greengrocer (BRIT), produce dealer (US); **marchand de poissons** fishmonger (BRIT), fish seller (US); **marchander** vi to bargain, haggle; **marchandise** nf goods pl, merchandise no pl

marche [maʀʃ] nf (d'escalier) step; (activité) walking; (promenade, trajet, allure) walk; (démarche) walk, gait; (Mil etc, Mus) march; (fonctionnement) running; (des événements) course; **dans le sens de la ~** (Rail) facing the engine; **en ~** (monter etc) while the vehicle is moving ou in motion; **mettre en ~** to start; **se mettre en ~** (personne) to get moving; (machine) to start; **être en état de ~** to be in working order; **marche à suivre** (correct) procedure; **marche arrière** reverse (gear); **faire marche arrière** to reverse; (fig) to backtrack, back-pedal

marché [maʀʃe] nm market; (transaction) bargain, deal; **faire du ~ noir** to buy and sell on the black market; **marché aux puces** flea market

marcher [maʀʃe] vi to walk; (Mil) to march; (aller: voiture, train, affaires) to go; (prospérer) to go well; (fonctionner) to work, run; (fam: consentir) to go along, agree; (: croire naïvement) to be taken in; **faire ~ qn** (taquiner) to pull sb's leg; (tromper) to lead sb up the garden path;

comment est-ce que ça marche? how does this work?; **marcheur, -euse** nm/f walker

mardi [maʀdi] nm Tuesday; **Mardi gras** Shrove Tuesday

mare [maʀ] nf pond; (flaque) pool

marécage [maʀekaʒ] nm marsh, swamp; **marécageux, -euse** adj marshy

maréchal, -aux [maʀeʃal, o] nm marshal

marée [maʀe] nf tide; (poissons) fresh (sea) fish; **marée haute/basse** high/low tide; **marée noire** oil slick

marelle [maʀɛl] nf: **(jouer à) la ~** (to play) hopscotch

margarine [maʀgaʀin] nf margarine

marge [maʀʒ] nf margin; **en ~ de** (fig) on the fringe of; **marge bénéficiaire** profit margin

marginal, e, -aux [maʀʒinal, o] nm/f (original) eccentric; (déshérité) dropout

marguerite [maʀgəʀit] nf marguerite, (oxeye) daisy; (d'imprimante) daisy-wheel

mari [maʀi] nm husband

mariage [maʀjaʒ] nm marriage; (noce) wedding; **mariage civil/religieux** registry office (BRIT) ou civil wedding/church wedding

marié, e [maʀje] adj married ▷ nm (bride)groom; **les ~s** the bride and groom; **les (jeunes) ~s** the newly-weds

marier [maʀje] vt to marry; (fig) to blend; **se ~ (avec)** to marry, get married (to)

marin, e [maʀɛ̃, in] adj sea cpd, marine ▷ nm sailor

marine [maʀin] adj voir **marin** ▷ adj inv navy (blue) ▷ nm (Mil) marine ▷ nf navy; **marine marchande** merchant navy

mariner [maʀine] vt: **faire ~** to marinade

marionnette [maʀjɔnɛt] nf puppet

maritalement [maʀitalmɑ̃] adv: **vivre ~** to live as husband and wife

maritime [maʀitim] adj sea cpd, maritime

mark [maʀk] nm mark

marmelade [maʀməlad] nf stewed fruit, compote; **marmelade d'oranges** marmalade

marmite [maʀmit] nf (cooking-)pot

marmonner [maʀmɔne] vt, vi to mumble, mutter

marmotter [maʀmɔte] vt to mumble

Maroc [maʀɔk] nm: **le ~** Morocco; **marocain, e** [maʀɔkɛ̃, ɛn] adj Moroccan ▷ nm/f: **Marocain, e** Moroccan

maroquinerie [maʀɔkinʀi] nf (articles) fine leather goods pl; (boutique) shop selling fine leather goods

marquant, e [maʀkɑ̃, ɑ̃t] adj outstanding

marque [maʀk] nf mark; (Comm: de nourriture) brand; (: de voiture, produits manufacturés) make; (de disques) label; **de ~** (produits) high-class; (visiteur etc) distinguished, well-known; **une grande ~ de vin** a well-known brand of wine; **marque de fabrique** trademark;

marque déposée registered trademark

marquer [maʀke] vt to mark; (inscrire) to write down; (bétail) to brand; (Sport: but etc) to score; (: joueur) to mark; (accentuer: taille etc) to emphasize; (manifester: refus, intérêt) to show ▷ vi (événement) to stand out, be outstanding; (Sport) to score; **~ les points** to keep the score

marqueterie [maʀketʀi] nf inlaid work, marquetry

marquis, e [maʀki] nm marquis, marquess

marraine [maʀɛn] nf godmother

marrant, e [maʀɑ̃, ɑ̃t] (fam) adj funny

marre [maʀ] (fam) adv: **en avoir ~ de** to be fed up with

marrer [maʀe]: **se ~** (fam) vi to have a (good) laugh

marron [maʀɔ̃] nm (fruit) chestnut ▷ adj inv brown; **marrons glacés** candied chestnuts; **marronnier** nm chestnut (tree)

mars [maʀs] nm March

Marseille [maʀsɛj] n Marseilles

marteau, x [maʀto] nm hammer; **être ~** (fam) to be nuts; **marteau-piqueur** nm pneumatic drill

marteler [maʀtəle] vt to hammer

martien, ne [maʀsjɛ̃, jɛn] adj Martian, of ou from Mars

martyr, e [maʀtiʀ] nm/f martyr ▷ adj: **enfants ~s** battered children; **martyre** nm martyrdom; (fig: sens affaibli) agony, torture; **martyriser** vt (Rel) to martyr; (fig) to bully; (enfant) to batter, beat

marxiste [maʀksist] adj, nm/f Marxist

mascara [maskaʀa] nm mascara

masculin, e [maskylɛ̃, in] adj masculine; (sexe, population) male; (équipe, vêtements) men's; (viril) manly ▷ nm masculine

masochiste [mazɔʃist] adj masochistic

masque [mask] nm mask; **masque de beauté** face pack ou mask; **masque de plongée** diving mask; **masquer** vt (cacher: paysage, porte) to hide, conceal; (dissimuler: vérité, projet) to mask, obscure

massacre [masakʀ] nm massacre, slaughter; **massacrer** vt to massacre, slaughter; (fam: texte etc) to murder

massage [masaʒ] nm massage

masse [mas] nf mass; (Élec) earth; (maillet) sledgehammer; (péj): **la ~** the masses pl; **une ~ de** (fam) masses ou loads of; **en ~** adv (acheter) in bulk; (en foule) en masse ▷ adj (exécutions, production) mass cpd

masser [mase] vt (assembler: gens) to gather; (pétrir) to massage; **se masser** vi (foule) to gather; **masseur, -euse** nm/f masseur(-euse)

massif, -ive [masif, iv] adj (porte) solid, massive; (visage) heavy, large; (bois, or) solid; (dose) massive; (déportations etc) mass cpd ▷ nm (montagneux) massif; (de fleurs) clump, bank; **le**

M~ Central the Massif Central

massue [masy] nf club, bludgeon

mastic [mastik] nm (pour vitres) putty; (pour fentes) filler

mastiquer [mastike] vt (aliment) to chew, masticate

mat, e [mat] adj (couleur, métal) mat(t); (bruit, son) dull ▷ adj inv (Échecs): **être ~** to be checkmate

mât [mɑ] nm (Navig) mast; (poteau) pole, post

match [matʃ] nm match; **faire ~ nul** to draw; **match aller** first leg; **match retour** second leg, return match

matelas [mat(ə)la] nm mattress; **matelas pneumatique** air bed ou mattress

matelot [mat(ə)lo] nm sailor, seaman

mater [mate] vt (personne) to bring to heel, subdue; (révolte) to put down

matérialiser [mateʀjalize]: **se matérialiser** vi to materialize

matérialiste [mateʀjalist] adj materialistic

matériau [mateʀjo] nm material; **matériaux** nmpl material(s)

matériel, le [mateʀjɛl] adj material ▷ nm equipment no pl; (de camping etc) gear no pl; (Inform) hardware

maternel, le [mateʀnɛl] adj (amour, geste) motherly, maternal; (grand-père, oncle) maternal; **maternelle** nf (aussi: **école maternelle**) (state) nursery school

maternité [mateʀnite] nf (établissement) maternity hospital; (état de mère) motherhood, maternity; (grossesse) pregnancy; **congé de ~** maternity leave

mathématique [matematik] adj mathematical; **mathématiques** nfpl (science) mathematics sg

maths [mat] nfpl maths

matière [matjɛʀ] nf matter; (Comm, Tech) material, matter no pl; (fig: d'un livre etc) subject matter, material; (Scol) subject; **en ~ de** as regards; **matières grasses** fat content sg; **matières premières** raw materials

Matignon [matiɲɔ̃] nm: **(l'hôtel) ~** the French Prime Minister's residence

matin [matɛ̃] nm, adv morning; **le ~** (pendant le matin) in the morning; **demain/hier/dimanche ~** tomorrow/yesterday/Sunday morning; **tous les ~s** every morning; **une heure du ~** one o'clock in the morning; **du ~ au soir** from morning till night; **de bon ou grand ~** early in the morning; **matinal, e, -aux** adj (toilette, gymnastique) morning cpd; **être matinal** (personne) to be up early; to be an early riser; **matinée** nf morning; (spectacle) matinée

matou [matu] nm tom(cat)

matraque [matʀak] nf (de policier) truncheon (BRIT), billy (US)

matricule [matʀikyl] *nm* (*Mil*) regimental number; (*Admin*) reference number

matrimonial, e, -aux [matʀimɔnjal, jo] *adj* marital, marriage *cpd*

maudit, e [modi, -it] (*fam*) *adj* (*satané*) blasted, confounded

maugréer [mogʀee] *vi* to grumble

maussade [mosad] *adj* sullen; (*temps*) gloomy

mauvais, e [mɔvɛ, ɛz] *adj* bad; (*faux*): **le ~ numéro/moment** the wrong number/moment; (*méchant, malveillant*) malicious, spiteful ▷ *adv*: **il fait ~** the weather is bad; **sentir ~** to have a nasty smell, smell nasty; **la mer est ~e** the sea is rough; **mauvais joueur** bad loser; **mauvaise herbe** weed; **mauvaise langue** gossip, scandalmonger (BRIT); **mauvaise plaisanterie** nasty trick

mauve [mov] *adj* mauve

maux [mo] *nmpl de* **mal**

maximum [maksimɔm] *adj, nm* maximum; **au ~** (*le plus possible*) as much as one can; (*tout au plus*) at the (very) most *ou* maximum; **faire le ~** to do one's level best

mayonnaise [majɔnɛz] *nf* mayonnaise

mazout [mazut] *nm* (fuel) oil

me, m' [m(ə)] *pron* (*direct: téléphoner, attendre etc*) me; (*indirect: parler, donner etc*) (to) me; (*réfléchi*) myself

mec [mɛk] (*fam*) *nm* bloke, guy

mécanicien, ne [mekanisjɛ̃, jɛn] *nm/f* mechanic; (*Rail*) (train *ou* engine) driver; **pouvez-vous nous envoyer un ~?** can you send a mechanic?

mécanique [mekanik] *adj* mechanical ▷ *nf* (*science*) mechanics *sg*; (*mécanisme*) mechanism; **ennui ~** engine trouble *no pl*

mécanisme [mekanism] *nm* mechanism

méchamment [meʃamɑ̃] *adv* nastily, maliciously, spitefully

méchanceté [meʃɑ̃ste] *nf* nastiness, maliciousness; **dire des ~s à qn** to say spiteful things to sb

méchant, e [meʃɑ̃, ɑ̃t] *adj* nasty, malicious, spiteful; (*enfant: pas sage*) naughty; (*animal*) vicious

mèche [mɛʃ] *nf* (*de cheveux*) lock; (*de lampe, bougie*) wick; (*d'un explosif*) fuse; **se faire faire des ~s** to have highlights put in one's hair; **de ~ avec** in league with

méchoui [meʃwi] *nm* barbecue of a whole roast sheep

méconnaissable [mekɔnɛsabl] *adj* unrecognizable

méconnaître [mekɔnɛtʀ] *vt* (*ignorer*) to be unaware of; (*mésestimer*) to misjudge

mécontent, e [mekɔ̃tɑ̃, ɑ̃t] *adj*: **~ (de)** discontented *ou* dissatisfied *ou* displeased (with); (*contrarié*) annoyed (at);

mécontentement *nm* dissatisfaction, discontent, displeasure; (*irritation*) annoyance

Mecque [mɛk] *nf*: **la ~** Mecca

médaille [medaj] *nf* medal

médaillon [medajɔ̃] *nm* (*bijou*) locket

médecin [med(ə)sɛ̃] *nm* doctor

médecine [med(ə)sin] *nf* medicine

média [medja] *nmpl*: **les ~** the media; **médiatique** *adj* media *cpd*

médical, e, -aux [medikal, o] *adj* medical; **passer une visite ~e** to have a medical

médicament [medikamɑ̃] *nm* medicine, drug

médiéval, e, -aux [medjeval, o] *adj* medieval

médiocre [medjɔkʀ] *adj* mediocre, poor

méditer [medite] *vi* to meditate

Méditerranée [mediteʀane] *nf*: **la (mer) ~** the Mediterranean (Sea); **méditerranéen, ne** *adj* Mediterranean ▷ *nm/f*: **Méditerranéen, ne** native *ou* inhabitant of a Mediterranean country

méduse [medyz] *nf* jellyfish

méfait [mefɛ] *nm* (*faute*) misdemeanour, wrongdoing; **méfaits** *nmpl* (*ravages*) ravages, damage *sg*

méfiance [mefjɑ̃s] *nf* mistrust, distrust

méfiant, e [mefjɑ̃, jɑ̃t] *adj* mistrustful, distrustful

méfier [mefje]: **se méfier** *vi* to be wary; to be careful; **se ~ de** to mistrust, distrust, be wary of

mégaoctet [megaɔktɛ] *nm* megabyte

mégarde [megaʀd] *nf*: **par ~** (*accidentellement*) accidentally; (*par erreur*) by mistake

mégère [meʒɛʀ] *nf* shrew

mégot [mego] (*fam*) *nm* cigarette end

meilleur, e [mejœʀ] *adj, adv* better ▷ *nm*: **le ~** the best; **le ~ des deux** the better of the two; **il fait ~ qu'hier** it's better weather than yesterday; **meilleur marché** (*inv*) cheaper

mél [mɛl] *nm* e-mail

mélancolie [melɑ̃kɔli] *nf* melancholy, gloom; **mélancolique** *adj* melancholic, melancholy

mélange [melɑ̃ʒ] *nm* mixture; **mélanger** *vt* to mix; (*vins, couleurs*) to blend; (*mettre en désordre*) to mix up, muddle (up)

mêlée [mele] *nf* mêlée, scramble; (*Rugby*) scrum(mage)

mêler [mele] *vt* (*unir*) to mix; (*embrouiller*) to muddle (up), mix up; **se mêler** *vi* to mix, mingle; **se ~ à** (*personne: se joindre*) to join; (: *s'associer à*) to mix with; **se ~ de** (*suj: personne*) to meddle with, interfere in; **mêle-toi de ce qui te regarde** *ou* **de tes affaires!** mind your own business!

mélodie [melɔdi] *nf* melody; **mélodieux, -euse** *adj* melodious

melon [m(ə)lɔ̃] *nm* (*Bot*) (honeydew) melon;

(*aussi*: **chapeau ~**) bowler (hat)
membre [mɑ̃bʀ] *nm* (*Anat*) limb; (*personne, pays, élément*) member ▷ *adj* member *cpd*
mémé [meme] (*fam*) *nf* granny

 MOT-CLÉ

même [mɛm] *adj* **1** (*avant le nom*) same; **en même temps** at the same time; **ils ont les mêmes goûts** they have the same *ou* similar tastes
2 (*après le nom: renforcement*): **il est la loyauté même** he is loyalty itself; **ce sont ses paroles mêmes** they are his very words
▷ *pron*: **le(la) même** the same one
▷ *adv* **1** (*renforcement*): **il n'a même pas pleuré** he didn't even cry; **même lui l'a dit** even HE said it; **ici même** at this very place; **même si** even if
2: **à même**: **à même la bouteille** straight from the bottle; **à même la peau** next to the skin; **être à même de faire** to be in a position to do, be able to do
3: **de même**: **faire de même** to do likewise; **lui de même** so does (*ou* did *ou* is) he; **de même que** just as; **il en va de même pour** the same goes for

mémoire [memwaʀ] *nf* memory ▷ *nm* (*Scol*) dissertation, paper; **mémoires** *nmpl* (*souvenirs*) memoirs; **à la ~ de** to the *ou* in memory of; **de ~** from memory; **mémoire morte** read-only memory, ROM; **mémoire vive** random access memory, RAM
mémorable [memɔʀabl] *adj* memorable, unforgettable
menace [mənas] *nf* threat; **menacer** *vt* to threaten
ménage [menaʒ] *nm* (*travail*) housework; (*couple*) (married) couple; (*famille*, *Admin*) household; **faire le ~** to do the housework; **ménagement** *nm* care and attention; **ménager, -ère** *adj* household *cpd*, domestic ▷ *vt* (*traiter: personne*) to handle with tact; (*utiliser*) to use sparingly; (*prendre soin de*) to take (great) care of, look after; (*organiser*) to arrange; **ménagère** *nf* housewife
mendiant, e [mɑ̃djɑ̃, jɑ̃t] *nm/f* beggar
mendier [mɑ̃dje] *vi* to beg ▷ *vt* to beg (for)
mener [m(ə)ne] *vt* to lead; (*enquête*) to conduct; (*affaires*) to manage ▷ *vi*: **~ à/dans** (*emmener*) to take to/into; **~ qch à bien** to see sth through (to a successful conclusion), complete sth successfully
meneur, -euse [mənœʀ, øz] *nm/f* leader; (*péj*) agitator
méningite [menɛ̃ʒit] *nf* meningitis *no pl*
ménopause [menopoz] *nf* menopause
menottes [mənɔt] *nfpl* handcuffs

mensonge [mɑ̃sɔ̃ʒ] *nm* lie; (*action*) lying *no pl*; **mensonger, -ère** *adj* false
mensualité [mɑ̃sɥalite] *nf* (*traite*) monthly payment
mensuel, le [mɑ̃sɥɛl] *adj* monthly
mensurations [mɑ̃syʀasjɔ̃] *nfpl* measurements
mental, e, -aux [mɑ̃tal, o] *adj* mental; **mentalité** *nf* mentality
menteur, -euse [mɑ̃tœʀ, øz] *nm/f* liar
menthe [mɑ̃t] *nf* mint
mention [mɑ̃sjɔ̃] *nf* (*annotation*) note, comment; (*Scol*) grade; **~ bien** ≈ grade B, ≈ good pass; (*Université*) ≈ upper 2nd class pass (*BRIT*), ≈ pass with (high) honors (*US*); (*Admin*): **"rayer les ~s inutiles"** "delete as appropriate"; **mentionner** *vt* to mention
mentir [mɑ̃tiʀ] *vi* to lie
menton [mɑ̃tɔ̃] *nm* chin
menu, e [məny] *adj* (*personne*) slim, slight; (*frais, difficulté*) minor ▷ *adv* (*couper, hacher*) very fine ▷ *nm* menu; **~ touristique/gastronomique** economy/gourmet's menu
menuiserie [mənɥizʀi] *nf* (*métier*) joinery, carpentry; (*passe-temps*) woodwork; **menuisier** *nm* joiner, carpenter
méprendre [mepʀɑ̃dʀ]: **se méprendre** *vi*: **se ~ sur** to be mistaken (about)
mépris [mepʀi] *nm* (*dédain*) contempt, scorn; **au ~ de** regardless of, in defiance of; **méprisable** *adj* contemptible, despicable; **méprisant, e** *adj* scornful; **méprise** *nf* mistake, error; **mépriser** *vt* to scorn, despise; (*gloire, danger*) to scorn, spurn
mer [mɛʀ] *nf* sea; (*marée*) tide; **en ~** at sea; **en haute** *ou* **pleine ~** off shore, on the open sea; **la ~ du Nord/Rouge/Noire/Morte** the North/Red/Black/Dead Sea
mercenaire [mɛʀsənɛʀ] *nm* mercenary, hired soldier
mercerie [mɛʀsəʀi] *nf* (*boutique*) haberdasher's shop (*BRIT*), notions store (*US*)
merci [mɛʀsi] *excl* thank you ▷ *nf*: **à la ~ de qn/qch** at sb's mercy/the mercy of sth; **~ beaucoup** thank you very much; **~ de** thank you for; **sans ~** merciless(ly)
mercredi [mɛʀkʀədi] *nm* Wednesday; **~ des Cendres** Ash Wednesday; *voir aussi* **lundi**
mercure [mɛʀkyʀ] *nm* mercury
merde [mɛʀd] (*fam!*) *nf* shit (!) ▷ *excl* (bloody) hell (!)
mère [mɛʀ] *nf* mother; **mère célibataire** single parent, unmarried mother; **mère de famille** housewife, mother
merguez [mɛʀgɛz] *nf* merguez sausage (*type of spicy sausage from N Africa*)
méridional, e, -aux [meʀidjɔnal, o] *adj* southern ▷ *nm/f* Southerner
meringue [məʀɛ̃g] *nf* meringue

mérite [merit] *nm* merit; **avoir du ~ (à faire qch)** to deserve credit (for doing sth); **mériter** *vt* to deserve

merle [mɛrl] *nm* blackbird

merveille [mɛrvej] *nf* marvel, wonder; **faire ~** to work wonders; **à ~** perfectly, wonderfully; **merveilleux, -euse** *adj* marvellous, wonderful

mes [me] *adj voir* **mon**

mésange [mezɑ̃ʒ] *nf* tit(mouse)

mésaventure [mezavɑ̃tyr] *nf* misadventure, misfortune

Mesdames [medam] *nfpl de* **Madame**

Mesdemoiselles [medmwazɛl] *nfpl de* **Mademoiselle**

mesquin, e [mɛskɛ̃, in] *adj* mean, petty; **mesquinerie** *nf* meanness; (*procédé*) mean trick

message [mesaʒ] *nm* message; **est-ce que je peux laisser un ~?** can I leave a message?; **~ SMS** text message; **messager, -ère** *nm/f* messenger; **messagerie** *nf* (*Internet*): **messagerie électronique** e-mail; **messagerie vocale** (*service*) voice mail; **messagerie instantanée** instant messenger

messe [mɛs] *nf* mass; **aller à la ~** to go to mass

Messieurs [mesjø] *nmpl de* **Monsieur**

mesure [m(ə)zyr] *nf* (*évaluation, dimension*) measurement; (*récipient*) measure; (*Mus: cadence*) time, tempo; (*: division*) bar; (*retenue*) moderation; (*disposition*) measure, step; **sur ~** (*costume*) made-to-measure; **dans la ~ où** insofar as, inasmuch as; **à ~ que** as; **être en ~ de** to be in a position to; **dans une certaine ~** to a certain extent

mesurer [məzyre] *vt* to measure; (*juger*) to weigh up, assess; (*modérer: ses paroles etc*) to moderate

métal, -aux [metal, o] *nm* metal; **métallique** *adj* metallic

météo [meteo] *nf* (*bulletin*) weather report

météorologie [meteˋlɔʒi] *nf* meteorology

méthode [metɔd] *nf* method; (*livre, ouvrage*) manual, tutor

méticuleux, -euse [metikylø, øz] *adj* meticulous

métier [metje] *nm* (*profession: gén*) job; (*: manuel*) trade; (*artisanal*) craft; (*technique, expérience*) (acquired) skill *ou* technique; (*aussi:* **~ à tisser**) (weaving) loom

métis, se [metis] *adj, nm/f* half-caste, half-breed

métrage [metraʒ] *nm*: **long/moyen/court ~** full-length/medium-length/short film

mètre [mɛtr] *nm* metre; (*règle*) (metre) rule; (*ruban*) tape measure; **métrique** *adj* metric

métro [metro] *nm* underground (brit), subway

métropole [metrɔpɔl] *nf* (*capitale*) metropolis; (*pays*) home country

mets [mɛ] *nm* dish

metteur [metœr] *nm*: **~ en scène** (*Théâtre*) producer; (*Cinéma*) director

 MOT-CLÉ

mettre [mɛtr] *vt* **1** (*placer*) to put; **mettre en bouteille/en sac** to bottle/put in bags *ou* sacks

2 (*vêtements: revêtir*) to put on; (*: porter*) to wear; **mets ton gilet** put your cardigan on; **je ne mets plus mon manteau** I no longer wear my coat

3 (*faire fonctionner: chauffage, électricité*) to put on; (*: réveil, minuteur*) to set; (*installer: gaz, eau*) to put in, lay on; **mettre en marche** to start up

4 (*consacrer*): **mettre du temps à faire qch** to take time to do sth *ou* over sth

5 (*noter, écrire*) to say, put; **qu'est-ce qu'il a mis sur la carte?** what did he say *ou* write on the card?; **mettez au pluriel ...** put ... into the plural

6 (*supposer*): **mettons que ...** let's suppose *ou* say that ...

7: **y mettre du sien** to pull one's weight

se mettre *vi* **1** (*se placer*): **vous pouvez vous mettre là** you can sit (*ou* stand) there; **où ça se met?** where does it go?; **se mettre au lit** to get into bed; **se mettre au piano** to sit down at the piano; **se mettre de l'encre sur les doigts** to get ink on one's fingers

2 (*s'habiller*): **se mettre en maillot de bain** to get into *ou* put on a swimsuit; **n'avoir rien à se mettre** to have nothing to wear

3: **se mettre à** to begin, start; **se mettre à faire** to begin *ou* start doing *ou* to do; **se mettre au piano** to start learning the piano; **se mettre au régime** to go on a diet; **se mettre au travail/à l'étude** to get down to work/one's studies

meuble [mœbl] *nm* piece of furniture; **des ~s** furniture; **meublé** *nm* furnished flatlet (brit) *ou* room; **meubler** *vt* to furnish

meuf [mœf] *nf* (*fam*) woman

meugler [møgle] *vi* to low, moo

meule [møl] *nf* (*de foin, blé*) stack; (*de fromage*) round; (*à broyer*) millstone

meunier [mønje] *nm* miller

meurs *etc* [mœr] *vb voir* **mourir**

meurtre [mœrtr] *nm* murder; **meurtrier, -ière** *adj* (*arme etc*) deadly; (*fureur, instincts*) murderous ▷ *nm/f* murderer(-eress)

meurtrir [mœrtrir] *vt* to bruise; (*fig*) to wound

meus *etc* [mœ] *vb voir* **mouvoir**

meute[møt] *nf* pack
mexicain, e[mɛksikɛ̃, ɛn] *adj* Mexican
▷ *nm/f*: **M~, e** Mexican
Mexico[mɛksiko] *n* Mexico City
Mexique[mɛksik] *nm*: **le ~** Mexico
mi[mi] *nm* (Mus) E; (en chantant la gamme) mi
▷ *préfixe*: **mi...** half(-); (en cantant) mid-: **à la mi-janvier**
in mid-January; **à mi-jambes/corps** (up *ou*
down) to the knees/waist; **à mi-hauteur**
halfway up
miauler[mjole] *vi* to mew
miche[miʃ] *nf* round *ou* cob loaf
mi-chemin[miʃmɛ̃]: **à ~** *adv* halfway, midway
mi-clos, e[miklo, kloz] *adj* half-closed
micro[mikro] *nm* mike, microphone; (Inform)
micro
microbe[mikrɔb] *nm* germ, microbe
micro...: **micro-onde** *nf*: **four à micro-ondes**
microwave oven; **micro-ordinateur** *nm*
microcomputer; **microscope** *nm* microscope;
microscopique *adj* microscopic
midi[midi] *nm* midday, noon; (moment du
déjeuner) lunchtime; (sud) south; **à ~** at 12
(o'clock) *ou* midday *ou* noon; **le M~** the South
(of France), the Midi
mie[mi] *nf* crumb (of the loaf)
miel[mjɛl] *nm* honey; **mielleux, -euse** *adj*
(personne) unctuous, syrupy
mien, ne[mjɛ̃, mjɛn] *pron*: **le(la) ~(ne), les**
~(ne)s mine; **les ~s** my family
miette[mjɛt] *nf* (de pain, gâteau) crumb; (fig:
de la conversation etc) scrap; **en ~s** in pieces
ou bits

MOT-CLÉ

mieux[mjø] *adv* **1** (d'une meilleure façon):
mieux (que) better (than); **elle travaille/**
mange mieux she works/eats better; **aimer**
mieux to prefer; **elle va mieux** she is better;
de mieux en mieux better and better
2 (de la meilleure façon) best; **ce que je**
connais le mieux what I know best; **les**
livres les mieux faits the best-made books
▷ *adj* **1** (plus à l'aise, en meilleure forme) better;
se sentir mieux to feel better
2 (plus satisfaisant) better; **c'est mieux ainsi**
it's better like this; **c'est le mieux des deux**
it's the better of the two; **le(la) mieux, les**
mieux the best; **demandez-lui, c'est le**
mieux ask him, it's the best thing
3 (plus joli) better-looking; **il est mieux que**
son frère (plus beau) he's better-looking than
his brother; (plus gentil) he's nicer than his
brother; **il est mieux sans moustache** he
looks better without a moustache
4: **au mieux** at best; **au mieux avec** on the
best of terms with; **pour le mieux** for the
best

▷ *nm* **1** (progrès) improvement
2: **de mon/ton mieux** as best I/you can (*ou*
could); **faire de son mieux** to do one's best

mignon, ne[miɲɔ̃, ɔn] *adj* sweet, cute
migraine[migrɛn] *nf* headache; (Méd)
migraine
mijoter[miʒɔte] *vt* to simmer; (préparer avec
soin) to cook lovingly; (fam: tramer) to plot,
cook up ▷ *vi* to simmer
milieu, x[miljø] *nm* (centre) middle; (Bio,
Géo) environment; (entourage social) milieu;
(provenance) background; (pègre): **le ~** the
underworld; **au ~ de** in the middle of; **au beau**
ou **en plein ~ (de)** right in the middle (of); **un**
juste ~ a happy medium
militaire[militɛr] *adj* military, army *cpd* ▷ *nm*
serviceman
militant, e[militɑ̃, ɑ̃t] *adj, nm/f* militant
militer[milite] *vi* to be a militant
mille[mil] *num* a *ou* one thousand ▷ *nm*
(mesure): **~ (marin)** nautical mile; **mettre**
dans le ~ (fig) to be bang on target;
millefeuille *nm* cream *ou* vanilla slice;
millénaire *nm* millennium ▷ *adj* thousand-
year-old; (fig) ancient; **mille-pattes** *nm inv*
centipede
millet[mijɛ] *nm* millet
milliard[miljar] *nm* milliard, thousand
million (BRIT), billion (US); **milliardaire** *nm/f*
multimillionaire (BRIT), billionaire (US)
millier[milje] *nm* thousand; **un ~ (de)** a
thousand or so, about a thousand; **par ~s** in
(their) thousands, by the thousand
milligramme[miligram] *nm* milligramme
millimètre[milimɛtr] *nm* millimetre
million[miljɔ̃] *nm* million; **deux ~s de** two
million; **millionnaire** *nm/f* millionaire
mime[mim] *nm/f* (acteur) mime(r) ▷ *nm* (art)
mime, miming; **mimer** *vt* to mime; (singer) to
mimic, take off
minable[minabl] *adj* (décrépit) shabby(-
looking); (médiocre) pathetic
mince[mɛ̃s] *adj* thin; (personne, taille) slim,
slender; (fig: profit, connaissances) slight, small,
weak ▷ *excl*: **~ alors!** drat it!, darn it! (US);
minceur *nf* thinness; (d'une personne) slimness,
slenderness; **mincir** *vi* to get slimmer
mine[min] *nf* (physionomie) expression, look;
(allure) exterior, appearance; (de crayon) lead;
(gisement, explosif, fig: source) mine; **avoir**
bonne ~ (personne) to look well; (ironique) to
look an utter idiot; **avoir mauvaise ~** to look
unwell *ou* poorly; **faire ~ de faire** to make a
pretence of doing; **~ de rien** although they
wouldn't think so
miner[mine] *vt* (saper) to undermine, erode;
(Mil) to mine
minerai[minrɛ] *nm* ore

minéral, e, -aux [mineʀal, o] *adj, nm* mineral

minéralogique [mineʀalɔʒik] *adj*: **plaque ~** number (BRIT) *ou* license (US) plate; **numéro ~** registration (BRIT) *ou* license (US) number

minet, te [mine, ɛt] *nm/f (chat)* pussy-cat; *(péj)* young trendy

mineur, e [minœʀ] *adj* minor ▷ *nm/f (Jur)* minor, person under age ▷ *nm (travailleur)* miner

miniature [minjatyʀ] *adj, nf* miniature

minibus [minibys] *nm* minibus

minier, -ière [minje, jɛʀ] *adj* mining

mini-jupe [miniʒyp] *nf* mini-skirt

minime [minim] *adj* minor, minimal

minimessage [minimesaʒ] *nm* text message

minimiser [minimize] *vt* to minimize; *(fig)* to play down

minimum [minimɔm] *adj, nm* minimum; **au ~** *(au moins)* at the very least

ministère [ministɛʀ] *nm (aussi Rel)* ministry; *(cabinet)* government

ministre [ministʀ] *nm (aussi Rel)* minister; **ministre d'État** senior minister *ou* secretary

Minitel® [minitɛl] *nm* videotext terminal and service

minoritaire [minɔʀitɛʀ] *adj* minority

minorité [minɔʀite] *nf* minority; **être en ~** to be in the *ou* a minority

minuit [minɥi] *nm* midnight

minuscule [minyskyl] *adj* minute, tiny ▷ *nf*: **(lettre) ~** small letter

minute [minyt] *nf* minute; **à la ~** (just) this instant; *(faire)* there and then; **minuter** *vt* to time; **minuterie** *nf* time switch

minutieux, -euse [minysjø, jøz] *adj (personne)* meticulous; *(travail)* minutely detailed

mirabelle [miʀabɛl] *nf* (cherry) plum

miracle [miʀakl] *nm* miracle

mirage [miʀaʒ] *nm* mirage

mire [miʀ] *nf*: **point de ~** *(fig)* focal point

miroir [miʀwaʀ] *nm* mirror

miroiter [miʀwate] *vi* to sparkle, shimmer; **faire ~ qch à qn** to paint sth in glowing colours for sb, dangle sth in front of sb's eyes

mis, e [mi, miz] *pp de* **mettre** ▷ *adj*: **bien ~** well-dressed

mise [miz] *nf (argent: au jeu)* stake; *(tenue)* clothing, attire; **être de ~** to be acceptable *ou* in season; **mise à jour** updating; **mise au point** *(fig)* clarification; **mise de fonds** capital outlay; **mise en plis** set; **mise en scène** production

miser [mize] *vt (enjeu)* to stake, bet; **~ sur** *(cheval, numéro)* to bet on; *(fig)* to bank *ou* count on

misérable [mizeʀabl] *adj (lamentable, malheureux)* pitiful, wretched; *(pauvre)* poverty-stricken; *(insignifiant, mesquin)* miserable ▷ *nm/f* wretch

misère [mizeʀ] *nf (extreme)* poverty, destitution; **misères** *nfpl (malheurs)* woes, miseries; *(ennuis)* little troubles; **salaire de ~** starvation wage

missile [misil] *nm* missile

mission [misjɔ̃] *nf* mission; **partir en ~** *(Admin, Pol)* to go on an assignment; **missionnaire** *nm/f* missionary

mité, e [mite] *adj* moth-eaten

mi-temps [mitɑ̃] *nf inv (Sport: période)* half; *(: pause)* half-time; **à ~** part-time

miteux, -euse [mitø, øz] *adj (lieu)* seedy

mitigé, e [mitiʒe] *adj*: **sentiments ~s** mixed feelings

mitoyen, ne [mitwajɛ̃, jɛn] *adj (mur)* common, party *cpd*; **maisons ~nes** semi-detached houses; *(plus de deux)* terraced (BRIT) *ou* row (US) houses

mitrailler [mitʀaje] *vt* to machine-gun; *(fig)* to pelt, bombard; *(: photographier)* to take shot after shot of; **mitraillette** *nf* submachine gun; **mitrailleuse** *nf* machine gun

mi-voix [mivwa]: **à ~** *adv* in a low *ou* hushed voice

mixage [miksaʒ] *nm (Cinéma)* (sound) mixing

mixer [miksœʀ] *nm (food)* mixer

mixte [mikst] *adj (gén)* mixed; *(Scol)* mixed, coeducational; **cuisinière ~** combined gas and electric cooker (BRIT) *ou* stove (US)

mixture [mikstyʀ] *nf* mixture; *(fig)* concoction

Mlle *(pl ~s)* *abr* = **Mademoiselle**

MM *abr* = **Messieurs**

Mme *(pl ~s)* *abr* = **Madame**

mobile [mɔbil] *adj* mobile; *(pièce de machine)* moving ▷ *nm (motif)* motive; *(œuvre d'art)* mobile; **(téléphone) ~** mobile (phone)

mobilier, -ière [mɔbilje, jɛʀ] *nm* furniture

mobiliser [mɔbilize] *vt* to mobilize

mocassin [mɔkasɛ̃] *nm* moccasin

moche [mɔʃ] *(fam) adj (laid)* ugly; *(mauvais)*

rotten

modalité[mɔdalite] nf form, mode

mode[mɔd] nf fashion ▷ nm (manière) form, mode; (Ling) mood; (Mus, Inform) mode; **à la ~** fashionable, in fashion; **mode d'emploi** directions pl (for use); **mode de paiement** method of payment; **mode de vie** lifestyle

modèle[mɔdɛl] adj, nm model; (qui pose: de peintre) sitter; **modèle déposé** registered design; **modèle réduit** small-scale model; **modeler** vt to model

modem[mɔdɛm] nm modem

modéré, e[mɔdeʀe] adj, nm/f moderate

modérer[mɔdeʀe] vt to moderate; **se modérer** vi to restrain o.s.

moderne[mɔdɛʀn] adj modern ▷ nm (style) modern style; (meubles) modern furniture; **moderniser** vt to modernize

modeste[mɔdɛst] adj modest; **modestie** nf modesty

modifier[mɔdifje] vt to modify, alter; **se modifier** vi to alter

modique[mɔdik] adj modest

module[mɔdyl] nm module

moelle[mwal] nf marrow

moelleux, -euse[mwalø, øz] adj soft; (gâteau) light and moist

mœurs[mœʀ] nfpl (conduite) morals; (manières) manners; (pratiques sociales, mode de vie) habits

moi[mwa] pron me; (emphatique): **~, je ...** for my part, I ...; I myself ...; **c'est ~ qui l'ai fait** I did it, it was me who did it; **apporte-le-~** bring it to me; **à ~** mine; (dans un jeu) my turn; **moi-même** pron myself; (emphatique) I myself

moindre[mwɛdʀ] adj lesser; lower; **le(la) ~, les ~s** the least, the slightest; **merci — c'est la ~ des choses!** thank you — it's a pleasure!

moine[mwan] nm monk, friar

moineau, x[mwano] nm sparrow

 MOT-CLÉ

moins[mwɛ] adv 1 (comparatif): **moins (que)** less (than); **moins grand que** less tall than, not as tall as; **il a 3 ans de moins que moi** he's 3 years younger than me; **moins je travaille, mieux je me porte** the less I work, the better I feel

2 (superlatif): **le moins** (the) least; **c'est ce que j'aime le moins** it's what I like (the) least; **le(la) moins doué(e)** the least gifted; **au moins, du moins** at least; **pour le moins** at the very least

3: **moins de** (quantité) less (than); (nombre) fewer (than); **moins de sable/d'eau** less sand/water; **moins de livres/gens** fewer books/people; **moins de 2 ans** less than 2 years; **moins de midi** not yet midday

4: **de moins, en moins**: **100 euros/3 jours de moins** 100 euros/3 days less; **3 livres en moins** 3 books fewer; 3 books too few; **de l'argent en moins** less money; **le soleil en moins** but for the sun, minus the sun; **de moins en moins** less and less

5: **à moins de, à moins que** unless; **à moins de faire** unless we do (ou he does etc); **à moins que tu ne fasses** unless you do; **à moins d'un accident** barring any accident

▷ prép: **4 moins 2** 4 minus 2; **il est moins 5** it's 5 to; **il fait moins 5** it's 5 (degrees) below (freezing), it's minus 5

mois[mwa] nm month

moisi[mwazi] nm mould, mildew; **odeur de ~** musty smell; **moisir** vi to go mouldy; **moisissure** nf mould no pl

moisson[mwasɔ] nf harvest; **moissonner** vt to harvest, reap; **moissonneuse** nf (machine) harvester

moite[mwat] adj sweaty, sticky

moitié[mwatje] nf half; **la ~** half; **la ~ de** half (of); **la ~ du temps** half the time; **à la ~ de** halfway through; (avant le verbe) half; (avant l'adjectif) half-; **à ~ prix** (at) half-price

molaire[mɔlɛʀ] nf molar

molester[mɔlɛste] vt to manhandle, maul (about)

molle[mɔl] adj voir **mou**; **mollement** adv (péj: travailler) sluggishly; (protester) feebly

mollet[mɔlɛ] nm calf ▷ adj m: **œuf ~** soft-boiled egg

molletonné, e[mɔltɔne] adj fleece-lined

mollir[mɔliʀ] vi (fléchir) to relent; (substance) to go soft

mollusque[mɔlysk] nm mollusc

môme[mom] (fam) nm/f (enfant) brat

moment[mɔmɑ] nm moment; **ce n'est pas le ~** this is not the (right) time; **au même ~** at the same time; (instant) at the same moment; **pour un bon ~** for a good while; **pour le ~** for the moment, for the time being; **au ~ de** at the time of; **au ~ où** just as; **à tout ~** (peut arriver etc) at any time ou moment; (constamment) constantly, continually; **en ce ~** at the moment; at present; **sur le ~** at the time; **par ~s** now and then, at times; **d'un ~ à l'autre** any time (now); **du ~ où ou que** seeing that, since; **momentané, e** adj temporary, momentary; **momentanément** adv (court instant) for a short while

momie[mɔmi] nf mummy

mon, ma[mɔ, ma] (pl **mes**) adj my

Monaco[mɔnako] nf Monaco

monarchie[mɔnaʀʃi] nf monarchy

monastère[mɔnastɛʀ] nm monastery

mondain, e[mɔdɛ, ɛn] adj (vie) society cpd

monde[mɔd] nm world; (haute société): **le ~**

(high) society; **il y a du ~** (beaucoup de gens) there are a lot of people; (quelques personnes) there are some people; **beaucoup/peu de ~** many/few people; **mettre au ~** to bring into the world; **pas le moins du ~** not in the least; **mondial, e, -aux** adj (population) world cpd; (influence) world-wide; **mondialement** adv throughout the world; **mondialisation** nf globalization

monégasque [mɔnegask] adj Monegasque, of ou from Monaco ▷ nm/f: **M~** Monegasque, person from ou inhabitant of Monaco

monétaire [mɔnetɛʀ] adj monetary

moniteur, -trice [mɔnitœʀ, tʀis] nm/f (Sport) instructor(-tress); (de colonie de vacances) supervisor ▷ nm (écran) monitor

monnaie [mɔnɛ] nf (Écon, gén: moyen d'échange) currency; (petites pièces): **avoir de la ~** to have (some) change; **une pièce de ~ a coin**; **faire de la ~** to get (some) change; **avoir/faire la ~ de 20 euros** to have change of/get change for 20 euros; **rendre à qn la ~ (sur 20 euros)** to give sb the change (out of ou from 20 euros); **gardez la ~** keep the change; **désolé, je n'ai pas de ~** sorry, I don't have any change; **avez-vous de la ~?** do you have any change?

monologue [mɔnɔlɔg] nm monologue, soliloquy; **monologuer** vi to soliloquize

monopole [mɔnɔpɔl] nm monopoly

monotone [mɔnɔtɔn] adj monotonous

Monsieur [məsjø] (pl **Messieurs**) titre Mr ▷ nm (homme quelconque): **un/le monsieur** a/the gentleman; **~, ...** (en tête de lettre) Dear Sir, ...; voir aussi **Madame**

monstre [mɔ̃stʀ] nm monster ▷ adj (fam: colossal) monstrous; **un travail ~** a fantastic amount of work; **monstrueux, -euse** adj monstrous

mont [mɔ̃] nm: **par ~s et par vaux** up hill and down dale; **le Mont Blanc** Mont Blanc

montage [mɔ̃taʒ] nm (assemblage d'appareil) assembly; (Photo) photomontage; (Cinéma) editing

montagnard, e [mɔ̃taɲaʀ, aʀd] adj mountain cpd ▷ nm/f mountain-dweller

montagne [mɔ̃taɲ] nf (cime) mountain; (région): **la ~** the mountains pl; **montagnes russes** big dipper sg, switchback sg; **montagneux, -euse** adj mountainous; (basse montagne) hilly

montant, e [mɔ̃tɑ̃, ɑ̃t] adj rising; **pull à col ~** high-necked jumper ▷ nm (somme, total) (sum) total, (total) amount; (de fenêtre) upright; (de lit) post

monte-charge [mɔ̃tʃaʀʒ] nm inv goods lift, hoist

montée [mɔ̃te] nf (des prix, hostilités) rise; (escalade) climb; (côte) hill; **au milieu de la ~** halfway up

monter [mɔ̃te] vt (escalier, côte) to go (ou come) up; (valise, paquet) to take (ou bring) up; (étagère) to raise; (tente, échafaudage) to put up; (machine) to assemble; (Cinéma) to edit; (Théâtre) to put on, stage; (société etc) to set up ▷ vi to go (ou come) up; (prix, niveau, température) to go up, rise; (passager) to get on; **~ à cheval** (faire du cheval) to ride (a horse); **~ sur** to climb up onto; **~ sur ou à un arbre/une échelle** to climb (up) a tree/ladder; **se monter à** (frais etc) to add up to, come to

montgolfière [mɔ̃gɔlfjɛʀ] nf hot-air balloon

montre [mɔ̃tʀ] nf watch; **contre la ~** (Sport) against the clock

Montréal [mɔ̃ʀeal] n Montreal

montrer [mɔ̃tʀe] vt to show; **~ qch à qn** to show sb sth; **pouvez-vous me ~ où c'est?** can you show me where it is?

monture [mɔ̃tyʀ] nf (cheval) mount; (de lunettes) frame; (d'une bague) setting

monument [mɔnymɑ̃] nm monument; **monument aux morts** war memorial

moquer [mɔke]: **se moquer de** vt to make fun of, laugh at; (fam: se désintéresser de) not to care about; (tromper): **se ~ de qn** to take sb for a ride

moquette [mɔkɛt] nf fitted carpet

moqueur, -euse [mɔkœʀ, øz] adj mocking

moral, e, -aux [mɔʀal, o] adj moral ▷ nm morale; **avoir le ~** (fam) to be in good spirits; **avoir le ~ à zéro** (fam) to be really down; **morale** nf (mœurs) morals pl; (valeurs) moral standards pl, morality; (d'une fable etc) moral; **faire la morale à** to lecture, preach at; **moralité** nf morality; (de fable) moral

morceau, x [mɔʀso] nm piece, bit; (d'une œuvre) passage, extract; (Mus) piece; (Culin: de viande) cut; (de sucre) lump; **mettre en ~x** to pull to pieces ou bits; **manger un ~** to have a bite (to eat)

morceler [mɔʀsəle] vt to break up, divide up

mordant, e [mɔʀdɑ̃, ɑ̃t] adj (ton, remarque) scathing, cutting; (ironie, froid) biting ▷ nm (style) bite, punch

mordiller [mɔʀdije] vt to nibble at, chew at

mordre [mɔʀdʀ] vt to bite ▷ vi (poisson) to bite; **~ sur** (fig) to go over into, overlap into; **~ à l'hameçon** to bite, rise to the bait

mordu, e [mɔʀdy] (fam) nm/f enthusiast; **un ~ de jazz** a jazz fanatic

morfondre [mɔʀfɔ̃dʀ]: **se morfondre** vi to mope

morgue [mɔʀg] nf (arrogance) haughtiness; (lieu: de la police) morgue; (: à l'hôpital) mortuary

morne [mɔʀn] adj dismal, dreary

morose [mɔʀoz] adj sullen, morose

mors [mɔʀ] nm bit

morse [mɔʀs] nm (Zool) walrus; (Tél) Morse (code)

morsure [mɔʀsyʀ] nf bite

mort[1] [mɔʀ] nf death

mort[2]**, e** [mɔʀ, mɔʀt] pp de **mourir** ▷ adj dead ▷ nm/f (défunt) dead man ou woman; (victime): **il y a eu plusieurs ~s** several people were killed, there were several killed; **~ de peur/ fatigue** frightened to death/dead tired

mortalité [mɔʀtalite] nf mortality, death rate

mortel, le [mɔʀtɛl] adj (poison etc) deadly, lethal; (accident, blessure) fatal; (silence, ennemi) deadly; (péché) mortal; (fam: ennuyeux) deadly boring

mort-né, e [mɔʀne] adj (enfant) stillborn

mortuaire [mɔʀtɥɛʀ] adj: **avis ~** death announcement

morue [mɔʀy] nf (Zool) cod inv

mosaïque [mɔzaik] nf mosaic

Moscou [mɔsku] n Moscow

mosquée [mɔske] nf mosque

mot [mo] nm word; (message) line, note; **~ à ~** word for word; **mot de passe** password; **mots croisés** crossword (puzzle) sg

motard [mɔtaʀ] nm biker; (policier) motorcycle cop

motel [mɔtɛl] nm motel

moteur, -trice [mɔtœʀ, tʀis] adj (Anat, Physiol) motor; (Tech) driving; (Auto): **à 4 roues motrices** 4-wheel drive ▷ nm engine, motor; **à ~** power-driven, motor cpd; **moteur de recherche** search engine

motif [mɔtif] nm (cause) motive; (décoratif) design, pattern, motif; **sans ~** groundless

motivation [mɔtivasjɔ̃] nf motivation

motiver [mɔtive] vt to motivate; (justifier) to justify, account for

moto [mɔto] nf (motor)bike; **motocycliste** nm/f motorcyclist

motorisé, e [mɔtɔʀize] adj (personne) having transport ou a car

motrice [mɔtʀis] adj voir **moteur**

motte [mɔt] nf: **~ de terre** lump of earth, clod (of earth); **motte de beurre** lump of butter

mou (mol), molle [mu, mɔl] adj soft; (personne) lethargic; (protestations) weak ▷ nm: **avoir du mou** to be slack

mouche [muʃ] nf fly

moucher [muʃe]: **se moucher** vi to blow one's nose

moucheron [muʃʀɔ̃] nm midge

mouchoir [muʃwaʀ] nm handkerchief, hanky; **mouchoir en papier** tissue, paper hanky

moudre [mudʀ] vt to grind

moue [mu] nf pout; **faire la ~** to pout; (fig) to pull a face

mouette [mwɛt] nf (sea)gull

moufle [mufl] nf (gant) mitt(en)

mouillé, e [muje] adj wet

mouiller [muje] vt (humecter) to wet, moisten; (tremper): **~ qn/qch** to make sb/sth wet ▷ vi (Navig) to lie ou be at anchor; **se mouiller** to get wet; (fam: prendre des risques) to commit o.s.

moulant, e [mulɑ̃, ɑ̃t] adj figure-hugging

moule [mul] nf mussel ▷ nm (Culin) mould; **moule à gâteaux** nm cake tin (BRIT) ou pan (US)

mouler [mule] vt (suj: vêtement) to hug, fit closely round

moulin [mulɛ̃] nm mill; **moulin à café** coffee mill; **moulin à eau** watermill; **moulin à légumes** (vegetable) shredder; **moulin à paroles** (fig) chatterbox; **moulin à poivre** pepper mill; **moulin à vent** windmill

moulinet [mulinɛ] nm (de canne à pêche) reel; (mouvement): **faire des ~s avec qch** to whirl sth around

moulinette® [mulinɛt] nf (vegetable) shredder

moulu, e [muly] pp de **moudre**

mourant, e [muʀɑ̃, ɑ̃t] adj dying

mourir [muʀiʀ] vi to die; (civilisation) to die out; **~ de froid/faim** to die of exposure/ hunger; **~ de faim/d'ennui** (fig) to be starving/be bored to death; **~ d'envie de faire** to be dying to do

mousse [mus] nf (Bot) moss; (de savon) lather; (écume: sur eau, bière) froth, foam; (Culin) mousse ▷ nm (Navig) ship's boy; **mousse à raser** shaving foam

mousseline [muslin] nf muslin; **pommes ~** mashed potatoes

mousser [muse] vi (bière, détergent) to foam; (savon) to lather; **mousseux, -euse** adj frothy ▷ nm: **(vin) mousseux** sparkling wine

mousson [musɔ̃] nf monsoon

moustache [mustaʃ] nf moustache; **moustaches** nfpl (du chat) whiskers pl; **moustachu, e** adj with a moustache

moustiquaire [mustikɛʀ] nf mosquito net

moustique [mustik] nm mosquito

moutarde [mutaʀd] nf mustard

mouton [mutɔ̃] nm sheep inv; (peau) sheepskin; (Culin) mutton

mouvement [muvmɑ̃] nm movement; (fig: impulsion) gesture; **avoir un bon ~** to make a nice gesture; **en ~** in motion; on the move; **mouvementé, e** adj (vie, poursuite) eventful; (réunion) turbulent

mouvoir [muvwaʀ]: **se mouvoir** vi to move

moyen, ne [mwajɛ̃, jɛn] adj average; (tailles, prix) medium; (de grandeur moyenne) medium-sized ▷ nm (façon) means sg, way; **moyens** nmpl (capacités) means; **très ~** (résultats) pretty poor; **je n'en ai pas les ~s** I can't afford it; **au ~ de** by means of; **par tous les ~s** by every possible means, every possible way; **par**

ses propres ~s all by oneself; **moyen âge** Middle Ages pl; **moyen de transport** means of transport

moyennant [mwajɛnɑ̃] prép (somme) for; (service, conditions) in return for; (travail, effort) with

moyenne [mwajɛn] nf average; (Math) mean; (Scol) pass mark; **en ~** on (an) average; **moyenne d'âge** average age

Moyen-Orient [mwajɛnɔrjɑ̃] nm: **le ~** the Middle East

moyeu, x [mwajø] nm hub

MST sigle f (= maladie sexuellement transmissible) STD

mû, mue [my] pp de **mouvoir**

muer [mɥe] vi (oiseau, mammifère) to moult; (serpent) to slough; (jeune garçon): **il mue** his voice is breaking

muet, te [mɥɛ, mɥɛt] adj dumb; (fig): **~ d'admiration** etc speechless with admiration etc; (Cinéma) silent ▷ nm/f mute

mufle [myfl] nm muzzle; (fam: goujat) boor

mugir [myʒir] vi (taureau) to bellow; (vache) to low; (fig) to howl

muguet [mygɛ] nm lily of the valley

mule [myl] nf (Zool) (she-)mule

mulet [mylɛ] nm (Zool) (he-)mule

multinationale [myltinasjɔnal] nf multinational

multiple [myltipl] adj multiple, numerous; (varié) many, manifold; **multiplication** nf multiplication; **multiplier** vt to multiply; **se multiplier** vi to multiply

municipal, e, -aux [mynisipal, o] adj (élections, stade) municipal; (conseil) town cpd; **piscine/bibliothèque ~e** public swimming pool/library; **municipalité** nf (ville) municipality; (conseil) town council

munir [mynir] vt: **~ qch de** to equip sth with; **se ~ de** to arm o.s. with

munitions [mynisjɔ̃] nfpl ammunition sg

mur [myr] nm wall; **mur du son** sound barrier

mûr, e [myr] adj ripe; (personne) mature

muraille [myraj] nf (high) wall

mural, e, -aux [myral, o] adj wall cpd; (art) mural

mûre [myr] nf blackberry

muret [myrɛ] nm low wall

mûrir [myrir] vi (fruit, blé) to ripen; (abcès) to come to a head; (fig: idée, personne) to mature ▷ vt (projet) to nurture; (personne) to (make) mature

murmure [myrmyr] nm murmur; **murmurer** vi to murmur

muscade [myskad] nf (aussi: **noix (de) ~**) nutmeg

muscat [myska] nm (raisins) muscat grape; (vin) muscatel (wine)

muscle [myskl] nm muscle; **musclé, e** adj muscular; (fig) strong-arm

museau, x [myzo] nm muzzle; (Culin) brawn

musée [myze] nm museum; (de peinture) art gallery

museler [myz(ə)le] vt to muzzle; **muselière** nf muzzle

musette [myzɛt] nf (sac) lunchbag

musical, e, -aux [myzikal, o] adj musical

music-hall [myzikol] nm (salle) variety theatre; (genre) variety

musicien, ne [myzisjɛ̃, jɛn] adj musical ▷ nm/f musician

musique [myzik] nf music

musulman, e [myzylmɑ̃, an] adj, nm/f Moslem, Muslim

mutation [mytasjɔ̃] nf (Admin) transfer

muter [myte] vt to transfer, move

mutilé, e [mytile] nm/f disabled person (through loss of limbs)

mutiler [mytile] vt to mutilate, maim

mutin, e [mytɛ̃, in] adj (air, ton) mischievous, impish ▷ nm/f (Mil, Navig) mutineer; **mutinerie** nf mutiny

mutisme [mytism] nm silence

mutuel, le [mytɥɛl] adj mutual; **mutuelle** nf voluntary insurance premiums for back-up health cover

myope [mjɔp] adj short-sighted

myosotis [mjɔzɔtis] nm forget-me-not

myrtille [mirtij] nf bilberry

mystère [mistɛr] nm mystery; **mystérieux, -euse** adj mysterious

mystifier [mistifje] vt to fool

mythe [mit] nm myth

mythologie [mitɔlɔʒi] nf mythology

n

n' [n] *adv voir* **ne**

nacre [nakʀ] *nf* mother of pearl

nage [naʒ] *nf* swimming; (*manière*) style of swimming, stroke; **traverser/s'éloigner à la ~** to swim across/away; **en ~** bathed in sweat; **nageoire** *nf* fin; **nager** *vi* to swim; **nageur, -euse** *nm/f* swimmer

naïf, -ïve [naif, naiv] *adj* naïve

nain, e [nɛ̃, nɛn] *nm/f* dwarf

naissance [nɛsɑ̃s] *nf* birth; **donner ~ à** to give birth to; (*fig*) to give rise to; **lieu de ~** place of birth

naître [nɛtʀ] *vi* to be born; (*fig*): **~ de** to arise from, be born out of; **il est né en 1960** he was born in 1960; **faire ~** (*fig*) to give rise to, arouse

naïveté [naivte] *nf* naïvety

nana [nana] (*fam*) *nf* (*fille*) chick, bird (BRIT)

nappe [nap] *nf* tablecloth; (*de pétrole, gaz*) layer; **napperon** *nm* table-mat

naquit *etc* [naki] *vb voir* **naître**

narguer [naʀge] *vt* to taunt

narine [naʀin] *nf* nostril

natal, e [natal] *adj* native; **natalité** *nf* birth rate

natation [natasjɔ̃] *nf* swimming

natif, -ive [natif, iv] *adj* native

nation [nasjɔ̃] *nf* nation; **national, e, -aux** *adj* national; **nationale** *nf*: **(route) nationale** ≈ A road (BRIT), ≈ state highway (US);

nationaliser *vt* to nationalize; **nationalisme** *nm* nationalism; **nationalité** *nf* nationality

natte [nat] *nf* (*cheveux*) plait; (*tapis*) mat

naturaliser [natyʀalize] *vt* to naturalize

nature [natyʀ] *nf* nature ▷ *adj, adv* (*Culin*) plain, without seasoning or sweetening; (*café, thé*) black, without sugar; (*yaourt*) natural; **payer en ~** to pay in kind; **nature morte** still life; **naturel, le** *adj* (*gén, aussi enfant*) natural ▷ *nm* (*absence d'affectation*) naturalness; (*caractère*) disposition, nature; **naturellement** *adv* naturally; (*bien sûr*) of course

naufrage [nofʀaʒ] *nm* (*ship*)wreck; **faire ~** to be shipwrecked

nausée [noze] *nf* nausea; **avoir la ~** to feel sick

nautique [notik] *adj* nautical, water *cpd*; **sports ~s** water sports

naval, e [naval] *adj* naval; (*industrie*) shipbuilding

navet [navɛ] *nm* turnip; (*péj: film*) rubbishy film

navette [navɛt] *nf* shuttle; **faire la ~ (entre)** to go to and fro *ou* shuttle (between)

navigateur [navigatœʀ] *nm* (*Navig*) seafarer; (*Inform*) browser

navigation [navigasjɔ̃] *nf* navigation, sailing

naviguer [navige] *vi* to navigate, sail; **~ sur Internet** to browse the Internet

navire [naviʀ] *nm* ship

navrer [navʀe] *vt* to upset, distress; **je suis navré** I'm so sorry

ne, n' [n(ə)] *adv voir* **pas; plus; jamais** *etc*; (*sans valeur négative: non traduit*): **c'est plus loin que je ne le croyais** it's further than I thought

né, e [ne] *pp* (*voir* **naître**): **né en 1960** born in 1960; **née Scott** née Scott

néanmoins [neɑ̃mwɛ̃] *adv* nevertheless

néant [neɑ̃] *nm* nothingness; **réduire à ~** to bring to nought; (*espoir*) to dash

nécessaire [neseseʀ] *adj* necessary ▷ *nm* necessary; (*sac*) kit; **je vais faire le ~** I'll see to it; **nécessaire de couture** sewing kit; **nécessaire de toilette** toilet bag; **nécessité** *nf* necessity; **nécessiter** *vt* to require

nectar [nɛktaʀ] *nm* nectar

néerlandais, e [neɛʀlɑ̃dɛ, ɛz] *adj* Dutch

nef [nɛf] *nf* (*d'église*) nave

néfaste [nefast] *adj* (*nuisible*) harmful; (*funeste*) ill-fated

négatif, -ive [negatif, iv] *adj* negative ▷ *nm* (*Photo*) negative

négligé, e [negliʒe] *adj* (*en désordre*) slovenly ▷ *nm* (*tenue*) negligee

négligeable [negliʒabl] *adj* negligible

négligent, e [negliʒɑ̃, ɑ̃t] *adj* careless, negligent

négliger [negliʒe] *vt* (*tenue*) to be careless

about; (*avis, précautions*) to disregard; (*épouse, jardin*) to neglect; **~ de faire** to fail to do, not bother to do

négociant, e [negɔsjɑ̃, jɑ̃t] *nm/f* merchant

négociation [negɔsjasjɔ̃] *nf* negotiation

négocier [negɔsje] *vi, vt* to negotiate

nègre [nɛgʀ] (*péj*) *nm* (*écrivain*) ghost (writer)

neige [nɛʒ] *nf* snow; **neiger** *vi* to snow

nénuphar [nenyfaʀ] *nm* water-lily

néon [neɔ̃] *nm* neon

néo-zélandais, e [neozelɑ̃dɛ, ɛz] *adj* New Zealand *cpd* ▷ *nm/f*: **Néo-Zélandais, e** New Zealander

Népal [nepal] *nm*: **le ~** Nepal

nerf [nɛʀ] *nm* nerve; **être sur les ~s** to be all keyed up; **nerveux, -euse** *adj* nervous; (*irritable*) touchy, nervy; (*voiture*) nippy, responsive; **nervosité** *nf* excitability, tenseness; (*irritabilité passagère*) irritability, nerviness

n'est-ce pas? [nɛspa] *adv* isn't it?, won't you? *etc, selon le verbe qui précède*

Net [nɛt] *nm* (Internet): **le ~** the Net

net, nette [nɛt] *adj* (*sans équivoque, distinct*) clear; (*évident: amélioration, différence*) marked, distinct; (*propre*) neat, clean; (*Comm: prix, salaire*) net ▷ *adv* (*refuser*) flatly ▷ *nm*: **mettre au ~** to copy out; **s'arrêter ~** to stop dead; **nettement** *adv* clearly, distinctly; (*incontestablement*) decidedly; **netteté** *nf* clearness

nettoyage [netwajaʒ] *nm* cleaning; **nettoyage à sec** dry cleaning

nettoyer [netwaje] *vt* to clean

neuf¹ [nœf] *num* nine

neuf², neuve [nœf, nœv] *adj* new; **remettre à ~** to do up (as good as new), refurbish; **quoi de ~?** what's new?

neutre [nøtʀ] *adj* neutral; (*Ling*) neuter

neuve [nœv] *adj voir* **neuf²**

neuvième [nœvjɛm] *num* ninth

neveu, x [n(ə)vø] *nm* nephew

New York [njujɔʀk] *n* New York

nez [ne] *nm* nose; **~ à ~ avec** face to face with; **avoir du ~** to have flair

ni [ni] *conj*: **ni ... ni** neither ... nor; **je n'aime ni les lentilles ni les épinards** I like neither lentils nor spinach; **il n'a dit ni oui ni non** he didn't say either yes or no; **elles ne sont venues ni l'une ni l'autre** neither of them came; **il n'a rien vu ni entendu** he didn't see or hear anything

niche [niʃ] *nf* (*du chien*) kennel; (*de mur*) recess, niche; **nicher** *vi* to nest

nid [ni] *nm* nest; **nid de poule** pothole

nièce [njɛs] *nf* niece

nier [nje] *vt* to deny

Nil [nil] *nm*: **le ~** the Nile

n'importe [nɛ̃pɔʀt] *adv*: **n'importe qui/quoi/où** anybody/anything/anywhere; **n'importe quand** any time; **n'importe quel/quelle** any; **n'importe lequel/laquelle** any (one); **n'importe comment** (*sans soin*) carelessly

niveau, x [nivo] *nm* level; (*des élèves, études*) standard; **niveau de vie** standard of living

niveler [niv(ə)le] *vt* to level

noble [nɔbl] *adj* noble; **noblesse** *nf* nobility; (*d'une action etc*) nobleness

noce [nɔs] *nf* wedding; (*gens*) wedding party (*ou* guests *pl*); **faire la ~** (*fam*) to go on a binge; **noces d'argent/d'or/de diamant** silver/golden/diamond wedding (anniversary)

nocif, -ive [nɔsif, iv] *adj* harmful

nocturne [nɔktyʀn] *adj* nocturnal ▷ *nf* late-night opening

Noël [nɔɛl] *nm* Christmas

nœud [nø] *nm* knot; (*ruban*) bow; **nœud papillon** bow tie

noir, e [nwaʀ] *adj* black; (*obscur, sombre*) dark ▷ *nm/f* black man/woman ▷ *nm*: **dans le ~** in the dark; **travail au ~** moonlighting; **travailler au ~** to work on the side; **noircir** *vt*, *vi* to blacken; **noire** *nf* (*Mus*) crotchet (BRIT), quarter note (US)

noisette [nwazɛt] *nf* hazelnut

noix [nwa] *nf* walnut; (*Culin*): **une ~ de beurre** a knob of butter; **à la ~** (*fam*) worthless; **noix de cajou** cashew nut; **noix de coco** coconut; **noix muscade** nutmeg

nom [nɔ̃] *nm* name; (*Ling*) noun; **nom de famille** surname; **nom de jeune fille** maiden name

nomade [nɔmad] *nm/f* nomad

nombre [nɔ̃bʀ] *nm* number; **venir en ~** to come in large numbers; **depuis ~ d'années** for many years; **au ~ de mes amis** among my friends; **nombreux, -euse** *adj* many, numerous; (*avec nom sg: foule etc*) large; **peu nombreux** few; **de nombreux cas** many cases

nombril [nɔ̃bʀi(l)] *nm* navel

nommer [nɔme] *vt* to name; (*élire*) to appoint, nominate; **se nommer**: **il se nomme Pascal** his name's Pascal, he's called Pascal

non [nɔ̃] *adv* (*réponse*) no; (*avec loin, sans, seulement*) not; **~ (pas) que** not that; **moi ~ plus** neither do I, I don't either; **c'est bon ~?** (*exprimant le doute*) it's good, isn't it?; **je pense que ~** I don't think so

non alcoolisé, e [nɔ̃alkɔlize] *adj* non alcoholic

nonchalant, e [nɔ̃ʃalɑ̃, ɑ̃t] *adj* nonchalant

non-fumeur, -euse [nɔ̃fymœʀ, øz] *nm/f* non-smoker

non-sens [nɔ̃sɑ̃s] *nm* absurdity

nord[nɔʀ] nm North ▷ adj northern; north;
au ~ (situation) in the north; (direction) to the
north; **au ~ de** (to the) north of; **nord-africain,
e** adj North-African ▷ nm/f: **Nord-Africain, e**
North African; **nord-est** nm North-East; **nord-
ouest** nm North-West

normal, e, -aux[nɔʀmal, o] adj normal;
c'est tout à fait ~ it's perfectly natural;
vous trouvez ça ~? does it seem right to
you?; **normale** nf: **la normale** the norm,
the average; **normalement** adv (en général)
normally

normand, e[nɔʀmã, ãd] adj of Normandy
▷ nm/f: **N~, e** (de Normandie) Norman

Normandie[nɔʀmãdi] nf Normandy

norme[nɔʀm] nf norm; (Tech) standard

Norvège[nɔʀvɛʒ] nf Norway; **norvégien,
ne** adj Norwegian ▷ nm/f: **Norvégien, ne**
Norwegian ▷ nm (Ling) Norwegian

nos[no] adj voir **notre**

nostalgie[nɔstalʒi] nf nostalgia;
nostalgique adj nostalgic

notable[nɔtabl] adj (fait) notable,
noteworthy; (marqué) noticeable, marked
▷ nm prominent citizen

notaire[nɔtɛʀ] nm solicitor

notamment[nɔtamã] adv in particular,
among others

note[nɔt] nf (écrite, Mus) note; (Scol) mark
(BRIT), grade; (facture) bill; **note de service**
memorandum

noter[nɔte] vt (écrire) to write down;
(remarquer) to note, notice; (devoir) to mark,
grade

notice[nɔtis] nf summary, short article;
(brochure) leaflet, instruction book

notifier[nɔtifje] vt: **~ qch à qn** to notify sb of
sth, notify sth to sb

notion[nosjõ] nf notion, idea

notoire[nɔtwaʀ] adj widely known; (en mal)
notorious

notre[nɔtʀ] adj voir **notre**

nôtre[notʀ] pron: **le ~, la ~, les ~s** ours ▷ adj
ours; **les ~s** ours; (alliés etc) our own people;
soyez des ~s join us

nouer[nwe] vt to tie, knot; (fig: alliance etc)
to strike up

noueux, -euse[nwø, øz] adj gnarled

nourrice[nuʀis] nf (gardienne) child-minder

nourrir[nuʀiʀ] vt to feed; (fig: espoir) to
harbour, nurse; **nourrissant, e** adj nourishing,
nutritious; **nourrisson** nm (unweaned)
infant; **nourriture** nf food

nous[nu] pron (sujet) we; (objet) us; **nous-
mêmes** pron ourselves

nouveau (nouvel), -elle, x[nuvo, nuvɛl]
adj new ▷ nm: **y a-t-il du nouveau?** is there
anything new on this? ▷ nm/f new pupil (ou
employee); **de nouveau, à nouveau** again;

nouveau venu, nouvelle venue newcomer;
nouveaux mariés newly-weds; **nouveau-né,
e** nm/f newborn baby; **nouveauté** nf novelty;
(objet) new thing ou article

nouvel[nuvɛl] adj voir **nouveau**; **Nouvel An**
New Year

nouvelle[nuvɛl] adj voir **nouveau** ▷ nf (piece
of) news sg; (Littérature) short story; **les ~s**
(Presse, TV) the news; **je suis sans ~s de lui** I
haven't heard from him; **Nouvelle-Calédonie**
nf New Caledonia; **Nouvelle-Zélande** nf New
Zealand

novembre[nɔvãbʀ] nm November

⬤ **NOVEMBRE**
⬤
⬤ **Le 11 novembre** is a public holiday in
⬤ France commemorating the signing of the
⬤ armistice, near Compiègne, at the end of
⬤ World War I.

noyade[nwajad] nf drowning no pl

noyau, x[nwajo] nm (de fruit) stone; (Bio,
Physique) nucleus; (fig: centre) core

noyer[nwaje] nm walnut (tree); (bois) walnut
▷ vt to drown; (moteur) to flood; **se noyer** vi to
be drowned, drown; (suicide) to drown o.s.

nu, e[ny] adj naked; (membres) naked, bare;
(pieds, mains, chambre, fil électrique) bare ▷ nm
(Art) nude; **tout nu** stark naked; **se mettre
nu** to strip

nuage[nɥaʒ] nm cloud; **nuageux, -euse** adj
cloudy

nuance[nɥãs] nf (de couleur, sens) shade; **il
y a une ~ (entre)** there's a slight difference
(between); **nuancer** vt (opinion) to bring some
reservations ou qualifications to

nucléaire[nykleɛʀ] adj nuclear ▷ nm: **le ~**
nuclear energy

nudiste[nydist] nm/f nudist

nuée[nɥe] nf: **une ~ de** a cloud ou host ou
swarm of

nuire[nɥiʀ] vi to be harmful; **~ à** to harm, do
damage to; **nuisible** adj harmful; **animal
nuisible** pest

nuit[nɥi] nf night; **il fait ~** it's dark; **cette
~** (hier) last night; (aujourd'hui) tonight; **de ~**
(vol, service) night cpd; **nuit blanche** sleepless
night

nul, nulle[nyl] adj (aucun) no; (minime) nil,
non-existent; (non valable) null; (péj): **être ~
(en)** to be useless ou hopeless (at) ▷ pron none,
no one; **match ou résultat ~** draw; **~ le part**
nowhere; **nullement** adv by no means

numérique[nymeʀik] adj numerical;
(affichage, son, télévision) digital

numéro[nymeʀo] nm number; (spectacle)
act, turn; (Presse) issue, number; **numéro de
téléphone** (tele)phone number; **numéro**

vert ≈ freefone® number (*BRIT*), ≈ toll-free
number (*US*); **numéroter** *vt* to number
nuque [nyk] *nf* nape of the neck
nu-tête [nytɛt] *adj inv, adv* bareheaded
nutritif, -ive [nytʀitif, iv] *adj* (*besoins, valeur*)
nutritional; (*nourrissant*) nutritious
nylon [nilɔ̃] *nm* nylon

oasis [ɔazis] *nf* oasis
obéir [ɔbeiʀ] *vi* to obey; **~ à** to obey;
  obéissance *nf* obedience; **obéissant, e** *adj*
  obedient
obèse [ɔbɛz] *adj* obese; **obésité** *nf* obesity
objecter [ɔbʒɛkte] *vt*: **~ que** to object that;
  objecteur *nm*: **objecteur de conscience**
  conscientious objector
objectif, -ive [ɔbʒɛktif, iv] *adj* objective ▷ *nm*
  objective; (*Photo*) lens *sg*, objective
objection [ɔbʒɛksjɔ̃] *nf* objection
objectivité [ɔbʒɛktivite] *nf* objectivity
objet [ɔbʒɛ] *nm* object; (*d'une discussion,
  recherche*) subject; **être** *ou* **faire l'~ de**
  (*discussion*) to be the subject of; (*soins*) to be
  given *ou* shown; **sans ~** purposeless; (*craintes*)
  groundless; **(bureau des) ~s trouvés** lost
  property *sg* (*BRIT*), lost-and-found *sg* (*US*);
  objet d'art objet d'art; **objets de valeur**
  valuables; **objets personnels** personal items
obligation [ɔbligasjɔ̃] *nf* obligation; (*Comm*)
  bond, debenture; **obligatoire** *adj* compulsory,
  obligatory; **obligatoirement** *adv* necessarily;
  (*fam: sans aucun doute*) inevitably
obliger [ɔbliʒe] *vt* (*contraindre*): **~ qn à faire**
  to force *ou* oblige sb to do; **je suis bien obligé
  (de le faire)** I have to (do it)
oblique [ɔblik] *adj* oblique; **en ~** diagonally
oblitérer [ɔbliteʀe] *vt* (*timbre-poste*) to cancel
obnubiler [ɔbnybile] *vt* to obsess

obscène [ɔpsɛn] *adj* obscene

obscur, e [ɔpskyʀ] *adj* dark; (*méconnu*) obscure; **obscurcir** *vt* to darken; (*fig*) to obscure; **s'obscurcir** *vi* to grow dark; **obscurité** *nf* darkness; **dans l'obscurité** in the dark, in darkness

obsédé, e [ɔpsede] *nm/f*: **un ~ de jazz** a jazz fanatic; **obsédé sexuel** sex maniac

obséder [ɔpsede] *vt* to obsess, haunt

obsèques [ɔpsɛk] *nfpl* funeral *sg*

observateur, -trice [ɔpsɛʀvatœʀ, tʀis] *adj* observant, perceptive ▷ *nm/f* observer

observation [ɔpsɛʀvasjɔ̃] *nf* observation; (*d'un règlement etc*) observance; (*reproche*) reproof; **être en ~** (*Méd*) to be under observation

observatoire [ɔpsɛʀvatwaʀ] *nm* observatory

observer [ɔpsɛʀve] *vt* (*regarder*) to observe, watch; (*scientifiquement; aussi règlement etc*) to observe; (*surveiller*) to watch; (*remarquer*) to observe, notice; **faire ~ qch à qn** (*dire*) to point out sth to sb

obsession [ɔpsesjɔ̃] *nf* obsession

obstacle [ɔpstakl] *nm* obstacle; (*Équitation*) jump, hurdle; **faire ~ à** (*projet*) to hinder, put obstacles in the path of

obstiné, e [ɔpstine] *adj* obstinate

obstiner [ɔpstine]: **s'obstiner** *vi* to insist, dig one's heels in; **s'~ à faire** to persist (obstinately) in doing

obstruer [ɔpstʀye] *vt* to block, obstruct

obtenir [ɔptəniʀ] *vt* to obtain, get; (*résultat*) to achieve, obtain; **~ de pouvoir faire** to obtain permission to do

obturateur [ɔptyʀatœʀ] *nm* (*Photo*) shutter

obus [ɔby] *nm* shell

occasion [ɔkazjɔ̃] *nf* (*aubaine, possibilité*) opportunity; (*circonstance*) occasion; (*Comm: article non neuf*) secondhand buy; (: *acquisition avantageuse*) bargain; **à plusieurs ~s** on several occasions; **à l'~** sometimes, on occasions; **d'~** secondhand; **occasionnel, le** *adj* (*non régulier*) occasional

occasionner [ɔkazjɔne] *vt* to cause

occident [ɔksidɑ̃] *nm*: **l'O~** the West; **occidental, e, -aux** *adj* western; (*Pol*) Western ▷ *nm/f* Westerner

occupation [ɔkypasjɔ̃] *nf* occupation

occupé, e [ɔkype] *adj* (*personne*) busy; (*place, sièges*) taken; (*toilettes*) engaged; (*Mil, Pol*) occupied; **la ligne est ~e** the line's engaged (*brit*) ou busy (*us*)

occuper [ɔkype] *vt* to occupy; (*poste*) to hold; **s'occuper de** (*être responsable de*) to be in charge of; (*se charger de: affaire*) to take charge of, deal with; (: *clients etc*) to attend to; **s'~ (à qch)** to occupy o.s. *ou* keep o.s. busy (with sth)

occurrence [ɔkyʀɑ̃s] *nf*: **en l'~** in this case

océan [ɔseɑ̃] *nm* ocean

octet [ɔktɛ] *nm* byte

octobre [ɔktɔbʀ] *nm* October

oculiste [ɔkylist] *nm/f* eye specialist

odeur [ɔdœʀ] *nf* smell

odieux, -euse [ɔdjø, jøz] *adj* hateful

odorant, e [ɔdɔʀɑ̃, ɑ̃t] *adj* sweet-smelling, fragrant

odorat [ɔdɔʀa] *nm* (sense of) smell

œil [œj] (*pl* **yeux**) *nm* eye; **avoir un ~ au beurre noir** *ou* **poché** to have a black eye; **à l'~** (*fam*) for free; **à l'~ nu** with the naked eye; **ouvrir l'~** (*fig*) to keep one's eyes open *ou* an eye out; **fermer les yeux (sur)** (*fig*) to turn a blind eye (to); **les yeux fermés** (*aussi fig*) with one's eyes shut

œillères [œjɛʀ] *nfpl* blinkers (*brit*), blinders (*us*)

œillet [œjɛ] *nm* (*Bot*) carnation

œuf [œf, *pl* ø] *nm* egg; **œuf à la coque** boiled egg; **œuf au plat** fried egg; **œuf dur** hard-boiled egg; **œuf de Pâques** Easter egg; **œufs brouillés** scrambled eggs

œuvre [œvʀ] *nf* (*tâche*) task, undertaking; (*livre, tableau etc*) work; (*ensemble de la production artistique*) works *pl* ▷ *nm* (*Constr*): **le gros ~** the shell; **mettre en ~** (*moyens*) to make use of; **œuvre de bienfaisance** charity; **œuvre d'art** work of art

offense [ɔfɑ̃s] *nf* insult; **offenser** *vt* to offend, hurt; **s'offenser de qch** to take offence (*brit*) *ou* offense (*us*) at sth

offert, e [ɔfɛʀ, ɛʀt] *pp de* **offrir**

office [ɔfis] *nm* (*agence*) bureau, agency; (*Rel*) service ▷ *nm ou nf* (*pièce*) pantry; **faire ~ de** to act as; **d'~** automatically; **office du tourisme** tourist bureau

officiel, le [ɔfisjɛl] *adj, nm/f* official

officier [ɔfisje] *nm* officer

officieux, -euse [ɔfisjø, jøz] *adj* unofficial

offrande [ɔfʀɑ̃d] *nf* offering

offre [ɔfʀ] *nf* offer; (*aux enchères*) bid; (*Admin: soumission*) tender; (*Écon*): **l'~ et la demande** supply and demand; **"~s d'emploi"** "situations vacant"; **offre d'emploi** job advertised; **offre publique d'achat** takeover bid

offrir [ɔfʀiʀ] *vt*: **~ (à qn)** to offer (to sb); (*faire cadeau de*) to give (to sb); **s'offrir** *vt* (*vacances, voiture*) to treat o.s. to; **~ (à qn) de faire qch** to offer to do sth (for sb); **~ à boire à qn** (*chez soi*) to offer sb a drink; **je vous offre un verre** I'll buy you a drink

OGM *sigle m* (= *organisme génétiquement modifié*) GMO

oie [wa] *nf* (*Zool*) goose

oignon [ɔɲɔ̃] *nm* onion; (*de tulipe etc*) bulb

oiseau, x [wazo] *nm* bird; **oiseau de proie** bird of prey

oisif, -ive [wazif, iv] *adj* idle

oléoduc [ɔleɔdyk] nm (oil) pipeline
olive [ɔliv] nf (Bot) olive; **olivier** nm olive (tree)
OLP sigle f (= Organisation de libération de la Palestine) PLO
olympique [ɔlɛ̃pik] adj Olympic
ombragé, e [ɔ̃braʒe] adj shaded, shady
ombre [ɔ̃br] nf (espace non ensoleillé) shade; (ombre portée, tache) shadow; **à l'~** in the shade; **dans l'~** (fig) in the dark; **ombre à paupières** eyeshadow
omelette [ɔmlɛt] nf omelette; **omelette norvégienne** baked Alaska
omettre [ɔmɛtr] vt to omit, leave out
omoplate [ɔmɔplat] nf shoulder blade

MOT-CLÉ

on [ɔ̃] pron **1** (indéterminé) you, one; **on peut le faire ainsi** you ou one can do it like this, it can be done like this
2 (quelqu'un): **on les a attaqués** they were attacked; **on vous demande au téléphone** there's a phone call for you, you're wanted on the phone
3 (nous) we; **on va y aller demain** we're going tomorrow
4 (les gens) they; **autrefois, on croyait ...** they used to believe ...
5: **on ne peut plus** adv: **~ on ne peut plus stupide** as stupid as can be

oncle [ɔ̃kl] nm uncle
onctueux, -euse [ɔ̃ktɥø, øz] adj creamy, smooth
onde [ɔ̃d] nf wave; **~s courtes/moyennes** short/medium wave sg; **grandes ~s** long wave sg
ondée [ɔ̃de] nf shower
on-dit [ɔ̃di] nm inv rumour
onduler [ɔ̃dyle] vi to undulate; (cheveux) to wave
onéreux, -euse [ɔnerø, øz] adj costly
ongle [ɔ̃gl] nm nail
ont [ɔ̃] vb voir **avoir**
ONU sigle f (= Organisation des Nations Unies) UN
onze [ɔ̃z] num eleven; **onzième** num eleventh
OPA sigle f = **offre publique d'achat**
opaque [ɔpak] adj opaque
opéra [ɔpera] nm opera; (édifice) opera house
opérateur, -trice [ɔperatœr, tris] nm/f operator; **opérateur (de prise de vues)** cameraman
opération [ɔperasjɔ̃] nf operation; (Comm) dealing
opératoire [ɔperatwar] adj (choc etc) post-operative
opérer [ɔpere] vt (personne) to operate on; (faire, exécuter) to carry out, make ▷ vi (remède:

faire effet) to act, work; (Méd) to operate; **s'opérer** vi (avoir lieu) to occur, take place; **se faire ~** to have an operation
opérette [ɔperɛt] nf operetta, light opera
opinion [ɔpinjɔ̃] nf opinion; **l'opinion (publique)** public opinion
opportun, e [ɔpɔrtœ̃, yn] adj timely, opportune; **opportuniste** nm/f opportunist
opposant, e [ɔpozɑ̃, ɑ̃t] nm/f opponent
opposé, e [ɔpoze] adj (direction) opposite; (faction) opposing; (opinions, intérêts) conflicting; (contre): **~ à** opposed to, against ▷ nm: **l'~** the other ou opposite side (ou direction); (contraire) the opposite; **à l'~** (fig) on the other hand; **à l'~ de** (fig) contrary to, unlike
opposer [ɔpoze] vt (personnes, équipes) to oppose; (couleurs) to contrast; **s'opposer** vi (équipes) to confront each other; (opinions) to conflict; (couleurs, styles) to contrast; **s'~ à** (interdire) to oppose; **~ qch à** (comme obstacle, défense) to set sth against; (comme objection) to put sth forward against
opposition [ɔpozisjɔ̃] nf opposition; **par ~ à** as opposed to; **entrer en ~ avec** to come into conflict with; **faire ~ à un chèque** to stop a cheque
oppressant, e [ɔpresɑ̃, ɑ̃t] adj oppressive
oppresser [ɔprese] vt to oppress; **oppression** nf oppression
opprimer [ɔprime] vt to oppress
opter [ɔpte] vi: **~ pour** to opt for
opticien, ne [ɔptisjɛ̃, jɛn] nm/f optician
optimisme [ɔptimism] nm optimism; **optimiste** nm/f optimist ▷ adj optimistic
option [ɔpsjɔ̃] nf option; **matière à ~** (Scol) optional subject
optique [ɔptik] adj (nerf) optic; (verres) optical ▷ nf (fig: manière de voir) perspective
or [ɔr] nm gold ▷ conj now, but; **en or** (objet) gold cpd; **une affaire en or** a real bargain; **il croyait gagner ou il a perdu** he was sure he would win and yet he lost
orage [ɔraʒ] nm (thunder)storm; **orageux, -euse** adj stormy
oral, e, -aux [ɔral, o] adj, nm oral; **par voie ~e** (Méd) orally
orange [ɔrɑ̃ʒ] nf orange ▷ adj inv orange; **orangé, e** adj orangey, orange-coloured; **orangeade** nf orangeade; **oranger** nm orange tree
orateur [ɔratœr] nm speaker
orbite [ɔrbit] nf (Anat) (eye-)socket; (Physique) orbit
Orcades [ɔrkad] nfpl: **les ~** the Orkneys, the Orkney Islands
orchestre [ɔrkɛstr] nm orchestra; (de jazz) band; (places) stalls pl (Brit), orchestra (US)
orchidée [ɔrkide] nf orchid

ordinaire [ɔʀdinɛʀ] *adj* ordinary; (*qualité*) standard; (*péj: commun*) common ▷ *nm* ordinary; (*menus*) everyday fare ▷ *nf* (*essence*) ≈ two-star (petrol) (BRIT), ≈ regular gas (US); **d'~** usually, normally; **comme à l'~** as usual

ordinateur [ɔʀdinatœʀ] *nm* computer; **ordinateur individuel** *ou* **personnel** personal computer; **ordinateur portable** laptop (computer)

ordonnance [ɔʀdɔnɑ̃s] *nf* (*Méd*) prescription; (*Mil*) orderly, batman (BRIT); **pouvez-vous me faire une ~?** can you write me a prescription?

ordonné, e [ɔʀdɔne] *adj* tidy, orderly

ordonner [ɔʀdɔne] *vt* (*agencer*) to organize, arrange; (*donner un ordre*): **~ à qn de faire** to order sb to do; (*Rel*) to ordain; (*Méd*) to prescribe

ordre [ɔʀdʀ] *nm* order; (*propreté et soin*) orderliness, tidiness; (*nature*): **d'~ pratique** of a practical nature; **ordres** *nmpl* (*Rel*) holy orders; **mettre en ~** to tidy (up), put in order; **par ~ alphabétique/d'importance** in alphabetical order/in order of importance; **à l'~ de qn** payable to sb; **être aux ~s de qn/sous les ~s de qn** to be at sb's disposal/under sb's command; **jusqu'à nouvel ~** until further notice; **de premier ~** first-rate; **ordre du jour** (*d'une réunion*) agenda; **à l'ordre du jour** (*fig*) topical; **ordre public** law and order

ordure [ɔʀdyʀ] *nf* filth *no pl*; **ordures** *nfpl* (*balayures, déchets*) rubbish *sg*, refuse *sg*; **ordures ménagères** household refuse

oreille [ɔʀɛj] *nf* ear; **avoir de l'~** to have a good ear (for music)

oreiller [ɔʀeje] *nm* pillow

oreillons [ɔʀejɔ̃] *nmpl* mumps *sg*

ores [ɔʀ]: **d'~ et déjà** *adv* already

orfèvrerie [ɔʀfɛvʀəʀi] *nf* goldsmith's (*ou* silversmith's) trade; (*ouvrage*) gold (*ou* silver) plate

organe [ɔʀgan] *nm* organ; (*porte-parole*) representative, mouthpiece

organigramme [ɔʀganigʀam] *nm* (*tableau hiérarchique*) organization chart; (*schéma*) flow chart

organique [ɔʀganik] *adj* organic

organisateur, -trice [ɔʀganizatœʀ, tʀis] *nm/f* organizer

organisation [ɔʀganizasjɔ̃] *nf* organization; **Organisation des Nations Unies** United Nations (Organization)

organiser [ɔʀganize] *vt* to organize; (*mettre sur pied: service etc*) to set up; **s'organiser** to get organized

organisme [ɔʀganism] *nm* (*Bio*) organism; (*corps, Admin*) body

organiste [ɔʀganist] *nm/f* organist

orgasme [ɔʀgasm] *nm* orgasm, climax

orge [ɔʀʒ] *nf* barley

orgue [ɔʀg] *nm* organ

orgueil [ɔʀgœj] *nm* pride; **orgueilleux, -euse** *adj* proud

oriental, e, -aux [ɔʀjɑ̃tal, -o] *adj* (*langue, produit*) oriental; (*frontière*) eastern

orientation [ɔʀjɑ̃tasjɔ̃] *nf* (*de recherches*) orientation; (*d'une maison etc*) aspect; (*d'un journal*) leanings *pl*; **avoir le sens de l'~** to have a (good) sense of direction; **orientation professionnelle** careers advisory service

orienté, e [ɔʀjɑ̃te] *adj* (*fig: article, journal*) slanted; **bien/mal ~** (*appartement*) well/badly positioned; **~ au sud** facing south, with a southern aspect

orienter [ɔʀjɑ̃te] *vt* (*tourner: antenne*) to direct, turn; (*personne, recherches*) to direct; (*fig: élève*) to orientate; **s'orienter** (*se repérer*) to find one's bearings; **s'~ vers** (*fig*) to turn towards

origan [ɔʀigɑ̃] *nm* oregano

originaire [ɔʀiʒinɛʀ] *adj*: **être ~ de** to be a native of

original, e, -aux [ɔʀiʒinal, o] *adj* original; (*bizarre*) eccentric ▷ *nm/f* eccentric ▷ *nm* (*document etc, Art*) original

origine [ɔʀiʒin] *nf* origin; **origines** *nfpl* (*d'une personne*) origins; **d'~** (*pays*) of origin; **d'~ suédoise** of Swedish origin; (*pneus etc*) original; **à l'~** originally; **originel, le** *adj* original

orme [ɔʀm] *nm* elm

ornement [ɔʀnəmɑ̃] *nm* ornament

orner [ɔʀne] *vt* to decorate, adorn

ornière [ɔʀnjɛʀ] *nf* rut

orphelin, e [ɔʀfəlɛ̃, in] *adj* orphan(ed) ▷ *nm/f* orphan; **orphelin de mère/de père** motherless/fatherless; **orphelinat** *nm* orphanage

orteil [ɔʀtɛj] *nm* toe; **gros ~** big toe

orthographe [ɔʀtɔgʀaf] *nf* spelling

ortie [ɔʀti] *nf* (stinging) nettle

os [ɔs] *nm* bone; **os à moelle** marrowbone

osciller [ɔsile] *vi* (*au vent etc*) to rock; (*fig*): **~ entre** to waver *ou* fluctuate between

osé, e [oze] *adj* daring, bold

oseille [ozɛj] *nf* sorrel

oser [oze] *vi, vt* to dare; **~ faire** to dare (to) do

osier [ozje] *nm* willow; **d'~, en ~** wicker(work)

osseux, -euse [ɔsø, øz] *adj* bony; (*tissu, maladie, greffe*) bone *cpd*

otage [ɔtaʒ] *nm* hostage; **prendre qn comme ~** to take sb hostage

OTAN *sigle f* (= *Organisation du traité de l'Atlantique Nord*) NATO

otarie [ɔtaʀi] *nf* sea-lion

ôter [ote] *vt* to remove; (*soustraire*) to take away; **~ qch à qn** to take sth (away) from sb; **~ qch de** to remove sth from

otite [ɔtit] *nf* ear infection

ou [u] *conj* or; **ou ... ou** either ... or; **ou bien** or (else)

MOT-CLÉ

où [u] *pron relatif* **1** (*position, situation*) where, that (*souvent omis*); **la chambre où il était** the room (that) he was in, the room where he was; **la ville où je l'ai rencontré** the town where I met him; **la pièce d'où il est sorti** the room he came out of; **le village d'où je viens** the village I come from; **les villes par où il est passé** the towns he went through **2** (*temps, état*) that (*souvent omis*); **le jour où il est parti** the day (that) he left; **au prix où c'est** at the price it is
▷ *adv* **1** (*interrogation*) where; **où est-il/va-t-il?** where is he/is he going?; **par où?** which way?; **d'où vient que ...?** how come ...?
2 (*position*) where; **je sais où il est** I know where he is; **où que l'on aille** wherever you go

ouate ['wat] *nf* cotton wool (*BRIT*), cotton (*US*)
oubli [ubli] *nm* (*acte*): **l'~ de** forgetting; (*trou de mémoire*) lapse of memory; (*négligence*) omission, oversight; **tomber dans l'~** to sink into oblivion
oublier [ublije] *vt* to forget; (*laisser quelque part: chapeau etc*) to leave behind; (*ne pas voir: erreurs etc*) to miss; **j'ai oublié ma clé/mon passeport** I've forgotten my key/passport
ouest [wɛst] *nm* west ▷ *adj inv* west; (*région*) western; **à l'~** in the west; (*direction*) (to the) west, westwards; **à l'~ de** (to the) west of
ouf ['uf] *excl* phew!
oui ['wi] *adv* yes
ouï-dire ['widiʀ]: **par ~** *adv* by hearsay
ouïe [wi] *nf* hearing; **ouïes** *nfpl* (*de poisson*) gills
ouragan [uʀagã] *nm* hurricane
ourlet [uʀlɛ] *nm* hem
ours [uʀs] *nm* bear; **ours blanc/brun** polar/brown bear; **ours (en peluche)** teddy (bear)
oursin [uʀsɛ̃] *nm* sea urchin
ourson [uʀsɔ̃] *nm* (bear-)cub
ouste [ust] *excl* hop it!
outil [uti] *nm* tool; **outiller** *vt* to equip
outrage [utʀaʒ] *nm* insult; **outrage à la pudeur** indecent conduct *no pl*
outrance [utʀãs]: **à ~** *adv* excessively, to excess
outre [utʀ] *prép* besides ▷ *adv*: **passer ~ à** to disregard, take no notice of; **en ~** besides, moreover; **~ mesure** (*manger, boire*) immoderately; **outre-Atlantique** *adv* across the Atlantic; **outre-mer** *adv* overseas
ouvert, e [uvɛʀ, ɛʀt] *pp de* **ouvrir** ▷ *adj* open; (*robinet, gaz etc*) on; **ouvertement** *adv* openly;

ouverture *nf* opening; (*Mus*) overture; **heures d'ouverture** (*Comm*) opening hours; **ouverture d'esprit** open-mindedness
ouvrable [uvʀabl] *adj*: **jour ~** working day, weekday
ouvrage [uvʀaʒ] *nm* (*tâche, de tricot etc*) work *no pl*; (*texte, livre*) work
ouvre-boîte(s) [uvʀəbwat] *nm inv* tin (*BRIT*) *ou* can opener
ouvre-bouteille(s) [uvʀəbutɛj] *nm inv* bottle-opener
ouvreuse [uvʀøz] *nf* usherette
ouvrier, -ière [uvʀije, ijɛʀ] *nm/f* worker ▷ *adj* working-class; (*conflit*) industrial; (*mouvement*) labour *cpd*; **classe ouvrière** working class
ouvrir [uvʀiʀ] *vt* (*gén*) to open; (*brèche, passage, Méd: abcès*) to open up; (*commencer l'exploitation de, créer*) to open (up); (*eau, électricité, chauffage, robinet*) to turn on ▷ *vi* to open; to open up; **s'ouvrir** *vi* to open; **s'~ à qn** to open one's heart to sb; **est-ce ouvert au public?** is it open to the public?; **quand est-ce que le musée est ouvert?** when is the museum open?; **à quelle heure ouvrez-vous?** what time do you open?; **~ l'appétit à qn** to whet sb's appetite
ovaire [ɔvɛʀ] *nm* ovary
ovale [ɔval] *adj* oval
OVNI [ɔvni] *sigle m* (= *objet volant non identifié*) UFO
oxyder [ɔkside]: **s'oxyder** *vi* to become oxidized
oxygène [ɔksiʒɛn] *nm* oxygen
oxygéné, e [ɔksiʒene] *adj*: **eau ~e** hydrogen peroxide
ozone [ozon] *nf* ozone; **la couche d'~** the ozone layer

pacifique [pasifik] *adj* peaceful ▷ *nm*: **le P~, l'océan P~** the Pacific (Ocean)

pack [pak] *nm* pack

pacotille [pakɔtij] *nf* cheap junk

PACS *sigle m* (= *pacte civil de solidarité*) contract of civil partnership; **pacser: se pacser** *vi* to sign a contract of civil partnership

pacte [pakt] *nm* pact, treaty

pagaille [pagaj] *nf* mess, shambles *sg*

page [paʒ] *nf* page ▷ *nm* page (boy); **à la ~** (*fig*) up-to-date; **page d'accueil** (*Inform*) home page; **page Web** (*Inform*) web page

paiement [pɛmɑ̃] *nm* payment

païen, ne [pajɛ̃, pajɛn] *adj, nm/f* pagan, heathen

paillasson [pajasɔ̃] *nm* doormat

paille [paj] *nf* straw

pain [pɛ̃] *nm* (*substance*) bread; (*unité*) loaf (of bread); (*morceau*): **~ de savon** *etc* bar of soap *etc*; **pain au chocolat** chocolate-filled pastry; **pain aux raisins** currant bun; **pain bis/complet** brown/wholemeal (*BRIT*) ou wholewheat (*US*) bread; **pain d'épice** ≈ gingerbread; **pain de mie** sandwich loaf; **pain grillé** toast

pair, e [pɛʀ] *adj* (*nombre*) even ▷ *nm* peer; **aller de ~** to go hand in hand ou together; **jeune fille au ~** au pair; **paire** *nf* pair

paisible [pezibl] *adj* peaceful, quiet

paix [pɛ] *nf* peace; **faire/avoir la ~** to make/have peace; **fiche-lui la ~!** (*fam*) leave him alone!

Pakistan [pakistɑ̃] *nm*: **le ~** Pakistan

palais [palɛ] *nm* palace; (*Anat*) palate

pâle [pal] *adj* pale; **bleu ~** pale blue

Palestine [palɛstin] *nf*: **la ~** Palestine

palette [palɛt] *nf* (*de peintre*) palette; (*produits*) range

pâleur [palœʀ] *nf* paleness

palier [palje] *nm* (*d'escalier*) landing; (*fig*) level, plateau; **par ~s** in stages

pâlir [paliʀ] *vi* to turn ou go pale; (*couleur*) to fade

pallier [palje] *vt* to offset, make up for

palme [palm] *nf* (*de plongeur*) flipper; **palmé, e** *adj* (*pattes*) webbed

palmier [palmje] *nm* palm tree; (*gâteau*) heart-shaped biscuit made of flaky pastry

pâlot, te [palo, ɔt] *adj* pale, peaky

palourde [paluʀd] *nf* clam

palper [palpe] *vt* to feel, finger

palpitant, e [palpitɑ̃, ɑ̃t] *adj* thrilling

palpiter [palpite] *vi* (*cœur, pouls*) to beat; (: *plus fort*) to pound, throb

paludisme [palydism] *nm* malaria

pamphlet [pɑ̃flɛ] *nm* lampoon, satirical tract

pamplemousse [pɑ̃pləmus] *nm* grapefruit

pan [pɑ̃] *nm* section, piece ▷ *excl* bang!

panache [panaʃ] *nm* plume; (*fig*) spirit, panache

panaché, e [panaʃe] *adj*: **glace ~e** mixed-flavour ice cream ▷ *nm* (*bière*) shandy

pancarte [pɑ̃kaʀt] *nf* sign, notice

pancréas [pɑ̃kreas] *nm* pancreas

pané, e [pane] *adj* fried in breadcrumbs

panier [panje] *nm* basket; **mettre au ~** to chuck away; **panier à provisions** shopping basket; **panier-repas** *nm* packed lunch

panique [panik] *nf, adj* panic; **paniquer** *vi* to panic

panne [pan] *nf* breakdown; **être/tomber en ~** to have broken down/break down; **être en ~ d'essence** ou **sèche** to have run out of petrol (*BRIT*) ou gas (*US*); **ma voiture est en ~** my car has broken down; **panne d'électricité** ou **de courant** power cut ou failure

panneau, x [pano] *nm* (*écriteau*) sign, notice; **panneau d'affichage** notice board; **panneau de signalisation** roadsign; **panneau indicateur** signpost

panoplie [panɔpli] *nf* (*jouet*) outfit; (*fig*) array

panorama [panɔrama] *nm* panorama

panse [pɑ̃s] *nf* paunch

pansement [pɑ̃smɑ̃] *nm* dressing, bandage; **pansement adhésif** sticking plaster

pantacourt [pɑ̃takuʀ] *nm* three-quarter length trousers *pl*

pantalon [pɑ̃talɔ̃] *nm* trousers *pl*, pair of trousers; **pantalon de ski** ski pants *pl*

panthère [pɑ̃tɛʀ] nf panther

pantin [pɑ̃tɛ̃] nm puppet

pantoufle [pɑ̃tufl] nf slipper

paon [pɑ̃] nm peacock

papa [papa] nm dad(dy)

pape [pap] nm pope

paperasse [papʀas] (péj) nf bumf no pl, papers pl; **paperasserie** (péj) nf paperwork no pl; (tracasserie) red tape no pl

papeterie [papetʀi] nf (magasin) stationer's (shop)

papi nm (fam) granddad

papier [papje] nm paper; (article) article; **papiers** nmpl (aussi: **~s d'identité**) (identity) papers; **papier à lettres** writing paper, notepaper; **papier (d')aluminium** aluminium (BRIT) ou aluminum (US) foil, tinfoil; **papier calque** tracing paper; **papier de verre** sandpaper; **papier hygiénique** ou **(de) toilette** toilet paper; **papier journal** newspaper; **papier peint** wallpaper

papillon [papijɔ̃] nm butterfly; (fam: contravention) (parking) ticket; **papillon de nuit** moth

papillote [papijɔt] nf: **en ~** cooked in tinfoil

papoter [papɔte] vi to chatter

paquebot [pak(ə)bo] nm liner

pâquerette [pakʀɛt] nf daisy

Pâques [pɑk] nm, nfpl Easter

* PÂQUES
*
* In France, Easter eggs are said to be brought
* by the Easter bells or **cloches de Pâques**
* which fly from Rome and drop them in
* people's gardens.

paquet [pakɛ] nm packet; (colis) parcel; (fig: tas): **~ de** pile ou heap of; **un ~ de cigarettes, s'il vous plaît** a packet of cigarettes, please; **paquet-cadeau** nm: **pouvez-vous me faire un paquet-cadeau, s'il vous plaît?** can you gift-wrap it for me, please?

par [paʀ] prép by; **finir** etc **~** to end etc with; **~ amour** out of love; **passer ~ Lyon/la côte** to go via ou through Lyons/along the coast; **~ la fenêtre** (jeter, regarder) out of the window; **3 ~ jour/personne** 3 a ou per day/person; **2 ~ 2** in twos; **~ ici** this way; (dans le coin) round here; **~-ci, ~-là** here and there; **~ temps de pluie** in wet weather

parabolique [paʀabɔlik] adj: **antenne ~** parabolic ou dish aerial

parachute [paʀaʃyt] nm parachute; **parachutiste** nm/f parachutist; (Mil) paratrooper

parade [paʀad] nf (spectacle, défilé) parade; (Escrime, Boxe) parry

paradis [paʀadi] nm heaven, paradise

paradoxe [paʀadɔks] nm paradox

paraffine [paʀafin] nf paraffin

parages [paʀaʒ] nmpl: **dans les ~ (de)** in the area ou vicinity (of)

paragraphe [paʀagʀaf] nm paragraph

paraître [paʀɛtʀ] vb +attrib to seem, look, appear ▷ vi to appear; (être visible) to show; (Presse, Édition) to be published, come out, appear ▷ vb impers: **il paraît que** it seems ou appears that, they say that

parallèle [paʀalɛl] adj parallel; (non officiel) unofficial ▷ nm (comparaison): **faire un ~ entre** to draw a parallel between ▷ nf parallel (line)

paralyser [paʀalize] vt to paralyse

paramédical, e, -aux [paʀamedikal, o] adj: **personnel ~** paramedics pl, paramedical workers pl

paraphrase [paʀafʀɑz] nf paraphrase

parapluie [paʀaplɥi] nm umbrella

parasite [paʀazit] nm parasite; **parasites** nmpl (Tél) interference sg

parasol [paʀasɔl] nm parasol, sunshade

paratonnerre [paʀatɔnɛʀ] nm lightning conductor

parc [paʀk] nm (public) park, gardens pl; (de château etc) grounds pl; (d'enfant) playpen; **parc à thème** theme park; **parc d'attractions** amusement park; **parc de stationnement** car park

parcelle [paʀsɛl] nf fragment, scrap; (de terrain) plot, parcel

parce que [paʀsk(ə)] conj because

parchemin [paʀʃəmɛ̃] nm parchment

parc(o)mètre [paʀkmɛtʀ] nm parking meter

parcourir [paʀkuʀiʀ] vt (trajet, distance) to cover; (article, livre) to skim ou glance through; (lieu) to go all over, travel up and down; (suj: frisson) to run through

parcours [paʀkuʀ] nm (trajet) journey; (itinéraire) route

par-dessous [paʀd(ə)su] prép, adv under(neath)

pardessus [paʀdəsy] nm overcoat

par-dessus [paʀd(ə)sy] prép over (the top of) ▷ adv over (the top); **~ le marché** on top of all that; **~ tout** above all; **en avoir ~ la tête** to have had enough

par-devant [paʀd(ə)vɑ̃] adv (passer) round the front

pardon [paʀdɔ̃] nm forgiveness no pl ▷ excl sorry!; (pour interpeller etc) excuse me!; **demander ~ à qn (de)** to apologize to sb (for); **je vous demande ~** I'm sorry; (pour interpeller) excuse me; **pardonner** vt to forgive; **pardonner qch à qn** to forgive sb for sth

pare...: **pare-brise** nm inv windscreen (BRIT), windshield (US); **pare-chocs** nm inv bumper;

pare-feu nm inv (de foyer) fireguard; (Inform) firewall

pareil, le [paʀɛj] adj (identique) the same, alike; (similaire) similar; (tel): **un courage/livre ~** such courage/a book, courage/a book like this; **de ~s livres** such books; **faire ~** to do the same (thing); **~ à** the same as; (similaire) similar to; **sans ~** unparalleled, unequalled

parent, e [paʀɑ̃, ɑ̃t] nm/f: **un(e) ~(e)** a relative ou relation; **parents** nmpl (père et mère) parents; **parenté** nf (lien) relationship

parenthèse [paʀɑ̃tɛz] nf (ponctuation) bracket, parenthesis; (digression) parenthesis, digression; **entre ~s** in brackets; (fig) incidentally

paresse [paʀɛs] nf laziness; **paresseux, -euse** adj lazy

parfait, e [paʀfɛ, ɛt] adj perfect ▷ nm (Ling) perfect (tense); **parfaitement** adv perfectly ▷ excl (most) certainly

parfois [paʀfwa] adv sometimes

parfum [paʀfœ̃] nm (produit) perfume, scent; (odeur: de fleur) scent, fragrance; (goût) flavour; **quels ~s avez-vous?** what flavours do you have?; **parfumé, e** adj (fleur, fruit) fragrant; (femme) perfumed; **parfumé au café** coffee-flavoured; **parfumer** vt (suj: odeur, bouquet) to perfume; (crème, gâteau) to flavour; **parfumerie** nf (produits) perfumes pl; (boutique) perfume shop

pari [paʀi] nm bet; **parier** vt to bet

Paris [paʀi] n Paris; **parisien, ne** adj Parisian; (Géo, Admin) Paris cpd ▷ nm/f: **Parisien, ne** Parisian

parité [paʀite] nf (Pol): **~ hommes-femmes** balanced representation of men and women

parjure [paʀʒyʀ] nm perjury

parking [paʀkiŋ] nm (lieu) car park

Attention à ne pas traduire **parking** par le mot anglais **parking**.

parlant, e [paʀlɑ̃, ɑ̃t] adj (regard) eloquent; (Cinéma) talking

parlement [paʀləmɑ̃] nm parliament; **parlementaire** adj parliamentary ▷ nm/f member of parliament

parler [paʀle] vi to speak, talk; (avouer) to talk; **~ (à qn) de** to talk ou speak (to sb) about; **~ le/en français** to speak French/in French; **~ affaires** to talk business; **sans ~ de** (fig) not to mention, to say nothing of; **tu parles!** (fam: bien sûr) you bet!; **parlez-vous français?** do you speak French?; **je ne parle pas anglais** I don't speak English; **est-ce que je peux ~ à ...?** can I speak to ...?

parloir [paʀlwaʀ] nm (de prison, d'hôpital) visiting room

parmi [paʀmi] prép among(st)

paroi [paʀwa] nf wall; (cloison) partition

paroisse [paʀwas] nf parish

parole [paʀɔl] nf (faculté): **la ~** speech; (mot, promesse) word; **paroles** nfpl (Mus) words, lyrics; **tenir ~** to keep one's word; **prendre la ~** to speak; **demander la ~** to ask for permission to speak; **je te crois sur ~** I'll take your word for it

parquet [paʀkɛ] nm (parquet) floor; (Jur): **le ~** the Public Prosecutor's department

parrain [paʀɛ̃] nm godfather; **parrainer** vt (suj: entreprise) to sponsor

pars [paʀ] vb voir **partir**

parsemer [paʀsəme] vt (suj: feuilles, papiers) to be scattered over; **~ qch de** to scatter sth with

part [paʀ] nf (qui revient à qn) share; (fraction, partie) part; **à ~** adv (séparément) separately; (de côté) aside ▷ prép apart from, except for; **prendre ~ à** (débat etc) to take part in; (soucis, douleur de qn) to share in; **faire ~ de qch à qn** to announce sth to, inform sb of sth; **pour ma ~** as for me, as far as I'm concerned; **à ~ entière** full; **de la ~ de** (au nom de) on behalf of; (donné par) from; **de toute(s) ~(s)** from all sides ou quarters; **de ~ et d'autre** on both sides, on either side; **d'une ~ ... d'autre ~** on the one hand ... on the other hand; **d'autre ~** (de plus) moreover; **faire la ~ des choses** to make allowances

partage [paʀtaʒ] nm (fractionnement) dividing up; (répartition) sharing (out) no pl, share-out

partager [paʀtaʒe] vt to share; (distribuer, répartir) to share (out); (morceler, diviser) to divide (up); **se partager** vt (héritage etc) to share between themselves (ou ourselves)

partenaire [paʀtənɛʀ] nm/f partner

parterre [paʀtɛʀ] nm (de fleurs) (flower) bed; (Théâtre) stalls pl

parti [paʀti] nm (Pol) party; (décision) course of action; (personne à marier) match; **tirer ~ de** to take advantage of, turn to good account; **prendre ~ (pour/contre)** to take sides ou a stand (for/against); **parti pris** bias

partial, e, -aux [paʀsjal, jo] adj biased, partial

participant, e [paʀtisipɑ̃, ɑ̃t] nm/f participant; (à un concours) entrant

participation [paʀtisipasjɔ̃] nf participation; (financière) contribution

participer [paʀtisipe]: **~ à** vt (course, réunion) to take part in; (frais etc) to contribute to; (chagrin, succès de qn) to share (in)

particularité [paʀtikylaʀite] nf (distinctive) characteristic

particulier, -ière [paʀtikylje, jɛʀ] adj (spécifique) particular; (spécial) special, particular; (personnel, privé) private; (étrange) peculiar, odd ▷ *nm* (*individu: Admin*) private individual; **~ à** peculiar to; **en ~** (*surtout*) in particular, particularly; (*en privé*) in private; **particulièrement** *adv* particularly

partie [paʁti] *nf* (*gén*) part; (*Jur etc: protagonistes*) party; (*de cartes, tennis etc*) game; **une ~ de pêche** a fishing party *ou* trip; **en ~** partly, in part; **faire ~ de** (*suj: chose*) to be part of; **prendre qn à ~** to take sb to task; **en grande ~** largely, in the main; **partie civile** (*Jur*) party claiming damages in a criminal case

partiel, le [paʁsjɛl] *adj* partial ▷ *nm* (*Scol*) class exam

partir [paʁtiʁ] *vi* (*gén*) to go; (*quitter*) to go, leave; (*tache*) to go, come out; **~ de** (*lieu: quitter*) to leave; (: *commencer à*) to start from; **~ pour/à** (*lieu, pays etc*) to leave for/go off to; **à ~ de** from; **le train/le bus part à quelle heure?** what time does the train/bus leave?

partisan, e [paʁtizã, an] *nm/f* partisan ▷ *adj*: **être ~ de qch/de faire** to be in favour of sth/doing

partition [paʁtisjɔ̃] *nf* (*Mus*) score

partout [paʁtu] *adv* everywhere; **~ où il allait** everywhere *ou* wherever he went

paru [paʁy] *pp de* **paraître**

parution [paʁysjɔ̃] *nf* publication

parvenir [paʁvəniʁ]: **~ à** *vt* (*atteindre*) to reach; (*réussir*): **~ à faire** to manage to do, succeed in doing; **faire ~ qch à qn** to have sth sent to sb

pas¹ [pa] *nm* (*enjambée, Danse*) step; (*allure, mesure*) pace; (*bruit*) (foot)step; (*trace*) footprint; **~ à ~** step by step; **au ~** at walking pace; **marcher à grands ~** to stride along; **à ~ de loup** stealthily; **faire les cent ~** to pace up and down; **faire le premier ~** to make the first move; **sur le ~ de la porte** on the doorstep

⊙ **MOT-CLÉ**

pas² [pa] *adv* **1** (*en corrélation avec ne, non etc*) not; **il ne pleure pas** (*habituellement*) he does not *ou* doesn't cry; (*maintenant*) he's not *ou* isn't crying; **il n'a pas pleuré/ne pleurera pas** he did not *ou* didn't/will not *ou* won't cry; **ils n'ont pas de voiture/ d'enfants** they don't have *ou* haven't got a car/any children; **il m'a dit de ne pas le faire** he told me not to do it; **non pas que ...** not that ...

2 (*employé sans ne etc*): **pas moi** not me, I don't (*ou* can't *etc*); **elle travaille, (mais) lui pas** *ou* **pas lui** she works but he doesn't *ou* does not; **une pomme pas mûre** an unripe apple; **pas du tout** not at all; **pas de sucre, merci** no sugar, thanks; **ceci est à vous**

ou pas? is this yours or not?, is this yours or isn't it?

3: **pas mal** (*joli: personne, maison*) not bad; **pas mal fait** not badly done *ou* made; **comment ça va? — pas mal** how are things? — not bad; **pas mal de** quite a lot of

passage [pasaʒ] *nm* (*fait de passer*) *voir* **passer**; (*lieu, prix de la traversée, extrait*) passage; (*chemin*) way; **de ~** (*touristes*) passing through; **passage à niveau** level crossing; **passage clouté** pedestrian crossing; **passage interdit** no entry; **passage souterrain** subway (BRIT), underpass

passager, -ère [pasaʒe, ɛʁ] *adj* passing ▷ *nm/f* passenger

passant, e [pasã, ãt] *adj* (*rue, endroit*) busy ▷ *nm/f* passer-by; **en ~** in passing

passe [pas] *nf* (*Sport, Navig*) pass; **être en ~ de faire** to be on the way to doing; **être dans une mauvaise ~** to be going through a rough patch

passé, e [pase] *adj* (*révolu*) past; (*dernier: semaine etc*) last; (*couleur*) faded ▷ *prép* after ▷ *nm* past; (*Ling*) past (tense); **~ de mode** out of fashion; **passé composé** perfect (tense); **passé simple** past historic (tense)

passe-partout [paspaʁtu] *nm inv* master *ou* skeleton key ▷ *adj inv* all-purpose

passeport [paspɔʁ] *nm* passport

passer [pase] *vi* (*aller*) to go; (*voiture, piétons: défiler*) to pass (by), go by; (*facteur, laitier etc*) to come, call; (*pour rendre visite*) to call *ou* drop in; (*film, émission*) to be on; (*temps, jours*) to pass, go by; (*couleur*) to fade; (*mode*) to die out; (*douleur*) to pass, go away; (*Scol*): **~ dans la classe supérieure** to go up to the next class ▷ *vt* (*frontière, rivière etc*) to cross; (*douane*) to go through; (*examen*) to sit, take; (*visite médicale etc*) to have; (*journée, temps*) to spend; (*enfiler: vêtement*) to slip on; (*film, pièce*) to show, put on; (*disque*) to play, put on; (*commande*) to place; (*marché, accord*) to agree on; **se passer** *vi* (*avoir lieu: scène, action*) to take place; (*se dérouler: entretien etc*) to go; (*s'écouler: semaine etc*) to pass, go by; (*arriver*): **que s'est-il passé?** what happened?; **~ qch à qn** (*sel etc*) to pass sth to sb; (*prêter*) to lend sb sth; (*lettre, message*) to pass sth on to sb; (*tolérer*) to let sb get away with sth; **~ par** to go through; **~ avant qch/qn** (*fig*) to come before sth/sb; **~ un coup de fil à qn** (*fam*) to give sb a ring; **laisser ~** (*air, lumière, personne*) to let through; (*occasion*) to let slip, miss; (*erreur*) to overlook; **~ à la radio/télévision** to be on the radio/on television; **~ à table** to sit down to eat; **~ au salon** to go into the sitting-room; **~ son tour** to miss one's turn; **~ la seconde** (*Auto*) to change into second; **~**

le balai/l'aspirateur to sweep up/hoover;
je vous passe M. Dupont (*je vous mets
en communication avec lui*) I'm putting you
through to Mr Dupont; (*je lui passe l'appareil*)
here is Mr Dupont, I'll hand you over to Mr
Dupont; **se ~ de** to go ou do without

passerelle [pɑsʀɛl] *nf* footbridge; (*de navire,
avion*) gangway

passe-temps [pɑstɑ̃] *nm inv* pastime

passif, -ive [pasif, iv] *adj* passive

passion [pasjɔ̃] *nf* passion; **passionnant,
e** *adj* fascinating; **passionné, e** *adj*
(*personne*) passionate; (*récit*) impassioned;
être passionné de to have a passion for;
passionner *vt* (*personne*) to fascinate, grip

passoire [pɑswaʀ] *nf* sieve; (*à légumes*)
colander; (*à thé*) strainer

pastèque [pastɛk] *nf* watermelon

pasteur [pastœʀ] *nm* (*protestant*) minister,
pastor

pastille [pastij] *nf* (*à sucer*) lozenge, pastille

patate [patat] *nf* (*fam: pomme de terre*) spud;
patate douce sweet potato

patauger [patoʒe] *vi* to splash about

pâte [pɑt] *nf* (*à tarte*) pastry; (*à pain*) dough; (*à
frire*) batter; **pâtes** *nfpl* (*macaroni etc*) pasta *sg*;
pâte à modeler modelling clay, Plasticine®
(BRIT); **pâte brisée** shortcrust pastry; **pâte
d'amandes** almond paste, marzipan; **pâte de
fruits** crystallized fruit *no pl*; **pâte feuilletée**
puff ou flaky pastry

pâté [pɑte] *nm* (*charcuterie*) pâté; (*tache*) ink
blot; **pâté de maisons** block (of houses); **pâté
(de sable)** sandpie; **pâté en croûte** ≈ pork pie

pâtée [pɑte] *nf* mash, feed

patente [patɑ̃t] *nf* (*Comm*) trading licence

paternel, le [patɛʀnɛl] *adj* (*amour, soins*)
fatherly; (*ligne, autorité*) paternal

pâteux, -euse [pɑtø, øz] *adj* pasty; (*langue*)
coated

pathétique [patetik] *adj* moving

patience [pasjɑ̃s] *nf* patience

patient, e [pasjɑ̃, jɑ̃t] *adj, nm/f* patient;
patienter *vi* to wait

patin [patɛ̃] *nm* skate; (*sport*) skating; **patins
(à glace)** (ice) skates; **patins à roulettes**
roller skates

patinage [patinaʒ] *nm* skating

patiner [patine] *vi* to skate; (*roue, voiture*) to
spin; **se patiner** *vi* (*meuble, cuir*) to acquire
a sheen; **patineur, -euse** *nm/f* skater;
patinoire *nf* skating rink, (ice) rink

pâtir [pɑtiʀ]: **~ de** *vt* to suffer because of

pâtisserie [pɑtisʀi] *nf* (*boutique*) cake shop;
(*gâteau*) cake, pastry; (*à la maison*) pastry- ou
cake-making, baking; **pâtissier, -ière** *nm/f*
pastrycook

patois [patwa] *nm* dialect, patois

patrie [patʀi] *nf* homeland

patrimoine [patʀimwan] *nm* (*culture*)
heritage

patriotique [patʀijɔtik] *adj* patriotic

patron, ne [patʀɔ̃, ɔn] *nm/f* boss; (*Rel*) patron
saint ▷ *nm* (*Couture*) pattern; **patronat**
nm employers *pl*; **patronner** *vt* to sponsor,
support

patrouille [patʀuj] *nf* patrol

patte [pat] *nf* (*jambe*) leg; (*pied: de chien, chat*)
paw; (: *d'oiseau*) foot

pâturage [pɑtyʀaʒ] *nm* pasture

paume [pom] *nf* palm

paumé, e [pome] (*fam*) *nm/f* drop-out

paupière [popjɛʀ] *nf* eyelid

pause [poz] *nf* (*arrêt*) break; (*en parlant, Mus*)
pause

pauvre [povʀ] *adj* poor; **les pauvres** *nmpl* the
poor; **pauvreté** *nf* (*état*) poverty

pavé, e [pave] *adj* (*cour*) paved; (*chaussée*)
cobbled ▷ *nm* (*bloc*) paving stone; cobblestone

pavillon [pavijɔ̃] *nm* (*de banlieue*) small
(detached) house; pavilion; (*drapeau*) flag

payant, e [pɛjɑ̃, ɑ̃t] *adj* (*spectateurs etc*)
paying; (*fig: entreprise*) profitable; (*effort*)
which pays off; **c'est ~** you have to pay, there
is a charge

paye [pɛj] *nf* pay, wages *pl*

payer [peje] *vt* (*créancier, employé, loyer*) to pay;
(*achat, réparations, fig: faute*) to pay for ▷ *vi* to
pay; (*métier*) to be well-paid; (*tactique etc*) to
pay off; **il me l'a fait ~ 10 euros** he charged
me 10 euros for it; **~ qch à qn** to buy sth for sb,
buy sb sth; **se ~ la tête de qn** (*fam*) to take the
mickey out of sb; **est-ce que je peux ~ par
carte de crédit?** can I pay by credit card?

pays [pei] *nm* country; (*région*) region; **du ~**
local

paysage [peizaʒ] *nm* landscape

paysan, ne [peizɑ̃, an] *nm/f* farmer; (*péj*)
peasant ▷ *adj* (*agricole*) farming; (*rural*)
country

Pays-Bas [peiba] *nmpl*: **les ~** the Netherlands

PC *nm* (*Inform*) PC

PDA *sigle m* (= *personal digital assistant*) PDA

PDG *sigle m* = **président directeur général**

péage [peaʒ] *nm* toll; (*endroit*) tollgate

peau, x [po] *nf* skin; **gants de ~** fine leather
gloves; **être bien/mal dans sa ~** to be quite
at ease/ill-at-ease; **peau de chamois** (*chiffon*)
chamois leather, shammy

pêche[pɛʃ] nf (fruit) peach; (sport, activité) fishing; (poissons pêchés) catch; **pêche à la ligne**(en rivière) angling

péché[peʃe] nm sin

pécher[peʃe] vi (Rel) to sin

pêcher[peʃe] nm peach tree ▷ vi to go fishing ▷ vt (attraper) to catch; (être pêcheur de) to fish for

pécheur, -eresse[peʃœʀ, peʃʀɛs] nm/f sinner

pêcheur[pɛʃœʀ] nm fisherman; (à la ligne) angler

pédagogie[pedaɡɔʒi] nf educational methods pl, pedagogy; **pédagogique** adj educational

pédale[pedal] nf pedal

pédalo[pedalo] nm pedal-boat

pédant, e[pedã, ãt] (péj) adj pedantic

pédestre[pedɛstʀ] adj: **randonnée ~** ramble; **sentier ~** pedestrian footpath

pédiatre[pedjatʀ] nm/f paediatrician, child specialist

pédicure[pedikyʀ] nm/f chiropodist

pègre[pɛɡʀ] nf underworld

peigne[pɛɲ] nm comb; **peigner** vt to comb (the hair of); **se peigner** vi to comb one's hair; **peignoir** nm dressing gown; **peignoir de bain**bathrobe

peindre[pɛ̃dʀ] vt to paint; (fig) to portray, depict

peine[pɛn] nf (affliction) sorrow, sadness no pl; (mal, effort) trouble no pl, effort; (difficulté) difficulty; (Jur) sentence; **avoir de la ~** to be sad; **faire de la ~ à qn** to distress ou upset sb; **prendre la ~ de faire** to go to the trouble of doing; **se donner de la ~** to make an effort; **ce n'est pas la ~ de faire** there's no point in doing, it's not worth doing; **à ~** scarcely, barely; **à ~ ... que** hardly ... than, no sooner ... than; **peine capitale**capital punishment; **peine de mort**death sentence ou penalty; **peiner** vi (personne) to work hard; (moteur, voiture) to labour ▷ vt to grieve, sadden

peintre[pɛ̃tʀ] nm painter; **peintre en bâtiment**painter (and decorator)

peinture[pɛ̃tyʀ] nf painting; (matière) paint; (surfaces peintes: aussi: **~s**) paintwork; **"~ fraîche"**"wet paint"

péjoratif, -ive[peʒɔʀatif, iv] adj pejorative, derogatory

Pékin[pekɛ̃] n Beijing

pêle-mêle[pɛlmɛl] adv higgledy-piggledy

peler[pəle] vt, vi to peel

pèlerin[pɛlʀɛ̃] nm pilgrim

pèlerinage[pɛlʀinaʒ] nm pilgrimage

pelle[pɛl] nf shovel; (d'enfant, de terrassier) spade

pellicule[pelikyl] nf film; **pellicules** nfpl (Méd) dandruff sg; **je voudrais une ~ de 36 poses** I'd like a 36-exposure film

pelote[p(ə)lɔt] nf (de fil, laine) ball; **pelote basque**pelota

peloton[p(ə)lɔtɔ̃] nm group, squad; (Cyclisme) pack

pelotonner[p(ə)lɔtɔne]: **se pelotonner** vi to curl (o.s.) up

pelouse[p(ə)luz] nf lawn

peluche[p(ə)lyʃ] nf: **(animal en) ~** fluffy animal, soft toy; **chien/lapin en ~** fluffy dog/rabbit

pelure[p(ə)lyʀ] nf peeling, peel no pl

pénal, e, -aux[penal, o] adj penal; **pénalité** nf penalty

penchant[pãʃã] nm (tendance) tendency, propensity; (faible) liking, fondness

pencher[pãʃe] vi to tilt, lean over ▷ vt to tilt; **se pencher** vi to lean over; (se baisser) to bend down; **se ~ sur** (fig: problème) to look into; **~ pour** to be inclined to favour

pendant[pãdã] prép (au cours de) during; (indique la durée) for; **~ que** while

pendentif[pãdãtif] nm pendant

penderie[pãdʀi] nf wardrobe

pendre[pãdʀ] vt, vi to hang; **se ~** (se suicider) to hang o.s.; **~ qch à** (mur) to hang sth (up) on; (plafond) to hang sth (up) from

pendule[pãdyl] nf clock ▷ nm pendulum

pénétrer[penetʀe] vi, vt to penetrate; **~ dans** to enter

pénible[penibl] adj (travail) hard; (sujet) painful; (personne) tiresome; **péniblement** adv with difficulty

péniche[peniʃ] nf barge

pénicilline[penisilin] nf penicillin

péninsule[penɛ̃syl] nf peninsula

pénis[penis] nm penis

pénitence[penitãs] nf (peine) penance; (repentir) penitence; **pénitencier** nm penitentiary

pénombre[penɔ̃bʀ] nf (faible clarté) half-light; (obscurité) darkness

pensée[pãse] nf thought; (démarche, doctrine) thinking no pl; (fleur) pansy; **en ~** in one's mind

penser[pãse] vi, vt to think; **~ à** (ami, vacances) to think of ou about; (réfléchir à: problème, offre) to think about ou over; (prévoir) to think of; **faire ~ à** to remind one of; **~ faire qch** to be thinking of doing sth, intend to do sth; **pensif, -ive** adj pensive, thoughtful

pension[pãsjɔ̃] nf (allocation) pension; (prix du logement) board and lodgings, bed and board; (école) boarding school; **pension alimentaire** (de divorcée) maintenance allowance, alimony; **pension complète**full board; **pension de famille**boarding house, guesthouse; **pensionnaire** nm/f (Scol) boarder; **pensionnat** nm boarding school

pente[pãt] nf slope; **en ~** sloping

Pentecôte [pɑ̃tkot] *nf*: **la ~** Whitsun (BRIT), Pentecost

pénurie [penyʀi] *nf* shortage

pépé [pepe] (*fam*) *nm* grandad

pépin [pepɛ̃] *nm* (*Bot: graine*) pip; (*ennui*) snag, hitch

pépinière [pepinjɛʀ] *nf* nursery

perçant, e [pɛʀsɑ̃, ɑ̃t] *adj* (*cri*) piercing, shrill; (*regard*) piercing

percepteur, -trice [pɛʀsɛptœʀ, tʀis] *nm/f* tax collector

perception [pɛʀsɛpsjɔ̃] *nf* perception; (*bureau*) tax office

percer [pɛʀse] *vt* to pierce; (*ouverture etc*) to make; (*mystère, énigme*) to penetrate ▷ *vi* to break through; **perceuse** *nf* drill

percevoir [pɛʀsəvwaʀ] *vt* (*distinguer*) to perceive, detect; (*taxe, impôt*) to collect; (*revenu, indemnité*) to receive

perche [pɛʀʃ] *nf* (*bâton*) pole

percher [pɛʀʃe] *vt, vi* to perch; **se percher** *vi* to perch; **perchoir** *nm* perch

perçois *etc* [pɛʀswa] *vb voir* **percevoir**

perçu, e [pɛʀsy] *pp de* **percevoir**

percussion [pɛʀkysjɔ̃] *nf* percussion

percuter [pɛʀkyte] *vt* to strike; (*suj: véhicule*) to crash into

perdant, e [pɛʀdɑ̃, ɑ̃t] *nm/f* loser

perdre [pɛʀdʀ] *vt* to lose; (*gaspiller: temps, argent*) to waste; (*personne: moralement etc*) to ruin ▷ *vi* to lose; (*sur une vente etc*) to lose out; **se perdre** *vi* (*s'égarer*) to get lost, lose one's way; (*denrées*) to go to waste; **j'ai perdu mon portefeuille/passeport** I've lost my wallet/ passport; **je me suis perdu** (*et je le suis encore*) I'm lost; (*et je ne le suis plus*) I got lost

perdrix [pɛʀdʀi] *nf* partridge

perdu, e [pɛʀdy] *pp de* **perdre** ▷ *adj* (*isolé*) out-of-the-way; (*Comm: emballage*) non-returnable; (*malade*): **il est ~** there's no hope left for him; **à vos moments ~s** in your spare time

père [pɛʀ] *nm* father; **père de famille** father; **le père Noël** Father Christmas

perfection [pɛʀfɛksjɔ̃] *nf* perfection; **à la ~** to perfection; **perfectionné, e** *adj* sophisticated; **perfectionner** *vt* to improve, perfect; **se perfectionner en anglais** to improve one's English

perforer [pɛʀfɔʀe] *vt* (*poinçonner*) to punch

performant, e [pɛʀfɔʀmɑ̃, ɑ̃t] *adj*: **très ~** high-performance *cpd*

perfusion [pɛʀfyzjɔ̃] *nf*: **faire une ~ à qn** to put sb on a drip

péril [peʀil] *nm* peril

périmé, e [peʀime] *adj* (*Admin*) out-of-date, expired

périmètre [peʀimɛtʀ] *nm* perimeter

période [peʀjɔd] *nf* period; **périodique** *adj* periodic ▷ *nm* periodical; **garniture** *ou* **serviette périodique** sanitary towel (BRIT) *ou* napkin (US)

périphérique [peʀifeʀik] *adj* (*quartiers*) outlying ▷ *nm* (*Auto*): **boulevard ~** ring road (BRIT), beltway (US)

périr [peʀiʀ] *vi* to die, perish

périssable [peʀisabl] *adj* perishable

perle [pɛʀl] *nf* pearl; (*de plastique, métal, sueur*) bead

permanence [pɛʀmanɑ̃s] *nf* permanence; (*local*) (duty) office; **assurer une ~** (*service public, bureaux*) to operate *ou* maintain a basic service; **être de ~** to be on call *ou* duty; **en ~** continuously

permanent, e [pɛʀmanɑ̃, ɑ̃t] *adj* permanent; (*spectacle*) continuous; **permanente** *nf* perm

perméable [pɛʀmeabl] *adj* (*terrain*) permeable; **~ à** (*fig*) receptive *ou* open to

permettre [pɛʀmɛtʀ] *vt* to allow, permit; **~ à qn de faire/qch** to allow sb to do/sth; **se ~ de faire** to take the liberty of doing

permis [pɛʀmi] *nm* permit, licence; **permis de conduire** driving licence (BRIT), driver's license (US); **permis de construire** planning permission (BRIT), building permit (US); **permis de séjour** residence permit; **permis de travail** work permit

permission [pɛʀmisjɔ̃] *nf* permission; (*Mil*) leave; **avoir la ~ de faire** to have permission to do; **en ~** on leave

Pérou [peʀu] *nm* Peru

perpétuel, le [pɛʀpetɥɛl] *adj* perpetual; **perpétuité** *nf*: **à perpétuité** for life; **être condamné à perpétuité** to receive a life sentence

perplexe [pɛʀplɛks] *adj* perplexed, puzzled

perquisitionner [pɛʀkizisjɔne] *vi* to carry out a search

perron [pɛʀɔ̃] *nm* steps *pl* (*leading to entrance*)

perroquet [pɛʀɔkɛ] *nm* parrot

perruche [pɛʀyʃ] *nf* budgerigar (BRIT), budgie (BRIT), parakeet (US)

perruque [pɛʀyk] *nf* wig

persécuter [pɛʀsekyte] *vt* to persecute

persévérer [pɛʀsevere] *vi* to persevere

persil [pɛʀsi] *nm* parsley

Persique [pɛʀsik] *adj*: **le golfe ~** the (Persian) Gulf

persistant, e [pɛʀsistɑ̃, ɑ̃t] *adj* persistent

persister [pɛʀsiste] *vi* to persist; **~ à faire qch** to persist in doing sth

personnage [pɛʀsɔnaʒ] *nm* (*individu*) character, individual; (*célébrité*) important person; (*de roman, film*) character; (*Peinture*) figure

personnalité [pɛʀsɔnalite] *nf* personality; (*personnage*) prominent figure

personne [pɛʀsɔn] *nf* person ▷ *pron* nobody,

no one; (*avec négation en anglais*) anybody,
anyone; **personne âgée** elderly person;
personnel, le *adj* personal; (*égoïste*) selfish
▷ *nm* staff, personnel; **personnellement** *adv*
personally

perspective [pɛʀspɛktiv] *nf* (*Art*)
perspective; (*vue*) view; (*point de vue*)
viewpoint, angle; (*chose envisagée*) prospect;
en ~ in prospect

perspicace [pɛʀspikas] *adj* clear-sighted,
gifted with (*ou* showing) insight; **perspicacité**
nf clear-sightedness

persuader [pɛʀsɥade] *vt*: **~ qn (de faire)**
to persuade sb (to do); **persuasif, -ive** *adj*
persuasive

perte [pɛʀt] *nf* loss; (*de temps*) waste; (*fig:
morale*) ruin; **à ~ de vue** as far as the eye can
(*ou* could) see; **pertes blanches** (vaginal)
discharge *sg*

pertinent, e [pɛʀtinɑ̃, ɑ̃t] *adj* apt, relevant

perturbation [pɛʀtyʀbasjɔ̃] *nf*:
perturbation (atmosphérique) atmospheric
disturbance

perturber [pɛʀtyʀbe] *vt* to disrupt; (*Psych*) to
perturb, disturb

pervers, e [pɛʀvɛʀ, ɛʀs] *adj* perverted

pervertir [pɛʀvɛʀtiʀ] *vt* to pervert

pesant, e [pəzɑ̃, ɑ̃t] *adj* heavy; (*fig: présence*)
burdensome

pèse-personne [pɛzpɛʀsɔn] *nm* (bathroom)
scales *pl*

peser [pəze] *vt* to weigh ▷ *vi* to weigh; (*fig:
avoir de l'importance*) to carry weight; **~ lourd**
to be heavy

pessimiste [pesimist] *adj* pessimistic ▷ *nm/f*
pessimist

peste [pɛst] *nf* plague

pétale [petal] *nm* petal

pétanque [petɑ̃k] *nf* type of bowls

PÉTANQUE

Pétanque is a version of the game
of 'boules', played on a variety of hard
surfaces. Standing with their feet together,
players throw steel bowls at a wooden
jack. **Pétanque** originated in the South
of France and is still very much associated
with that area.

pétard [petaʀ] *nm* banger (BRIT), firecracker

péter [pete] *vi* (*fam: casser*) to bust; (*fam!*) to
fart (!)

pétillant, e [petijɑ̃, ɑ̃t] *adj* (*eau etc*) sparkling

pétiller [petije] *vi* (*feu*) to crackle; (*champagne*)
to bubble; (*yeux*) to sparkle

petit, e [p(ə)ti, it] *adj* small; (*avec nuance
affective*) little; (*voyage*) short, little; (*bruit etc*)
faint, slight ▷ *nm/f* (*petit enfant*) little boy/girl,

child; **petits** *nmpl* (*d'un animal*) young *no pl*;
faire des ~s to have kittens (*ou* puppies *etc*);
la classe des ~s the infant class; **les tout-~s**
the little ones, the tiny tots (*fam*); **~ à ~** bit by
bit, gradually; **petit(e) ami(e)** boyfriend/
girlfriend; **petit déjeuner** breakfast; **le petit
déjeuner est à quelle heure?** what time is
breakfast?; **petit four** petit four; **petit pain**
(bread) roll; **les petites annonces** the small
ads; **petits pois** (garden) peas; **petite-fille** *nf*
granddaughter; **petit-fils** *nm* grandson

pétition [petisjɔ̃] *nf* petition

petits-enfants [pətizɑ̃fɑ̃] *nmpl*
grandchildren

pétrin [petʀɛ̃] *nm* (*fig*): **dans le ~** (*fam*) in a
jam *ou* fix

pétrir [petʀiʀ] *vt* to knead

pétrole [petʀɔl] *nm* oil; (*pour lampe, réchaud
etc*) paraffin (oil); **pétrolier, -ière** *nm* oil tanker

 Attention à ne pas traduire *pétrole* par le
mot anglais *petrol*.

 MOT-CLÉ

peu [pø] *adv* **1** (*modifiant verbe, adjectif, adverbe*):
il boit peu he doesn't drink (very) much; **il
est peu bavard** he's not very talkative; **peu
avant/après** shortly before/afterwards
2 (*modifiant nom*): **peu de**: **peu de gens/
d'arbres** few *ou* not (very) many people/trees;
il a peu d'espoir he hasn't (got) much hope,
he has little hope; **pour peu de temps** for
(only) a short while
3: **peu à peu** little by little; **à peu près** just
about, more or less; **à peu près 10 kg/10
euros** approximately 10 kg/10 euros
▷ *nm* **1**: **le peu de gens qui** the few people
who; **le peu de sable qui** what little sand, the
little sand which
2: **un peu** a little; **un petit peu** a little bit;
un peu d'espoir a little hope; **elle est un
peu bavarde** she's quite *ou* rather talkative;
un peu plus de slightly more than; **un peu
moins de** slightly less than; (*avec pluriel*)
slightly fewer than
▷ *pron*: **peu le savent** few know (it); **de peu**
(only) just

peuple [pœpl] *nm* people; **peupler** *vt* (*pays,
région*) to populate; (*étang*) to stock; (*suj:
hommes, poissons*) to inhabit

peuplier [pœplije] *nm* poplar (tree)

peur [pœʀ] *nf* fear; **avoir ~ (de/de faire/que)**
to be frightened *ou* afraid (of/of doing/that);
faire ~ à to frighten; **de ~ de/que** for fear
of/that; **peureux, -euse** *adj* fearful, timorous

peut [pø] *vb voir* **pouvoir**

peut-être [pøtɛtʀ] *adv* perhaps, maybe; **~
que** perhaps, maybe; **~ bien qu'il fera/est** he

may well do/be

phare [faʀ] nm (en mer) lighthouse; (de véhicule) headlight

pharmacie [faʀmasi] nf (magasin) chemist's (BRIT), pharmacy; (de salle de bain) medicine cabinet; **pharmacien, ne** nm/f pharmacist, chemist (BRIT)

phénomène [fenɔmɛn] nm phenomenon

philosophe [filɔzɔf] nm/f philosopher ▷ adj philosophical

philosophie [filɔzɔfi] nf philosophy

phobie [fɔbi] nf phobia

phoque [fɔk] nm seal

phosphorescent, e [fɔsfɔʀesɑ̃, ɑ̃t] adj luminous

photo [fɔto] nf photo(graph); **prendre en ~** to take a photo of; **pourriez-vous nous prendre en ~, s'il vous plaît?** would you take a picture of us, please?; **faire de la ~** to take photos; **photo d'identité** passport photograph; **photocopie** nf photocopy; **photocopier** vt to photocopy; **photocopieuse** nf photocopier; **photographe** nm/f photographer; **photographie** nf (technique) photography; (cliché) photograph; **photographier** vt to photograph

phrase [fʀɑz] nf sentence

physicien, ne [fizisjɛ̃, jɛn] nm/f physicist

physique [fizik] adj physical ▷ nm physique ▷ nf physics sg; **au ~** physically; **physiquement** adv physically

pianiste [pjanist] nm/f pianist

piano [pjano] nm piano; **pianoter** vi to tinkle away (at the piano)

pic [pik] nm (instrument) pick(axe); (montagne) peak; (Zool) woodpecker; **à ~** vertically; (fig: tomber, arriver) just at the right time

pichet [piʃɛ] nm jug

picorer [pikɔʀe] vt to peck

pie [pi] nf magpie

pièce [pjɛs] nf (d'un logement) room; (Théâtre) play; (de machine) part; (de monnaie) coin; (document) document; (fragment, de collection) piece; **dix euros ~** ten euros each; **vendre à la ~** to sell separately; **travailler à la ~** to do piecework; **un maillot une ~** a one-piece swimsuit; **un deux-~s cuisine** a two-room(ed) flat (BRIT) ou apartment (US) with kitchen; **pièce à conviction** exhibit; **pièce d'eau** ornamental lake ou pond; **pièce de rechange** spare (part); **pièce d'identité: avez-vous une pièce d'identité?** have you got any (means of) identification?; **pièce jointe** (Comput) attachment; **pièce montée** tiered cake; **pièces détachées** spares, (spare) parts; **pièces justificatives** supporting documents

pied [pje] nm foot; (de table) leg; (de lampe) base; **~s nus** ou **nus-~s** barefoot; **à ~** on foot;

au ~ de la lettre literally; **avoir ~** to be able to touch the bottom, not to be out of one's depth; **avoir le ~ marin** to be a good sailor; **sur ~** (debout, rétabli) up and about; **mettre sur ~** (entreprise) to set up; **c'est le ~** (fam) it's brilliant; **mettre les ~s dans le plat** (fam) to put one's foot in it; **il se débrouille comme un ~** (fam) he's completely useless; **pied-noir** nm Algerian-born Frenchman

piège [pjɛʒ] nm trap; **prendre au ~** to trap; **piéger** vt (avec une bombe) to booby-trap; **lettre/voiture piégée** letter-/car-bomb

piercing [pjɛʀsiŋ] nm body piercing

pierre [pjɛʀ] nf stone; **pierre tombale** tombstone; **pierreries** nfpl gems, precious stones

piétiner [pjetine] vi (trépigner) to stamp (one's foot); (fig) to be at a standstill ▷ vt to trample on

piéton, ne [pjetɔ̃, ɔn] nm/f pedestrian; **piétonnier, -ière** adj: **rue** ou **zone piétonnière** pedestrian precinct

pieu, x [pjø] nm post; (pointu) stake

pieuvre [pjœvʀ] nf octopus

pieux, -euse [pjø, pjøz] adj pious

pigeon [piʒɔ̃] nm pigeon

piger [piʒe] (fam) vi, vt to understand

pigiste [piʒist] nm/f freelance(r)

pignon [piɲɔ̃] nm (de mur) gable

pile [pil] nf (tas) pile; (Élec) battery ▷ adv (fam: s'arrêter etc) dead; **à deux heures ~** at two on the dot; **jouer à ~ ou face** to toss up (for it); **~ ou face?** heads or tails?

piler [pile] vt to crush, pound

pilier [pilje] nm pillar

piller [pije] vt to pillage, plunder, loot

pilote [pilɔt] nm pilot; (de voiture) driver ▷ adj pilot cpd; **pilote de course** racing driver; **pilote de ligne** airline pilot; **piloter** vt (avion) to pilot, fly; (voiture) to drive

pilule [pilyl] nf pill; **prendre la ~** to be on the pill

piment [pimɑ̃] nm (aussi: **~ rouge**) chilli; (fig) spice, piquancy; **~ doux** pepper, capsicum; **pimenté, e** adj (plat) hot, spicy

pin [pɛ̃] nm pine

pinard [pinaʀ] (fam) nm (cheap) wine, plonk (BRIT)

pince [pɛ̃s] nf (outil) pliers pl; (de homard, crabe) pincer, claw; (Couture: pli) dart; **pince à épiler** tweezers pl; **pince à linge** clothes peg (BRIT) ou pin (US)

pincé, e [pɛ̃se] adj (air) stiff

pinceau, x [pɛ̃so] nm (paint)brush

pincer [pɛ̃se] vt to pinch; (fam) to nab

pinède [pined] nf pinewood, pine forest

pingouin [pɛ̃gwɛ̃] nm penguin

ping-pong® [piŋpɔ̃g] nm table tennis

pinson [pɛ̃sɔ̃] nm chaffinch

pintade [pɛ̃tad] *nf* guinea-fowl

pion [pjɔ̃] *nm* (*Échecs*) pawn; (*Dames*) piece; (*Scol*) supervisor

pionnier [pjɔnje] *nm* pioneer

pipe [pip] *nf* pipe; **fumer la ~** to smoke a pipe

piquant, e [pikɑ̃, ɑ̃t] *adj* (*barbe, rosier etc*) prickly; (*saveur, sauce*) hot, pungent; (*détail*) titillating; (*froid*) biting ▷ *nm* (*épine*) thorn, prickle; (*fig*) spiciness, spice

pique [pik] *nf* pike; (*fig*) cutting remark ▷ *nm* (*Cartes*) spades *pl*

pique-nique [piknik] *nm* picnic; **pique-niquer** *vi* to have a picnic

piquer [pike] *vt* (*suj: guêpe, fumée, orties*) to sting; (: *moustique*) to bite; (: *barbe*) to prick; (: *froid*) to bite; (*Méd*) to give a jab to; (*chien, chat*) to put to sleep; (*intérêt*) to arouse; (*fam: voler*) to pinch ▷ *vi* (*avion*) to go into a dive

piquet [pikɛ] *nm* (*pieu*) post, stake; (*de tente*) peg

piqûre [pikyʀ] *nf* (*d'épingle*) prick; (*d'ortie*) sting; (*de moustique*) bite; (*Méd*) injection, shot (*us*); **faire une ~ à qn** to give sb an injection

pirate [piʀat] *nm, adj* pirate; **pirate de l'air** hijacker

pire [piʀ] *adj* worse; (*superlatif*): **le(la) ~ ...** the worst ... ▷ *nm*: **le ~ (de)** the worst (of); **au ~** at (the very) worst

pis [pi] *nm* (*de vache*) udder ▷ *adj, adv* worse; **de mal en ~** from bad to worse

piscine [pisin] *nf* (*swimming*) pool; **piscine couverte** indoor (swimming) pool

pissenlit [pisɑ̃li] *nm* dandelion

pistache [pistaʃ] *nf* pistachio (nut)

piste [pist] *nf* (*d'un animal, sentier*) track, trail; (*indice*) lead; (*de stade*) track; (*de cirque*) ring; (*de danse*) floor; (*de patinage*) rink; (*de ski*) run; (*Aviat*) runway; **piste cyclable** cycle track

pistolet [pistɔlɛ] *nm* (*arme*) pistol, gun; (*à peinture*) spray gun; **pistolet-mitrailleur** *nm* submachine gun

piston [pistɔ̃] *nm* (*Tech*) piston; **avoir du ~** (*fam*) to have friends in the right places; **pistonner** *vt* (*candidat*) to pull strings for

piteux, -euse [pitø, øz] *adj* pitiful, sorry (*avant le nom*); **en ~ état** in a sorry state

pitié [pitje] *nf* pity; **il me fait ~** I feel sorry for him; **avoir ~ de** (*compassion*) to pity, feel sorry for; (*merci*) to have pity ou mercy on

pitoyable [pitwajabl] *adj* pitiful

pittoresque [pitɔʀɛsk] *adj* picturesque

PJ *sigle f* (= *police judiciaire*) ≈ CID (*BRIT*), ≈ FBI (*us*)

placard [plakaʀ] *nm* (*armoire*) cupboard; (*affiche*) poster, notice

place [plas] *nf* (*emplacement, classement*) place; (*de ville, village*) square; (*espace libre*) room, space; (*de parking*) space; (*siège: de train, cinéma, voiture*) seat; (*emploi*) job; **en ~** (*mettre*) in its place; **sur ~** on the spot; **faire ~ à** to give way to; **ça prend de la ~** it takes up a lot of room ou space; **à la ~ de** instead of, in place of; **à votre ~ ...** if I were you ...; **je voudrais réserver deux ~s** I'd like to book two seats; **la ~ est prise?** is this seat taken?; **se mettre à la ~ de qn** to put o.s. in sb's place ou in sb's shoes

placé, e [plase] *adj*: **haut ~** (*fig*) high-ranking; **être bien/mal ~** (*spectateur*) to have a good/a poor seat; (*concurrent*) to be in a good/bad position; **il est bien ~ pour le savoir** he is in a position to know

placement [plasmɑ̃] *nm* (*Finance*) investment; **agence** ou **bureau de ~** employment agency

placer [plase] *vt* to place; (*convive, spectateur*) to seat; (*argent*) to place, invest; **se ~ au premier rang** to go and stand (ou sit) in the first row

plafond [plafɔ̃] *nm* ceiling

plage [plaʒ] *nf* beach; **plage arrière** (*Auto*) parcel ou back shelf

plaider [plede] *vi* (*avocat*) to plead ▷ *vt* to plead; **~ pour** (*fig*) to speak for; **plaidoyer** *nm* (*Jur*) speech for the defence; (*fig*) plea

plaie [plɛ] *nf* wound

plaignant, e [plɛɲɑ̃, ɑ̃t] *nm/f* plaintiff

plaindre [plɛ̃dʀ] *vt* to pity, feel sorry for; **se plaindre** *vi* (*gémir*) to moan; (*protester*): **se ~ (à qn) (de)** to complain (to sb) (about); (*souffrir*): **se ~ de** to complain of

plaine [plɛn] *nf* plain

plain-pied [plɛ̃pje] *adv*: **de ~ (avec)** on the same level (as)

plainte [plɛ̃t] *nf* (*gémissement*) moan, groan; (*doléance*) complaint; **porter ~** to lodge a complaint

plaire [plɛʀ] *vi* to be a success, be successful; **ça plaît beaucoup aux jeunes** it's very popular with young people; **~ à: cela me plaît** I like it; **se ~ quelque part** to like being somewhere ou like it somewhere; **s'il vous plaît** please

plaisance [plɛzɑ̃s] *nf* (*aussi*: **navigation de ~**) (pleasure) sailing, yachting

plaisant, e [plɛzɑ̃, ɑ̃t] *adj* pleasant; (*histoire, anecdote*) amusing

plaisanter [plɛzɑ̃te] *vi* to joke; **plaisanterie** *nf* joke

plaisir [pleziʀ] *nm* pleasure; **faire ~ à qn** (*délibérément*) to be nice to sb, please sb; **ça me fait ~** I like (doing) it; **j'espère que ça te fera ~** I hope you'll like it; **pour le ~** for pleasure

plaît [plɛ] *vb voir* **plaire**

plan, e [plɑ̃, an] *adj* flat ▷ *nm* plan; (*fig*) level, plane; (*Cinéma*) shot; **au premier/second ~** in the foreground/middle distance; **à l'arrière ~** in the background; **plan d'eau** lake

planche [plɑ̃ʃ] *nf* (*pièce de bois*) plank,

(wooden) board; (*illustration*) plate; **planche à repasser** ironing board; **planche (à roulettes)** skateboard; **planche (à voile)** (*sport*) windsurfing

plancher [plɑ̃ʃe] *nm* floor; floorboards *pl* ▷ *vi* (*fam*) to work hard

planer [plane] *vi* to glide; (*fam: rêveur*) to have one's head in the clouds; **~ sur** (*fig: danger*) to hang over

planète [planɛt] *nf* planet

planeur [plancœr] *nm* glider

planifier [planifje] *vt* to plan

planning [planiŋ] *nm* programme, schedule; **planning familial** family planning

plant [plɑ̃] *nm* seedling, young plant

plante [plɑ̃t] *nf* plant; **la plante du pied** the sole (of the foot); **plante verte** *ou* **d'appartement** house plant

planter [plɑ̃te] *vt* (*plante*) to plant; (*enfoncer*) to hammer ou drive in; (*tente*) to put up, pitch; (*fam: personne*) to dump; **se planter** (*fam: se tromper*) to get it wrong

plaque [plak] *nf* plate; (*de verglas, d'eczéma*) patch; (*avec inscription*) plaque; **plaque chauffante** hotplate; **plaque de chocolat** bar of chocolate; **plaque tournante** (*fig*) centre

plaqué, e [plake] *adj*: **~ or/argent** gold-/silver-plated

plaquer [plake] *vt* (*Rugby*) to bring down; (*fam: laisser tomber*) to drop

plaquette [plakɛt] *nf* (*de chocolat*) bar; (*beurre*) pack(et); **plaquette de frein** brake pad

plastique [plastik] *adj, nm* plastic; **plastiquer** *vt* to blow up (*with a plastic bomb*)

plat, e [pla, -at] *adj* flat; (*cheveux*) straight; (*style*) flat, dull ▷ *nm* (*récipient, Culin*) dish; (*d'un repas*) course; **à ~ ventre** face down; **à ~** (*pneu, batterie*) flat; (*fam: personne*) dead beat; **plat cuisiné** pre-cooked meal; **plat de résistance** main course; **plat du jour** dish of the day

platane [platan] *nm* plane tree

plateau, x [plato] *nm* (*support*) tray; (*Géo*) plateau; (*Cinéma*) set; **plateau à fromages** cheese board

plate-bande [platbɑ̃d] *nf* flower bed

plate-forme [platfɔrm] *nf* platform; **plate-forme de forage/pétrolière** drilling/oil rig

platine [platin] *nm* platinum ▷ *nf* (*d'un tourne-disque*) turntable; **platine laser** compact disc ou CD player

plâtre [plɑtr] *nm* (*matériau*) plaster; (*statue*) plaster statue; (*Méd*) (plaster) cast; **avoir un bras dans le ~** to have an arm in plaster

plein, e [plɛ̃, plɛn] *adj* full ▷ *nm*: **faire le ~ (d'essence)** to fill up (with petrol); **à ~es mains** (*ramasser*) in handfuls; **à ~ temps** full-time; **en ~ air** in the open air; **en ~ soleil** in direct sunlight; **en ~e nuit/rue** in the middle of the night/street; **en ~ jour** in broad daylight; **le ~, s'il vous plaît** fill it up, please

pleurer [plœre] *vi* to cry; (*yeux*) to water ▷ *vt* to mourn (for); **~ sur** to lament (over), to bemoan

pleurnicher [plœrniʃe] *vi* to snivel, whine

pleurs [plœr] *nmpl*: **en ~** in tears

pleut [plø] *vb voir* **pleuvoir**

pleuvoir [pløvwar] *vb impers* to rain ▷ *vi* (*coups*) to rain down; (*critiques, invitations*) to shower down; **il pleut** it's raining; **il pleut des cordes** it's pouring (down), it's raining cats and dogs

pli [pli] *nm* fold; (*de jupe*) pleat; (*de pantalon*) crease

pliant, e [plijɑ̃, plijɑ̃t] *adj* folding

plier [plije] *vt* to fold; (*pour ranger*) to fold up; (*genou, bras*) to bend ▷ *vi* to bend; (*fig*) to yield; **se ~ à** to submit to

plisser [plise] *vt* (*jupe*) to put pleats in; (*yeux*) to screw up; (*front*) to crease

plomb [plɔ̃] *nm* (*métal*) lead; (*d'une cartouche*) (lead) shot; (*Pêche*) sinker; (*Élec*) fuse; **sans ~** (*essence etc*) unleaded

plomberie [plɔ̃bri] *nf* plumbing

plombier [plɔ̃bje] *nm* plumber

plonge [plɔ̃ʒ] *nf* washing-up

plongeant, e [plɔ̃ʒɑ̃, ɑ̃t] *adj* (*vue*) from above; (*décolleté*) plunging

plongée [plɔ̃ʒe] *nf* (*Sport*) diving *no pl*; (*sans scaphandre*) skin diving; **~ sous-marine** diving

plongeoir [plɔ̃ʒwar] *nm* diving board

plongeon [plɔ̃ʒɔ̃] *nm* dive

plonger [plɔ̃ʒe] *vi* to dive ▷ *vt*: **~ qch dans** to plunge sth into; **se ~ dans** (*études, lecture*) to bury ou immerse o.s. in; **plongeur** *nm* diver

plu [ply] *pp de* **plaire**; *de* **pleuvoir**

pluie [plɥi] *nf* rain

plume [plym] *nf* feather; (*pour écrire*) (pen) nib; (*fig*) pen

plupart [plypar]: **la ~** *pron* the majority, most (of them); **la ~ des** most, the majority of; **la ~ du temps/d'entre nous** most of the time/of us; **pour la ~** for the most part, mostly

pluriel [plyrjɛl] *nm* plural

plus¹ [ply] *vb voir* **plaire**

 MOT-CLÉ

plus² [ply] *adv* **1** (*forme négative*): **ne ... plus** no more, no longer; **je n'ai plus d'argent** I've got no more money ou no money left; **il ne travaille plus** he's no longer working, he doesn't work any more

2 [ply, plyz + voyelle] (*comparatif*) more, ...+er; (*superlatif*): **le plus** the most, the ...+est; **plus grand/intelligent (que)** bigger/more intelligent (than); **le plus grand/intelligent** the biggest/most intelligent; **tout au plus** at the very most

3 [plys, plyz + *voyelle*] (*davantage*) more; **il travaille plus (que)** he works more (than); **plus il travaille, plus il est heureux** the more he works, the happier he is; **plus de 10 personnes/3 heures** more than *ou* over 10 people/3 hours; **3 heures de plus que** 3 hours more than; **de plus** what's more, moreover; **il a 3 ans de plus que moi** he's 3 years older than me; **3 kilos en plus** 3 kilos more; **en plus de** in addition to; **de plus en plus** more and more; **plus ou moins** more or less; **ni plus ni moins** no more, no less
▷ *prép* [plys]: **4 plus 2** 4 plus 2

plusieurs [plyzjœr] *dét, pron* several; **ils sont ~** there are several of them

plus-value [plyvaly] *nf* (*bénéfice*) surplus

plutôt [plyto] *adv* rather; **je préfère ~ celui-ci** I'd rather have this one; **~ que (de) faire** rather than *ou* instead of doing

pluvieux, -euse [plyvjø, jøz] *adj* rainy, wet

PME *sigle f* (= petite(s) et moyenne(s) entreprise(s)) small business(es)

PMU *sigle m* (= Pari mutuel urbain) system of betting on horses; (*café*) betting agency

PNB *sigle m* (= produit national brut) GNP

pneu [pnø] *nm* tyre (BRIT), tire (US); **j'ai un ~ crevé** I've got a flat tyre

pneumonie [pnømɔni] *nf* pneumonia

poche [pɔʃ] *nf* pocket; (*sous les yeux*) bag, pouch; **argent de ~** pocket money

pochette [pɔʃɛt] *nf* (*d'aiguilles etc*) case; (*mouchoir*) breast pocket handkerchief; (*sac à main*) clutch bag; **pochette de disque** record sleeve

poêle [pwal] *nm* stove ▷ *nf*: **~ (à frire)** frying pan

poème [pɔɛm] *nm* poem

poésie [pɔezi] *nf* (*poème*) poem; (*art*): **la ~** poetry

poète [pɔɛt] *nm* poet

poids [pwa] *nm* weight; (*Sport*) shot; **vendre au ~** to sell by weight; **perdre/prendre du ~** to lose/put on weight; **poids lourd** (*camion*) lorry (BRIT), truck (US)

poignant, e [pwaɲɑ̃, ɑ̃t] *adj* poignant

poignard [pwaɲar] *nm* dagger; **poignarder** *vt* to stab, knife

poigne [pwaɲ] *nf* grip; **avoir de la ~** (*fig*) to rule with a firm hand

poignée [pwaɲe] *nf* (*de sel etc, fig*) handful; (*de couvercle, porte*) handle; **poignée de main** handshake

poignet [pwaɲɛ] *nm* (*Anat*) wrist; (*de chemise*) cuff

poil [pwal] *nm* (*Anat*) hair; (*de pinceau, brosse*) bristle; (*de tapis*) strand; (*pelage*) coat; **à ~** (*fam*) starkers; **au ~** (*fam*) hunky-dory; **poilu, e** *adj* hairy

poinçonner [pwɛ̃sɔne] *vt* (*bijou*) to hallmark; (*billet*) to punch

poing [pwɛ̃] *nm* fist; **coup de ~** punch

point [pwɛ̃] *nm* point; (*endroit*) spot; (*marque, signe*) dot; (: *de ponctuation*) full stop, period (US); (*Couture, Tricot*) stitch ▷ *adv* = **pas²**; **faire le ~** (*fig*) to take stock (of the situation); **sur le ~ de faire** (just) about to do; **à tel ~ que** so much so that; **mettre au ~** (*procédé*) to develop; (*affaire*) to settle; **à ~** (*Culin: viande*) medium; **à ~ (nommé)** just at the right time; **deux ~s** colon; **point de côté** stitch (*pain*); **point d'exclamation/d'interrogation** exclamation/question mark; **point de repère** landmark; (*dans le temps*) point of reference; **point de vente** retail outlet; **point de vue** viewpoint; (*fig: opinion*) point of view; **point faible** weak spot; **point final** full stop, period (US); **point mort**: **au point mort** (*Auto*) in neutral; **points de suspension** suspension points

pointe [pwɛ̃t] *nf* point; (*clou*) tack; (*fig*): **une ~ de** a hint of; **être à la ~ de** (*fig*) to be in the forefront of; **sur la ~ des pieds** on tiptoe; **en ~** pointed, tapered; **de ~** (*technique etc*) leading; **heures de ~** peak hours

pointer [pwɛ̃te] *vt* (*diriger: canon, doigt*): **~ sur qch** to point at sth ▷ *vi* (*employé*) to clock in

pointillé [pwɛ̃tije] *nm* (*trait*) dotted line

pointilleux, -euse [pwɛ̃tijø, øz] *adj* particular, pernickety

pointu, e [pwɛ̃ty] *adj* pointed; (*voix*) shrill; (*analyse*) precise

pointure [pwɛ̃tyr] *nf* size

point-virgule [pwɛ̃virgyl] *nm* semi-colon

poire [pwar] *nf* pear; (*fam: péj*) mug

poireau, x [pwaro] *nm* leek

poirier [pwarje] *nm* pear tree

pois [pwa] *nm* (*Bot*) pea; (*sur une étoffe*) dot, spot; **~ chiche** chickpea; **à ~** (*cravate etc*) spotted, polka-dot *cpd*

poison [pwazɔ̃] *nm* poison

poisseux, -euse [pwasø, øz] *adj* sticky

poisson [pwasɔ̃] *nm* fish *gén inv*; (*Astrol*): **P~s** Pisces; **~ d'avril** April fool; (*blague*) April Fool's Day trick; *see note*; **poisson rouge** goldfish; **poissonnerie** *nf* fish-shop; **poissonnier, -ière** *nm/f* fishmonger (BRIT), fish merchant (US)

● **POISSON D'AVRIL**
●
●
● The traditional April Fools' Day prank in
● France involves attaching a cut-out paper
● fish, known as a 'poisson d'avril', to the back
● of one's victim, without being caught.

poitrine [pwatrin] *nf* chest; (*seins*) bust,

bosom; (*Culin*) breast
poivre [pwavʀ] *nm* pepper
poivron [pwavʀɔ̃] *nm* pepper, capsicum
polaire [pɔlɛʀ] *adj* polar
pôle [pol] *nm* (*Géo*, *Élec*) pole; **le ~ Nord/Sud** the North/South Pole
poli, e [pɔli] *adj* polite; (*lisse*) smooth
police [pɔlis] *nf* police; **police judiciaire** ≈ Criminal Investigation Department (*BRIT*), ≈ Federal Bureau of Investigation (*US*); **police secours** ≈ emergency services *pl* (*BRIT*), ≈ paramedics *pl* (*US*); **policier, -ière** *adj* police *cpd* ▷ *nm* policeman; (*aussi:* **roman policier**) detective novel
polir [pɔliʀ] *vt* to polish
politesse [pɔlites] *nf* politeness
politicien, ne [pɔlitisjɛ̃, jɛn] (*péj*) *nm/f* politician
politique [pɔlitik] *adj* political ▷ *nf* politics *sg*; (*mesures, méthode*) policies *pl*
politiquement [pɔlitikmɑ̃] *adv* politically; **~ correct** politically correct
pollen [pɔlɛn] *nm* pollen
polluant, e [pɔlɥɑ̃, ɑ̃t] *adj* polluting ▷ *nm* (*produit*) ~ pollutant; **non ~** non-polluting
polluer [pɔlɥe] *vt* to pollute; **pollution** *nf* pollution
polo [pɔlo] *nm* (*chemise*) polo shirt
Pologne [pɔlɔɲ] *nf*: **la ~** Poland; **polonais, e** *adj* Polish ▷ *nm/f*: **Polonais, e** Pole ▷ *nm* (*Ling*) Polish
poltron, ne [pɔltʀɔ̃, ɔn] *adj* cowardly
polycopier [pɔlikɔpje] *vt* to duplicate
Polynésie [pɔlinezi] *nf*: **la ~** Polynesia; **la ~ française** French Polynesia
polyvalent, e [pɔlivalɑ̃, ɑ̃t] *adj* (*rôle*) varied; (*salle*) multi-purpose
pommade [pɔmad] *nf* ointment, cream
pomme [pɔm] *nf* apple; **tomber dans les ~s** (*fam*) to pass out; **pomme d'Adam** Adam's apple; **pomme de pin** pine *ou* fir cone; **pomme de terre** potato
pommette [pɔmɛt] *nf* cheekbone
pommier [pɔmje] *nm* apple tree
pompe [pɔ̃p] *nf* pump; (*faste*) pomp (and ceremony); **pompe (à essence)** petrol pump; **pompes funèbres** funeral parlour *sg*, undertaker's *sg*; **pomper** *vt* to pump; (*aspirer*) to pump up; (*absorber*) to soak up
pompeux, -euse [pɔ̃pø, øz] *adj* pompous
pompier [pɔ̃pje] *nm* fireman
pompiste [pɔ̃pist] *nm/f* petrol (*BRIT*) *ou* gas (*US*) pump attendant
poncer [pɔ̃se] *vt* to sand (down)
ponctuation [pɔ̃ktɥasjɔ̃] *nf* punctuation
ponctuel, le [pɔ̃ktɥɛl] *adj* punctual
pondéré, e [pɔ̃deʀe] *adj* level-headed, composed
pondre [pɔ̃dʀ] *vt* to lay

poney [pɔnɛ] *nm* pony
pont [pɔ̃] *nm* bridge; (*Navig*) deck; **faire le ~** to take the extra day off; *see note*; **pont suspendu** suspension bridge; **pont-levis** *nm* drawbridge

PONT

The expression 'faire le pont' refers to the practice of taking a Monday or Friday off to make a long weekend if a public holiday falls on a Tuesday or Thursday. The French commonly take an extra day off work to give four consecutive days' holiday at 'l'Ascension', 'le 14 juillet' and 'le 15 août'.

pop [pɔp] *adj inv* pop
populaire [pɔpylɛʀ] *adj* popular; (*manifestation*) mass *cpd*; (*milieux, quartier*) working-class; (*expression*) vernacular
popularité [pɔpylaʀite] *nf* popularity
population [pɔpylasjɔ̃] *nf* population
populeux, -euse [pɔpylø, øz] *adj* densely populated
porc [pɔʀ] *nm* pig; (*Culin*) pork
porcelaine [pɔʀsəlɛn] *nf* porcelain, china; piece of china(ware)
porc-épic [pɔʀkepik] *nm* porcupine
porche [pɔʀʃ] *nm* porch
porcherie [pɔʀʃəʀi] *nf* pigsty
pore [pɔʀ] *nm* pore
porno [pɔʀno] *adj* porno ▷ *nm* porn
port [pɔʀ] *nm* harbour, port; (*ville*) port; (*de l'uniforme etc*) wearing; (*pour lettre*) postage; (*pour colis, aussi: posture*) carriage; **port d'arme** (*Jur*) carrying of a firearm; **port payé** postage paid
portable [pɔʀtabl] *adj* (*portatif*) portable; (*téléphone*) mobile ▷ *nm* (*Comput*) laptop (computer); (*téléphone*) mobile (phone)
portail [pɔʀtaj] *nm* gate
portant, e [pɔʀtɑ̃, ɑ̃t] *adj*: **bien/mal ~** in good/poor health
portatif, -ive [pɔʀtatif, iv] *adj* portable
porte [pɔʀt] *nf* door; (*de ville, jardin*) gate; **mettre à la ~** to throw out; **porte-avions** *nm inv* aircraft carrier; **porte-bagages** *nm inv* luggage rack; **porte-bonheur** *nm inv* lucky charm; **porte-clefs** *nm inv* key ring; **porte-documents** *nm inv* attaché *ou* document case
porté, e [pɔʀte] *adj*: **être ~ à faire** to be inclined to do; **être ~ sur qch** to be keen on sth; **portée** *nf* (*d'une arme*) range; (*fig: effet*) impact, import; (: *capacité*) scope, capability; (*de chatte etc*) litter; (*Mus*) stave, staff; **à/hors de portée (de)** within/out of reach (of); **à portée de (la) main** within (arm's) reach; **à la portée de qn** (*fig*) at sb's level, within sb's

capabilities

porte...: portefeuille nm wallet;
portemanteau, x nm (cintre) coat hanger; (au
mur) coat rack; **porte-monnaie** nm inv purse;
porte-parole nm inv spokesman

porter [pɔʀte] vt to carry; (sur soi: vêtement,
barbe, bague) to wear; (fig: responsabilité etc)
to bear, carry; (inscription, nom, fruits) to bear;
(coup) to deal; (attention) to turn; (apporter): **~
qch à qn** to take sth to sb ▷ vi (voix) to carry;
(coup, argument) to hit home; **se porter** vi (se
sentir): **se ~ bien/mal** to be well/unwell; **~ sur**
(recherches) to be concerned with; **se faire ~
malade** to report sick

porteur, -euse [pɔʀtœʀ, øz] nm/f (de
bagages) porter; (de chèque) bearer

porte-voix [pɔʀtəvwa] nm inv megaphone

portier [pɔʀtje] nm doorman

portière [pɔʀtjɛʀ] nf door

portion [pɔʀsjɔ̃] nf (part) portion, share;
(partie) portion, section

porto [pɔʀto] nm port (wine)

portrait [pɔʀtʀɛ] nm (peinture) portrait;
(photo) photograph; **portrait-robot** nm
Identikit® ou photo-fit® picture

portuaire [pɔʀtɥɛʀ] adj port cpd,
harbour cpd

portugais, e [pɔʀtygɛ, ɛz] adj Portuguese
▷ nm/f: **P~, e** Portuguese ▷ nm (Ling)
Portuguese

Portugal [pɔʀtygal] nm: **le ~** Portugal

pose [poz] nf (de moquette) laying; (attitude, d'un
modèle) pose; (Photo) exposure

posé, e [poze] adj serious

poser [poze] vt to put; (installer: moquette,
carrelage) to lay; (rideaux, papier peint) to hang;
(question) to ask; (principe, conditions) to lay
ou set down; (difficulté) to pose; (formuler:
problème) to formulate ▷ vi (modèle) to pose;
se poser vi (oiseau, avion) to land; (question)
to arise; **~ qch (sur)** (déposer) to put sth down
(on); **~ qch sur/quelque part** (placer) to put
sth on/somewhere; **~ sa candidature à un
poste** to apply for a post

positif, -ive [pozitif, iv] adj positive

position [pozisjɔ̃] nf position; **prendre ~** (fig)
to take a stand

posologie [pozɔlɔʒi] nf dosage

posséder [posede] vt to own, possess;
(qualité, talent) to have, possess; (sexuellement)
to possess; **possession** nf ownership no pl,
possession; **prendre possession de qch** to
take possession of sth

possibilité [posibilite] nf possibility;
possibilités nfpl (potentiel) potential sg

possible [posibl] adj possible; (projet,
entreprise) feasible ▷ nm: **faire son ~** to do all
one can, do one's utmost; **le plus/moins de
livres ~** as many/few books as possible; **le**

plus vite ~ as quickly as possible; **aussitôt/
dès que ~** as soon as possible

postal, e, -aux [pɔstal, o] adj postal

poste¹ [pɔst] nf (service) post, postal service;
(administration, bureau) post office; **mettre à
la ~** to post; **poste restante** poste restante
(BRIT), general delivery (US)

poste² [pɔst] nm (fonction, Mil) post; (Tél)
extension; (de radio etc) set; **poste (de police)**
police station; **poste de secours** first-aid
post; **poste d'essence** filling station; **poste
d'incendie** fire point; **poste de pilotage**
cockpit, flight deck

poster [pɔste] vt to post; **où est-ce que je
peux ~ ces cartes postales?** where can I post
these cards?

postérieur, e [pɔsteʀjœʀ] adj (date) later;
(partie) back ▷ nm (fam) behind

postuler [pɔstyle] vi: **~ à** ou **pour un emploi**
to apply for a job

pot [po] nm (en verre) jar; (en terre) pot; (en
plastique, carton) carton; (en métal) tin; (fam:
chance) luck; **avoir du ~** (fam) to be
lucky; **boire** ou **prendre un ~** (fam) to have
a drink; **petit ~ (pour bébé)** (jar of) baby
food; **~ catalytique** catalytic converter; **pot
d'échappement** exhaust pipe

potable [pɔtabl] adj: **eau (non) ~**
(non-)drinking water

potage [pɔtaʒ] nm soup; **potager, -ère**
adj: **(jardin) potager** kitchen ou vegetable
garden

pot-au-feu [pɔtofø] nm inv (beef) stew

pot-de-vin [podvɛ̃] nm bribe

pote [pɔt] (fam) nm pal

poteau, x [pɔto] nm post; **poteau indicateur**
signpost

potelé, e [pɔt(ə)le] adj plump, chubby

potentiel, le [pɔtɑ̃sjɛl] adj, nm potential

poterie [pɔtʀi] nf pottery; (objet) piece of
pottery

potier, -ière [pɔtje, jɛʀ] nm/f potter

potiron [pɔtiʀɔ̃] nm pumpkin

pou, x [pu] nm louse

poubelle [pubɛl] nf (dust)bin

pouce [pus] nm thumb

poudre [pudʀ] nf powder; (fard) (face)
powder; (explosif) gunpowder; **en ~**: **café en
~** instant coffee; **lait en ~** dried ou powdered
milk; **poudreuse** nf powder snow; **poudrier**
nm (powder) compact

pouffer [pufe] vi: **~ (de rire)** to burst out
laughing

poulailler [pulaje] nm henhouse

poulain [pulɛ̃] nm foal; (fig) protégé

poule [pul] nf hen; (Culin) (boiling) fowl; **poule
mouillée** coward

poulet [pulɛ] nm chicken; (fam) cop

poulie [puli] nf pulley

pouls [pu] *nm* pulse; **prendre le ~ de qn** to feel sb's pulse

poumon [pumɔ̃] *nm* lung

poupée [pupe] *nf* doll

pour [puʀ] *prép* for ▷ *nm*: **le ~ et le contre** the pros and cons; **~ faire** (so as) to do, in order to do; **~ avoir fait** for having done; **~ que** so that, in order that; **fermé ~ (cause de) travaux** closed for refurbishment *ou* alterations; **c'est ~ ça que ...** that's why ...; **~ quoi faire?** what for?; **~ 20 euros d'essence** 20 euros' worth of petrol; **~ cent** per cent; **~ ce qui est de** as for

pourboire [puʀbwaʀ] *nm* tip; **combien de ~ est-ce qu'il faut laisser?** how much should I tip?

pourcentage [puʀsɑ̃taʒ] *nm* percentage

pourchasser [puʀʃase] *vt* to pursue

pourparlers [puʀpaʀle] *nmpl* talks, negotiations

pourpre [puʀpʀ] *adj* crimson

pourquoi [puʀkwa] *adv, conj* why ▷ *nm inv*: **le ~ (de)** the reason (for)

pourrai *etc* [puʀe] *vb voir* **pouvoir**

pourri, e [puʀi] *adj* rotten

pourrir [puʀiʀ] *vi* to rot; (*fruit*) to go rotten *ou* bad ▷ *vt* to rot; (*fig*) to spoil thoroughly; **pourriture** *nf* rot

poursuite [puʀsɥit] *nf* pursuit, chase; **poursuites** *nfpl* (*Jur*) legal proceedings

poursuivre [puʀsɥivʀ] *vt* to pursue, chase (after); (*obséder*) to haunt; (*Jur*) to bring proceedings against, prosecute; (: *au civil*) to sue; (*but*) to strive towards; (*continuer: études etc*) to carry on with, continue; **se poursuivre** *vi* to go on, continue

pourtant [puʀtɑ̃] *adv* yet; **c'est ~ facile** (and) yet it's easy

pourtour [puʀtuʀ] *nm* perimeter

pourvoir [puʀvwaʀ] *vt*: **~ qch/qn de** to equip sth/sb with ▷ *vi*: **~ à** to provide for; **pourvu, e** *adj*: **pourvu de** equipped with; **pourvu que** (*si*) provided that, so long as; (*espérons que*) let's hope (that)

pousse [pus] *nf* growth; (*bourgeon*) shoot

poussée [puse] *nf* thrust; (*d'acné*) eruption; (*fig: prix*) upsurge

pousser [puse] *vt* to push; (*émettre: cri, soupir*) to give; (*stimuler: élève*) to urge on; (*poursuivre: études, discussion*) to carry on (further) ▷ *vi* to push; (*croître*) to grow; **se pousser** *vi* to move over; **~ qn à** (*inciter*) to urge *ou* press sb to; (*acculer*) to drive sb to; **faire ~** (*plante*) to grow

poussette [puset] *nf* push chair (BRIT), stroller (US)

poussière [pusjɛʀ] *nf* dust; **poussiéreux, -euse** *adj* dusty

poussin [pusɛ̃] *nm* chick

poutre [putʀ] *nf* beam

 MOT-CLÉ

pouvoir [puvwaʀ] *nm* power; (*Pol: dirigeants*): **le pouvoir** those in power; **les pouvoirs publics** the authorities; **pouvoir d'achat** purchasing power
▷ *vb semi-aux* **1** (*être en état de*) can, be able to; **je ne peux pas le réparer** I can't *ou* I am not able to repair it; **déçu de ne pas pouvoir le faire** disappointed not to be able to do it
2 (*avoir la permission*) can, may, be allowed to; **vous pouvez aller au cinéma** you can *ou* may go to the pictures
3 (*probabilité, hypothèse*) may, might, could; **il a pu avoir un accident** he may *ou* might *ou* could have had an accident; **il aurait pu le dire!** he might *ou* could have said (so)!
▷ *vb impers* may, might, could; **il peut arriver que** it may *ou* might *ou* could happen that; **il pourrait pleuvoir** it might rain
▷ *vt* can, be able to; **j'ai fait tout ce que j'ai pu** I did all I could; **je n'en peux plus** (*épuisé*) I'm exhausted; (*à bout*) I can't take any more
▷ *vi*: **se pouvoir**: **il se peut que** it may *ou* might be that; **cela se pourrait** that's quite possible

prairie [pʀeʀi] *nf* meadow

praline [pʀalin] *nf* sugared almond

praticable [pʀatikabl] *adj* passable, practicable

pratiquant, e [pʀatikɑ̃, ɑ̃t] *nm/f* (regular) churchgoer

pratique [pʀatik] *nf* practice ▷ *adj* practical; **pratiquement** *adv* (*pour ainsi dire*) practically, virtually; **pratiquer** *vt* to practise; (*l'équitation, la pêche*) to go in for; (*le golf, football*) to play; (*intervention, opération*) to carry out

pré [pʀe] *nm* meadow

préalable [pʀealabl] *adj* preliminary; **au ~** beforehand

préambule [pʀeɑ̃byl] *nm* preamble; (*fig*) prelude; **sans ~** straight away

préau [pʀeo] *nm* (*Scol*) covered playground

préavis [pʀeavi] *nm* notice

précaution [pʀekosjɔ̃] *nf* precaution; **avec ~** cautiously; **par ~** as a precaution

précédemment [pʀesedamɑ̃] *adv* before, previously

précédent, e [pʀesedɑ̃, ɑ̃t] *adj* previous ▷ *nm* precedent; **sans ~** unprecedented; **le jour ~** the day before, the previous day

précéder [pʀesede] *vt* to precede

prêcher [pʀeʃe] *vt* to preach

précieux, -euse [pʀesjø, jøz] *adj* precious; (*aide, conseil*) invaluable

précipice [pʀesipis] *nm* drop, chasm

précipitamment [presipitamã] *adv* hurriedly, hastily

précipitation [presipitasjõ] *nf* (*hâte*) haste

précipité, e [presipite] *adj* hurried, hasty

précipiter [presipite] *vt* (*hâter: départ*) to hasten; (*faire tomber*): **~ qn/qch du haut de** to throw *ou* hurl sb/sth off *ou* from; **se précipiter** *vi* to speed up; **se ~ sur/vers** to rush at/towards

précis, e [presi, iz] *adj* precise; (*mesures*) accurate, precise; **à 4 heures ~es** at 4 o'clock sharp; **précisément** *adv* precisely; **préciser** *vt* (*expliquer*) to be more specific about, clarify; (*spécifier*) to state, specify; **se préciser** *vi* to become clear(er); **précision** *nf* precision; (*détail*) point *ou* detail; **demander des précisions** to ask for further explanation

précoce [prekɔs] *adj* early; (*enfant*) precocious

préconçu, e [prekõsy] *adj* preconceived

préconiser [prekɔnize] *vt* to advocate

prédécesseur [predesesœr] *nm* predecessor

prédilection [predilɛksjõ] *nf*: **avoir une ~ pour** to be partial to

prédire [predir] *vt* to predict

prédominer [predɔmine] *vi* to predominate

préface [prefas] *nf* preface

préfecture [prefɛktyr] *nf* prefecture; **préfecture de police** police headquarters *pl*

préférable [preferabl] *adj* preferable

préféré, e [prefere] *adj, nm/f* favourite

préférence [preferãs] *nf* preference; **de ~** preferably

préférer [prefere] *vt*: **~ qn/qch (à)** to prefer sb/sth (to), like sb/sth better (than); **~ faire** to prefer to do; **je préférerais du thé** I would rather have tea, I'd prefer tea

préfet [prefe] *nm* prefect

préhistorique [preistɔrik] *adj* prehistoric

préjudice [preʒydis] *nm* (*matériel*) loss; (*moral*) harm *no pl*; **porter ~ à** to harm, be detrimental to; **au ~ de** at the expense of

préjugé [preʒyʒe] *nm* prejudice; **avoir un ~ contre** to be prejudiced *ou* biased against

prélasser [prelase]: **se prélasser** *vi* to lounge

prélèvement [prelɛvmã] *nm* (*montant*) deduction; **faire un ~ de sang** to take a blood sample

prélever [prel(ə)ve] *vt* (*échantillon*) to take; **~ (sur)** (*montant*) to deduct (from); (*argent: sur son compte*) to withdraw (from)

prématuré, e [prematyre] *adj* premature ▷ *nm* premature baby

premier, -ière [prəmje, jɛr] *adj* first; (*rang*) front; (*fig: objectif*) basic; **le ~ venu** the first person to come along; **de ~ ordre** first-rate; **Premier ministre** Prime Minister; **première** *nf* (*Scol*) year 12 (BRIT), eleventh grade (US); (*Aviat, Rail etc*) first class; **premièrement** *adv* firstly

prémonition [premɔnisjõ] *nf* premonition

prenant, e [prənã, ãt] *adj* absorbing, engrossing

prénatal, e [prenatal] *adj* (*Méd*) antenatal

prendre [prãdr] *vt* to take; (*repas*) to have; (*se procurer*) to get; (*malfaiteur, poisson*) to catch; (*passager*) to pick up; (*personnel*) to take on; (*traiter: personne*) to handle; (*voix, ton*) to put on; (*ôter*): **~ qch à** to take sth from; (*coincer*): **se ~ les doigts dans** to get one's fingers caught in ▷ *vi* (*liquide, ciment*) to set; (*greffe, vaccin*) to take; (*feu: foyer*) to go; (*se diriger*): **~ à gauche** to turn (to the) left; **~ froid** to catch cold; **se ~ pour** to think one is; **s'en ~ à** to attack; **se ~ d'amitié pour** to befriend; **s'y ~** (*procéder*) to set about it

preneur [prənœr] *nm*: **être/trouver ~** to be willing to buy/find a buyer

prénom [prenõ] *nm* first *ou* Christian name

préoccupation [preɔkypasjõ] *nf* (*souci*) concern; (*idée fixe*) preoccupation

préoccuper [preɔkype] *vt* (*inquiéter*) to worry; (*absorber*) to preoccupy; **se ~ de** to be concerned with

préparatifs [preparatif] *nmpl* preparations

préparation [preparasjõ] *nf* preparation

préparer [prepare] *vt* to prepare; (*café, thé*) to make; (*examen*) to prepare for; (*voyage, entreprise*) to plan; **se préparer** *vi* (*orage, tragédie*) to brew, be in the air; **~ qch à qn** (*surprise etc*) to have sth in store for sb; **se ~ (à qch/faire)** to prepare (o.s.) *ou* get ready (for sth/to do)

prépondérant, e [prepõderã, ãt] *adj* major, dominating

préposé, e [prepoze] *nm/f* employee; (*facteur*) postman

préposition [prepozisjõ] *nf* preposition

près [pre] *adv* near, close; **~ de** near (to), close to; (*environ*) nearly, almost; **de ~** closely; **à 5 kg ~** to within about 5 kg; **il n'est pas à 10 minutes ~** he can spare 10 minutes; **est-ce qu'il y a une banque ~ d'ici?** is there a bank nearby?

présage [prezaʒ] *nm* omen

presbyte [presbit] *adj* long-sighted

presbytère [presbiter] *nm* presbytery

prescription [preskripsjõ] *nf* prescription

prescrire [preskrir] *vt* to prescribe

présence [prezãs] *nf* presence; (*au bureau, à l'école*) attendance

présent, e [prezã, ãt] *adj, nm* present; **à ~ (que)** now (that)

présentation [prezãtasjõ] *nf* presentation; (*de nouveau venu*) introduction; (*allure*) appearance; **faire les ~s** to do the introductions

présenter [prezãte] *vt* to present; (*excuses, condoléances*) to offer; (*invité, conférencier*):

~ qn (à) to introduce sb (to) ▷ *vi*: **~ bien** to have a pleasing appearance; **se présenter** *vi* (*occasion*) to arise; **se ~ à** (*examen*) to sit; (*élection*) to stand at, run for; **je vous présente Nadine** this is Nadine, could I introduce you to Nadine?

préservatif [prezervatif] *nm* condom, sheath

préserver [prezerve] *vt*: **~ de** (*protéger*) to protect from

président [prezidã] *nm* (*Pol*) president; (*d'une assemblée, Comm*) chairman; **président directeur général** chairman and managing director; **présidentielles** *nfpl* presidential elections

présider [prezide] *vt* to preside over; (*dîner*) to be the guest of honour at

presque [presk] *adv* almost, nearly; **~ personne** hardly anyone; **~ rien** hardly anything; **~ pas** hardly (at all); **~ pas (de)** hardly any

presqu'île [preskil] *nf* peninsula

pressant, e [presã, ãt] *adj* urgent

presse [pres] *nf* press; (*affluence*): **heures de ~** busy times

pressé, e [prese] *adj* in a hurry; (*travail*) urgent; **orange ~e** freshly-squeezed orange juice

pressentiment [presãtimã] *nm* foreboding, premonition

pressentir [presãtir] *vt* to sense

presse-papiers [prespapje] *nm inv* paperweight

presser [prese] *vt* (*fruit, éponge*) to squeeze; (*bouton*) to press; (*allure*) to speed up; (*inciter*): **~ qn de faire** to urge ou press sb to do ▷ *vi* to be urgent; **se presser** *vi* (*se hâter*) to hurry (up); **se ~ contre qn** to squeeze up against sb; **le temps presse** there's not much time; **rien ne presse** there's no hurry

pressing [presiŋ] *nm* (*magasin*) dry-cleaner's

pression [presjõ] *nf* pressure; (*bouton*) press stud; (*fam: bière*) draught beer; **faire ~ sur** to put pressure on; **sous ~** pressurized, under pressure; (*fig*) under pressure; **pression artérielle** blood pressure

prestataire [prestater] *nm/f* supplier

prestation [prestasjõ] *nf* (*allocation*) benefit; (*d'une entreprise*) service provided; (*d'un artiste*) performance

prestidigitateur, -trice [prestidiʒitatœr, tris] *nm/f* conjurer

prestige [prestiʒ] *nm* prestige; **prestigieux, -euse** *adj* prestigious

présumer [prezyme] *vt*: **~ que** to presume ou assume that

prêt, e [pre, pret] *adj* ready ▷ *nm* (*somme*) loan; **quand est-ce que mes photos seront ~es?** when will my photos be ready?; **prêt-à-porter** *nm* ready-to-wear ou off-the-peg (*BRIT*) clothes *pl*

prétendre [pretãdr] *vt* (*affirmer*): **~ que** to claim that; (*avoir l'intention de*): **~ faire qch** to mean ou intend to do sth; **prétendu, e** *adj* (*supposé*) so-called

> Attention à ne pas traduire **prétendre** par *to pretend*.

prétentieux, -euse [pretãsjø, jøz] *adj* pretentious

prétention [pretãsjõ] *nf* claim; (*vanité*) pretentiousness

prêter [prete] *vt* (*livres, argent*): **~ qch (à)** to lend sth (to); (*supposer*): **~ à qn** (*caractère, propos*) to attribute to sb; **pouvez-vous me ~ de l'argent?** can you lend me some money?

prétexte [pretekst] *nm* pretext, excuse; **sous aucun ~** on no account; **prétexter** *vt* to give as a pretext ou an excuse

prêtre [pretr] *nm* priest

preuve [prœv] *nf* proof; (*indice*) proof, evidence *no pl*; **faire ~ de** to show; **faire ses ~s** to prove o.s. (ou itself)

prévaloir [prevalwar] *vi* to prevail

prévenant, e [prev(ə)nã, ãt] *adj* thoughtful, kind

prévenir [prev(ə)nir] *vt* (*éviter: catastrophe etc*) to avoid, prevent; (*anticiper: désirs, besoins*) to anticipate; **~ qn (de)** (*avertir*) to warn sb (about); (*informer*) to tell ou inform sb (about)

préventif, -ive [prevãtif, iv] *adj* preventive

prévention [prevãsjõ] *nf* prevention; **prévention routière** road safety

prévenu, e [prev(ə)ny] *nm/f* (*Jur*) defendant, accused

prévision [previzjõ] *nf*: **~s** predictions; (*Écon*) forecast *sg*; **en ~ de** in anticipation of; **prévisions météorologiques** weather forecast *sg*

prévoir [prevwar] *vt* (*anticiper*) to foresee; (*s'attendre à*) to expect, reckon on; (*organiser: voyage etc*) to plan; (*envisager*) to allow; **comme prévu** as planned; **prévoyant, e** *adj* gifted with (ou showing) foresight; **prévu, e** *pp de* **prévoir**

prier [prije] *vi* to pray ▷ *vt* (*Dieu*) to pray to; (*implorer*) to beg; (*demander*): **~ qn de faire** to ask sb to do; **se faire ~** to need coaxing ou persuading; **je vous en prie** (*allez-y*) please do; (*de rien*) don't mention it; **prière** *nf* prayer; **"prière de ..."** "please ..."

primaire [primer] *adj* primary ▷ *nm* (*Scol*) primary education

prime [prim] *nf* (*bonus*) bonus; (*subvention*) premium; (*Comm: cadeau*) free gift; (*Assurances, Bourse*) premium ▷ *adj*: **de ~ abord** at first glance; **primer** *vt* (*récompenser*) to award a prize to ▷ *vi* to dominate; to be most important

primevère [pʀimvɛʀ] nf primrose

primitif, -ive [pʀimitif, iv] adj primitive; (originel) original

prince [pʀɛ̃s] nm prince; **princesse** nf princess

principal, e, -aux [pʀɛ̃sipal, o] adj principal, main ▷ nm (Scol) principal, head(master); (essentiel) main thing

principe [pʀɛ̃sip] nm principle; **par ~** on principle; **en ~** (habituellement) as a rule; (théoriquement) in principle

printemps [pʀɛ̃tɑ̃] nm spring

priorité [pʀijɔʀite] nf priority; (Auto) right of way; **priorité à droite** right of way to vehicles coming from the right

pris, e [pʀi, pʀiz] pp de **prendre** ▷ adj (place) taken; (mains) full; (personne) busy; **avoir le nez/la gorge ~(e)** to have a stuffy nose/a hoarse throat; **être ~ de panique** to be panic-stricken

prise [pʀiz] nf (d'une ville) capture; (Pêche, Chasse) catch; (point d'appui ou pour empoigner) hold; (Élec: fiche) plug; (: femelle) socket; **être aux ~s avec** to be grappling with; **prise de courant** power point; **prise de sang** blood test; **prise multiple** adaptor

priser [pʀize] vt (estimer) to prize, value

prison [pʀizɔ̃] nf prison; **aller/être en ~** to go to/be in prison ou jail; **prisonnier, -ière** nm/f prisoner ▷ adj captive

privé, e [pʀive] adj private; (en punition): **tu es ~ de télé!** no TV for you! ▷ nm (Comm) private sector; **en ~** in private

priver [pʀive] vt: **~ qn de** to deprive sb of; **se priver de** to go ou do without

privilège [pʀivilɛʒ] nm privilege

prix [pʀi] nm price; (récompense, Scol) prize; **hors de ~** exorbitantly priced; **à aucun ~** not at any price; **à tout ~** at all costs

probable [pʀɔbabl] adj likely, probable; **probablement** adv probably

problème [pʀɔblɛm] nm problem

procédé [pʀɔsede] nm (méthode) process; (comportement) behaviour no pl

procéder [pʀɔsede] vi to proceed; (moralement) to behave; **~ à** to carry out

procès [pʀɔsɛ] nm trial; (poursuites) proceedings pl; **être en ~ avec** to be involved in a lawsuit with

processus [pʀɔsesys] nm process

procès-verbal, -aux [pʀɔsɛvɛʀbal, o] nm (de réunion) minutes pl; (aussi: **P.-V.**) parking ticket

prochain, e [pʀɔʃɛ̃, ɛn] adj next; (proche: départ, arrivée) impending ▷ nm fellow man; **la ~e fois/semaine ~e** next time/week; **prochainement** adv soon, shortly

proche [pʀɔʃ] adj nearby; (dans le temps) imminent; (parent, ami) close; **proches** nmpl (parents) close relatives; **être ~ (de)** to be near, be close (to)

proclamer [pʀɔklame] vt to proclaim

procuration [pʀɔkyʀasjɔ̃] nf proxy

procurer [pʀɔkyʀe] vt: **~ qch à qn** (fournir) to obtain sth for sb; (causer: plaisir etc) to bring sb sth; **se procurer** vt to get; **procureur** nm public prosecutor

prodige [pʀɔdiʒ] nm marvel, wonder; (personne) prodigy; **prodiguer** vt (soins, attentions): **prodiguer qch à qn** to give sb sth

producteur, -trice [pʀɔdyktœʀ, tʀis] nm/f producer

productif, -ive [pʀɔdyktif, iv] adj productive

production [pʀɔdyksjɔ̃] nf production; (rendement) output

productivité [pʀɔdyktivite] nf productivity

produire [pʀɔdɥiʀ] vt to produce; **se produire** vi (événement) to happen, occur; (acteur) to perform, appear

produit [pʀɔdɥi] nm product; **produit chimique** chemical; **produits agricoles** farm produce sg; **produits de beauté** beauty products, cosmetics; **produits d'entretien** cleaning products

prof [pʀɔf] (fam) nm teacher

proférer [pʀɔfeʀe] vt to utter

professeur, e [pʀɔfesœʀ] nm/f teacher; (de faculté) (university) lecturer; (: titulaire d'une chaire) professor

profession [pʀɔfesjɔ̃] nf occupation; **~ libérale** (liberal) profession; **sans ~** unemployed; **professionnel, le** adj, nm/f professional

profil [pʀɔfil] nm profile; **de ~** in profile

profit [pʀɔfi] nm (avantage) benefit, advantage; (Comm, Finance) profit; **au ~ de** in aid of; **tirer ~ de** to profit from; **profitable** adj (utile) beneficial; (lucratif) profitable; **profiter** vi: **profiter de** (situation, occasion) to take advantage of; (vacances, jeunesse etc) to make the most of

profond, e [pʀɔfɔ̃, ɔ̃d] adj deep; (sentiment, intérêt) profound; **profondément** adv deeply; **il dort profondément** he is sound asleep; **profondeur** nf depth; **l'eau à quelle profondeur?** how deep is the water?

programme [pʀɔgʀam] nm programme; (Scol) syllabus, curriculum; (Inform) program; **programmer** vt (émission) to schedule; (Inform) to program; **programmeur, -euse** nm/f programmer

progrès [pʀɔgʀɛ] nm progress no pl; **faire des ~** to make progress; **progresser** vi to progress; **progressif, -ive** adj progressive

proie [pʀwa] nf prey no pl

projecteur [pʀɔʒɛktœʀ] nm (pour film) projector; (de théâtre, cirque) spotlight

projectile [pʀɔʒɛktil] nm missile

projection [prɔʒɛksjɔ̃] nf projection; (séance) showing

projet [prɔʒɛ] nm plan; (ébauche) draft; **projet de loi** bill; **projeter** vt (envisager) to plan; (film, photos) to project; (ombre, lueur) to throw, cast; (jeter) to throw up (ou off ou out)

prolétaire [prɔletɛr] adj, nmf proletarian

prolongement [prɔlɔ̃ʒmɑ̃] nm extension; **dans le ~ de** running on from

prolonger [prɔlɔ̃ʒe] vt (débat, séjour) to prolong; (délai, billet, rue) to extend; **se prolonger** vi to go on

promenade [prɔm(ə)nad] nf walk (ou drive ou ride); **faire une ~** to go for a walk; **une ~ en voiture/à vélo** a drive-/(bicycle) ride

promener [prɔm(ə)ne] vt (chien) to take out for a walk; (doigts, regard): **~ qch sur** to run sth over; **se promener** vi to go for (ou be out for) a walk

promesse [prɔmɛs] nf promise

promettre [prɔmɛtr] vt to promise ▷ vi to be ou look promising; **~ à qn de faire** to promise sb that one will do

promiscuité [prɔmiskɥite] nf (chambre) lack of privacy

promontoire [prɔmɔ̃twar] nm headland

promoteur, -trice [prɔmɔtœr, tris] nm/f: **promoteur (immobilier)** property developer (brit), real estate promoter (us)

promotion [prɔmɔsjɔ̃] nf promotion; **en ~** on special offer

promouvoir [prɔmuvwar] vt to promote

prompt, e [prɔ̃(pt), prɔ̃(p)t] adj swift, rapid

prôner [prone] vt (préconiser) to advocate

pronom [prɔnɔ̃] nm pronoun

prononcer [prɔnɔ̃se] vt to pronounce; (dire) to utter; (discours) to deliver; **se prononcer** vi to be pronounced; **comment est-ce que ça se prononce?** how do you pronounce ou say it?; **se ~ (sur)** (se décider) to reach a decision (on ou about), give a verdict (on); **prononciation** nf pronunciation

pronostic [prɔnɔstik] nm (Méd) prognosis; (fig: aussi: **~s**) forecast

propagande [prɔpagɑ̃d] nf propaganda

propager [prɔpaʒe] vt to spread; **se propager** vi to spread

prophète [prɔfɛt] nm prophet

prophétie [prɔfesi] nf prophecy

propice [prɔpis] adj favourable

proportion [prɔpɔrsjɔ̃] nf proportion; **toute(s) ~(s) gardée(s)** making due allowance(s)

propos [prɔpo] nm (intention) intention, aim; (sujet): **à quel ~?** what about? ▷ nmpl (paroles) talk no pl, remarks; **à ~ de** about, regarding; **à tout ~** for the slightest thing ou reason; **à ~** by the way; (opportunément) at the right moment

proposer [prɔpoze] vt to propose; **~ qch**

(à qn) (suggérer) to suggest sth (to sb), propose sth (to sb); (offrir) to offer (sb) sth; **se ~ (pour faire)** to offer one's services (to do); **proposition** (suggestion) nf proposal, suggestion; (Ling) clause

propre [prɔpr] adj clean; (net) neat, tidy; (possessif) own; (sens) literal; (particulier): **~ à** peculiar to; (approprié): **~ à** suitable for ▷ nm: **recopier au ~** to make a fair copy of; **proprement** adv (avec propreté) cleanly; **le village proprement dit** the village itself; **à proprement parler** strictly speaking; **propreté** nf cleanliness

propriétaire [prɔprijetɛr] nm/f owner; (pour le locataire) landlord(-lady)

propriété [prɔprijete] nf property; (droit) ownership

propulser [prɔpylse] vt to propel

prose [proz] nf (style) prose

prospecter [prɔspɛkte] vt to prospect; (Comm) to canvass

prospectus [prɔspɛktys] nm leaflet

prospère [prɔspɛr] adj prosperous; **prospérer** vi to prosper

prosterner [prɔstɛrne]: **se prosterner** vi to bow low, prostrate o.s.

prostituée [prɔstitɥe] nf prostitute

prostitution [prɔstitysjɔ̃] nf prostitution

protecteur, -trice [prɔtɛktœr, tris] adj protective; (air, ton: péj) patronizing ▷ nm/f protector

protection [prɔtɛksjɔ̃] nf protection; (d'un personnage influent: aide) patronage

protéger [prɔteʒe] vt to protect; **se ~ de/ contre** to protect o.s. from

protège-slip [prɔtɛʒslip] nm panty liner

protéine [prɔtein] nf protein

protestant, e [prɔtɛstɑ̃, ɑ̃t] adj, nm/f Protestant

protestation [prɔtɛstasjɔ̃] nf (plainte) protest

protester [prɔtɛste] vi: **~ (contre)** to protest (against ou about); **~ de** (son innocence) to protest

prothèse [prɔtɛz] nf: **prothèse dentaire** denture

protocole [prɔtɔkɔl] nm (fig) etiquette

proue [pru] nf bow(s pl), prow

prouesse [prues] nf feat

prouver [pruve] vt to prove

provenance [prɔv(ə)nɑ̃s] nf origin; **avion en ~ de** plane (arriving) from

provenir [prɔv(ə)nir]: **~ de** vt to come from

proverbe [prɔvɛrb] nm proverb

province [prɔvɛ̃s] nf province

proviseur [prɔvizœr] nm ≈ head(teacher) (brit), ≈ principal (us)

provision [prɔvizjɔ̃] nf (réserve) stock, supply;

provisions nfpl (vivres) provisions, food no pl
provisoire [pʀɔvizwaʀ] adj temporary;
provisoirement adv temporarily
provocant, e [pʀɔvɔkɑ̃, ɑ̃t] adj provocative
provoquer [pʀɔvɔke] vt (défier) to provoke;
(causer) to cause, bring about; (inciter): ~ qn à
to incite sb to
proxénète [pʀɔksenɛt] nm procurer
proximité [pʀɔksimite] nf nearness,
closeness; (dans le temps) imminence,
closeness; à ~ near ou close by; à ~ de near
(to), close to
prudemment [pʀydamɑ̃] adv carefully;
wisely, sensibly
prudence [pʀydɑ̃s] nf carefulness; avec ~
carefully; par ~ as a precaution
prudent, e [pʀydɑ̃, ɑ̃t] adj (pas téméraire)
careful; (: en général) safety-conscious; (sage,
conseillé) wise, sensible; c'est plus ~ it's wiser
prune [pʀyn] nf plum
pruneau, x [pʀyno] nm prune
prunier [pʀynje] nm plum tree
PS sigle m = **parti socialiste**
pseudonyme [psødɔnim] nm (gén) fictitious
name; (d'écrivain) pseudonym, pen name
psychanalyse [psikanaliz] nf
psychoanalysis
psychiatre [psikjatʀ] nm/f psychiatrist;
psychiatrique adj psychiatric
psychique [psiʃik] adj psychological
psychologie [psikɔlɔʒi] nf psychology;
psychologique adj psychological;
psychologue nm/f psychologist
pu [py] pp de **pouvoir**
puanteur [pɥɑ̃tœʀ] nf stink, stench
pub [pyb] nf (fam: annonce) ad, advert;
(pratique) advertising
public, -ique [pyblik] adj public; (école,
instruction) state cpd ▷ nm public; (assistance)
audience; en ~ in public
publicitaire [pyblisitɛʀ] adj advertising cpd;
(film) publicity cpd
publicité [pyblisite] nf (méthode, profession)
advertising; (annonce) advertisement;
(révélations) publicity
publier [pyblije] vt to publish
publipostage [pyblipostaʒ] nm mailing m
publique [pyblik] adj voir **public**
puce [pys] nf flea; (Inform) chip; carte à ~
smart card; (marché aux) ~s flea market sg
pudeur [pydœʀ] nf modesty; **pudique** adj
(chaste) modest; (discret) discreet
puer [pɥe] (péj) vi to stink
puéricultrice [pɥeʀikyltʀis] nf p(a)ediatric
nurse
puéril, e [pɥeʀil] adj childish
puis [pɥi] vb voir **pouvoir** ▷ adv then
puiser [pɥize] vt: ~ (dans) to draw (from)
puisque [pɥisk] conj since

puissance [pɥisɑ̃s] nf power; en ~ adj
potential
puissant, e [pɥisɑ̃, ɑ̃t] adj powerful
puits [pɥi] nm well
pull(-over) [pyl(ɔvɛʀ)] nm sweater
pulluler [pylyle] vi to swarm
pulpe [pylp] nf pulp
pulvériser [pylveʀize] vt to pulverize;
(liquide) to spray
punaise [pynɛz] nf (Zool) bug; (clou) drawing
pin (BRIT), thumbtack (US)
punch [pɔ̃ʃ] nm (boisson) punch
punir [pyniʀ] vt to punish; **punition** nf
punishment
pupille [pypij] nf (Anat) pupil ▷ nm/f (enfant)
ward
pupitre [pypitʀ] nm (Scol) desk
pur, e [pyʀ] adj pure; (vin) undiluted; (whisky)
neat; en ~e perte to no avail; c'est de la folie
~e it's sheer madness
purée [pyʀe] nf: ~ (de pommes de terre)
mashed potatoes pl; **purée de marrons**
chestnut purée
purement [pyʀmɑ̃] adv purely
purgatoire [pyʀgatwaʀ] nm purgatory
purger [pyʀʒe] vt (Méd, Pol) to purge; (Jur:
peine) to serve
pur-sang [pyʀsɑ̃] nm inv thoroughbred
pus [py] nm pus
putain [pytɛ̃] (fam!) nf whore (!)
puzzle [pœzl] nm jigsaw (puzzle)
P.-V. [peve] sigle m = **procès-verbal**
pyjama [piʒama] nm pyjamas pl (BRIT),
pajamas pl (US)
pyramide [piʀamid] nf pyramid
Pyrénées [piʀene] nfpl: les ~ the Pyrenees

QI *sigle m* (= *quotient intellectuel*) IQ

quadragénaire[k(w)adraʒenɛʀ] *nm/f* man/ woman in his/her forties

quadruple[k(w)adʀypl] *nm*: **le ~ de** four times as much as

quai[ke] *nm* (*de port*) quay; (*de gare*) platform; **être à ~** (*navire*) to be alongside; **de quel ~ part le train pour Paris?** which platform does the Paris train go from?

qualification[kalifikasjɔ̃] *nf* (*aptitude*) qualification

qualifier[kalifje] *vt* to qualify; **se qualifier** *vi* to qualify; **~ qch/qn de** to describe sth/sb as

qualité[kalite] *nf* quality

quand[kɑ̃] *conj, adv* when; **~ je serai riche** when I'm rich; **~ même** all the same; **~ même, il exagère!** really, he overdoes it!; **~ bien même** even though

quant[kɑ̃]: **~ à** *prép* (*pour ce qui est de*) as for, as to; (*au sujet de*) regarding

quantité[kɑ̃tite] *nf* quantity, amount; (*grand nombre*): **une** ou **des ~(s) de** a great deal of

quarantaine[kaʀɑ̃tɛn] *nf* (*Méd*) quarantine; **avoir la ~** (*âge*) to be around forty; **une ~ (de)** forty or so, about forty

quarante[kaʀɑ̃t] *num* forty

quart[kaʀ] *nm* (*fraction*) quarter; (*surveillance*) watch; **un ~ de vin** a quarter

litre of wine; **le ~ de** a quarter of; **quart d'heure** quarter of an hour; **quarts de finale** quarter finals

quartier[kaʀtje] *nm* (*de ville*) district, area; (*de bœuf*) quarter; (*de fruit*) piece; **cinéma de ~** local cinema; **avoir ~ libre** (*fig*) to be free; **quartier général** headquarters *pl*

quartz[kwaʀts] *nm* quartz

quasi[kazi] *adv* almost, nearly; **quasiment** *adv* almost, nearly; **quasiment jamais** hardly ever

quatorze[katɔʀz] *num* fourteen

quatorzième[katɔʀzjɛm] *num* fourteenth

quatre[katʀ] *num* four; **à ~ pattes** on all fours; **se mettre en ~ pour qn** to go out of one's way for sb; **~ à ~** (*monter, descendre*) four at a time; **quatre-vingt-dix** *num* ninety; **quatre-vingts** *num* eighty; **quatrième** *num* fourth ▷ *nf* (*Scol*) year 9 (*BRIT*), eighth grade (*US*)

quatuor[kwatɥɔʀ] *nm* quartet(te)

 MOT-CLÉ

que[kə] *conj* **1** (*introduisant complétive*) that; **il sait que tu es là** he knows (that) you're here; **je veux que tu acceptes** I want you to accept; **il a dit que oui** he said he would (*ou* it was *etc*)

2 (*reprise d'autres conjonctions*): **quand il rentrera et qu'il aura mangé** when he gets back and (when) he has eaten; **si vous y allez et que vous …** if you go there and if you …

3 (*en tête de phrase: hypothèse, souhait etc*): **qu'il le veuille ou non** whether he likes it or not; **qu'il fasse ce qu'il voudra!** let him do as he pleases!

4 (*après comparatif*) than, as; *voir aussi* **plus**, **aussi**; **autant** *etc*

5 (*seulement*): **ne … que** only; **il ne boit que de l'eau** he only drinks water

6 (*temps*): **il y a 4 ans qu'il est parti** it is 4 years since he left, he left 4 years ago

▷ *adv* (*exclamation*): **qu'il** ou **qu'est-ce qu'il est bête/court vite!** he's so silly!/he runs so fast!; **que de livres!** what a lot of books!

▷ *pron* **1** (*relatif: personne*) whom; (: *chose*) that, which; **l'homme que je vois** the man (whom) I see; **le livre que tu vois** the book (that ou which) you see; **un jour que j'étais …** a day when I was …

2 (*interrogatif*) what; **que fais-tu?**, **qu'est-ce que tu fais?** what are you doing?; **qu'est-ce que c'est?** what is it?, what's that?; **que faire?** what can one do?

Québec[kebɛk] *n*: **le ~** Quebec; **québecois, e** *adj* Quebec ▷ *nm/f*: **Québecois, e** Quebecker

▷ nm (Ling) Quebec French

MOT-CLÉ

quel, quelle [kɛl] adj **1** (interrogatif: personne)
who; (: chose) what; **quel est cet homme?**
who is this man?; **quel est ce livre?** what
is this book?; **quel livre/homme?** what
book/man?; (parmi un certain choix) which
book/man?; **quels acteurs préférez-vous?**
which actors do you prefer?; **dans quels pays
êtes-vous allé?** which ou what countries did
you go to?
2 (exclamatif): **quelle surprise!** what a
surprise!
3: **quel que soit le coupable** whoever is
guilty; **quel que soit votre avis** whatever
your opinion

quelconque [kɛlkɔ̃k] adj (indéfini): **un
ami/prétexte ~** some friend/pretext or
other; (médiocre: repas) indifferent, poor; (laid:
personne) plain-looking

MOT-CLÉ

quelque [kɛlk] adj **1** (au singulier) some; (au
pluriel) a few, some; (tournure interrogative) any;
quelque espoir some hope; **il a quelques
amis** he has a few ou some friends; **a-t-il
quelques amis?** does he have any friends?; **les
quelques livres qui** the few books which; **20
kg et quelque(s)** a bit over 20 kg
2: **quelque ... que**: **quelque livre qu'il
choisisse** whatever (ou whichever) book he
chooses
3: **quelque chose** something; (tournure
interrogative) anything; **quelque chose
d'autre** something else; anything else;
quelque part somewhere; anywhere; **en
quelque sorte** as it were
▷ adv **1** (environ): **quelque 100 mètres** some
100 metres
2: **quelque peu** rather, somewhat

quelquefois [kɛlkəfwa] adv sometimes
quelques-uns, -unes [kɛlkəzœ̃, yn] pron a
few, some
quelqu'un [kɛlkœ̃] pron someone, somebody;
(+ tournure interrogative) anyone, anybody;
quelqu'un d'autre someone ou somebody
else; (+ tournure interrogative) anybody else
qu'en dira-t-on [kɑ̃diʁatɔ̃] nm inv: **le qu'en
dira-t-on** gossip, what people say
querelle [kaʁɛl] nf quarrel; **quereller**: **se
quereller** vi to quarrel
qu'est-ce que [kɛskə] vb + conj voir **que**
qu'est-ce qui [kɛski] vb + conj voir **qui**
question [kɛstjɔ̃] nf question; (fig) matter,

issue; **il a été ~ de** we (ou they) spoke about;
de quoi est-il ~? what is it about?; **il n'en
est pas ~** there's no question of it; **en ~** in
question; **hors de ~** out of the question;
remettre en ~ to question; **questionnaire**
nm questionnaire; **questionner** vt to
question
quête [kɛt] nf collection; (recherche) quest,
search; **faire la ~** (à l'église) to take the
collection; (artiste) to pass the hat round
quetsche [kwɛtʃ] nf kind of dark-red plum
queue [kø] nf tail; (fig: du classement) bottom;
(: de poêle) handle; (: de fruit, feuille) stalk; (: de
train, colonne, file) rear; **faire la ~** to queue (up)
(BRIT), line up (US); **queue de cheval** ponytail;
queue de poisson (Auto): **faire une queue de
poisson à qn** to cut in front of sb

MOT-CLÉ

qui [ki] pron **1** (interrogatif: personne) who; (:
chose): **qu'est-ce qui est sur la table?** what
is on the table?; **qui est-ce qui?** who?; **qui est-
ce que?** who?; **à qui est ce sac?** whose bag is
this?; **à qui parlais-tu?** who were you talking
to?, to whom were you talking?; **chez qui
allez-vous?** whose house are you going to?
2 (relatif: personne) who; (+ prép) whom; **l'ami
de qui je vous ai parlé** the friend I told you
about; **la dame chez qui je suis allé** the lady
whose house I went to
3 (sans antécédent): **amenez qui vous voulez**
bring who you like; **qui que ce soit** whoever
it may be

quiconque [kikɔ̃k] pron (celui qui) whoever,
anyone who; (n'importe qui) anyone, anybody
quille [kij] nf: **(jeu de) ~s** skittles sg (BRIT),
bowling (US)
quincaillerie [kɛ̃kajʁi] nf (ustensiles)
hardware; (magasin) hardware shop
quinquagénaire [kɛ̃kaʒenɛʁ] nm/f man/
woman in his/her fifties
quinquennat [kɛ̃kena] nm five year term of
office (of French President)
quinte [kɛ̃t] nf: **~ (de toux)** coughing fit
quintuple [kɛ̃typl] nm: **le ~ de** five times as
much as
quinzaine [kɛ̃zɛn] nf: **une ~ (de)** about
fifteen, fifteen or so; **une ~ (de jours)** a
fortnight (BRIT), two weeks
quinze [kɛ̃z] num fifteen; **dans ~ jours** in a
fortnight('s time), in two weeks(' time)
quinzième [kɛ̃zjɛm] num fifteenth
quiproquo [kipʁɔko] nm misunderstanding
quittance [kitɑ̃s] nf (reçu) receipt
quitte [kit] adj: **être ~ envers qn** to be no
longer in sb's debt; (fig) to be quits with sb; **~ à
faire** even if it means doing

quitter [kite] *vt* to leave; (*vêtement*) to take off;
  se quitter *vi* (*couples, interlocuteurs*) to part;
  ne quittez pas (*au téléphone*) hold the line
qui-vive [kiviv] *nm*: **être sur le ~** to be on
  the alert

 MOT-CLÉ

quoi [kwa] *pron interrog* **1** what; **quoi de neuf?**
what's new?; **quoi?** (*qu'est-ce que tu dis?*) what?
2 (*avec prép*): **à quoi tu penses?** what are you
thinking about?; **de quoi parlez-vous?** what
are you talking about?; **à quoi bon?** what's
the use?
▷ *pron rel*: **as-tu de quoi écrire?** do you have
anything to write with?; **il n'y a pas de quoi**
(please) don't mention it; **il n'y a pas de quoi
rire** there's nothing to laugh about
▷ *pron* (*locutions*): **quoi qu'il arrive** whatever
happens; **quoi qu'il en soit** be that as it may;
quoi que ce soit anything at all
▷ *excl* what!

quoique [kwak] *conj* (al)though
quotidien, ne [kɔtidjɛ̃, jɛn] *adj* daily;
(*banal*) everyday ▷ *nm* (*journal*) daily (paper);
  quotidiennement *adv* daily

r. *abr* = **route**; **rue**
rab [ʀab] (*fam*) *nm* (*nourriture*) extra; **est-ce
qu'il y a du ~?** are there any seconds?
rabâcher [ʀabɑʃe] *vt* to keep on repeating
rabais [ʀabɛ] *nm* reduction, discount;
  rabaisser *vt* (*dénigrer*) to belittle; (*rabattre:
prix*) to reduce
Rabat [ʀaba(t)] *n* Rabat
rabattre [ʀabatʀ] *vt* (*couvercle, siège*) to pull
down; (*déduire*) to reduce; **se rabattre** *vi*
(*se refermer: couvercle*) to fall shut; (*véhicule,
coureur*) to cut in; **se ~ sur** to fall back on
rabbin [ʀabɛ̃] *nm* rabbi
rabougri, e [ʀabugʀi] *adj* stunted
raccommoder [ʀakɔmɔde] *vt* to mend,
repair
raccompagner [ʀakɔ̃paɲe] *vt* to take *ou*
see back
raccord [ʀakɔʀ] *nm* link; (*retouche*) touch up;
  raccorder *vt* to join (up), link up; (*suj: pont etc*)
to connect, link
raccourci [ʀakuʀsi] *nm* short cut
raccourcir [ʀakuʀsiʀ] *vt* to shorten ▷ *vi*
(*jours*) to grow shorter, draw in
raccrocher [ʀakʀɔʃe] *vt* (*tableau*) to hang
back up; (*récepteur*) to put down ▷ *vi* (*Tél*) to
hang up, ring off
race [ʀas] *nf* race; (*d'animaux, fig*) breed; **de ~**
purebred, pedigree
rachat [ʀaʃa] *nm* buying; (*du même objet*)

buying back

racheter [Raʃ(ə)te] vt (article perdu) to buy another; (après avoir vendu) to buy back; (d'occasion) to buy; (Comm: part, firme) to buy up; (davantage): **~ du lait/3 œufs** to buy more milk/another 3 eggs ou 3 more eggs; **se racheter** vi (fig) to make amends

racial, e, -aux [Rasjal, jo] adj racial

racine [Rasin] nf root; **racine carrée/ cubique** square/cube root

racisme [Rasism] nm racism

raciste [Rasist] adj, nm/f racist

racket [Raket] nm racketeering no pl

raclée [Rakle] (fam) nf hiding, thrashing

racler [Rakle] vt (surface) to scrape; **se ~ la gorge** to clear one's throat

racontars [Rakɔ̃tar] nmpl story, lie

raconter [Rakɔ̃te] vt: **~ (à qn)** (décrire) to relate (to sb), tell (sb) about; (dire de mauvaise foi) to tell (sb); **~ une histoire** to tell a story

radar [Radar] nm radar

rade [Rad] nf (natural) harbour; **rester en ~** (fig) to be left stranded

radeau, x [Rado] nm raft

radiateur [Radjatœr] nm radiator, heater; (Auto) radiator; **radiateur électrique** electric heater ou fire

radiation [Radjasjɔ̃] nf (Physique) radiation

radical, e, -aux [Radikal, o] adj radical

radieux, -euse [Radjø, jøz] adj radiant

radin, e [Radɛ̃, in] (fam) adj stingy

radio [Radjo] nf radio; (Méd) X-ray ▷ nm radio operator; **à la ~** on the radio; **radioactif, -ive** adj radioactive; **radiocassette** nm cassette radio, radio cassette player; **radiographie** nf radiography; (photo) X-ray photograph; **radiophonique** adj radio cpd; **radio-réveil** (pl **radios-réveils**) nm radio alarm clock

radis [Radi] nm radish

radoter [Radote] vi to ramble on

radoucir [Radusir]: **se radoucir** vi (temps) to become milder; (se calmer) to calm down

rafale [Rafal] nf (vent) gust (of wind); (tir) burst of gunfire

raffermir [Rafɛrmir] vt to firm up

raffiner [Rafine] vt to refine; **raffinerie** nf refinery

raffoler [Rafole]: **~ de** vt to be very keen on

rafle [Rafl] nf (de police) raid; **rafler** (fam) vt to swipe, nick

rafraîchir [Rafreʃir] vt (atmosphère, température) to cool (down); (aussi: **mettre à ~**) to chill; (fig: rénover) to brighten up; **se rafraîchir** vi (temps) to grow cooler; (en se lavant) to freshen up; (en buvant) to refresh o.s.; **rafraîchissant, e** adj refreshing; **rafraîchissement** nm (boisson) cool drink; **rafraîchissements** nmpl (boissons, fruits etc) refreshments

rage [Raʒ] nf (Méd): **la ~** rabies; (fureur) rage, fury; **faire ~** to rage; **rage de dents** (raging) toothache

ragot [Rago] (fam) nm malicious gossip no pl

ragoût [Ragu] nm stew

raide [Rɛd] adj stiff; (câble) taut, tight; (escarpé) steep; (droit: cheveux) straight; (fam: sans argent) flat broke; (osé) daring, bold ▷ adv (en pente) steeply; **~ mort** stone dead; **raideur** nf (rigidité) stiffness; **avec raideur** (répondre) stiffly, abruptly; **raidir** vt (muscles) to stiffen; **se raidir** vi (tissu) to stiffen; (personne) to tense up; (: se préparer moralement) to brace o.s.; (fig: position) to harden

raie [Rɛ] nf (Zool) skate, ray; (rayure) stripe; (des cheveux) parting

raifort [Rɛfɔr] nm horseradish

rail [Raj] nm rail; (chemins de fer) railways pl; **par ~** by rail

railler [Raje] vt to scoff at, jeer at

rainure [Renyr] nf groove

raisin [Rɛzɛ̃] nm (aussi: **~s**) grapes pl; **raisins secs** raisins

raison [Rɛzɔ̃] nf reason; **avoir ~** to be right; **donner ~ à qn** to agree with sb; (événement) to prove sb right; **perdre la ~** to become insane; **se faire une ~** to learn to live with it; **~ de plus** all the more reason; **à plus forte ~** all the more so; **en ~ de** because of; **à ~ de** at the rate of; **sans ~** for no reason; **raison sociale** corporate name; **raisonnable** adj reasonable, sensible

raisonnement [Rɛzɔnmã] nm (façon de réfléchir) reasoning; (argumentation) argument

raisonner [Rɛzɔne] vi (penser) to reason; (argumenter, discuter) to argue ▷ vt (personne) to reason with

rajeunir [Raʒœnir] vt (suj: coiffure, robe): **~ qn** to make sb look younger; (fig: personnel) to inject new blood into ▷ vi to become (ou look) younger

rajouter [Raʒute] vt to add

rajuster [Raʒyste] vt (vêtement) to straighten, tidy; (salaires) to adjust

ralenti [Ralãti] nm: **au ~** (fig) at a slower pace; **tourner au ~** (Auto) to tick over, idle

ralentir [Ralãtir] vt to slow down

râler [Rale] vi to groan; (fam) to grouse, moan (and groan)

rallier [Ralje] vt (rejoindre) to rejoin; (gagner à sa cause) to win over

rallonge [Ralɔ̃ʒ] nf (de table) (extra) leaf

rallonger [Ralɔ̃ʒe] vt to lengthen

rallye [Rali] nm rally; (Pol) march

ramassage [Ramasaʒ] nm: **ramassage scolaire** school bus service

ramasser [Ramase] vt (objet tombé ou par terre, fam) to pick up; (recueillir: copies, ordures) to collect; (récolter) to gather; **ramassis** (péj) nm

(*de voyous*) bunch; (*d'objets*) jumble
rambarde [ʀɑ̃baʀd] *nf* guardrail
rame [ʀam] *nf* (*aviron*) oar; (*de métro*) train; (*de papier*) ream
rameau, x [ʀamo] *nm* (small) branch; **les Rameaux** (*Rel*) Palm Sunday *sg*
ramener [ʀam(ə)ne] *vt* to bring back; (*reconduire*) to take back; **~ qch à** (*réduire à*) to reduce sth to
ramer [ʀame] *vi* to row
ramollir [ʀamɔliʀ] *vt* to soften; **se ramollir** *vi* to go soft
rampe [ʀɑ̃p] *nf* (*d'escalier*) banister(s *pl*); (*dans un garage*) ramp; (*Théâtre*): **la ~** the footlights *pl*; **rampe de lancement** launching pad
ramper [ʀɑ̃pe] *vi* to crawl
rancard [ʀɑ̃kaʀ] (*fam*) *nm* (*rendez-vous*) date
rancart [ʀɑ̃kaʀ] *nm*: **mettre au ~** (*fam*) to scrap
rance [ʀɑ̃s] *adj* rancid
rancœur [ʀɑ̃kœʀ] *nf* rancour
rançon [ʀɑ̃sɔ̃] *nf* ransom
rancune [ʀɑ̃kyn] *nf* grudge, rancour; **garder ~ à qn (de qch)** to bear sb a grudge (for sth); **sans ~!** no hard feelings!; **rancunier, -ière** *adj* vindictive, spiteful
randonnée [ʀɑ̃dɔne] *nf* (*pédestre*) walk, ramble; (: *en montagne*) hike, hiking *no pl*; **la ~** (*activité*) hiking, walking; **une ~ à cheval** a pony trek
rang [ʀɑ̃] *nm* (*rangée*) row; (*grade, classement*) rank; **rangs** *nmpl* (*Mil*) ranks; **se mettre en ~s** to get into *ou* form rows; **au premier ~** in the first row; (*fig*) ranking first
rangé, e [ʀɑ̃ʒe] *adj* (*vie*) well-ordered; (*personne*) steady
rangée [ʀɑ̃ʒe] *nf* row
ranger [ʀɑ̃ʒe] *vt* (*mettre de l'ordre dans*) to tidy up; (*classer, grouper*) to order, arrange; (*mettre à sa place*) to put away; (*fig: classer*): **~ qn/qch parmi** to rank sb/sth among; **se ranger** *vi* (*véhicule, conducteur*) to pull over *ou* in; (*piéton*) to step aside; (*s'assagir*) to settle down; **se ~ à** (*avis*) to come round to
ranimer [ʀanime] *vt* (*personne*) to bring round; (*douleur, souvenir*) to revive; (*feu*) to rekindle
rapace [ʀapas] *nm* bird of prey
râpe [ʀɑp] *nf* (*Culin*) grater; **râper** *vt* (*Culin*) to grate
rapide [ʀapid] *adj* fast; (*prompt: coup d'œil, mouvement*) quick ▷ *nm* express (train); (*de cours d'eau*) rapid; **rapidement** *adv* fast; quickly
rapiécer [ʀapjese] *vt* to patch
rappel [ʀapɛl] *nm* (*Théâtre*) curtain call; (*Méd: vaccination*) booster; (*deuxième avis*) reminder; **rappeler** *vt* to call back; (*ambassadeur, Mil*) to recall; (*faire se souvenir*): **rappeler qch à qn** to

remind sb of sth; **se rappeler** *vt* (*se souvenir de*) to remember, recall; **pouvez-vous rappeler plus tard?** can you call back later?
rapport [ʀapɔʀ] *nm* (*lien, analogie*) connection; (*compte rendu*) report; (*profit*) yield, return; **rapports** *nmpl* (*entre personnes, pays*) relations; **avoir ~ à** to have something to do with; **être/se mettre en ~ avec qn** to be/get in touch with sb; **par ~ à** in relation to; **rapports (sexuels)** (sexual) intercourse *sg*; **rapport qualité-prix** value (for money)
rapporter [ʀapɔʀte] *vt* (*rendre, ramener*) to bring back; (*bénéfice*) to yield, bring in; (*mentionner, répéter*) to report ▷ *vi* (*investissement*) to give a good return *ou* yield; (*activité*) to be very profitable; **se ~ à** to relate to
rapprochement [ʀapʀɔʃmɑ̃] *nm* (*de nations*) reconciliation; (*rapport*) parallel
rapprocher [ʀapʀɔʃe] *vt* (*deux objets*) to bring closer together; (*fig: ennemis, partis etc*) to bring together; (*comparer*) to establish a parallel between; (*chaise d'une table*): **~ qch (de)** to bring sth closer (to); **se rapprocher** *vi* to draw closer *ou* nearer; **se ~ de** to come closer to; (*présenter une analogie avec*) to be close to
raquette [ʀakɛt] *nf* (*de tennis*) racket; (*de ping-pong*) bat
rare [ʀɑʀ] *adj* rare; **se faire ~** to become scarce; **rarement** *adv* rarely, seldom
ras, e [ʀɑ, ʀɑz] *adj* (*poil, herbe*) short; (*tête*) close-cropped ▷ *adv* short; **en ~e campagne** in open country; **à ~ bords** to the brim; **en avoir ~ le bol** (*fam*) to be fed up
raser [ʀaze] *vt* (*barbe, cheveux*) to shave off; (*menton, personne*) to shave; (*fam: ennuyer*) to bore; (*démolir*) to raze (to the ground); (*frôler*) to graze, skim; **se raser** *vi* to shave; (*fam*) to be bored (to tears); **rasoir** *nm* razor
rassasier [ʀasazje] *vt*: **être rassasié** to have eaten one's fill
rassemblement [ʀasɑ̃bləmɑ̃] *nm* (*groupe*) gathering; (*Pol*) union
rassembler [ʀasɑ̃ble] *vt* (*réunir*) to assemble, gather; (*documents, notes*) to gather together, collect; **se rassembler** *vi* to gather
rassurer [ʀasyʀe] *vt* to reassure; **se rassurer** *vi* to reassure o.s.; **rassure-toi** don't worry
rat [ʀa] *nm* rat
rate [ʀat] *nf* spleen
raté, e [ʀate] *adj* (*tentative*) unsuccessful, failed ▷ *nm/f* (*fam: personne*) failure
râteau, x [ʀɑto] *nm* rake
rater [ʀate] *vi* (*affaire, projet etc*) to go wrong, fail ▷ *vt* (*fam: cible, train, occasion*) to miss; (*plat*) to spoil; (*fam: examen*) to fail; **nous avons raté notre train** we missed our train
ration [ʀasjɔ̃] *nf* ration

RATP sigle f (= Régie autonome des transports parisiens) Paris transport authority

rattacher [Rataʃe] vt (animal, cheveux) to tie up again; (fig: relier): **~ qch à** to link sth with

rattraper [RatRape] vt (fugitif) to recapture; (empêcher de tomber) to catch (hold of); (atteindre, rejoindre) to catch up with; (réparer: erreur) to make up for; **se rattraper** vi to make up for it; **se ~ (à)** (se raccrocher) to stop o.s. falling (by catching hold of)

rature [RatyR] nf deletion, erasure

rauque [Rok] adj (voix) hoarse

ravages [Ravaʒ] nmpl: **faire des ~** to wreak havoc

ravi, e [Ravi] adj: **être ~ de/que** to be delighted with/that

ravin [Ravɛ̃] nm gully, ravine

ravir [RaviR] vt (enchanter) to delight; **à ~** adv beautifully

raviser [Ravize]: **se raviser** vi to change one's mind

ravissant, e [Ravisɑ̃, ɑ̃t] adj delightful

ravisseur, -euse [RavisœR, øz] nm/f abductor, kidnapper

ravitailler [Ravitaje] vt (en vivres, munitions) to provide with fresh supplies; (avion) to refuel; **se ~ (en)** to get fresh supplies (of)

raviver [Ravive] vt (feu, douleur) to revive; (couleurs) to brighten up

rayé, e [Reje] adj (à rayures) striped

rayer [Reje] vt (érafler) to scratch; (barrer) to cross out; (d'une liste) to cross off

rayon [Rejɔ̃] nm (de soleil etc) ray; (Géom) radius; (de roue) spoke; (étagère) shelf; (de grand magasin) department; **dans un ~ de** within a radius of; **rayon de soleil** sunbeam; **rayons X** X-rays

rayonnement [Rejɔnmɑ̃] nm (fig: d'une culture) influence

rayonner [Rejɔne] vi (fig) to shine forth; (personne: de joie, de beauté) to be radiant; (touriste) to go touring (from one base)

rayure [RejyR] nf (motif) stripe; (éraflure) scratch; **à ~s** striped

raz-de-marée [RadmaRe] nm inv tidal wave

ré [Re] nm (Mus) D; (en chantant la gamme) re

réaction [Reaksjɔ̃] nf reaction

réadapter [Readapte]: **se réadapter (à)** vi to readjust (to)

réagir [ReaʒiR] vi to react

réalisateur, -trice [RealizatœR, tRis] nm/f (TV, Cinéma) director

réalisation [Realizasjɔ̃] nf realization; (cinéma) production; **en cours de ~** under way

réaliser [Realize] vt (projet, opération) to carry out, realize; (rêve, souhait) to realize, fulfil; (exploit) to achieve; (film) to produce; (se rendre compte de) to realize; **se réaliser** vi to be realized

réaliste [Realist] adj realistic

réalité [Realite] nf reality; **en ~** in (actual) fact; **dans la ~** in reality

réanimation [Reanimasjɔ̃] nf resuscitation; **service de ~** intensive care unit

rébarbatif, -ive [RebaRbatif, iv] adj forbidding

rebattu, e [R(ə)baty] adj hackneyed

rebelle [Rəbɛl] nm/f rebel ▷ adj (troupes) rebel; (enfant) rebellious; (mèche etc) unruly

rebeller [R(ə)bele]: **se rebeller** vi to rebel

rebondir [R(ə)bɔ̃diR] vi (ballon: au sol) to bounce; (: contre un mur) to rebound; (fig) to get moving again

rebord [R(ə)bɔR] nm edge; **le ~ de la fenêtre** the windowsill

rebours [R(ə)buR]: **à ~** adv the wrong way

rebrousser [R(ə)bRuse] vt: **~ chemin** to turn back

rebuter [Rəbyte] vt to put off

récalcitrant, e [Rekalsitrɑ̃, ɑ̃t] adj refractory

récapituler [Rekapityle] vt to recapitulate, sum up

receler [R(ə)səle] vt (produit d'un vol) to receive; (fig) to conceal; **receleur, -euse** nm/f receiver

récemment [Resamɑ̃] adv recently

recensement [R(ə)sɑ̃smɑ̃] nm (population) census

recenser [R(ə)sɑ̃se] vt (population) to take a census of; (inventorier) to list

récent, e [Resɑ̃, ɑ̃t] adj recent

récépissé [Resepise] nm receipt

récepteur [ReseptœR] nm receiver

réception [Resepsjɔ̃] nf receiving no pl; (accueil) reception, welcome; (bureau) reception desk; (réunion mondaine) reception, party; **réceptionniste** nm/f receptionist

recette [R(ə)sɛt] nf recipe; (Comm) takings pl; **recettes** nfpl (Comm: rentrées) receipts; **faire ~** (spectacle, exposition) to be a winner

recevoir [R(ə)səvwaR] vt to receive; (client, patient) to see; **être reçu (à un examen)** to pass

rechange [R(ə)ʃɑ̃ʒ]: **de ~** adj (pièces, roue) spare; (fig: solution) alternative; **des vêtements de ~** a change of clothes

recharge [R(ə)ʃaRʒ] nf refill; **rechargeable** adj (stylo etc) refillable; **recharger** vt (stylo) to refill; (batterie) to recharge

réchaud [Reʃo] nm (portable) stove

réchauffer [Reʃofe] vt (plat) to reheat; (mains, personne) to warm; **se réchauffer** vi (température) to get warmer; (personne) to warm o.s. (up)

rêche [Rɛʃ] adj rough

recherche [R(ə)ʃɛRʃ] nf (action) search; (raffinement) studied elegance; (scientifique etc): **la ~** research; **recherches** nfpl (de la police) investigations; (scientifiques) research sg; **la ~ de** the search for; **être à la ~ de qch** to be looking for sth

recherché, e[R(ə)ʃɛRʃe] adj (rare, demandé) much sought-after; (raffiné: style) mannered; (: tenue) elegant

rechercher[R(ə)ʃɛRʃe] vt (objet égaré, personne) to look for; (causes, nouveau procédé) to try to find; (bonheur, compliments) to seek

rechute[R(ə)ʃyt] nf (Méd) relapse

récidiver[Residive] vi to commit a subsequent offence; (fig) to do it again

récif[Resif] nm reef

récipient[Resipjɑ̃] nm container

réciproque[Resiprɔk] adj reciprocal

récit[Resi] nm story; **récital** nm recital; **réciter** vt to recite

réclamation[Reklamasjɔ̃] nf complaint; **(service des) ~s** complaints department

réclame[Reklam] nf ad, advert(isement); **en ~** on special offer; **réclamer** vt to ask for; (revendiquer) to claim, demand ▷ vi to complain

réclusion[Reklyzjɔ̃] nf imprisonment

recoin[Rəkwɛ̃] nm nook, corner

reçois etc [Rəswa] vb voir **recevoir**

récolte[Rekɔlt] nf harvesting, gathering; (produits) harvest, crop; **récolter** vt to harvest, gather (in); (fig) to collect

recommandé[R(ə)kɔmɑ̃de] nm (Postes): **en ~** by registered mail

recommander[R(ə)kɔmɑ̃de] vt to recommend; (Postes) to register

recommencer[R(ə)kɔmɑ̃se] vt (reprendre: lutte, séance) to resume, start again; (refaire: travail, explications) to start afresh, start (over) again ▷ vi to start again; (récidiver) to do it again

récompense[Rekɔ̃pɑ̃s] nf reward; (prix) award; **récompenser** vt: **récompenser qn (de** ou **pour)** to reward sb (for)

réconcilier[Rekɔ̃silje] vt to reconcile; **se réconcilier (avec)** to make up (with)

reconduire[R(ə)kɔ̃dɥiR] vt (raccompagner) to take ou see back; (renouveler) to renew

réconfort[Rekɔ̃fɔR] nm comfort; **réconforter** vt (consoler) to comfort

reconnaissance[R(ə)kɔnɛsɑ̃s] nf (gratitude) gratitude, gratefulness; (action de reconnaître) recognition; (Mil) reconnaissance, recce; **reconnaissant, e** adj grateful; **je vous serais reconnaissant de bien vouloir ...** I would be most grateful if you would (kindly) ...

reconnaître[R(ə)kɔnɛtR] vt to recognize; (Mil: lieu) to reconnoitre; (Jur: enfant, torts) to acknowledge; **~ que** to admit ou acknowledge that; **~ qn/qch à** (l'identifier grâce à) to recognize sb/sth by; **reconnu, e** adj (indiscuté, connu) recognized

reconstituer[R(ə)kɔ̃stitɥe] vt (événement, accident) to reconstruct; (fresque, vase brisé) to

piece together, reconstitute

reconstruire[R(ə)kɔ̃stRɥiR] vt to rebuild

reconvertir[R(ə)kɔ̃vɛRtiR]: **se reconvertir dans** vr (un métier, une branche) to go into

record[R(ə)kɔR] nm, adj record

recoupement[R(ə)kupmɑ̃] nm: **par ~** by cross-checking

recouper[R(ə)kupe]: **se recouper** vi (témoignages) to tie ou match up

recourber[R(ə)kuRbe]: **se recourber** vi to curve (up), bend (up)

recourir[R(ə)kuRiR]: **~ à** vt (ami, agence) to turn ou appeal to; (force, ruse, emprunt) to resort to

recours[R(ə)kuR] nm: **avoir ~ à** = **recourir à**; **en dernier ~** as a last resort

recouvrer[R(ə)kuvRe] vt (vue, santé etc) to recover, regain

recouvrir[R(ə)kuvRiR] vt (couvrir à nouveau) to re-cover; (couvrir entièrement, aussi fig) to cover

récréation[RekReasjɔ̃] nf (Scol) break

recroqueviller[R(ə)kRɔk(ə)vije]: **se recroqueviller** vi (personne) to huddle up

recrudescence[R(ə)kRydesɑ̃s] nf fresh outbreak

recruter[R(ə)kRyte] vt to recruit

rectangle[Rɛktɑ̃gl] nm rectangle; **rectangulaire** adj rectangular

rectificatif[Rɛktifikatif] nm correction

rectifier[Rɛktifje] vt (calcul, adresse, paroles) to correct; (erreur) to rectify

rectiligne[Rɛktiliɲ] adj straight

recto[Rɛkto] nm front (of a page); **~ verso** on both sides (of the page)

reçu, e[R(ə)sy] pp de **recevoir** ▷ adj (candidat) successful; (admis, consacré) accepted ▷ nm (Comm) receipt; **je peux avoir un ~, s'il vous plaît?** can I have a receipt, please?

recueil[Rəkœj] nm collection; **recueillir** vt to collect; (voix, suffrages) to win; (accueillir: réfugiés, chat) to take in; **se recueillir** vi to gather one's thoughts, meditate

recul[R(ə)kyl] nm (éloignement) distance; (déclin) decline; **être en ~** to be on the decline; **avec du ~** with hindsight; **avoir un mouvement de ~** to recoil; **prendre du ~** to stand back; **reculé, e** adj remote; **reculer** vi to move back, back away; (Auto) to reverse, back (up); (fig) to (be on the) decline ▷ vt to move back; (véhicule) to reverse, back (up); (date, décision) to postpone; **reculer devant** (danger, difficulté) to shrink from; **reculons: à reculons** adv backwards

récupérer[Rekypere] vt to recover, get back; (heures de travail) to make up; (déchets) to salvage ▷ vi to recover

récurer[RekyRe] vt to scour; **poudre à ~** scouring powder

reçut [Rəsy] vb voir **recevoir**
recycler [R(ə)sikle] vt (*Tech*) to recycle; **se recycler** vi to retrain
rédacteur, -trice [Redaktœr, tRis] nm/f (*journaliste*) writer; subeditor; (*d'ouvrage de référence*) editor, compiler
rédaction [Redaksjɔ̃] nf writing; (*rédacteurs*) editorial staff; (*Scol: devoir*) essay, composition
redescendre [R(ə)desɑ̃dR] vi to go back down ▷ vt (*pente etc*) to go down
rédiger [Redize] vt to write; (*contrat*) to draw up
redire [R(ə)diR] vt to repeat; **trouver à ~ à** to find fault with
redoubler [R(ə)duble] vi (*tempête, violence*) to intensify; (*Scol*) to repeat a year; **~ de patience/prudence** to be doubly patient/careful
redoutable [R(ə)dutabl] adj formidable, fearsome
redouter [R(ə)dute] vt to dread
redressement [R(ə)dResmɑ̃] nm (*économique*) recovery
redresser [R(ə)dRese] vt (*relever*) to set upright; (*pièce tordue*) to straighten out; (*situation, économie*) to put right; **se redresser** vi (*personne*) to sit (*ou* stand) up (straight); (*économie*) to recover
réduction [Redyksjɔ̃] nf reduction; **y a-t-il une ~ pour les étudiants?** is there a reduction for students?
réduire [RedɥiR] vt to reduce; (*prix, dépenses*) to cut, reduce; **réduit** nm (*pièce*) tiny room
rééducation [Reedykasjɔ̃] nf (*d'un membre*) re-education; (*de délinquants, d'un blessé*) rehabilitation
réel, le [Reɛl] adj real; **réellement** adv really
réexpédier [Reɛkspedje] vt (*à l'envoyeur*) to return, send back; (*au destinataire*) to send on, forward
refaire [R(ə)fɛR] vt to do again; (*faire de nouveau: sport*) to take up again; (*réparer, restaurer*) to do up
réfectoire [RefɛktwaR] nm refectory
référence [RefeRɑ̃s] nf reference; **références** nfpl (*recommandations*) reference sg
référer [Refere]: **se référer à** vt to refer to
refermer [R(ə)fɛRme] vt to close *ou* shut again; **se refermer** vi (*porte*) to close *ou* shut (again)
refiler [R(ə)file] vi (*fam*) to palm off
réfléchi, e [Refleʃi] adj (*caractère*) thoughtful; (*action*) well-thought-out; (*Ling*) reflexive; **c'est tout ~** my mind's made up
réfléchir [RefleʃiR] vt to reflect ▷ vi to think; **~ à** to think about
reflet [R(ə)flɛ] nm reflection; (*sur l'eau etc*) sheen no pl, glint; **refléter** vt to reflect; **se refléter** vi to be reflected

réflexe [Reflɛks] nm, adj reflex
réflexion [Refleksjɔ̃] nf (*de la lumière etc*) reflection; (*fait de penser*) thought; (*remarque*) remark; **~ faite, à la ~** on reflection
réflexologie [Refleksɔlɔʒi] nf reflexology
réforme [RefɔRm] nf reform; (*Rel*): **la R~** the Reformation; **réformer** vt to reform; (*Mil*) to declare unfit for service
refouler [R(ə)fule] vt (*envahisseurs*) to drive back; (*larmes*) to force back; (*désir, colère*) to repress
refrain [R(ə)fRɛ̃] nm refrain, chorus
refréner [Rəfrene], **réfréner** [Refrene] vt to curb, check
réfrigérateur [RefriʒeRatœR] nm refrigerator, fridge
refroidir [R(ə)fRwadiR] vt to cool; (*fig: personne*) to put off ▷ vi to cool (down); **se refroidir** vi (*temps*) to get cooler *ou* colder; (*fig: ardeur*) to cool (off); **refroidissement** nm (*grippe etc*) chill
refuge [R(ə)fyʒ] nm refuge; **réfugié, e** adj, nm/f refugee; **se réfugier** vi to take refuge
refus [R(ə)fy] nm refusal; **ce n'est pas de ~** I won't say no, it's welcome; **refuser** vt to refuse; (*Scol: candidat*) to fail; **refuser qch à qn** to refuse sb sth; **refuser du monde** to have to turn people away; **se refuser à faire** to refuse to do
regagner [R(ə)gaɲe] vt (*faveur*) to win back; (*lieu*) to get back to
régal [Regal] nm treat; **régaler: se régaler** vi to have a delicious meal; (*fig*) to enjoy o.s.
regard [R(ə)gaR] nm (*coup d'œil*) look, glance; (*expression*) look (in one's eye); **au ~ de** (*loi, morale*) from the point of view of; **en ~ de** in comparison with
regardant, e [R(ə)gaRdɑ̃, ɑ̃t] adj (*économe*) tight-fisted; **peu ~ (sur)** very free (about)
regarder [R(ə)gaRde] vt to look at; (*film, télévision, match*) to watch; (*concerner*) to concern ▷ vi to look; **ne pas ~ à la dépense** to spare no expense; **~ qn/qch comme** to regard sb/sth as
régie [Reʒi] nf (*Comm, Industrie*) state-owned company; (*Théâtre, Cinéma*) production; (*Radio, TV*) control room
régime [Reʒim] nm (*Pol*) régime; (*Méd*) diet; (*Admin: carcéral, fiscal etc*) system; (*de bananes, dattes*) bunch; **se mettre au/suivre un ~** to go on/be on a diet
régiment [Reʒimɑ̃] nm regiment
région [Reʒjɔ̃] nf region; **régional, e, -aux** adj regional
régir [ReʒiR] vt to govern
régisseur [ReʒisœR] nm (*d'un domaine*) steward; (*Cinéma, TV*) assistant director; (*Théâtre*) stage manager

registre[ʀəʒistʀ] nm register

réglage[ʀeglaʒ] nm adjustment

règle[ʀɛgl] nf (instrument) ruler; (loi) rule; **règles** nfpl (menstruation) period sg; **en ~** (papiers d'identité) in order; **en ~ générale** as a (general) rule

réglé, e[ʀegle] adj (vie) well-ordered; (arrangé) settled

règlement[ʀɛgləmɑ̃] nm (paiement) settlement; (arrêté) regulation; (règles, statuts) regulations pl, rules pl; **réglementaire** adj conforming to the regulations; (tenue) regulation cpd; **réglementation** nf (règles) regulations; **réglementer** vt to regulate

régler[ʀegle] vt (conflit, facture) to settle; (personne) to settle up with; (mécanisme, machine) to regulate, adjust; (thermostat etc) to set, adjust

réglisse[ʀeglis] nf liquorice

règne[ʀɛɲ] nm (d'un roi etc, fig) reign; **le ~ végétal/animal** the vegetable/animal kingdom; **régner** vi (roi) to rule, reign; (fig) to reign

regorger[ʀ(ə)gɔʀʒe] vi: **~ de** to overflow with, be bursting with

regret[ʀ(ə)gʀɛ] nm regret; **à ~** with regret; **sans ~** with no regrets; **regrettable** adj regrettable; **regretter** vt to regret; (personne) to miss; **je regrette mais ...** I'm sorry but ...

regrouper[ʀ(ə)gʀupe] vt (grouper) to group together; (contenir) to include, comprise; **se regrouper** vi to gather (together)

régulier, -ière[ʀegylje, jɛʀ] adj (gén) regular; (vitesse, qualité) steady; (égal: couche, ligne) even; (Transports: ligne, service) scheduled, regular; (légal) lawful, in order; (honnête) straight, on the level; **régulièrement** adv regularly; (uniformément) evenly

rehausser[ʀəose] vt (relever) to heighten, raise; (fig: souligner) to set off, enhance

rein[ʀɛ̃] nm kidney; **reins** nmpl (dos) back sg

reine[ʀɛn] nf queen

reine-claude[ʀɛnklod] nf greengage

réinscriptible[ʀeɛ̃skʀiptibl] adj (CD, DVD) rewritable

réinsertion[ʀeɛ̃sɛʀsjɔ̃] nf (de délinquant) reintegration, rehabilitation

réintégrer[ʀeɛ̃tegʀe] vt (lieu) to return to; (fonctionnaire) to reinstate

rejaillir[ʀ(ə)ʒajiʀ] vi to splash up; **~ sur** (fig: scandale) to rebound on; (: gloire) to be reflected on

rejet[ʀəʒɛ] nm rejection; **rejeter** vt (relancer) to throw back; (écarter) to reject; (déverser) to throw out, discharge; (vomir) to bring ou throw up; **rejeter la responsabilité de qch sur qn** to lay the responsibility for sth at sb's door

rejoindre[ʀ(ə)ʒwɛ̃dʀ] vt (famille, régiment) to rejoin, return to; (lieu) to get (back) to; (suj:

route etc) to meet, join; (rattraper) to catch up (with); **se rejoindre** vi to meet; **je te rejoins à la gare** I'll see ou meet you at the station

réjouir[ʀeʒwiʀ] vt to delight; **se ~ (de qch/de faire)** to be delighted (about sth/to do); **réjouissances** nfpl (fête) festivities

relâche[ʀəlɑʃ] nm ou nf: **sans ~** without respite ou a break; **relâché, e** adj loose, lax; **relâcher** vt (libérer) to release; (desserrer) to loosen; **se relâcher** vi (discipline) to become slack ou lax; (élève etc) to slacken off

relais[ʀ(ə)lɛ] nm (Sport): **(course de) ~** relay (race); **prendre le ~ (de)** to take over (from); **relais routier** ≈ transport café (BRIT), ≈ truck stop (US)

relancer[ʀ(ə)lɑ̃se] vt (balle) to throw back; (moteur) to restart; (fig) to boost, revive; (harceler): **~ qn** to pester sb

relatif, -ive[ʀ(ə)latif, iv] adj relative

relation[ʀ(ə)lasjɔ̃] nf (rapport) relation(ship); (connaissance) acquaintance; **relations** nfpl (rapports) relations; (connaissances) connections; **être/entrer en ~(s) avec** to be/get in contact with

relaxer[ʀəlakse]: **se relaxer** vi to relax

relayer[ʀ(ə)leje] vt (collaborateur, coureur etc) to relieve; **se relayer** vi (dans une activité) to take it in turns

reléguer[ʀ(ə)lege] vt to relegate

relevé, e[ʀəl(ə)ve] adj (manches) rolled-up; (sauce) highly-seasoned ▷ nm (de compteur) reading; **relevé bancaire** ou **de compte** bank statement

relève[ʀəlɛv] nf (personne) relief; **prendre la ~** to take over

relever[ʀəl(ə)ve] vt (meuble) to stand up again; (personne tombée) to help up; (vitre, niveau de vie) to raise; (inf) to turn up; (style) to elevate; (plat, sauce) to season; (sentinelle, équipe) to relieve; (fautes) to pick out; (défi) to accept, take up; (noter: adresse etc) to take down, note; (: plan) to sketch; (compteur) to read; (ramasser: cahiers) to collect, take in; **se relever** vi (se remettre debout) to get up; **~ de** (maladie) to be recovering from; (être du ressort de) to be a matter for; (fig) to pertain to; **~ qn de** (fonctions) to relieve sb of; **~ la tête** to look up

relief[ʀəljɛf] nm relief; **mettre en ~** (fig) to bring out, highlight

relier[ʀəlje] vt to link up; (livre) to bind; **~ qch à** to link sth to

religieux, -euse[ʀ(ə)liʒjø, jøz] adj religious ▷ nm monk

religion[ʀ(ə)liʒjɔ̃] nf religion

relire[ʀ(ə)liʀ] vt (à nouveau) to reread, read again; (vérifier) to read over

reluire[ʀ(ə)lɥiʀ] vi to gleam

remanier[ʀ(ə)manje] vt to reshape, recast;

(Pol) to reshuffle

remarquable [ʀ(ə)maʀkabl] adj remarkable

remarque [ʀ(ə)maʀk] nf remark; (écrite) note

remarquer [ʀ(ə)maʀke] vt (voir) to notice;
se remarquer vi to be noticeable; **faire ~ (à qn) que** to point out (to sb) that; **faire ~ qch (à qn)** to point sth out (to sb); **remarquez, ...** mind you ...; **se faire ~** to draw attention to o.s.

rembourrer [ʀɑ̃buʀe] vt to stuff

remboursement [ʀɑ̃buʀsəmɑ̃] nm (de dette, d'emprunt) repayment; (de frais) refund; **rembourser** vt to pay back, repay; (frais, billet etc) to refund; **se faire rembourser** to get a refund

remède [ʀ(ə)mɛd] nm (médicament) medicine; (traitement, fig) remedy, cure

remémorer [ʀ(ə)memɔʀe]: **se remémorer** vt to recall, recollect

remerciements [ʀəmɛʀsimɑ̃] nmpl thanks; **(avec) tous mes ~** (with) grateful ou many thanks

remercier [ʀ(ə)mɛʀsje] vt to thank; (congédier) to dismiss; **~ qn de/d'avoir fait** to thank sb for/for having done

remettre [ʀ(ə)mɛtʀ] vt (replacer) to put back; (vêtement) to put back on; (ajouter) to add; (ajourner): **~ qch (à)** to postpone sth (until); **se remettre** vi: **se ~ (de)** to recover (from); **~ qch à qn** (donner: lettre, clé etc) to hand over sth to sb; (: prix, décoration) to present sb with sth; **se ~ à faire qch** to start doing sth again; **s'en ~ à** to leave it (up) to

remise [ʀ(ə)miz] nf (rabais) discount; (local) shed; **remise de peine** reduction of sentence; **remise des prix** prize-giving; **remise en cause** ou **question** calling into question, challenging; **remise en jeu** (Football) throw-in

remontant [ʀ(ə)mɔ̃tɑ̃] nm tonic, pick-me-up

remonte-pente [ʀ(ə)mɔ̃tpɑ̃t] nm ski-lift

remonter [ʀ(ə)mɔ̃te] vi to go back up; (prix, température) to go up again ▷ vt (pente) to go up; (fleuve) to sail (ou swim etc) up; (manches, pantalon) to roll up; (col) to turn up; (niveau, limite) to raise; (fig: personne) to buck up; (qch de démonté) to put back together, reassemble; (montre) to wind up; **~ le moral à qn** to raise sb's spirits; **~ à** (dater de) to date ou go back to

remords [ʀ(ə)mɔʀ] nm remorse no pl; **avoir des ~** to feel remorse

remorque [ʀ(ə)mɔʀk] nf trailer; **remorquer** vt to tow; **remorqueur** nm tug(boat)

remous [ʀəmu] nm (d'un navire) (back)wash no pl; (de rivière) swirl, eddy ▷ nmpl (fig) stir sg

remparts [ʀɑ̃paʀ] nmpl walls, ramparts

remplaçant, e [ʀɑ̃plasɑ̃, ɑ̃t] nm/f replacement, stand-in; (Scol) supply teacher

remplacement [ʀɑ̃plasmɑ̃] nm replacement; **faire des ~s** (professeur) to do supply teaching; (secrétaire) to temp

remplacer [ʀɑ̃plase] vt to replace; **~ qch/qn par** to replace sth/sb with

rempli, e [ʀɑ̃pli] adj (emploi du temps) full, busy; **~ de** full of, filled with

remplir [ʀɑ̃pliʀ] vt to fill (up); (questionnaire) to fill out ou up; (obligations, fonction, condition) to fulfil; **se remplir** vi to fill up

remporter [ʀɑ̃pɔʀte] vt (marchandise) to take away; (fig) to win, achieve

remuant, e [ʀəmɥɑ̃, ɑ̃t] adj restless

remue-ménage [ʀ(ə)mymena3] nm inv commotion

remuer [ʀəmɥe] vt to move; (café, sauce) to stir ▷ vi to move; **se remuer** vi to move; (fam: s'activer) to get a move on

rémunérer [ʀemyneʀe] vt to remunerate

renard [ʀ(ə)naʀ] nm fox

renchérir [ʀɑ̃feʀiʀ] vi (fig): **~ (sur)** (en paroles) to add something (to)

rencontre [ʀɑ̃kɔ̃tʀ] nf meeting; (imprévue) encounter; **aller à la ~ de qn** to go and meet sb; **rencontrer** vt to meet; (mot, expression) to come across; (difficultés) to meet with; **se rencontrer** vi to meet

rendement [ʀɑ̃dmɑ̃] nm (d'un travailleur, d'une machine) output; (d'un champ) yield

rendez-vous [ʀɑ̃devu] nm appointment; (d'amoureux) date; (lieu) meeting place; **donner ~ à qn** to arrange to meet sb; **avoir/prendre ~ (avec)** to have/make an appointment (with); **j'ai ~ avec ...** I have an appointment with ...; **je voudrais prendre ~** I'd like to make an appointment

rendre [ʀɑ̃dʀ] vt (restituer) to give back, return; (invitation) to return, repay; (vomir) to bring up; (exprimer, traduire) to render; (faire devenir): **~ qn célèbre/qch possible** to make sb famous/sth possible; **se rendre** vi (capituler) to surrender, give o.s. up; (aller): **se ~ quelque part** to go somewhere; **~ la monnaie à qn** to give sb his change; **se ~ compte de qch** to realize sth

rênes [ʀɛn] nfpl reins

renfermé, e [ʀɑ̃fɛʀme] adj (fig) withdrawn ▷ nm: **sentir le ~** to smell stuffy

renfermer [ʀɑ̃fɛʀme] vt to contain

renforcer [ʀɑ̃fɔʀse] vt to reinforce; **renfort**: **renforts** nmpl reinforcements; **à grand renfort de** with a great deal of

renfrogné, e [ʀɑ̃fʀɔɲe] adj sullen

renier [ʀənje] vt (personne) to disown, repudiate; (foi) to renounce

renifler [ʀ(ə)nifle] vi, vt to sniff

renne [ʀɛn] nm reindeer inv

renom [ʀənɔ̃] nm reputation; (célébrité) renown; **renommé, e** adj celebrated, renowned; **renommée** nf fame

renoncer [ʀənɔ̃se]: **~ à** vt to give up; **~ à faire** to give up the idea of doing

renouer [ʀənwe] vt: **~ avec** (habitude) to take

up again

renouveler [ʀ(ə)nuv(ə)le] vt to renew; (exploit, méfait) to repeat; **se renouveler** vi (incident) to recur, happen again; **renouvellement** nm (remplacement) renewal

rénover [ʀenɔve] vt (immeuble) to renovate, do up; (quartier) to redevelop

renseignement [ʀɑ̃sɛɲmɑ̃] nm information no pl, piece of information; **(guichet des) ~s** information office; **(service des) ~s** (Tél) directory enquiries (BRIT), information (US)

renseigner [ʀɑ̃seɲe] vt: **~ qn (sur)** to give information to sb (about); **se renseigner** vi to ask for information, make inquiries

rentabilité [ʀɑ̃tabilite] nf profitability

rentable [ʀɑ̃tabl] adj profitable

rente [ʀɑ̃t] nf private income; (pension) pension

rentrée [ʀɑ̃tʀe] nf: **~ (d'argent)** cash no pl coming in; **la ~ (des classes)** the start of the new school year

rentrer [ʀɑ̃tʀe] vi (revenir chez soi) to go (ou come) (back) home; (entrer de nouveau) to go (ou come) back in; (entrer) to go (ou come) in; (air, clou: pénétrer) to go in; (revenu) to come in ▷ vt to bring in; (véhicule) to put away; (chemise dans pantalon etc) to tuck in; (griffes) to draw in; **~ le ventre** to pull in one's stomach; **~ dans** (heurter) to crash into; **~ dans l'ordre** to be back to normal; **~ dans ses frais** to recover one's expenses; **je rentre mardi** I'm going ou coming home on Tuesday

renverse [ʀɑ̃vɛʀs]: **à la ~** adv backwards

renverser [ʀɑ̃vɛʀse] vt (faire tomber: chaise, verre) to knock over, overturn; (liquide, contenu) to spill, upset; (piéton) to knock down; (retourner) to turn upside down; (: ordre des mots etc) to reverse; (fig: gouvernement etc) to overthrow; (stupéfier) to bowl over; **se renverser** vi (verre, vase) to fall over; (contenu) to spill

renvoi [ʀɑ̃vwa] nm (d'employé) dismissal; (d'élève) expulsion; (référence) cross-reference; (éructation) belch; **renvoyer** vt to send back; (congédier) to dismiss; (élève: définitivement) to expel; (lumière) to reflect; (ajourner): **renvoyer qch (à)** to put sth off ou postpone sth (until)

repaire [ʀ(ə)pɛʀ] nm den

répandre [ʀepɑ̃dʀ] vt (renverser) to spill; (étaler, diffuser) to spread; (odeur) to give off; **se répandre** vi to spill; (se propager) to spread; **répandu, e** adj (opinion, usage) widespread

réparation [ʀepaʀasjɔ̃] nf repair

réparer [ʀepaʀe] vt to repair; (fig: offense) to make up for, atone for; (: oubli, erreur) to put right; **où est-ce que je peux le faire ~?** where can I get it fixed?

repartie [ʀepaʀti] nf retort; **avoir de la ~** to be quick at repartee

repartir [ʀ(ə)paʀtiʀ] vi to leave again; (voyageur) to set off again; (fig) to get going again; **~ à zéro** to start from scratch (again)

répartir [ʀepaʀtiʀ] vt (pour attribuer) to share out; (pour disperser, disposer) to divide up; (poids) to distribute; **se répartir** vt (travail, rôles) to share out between themselves; **répartition** nf (des richesses etc) distribution

repas [ʀ(ə)pɑ] nm meal

repassage [ʀ(ə)pasaʒ] nm ironing

repasser [ʀ(ə)pase] vi to come (ou go) back ▷ vt (vêtement, tissu) to iron; (examen) to retake, resit; (film) to show again; (leçon: revoir) to go over (again)

repentir [ʀəpɑ̃tiʀ] nm repentance; **se repentir** vi to repent; **se ~ d'avoir fait qch** (regretter) to regret having done sth

répercussions [ʀepɛʀkysjɔ̃] nfpl (fig) repercussions

répercuter [ʀepɛʀkyte]: **se répercuter** vi (bruit) to reverberate; (fig): **se ~ sur** to have repercussions on

repère [ʀ(ə)pɛʀ] nm mark; (monument, événement) landmark

repérer [ʀ(ə)peʀe] vt (fam: erreur, personne) to spot; (: endroit) to locate; **se repérer** vi to find one's way about

répertoire [ʀepɛʀtwaʀ] nm (liste) (alphabetical) list; (carnet) index notebook; (Inform) folder, directory; (d'un artiste) repertoire

répéter [ʀepete] vt to repeat; (préparer: leçon) to learn, go over; (Théâtre) to rehearse; **se répéter** vi (redire) to repeat o.s.; (se reproduire) to be repeated, recur; **pouvez-vous ~, s'il vous plaît?** can you repeat that, please?

répétition [ʀepetisjɔ̃] nf repetition; (Théâtre) rehearsal; **~ générale** (final) dress rehearsal

répit [ʀepi] nm respite; **sans ~** without letting up

replier [ʀ(ə)plije] vt (rabattre) to fold down ou over; **se replier** vi (troupes, armée) to withdraw, fall back; (sur soi-même) to withdraw into o.s.

réplique [ʀeplik] nf (repartie, fig) reply; (Théâtre) line; (copie) replica; **répliquer** vi to reply; (riposter) to retaliate

répondeur [ʀepɔ̃dœʀ] nm: **~ (automatique)** (Tél) answering machine

répondre [ʀepɔ̃dʀ] vi to answer, reply; (freins) to respond; **~ à** to reply to, answer; (affection, salut) to return; (provocation) to respond to; (correspondre à: besoin) to answer; (: conditions) to meet; (: description) to match; (avec impertinence): **~ à qn** to answer sb back; **~ de** to answer for

réponse [ʀepɔ̃s] nf answer, reply; **en ~ à** in reply to

reportage [ʀ(ə)pɔʀtaʒ] nm report

reporter¹ [ʀəpɔʀtɛʀ] nm reporter

reporter² [ʀəpɔʀte] *vt* (*ajourner*): **~ qch (à)** to postpone sth (until); (*transférer*): **~ qch sur** to transfer sth to; **se reporter à** (*époque*) to think back to; (*document*) to refer to

repos [ʀ(ə)po] *nm* rest; (*tranquillité*) peace (and quiet); (*Mil*): **~!** stand at ease!; **ce n'est pas de tout ~!** it's no picnic!

reposant, e [ʀ(ə)pozɑ̃, ɑ̃t] *adj* restful

reposer [ʀ(ə)poze] *vt* (*verre, livre*) to put down; (*délasser*) to rest ▷ *vi*: **laisser ~** (*pâte*) to leave to stand; **se reposer** *vi* to rest; **se ~ sur qn** to rely on sb; **~ sur** (*fig*) to rest on

repoussant, e [ʀ(ə)pusɑ̃, ɑ̃t] *adj* repulsive

repousser [ʀ(ə)puse] *vi* to grow again ▷ *vt* to repel, repulse; (*offre*) to turn down, reject; (*personne*) to push back; (*différer*) to put back

reprendre [ʀ(ə)pʀɑ̃dʀ] *vt* (*objet prêté, donné*) to take back; (*prisonnier, ville*) to recapture; (*firme, entreprise*) to take over; (*le travail*) to resume; (*emprunter: argument, idée*) to take up, use; (*refaire: article etc*) to go over again; (*vêtement*) to alter; (*réprimander*) to tell off; (*corriger*) to correct; (*chercher*): **je viendrai te ~ à 4 h** I'll come and fetch you at 4; (*se resservir de*): **~ du pain/un œuf** to take (*ou* eat) more bread/another egg ▷ *vi* (*classes, pluie*) to start (up) again; (*activités, travaux, combats*) to resume, start (up) again; (*affaires*) to pick up; (*dire*): **reprit-il** he went on; **~ des forces** to recover one's strength; **~ courage** to take new heart; **~ la route** to resume one's journey, set off again; **~ haleine** *ou* **son souffle** to get one's breath back

représentant, e [ʀ(ə)pʀezɑ̃tɑ̃, ɑ̃t] *nm/f* representative

représentation [ʀ(ə)pʀezɑ̃tasjɔ̃] *nf* (*symbole, image*) representation; (*spectacle*) performance

représenter [ʀ(ə)pʀezɑ̃te] *vt* to represent; (*donner: pièce, opéra*) to perform; **se représenter** *vt* (*se figurer*) to imagine

répression [ʀepʀesjɔ̃] *nf* repression

réprimer [ʀepʀime] *vt* (*émotions*) to suppress; (*peuple etc*) to repress

repris [ʀ(ə)pʀi] *nm*: **~ de justice** ex-prisoner, ex-convict

reprise [ʀ(ə)pʀiz] *nf* (*recommencement*) resumption; (*économique*) recovery; (*TV*) repeat; (*Comm*) trade-in, part exchange; (*raccommodage*) mend; **à plusieurs ~s** on several occasions

repriser [ʀ(ə)pʀize] *vt* (*chaussette, lainage*) to darn; (*tissu*) to mend

reproche [ʀ(ə)pʀɔʃ] *nm* (*remontrance*) reproach; **faire des ~s à qn** to reproach sb; **sans ~(s)** beyond reproach; **reprocher** *vt*: **reprocher qch à qn** to reproach *ou* blame sb for sth; **reprocher qch à** (*critiquer*) to have sth against

reproduction [ʀ(ə)pʀɔdyksjɔ̃] *nf* reproduction

reproduire [ʀ(ə)pʀɔdɥiʀ] *vt* to reproduce; **se reproduire** *vi* (*Bio*) to reproduce; (*recommencer*) to recur, re-occur

reptile [ʀɛptil] *nm* reptile

république [ʀepyblik] *nf* republic

répugnant, e [ʀepyɲɑ̃, ɑ̃t] *adj* disgusting

répugner [ʀepyɲe]: **~ à** *vt*: **~ à qn** to repel *ou* disgust sb; **~ à faire** to be loath *ou* reluctant to do

réputation [ʀepytasjɔ̃] *nf* reputation; **réputé, e** *adj* renowned

requérir [ʀəkeʀiʀ] *vt* (*nécessiter*) to require, call for

requête [ʀəkɛt] *nf* request

requin [ʀəkɛ̃] *nm* shark

requis, e [ʀəki, iz] *adj* required

RER *sigle m* (= *réseau express régional*) *Greater Paris high-speed train service*

rescapé, e [ʀɛskape] *nm/f* survivor

rescousse [ʀɛskus] *nf*: **aller à la ~ de qn** to go to sb's aid *ou* rescue

réseau, x [ʀezo] *nm* network

réservation [ʀezɛʀvasjɔ̃] *nf* booking, reservation; **j'ai confirmé ma ~ par fax/e-mail** I confirmed my booking by fax/e-mail

réserve [ʀezɛʀv] *nf* (*retenue*) reserve; (*entrepôt*) storeroom; (*restriction, d'Indiens*) reservation; (*de pêche, chasse*) preserve; **de ~** (*provisions etc*) in reserve

réservé, e [ʀezɛʀve] *adj* reserved; **chasse/pêche ~e** private hunting/fishing

réserver [ʀezɛʀve] *vt* to reserve; (*chambre, billet etc*) to book, reserve; (*fig: destiner*) to have in store; (*garder*): **~ qch pour/à** to keep *ou* save sth for; **je voudrais ~ une chambre pour deux personnes** I'd like to book a double room; **j'ai réservé une table au nom de ...** I booked a table in the name of ...

réservoir [ʀezɛʀvwaʀ] *nm* tank

résidence [ʀezidɑ̃s] *nf* residence; **résidence secondaire** second home; **résidence universitaire** hall of residence (*Brit*), dormitory (*us*); **résidentiel, le** *adj* residential; **résider** *vi*: **résider à/dans/en** to reside in; **résider dans** (*fig*) to lie in

résidu [ʀezidy] *nm* residue *no pl*

résigner [ʀeziɲe]: **se résigner** *vi*: **se ~ (à qch/à faire)** to resign o.s. (to sth/to doing)

résilier [ʀezilje] *vt* to terminate

résistance [ʀezistɑ̃s] *nf* resistance; (*de réchaud, bouilloire: fil*) element

résistant, e [ʀezistɑ̃, ɑ̃t] *adj* (*personne*) robust, tough; (*matériau*) strong, hard-wearing

résister [ʀeziste] *vi* to resist; **~ à** (*assaut, tentation*) to resist; (*supporter: gel etc*) to withstand; (*désobéir à*) to stand up to, oppose

résolu, e [ʀezɔly] *pp de* **résoudre** ▷ *adj*: **être ~ à qch/faire** to be set upon sth/doing

résolution [Rezɔlysjɔ̃] nf (fermeté, décision) resolution; (d'un problème) solution

résolve etc [Rezɔlv] vb voir **résoudre**

résonner [Rezone] vi (cloche, pas) to reverberate, resound; (salle) to be resonant

résorber [RezɔRbe]: **se résorber** vi (fig: chômage) to be reduced; (: déficit) to be absorbed

résoudre [Rezudr] vt to solve; **se ~ à faire** to bring o.s. to do

respect [Respe] nm respect; **tenir en ~** to keep at bay; **présenter ses ~s à qn** to pay one's respects to sb; **respecter** vt to respect; **respectueux, -euse** adj respectful

respiration [Respirasjɔ̃] nf breathing no pl

respirer [Respire] vi to breathe; (fig: se détendre) to get one's breath; (: se rassurer) to breathe again ▷ vt to breathe (in), inhale; (manifester: santé, calme etc) to exude

resplendir [Resplɑ̃dir] vi to shine; (fig): **~ (de)** to be radiant (with)

responsabilité [Respɔ̃sabilite] nf responsibility; (légale) liability

responsable [Respɔ̃sabl] adj responsible ▷ nm/f (coupable) person responsible; (personne compétente) person in charge; (de parti, syndicat) official; **~ de** responsible for

ressaisir [R(ə)sezir]: **se ressaisir** vi to regain one's self-control

ressasser [R(ə)sase] vt to keep going over

ressemblance [R(ə)sɑ̃blɑ̃s] nf resemblance, similarity, likeness

ressemblant, e [R(ə)sɑ̃blɑ̃, ɑ̃t] adj (portrait) lifelike, true to life

ressembler [R(ə)sɑ̃ble]: **~ à** vt to be like, resemble; (visuellement) to look like; **se ressembler** vi to be (ou look) alike

ressentiment [R(ə)sɑ̃timɑ̃] nm resentment

ressentir [R(ə)sɑ̃tir] vt to feel; **se ~ de** to feel (ou show) the effects of

resserrer [R(ə)sere] vt (nœud, boulon) to tighten (up); (fig: liens) to strengthen

resservir [R(ə)servir] vi to do ou serve again; **~ qn (d'un plat)** to give sb a second helping (of a dish); **se ~ de** (plat) to take a second helping of; (outil etc) to use again

ressort [Rəsɔr] nm (pièce) spring; (énergie) spirit; (recours): **en dernier ~** as a last resort; (compétence): **être du ~ de** to fall within the competence of

ressortir [Rəsɔrtir] vi to go (ou come) out (again); (contraster) to stand out; **~ de** to emerge from; **faire ~** (fig: souligner) to bring out

ressortissant, e [R(ə)sɔrtisɑ̃, ɑ̃t] nm/f national

ressources [R(ə)surs] nfpl (moyens) resources

ressusciter [Resysite] vt (fig) to revive, bring back ▷ vi to rise (from the dead)

restant, e [Restɑ̃, ɑ̃t] adj remaining ▷ nm:

le ~ (de) the remainder (of); **un ~ de** (de trop) some left-over

restaurant [Restɔrɑ̃] nm restaurant; **pouvez-vous m'indiquer un bon ~?** can you recommend a good restaurant?

restauration [Restɔrasjɔ̃] nf restoration; (hôtellerie) catering; **restauration rapide** fast food

restaurer [Restɔre] vt to restore; **se restaurer** vi to have something to eat

reste [Rest] nm (restant): **le ~ (de)** the rest (of); (de trop): **un ~ (de)** some left-over; **restes** nmpl (nourriture) left-overs; (d'une cité etc, dépouille mortelle) remains; **du ~, au ~** besides, moreover

rester [Reste] vi to stay, remain; (subsister) to remain, be left; (durer) to last, live on ▷ vb impers: **il reste du pain/2 œufs** there's some bread/there are 2 eggs left (over); **restons-en là** let's leave it at that; **il me reste assez de temps** I have enough time left; **il ne me reste plus qu'à ...** I've just got to ...

restituer [Restitɥe] vt (objet, somme): **~ qch (à qn)** to return sth (to sb)

restreindre [Restrɛ̃dr] vt to restrict, limit

restriction [Restriksjɔ̃] nf restriction

résultat [Rezylta] nm result; **résultats** nmpl (d'examen, d'élection) results pl

résulter [Rezylte]: **~ de** vt to result from, be the result of

résumé [Rezyme] nm summary, résumé; **en ~** in brief; (pour conclure) to sum up

résumer [Rezyme] vt (texte) to summarize; (récapituler) to sum up

⬛ Attention à ne pas traduire **résumer** par **to resume**.

résurrection [Rezyrɛksjɔ̃] nf resurrection

rétablir [Retablir] vt to restore, re-establish; **se rétablir** vi (guérir) to recover; (silence, calme) to return, be restored; **rétablissement** nm restoring; (guérison) recovery

retaper [R(ə)tape] (fam) vt (maison, voiture etc) to do up; (revigorer) to buck up

retard [R(ə)tar] nm (d'une personne attendue) lateness no pl; (sur l'horaire, un programme) delay; (fig: scolaire, mental etc) backwardness; **en ~ (de 2 heures)** (2 hours) late; **avoir du ~** to be late; (sur un programme) to be behind (schedule); **prendre du ~** (train, avion) to be delayed; **sans ~** without delay; **désolé d'être en ~** sorry I'm late; **le vol a deux heures de ~** the flight is two hours late

retardataire [R(ə)tardater] nm/f latecomer

retardement [R(ə)tardəmɑ̃]: **à ~** adj delayed action cpd; **bombe à ~** time bomb

retarder [R(ə)tarde] vt to delay; (montre) to put back ▷ vi (montre) to be slow; **~ qn (d'une heure)** (sur un horaire) to delay sb (an hour); **~ qch (de 2 jours)** (départ, date) to put sth back

(2 days)

retenir [Rət(ə)niR] vt (garder, retarder) to keep, detain; (maintenir: objet qui glisse, fig: colère, larmes) to hold back; (se rappeler) to retain; (réserver) to reserve; (accepter: proposition etc) to accept; (fig: empêcher d'agir): **~ qn (de faire)** to hold sb back (from doing); (prélever): **~ qch (sur)** to deduct sth (from); **se retenir** vi (se raccrocher): **se ~ à** to hold onto; (se contenir): **se ~ de faire** to restrain o.s. from doing; **~ son souffle** to hold one's breath

retentir [R(ə)tãtiR] vi to ring out; **retentissant, e** adj resounding

retenue [Rət(ə)ny] nf (prélèvement) deduction; (Scol) detention; (modération) (self-)restraint

réticence [Retisãs] nf hesitation, reluctance no pl; **réticent, e** adj hesitant, reluctant

rétine [Retin] nf retina

retiré, e [R(ə)tiRe] adj (vie) secluded; (lieu) remote

retirer [R(ə)tiRe] vt (vêtement, lunettes) to take off, remove; (argent, plainte) to withdraw; (reprendre: bagages, billets) to collect, pick up; (extraire): **~ qch de** to take sth out of, remove sth from

retomber [R(ə)tõbe] vi (à nouveau) to fall again; (atterrir: après un saut etc) to land; (échoir): **~ sur qn** to fall on sb

rétorquer [RetoRke] vt: **~ (à qn) que** to retort (to sb) that

retouche [R(ə)tuʃ] nf (sur vêtement) alteration; **retoucher** vt (photographie) to touch up; (texte, vêtement) to alter

retour [R(ə)tuR] nm return; **au ~** (en route) on the way back; **à mon ~** when I get/got back; **être de ~ (de)** to be back (from); **par ~ du courrier** by return of post; **quand serons-nous de ~?** when do we get back?

retourner [R(ə)tuRne] vt (dans l'autre sens: matelas, crêpe etc) to turn (over); (: sac, vêtement) to turn inside out; (fam: bouleverser) to shake; (renvoyer, restituer): **~ qch à qn** to return sth to sb ▷ vi (aller, revenir): **~ quelque part/à** to go back ou return somewhere/to; **se retourner** vi (tourner la tête) to turn round; **~ à** (état, activité) to return to, go back to; **se ~ contre** (fig) to turn against

retrait [R(ə)tRɛ] nm (d'argent) withdrawal; **en ~** set back; **retrait du permis (de conduire)** disqualification from driving (BRIT), revocation of driver's license (us)

retraite [R(ə)tRɛt] nf (d'un employé) retirement; (revenu) pension; (d'une armée, Rel) retreat; **prendre sa ~** to retire; **retraite anticipée** early retirement; **retraité, e** adj retired ▷ nm/f pensioner

retrancher [R(ə)tRãʃe] vt (nombre, somme):

~ qch de to take ou deduct sth from; **se ~ derrière/dans** to take refuge behind/in

rétrécir [RetResiR] vt (vêtement) to take in ▷ vi to shrink; **se rétrécir** (route, vallée) to narrow

rétro [RetRo] adj inv: **la mode ~** the nostalgia vogue

rétroprojecteur [RetRopRɔʒɛktœR] nm overhead projector

rétrospective [RetRɔspɛktiv] nf (Art) retrospective; (Cinéma) season, retrospective; **rétrospectivement** adv in retrospect

retrousser [R(ə)tRuse] vt to roll up

retrouvailles [R(ə)tRuvaj] nfpl reunion sg

retrouver [R(ə)tRuve] vt (fugitif, objet perdu) to find; (calme, santé) to regain; (revoir) to see again; (rejoindre) to meet (again), join; **se retrouver** vi to meet; (s'orienter) to find one's way; **se ~ quelque part** to find o.s. somewhere; **s'y ~** (y voir clair) to make sense of it; (rentrer dans ses frais) to break even; **je ne retrouve plus mon portefeuille** I can't find my wallet (BRIT) ou billfold (us)

rétroviseur [RetRovizœR] nm (rear-view) mirror

réunion [Reynjõ] nf (séance) meeting

réunir [ReyniR] vt (rassembler) to gather together; (inviter: amis, famille) to have round, have in; (cumuler: qualités etc) to combine; (rapprocher: ennemis) to bring together (again), reunite; (rattacher: parties) to join (together); **se réunir** vi (se rencontrer) to meet

réussi, e [Reysi] adj successful

réussir [ReysiR] vi to succeed, be successful; (à un examen) to pass ▷ vt to make a success of; **~ à faire** to succeed in doing; **~ à qn** (être bénéfique à) to agree with sb; **réussite** nf success; (Cartes) patience

revaloir [R(ə)valwaR] vt: **je vous revaudrai cela** I'll repay you some day; (en mal) I'll pay you back for this

revanche [R(ə)vãʃ] nf revenge; (sport) revenge match; **en ~** on the other hand

rêve [Rɛv] nm dream; **de ~** dream cpd; **faire un ~** to have a dream

réveil [Revɛj] nm waking up no pl; (fig) awakening; (pendule) alarm (clock); **au ~** on waking (up); **réveiller** vt (personne) to wake up; (fig) to awaken, revive; **se réveiller** vi to wake up; **pouvez-vous me réveiller à 7 heures, s'il vous plaît?** could I have an alarm call at 7am, please?

réveillon [Revɛjõ] nm Christmas Eve; (de la Saint-Sylvestre) New Year's Eve; **réveillonner** vi to celebrate Christmas Eve (ou New Year's Eve)

révélateur, -trice [RevelatœR, tRis] adj: **~ (de qch)** revealing (sth)

révéler [Revele] vt to reveal; **se révéler** vi to be revealed, reveal itself ▷ vb +attrib: **se ~**

difficile/aisé to prove difficult/easy
revenant, e[ʀ(ə)vənɑ̃, ɑ̃t] *nm/f* ghost
revendeur, -euse[ʀ(ə)vɑ̃dœʀ, øz] *nm/f*
(*détaillant*) retailer; (*de drogue*) (drug-)dealer
revendication[ʀ(ə)vɑ̃dikasjɔ̃] *nf* claim,
demand
revendiquer[ʀ(ə)vɑ̃dike] *vt* to claim,
demand; (*responsabilité*) to claim
revendre[ʀ(ə)vɑ̃dʀ] *vt* (*d'occasion*) to resell;
(*détailler*) to sell; **à ~** (*en abondance*) to spare
revenir[ʀəv(ə)niʀ] *vi* to come back; (*coûter*):
~ cher/à 100 euros (à qn) to cost (sb) a
lot/100 euros; **~ à** (*reprendre: études, projet*) to
return to, go back to; (*équivaloir à*) to amount
to; **~ à qn** (*part, honneur*) to go to sb, be sb's;
(*souvenir, nom*) to come back to sb; **~ sur**
(*question, sujet*) to go back over; (*engagement*)
to go back on; **~ à soi** to come round; **n'en
pas ~: je n'en reviens pas** I can't get over
it; **~ sur ses pas** to retrace one's steps; **cela
revient à dire que/au même** it amounts to
saying that/the same thing; **faire ~** (*Culin*)
to brown
revenu[ʀəv(ə)ny] *nm* income; **revenus** *nmpl*
income *sg*
rêver[ʀeve] *vi, vt* to dream; **~ de/à** to dream of
réverbère[ʀeveʀbɛʀ] *nm* street lamp *ou* light;
réverbérer *vt* to reflect
revers[ʀ(ə)vɛʀ] *nm* (*de feuille, main*) back;
(*d'étoffe*) wrong side; (*de pièce, médaille*) back,
reverse; (*Tennis, Ping-Pong*) backhand; (*de veste*)
lapel; (*fig: échec*) setback
revêtement[ʀ(ə)vɛtmɑ̃] *nm* (*des sols*)
flooring; (*de chaussée*) surface
revêtir[ʀ(ə)vetiʀ] *vt* (*habit*) to don, put on;
(*prendre: importance, apparence*) to take on; **~
qch de** to cover sth with
rêveur, -euse[ʀɛvœʀ, øz] *adj* dreamy ▷ *nm/f*
dreamer
revient[ʀəvjɛ̃] *vb voir* **revenir**
revigorer[ʀ(ə)vigɔʀe] *vt* (*air frais*) to
invigorate, brace up; (*repas, boisson*) to revive,
buck up
revirement[ʀ(ə)viʀmɑ̃] *nm* change of mind;
(*d'une situation*) reversal
réviser[ʀevize] *vt* to revise; (*machine*) to
overhaul, service
révision[ʀevizjɔ̃] *nf* revision; (*de voiture*)
servicing *no pl*
revivre[ʀ(ə)vivʀ] *vi* (*reprendre des forces*) to
come alive again ▷ *vt* (*épreuve, moment*) to
relive
revoir[ʀəvwaʀ] *vt* to see again; (*réviser*) to
revise ▷ *nm*: **au ~** goodbye
révoltant, e[ʀevɔltɑ̃, ɑ̃t] *adj* revolting,
appalling
révolte[ʀevɔlt] *nf* rebellion, revolt
révolter[ʀevɔlte] *vt* to revolt; **se révolter
(contre)** to rebel (against)

révolu, e[ʀevɔly] *adj* past; (*Admin*): **âgé de 18
ans ~s** over 18 years of age
révolution[ʀevɔlysjɔ̃] *nf* revolution;
révolutionnaire *adj, nm/f* revolutionary
revolver[ʀevɔlvɛʀ] *nm* gun; (*à barillet*)
revolver
révoquer[ʀevɔke] *vt* (*fonctionnaire*) to
dismiss; (*arrêt, contrat*) to revoke
revue[ʀ(ə)vy] *nf* review; (*périodique*) review,
magazine; (*de music-hall*) variety show; **passer
en ~** (*mentalement*) to go through
rez-de-chaussée[ʀed(ə)ʃose] *nm inv* ground
floor
RF *sigle f* = **République française**
Rhin[ʀɛ̃] *nm* Rhine
rhinocéros[ʀinɔseʀɔs] *nm* rhinoceros
Rhône[ʀon] *nm* Rhone
rhubarbe[ʀybaʀb] *nf* rhubarb
rhum[ʀɔm] *nm* rum
rhumatisme[ʀymatism] *nm*
rheumatism *no pl*
rhume[ʀym] *nm* cold; **rhume de cerveau**
head cold; **le rhume des foins** hay fever
ricaner[ʀikane] *vi* (*avec méchanceté*) to
snigger; (*bêtement*) to giggle
riche[ʀiʃ] *adj* rich; (*personne, pays*) rich,
wealthy; **~ en** rich in; **richesse** *nf* wealth;
(*fig: de sol, musée etc*) richness; **richesses** *nfpl*
(*ressources, argent*) wealth *sg*; (*fig: trésors*)
treasures
ricochet[ʀikɔʃɛ] *nm*: **faire des ~s** to skip
stones
ride[ʀid] *nf* wrinkle
rideau, x[ʀido] *nm* curtain; **rideau de fer**
(*boutique*) metal shutter(s)
rider[ʀide] *vt* to wrinkle; **se rider** *vi* to
become wrinkled
ridicule[ʀidikyl] *adj* ridiculous ▷ *nm*:
le ~ ridicule; **ridiculiser** *vt* to ridicule; **se
ridiculiser** *vi* to make a fool of o.s.

 MOT-CLÉ

rien[ʀjɛ̃] *pron* **1** **(ne) ... rien** nothing, *tournure
négative + anything*; **qu'est-ce que vous avez?
— rien** what have you got? — nothing; **il n'a
rien dit/fait** he said/did nothing; he hasn't
said/done anything; **n'avoir peur de rien** to
be afraid *ou* frightened of nothing, not to be
afraid *ou* frightened of anything; **il n'a rien**
(*n'est pas blessé*) he's all right; **ça ne fait rien** it
doesn't matter; **de rien!** not at all!
2 rien de: rien d'intéressant nothing
interesting; **rien d'autre** nothing else; **rien du
tout** nothing at all
3 rien que just, only; nothing but; **rien que
pour lui faire plaisir** only *ou* just to please
him; **rien que la vérité** nothing but the truth;
rien que cela that alone

▷ *nm*: **un petit rien** (*cadeau*) a little something; **des riens** trivia *pl*; **un rien de** a hint of; **en un rien de temps** in no time at all

rieur, -euse [ʀ(i)jœʀ, ʀ(i)jøz] *adj* cheerful
rigide [ʀiʒid] *adj* stiff; (*fig*) rigid; strict
rigoler [ʀiɡɔle] *vi* (*fam: rire*) to laugh; (*s'amuser*) to have (some) fun; (*plaisanter*) to be joking *ou* kidding; **rigolo, -ote** (*fam*) *adj* funny ▷ *nm/f* comic; (*péj*) fraud, phoney
rigoureusement [ʀiɡuʀøzmɑ̃] *adv* (*vrai*) absolutely; (*interdit*) strictly
rigoureux, -euse [ʀiɡuʀø, øz] *adj* rigorous; (*hiver*) hard, harsh
rigueur [ʀiɡœʀ] *nf* rigour; **"tenue de soirée de ~"** "formal dress only"; **à la ~** at a pinch; **tenir ~ à qn de qch** to hold sth against sb
rillettes [ʀijɛt] *nfpl* potted meat (*made from pork or goose*)
rime [ʀim] *nf* rhyme
rinçage [ʀɛ̃saʒ] *nm* rinsing (out); (*opération*) rinse
rincer [ʀɛ̃se] *vt* to rinse; (*récipient*) to rinse out
ringard, e [ʀɛ̃ɡaʀ, aʀd] (*fam*) *adj* old-fashioned
riposter [ʀipɔste] *vi* to retaliate ▷ *vt*: **~ que** to retort that
rire [ʀiʀ] *vi* to laugh; (*se divertir*) to have fun ▷ *nm* laugh; **le ~** laughter; **~ de** to laugh at; **pour ~** (*pas sérieusement*) for a joke *ou* a laugh
risible [ʀizibl] *adj* laughable
risque [ʀisk] *nm* risk; **le ~** danger; **à ses ~s et périls** at his own risk; **risqué, e** *adj* risky; (*plaisanterie*) risqué, daring; **risquer** *vt* to risk; (*allusion, question*) to venture, hazard; **ça ne risque rien** it's quite safe; **risquer de: il risque de se tuer** he could get himself killed; **ce qui risque de se produire** what might *ou* could well happen; **il ne risque pas de recommencer** there's no chance of him doing that again; **se risquer à faire** (*tenter*) to venture *ou* dare to do
rissoler [ʀisɔle] *vi, vt*: **(faire) ~** to brown
ristourne [ʀistuʀn] *nf* discount
rite [ʀit] *nm* rite; (*fig*) ritual
rivage [ʀivaʒ] *nm* shore
rival, e, -aux [ʀival, o] *adj, nm/f* rival; **rivaliser** *vi*: **rivaliser avec** (*personne*) to rival, vie with; **rivalité** *nf* rivalry
rive [ʀiv] *nf* shore; (*de fleuve*) bank; **riverain, e** *nm/f* riverside (*ou* lakeside) resident; (*d'une route*) local resident
rivière [ʀivjɛʀ] *nf* river
riz [ʀi] *nm* rice; **rizière** *nf* paddy-field, ricefield
RMI *sigle m* (= *revenu minimum d'insertion*) ≈ income support (*BRIT*), ≈ welfare (*US*)
RN *sigle f* = **route nationale**
robe [ʀɔb] *nf* dress; (*de juge*) robe; (*pelage*) coat; **robe de chambre** dressing gown; **robe**

de mariée wedding dress; **robe de soirée** evening dress
robinet [ʀɔbinɛ] *nm* tap (*BRIT*), faucet (*US*)
robot [ʀɔbo] *nm* robot; **robot de cuisine** food processor
robuste [ʀɔbyst] *adj* robust, sturdy; **robustesse** *nf* robustness, sturdiness
roc [ʀɔk] *nm* rock
rocade [ʀɔkad] *nf* bypass
rocaille [ʀɔkaj] *nf* loose stones *pl*; (*jardin*) rockery, rock garden
roche [ʀɔʃ] *nf* rock
rocher [ʀɔʃe] *nm* rock
rocheux, -euse [ʀɔʃø, øz] *adj* rocky
rodage [ʀɔdaʒ] *nm*: **en ~** running in
rôder [ʀode] *vi* to roam about; (*de façon suspecte*) to lurk (about *ou* around); **rôdeur, -euse** *nm/f* prowler
rogne [ʀɔɲ] (*fam*) *nf*: **être en ~** to be in a temper
rogner [ʀɔɲe] *vt* to clip; **~ sur** (*fig*) to cut down *ou* back on
rognons [ʀɔɲɔ̃] *nmpl* (*Culin*) kidneys
roi [ʀwa] *nm* king; **la fête des Rois, les Rois** Twelfth Night
rôle [ʀol] *nm* role, part
rollers [ʀɔlœʀ] *nmpl* Rollerblades®
romain, e [ʀɔmɛ̃, ɛn] *adj* Roman ▷ *nm/f*: **R~, e** Roman
roman, e [ʀɔmɑ̃, an] *adj* (*Archit*) Romanesque ▷ *nm* novel; **roman policier** detective story
romancer [ʀɔmɑ̃se] *vt* (*agrémenter*) to romanticize; **romancier, -ière** *nm/f* novelist; **romanesque** *adj* (*amours, aventures*) storybook *cpd*; (*sentimental: personne*) romantic
roman-feuilleton [ʀɔmɑ̃fœjtɔ̃] *nm* serialized novel
romanichel, le [ʀɔmaniʃɛl] (*péj*) *nm/f* gipsy
romantique [ʀɔmɑ̃tik] *adj* romantic
romarin [ʀɔmaʀɛ̃] *nm* rosemary
Rome [ʀɔm] *n* Rome
rompre [ʀɔ̃pʀ] *vt* to break; (*entretien, fiançailles*) to break off ▷ *vi* (*fiancés*) to break it off; **se rompre** *vi* to break; **rompu, e** *adj* (*fourbu*) exhausted
ronces [ʀɔ̃s] *nfpl* brambles
ronchonner [ʀɔ̃ʃɔne] (*fam*) *vi* to grouse, grouch
rond, e [ʀɔ̃, ʀɔ̃d] *adj* round; (*joues, mollets*) well-rounded; (*fam: ivre*) tight ▷ *nm* (*cercle*) ring; (*fam: sou*): **je n'ai plus un ~** I haven't a penny left; **en ~** (*s'asseoir, danser*) in a ring; **ronde** *nf* (*gén: de surveillance*) rounds *pl*, patrol; (*danse*) round (dance); (*Mus*) semibreve (*BRIT*), whole note (*US*); **à la ronde** (*alentour*): **à 10 km à la ronde** for 10 km round; **rondelet, te** *adj* plump
rondelle [ʀɔ̃dɛl] *nf* (*tranche*) slice, round; (*Tech*) washer

rond-point[Rɔ̃pwɛ̃] nm roundabout
ronflement[Rɔ̃fləmɑ̃] nm snore, snoring
ronfler[Rɔ̃fle] vi to snore; (moteur, poêle) to hum
ronger[Rɔ̃ʒe] vt to gnaw (at); (suj: vers, rouille) to eat into; **se ~ les ongles** to bite one's nails; **se ~ les sangs** to worry o.s. sick; **rongeur** nm rodent
ronronner[Rɔ̃Rɔne] vi to purr
rosbif[Rɔsbif] nm: **du ~** roasting beef; (cuit) roast beef
rose[Roz] nf rose ▷ adj pink; **rose bonbon** adj inv candy pink
rosé, e[Roze] adj pinkish; **(vin) ~** rosé
roseau, x[Rozo] nm reed
rosée[Roze] nf dew
rosier[Rozje] nm rosebush, rose tree
rossignol[Rɔsiɲɔl] nm (Zool) nightingale
rotation[Rɔtasjɔ̃] nf rotation
roter[Rɔte] (fam) vi to burp, belch
rôti[Roti] nm: **du ~** roasting meat; (cuit) roast meat; **un ~ de bœuf/porc** a joint of beef/pork
rotin[Rɔtɛ̃] nm rattan (cane); **fauteuil en ~** cane (arm)chair
rôtir[RotiR] vi, vt (aussi: **faire ~**) to roast; **rôtisserie** nf (restaurant) steakhouse; (traiteur) roast meat shop; **rôtissoire** nf (roasting) spit
rotule[Rɔtyl] nf kneecap
rouage[Rwaʒ] nm cog(wheel), gearwheel; **les ~s de l'État** the wheels of State
roue[Ru] nf wheel; **roue de secours** spare wheel
rouer[Rwe] vt: **~ qn de coups** to give sb a thrashing
rouge[Ruʒ] adj, nm/f red ▷ nm red; **(vin) ~** red wine; **sur la liste ~** ex-directory (BRIT), unlisted (US); **passer au ~** (signal) to go red; (automobiliste) to go through a red light; **rouge à joue** blusher; **rouge (à lèvres)** lipstick; **rouge-gorge** nm robin (redbreast)
rougeole[Ruʒɔl] nf measles sg
rougeoyer[Ruʒwaje] vi to glow red
rouget[Ruʒɛ] nm mullet
rougeur[RuʒœR] nf redness; (Méd: tache) red blotch
rougir[RuʒiR] vi to turn red; (de honte, timidité) to blush, flush; (de plaisir, colère) to flush
rouille[Ruj] nf rust; **rouillé, e** adj rusty; **rouiller** vt to rust ▷ vi to rust, go rusty
roulant, e[Rulɑ̃, ɑ̃t] adj (meuble) on wheels; (tapis etc) moving; **escalier ~** escalator
rouleau, x[Rulo] nm roll; (à mise en plis, à peinture, vague) roller; **rouleau à pâtisserie** rolling pin
roulement[Rulmɑ̃] nm (rotation) rotation; (bruit) rumbling no pl, rumble; **travailler par ~** to work on a rota (BRIT) ou rotation (US) basis; **roulement (à billes)** ball bearings pl;

roulement de tambour drum roll
rouler[Rule] vt to roll; (papier, tapis) to roll up; (Culin: pâte) to roll out; (fam: duper) to do, con ▷ vi (bille, boule) to roll; (voiture, train) to go, run; (automobiliste) to drive; (bateau) to roll; **se ~ dans** (boue) to roll in; (couverture) to roll o.s. (up) in
roulette[Rulɛt] nf (de table, fauteuil) castor; (de dentiste) drill; (jeu) roulette; **à ~s** on castors; **ça a marché comme sur des ~s** (fam) it went off very smoothly
roulis[Ruli] nm roll(ing)
roulotte[Rulɔt] nf caravan
roumain, e[Rumɛ̃, ɛn] adj Rumanian ▷ nm/f: **R~, e** Rumanian
Roumanie[Rumani] nf Rumania
rouquin, e[Rukɛ̃, in] (péj) nm/f redhead
rouspéter[Ruspete] (fam) vi to moan
rousse[Rus] adj voir **roux**
roussir[RusiR] vt to scorch ▷ vi (Culin): **faire ~** to brown
route[Rut] nf road; (fig: chemin) way; (itinéraire, parcours) route; (fig: voie) road, path; **il y a 3h de ~** it's a 3-hour ride ou journey; **en ~** on the way; **en ~!** let's go!; **mettre en ~** to start up; **se mettre en ~** to set off; **quelle ~ dois-je prendre pour aller à ...?** which road do I take for ...?; **route nationale** ≈ A road (BRIT), ≈ state highway (US); **routier, -ière** adj road cpd ▷ nm (camionneur) (long-distance) lorry (BRIT) ou truck (US) driver; (restaurant) ≈ transport café (BRIT), ≈ truck stop (US)
routine[Rutin] nf routine; **routinier, -ière** (péj) adj (activité) humdrum; (personne) addicted to routine
rouvrir[RuvRiR] vt, vi to reopen, open again; **se rouvrir** vi to reopen, open again
roux, rousse[Ru, Rus] adj red; (personne) red-haired ▷ nm/f redhead
royal, e, -aux[Rwajal, o] adj royal; (cadeau etc) fit for a king
royaume[Rwajom] nm kingdom; (fig) realm; **le Royaume-Uni** the United Kingdom
royauté[Rwajote] nf (régime) monarchy
ruban[Rybɑ̃] nm ribbon; **ruban adhésif** adhesive tape
rubéole[Rybeɔl] nf German measles sg, rubella
rubis[Rybi] nm ruby
rubrique[RybRik] nf (titre, catégorie) heading; (Presse: article) column
ruche[Ryʃ] nf hive
rude[Ryd] adj (au toucher) rough; (métier, tâche) hard, tough; (climat) severe, harsh; (bourru) harsh, rough; (fruste: manières) rugged, tough; (fam: fameux) jolly good; **rudement** (fam) adv (très) terribly
rudimentaire[Rydimɑ̃tɛR] adj rudimentary, basic

rudiments [ʀydimɑ̃] *nmpl*: **avoir des ~ d'anglais** to have a smattering of English

rue [ʀy] *nf* street

ruée [ʀɥe] *nf* rush

ruelle [ʀɥɛl] *nf* alley(-way)

ruer [ʀɥe] *vi* (*cheval*) to kick out; **se ruer** *vi*: **se ~ sur** to pounce on; **se ~ vers/dans/hors de** to rush *ou* dash towards/into/out of

rugby [ʀygbi] *nm* rugby (football)

rugir [ʀyʒiʀ] *vi* to roar

rugueux, -euse [ʀygø, øz] *adj* rough

ruine [ʀɥin] *nf* ruin; **ruiner** *vt* to ruin; **ruineux, -euse** *adj* ruinous

ruisseau, x [ʀɥiso] *nm* stream, brook

ruisseler [ʀɥis(ə)le] *vi* to stream

rumeur [ʀymœʀ] *nf* (*nouvelle*) rumour; (*bruit confus*) rumbling

ruminer [ʀymine] *vt* (*herbe*) to ruminate; (*fig*) to ruminate on *ou* over, chew over

rupture [ʀyptyʀ] *nf* (*séparation, désunion*) break-up, split; (*de négociations etc*) breakdown; (*de contrat*) breach; (*dans continuité*) break

rural, e, -aux [ʀyʀal, o] *adj* rural, country *cpd*

ruse [ʀyz] *nf*: **la ~** cunning, craftiness; (*pour tromper*) trickery; **une ~** a trick, a ruse; **rusé, e** *adj* cunning, crafty

russe [ʀys] *adj* Russian ▷ *nm/f*: **R~** Russian ▷ *nm* (*Ling*) Russian

Russie [ʀysi] *nf*: **la ~** Russia

rustine® [ʀystin] *nf* rubber repair patch (*for bicycle tyre*)

rustique [ʀystik] *adj* rustic

rythme [ʀitm] *nm* rhythm; (*vitesse*) rate; (: *de la vie*) pace, tempo; **rythmé, e** *adj* rhythmic(al)

S

s' [s] *pron voir* **se**

sa [sa] *adj voir* **son¹**

sable [sabl] *nm* sand

sablé [sable] *nm* shortbread biscuit

sabler [sable] *vt* (*contre le verglas*) to grit; **~ le champagne** to drink champagne

sabot [sabo] *nm* clog; (*de cheval*) hoof; **sabot de frein** brake shoe

saboter [sabɔte] *vt* to sabotage; (*bâcler*) to make a mess of, botch

sac [sak] *nm* bag; (*à charbon etc*) sack; **mettre à ~** to sack; **sac à dos** rucksack; **sac à main** handbag; **sac de couchage** sleeping bag; **sac de voyage** travelling bag

saccadé, e [sakade] *adj* jerky; (*respiration*) spasmodic

saccager [sakaʒe] *vt* (*piller*) to sack; (*dévaster*) to create havoc in

saccharine [sakaʀin] *nf* saccharin

sachet [saʃɛ] *nm* (small) bag; (*de sucre, café*) sachet; **du potage en ~** packet soup; **sachet de thé** tea bag

sacoche [sakɔʃ] *nf* (*gén*) bag; (*de bicyclette*) saddlebag

sacré, e [sakʀe] *adj* sacred; (*fam: satané*) blasted; (: *fameux*): **un ~ toupet** a heck of a cheek

sacrement [sakʀəmɑ̃] *nm* sacrament

sacrifice [sakʀifis] *nm* sacrifice; **sacrifier** *vt* to sacrifice

sacristie [sakʀisti] nf (catholique) sacristy; (protestante) vestry

sadique [sadik] adj sadistic

safran [safʀɑ̃] nm saffron

sage [saʒ] adj wise; (enfant) good

sage-femme [saʒfam] nf midwife

sagesse [saʒɛs] nf wisdom

Sagittaire [saʒiteʀ] nm: **le ~** Sagittarius

Sahara [saaʀa] nm: **le ~** the Sahara (desert)

saignant, e [sɛɲɑ̃, ɑ̃t] adj (viande) rare

saigner [seɲe] vi to bleed ▷ vt to bleed; (animal) to kill (by bleeding); **~ du nez** to have a nosebleed

saillir [sajiʀ] vi to project, stick out; (veine, muscle) to bulge

sain, e [sɛ̃, sɛn] adj healthy; **~ et sauf** safe and sound, unharmed; **~ d'esprit** sound in mind, sane

saindoux [sɛ̃du] nm lard

saint, e [sɛ̃, sɛt] adj holy ▷ nm/f saint; **le Saint Esprit** the Holy Spirit ou Ghost; **la Sainte Vierge** the Blessed Virgin; **la Saint-Sylvestre** New Year's Eve; **sainteté** nf holiness

sais etc [sɛ] vb voir **savoir**

saisie [sezi] nf seizure; **saisie (de données)** (data) capture

saisir [seziʀ] vt to take hold of, grab; (fig: occasion) to seize; (comprendre) to grasp; (entendre) to get, catch; (données) to capture; (Culin) to fry quickly; (Jur: biens, publication) to seize; **saisissant, e** adj startling, striking

saison [sɛzɔ̃] nf season; **haute/basse/morte ~** high/low/slack season; **saisonnier, -ière** adj seasonal

salade [salad] nf (Bot) lettuce etc; (Culin) (green) salad; (fam: confusion) tangle, muddle; **salade composée** mixed salad; **salade de fruits** fruit salad; **saladier** nm (salad) bowl

salaire [saleʀ] nm (annuel, mensuel) salary; (hebdomadaire, journalier) pay, wages pl; **salaire minimum interprofessionnel de croissance** index-linked guaranteed minimum wage

salarié, e [salaʀje] nm/f salaried employee; wage-earner

salaud [salo] (fam!) nm sod (!), bastard (!)

sale [sal] adj dirty, filthy; (fam: mauvais) nasty

salé, e [sale] adj (mer, goût) salty; (Culin: amandes, beurre etc) salted; (: gâteaux) savoury; (fam: grivois) spicy; (: facture) steep

saler [sale] vt to salt

saleté [salte] nf (état) dirtiness; (crasse) dirt, filth; (tache etc) dirt no pl; (fam: méchanceté) dirty trick; (: camelote) rubbish no pl; (: obscénité) filthy thing (to say)

salière [saljɛʀ] nf saltcellar

salir [saliʀ] vt to (make) dirty; (fig: quelqu'un) to soil the reputation of; **se salir** vi to get dirty; **salissant, e** adj (tissu) which shows the dirt;

(travail) dirty, messy

salle [sal] nf room; (d'hôpital) ward; (de restaurant) dining room; (d'un cinéma) auditorium; (: public) audience; **salle à manger** dining room; **salle d'attente** waiting room; **salle de bain(s)** bathroom; **salle de classe** classroom; **salle de concert** concert hall; **salle d'eau** shower-room; **salle d'embarquement** (à l'aéroport) departure lounge; **salle de jeux** (pour enfants) playroom; **salle de séjour** living room; **salle des ventes** saleroom

salon [salɔ̃] nm lounge, sitting room; (mobilier) lounge suite; (exposition) exhibition, show; **salon de coiffure** hairdressing salon; **salon de thé** tearoom

salope [salɔp] (fam!) nf bitch (!); **saloperie** (fam!) nf (action) dirty trick; (chose sans valeur) rubbish no pl

salopette [salɔpɛt] nf dungarees pl; (d'ouvrier) overall(s)

salsifis [salsifi] nm salsify

salubre [salybʀ] adj healthy, salubrious

saluer [salɥe] vt (pour dire bonjour, fig) to greet; (pour dire au revoir) to take one's leave; (Mil) to salute

salut [saly] nm (geste) wave; (parole) greeting; (Mil) salute; (sauvegarde) safety; (Rel) salvation ▷ excl (fam: bonjour) hi (there); (: au revoir) see you, bye

salutations [salytasjɔ̃] nfpl greetings; **Veuillez agréer, Monsieur, mes ~ distinguées** yours faithfully

samedi [samdi] nm Saturday

SAMU [samy] sigle m (= service d'assistance médicale d'urgence) ≈ ambulance (service) (BRIT), ≈ paramedics pl (US)

sanction [sɑ̃ksjɔ̃] nf sanction; **sanctionner** vt (loi, usage) to sanction; (punir) to punish

sandale [sɑ̃dal] nf sandal

sandwich [sɑ̃dwi(t)ʃ] nm sandwich; **je voudrais un ~ au jambon/fromage** I'd like a ham/cheese sandwich

sang [sɑ̃] nm blood; **en ~** covered in blood; **se faire du mauvais ~** to fret, get in a state; **sang-froid** nm calm, sangfroid; **de sang-froid** in cold blood; **sanglant, e** adj bloody

sangle [sɑ̃gl] nf strap

sanglier [sɑ̃glije] nm (wild) boar

sanglot [sɑ̃glo] nm sob; **sangloter** vi to sob

sangsue [sɑ̃sy] nf leech

sanguin, e [sɑ̃gɛ̃, in] adj blood cpd

sanitaire [saniteʀ] adj health cpd; **sanitaires** nmpl (lieu) bathroom sg

sans [sɑ̃] prép without; **un pull ~ manches** a sleeveless jumper; **~ faute** without fail; **~ arrêt** without a break; **~ ça** (fam) otherwise; **~ qu'il s'en aperçoive** without him ou his noticing; **sans-abri** nmpl homeless; **sans-**

emploi nm/f inv unemployed person; **les sans-emploi** the unemployed; **sans-gêne** adj inv inconsiderate

santé [sɑ̃te] nf health; **en bonne ~** in good health; **boire à la ~ de qn** to drink (to) sb's health; **à ta/votre ~!** cheers!

saoudien, ne [saudjɛ̃, jɛn] adj Saudi Arabian ▷ nm/f: **S~, ne** Saudi Arabian

saoul, e [su, sul] adj = **soûl**

saper [sape] vt to undermine, sap

sapeur-pompier [sapœʀpɔ̃pje] nm fireman

saphir [safiʀ] nm sapphire

sapin [sapɛ̃] nm fir (tree); (bois) fir; **sapin de Noël** Christmas tree

sarcastique [saʀkastik] adj sarcastic

Sardaigne [saʀdɛɲ] nf: **la ~** Sardinia

sardine [saʀdin] nf sardine

SARL sigle f (= société à responsabilité limitée) ≈ plc (BRIT), ≈ Inc. (US)

sarrasin [saʀazɛ̃] nm buckwheat

satané, e [satane] (fam) adj confounded

satellite [satelit] nm satellite

satin [satɛ̃] nm satin

satire [satiʀ] nf satire; **satirique** adj satirical

satisfaction [satisfaksjɔ̃] nf satisfaction

satisfaire [satisfɛʀ] vt to satisfy; **~ à** (conditions) to meet; **satisfaisant, e** adj (acceptable) satisfactory; **satisfait, e** adj satisfied; **satisfait de** happy ou satisfied with

saturer [satyʀe] vt to saturate

sauce [sos] nf sauce; (avec un rôti) gravy; **sauce tomate** tomato sauce; **saucière** nf sauceboat

saucisse [sosis] nf sausage

saucisson [sosisɔ̃] nm (slicing) sausage

sauf, sauve [sof, sov] adj unharmed, unhurt; (fig: honneur) intact, saved ▷ prép except; **laisser la vie sauve à qn** to spare sb's life; **~ si** (à moins que) unless; **~ erreur** if I'm not mistaken; **~ avis contraire** unless you hear to the contrary

sauge [soʒ] nf sage

saugrenu, e [sogʀəny] adj preposterous

saule [sol] nm willow (tree)

saumon [somɔ̃] nm salmon inv

saupoudrer [sopudʀe] vt: **~ qch de** to sprinkle sth with

saur [sɔʀ] adj m: **hareng ~** smoked herring, kipper

saut [so] nm jump; (discipline sportive) jumping; **faire un ~ chez qn** to pop over to sb's (place); **saut à l'élastique** bungee jumping; **saut à la perche** pole vaulting; **saut en hauteur/longueur** high/long jump; **saut périlleux** somersault

sauter [sote] vi to jump, leap; (exploser) to blow up, explode; (: fusibles) to blow; (se détacher) to pop out (ou off) ▷ vt to jump (over), leap (over); (fig: omettre) to skip, miss

(out); **faire ~** to blow up; (Culin) to sauté; **~ à la corde** to skip; **~ au cou de qn** to fly into sb's arms; **~ sur une occasion** to jump at an opportunity; **~ aux yeux** to be (quite) obvious

sauterelle [sotʀɛl] nf grasshopper

sautiller [sotije] vi (oiseau) to hop; (enfant) to skip

sauvage [sovaʒ] adj (gén) wild; (peuplade) savage; (farouche: personne) unsociable; (barbare) wild, savage; (non officiel) unauthorized, unofficial; **faire du camping ~** to camp in the wild ▷ nm/f savage; (timide) unsociable type

sauve [sov] adj f voir **sauf**

sauvegarde [sovgaʀd] nf safeguard; (Inform) backup; **sauvegarder** vt to safeguard; (Inform: enregistrer) to save; (: copier) to back up

sauve-qui-peut [sovkipø] excl run for your life!

sauver [sove] vt to save; (porter secours à) to rescue; (récupérer) to salvage, rescue; **se sauver** vi (s'enfuir) to run away; (fam: partir) to be off; **sauvetage** nm rescue; **sauveteur** nm rescuer; **sauvette: à la sauvette** adv (se marier etc) hastily, hurriedly; **sauveur** nm saviour (BRIT), savior (US)

savant, e [savɑ̃, ɑ̃t] adj scholarly, learned ▷ nm scientist

saveur [savœʀ] nf flavour; (fig) savour

savoir [savwaʀ] vt to know; (être capable de): **il sait nager** he can swim ▷ nm knowledge; **se savoir** vi (être connu) to be known; **je ne sais pas** I don't know; **je ne sais pas parler français** I don't speak French; **savez-vous où je peux ...?** do you know where I can ...?; **je n'en sais rien** I (really) don't know; **à ~** that is, namely; **faire ~ qch à qn** to let sb know sth; **pas que je sache** not as far as I know

savon [savɔ̃] nm (produit) soap; (morceau) bar of soap; (fam): **passer un ~ à qn** to give sb a good dressing-down; **savonner** vt to soap; **savonnette** nf bar of soap

savourer [savuʀe] vt to savour; **savoureux, -euse** adj tasty; (fig: anecdote) spicy, juicy

saxo(phone) [saksɔ(fɔn)] nm sax(ophone)

scabreux, -euse [skabʀø, øz] adj risky; (indécent) improper, shocking

scandale [skɑ̃dal] nm scandal; **faire un ~** (scène) to make a scene; (Jur) to create a disturbance; **faire ~** to scandalize people; **scandaleux, -euse** adj scandalous, outrageous

scandinave [skɑ̃dinav] adj Scandinavian ▷ nm/f: **S~** Scandinavian

Scandinavie [skɑ̃dinavi] nf Scandinavia

scarabée [skaʀabe] nm beetle

scarlatine [skaʀlatin] nf scarlet fever

scarole [skaʀɔl] nf endive

sceau, x [so] nm seal

sceller [sele] *vt* to seal

scénario [senarjo] *nm* scenario

scène [sɛn] *nf* (*gén*) scene; (*estrade, fig: théâtre*) stage; **entrer en ~** to come on stage; **mettre en ~** (*Théâtre*) to stage; (*Cinéma*) to direct; **faire une ~ (à qn)** to make a scene (with sb); **scène de ménage** domestic scene

sceptique [sɛptik] *adj* sceptical

schéma [ʃema] *nm* (*diagramme*) diagram, sketch; **schématique** *adj* diagrammatic(al), schematic; (*fig*) oversimplified

sciatique [sjatik] *nf* sciatica

scie [si] *nf* saw

sciemment [sjamɑ̃] *adv* knowingly

science [sjɑ̃s] *nf* science; (*savoir*) knowledge; **sciences humaines/sociales** social sciences; **sciences naturelles** (*Scol*) natural science *sg*, biology *sg*; **sciences po** political science *ou* studies *pl*; **science-fiction** *nf* science fiction; **scientifique** *adj* scientific ▷ *nm/f* scientist; (*étudiant*) science student

scier [sje] *vt* to saw; (*retrancher*) to saw off; **scierie** *nf* sawmill

scintiller [sɛ̃tije] *vi* to sparkle; (*étoile*) to twinkle

sciure [sjyr] *nf*: **~ (de bois)** sawdust

sclérose [skleroz] *nf*: **sclérose en plaques** multiple sclerosis

scolaire [skɔlɛr] *adj* school *cpd*; **scolariser** *vt* to provide with schooling/schools; **scolarité** *nf* schooling

scooter [skutœr] *nm* (motor) scooter

score [skɔr] *nm* score

scorpion [skɔrpjɔ̃] *nm* (*signe*): **le S~** Scorpio

scotch [skɔtʃ] *nm* (*whisky*) scotch, whisky; **S~®** (*adhésif*) Sellotape® (BRIT), Scotch® tape (US)

scout, e [skut] *adj, nm* scout

script [skript] *nm* (*écriture*) printing; (*Cinéma*) (shooting) script

scrupule [skrypyl] *nm* scruple

scruter [skryte] *vt* to scrutinize; (*l'obscurité*) to peer into

scrutin [skrytɛ̃] *nm* (*vote*) ballot; (*ensemble des opérations*) poll

sculpter [skylte] *vt* to sculpt; (*bois*) to carve; **sculpteur** *nm* sculptor; **sculpture** *nf* sculpture

SDF *sigle m*: **sans domicile fixe** homeless person; **les ~** the homeless

 MOT-CLÉ

se [sə], **s'** *pron* **1** (*emploi réfléchi*) oneself; (: *masc*) himself; (: *fém*) herself; (: *sujet non humain*) itself; (: *pl*) themselves; **se savonner** to soap o.s.
2 (*réciproque*) one another, each other; **ils s'aiment** they love one another *ou* each other
3 (*passif*): **cela se répare facilement** it is easily repaired
4 (*possessif*): **se casser la jambe/se laver les mains** to break one's leg/wash one's hands

séance [seɑ̃s] *nf* (*d'assemblée*) meeting, session; (*de tribunal*) sitting, session; (*musicale, Cinéma, Théâtre*) performance

seau, x [so] *nm* bucket, pail

sec, sèche [sɛk, sɛʃ] *adj* dry; (*raisins, figues*) dried; (*cœur: insensible*) hard, cold ▷ *nm*: **tenir au ~** to keep in a dry place ▷ *adv* hard; **je le bois ~** I drink it straight *ou* neat; **à ~** (*puits*) dried up

sécateur [sekatœr] *nm* secateurs *pl* (BRIT), shears *pl*

sèche [sɛʃ] *adj f voir* **sec**; **sèche-cheveux** *nm inv* hair-drier; **sèche-linge** *nm inv* tumble dryer; **sèchement** *adv* (*répondre*) drily

sécher [seʃe] *vt* to dry; (*dessécher: peau, figues*) to dry (out); (: *étang*) to dry up; (*fam: cours*) to skip ▷ *vi* to dry; to dry out; to dry up; (*fam: candidat*) to be stumped; **se sécher** (*après le bain*) to dry o.s.; **sécheresse** *nf* dryness; (*absence de pluie*) drought; **séchoir** *nm* drier

second, e¹ [s(ə)ɡɔ̃, ɔ̃d] *adj* second ▷ *nm* (*assistant*) second in command; (*Navig*) first mate ▷ *nf* (*Scol*) year 11 (BRIT), tenth grade (US); (*Aviat, Rail etc*) second class; **voyager en ~e** to travel second-class; **secondaire** *adj* secondary; **seconde²** *nf* second; **seconder** *vt* to assist

secouer [s(ə)kwe] *vt* to shake; (*passagers*) to rock; (*traumatiser*) to shake (up)

secourir [s(ə)kurir] *vt* (*venir en aide à*) to assist, aid; **secourisme** *nm* first aid; **secouriste** *nm/f* first-aid worker

secours [s(ə)kur] *nm* help, aid, assistance ▷ *nmpl* aid *sg*; **au ~!** help!; **appeler au ~** to shout *ou* call for help; **porter ~ à qn** to give sb assistance, help sb; **les premiers ~** first aid *sg*

● **ÉQUIPES DE SECOURS**
●
● Emergency phone numbers can be dialled
● free from public phones. For the police
● ('la police') dial 17; for medical services ('le
● SAMU') dial 15; for the fire brigade ('les
● sapeurs pompiers'), dial 18.

secousse [s(ə)kus] *nf* jolt, bump; (*électrique*) shock; (*fig: psychologique*) jolt, shock

secret, -ète [səkrɛ, ɛt] *adj* secret; (*fig: renfermé*) reticent, reserved ▷ *nm* secret; (*discrétion absolue*): **le ~** secrecy; **en ~** in secret, secretly; **secret professionel** professional secrecy

secrétaire [s(ə)kretɛr] *nm/f* secretary ▷ *nm* (*meuble*) writing desk; **secrétaire de direction** private *ou* personal secretary; **secrétaire**

d'État junior minister; **secrétariat** nm
(profession) secretarial work; (bureau) office;
(: d'organisation internationale) secretariat

secteur [sɛktœʀ] nm sector; (zone) area;
(Élec): **branché sur ~** plugged into the mains
(supply)

section [sɛksjɔ̃] nf section; (de parcours
d'autobus) fare stage; (Mil: unité) platoon;
sectionner vt to sever

sécu [seky] abrf = **sécurité sociale**

sécurité [sekyʀite] nf (absence de danger)
safety; (absence de troubles) security; **système
de ~** security system; **être en ~** to be safe; **la
sécurité routière** road safety; **la sécurité
sociale** ≈ (the) Social Security (BRIT), ≈ Welfare
(US)

sédentaire [sedɑ̃tɛʀ] adj sedentary

séduction [sedyksjɔ̃] nf seduction; (charme,
attrait) appeal, charm

séduire [seduiʀ] vt to charm; (femme: abuser
de) to seduce; **séduisant, e** adj (femme)
seductive; (homme, offre) very attractive

ségrégation [segʀegasjɔ̃] nf segregation

seigle [sɛgl] nm rye

seigneur [sɛɲœʀ] nm lord

sein [sɛ̃] nm breast; (entrailles) womb; **au ~ de**
(équipe, institution) within

séisme [seism] nm earthquake

seize [sɛz] num sixteen; **seizième** num
sixteenth

séjour [seʒuʀ] nm stay; (pièce) living room;
séjourner vi to stay

sel [sɛl] nm salt; (fig: piquant) spice

sélection [selɛksjɔ̃] nf selection;
sélectionner vt to select

self-service [sɛlfsɛʀvis] adj, nm self-service

selle [sɛl] nf saddle; **selles** nfpl (Méd) stools;
seller vt to saddle

selon [s(ə)lɔ̃] prép according to; (en se
conformant à) in accordance with; **~ que**
according to whether; **~ moi** as I see it

semaine [s(ə)mɛn] nf week; **en ~** during the
week, on weekdays

semblable [sɑ̃blabl] adj similar; (de ce genre):
de ~s mésaventures such mishaps ▷ nm
fellow creature ou man; **~ à** similar to, like

semblant [sɑ̃blɑ̃] nm: **un ~ de ...** a semblance
of ...; **faire ~ (de faire)** to pretend (to do)

sembler [sɑ̃ble] vb +attrib to seem ▷ vb impers:
il semble (bien) que/inutile de it (really)
seems ou appears that/useless to; **il me
semble que** it seems to me that; **comme bon
lui semble** as he sees fit

semelle [s(ə)mɛl] nf sole; (intérieure) insole,
inner sole

semer [s(ə)me] vt to sow; (fig: éparpiller)
to scatter; (: confusion) to spread; (fam:
poursuivants) to lose, shake off; **semé de**
(difficultés) riddled with

semestre [s(ə)mɛstʀ] nm half-year; (Scol)
semester

séminaire [seminɛʀ] nm seminar

semi-remorque [səmiʀəmɔʀk] nm
articulated lorry (BRIT), semi(trailer) (US)

semoule [s(ə)mul] nf semolina

sénat [sena] nm senate; **sénateur** nm senator

Sénégal [senegal] nm: **le ~** Senegal

sens [sɑ̃s] nm (Physiol.) sense; (signification)
meaning, sense; (direction) direction; **à mon
~** to my mind; **dans le ~ des aiguilles d'une
montre** clockwise; **dans le ~ contraire des
aiguilles d'une montre** anticlockwise; **dans
le mauvais ~** (aller) the wrong way, in the
wrong direction; **le bon ~** common sense;
sens dessus dessous upside down; **sens
interdit/unique** one-way street

sensation [sɑ̃sasjɔ̃] nf sensation; **à ~** (péj)
sensational; **faire ~** to cause ou create
a sensation; **sensationnel, le** adj (fam)
fantastic, terrific

sensé, e [sɑ̃se] adj sensible

sensibiliser [sɑ̃sibilize] vt: **~ qn à** to make sb
sensitive to

sensibilité [sɑ̃sibilite] nf sensitivity

sensible [sɑ̃sibl] adj sensitive; (aux sens)
perceptible; (appréciable: différence, progrès)
appreciable, noticeable; **~ à** sensitive to;
sensiblement adv (à peu près): **ils sont
sensiblement du même âge** they are
approximately the same age; **sensiblerie** nf
sentimentality

> Attention à ne pas traduire **sensible** par
> le mot anglais **sensible**.

sensuel, le [sɑ̃suɛl] adj (personne) sensual;
(musique) sensuous

sentence [sɑ̃tɑ̃s] nf (jugement) sentence

sentier [sɑ̃tje] nm path

sentiment [sɑ̃timɑ̃] nm feeling; **recevez
mes ~s respectueux** (personne nommée)
yours sincerely; (personne non nommée)
yours faithfully; **sentimental, e, -aux** adj
sentimental; (vie, aventure) love cpd

sentinelle [sɑ̃tinɛl] nf sentry

sentir [sɑ̃tiʀ] vt (par l'odorat) to smell; (par le
goût) to taste; (au toucher, fig) to feel; (répandre
une odeur de) to smell of; (: ressemblance) to
smell like ▷ vi to smell; **~ mauvais** to smell
bad; **se ~ bien** to feel good; **se ~ mal** (être
indisposé) to feel unwell ou ill; **se ~ le courage/
la force de faire** to feel brave/strong enough
to do; **il ne peut pas le ~** (fam) he can't stand
him; **je ne me sens pas bien** I don't feel well

séparation [sepaʀasjɔ̃] nf separation;
(cloison) division, partition

séparé, e [sepaʀe] adj (distinct) separate;
(époux) separated; **séparément** adv
separately

séparer [sepaʀe] vt to separate; (désunir) to

drive apart; *(détacher):* **~ qch de** to pull sth (off) from; **se séparer** *vi (époux, amis)* to separate, part; *(se diviser: route etc)* to divide; **se ~ de** *(époux)* to separate *ou* part from; *(employé, objet personnel)* to part with

sept[sɛt] *num* seven; **septante**(BELGIQUE, SUISSE) *adj inv* seventy

septembre[sɛptɑ̃br] *nm* September

septicémie[sɛptisemi] *nf* blood poisoning, septicaemia

septième[sɛtjɛm] *num* seventh

séquelles[sekɛl] *nfpl* after-effects; *(fig)* aftermath *sg*

serbe[sɛrb(ə)] *adj* Serbian

Serbie[sɛrbi] *nf:* **la ~** Serbia

serein, e[sərɛ̃, ɛn] *adj* serene

sergent[sɛrʒɑ̃] *nm* sergeant

série[seri] *nf* series *inv; (de clés, casseroles, outils)* set; *(catégorie: Sport)* rank; **en ~** in quick succession; *(Comm)* mass *cpd;* **de ~** *(voiture)* standard; **hors ~** *(Comm)* custom-built; **série noire**(crime) thriller

sérieusement[serjøzmɑ̃] *adv* seriously

sérieux, -euse[serjø, jøz] *adj* serious; *(élève, employé)* reliable, responsible; *(client, maison)* reliable, dependable ▷ *nm* seriousness; *(d'une entreprise etc)* reliability; **garder son ~** to keep a straight face; **prendre qch/qn au ~** to take sth/sb seriously

serin[s(ə)rɛ̃] *nm* canary

seringue[s(ə)rɛ̃g] *nf* syringe

serment[sɛrmɑ̃] *nm (juré)* oath; *(promesse)* pledge, vow

sermon[sɛrmɔ̃] *nm* sermon

séropositif, -ive[seropozitif, iv] *adj (Méd)* HIV positive

serpent[sɛrpɑ̃] *nm* snake; **serpenter** *vi* to wind

serpillière[sɛrpijɛr] *nf* floorcloth

serre[sɛr] *nf (Agr)* greenhouse; **serres** *nfpl* *(griffes)* claws, talons

serré, e[sere] *adj (habits)* tight; *(fig: lutte, match)* tight, close-fought; *(passagers etc)* (tightly) packed; *(réseau)* dense; **avoir le cœur ~** to have a heavy heart

serrer[sere] *vt (tenir)* to grip *ou* hold tight; *(comprimer, coincer)* to squeeze; *(poings, mâchoires)* to clench; *(suj: vêtement)* to be too tight for; *(ceinture, nœud, vis)* to tighten ▷ *vi:* **~ à droite** to keep *ou* get over to the right

serrure[seryr] *nf* lock; **serrurier** *nm* locksmith

sert *etc* [sɛr] *vb voir* **servir**

servante[sɛrvɑ̃t] *nf (maid)*servant

serveur, -euse[sɛrvœr, øz] *nm/f* waiter (waitress)

serviable[sɛrvjabl] *adj* obliging, willing to help

service[sɛrvis] *nm* service; *(assortiment de* vaisselle) set, service; *(bureau: de la vente etc)* department, section; *(travail)* duty; **premier ~** *(série de repas)* first sitting; **être de ~** to be on duty; **faire le ~** to serve; **rendre un ~ à qn** to do sb a favour; *(objet: s'avérer utile)* to come in useful *ou* handy for sb; **mettre en ~** to put into service *ou* operation; **~ compris/non compris** service included/not included; **hors ~** out of order; **service après vente**after sales service; **service d'ordre**police *(ou* stewards) in charge of maintaining order; **service militaire** military service; *see note;* **services secrets** secret service *sg*

serviette[sɛrvjɛt] *nf (de table)* (table) napkin, serviette; *(de toilette)* towel; *(porte-documents)* briefcase; **serviette hygiénique**sanitary towel

servir[sɛrvir] *vt* to serve; *(au restaurant)* to wait on; *(au magasin)* to serve, attend to ▷ *vi* *(Tennis)* to serve; *(Cartes)* to deal; **se servir** *vi* *(prendre d'un plat)* to help o.s.; **vous êtes servi?** are you being served?; **~ à qn** *(diplôme, livre)* to be of use to sb; **~ à qch/faire** *(outil etc)* to be used for sth/doing; **ça ne sert à rien** it's no use; **~ (à qn) de** to serve as (for sb); **se ~ de** *(plat)* to help o.s. to; *(voiture, outil, relations)* to use; **sers-toi!** help yourself!

serviteur[sɛrvitœr] *nm* servant

ses[se] *adj voir* **son**

seuil[sœj] *nm* doorstep; *(fig)* threshold

seul, e[sœl] *adj (sans compagnie)* alone; *(unique)* **un ~ livre** only one book, a single book ▷ *adv (vivre)* alone, on one's own ▷ *nm,* *nf:* **il en reste un(e) ~(e)** there's only one left; **le ~ livre** the only book; **parler tout ~** to talk to oneself; **faire qch (tout) ~** to do sth (all) on one's own *ou* (all) by oneself; **à**

lui (tout) ~ single-handed, on his own; **se sentir ~** to feel lonely; **seulement** adv only; **non seulement ... mais aussi** ou **encore** not only ... but also
sève [sɛv] nf sap
sévère [sevɛʀ] adj severe
sexe [sɛks] nm sex; (organes génitaux) genitals, sex organs; **sexuel, le** adj sexual
shampooing [ʃɑ̃pwɛ̃] nm shampoo
Shetland [ʃɛtlɑ̃d] n: **les îles ~** the Shetland Islands, Shetland
short [ʃɔʀt] nm (pair of) shorts pl

MOT-CLÉ

si [si] adv 1 (oui) yes; **"Paul n'est pas venu" — "si!"** "Paul hasn't come" — "yes, he has!"; **je vous assure que si** I assure you he did ou she is etc
2 (tellement) so; **si gentil/rapidement** so kind/fast; **(tant et) si bien que** so much so that; **si rapide qu'il soit** however fast he may be
▷ conj if; **si tu veux** if you want; **je me demande si** I wonder if ou whether; **si seulement** if only
▷ nm (Mus) B; (en chantant la gamme) ti

Sicile [sisil] nf: **la ~** Sicily
SIDA [sida] sigle m (= syndrome immuno-déficitaire acquis) AIDS sg
sidéré, e [sidere] adj staggered
sidérurgie [sideʀyʀʒi] nf steel industry
siècle [sjɛkl] nm century
siège [sjɛʒ] nm seat; (d'entreprise) head office; (d'organisation) headquarters pl; (Mil) siege; **siège social** registered office; **siéger** vi to sit
sien, ne [sjɛ̃, sjɛn] pron: **le(la) ~(ne), les ~(ne)s** (homme) his; (femme) hers; (chose, animal) its
sieste [sjɛst] nf (afternoon) snooze ou nap; **faire la ~** to have a snooze ou nap
sifflement [sifləmɑ̃] nm: **un ~** a whistle
siffler [sifle] vi (gén) to whistle; (en respirant) to wheeze; (serpent, vapeur) to hiss ▷ vt (chanson) to whistle; (chien etc) to whistle for; (fille) to whistle at; (pièce, orateur) to hiss, boo; (fin du match, départ) to blow one's whistle for; (fam: verre) to guzzle
sifflet [siflɛ] nm whistle; **coup de ~** whistle
siffloter [siflɔte] vi, vt to whistle
sigle [sigl] nm acronym
signal, -aux [siɲal, o] nm signal; (indice, écriteau) sign; **donner le ~ de** to give the signal for; **signal d'alarme** alarm signal; **signalement** nm description, particulars pl
signaler [siɲale] vt to indicate; (personne: faire un signe) to signal; (vol, perte) to report; (faire remarquer): **~ qch à qn/(à qn) que** to point out

sth to sb/(to sb) that; **je voudrais ~ un vol** I'd like to report a theft
signature [siɲatyʀ] nf signature; (action) signing
signe [siɲ] nm sign; (Typo) mark; **faire un ~ de la main** to give a sign with one's hand; **faire ~ à qn** (fig: contacter) to get in touch with sb; **faire ~ à qn d'entrer** to motion (to) sb to come in; **signer** vt to sign; **se signer** vi to cross o.s.; **où dois-je signer?** where do I sign?
significatif, -ive [siɲifikatif, iv] adj significant
signification [siɲifikasjɔ̃] nf meaning
signifier [siɲifje] vt (vouloir dire) to mean; (faire connaître): **~ qch (à qn)** to make sth known (to sb)
silence [silɑ̃s] nm silence; (Mus) rest; **garder le ~** to keep silent, say nothing; **silencieux, -euse** adj quiet, silent ▷ nm silencer
silhouette [silwɛt] nf outline, silhouette; (allure) figure
sillage [sijaʒ] nm wake
sillon [sijɔ̃] nm furrow; (de disque) groove; **sillonner** vt to criss-cross
simagrées [simagʀe] nfpl fuss sg
similaire [similɛʀ] adj similar; **similicuir** nm imitation leather; **similitude** nf similarity
simple [sɛ̃pl] adj simple; (non multiple) single ▷ nm: **~ messieurs/dames** men's/ladies' singles sg ▷ nm/f: **~ d'esprit** simpleton
simplicité [sɛ̃plisite] nf simplicity; **en toute ~** quite simply
simplifier [sɛ̃plifje] vt to simplify
simuler [simyle] vt to sham, simulate
simultané, e [simyltane] adj simultaneous
sincère [sɛ̃sɛʀ] adj sincere; **sincèrement** adv sincerely; (pour parler franchement) honestly, really; **sincérité** nf sincerity
Singapour [sɛ̃gapuʀ] nm Singapore
singe [sɛ̃ʒ] nm monkey; (de grande taille) ape; **singer** vt to ape, mimic; **singeries** nfpl antics
singulariser [sɛ̃gylaʀize]: **se singulariser** vi to call attention to o.s.
singularité [sɛ̃gylaʀite] nf peculiarity
singulier, -ière [sɛ̃gylje, jɛʀ] adj remarkable, singular ▷ nm singular
sinistre [sinistʀ] adj sinister ▷ nm (incendie) blaze; (catastrophe) disaster; (Assurances) damage (giving rise to a claim); **sinistré, e** adj disaster-stricken ▷ nm/f disaster victim
sinon [sinɔ̃] conj (autrement, sans quoi) otherwise, or else; (sauf) except, other than; (si ce n'est) if not
sinueux, -euse [sinɥø, øz] adj winding
sinus [sinys] nm (Anat) sinus; (Géom) sine; **sinusite** nf sinusitis
sirène [siʀɛn] nf siren; **sirène d'alarme** fire alarm; (en temps de guerre) air-raid siren
sirop [siʀo] nm (à diluer: de fruit etc) syrup;

(*pharmaceutique*) syrup, mixture; **~ pour la toux** cough mixture

siroter [siʀɔte] vt to sip

sismique [sismik] adj seismic

site [sit] nm (*paysage, environnement*) setting; (*d'une ville etc: emplacement*) site; **site (pittoresque)** beauty spot; **sites touristiques** places of interest; **site Web** (*Inform*) website

sitôt [sito] adv: **~ parti** as soon as he *etc* had left; **~ que** as soon as; **pas de ~** not for a long time

situation [situasjɔ̃] nf situation; (*d'un édifice, d'une ville*) position, location; **situation de famille** marital status

situé, e [situe] adj situated

situer [situe] vt to site, situate; (*en pensée*) to set, place; **se situer** vi to be situated

six [sis] num six; **sixième** num sixth ▷ nf (*Scol*) year 7 (*BRIT*), sixth grade (*US*)

skaï® [skaj] nm Leatherette®

ski [ski] nm (*objet*) ski; (*sport*) skiing; **faire du ~** to ski; **ski de fond** cross-country skiing; **ski nautique** water-skiing; **ski de piste** downhill skiing; **ski de randonnée** cross-country skiing; **skier** vi to ski; **skieur, -euse** nm/f skier

slip [slip] nm (*sous-vêtement*) pants pl, briefs pl; (*de bain: d'homme*) trunks pl; (: *du bikini*) (bikini) briefs pl

slogan [slɔgɑ̃] nm slogan

Slovaquie [slɔvaki] nf: **la ~** Slovakia

SMIC [smik] sigle m = **salaire minimum interprofessionnel de croissance**

smoking [smɔkiŋ] nm dinner *ou* evening suit

SMS sigle m (= *short message service*) (*service*) SMS; (*message*) text message

SNCF sigle f (= *Société nationale des chemins de fer français*) French railways

snob [snɔb] adj snobbish ▷ nm/f snob; **snobisme** nm snobbery, snobbishness

sobre [sɔbʀ] adj (*personne*) temperate, abstemious; (*élégance, style*) sober

sobriquet [sɔbʀikɛ] nm nickname

social, e, -aux [sɔsjal, jo] adj social

socialisme [sɔsjalism] nm socialism; **socialiste** nm/f socialist

société [sɔsjete] nf society; (*sportive*) club; (*Comm*) company; **la ~ de consommation** the consumer society; **société anonyme** ≈ limited (*BRIT*) *ou* incorporated (*US*) company

sociologie [sɔsjɔlɔʒi] nf sociology

socle [sɔkl] nm (*de colonne, statue*) plinth, pedestal; (*de lampe*) base

socquette [sɔkɛt] nf ankle sock

sœur [sœʀ] nf sister; (*religieuse*) nun, sister

soi [swa] pron oneself; **en ~** (*intrinsèquement*) in itself; **cela va de ~** that *ou* it goes without saying; **soi-disant** adj inv so-called ▷ adv supposedly

soie [swa] nf silk; **soierie** nf (*tissu*) silk

soif [swaf] nf thirst; **avoir ~** to be thirsty; **donner ~ à qn** to make sb thirsty

soigné, e [swaɲe] adj (*tenue*) well-groomed, neat; (*travail*) careful, meticulous

soigner [swaɲe] vt (*malade, maladie: suj: docteur*) to treat; (*suj: infirmière, mère*) to nurse, look after; (*travail, détails*) to take care over; (*jardin, invités*) to look after; **soigneux, -euse** adj (*propre*) tidy, neat; (*appliqué*) painstaking, careful

soi-même [swamɛm] pron oneself

soin [swɛ̃] nm (*application*) care; (*propreté, ordre*) tidiness, neatness; **soins** nmpl (*à un malade, blessé*) treatment sg, medical attention sg; (*hygiène*) care sg; **prendre ~ de** to take care of, look after; **prendre ~ de faire** to take care to do; **les premiers ~s** first aid sg

soir [swaʀ] nm evening; **ce ~** this evening, tonight; **à ce ~!** see you this evening (*ou* tonight)!; **sept/dix heures du ~** seven in the evening/ten at night; **demain ~** tomorrow evening, tomorrow night; **soirée** nf evening; (*réception*) party

soit¹ [swa] vb voir **être** ▷ conj (*à savoir*) namely; (*ou*): **~ ... ~** either ... or; **~ que ... ~ que** *ou* **ou que** whether ... or whether

soit² [swat] adv so be it, very well

soixantaine [swasɑ̃tɛn] nf: **une ~ (de)** sixty or so, about sixty; **avoir la ~** (*âge*) to be around sixty

soixante [swasɑ̃t] num sixty; **soixante-dix** num seventy

soja [sɔʒa] nm soya; (*graines*) soya beans pl; **germes de ~** beansprouts

sol [sɔl] nm ground; (*de logement*) floor; (*Agr*) soil; (*Mus*) G; (: *en chantant la gamme*) so(h)

solaire [sɔlɛʀ] adj (*énergie etc*) solar; (*crème etc*) sun cpd

soldat [sɔlda] nm soldier

solde [sɔld] nf pay ▷ nm (*Comm*) balance; **soldes** nm *ou* f pl (*articles*) sale goods; (*vente*) sales; **en ~** at sale price; **solder** vt (*marchandise*) to sell at sale price, sell off

sole [sɔl] nf sole inv (*fish*)

soleil [sɔlej] nm sun; (*lumière*) sun(light); (*temps ensoleillé*) sun(shine); **il fait du ~** it's sunny; **au ~** in the sun

solennel, le [sɔlanɛl] adj solemn

solfège [sɔlfɛʒ] nm musical theory

solidaire [sɔlidɛʀ] adj: **être ~s** to show solidarity, stand *ou* stick together; **être ~ de** (*collègues*) to stand by; **solidarité** nf solidarity; **par solidarité (avec)** in sympathy (with)

solide [sɔlid] adj solid; (*mur, maison, meuble*) solid, sturdy; (*connaissances, argument*) sound; (*personne, estomac*) robust, sturdy ▷ nm solid

soliste [sɔlist] nm/f soloist

solitaire [sɔlitɛʀ] adj (*sans compagnie*) solitary,

lonely; (*lieu*) lonely ▷ *nm/f* (*ermite*) recluse; (*fig: ours*) loner

solitude [sɔlityd] *nf* loneliness; (*tranquillité*) solitude

solliciter [sɔlisite] *vt* (*personne*) to appeal to; (*emploi, faveur*) to seek

sollicitude [sɔlisityd] *nf* concern

soluble [sɔlybl] *adj* soluble

solution [sɔlysjɔ̃] *nf* solution; **solution de facilité** easy way out

solvable [sɔlvabl] *adj* solvent

sombre [sɔ̃bʀ] *adj* dark; (*fig*) gloomy; **sombrer** *vi* (*bateau*) to sink; **sombrer dans** (*misère, désespoir*) to sink into

sommaire [sɔmɛʀ] *adj* (*simple*) basic; (*expéditif*) summary ▷ *nm* summary

somme [sɔm] *nf* (*Math*) sum; (*quantité*) amount; (*argent*) sum, amount ▷ *nm*: **faire un ~** to have a (short) nap; **en ~** all in all; **~ toute** all in all

sommeil [sɔmɛj] *nm* sleep; **avoir ~** to be sleepy; **sommeiller** *vi* to doze

sommet [sɔmɛ] *nm* top; (*d'une montagne*) summit, top; (*fig: de la perfection, gloire*) height

sommier [sɔmje] *nm* (*bed*) base

somnambule [sɔmnɑ̃byl] *nm/f* sleepwalker

somnifère [sɔmnifɛʀ] *nm* sleeping drug *no pl* (*ou* pill)

somnoler [sɔmnɔle] *vi* to doze

somptueux, -euse [sɔ̃ptɥø, øz] *adj* sumptuous

son¹, sa [sɔ̃, sa] (*pl* **ses**) *adj* (*antécédent humain: mâle*) his; (: *femelle*) her; (: *valeur indéfinie*) one's, his/her; (*antécédent non humain*) its

son² [sɔ̃] *nm* sound; (*de blé*) bran

sondage [sɔ̃daʒ] *nm*: **sondage (d'opinion)** (opinion) poll

sonde [sɔ̃d] *nf* (*Navig*) lead *ou* sounding line; (*Méd*) probe; (*Tech: de forage*) borer, driller

sonder [sɔ̃de] *vt* (*Navig*) to sound; (*Tech*) to bore, drill; (*fig: personne*) to sound out; **~ le terrain** (*fig*) to test the ground

songe [sɔ̃ʒ] *nm* dream; **songer** *vi*: **songer à** (*penser à*) to think over; (*envisager*) to consider, think of; **songer que** to think that; **songeur, -euse** *adj* pensive

sonnant, e [sɔnɑ̃, ɑ̃t] *adj*: **à 8 heures ~es** on the stroke of 8

sonné, e [sɔne] *adj* (*fam*) cracked; **il est midi ~** it's gone twelve

sonner [sɔne] *vi* to ring ▷ *vt* (*cloche*) to ring; (*glas, tocsin*) to sound; (*portier, infirmière*) to ring for; **~ faux** (*instrument*) to sound out of tune; (*rire*) to ring false

sonnerie [sɔnʀi] *nf* (*son*) ringing; (*sonnette*) bell; (*de portable*) ringtone; **sonnerie d'alarme** alarm bell

sonnette [sɔnɛt] *nf* bell; **sonnette d'alarme** alarm bell

sonore [sɔnɔʀ] *adj* (*voix*) sonorous, ringing; (*salle*) resonant; (*film, signal*) sound *cpd*; **sonorisation** *nf* (*équipement: de salle de conférences*) public address system, P.A. system; (: *de discothèque*) sound system; **sonorité** *nf* (*de piano, violon*) tone; (*d'une salle*) acoustics *pl*

sophistiqué, e [sɔfistike] *adj* sophisticated

sorbet [sɔʀbɛ] *nm* water ice, sorbet

sorcier [sɔʀsje] *nm* sorcerer

sordide [sɔʀdid] *adj* (*lieu*) squalid; (*action*) sordid

sort [sɔʀ] *nm* (*destinée*) fate; (*condition*) lot; (*magique*) curse, spell; **tirer au ~** to draw lots

sorte [sɔʀt] *nf* sort, kind; **de la ~** in that way; **de (telle) ~ que; en quelque ~** in a way; **faire en ~ que** to see to it that; **quelle ~ de …?** what kind of …?

sortie [sɔʀti] *nf* (*issue*) way out, exit; (*remarque drôle*) sally; (*promenade*) outing; (*le soir: au restaurant etc*) night out; (*Comm: d'un disque*) release; (: *d'un livre*) publication; (: *d'un modèle*) launching; **où est la ~?** where's the exit?; **sortie de bain** (*vêtement*) bathrobe

sortilège [sɔʀtilɛʒ] *nm* (*magic*) spell

sortir [sɔʀtiʀ] *vi* (*gén*) to come out; (*partir, se promener, aller au spectacle*) to go out; (*numéro gagnant*) to come up ▷ *vt* (*gén*) to take out; (*produit, modèle*) to bring out; (*fam: dire*) to come out with; **~ avec qn** to be going out with sb; **s'en ~** (*malade*) to pull through; (*d'une difficulté etc*) to get through; **~ de** (*endroit*) to go (*ou* come) out of, leave; (*provenir de*) to come from; (*compétence*) to be outside

sosie [sɔzi] *nm* double

sot, sotte [so, sɔt] *adj* silly, foolish ▷ *nm/f* fool; **sottise** *nf* (*caractère*) silliness, foolishness; (*action*) silly *ou* foolish thing

sou [su] *nm*: **près de ses ~s** tight-fisted; **sans le ~** penniless

soubresaut [subʀəso] *nm* start; (*cahot*) jolt

souche [suʃ] *nf* (*d'arbre*) stump; (*de carnet*) counterfoil (BRIT), stub

souci [susi] *nm* (*inquiétude*) worry; (*préoccupation*) concern; (*Bot*) marigold; **se faire du ~** to worry; **soucier: se soucier de** *vt* to care about; **soucieux, -euse** *adj* concerned, worried

soucoupe [sukup] *nf* saucer; **soucoupe volante** flying saucer

soudain, e [sudɛ̃, ɛn] *adj* (*douleur, mort*) sudden ▷ *adv* suddenly, all of a sudden

Soudan [sudɑ̃] *nm*: **le ~** Sudan

soude [sud] *nf* soda

souder [sude] *vt* (*avec fil à souder*) to solder; (*par soudure autogène*) to weld; (*fig*) to bind together

soudure [sudyʀ] *nf* soldering; welding; (*joint*) soldered joint; weld

souffle [sufl] nm (en expirant) breath; (en soufflant) puff, blow; (respiration) breathing; (d'explosion, de ventilateur) blast; (du vent) blowing; **être à bout de ~** to be out of breath; **un ~ d'air** a breath of air

soufflé, e [sufle] adj (fam: stupéfié) staggered ▷ nm (Culin) soufflé

souffler [sufle] vi (gén) to blow; (haleter) to puff (and blow) ▷ vt (feu, bougie) to blow out; (chasser: poussière etc) to blow away; (Tech: verre) to blow; (dire): **~ qch à qn** to whisper sth to sb

souffrance [sufrɑ̃s] nf suffering; **en ~** (affaire) pending

souffrant, e [sufrɑ̃, ɑ̃t] adj unwell

souffre-douleur [sufrədulœr] nm inv butt, underdog

souffrir [sufrir] vi to suffer, be in pain ▷ vt to suffer, endure; (supporter) to bear, stand; **~ de** (maladie, froid) to suffer from; **elle ne peut pas le ~** she can't stand ou bear him

soufre [sufr] nm sulphur

souhait [swɛ] nm wish; **tous nos ~s pour la nouvelle année** (our) best wishes for the New Year; **à vos ~s!** bless you!; **souhaitable** adj desirable

souhaiter [swete] vt to wish for; **~ la bonne année à qn** to wish sb a happy New Year; **~ que** to hope that

soûl, e [su, sul] adj drunk ▷ nm: **tout son ~** to one's heart's content

soulagement [sulaʒmɑ̃] nm relief

soulager [sulaʒe] vt to relieve

soûler [sule] vt: **~ qn** to get sb drunk; (suj: boisson) to make sb drunk; (fig) to make sb's head spin ou reel; **se soûler** vi to get drunk

soulever [sul(ə)ve] vt to lift; (poussière) to send up; (enthousiasme) to arouse; (question, débat) to raise; **se soulever** vi (peuple) to rise up; (personne couchée) to lift o.s. up

soulier [sulje] nm shoe

souligner [suliɲe] vt to underline; (fig) to emphasize, stress

soumettre [sumɛtr] vt (pays) to subject, subjugate; (rebelle) to put down, subdue; **~ qch à qn** (projet etc) to submit sth to sb; **se soumettre (à)** to submit (to)

soumis, e [sumi, iz] adj submissive; **soumission** nf submission

soupçon [supsɔ̃] nm suspicion; (petite quantité): **un ~ de** a hint ou touch of; **soupçonner** vt to suspect; **soupçonneux, -euse** adj suspicious

soupe [sup] nf soup

souper [supe] vi to have supper ▷ nm supper

soupeser [supəze] vt to weigh in one's hand(s); (fig) to weigh up

soupière [supjɛr] nf (soup) tureen

soupir [supir] nm sigh; **pousser un ~ de**

soulagement to heave a sigh of relief

soupirer [supire] vi to sigh

souple [supl] adj supple; (fig: règlement, caractère) flexible; (: démarche, taille) lithe, supple; **souplesse** nf suppleness; (de caractère) flexibility

source [surs] nf (point d'eau) spring; (d'un cours d'eau, fig) source; **de bonne ~** on good authority

sourcil [sursi] nm (eye)brow; **sourciller** vi: **sans sourciller** without turning a hair ou batting an eyelid

sourd, e [sur, surd] adj deaf; (bruit) muffled; (douleur) dull ▷ nm/f deaf person; **faire la ~e oreille** to turn a deaf ear; **sourdine** nf (Mus) mute; **en sourdine** softly, quietly; **sourd-muet, sourde-muette** adj deaf-and-dumb ▷ nm/f deaf-mute

souriant, e [surjɑ̃, jɑ̃t] adj cheerful

sourire [surir] nm smile ▷ vi to smile; **~ à qn** to smile at sb; (fig: plaire à) to appeal to sb; (suj: chance) to smile on sb; **garder le ~** to keep smiling

souris [suri] nf mouse

sournois, e [surnwa, waz] adj deceitful, underhand

sous [su] prép under; **~ la pluie** in the rain; **~ terre** underground; **~ peu** shortly, before long; **sous-bois** nm inv undergrowth

souscrire [suskrir] : **~ à** vt to subscribe to

sous...: **sous-directeur, -trice** nm/f assistant manager(-manageress); **sous-entendre** vt to imply, infer; **sous-entendu, e** adj implied ▷ nm innuendo, insinuation; **sous-estimer** vt to underestimate; **sous-jacent, e** adj underlying; **sous-louer** vt to sublet; **sous-marin, e** adj (flore, faune) submarine; (pêche) underwater ▷ nm submarine; **sous-pull** nm thin poloneck jersey; **soussigné, e** adj: **je soussigné** I the undersigned; **sous-sol** nm basement; **sous-titre** nm subtitle

soustraction [sustraksjɔ̃] nf subtraction

soustraire [sustrer] vt to subtract, take away; (dérober): **~ qch à qn** to remove sth from sb; **se soustraire à** (autorité etc) to elude, escape from

sous...: **sous-traitant** nm sub-contractor; **sous-traiter** vt to sub-contract; **sous-vêtements** nmpl underwear sg

soutane [sutan] nf cassock, soutane

soute [sut] nf hold

soutenir [sut(ə)nir] vt to support; (assaut, choc) to stand up to, withstand; (intérêt, effort) to keep up; (assurer): **~ que** to maintain that; **soutenu, e** adj (efforts) sustained, unflagging; (style) elevated

souterrain, e [suterɛ̃, ɛn] adj underground ▷ nm underground passage

soutien [sutjɛ̃] nm support; **soutien-gorge**

nm bra
soutirer [sutiʀe] *vt*: **~ qch à qn** to squeeze *ou* get sth out of sb
souvenir [suv(ə)niʀ] *nm* (*réminiscence*) memory; (*objet*) souvenir ▷ *vb*: **se ~ de** to remember; **se ~ que** to remember that; **en ~ de** in memory *ou* remembrance of; **avec mes affectueux/meilleurs ~s, ...** with love from, .../regards, ...
souvent [suvɑ̃] *adv* often; **peu ~** seldom, infrequently
souverain, e [suv(ə)ʀɛ̃, ɛn] *nm/f* sovereign, monarch
soyeux, -euse [swajø, øz] *adj* silky
spacieux, -euse [spasjø, jøz] *adj* spacious, roomy
spaghettis [spageti] *nmpl* spaghetti *sg*
sparadrap [spaʀadʀa] *nm* sticking plaster (*BRIT*), Bandaid® (*US*)
spatial, e, -aux [spasjal, jo] *adj* (*Aviat*) space *cpd*
speaker, ine [spikœʀ, kʀin] *nm/f* announcer
spécial, e, -aux [spesjal, jo] *adj* special; (*bizarre*) peculiar; **spécialement** *adv* especially, particularly; (*tout exprès*) specially; **spécialiser: se spécialiser** *vi* to specialize; **spécialiste** *nm/f* specialist; **spécialité** *nf* speciality; (*branche*) special field
spécifier [spesifje] *vt* to specify, state
spécimen [spesimɛn] *nm* specimen
spectacle [spɛktakl] *nm* (*scène*) sight; (*représentation*) show; (*industrie*) show business; **spectaculaire** *adj* spectacular
spectateur, -trice [spɛktatœʀ, tʀis] *nm/f* (*Cinéma etc*) member of the audience; (*Sport*) spectator; (*d'un événement*) onlooker, witness
spéculer [spekyle] *vi* to speculate
spéléologie [speleɔlɔʒi] *nf* potholing
sperme [spɛʀm] *nm* semen, sperm
sphère [sfɛʀ] *nf* sphere
spirale [spiʀal] *nf* spiral
spirituel, le [spiʀitɥel] *adj* spiritual; (*fin, piquant*) witty
splendide [splɑ̃did] *adj* splendid
spontané, e [spɔ̃tane] *adj* spontaneous; **spontanéité** *nf* spontaneity
sport [spɔʀ] *nm* sport ▷ *adj inv* (*vêtement*) casual; **faire du ~** to do sport; **sports d'hiver** winter sports; **sportif, -ive** *adj* (*journal, association, épreuve*) sports *cpd*; (*allure, démarche*) athletic; (*attitude, esprit*) sporting
spot [spɔt] *nm* (*lampe*) spot(light); (*annonce*): **spot (publicitaire)** commercial (break)
square [skwaʀ] *nm* public garden(s)
squelette [skəlɛt] *nm* skeleton; **squelettique** *adj* scrawny
SRAS [sʀas] *sigle m* (= *syndrome respiratoire aigu sévère*) SARS
Sri Lanka [sʀilɑ̃ka] *nm*: **le ~** Sri Lanka

stabiliser [stabilize] *vt* to stabilize
stable [stabl] *adj* stable, steady
stade [stad] *nm* (*Sport*) stadium; (*phase, niveau*) stage
stage [staʒ] *nm* (*cours*) training course; **~ de formation (professionnelle)** vocational (training) course; **~ de perfectionnement** advanced training course; **stagiaire** *nm/f, adj* trainee

Attention à ne pas traduire *stage* par le mot anglais *stage*.

stagner [stagne] *vi* to stagnate
stand [stɑ̃d] *nm* (*d'exposition*) stand; (*de foire*) stall; **stand de tir** (*à la foire, Sport*) shooting range
standard [stɑ̃daʀ] *adj inv* standard ▷ *nm* switchboard; **standardiste** *nm/f* switchboard operator
standing [stɑ̃diŋ] *nm* standing; **de grand ~** luxury
starter [staʀtɛʀ] *nm* (*Auto*) choke
station [stasjɔ̃] *nf* station; (*de bus*) stop; (*de villégiature*) resort; **station de ski** ski resort; **station de taxis** taxi rank (*BRIT*) *ou* stand (*US*); **stationnement** *nm* parking; **stationner** *vi* to park; **station-service** *nf* service station
statistique [statistik] *nf* (*science*) statistics *sg*; (*rapport, étude*) statistic ▷ *adj* statistical
statue [staty] *nf* statue
statu quo [statykwo] *nm* status quo
statut [staty] *nm* status; **statuts** *nmpl* (*Jur, Admin*) statutes; **statutaire** *adj* statutory
Sté *abr* = **société**
steak [stɛk] *nm* steak; **~ haché** hamburger
sténo(graphie) [stenɔ(gʀafi)] *nf* shorthand
stérile [steʀil] *adj* sterile
stérilet [steʀilɛ] *nm* coil, loop
stériliser [steʀilize] *vt* to sterilize
stimulant [stimylɑ̃] *nm* (*fig*) stimulus, incentive; (*physique*) stimulant
stimuler [stimyle] *vt* to stimulate
stipuler [stipyle] *vt* to stipulate
stock [stɔk] *nm* stock; **stocker** *vt* to stock
stop [stɔp] *nm* (*Auto: écriteau*) stop sign; (: *feu arrière*) brake-light; **faire du ~** (*fam*) to hitch(hike); **stopper** *vt, vi* to stop, halt
store [stɔʀ] *nm* blind; (*de magasin*) shade, awning
strabisme [stʀabism] *nm* squinting
strapontin [stʀapɔ̃tɛ̃] *nm* jump *ou* foldaway seat
stratégie [stʀateʒi] *nf* strategy; **stratégique** *adj* strategic
stress [stʀɛs] *nm* stress; **stressant, e** *adj* stressful; **stresser** *vt*: **stresser qn** to make sb (feel) tense
strict, e [stʀikt] *adj* strict; (*tenue, décor*) severe, plain; **le ~ nécessaire/minimum** the bare essentials/minimum

strident, e[stridɑ̃, ɑ̃t] adj shrill, strident
strophe[strɔf] nf verse, stanza
structure[stryktyr] nf structure; **~s d'accueil** reception facilities
studieux, -euse[stydjø, jøz] adj studious
studio[stydjo] nm (logement) (one-roomed) flatlet (BRIT) ou apartment (US); (d'artiste, TV etc) studio
stupéfait, e[stypefɛ, ɛt] adj astonished
stupéfiant, e[stypefjɑ̃, jɑ̃t] adj (étonnant) stunning, astounding ▷ nm (Méd) drug, narcotic
stupéfier[stypefje] vt (étonner) to stun, astonish
stupeur[stypœr] nf astonishment
stupide[stypid] adj stupid; **stupidité** nf stupidity; (parole, acte) stupid thing (to do ou say)
style[stil] nm style
stylé, e[stile] adj well-trained
styliste[stilist] nm/f designer
stylo[stilo] nm: **~ (à encre)** (fountain) pen; **stylo (à) bille**ball-point pen
su, e[sy] pp de **savoir** ▷ nm: **au su de** with the knowledge of
suave[sɥav] adj sweet
subalterne[sybaltɛrn] adj (employé, officier) junior; (rôle) subordinate, subsidiary ▷ nm/f subordinate
subconscient[sybkɔ̃sjɑ̃] nm subconscious
subir[sybir] vt (affront, dégâts) to suffer; (opération, châtiment) to undergo
subit, e[sybi, it] adj sudden; **subitement** adv suddenly, all of a sudden
subjectif, -ive[sybʒɛktif, iv] adj subjective
subjonctif[sybʒɔ̃ktif] nm subjunctive
subjuguer[sybʒyge] vt to captivate
submerger[sybmɛrʒe] vt to submerge; (fig) to overwhelm
subordonné, e[sybɔrdɔne] adj, nm/f subordinate
subrepticement[sybrɛptismɑ̃] adv surreptitiously
subside[sybzid] nm grant
subsidiaire[sybzidjɛr] adj: **question ~** deciding question
subsister[sybziste] vi (rester) to remain, subsist; (survivre) to live on
substance[sypstɑ̃s] nf substance
substituer[sypstitɥe] vt: **~ qn/qch à** to substitute sb/sth for; **se ~ à qn** (évincer) to substitute o.s. for sb
substitut[sypstity] nm (succédané) substitute
subterfuge[sybtɛrfyʒ] nm subterfuge
subtil, e[syptil] adj subtle
subvenir[sybvənir] vi: **~ à** vt to meet
subvention[sybvɑ̃sjɔ̃] nf subsidy, grant; **subventionner** vt to subsidize
suc[syk] nm (Bot) sap; (de viande, fruit) juice

succéder[syksede]: **~ à** vt to succeed; **se succéder** vi (accidents, années) to follow one another
succès[syksɛ] nm success; **avoir du ~** to be a success, be successful; **à ~** successful; **succès de librairie**bestseller
successeur[syksesœr] nm successor
successif, -ive[syksesif, iv] adj successive
succession[syksesjɔ̃] nf (série, Pol) succession; (Jur: patrimoine) estate, inheritance
succomber[sykɔ̃be] vi to die, succumb; (fig): **~ à** to succumb to
succulent, e[sykylɑ̃, ɑ̃t] adj (repas, mets) delicious
succursale[sykyrsal] nf branch
sucer[syse] vt to suck; **sucette** nf (bonbon) lollipop; (de bébé) dummy (BRIT), pacifier (US)
sucre[sykr] nm (substance) sugar; (morceau) lump of sugar, sugar lump ou cube; **sucre d'orge**barley sugar; **sucre en morceaux/cristallisé/en poudre**lump/granulated/caster sugar; **sucre glace**icing sugar (BRIT), confectioner's sugar (US); **sucré, e** adj (produit alimentaire) sweetened; (au goût) sweet; **sucrer** vt (thé, café) to sweeten, put sugar in; **sucreries** nfpl (bonbons) sweets, sweet things; **sucrier** nm (récipient) sugar bowl
sud[syd] nm: **le ~** the south ▷ adj inv south; (côte) south, southern; **au ~** (situation) in the south; (direction) to the south; **au ~ de** (to the) south of; **sud-africain, e** adj South African ▷ nm/f: **Sud-Africain, e** South African; **sud-américain, e** adj South American ▷ nm/f: **Sud-Américain, e** South American; **sud-est** nm, adj inv south-east; **sud-ouest** nm, adj inv south-west
Suède[sɥɛd] nf: **la ~** Sweden; **suédois, e** adj Swedish ▷ nm/f: **Suédois, e** Swede ▷ nm (Ling) Swedish
suer[sɥe] vi to sweat; (suinter) to ooze; **sueur** nf sweat; **en sueur** sweating, in a sweat; **donner des sueurs froides à qn** to put sb in(to) a cold sweat
suffire[syfir] vi (être assez): **~ (à qn/pour qch/pour faire)** to be enough ou sufficient (for sb/for sth/to do); **il suffit d'une négligence ...** it only takes one act of carelessness ...; **il suffit qu'on oublie pour que ...** one only needs to forget for ...; **ça suffit!** that's enough!
suffisamment[syfizamɑ̃] adv sufficiently, enough; **~ de** sufficient, enough
suffisant, e[syfizɑ̃, ɑ̃t] adj sufficient; (résultats) satisfactory; (vaniteux) self-important, bumptious
suffixe[syfiks] nm suffix
suffoquer[syfɔke] vt to choke, suffocate; (stupéfier) to stagger, astound ▷ vi to choke, suffocate

suffrage [syfʀaʒ] nm (Pol: voix) vote

suggérer [sygʒeʀe] vt to suggest; **suggestion** nf suggestion

suicide [sɥisid] nm suicide; **suicider: se suicider** vi to commit suicide

suie [sɥi] nf soot

suisse [sɥis] adj Swiss ▷ nm: **S~** Swiss pl inv ▷ nf: **la S~** Switzerland; **la S~ romande/ allemande** French-speaking/German-speaking Switzerland

suite [sɥit] nf (continuation: d'énumération etc) rest, remainder; (: de feuilleton) continuation; (: film etc sur le même thème) sequel; (série) series, succession; (conséquence) result; (ordre, liaison logique) coherence; (appartement, Mus) suite; (escorte) retinue, suite; **suites** nfpl (d'une maladie etc) effects; **prendre la ~ de** (directeur etc) to succeed, take over from; **donner ~ à** (requête, projet) to follow up; **faire ~ à** (faisant) ~ **à votre lettre du ...** further to your letter of the ...; **de ~** (d'affilée) in succession; (immédiatement) at once; **par la ~** afterwards, subsequently; **à la ~** one after the other; **à la ~ de** (derrière) behind; (en conséquence de) following

suivant, e [sɥivã, ãt] adj next, following ▷ prép (selon) according to; **au ~!** next!

suivi, e [sɥivi] adj (effort, qualité) consistent; (cohérent) coherent; **très/peu ~** (cours) well-/poorly-attended

suivre [sɥivʀ] vt (gén) to follow; (Scol: cours) to attend; (comprendre) to keep up with; (Comm: article) to continue to stock ▷ vi to follow; (élève: assimiler) to keep up; **se suivre** vi (accidents etc) to follow one after the other; **faire ~** (lettre) to forward; **"à ~"** "to be continued"

sujet, te [syʒɛ, ɛt] adj: **être ~ à** (vertige etc) to be liable ou subject to ▷ nm/f (d'un souverain) subject ▷ nm subject; **au ~ de** about; **sujet de conversation** topic ou subject of conversation; **sujet d'examen** (Scol) examination question

super [sypɛʀ] (fam) adj inv terrific, great, fantastic, super

superbe [sypɛʀb] adj magnificent, superb

superficie [sypɛʀfisi] nf (surface) area

superficiel, le [sypɛʀfisjɛl] adj superficial

superflu, e [sypɛʀfly] adj superfluous

supérieur, e [sypeʀjœʀ] adj (lèvre, étages, classes) upper; (plus élevé: température, niveau, enseignement): **~ (à)** higher (than); (meilleur: qualité, produit): **~ (à)** superior (to); (excellent, hautain) superior ▷ nm, nf superior; **supériorité** nf superiority

supermarché [sypɛʀmaʀʃe] nm supermarket

superposer [sypɛʀpoze] vt (faire chevaucher) to superimpose; **lits superposés** bunk beds

superpuissance [sypɛʀpɥisɑ̃s] nf super-power

superstitieux, -euse [sypɛʀstisjø, jøz] adj superstitious

superviser [sypɛʀvize] vt to supervise

supplanter [syplãte] vt to supplant

suppléant, e [sypleã, -ãt] adj (professeur) supply cpd; (juge, fonctionnaire) deputy cpd ▷ nm/f (professeur) supply teacher

suppléer [syplee] vt (ajouter: mot manquant etc) to supply, provide; (compenser: lacune) to fill in; **~ à** to make up for

supplément [syplemã] nm supplement; (de frites etc) extra portion; **un ~ de travail** extra ou additional work; **payer un ~** to pay an additional charge; **le vin est en ~** wine is extra; **supplémentaire** adj additional, further; (train, bus) relief cpd, extra

supplications [syplikasjõ] nfpl pleas, entreaties

supplice [syplis] nm torture no pl

supplier [syplije] vt to implore, beseech

support [sypɔʀ] nm support; (publicitaire) medium; (audio-visuel) aid

supportable [sypɔʀtabl] adj (douleur) bearable

supporter¹ [sypɔʀtɛʀ] nm supporter, fan

supporter² [sypɔʀte] vt (conséquences, épreuve) to bear, endure; (défauts, défense) to put up with; (suj: chose: chaleur etc) to withstand; (: personne: chaleur, vin) to be able to take

 Attention à ne pas traduire **supporter** par **to support**.

supposer [sypoze] vt to suppose; (impliquer) to presuppose; **à ~ que** supposing (that)

suppositoire [sypozitwaʀ] nm suppository

suppression [sypʀesjõ] nf (voir supprimer) cancellation; removal; deletion

supprimer [sypʀime] vt (congés, service d'autobus etc) to cancel; (emplois, privilèges, témoin gênant) to do away with; (cloison, cause, anxiété) to remove; (clause, mot) to delete

suprême [sypʀɛm] adj supreme

⊙ MOT-CLÉ

sur [syʀ] prép **1** (position) on; (par-dessus) over; (au-dessus) above; **pose-la sur la table** put it on the table; **je n'ai pas d'argent sur moi** I haven't any money on me

2 (direction) towards; **en allant sur Paris** going towards Paris; **sur votre droite** on ou to your right

3 (à propos de) on, about; **un livre/une conférence sur Balzac** a book/lecture on ou about Balzac

4 (proportion) out of; **un sur 10** one in 10; (Scol) one out of 10

5 (*mesures*) by; **4 m sur 2** 4 m by 2
6 (*succession*): **avoir accident sur accident** to have one accident after the other

sûr, e [syr] *adj* sure, certain; (*digne de confiance*) reliable; (*sans danger*) safe; (*diagnostic, goût*) reliable; **le plus ~ est de** the safest thing is to; **sûr de soi** self-assured, self-confident
surcharge [syrʃarʒ] *nf* (*de passagers, marchandises*) excess load; **surcharger** *vt* to overload
surcroît [syrkrwa] *nm*: **un ~ de** additional +*nom*; **par ou de ~** moreover; **en ~** in addition
surdité [syrdite] *nf* deafness
sûrement [syrmɑ̃] *adv* (*certainement*) certainly; (*sans risques*) safely
surenchère [syrɑ̃ʃɛr] *nf* (*aux enchères*) higher bid; **surenchérir** *vi* to bid higher; (*fig*) to try and outbid each other
surestimer [syrɛstime] *vt* to overestimate
sûreté [syrte] *nf* (*sécurité*) safety; (*exactitude: de renseignements etc*) reliability; (*d'un geste*) steadiness; **mettre en ~** to put in a safe place; **pour plus de ~** as an extra precaution, to be on the safe side
surf [sœrf] *nm* surfing
surface [syrfas] *nf* surface; (*superficie*) surface area; **une grande ~** a supermarket; **faire ~** to surface; **en ~** near the surface; (*fig*) superficially
surfait, e [syrfɛ, ɛt] *adj* overrated
surfer [syrfe] *vi*: **~ sur Internet** to surf *ou* browse the Internet
surgelé, e [syrʒəle] *adj* (deep-)frozen ▷ *nm*: **les ~s** (deep-)frozen food
surgir [syrʒir] *vi* to appear suddenly; (*fig: problème, conflit*) to arise
sur...: **surhumain, e** *adj* superhuman; **sur-le-champ** *adv* immediately; **surlendemain** *nm*: **le surlendemain (soir)** two days later (in the evening); **le surlendemain de** two days after; **surmenage** *nm* overwork(ing); **surmener**; **se surmener** *vi* to overwork
surmonter [syrmɔ̃te] *vt* (*vaincre*) to overcome; (*être au-dessus de*) to top
surnaturel, le [syrnatyrɛl] *adj, nm* supernatural
surnom [syrnɔ̃] *nm* nickname
surnombre [syrnɔ̃br] *nm*: **être en ~** to be too many (*ou* one too many)
surpeuplé, e [syrpœple] *adj* overpopulated
surplace [syrplas] *nm*: **faire du ~** to mark time
surplomber [syrplɔ̃be] *vt, vi* to overhang
surplus [syrply] *nm* (*Comm*) surplus; (*reste*): **~ de bois** wood left over
surprenant, e [syrprənɑ̃, ɑ̃t] *adj* amazing
surprendre [syrprɑ̃dr] *vt* (*étonner*) to surprise; (*tomber sur: intrus etc*) to catch;

(*entendre*) to overhear
surpris, e [syrpri, iz] *adj*: **~ (de/que)** surprised (at/that); **surprise** *nf* surprise; **faire une surprise à qn** to give sb a surprise; **surprise-partie** *nf* party
sursaut [syrso] *nm* start, jump; **~ de** (*énergie, indignation*) sudden fit ou burst of; **en ~** with a start; **sursauter** *vi* to (give a) start, jump
sursis [syrsi] *nm* (*Jur: gén*) suspended sentence; (*fig*) reprieve
surtout [syrtu] *adv* (*avant tout, d'abord*) above all; (*spécialement, particulièrement*) especially; **~, ne dites rien!** whatever you do don't say anything!; **~ pas!** certainly ou definitely not!; **~ que ...** especially as ...
surveillance [syrvɛjɑ̃s] *nf* watch; (*Police, Mil*) surveillance; **sous ~ médicale** under medical supervision
surveillant, e [syrvɛjɑ̃, ɑ̃t] *nm/f* (*de prison*) warder; (*Scol*) monitor
surveiller [syrveje] *vt* (*enfant, élèves, bagages*) to watch, keep an eye on; (*prisonnier, suspect*) to keep (a) watch on; (*territoire, bâtiment*) to (keep) watch over; (*travaux, cuisson*) to supervise; (*Scol: examen*) to invigilate; **~ son langage/sa ligne** to watch one's language/figure
survenir [syrvənir] *vi* (*incident, retards*) to occur, arise; (*événement*) to take place
survêtement [syrvɛtmɑ̃] *nm* tracksuit
survie [syrvi] *nf* survival; **survivant, e** *nm/f* survivor; **survivre** *vi* to survive; **survivre à** (*accident etc*) to survive
survoler [syrvole] *vt* to fly over; (*fig: livre*) to skim through
survolté, e [syrvɔlte] *adj* (*fig*) worked up
sus [sy(s)]: **en ~ de** *prép* in addition to, over and above; **en ~** in addition
susceptible [syseptibl] *adj* touchy, sensitive; **~ de faire** (*hypothèse*) liable to do
susciter [sysite] *vt* (*admiration*) to arouse; (*ennuis*): **~ (à qn)** to create (for sb)
suspect, e [syspɛ(kt), ɛkt] *adj* suspicious; (*témoignage, opinions*) suspect ▷ *nm/f* suspect; **suspecter** *vt* to suspect; (*honnêteté de qn*) to question, have one's suspicions about
suspendre [syspɑ̃dr] *vt* (*accrocher: vêtement*): **~ qch (à)** to hang sth up (on); (*interrompre, démettre*) to suspend
suspendu, e [syspɑ̃dy] *adj* (*accroché*): **~ à** hanging on (*ou* from); (*perché*): **~ au-dessus de** suspended over
suspens [syspɑ̃]: **en ~** *adv* (*affaire*) in abeyance; **tenir en ~** to keep in suspense
suspense [syspɛns, syspɑ̃s] *nm* suspense
suspension [syspɑ̃sjɔ̃] *nf* suspension; (*lustre*) light fitting ou fitment
suture [sytyr] *nf* (*Méd*): **point de ~** stitch
svelte [svɛlt] *adj* slender, svelte

SVP abr (= s'il vous plaît) please
sweat [swit] nm (fam) sweatshirt
sweat-shirt [switʃœʀt] (pl **-s**) nm sweatshirt
syllabe [si(l)lab] nf syllable
symbole [sɛ̃bɔl] nm symbol; **symbolique**
adj symbolic(al); (geste, offrande) token cpd;
symboliser vt to symbolize
symétrique [simetʀik] adj symmetrical
sympa [sɛ̃pa] (fam) adj inv nice; **sois ~, prête-
le moi** be a pal and lend it to me
sympathie [sɛ̃pati] nf (inclination) liking;
(affinité) friendship; (condoléances) sympathy;
j'ai beaucoup de ~ pour lui I like him a lot;
sympathique adj nice, friendly

> Attention à ne pas traduire *sympathique*
> par *sympathetic*.

sympathisant, e [sɛ̃patizɑ̃, ɑ̃t] nm/f
sympathizer
sympathiser [sɛ̃patize] vi (voisins etc:
s'entendre) to get on (BRIT) ou along (US) (well)
symphonie [sɛ̃fɔni] nf symphony
symptôme [sɛ̃ptom] nm symptom
synagogue [sinagɔg] nf synagogue
syncope [sɛ̃kɔp] nf (Méd) blackout; **tomber
en ~** to faint, pass out
syndic [sɛ̃dik] nm (d'immeuble) managing
agent
syndical, e, -aux [sɛ̃dikal, o] adj (trade)
union cpd; **syndicaliste** nm/f trade unionist
syndicat [sɛ̃dika] nm (d'ouvriers, employés)
(trade) union; **syndicat d'initiative** tourist
office; **syndiqué, e** adj belonging to a (trade)
union; **syndiquer: se syndiquer** vi to form a
trade union; (adhérer) to join a trade union
synonyme [sinɔnim] adj synonymous ▷ nm
synonym; **~ de** synonymous with
syntaxe [sɛ̃taks] nf syntax
synthèse [sɛ̃tɛz] nf synthesis
synthétique [sɛ̃tetik] adj synthetic
Syrie [siʀi] nf: **la ~** Syria
systématique [sistematik] adj systematic
système [sistɛm] nm system; **le ~ D**
resourcefulness

t

t' [t] pron voir **te**
ta [ta] adj voir **ton**[1]
tabac [taba] nm tobacco; (magasin)
tobacconist's (shop)
tabagisme [tabaʒism] nm: **tabagisme
passif** passive smoking
table [tabl] nf table; **à ~!** dinner etc is ready!;
se mettre à ~ to sit down to eat; **mettre la ~**
to lay the table; **une ~ pour 4, s'il vous plaît**
a table for 4, please; **table à repasser** ironing
board; **table de cuisson** hob; **table de nuit** ou
de chevet bedside table; **table des matières**
(table of) contents pl; **table d'orientation**
viewpoint indicator; **table roulante** trolley
(BRIT), tea wagon (US)
tableau, x [tablo] nm (peinture) painting;
(reproduction, fig) picture; (panneau) board;
(schéma) table, chart; **tableau d'affichage**
notice board; **tableau de bord** dashboard;
(Aviat) instrument panel; **tableau noir**
blackboard
tablette [tablɛt] nf (planche) shelf; **tablette
de chocolat** bar of chocolate
tablier [tablije] nm apron
tabou [tabu] nm taboo
tabouret [tabuʀɛ] nm stool
tac [tak] nm: **il m'a répondu du ~ au ~** he
answered me right back
tache [taʃ] nf (saleté) stain, mark; (Art, de
couleur, lumière) spot; **tache de rousseur**

freckle

tâche [taʃ] nf task

tacher [taʃe] vt to stain, mark

tâcher [taʃe] vi: **~ de faire** to try ou endeavour to do

tacheté, e [taʃte] adj spotted

tact [takt] nm tact; **avoir du ~** to be tactful

tactique [taktik] adj tactical ▷ nf (technique) tactics sg; (plan) tactic

taie [tɛ] nf: **~ (d'oreiller)** pillowslip, pillowcase

taille [taj] nf cutting; (d'arbre etc) pruning; (milieu du corps) waist; (hauteur) height; (grandeur) size; **de ~ à faire** capable of doing; **de ~** sizeable; **taille-crayon(s)** nm pencil sharpener

tailler [taje] vt (pierre, diamant) to cut; (arbre, plante) to prune; (vêtement) to cut out; (crayon) to sharpen

tailleur [tajœʀ] nm (couturier) tailor; (vêtement) suit; **en ~** (assis) cross-legged

taillis [taji] nm copse

taire [tɛʀ] vi: **faire ~ qn** to make sb be quiet; **se taire** vi to be silent ou quiet; **taisez-vous!** be quiet!

Taiwan [tajwan] nf Taiwan

talc [talk] nm talc, talcum powder

talent [talɑ̃] nm talent

talkie-walkie [tokiwoki] nm walkie-talkie

talon [talɔ̃] nm heel; (de chèque, billet) stub, counterfoil (BRIT); **talons plats/aiguilles** flat/stiletto heels

talus [taly] nm embankment

tambour [tɑ̃buʀ] nm (Mus, aussi Tech) drum; (musicien) drummer; (porte) revolving door(s pl); **tambourin** nm tambourine

Tamise [tamiz] nf: **la ~** the Thames

tamisé, e [tamize] adj (fig) subdued, soft

tampon [tɑ̃pɔ̃] nm (de coton, d'ouate) wad, pad; (amortisseur) buffer; (bouchon) plug, stopper; (cachet, timbre) stamp; (mémoire) ~ (Inform) buffer; **tampon (hygiénique)** tampon; **tamponner** vt (timbres) to stamp; (heurter) to crash ou bump into; **tamponneuse** adj f: **autos tamponneuses** dodgems

tandem [tɑ̃dɛm] nm tandem

tandis [tɑ̃di]: **~ que** conj while

tanguer [tɑ̃ge] vi to pitch (and toss)

tant [tɑ̃] adv so much; **~ de** (sable, eau) so much; (gens, livres) so many; **~ que** as long as; (autant que) as much as; **~ mieux** that's great; (avec une certaine réserve) so much the better; **~ pis** too bad; (conciliant) never mind; **~ bien que mal** as well as can be expected

tante [tɑ̃t] nf aunt

tantôt [tɑ̃to] adv (parfois): **~ ... ~** now ... now; (cet après-midi) this afternoon

taon [tɑ̃] nm horsefly

tapage [tapaʒ] nm uproar, din

tapageur, -euse [tapaʒœʀ, øz] adj noisy; (voyant) loud, flashy

tape [tap] nf slap

tape-à-l'œil [tapalœj] adj inv flashy, showy

taper [tape] vt (porte) to bang, slam; (enfant) to slap; (dactylographier) to type (out); (fam: emprunter): **~ qn de 10 euros** to touch sb for 10 euros ▷ vi (soleil) to beat down; **se taper** vt (repas) to put away; (fam: corvée) to get landed with; **~ sur qn** to thump sb; (fig) to run sb down; **~ sur un clou** to hit a nail; **~ sur la table** to bang on the table; **~ à** (porte etc) to knock on; **~ dans** (se servir) to dig into; **~ des mains/pieds** to clap one's hands/stamp one's feet; **~ (à la machine)** to type

tapi, e [tapi] adj (blotti) crouching; (caché) hidden away

tapis [tapi] nm carpet; (petit) rug; **tapis de sol** (de tente) groundsheet; **tapis de souris** (Inform) mouse mat; **tapis roulant** (pour piétons) moving walkway; (pour bagages) carousel

tapisser [tapise] vt (avec du papier peint) to paper; (recouvrir): **~ qch (de)** to cover sth (with); **tapisserie** nf (tenture, broderie) tapestry; (papier peint) wallpaper; **tapissier-décorateur** nm interior decorator

tapoter [tapɔte] vt (joue, main) to pat; (objet) to tap

taquiner [takine] vt to tease

tard [taʀ] adv late; **plus ~** later (on); **au plus ~** at the latest; **sur le ~** late in life; **il est trop ~** it's too late

tarder [taʀde] vi (chose) to be a long time coming; (personne): **~ à faire** to delay doing; **il me tarde d'être** I am longing to be; **sans (plus) ~** without further delay

tardif, -ive [taʀdif, iv] adj late

tarif [taʀif] nm: **~ des consommations** price list; **~s postaux/douaniers** postal/customs rates; **~ des taxis** taxi fares; **~ plein/réduit** (train) full/reduced fare; (téléphone) peak/off-peak rate

tarir [taʀiʀ] vi to dry up, run dry

tarte [taʀt] nf tart; **~ aux fraises** strawberry tart; **~ Tatin** ≈ apple upside-down tart

tartine [taʀtin] nf slice of bread; **tartine de miel** slice of bread and honey; **tartiner** vt to spread; **fromage à tartiner** cheese spread

tartre [taʀtʀ] nm (des dents) tartar; (de bouilloire) fur, scale

tas [tɑ] nm heap, pile; (fig): **un ~ de** heaps of, lots of; **en ~** in a heap ou pile; **formé sur le ~** trained on the job

tasse [tɑs] nf cup; **tasse à café** coffee cup

tassé, e [tɑse] adj: **bien ~** (café etc) strong

tasser [tɑse] vt (terre, neige) to pack down; (entasser): **~ qch dans** to cram sth into; **se tasser** vi (se serrer) to squeeze up; (s'affaisser) to settle; (fig) to settle down

tâter [tɑte] vt to feel; (fig) to try out; **se tâter** (hésiter) to be in two minds; **~ de** (prison etc) to have a taste of

tatillon, ne [tatijɔ̃, ɔn] adj pernickety

tâtonnement [tɑtɔnmɑ̃] nm: **par ~s** (fig) by trial and error

tâtonner [tɑtɔne] vi to grope one's way along

tâtons [tɑtɔ̃]: **à ~** adv: **chercher/avancer à ~** to grope around for/grope one's way forward

tatouage [tatwaʒ] nm tattoo

tatouer [tatwe] vt to tattoo

taudis [todi] nm hovel, slum

taule [tol] (fam) nf (fam) nick (fam), prison

taupe [top] nf mole

taureau, x [tɔʁo] nm bull; (signe): **le T~** Taurus

taux [to] nm rate; (d'alcool) level; **taux d'intérêt** interest rate

taxe [taks] nf tax; (douanière) duty; **toutes ~s comprises** inclusive of tax; **la boutique hors ~s** the duty-free shop; **taxe à la valeur ajoutée** value-added tax; **taxe de séjour** tourist tax

taxer [takse] vt (personne) to tax; (produit) to put a tax on, tax

taxi [taksi] nm taxi; (chauffeur: fam) taxi driver; **pouvez-vous m'appeler un ~, s'il vous plaît?** can you call me a taxi, please?

Tchécoslovaquie [tʃekɔslɔvaki] nf Czechoslovakia; **tchèque** adj Czech ▷ nm/f: **Tchèque** Czech ▷ nm (Ling) Czech; **la République tchèque** the Czech Republic

Tchétchénie [tʃetʃeni] nf: **la ~** Chechnya

te, t' [tə] pron you; (réfléchi) yourself

technicien, ne [tɛknisjɛ̃, jɛn] nm/f technician

technico-commercial, e, -aux [tɛknikɔkɔmɛʁsjal, jo] adj: **agent ~** sales technician

technique [tɛknik] adj technical ▷ nf technique; **techniquement** adv technically

techno [tɛkno] nf (Mus) techno (music)

technologie [tɛknɔlɔʒi] nf technology; **technologique** adj technological

teck [tɛk] nm teak

tee-shirt [tiʃœʁt] nm T-shirt, tee-shirt

teindre [tɛ̃dʁ] vt to dye; **se ~ les cheveux** to dye one's hair; **teint, e** adj dyed ▷ nm (du visage) complexion; (momentané) colour ▷ nf shade; **grand teint** colourfast

teinté, e [tɛ̃te] adj: **~ de** (fig) tinged with

teinter [tɛ̃te] vt (verre, papier) to tint; (bois) to stain

teinture [tɛ̃tyʁ] nf dye; **teinture d'iode** tincture of iodine; **teinturerie** nf dry cleaner's; **teinturier** nm dry cleaner

tel, telle [tɛl] adj (pareil) such; (comme): **~ un/ des ...** like a/like ...; (indéfini) such-and-such a; (intensif): **un ~/de ~s ...** such (a)/such ...; **rien de ~** nothing like it; **~ que** like, such as; **~ quel**

as it is ou stands (ou was etc); **venez ~ jour** come on such-and-such a day

télé [tele] (fam) nf TV; **à la ~** on TV ou telly

télé...: **télécabine** nf (benne) cable car; **télécarte** nf phonecard; **téléchargeable** adj downloadable; **téléchargement** nm (action) downloading; (fichier) download; **télécharger** vt to download; **télécommande** nf remote control; **télécopieur** nm fax machine; **télédistribution** nf cable TV; **télégramme** nm telegram; **télégraphier** vt to telegraph, cable; **téléguider** vt to radio-control; **télématique** nf telematics sg; **téléobjectif** nm telephoto lens sg; **télépathie** nf telepathy; **téléphérique** nm cable car

téléphone [telefɔn] nm telephone; **avoir le ~** to be on the (tele)phone; **au ~** on the phone; **téléphoner** vi to make a phone call; **téléphoner à** to phone, call up; **est-ce que je peux téléphoner d'ici?** can I make a call from here?; **téléphonique** adj (tele)phone cpd

télé...: **téléréalité** nf reality TV

télescope [telɛskɔp] nm telescope

télescoper [telɛskɔpe] vt to smash up; **se télescoper** (véhicules) to concertina

télé...: **téléscripteur** nm teleprinter; **télésiège** nm chairlift; **téléski** nm ski-tow; **téléspectateur, -trice** nm/f (television) viewer; **télétravail** nm telecommuting; **télévente** nf telesales; **téléviseur** nm television set; **télévision** nf television; **à la télévision** on television; **télévision numérique** digital TV; **télévision par câble/ satellite** cable/satellite television

télex [telɛks] nm telex

telle [tɛl] adj voir **tel**; **tellement** adv (tant) so much; (si) so; **tellement de** (sable, eau) so much; (gens, livres) so many; **il s'est endormi tellement il était fatigué** he was so tired (that) he fell asleep; **pas tellement** not (all) that much; not (all) that +adjectif

téméraire [temeʁɛʁ] adj reckless, rash

témoignage [temwaɲaʒ] nm (Jur: déclaration) testimony no pl, evidence no pl; (rapport, récit) account; (fig: d'affection etc: cadeau) token, mark; (: geste) expression

témoigner [temwaɲe] vt (intérêt, gratitude) to show ▷ vi (Jur) to testify, give evidence; **~ de** to bear witness to, testify to

témoin [temwɛ̃] nm witness ▷ adj: **appartement ~** show flat (BRIT); **être ~ de** to witness; **témoin oculaire** eyewitness

tempe [tɑ̃p] nf temple

tempérament [tɑ̃peʁamɑ̃] nm temperament, disposition; **à ~** (vente) on deferred (payment) terms; (achat) by instalments, hire purchase cpd

température [tɑ̃peʁatyʁ] nf temperature; **avoir** ou **faire de la ~** to be running ou have a temperature

tempête [tɑ̃pɛt] *nf* storm; **tempête de sable/neige** sand/snowstorm

temple [tɑ̃pl] *nm* temple; (*protestant*) church

temporaire [tɑ̃pɔʀɛʀ] *adj* temporary

temps [tɑ̃] *nm* (*atmosphérique*) weather; (*durée*) time, times *pl*; (*Ling*) tense; (*Mus*) beat; (*Tech*) stroke; **un ~ de chien** (*fam*) rotten weather; **quel ~ fait-il?** what's the weather like?; **il fait beau/mauvais** ~ the weather is fine/bad; **avoir le ~/tout son** ~ to have time/plenty of time; **en ~ de paix/ guerre** in peacetime/wartime; **en ~ utile** *ou* **voulu** in due time *ou* course; **ces derniers** ~ lately; **dans quelque** ~ in a (little) while; **de ~ en ~, de ~ à autre** from time to time; **à ~** (*partir, arriver*) in time; **à ~ complet, à plein** ~ full-time; **à ~ partiel, à mi-~** part-time; **dans le ~** at one time; **temps d'arrêt** pause, halt; **temps libre** free *ou* spare time; **temps mort** (*Comm*) slack period

tenable [t(ə)nabl] *adj* bearable

tenace [tənas] *adj* persistent

tenant, e [tənɑ̃, ɑ̃t] *nm/f* (*Sport*): **~ du titre** title-holder

tendance [tɑ̃dɑ̃s] *nf* tendency; (*opinions*) leanings *pl*, sympathies *pl*; (*évolution*) trend; **avoir ~ à** to have a tendency to, tend to

tendeur [tɑ̃dœʀ] *nm* (*attache*) elastic strap

tendre [tɑ̃dʀ] *adj* tender; (*bois, roche, couleur*) soft ▷ *vt* (*élastique, peau*) to stretch; (*corde*) to tighten; (*muscle*) to tense; (*fig: piège*) to set, lay; (*donner*): **~ qch à qn** to hold sth out to sb; (*offrir*) to offer sb sth; **se tendre** *vi* (*corde*) to tighten; (*relations*) to become strained; **~ à qch/à faire** to tend towards sth/to do; **~ l'oreille** to prick up one's ears; **~ la main/le bras** to hold out one's hand/stretch out one's arm; **tendrement** *adv* tenderly; **tendresse** *nf* tenderness

tendu, e [tɑ̃dy] *pp de* **tendre** ▷ *adj* (*corde*) tight; (*muscles*) tensed; (*relations*) strained

ténèbres [tenɛbʀ] *nfpl* darkness *sg*

teneur [tənœʀ] *nf* content; (*d'une lettre*) terms *pl*, content

tenir [t(ə)niʀ] *vt* to hold; (*magasin, hôtel*) to run; (*promesse*) to keep ▷ *vi* to hold; (*neige, gel*) to last; **se tenir** *vi* (*avoir lieu*) to be held, take place; (*être: personne*) to stand; **~ à** (*personne, objet*) to be attached to; (*réputation*) to care about; **~ à faire** to be determined to do; **~ de** (*ressembler à*) to take after; **ça ne tient qu'à lui** it is entirely up to him; **~ qn pour** to regard sb as; **~ qch de qn** (*histoire*) to have heard *ou* learnt sth from sb; (*qualité, défaut*) to have inherited *ou* got sth from sb; **~ dans** to fit into; **~ compte de qch** to take sth into account; **~ les comptes** to keep the books; **~ bon** to stand fast; **~ le coup** to hold out; **~ au chaud**

(*café, plat*) to keep hot; **un manteau qui tient chaud** a warm coat; **tiens/tenez, voilà le stylo** there's the pen!; **tiens, voilà Alain!** look, here's Alain!; **tiens?** (*surprise*) really?; **se droit** to stand (*ou* sit) up straight; **bien se ~** to behave well; **se ~ à qch** to hold on to sth; **s'en ~ à qch** to confine o.s. to sth

tennis [tenis] *nm* tennis; (*court*) tennis court ▷ *nm ou f pl* (*aussi*: **chaussures de ~**) tennis *ou* gym shoes; **tennis de table** table tennis; **tennisman** *nm* tennis player

tension [tɑ̃sjɔ̃] *nf* tension; (*Méd*) blood pressure; **avoir de la ~** to have high blood pressure

tentation [tɑ̃tasjɔ̃] *nf* temptation

tentative [tɑ̃tativ] *nf* attempt

tente [tɑ̃t] *nf* tent

tenter [tɑ̃te] *vt* (*éprouver, attirer*) to tempt; (*essayer*): **~ qch/de faire** to attempt *ou* try sth/to do; **~ sa chance** to try one's luck

tenture [tɑ̃tyʀ] *nf* hanging

tenu, e [t(ə)ny] *pp de* **tenir** ▷ *adj* (*maison, comptes*): **bien ~** well-kept; (*obligé*): **~ de faire** obliged to do ▷ *nf* (*vêtements*) clothes *pl*; (*comportement*) (good) manners *pl*, good behaviour; (*d'une maison*) upkeep; **en petite ~e** scantily dressed *ou* clad

ter [tɛʀ] *adj*: **16** = 16b *ou* B

terme [tɛʀm] *nm* term; (*fin*) end; **à court/ long** ~ *adj* short-/long-term ▷ *adv* in the short/long term; **avant** ~ (*Méd*) prematurely; **mettre un ~ à** to put an end *ou* a stop to; **en bons ~s** on good terms

terminaison [tɛʀminɛzɔ̃] *nf* (*Ling*) ending

terminal, -aux [tɛʀminal, o] *nm* terminal; **terminale** *nf* (*Scol*) ≈ year 13 (*BRIT*), ≈ twelfth grade (*US*)

terminer [tɛʀmine] *vt* to finish; **se terminer** *vi* to end; **quand est-ce que le spectacle se termine?** when does the show finish?

terne [tɛʀn] *adj* dull

ternir [tɛʀniʀ] *vt* to dull; (*fig*) to sully, tarnish; **se ternir** *vi* to become dull

terrain [tɛʀɛ̃] *nm* (*sol, fig*) ground; (*Comm: étendue de terre*) land *no pl*; (*parcelle*) plot (of land); (*à bâtir*) site; **sur le ~** (*fig*) on the field; **terrain d'aviation** airfield; **terrain de camping** campsite; **terrain de football/ rugby** football/rugby pitch (*BRIT*) *ou* field (*US*); **terrain de golf** golf course; **terrain de jeu** games field; (*pour les petits*) playground; **terrain de sport** sports ground; **terrain vague** waste ground *no pl*

terrasse [tɛʀas] *nf* terrace; **à la ~** (*café*) outside; **terrasser** *vt* (*adversaire*) to floor; (*suj: maladie etc*) to strike down

terre [tɛʀ] *nf* (*gén, aussi Élec*) earth; (*substance*) soil, earth; (*opposé à mer*) land *no pl*; (*contrée*) land; **terres** *nfpl* (*terrains*) lands, land *sg*; **en ~**

(*pipe, poterie*) clay *cpd*; **à ~ ou par ~** (*mettre, être, s'asseoir*) on the ground (*ou* floor); (*jeter, tomber*) to the ground, down; **terre à terre** *adj inv* (*considération, personne*) down-to-earth; **terre cuite** terracotta; **la terre ferme** dry land; **terre glaise** clay

terreau [tεro] *nm* compost

terre-plein [tεrplε̃] *nm* platform; (*sur chaussée*) central reservation

terrestre [tεrεstr] *adj* (*surface*) earth's, of the earth; (*Bot, Zool, Mil*) land *cpd*; (*Rel*) earthly

terreur [tεrœr] *nf* terror *no pl*

terrible [tεribl] *adj* terrible, dreadful; (*fam*) terrific; **pas ~** nothing special

terrien, ne [tεrjε̃, jεn] *adj*: **propriétaire ~** landowner ▷ *nm/f* (*non martien etc*) earthling

terrier [tεrje] *nm* burrow, hole; (*chien*) terrier

terrifier [tεrifje] *vt* to terrify

terrine [tεrin] *nf* (*récipient*) terrine; (*Culin*) pâté

territoire [tεritwar] *nm* territory

terroriser [tεrorize] *vt* to terrorize

terrorisme [tεrorism] *nm* terrorism; **terroriste** *nm/f* terrorist

tertiaire [tεrsjεr] *adj* tertiary ▷ *nm* (*Écon*) service industries *pl*

tes [te] *adj voir* **ton¹**

test [tεst] *nm* test

testament [tεstamã] *nm* (*Jur*) will; (*Rel*) Testament; (*fig*) legacy

tester [tεste] *vt* to test

testicule [tεstikyl] *nm* testicle

tétanos [tetanos] *nm* tetanus

têtard [tεtar] *nm* tadpole

tête [tεt] *nf* head; (*cheveux*) hair *no pl*; (*visage*) face; **de ~** (*comme adj: wagon etc*) front *cpd*; (*comme adv: calculer*) in one's head, mentally; **perdre la ~** (*fig: s'affoler*) to lose one's head; (: *devenir fou*) to go off one's head; **tenir ~ à qn** to stand up to sb; **la ~ en bas** with one's head down; **la ~ la première** (*tomber*) headfirst; **faire une ~** (*Football*) to head the ball; **faire la ~** (*fig*) to sulk; **en ~** at the front; (*Sport*) in the lead; **à la ~ de** at the head of; **à ~ reposée** in a more leisurely moment; **n'en faire qu'à sa ~** to do as one pleases; **en avoir par-dessus la ~** to be fed up; **en ~ à ~** in private, alone together; **de la ~ aux pieds** from head to toe; **tête de lecture** (*playback*) head; **tête de liste** (*Pol*) chief candidate; **tête de mort** skull and crossbones; **tête de série** (*Tennis*) seeded player, seed; **tête de Turc** (*fig*) whipping boy (*BRIT*), butt; **tête-à-queue** *nm inv*: **faire un tête-à-queue** to spin round

téter [tete] *vt*: **~ (sa mère)** to suck at one's mother's breast, feed

tétine [tetin] *nf* teat; (*sucette*) dummy (*BRIT*), pacifier (*US*)

têtu, e [tety] *adj* stubborn, pigheaded

texte [tεkst] *nm* text; (*morceau choisi*) passage

textile [tεkstil] *adj* textile *cpd* ▷ *nm* textile; **le ~** the textile industry

Texto® [tεksto] *nm* text message

texture [tεkstyr] *nf* texture

TGV *sigle m* (= *train à grande vitesse*) high-speed train

thaïlandais, e [tajlãdε, εz] *adj* Thai ▷ *nm/f*: **T~, e** Thai

Thaïlande [tailãd] *nf* Thailand

thé [te] *nm* tea; **~ au citron** lemon tea; **~ au lait** tea with milk; **prendre le ~** to have tea; **faire le ~** to make the tea

théâtral, e, -aux [teatral, o] *adj* theatrical

théâtre [teatr] *nm* theatre; (*péj: simulation*) playacting; (*fig: lieu*): **le ~ de** the scene of; **faire du ~** to act

théière [tejεr] *nf* teapot

thème [tεm] *nm* theme; (*Scol: traduction*) prose (composition)

théologie [teoloʒi] *nf* theology

théorie [teori] *nf* theory; **théorique** *adj* theoretical

thérapie [terapi] *nf* therapy

thermal, e, -aux [tεrmal, o] *adj*: **station ~e** spa; **cure ~e** water cure

thermomètre [tεrmɔmεtr] *nm* thermometer

thermos® [tεrmos] *nm ou nf*: **(bouteille) thermos** vacuum *ou* Thermos® flask

thermostat [tεrmosta] *nm* thermostat

thèse [tεz] *nf* thesis

thon [tɔ̃] *nm* tuna (fish)

thym [tε̃] *nm* thyme

Tibet [tibε] *nm*: **le ~** Tibet

tibia [tibja] *nm* shinbone, tibia; (*partie antérieure de la jambe*) shin

TIC *sigle fpl* (= *technologies de l'information et de la communication*) ICT *sg*

tic [tik] *nm* tic, (*nervous*) twitch; (*de langage etc*) mannerism

ticket [tikε] *nm* ticket; **ticket de caisse** receipt; **je peux avoir un ticket de caisse, s'il vous plaît?** can I have a receipt, please?

tiède [tjεd] *adj* lukewarm; (*vent, air*) mild, warm; **tiédir** *vi* to cool; (*se réchauffer*) to grow warmer

tien, ne [tjε̃, tjεn] *pron*: **le(la) ~(ne), les ~(ne)s** yours; **à la ~ne!** cheers!

tiens [tjε̃] *vb, excl voir* **tenir**

tiercé [tjεrse] *nm* system of forecast betting giving first 3 horses

tiers, tierce [tjεr, tjεrs] *adj* third ▷ *nm* (*Jur*) third party; (*fraction*) third; **le tiers monde** the Third World

tige [tiʒ] *nf* stem; (*baguette*) rod

tignasse [tiɲas] (*péj*) *nf* mop of hair

tigre [tigr] *nm* tiger; **tigré, e** *adj* (*rayé*) striped; (*tacheté*) spotted; (*chat*) tabby; **tigresse** *nf* tigress

tilleul [tijœl] nm lime (tree), linden (tree); (boisson) lime(-blossom) tea

timbre [tɛ̃bʀ] nm (tampon) stamp; (aussi: **~-poste**) (postage) stamp; (Mus: de voix, instrument) timbre, tone

timbré, e [tɛ̃bʀe] (fam) adj cracked

timide [timid] adj shy; (timoré) timid; **timidement** adv shyly; timidly; **timidité** nf shyness; timidity

tintamarre [tɛ̃tamaʀ] nm din, uproar

tinter [tɛ̃te] vi to ring, chime; (argent, clefs) to jingle

tique [tik] nf (parasite) tick

tir [tiʀ] nm (sport) shooting; (fait ou manière de tirer) firing no pl; (rafale) fire; (stand) shooting gallery; **tir à l'arc** archery

tirage [tiʀaʒ] nm (action) printing; (Photo) print; (de journal) circulation; (de livre: nombre d'exemplaires) (print) run; (: édition) edition; (de loterie) draw; **par ~ au sort** by drawing lots

tire [tiʀ] nf: **vol à la ~** pickpocketing

tiré, e [tiʀe] adj (traits) drawn; **~ par les cheveux** far-fetched

tire-bouchon [tiʀbuʃɔ̃] nm corkscrew

tirelire [tiʀliʀ] nf moneybox

tirer [tiʀe] vt (gén) to pull; (trait, rideau, carte, conclusion, chèque) to draw; (langue) to stick out; (en faisant feu: balle, coup) to fire; (: animal) to shoot; (journal, livre, photo) to print; (Football: corner etc) to take ▷ vi (faire feu) to fire; (faire du tir, Football) to shoot; **se tirer** vi (fam) to push off; **s'en ~** (éviter le pire) to get off; (survivre) to pull through; (se débrouiller) to manage; **~ qch de** (extraire) to take ou pull sth out of; **~ qn de** (embarras etc) to help ou get sb out of; **~ sur** (corde) to pull on ou at; (faire feu sur) to shoot ou fire at; (pipe) to draw on; (approcher de: couleur) to verge ou border on; **~ à l'arc/la carabine** to shoot with a bow and arrow/with a rifle; **~ à sa fin** to be drawing to a close; **~ qch au clair** to clear sth up; **~ au sort** to draw lots; **~ parti de** to take advantage of; **~ profit de** to profit from; **~ les cartes** to read ou tell the cards

tiret [tiʀɛ] nm dash

tireur [tiʀœʀ] nm gunman; **tireur d'élite** marksman

tiroir [tiʀwaʀ] nm drawer; **tiroir-caisse** nm till

tisane [tizan] nf herb tea

tisser [tise] vt to weave

tissu [tisy] nm fabric, material, cloth no pl; (Anat, Bio) tissue; **tissu-éponge** nm (terry) towelling no pl

titre [titʀ] nm (gén) title; (de journal) headline; (diplôme) qualification; (Comm) security; **en ~** (champion) official; **à juste ~** rightly; **à quel ~?** on what grounds?; **à aucun ~** on no account; **au même ~ (que)** in the same way (as); **à ~ d'information** for (your) information; **à ~ gracieux** free of charge; **à ~ d'essai** on a trial basis; **à ~ privé** in a private capacity; **titre de propriété** title deed; **titre de transport** ticket

tituber [titybe] vi to stagger (along)

titulaire [titylɛʀ] adj (Admin) with tenure ▷ nm/f (de permis) holder; **être ~ de** (diplôme, permis) to hold

toast [tost] nm slice ou piece of toast; (de bienvenue) (welcoming) toast; **porter un ~ à qn** to propose ou drink a toast to sb

toboggan [tɔbɔgɑ̃] nm slide; (Auto) flyover

toc [tɔk] excl: **~, ~** knock knock ▷ nm: **en ~** fake

tocsin [tɔksɛ̃] nm alarm (bell)

tohu-bohu [tɔyboy] nm hubbub

toi [twa] pron you

toile [twal] nf (tableau) canvas; **de** ou **en ~** (pantalon) cotton; (sac) canvas; **la T~** (Internet) the Web; **toile cirée** oilcloth; **toile d'araignée** cobweb; **toile de fond** (fig) backdrop

toilette [twalɛt] nf (habits) outfit; **toilettes** nfpl (w.-c.) toilet sg; **faire sa ~** to have a wash, get washed; **articles de ~** toiletries; **où sont les ~s?** where's the toilet?

toi-même [twamɛm] pron yourself

toit [twa] nm roof; **toit ouvrant** sunroof

toiture [twatyʀ] nf roof

Tokyo [tɔkjo] n Tokyo

tôle [tol] nf (plaque) steel ou iron sheet; **tôle ondulée** corrugated iron

tolérable [tɔleʀabl] adj tolerable

tolérant, e [tɔleʀɑ̃, ɑ̃t] adj tolerant

tolérer [tɔleʀe] vt to tolerate; (Admin: hors taxe etc) to allow

tollé [tɔ(l)le] nm outcry

tomate [tɔmat] nf tomato; **~s farcies** stuffed tomatoes

tombe [tɔ̃b] nf (sépulture) grave; (avec monument) tomb

tombeau, x [tɔ̃bo] nm tomb

tombée [tɔ̃be] nf: **à la ~ de la nuit** at nightfall

tomber [tɔ̃be] vi to fall; (fièvre, vent) to drop; **laisser ~** (objet) to drop; (personne) to let down; (activité) to give up; **laisse ~!** forget it!; **faire ~** to knock over; **~ sur** (rencontrer) to bump into; **~ de fatigue/sommeil** to drop from exhaustion/be falling asleep on one's feet; **ça tombe bien** that's come at the right time; **il est bien tombé** he's been lucky; **~ à l'eau** (projet) to fall through; **~ en panne** to break down

tombola [tɔ̃bɔla] nf raffle

tome [tɔm] nm volume

ton¹, ta [tɔ̃, ta] (pl **tes**) adj your

ton² [tɔ̃] nm (gén) tone; (couleur) shade, tone; **de bon ~** in good taste

tonalité [tɔnalite] nf (au téléphone) dialling tone

tondeuse [tɔ̃døz] nf (à gazon) (lawn)mower;

(*du coiffeur*) clippers pl; (*pour les moutons*) shears pl

tondre [tɔ̃dʀ] vt (*pelouse, herbe*) to mow; (*haie*) to cut, clip; (*mouton, toison*) to shear; (*cheveux*) to crop

tongs [tɔ̃g] nfpl flip-flops

tonifier [tɔnifje] vt (*peau, organisme*) to tone up

tonique [tɔnik] adj fortifying ▷ nm tonic

tonne [tɔn] nf metric ton, tonne

tonneau, x [tɔno] nm (*à vin, cidre*) barrel; **faire des ~x** (*voiture, avion*) to roll over

tonnelle [tɔnɛl] nf bower, arbour

tonner [tɔne] vi to thunder; **il tonne** it is thundering, there's some thunder

tonnerre [tɔnɛʀ] nm thunder

tonus [tɔnys] nm energy

top [tɔp] nm: **au 3ème ~** at the 3rd stroke ▷ adj: **~ secret** top secret

topinambour [tɔpinɑ̃buʀ] nm Jerusalem artichoke

torche [tɔʀʃ] nf torch

torchon [tɔʀʃɔ̃] nm cloth; (*à vaisselle*) tea towel ou cloth

tordre [tɔʀdʀ] vt (*chiffon*) to wring; (*barre, fig: visage*) to twist; **se tordre** vi: **se ~ le poignet/ la cheville** to twist one's wrist/ankle; **se ~ de douleur/rire** to be doubled up with pain/ laughter; **tordu, e** adj bent; (*fig*) crazy

tornade [tɔʀnad] nf tornado

torrent [tɔʀɑ̃] nm mountain stream

torsade [tɔʀsad] nf: **un pull à ~s** a cable sweater

torse [tɔʀs] nm chest; (*Anat, Sculpture*) torso; **~ nu** stripped to the waist

tort [tɔʀ] nm (*défaut*) fault; **torts** nmpl (*Jur*) fault sg; **avoir ~** to be wrong; **être dans son ~** to be in the wrong; **donner ~ à qn** to lay the blame on sb; **causer du ~ à qn** to harm sb; **à ~** wrongly; **à ~ et à travers** wildly

torticolis [tɔʀtikɔli] nm stiff neck

tortiller [tɔʀtije] vt to twist; (*moustache*) to twirl; **se tortiller** vi to wriggle; (*en dansant*) to wiggle

tortionnaire [tɔʀsjɔnɛʀ] nm torturer

tortue [tɔʀty] nf tortoise; (*d'eau douce*) terrapin; (*d'eau de mer*) turtle

tortueux, -euse [tɔʀtɥø, øz] adj (*rue*) twisting; (*fig*) tortuous

torture [tɔʀtyʀ] nf torture; **torturer** vt to torture; (*fig*) to torment

tôt [to] adv early; **~ ou tard** sooner or later; **si ~** so early; (*déjà*) so soon; **plus ~** earlier; **au plus ~** at the earliest

total, e, -aux [tɔtal, o] adj, nm total; **au ~** in total; (*fig*) on the whole; **faire le ~** to work out
· the total; **totalement** adv totally; **totaliser** vt to total; **totalitaire** adj totalitarian; **totalité** nf: **la totalité de** all (of); the whole

+sg; **en totalité** entirely

toubib [tubib] (*fam*) nm doctor

touchant, e [tuʃɑ̃, ɑ̃t] adj touching

touche [tuʃ] nf (*de piano, de machine à écrire*) key; (*de téléphone*) button; (*Peinture etc*) stroke, touch; (*fig: de nostalgie*) touch; (*Football: aussi:* **remise en ~**) throw-in; (*aussi:* **ligne de ~**) touch-line; **touche dièse** (*de téléphone, clavier*) hash key

toucher [tuʃe] nm touch ▷ vt to touch; (*palper*) to feel; (*atteindre: d'un coup de feu etc*) to hit; (*concerner*) to concern, affect; (*contacter*) to reach, contact; (*recevoir: récompense*) to receive, get; (*: salaire*) to draw, get; (*: chèque*) to cash; **se toucher** (*être en contact*) to touch; **au ~** to the touch; **~ à** to touch; (*concerner*) to concern; **je vais lui en ~ un mot** I'll have a word with him about it; **~ au but** (*fig*) to near one's goal; **~ à sa fin** to be drawing to a close

touffe [tuf] nf tuft

touffu, e [tufy] adj thick, dense

toujours [tuʒuʀ] adv always; (*encore*) still; (*constamment*) forever; **~ plus** more and more; **pour ~** forever; **~ est-il que** the fact remains that; **essaie ~** (you can) try anyway

toupie [tupi] nf (spinning) top

tour¹ [tuʀ] nf tower; (*immeuble*) high-rise block (*BRIT*) ou building (*US*); (*Échecs*) castle, rook; **tour de contrôle** nf control tower; **la tour Eiffel** the Eiffel Tower

tour² [tuʀ] nm (*excursion*) trip; (*à pied*) stroll, walk; (*en voiture*) run, ride; (*Sport: aussi:* **~ de piste**) lap; (*d'être servi ou de jouer etc*) turn; (*de roue etc*) revolution; (*Pol: aussi:* **~ de scrutin**) ballot; (*ruse, de prestidigitation*) trick; (*de potier*) wheel; (*à bois, métaux*) lathe; (*circonférence*): **de 3 m de ~** 3 m round, with a circumference ou girth of 3 m; **faire le ~ de** to go round; (*à pied*) to walk round; **c'est au ~ de Renée** it's Renée's turn; **à ~ de rôle, ~ à ~** in turn; **tour de chant** nm song recital; **tour de force** tour de force; **tour de garde** nm spell of duty; **tour d'horizon** nm (*fig*) general survey; **tour de taille/tête** nm waist/head measurement; **un 33 tours** an LP; **un 45 tours** a single

tourbe [tuʀb] nf peat

tourbillon [tuʀbijɔ̃] nm whirlwind; (*d'eau*) whirlpool; (*fig*) whirl, swirl; **tourbillonner** vi to whirl (round)

tourelle [tuʀɛl] nf turret

tourisme [tuʀism] nm tourism; **agence de ~** tourist agency; **faire du ~** to go touring; (*en ville*) to go sightseeing; **touriste** nm/f tourist; **touristique** adj tourist cpd; (*région*) touristic

tourment [tuʀmɑ̃] nm torment; **tourmenter** vt to torment; **se tourmenter** to fret, worry o.s.

tournage [tuʀnaʒ] nm (*Cinéma*) shooting

tournant [tuʀnɑ̃] nm (*de route*) bend; (*fig*)

turning point

tournée [turne] nf (du facteur etc) round; (d'artiste, politicien) tour; (au café) round (of drinks)

tourner [turne] vt to turn; (sauce, mélange) to stir; (Cinéma: faire les prises de vues) to shoot; (: produire) to make ▷ vi to turn; (moteur) to run; (taximètre) to tick away; (lait etc) to turn (sour); **se tourner** vi to turn round; **tournez à gauche/droite au prochain carrefour** turn left/right at the next junction; **mal ~** to go wrong; **~ autour de** to go round; (péj) to hang round; **~ à/en** to turn into; **~ qn en ridicule** to ridicule sb; **~ le dos à** (mouvement) to turn one's back on; (position) to have one's back to; **~ de l'œil** to pass out; **se ~ vers** to turn towards; (fig) to turn to; **se ~ les pouces** to twiddle one's thumbs

tournesol [turnəsɔl] nm sunflower
tournevis [turnəvis] nm screwdriver
tournoi [turnwa] nm tournament
tournure [turnyr] nf (Ling) turn of phrase; (évolution): **la ~ de qch** the way sth is developing; **tournure d'esprit** turn ou cast of mind

tourte [turt] nf pie
tourterelle [turtərɛl] nf turtledove
tous [tu] adj, pron voir **tout**
Toussaint [tusɛ̃] nf: **la ~** All Saints' Day

tousser [tuse] vi to cough

 MOT-CLÉ

tout, e [tu, tut] (mpl **tous**, fpl **toutes**) adj
1 (avec article singulier) all; **tout le lait** all the milk; **toute la nuit** all night, the whole night; **tout le livre** the whole book; **tout un pain** a whole loaf; **tout le temps** all the time; the whole time; **tout le monde** everybody; **c'est tout le contraire** it's quite the opposite
2 (avec article pluriel) every, all; **tous les livres** all the books; **toutes les nuits** every night; **toutes les fois** every time; **toutes les trois/deux semaines** every third/other ou second week, every three/two weeks; **tous les deux** both ou each of us (ou them ou you); **toutes les trois** all three of us (ou them ou you)
3 (sans article): **à tout âge** at any age; **pour toute nourriture, il avait ...** his only food was ...
▷ pron everything, all; **il a tout fait** he's done everything; **je les vois tous** I can see them all ou all of them; **nous y sommes tous allés** all of us went, we all went; **c'est tout** that's all; **en tout** in all; **tout ce qu'il sait** all he knows
▷ nm whole; **le tout** all of it (ou them); **le tout est de ...** the main thing is to ...; **pas du tout** not at all
▷ adv **1** (très, complètement) very; **tout près** very near; **le tout premier** the very first; **tout seul** all alone; **le livre tout entier** the whole book; **tout en haut** right at the top; **tout droit** straight ahead
2: **tout en** while; **tout en travaillant** while working, as he etc works ou worked
3: **tout d'abord** first of all; **tout à coup** suddenly; **tout à fait** absolutely; **tout à l'heure** a short while ago; (futur) in a short while, shortly; **à tout à l'heure!** see you later!; **tout de même** all the same; **tout de suite** immediately, straight away; **tout simplement** quite simply

toutefois [tutfwa] adv however
toutes [tut] adj, pron voir **tout**
tout-terrain [tuterɛ̃] adj: **vélo ~** mountain bike; **véhicule ~** four-wheel drive
toux [tu] nf cough
toxicomane [tɔksikɔman] nm/f drug addict
toxique [tɔksik] adj toxic
trac [trak] nm (au théâtre, en public) stage fright; (aux examens) nerves pl; **avoir le ~** (au théâtre, en public) to have stage fright; (aux examens) to be feeling nervous
tracasser [trakase] vt to worry, bother; **se tracasser** to worry
trace [tras] nf (empreintes) tracks pl; (marques, aussi fig) mark; (quantité infime, indice, vestige) trace; **traces de pas** footprints
tracer [trase] vt to draw; (piste) to open up
tract [trakt] nm tract, pamphlet
tracteur [traktœr] nm tractor
traction [traksjɔ̃] nf: **~ avant/arrière** front-wheel/rear-wheel drive
tradition [tradisjɔ̃] nf tradition; **traditionnel, le** adj traditional
traducteur, -trice [tradyktœr, tris] nm/f translator
traduction [tradyksjɔ̃] nf translation
traduire [traduir] vt to translate; (exprimer) to convey; **~ qn en justice** to bring sb before the courts; **pouvez-vous me ~ ceci?** can you translate this for me?
trafic [trafik] nm traffic; **trafic d'armes** arms dealing; **trafiquant, e** nm/f trafficker; (d'armes) dealer; **trafiquer** (péj) vt (vin) to doctor; (moteur, document) to tamper with
tragédie [traʒedi] nf tragedy; **tragique** adj tragic

trahir[traiʀ] vt to betray; **trahison** nf betrayal; (Jur) treason

train[trɛ̃] nm (Rail) train; (allure) pace; **être en ~ de faire qch** to be doing sth; **c'est bien le ~ pour ...?** is this the train for ...?; **train d'atterrissage** undercarriage; **train de vie** lifestyle; **train électrique** (jouet) (electric) train set

traîne[trɛn] nf (de robe) train; **être à la ~** to lag behind

traîneau, x[trɛno] nm sleigh, sledge

traîner[trene] vt (remorque) to pull; (enfant, chien) to drag ou trail along ▷ vi (robe, manteau) to trail; (être en désordre) to lie around; (aller lentement) to dawdle (along); (vagabonder, agir lentement) to hang about; (durer) to drag on; **se traîner** vi: **se ~ par terre** to crawl (on the ground); **~ les pieds** to drag one's feet

train-train[trɛ̃trɛ̃] nm humdrum routine

traire[trɛʀ] vt to milk

trait[trɛ] nm (ligne) line; (de dessin) stroke; (caractéristique) feature, trait; **traits** nmpl (du visage) features; **d'un ~** (boire) in one gulp; **de ~** (animal) draught; **avoir ~ à** to concern; **trait d'union** hyphen

traitant, e[trɛtɑ̃, ɑ̃t] adj (shampooing) medicated; **votre médecin ~** your usual ou family doctor

traite[trɛt] nf (Comm) draft; (Agr) milking; **d'une ~** without stopping

traité[trete] nm treaty

traitement[trɛtmɑ̃] nm treatment; (salaire) salary; **traitement de données** data processing; **traitement de texte** word processing; (logiciel) word processing package

traiter[trete] vt to treat; (qualifier): **~ qn d'idiot** to call sb a fool ▷ vi to deal; **~ de** to deal with

traiteur[trɛtœr] nm caterer

traître, -esse[trɛtr, trɛtrɛs] adj (dangereux) treacherous ▷ nm traitor

trajectoire[traʒɛktwar] nf path

trajet[traʒɛ] nm (parcours, voyage) journey; (itinéraire) route; (distance à parcourir) distance; **il y a une heure de ~** the journey takes one hour

trampoline[trɑ̃pɔlin] nm trampoline

tramway[tramwɛ] nm tram(way); (voiture) tram(car) (BRIT), streetcar (US)

tranchant, e[trɑ̃ʃɑ̃, ɑ̃t] adj sharp; (fig) peremptory ▷ nm (d'un couteau) cutting edge; (de la main) edge; **à double ~** double-edged

tranche[trɑ̃ʃ] nf (morceau) slice; (arête) edge; **~ d'âge/de salaires** age/wage bracket

tranché, e[trɑ̃ʃe] adj (couleurs) distinct; (opinions) clear-cut

trancher[trɑ̃ʃe] vt to cut, sever ▷ vi to take a decision; **~ avec** to contrast sharply with

tranquille[trɑ̃kil] adj quiet; (rassuré) easy in one's mind, with one's mind at rest; **se tenir ~** (enfant) to be quiet; **laisse-moi/laisse-ça ~** leave me/it alone; **avoir la conscience ~** to have a clear conscience; **tranquillisant** nm tranquillizer; **tranquillité** nf peace (and quiet); (d'esprit) peace of mind

transférer[trɑ̃sfere] vt to transfer; **transfert** nm transfer

transformation[trɑ̃sfɔrmasjɔ̃] nf change, alteration; (radicale) transformation; (Rugby) conversion; **transformations** nfpl (travaux) alterations

transformer[trɑ̃sfɔrme] vt to change; (radicalement) to transform; (vêtement) to alter; (matière première, appartement, Rugby) to convert; **(se) en** to turn into

transfusion[trɑ̃sfyzjɔ̃] nf: **~ sanguine** blood transfusion

transgénique[trɑ̃sʒenik] adj transgenic

transgresser[trɑ̃sgrese] vt to contravene

transi, e[trɑ̃zi] adj numb (with cold), chilled to the bone

transiger[trɑ̃ziʒe] vi to compromise

transit[trɑ̃zit] nm transit; **transiter** vi to pass in transit

transition[trɑ̃zisjɔ̃] nf transition; **transitoire** adj transitional

transmettre[trɑ̃smɛtr] vt (passer): **~ qch à qn** to pass sth on to sb; (Tech, Tél, Méd) to transmit; (TV, Radio: retransmettre) to broadcast; **transmission** nf transmission

transparent, e[trɑ̃sparɑ̃, ɑ̃t] adj transparent

transpercer[trɑ̃sperse] vt (froid, pluie) to go through, pierce; (balle) to go through

transpiration[trɑ̃spirasjɔ̃] nf perspiration

transpirer[trɑ̃spire] vi to perspire

transplanter[trɑ̃splɑ̃te] vt (Méd, Bot) to transplant

transport[trɑ̃spɔr] nm transport; **transports en commun** public transport sg; **transporter** vt to carry, move; (Comm) to transport, convey; **transporteur** nm haulage contractor (BRIT), trucker (US)

transvaser[trɑ̃svaze] vt to decant

transversal, e, -aux[trɑ̃svɛrsal, o] adj (rue) which runs across; **coupe ~e** cross section

trapèze[trapɛz] nm (au cirque) trapeze

trappe[trap] nf trap door

trapu, e[trapy] adj squat, stocky

traquenard[traknar] nm trap

traquer[trake] vt to track down; (harceler) to hound

traumatiser[tromatize] vt to traumatize

travail, -aux[travaj] nm (gén) work; (tâche, métier) work no pl, job; (Écon, Méd) labour; **être sans ~** (employé) to be unemployed; voir aussi **travaux; travail (au) noir** moonlighting

travailler[travaje] vi to work; (bois) to warp

▷ *vt* (*bois, métal*) to work; (*objet d'art, discipline*) to work on; **cela le travaille** it is on his mind; **travailleur, -euse** *adj* hard-working ▷ *nm/f* worker; **travailleur social** social worker; **travailliste** *adj* ≈ Labour *cpd*

travaux [tʀavo] *nmpl* (*de réparation, agricoles etc*) work *sg*; (*sur route*) roadworks *pl*; (*de construction*) building (work); **travaux des champs** farmwork *sg*; **travaux dirigés** (*Scol*) tutorial *sg*; **travaux forcés** hard labour *no pl*; **travaux manuels** (*Scol*) handicrafts; **travaux ménagers** housework *no pl*; **travaux pratiques** (*Scol*) practical work; (*en laboratoire*) lab work

travers [tʀavɛʀ] *nm* fault, failing; **en ~ (de)** across; **au ~ (de)/à ~** through; **de ~** (*nez, bouche*) crooked; (*chapeau*) askew; **comprendre de ~** to misunderstand; **regarder de ~** (*fig*) to look askance at

traverse [tʀavɛʀs] *nf* (*de voie ferrée*) sleeper; **chemin de ~** shortcut

traversée [tʀavɛʀse] *nf* crossing; **combien de temps dure la ~?** how long does the crossing take?

traverser [tʀavɛʀse] *vt* (*gén*) to cross; (*ville, tunnel, aussi: percer, fig*) to go through; (*suj: ligne, trait*) to run across

traversin [tʀavɛʀsɛ̃] *nm* bolster

travesti [tʀavɛsti] *nm* transvestite

trébucher [tʀebyʃe] *vi*: **~ (sur)** to stumble (over), trip (against)

trèfle [tʀɛfl] *nm* (*Bot*) clover; (*Cartes: couleur*) clubs *pl*; (: *carte*) club; **~ à quatre feuilles** four-leaf clover

treize [tʀɛz] *num* thirteen; **treizième** *num* thirteenth

tréma [tʀema] *nm* diaeresis

tremblement [tʀɑ̃bləmɑ̃] *nm*: **tremblement de terre** earthquake

trembler [tʀɑ̃ble] *vi* to tremble, shake; **~ de** (*froid, fièvre*) to shiver *ou* tremble with; (*peur*) to shake *ou* tremble with; **~ pour qn** to fear for sb

trémousser [tʀemuse]: **se trémousser** *vi* to jig about, wriggle about

trempé, e [tʀɑ̃pe] *adj* soaking (wet), drenched; (*Tech*) tempered

tremper [tʀɑ̃pe] *vt* to soak, drench; (*aussi:* **faire ~, mettre à ~**) to soak; (*plonger*): **~ qch dans** to dip sth in(to) ▷ *vi* to soak; (*fig*): **~ dans** to be involved *ou* have a hand in; **se tremper** *vi* to have a quick dip

tremplin [tʀɑ̃plɛ̃] *nm* springboard; (*Ski*) ski-jump

trentaine [tʀɑ̃tɛn] *nf*: **une ~ (de)** thirty or so, about thirty; **avoir la ~** (*âge*) to be around thirty

trente [tʀɑ̃t] *num* thirty; **être sur son ~ et un** to be wearing one's Sunday best; **trentième** *num* thirtieth

trépidant, e [tʀepidɑ̃, ɑ̃t] *adj* (*fig: rythme*) pulsating; (: *vie*) hectic

trépigner [tʀepiɲe] *vi* to stamp (one's feet)

très [tʀɛ] *adv* very; much +*pp*, highly +*pp*

trésor [tʀezɔʀ] *nm* treasure; **Trésor (public)** public revenue; **trésorerie** *nf* (*gestion*) accounts *pl*; (*bureaux*) accounts department; **difficultés de trésorerie** cash problems, shortage of cash *ou* funds; **trésorier, -ière** *nm/f* treasurer

tressaillir [tʀesajiʀ] *vi* to shiver, shudder

tressauter [tʀesote] *vi* to start, jump

tresse [tʀɛs] *nf* braid, plait; **tresser** *vt* (*cheveux*) to braid, plait; (*fil, jonc*) to plait; (*corbeille*) to weave; (*corde*) to twist

tréteau, x [tʀeto] *nm* trestle

treuil [tʀœj] *nm* winch

trêve [tʀɛv] *nf* (*Mil, Pol*) truce; (*fig*) respite; **~ de ...** enough of this ...

tri [tʀi] *nm*: **faire le ~ (de)** to sort out; **le (bureau de) ~** (*Postes*) the sorting office

triangle [tʀijɑ̃gl] *nm* triangle; **triangulaire** *adj* triangular

tribord [tʀibɔʀ] *nm*: **à ~** to starboard, on the starboard side

tribu [tʀiby] *nf* tribe

tribunal, -aux [tʀibynal, o] *nm* (*Jur*) court; (*Mil*) tribunal

tribune [tʀibyn] *nf* (*estrade*) platform, rostrum; (*débat*) forum; (*d'église, de tribunal*) gallery; (*de stade*) stand

tribut [tʀiby] *nm* tribute

tributaire [tʀibytɛʀ] *adj*: **être ~ de** to be dependent on

tricher [tʀiʃe] *vi* to cheat; **tricheur, -euse** *nm/f* cheat(er)

tricolore [tʀikɔlɔʀ] *adj* three-coloured; (*français*) red, white and blue

tricot [tʀiko] *nm* (*technique, ouvrage*) knitting *no pl*; (*vêtement*) jersey, sweater; **~ de peau** vest; **tricoter** *vt* to knit

tricycle [tʀisikl] *nm* tricycle

trier [tʀije] *vt* to sort out; (*Postes, fruits*) to sort

trimestre [tʀimɛstʀ] *nm* (*Scol*) term; (*Comm*) quarter; **trimestriel, le** *adj* quarterly; (*Scol*) end-of-term

trinquer [tʀɛ̃ke] *vi* to clink glasses

triomphe [tʀijɔ̃f] *nm* triumph; **triompher** *vi* to triumph, win; (*Postes, fruits*) to sort **triompher de** to triumph over, overcome

tripes [tʀip] *nfpl* (*Culin*) tripe *sg*

triple [tʀipl] *adj* triple ▷ *nm*: **le ~ (de)** (*comparaison*) three times as much (as); **en ~ exemplaire** in triplicate; **tripler** *vi, vt* to triple, treble

triplés, -ées [tʀiple] *nm/fpl* triplets

tripoter [tʀipɔte] *vt* to fiddle with

triste [tʀist] *adj* sad; (*couleur, temps, journée*) dreary; (*péj*): **~ personnage/affaire** sorry individual/affair; **tristesse** nf sadness

trivial, e, -aux [tʀivjal, jo] adj coarse, crude; (commun) mundane

troc [tʀɔk] nm barter

trognon [tʀɔɲɔ̃] nm (de fruit) core; (de légume) stalk

trois [tʀwa] num three; **troisième** num third ▷ nf (Scol) year 10 (BRIT), ninth grade (US); **le troisième âge** (période de vie) one's retirement years; (personnes âgées) senior citizens pl

trombe [tʀɔ̃b] nf: **des ~s d'eau** a downpour; **en ~** like a whirlwind

trombone [tʀɔ̃bɔn] nm (Mus) trombone; (de bureau) paper clip

trompe [tʀɔ̃p] nf (d'éléphant) trunk; (Mus) trumpet, horn

tromper [tʀɔ̃pe] vt to deceive; (vigilance, poursuivants) to elude; **se tromper** vi to make a mistake, be mistaken; **se ~ de voiture/jour** to take the wrong car/get the day wrong; **se ~ de 3 cm/20 euros** to be out by 3 cm/20 euros; **je me suis trompé de route** I took the wrong road

trompette [tʀɔ̃pɛt] nf trumpet; **en ~** (nez) turned-up

trompeur, -euse [tʀɔ̃pœʀ, øz] adj deceptive

tronc [tʀɔ̃] nm (Bot, Anat) trunk; (d'église) collection box

tronçon [tʀɔ̃sɔ̃] nm section; **tronçonner** vt to saw up; **tronçonneuse** nf chainsaw

trône [tʀon] nm throne

trop [tʀo] adv (+vb) too much; (+adjectif, adverbe) too; **~ (nombreux)** too many; **~ peu (nombreux)** too few; **~ (souvent)** too often; **~ (longtemps)** (for) too long; **~ de** (nombre) too many; (quantité) too much; **de ~, en ~:** des livres en ~ a few books too many; **du lait en ~** too much milk; **3 livres/3 euros de ~** 3 books too many/3 euros too much; **ça coûte ~ cher** it's too expensive

tropical, e, -aux [tʀɔpikal, o] adj tropical

tropique [tʀɔpik] nm tropic

trop-plein [tʀoplɛ̃] nm (tuyau) overflow ou outlet (pipe); (liquide) overflow

troquer [tʀɔke] vt: **~ qch contre** to barter ou trade sth for; (fig) to swap sth for

trot [tʀo] nm trot; **trotter** vi to trot

trottinette [tʀɔtinɛt] nf (child's) scooter

trottoir [tʀɔtwaʀ] nm pavement (BRIT), sidewalk (US); **faire le ~** (péj) to walk the streets; **trottoir roulant** moving walkway, travellator

trou [tʀu] nm hole; (fig) gap; (Comm) deficit; **trou d'air** air pocket; **trou de mémoire** blank, lapse of memory

troublant, e [tʀublɑ̃, ɑ̃t] adj disturbing

trouble [tʀubl] adj (liquide) cloudy; (image, photo) blurred; (affaire) shady, murky ▷ adv: **voir ~** to have blurred vision ▷ nm agitation;

troubles nmpl (Pol) disturbances, troubles, unrest sg; (Méd) trouble sg, disorders; **trouble-fête** nm spoilsport

troubler [tʀuble] vt to disturb; (liquide) to make cloudy; (intriguer) to bother; **se troubler** vi (personne) to become flustered ou confused

trouer [tʀue] vt to make a hole (ou holes) in

trouille [tʀuj] (fam) nf: **avoir la ~** to be scared to death

troupe [tʀup] nf troop; **troupe (de théâtre)** (theatrical) company

troupeau, x [tʀupo] nm (de moutons) flock; (de vaches) herd

trousse [tʀus] nf case, kit; (d'écolier) pencil case; **aux ~s de** (fig) on the heels ou tail of; **trousse à outils** toolkit; **trousse de toilette** toilet bag

trousseau, x [tʀuso] nm (de mariée) trousseau; **trousseau de clefs** bunch of keys

trouvaille [tʀuvaj] nf find

trouver [tʀuve] vt to find; (rendre visite): **aller/ venir ~ qn** to go/come and see sb; **se trouver** vi (être) to be; **je trouve que** I find ou think that; **~ à boire/critiquer** to find something to drink/criticize; **se ~ mal** to pass out

truand [tʀyɑ̃] nm gangster; **truander** vt: **se faire truander** to be swindled

truc [tʀyk] nm (astuce) way, trick; (de cinéma, prestidigitateur) trick, effect; (chose) thing, thingumajig; **avoir le ~** to have the knack; **c'est pas mon ~** (fam) it's not really my thing

truffe [tʀyf] nf truffle; (nez) nose

truffé, e [tʀyfe] adj (Culin) garnished with truffles; **~ de** (fig: citations) peppered with; (: fautes) riddled with; (: pièges) bristling with

truie [tʀyi] nf sow

truite [tʀyit] nf trout inv

truquage [tʀykaʒ] nm special effects pl

truquer [tʀyke] vt (élections, serrure, dés) to fix

TSVP sigle (= tournez svp) PTO

TTC sigle (= toutes taxes comprises) inclusive of tax

tu¹ [ty] pron you; **dire tu à qn** to use the "tu" form to sb

tu², e [ty] pp de **taire**

tuba [tyba] nm (Mus) tuba; (Sport) snorkel

tube [tyb] nm tube; (chanson) hit

tuberculose [tybɛʀkyloz] nf tuberculosis

tuer [tɥe] vt to kill; **se tuer** vi to be killed; (suicide) to kill o.s.; **se ~ au travail** (fig) to work o.s. to death; **tuerie** nf slaughter no pl

tue-tête [tytɛt]: **à ~** adv at the top of one's voice

tueur [tɥœʀ] nm killer; **tueur à gages** hired killer

tuile [tɥil] nf tile; (fam) spot of bad luck, blow

tulipe [tylip] nf tulip

tuméfié, e [tymefje] adj puffed-up, swollen

tumeur [tymœʀ] nf growth, tumour

tumulte [tymylt] *nm* commotion;
  tumultueux, -euse *adj* stormy, turbulent
tunique [tynik] *nf* tunic
Tunis [tynis] *n* Tunis
Tunisie [tynizi] *nf*: **la ~** Tunisia; **tunisien, ne**
  adj Tunisian ▷ *nm/f*: **Tunisien, ne** Tunisian
tunnel [tynɛl] *nm* tunnel; **le ~ sous la**
  Manche the Channel Tunnel
turbulent, e [tyʀbylɑ̃, ɑ̃t] *adj* boisterous,
  unruly
turc, turque [tyʀk] *adj* Turkish ▷ *nm/f*: **T~,**
  Turque Turk/Turkish woman ▷ *nm* (*Ling*)
  Turkish
turf [tyʀf] *nm* racing; **turfiste** *nm/f* racegoer
Turquie [tyʀki] *nf*: **la ~** Turkey
turquoise [tyʀkwaz] *nf* turquoise ▷ *adj inv*
  turquoise
tutelle [tytɛl] *nf* (*Jur*) guardianship; (*Pol*)
  trusteeship; **sous la ~ de** (*fig*) under the
  supervision of
tuteur [tytœʀ] *nm* (*Jur*) guardian; (*de plante*)
  stake, support
tutoyer [tytwaje] *vt*: **~ qn** to address sb as "tu"
tuyau, x [tɥijo] *nm* pipe; (*flexible*) tube; (*fam*)
  tip; **tuyau d'arrosage** hosepipe; **tuyau**
  d'échappement exhaust pipe; **tuyauterie**
  nf piping *no pl*
TVA *sigle f* (= *taxe à la valeur ajoutée*) VAT
tympan [tɛ̃pɑ̃] *nm* (*Anat*) eardrum
type [tip] *nm* type; (*fam*) chap, guy ▷ *adj*
  typical, classic
typé, e [tipe] *adj* ethnic
typique [tipik] *adj* typical
tyran [tiʀɑ̃] *nm* tyrant; **tyrannique** *adj*
  tyrannical
tzigane [dzigan] *adj* gipsy, tzigane

ulcère [ylsɛʀ] *nm* ulcer
ultérieur, e [ylteʀjœʀ] *adj* later, subsequent;
  remis à une date ~e postponed to a later
  date; **ultérieurement** *adv* later, subsequently
ultime [yltim] *adj* final

 MOT-CLÉ

un, une [œ̃, yn] *art indéf* a; (*devant voyelle*) an;
  un garçon/vieillard a boy/an old man; **une**
  fille a girl
  ▷ *pron* one; **l'un des meilleurs** one of the
  best; **l'un ..., l'autre** (the) one ..., the other;
  les uns ..., les autres some ..., others; **l'un et**
  l'autre both
  (of them); **l'un ou l'autre** either (of them);
  l'un l'autre each other; **les**
  uns les autres one another; **pas un seul** not a
  single one; **un par un** one by one
  ▷ *num* one; **un pamplemousse seulement**
  one grapefruit only, just one grapefruit
  ▷ *nf*: **la une** (*Presse*) the front page

unanime [ynanim] *adj* unanimous;
  unanimité *nf*: **à l'unanimité** unanimously
uni, e [yni] *adj* (*ton, tissu*) plain; (*surface*)
  smooth, even; (*famille*) close(-knit); (*pays*)
  united
unifier [ynifje] *vt* to unite, unify
uniforme [ynifɔʀm] *adj* uniform; (*surface,*

ton) even ▷ *nm* uniform; **uniformiser** *vt*
(*systèmes*) to standardize
union [ynjɔ̃] *nf* union; **union de**
consommateurs consumers' association;
union libre: **vivre en union libre** (*en*
concubinage) to cohabit; **Union européenne**
European Union; **Union soviétique** Soviet
Union
unique [ynik] *adj* (*seul*) only; (*exceptionnel*)
unique; (*le même*): **un prix/système ~** a
single price/system; **fils/fille ~** only son/
daughter, only child; **sens ~** one-way street;
uniquement *adv* only, solely; (*juste*) only,
merely
unir [yniʀ] *vt* (*nations*) to unite; (*en mariage*)
to unite, join together; **s'unir** *vi* to unite; (*en*
mariage) to be joined together
unitaire [yniteʀ] *adj*: **prix ~** unit price
unité [ynite] *nf* unit; (*harmonie, cohésion*) unity
univers [yniveʀ] *nm* universe; **universel, le**
adj universal
universitaire [yniveʀsiteʀ] *adj* university
cpd; (*diplôme, études*) academic, university *cpd*
▷ *nm/f* academic
université [yniveʀsite] *nf* university
urbain, e [yʀbɛ̃, ɛn] *adj* urban, city *cpd*,
town *cpd*; **urbanisme** *nm* town planning
urgence [yʀʒɑ̃s] *nf* urgency; (*Méd etc*)
emergency; **d'~** *adj* emergency *cpd* ▷ *adv* as a
matter of urgency; (**service des**) **~s** casualty
urgent, e [yʀʒɑ̃, ɑ̃t] *adj* urgent
urine [yʀin] *nf* urine; **urinoir** *nm* (public)
urinal
urne [yʀn] *nf* (*électorale*) ballot box; (*vase*) urn
urticaire [yʀtikeʀ] *nf* nettle rash
us [ys] *nmpl*: **us et coutumes** (habits and)
customs
usage [yzaʒ] *nm* (*emploi, utilisation*) use;
(*coutume*) custom; **à l'~** with use; **à l'~ de** (*pour*)
for (use of); **en ~** in use; **hors d'~** out of service;
à ~ interne (*Méd*) to be taken (internally); **à ~**
externe (*Méd*) for external use only; **usagé, e**
adj (*usé*) worn; **usager, -ère** *nm/f* user
usé, e [yze] *adj* worn; (*banal: argument etc*)
hackneyed
user [yze] *vt* (*outil*) to wear down; (*vêtement*) to
wear out; (*matière*) to wear away; (*consommer*:
charbon etc) to use; **s'user** *vi* (*tissu, vêtement*) to
wear out; **~ de** (*moyen, procédé*) to use, employ;
(*droit*) to exercise
usine [yzin] *nf* factory
usité, e [yzite] *adj* common
ustensile [ystɑ̃sil] *nm* implement; **ustensile**
de cuisine kitchen utensil
usuel, le [yzɥɛl] *adj* everyday, common
usure [yzyʀ] *nf* wear
utérus [yteʀys] *nm* uterus, womb
utile [ytil] *adj* useful
utilisation [ytilizasjɔ̃] *nf* use

utiliser [ytilize] *vt* to use
utilitaire [ytiliteʀ] *adj* utilitarian
utilité [ytilite] *nf* usefulness *no pl*; **de peu d'~**
of little use *ou* help
utopie [ytɔpi] *nf* utopia

va [va] *vb voir* **aller**

vacance [vakɑ̃s] *nf* (*Admin*) vacancy; **vacances** *nfpl* holiday(s *pl* (BRIT)), vacation *sg* (US); **les grandes ~s** the summer holidays; **prendre des/ses ~s** to take a holiday/one's holiday(s); **aller en ~s** to go on holiday; **je suis ici en ~s** I'm here on holiday; **vacancier, -ière** *nm/f* holiday-maker

vacant, e [vakɑ̃, ɑ̃t] *adj* vacant

vacarme [vakaʀm] *nm* (*bruit*) racket

vaccin [vaksɛ̃] *nm* vaccine; (*opération*) vaccination; **vaccination** *nf* vaccination; **vacciner** *vt* to vaccinate; **être vacciné contre qch** (*fam*) to be cured of sth

vache [vaʃ] *nf* (*Zool*) cow; (*cuir*) cowhide ▷ *adj* (*fam*) rotten, mean; **vachement** (*fam*) *adv* (*très*) really; (*pleuvoir, travailler*) a hell of a lot; **vacherie** (*fam*) *nf* (*action*) dirty trick; (*remarque*) nasty remark

vaciller [vasije] *vi* to sway, wobble; (*bougie, lumière*) to flicker; (*fig*) to be failing, falter

va-et-vient [vaevjɛ̃] *nm inv* (*de personnes, véhicules*) comings and goings *pl*, to-ings and fro-ings *pl*

vagabond [vagabɔ̃] *nm* (*rôdeur*) tramp, vagrant; (*voyageur*) wanderer; **vagabonder** *vi* to roam, wander

vagin [vaʒɛ̃] *nm* vagina

vague [vag] *nf* wave ▷ *adj* vague; (*regard*) faraway; (*manteau, robe*) loose(-fitting); (*quelconque*): **un ~ bureau/cousin** some office/cousin or other; **vague de fond** ground swell; **vague de froid** cold spell

vaillant, e [vajɑ̃, ɑ̃t] *adj* (*courageux*) gallant; (*robuste*) hale and hearty

vain, e [vɛ̃, vɛn] *adj* vain; **en ~** in vain

vaincre [vɛ̃kʀ] *vt* to defeat; (*fig*) to conquer, overcome; **vaincu, e** *nm/f* defeated party; **vainqueur** *nm* victor; (*Sport*) winner

vaisseau, x [veso] *nm* (*Anat*) vessel; (*Navig*) ship, vessel; **vaisseau spatial** spaceship

vaisselier [vesəlje] *nm* dresser

vaisselle [vesɛl] *nf* (*service*) crockery; (*plats etc à laver*) (dirty) dishes *pl*; **faire la ~** to do the washing-up (BRIT) *ou* the dishes

valable [valabl] *adj* valid; (*acceptable*) decent, worthwhile

valet [valɛ] *nm* manservant; (*Cartes*) jack

valeur [valœʀ] *nf* (*gén*) value; (*mérite*) worth, merit; (*Comm: titre*) security; **valeurs** *nfpl* (*morales*) values; **mettre en ~** (*détail*) to highlight; (*objet décoratif*) to show off to advantage; **avoir de la ~** to be valuable; **sans ~** worthless; **prendre de la ~** to go up *ou* gain in value

valide [valid] *adj* (*en bonne santé*) fit; (*valable*) valid; **valider** *vt* to validate

valise [valiz] *nf* (suit)case; **faire ses ~s** to pack one's bags

vallée [vale] *nf* valley

vallon [valɔ̃] *nm* small valley

valoir [valwaʀ] *vi* (*être valable*) to hold, apply ▷ *vt* (*prix, valeur, effort*) to be worth; (*causer*): **~ qch à qn** to earn sb sth; **se valoir** *vi* to be of equal merit; (*péj*) to be two of a kind; **faire ~** (*droits, prérogatives*) to assert; **se faire ~** to make the most of o.s.; **à ~ sur** to be deducted from; **vaille que vaille** somehow or other; **cela ne me dit rien qui vaille** I don't like the look of it at all; **ce climat ne me vaut rien** this climate doesn't suit me; **~ le coup** *ou* **la peine** to be worth the trouble *ou* worth it; **~ mieux**: **il vaut mieux se taire** it's better to say nothing; **ça ne vaut rien** it's worthless; **que vaut ce candidat?** how good is this applicant?

valse [vals] *nf* waltz

vandalisme [vɑ̃dalism] *nm* vandalism

vanille [vanij] *nf* vanilla

vanité [vanite] *nf* vanity; **vaniteux, -euse** *adj* vain, conceited

vanne [van] *nf* gate; (*fig*) joke

vannerie [vanʀi] *nf* basketwork

vantard, e [vɑ̃taʀ, aʀd] *adj* boastful

vanter [vɑ̃te] *vt* to speak highly of, praise; **se vanter** *vi* to boast, brag; **se ~ de** to pride o.s. on; (*péj*) to boast of

vapeur [vapœʀ] *nf* steam; (*émanation*) vapour, fumes *pl*; **vapeurs** *nfpl* (*bouffées*) vapours; **à ~** steam-powered, steam *cpd*; **cuit à la ~**

steamed; **vaporeux, -euse** adj (flou) hazy, misty; (léger) filmy; **vaporisateur** nm spray; **vaporiser** vt (parfum etc) to spray

varappe [vaʀap] nf rock climbing

vareuse [vaʀøz] nf (blouson) pea jacket; (d'uniforme) tunic

variable [vaʀjabl] adj variable; (temps, humeur) changeable; (divers: résultats) varied, various

varice [vaʀis] nf varicose vein

varicelle [vaʀisɛl] nf chickenpox

varié, e [vaʀje] adj varied; (divers) various; **hors d'œuvre ~s** selection of hors d'œuvres

varier [vaʀje] vi to vary; (temps, humeur) to change ▷ vt to vary; **variété** nf variety; **variétés** nfpl: **spectacle/émission de variétés** variety show

variole [vaʀjɔl] nf smallpox

Varsovie [vaʀsɔvi] n Warsaw

vas [va] vb voir **aller; ~-y!** [vazi] go on!

vase [vaz] nm vase ▷ nf silt, mud; **vaseux, -euse** adj silty, muddy; (fig: confus) woolly, hazy; (: fatigué) woozy

vasistas [vazistas] nm fanlight

vaste [vast] adj vast, immense

vautour [votuʀ] nm vulture

vautrer [votʀe] vb: **se ~ dans/sur** to wallow in/sprawl on

va-vite [vavit]: **à la ~** adv in a rush ou hurry

VDQS sigle (= vin délimité de qualité supérieure) label guaranteeing the quality of wine

veau, x [vo] nm (Zool) calf; (Culin) veal; (peau) calfskin

vécu, e [veky] pp de **vivre**

vedette [vədɛt] nf (artiste etc) star; (canot) motor boat; (police) launch

végétal, e, -aux [veʒetal, o] adj vegetable ▷ nm vegetable, plant; **végétalien, ne** adj, nm/f vegan

végétarien, ne [veʒetaʀjɛ̃, jɛn] adj, nm/f vegetarian; **avez-vous des plats ~s?** do you have any vegetarian dishes?

végétation [veʒetasjɔ̃] nf vegetation; **végétations** nfpl (Méd) adenoids

véhicule [veikyl] nm vehicle; **véhicule utilitaire** commercial vehicle

veille [vɛj] nf (état) wakefulness; (jour): **la ~ (de)** the day before; **la ~ au soir** the previous evening; **à la ~ de** on the eve of; **la ~ de Noël** Christmas Eve; **la ~ du jour de l'An** New Year's Eve

veillée [veje] nf (soirée) evening; (réunion) evening gathering; **veillée (funèbre)** wake

veiller [veje] vi to stay up ▷ vt (malade, mort) to watch over, sit up with; **~ à** to attend to, see to; **~ à ce que** to make sure that; **~ sur** to watch over; **veilleur** nm: **veilleur de nuit** night watchman; **veilleuse** nf (lampe) night light; (Auto) sidelight; (flamme) pilot light

veinard, e [vɛnaʀ, aʀd] nm/f lucky devil

veine [vɛn] nf (Anat, du bois etc) vein; (filon) vein, seam; (fam: chance): **avoir de la ~** to be lucky

véliplanchiste [veliplɑ̃ʃist] nm/f windsurfer

vélo [velo] nm bike, cycle; **faire du ~** to go cycling; **vélomoteur** nm moped

velours [v(ə)luʀ] nm velvet; **velours côtelé** corduroy; **velouté, e** adj velvety ▷ nm: **velouté de tomates** cream of tomato soup

velu, e [vəly] adj hairy

vendange [vɑ̃dɑ̃ʒ] nf (aussi: ~s) grape harvest; **vendanger** vi to harvest the grapes

vendeur, -euse [vɑ̃dœʀ, øz] nm/f shop assistant ▷ nm (Jur) vendor, seller

vendre [vɑ̃dʀ] vt to sell; **~ qch à qn** to sell sb sth; **"à ~"** "for sale"

vendredi [vɑ̃dʀədi] nm Friday; **vendredi saint** Good Friday

vénéneux, -euse [venenø, øz] adj poisonous

vénérien, ne [veneʀjɛ̃, jɛn] adj venereal

vengeance [vɑ̃ʒɑ̃s] nf vengeance no pl, revenge no pl

venger [vɑ̃ʒe] vt to avenge; **se venger** vi to avenge o.s.; **se ~ de qch** to avenge o.s. for sth, take one's revenge for sth; **se ~ de qn** to take revenge on sb; **se ~ sur** to take revenge on

venimeux, -euse [vənimø, øz] adj poisonous, venomous; (fig: haineux) venomous, vicious

venin [vənɛ̃] nm venom, poison

venir [v(ə)niʀ] vi to come; **~ de** to come from; **~ de faire: je viens d'y aller/de le voir** I've just been there/seen him; **s'il vient à pleuvoir** if it should rain; **j'en viens à croire que** I have come to believe that; **où veux-tu en ~?** what are you getting at?; **faire ~** (docteur, plombier) to call (out)

vent [vɑ̃] nm wind; **il y a du ~** it's windy; **c'est du ~** it's all hot air; **dans le ~** (fam) trendy

vente [vɑ̃t] nf sale; **la ~** (activité) selling; (secteur) sales pl; **mettre en ~** (produit) to put on sale; (maison, objet personnel) to put up for sale; **vente aux enchères** auction sale; **vente de charité** jumble sale

venteux, -euse [vɑ̃tø, øz] adj windy

ventilateur [vɑ̃tilatœʀ] nm fan

ventiler [vɑ̃tile] vt to ventilate

ventouse [vɑ̃tuz] nf (de caoutchouc) suction pad

ventre [vɑ̃tʀ] nm (Anat) stomach; (légèrement péj) belly; (utérus) womb; **avoir mal au ~** to have stomach ache (BRIT) ou a stomach ache (US)

venu, e [v(ə)ny] pp de **venir** ▷ adj: **bien ~** timely; **mal ~** out of place; **être mal ~ à ou de faire** to have no grounds for doing, be in no position to do

ver [vɛʀ] nm worm; (des fruits etc) maggot; (du

bois) woodworm *no pl*; *voir aussi* **vers**; **ver à soie** silkworm; **ver de terre** earthworm; **ver luisant** glow-worm; **ver solitaire** tapeworm

verbe [vɛʀb] *nm* verb

verdâtre [vɛʀdɑtʀ] *adj* greenish

verdict [vɛʀdik(t)] *nm* verdict

verdir [vɛʀdiʀ] *vi, vt* to turn green; **verdure** *nf* greenery

véreux, -euse [veʀø, øz] *adj* worm-eaten; (*malhonnête*) shady, corrupt

verge [vɛʀʒ] *nf* (*Anat*) penis

verger [vɛʀʒe] *nm* orchard

verglacé, e [vɛʀɡlase] *adj* icy, iced-over

verglas [vɛʀɡlɑ] *nm* (black) ice

véridique [veʀidik] *adj* truthful

vérification [veʀifikasjɔ̃] *nf* (*action*) checking *no pl*; (*contrôle*) check

vérifier [veʀifje] *vt* to check; (*corroborer*) to confirm, bear out

véritable [veʀitabl] *adj* real; (*ami, amour*) true; **un ~ désastre** an absolute disaster

vérité [veʀite] *nf* truth; **en ~** really, actually

verlan [vɛʀlɑ̃] *nm* (*fam*) (back) slang

vermeil, le [vɛʀmɛj] *adj* ruby red

vermine [vɛʀmin] *nf* vermin *pl*

vermoulu, e [vɛʀmuly] *adj* worm-eaten

verni, e [vɛʀni] *adj* (*fam*) lucky; **cuir ~** patent leather

vernir [vɛʀniʀ] *vt* (*bois, tableau, ongles*) to varnish; (*poterie*) to glaze; **vernis** *nm* (*enduit*) varnish; glaze; (*fig*) veneer; **vernis à ongles** nail polish *ou* varnish; **vernissage** *nm* (*d'une exposition*) preview

vérole [veʀɔl] *nf* (*variole*) smallpox

verre [vɛʀ] *nm* glass; (*de lunettes*) lens *sg*; **boire ou prendre un ~** to have a drink; **verres de contact** contact lenses; **verrière** *nf* (*paroi vitrée*) glass wall; (*toit vitré*) glass roof

verrou [veʀu] *nm* (*targette*) bolt; **mettre qn sous les ~s** to put sb behind bars; **verrouillage** *nm* locking; **verrouillage centralisé** central locking; **verrouiller** *vt* (*porte*) to bolt; (*ordinateur*) to lock

verrue [veʀy] *nf* wart

vers [vɛʀ] *nm* line *ou* *nmpl* (*poésie*) verse *sg* ▷ *prép* (*en direction de*) toward(s); (*près de*) around (about); (*temporel*) about, around

versant [vɛʀsɑ̃] *nm* slopes *pl*, side

versatile [vɛʀsatil] *adj* fickle, changeable

verse [vɛʀs]: **à ~** *adv*: **il pleut à ~** it's pouring (with rain)

Verseau [vɛʀso] *nm*: **le ~** Aquarius

versement [vɛʀsəmɑ̃] *nm* payment; **en 3 ~s** in 3 instalments

verser [vɛʀse] *vt* (*liquide, grains*) to pour; (*larmes, sang*) to shed; (*argent*) to pay; **~ qch sur un compte** to pay sth into an account

version [vɛʀsjɔ̃] *nf* version; (*Scol*) translation (*into the mother tongue*); **film en ~ originale** film in the original language

verso [vɛʀso] *nm* back; **voir au ~** see over(leaf)

vert, e [vɛʀ, vɛʀt] *adj* green; (*vin*) young; (*vigoureux*) sprightly ▷ *nm* green; **les V~s** (*Pol*) the Greens

vertèbre [vɛʀtɛbʀ] *nf* vertebra

vertement [vɛʀtəmɑ̃] *adv* (*réprimander*) sharply

vertical, e, -aux [vɛʀtikal, o] *adj* vertical; **verticale** *nf* vertical; **à la verticale** vertically; **verticalement** *adv* vertically

vertige [vɛʀtiʒ] *nm* (*peur du vide*) vertigo; (*étourdissement*) dizzy spell; (*fig*) fever; **vertigineux, -euse** *adj* breathtaking

vertu [vɛʀty] *nf* virtue; **en ~ de** in accordance with; **vertueux, -euse** *adj* virtuous

verve [vɛʀv] *nf* witty eloquence; **être en ~** to be in brilliant form

verveine [vɛʀvɛn] *nf* (*Bot*) verbena, vervain; (*infusion*) verbena tea

vésicule [vezikyl] *nf* vesicle; **vésicule biliaire** gall-bladder

vessie [vesi] *nf* bladder

veste [vɛst] *nf* jacket; **veste droite/croisée** single-/double-breasted jacket

vestiaire [vɛstjɛʀ] *nm* (*au théâtre etc*) cloakroom; (*de stade etc*) changing-room (BRIT), locker-room (US)

vestibule [vɛstibyl] *nm* hall

vestige [vɛstiʒ] *nm* relic; (*fig*) vestige; **vestiges** *nmpl* (*de ville*) remains

vestimentaire [vɛstimɑ̃tɛʀ] *adj* (*détail*) of dress; (*élégance*) sartorial; **dépenses ~s** clothing expenditure

veston [vɛstɔ̃] *nm* jacket

vêtement [vɛtmɑ̃] *nm* garment, item of clothing; **vêtements** *nmpl* clothes

vétérinaire [veteʀinɛʀ] *nm/f* vet, veterinary surgeon

vêtir [vetiʀ] *vt* to clothe, dress

vêtu, e [vety] *pp de* **vêtir** ▷ *adj*: **~ de** dressed in, wearing

vétuste [vetyst] *adj* ancient, timeworn

veuf, veuve [vœf, vœv] *adj* widowed ▷ *nm* widower

veuve [vœv] *nf* widow

vexant, e [vɛksɑ̃, ɑ̃t] *adj* (*contrariant*) annoying; (*blessant*) hurtful

vexation [vɛksasjɔ̃] *nf* humiliation

vexer [vɛkse] *vt*: **~ qn** to hurt sb's feelings; **se vexer** *vi* to be offended

viable [vjabl] *adj* viable; (*économie, industrie etc*) sustainable

viande [vjɑ̃d] *nf* meat; **je ne mange pas de ~** I don't eat meat

vibrer [vibʀe] *vi* to vibrate; (*son, voix*) to be vibrant; (*fig*) to be stirred; **faire ~** to (cause to) vibrate; (*fig*) to stir, thrill

vice [vis] *nm* vice; (*défaut*) fault ▷ *préfixe*: **~...** vice-; **vice de forme** legal flaw *ou* irregularity

vicié, e [visje] *adj* (*air*) polluted, tainted; (*Jur*) invalidated

vicieux, -euse [visjø, jøz] *adj* (*pervers*) lecherous; (*rétif*) unruly ▷ *nm/f* lecher

vicinal, e, -aux [visinal, o] *adj*: **chemin ~** by-road, byway

victime [viktim] *nf* victim; (*d'accident*) casualty

victoire [viktwaR] *nf* victory

victuailles [viktɥaj] *nfpl* provisions

vidange [vidɑ̃ʒ] *nf* (*d'un fossé, réservoir*) emptying; (*Auto*) oil change; (*de lavabo: bonde*) waste outlet; **vidanges** *nfpl* (*matières*) sewage *sg*; **vidanger** *vt* to empty

vide [vid] *adj* empty ▷ *nm* (*Physique*) vacuum; (*espace*) (empty) space, gap; (*futilité, néant*) void; **avoir peur du ~** to be afraid of heights; **emballé sous ~** vacuum packed; **à ~** (*sans occupants*) empty; (*sans charge*) unladen

vidéo [video] *nf* video ▷ *adj*: **cassette ~** video cassette; **jeu ~** video game; **vidéoclip** *nm* music video; **vidéoconférence** *nf* videoconference

vide-ordures [vidɔRdyR] *nm inv* (rubbish) chute

vider [vide] *vt* to empty; (*Culin: volaille, poisson*) to gut, clean out; **se vider** *vi* to empty; **~ les lieux** to quit *ou* vacate the premises; **videur** *nm* (*de boîte de nuit*) bouncer, doorman

vie [vi] *nf* life; **être en ~** to be alive; **sans ~** lifeless; **à ~** for life; **que faites-vous dans la ~?** what do you do?

vieil [vjɛj] *adj m voir* **vieux**; **vieillard** *nm* old man; **vieille** *adj, nf voir* **vieux**; **vieilleries** *nfpl* old things; **vieillesse** *nf* old age; **vieillir** *vi* (*prendre de l'âge*) to grow old; (*population, vin*) to age; (*doctrine, auteur*) to become dated ▷ *vt* to age; **vieillissement** *nm* growing old; ageing

Vienne [vjɛn] *nf* Vienna

viens [vjɛ̃] *vb voir* **venir**

vierge [vjɛRʒ] *adj* virgin; (*page*) clean, blank ▷ *nf* virgin; (*signe*): **la V~** Virgo

Vietnam, Viet-Nam [vjɛtnam] *nm* Vietnam; **vietnamien, ne** *adj* Vietnamese ▷ *nm/f*: **Vietnamien, ne** Vietnamese

vieux, vieil, vieille [vjø, vjɛj] *adj* old ▷ *nm/f* old man (woman); **les vieux** *nmpl* old people; **un petit ~** a little old man; **mon ~/ma vieille** (*fam*) old man/girl; **prendre un coup de ~** to put years on; **vieux garçon** bachelor; **vieux jeu** *adj inv* old-fashioned

vif, vive [vif, viv] *adj* (*animé*) lively; (*alerte, brusque, aigu*) sharp; (*lumière, couleur*) bright; (*air*) crisp; (*vent, émotion*) keen; (*fort: regret, déception*) great, deep; (*vivant*): **brûlé ~** burnt alive; **de vive voix** personally; **avoir l'esprit ~** to be quick-witted; **piquer qn au ~** to cut sb to the quick; **à ~** (*plaie*) open; **avoir les nerfs à ~** to be on edge

vigne [viɲ] *nf* (*plante*) vine; (*plantation*) vineyard; **vigneron** *nm* wine grower

vignette [viɲɛt] *nf* (*Admin*) ≈ (road) tax disc (BRIT), ≈ license plate sticker (US); (*de médicament*) price label (*used for reimbursement*)

vignoble [viɲɔbl] *nm* (*plantation*) vineyard; (*vignes d'une région*) vineyards *pl*

vigoureux, -euse [viguRø, øz] *adj* vigorous, robust

vigueur [vigœR] *nf* vigour; **entrer en ~** to come into force; **en ~** current

vilain, e [vilɛ̃, ɛn] *adj* (*laid*) ugly; (*affaire, blessure*) nasty; (*pas sage: enfant*) naughty; **vilain mot** naughty *ou* bad word

villa [villa] *nf* (detached) house; **~ en multipropriété** time-share villa

village [vilaʒ] *nm* village; **villageois, e** *adj* village *cpd* ▷ *nm/f* villager

ville [vil] *nf* town; (*importante*) city; (*administration*): **la ~** the (town) council, the local authority; **ville d'eaux** spa; **ville nouvelle** new town

vin [vɛ̃] *nm* wine; **avoir le ~ gai** to get happy after a few drinks; **vin d'honneur** reception (with wine and snacks); **vin de pays** local wine; **vin ordinaire** *ou* **de table** table wine

vinaigre [vinɛgR] *nm* vinegar; **vinaigrette** *nf* vinaigrette, French dressing

vindicatif, -ive [vɛ̃dikatif, iv] *adj* vindictive

vingt [vɛ̃] *num* twenty; **~-quatre heures sur ~-quatre** twenty-four hours a day, round the clock; **vingtaine** *nf*: **une vingtaine (de)** about twenty, twenty or so; **vingtième** *num* twentieth

vinicole [vinikɔl] *adj* wine *cpd*, wine-growing

vinyle [vinil] *nm* vinyl

viol [vjɔl] *nm* (*d'une femme*) rape; (*d'un lieu sacré*) violation

violacé, e [vjɔlase] *adj* purplish, mauvish

violemment [vjɔlamɑ̃] *adv* violently

violence [vjɔlɑ̃s] *nf* violence

violent, e [vjɔlɑ̃, ɑ̃t] *adj* violent; (*remède*) drastic

violer [vjɔle] *vt* (*femme*) to rape; (*sépulture, loi, traité*) to violate

violet, te [vjɔlɛ, ɛt] *adj, nm* purple, mauve; **violette** *nf* (*fleur*) violet

violon [vjɔlɔ̃] *nm* violin; (*fam: prison*) lock-up; **violon d'Ingres** hobby; **violoncelle** *nm* cello; **violoniste** *nm/f* violinist

vipère [vipɛR] *nf* viper, adder

virage [viRaʒ] *nm* (*d'un véhicule*) turn; (*d'une route, piste*) bend

virée [viRe] *nf* trip; (*à pied*) walk; (*longue*) walking tour; (*dans les cafés*) tour

virement[viʀmã] nm (Comm) transfer
virer[viʀe] vt (Comm): **~ qch (sur)** to transfer sth (into); (fam: expulser): **~ qn** to kick sb out ▷ vi to turn; (Chimie) to change colour; **~ au bleu/rouge** to turn blue/red; **~ de bord** to tack
virevolter[viʀvɔlte] vi to twirl around
virgule[viʀgyl] nf comma; (Math) point
viril, e[viʀil] adj (propre à l'homme) masculine; (énergique, courageux) manly, virile
virtuel, le[viʀtɥɛl] adj potential; (théorique) virtual
virtuose[viʀtɥoz] nm/f (Mus) virtuoso; (gén) master
virus[viʀys] nm virus
vis¹[vi] vb voir **voir**; **vivre**
vis²[vis] nf screw
visa[viza] nm (sceau) stamp; (validation de passeport) visa
visage[vizaʒ] nm face
vis-à-vis[vizavi] prép: **~ de qn** to(wards) sb; **en ~** facing each other
visées[vize] nfpl (intentions) designs
viser[vize] vi to aim ▷ vt to aim at; (concerner) to be aimed ou directed at; (apposer un visa sur) to stamp, visa; **~ à qch/faire** to aim at sth/at doing ou to do
visibilité[vizibilite] nf visibility
visible[vizibl] adj visible; (disponible): **est-il ~?** can he see me?, will he see visitors?
visière[vizjɛʀ] nf (de casquette) peak; (qui s'attache) eyeshade
vision[vizjɔ̃] nf vision; (sens) (eye)sight, vision; (fait de voir): **la ~ de** the sight of; **visionneuse** nf viewer
visiophone[vizjɔfɔn] nm videophone
visite[vizit] nf visit; **~ médicale** medical examination; **~ accompagnée** ou **guidée** guided tour; **la ~ guidée commence à quelle heure?** what time does the guided tour start?; **faire une ~ à qn** to call on sb, pay sb a visit; **rendre ~ à qn** to visit sb, pay sb a visit; **être en ~ (chez qn)** to be visiting (sb); **avoir de la ~** to have visitors; **heures de ~** (hôpital, prison) visiting hours
visiter[vizite] vt to visit; **visiteur, -euse** nm/f visitor
vison[vizɔ̃] nm mink
visser[vise] vt: **~ qch** (fixer, serrer) to screw sth on
visuel, le[vizɥɛl] adj visual
vital, e, -aux[vital, o] adj vital
vitamine[vitamin] nf vitamin
vite[vit] adv (rapidement) quickly, fast; (sans délai) quickly; (sous peu) soon; **~!** quick!; **faire ~** to be quick; **le temps passe ~** time flies
vitesse[vitɛs] nf speed; (Auto: dispositif) gear; **prendre de la ~** to pick up ou gather speed; **à toute ~** at full ou top speed; **en ~** (rapidement)

quickly; (en hâte) in a hurry

● **LIMITE DE VITESSE**
●
● The speed limit in France is 50 km/h in
● built-up areas, 90 km/h on main roads, and
● 130 km/h on motorways (110 km/h when
● it is raining).

viticulteur[vitikyltœʀ] nm wine grower
vitrage[vitʀaʒ] nm: **double ~** double glazing
vitrail, -aux[vitʀaj, o] nm stained-glass window
vitre[vitʀ] nf (window) pane; (de portière, voiture) window; **vitré, e** adj glass cpd
vitrine[vitʀin] nf (shop) window; (petite armoire) display cabinet; **en ~** in the window
vivable[vivabl] adj (personne) livable-with; (maison) fit to live in
vivace[vivas] adj (arbre, plante) hardy; (fig) indestructible, inveterate
vivacité[vivasite] nf liveliness, vivacity
vivant, e[vivã, ãt] adj (qui vit) living, alive; (animé) lively; (preuve, exemple) living ▷ nm: **du ~ de qn** in sb's lifetime; **les ~s** the living
vive[viv] adj voir **vif** ▷ vb voir **vivre** ▷ excl: **~ le roi!** long live the king!; **vivement** adv deeply ▷ excl: **vivement les vacances!** roll on the holidays!
vivier[vivje] nm (étang) fish tank; (réservoir) fishpond
vivifiant, e[vivifjã, jãt] adj invigorating
vivoter[vivɔte] vi (personne) to scrape a living, get by; (fig: affaire etc) to struggle along
vivre[vivʀ] vi, vt to live; (période) to live through; **vivres** nmpl provisions, food supplies; **~ de** to live on; **il vit encore** he is still alive; **se laisser ~** to take life as it comes; **ne plus ~** (être anxieux) to live on one's nerves; **il a vécu** (eu une vie aventureuse) he has seen life; **être facile à ~** to be easy to get on with; **faire ~ qn** (pourvoir à sa subsistance) to provide (a living) for sb
vlan[vlã] excl wham!, bang!
VO[veo] nf: **film en VO** film in the original version; **en VO sous-titrée** in the original version with subtitles
vocabulaire[vɔkabylɛʀ] nm vocabulary
vocation[vɔkasjɔ̃] nf vocation, calling
vœu, x[vø] nm wish; (promesse) vow; **faire ~ de** to take a vow of; **tous nos ~x de bonne année, meilleurs ~x** best wishes for the New Year
vogue[vɔg] nf fashion, vogue; **en ~** in fashion, in vogue
voici[vwasi] prép (pour introduire, désigner) here is +sg, here are +pl; **et ~ que ...** and now it (ou he) ...; voir aussi **voilà**
voie[vwa] nf way; (Rail) track, line; (Auto) lane;

être en bonne ~ to be going well; **mettre qn sur la ~** to put sb on the right track; **pays en ~ de développement** developing country; **être en ~ d'achèvement/de rénovation** to be nearing completion/in the process of renovation; **par ~ buccale** ou **orale** orally; **route à ~ unique** single-track road; **route à 2/3 ~s** 2-/3-lane road; **voie de garage** (Rail) siding; **voie express** expressway; **voie ferrée** track; railway line (BRIT), railroad (US); **la voie lactée** the Milky Way; **la voie publique** the public highway

voilà [vwala] *prép* (*en désignant*) there is +*sg*, there are +*pl*; **les ~** ou **voici** here ou there they are; **en ~** ou **voici un** here's one, there's one; **voici mon frère et ~ ma sœur** this is my brother and that's my sister; **~** ou **voici deux ans** two years ago; **~** ou **voici deux ans que** it's two years since; **et ~!** there we are!; **~ tout** that's all; **~** ou **voici** (*en offrant etc*) there ou here you are; **tiens! ~ Paul** look! there's Paul

voile [vwal] *nm* veil; (*tissu léger*) net ▷ *nf* sail; (*sport*) sailing; **voiler** *vt* to veil; (*fausser: roue*) to buckle; (: *bois*) to warp; **se voiler** *vi* (*lune, regard*) to mist over; (*voix*) to become husky; (*roue, disque*) to buckle; (*planche*) to warp; **voilier** *nm* sailing ship; (*de plaisance*) sailing boat; **voilure** *nf* (*de voilier*) sails *pl*

voir [vwaʀ] *vi, vt* to see; **se voir** *vi* (*être visible*) to show; (*se fréquenter*) to see each other; (*se produire*) to happen; **cela se voit** (*c'est visible*) that's obvious, it shows; **faire ~ qch à qn** to show sb sth; **en faire ~ à qn** (*fig*) to give sb a hard time; **ne pas pouvoir ~ qn** not to be able to stand sb; **voyons!** let's see now; (*indignation etc*) come on!; **ça n'a rien à ~ avec lui** that has nothing to do with him

voire [vwaʀ] *adv* even

voisin, e [vwazɛ̃, in] *adj* (*proche*) neighbouring; (*contigu*) next; (*ressemblant*) connected ▷ *nm/f* neighbour; **voisinage** *nm* (*proximité*) proximity; (*environs*) vicinity; (*quartier, voisins*) neighbourhood

voiture [vwatyʀ] *nf* car; (*wagon*) coach, carriage; **voiture de course** racing car; **voiture de sport** sports car

voix [vwa] *nf* voice; (*Pol*) vote; **à haute ~** aloud; **à ~ basse** in a low voice; **à 2/4 ~** (*Mus*) in 2/4 parts; **avoir ~ au chapitre** to have a say in the matter

vol [vɔl] *nm* (*d'oiseau, d'avion*) flight; (*larcin*) theft; **~ régulier** scheduled flight; **à ~ d'oiseau** as the crow flies; **au ~: attraper qch au ~** to catch sth as it flies past; **en ~** in flight; **je voudrais signaler un ~** I'd like to report a theft; **vol à main armée** armed robbery; **vol à voile** gliding; **vol libre** hang-gliding

volage [vɔlaʒ] *adj* fickle

volaille [vɔlaj] *nf* (*oiseaux*) poultry *pl*; (*viande*)

poultry *no pl*; (*oiseau*) fowl

volant, e [vɔlɑ̃, ɑ̃t] *adj voir* **feuille** *etc* ▷ *nm* (*d'automobile*) (steering) wheel; (*de commande*) wheel; (*objet lancé*) shuttlecock; (*bande de tissu*) flounce

volcan [vɔlkɑ̃] *nm* volcano

volée [vɔle] *nf* (*Tennis*) volley; **à la ~: rattraper à la ~** to catch in mid-air; **à toute ~** (*sonner les cloches*) vigorously; (*lancer un projectile*) with full force

voler [vɔle] *vi* (*avion, oiseau, fig*) to fly; (*voleur*) to steal ▷ *vt* (*objet*) to steal; (*personne*) to rob; **~ qch à qn** to steal sth from sb; **on m'a volé mon portefeuille** my wallet ou billfold (US) has been stolen; **il ne l'a pas volé!** he asked for it!

volet [vɔlɛ] *nm* (*de fenêtre*) shutter; (*de feuillet, document*) section

voleur, -euse [vɔlœʀ, øz] *nm/f* thief ▷ *adj* thieving; **"au ~!"** "stop thief!"

volontaire [vɔlɔ̃tɛʀ] *adj* (*acte, enrôlement, prisonnier*) voluntary; (*oubli*) intentional; (*caractère, personne: décidé*) self-willed ▷ *nm/f* volunteer

volonté [vɔlɔ̃te] *nf* (*faculté de vouloir*) will; (*énergie, fermeté*) will(power); (*souhait, désir*) wish; **à ~** as much as one likes; **bonne ~** goodwill, willingness; **mauvaise ~** lack of goodwill, unwillingness

volontiers [vɔlɔ̃tje] *adv* (*avec plaisir*) willingly, gladly; (*habituellement, souvent*) readily, willingly; **voulez-vous boire quelque chose? — ~!** would you like something to drink? — yes, please!

volt [vɔlt] *nm* volt

volte-face [vɔltəfas] *nf inv*: **faire ~** to turn round

voltige [vɔltiʒ] *nf* (*Équitation*) trick riding; (*au cirque*) acrobatics *sg*; **voltiger** *vi* to flutter (about)

volubile [vɔlybil] *adj* voluble

volume [vɔlym] *nm* volume; (*Géom: solide*) solid; **volumineux, -euse** *adj* voluminous, bulky

volupté [vɔlypte] *nf* sensual delight ou pleasure

vomi [vɔmi] *nm* vomit; **vomir** *vi* to vomit, be sick ▷ *vt* to vomit, bring up; (*fig*) to belch out, spew out; (*exécrer*) to loathe, abhor

vorace [vɔʀas] *adj* voracious

vos [vo] *adj voir* **votre**

vote [vɔt] *nm* vote; **vote par correspondance/procuration** postal/proxy vote; **voter** *vi* to vote ▷ *vt* (*projet de loi*) to vote for; (*loi, réforme*) to pass

votre [vɔtʀ] (*pl* **vos**) *adj* your

vôtre [votʀ] *pron*: **le ~, la ~, les ~s** yours; **les ~s** (*fig*) your family ou folks; **à la ~** (*toast*) your (good) health!

vouer [vwe] *vt*: **~ sa vie à** (*étude, cause etc*) to devote one's life to; **~ une amitié éternelle à qn** to vow undying friendship to sb

○ **MOT-CLÉ**

vouloir [vulwaʀ] *nm*: **le bon vouloir de qn** sb's goodwill; sb's pleasure
▷ *vt* **1** (*exiger, désirer*) to want; **vouloir faire/que qn fasse** to want to do/sb to do; **voulez-vous du thé?** would you like *ou* do you want some tea?; **que me veut-il?** what does he want with me?; **sans le vouloir** (*involontairement*) without meaning to, unintentionally; **je voudrais ceci/faire** I would *ou* I'd like this/to do; **le hasard a voulu que ...** as fate would have it ...; **la tradition veut que ...** it is a tradition that ...
2 (*consentir*): **je veux bien** (*bonne volonté*) I'll be happy to; (*concession*) fair enough, that's fine; **je peux le faire, si vous voulez** I can do it if you like; **oui, si on veut** (*en quelque sorte*) yes, if you like; **veuillez attendre** please wait; **veuillez agréer ...** (*formule épistolaire: personne nommée*) yours sincerely; (*personne non nommée*) yours faithfully
3: **en vouloir à qn** to bear sb a grudge; **s'en vouloir (de)** to be annoyed with o.s. (for); **il en veut à mon argent** he's after my money
4: **vouloir de: l'entreprise ne veut plus de lui** the firm doesn't want him any more; **elle ne veut pas de son aide** she doesn't want his help
5: **vouloir dire** to mean

voulu, e [vuly] *adj* (*requis*) required, requisite; (*délibéré*) deliberate, intentional; *voir aussi* **vouloir**

vous [vu] *pron* you; (*objet indirect*) (to) you; (*réfléchi: sg*) yourself; (: *pl*) yourselves; (*réciproque*) each other ▷ *nm*: **employer le ~** (*vouvoyer*) to use the "vous" form; **~-même** yourself; **~-mêmes** yourselves

vouvoyer [vuvwaje] *vt*: **~ qn** to address sb as "vous"

voyage [vwajaʒ] *nm* journey, trip; (*fait de voyager*): **le ~** travel(ling); **partir/être en ~** to go off/be away on a journey *ou* trip; **faire bon ~** to have a good journey; **votre ~ s'est bien passé?** how was your journey?; **voyage d'affaires/d'agrément** business/pleasure trip; **voyage de noces** honeymoon; **nous sommes en voyage de noces** we're on honeymoon; **voyage organisé** package tour

voyager [vwajaʒe] *vi* to travel; **voyageur, -euse** *nm/f* traveller; (*passager*) passenger; **voyageur de commerce** sales representative, commercial traveller

voyant, e [vwajā, āt] *adj* (*couleur*) loud, gaudy

▷ *nm* (*signal*) (warning) light

voyelle [vwajɛl] *nf* vowel

voyou [vwaju] *nm* hooligan

vrac [vʀak]: **en ~** *adv* (*au détail*) loose; (*en gros*) in bulk; (*en désordre*) in a jumble

vrai, e [vʀe] *adj* (*véridique: récit, faits*) true; (*non factice, authentique*) real; **à ~ dire** to tell the truth; **vraiment** *adv* really; **vraisemblable** *adj* likely; (*excuse*) convincing; **vraisemblablement** *adj* probably; **vraisemblance** *nf* likelihood; (*romanesque*) verisimilitude

vrombir [vʀɔ̃biʀ] *vi* to hum

VRP *sigle m* (= *voyageur, représentant, placier*) sales rep (*fam*)

VTT *sigle m* (= *vélo tout-terrain*) mountain bike

vu, e [vy] *pp de* **voir** ▷ *adj*: **bien/mal vu** (*fig: personne*) popular/unpopular; (: *chose*) approved/disapproved of ▷ *prép* (*en raison de*) in view of; **vu que** in view of the fact that

vue [vy] *nf* (*fait de voir*): **la ~ de** the sight of; (*sens, faculté*) (eye)sight; (*panorama, image, photo*) view; **vues** *nfpl* (*idées*) views; (*dessein*) designs; **hors de ~** out of sight; **avoir en ~** to have in mind; **tirer à ~** to shoot on sight; **à ~ d'œil** visibly; **à première ~** at first sight; **de ~** by sight; **perdre de ~** to lose sight of; **en ~** (*visible*) in sight; (*célèbre*) in the public eye; **en ~ de faire** with a view to doing; **perdre la ~** to lose one's (eye)sight; **avoir ~ sur** (*suj: fenêtre*) to have a view of; **vue d'ensemble** overall view

vulgaire [vylgɛʀ] *adj* (*grossier*) vulgar, coarse; (*ordinaire*) commonplace, mundane; (*péj: quelconque*): **de ~s touristes** common tourists; (*Bot, Zool: non latin*) common; **vulgariser** *vt* to popularize

vulnérable [vylneʀabl] *adj* vulnerable

wagon [vagɔ̃] *nm (de voyageurs)* carriage; *(de marchandises)* truck, wagon; **wagon-lit** *nm* sleeper, sleeping car; **wagon-restaurant** *nm* restaurant *ou* dining car

wallon, ne [walɔ̃, ɔn] *adj* Walloon ▷ *nm (Ling)* Walloon ▷ *nm/f:* **W~, ne** Walloon

watt [wat] *nm* watt

w-c *sigle mpl (= water-closet(s))* toilet

Web [wɛb] *nm inv:* **le ~** the (World Wide) Web; **webmaster** [-mastœr], **webmestre** [-mɛstʀ] *nm/f* webmaster

week-end [wikɛnd] *nm* weekend

western [wɛstɛʀn] *nm* western

whisky [wiski] *(pl* **whiskies)** *nm* whisky

xénophobe [gzenɔfɔb] *adj* xenophobic ▷ *nm/f* xenophobe

xérès [gzeʀɛs] *nm* sherry

xylophone [gzilɔfɔn] *nm* xylophone

y z

y [i] *adv* (*à cet endroit*) there; (*dessus*) on it (*ou* them); (*dedans*) in it (*ou* them) ▷ *pron* (about *ou* on *ou* of) it (*d'après le verbe employé*); **j'y pense** I'm thinking about it; **ça y est!** that's it!; *voir aussi* **aller**; **avoir**

yacht [jɔt] *nm* yacht

yaourt [jauʀt] *nm* yoghourt; **~ nature/aux fruits** plain/fruit yogurt

yeux [jø] *nmpl de* **œil**

yoga [jɔga] *nm* yoga

yoghourt [jɔguʀt] *nm* = **yaourt**

yougoslave [jugɔslav] (*Histoire*) *adj* Yugoslav(ian) ▷ *nm/f*: **Y~** Yugoslav

Yougoslavie [jugɔslavi] *nf* (*Histoire*) Yugoslavia; **l'ex-~** the former Yugoslavia

zapper [zape] *vi* to zap

zapping [zapiŋ] *nm*: **faire du ~** to flick through the channels

zèbre [zebʀ(ə)] *nm* (*Zool*) zebra; **zébré, e** *adj* striped, streaked

zèle [zɛl] *nm* zeal; **faire du ~** (*péj*) to be over-zealous; **zélé, e** *adj* zealous

zéro [zeʀo] *nm* zero, nought (*BRIT*); **au-dessous de ~** below zero (Centigrade) *ou* freezing; **partir de ~** to start from scratch; **trois (buts) à ~** 3 (goals to) nil

zeste [zɛst] *nm* peel, zest

zézayer [zezeje] *vi* to have a lisp

zigzag [zigzag] *nm* zigzag; **zigzaguer** *vi* to zigzag

Zimbabwe [zimbabwe] *nm*: **le ~** Zimbabwe

zinc [zɛ̃g] *nm* (*Chimie*) zinc

zipper [zipe] *vt* (*Inform*) to zip

zizi [zizi] *nm* (*langage enfantin*) willy

zodiaque [zɔdjak] *nm* zodiac

zona [zona] *nm* shingles *sg*

zone [zon] *nf* zone, area; (*fam: quartiers pauvres*): **la ~** the slums; **zone bleue** ≈ restricted parking area; **zone industrielle** industrial estate

zoo [zo(o)] *nm* zoo

zoologie [zɔɔlɔʒi] *nf* zoology; **zoologique** *adj* zoological

zut [zyt] *excl* dash (it)! (*BRIT*), nuts! (*US*)

**ENGLISH | FRENCH
ANGLAIS | FRANÇAIS**

A[eɪ] n (Mus) la m

KEYWORD

a[eɪ, ə] (before vowel or silent h **an**) indef art
1 un(e); **a book** un livre; **an apple** une pomme;
she's a doctor elle est médecin
2 (instead of the number "one") un(e); **a year ago**
il y a un an; **a hundred/thousand** etc **pounds**
cent/mille etc livres
3 (in expressing ratios, prices etc): **3 a day/week**
3 par jour/semaine; **10 km an hour** 10 km à
l'heure; **£5 a person** 5£ par personne; **30p a
kilo** 30p le kilo

A2 n (BRIT: Scol) deuxième partie de l'examen
équivalent au baccalauréat
A.A. n abbr (BRIT: = Automobile Association)
≈ ACF m; (= Alcoholics Anonymous) AA
A.A.A. n abbr (= American Automobile
Association) ≈ ACF m
aback[ə'bæk] adv: **to be taken ~** être
décontenancé(e)
abandon[ə'bændən] vt abandonner
abattoir['æbətwɑ:ʳ] n (BRIT) abattoir m
abbey['æbɪ] n abbaye f
abbreviation[əbri:vɪ'eɪʃən] n abréviation f
abdomen['æbdəmən] n abdomen m
abduct[æb'dʌkt] vt enlever
abide[ə'baɪd] vt souffrir, supporter; **I can't ~**

it/him je ne le supporte pas; **abide by** vt fus
observer, respecter
ability[ə'bɪlɪtɪ] n compétence f; capacité f;
(skill) talent m
able['eɪbl] adj compétent(e); **to be ~ to do sth**
pouvoir faire qch, être capable de faire qch
abnormal[æb'nɔ:məl] adj anormal(e)
aboard[ə'bɔ:d] adv à bord ▷ prep à bord de;
(train) dans
abolish[ə'bɔlɪʃ] vt abolir
abolition[æbə'lɪʃən] n abolition f
abort[ə'bɔ:t] vt (Med) faire avorter; (Comput,
fig) abandonner; **abortion**[ə'bɔ:ʃən] n
avortement m; **to have an abortion** se faire
avorter

KEYWORD

about[ə'baut] adv **1** (approximately) environ,
à peu près; **about a hundred/thousand** etc
environ cent/mille etc, une centaine (de)/un
millier (de) etc; **it takes about 10 hours** ça
prend environ or à peu près 10 heures; **at
about 2 o'clock** vers 2 heures; **I've just about
finished** j'ai presque fini
2 (referring to place) çà et là, de-ci de-là; **to
run about** courir çà et là; **to walk about** se
promener, aller et venir; **they left all their
things lying about** ils ont laissé traîner
toutes leurs affaires
3: **to be about to do sth** être sur le point de
faire qch
▷ prep **1** (relating to) au sujet de, à propos de;
a book about London un livre sur Londres;
what is it about? de quoi s'agit-il?; **we talked
about it** nous en avons parlé; **what or how
about doing this?** et si nous faisions ceci?
2 (referring to place) dans; **to walk about the
town** se promener dans la ville

above[ə'bʌv] adv au-dessus ▷ prep au-
dessus de; (more than) plus de; **mentioned ~**
mentionné ci-dessus; **~ all** par-dessus tout,
surtout
abroad[ə'brɔ:d] adv à l'étranger
abrupt[ə'brʌpt] adj (steep, blunt) abrupt(e);
(sudden, gruff) brusque
abscess['æbsɪs] n abcès m
absence['æbsəns] n absence f
absent['æbsənt] adj absent(e); **absent-
minded** adj distrait(e)
absolute['æbsəlu:t] adj absolu(e);
absolutely[æbsə'lu:tlɪ] adv absolument
absorb[əb'zɔ:b] vt absorber; **to be ~ed in a
book** être plongé(e) dans un livre; **absorbent
cotton** n (US) coton m hydrophile; **absorbing**
adj absorbant(e); (book, film etc) captivant(e)
abstain[əb'steɪn] vi: **to ~ (from)** s'abstenir
(de)

abstract ['æbstrækt] *adj* abstrait(e)

absurd [əb'sə:d] *adj* absurde

abundance [ə'bʌndəns] *n* abondance *f*

abundant [ə'bʌndənt] *adj* abondant(e)

abuse *n* [ə'bju:s] (*insults*) insultes *fpl*, injures *fpl*; (*ill-treatment*) mauvais traitements *mpl*; (*of power etc*) abus *m* ▷ *vt* [ə'bju:z] (*insult*) insulter; (*ill-treat*) malmener; (*power etc*) abuser de; **abusive** *adj* grossier(-ière), injurieux(-euse)

abysmal [ə'bɪzməl] *adj* exécrable; (*ignorance etc*) sans bornes

academic [ækə'dɛmɪk] *adj* universitaire; (*person: scholarly*) intellectuel(-le); (*pej: issue*) oiseux(-euse), purement théorique ▷ *n* universitaire *m/f*; **academic year** *n* (*University*) année *f* universitaire; (*Scol*) année scolaire

academy [ə'kædəmɪ] *n* (*learned body*) académie *f*; (*school*) collège *m*; **~ of music** conservatoire *m*

accelerate [æk'sɛləreɪt] *vt, vi* accélérer; **acceleration** [æksɛlə'reɪʃən] *n* accélération *f*; **accelerator** *n* (*BRIT*) accélérateur *m*

accent ['æksɛnt] *n* accent *m*

accept [ək'sɛpt] *vt* accepter; **acceptable** *adj* acceptable; **acceptance** *n* acceptation *f*

access ['æksɛs] *n* accès *m*; **to have ~ to** (*information, library etc*) avoir accès à, pouvoir utiliser *or* consulter; (*person*) avoir accès auprès de; **accessible** [æk'sɛsəbl] *adj* accessible

accessory [æk'sɛsərɪ] *n* accessoire *m*; **~ to** (*Law*) accessoire à

accident ['æksɪdənt] *n* accident *m*; (*chance*) hasard *m*; **I've had an ~** j'ai eu un accident; **by ~** (*by chance*) par hasard; (*not deliberately*) accidentellement; **accidental** [æksɪ'dɛntl] *adj* accidentel(le); **accidentally** [æksɪ'dɛntəlɪ] *adv* accidentellement; **Accident and Emergency Department** *n* (*BRIT*) service *m* des urgences; **accident insurance** *n* assurance *f* accident

acclaim [ə'kleɪm] *vt* acclamer ▷ *n* acclamations *fpl*

accommodate [ə'kɔmədeɪt] *vt* loger, recevoir; (*oblige, help*) obliger; (*car etc*) contenir; **accommodation** (*us* **accommodations**) [əkɔmə'deɪʃən(z)] *n(pl)* logement *m*

accompaniment [ə'kʌmpənɪmənt] *n* accompagnement *m*

accompany [ə'kʌmpənɪ] *vt* accompagner

accomplice [ə'kʌmplɪs] *n* complice *m/f*

accomplish [ə'kʌmplɪʃ] *vt* accomplir; **accomplishment** *n* (*skill: gen pl*) talent *m*; (*completion*) accomplissement *m*; (*achievement*) réussite *f*

accord [ə'kɔ:d] *n* accord *m* ▷ *vt* accorder; **of his own ~** de son plein gré; **accordance** *n*: **in accordance with** conformément à; **according**: **according to** *prep* selon;

accordingly *adv* (*appropriately*) en conséquence; (*as a result*) par conséquent

account [ə'kaunt] *n* (*Comm*) compte *m*; (*report*) compte rendu, récit *m*; **accounts** *npl* (*Comm: records*) comptabilité *f*, comptes; **of no ~** sans importance; **on ~** en acompte; **to buy sth on ~** acheter qch à crédit; **on no ~** en aucun cas; **on ~ of** à cause de; **to take into ~**, **take ~ of** tenir compte de; **account for** *vt fus* (*explain*) expliquer, rendre compte de; (*represent*) représenter; **accountable** *adj*: **accountable (to)** responsable (devant); **accountant** *n* comptable *m/f*; **account number** *n* numéro *m* de compte

accumulate [ə'kju:mjuleɪt] *vt* accumuler, amasser ▷ *vi* s'accumuler, s'amasser

accuracy ['ækjurəsɪ] *n* exactitude *f*, précision *f*

accurate ['ækjurɪt] *adj* exact(e), précis(e); (*device*) précis; **accurately** *adv* avec précision

accusation [ækju'zeɪʃən] *n* accusation *f*

accuse [ə'kju:z] *vt*: **to ~ sb (of sth)** accuser qn (de qch); **accused** *n* (*Law*) accusé(e)

accustomed [ə'kʌstəmd] *adj*: **~ to** habitué(e) *or* accoutumé(e) à

ace [eɪs] *n* as *m*

ache [eɪk] *n* mal *m*, douleur *f* ▷ *vi* (*be sore*) faire mal, être douloureux(-euse); **my head ~s** j'ai mal à la tête

achieve [ə'tʃi:v] *vt* (*aim*) atteindre; (*victory, success*) remporter, obtenir; **achievement** *n* exploit *m*, réussite *f*; (*of aims*) réalisation *f*

acid ['æsɪd] *adj, n* acide (*m*)

acknowledge [ək'nɔlɪdʒ] *vt* (*also*: **~ receipt of**) accuser réception de; (*fact*) reconnaître; **acknowledgement** *n* (*of letter*) accusé *m* de réception

acne ['æknɪ] *n* acné *m*

acorn ['eɪkɔ:n] *n* gland *m*

acoustic [ə'ku:stɪk] *adj* acoustique

acquaintance [ə'kweɪntəns] *n* connaissance *f*

acquire [ə'kwaɪər] *vt* acquérir; **acquisition** [ækwɪ'zɪʃən] *n* acquisition *f*

acquit [ə'kwɪt] *vt* acquitter; **to ~ o.s. well** s'en tirer très honorablement

acre ['eɪkər] *n* acre *f* (= 4047 *m²*)

acronym ['ækrənɪm] *n* acronyme *m*

across [ə'krɔs] *prep* (*on the other side*) de l'autre côté de; (*crosswise*) en travers de ▷ *adv* de l'autre côté; en travers; **to run/swim ~** traverser en courant/à la nage; **~ from** en face de

acrylic [ə'krɪlɪk] *adj, n* acrylique (*m*)

act [ækt] *n* acte *m*, action *f*; (*Theat: part of play*) acte; (*: of performer*) numéro *m*; (*Law*) loi *f* ▷ *vi* agir; (*Theat*) jouer; (*pretend*) jouer la comédie ▷ *vt* (*role*) jouer, tenir; **to catch sb in the ~** prendre qn sur le fait *or* en flagrant délit; **to ~ as** servir de; **act up** (inf) ▷ vi (person) se conduire mal; (knee, back, injury) jouer des tours; (machine) être capricieux(-ieuse); **acting** adj suppléant(e), par intérim ▷ n (activity): **to do some acting** faire du théâtre (or du cinéma)

action ['ækʃən] n action f; (Mil) combat(s) m(pl); (Law) procès m, action en justice; **out of ~** hors de combat; (machine etc) hors d'usage; **to take ~** agir, prendre des mesures; **action replay** n (BRIT TV) ralenti m

activate ['æktɪveɪt] vt (mechanism) actionner, faire fonctionner

active ['æktɪv] adj actif(-ive); (volcano) en activité; **actively** adv activement; (discourage) vivement

activist ['æktɪvɪst] n activiste m/f

activity [æk'tɪvɪtɪ] n activité f; **activity holiday** n vacances actives

actor ['æktə'] n acteur m

actress ['æktrɪs] n actrice f

actual ['æktjʊəl] adj réel(le), véritable; (emphatic use) lui-même (elle-même)

> Be careful not to translate *actual* by the French word *actuel*.

actually ['æktjʊəlɪ] adv réellement, véritablement; (in fact) en fait

> Be careful not to translate *actually* by the French word *actuellement*.

acupuncture ['ækjʊpʌŋktʃə'] n acuponcture f

acute [ə'kjuːt] adj aigu(ë); (mind, observer) pénétrant(e)

A.D. adv abbr (= Anno Domini) ap. J.-C.

ad [æd] n abbr = **advertisement**

adamant ['ædəmənt] adj inflexible

adapt [ə'dæpt] vt adapter ▷ vi: **to ~ (to)** s'adapter (à); **adapter, adaptor** n (Elec) adaptateur m; (for several plugs) prise f multiple

add [æd] vt ajouter; (figures: also: **to ~ up**) additionner ▷ vi (fig): **it doesn't ~ up** cela ne rime à rien; **add up to** vt fus (Math) s'élever à; (fig: mean) signifier

addict ['ædɪkt] n toxicomane m/f; (fig) fanatique m/f; **addicted** [ə'dɪktɪd] adj: **to be addicted to** (drink, drugs) être adonné(e) à; (fig: football etc) être un(e) fanatique de; **addiction** [ə'dɪkʃən] n (Med) dépendance f; **addictive** [ə'dɪktɪv] adj qui crée une dépendance

addition [ə'dɪʃən] n (adding up) addition f; (thing added) ajout m; **in ~** de plus, de surcroît; **in ~ to** en plus de; **additional** adj supplémentaire

additive ['ædɪtɪv] n additif m

address [ə'drɛs] n adresse f; (talk) discours m, allocution f ▷ vt adresser; (speak to) s'adresser à; **my ~ is ...** mon adresse, c'est ...; **address book** n carnet m d'adresses

adequate ['ædɪkwɪt] adj (enough) suffisant(e); (satisfactory) satisfaisant(e)

adhere [əd'hɪə'] vi: **to ~ to** adhérer à; (fig: rule, decision) se tenir à

adhesive [əd'hiːzɪv] n adhésif m; **adhesive tape** n (BRIT) ruban m adhésif; (US Med) sparadrap m

adjacent [ə'dʒeɪsənt] adj adjacent(e), contigu(ë); **~ to** adjacent à

adjective ['ædʒɛktɪv] n adjectif m

adjoining [ə'dʒɔɪnɪŋ] adj voisin(e), adjacent(e), attenant(e)

adjourn [ə'dʒəːn] vt ajourner ▷ vi suspendre la séance; lever la séance; clore la session

adjust [ə'dʒʌst] vt (machine) ajuster, régler; (prices, wages) rajuster ▷ vi: **to ~ (to)** s'adapter (à); **adjustable** adj réglable; **adjustment** n (of machine) ajustage m, réglage m; (of prices, wages) rajustement m; (of person) adaptation f

administer [əd'mɪnɪstə'] vt administrer; **administration** [ədmɪnɪs'treɪʃən] n (management) administration f; (government) gouvernement m; **administrative** [əd'mɪnɪstrətɪv] adj administratif(-ive)

administrator [əd'mɪnɪstreɪtə'] n administrateur(-trice)

admiral ['ædmərəl] n amiral m

admiration [ædmə'reɪʃən] n admiration f

admire [əd'maɪə'] vt admirer; **admirer** n (fan) admirateur(-trice)

admission [əd'mɪʃən] n admission f; (to exhibition, night club etc) entrée f; (confession) aveu m

admit [əd'mɪt] vt laisser entrer; admettre; (agree) reconnaître, admettre; (crime) reconnaître avoir commis; **"children not ~ted"** "entrée interdite aux enfants"; **admit to** vt fus reconnaître, avouer; **admittance** n admission f, (droit m d')entrée f; **admittedly** adv il faut en convenir

adolescent [ædəʊ'lɛsnt] adj, n adolescent(e)

adopt [ə'dɔpt] vt adopter; **adopted** adj adoptif(-ive), adopté(e); **adoption** [ə'dɔpʃən] n adoption f

adore [ə'dɔː'] vt adorer

adorn [ə'dɔːn] vt orner

Adriatic (Sea) [eɪdrɪ'ætɪk-] n, adj: **the Adriatic (Sea)** la mer Adriatique, l'Adriatique f

adrift [ə'drɪft] adv à la dérive

adult ['ædʌlt] n adulte m/f ▷ adj (grown-up) adulte; (for adults) pour adultes; **adult education** n éducation f des adultes

adultery [ə'dʌltərɪ] n adultère m

advance [əd'vɑːns] n avance f ▷ vt avancer ▷ vi s'avancer; **in ~** en avance, d'avance; **to make ~s to sb** (gen) faire des propositions à qn; (amorously) faire des avances à qn; **~ booking** location f; **~ notice, ~ warning** préavis m; (verbal) avertissement m; **do I**

need to book in ~? est-ce qu'il faut réserver à l'avance?; **advanced** adj avancé(e); (Scol: studies) supérieur(e)

advantage [əd'vɑːntɪdʒ] n (also Tennis) avantage m; **to take ~ of** (person) exploiter; (opportunity) profiter de

advent ['ædvənt] n avènement m, venue f; **A~** (Rel) avent m

adventure [əd'ventʃər] n aventure f; **adventurous** [əd'ventʃərəs] adj aventureux(-euse)

adverb ['ædvəːb] n adverbe m

adversary ['ædvəsərɪ] n adversaire m/f

adverse ['ædvəːs] adj adverse; (effect) négatif(-ive); (weather, publicity) mauvais(e); (wind) contraire

advert ['ædvəːt] n abbr (BRIT) = **advertisement**

advertise ['ædvətaɪz] vi faire de la publicité or de la réclame; (in classified ads etc) mettre une annonce ▷ vt faire de la publicité or de la réclame pour; (in classified ads etc) mettre une annonce pour vendre; **to ~ for** (staff) recruter par (voie d')annonce; **advertisement** [əd'vəːtɪsmənt] n (Comm) publicité f, réclame f; (in classified ads etc) annonce f; **advertiser** n annonceur m; **advertising** n publicité f

advice [əd'vaɪs] n conseils mpl; (notification) avis m; **a piece of ~** un conseil; **to take legal ~** consulter un avocat

advisable [əd'vaɪzəbl] adj recommandable, indiqué(e)

advise [əd'vaɪz] vt conseiller; **to ~ sb of sth** aviser or informer qn de qch; **to ~ against sth/doing sth** déconseiller qch/conseiller de ne pas faire qch; **adviser, advisor** n conseiller(-ère); **advisory** adj consultatif(-ive)

advocate n ['ædvəkɪt] (lawyer) avocat (plaidant); (upholder) défenseur m, avocat(e) ▷ vt ['ædvəkeɪt] recommander, prôner; **to be an ~ of** être partisan(e) de

Aegean [iː'dʒiːən] n, adj: **the ~ (Sea)** la mer Égée, l'Égée f

aerial ['ɛərɪəl] n antenne f ▷ adj aérien(ne)

aerobics [ɛə'rəubɪks] n aérobic m

aeroplane ['ɛərəpleɪn] n (BRIT) avion m

aerosol ['ɛərəsɔl] n aérosol m

affair [ə'fɛər] n affaire f; (also: **love ~**) liaison f, aventure f

affect [ə'fɛkt] vt affecter; (subj: disease) atteindre; **affected** adj affecté(e); **affection** n affection f; **affectionate** adj affectueux(-euse)

afflict [ə'flɪkt] vt affliger

affluent ['æfluənt] adj (person, family, surroundings) aisé(e), riche; **the ~ society** la société d'abondance

afford [ə'fɔːd] vt (behaviour) se permettre; (provide) fournir, procurer; **can we ~ a car?**

avons-nous de quoi acheter or les moyens d'acheter une voiture?; **affordable** adj abordable

Afghanistan [æf'gænɪstæn] n Afghanistan m

afraid [ə'freɪd] adj effrayé(e); **to be ~ of** or **to** avoir peur de; **I am ~ that** je crains que + sub; **I'm ~ so/not** oui/non, malheureusement

Africa ['æfrɪkə] n Afrique f; **African** adj africain(e) ▷ n Africain(e); **African-American** adj afro-américain(e) ▷ n Afro-Américain(e)

after ['ɑːftər] prep, adv après ▷ conj après que; **it's quarter ~ two** (US) il est deux heures et quart; **~ having done/~ he left** après avoir fait/après son départ; **to name sb ~ sb** donner à qn le nom de qn; **to ask ~ sb** demander des nouvelles de qn; **what/who are you ~?** que/qui cherchez-vous?; **~ you!** après vous!; **~ all** après tout; **after-effects** npl (of disaster, radiation, drink etc) répercussions fpl; (of illness) séquelles fpl, suites fpl; **aftermath** n conséquences fpl; **afternoon** n après-midi m or f; **after-shave (lotion)** n lotion f après-rasage; **aftersun (lotion/cream)** n après-soleil m inv; **afterwards** (US **afterward**) adv après

again [ə'gɛn] adv de nouveau, encore (une fois); **to do sth ~** refaire qch; **~ and ~** à plusieurs reprises

against [ə'gɛnst] prep contre; (compared to) par rapport à

age [eɪdʒ] n âge m ▷ vt, vi vieillir; **he is 20 years of ~** il a 20 ans; **to come of ~** atteindre sa majorité; **it's been ~s since I saw you** ça fait une éternité que je ne t'ai pas vu; **~d 10** âgé(e) de 10 ans; **age group** n tranche f d'âge; **age limit** n limite f d'âge

agency ['eɪdʒənsɪ] n agence f

agenda [ə'dʒɛndə] n ordre m du jour

> Be careful not to translate **agenda** by the French word **agenda**.

agent ['eɪdʒənt] n agent m; (firm) concessionnaire m

aggravate ['ægrəveɪt] vt (situation) aggraver; (annoy) exaspérer, agacer

aggression [ə'grɛʃən] n agression f

aggressive [ə'grɛsɪv] adj agressif(-ive)

agile ['ædʒaɪl] adj agile

agitated ['ædʒɪteɪtɪd] adj inquiet(-ète)

AGM n abbr (= annual general meeting) AG f

ago [ə'gəu] adv: **2 days ~** il y a 2 jours; **not long ~** il n'y a pas longtemps; **how long ~?** il y a combien de temps (de cela)?

agony ['ægənɪ] n (pain) douleur f atroce; (distress) angoisse f; **to be in ~** souffrir le martyre

agree [ə'griː] vt (price) convenir de ▷ vi: **to ~ with** (person) être d'accord avec; (statements etc) concorder avec; (Ling) s'accorder avec; **to ~ to do** accepter de or consentir à faire;

to ~ **to sth** consentir à qch; **to** ~ **that** (admit) convenir or reconnaître que; **garlic doesn't** ~ **with me** je ne supporte pas l'ail; **agreeable** adj (pleasant) agréable; (willing) consentant(e), d'accord; **agreed** adj (time, place) convenu(e); **agreement** n accord m; **in agreement** d'accord

agricultural [ægrɪˈkʌltʃərəl] adj agricole

agriculture [ˈægrɪkʌltʃəʳ] n agriculture f

ahead [əˈhɛd] adv en avant; devant; **go right** or **straight** ~ (direction) allez tout droit; **go** ~! (permission) allez-y!; ~ **of** devant; (fig: schedule etc) en avance sur; ~ **of time** en avance

aid [eɪd] n aide f; (device) appareil m ▷ vt aider; **in** ~ **of** en faveur de

aide [eɪd] n (person) assistant(e)

AIDS [eɪdz] n abbr (= acquired immune (or immuno-)deficiency syndrome) SIDA m

ailing [ˈeɪlɪŋ] adj (person) souffreteux(euse); (economy) malade

ailment [ˈeɪlmənt] n affection f

aim [eɪm] vt: **to** ~ **sth (at)** (gun, camera) braquer or pointer qch (sur); (missile) lancer qch (à or contre or en direction de); (remark, blow) destiner or adresser qch (à) ▷ vi (also: **to take** ~) viser ▷ n (objective) but m; (skill): **his** ~ **is bad** il vise mal; **to** ~ **at** viser (à); (fig) viser (à); **to** ~ **to do** avoir l'intention de faire

ain't [eɪnt] (inf) = **am not**; **aren't**; **isn't**

air [eəʳ] n air m ▷ vt aérer; (idea, grievance, views) mettre sur le tapis ▷ cpd (currents, attack etc) aérien(ne); **to throw sth into the** ~ (ball etc) jeter qch en l'air; **by** ~ par avion; **to be on the** ~ (Radio, TV: programme) être diffusé(e); (: station) émettre; **airbag** n airbag m; **airbed** n (BRIT) matelas m pneumatique; **airborne** adj (plane) en vol; **as soon as the plane was airborne** dès que l'avion eut décollé; **air-conditioned** adj climatisé(e), à air conditionné; **air conditioning** n climatisation f; **aircraft** n inv avion m; **airfield** n terrain m d'aviation; **Air Force** n Armée f de l'air; **air hostess** n (BRIT) hôtesse f de l'air; **airing cupboard** n (BRIT) placard qui contient la chaudière et dans lequel on met le linge à sécher; **airlift** n pont aérien; **airline** n ligne aérienne, compagnie aérienne; **airliner** n avion m de ligne; **airmail** n: **by airmail** par avion; **airplane** n (US) avion m; **airport** n aéroport m; **air raid** n attaque aérienne; **airsick** adj: **to be airsick** avoir le mal de l'air; **airspace** n espace m aérien; **airstrip** n terrain m d'atterrissage; **air terminal** n aérogare f; **airtight** adj hermétique; **air-traffic controller** n aiguilleur m du ciel; **airy** adj bien aéré(e); (manners) dégagé(e)

aisle [aɪl] n (of church: central) allée f centrale; (: side) nef f latérale, bas-côté m; (in theatre, supermarket) allée f; (on plane) couloir m; **aisle seat** n place f côté couloir

ajar [əˈdʒɑːʳ] adj entrouvert(e)

à la carte [ælæˈkɑːt] adv à la carte

alarm [əˈlɑːm] n alarme f ▷ vt alarmer; **alarm call** n coup m de fil pour réveiller; **could I have an alarm call at 7 am, please?** pouvez-vous me réveiller à 7 heures, s'il vous plaît?; **alarm clock** n réveille-matin m inv, réveil m; **alarmed** adj (frightened) alarmé(e); (protected by an alarm) protégé(e) par un système d'alarme; **alarming** adj alarmant(e)

Albania [ælˈbeɪnɪə] n Albanie f

albeit [ɔːlˈbiːɪt] conj bien que + sub, encore que + sub

album [ˈælbəm] n album m

alcohol [ˈælkəhɔl] n alcool m; **alcohol-free** adj sans alcool; **alcoholic** [ælkəˈhɔlɪk] adj, n alcoolique (m/f)

alcove [ˈælkəuv] n alcôve f

ale [eɪl] n bière f

alert [əˈləːt] adj alerte, vif (vive); (watchful) vigilant(e) ▷ n alerte f ▷ vt alerter; **on the** ~ sur le qui-vive; (Mil) en état d'alerte

algebra [ˈældʒɪbrə] n algèbre m

Algeria [ælˈdʒɪərɪə] n Algérie f

Algerian [ælˈdʒɪərɪən] adj algérien(ne) ▷ n Algérien(ne)

Algiers [ælˈdʒɪəz] n Alger

alias [ˈeɪlɪəs] adv alias ▷ n faux nom, nom d'emprunt

alibi [ˈælɪbaɪ] n alibi m

alien [ˈeɪlɪən] n (from abroad) étranger(-ère); (from outer space) extraterrestre ▷ adj: ~ **(to)** étranger(-ère) (à); **alienate** vt aliéner; (subj: person) s'aliéner

alight [əˈlaɪt] adj en feu ▷ vi mettre pied à terre; (passenger) descendre; (bird) se poser

align [əˈlaɪn] vt aligner

alike [əˈlaɪk] adj semblable, pareil(le) ▷ adv de même; **to look** ~ se ressembler

alive [əˈlaɪv] adj vivant(e); (active) plein(e) de vie

O **KEYWORD**

all [ɔːl] adj (singular) tout(e); (plural) tous (toutes); **all day** toute la journée; **all night** toute la nuit; **all men** tous les hommes; **all five** tous les cinq; **all the books** tous les livres; **all his life** toute sa vie

▷ pron **1** tout; **I ate it all, I ate all of it** j'ai tout mangé; **all of us went** nous y sommes tous allés; **all of the boys went** tous les garçons y sont allés; **is that all?** c'est tout?; (in shop) ce sera tout?

2 (in phrases): **above all** surtout, par-dessus tout; **after all** après tout; **at all**: (in answer to question) pas du tout; (in answer to thanks) je vous en prie!; **I'm not at all tired** je ne suis pas du tout fatigué(e); **anything at all**

will do n'importe quoi fera l'affaire; **all in all** tout bien considéré, en fin de compte ▷ adv: **all alone** tout(e) seul(e); **it's not as hard as all that** ce n'est pas si difficile que ça; **all the more/the better** d'autant plus/mieux; **all but** presque, pratiquement; **the score is 2 all** le score est de 2 partout

Allah ['ælə] n Allah m
allegation [ælɪ'ɡeɪʃən] n allégation f
alleged [ə'lɛdʒd] adj prétendu(e); **allegedly** adv à ce que l'on prétend, paraît-il
allegiance [ə'li:dʒəns] n fidélité f, obéissance f
allergic [ə'lə:dʒɪk] adj: **~ to** allergique à; **I'm ~ to penicillin** je suis allergique à la pénicilline
allergy ['ælədʒɪ] n allergie f
alleviate [ə'li:vɪeɪt] vt soulager, adoucir
alley ['ælɪ] n ruelle f
alliance [ə'laɪəns] n alliance f
allied ['ælaɪd] adj allié(e)
alligator ['ælɪɡeɪtə'] n alligator m
all-in ['ɔ:lɪn] adj, adv (BRIT: charge) tout compris
allocate ['æləkeɪt] vt (share out) répartir, distribuer; **to ~ sth to** (duties) assigner or attribuer qch à; (sum, time) allouer qch à
allot [ə'lɔt] vt (share out) répartir, distribuer; **to ~ sth to** (time) allouer qch à; (duties) assigner qch à
all-out ['ɔ:laut] adj (effort etc) total(e)
allow [ə'lau] vt (practice, behaviour) permettre, autoriser; (sum to spend etc) accorder, allouer; (sum, time estimated) compter, prévoir; (claim, goal) admettre; (concede): **to ~ that** convenir que; **to ~ sb to do** permettre à qn de faire, autoriser qn à faire; **he is ~ed to** ... on lui permet de ...; **allow for** vt fus tenir compte de; **allowance** n (money received) allocation f; (: from parent etc) subside m; (: for expenses) indemnité f; (US: pocket money) argent m de poche; (Tax) somme f déductible du revenu imposable, abattement m; **to make allowances for** (person) essayer de comprendre; (thing) tenir compte de
all right adv (feel, work) bien; (as answer) d'accord
ally n ['ælaɪ] allié m ▷ vt [ə'laɪ]: **to ~ o.s. with** s'allier avec
almighty [ɔ:l'maɪtɪ] adj tout(e)-puissant(e); (tremendous) énorme
almond ['ɑ:mənd] n amande f
almost ['ɔ:lməust] adv presque
alone [ə'ləun] adj, adv seul(e); **to leave sb ~** laisser qn tranquille; **to leave sth ~** ne pas toucher à qch; **let ~ ...** sans parler de ...; encore moins ...
along [ə'lɔŋ] prep le long de ▷ adv: **is he coming ~ with us?** vient-il avec nous?; **he was hopping/limping ~** il venait or avançait

en sautillant/boitant; **~ with** avec, en plus de; (person) en compagnie de; **all ~** (all the time) depuis le début; **alongside** prep (along) le long de; (beside) à côté de ▷ adv bord à bord; côte à côte
aloof [ə'lu:f] adj distant(e) ▷ adv: **to stand ~** se tenir à l'écart or à distance
aloud [ə'laud] adv à haute voix
alphabet ['ælfəbɛt] n alphabet m
Alps [ælps] npl: **the ~** les Alpes fpl
already [ɔ:l'rɛdɪ] adv déjà
alright ['ɔ:l'raɪt] adv (BRIT) = **all right**
also ['ɔ:lsəu] adv aussi
altar ['ɔltə'] n autel m
alter ['ɔltə'] vt, vi changer; **alteration** [ɔltə'reɪʃən] n changement m, modification f; **alterations** npl (Sewing) retouches fpl; (Archit) modifications fpl
alternate adj [ɔl'tə:nɪt] alterné(e), alternant(e), alternatif(-ive); (US) = **alternative** ▷ vi ['ɔltə:neɪt] alterner; **to ~ with** alterner avec; **on ~ days** un jour sur deux, tous les deux jours
alternative [ɔl'tə:nətɪv] adj (solution, plan) autre, de remplacement; (lifestyle) parallèle ▷ n (choice) alternative f; (other possibility) autre possibilité f; **~ medicine** médecine alternative, médecine douce; **alternatively** adv: **alternatively one could ...** une autre or l'autre solution serait de ...
although [ɔ:l'ðəu] conj bien que + sub
altitude ['æltɪtju:d] n altitude f
altogether [ɔ:ltə'ɡɛðə'] adv entièrement, tout à fait; (on the whole) tout compte fait; (in all) en tout
aluminium [ælju'mɪnɪəm] (BRIT **aluminum**) [ə'lu:mɪnəm] (US) n aluminium m
always ['ɔ:lweɪz] adv toujours
Alzheimer's (disease) ['æltshaɪməz-] n maladie f d'Alzheimer
am [æm] vb see **be**
a.m. adv abbr (= ante meridiem) du matin
amalgamate [ə'mælɡəmeɪt] vt, vi fusionner
amass [ə'mæs] vt amasser
amateur ['æmətə'] n amateur m
amaze [ə'meɪz] vt stupéfier; **to be ~d (at)** être stupéfait(e) (de); **amazed** adj stupéfait(e); **amazement** n surprise f, étonnement m; **amazing** adj étonnant(e), incroyable; (bargain, offer) exceptionnel(le)
Amazon ['æməzən] n (Geo) Amazone f
ambassador [æm'bæsədə'] n ambassadeur m
amber ['æmbə'] n ambre m; **at ~** (BRIT Aut) à l'orange
ambiguous [æm'bɪɡjuəs] adj ambigu(ë)
ambition [æm'bɪʃən] n ambition f; **ambitious** [æm'bɪʃəs] adj ambitieux(-euse)
ambulance ['æmbjuləns] n ambulance f;

call an ~! appelez une ambulance!
ambush ['æmbʊʃ] n embuscade f ▷ vt tendre une embuscade à
amen ['ɑːˈmɛn] excl amen
amend [əˈmɛnd] vt (law) amender; (text) corriger; **to make ~s** réparer ses torts, faire amende honorable; **amendment** n (to law) amendement m; (to text) correction f
amenities [əˈmiːnɪtiz] npl aménagements mpl, équipements mpl
America [əˈmɛrɪkə] n Amérique f; **American** adj américain(e) ▷ n Américain(e); **American football** n (BRIT) football m américain
amicable ['æmɪkəbl] adj amical(e); (Law) à l'amiable
amid(st) [əˈmɪd(st)] prep parmi, au milieu de
ammunition [æmjuˈnɪʃən] n munitions fpl
amnesty ['æmnɪstɪ] n amnistie f
among(st) [əˈmʌŋ(st)] prep parmi, entre
amount [əˈmaʊnt] n (sum of money) somme f; (total) montant m; (quantity) quantité f; nombre m ▷ vi: **to ~ to** (total) s'élever à; (be same as) équivaloir à, revenir à
amp(ère) ['æmp(ɛəʳ)] n ampère m
ample ['æmpl] adj ample, spacieux(-euse); (enough): **this is ~** c'est largement suffisant; **to have ~ time/room** avoir bien assez de temps/place
amplifier ['æmplɪfaɪəʳ] n amplificateur m
amputate ['æmpjuteɪt] vt amputer
Amtrak ['æmtræk] (US) n société mixte de transports ferroviaires interurbains pour voyageurs
amuse [əˈmjuːz] vt amuser; **amusement** n amusement m; (pastime) distraction f; **amusement arcade** n salle f de jeu; **amusement park** n parc m d'attractions
amusing [əˈmjuːzɪŋ] adj amusant(e), divertissant(e)
an [æn, ən, n] indef art see a
anaemia [əˈniːmɪə] (US anemia) n anémie f
anaemic [əˈniːmɪk] (US anemic) adj anémique
anaesthetic [ænɪsˈθɛtɪk] (US anesthetic) n anesthésique m
analog(ue) ['ænəlɔg] adj (watch, computer) analogique
analogy [əˈnælədʒɪ] n analogie f
analyse ['ænəlaɪz] (US analyze) vt analyser; **analysis** (pl analyses) [əˈnæləsɪs, -siːz] n analyse f; **analyst** ['ænəlɪst] n (political analyst etc) analyste m/f; (US) psychanalyste m/f
analyze ['ænəlaɪz] vt (US) = analyse
anarchy ['ænəkɪ] n anarchie f
anatomy [əˈnætəmɪ] n anatomie f
ancestor ['ænsɪstəʳ] n ancêtre m, aïeul m
anchor ['æŋkəʳ] n ancre f ▷ vi (also: **to drop ~**) jeter l'ancre, mouiller ▷ vt mettre à l'ancre;

(fig): **to ~ sth** fixer qch à
anchovy ['æntʃəvɪ] n anchois m
ancient ['eɪnʃənt] adj ancien(ne), antique; (person) d'un âge vénérable; (car) antédiluvien(ne)
and [ænd] conj et; **~ so on** et ainsi de suite; **try ~ come** tâchez de venir; **come ~ sit here** venez vous asseoir ici; **he talked ~ talked** il a parlé pendant des heures; **better ~ better** de mieux en mieux; **more ~ more** de plus en plus
Andorra [ænˈdɔːrə] n (principauté f d')Andorre f
anemia etc [əˈniːmɪə] (US) = anaemia etc
anesthetic [ænɪsˈθɛtɪk] (US) = anaesthetic
angel ['eɪndʒəl] n ange m
anger ['æŋgəʳ] n colère f
angina [ænˈdʒaɪnə] n angine f de poitrine
angle ['æŋgl] n angle m; **from their ~** de leur point de vue
angler ['æŋgləʳ] n pêcheur(-euse) à la ligne
Anglican ['æŋglɪkən] adj, n anglican(e)
angling ['æŋglɪŋ] n pêche f à la ligne
angrily ['æŋgrɪlɪ] adv avec colère
angry ['æŋgrɪ] adj en colère, furieux(-euse); (wound) enflammé(e); **to be ~ with sb/at sth** être furieux contre qn/de qch; **to get ~** se fâcher, se mettre en colère
anguish ['æŋgwɪʃ] n angoisse f
animal ['ænɪməl] n animal m ▷ adj animal(e)
animated ['ænɪmeɪtɪd] adj animé(e)
animation [ænɪˈmeɪʃən] n (of person) entrain m; (of street, Cine) animation f
aniseed ['ænɪsiːd] n anis m
ankle ['æŋkl] n cheville f
annex ['ænɛks] n (BRIT: also: ~e) annexe f ▷ vt [əˈnɛks] annexer
anniversary [ænɪˈvɜːsərɪ] n anniversaire m
announce [əˈnaʊns] vt annoncer; (birth, death) faire part de; **announcement** n annonce f; (for births etc: in newspaper) avis m de faire-part; (: letter, card) faire-part m; **announcer** n (Radio, TV: between programmes) speaker(ine); (: in a programme) présentateur(-trice)
annoy [əˈnɔɪ] vt agacer, ennuyer, contrarier; **don't get ~ed!** ne vous fâchez pas!; **annoying** adj agaçant(e), contrariant(e)
annual ['ænjuəl] adj annuel(le) ▷ n (Bot) plante annuelle; (book) album m; **annually** adv annuellement
annum ['ænəm] n see per
anonymous [əˈnɔnɪməs] adj anonyme
anorak ['ænəræk] n anorak m
anorexia [ænəˈrɛksɪə] n (also: ~ nervosa) anorexie f
anorexic [ænəˈrɛksɪk] adj, n anorexique (m/f)
another [əˈnʌðəʳ] adj: **~ book** (one more) un

autre livre, encore un livre, un livre de plus; (a different one) un autre livre ▷ pron un(e) autre, encore un(e), un(e) de plus; see also **one**

answer ['ɑːnsə'] n réponse f; (to problem) solution f ▷ vi répondre ▷ vt (reply to) répondre à; (problem) résoudre; (prayer) exaucer; **in ~ to your letter** suite à or en réponse à votre lettre; **to ~ the phone** répondre (au téléphone); **to ~ the bell** or **the door** aller or venir ouvrir (la porte); **answer back** vi répondre, répliquer; **answerphone** n (esp BRIT) répondeur m (téléphonique)

ant [ænt] n fourmi f

Antarctic [ænt'ɑːktɪk] n: **the ~** l'Antarctique m

antelope ['æntɪləʊp] n antilope f

antenatal ['æntɪ'neɪtl] adj prénatal(e)

antenna (pl ~e) [æn'tenə, -niː] n antenne f

anthem ['ænθəm] n: **national ~** hymne national

anthology [æn'θɒlədʒɪ] n anthologie f

anthrax ['ænθræks] n anthrax m

anthropology [ænθrə'pɒlədʒɪ] n anthropologie f

anti ['æntɪ] prefix anti-; **antibiotic** ['æntɪbaɪ'ɒtɪk] n antibiotique m; **antibody** ['æntɪbɒdɪ] n anticorps m

anticipate [æn'tɪsɪpeɪt] vt s'attendre à, prévoir; (wishes, request) aller au devant de, devancer; **anticipation** [æntɪsɪ'peɪʃən] n attente f

anticlimax ['æntɪ'klaɪmæks] n déception f

anticlockwise ['æntɪ'klɒkwaɪz] (BRIT) adv dans le sens inverse des aiguilles d'une montre

antics ['æntɪks] npl singeries fpl

anti: **antidote** ['æntɪdəʊt] n antidote m, contrepoison m; **antifreeze** ['æntɪfriːz] n antigel m; **anti-globalization** [æntɪgləʊbəlaɪ'zeɪʃən] n antimondialisation f; **antihistamine** [æntɪ'hɪstəmɪn] n antihistaminique m; **antiperspirant** [æntɪ'pəːspɪrənt] n déodorant m

antique [æn'tiːk] n (ornament) objet m d'art ancien; (furniture) meuble ancien ▷ adj ancien(ne); **antique shop** n magasin m d'antiquités

antiseptic [æntɪ'septɪk] adj, n antiseptique (m)

antisocial ['æntɪ'səʊʃəl] adj (unfriendly) peu liant(e), insociable; (against society) antisocial(e)

antlers ['æntləz] npl bois mpl, ramure f

anxiety [æŋ'zaɪətɪ] n anxiété f; (keenness): **~ to do** grand désir or impatience f de faire

anxious ['æŋkʃəs] adj (très) inquiet(-ète); (always worried) anxieux(-euse); (worrying) angoissant(e); (keen): **~ to do/that** qui tient

beaucoup à faire/à ce que + sub; impatient(e) de faire/que + sub

 KEYWORD

any ['enɪ] adj 1 (in questions etc: singular) du, de l', de la; (: plural) des; **do you have any butter/children/ink?** avez-vous du beurre/des enfants/de l'encre?

2 (with negative) de, d'; **I don't have any money/books** je n'ai pas d'argent/de livres

3 (no matter which) n'importe quel(le); (each and every) tout(e), chaque; **choose any book you like** vous pouvez choisir n'importe quel livre; **any teacher you ask will tell you** n'importe quel professeur vous le dira

4 (in phrases): **in any case** de toute façon; **any day now** d'un jour à l'autre; **at any moment** à tout moment, d'un instant à l'autre; **at any rate** en tout cas; **any time** n'importe quand; **he might come (at) any time** il pourrait venir n'importe quand; **come (at) any time** venez quand vous voulez

▷ pron 1 (in questions etc) en; **have you got any?** est-ce que vous en avez?; **can any of you sing?** est-ce que parmi vous il y en a qui savent chanter?

2 (with negative) en; **I don't have any (of them)** je n'en ai pas, je n'en ai aucun

3 (no matter which one(s)) n'importe lequel (or laquelle); (anybody) n'importe qui; **take any of those books (you like)** vous pouvez prendre n'importe lequel de ces livres

▷ adv 1 (in questions etc): **do you want any more soup/sandwiches?** voulez-vous encore de la soupe/des sandwichs?; **are you feeling any better?** est-ce que vous vous sentez mieux?

2 (with negative): **I can't hear him any more** je ne l'entends plus; **don't wait any longer** n'attendez pas plus longtemps; **anybody** pron n'importe qui; (in interrogative sentences) quelqu'un; (in negative sentences): **I don't see anybody** je ne vois personne; **if anybody should phone ...** si quelqu'un téléphone ...; **anyhow** adv quoi qu'il en soit; (haphazardly) n'importe comment; **do it anyhow you like** faites-le comme vous voulez; **she leaves things just anyhow** elle laisse tout traîner; **I shall go anyhow** j'irai de toute façon; **anyone** pron = **anybody**; **anything** pron (no matter what) n'importe quoi; (in questions) quelque chose; (with negative) ne ... rien; **can you see anything?** tu vois quelque chose?; **if anything happens to me ...** s'il m'arrive quoi que ce soit ...; **you can say anything you like** vous pouvez dire ce que vous voulez; **anything will do** n'importe quoi fera l'affaire; **he'll eat anything** il mange de tout; **anytime**

adv (*at any moment*) d'un moment à l'autre; (*whenever*) n'importe quand; **anyway** *adv* de toute façon; **anyway, I couldn't come even if I wanted to** de toute façon, je ne pouvais pas venir même si je le voulais; **I shall go anyway** j'irai quand même; **why are you phoning, anyway?** au fait, pourquoi tu me téléphones?; **anywhere** *adv* n'importe où; (*in interrogative sentences*) quelque part; (*in negative sentences*): **I can't see him anywhere** je ne le vois nulle part; **can you see him anywhere?** tu le vois quelque part?; **put the books down anywhere** pose les livres n'importe où; **anywhere in the world** (*no matter where*) n'importe où dans le monde

apart[ə'pɑːt] *adv* (*to one side*) à part; de côté; à l'écart; (*separately*) séparément; **to take/pull ~** démonter; **10 miles/a long way ~** à 10 miles/très éloignés l'un de l'autre; **~ from** *prep* à part, excepté

apartment[ə'pɑːtmənt] *n* (*US*) appartement *m*, logement *m*; (*room*) chambre *f*; **apartment building** *n* (*US*) immeuble *m*; maison divisée en appartements

apathy['æpəθɪ] *n* apathie *f*, indifférence *f*

ape[eɪp] *n* (grand) singe ▷ *vt* singer

aperitif[ə'perɪtɪf] *n* apéritif *m*

aperture['æpətʃuə⁺] *n* orifice *m*, ouverture *f*; (*Phot*) ouverture (du diaphragme)

APEX['eɪpɛks] *n abbr* (*Aviat*: = *advance purchase excursion*) APEX *m*

apologize[ə'pɔlədʒaɪz] *vi*: **to ~ (for sth to sb)** s'excuser (de qch auprès de qn), présenter des excuses (à qn pour qch)

apology[ə'pɔlədʒɪ] *n* excuses *fpl*

apostrophe[ə'pɔstrəfɪ] *n* apostrophe *f*

appal[ə'pɔːl] (*US* **appall**) *vt* consterner, atterrer; horrifier; **appalling** *adj* épouvantable; (*stupidity*) consternant(e)

apparatus[æpə'reɪtəs] *n* appareil *m*, dispositif *m*; (*in gymnasium*) agrès *mpl*

apparent[ə'pærənt] *adj* apparent(e); **apparently** *adv* apparemment

appeal[ə'piːl] *vi* (*Law*) faire or interjeter appel ▷ *n* (*Law*) appel *m*; (*request*) appel; prière *f*; (*charm*) attrait *m*, charme *m*; **to ~ for** demander (instamment); implorer; **to ~ to** (*beg*) faire appel à; (*be attractive*) plaire à; **it doesn't ~ to me** cela ne m'attire pas; **appealing** *adj* (*attractive*) attrayant(e)

appear[ə'pɪə⁺] *vi* apparaître, se montrer; (*Law*) comparaître; (*publication*) paraître, sortir, être publié(e); (*seem*) paraître, sembler; **it would ~ that** il semble que; **to ~ in Hamlet** jouer dans Hamlet; **to ~ on TV** passer à la télé; **appearance** *n* apparition *f*; parution *f*; (*look, aspect*) apparence *f*, aspect *m*

appendices[ə'pɛndɪsiːz] *npl of* **appendix**

appendicitis[əpɛndɪ'saɪtɪs] *n* appendicite *f*

appendix(*pl* **appendices**) [ə'pɛndɪks, -siːz] *n* appendice *m*

appetite['æpɪtaɪt] *n* appétit *m*

appetizer['æpɪtaɪzə⁺] *n* (*food*) amuse-gueule *m*; (*drink*) apéritif *m*

applaud[ə'plɔːd] *vt, vi* applaudir

applause[ə'plɔːz] *n* applaudissements *mpl*

apple['æpl] *n* pomme *f*; **apple pie** *n* tarte *f* aux pommes

appliance[ə'plaɪəns] *n* appareil *m*

applicable[ə'plɪkəbl] *adj* applicable; **to be ~ to** (*relevant*) valoir pour

applicant['æplɪkənt] *n*: **~ (for)** candidat *m* (à)

application[æplɪ'keɪʃən] *n* application *f*; (*for a job, a grant etc*) demande *f*; candidature *f*; **application form** *n* formulaire *m* de demande

apply[ə'plaɪ] *vt*: **to ~ (to)** (*paint, ointment*) appliquer (sur); (*law, etc*) appliquer (à) ▷ *vi*: **to ~ to** (*ask*) s'adresser à; (*be suitable for, relevant to*) s'appliquer à; **to ~ (for)** (*permit, grant*) faire une demande (en vue d'obtenir); (*job*) poser sa candidature (pour), faire une demande d'emploi (concernant); **to ~ o.s. to** s'appliquer à

appoint[ə'pɔɪnt] *vt* (*to post*) nommer, engager; (*date, place*) fixer, désigner; **appointment** *n* (*to post*) nomination *f*; (*job*) poste *m*; (*arrangement to meet*) rendez-vous *m*; **to have an appointment** avoir un rendez-vous; **to make an appointment (with)** prendre rendez-vous (avec); **I'd like to make an appointment** je voudrais prendre rendez-vous

appraisal[ə'preɪzl] *n* évaluation *f*

appreciate[ə'priːʃɪeɪt] *vt* (*like*) apprécier, faire cas de; (*be grateful for*) être reconnaissant(e) de; (*be aware of*) comprendre, se rendre compte de ▷ *vi* (*Finance*) prendre de la valeur; **appreciation**[əpriːʃɪ'eɪʃən] *n* appréciation *f*; (*gratitude*) reconnaissance *f*; (*Finance*) hausse *f*, valorisation *f*

apprehension[æprɪ'hɛnʃən] *n* appréhension *f*, inquiétude *f*

apprehensive[æprɪ'hɛnsɪv] *adj* inquiet(-ète), appréhensif(-ive)

apprentice[ə'prɛntɪs] *n* apprenti *m*

approach[ə'prəutʃ] *vi* approcher ▷ *vt* (*come near*) approcher de; (*ask, apply to*) s'adresser à; (*subject, passer-by*) aborder ▷ *n* approche *f*; accès *m*, abord *m*; démarche *f* (*intellectuelle*)

appropriate *adj* [ə'prəuprɪɪt] (*tool etc*) qui convient, approprié(e); (*moment, remark*) opportun(e) ▷ *vt* [ə'prəuprɪeɪt] (*take*) s'approprier

approval[ə'pruːvəl] *n* approbation *f*; **on ~** (*Comm*) à l'examen

approve[ə'pruːv] *vt* approuver; **approve of**

vt fus (thing) approuver; *(person):* **they don't ~ of her** ils n'ont pas bonne opinion d'elle

approximate [ə'prɒksɪmɪt] *adj* approximatif(-ive); **approximately** *adv* approximativement

Apr. *abbr* = **April**

apricot ['eɪprɪkɒt] *n* abricot *m*

April ['eɪprəl] *n* avril *m*; **April Fools' Day** *n* le premier avril

○ **APRIL FOOLS' DAY**
○
○ **April Fools' Day** est le 1er avril, à l'occasion
○ duquel on fait des farces de toutes sortes.
○ Les victimes de ces farces sont les "April
○ fools". Traditionnellement, on n'est censé
○ faire des farces que jusqu'à midi.

apron ['eɪprən] *n* tablier *m*

apt [æpt] *adj (suitable)* approprié(e); *(likely):* **~ to do** susceptible de faire; ayant tendance à faire

aquarium [ə'kwɛərɪəm] *n* aquarium *m*

Aquarius [ə'kwɛərɪəs] *n* le Verseau

Arab ['ærəb] *n* Arabe *m/f* ▷ *adj* arabe

Arabia [ə'reɪbɪə] *n* Arabie *f*; **Arabian** *adj* arabe; **Arabic** ['ærəbɪk] *adj*, *n* arabe (*m*)

arbitrary ['ɑ:bɪtrərɪ] *adj* arbitraire

arbitration [ɑ:bɪ'treɪʃən] *n* arbitrage *m*

arc [ɑ:k] *n* arc *m*

arcade [ɑ:'keɪd] *n* arcade *f*; *(passage with shops)* passage *m*, galerie *f*; *(with games)* salle *f* de jeu

arch [ɑ:tʃ] *n* arche *f*; *(of foot)* cambrure *f*, voûte *f* plantaire ▷ *vt* arquer, cambrer

archaeology [ɑ:kɪ'ɒlədʒɪ] *(us* **archeology**) *n* archéologie *f*

archbishop [ɑ:tʃ'bɪʃəp] *n* archevêque *m*

archeology [ɑ:kɪ'ɒlədʒɪ] *(us)* = **archaeology**

architect ['ɑ:kɪtɛkt] *n* architecte *m*; **architectural** [ɑ:kɪ'tɛktʃərəl] *adj* architectural(e); **architecture** *n* architecture *f*

archive ['ɑ:kaɪv] *n (often pl)* archives *fpl*

Arctic ['ɑ:ktɪk] *adj* arctique ▷ *n*: **the ~** l'Arctique *m*

are [ɑ:*] *vb see* **be**

area ['ɛərɪə] *n (Geom)* superficie *f*; *(zone)* région *f*; *(: smaller)* secteur *m*; *(in room)* coin *m*; *(knowledge, research)* domaine *m*; **area code** *(us) (Tel)* indicatif *m* de zone

arena [ə'ri:nə] *n* arène *f*

aren't [ɑ:nt] = **are not**

Argentina [ɑ:dʒən'ti:nə] *n* Argentine *f*; **Argentinian** [ɑ:dʒən'tɪnɪən] *adj* argentin(e) ▷ *n* Argentin(e)

arguably ['ɑ:gjuəblɪ] *adv*: **it is ~ ...** on peut soutenir que c'est ...

argue ['ɑ:gju:] *vi (quarrel)* se disputer; *(reason)* argumenter; **to ~ that** objecter *or* alléguer que, donner comme argument que

argument ['ɑ:gjumənt] *n (quarrel)* dispute *f*, discussion *f*; *(reasons)* argument *m*

Aries ['ɛərɪz] *n* le Bélier

arise *(pt* **arose**, *pp* **~n)** [ə'raɪz, ə'rəuz, ə'rɪzn] *vi* survenir, se présenter

arithmetic [ə'rɪθmətɪk] *n* arithmétique *f*

arm [ɑ:m] *n* bras *m* ▷ *vt* armer; **arms** *npl (weapons, Heraldry)* armes *fpl*; **~ in ~** bras dessus bras dessous; **armchair** ['ɑ:mtʃɛə*] *n* fauteuil *m*

armed [ɑ:md] *adj* armé(e); **armed forces** *npl*: **the armed forces** les forces armées; **armed robbery** *n* vol *m* à main armée

armour *(us* **armor)** ['ɑ:mə*] *n* armure *f*; *(Mil: tanks)* blindés *mpl*

armpit ['ɑ:mpɪt] *n* aisselle *f*

armrest ['ɑ:mrɛst] *n* accoudoir *m*

army ['ɑ:mɪ] *n* armée *f*

A road *n (BRIT)* ≈ route nationale

aroma [ə'rəumə] *n* arôme *m*; **aromatherapy** *n* aromathérapie *f*

arose [ə'rəuz] *pt of* **arise**

around [ə'raund] *adv (tout)* autour; *(nearby)* dans les parages ▷ *prep* autour de; *(near)* près de; *(fig: about)* environ; *(: date, time)* vers; **is he ~?** est-il dans les parages *or* là?

arouse [ə'rauz] *vt (sleeper)* éveiller; *(curiosity, passions)* éveiller, susciter; *(anger)* exciter

arrange [ə'reɪndʒ] *vt* arranger; **to ~ to do sth** prévoir de faire qch; **arrangement** *n* arrangement *m*; **arrangements** *npl (plans etc)* arrangements *mpl*, dispositions *fpl*

array [ə'reɪ] *n (of objects)* déploiement *m*, étalage *m*

arrears [ə'rɪəz] *npl* arriéré *m*; **to be in ~ with one's rent** devoir un arriéré de loyer

arrest [ə'rɛst] *vt* arrêter; *(sb's attention)* retenir, attirer ▷ *n* arrestation *f*; **under ~** en état d'arrestation

arrival [ə'raɪvl] *n* arrivée *f*; **new ~** nouveau venu/nouvelle venue; *(baby)* nouveau-né(e)

arrive [ə'raɪv] *vi* arriver; **arrive at** *vt fus (decision, solution)* parvenir à

arrogance ['ærəgəns] *n* arrogance *f*

arrogant ['ærəgənt] *adj* arrogant(e)

arrow ['ærəu] *n* flèche *f*

arse [ɑ:s] *n (BRIT infl)* cul *m (!)*

arson ['ɑ:sn] *n* incendie criminel

art [ɑ:t] *n* art *m*; **Arts** *npl (Scol)* les lettres *fpl*; **art college** *n* école *f* des beaux-arts

artery ['ɑ:tərɪ] *n* artère *f*

art gallery *n* musée *m* d'art; *(saleroom)* galerie *f* de peinture

arthritis [ɑ:'θraɪtɪs] *n* arthrite *f*

artichoke ['ɑ:tɪtʃəuk] *n* artichaut *m*; **Jerusalem ~** topinambour *m*

article ['ɑ:tɪkl] *n* article *m*

articulate *adj* [ɑ:'tɪkjulɪt] *(person)* qui s'exprime clairement et aisément; *(speech)*

bien articulé(e), prononcé(e) clairement
▷ *vb* [ɑːˈtɪkjuleɪt] ▷ *vi* articuler, parler
distinctement ▷ *vt* articuler
artificial [ɑːtɪˈfɪʃəl] *adj* artificiel(le)
artist [ˈɑːtɪst] *n* artiste *m/f*; **artistic** [ɑːˈtɪstɪk]
adj artistique
art school *n* ≈ école *f* des beaux-arts

KEYWORD

as [æz] *conj* **1** (*time: moment*) comme, alors que;
à mesure que; **he came in as I was leaving**
il est arrivé comme je partais; **as the years
went by** à mesure que les années passaient;
as from tomorrow à partir de demain
2 (*since, because*) comme, puisque; **he left
early as he had to be home by 10** comme il or
puisqu'il devait être de retour avant 10h, il est
parti de bonne heure
3 (*referring to manner, way*) comme; **do as you
wish** faites comme vous voudrez; **as she said**
comme elle disait
▷ *adv* **1** (*in comparisons*): **as big as** aussi grand
que; **twice as big as** deux fois plus grand que;
as much or **many as** autant que; **as much
money/many books as** autant d'argent/de
livres que; **as soon as** dès que
2 (*concerning*): **as for** or **to that** quant à cela,
pour ce qui est de cela
3: **as if** or **though** comme si; **he looked as if
he was ill** il avait l'air d'être malade; *see also*
long; such; well
▷ *prep* (*in the capacity of*) en tant que, en qualité
de; **he works as a driver** il travaille comme
chauffeur; **as chairman of the company,
he ...** en tant que président de la société, il ...;
he gave me it as a present il me l'a offert, il
m'en a fait cadeau

a.s.a.p. *abbr* = **as soon as possible**
asbestos [æzˈbɛstəs] *n* asbeste *m*, amiante *m*
ascent [əˈsɛnt] *n* (*climb*) ascension *f*
ash [æʃ] *n* (*dust*) cendre *f*; (*also:* ~ **tree**) frêne *m*
ashamed [əˈʃeɪmd] *adj* honteux(-euse),
confus(e); **to be ~ of** avoir honte de
ashore [əˈʃɔːʳ] *adv* à terre
ashtray [ˈæʃtreɪ] *n* cendrier *m*
Ash Wednesday *n* mercredi *m* des Cendres
Asia [ˈeɪʃə] *n* Asie *f*; **Asian** *n* (*from Asia*)
Asiatique *m/f*; (*BRIT: from Indian subcontinent*)
Indo-Pakistanais(-e) ▷ *adj* asiatique; indo-
pakistanais(-e)
aside [əˈsaɪd] *adv* de côté; à l'écart ▷ *n*
aparté *m*
ask [ɑːsk] *vt* demander; (*invite*) inviter; **to ~ sb
sth/to do sth** demander à qn qch/de faire
qch; **to ~ sb about sth** questionner qn au
sujet de qch; se renseigner auprès de qn au
sujet de qch; **to ~ (sb) a question** poser une

question (à qn); **to ~ sb out to dinner** inviter
qn au restaurant; **ask for** *vt fus* demander;
it's just ~ing for trouble or **for it** ce serait
chercher des ennuis
asleep [əˈsliːp] *adj* endormi(e); **to fall ~**
s'endormir
AS level *n abbr* (= *Advanced Subsidiary level*)
*première partie de l'examen équivalent au
baccalauréat*
asparagus [əsˈpærəgəs] *n* asperges *fpl*
aspect [ˈæspɛkt] *n* aspect *m*; (*direction in which
a building etc faces*) orientation *f*, exposition *f*
aspirations [æspəˈreɪʃənz] *npl* (*hopes,
ambition*) aspirations *fpl*
aspire [əsˈpaɪəʳ] *vi*: **to ~ to** aspirer à
aspirin [ˈæsprɪn] *n* aspirine *f*
ass [æs] *n* âne *m*; (*inf*) imbécile *m/f*; (*us infl*)
cul *m* (!)
assassin [əˈsæsɪn] *n* assassin *m*; **assassinate**
vt assassiner
assault [əˈsɔːlt] *n* (*Mil*) assaut *m*; (*gen: attack*)
agression *f* ▷ *vt* attaquer; (*sexually*) violenter
assemble [əˈsɛmbl] *vt* assembler ▷ *vi*
s'assembler, se rassembler
assembly [əˈsɛmblɪ] *n* (*meeting*)
rassemblement *m*; (*parliament*) assemblée *f*;
(*construction*) assemblage *m*
assert [əˈsəːt] *vt* affirmer, déclarer; (*authority*)
faire valoir; (*innocence*) protester de; **assertion**
[əˈsəːʃən] *n* assertion *f*, affirmation *f*
assess [əˈsɛs] *vt* évaluer, estimer; (*tax,
damages*) établir or fixer le montant de; (*person*)
juger la valeur de; **assessment** *n* évaluation *f*,
estimation *f*; (*of tax*) fixation *f*
asset [ˈæsɛt] *n* avantage *m*, atout *m*; (*person*)
atout; **assets** *npl* (*Comm*) capital *m*; avoir(s)
m(pl); actif *m*
assign [əˈsaɪn] *vt* (*date*) fixer, arrêter; **to ~ sth
to** (*task*) assigner qch à; (*resources*) affecter qch
à; **assignment** *n* (*task*) mission *f*; (*homework*)
devoir *m*
assist [əˈsɪst] *vt* aider, assister; **assistance** *n*
aide *f*, assistance *f*; **assistant** *n* assistant(e),
adjoint(e); (*BRIT: also:* **shop assistant**)
vendeur(-euse)
associate *adj, n* [əˈsəʊʃiɪt] associé(e) ▷ *vb*
[əˈsəʊʃieɪt] ▷ *vt* associer ▷ *vi*: **to ~ with sb**
fréquenter qn
association [əsəʊsɪˈeɪʃən] *n* association *f*
assorted [əˈsɔːtɪd] *adj* assorti(e)
assortment [əˈsɔːtmənt] *n* assortiment *m*;
(*of people*) mélange *m*
assume [əˈsjuːm] *vt* supposer; (*responsibilities
etc*) assumer; (*attitude, name*) prendre, adopter
assumption [əˈsʌmpʃən] *n* supposition *f*,
hypothèse *f*; (*of power*) assomption *f*, prise *f*
assurance [əˈʃʊərəns] *n* assurance *f*
assure [əˈʃʊəʳ] *vt* assurer
asterisk [ˈæstərɪsk] *n* astérisque *m*

asthma ['æsmə] n asthme m

astonish [ə'stɒnɪʃ] vt étonner, stupéfier; **astonished** adj étonné(e); **to be astonished at** être étonné(e) de; **astonishing** adj étonnant(e), stupéfiant(e); **I find it astonishing that ...** je trouve incroyable que ... + sub; **astonishment** n (grand) étonnement, stupéfaction f

astound [ə'staund] vt stupéfier, sidérer

astray [ə'streɪ] adv: **to go ~** s'égarer; (fig) quitter le droit chemin; **to lead ~** (morally) détourner du droit chemin

astrology [ə'strɒlədʒɪ] n astrologie f

astronaut ['æstrənɔːt] n astronaute m/f

astronomer [əs'trɒnəmə^r] n astronome m

astronomical [æstrə'nɒmɪkl] adj astronomique

astronomy [əs'trɒnəmɪ] n astronomie f

astute [əs'tjuːt] adj astucieux(-euse), malin(-igne)

asylum [ə'saɪləm] n asile m; **asylum seeker** [-siːkə^r] n demandeur(-euse) d'asile

KEYWORD

at [æt] prep **1** (referring to position, direction) à; **at the top** au sommet; **at home/school** à la maison or chez soi/à l'école; **at the baker's** à la boulangerie, chez le boulanger; **to look at sth** regarder qch

2 (referring to time): **at 4 o'clock** à 4 heures; **at Christmas** à Noël; **at night** la nuit; **at times** par moments, parfois

3 (referring to rates, speed etc) à; **at £1 a kilo** une livre le kilo; **two at a time** deux à la fois; **at 50 km/h** à 50 km/h

4 (referring to manner): **at a stroke** d'un seul coup; **at peace** en paix

5 (referring to activity): **to be at work** (in the office etc) être au travail; (working) travailler; **to play at cowboys** jouer aux cowboys; **to be good at sth** être bon en qch

6 (referring to cause): **shocked/surprised/ annoyed at sth** choqué par/étonné de/agacé par qch; **I went at his suggestion** j'y suis allé sur son conseil

7 (symbol) arobase f

ate [eɪt] pt of **eat**

atheist ['eɪθɪɪst] n athée m/f

Athens ['æθɪnz] n Athènes

athlete ['æθliːt] n athlète m/f

athletic [æθ'lɛtɪk] adj athlétique; **athletics** n athlétisme m

Atlantic [ət'læntɪk] adj atlantique ▷ n: **the ~ (Ocean)** l'(océan m) Atlantique m

atlas ['ætləs] n atlas m

A.T.M. n abbr (= Automated Telling Machine) guichet m automatique

atmosphere ['ætməsfɪə^r] n (air) atmosphère f; (fig: of place etc) atmosphère, ambiance f

atom ['ætəm] n atome m; **atomic** [ə'tɒmɪk] adj atomique; **atom(ic) bomb** n bombe f atomique

A to Z® n (map) plan m des rues

atrocity [ə'trɒsɪtɪ] n atrocité f

attach [ə'tætʃ] vt (gen) attacher; (document, letter) joindre; **to be ~ed to sb/sth** (to like) être attaché à qn/qch; **attachment** n (tool) accessoire m; (Comput) fichier m joint; (love): **attachment (to)** affection f(pour), attachement m (à)

attack [ə'tæk] vt attaquer; (task etc) s'attaquer à ▷ n attaque f; **heart ~** crise f cardiaque; **attacker** n attaquant m; agresseur m

attain [ə'teɪn] vt (also: **to ~ to**) parvenir à, atteindre; (knowledge) acquérir

attempt [ə'tɛmpt] n tentative f ▷ vt essayer, tenter

attend [ə'tɛnd] vt (course) suivre; (meeting, talk) assister à; (school, church) aller à, fréquenter; (patient) soigner, s'occuper de; **attend to** vt fus (needs, affairs etc) s'occuper de; (customer) s'occuper de, servir; **attendance** n (being present) présence f; (people present) assistance f; **attendant** n employé(e); gardien(ne) ▷ adj concomitant(e), qui accompagne or s'ensuit

Be careful not to translate **to attend** by the French word **attendre**.

attention [ə'tɛnʃən] n attention f ▷ excl (Mil) garde-à-vous!; **for the ~ of** (Admin) à l'attention de

attic ['ætɪk] n grenier m, combles mpl

attitude ['ætɪtjuːd] n attitude f

attorney [ə'təːnɪ] n (US: lawyer) avocat m; **Attorney General** n (BRIT) ≈ procureur général; (US) ≈ garde m des Sceaux, ministre m de la Justice

attract [ə'trækt] vt attirer; **attraction** [ə'trækʃən] n (gen pl: pleasant things) attraction f, attrait m; (Physics) attraction f; (fig: towards sb, sth) attirance f; **attractive** adj séduisant(e), attrayant(e)

attribute n ['ætrɪbjuːt] attribut m ▷ vt [ə'trɪbjuːt]: **to ~ sth to** attribuer qch à

aubergine ['əubəʒiːn] n aubergine f

auburn ['ɔːbən] adj auburn inv, châtain roux inv

auction ['ɔːkʃən] n (also: **sale by ~**) vente f aux enchères ▷ vt (also: **to sell by ~**) vendre aux enchères

audible ['ɔːdɪbl] adj audible

audience ['ɔːdɪəns] n (people) assistance f, public m; (on radio) auditeurs mpl; (at theatre) spectateurs mpl; (interview) audience f

audit ['ɔːdɪt] vt vérifier

audition [ɔː'dɪʃən] n audition f

auditor ['ɔːdɪtəʳ] n vérificateur m des comptes
auditorium [ɔːdɪ'tɔːrɪəm] n auditorium m, salle f de concert or de spectacle
Aug. abbr = **August**
August ['ɔːgəst] n août m
aunt [ɑːnt] n tante f; **auntie, aunty** n diminutive of **aunt**
au pair ['əʊ'pεəʳ] n (also: **~ girl**) jeune fille f au pair
aura ['ɔːrə] n atmosphère f; (of person) aura f
austerity [ɔs'tεrɪtɪ] n austérité f
Australia [ɔs'treɪlɪə] n Australie f; **Australian** adj australien(ne) ⊳ n Australien(ne)
Austria ['ɔstrɪə] n Autriche f; **Austrian** adj autrichien(ne) ⊳ n Autrichien(ne)
authentic [ɔː'θεntɪk] adj authentique
author ['ɔːθəʳ] n auteur m
authority [ɔː'θɔrɪtɪ] n autorité f; (permission) autorisation (formelle); **the authorities** les autorités fpl, l'administration f
authorize ['ɔːθəraɪz] vt autoriser
auto ['ɔːtəʊ] n (us) auto f, voiture f;
autobiography [ɔːtəbaɪ'ɔgrəfɪ] n autobiographie f; **autograph** ['ɔːtəgrɑːf] n autographe m ⊳ vt signer, dédicacer;
automatic [ɔːtə'mætɪk] adj automatique ⊳ n (gun) automatique m; (car) voiture f à transmission automatique; **automatically** adv automatiquement; **automobile** ['ɔːtəməbiːl] n (us) automobile f; **autonomous** [ɔː'tɔnəməs] adj autonome; **autonomy** [ɔː'tɔnəmɪ] n autonomie f
autumn ['ɔːtəm] n automne m
auxiliary [ɔːg'zɪlɪərɪ] adj, n auxiliaire (m/f)
avail [ə'veɪl] vt: **to ~ o.s. of** user de; profiter de ⊳ n: **to no ~** sans résultat, en vain, en pure perte
availability [əveɪlə'bɪlɪtɪ] n disponibilité f
available [ə'veɪləbl] adj disponible
avalanche ['ævəlɑːnʃ] n avalanche f
Ave. abbr = **avenue**
avenue ['ævənjuː] n avenue f; (fig) moyen m
average ['ævərɪdʒ] n moyenne f ⊳ adj moyen(ne) ⊳ vt (a certain figure) atteindre or faire etc en moyenne; **on ~** en moyenne
avert [ə'vɜːt] vt (danger) prévenir, écarter; (one's eyes) détourner
avid ['ævɪd] adj avide
avocado [ævə'kɑːdəʊ] n (BRIT: also: **~ pear**) avocat m
avoid [ə'vɔɪd] vt éviter
await [ə'weɪt] vt attendre
awake [ə'weɪk] adj éveillé(e) ⊳ vb (pt awoke, pp awoken) ⊳ vt éveiller ⊳ vi s'éveiller; **to be ~** être réveillé(e)
award [ə'wɔːd] n (for bravery) récompense f; (prize) prix m; (Law: damages) dommages-intérêts mpl ⊳ vt (prize) décerner; (Law: damages) accorder

aware [ə'wεəʳ] adj: **~ of** (conscious) conscient(e) de; (informed) au courant de; **to become ~ of/that** prendre conscience de/que; se rendre compte de/que; **awareness** n conscience f, connaissance f
away [ə'weɪ] adv (au) loin; (movement): **she went ~** elle est partie ⊳ adj (not in, not here) absent(e); **far ~** (au) loin; **two kilometres ~** à (une distance de) deux kilomètres, à deux kilomètres de distance; **two hours ~ by car** à deux heures de voiture or de route; **the holiday was two weeks ~** il restait deux semaines jusqu'aux vacances; **he's ~ for a week** il est parti (pour) une semaine; **to take sth ~ from sb** prendre qch à qn; **to take sth ~ from sth** (subtract) ôter qch de qch; **to work/pedal ~** travailler/pédaler à cœur joie; **to fade ~** (colour) s'estomper; (sound) s'affaiblir
awe [ɔː] n respect mêlé de crainte, effroi mêlé d'admiration; **awesome** ['ɔːsəm] (us) adj (inf: excellent) génial(e)
awful ['ɔːfəl] adj affreux(-euse); **an ~ lot of** énormément de; **awfully** adv (very) terriblement, vraiment
awkward ['ɔːkwəd] adj (clumsy) gauche, maladroit(e); (inconvenient) peu pratique; (embarrassing) gênant
awoke [ə'wəʊk] pt of **awake**
awoken [ə'wəʊkən] pp of **awake**
axe [æks] (us **ax**) n hache f ⊳ vt (project etc) abandonner; (jobs) supprimer
axle ['æksl] n essieu m
ay(e) [aɪ] excl (yes) oui
azalea [ə'zeɪlɪə] n azalée f

B [biː] *n* (*Mus*): **B** si *m*

B.A. *abbr* (*Scol*) = **Bachelor of Arts**

baby ['beɪbɪ] *n* bébé *m*; **baby carriage** *n* (*US*) voiture *f* d'enfant; **baby-sit** *vi* garder les enfants; **baby-sitter** *n* baby-sitter *m/f*; **baby wipe** *n* lingette *f* (*pour bébé*)

bachelor ['bætʃələʳ] *n* célibataire *m*; **B~ of Arts/Science (BA/BSc)** ≈ licencié(e) ès *or* en lettres/sciences

back [bæk] *n* (*of person, horse*) dos *m*; (*of hand*) dos, revers *m*; (*of house*) derrière *m*; (*of car, train*) arrière *m*; (*of chair*) dossier *m*; (*of page*) verso *m*; (*of crowd*): **can the people at the ~ hear me properly?** est-ce que les gens du fond peuvent m'entendre?; (*Football*) arrière *m*; **~ to front** à l'envers ▷ *vt* (*financially*) soutenir (financièrement); (*candidate: also*: **~ up**) soutenir, appuyer; (*horse: at races*) parier *or* miser sur; (*car*) (faire) reculer ▷ *vi* reculer; (*car etc*) faire marche arrière ▷ *adj* (*in compounds*) de derrière, à l'arrière, **~ seat/wheel** (*Aut*) siège *m*/roue *f* arrière *inv*; **~ payments/rent** arriéré *m* de paiements/loyer; **~ garden/room** jardin/pièce sur l'arrière ▷ *adv* (*not forward*) en arrière; (*returned*): **he's ~** il est rentré, il est de retour; **he ran ~** il est revenu en courant; (*restitution*): **throw the ball ~** renvoie la balle; **can I have it ~?** puis-je le ravoir?, peux-tu me le rendre?; (*again*): **he called ~** il a rappelé;

back down *vi* rabattre de ses prétentions; **back out** *vi* (*of promise*) se dédire; **back up** *vt* (*person*) soutenir; (*Comput*) faire une copie de sauvegarde de; **backache** *n* mal *m* au dos; **backbencher** (*BRIT*) *n* membre du parlement *sans portefeuille*; **backbone** *n* colonne vertébrale, épine dorsale; **back door** *n* porte *f* de derrière; **backfire** *vi* (*Aut*) pétarader; (*plans*) mal tourner; **backgammon** *n* trictrac *m*; **background** *n* arrière-plan *m*; (*of events*) situation *f*, conjoncture *f*; (*basic knowledge*) éléments *mpl* de base; (*experience*) formation *f*; **family background** milieu familial; **backing** *n* (*fig*) soutien *m*, appui *m*; **backlog** *n*: **backlog of work** travail *m* en retard; **backpack** *n* sac *m* à dos; **backpacker** *n* randonneur(-euse); **backslash** *n* barre oblique inversée; **backstage** *adv* dans les coulisses; **backstroke** *n* dos crawlé; **backup** *adj* (*train, plane*) supplémentaire, de réserve; (*Comput*) de sauvegarde ▷ *n* (*support*) appui *m*, soutien *m*; (*Comput: also*: **backup file**) sauvegarde *f*; **backward** *adj* (*movement*) en arrière; (*person, country*) arriéré(e), attardé(e); **backwards** *adv* (*move, go*) en arrière; (*read a list*) à l'envers, à rebours; (*fall*) se la renverse; (*walk*) à reculons; **backyard** *n* arrière-cour *f*

bacon ['beɪkən] *n* bacon *m*, lard *m*

bacteria [bæk'tɪərɪə] *npl* bactéries *fpl*

bad [bæd] *adj* mauvais(e); (*child*) vilain(e); (*mistake, accident*) grave; (*meat, food*) gâté(e), avarié(e); **his ~ leg** sa jambe malade; **to go ~** (*meat, food*) se gâter; (*milk*) tourner

bade [bæd] *pt of* **bid**

badge [bædʒ] *n* insigne *m*; (*of policeman*) plaque *f*; (*stick-on, sew-on*) badge *m*

badger ['bædʒəʳ] *n* blaireau *m*

badly ['bædlɪ] *adv* (*work, dress etc*) mal; **to reflect ~ on sb** donner une mauvaise image de qn; **~ wounded** grièvement blessé; **he needs it ~** il en a absolument besoin; **~ off** *adj*, *adv* dans la gêne

bad-mannered ['bæd'mænəd] *adj* mal élevé(e)

badminton ['bædmɪntən] *n* badminton *m*

bad-tempered ['bæd'tɛmpəd] *adj* (*by nature*) ayant mauvais caractère; (*on one occasion*) de mauvaise humeur

bag [bæg] *n* sac *m*; **~s of** (*inf: lots of*) des tas de; **baggage** *n* bagages *mpl*; **baggage allowance** *n* franchise *f* de bagages; **baggage reclaim** *n* (*at airport*) livraison *f* des bagages; **baggy** *adj* avachi(e), qui fait des poches; **bagpipes** *npl* cornemuse *f*

bail [beɪl] *n* caution *f* ▷ *vt* (*prisoner: also*: **grant ~ to**) mettre en liberté sous caution; (*boat: also*: **~ out**) écoper; **to be released on ~** être libéré(e) sous caution; **bail out** *vt* (*prisoner*) payer la caution de

bait[beɪt] n appât m ▷ vt appâter; (fig: tease) tourmenter

bake[beɪk] vt (faire) cuire au four ▷ vi (bread etc) cuire (au four); (make cakes etc) faire de la pâtisserie; **baked beans** npl haricots blancs à la sauce tomate; **baked potato** n pomme f de terre en robe des champs; **baker** n boulanger m; **bakery** n boulangerie f; **baking** n (process) cuisson f; **baking powder** n levure f (chimique)

balance['bæləns] n équilibre m; (Comm: sum) solde m; (remainder) reste m; (scales) balance f ▷ vt mettre or faire tenir en équilibre; (pros and cons) peser; (budget) équilibrer; (account) balancer; (compensate) compenser, contrebalancer; **~ of trade/payments** balance commerciale/des comptes or paiements; **balanced** adj (personality, diet) équilibré(e); (report) objectif(-ive); **balance sheet** n bilan m

balcony['bælkənɪ] n balcon m; **do you have a room with a ~?** avez-vous une chambre avec balcon?

bald[bɔːld] adj chauve; (tyre) lisse

ball[bɔːl] n boule f; (football) ballon m; (for tennis, golf) balle f; (dance) bal m; **to play ~** jouer au ballon (or à la balle); (fig) coopérer

ballerina[bælə'riːnə] n ballerine f

ballet['bæleɪ] n ballet m; (art) danse f (classique); **ballet dancer** n danseur(-euse) de ballet

balloon[bə'luːn] n ballon m

ballot['bælət] n scrutin m

ballpoint (pen)['bɔːlpɔɪnt-] n stylo m à bille

ballroom['bɔːlrum] n salle f de bal

Baltic[bɔːltɪk] n: **the ~ (Sea)** la (mer) Baltique

bamboo[bæm'buː] n bambou m

ban[bæn] n interdiction f ▷ vt interdire

banana[bə'nɑːnə] n banane f

band[bænd] n bande f; (at a dance) orchestre m; (Mil) musique f, fanfare f

bandage['bændɪdʒ] n bandage m, pansement m ▷ vt (wound, leg) mettre un pansement or un bandage sur

Band-Aid®['bændeɪd] n (us) pansement adhésif

B. & B. n abbr = **bed and breakfast**

bandit['bændɪt] n bandit m

bang[bæŋ] n détonation f; (of door) claquement m; (blow) coup (violent) ▷ vt frapper (violemment); (door) claquer ▷ vi détoner; claquer

Bangladesh[bæŋglə'deʃ] n Bangladesh m

Bangladeshi[bæŋglə'deʃɪ] adj du Bangladesh ▷ n habitant(e) du Bangladesh

bangle['bæŋgl] n bracelet m

bangs[bæŋz] npl (us: fringe) frange f

banish['bænɪʃ] vt bannir

banister(s)['bænɪstə(z)] n(pl) rampe f (d'escalier)

banjo(pl **~es** or **~s**) ['bændʒəu] n banjo m

bank[bæŋk] n banque f; (of river, lake) bord m, rive f; (of earth) talus m, remblai m ▷ vi (Aviat) virer sur l'aile; **bank on** vt fus miser or tabler sur; **bank account** n compte m en banque; **bank balance** n solde m bancaire; **bank card** (BRIT) n carte f d'identité bancaire; **bank charges** npl (BRIT) frais mpl de banque; **banker** n banquier m; **bank holiday** n (BRIT) jour férié (où les banques sont fermées); voir encadré; **banking** n opérations fpl bancaires; profession f de banquier; **bank manager** n directeur m d'agence (bancaire); **banknote** n billet m de banque

⬤ **BANK HOLIDAY**
⬤
⬤ Le terme **bank holiday** s'applique au
⬤ Royaume-Uni aux jours fériés pendant
⬤ lesquels banques et commerces sont
⬤ fermés. Les principaux **bank holidays** à
⬤ part Noël et Pâques se situent au mois de
⬤ mai et fin août, et contrairement aux pays
⬤ de tradition catholique, ne coïncident pas
⬤ nécessairement avec une fête religieuse.

bankrupt['bæŋkrʌpt] adj en faillite; **to go ~** faire faillite; **bankruptcy** n faillite f

bank statement n relevé m de compte

banner['bænər] n bannière f

bannister(s)['bænɪstə(z)] n(pl) = **banister(s)**

banquet['bæŋkwɪt] n banquet m, festin m

baptism['bæptɪzəm] n baptême m

baptize[bæp'taɪz] vt baptiser

bar[bɑːr] n (pub) bar m; (counter) comptoir m, bar; (rod: of metal etc) barre f; (of window etc) barreau m; (of chocolate) tablette f, plaque f; (fig: obstacle) obstacle m; (prohibition) mesure f d'exclusion; (Mus) mesure f ▷ vt (road) barrer; (person) exclure; (activity) interdire; **~ of soap** savonnette f; **behind ~s** (prisoner) derrière les barreaux; **the B~** (Law) le barreau; **~ none** sans exception

barbaric[bɑː'bærɪk] adj barbare

barbecue['bɑːbɪkjuː] n barbecue m

barbed wire['bɑːbd-] n fil m de fer barbelé

barber['bɑːbər] n coiffeur m (pour hommes); **barber's (shop)**(us **barber (shop)**) n salon m de coiffure (pour hommes)

bar code n code m à barres, code-barre m

bare[beər] adj nu(e) ▷ vt mettre à nu, dénuder; (teeth) montrer; **barefoot** adj, adv nu-pieds, (les) pieds nus; **barely** adv à peine

bargain['bɑːgɪn] n (transaction) marché m; (good buy) affaire f, occasion f ▷ vi (haggle) marchander; (negotiate) négocier, traiter; **into the ~** par-dessus le marché; **bargain for** vt fus (*inf*): **he got more than he ~ed for!** il en a eu pour son argent!

barge [bɑːdʒ] *n* péniche *f*; **barge in** *vi* (*walk in*) faire irruption; (*interrupt talk*) intervenir mal à propos

bark [bɑːk] *n* (*of tree*) écorce *f*; (*of dog*) aboiement *m* ▷ *vi* aboyer

barley ['bɑːlɪ] *n* orge *f*

barmaid ['bɑːmeɪd] *n* serveuse *f* (de bar), barmaid *f*

barman ['bɑːmən] *n* serveur *m* (de bar), barman *m*

barn [bɑːn] *n* grange *f*

barometer [bə'rɒmɪtə'] *n* baromètre *m*

baron ['bærən] *n* baron *m*; **baroness** *n* baronne *f*

barracks ['bærəks] *npl* caserne *f*

barrage ['bærɑːʒ] *n* (*Mil*) tir *m* de barrage; (*dam*) barrage *m*; (*of criticism*) feu *m*

barrel ['bærəl] *n* tonneau *m*; (*of gun*) canon *m*

barren ['bærən] *adj* stérile

barrette [bə'rɛt] (*us*) *n* barrette *f*

barricade [bærɪ'keɪd] *n* barricade *f*

barrier ['bærɪə'] *n* barrière *f*

barring ['bɑːrɪŋ] *prep* sauf

barrister ['bærɪstə'] *n* (*BRIT*) avocat *m* (plaidant)

barrow ['bærəu] *n* (*cart*) charrette *f* à bras

bartender ['bɑːtɛndə'] *n* (*us*) serveur *m* (*de bar*), barman *m*

base [beɪs] *n* base *f* ▷ *vt* (*opinion, belief*): **to ~ sth on** baser *or* fonder qch sur ▷ *adj* vil(e), bas(se)

baseball ['beɪsbɔːl] *n* base-ball *m*; **baseball cap** *n* casquette *f* de base-ball

Basel [bɑːl] *n* = **Basle**

basement ['beɪsmənt] *n* sous-sol *m*

bases ['beɪsiːz] *npl of* **basis**

bash [bæʃ] *n* (*inf*) frapper, cogner

basic ['beɪsɪk] *adj* (*precautions, rules*) élémentaire; (*principles, research*) fondamental(e); (*vocabulary, salary*) de base; (*minimal*) réduit(e) au minimum, rudimentaire; **basically** *adv* (*in fact*) en fait; (*essentially*) fondamentalement; **basics** *npl*: **the basics** l'essentiel *m*

basil ['bæzl] *n* basilic *m*

basin ['beɪsn] *n* (*vessel, also Geo*) cuvette *f*, bassin *m*; (*BRIT: for food*) bol *m*; (*also:* **wash~**) lavabo *m*

basis (*pl* **bases**) ['beɪsɪs, -siːz] *n* base *f*; **on a part-time/trial ~** à temps partiel/à l'essai

basket ['bɑːskɪt] *n* corbeille *f*; (*with handle*) panier *m*; **basketball** *n* basket-ball *m*

Basle [bɑːl] *n* Bâle

Basque [bæsk] *adj* basque ▷ *n* Basque *m/f*; **the ~ Country** le Pays basque

bass [beɪs] *n* (*Mus*) basse *f*

bastard ['bɑːstəd] *n* enfant naturel(le),

bâtard(e); (*inf!*) salaud *m* (!)

bat [bæt] *n* chauve-souris *f*; (*for baseball etc*) batte *f*; (*BRIT: for table tennis*) raquette *f* ▷ *vt*: **he didn't ~ an eyelid** il n'a pas sourcillé *or* bronché

batch [bætʃ] *n* (*of bread*) fournée *f*; (*of papers*) liasse *f*; (*of applicants, letters*) paquet *m*

bath (*pl* **~s**) [bɑːθ, bɑːðz] *n* bain *m*; (*bathtub*) baignoire *f* ▷ *vt* baigner, donner un bain à; **to have a ~** prendre un bain; *see also* **baths**

bathe [beɪð] *vi* se baigner ▷ *vt* baigner; (*wound etc*) laver

bathing ['beɪðɪŋ] *n* baignade *f*; **bathing costume** (*us* **bathing suit**) *n* maillot *m* (de bain)

bath: **bathrobe** *n* peignoir *m* de bain; **bathroom** *n* salle *f* de bains; **baths** [bɑːðz] *npl* (*BRIT: also:* **swimming baths**) piscine *f*; **bath towel** *n* serviette *f* de bain; **bathtub** *n* baignoire *f*

baton ['bætən] *n* bâton *m*; (*Mus*) baguette *f*; (*club*) matraque *f*

batter ['bætə'] *vt* battre ▷ *n* pâte *f* à frire; **battered** *adj* (*hat, pan*) cabossé(e); **battered wife/child** épouse/enfant maltraité(e) *or* martyr(e)

battery ['bætərɪ] *n* (*for torch, radio*) pile *f*; (*Aut, Mil*) batterie *f*; **battery farming** *n* élevage *m* en batterie

battle ['bætl] *n* bataille *f*, combat *m* ▷ *vi* se battre, lutter; **battlefield** *n* champ *m* de bataille

bay [beɪ] *n* (*of sea*) baie *f*; (*BRIT: for parking*) place *f* de stationnement; (*: for loading*) aire *f* de chargement; **B~ of Biscay** golfe *m* de Gascogne; **to hold sb at ~** tenir qn à distance *or* en échec

bay leaf *n* laurier *m*

bazaar [bə'zɑː'] *n* (*shop, market*) bazar *m*; (*sale*) vente *f* de charité

BBC *n abbr* (= British Broadcasting Corporation) office de la radiodiffusion et télévision britannique

B.C. *adv abbr* (= before Christ) av. J.-C.

 KEYWORD

be [biː] (*pt* **was, were**, *pp* **been**) *aux vb* **1** (*with present participle: forming continuous tenses*): **what are you doing?** que faites-vous?; **they're coming tomorrow** ils viennent demain; **I've been waiting for you for 2 hours** je t'attends depuis 2 heures

2 (*with pp: forming passives*) être; **to be killed** être tué(e); **the box had been opened** la boîte avait été ouverte; **he was nowhere to be seen** on ne le voyait nulle part

3 (*in tag questions*): **it was fun, wasn't it?** c'était drôle, n'est-ce pas?; **he's good-**

looking, isn't he? il est beau, n'est-ce pas?; **she's back, is she?** elle est rentrée, n'est-ce pas *or* alors?

4 (+*to* +*infinitive*): **the house is to be sold** (*necessity*) la maison doit être vendue; (*future*) la maison va être vendue; **he's not to open it** il ne doit pas l'ouvrir
▷ *vb* + *complement* **1** (*gen*) être; **I'm English** je suis anglais(e); **I'm tired** je suis fatigué(e); **I'm hot/cold** j'ai chaud/froid; **he's a doctor** il est médecin; **be careful/good/quiet!** faites attention/soyez sages/taisez-vous!; **2 and 2 are 4** 2 et 2 font 4

2 (*of health*) aller; **how are you?** comment allez-vous?; **I'm better now** je vais mieux maintenant; **he's very ill** il est très malade **3** (*of age*) avoir; **how old are you?** quel âge avez-vous?; **I'm sixteen (years old)** j'ai seize ans

4 (*cost*) coûter; **how much was the meal?** combien a coûté le repas?; **that'll be £5, please** ça fera 5 livres, s'il vous plaît; **this shirt is £17** cette chemise coûte 17 livres
▷ *vi* **1** (*exist, occur etc*) être, exister; **the prettiest girl that ever was** la fille la plus jolie qui ait jamais existé; **is there a God?** y a-t-il un dieu?; **be that as it may** quoi qu'il en soit; **so be it** soit

2 (*referring to place*) être, se trouver; **I won't be here tomorrow** je ne serai pas là demain **3** (*referring to movement*) aller; **where have you been?** où êtes-vous allé(s)?
▷ *impers vb* **1** (*referring to time*) être; **it's 5 o'clock** il est 5 heures; **it's the 28th of April** c'est le 28 avril

2 (*referring to distance*): **it's 10 km to the village** le village est à 10 km
3 (*referring to the weather*) faire; **it's too hot/cold** il fait trop chaud/froid; **it's windy today** il y a du vent aujourd'hui
4 (*emphatic*): **it's me/the postman** c'est moi/le facteur; **it was Maria who paid the bill** c'est Maria qui a payé la note

beach [biːtʃ] *n* plage *f* ▷ *vt* échouer
beacon ['biːkən] *n* (*lighthouse*) fanal *m*; (*marker*) balise *f*
bead [biːd] *n* perle *f*; (*of dew, sweat*) goutte *f*; **beads** *npl* (*necklace*) collier *m*
beak [biːk] *n* bec *m*
beam [biːm] *n* (*Archit*) poutre *f*; (*of light*) rayon *m* ▷ *vi* rayonner
bean [biːn] *n* haricot *m*; (*of coffee*) grain *m*; **beansprouts** *npl* pousses *fpl or* germes *mpl* de soja
bear [bɛəʳ] *n* ours *m* ▷ *vb* (*pt* **bore**, *pp* **borne**)
▷ *vt* porter; (*endure*) supporter, rapporter ▷ *vi*: **to ~ right/left** obliquer à droite/gauche, se diriger vers la droite/gauche

beard [bɪəd] *n* barbe *f*
bearer ['bɛərəʳ] *n* porteur *m*; (*of passport etc*) titulaire *m/f*
bearing ['bɛərɪŋ] *n* maintien *m*, allure *f*; (*connection*) rapport *m*; (*Tech*): **(ball) bearings** *npl* roulement *m* (à billes)
beast [biːst] *n* bête *f*; (*inf: person*) brute *f*
beat [biːt] *n* battement *m*; (*Mus*) temps *m*, mesure *f*; (*of policeman*) ronde *f* ▷ *vt, vi* (*pt* ~, *pp* ~**en**) battre; **off the ~en track** hors des chemins *or* sentiers battus; **to ~ it** (*inf*) ficher le camp; **beat up** *vt* (*inf: person*) tabasser; **beating** *n* raclée *f*
beautiful ['bjuːtɪful] *adj* beau (belle); **beautifully** *adv* admirablement
beauty ['bjuːtɪ] *n* beauté *f*; **beauty parlour** (*us* **beauty parlor**) [-'pɑːləʳ] *n* institut *m* de beauté; **beauty salon** *n* institut *m* de beauté; **beauty spot** *n* (*on skin*) grain *m* de beauté; (*BRIT Tourism*) site naturel (d'une grande beauté)
beaver ['biːvəʳ] *n* castor *m*
became [bɪ'keɪm] *pt of* **become**
because [bɪ'kɔz] *conj* parce que; **~ of** *prep* à cause de
beckon ['bɛkən] *vt* (*also:* **~ to**) faire signe (de venir) à
become [bɪ'kʌm] *vi* devenir; **to ~ fat/thin** grossir/maigrir; **to ~ angry** se mettre en colère
bed [bɛd] *n* lit *m*; (*of flowers*) parterre *m*; (*of coal, clay*) couche *f*; (*of sea, lake*) fond *m*; **to go to ~** aller se coucher; **bed and breakfast** *n* (*terms*) chambre et petit déjeuner; (*place*) ≈ chambre *f* d'hôte; *voir encadré*; **bedclothes** *npl* couvertures *fpl* et draps *mpl*; **bedding** *n* literie *f*; **bed linen** *n* draps *mpl* de lit (et taies *fpl* d'oreillers), literie *f*; **bedroom** *n* chambre *f* (à coucher); **bedside** *n*: **at sb's bedside** au chevet de qn; **bedside lamp** *n* lampe *f* de chevet; **bedside table** *n* table *f* de chevet; **bedsit(ter)** *n* (*BRIT*) chambre meublée, studio *m*; **bedspread** *n* couvre-lit *m*, dessus-de-lit *m*; **bedtime** *n*: **it's bedtime** c'est l'heure de se coucher

BED AND BREAKFAST

Un **bed and breakfast** est une petite pension dans une maison particulière ou une ferme où l'on peut louer une chambre avec petit déjeuner compris pour un prix modique par rapport à ce que l'on paierait dans un hôtel. Ces établissements sont communément appelés "B & B", et sont signalés par une pancarte dans le jardin ou au-dessus de la porte.

bee [biː] *n* abeille *f*

beech [biːtʃ] *n* hêtre *m*
beef [biːf] *n* bœuf *m*; **roast ~** rosbif *m*;
beefburger *n* hamburger *m*; **Beefeater** *n*
hallebardier *m* (de la tour de Londres)
been [biːn] *pp of* **be**
beer [bɪəʳ] *n* bière *f*; **beer garden** *n* (BRIT)
jardin *m* d'un pub (*où l'on peut emmener ses
consommations*)
beet [biːt] *n* (*vegetable*) betterave *f*; (US: *also*:
red ~) betterave (potagère)
beetle [ˈbiːtl] *n* scarabée *m*, coléoptère *m*
beetroot [ˈbiːtruːt] *n* (BRIT) betterave *f*
before [bɪˈfɔːʳ] *prep* (*of time*) avant; (*of space*)
devant ▷ *conj* avant que + *sub*; avant de
▷ *adv* avant; **~ going** avant de partir; **~ she
goes** avant qu'elle (ne) parte; **the week ~** la
semaine précédente *or* d'avant; **I've never
seen it ~** c'est la première fois que je le vois;
beforehand *adv* au préalable, à l'avance
beg [bɛg] *vi* mendier ▷ *vt* (*forgiveness*,
mercy etc) demander; (*entreat*) supplier; **to ~
sb to do sth** supplier qn de faire qch; *see also*
pardon
began [bɪˈgæn] *pt of* **begin**
beggar [ˈbɛgəʳ] *n* mendiant(e)
begin [bɪˈgɪn] (*pt* **began**, *pp* **begun**) *vt*,
vi commencer; **to ~ doing** *or* **to do sth**
commencer à faire qch; **beginner** *n*
débutant(e); **beginning** *n* commencement
m, début *m*
begun [bɪˈgʌn] *pp of* **begin**
behalf [bɪˈhɑːf] *n*: **on ~ of**, (US) **in ~ of**
(*representing*) de la part de; (*for benefit of*)
pour le compte de; **on my/his ~** de ma/sa
part
behave [bɪˈheɪv] *vi* se conduire, se comporter;
(*well: also*: **~ o.s.**) se conduire bien *or*
comme il faut; **behaviour** (US **behavior**) *n*
comportement *m*, conduite *f*
behind [bɪˈhaɪnd] *prep* derrière; (*time*) en
retard sur; (*supporting*): **to be ~ sb** soutenir qn
▷ *adv* derrière; en retard ▷ *n* derrière *m*; **~ the
scenes** dans les coulisses; **to be ~ (schedule)
with sth** être en retard dans qch
beige [beɪʒ] *adj* beige
Beijing [ˈbeɪˈdʒɪŋ] *n* Pékin
being [ˈbiːɪŋ] *n* être *m*; **to come into ~** prendre
naissance
belated [bɪˈleɪtɪd] *adj* tardif(-ive)
belch [bɛltʃ] *vi* avoir un renvoi, roter ▷ *vt* (*also*:
~ out: *smoke etc*) vomir, cracher
Belgian [ˈbɛldʒən] *adj* belge, de Belgique ▷ *n*
Belge *m/f*
Belgium [ˈbɛldʒəm] *n* Belgique *f*
belief [bɪˈliːf] *n* (*opinion*) conviction *f*; (*trust*,
faith) foi *f*
believe [bɪˈliːv] *vt*, *vi* croire, estimer; **to ~
in** (*God*) croire en; (*ghosts*, *method*) croire à;
believer *n* (*in idea*, *activity*) partisan(e); (*Rel*)

croyant(e)
bell [bɛl] *n* cloche *f*; (*small*) clochette *f*, grelot *m*;
(*on door*) sonnette *f*; (*electric*) sonnerie *f*
bellboy [ˈbɛlbɔɪ] (US **bellhop** [ˈbɛlhɔp]) *n*
groom *m*, chasseur *m*
bellow [ˈbɛləu] *vi* (*bull*) meugler; (*person*)
brailler
bell pepper *n* (*esp* US) poivron *m*
belly [ˈbɛlɪ] *n* ventre *m*; **belly button** (*inf*) *n*
nombril *m*
belong [bɪˈlɔŋ] *vi*: **to ~** appartenir à; (*club
etc*) faire partie de; **this book ~s here** ce livre
va ici, la place de ce livre est ici; **belongings** *npl*
affaires *fpl*, possessions *fpl*
beloved [bɪˈlʌvɪd] *adj* (bien-)aimé(e), chéri(e)
below [bɪˈləu] *prep* sous, au-dessous de ▷ *adv*
en dessous; en contre-bas; **see ~** voir plus bas
or plus loin *or* ci-dessous
belt [bɛlt] *n* ceinture *f*; (*Tech*) courroie *f* ▷ *vt*
(*thrash*) donner une raclée à; **beltway** *n*
(US *Aut*) route *f* de ceinture; (: *motorway*)
périphérique *m*
bemused [bɪˈmjuːzd] *adj* médusé(e)
bench [bɛntʃ] *n* banc *m*; (*in workshop*) établi
m; **the B~** (*Law*: *judges*) la magistrature, la
Cour
bend [bɛnd] *vb* (*pt*, *pp* **bent**) ▷ *vt* courber; (*leg*,
arm) plier ▷ *vi* se courber ▷ *n* (BRIT: *in road*)
virage *m*, tournant *m*; (*in pipe*, *river*) coude *m*;
bend down *vi* se baisser; **bend over** *vi* se
pencher
beneath [bɪˈniːθ] *prep* sous, au-dessous de;
(*unworthy of*) indigne de ▷ *adv* dessous, au-
dessous, en bas
beneficial [bɛnɪˈfɪʃəl] *adj*: **~ (to)** salutaire
(pour), bénéfique (à)
benefit [ˈbɛnɪfɪt] *n* avantage *m*, profit *m*;
(*allowance of money*) allocation *f* ▷ *vt* faire
du bien à, profiter à ▷ *vi*: **he'll ~ from it**
cela lui fera du bien, il y gagnera *or* s'en
trouvera bien
Benelux [ˈbɛnɪlʌks] *n* Bénélux *m*
benign [bɪˈnaɪn] *adj* (*person*, *smile*)
bienveillant(e), affable; (*Med*) bénin(-igne)
bent [bɛnt] *pt*, *pp of* **bend** ▷ *n* inclination
f, penchant *m* ▷ *adj*: **to be ~ on** être
résolu(e) à
bereaved [bɪˈriːvd] *n*: **the ~** la famille du
disparu
beret [ˈbɛreɪ] *n* béret *m*
Berlin [bəːˈlɪn] *n* Berlin
Bermuda [bəːˈmjuːdə] *n* Bermudes *fpl*
Bern [bəːn] *n* Berne
berry [ˈbɛrɪ] *n* baie *f*
berth [bəːθ] *n* (*bed*) couchette *f*; (*for ship*) poste
m d'amarrage, mouillage *m* ▷ *vi* (*in harbour*)
venir à quai; (*at anchor*) mouiller
beside [bɪˈsaɪd] *prep* à côté de; (*compared with*)
par rapport à; **that's ~ the point** ça n'a rien à

voir; **to be ~ o.s. (with anger)** être hors de soi; **besides** adv en outre, de plus ▷ prep en plus de; (except) excepté

best [bɛst] adj meilleur(e) ▷ adv le mieux; **the ~ part of** (quantity) le plus clair de, la plus grande partie de; **at ~** au mieux; **to make the ~ of sth** s'accommoder de qch (du mieux que l'on peut); **to do one's ~** faire de son mieux; **to the ~ of my knowledge** pour autant que je sache; **to the ~ of my ability** du mieux que je pourrai; **best man** (irreg) n garçon m d'honneur; **bestseller** n best-seller m, succès m de librairie

best-before date n date f de limite d'utilisation or de consommation;

bet [bɛt] n pari m ▷ vt, vi (pt, pp ~ or ~ted) parier; **to ~ sb sth** parier qch à qn

betray [bɪˈtreɪ] vt trahir

better [ˈbɛtər] adj meilleur(e) ▷ adv mieux ▷ vt améliorer ▷ n: **to get the ~ of** triompher de, l'emporter sur; **you had ~ do it** vous feriez mieux de le faire; **he thought ~ of it** il s'est ravisé; **to get ~** (Med) aller mieux; (improve) s'améliorer

betting [ˈbɛtɪŋ] n paris mpl; **betting shop** n (BRIT) bureau m de paris

between [bɪˈtwiːn] prep entre ▷ adv au milieu, dans l'intervalle

beverage [ˈbɛvərɪdʒ] n boisson f (gén sans alcool)

beware [bɪˈwɛər] vi: **to ~ (of)** prendre garde (à); **"~ of the dog"** "(attention) chien méchant"

bewildered [bɪˈwɪldəd] adj dérouté(e), ahuri(e)

beyond [bɪˈjɔnd] prep (in space, time) au-delà de; (exceeding) au-dessus de ▷ adv au-delà; **~ doubt** hors de doute; **~ repair** irréparable

bias [ˈbaɪəs] n (prejudice) préjugé m, parti pris; (preference) prévention f; **bias(s)ed** adj partial(e), montrant un parti pris

bib [bɪb] n bavoir m

Bible [ˈbaɪbl] n Bible f

bicarbonate of soda [baɪˈkɑːbənɪt-] n bicarbonate m de soude

biceps [ˈbaɪsɛps] n biceps m

bicycle [ˈbaɪsɪkl] n bicyclette f; **bicycle pump** n pompe f à vélo

bid [bɪd] n offre f; (at auction) enchère f; (attempt) tentative f ▷ vb (pt ~ or **bade**, pp ~ or ~den) ▷ vi faire une enchère or offre ▷ vt faire une enchère or offre de; **to ~ sb good day** souhaiter le bonjour à qn; **bidder** n: **the highest bidder** le plus offrant

bidet [ˈbiːdeɪ] n bidet m

big [bɪg] adj (in height: person, building, tree) grand(e); (in bulk, amount: person, parcel, book) gros(se); **bigheaded** adj prétentieux(-euse);

big toe n gros orteil

bike [baɪk] n vélo m; **bike lane** n piste f cyclable

bikini [bɪˈkiːnɪ] n bikini m

bilateral [baɪˈlætərl] adj bilatéral(e)

bilingual [baɪˈlɪŋgwəl] adj bilingue

bill [bɪl] n note f, facture f; (in restaurant) addition f, note f; (Pol) projet m de loi; (US: banknote) billet m (de banque); (notice) affiche f; (of bird) bec m; **put it on my ~** mettez-le sur mon compte; **"post no ~s"** "défense d'afficher"; **to fit** or **fill the ~** (fig) faire l'affaire; **billboard** (US) n panneau m d'affichage; **billfold** [ˈbɪlfəʊld] n (US) portefeuille m

billiards [ˈbɪljədz] n (jeu m de) billard m

billion [ˈbɪljən] n (BRIT) billion m (million de millions); (US) milliard m

bin [bɪn] n boîte f; (BRIT: also: **dust~**, **litter ~**) poubelle f; (for coal) coffre m

bind (pt, pp **bound**) [baɪnd, baʊnd] vt attacher; (book) relier; (oblige) obliger, contraindre ▷ n (inf: nuisance) scie f

binge [bɪndʒ] n (inf): **to go on a ~** faire la bringue

bingo [ˈbɪŋgəʊ] n sorte de jeu de loto pratiqué dans des établissements publics

binoculars [bɪˈnɔkjuləz] npl jumelles fpl

bio... [baɪə] prefix: **biochemistry** n biochimie f; **biodegradable** [ˈbaɪəʊdɪˈgreɪdəbl] adj biodégradable; **biography** [baɪˈɔgrəfɪ] n biographie f; **biological** adj biologique; **biology** [baɪˈɔlədʒɪ] n biologie f; **biometric** [baɪəˈmɛtrɪk] adj biométrique

birch [bəːtʃ] n bouleau m

bird [bəːd] n oiseau m; (BRIT inf: girl) nana f; **bird flu** n grippe f aviaire; **bird of prey** n oiseau m de proie; **birdwatching** n ornithologie f (d'amateur)

Biro® [ˈbaɪərəʊ] n stylo m à bille

birth [bəːθ] n naissance f; **to give ~ to** donner naissance à, mettre au monde; (subj: animal) mettre bas; **birth certificate** n acte m de naissance; **birth control** n (policy) limitation f des naissances; (*methods*) méthode(s) contraceptive(s); **birthday** *n* anniversaire *m* ▷ *cpd* (*cake, card etc*) d'anniversaire; **birthmark** *n* envie *f*, tache *f* de vin; **birthplace** *n* lieu *m* de naissance

biscuit ['bɪskɪt] *n* (BRIT) biscuit *m*; (US) petit pain au lait

bishop ['bɪʃəp] *n* évêque *m*; (*Chess*) fou *m*

bistro ['bi:strəu] *n* petit restaurant *m*, bistrot *m*

bit [bɪt] *pt of* **bite** ▷ *n* morceau *m*; (*Comput*) bit *m*, élément *m* binaire; (*of tool*) mèche *f*; (*of horse*) mors *m*; **a ~ of** un peu de; **a ~ mad/dangerous** un peu fou/risqué; **~ by ~** petit à petit

bitch [bɪtʃ] *n* (*dog*) chienne *f*; (*inf!*) salope *f*(!), garce *f*

bite [baɪt] *vt, vi* (*pt* **bit**, *pp* **bitten**) mordre; (*insect*) piquer ▷ *n* morsure *f*; (*insect bite*) piqûre *f*; (*mouthful*) bouchée *f*; **let's have a ~ (to eat)** mangeons un morceau; **to ~ one's nails** se ronger les ongles

bitten ['bɪtn] *pp of* **bite**

bitter ['bɪtəʳ] *adj* amer(-ère); (*criticism*) cinglant(e); (*icy: weather, wind*) glacial(e) ▷ *n* (BRIT: *beer*) bière *f* (*à forte teneur en houblon*)

bizarre [bɪ'zɑːʳ] *adj* bizarre

black [blæk] *adj* noir(e) ▷ *n* (*colour*) noir *m*; (*person*): **B~** noir(e) ▷ *vt* (BRIT *Industry*) boycotter; **to give sb a ~ eye** pocher l'œil à qn, faire un œil au beurre noir à qn; **to be in the ~** (*in credit*) avoir un compte créditeur; **~ and blue** (*bruised*) couvert(e) de bleus; **black out** *vi* (*faint*) s'évanouir; **blackberry** *n* mûre *f*; **blackbird** *n* merle *m*; **blackboard** *n* tableau noir; **black coffee** *n* café noir; **blackcurrant** *n* cassis *m*; **black ice** *n* verglas *m*; **blackmail** *n* chantage *m* ▷ *vt* faire chanter, soumettre au chantage; **black market** *n* marché noir; **blackout** *n* (*loss of electricity*) panne *f* d'électricité; (*in wartime*) black-out *m*; (*TV*) interruption *f* d'émission; (*fainting*) syncope *f*; **black pepper** *n* poivre noir; **black pudding** *n* boudin (noir); **Black Sea** *n*: **the Black Sea** la mer Noire

bladder ['blædəʳ] *n* vessie *f*

blade [bleɪd] *n* lame *f*; (*of propeller*) pale *f*; **a ~ of grass** un brin d'herbe

blame [bleɪm] *n* faute *f*, blâme *m* ▷ *vt*: **to ~ sb/sth for sth** attribuer à qn/qch la responsabilité de qch; reprocher qch à qn/qch; **I'm not to ~** ce n'est pas ma faute

bland [blænd] *adj* (*taste, food*) doux (douce), fade

blank [blæŋk] *adj* blanc (blanche); (*look*) sans expression, dénué(e) d'expression ▷ *n* espace *m* vide, blanc *m*; (*cartridge*) cartouche *f* à blanc; **his mind was a ~** il avait la tête vide

blanket ['blæŋkɪt] *n* couverture *f*; (*of snow, cloud*) couche *f*

blast [blɑːst] *n* explosion *f*; (*shock wave*) souffle *m*; (*of air, steam*) bouffée *f* ▷ *vt* faire sauter or exploser

blatant ['bleɪtənt] *adj* flagrant(e), criant(e)

blaze [bleɪz] *n* (*fire*) incendie *m*; (*fig*) flamboiement *m* ▷ *vi* (*fire*) flamber; (*fig*) flamboyer, resplendir ▷ *vt*: **to ~ a trail** (*fig*) montrer la voie; **in a ~ of publicity** à grand renfort de publicité

blazer ['bleɪzəʳ] *n* blazer *m*

bleach [bliːtʃ] *n* (*also:* **household ~**) eau *f* de Javel ▷ *vt* (*linen*) blanchir; **bleachers** *npl* (US *Sport*) gradins *mpl* (*en plein soleil*)

bleak [bliːk] *adj* morne, désolé(e); (*weather*) triste, maussade; (*smile*) lugubre; (*prospect, future*) morose

bled [bled] *pt, pp of* **bleed**

bleed [bliːd] (*pt, pp* **bled**) [bliːd, bled] *vt* saigner; (*brakes, radiator*) purger ▷ *vi* saigner; **my nose is ~ing** je saigne du nez

blemish ['blemɪʃ] *n* défaut *m*; (*on reputation*) tache *f*

blend [blend] *n* mélange *m* ▷ *vt* mélanger ▷ *vi* (*colours etc: also:* **~ in**) se mélanger, se fondre, s'allier; **blender** *n* (*Culin*) mixeur *m*

bless (*pt, pp* **~ed** *or* **blest**) [bles, blest] *vt* bénir; **~ you!** (*after sneeze*) à tes souhaits!; **blessing** *n* bénédiction *f*; (*godsend*) bienfait *m*

blew [bluː] *pt of* **blow**

blight [blaɪt] *vt* (*hopes etc*) anéantir, briser

blind [blaɪnd] *adj* aveugle ▷ *n* (*for window*) store *m* ▷ *vt* aveugler; **the blind** *npl* les aveugles *mpl*; **blind alley** *n* impasse *f*; **blindfold** *n* bandeau *m* ▷ *adj, adv* les yeux bandés ▷ *vt* bander les yeux à

blink [blɪŋk] *vi* cligner des yeux; (*light*) clignoter

bliss [blɪs] *n* félicité *f*, bonheur *m* sans mélange

blister ['blɪstəʳ] *n* (*on skin*) ampoule *f*, cloque *f*; (*on paintwork*) boursouflure *f* ▷ *vi* (*paint*) se boursoufler, se cloquer

blizzard ['blɪzəd] *n* blizzard *m*, tempête *f* de neige

bloated ['bləutɪd] *adj* (*face*) bouffi(e); (*stomach, person*) gonflé(e)

blob [blɔb] *n* (*drop*) goutte *f*; (*stain, spot*) tache *f*

block [blɔk] *n* bloc *m*; (*in pipes*) obstruction *f*; (*toy*) cube *m*; (*of buildings*) pâté *m* (*de maisons*) ▷ *vt* bloquer; (*fig*) faire obstacle à; **the sink is ~ed** l'évier est bouché; **~ of flats** (BRIT) immeuble (locatif); **mental ~** blocage *m*; **block up** *vt* boucher; **blockade** [blɔ'keɪd] *n* blocus *m* ▷ *vt* faire le blocus de; **blockage** *n* obstruction *f*; **blockbuster** *n* (*film, book*) grand succès; **block capitals** *npl* majuscules *fpl* d'imprimerie; **block letters** *npl* majuscules *fpl*

blog [blɔg] *n* blog *m*, blogue *m*

bloke [bləuk] *n* (BRIT *inf*) type *m*

blond(e) [blɔnd] *adj, n* blond(e)

blood [blʌd] n sang m; **blood donor** n
donneur(-euse) de sang; **blood group**
n groupe sanguin; **blood poisoning**
n empoisonnement m du sang; **blood
pressure** n tension (artérielle); **bloodshed**
n effusion f de sang, carnage m; **bloodshot**
adj: **bloodshot eyes** yeux injectés de sang;
bloodstream n sang m, système sanguin;
blood test n analyse f de sang; **blood
transfusion** n transfusion f de sang; **blood
type** n groupe sanguin; **blood vessel** n
vaisseau sanguin; **bloody** adj sanglant(e);
(BRIT inf!): **this bloody ...** ce foutu ..., ce putain
de ... (!) ▷ adv: **bloody strong/good** (BRIT: inf!)
vachement or sacrément fort/bon

bloom [blu:m] n fleur f ▷ vi être en fleur

blossom ['blɔsəm] n fleur(s) f(pl) ▷ vi être en
fleurs; (fig) s'épanouir

blot [blɔt] n tache f ▷ vt tacher; (ink) sécher

blouse [blauz] n (feminine garment) chemisier
m, corsage m

blow [bləu] n coup m ▷ vb (pt **blew**, pp **~n**) ▷ vi
souffler ▷ vt (instrument) jouer de; (fuse) faire
sauter; **to ~ one's nose** se moucher; **blow
away** vi s'envoler ▷ vt chasser, faire s'envoler;
blow out vi (fire, flame) s'éteindre; (tyre)
éclater; (fuse) sauter; **blow up** vi exploser,
sauter ▷ vt faire sauter; (tyre) gonfler; (Phot)
agrandir; **blow-dry** n (hairstyle) brushing m

blown [bləun] pp of **blow**

blue [blu:] adj bleu(e); (depressed) triste; **~
film/joke** film m/histoire f pornographique;
out of the ~ (fig) à l'improviste, sans qu'on
s'y attende; **bluebell** n jacinthe f des bois;
blueberry n myrtille f, airelle f; **blue cheese** n
(fromage) bleu m; **blues** npl: **the blues** (Mus)
le blues; **to have the blues** (inf: feeling) avoir le
cafard; **bluetit** n mésange bleue

bluff [blʌf] vi bluffer ▷ n bluff m; **to call sb's ~**
mettre qn au défi d'exécuter ses menaces

blunder ['blʌndər] n gaffe f, bévue f ▷ vi faire
une gaffe or une bévue

blunt [blʌnt] adj (knife) émoussé(e), peu
tranchant(e); (pencil) mal taillé(e); (person)
brusque, ne mâchant pas ses mots

blur [blə:r] n (shape): **to become a ~** devenir
flou ▷ vt brouiller, rendre flou(e); **blurred** adj
flou(e)

blush [blʌʃ] vi rougir ▷ n rougeur f; **blusher** n
rouge m à joues

board [bɔ:d] n (wooden) planche f; (on
wall) panneau m; (for chess etc) plateau m;
(cardboard) carton m; (committee) conseil m,
comité m; (in firm) conseil d'administration;
(Naut, Aviat): **on ~** à bord ▷ vt (ship) monter
à bord de; (train) monter dans; **full ~** (BRIT)
pension complète; **half ~** (BRIT) demi-
pension f; **~ and lodging** n chambre f avec
pension; **to go by the ~** (hopes, principles)

être abandonné(e); **board game** n jeu m de
société; **boarding card** n (Aviat, Naut) carte
f d'embarquement; **boarding pass** n (BRIT)
= **boarding card**; **boarding school** n internat
m, pensionnat m; **board room** n salle f du
conseil d'administration

boast [bəust] vi: **to ~ (about** or **of)** se vanter
(de)

boat [bəut] n bateau m; (small) canot m;
barque f

bob [bɔb] vi (boat, cork on water: also: **~ up and
down**) danser, se balancer

bobby pin ['bɔbɪ-] n (US) pince f à cheveux

body ['bɔdɪ] n corps m; (of car) carrosserie f;
(fig: society) organe m, organisme m; **body-
building** n body-building m, culturisme m;
bodyguard n garde m du corps; **bodywork** n
carrosserie f

bog [bɔg] n tourbière f ▷ vt: **to get ~ged down
(in)** (fig) s'enliser (dans)

bogus ['bəugəs] adj bidon inv; fantôme

boil [bɔɪl] vt (faire) bouillir ▷ vi bouillir ▷ n
(Med) furoncle m; **to come to the** or (US) **a ~**
bouillir; **boil down** vi (fig): **to ~ down to** se
réduire or ramener à; **boil over** vi déborder;
boiled egg n œuf m à la coque; **boiled
potatoes** npl pommes fpl à l'anglaise or à l'eau;
boiler n chaudière f; **boiling** ['bɔɪlɪŋ] adj: **I'm
boiling (hot)** (inf) je crève de chaud; **boiling
point** n point m d'ébullition

bold [bəuld] adj hardi(e), audacieux(-euse);
(pej) effronté(e); (outline, colour) franc (franche),
tranché(e), marqué(e)

bollard ['bɔləd] n (BRIT Aut) borne lumineuse
or de signalisation

bolt [bəult] n verrou m; (with nut) boulon m
▷ adv: **~ upright** droit(e) comme un piquet
▷ vt (door) verrouiller; (food) engloutir ▷ vi
se sauver, filer (comme une flèche); (horse)
s'emballer

bomb [bɔm] n bombe f ▷ vt bombarder;
bombard [bɔm'bɑ:d] vt bombarder; **bomber**
n (Aviat) bombardier m; (terrorist) poseur m de
bombes; **bomb scare** n alerte f à la bombe

bond [bɔnd] n lien m; (binding promise)
engagement m, obligation f; (Finance)
obligation; **bonds** npl (chains) chaînes fpl; **in ~**
(of goods) en entrepôt

bone [bəun] n os m; (of fish) arête f ▷ vt
désosser; ôter les arêtes de

bonfire ['bɔnfaɪər] n feu m (de joie); (for
rubbish) feu

bonnet ['bɔnɪt] n bonnet m; (BRIT: of car)
capot m

bonus ['bəunəs] n (money) prime f; (advantage)
avantage m

boo [bu:] excl hou!, peuh! ▷ vt huer

book [buk] n livre m; (of stamps, tickets etc)
carnet m; (Comm): **books** npl comptes mpl,

comptabilité f ▷ vt (ticket) prendre; (seat, room) réserver; (football player) prendre le nom de, donner un carton à; **I ~ed a table in the name of ...** j'ai réservé une table au nom de ...; **book in** vi (BRIT: at hotel) prendre sa chambre; **book up** vt réserver; **the hotel is ~ed up** l'hôtel est complet; **bookcase** n bibliothèque f (meuble); **booking** n (BRIT) réservation f; **I confirmed my booking by fax/e-mail** j'ai confirmé ma réservation par fax/e-mail; **booking office** n (BRIT) bureau m de location; **book-keeping** n comptabilité f; **booklet** n brochure f; **bookmaker** n bookmaker m; **bookmark** n (for book) marque-page m; (Comput) signet m; **bookseller** n libraire m/f; **bookshelf** n (single) étagère f (à livres); (bookcase) bibliothèque f; **bookshop, bookstore** n librairie f

boom [bu:m] n (noise) grondement m; (in prices, population) forte augmentation f; (busy period) boom m, vague f de prospérité ▷ vi gronder; prospérer

boost [bu:st] n stimulant m, remontant m ▷ vt stimuler

boot [bu:t] n botte f; (for hiking) chaussure f (de marche); (ankle boot) bottine f; (BRIT: of car) coffre m ▷ vt (Comput) lancer, mettre en route; **to ~** (in addition) par-dessus le marché, en plus

booth [bu:ð] n (at fair) baraque (foraine); (of telephone etc) cabine f; (also: **voting ~**) isoloir m

booze [bu:z] (inf) n boissons fpl alcooliques, alcool m

border ['bɔ:dər] n bordure f; bord m; (of a country) frontière f; **borderline** n (fig) ligne f de démarcation

bore [bɔ:r] pt of **bear** ▷ vt (person) ennuyer, raser; (hole) percer; (well, tunnel) creuser ▷ n (person) raseur(-euse); (of gun) calibre m; **bored** adj: **to be bored** s'ennuyer; **boredom** n ennui m

boring ['bɔ:rɪŋ] adj ennuyeux(-euse)

born [bɔ:n] adj: **to be ~** naître; **I was ~ in 1960** je suis né en 1960

borne [bɔ:n] pp of **bear**

borough ['bʌrə] n municipalité f

borrow ['bɔrəu] vt: **to ~ sth (from sb)** emprunter qch (à qn)

Bosnia(-Herzegovina) ['bɔ:snɪə(hɛrzə'gəuvi:nə)] n Bosnie-Herzégovine f; **Bosnian** ['bɔznɪən] adj bosniaque, bosnien(ne) ▷ n Bosniaque m/f, Bosnien(ne)

bosom ['buzəm] n poitrine f; (fig) sein m

boss [bɔs] n patron(ne) ▷ vt (also: **~ about**, **~ around**) mener à la baguette; **bossy** adj autoritaire

both [bəuθ] adj les deux, l'un(e) et l'autre ▷ pron: **~ (of them)** les deux, tous (toutes) (les) deux, l'un(e) et l'autre; **~ of us went, we ~ went** nous y sommes allés tous les deux ▷ adv: **~ A and B** A et B

bother ['bɔðər] vt (worry) tracasser; (needle, bait) importuner, ennuyer; (disturb) déranger ▷ vi (also: **~ o.s.**) se tracasser, se faire du souci ▷ n (trouble) ennuis mpl; **to ~ doing** prendre la peine de faire; **don't ~** ce n'est pas la peine; **it's no ~** aucun problème

bottle ['bɔtl] n bouteille f; (baby's) biberon m; (of perfume, medicine) flacon m ▷ vt mettre en bouteille(s); **bottle bank** n conteneur m (de bouteilles); **bottle-opener** n ouvre-bouteille m

bottom ['bɔtəm] n (of container, sea etc) fond m; (buttocks) derrière m; (of page, list) bas m; (of mountain, tree, hill) pied m ▷ adj (shelf, step) du bas

bought [bɔ:t] pt, pp of **buy**

boulder ['bəuldər] n gros rocher (gén lisse, arrondi)

bounce [bauns] vi (ball) rebondir; (cheque) être refusé (étant sans provision) ▷ vt faire rebondir ▷ n (rebound) rebond m; **bouncer** n (inf: at dance, club) videur m

bound [baund] pt, pp of **bind** ▷ n (gen pl) limite f; (leap) bond m ▷ vi (leap) bondir ▷ vt (limit) borner ▷ adj: **to be ~ to do sth** (obliged) être obligé(e) or avoir obligation de faire qch; **he's ~ to fail** (likely) il est sûr d'échouer, son échec est inévitable or assuré; **~ by** (law, regulation) engagé(e) par; **~ for** à destination de; **out of ~s** dont l'accès est interdit

boundary ['baundrɪ] n frontière f

bouquet ['bukeɪ] n bouquet m

bourbon ['buəbən] n (US: also: **~ whiskey**) bourbon m

bout [baut] n période f; (of malaria etc) accès m, crise f, attaque f; (Boxing etc) combat m, match m

boutique [bu:'ti:k] n boutique f

bow¹ [bəu] n nœud m; (weapon) arc m; (Mus) archet m

bow² [bau] n (with body) révérence f, inclination f (du buste or corps); (Naut: also: **~s**) proue f ▷ vi faire une révérence, s'incliner

bowels [bauəlz] npl intestins mpl; (fig) entrailles fpl

bowl [bəul] n (for eating) bol m; (for washing) cuvette f; (ball) boule f ▷ vi (Cricket) lancer (la balle); **bowler** n (Cricket) lanceur m (de la balle); (BRIT: also: **bowler hat**) (chapeau m) melon m; **bowling** n (game) jeu m de boules, jeu de quilles; **bowling alley** n bowling m; **bowling green** n terrain m de boules (gazonné et carré); **bowls** n (jeu m de) boules fpl

bow tie [bəu-] n nœud m papillon

box [bɔks] n boîte f; (also: **cardboard ~**) carton m; (Theat) loge f ▷ vt mettre en boîte ▷ vi boxer, faire de la boxe; **boxer** ['bɔksər] n (person) boxeur m; **boxer shorts** npl caleçon m;

boxing ['bɔksɪŋ] n (sport) boxe f; **Boxing Day** n (BRIT) le lendemain de Noël; voir encadré; **boxing gloves** npl gants mpl de boxe; **boxing ring** n ring m; **box junction** n (BRIT Aut) zone f (de carrefour) d'accès réglementé; **box office** n bureau m de location

● **BOXING DAY**
●
● **Boxing Day** est le lendemain de Noël, férié
● en Grande-Bretagne. Ce nom vient d'une
● coutume du XIXe siècle qui consistait à
● donner des cadeaux de Noël (dans des
● boîtes) à ses employés etc le 26 décembre.

boy [bɔɪ] n garçon m; **boy band** n boys band m

boycott ['bɔɪkɔt] n boycottage m ▷ vt boycotter

boyfriend ['bɔɪfrɛnd] n (petit) ami

bra [brɑː] n soutien-gorge m

brace [breɪs] n (support) attache f, agrafe f; (BRIT: also: **~s**: on teeth) appareil m (dentaire); (tool) vilebrequin m ▷ vt (support) consolider, soutenir; **braces** npl (BRIT: for trousers) bretelles fpl; **to ~ o.s.** (fig) se préparer mentalement

bracelet ['breɪslɪt] n bracelet m

bracket ['brækɪt] n (Tech) tasseau m, support m; (group) classe f, tranche f; (also: **brace ~**) accolade f; (also: **round ~**) parenthèse f; (also: **square ~**) crochet m ▷ vt mettre entre parenthèses; **in ~s** entre parenthèses or crochets

brag [bræg] vi se vanter

braid [breɪd] n (trimming) galon m; (of hair) tresse f, natte f

brain [breɪn] n cerveau m; **brains** npl (intellect, food) cervelle f

braise [breɪz] vt braiser

brake [breɪk] n frein m ▷ vt, vi freiner; **brake light** n feu m de stop

bran [bræn] n son m

branch [brɑːntʃ] n branche f; (Comm) succursale f; (: of bank) agence f; **branch off** vi (road) bifurquer; **branch out** vi diversifier ses activités

brand [brænd] n marque (commerciale) ▷ vt (cattle) marquer (au fer rouge); **brand name** n nom m de marque; **brand-new** adj tout(e) neuf (neuve), flambant neuf (neuve)

brandy ['brændɪ] n cognac m

brash [bræʃ] adj effronté(e)

brass [brɑːs] n cuivre m (jaune), laiton m; **the ~** (Mus) les cuivres; **brass band** n fanfare f

brat [bræt] n (pej) mioche m/f, môme m/f

brave [breɪv] adj courageux(-euse), brave ▷ vt braver, affronter; **bravery** n bravoure f, courage m

brawl [brɔːl] n rixe f, bagarre f

Brazil [brə'zɪl] n Brésil m; **Brazilian** adj brésilien(ne) ▷ n Brésilien(ne)

breach [briːtʃ] vt ouvrir une brèche dans ▷ n (gap) brèche f; (breaking): **~ of contract** rupture f de contrat; **~ of the peace** attentat m à l'ordre public

bread [brɛd] n pain m; **breadbin** n (BRIT) boîte f or huche f à pain; **breadbox** n (US) boîte f or huche f à pain; **breadcrumbs** npl miettes fpl de pain; (Culin) chapelure f, panure f

breadth [brɛtθ] n largeur f

break [breɪk] (pt **broke**, pp **broken**) vt casser, briser; (promise) rompre; (law) violer ▷ vi se casser, se briser; (weather) tourner; (storm) éclater; (day) se lever ▷ n (gap) brèche f; (fracture) cassure f; (rest) interruption f, arrêt m; (: short) pause f; (: at school) récréation f; (chance) chance f, occasion f favorable; **to ~ one's leg** etc se casser la jambe etc; **to ~ a record** battre un record; **to ~ the news to sb** annoncer la nouvelle à qn; **break down** vt (door etc) enfoncer; (figures, data) décomposer, analyser ▷ vi s'effondrer; (Med) faire une dépression (nerveuse); (Aut) tomber en panne; **my car has broken down** ma voiture est en panne; **break in** vt (horse etc) dresser ▷ vi (burglar) entrer par effraction; (interrupt) interrompre; **break into** vt fus (house) s'introduire or pénétrer par effraction dans; **break off** vi (speaker) s'interrompre; (branch) se rompre ▷ vt (talks, engagement) rompre; **break out** vi éclater, se déclarer; (prisoner) s'évader; **to ~ out in spots** se couvrir de boutons; **break up** vi (partnership) cesser, prendre fin; (marriage) se briser; (crowd, meeting) se séparer; (ship) se disloquer; (Scol: pupils) être en vacances; (line) couper; **the line's** or **you're ~ing up** ça coupe ▷ vt fracasser, casser; (fight etc) interrompre, faire cesser; (marriage) désunir; **breakdown** n (Aut) panne f; (in communications, marriage) rupture f; (Med: also: **nervous breakdown**) dépression (nerveuse); (of figures) ventilation f, répartition f; **breakdown truck** (US **breakdown van**) n dépanneuse f

breakfast ['brɛkfəst] n petit déjeuner m; **what time is ~?** le petit déjeuner est à quelle heure?

break: **break-in** n cambriolage m; **breakthrough** n percée f

breast [brɛst] n (of woman) sein m; (chest) poitrine f; (of chicken, turkey) blanc m; **breast-feed** vt, vi (irreg: like **feed**) allaiter; **breast-stroke** n brasse f

breath [brɛθ] n haleine f, souffle m; **to take a deep ~** respirer à fond; **out of ~** à bout de souffle, essoufflé(e)

Breathalyser® ['brɛθəlaɪzəʳ] (BRIT) n alcootest m

breathe [briːð] vt, vi respirer; **breathe in** vi inspirer ▷ vt aspirer; **breathe out** vt, vi expirer; **breathing** n respiration f

breath: **breathless** adj essoufflé(e), haletant(e); **breathtaking** adj stupéfiant(e), à vous couper le souffle; **breath test** n alcootest m

bred [bred] pt, pp of **breed**

breed [briːd] (pt, pp **bred**) vt élever, faire l'élevage de ▷ vi se reproduire ▷ n race f, variété f

breeze [briːz] n brise f

breezy ['briːzɪ] adj (day, weather) venteux(-euse); (manner) désinvolte; (person) jovial(e)

brew [bruː] vt (tea) faire infuser; (beer) brasser ▷ vi (fig) se préparer, couver; **brewery** n brasserie f (fabrique)

bribe [braɪb] n pot-de-vin m ▷ vt acheter; soudoyer; **bribery** n corruption f

bric-a-brac ['brɪkəbræk] n bric-à-brac m

brick [brɪk] n brique f; **bricklayer** n maçon m

bride [braɪd] n mariée f, épouse f; **bridegroom** n marié m, époux m; **bridesmaid** n demoiselle f d'honneur

bridge [brɪdʒ] n pont m; (Naut) passerelle f (de commandement); (of nose) arête f; (Cards, Dentistry) bridge m ▷ vt (gap) combler

bridle ['braɪdl] n bride f

brief [briːf] adj bref (brève) ▷ n (Law) dossier m, cause f; (gen) tâche f ▷ vt mettre au courant; **briefs** npl slip m; **briefcase** n serviette f; porte-documents m inv; **briefing** n instructions fpl; (Press) briefing m; **briefly** adv brièvement

brigadier [brɪgə'dɪə'] n brigadier général

bright [braɪt] adj brillant(e); (room, weather) clair(e); (person: clever) intelligent(e), doué(e); (: cheerful) gai(e); (idea) génial(e); (colour) vif (vive)

brilliant ['brɪljənt] adj brillant(e); (light, sunshine) éclatant(e); (inf: great) super

brim [brɪm] n bord m

brine [braɪn] n (Culin) saumure f

bring (pt, pp **brought**) [brɪŋ, brɔːt] vt (thing) apporter; (person) amener; **bring about** vt provoquer, entraîner; **bring back** vt rapporter; (person) ramener; **bring down** vt (lower) abaisser; (shoot down) abattre; (government) faire s'effondrer; **bring in** vt (person) faire entrer; (object) rentrer; (Pol: legislation) introduire; (produce: income) rapporter; **bring on** vt (illness, attack) provoquer; (player, substitute) amener; **bring out** vt (meaning) faire ressortir, mettre en relief; **bring up** vt élever; (carry up) monter; (question) soulever; (food: vomit) vomir, rendre

brink [brɪŋk] n bord m

brisk [brɪsk] adj vif (vive); (abrupt) brusque; (trade etc) actif(-ive)

bristle ['brɪsl] n poil m ▷ vi se hérisser

Brit [brɪt] n abbr (inf: = British person) Britannique m/f

Britain ['brɪtən] n (also: **Great ~**) la Grande-Bretagne

British ['brɪtɪʃ] adj britannique ▷ npl: **the ~** les Britanniques mpl; **British Isles** npl: **the British Isles** les îles fpl Britanniques

Briton ['brɪtən] n Britannique m/f

Brittany ['brɪtənɪ] n Bretagne f

brittle ['brɪtl] adj cassant(e), fragile

B road n (BRIT) ≈ route départementale

broad [brɔːd] adj large; (distinction) général(e); (accent) prononcé(e); **in ~ daylight** en plein jour; **broadband** n transmission f à haut débit; **broad bean** n fève f; **broadcast** n émission f ▷ vb (pt, pp **broadcast**) ▷ vt (Radio) radiodiffuser; (TV) téléviser ▷ vi émettre; **broaden** vt élargir; **to broaden one's mind** élargir ses horizons ▷ vi s'élargir; **broadly** adv en gros, généralement; **broad-minded** adj large d'esprit

broccoli ['brɔkəlɪ] n brocoli m

brochure ['brəʊʃjʊə'] n prospectus m, dépliant m

broil [brɔɪl] (us) vt rôtir

broiler ['brɔɪlə'] n (fowl) poulet m (à rôtir); (us: grill) gril m

broke [brəʊk] pt of **break** ▷ adj (inf) fauché(e)

broken ['brəʊkn] pp of **break** ▷ adj (stick, leg etc) cassé(e); (machine: also: **~ down**) fichu(e); **in ~ French/English** dans un français/anglais approximatif ou hésitant

broker ['brəʊkə'] n courtier m

bronchitis [brɔn'kaɪtɪs] n bronchite f

bronze [brɔnz] n bronze m

brooch [brəʊtʃ] n broche f

brood [bruːd] n couvée f ▷ vi (person) méditer (sombrement), ruminer

broom [brum] n balai m; (Bot) genêt m

Bros. abbr (Comm: = brothers) Frères

broth [brɔθ] n bouillon m de viande et de légumes

brothel ['brɔθl] n maison close, bordel m

brother ['brʌðə'] n frère m; **brother-in-law** n beau-frère m

brought [brɔːt] pt, pp of **bring**

brow [braʊ] n front m; (eyebrow) sourcil m; (of hill) sommet m

brown [braʊn] adj brun(e), marron inv; (hair) châtain inv; (tanned) bronzé(e) ▷ n (colour) brun m, marron m ▷ vt brunir; (Culin) faire dorer, faire roussir; **brown bread** n pain m bis

Brownie ['braʊnɪ] n jeannette f éclaireuse (cadette)

brown rice n riz m complet

brown sugar n cassonade f
browse [brauz] vi (in shop) regarder (sans acheter); **to ~ through a book** feuilleter un livre; **browser** n (Comput) navigateur m
bruise [bruːz] n bleu m, ecchymose f, contusion f ▷ vt contusionner, meurtrir
brunette [bruːˈnɛt] n (femme) brune
brush [brʌʃ] n brosse f; (for painting) pinceau m; (for shaving) blaireau m; (quarrel) accrochage m, prise f de bec ▷ vt brosser; (also: ~ **past**, ~ **against**) effleurer, frôler
Brussels [ˈbrʌslz] n Bruxelles
Brussels sprout [-spraut] n chou m de Bruxelles
brutal [ˈbruːtl] adj brutal(e)
B.Sc. n abbr = **Bachelor of Science**
BSE n abbr (= bovine spongiform encephalopathy) ESB f, BSE f
bubble [ˈbʌbl] n bulle f ▷ vi bouillonner, faire des bulles; (sparkle, fig) pétiller; **bubble bath** n bain moussant; **bubble gum** n chewing-gum m; **bubblejet printer** [ˈbʌbldʒet-] n imprimante f à bulle d'encre
buck [bʌk] n mâle m (d'un lapin, lièvre, daim etc); (us inf) dollar m ▷ vi ruer, lancer une ruade; **to pass the ~ (to sb)** se décharger de la responsabilité (sur qn)
bucket [ˈbʌkɪt] n seau m
buckle [ˈbʌkl] n boucle f ▷ vt (belt etc) boucler, attacher ▷ vi (warp) tordre, gauchir; (: wheel) se voiler
bud [bʌd] n bourgeon m; (of flower) bouton m ▷ vi bourgeonner; (flower) éclore
Buddhism [ˈbudɪzəm] n bouddhisme m
Buddhist [ˈbudɪst] adj bouddhiste ▷ n Bouddhiste m/f
buddy [ˈbʌdɪ] n (us) copain m
budge [bʌdʒ] vt faire bouger ▷ vi bouger
budgerigar [ˈbʌdʒərɪɡɑː] n perruche f
budget [ˈbʌdʒɪt] n budget m ▷ vi: **to ~ for sth** inscrire qch au budget
budgie [ˈbʌdʒɪ] n = **budgerigar**
buff [bʌf] adj (couleur f) chamois m ▷ n (inf: enthusiast) mordu(e)
buffalo (pl ~ or ~es) [ˈbʌfələu] n (BRIT) buffle m; (us) bison m
buffer [ˈbʌfəʳ] n tampon m; (Comput) mémoire f tampon
buffet n [ˈbufeɪ] (food BRIT: bar) buffet m ▷ vt [ˈbʌfɪt] secouer, ébranler; **buffet car** n (BRIT Rail) voiture-bar f
bug [bʌɡ] n (bedbug etc) punaise f; (esp us: any insect) insecte m, bestiole f; (fig: germ) virus m, microbe m; (spy device) dispositif m d'écoute (électronique), micro clandestin; (Comput: of program) erreur f ▷ vt (room) poser des micros dans; (inf: annoy) embêter
buggy [ˈbʌɡɪ] n poussette f
build [bɪld] n (of person) carrure f, charpente f ▷ vt (pt, pp **built**) construire, bâtir; **build up** vt accumuler, amasser; (business) développer; (reputation) bâtir; **builder** n entrepreneur m; **building** n (trade) construction f; (: structure) bâtiment m, construction; (: residential, offices) immeuble m; **building site** n chantier m (de construction); **building society** n (BRIT) société f de crédit immobilier
built [bɪlt] pt, pp of **build**; **built-in** adj (cupboard) encastré(e); (device) incorporé(e); intégré(e); **built-up** adj: **built-up area** zone urbanisée
bulb [bʌlb] n (Bot) bulbe m, oignon m; (Elec) ampoule f
Bulgaria [bʌlˈɡɛərɪə] n Bulgarie f; **Bulgarian** adj bulgare ▷ n Bulgare m/f
bulge [bʌldʒ] n renflement m, gonflement m ▷ vi faire saillie; présenter un renflement; (pocket, file): **to be bulging with** être plein(e) à craquer de
bulimia [bəˈlɪmɪə] n boulimie f
bulimic [bjuːˈlɪmɪk] adj, n boulimique (m/f)
bulk [bʌlk] n masse f, volume m; **in ~** (Comm) en gros, en vrac; **the ~ of** la plus grande or grosse partie de; **bulky** adj volumineux(-euse), encombrant(e)
bull [bul] n taureau m; (male elephant, whale) mâle m
bulldozer [ˈbuldəuzəʳ] n bulldozer m
bullet [ˈbulɪt] n balle f (de fusil etc)
bulletin [ˈbulɪtɪn] n bulletin m, communiqué m; (also: **news ~**) (bulletin d')informations fpl; **bulletin board** n (Comput) messagerie f (électronique)
bullfight [ˈbulfaɪt] n corrida f, course f de taureaux; **bullfighter** n torero m; **bullfighting** n tauromachie f
bully [ˈbulɪ] n brute f, tyran m ▷ vt tyranniser, rudoyer
bum [bʌm] n (inf: BRIT: backside) derrière m; (: esp us: tramp) vagabond(e), traîne-savates m/f inv; (: idler) glandeur m
bumblebee [ˈbʌmblbiː] n bourdon m
bump [bʌmp] n (blow) coup m, choc m; (jolt) cahot m; (on road etc, on head) bosse f ▷ vt heurter, cogner; (car) emboutir; **bump into** vt fus rentrer dans, tamponner; (inf: meet) tomber sur; **bumper** n pare-chocs m inv ▷ adj: **bumper crop/harvest** récolte/moisson exceptionnelle; **bumpy** adj (road) cahoteux(-euse); **it was a bumpy flight/ride** on a été secoués dans l'avion/la voiture
bun [bʌn] n (cake) petit gâteau; (bread) petit pain au lait; (of hair) chignon m
bunch [bʌntʃ] n (of flowers) bouquet m; (of keys) trousseau m; (of bananas) régime m; (of people) groupe m; **bunches** npl (in hair) couettes fpl; ~ **of grapes** grappe f de raisin
bundle [ˈbʌndl] n paquet m ▷ vt (also: ~ **up**)

faire un paquet de; (*put*): **to ~ sth/sb into** fourrer or enfourner qch/qn dans

bungalow ['bʌŋgələʊ] n bungalow m

bungee jumping ['bʌndʒiː'dʒʌmpɪŋ] n saut m à l'élastique

bunion ['bʌnjən] n oignon m (*au pied*)

bunk [bʌŋk] n couchette f; **bunk beds** npl lits superposés

bunker ['bʌŋkə^r] n (*coal store*) soute f à charbon; (*Mil*, *Golf*) bunker m

bunny ['bʌnɪ] n (*also*: **~ rabbit**) lapin m

buoy [bɔɪ] n bouée f; **buoyant** adj (*ship*) flottable; (*carefree*) gai(e), plein(e) d'entrain; (*Comm*: *market*, *economy*) actif(-ive)

burden ['bəːdn] n fardeau m, charge f ▷ vt charger; (*oppress*) accabler, surcharger

bureau (pl **~x**) ['bjʊərəʊ, -z] n (BRIT: *writing desk*) bureau m, secrétaire m; (US: *chest of drawers*) commode f; (*office*) bureau, office m

bureaucracy [bjʊə'rɔkrəsɪ] n bureaucratie f

bureaucrat ['bjʊərəkræt] n bureaucrate m/f, rond-de-cuir m

bureau de change [-də'ʃɑ̃ʒ] (pl **bureaux de change**) n bureau m de change

bureaux ['bjʊərəʊz] npl of **bureau**

burger ['bəːgə^r] n hamburger m

burglar ['bəːglə^r] n cambrioleur m; **burglar alarm** n sonnerie f d'alarme; **burglary** n cambriolage m

Burgundy ['bəːgəndɪ] n Bourgogne f

burial ['bɛrɪəl] n enterrement m

burn [bəːn] vt, vi (pt, pp **~ed** or **~t**) brûler ▷ n brûlure f; **burn down** vt incendier, détruire par le feu; **burn out** vt (*writer etc*): **to ~ o.s. out** s'user (à force de travailler); **burning** adj (*building*, *forest*) en flammes; (*issue*, *question*) brûlant(e); (*ambition*) dévorant(e)

Burns' Night [bəːnz-] n fête écossaise à la mémoire du poète Robert Burns

BURNS NIGHT

Burns Night est une fête qui a lieu le 25 janvier, à la mémoire du poète écossais Robert Burns (1759 - 1796), à l'occasion de laquelle les Écossais partout dans le monde organisent un souper, en général arrosé de whisky. Le plat principal est toujours le haggis, servi avec de la purée de pommes de terre et de la purée de rutabagas. On apporte le haggis au son des cornemuses et au cours du repas on lit des poèmes de Burns et on chante ses chansons.

burnt [bəːnt] pt, pp of **burn**

burp [bəːp] (*inf*) n rot m ▷ vi roter

burrow ['bʌrəʊ] n terrier m ▷ vi (*rabbit*) creuser un terrier; (*rummage*) fouiller

burst [bəːst] (pt, pp **~**) vt faire éclater; (*river*: *banks etc*) rompre ▷ vi éclater; (*tyre*) crever ▷ n explosion f; (*also*: **~ pipe**) fuite f (*due à une rupture*); **a ~ of enthusiasm/energy** un accès d'enthousiasme/d'énergie; **to ~ into flames** s'enflammer soudainement; **to ~ out laughing** éclater de rire; **to ~ into tears** fondre en larmes; **to ~ open** vi s'ouvrir violemment or soudainement; **to be ~ing with** (*container*) être plein(e) (à craquer) de, regorger de; (*fig*) être débordant(e) de; **burst into** vt fus (*room etc*) faire irruption dans

bury ['bɛrɪ] vt enterrer

bus (pl **~es**) [bʌs, 'bʌsɪz] n autobus m; **bus conductor** n receveur(-euse) m/f de bus

bush [bʊʃ] n buisson m; (*scrub land*) brousse f; **to beat about the ~** tourner autour du pot

business ['bɪznɪs] n (*matter*, *firm*) affaire f; (*trading*) affaires fpl; (*job*, *duty*) travail m; **to be away on ~** être en déplacement d'affaires; **it's none of my ~** cela ne me regarde pas, ce ne sont pas mes affaires; **he means ~** il ne plaisante pas, il est sérieux; **business class** n (*on plane*) classe f affaires; **businesslike** adj sérieux(-euse), efficace; **businessman** (*irreg*) n homme m d'affaires; **business trip** n voyage m d'affaires; **businesswoman** (*irreg*) n femme f d'affaires

busker ['bʌskə^r] n (BRIT) artiste ambulant(e)

bus: **bus pass** n carte f de bus; **bus shelter** n abribus m; **bus station** n gare routière; **bus-stop** n arrêt m d'autobus

bust [bʌst] n buste m; (*measurement*) tour m de poitrine ▷ adj (*inf*: *broken*) fichu(e), fini(e); **to go ~** faire faillite

bustling ['bʌslɪŋ] adj (*town*) très animé(e)

busy ['bɪzɪ] adj occupé(e); (*shop*, *street*) très fréquenté(e); (US: *telephone*, *line*) occupé ▷ vt: **to ~ o.s.** s'occuper; **busy signal** n (US) tonalité f occupé inv

KEYWORD

but [bʌt] conj mais; **I'd love to come, but I'm busy** j'aimerais venir mais je suis occupé; **he's not English but French** il n'est pas anglais mais français; **but that's far too expensive!** mais c'est bien trop cher!
▷ prep (*apart from*, *except*) sauf, excepté; **nothing but** rien d'autre que; **we've had nothing but trouble** nous n'avons eu que des ennuis; **no-one but him can do it** lui seul peut le faire; **who but a lunatic would do such a thing?** qui sinon un fou ferait une chose pareille?; **but for you/your help** sans toi/ton aide; **anything but that** tout sauf or excepté ça, tout mais pas ça
▷ adv (*just*, *only*) ne ... que; **she's but a child** elle n'est qu'une enfant; **had I but known**

si seulement j'avais su; **I can but try** je
peux toujours essayer; **all but finished**
pratiquement terminé

butcher ['butʃə^r] *n* boucher *m* ▷ *vt* massacrer;
(*cattle etc for meat*) tuer; **butcher's (shop)** *n*
boucherie *f*

butler ['bʌtlə^r] *n* maître *m* d'hôtel

butt [bʌt] *n* (*cask*) gros tonneau; (*of gun*) crosse
f; (*of cigarette*) mégot *m*; (*BRIT fig: target*) cible *f*
▷ *vt* donner un coup de tête à

butter ['bʌtə^r] *n* beurre *m* ▷ *vt* beurrer;
buttercup *n* bouton *m* d'or

butterfly ['bʌtəflaɪ] *n* papillon *m*; (*Swimming:
also:* ~ **stroke**) brasse *f* papillon

buttocks ['bʌtəks] *npl* fesses *fpl*

button ['bʌtn] *n* bouton *m*; (*us: badge*) pin *m*
▷ *vt* (*also:* ~ **up**) boutonner ▷ *vi* se boutonner

buy [baɪ] (*pt, pp* **bought**) *vt* acheter ▷ *n* achat
m; **to ~ sb sth/sth from sb** acheter qch à qn;
to ~ sb a drink offrir un verre *or* à boire à qn;
can I ~ you a drink? je vous offre un verre?;
where can I ~ some postcards? où est-ce que
je peux acheter des cartes postales?; **buy out**
vt (*partner*) désintéresser; **buy up** *vt* acheter
en bloc, rafler; **buyer** *n* acheteur(-euse) *m/f*

buzz [bʌz] *n* bourdonnement *m*; (*inf: phone
call*): **to give sb a ~** passer un coup de fil à
qn ▷ *vi* bourdonner; **buzzer** *n* timbre *m*
électrique

 KEYWORD

by [baɪ] *prep* **1** (*referring to cause, agent*) par,
de; **killed by lightning** tué par la foudre;
surrounded by a fence entouré d'une
barrière; **a painting by Picasso** un tableau
de Picasso

2 (*referring to method, manner, means*): **by
bus/car** en autobus/voiture; **by train** par le *or*
en train; **to pay by cheque** payer par chèque;
by moonlight/candlelight à la lueur de la
lune/d'une bougie; **by saving hard, he ...** à
force d'économiser, il ...

3 (*via, through*) par; **we came by Dover** nous
sommes venus par Douvres

4 (*close to, past*) à côté de; **the house by the
school** la maison à côté de l'école; **a holiday
by the sea** des vacances au bord de la mer;
she went by me elle est passée à côté de moi;
I go by the post office every day je passe
devant la poste tous les jours

5 (*with time: not later than*) avant; (: *during*):
by daylight à la lumière du jour; **by night** la
nuit, de nuit; **by 4 o'clock** avant 4 heures; **by
this time tomorrow** d'ici demain à la même
heure; **by the time I got here it was too late**
lorsque je suis arrivé il était déjà trop tard

6 (*amount*) à; **by the kilo/metre** au kilo/au

mètre; **paid by the hour** payé à l'heure

7 (*Math: measure*): **to divide/multiply by 3**
diviser/multiplier par 3; **a room 3 metres by 4**
une pièce de 3 mètres sur 4; **it's broader by a
metre** c'est plus large d'un mètre

8 (*according to*) d'après, selon; **it's 3 o'clock by
my watch** il est 3 heures à ma montre; **it's all
right by me** je n'ai rien contre

9: **(all) by oneself** *etc* tout(e) seul(e)
▷ *adv* **1** *see* **go**; **pass** *etc*

2: **by and by** un peu plus tard, bientôt; **by and
large** dans l'ensemble

bye(-bye) ['baɪ('baɪ)] *excl* au revoir!, salut!

by-election ['baɪɪlɛkʃən] *n* (*BRIT*) élection
(législative) partielle

bypass ['baɪpɑːs] *n* rocade *f*; (*Med*) pontage
m ▷ *vt* éviter

byte [baɪt] *n* (*Comput*) octet *m*

C [siː] n (Mus): **C** do m
cab [kæb] n taxi m; (of train, truck) cabine f
cabaret ['kæbəreɪ] n (show) spectacle m de cabaret
cabbage ['kæbɪdʒ] n chou m
cabin ['kæbɪn] n (house) cabane f, hutte f; (on ship) cabine f; (on plane) compartiment m; **cabin crew** n (Aviat) équipage m
cabinet ['kæbɪnɪt] n (Pol) cabinet m; (furniture) petit meuble à tiroirs et rayons; (also: **display ~**) vitrine f, petite armoire vitrée; **cabinet minister** n ministre m (membre du cabinet)
cable ['keɪbl] n câble m ▷ vt câbler, télégraphier; **cable car** n téléphérique m; **cable television** n télévision f par câble
cactus (pl **cacti**) ['kæktəs, -taɪ] n cactus m
café ['kæfeɪ] n ≈ café(-restaurant) m (sans alcool)
cafeteria [kæfɪ'tɪərɪə] n cafétéria f
caffein(e) ['kæfiːn] n caféine f
cage [keɪdʒ] n cage f
cagoule [kə'guːl] n K-way® m
Cairo ['kaɪərəʊ] n le Caire
cake [keɪk] n gâteau m; **~ of soap** savonnette f
calcium ['kælsɪəm] n calcium m
calculate ['kælkjuleɪt] vt calculer; (estimate: chances, effect) évaluer; **calculation** [kælkju'leɪʃən] n calcul m; **calculator** n

calculatrice f
calendar ['kæləndər] n calendrier m
calf (pl **calves**) [kɑːf, kɑːvz] n (of cow) veau m; (of other animals) petit m; (also: **~skin**) veau m, vachette f; (Anat) mollet m
calibre (US **caliber**) ['kælɪbər] n calibre m
call [kɔːl] vt appeler; (meeting) convoquer ▷ vi appeler; (visit: also: **~ in, ~ round**) passer ▷ n (shout) appel m, cri m; (also: **telephone ~**) coup m de téléphone; **to be on ~** être de permanence; **to be ~ed** s'appeler; **can I make a ~ from here?** est-ce que je peux téléphoner d'ici?; **call back** vi (return) repasser; (Tel) rappeler ▷ vt (Tel) rappeler; **can you ~ back later?** pouvez-vous rappeler plus tard?; **call for** vt fus (demand) demander; (fetch) passer prendre; **call in** vt (doctor, expert, police) appeler, faire venir; **call off** vt annuler; **call on** vt fus (visit) rendre visite à, passer voir; (request): **to ~ on sb to do** inviter qn à faire; **call out** vi pousser un cri or des cris; **call up** vt (Mil) appeler, mobiliser; (Tel) appeler; **callbox** n (BRIT) cabine f téléphonique; **call centre** (US **call center**) n centre m d'appels; **caller** n (Tel) personne f qui appelle; (visitor) visiteur m
callous ['kæləs] adj dur(e), insensible
calm [kɑːm] adj calme ▷ n calme m ▷ vt calmer, apaiser; **calm down** vi se calmer, s'apaiser ▷ vt calmer, apaiser; **calmly** ['kɑːmlɪ] adv calmement, avec calme
Calor gas® ['kælər-] n (BRIT) butane m, butagaz® m
calorie ['kælərɪ] n calorie f
calves [kɑːvz] npl of **calf**
Cambodia [kæm'bəʊdɪə] n Cambodge m
camcorder ['kæmkɔːdər] n caméscope m
came [keɪm] pt of **come**
camel ['kæməl] n chameau m
camera ['kæmərə] n appareil-photo m; (Cine, TV) caméra f; **in ~** à huis clos, en privé; **cameraman** n caméraman m; **camera phone** n téléphone m avec appareil photo numérique intégré
camouflage ['kæməflɑːʒ] n camouflage m ▷ vt camoufler
camp [kæmp] n camp m ▷ vi camper ▷ adj (man) efféminé(e)
campaign [kæm'peɪn] n (Mil, Pol etc) campagne f ▷ vi (also fig) faire campagne; **campaigner** n: **campaigner for** partisan(e) de; **campaigner against** opposant(e) à
camp: **campbed** n (BRIT) lit m de camp; **camper** n campeur(-euse); (vehicle) camping-car m; **campground** (US) n (terrain m de) camping m; **camping** n camping m; **to go camping** faire du camping; **campsite** n (terrain m de)

camping *m*

campus ['kæmpəs] *n* campus *m*

can¹ [kæn] *n* (*of milk, oil, water*) bidon *m*; (*tin*) boîte *f* (de conserve) ▷ *vt* mettre en conserve

 KEYWORD

can² [kæn] (*negative* **cannot, can't**, *conditional and pt* **could**) *aux vb* **1** (*be able to*) pouvoir; **you can do it if you try** vous pouvez le faire si vous essayez; **I can't hear you** je ne t'entends pas

2 (*know how to*) savoir; **I can swim/play tennis/drive** je sais nager/jouer au tennis/conduire; **can you speak French?** parlez-vous français?

3 (*may*) pouvoir; **can I use your phone?** puis-je me servir de votre téléphone?

4 (*expressing disbelief, puzzlement etc*): **it can't be true!** ce n'est pas possible!; **what can he want?** qu'est-ce qu'il peut bien vouloir?

5 (*expressing possibility, suggestion etc*): **he could be in the library** il est peut-être dans la bibliothèque; **she could have been delayed** il se peut qu'elle ait été retardée

Canada ['kænədə] *n* Canada *m*; **Canadian** [kə'neɪdɪən] *adj* canadien(ne) ▷ *n* Canadien(ne)

canal [kə'næl] *n* canal *m*

canary [kə'nεərɪ] *n* canari *m*, serin *m*

cancel ['kænsəl] *vt* annuler; (*train*) supprimer; (*party, appointment*) décommander; (*cross out*) barrer, rayer; (*cheque*) faire opposition à; **I would like to ~ my booking** je voudrais annuler ma réservation; **cancellation** [kænsə'leɪʃən] *n* annulation *f*; suppression *f*

Cancer ['kænsə'] *n* (*Astrology*) le Cancer

cancer ['kænsə'] *n* cancer *m*

candidate ['kændɪdeɪt] *n* candidat(e)

candle ['kændl] *n* bougie *f*; (*in church*) cierge *m*; **candlestick** *n* (*also:* **candle holder**) bougeoir *m*; (*bigger, ornate*) chandelier *m*

candy ['kændɪ] *n* sucre candi; (*US*) bonbon *m*; **candy bar** (*US*) *n* barre *f* chocolatée; **candyfloss** *n* (*BRIT*) barbe *f* à papa

cane [keɪn] *n* canne *f*; (*for baskets, chairs etc*) rotin *m* ▷ *vt* (*BRIT Scol*) administrer des coups de bâton à

canister ['kænɪstə'] *n* boîte *f* (gén en métal); (*of gas*) bombe *f*

cannabis ['kænəbɪs] *n* (*drug*) cannabis *m*

canned ['kænd] *adj* (*food*) en boîte, en conserve; (*inf: music*) enregistré(e); (*BRIT inf: drunk*) bourré(e); (*US inf: worker*) mis(e) à la porte

cannon (*pl* **~** *or* **~s**) ['kænən] *n* (*gun*)

canon *m*

cannot ['kænɔt] = **can not**

canoe [kə'nu:] *n* pirogue *f*; (*Sport*) canoë *m*; **canoeing** *n* (*sport*) canoë *m*

canon ['kænən] *n* (*clergyman*) chanoine *m*; (*standard*) canon *m*

can-opener [-'əupnə'] *n* ouvre-boîte *m*

can't [ka:nt] = **can not**

canteen [kæn'ti:n] *n* (*eating place*) cantine *f*; (*BRIT: of cutlery*) ménagère *f*

canter ['kæntə'] *vi* aller au petit galop

canvas ['kænvəs] *n* toile *f*

canvass ['kænvəs] *vi* (*Pol*): **to ~ for** faire campagne pour ▷ *vt* (*citizens, opinions*) sonder

canyon ['kænjən] *n* cañon *m*, gorge *f* (profonde)

cap [kæp] *n* casquette *f*; (*for swimming*) bonnet *m* de bain; (*of pen*) capuchon *m*; (*of bottle*) capsule *f*; (*BRIT: contraceptive: also:* **Dutch ~**) diaphragme *m* ▷ *vt* (*outdo*) surpasser; (*put limit on*) plafonner

capability [keɪpə'bɪlɪtɪ] *n* aptitude *f*, capacité *f*

capable ['keɪpəbl] *adj* capable

capacity [kə'pæsɪtɪ] *n* (*of container*) capacité *f*, contenance *f*; (*ability*) aptitude *f*

cape [keɪp] *n* (*garment*) cape *f*; (*Geo*) cap *m*

caper ['keɪpə'] *n* (*Culin: gen pl*) câpre *f*; (*prank*) farce *f*

capital ['kæpɪtl] *n* (*also:* **~ city**) capitale *f*; (*money*) capital *m*; (*also:* **~ letter**) majuscule *f*; **capitalism** *n* capitalisme *m*; **capitalist** *adj, n* capitaliste *m/f*; **capital punishment** *n* peine capitale

Capitol ['kæpɪtl] *n*: **the ~** le Capitole

Capricorn ['kæprɪkɔ:n] *n* le Capricorne

capsize [kæp'saɪz] *vt* faire chavirer ▷ *vi* chavirer

capsule ['kæpsju:l] *n* capsule *f*

captain ['kæptɪn] *n* capitaine *m*

caption ['kæpʃən] *n* légende *f*

captivity [kæp'tɪvɪtɪ] *n* captivité *f*

capture ['kæptʃə'] *vt* (*prisoner, animal*) capturer; (*town*) prendre; (*attention*) capter; (*Comput*) saisir ▷ *n* capture *f*; (*of data*) saisie *f* de données

car [ka:'] *n* voiture *f*, auto *f*; (*US Rail*) wagon *m*, voiture

carafe [kə'ræf] *n* carafe *f*

caramel ['kærəməl] *n* caramel *m*

carat ['kærət] *n* carat *m*

caravan ['kærəvæn] *n* caravane *f*; **caravan site** *n* (*BRIT*) camping *m* pour caravanes

carbohydrate [ka:bəu'haɪdreɪt] *n* hydrate *m* de carbone; (*food*) féculent *m*

carbon ['ka:bən] *n* carbone *m*; **carbon dioxide** [-daɪ'ɔksaɪd] *n* gaz *m* carbonique, dioxyde *m* de carbone; **carbon monoxide** [-mɔ'nɔksaɪd] *n* oxyde *m* de carbone

car boot sale n voir encadré

● **CAR BOOT SALE**
●
● Type de brocante très populaire, où chacun
● vide sa cave ou son grenier. Les articles
● sont présentés dans des coffres de voitures
● et la vente a souvent lieu sur un parking
● ou dans un champ. Les brocanteurs d'un
● jour doivent s'acquitter d'une petite
● contribution pour participer à la vente.

carburettor (US **carburetor**) [kɑ:bju'retə^r] n carburateur m

card [kɑ:d] n carte f; (material) carton m; **cardboard** n carton m; **card game** n jeu m de cartes

cardigan ['kɑ:dɪgən] n cardigan m

cardinal ['kɑ:dɪnl] adj cardinal(e); (importance) capital(e) ▷ n cardinal m

cardphone ['kɑ:dfəun] n téléphone m à carte (magnétique)

care [kɛə^r] n soin m, attention f; (worry) souci m ▷ vi: **to ~ about** (feel interest for) se soucier de, s'intéresser à; (person: love) être attaché(e) à; **in sb's ~** à la garde de qn, confié à qn; **~ of** (on letter) chez; **to take ~** faire attention (à faire); **to take ~ of** vt s'occuper de; **I don't ~** ça m'est bien égal, peu m'importe; **I couldn't ~ less** cela m'est complètement égal, je m'en fiche complètement; **care for** vt fus s'occuper de; (like) aimer

career [kə'rɪə^r] n carrière f ▷ vi (also: **~ along**) aller à toute allure

care: **carefree** adj sans souci, insouciant(e); **careful** adj soigneux(-euse); (cautious) prudent(e); **(be) careful!** (fais) attention!; **carefully** adv avec soin, soigneusement; prudemment; **caregiver** (US) n (professional) travailleur social; (unpaid) personne qui s'occupe d'un proche qui est malade; **careless** adj négligent(e); (heedless) insouciant(e); **carelessness** n manque m de soin, négligence f; insouciance f; **carer** ['kɛərə^r] n (professional) travailleur social; (unpaid) personne qui s'occupe d'un proche qui est malade; **caretaker** n gardien(ne), concierge m/f

car-ferry ['kɑ:fɛrɪ] n (on sea) ferry(-boat) m; (on river) bac m

cargo (pl **-es**) ['kɑ:gəu] n cargaison f, chargement m

car hire n (BRIT) location f de voitures

Caribbean [kærɪ'bi:ən] adj, n: **the ~ (Sea)** la mer des Antilles or des Caraïbes

caring ['kɛərɪŋ] adj (person) bienveillant(e); (society, organization) humanitaire

carnation [kɑ:'neɪʃən] n œillet m

carnival ['kɑ:nɪvl] n (public celebration) carnaval m; (US: funfair) fête foraine

carol ['kærəl] n: **(Christmas) ~** chant m de Noël

carousel [kærə'sɛl] n (for luggage) carrousel m; (US) manège m

car park (BRIT) n parking m, parc m de stationnement

carpenter ['kɑ:pɪntə^r] n charpentier m; (joiner) menuisier m

carpet ['kɑ:pɪt] n tapis m ▷ vt recouvrir (d'un tapis); **fitted ~** (BRIT) moquette f

car rental n (US) location f de voitures

carriage ['kærɪdʒ] n (BRIT Rail) wagon m; (horse-drawn) voiture f; (of goods) transport m; (: cost) port m; **carriageway** n (BRIT: part of road) chaussée f

carrier ['kærɪə^r] n transporteur m, camionneur m; (company) entreprise f de transport; (Med) porteur(-euse); **carrier bag** n (BRIT) sac m en papier or en plastique

carrot ['kærət] n carotte f

carry ['kærɪ] vt (subj: person) porter; (: vehicle) transporter; (involve: responsibilities etc) comporter, impliquer; (Med: disease) être porteur de ▷ vi (sound) porter; **to get carried away** (fig) s'emballer, s'enthousiasmer; **carry on** vi (continue) continuer ▷ vt (conduct: business) diriger; (: conversation) entretenir; (continue: business, conversation) continuer; **to ~ on with sth/doing** continuer qch/à faire; **carry out** vt (orders) exécuter; (investigation) effectuer

cart [kɑ:t] n charrette f ▷ vt (inf) transporter

carton ['kɑ:tən] n (box) carton m; (of yogurt) pot m (en carton)

cartoon [kɑ:'tu:n] n (Press) dessin m (humoristique); (satirical) caricature f; (comic strip) bande dessinée; (Cine) dessin animé

cartridge ['kɑ:trɪdʒ] n (for gun, pen) cartouche f

carve [kɑ:v] vt (meat: also: **~ up**) découper; (wood, stone) tailler, sculpter; **carving** n (in wood etc) sculpture f

car wash n station f de lavage (de voitures)

case [keɪs] n cas m; (Law) affaire f, procès m; (box) caisse f, boîte f; (for glasses) étui m; (BRIT: also: **suit~**) valise f; **in ~ of** en cas de; **in ~ he** au cas où il; **just in ~** à tout hasard; **in any ~** en tout cas, de toute façon

cash [kæʃ] n argent m; (Comm) (argent m) liquide m ▷ vt encaisser; **to pay (in) ~** payer (en argent) comptant or en espèces; **~ with order/on delivery** (Comm) payable or paiement à la commande/livraison; **I haven't got any ~** je n'ai pas de liquide; **cashback** n (discount) remise f; (at supermarket etc) retrait m (à la caisse); **cash card** n carte f de retrait; **cash desk** n (BRIT) caisse f; **cash dispenser** n distributeur m automatique de billets

cashew [kæ'ʃu:] n (also: **~ nut**) noix f de cajou

cashier [kæˈʃɪəʳ] n caissier(-ère)
cashmere [ˈkæʃmɪəʳ] n cachemire m
cash point n distributeur m automatique de billets
cash register n caisse enregistreuse
casino [kəˈsiːnəu] n casino m
casket [ˈkɑːskɪt] n coffret m; (US: coffin) cercueil m
casserole [ˈkæsərəul] n (pot) cocotte f; (food) ragoût m (en cocotte)
cassette [kæˈsɛt] n cassette f; **cassette player** n lecteur m de cassettes
cast [kɑːst] (vb: pt, pp **~**) vt (throw) jeter; (shadow: lit) projeter; (: fig) jeter; (glance) jeter ▷ n (Theat) distribution f; (also: **plaster ~**) plâtre m; **to ~ sb as Hamlet** attribuer à qn le rôle d'Hamlet; **to ~ one's vote** voter, exprimer son suffrage; **to ~ doubt on** jeter un doute sur; **cast off** vi (Naut) larguer les amarres; (Knitting) arrêter les mailles
castanets [kæstəˈnɛts] npl castagnettes fpl
caster sugar [ˈkɑːstə-] n (BRIT) sucre m semoule
cast-iron [ˈkɑːstaɪən] adj (lit) de or en fonte; (fig: will) de fer; (alibi) en béton
castle [ˈkɑːsl] n château m; (fortress) château-fort m; (Chess) tour f
casual [ˈkæʒjul] adj (by chance) de hasard, fait(e) au hasard, fortuit(e); (irregular: work etc) temporaire; (unconcerned) désinvolte; **~ wear** vêtements mpl sport inv
casualty [ˈkæʒjultɪ] n accidenté(e), blessé(e); (dead) victime f, mort(e); (BRIT: Med: department) urgences fpl
cat [kæt] n chat m
Catalan [ˈkætəlæn] adj catalan(e)
catalogue (US **catalog**) [ˈkætələɔg] n catalogue m ▷ vt cataloguer
catalytic converter [kætəˈlɪtɪkkənˈvəːtəʳ] n pot m catalytique
cataract [ˈkætərækt] n (also Med) cataracte f
catarrh [kəˈtɑːʳ] n rhume m chronique, catarrhe f
catastrophe [kəˈtæstrəfɪ] n catastrophe f
catch [kætʃ] (pt, pp **caught**) vt attraper; (person: by surprise) prendre, surprendre; (understand) saisir; (get entangled) accrocher ▷ vi (fire) prendre; (get entangled) s'accrocher ▷ n (fish etc) prise f; (hidden problem) attrape f; (Tech) loquet m; cliquet m; **to ~ sb's attention** or **eye** attirer l'attention de qn; **to ~ fire** prendre feu; **to ~ sight of** apercevoir; **catch up** vi (with work) se rattraper, combler son retard ▷ vt (also: **~ up with**) rattraper; **catching** [ˈkætʃɪŋ] adj (Med) contagieux(-euse)
category [ˈkætɪgərɪ] n catégorie f
cater [ˈkeɪtəʳ] vi: **to ~ for** (BRIT: needs) satisfaire, pourvoir à; (: readers, consumers) s'adresser à,

pourvoir aux besoins de; (Comm: parties etc) préparer des repas pour
caterpillar [ˈkætəpɪləʳ] n chenille f
cathedral [kəˈθiːdrəl] n cathédrale f
Catholic [ˈkæθəlɪk] (Rel) adj catholique ▷ n catholique m/f
Catseye® [ˈkætsˈaɪ] n (BRIT Aut) (clou m à) catadioptre m
cattle [ˈkætl] npl bétail m, bestiaux mpl
catwalk [ˈkætwɔːk] n passerelle f; (for models) podium m (de défilé de mode)
caught [kɔːt] pt, pp of **catch**
cauliflower [ˈkɔlɪflauəʳ] n chou-fleur m
cause [kɔːz] n cause f ▷ vt causer
caution [ˈkɔːʃən] n prudence f; (warning) avertissement m ▷ vt avertir, donner un avertissement à; **cautious** adj prudent(e)
cave [keɪv] n caverne f, grotte f; **cave in** vi (roof etc) s'effondrer
caviar(e) [ˈkævɪɑːʳ] n caviar m
cavity [ˈkævɪtɪ] n cavité f; (Med) carie f
cc abbr (= cubic centimetre) cm³; (on letter etc) = **carbon copy**
CCTV n abbr = **closed-circuit television**
CD n abbr (= compact disc) CD m; **CD burner** n graveur m de CD; **CD player** n platine f laser; **CD-ROM** [siːdiːˈrɔm] n abbr (= compact disc read-only memory) CD-ROM m inv; **CD writer** n graveur m de CD
cease [siːs] vt, vi cesser; **ceasefire** n cessez-le-feu m
cedar [ˈsiːdəʳ] n cèdre m
ceilidh [ˈkeɪlɪ] n bal m folklorique écossais or irlandais
ceiling [ˈsiːlɪŋ] n (also fig) plafond m
celebrate [ˈsɛlɪbreɪt] vt, vi célébrer; **celebration** [sɛlɪˈbreɪʃən] n célébration f
celebrity [sɪˈlɛbrɪtɪ] n célébrité f
celery [ˈsɛlərɪ] n céleri m (en branches)
cell [sɛl] n (gen) cellule f; (Elec) élément m (de pile)
cellar [ˈsɛləʳ] n cave f
cello [ˈtʃɛləu] n violoncelle m
Cellophane® [ˈsɛləfeɪn] n cellophane® f
cellphone [ˈsɛlfəun] n téléphone m cellulaire
Celsius [ˈsɛlsɪəs] adj Celsius inv
Celtic [ˈkɛltɪk, ˈsɛltɪk] adj celte, celtique
cement [səˈmɛnt] n ciment m
cemetery [ˈsɛmɪtrɪ] n cimetière m
censor [ˈsɛnsəʳ] n censeur m ▷ vt censurer; **censorship** n censure f
census [ˈsɛnsəs] n recensement m
cent [sɛnt] n (unit of dollar, euro) cent m (= un centième du dollar, de l'euro); see also **per**
centenary [sɛnˈtiːnərɪ] (US **centennial**) [sɛnˈtɛnɪəl] n centenaire m
center [ˈsɛntəʳ] (US) = **centre**
centi... [sɛntɪ] prefix: **centigrade** adj centigrade; **centimetre** (US **centimeter**) n

centimètre m; **centipede** ['sɛntɪpiːd] n mille-pattes m inv

central ['sɛntrəl] adj central(e); **Central America** n Amérique centrale; **central heating** n chauffage central; **central reservation** n (BRIT Aut) terre-plein central

centre (US **center**) ['sɛntə'] n centre m ▷ vt centrer; **centre-forward** n (Sport) avant-centre m; **centre-half** n (Sport) demi-centre m

century ['sɛntjurɪ] n siècle m; **in the twentieth ~** au vingtième siècle

CEO n abbr (US) = **chief executive officer**

ceramic [sɪ'ræmɪk] adj céramique

cereal ['siːrɪəl] n céréale f

ceremony ['sɛrɪmənɪ] n cérémonie f; **to stand on ~** faire des façons

certain ['səːtən] adj certain(e); **to make ~ of** s'assurer de; **for ~** certainement, sûrement; **certainly** adv certainement; **certainty** n certitude f

certificate [sə'tɪfɪkɪt] n certificat m

certify ['səːtɪfaɪ] vt certifier; (award diploma to) conférer un diplôme etc à; (declare insane) déclarer malade mental(e)

cf. abbr (= compare) cf., voir

CFC n abbr (= chlorofluorocarbon) CFC m

chain [tʃeɪn] n (gen) chaîne f ▷ vt (also: ~ **up**) enchaîner, attacher (avec une chaîne); **chain-smoke** vi fumer cigarette sur cigarette

chair [tʃɛə'] n chaise f; (armchair) fauteuil m; (of university) chaire f; (of meeting) présidence f ▷ vt (meeting) présider; **chairlift** n télésiège m; **chairman** n président m; **chairperson** n président(e); **chairwoman** n présidente f

chalet ['ʃæleɪ] n chalet m

chalk [tʃɔːk] n craie f; **chalkboard** (US) n tableau noir

challenge ['tʃælɪndʒ] n défi m ▷ vt défier; (statement, right) mettre en question, contester; **to ~ sb to do** mettre qn au défi de faire; **challenging** adj (task, career) qui représente un défi or une gageure; (tone, look) de défi, provocateur(-trice)

chamber ['tʃeɪmbə'] n chambre f; (BRIT Law: gen pl) cabinet m; **~ of commerce** chambre de commerce; **chambermaid** n femme f de chambre

champagne [ʃæm'peɪn] n champagne m

champion ['tʃæmpɪən] n (also of cause) champion(ne); **championship** n championnat m

chance [tʃɑːns] n (luck) hasard m; (opportunity) occasion f, possibilité f; (hope, likelihood) chance f; (risk) risque m ▷ vt (risk) risquer ▷ adj fortuit(e), de hasard; **to take a ~** prendre un risque; **by ~** par hasard; **to ~ it** risquer le coup, essayer

chancellor ['tʃɑːnsələ'] n chancelier m; **Chancellor of the Exchequer** [-ɪks'tʃɛkə']

(BRIT) n chancelier m de l'Échiquier

chandelier [ʃændə'lɪə'] n lustre m

change [tʃeɪndʒ] vt (alter, replace: Comm: money) changer; (switch, substitute: hands, trains, clothes, one's name etc) changer de ▷ vi (gen) changer; (change clothes) se changer; (be transformed): **to ~ into** se changer or transformer en ▷ n changement m; (money) monnaie f; **to ~ gear** (Aut) changer de vitesse; **to ~ one's mind** changer d'avis; **a ~ of clothes** des vêtements de rechange; **for a ~** pour changer; **do you have ~ for £10?** vous avez la monnaie de 10 livres?; **where can I ~ some money?** où est-ce que je peux changer de l'argent?; **keep the ~!** gardez la monnaie!; **change over** vi (swap) échanger; (change: drivers etc) changer; (change sides: players etc) changer de côté; **to ~ over from sth to sth** passer de qch à qch; **changeable** adj (weather) variable; **change machine** n distributeur m de monnaie; **changing room** n (BRIT: in shop) salon m d'essayage; (: Sport) vestiaire m

channel ['tʃænl] n (TV) chaîne f; (waveband, groove, fig: medium) canal m; (of river, sea) chenal m ▷ vt canaliser; **the (English) C~** la Manche; **Channel Islands** npl: **the Channel Islands** les îles fpl Anglo-Normandes; **Channel Tunnel** n: **the Channel Tunnel** le tunnel sous la Manche

chant [tʃɑːnt] n chant m; (Rel) psalmodie f ▷ vt chanter, scander

chaos ['keɪɔs] n chaos m

chaotic [keɪ'ɔtɪk] adj chaotique

chap [tʃæp] n (BRIT inf: man) type m

chapel ['tʃæpl] n chapelle f

chapped [tʃæpt] adj (skin, lips) gercé(e)

chapter ['tʃæptə'] n chapitre m

character ['kærɪktə'] n caractère m; (in novel, film) personnage m; (eccentric person) numéro m, phénomène m; **characteristic** ['kærɪktə'rɪstɪk] adj, n caractéristique (f); **characterize** ['kærɪktəraɪz] vt caractériser

charcoal ['tʃɑːkəul] n charbon m de bois; (Art) charbon

charge [tʃɑːdʒ] n (accusation) accusation f; (Law) inculpation f; (cost) prix (demandé) ▷ vt (gun, battery, Mil: enemy) charger; (customer, sum) faire payer ▷ vi foncer; **charges** npl (costs) frais mpl; (BRIT Tel): **to reverse the ~s** téléphoner en PCV; **to take ~ of** se charger de; **to be in ~ of** être responsable de, s'occuper de; **to ~ sb (with)** (Law) inculper qn (de); **charge card** n carte f de client (émise par un grand magasin); **charger** n (also: **battery charger**) chargeur m

charismatic [kærɪz'mætɪk] adj charismatique

charity ['tʃærɪtɪ] n charité f; (organization) institution f charitable or de bienfaisance, œuvre f (de charité); **charity shop** n (BRIT) boutique vendant des articles d'occasion au profit d'une organisation caritative

charm [tʃɑːm] n charme m; (on bracelet) breloque f ▷ vt charmer, enchanter; **charming** adj charmant(e)

chart [tʃɑːt] n tableau m, diagramme m; graphique m; (map) carte marine ▷ vt dresser or établir la carte de; (sales, progress) établir la courbe de; **charts** npl (Mus) hit-parade m; **to be in the ~s** (record, pop group) figurer au hit-parade

charter [ˈtʃɑːtəʳ] vt (plane) affréter ▷ n (document) charte f; **chartered accountant** n (BRIT) expert-comptable m; **charter flight** n charter m

chase [tʃeɪs] vt poursuivre, pourchasser; (also: **~ away**) chasser ▷ n poursuite f, chasse f

chat [tʃæt] vi (also: **have a ~**) bavarder, causer; (on Internet) chatter ▷ n conversation f; **chat up** vt (BRIT inf: girl) baratiner; **chat room** n (Internet) forum m de discussion; **chat show** n (BRIT) talk-show m

chatter [ˈtʃætəʳ] vi (person) bavarder, papoter ▷ n bavardage m, papotage m; **my teeth are ~ing** je claque des dents

chauffeur [ˈʃəʊfəʳ] n chauffeur m (de maître)

chauvinist [ˈʃəʊvɪnɪst] n (also: **male ~**) phallocrate m, macho m; (nationalist) chauvin(e)

cheap [tʃiːp] adj bon marché inv, pas cher (chère); (reduced: ticket) à prix réduit; (: fare) réduit(e); (joke) facile, d'un goût douteux; (poor quality) à bon marché, de qualité médiocre ▷ adv à bon marché, pour pas cher; **can you recommend a ~ hotel/restaurant, please?** pourriez-vous m'indiquer un hôtel/restaurant bon marché?; **cheap day return** n billet m d'aller et retour réduit (valable pour la journée); **cheaply** adv à bon marché, à bon compte

cheat [tʃiːt] vi tricher; (in exam) copier ▷ vt tromper, duper; (rob): **to ~ sb out of sth** escroquer qch à qn ▷ n tricheur(-euse) m/f; escroc m; **cheat on** vt fus tromper

Chechnya [tʃɪtʃˈnjɑː] n Tchétchénie f

check [tʃɛk] vt vérifier; (passport, ticket) contrôler; (halt) enrayer; (restrain) maîtriser ▷ vi (official etc) se renseigner ▷ n vérification f; contrôle m; (curb) frein m; (BRIT: bill) addition f; (US) = **cheque**; (pattern: gen pl) carreaux mpl; **to ~ with sb** demander à qn; **check in** vi (in hotel) remplir sa fiche (d'hôtel); (at airport) se présenter à l'enregistrement ▷ vt (luggage) (faire) enregistrer; **check off** vt (tick off) cocher; **check out** vi (in hotel) régler sa note ▷ vt (investigate: story) vérifier; **check up** vi: **to ~ up (on sth)** vérifier (qch); **to ~ up on sb** se renseigner sur le compte de qn; **checkbook** (US) = **chequebook**; **checked** adj

(pattern, cloth) à carreaux; **checkers** n (US) jeu m de dames; **check-in** n (also: **check-in desk**: at airport) enregistrement m; **checking account** n (US) compte courant; **checklist** n liste f de contrôle; **checkmate** n échec et mat m; **checkout** n (in supermarket) caisse f; **checkpoint** n contrôle m; **checkroom** (US) n consigne f; **checkup** n (Med) examen médical, check-up m

cheddar [ˈtʃɛdəʳ] n (also: **~ cheese**) cheddar m

cheek [tʃiːk] n joue f; (impudence) toupet m, culot m; **what a ~!** quel toupet!; **cheekbone** n pommette f; **cheeky** adj effronté(e), culotté(e)

cheer [tʃɪəʳ] vt acclamer, applaudir; (gladden) réjouir, réconforter ▷ vi applaudir ▷ n (gen pl) acclamations fpl, applaudissements mpl; bravos mpl, hourras mpl; **~s!** à la vôtre!; **cheer up** vi se dérider, reprendre courage ▷ vt remonter le moral à or de, dérider, égayer; **cheerful** adj gai(e), joyeux(-euse)

cheerio [tʃɪərɪˈəʊ] excl (BRIT) salut!, au revoir!

cheerleader [ˈtʃɪəliːdəʳ] n membre d'un groupe de majorettes qui chantent et dansent pour soutenir leur équipe pendant les matchs de football américain

cheese [tʃiːz] n fromage m; **cheeseburger** n cheeseburger m; **cheesecake** n tarte f au fromage

chef [ʃɛf] n chef (cuisinier)

chemical [ˈkɛmɪkl] adj chimique ▷ n produit m chimique

chemist [ˈkɛmɪst] n (BRIT: pharmacist) pharmacien(ne); (scientist) chimiste m/f; **chemistry** n chimie f; **chemist's (shop)** n (BRIT) pharmacie f

cheque (US **check**) [tʃɛk] n chèque m; **chequebook** (US **checkbook**) n chéquier m, carnet m de chèques; **cheque card** n (BRIT) carte f (d'identité) bancaire

cherry [ˈtʃɛrɪ] n cerise f; (also: **~ tree**) cerisier m

chess [tʃɛs] n échecs mpl

chest [tʃɛst] n poitrine f; (box) coffre m, caisse f

chestnut [ˈtʃɛsnʌt] n châtaigne f; (also: **~ tree**) châtaignier m

chest of drawers n commode f

chew [tʃuː] vt mâcher; **chewing gum** n chewing-gum m

chic [ʃiːk] adj chic inv, élégant(e)

chick [tʃɪk] n poussin m; (inf) pépée f

chicken [ˈtʃɪkɪn] n poulet m; (inf: coward) poule mouillée; **chicken out** vi (inf) se dégonfler; **chickenpox** n varicelle f

chickpea [ˈtʃɪkpiː] n pois m chiche

chief [tʃiːf] n chef m ▷ adj principal(e); **chief executive** (US **chief executive officer**) n directeur(-trice) général(e); **chiefly** adv principalement, surtout

child (pl **~ren**) [tʃaɪld, ˈtʃɪldrən] n enfant

m/f; **child abuse** *n* maltraitance *f* d'enfants; (*sexual*) abus *mpl* sexuels sur des enfants; **child benefit** *n* (BRIT) ≈ allocations familiales; **childbirth** *n* accouchement *m*; **child-care** *n* (*for working parents*) garde *f* des enfants (*pour les parents qui travaillent*); **childhood** *n* enfance *f*; **childish** *adj* puéril(e), enfantin(e); **child minder** *n* (BRIT) garde *f* d'enfants; **children** ['tʃɪldrən] *npl of* **child**

Chile ['tʃɪlɪ] *n* Chili *m*

chill [tʃɪl] *n* (*of water*) froid *m*; (*of air*) fraîcheur *f*; (*Med*) refroidissement *m*, coup *m* de froid ▷ *vt* (*person*) faire frissonner; (*Culin*) mettre au frais, rafraîchir; **chill out** *vi* (*inf: esp* US) se relaxer

chil(l)i ['tʃɪlɪ] *n* piment *m* (rouge)

chilly ['tʃɪlɪ] *adj* froid(e), glacé(e); (*sensitive to cold*) frileux(-euse)

chimney ['tʃɪmnɪ] *n* cheminée *f*

chimpanzee [tʃɪmpæn'ziː] *n* chimpanzé *m*

chin [tʃɪn] *n* menton *m*

China ['tʃaɪnə] *n* Chine *f*

china ['tʃaɪnə] *n* (*material*) porcelaine *f*; (*crockery*) (vaisselle *f* en) porcelaine

Chinese [tʃaɪ'niːz] *adj* chinois(e) ▷ *n* (*pl inv*) Chinois(e); (*Ling*) chinois *m*

chip [tʃɪp] *n* (*gen pl: Culin*: BRIT) frite *f*; (: US: also: **potato ~**) chip *m*; (*of wood*) copeau *m*; (*of glass, stone*) éclat *m*; (*also*: **micro~**) puce *f*; (*in gambling*) fiche *f* ▷ *vt* (*cup, plate*) ébrécher; **chip shop** *n* (BRIT) friterie *f*

◉ **CHIP SHOP**

◉
◉ Un **chip shop**, que l'on appelle également
◉ un "fish-and-chip shop", est un magasin
◉ où l'on vend des plats à emporter. Les
◉ **chip shops** sont d'ailleurs à l'origine des
◉ "takeaways". On y achète en particulier
◉ du poisson frit et des frites, mais on y
◉ trouve également des plats traditionnels
◉ britanniques ("steak pies", saucisses, etc).
◉ Tous les plats étaient à l'origine emballés
◉ dans du papier journal. Dans certains
◉ de ces magasins, on peut s'asseoir pour
◉ consommer sur place.

chiropodist [kɪ'rɔpədɪst] *n* (BRIT) pédicure *m/f*

chisel ['tʃɪzl] *n* ciseau *m*

chives [tʃaɪvz] *npl* ciboulette *f*, civette *f*

chlorine ['klɔːriːn] *n* chlore *m*

choc-ice ['tʃɔkaɪs] *n* (BRIT) esquimau® *m*

chocolate ['tʃɔklɪt] *n* chocolat *m*

choice [tʃɔɪs] *n* choix *m* ▷ *adj* de choix

choir ['kwaɪə'] *n* chœur *m*, chorale *f*

choke [tʃəuk] *vi* étouffer ▷ *vt* étrangler; étouffer; (*block*) boucher, obstruer ▷ *n* (*Aut*) starter *m*

cholesterol [kə'lɛstərɔl] *n* cholestérol *m*

choose (*pt* **chose**, *pp* **chosen**) [tʃuːz, tʃəuz, 'tʃəuzn] *vt* choisir; **to ~ to do** décider de faire, juger bon de faire

chop [tʃɔp] *vt* (*wood*) couper (à la hache); (*Culin: also*: **~ up**) couper (fin), émincer, hacher (en morceaux) ▷ *n* (*Culin*) côtelette *f*; **chop down** *vt* (*tree*) abattre; **chop off** *vt* trancher; **chopsticks** ['tʃɔpstɪks] *npl* baguettes *fpl*

chord [kɔːd] *n* (*Mus*) accord *m*

chore [tʃɔː'] *n* travail *m* de routine; **household ~s** travaux *mpl* du ménage

chorus ['kɔːrəs] *n* chœur *m*; (*repeated part of song, also fig*) refrain *m*

chose [tʃəuz] *pt of* **choose**

chosen ['tʃəuzn] *pp of* **choose**

Christ [kraɪst] *n* Christ *m*

christen ['krɪsn] *vt* baptiser; **christening** *n* baptême *m*

Christian ['krɪstɪən] *adj, n* chrétien(ne); **Christianity** [krɪstɪ'ænɪtɪ] *n* christianisme *m*; **Christian name** *n* prénom *m*

Christmas ['krɪsməs] *n* Noël *m or f*; **happy or merry ~!** joyeux Noël!; **Christmas card** *n* carte *f* de Noël; **Christmas carol** *n* chant *m* de Noël; **Christmas Day** *n* le jour de Noël; **Christmas Eve** *n* la veille de Noël; la nuit de Noël; **Christmas pudding** *n* (*esp* BRIT) Christmas *m* pudding; **Christmas tree** *n* arbre *m* de Noël

chrome [krəum] *n* chrome *m*

chronic ['krɔnɪk] *adj* chronique

chrysanthemum [krɪ'sænθəməm] *n* chrysanthème *m*

chubby ['tʃʌbɪ] *adj* potelé(e), rondelet(te)

chuck [tʃʌk] *vt* (*inf*) lancer, jeter; (BRIT: *also*: **~ up**: *job*) lâcher; **chuck out** *vt* (*inf: person*) flanquer dehors *or* à la porte; (: *rubbish etc*) jeter

chuckle ['tʃʌkl] *vi* glousser

chum [tʃʌm] *n* copain (copine)

chunk [tʃʌŋk] *n* gros morceau

church [tʃəːtʃ] *n* église *f*; **churchyard** *n* cimetière *m*

churn [tʃəːn] *n* (*for butter*) baratte *f*; (*also*: **milk ~**) (grand) bidon à lait

chute [ʃuːt] *n* goulotte *f*; (*also*: **rubbish ~**) vide-ordures *m inv*; (BRIT: *children's slide*) toboggan *m*

chutney ['tʃʌtnɪ] *n* chutney *m*

CIA *n abbr* (= Central Intelligence Agency) CIA *f*

CID *n abbr* (= Criminal Investigation Department) ≈ P.J. *f*

cider ['saɪdə'] *n* cidre *m*

cigar [sɪ'gɑː'] *n* cigare *m*

cigarette [sɪgə'rɛt] *n* cigarette *f*; **cigarette lighter** *n* briquet *m*

cinema ['sɪnəmə] *n* cinéma *m*

cinnamon ['sɪnəmən] *n* cannelle *f*

circle ['səːkl] *n* cercle *m*; (*in cinema*) balcon *m* ▷ *vi* faire *or* décrire des cercles ▷ *vt* (*surround*) entourer, encercler; (*move round*) faire le tour de, tourner autour de

circuit ['sə:kɪt] n circuit m; (lap) tour m

circular ['sə:kjulər] adj circulaire ▷ n circulaire f; (as advertisement) prospectus m

circulate ['sə:kjuleɪt] vi circuler ▷ vt faire circuler; **circulation** [sə:kju'leɪʃən] n circulation f; (of newspaper) tirage m

circumstances ['sə:kəmstənsɪz] npl circonstances fpl; (financial condition) moyens mpl, situation financière

circus ['sə:kəs] n cirque m

cite [saɪt] vt citer

citizen ['sɪtɪzn] n (Pol) citoyen(ne); (resident): **the ~s of this town** les habitants de cette ville; **citizenship** n citoyenneté f; (BRIT: Scol) ≈ éducation f civique

citrus fruits ['sɪtrəs-] npl agrumes mpl

city ['sɪtɪ] n (grande) ville f; **the C~** la Cité de Londres (centre des affaires); **city centre** n centre ville m; **city technology college** n (BRIT) établissement m d'enseignement technologique (situé dans un quartier défavorisé)

civic ['sɪvɪk] adj civique; (authorities) municipal(e)

civil ['sɪvɪl] adj civil(e); (polite) poli(e), civil(e); **civilian** [sɪ'vɪlɪən] adj, n civil(e)

civilization [sɪvɪlaɪ'zeɪʃən] n civilisation f

civilized ['sɪvɪlaɪzd] adj civilisé(e); (fig) où règnent les bonnes manières

civil: **civil law** n code civil; (study) droit civil; **civil rights** npl droits mpl civiques; **civil servant** n fonctionnaire m/f; **Civil Service** n fonction publique, administration f; **civil war** n guerre civile

CJD n abbr (= Creutzfeldt-Jakob disease) MCJ f

claim [kleɪm] vt (rights etc) revendiquer; (compensation) réclamer; (assert) déclarer, prétendre ▷ vi (for insurance) faire une déclaration de sinistre ▷ n revendication f; prétention f; (right) droit m; **(insurance) ~** demande f d'indemnisation, déclaration f de sinistre; **claim form** n (gen) formulaire m de demande

clam [klæm] n palourde f

clamp [klæmp] n crampon m; (on workbench) valet m; (on car) sabot m de Denver ▷ vt attacher; (car) mettre un sabot à; **clamp down on** vt fus sévir contre, prendre des mesures draconiennes à l'égard de

clan [klæn] n clan m

clap [klæp] vi applaudir

claret ['klærət] n (vin m de) bordeaux m (rouge)

clarify ['klærɪfaɪ] vt clarifier

clarinet [klærɪ'nɛt] n clarinette f

clarity ['klærɪtɪ] n clarté f

clash [klæʃ] n (sound) choc m, fracas m; (with police) affrontement m; (fig) conflit m ▷ vi se heurter; être or entrer en conflit; (colours) jurer;

(dates, events) tomber en même temps

clasp [klɑ:sp] n (of necklace, bag) fermoir m ▷ vt serrer, étreindre

class [klɑ:s] n (gen) classe f; (group, category) catégorie f ▷ vt classer, classifier

classic ['klæsɪk] adj classique ▷ n (author, work) classique m; **classical** adj classique

classification [klæsɪfɪ'keɪʃən] n classification f

classify ['klæsɪfaɪ] vt classifier, classer

classmate ['klɑ:smeɪt] n camarade m/f de classe

classroom ['klɑ:srum] n (salle f de) classe f; **classroom assistant** n assistant(-e) d'éducation

classy ['klɑ:sɪ] (inf) adj classe (inf)

clatter ['klætər] n cliquetis m ▷ vi cliqueter

clause [klɔ:z] n clause f; (Ling) proposition f

claustrophobic [klɔ:strə'fəubɪk] adj (person) claustrophobe; (place) où l'on se sent claustrophobe

claw [klɔ:] n griffe f; (of bird of prey) serre f; (of lobster) pince f

clay [kleɪ] n argile f

clean [kli:n] adj propre; (clear, smooth) net(te); (record, reputation) sans tache; (joke, story) correct(e) ▷ vt nettoyer; **clean up** vt nettoyer; (fig) remettre de l'ordre dans; **cleaner** n (person) nettoyeur(-euse), femme f de ménage; (product) détachant m; **cleaner's** n (also: **dry cleaner's**) teinturier m; **cleaning** n nettoyage m

cleanser ['klɛnzər] n (for face) démaquillant m

clear [klɪər] adj clair(e); (glass, plastic) transparent(e); (road, way) libre, dégagé(e); (profit, majority) net(te); (conscience) tranquille; (skin) frais (fraîche); (sky) dégagé(e) ▷ vt (road) dégager, déblayer; (table) débarrasser; (room etc: of people) faire évacuer; (cheque) compenser; (Law: suspect) innocenter; (obstacle) franchir or sauter sans heurter ▷ vi (weather) s'éclaircir; (fog) se dissiper ▷ adv: **~ of** à distance de, à l'écart de; **to ~ the table** débarrasser la table, desservir; **clear away** vt (things, clothes etc) enlever, retirer; **to ~ away the dishes** débarrasser la table; **clear up** vt ranger, mettre en ordre; (mystery) éclaircir, résoudre; **clearance** n (removal) déblayage m; (permission) autorisation f; **clear-cut** adj précis(e), nettement défini(e); **clearing** n (in forest) clairière f; **clearly** adv clairement; (obviously) de toute évidence; **clearway** n (BRIT) route f à stationnement interdit

clench [klɛntʃ] vt serrer

clergy ['klə:dʒɪ] n clergé m

clerk [klɑ:k, US klə:rk] n (BRIT) employé(e) de bureau; (US: salesman/woman) vendeur(-euse)

clever ['klɛvər] adj (intelligent) intelligent(e); (skilful) habile, adroit(e); (device, arrangement)

ingénieux(-euse), astucieux(-euse)
cliché ['kli:feɪ] *n* cliché *m*
click [klɪk] *n* (*Comput*) cliquer ▷ *vt*: **to ~ one's tongue** faire claquer sa langue; **to ~ one's heels** claquer des talons; **to ~ on an icon** cliquer sur une icône
client ['klaɪənt] *n* client(e)
cliff [klɪf] *n* falaise *f*
climate ['klaɪmɪt] *n* climat *m*; **climate change** *n* changement *m* climatique
climax ['klaɪmæks] *n* apogée *m*, point culminant; (*sexual*) orgasme *m*
climb [klaɪm] *vi* grimper, monter; (*plane*) prendre de l'altitude ▷ *vt* (*stairs*) monter; (*mountain*) escalader; (*tree*) grimper à ▷ *n* montée *f*, escalade *f*; **to ~ over a wall** passer par dessus un mur; **climb down** *vi* (re)descendre; (*BRIT fig*) rabattre de ses prétentions; **climber** *n* (*also*: **rock climber**) grimpeur(-euse), varappeur(-euse); (*plant*) plante grimpante; **climbing** *n* (*also*: **rock climbing**) escalade *f*, varappe *f*
clinch [klɪntʃ] *vt* (*deal*) conclure, sceller
cling (*pt*, *pp* **clung**) [klɪŋ, klʌŋ] *vi*: **to ~ (to)** se cramponner (à), s'accrocher (à); (*clothes*) coller (à)
Clingfilm® ['klɪŋfɪlm] *n* film *m* alimentaire
clinic ['klɪnɪk] *n* clinique *f*; centre médical
clip [klɪp] *n* (*for hair*) barrette *f*; (*also*: **paper ~**) trombone *m*; (*TV*, *Cinema*) clip *m* ▷ *vt* (*also*: **~ together**: *papers*) attacher; (*hair*, *nails*) couper; (*hedge*) tailler; **clipping** *n* (*from newspaper*) coupure *f* de journal
cloak [kləuk] *n* grande cape ▷ *vt* (*fig*) masquer, cacher; **cloakroom** *n* (*for coats etc*) vestiaire *m*; (*BRIT*: *W.C.*) toilettes *fpl*
clock [klɔk] *n* (*large*) horloge *f*; (*small*) pendule *f*; **clock in** *or* **on** (*BRIT*) *vi* (*with card*) pointer (en arrivant); (*start work*) commencer à travailler; **clock off** *or* **out** (*BRIT*) *vi* (*with card*) pointer (en partant); (*leave work*) quitter le travail; **clockwise** *adv* dans le sens des aiguilles d'une montre; **clockwork** *n* rouages *mpl*, mécanisme *m*; (*of clock*) mouvement *m* (d'horlogerie) ▷ *adj* (*toy*, *train*) mécanique
clog [klɔg] *n* sabot *m* ▷ *vt* boucher, encrasser ▷ *vi* (*also*: **~ up**) se boucher, s'encrasser
clone [kləun] *n* clone *m* ▷ *vt* cloner
close¹ [kləus] *adj* (*near*): **~ (to)** près (de), proche (de); (*contact*, *link*, *watch*) étroit(e); (*examination*) attentif(-ive), minutieux(-euse); (*contest*) très serré(e); (*weather*) lourd(e), étouffant(e) ▷ *adv* près, à proximité; **~ to** *prep* près de; **~ by**, **~ at hand** *adj*, *adv* tout(e) près; **a ~ friend** un ami intime; **to have a ~ shave** (*fig*) l'échapper belle
close² [kləuz] *vt* fermer ▷ *vi* (*shop etc*) fermer; (*lid*, *door etc*) se fermer; (*end*) se terminer, se conclure ▷ *n* (*end*) conclusion *f*; **what time**

do you ~? à quelle heure fermez-vous?; **close down** *vi* fermer (*définitivement*); **closed** *adj* (*shop etc*) fermé(e)
closely ['kləuslɪ] *adv* (*examine*, *watch*) de près
closet ['klɔzɪt] *n* (*cupboard*) placard *m*, réduit *m*
close-up ['kləusʌp] *n* gros plan
closing time *n* heure *f* de fermeture
closure ['kləuʒə'] *n* fermeture *f*
clot [klɔt] *n* (*of blood*, *milk*) caillot *m*; (*inf*: *person*) ballot *m* ▷ *vi* (: *external bleeding*) se coaguler
cloth [klɔθ] *n* (*material*) tissu *m*, étoffe *f*; (*BRIT*: *also*: **tea ~**) torchon *m*; lavette *f*; (*also*: **table~**) nappe *f*
clothes [kləuðz] *npl* vêtements *mpl*, habits *mpl*; **clothes line** *n* corde *f* (à linge); **clothes peg** (*US* **clothes pin**) *n* pince *f* à linge
clothing ['kləuðɪŋ] *n* = **clothes**
cloud [klaud] *n* nuage *m*; **cloud over** *vi* se couvrir; (*fig*) s'assombrir; **cloudy** *adj* nuageux(-euse), couvert(e); (*liquid*) trouble
clove [kləuv] *n* clou *m* de girofle; **a ~ of garlic** une gousse d'ail
clown [klaun] *n* clown *m* ▷ *vi* (*also*: **~ about**, **~ around**) faire le clown
club [klʌb] *n* (*society*) club *m*; (*weapon*) massue *f*, matraque *f*; (*also*: **golf ~**) club ▷ *vt* matraquer ▷ *vi*: **to ~ together** s'associer; **clubs** *npl* (*Cards*) trèfle *m*; **club class** *n* (*Aviat*) classe *f* club
clue [klu:] *n* indice *m*; (*in crosswords*) définition *f*; **I haven't a ~** je n'en ai pas la moindre idée
clump [klʌmp] *n*: **~ of trees** bouquet *m* d'arbres
clumsy ['klʌmzɪ] *adj* (*person*) gauche, maladroit(e); (*object*) malcommode, peu maniable
clung [klʌŋ] *pt*, *pp* of **cling**
cluster ['klʌstə'] *n* (*petit*) groupe; (*of flowers*) grappe *f* ▷ *vi* se rassembler
clutch [klʌtʃ] *n* (*Aut*) embrayage *m*; (*grasp*): **-es** étreinte *f*, prise *f* ▷ *vt* (*grasp*) agripper; (*hold tightly*) serrer fort; (*hold on to*) se cramponner à
cm *abbr* (= *centimetre*) cm
Co. *abbr* = **company**, **county**
c/o *abbr* (= *care of*) c/o, aux bons soins de
coach [kəutʃ] *n* (*bus*) autocar *m*; (*horse-drawn*) diligence *f*; (*of train*) voiture *f*, wagon *m*; (*Sport*: *trainer*) entraîneur(-euse); (*school*: *tutor*) répétiteur(-trice) ▷ *vt* (*Sport*) entraîner; (*student*) donner des leçons particulières à; **coach station** (*BRIT*) *n* gare routière; **coach trip** *n* excursion *f* en car
coal [kəul] *n* charbon *m*
coalition [kəuə'lɪʃən] *n* coalition *f*
coarse [kɔ:s] *adj* grossier(-ère), rude; (*vulgar*) vulgaire
coast [kəust] *n* côte *f* ▷ *vi* (*car*, *cycle*) descendre en roue libre; **coastal** *adj* côtier(-ère); **coastguard** *n* garde-côte *m*; **coastline** *n* côte *f*, littoral *m*

coat [kəʊt] n manteau m; (of animal) pelage m, poil m; (of paint) couche f ▷ vt couvrir, enduire; **coat hanger** n cintre m; **coating** n couche f, enduit m

coax [kəʊks] vt persuader par des cajoleries

cob [kɔb] n see **corn**

cobbled ['kɔbld] adj pavé(e)

cobweb ['kɔbwɛb] n toile f d'araignée

cocaine [kə'keɪn] n cocaïne f

cock [kɔk] n (rooster) coq m; (male bird) mâle m ▷ vt (gun) armer; **cockerel** n jeune coq m

cockney ['kɔknɪ] n cockney m/f (habitant des quartiers populaires de l'East End de Londres), ≈ faubourien(ne)

cockpit ['kɔkpɪt] n (in aircraft) poste m de pilotage, cockpit m

cockroach ['kɔkrəʊtʃ] n cafard m, cancrelat m

cocktail ['kɔkteɪl] n cocktail m

cocoa ['kəʊkəʊ] n cacao m

coconut ['kəʊkənʌt] n noix f de coco

C.O.D. abbr = **cash on delivery**

cod [kɔd] n morue fraîche, cabillaud m

code [kəʊd] n code m; (Tel: area code) indicatif m

coeducational ['kəʊɛdju'keɪʃənl] adj mixte

coffee ['kɔfɪ] n café m; **coffee bar** n (BRIT) café m; **coffee bean** n grain m de café; **coffee break** n pause-café f; **coffee maker** n cafetière f; **coffeepot** n cafetière f; **coffee shop** n café m; **coffee table** n (petite) table basse

coffin ['kɔfɪn] n cercueil m

cog [kɔg] n (wheel) roue dentée; (tooth) dent f (d'engrenage)

cognac ['kɔnjæk] n cognac m

coherent [kəʊ'hɪərənt] adj cohérent(e)

coil [kɔɪl] n rouleau m, bobine f; (contraceptive) stérilet m ▷ vt enrouler

coin [kɔɪn] n pièce f (de monnaie) ▷ vt (word) inventer

coincide [kəʊɪn'saɪd] vi coïncider; **coincidence** [kəʊ'ɪnsɪdəns] n coïncidence f

Coke® [kəʊk] n coca m

coke [kəʊk] n (coal) coke m

colander ['kɔləndər] n passoire f (à légumes)

cold [kəʊld] adj froid(e) ▷ n froid m; (Med) rhume m; **it's ~** il fait froid; **to be ~** (person) avoir froid; **to catch a ~** s'enrhumer, attraper un rhume; **in ~ blood** de sang-froid; **cold cuts** (US) npl viandes froides; **cold sore** n bouton m de fièvre

coleslaw ['kəʊlslɔː] n sorte de salade de chou cru

colic ['kɔlɪk] n colique(s) f(pl)

collaborate [kə'læbəreɪt] vi collaborer

collapse [kə'læps] vi s'effondrer, s'écrouler; (Med) avoir un malaise ▷ n effondrement m, écroulement m; (of government) chute f

collar ['kɔlər] n (of coat, shirt) col m; (for dog) collier m; **collarbone** n clavicule f

colleague ['kɔliːg] n collègue m/f

collect [kə'lɛkt] vt rassembler; (pick up) ramasser; (as a hobby) collectionner; (BRIT: call for) (passer) prendre; (mail) faire la levée de, ramasser; (money owed) encaisser; (donations, subscriptions) recueillir ▷ vi (people) se rassembler; (dust, dirt) s'amasser; **to call ~** (US Tel) téléphoner en PCV; **collection** [kə'lɛkʃən] n collection f; (of mail) levée f; (for money) collecte f, quête f; **collective** [kə'lɛktɪv] adj collectif(-ive); **collector** n collectionneur m

college ['kɔlɪdʒ] n collège m; (of technology, agriculture etc) institut m

collide [kə'laɪd] vi: **to ~ (with)** entrer en collision (avec)

collision [kə'lɪʒən] n collision f, heurt m

cologne [kə'ləʊn] n (also: **eau de ~**) eau f de cologne

colon ['kəʊlən] n (sign) deux-points mpl; (Med) côlon m

colonel ['kəːnl] n colonel m

colonial [kə'ləʊnɪəl] adj colonial(e)

colony ['kɔlənɪ] n colonie f

colour etc (US **color** etc) ['kʌlər] n couleur f ▷ vt colorer; (dye) teindre; (paint) peindre; (with crayons) colorier; (news) fausser, exagérer ▷ vi (blush) rougir; **I'd like a different ~** je le voudrais dans un autre coloris; **colour in** vt colorier; **colour-blind** adj daltonien(ne); **coloured** adj coloré(e); (photo) en couleur; **colour film** n (for camera) pellicule f (en) couleur; **colourful** adj coloré(e), vif (vive); (personality) pittoresque, haut(e) en couleurs; **colouring** n colorant m; (complexion) teint m; **colour television** n télévision f (en) couleur

column ['kɔləm] n colonne f; (fashion column, sports column etc) rubrique f

coma ['kəʊmə] n coma m

comb [kəʊm] n peigne m ▷ vt (hair) peigner; (area) ratisser, passer au peigne fin

combat ['kɔmbæt] n combat m ▷ vt combattre, lutter contre

combination [kɔmbɪ'neɪʃən] n (gen) combinaison f

combine vb [kəm'baɪn] ▷ vt combiner ▷ vi s'associer; (Chem) se combiner ▷ n ['kɔmbaɪn] (Econ) trust m; **to ~ sth with sth** (one quality with another) joindre ou allier qch à qch

come (pt **came**, pp **~**) [kʌm, keɪm] vi
1 (movement towards) venir; **to ~ running** arriver en courant; **he's ~ here to work** il est venu ici pour travailler; **~ with me** suivez-moi
2 (arrive) arriver; **to ~ home** rentrer (chez soi or à la maison); **we've just ~ from Paris** nous arrivons de Paris
3 (reach): **to ~ to** (decision etc) parvenir à, arriver à; **the bill came to £40** la note s'est élevée à 40 livres
4 (occur): **an idea came to me** il m'est venu

une idée
5 (be, become): **to ~ loose/undone** se
défaire/desserrer; **I've ~ to like him** j'ai fini par
bien l'aimer; **come across** vt fus rencontrer
par hasard, tomber sur; **come along** vi (BRIT:
pupil, work) faire des progrès, avancer; **come
back** vi revenir; **come down** vi descendre;
(prices) baisser; (buildings) s'écrouler; (: be
demolished) être démoli(e); **come from** vt fus
(source) venir de; (train) arriver; (fashion)
de; **come in** vi entrer; (train) arriver; (fashion)
entrer en vogue; (on deal etc) participer; **come
off** vi (button) se détacher; (attempt) réussir;
come on vi (lights, electricity) s'allumer;
(central heating) se mettre en marche; (pupil,
work, project) faire des progrès, avancer; **~ on!**
viens!; allons!, allez!; **come out** vi sortir; (sun)
se montrer; (book) paraître; (stain) s'enlever;
(strike) cesser le travail, se mettre en grève;
come round vi (after faint, operation) revenir
à soi, reprendre connaissance; **come to** vi
revenir à soi; **come up** vi monter; (sun) se
lever; (problem) se poser; (event) survenir; (in
conversation) être soulevé; **come up with** vt
fus (money) fournir; **he came up with an idea**
il a eu une idée, il a proposé quelque chose
comeback ['kʌmbæk] n (Theat etc) rentrée f
comedian [kə'miːdɪən] n (comic) comique m;
(Theat) comédien m
comedy ['kɔmɪdɪ] n comédie f; (humour)
comique m
comet ['kɔmɪt] n comète f
comfort ['kʌmfət] n confort m, bien-être
m; (solace) consolation f, réconfort m ▷ vt
consoler, réconforter; **comfortable** adj
confortable; (person) à l'aise; (financially)
aisé(e); (patient) dont l'état est stationnaire;
comfort station n (US) toilettes fpl
comic ['kɔmɪk] adj comique ▷ n (also: **~al**)
(person) comique m; (BRIT: magazine: for
children) magazine m de bandes dessinées or de
BD; (: for adults) illustré m; **comic book** (US) n
(for children) magazine m de bandes dessinées
or de BD; (for adults) illustré m; **comic strip** n
bande dessinée
comma ['kɔmə] n virgule f
command [kə'mɑːnd] n ordre m,
commandement m; (Mil: authority)
commandement m; (mastery) maîtrise
f ▷ vt (troops) commander; **to ~ sb to do**
donner l'ordre or commander à qn de faire;
commander n (Mil) commandant m
commemorate [kə'mɛməreɪt] vt
commémorer
commence [kə'mɛns] vt, vi commencer;
commencement (US) n (University) remise f
des diplômes
commend [kə'mɛnd] vt louer; (recommend)
recommander

comment ['kɔmɛnt] n commentaire m ▷ vi:
to ~ on faire des remarques sur; **"no ~"** je n'ai
rien à déclarer"; **commentary** ['kɔməntərɪ]
n commentaire m; (Sport) reportage m (en
direct); **commentator** ['kɔməntetɪər] n
commentateur m; (Sport) reporter m
commerce ['kɔməːs] n commerce m
commercial [kə'məːʃəl] adj commercial(e)
▷ n (Radio, TV) annonce f publicitaire, spot m
(publicitaire); **commercial break** n (Radio, TV)
spot m (publicitaire)
commission [kə'mɪʃən] n (committee, fee)
commission f ▷ vt (work of art) commander,
charger un artiste de l'exécution de; **out of
~** (machine) hors service; **commissioner** n
(Police) préfet m (de police)
commit [kə'mɪt] vt (act) commettre;
(resources) consacrer; (to sb's care) confier (à); **to
~ o.s. (to do)** s'engager (à faire); **to ~ suicide**
se suicider; **commitment** n engagement m;
(obligation) responsabilité(s) (fpl)
committee [kə'mɪtɪ] n comité m;
commission f
commodity [kə'mɔdɪtɪ] n produit m,
marchandise f, article m
common ['kɔmən] adj (gen) commun(e);
(usual) courant(e) ▷ n terrain communal;
commonly adv communément,
généralement; couramment; **commonplace**
adj banal(e), ordinaire; **Commons** npl (BRIT
Pol): **the (House of) Commons** la chambre
des Communes; **common sense** n bon sens;
Commonwealth n: **the Commonwealth** le
Commonwealth
communal ['kɔmjuːnl] adj (life)
communautaire; (for common use) commun(e)
commune n ['kɔmjuːn] (group) communauté
f ▷ vi [kə'mjuːn]: **to ~ with** (nature)
communier avec
communicate [kə'mjuːnɪkeɪt] vt
communiquer, transmettre ▷ vi: **to ~ (with)**
communiquer (avec)
communication [kəmjuːnɪ'keɪʃən] n
communication f
communion [kə'mjuːnɪən] n (also: **Holy C~**)
communion f
communism ['kɔmjunɪzəm] n
communisme m; **communist** adj, n
communiste m/f
community [kə'mjuːnɪtɪ] n communauté f;
community centre (US **community center**)
n foyer socio-éducatif, centre m de loisirs;
community service n ≈ travail m d'intérêt
général, TIG m
commute [kə'mjuːt] vi faire le trajet
journalier (de son domicile à un lieu de travail
assez éloigné) ▷ vt (Law) commuer; **commuter**
n banlieusard(e) (qui fait un trajet journalier pour
se rendre à son travail)

compact adj [kəm'pækt] compact(e) ▷ n ['kɔmpækt] (also: **powder ~**) poudrier m; **compact disc** n disque compact; **compact disc player** n lecteur m de disques compacts

companion [kəm'pænjən] n compagnon (compagne)

company ['kʌmpənɪ] n compagnie f; **to keep sb ~** tenir compagnie à qn; **company car** n voiture f de fonction; **company director** n administrateur(-trice)

comparable ['kɔmpərəbl] adj comparable

comparative [kəm'pærətɪv] adj (study) comparatif(-ive); (relative) relatif(-ive); **comparatively** adv (relatively) relativement

compare [kəm'pɛəʳ] vt: **to ~ sth/sb with** or **to** comparer qch/qn avec or à ▷ vi: **to ~ (with)** se comparer (à); être comparable (à); **comparison** [kəm'pærɪsn] n comparaison f

compartment [kəm'pɑ:tmənt] n (also Rail) compartiment m; **a non-smoking ~** un compartiment non-fumeurs

compass ['kʌmpəs] n boussole f; **compasses** npl (Math) compas m

compassion [kəm'pæʃən] n compassion f, humanité f

compatible [kəm'pætɪbl] adj compatible

compel [kəm'pɛl] vt contraindre, obliger; **compelling** adj (fig: argument) irrésistible

compensate ['kɔmpənseɪt] vt indemniser, dédommager ▷ vi: **to ~ for** compenser; **compensation** [kɔmpən'seɪʃən] n compensation f; (money) dédommagement m, indemnité f

compete [kəm'pi:t] vi (take part) concourir; (vie): **to ~ (with)** rivaliser (avec), faire concurrence (à)

competent ['kɔmpɪtənt] adj compétent(e), capable

competition [kɔmpɪ'tɪʃən] n (contest) compétition f, concours m; (Econ) concurrence f

competitive [kəm'pɛtɪtɪv] adj (Econ) concurrentiel(le); (sports) de compétition; (person) qui a l'esprit de compétition

competitor [kəm'pɛtɪtəʳ] n concurrent(e)

complacent [kəm'pleɪsnt] adj (trop) content(e) de soi

complain [kəm'pleɪn] vi: **to ~ (about)** se plaindre (de); (in shop etc) réclamer (au sujet de); **complaint** n plainte f; (in shop etc) réclamation f; (Med) affection f

complement ['kɔmplɪmənt] n complément m; (esp of ship's crew etc) effectif complet ▷ vt (enhance) compléter; **complementary** [kɔmplɪ'mɛntərɪ] adj complémentaire

complete [kəm'pli:t] adj complet(-ète); (finished) achevé(e) ▷ vt achever, parachever; (set, group) compléter; (a form) remplir; **completely** adv complètement; **completion**

[kəm'pli:ʃən] n achèvement m; (of contract) exécution f

complex ['kɔmplɛks] adj complexe ▷ n (Psych, buildings etc) complexe m

complexion [kəm'plɛkʃən] n (of face) teint m

compliance [kəm'plaɪəns] n (submission) docilité f; (agreement): **~ with** le fait de se conformer à; **in ~ with** en conformité avec, conformément à

complicate ['kɔmplɪkeɪt] vt compliquer; **complicated** adj compliqué(e); **complication** [kɔmplɪ'keɪʃən] n complication f

compliment n ['kɔmplɪmənt] compliment m ▷ vt ['kɔmplɪmɛnt] complimenter; **complimentary** [kɔmplɪ'mɛntərɪ] adj flatteur(-euse); (free) à titre gracieux

comply [kəm'plaɪ] vi: **to ~ with** se soumettre à, se conformer à

component [kəm'pəunənt] adj composant(e), constituant(e) ▷ n composant m, élément m

compose [kəm'pəuz] vt composer; (form): **to be ~d of** se composer de; **to ~ o.s.** se calmer, se maîtriser; **composer** n (Mus) compositeur m; **composition** [kɔmpə'zɪʃən] n composition f

composure [kəm'pəuʒəʳ] n calme m, maîtrise f de soi

compound ['kɔmpaund] n (Chem, Ling) composé m; (enclosure) enclos m, enceinte f ▷ adj composé(e); (fracture) compliqué(e)

comprehension [kɔmprɪ'hɛnʃən] n compréhension f

comprehensive [kɔmprɪ'hɛnsɪv] adj (très) complet(-ète); **~ policy** (Insurance) assurance f tous risques; **comprehensive (school)** n (BRIT) école secondaire non sélective avec libre circulation d'une section à l'autre, ≈ CES m

> Be careful not to translate *comprehensive* by the French word *compréhensif*.

compress vt [kəm'prɛs] comprimer; (text, information) condenser ▷ n ['kɔmprɛs] (Med) compresse f

comprise [kəm'praɪz] vt (also: **be ~d of**) comprendre; (constitute) constituer, représenter

compromise ['kɔmprəmaɪz] n compromis m ▷ vt compromettre ▷ vi transiger, accepter un compromis

compulsive [kəm'pʌlsɪv] adj (Psych) compulsif(-ive); (book, film etc) captivant(e)

compulsory [kəm'pʌlsərɪ] adj obligatoire

computer [kəm'pju:təʳ] n ordinateur m; **computer game** n jeu m vidéo; **computer-generated** adj de synthèse; **computerize** vt (data) traiter par ordinateur; (system, office) informatiser; **computer programmer**

n programmeur(-euse); **computer programming** *n* programmation *f*; **computer science** *n* informatique *f*; **computer studies** *npl* informatique *f*; **computing** [kəm'pju:tɪŋ] *n* informatique *f*

con [kɔn] *vt* duper; (*cheat*) escroquer ▷ *n* escroquerie *f*

conceal [kən'si:l] *vt* cacher, dissimuler

concede [kən'si:d] *vt* concéder ▷ *vi* céder

conceited [kən'si:tɪd] *adj* vaniteux(-euse), suffisant(e)

conceive [kən'si:v] *vt*, *vi* concevoir

concentrate ['kɔnsəntreɪt] *vi* se concentrer ▷ *vt* concentrer

concentration [kɔnsən'treɪʃən] *n* concentration *f*

concept ['kɔnsɛpt] *n* concept *m*

concern [kən'sə:n] *n* affaire *f*; (*Comm*) entreprise *f*, firme *f*; (*anxiety*) inquiétude *f*, souci *m* ▷ *vt* (*worry*) inquiéter; (*involve*) concerner; (*relate to*) se rapporter à; **to be ~ed (about)** s'inquiéter (de), être inquiet(-ète) (au sujet de); **concerning** *prep* en ce qui concerne, à propos de

concert ['kɔnsət] *n* concert *m*; **concert hall** *n* salle *f* de concert

concerto [kən'tʃə:təu] *n* concerto *m*

concession [kən'sɛʃən] *n* (*compromise*) concession *f*; (*reduced price*) réduction *f*; **tax ~** dégrèvement fiscal; **"~s"** tarif réduit

concise [kən'saɪs] *adj* concis(e)

conclude [kən'klu:d] *vt* conclure; **conclusion** [kən'klu:ʒən] *n* conclusion *f*

concrete ['kɔnkri:t] *n* béton *m* ▷ *adj* concret(-ète); (*Constr*) en béton

concussion [kən'kʌʃən] *n* (*Med*) commotion (cérébrale)

condemn [kən'dɛm] *vt* condamner

condensation [kɔndɛn'seɪʃən] *n* condensation *f*

condense [kən'dɛns] *vi* se condenser ▷ *vt* condenser

condition [kən'dɪʃən] *n* condition *f*; (*disease*) maladie *f* ▷ *vt* déterminer, conditionner; **on ~ that** à condition que + *sub*, à condition de; **conditional** [kən'dɪʃənl] *adj* conditionnel(le); **conditioner** *n* (*for hair*) baume démêlant; (*for fabrics*) assouplissant *m*

condo ['kɔndəu] *n* (*us inf*) = **condominium**

condom ['kɔndəm] *n* préservatif *m*

condominium [kɔndə'mɪnɪəm] *n* (*us: building*) immeuble *m* (en copropriété); (*: rooms*) appartement *m* (dans un immeuble en copropriété)

condone [kən'dəun] *vt* fermer les yeux sur, approuver (tacitement)

conduct *n* ['kɔndʌkt] conduite *f* ▷ *vt* [kən'dʌkt] conduire; (*manage*) mener, diriger; (*Mus*) diriger; **to ~ o.s.** se conduire, se comporter; **conducted tour** (*BRIT*) *n* voyage organisé; (*of building*) visite guidée; **conductor** *n* (*of orchestra*) chef *m* d'orchestre; (*on bus*) receveur *m*; (*us: on train*) chef *m* de train; (*Elec*) conducteur *m*

cone [kəun] *n* cône *m*; (*for ice-cream*) cornet *m*; (*Bot*) pomme *f* de pin, cône

confectionery [kən'fɛkʃənrɪ] *n* (*sweets*) confiserie *f*

confer [kən'fə:ʳ] *vt*: **to ~ sth on** conférer qch à ▷ *vi* conférer, s'entretenir

conference ['kɔnfərns] *n* conférence *f*

confess [kən'fɛs] *vt* confesser, avouer ▷ *vi* (*admit sth*) avouer; (*Rel*) se confesser; **confession** [kən'fɛʃən] *n* confession *f*

confide [kən'faɪd] *vi*: **to ~ in** s'ouvrir à, se confier à

confidence ['kɔnfɪdns] *n* confiance *f*; (*also:* **self-~**) assurance *f*, confiance en soi; (*secret*) confidence *f*; **in ~** (*speak, write*) en confidence, confidentiellement; **confident** *adj* (*self-assured*) sûr(e) de soi; (*sure*) sûr(e); **confidential** [kɔnfɪ'dɛnʃəl] *adj* confidentiel(le)

confine [kən'faɪn] *vt* limiter, borner; (*shut up*) confiner, enfermer; **confined** *adj* (*space*) restreint(e), réduit(e)

confirm [kən'fə:m] *vt* (*report, Rel*) confirmer; (*appointment*) ratifier; **confirmation** [kɔnfə'meɪʃən] *n* confirmation *f*; ratification *f*

confiscate ['kɔnfɪskeɪt] *vt* confisquer

conflict *n* ['kɔnflɪkt] conflit *m*, lutte *f* ▷ *vi* [kən'flɪkt] (*opinions*) s'opposer, se heurter

conform [kən'fɔ:m] *vi*: **to ~ (to)** se conformer (à)

confront [kən'frʌnt] *vt* (*two people*) confronter; (*enemy, danger*) affronter, faire face à; (*problem*) faire face à; **confrontation** [kɔnfrən'teɪʃən] *n* confrontation *f*

confuse [kən'fju:z] *vt* (*person*) troubler; (*situation*) embrouiller; (*one thing with another*) confondre; **confused** *adj* (*person*) dérouté(e), désorienté(e); (*situation*) embrouillé(e); **confusing** *adj* peu clair(e), déroutant(e); **confusion** [kən'fju:ʒən] *n* confusion *f*

congestion [kən'dʒɛstʃən] *n* (*Med*) congestion *f*; (*fig: traffic*) encombrement *m*

congratulate [kən'grætjuleɪt] *vt*: **to ~ sb (on)** féliciter qn (de); **congratulations** [kəngrætju'leɪʃənz] *npl*: **congratulations (on)** félicitations *fpl* (pour) ▷ *excl*: **congratulations!** (toutes mes) félicitations!

congregation [kɔŋgrɪ'geɪʃən] *n* assemblée *f* (des fidèles)

congress ['kɔŋgrɛs] *n* congrès *m*; (*Pol*): **C~** Congrès *m*; **congressman** *n* membre *m* du Congrès; **congresswoman** *n* membre *m* du Congrès

conifer ['kɔnɪfəʳ] *n* conifère *m*

conjugate ['kɔndʒugeɪt] *vt* conjuguer

conjugation [kɒndʒə'geɪʃən] n conjugaison f
conjunction [kən'dʒʌŋkʃən] n conjonction f;
in ~ with (conjointement) avec
conjure ['kʌndʒə'] vi faire des tours de
passe-passe
connect [kə'nɛkt] vt joindre, relier; (Elec)
connecter; (Tel: caller) mettre en connexion;
(: subscriber) brancher; (fig) établir un rapport
entre, faire un rapprochement entre ▷ vi
(train): **to ~ with** assurer la correspondance
avec; **to be ~ed with** avoir un rapport avec;
(have dealings with) avoir des rapports avec,
être en relation avec; **connecting flight** n
(vol m de) correspondance f; **connection**
[kə'nɛkʃən] n relation f, lien m; (Elec)
connexion f; (Tel) communication f; (train etc)
correspondance f
conquer ['kɒŋkə'] vt conquérir; (feelings)
vaincre, surmonter
conquest ['kɒŋkwɛst] n conquête f
cons [kɒnz] npl see **convenience**; **pro**
conscience ['kɒnʃəns] n conscience f
conscientious [kɒnʃɪ'ɛnʃəs] adj
consciencieux(-euse)
conscious ['kɒnʃəs] adj conscient(e);
(deliberate: insult, error) délibéré(e);
consciousness n conscience f; (Med)
connaissance f
consecutive [kən'sɛkjʊtɪv] adj
consécutif(-ive); **on three ~ occasions** trois
fois de suite
consensus [kən'sɛnsəs] n consensus m
consent [kən'sɛnt] n consentement m ▷ vi: **to
~ (to)** consentir (à)
consequence ['kɒnsɪkwəns] n suites fpl,
conséquence f; (significance) importance f
consequently ['kɒnsɪkwəntlɪ] adv par
conséquent, donc
conservation [kɒnsə'veɪʃən] n préservation
f, protection f; (also: **nature ~**) défense f de
l'environnement
conservative [kən'sə:vətɪv] adj
conservateur(-trice); (cautious)
prudent(e); **Conservative** adj, n (BRIT Pol)
conservateur(-trice)
conservatory [kən'sə:vətrɪ] n (room) jardin
m d'hiver; (Mus) conservatoire m
consider [kən'sɪdə'] vt (study) considérer,
réfléchir à; (take into account) penser à,
prendre en considération; (regard, judge)
considérer, estimer; **to ~ doing sth**
envisager de faire qch; **considerable** adj
considérable; **considerably** adv nettement;
considerate adj prévenant(e), plein(e)
d'égards; **consideration** [kənsɪdə'reɪʃən]
n considération f; (reward) rétribution
f, rémunération f; **considering** prep:
considering (that) étant donné (que)
consignment [kən'saɪnmənt] n arrivage

m, envoi m
consist [kən'sɪst] vi: **to ~ of** consister en, se
composer de
consistency [kən'sɪstənsɪ] n (thickness)
consistance f; (fig) cohérence f
consistent [kən'sɪstənt] adj logique,
cohérent(e)
consolation [kɒnsə'leɪʃən] n consolation f
console[1] [kən'səul] vt consoler
console[2] ['kɒnsəul] n console f
consonant ['kɒnsənənt] n consonne f
conspicuous [kən'spɪkjuəs] adj voyant(e),
qui attire l'attention
conspiracy [kən'spɪrəsɪ] n conspiration f,
complot m
constable ['kʌnstəbl] n (BRIT) ≈ agent m de
police, gendarme m; **chief ~** ≈ préfet m de
police
constant ['kɒnstənt] adj constant(e);
incessant(e); **constantly** adv constamment,
sans cesse
constipated ['kɒnstɪpeɪtɪd] adj constipé(e);
constipation [kɒnstɪ'peɪʃən] n constipation f
constituency [kən'stɪtjuənsɪ] n (Pol:
area) circonscription électorale; (: electors)
électorat m
constitute ['kɒnstɪtjuːt] vt constituer
constitution [kɒnstɪ'tjuːʃən] n constitution f
constraint [kən'streɪnt] n contrainte f
construct [kən'strʌkt] vt construire;
construction [kən'strʌkʃən] n construction f;
constructive adj constructif(-ive)
consul ['kɒnsl] n consul m; **consulate**
['kɒnsjulɪt] n consulat m
consult [kən'sʌlt] vt consulter;
consultant n (Med) médecin consultant;
(other specialist) consultant m, (expert-
)conseil m; **consultation** [kɒnsəl'teɪʃən] n
consultation f; **consulting room** n (BRIT)
cabinet m de consultation
consume [kən'sjuːm] vt consommer; (subj:
flames, hatred, desire) consumer; **consumer** n
consommateur(-trice)
consumption [kən'sʌmpʃən] n
consommation f
cont. abbr (= continued) suite
contact ['kɒntækt] n contact m; (person)
connaissance f, relation f ▷ vt se mettre en
contact or en rapport avec; **contact lenses**
npl verres mpl de contact
contagious [kən'teɪdʒəs] adj
contagieux(-euse)
contain [kən'teɪn] vt contenir; **to ~ o.s.** se
contenir, se maîtriser; **container** n récipient
m; (for shipping etc) conteneur m
contaminate [kən'tæmɪneɪt] vt contaminer
cont'd abbr (= continued) suite
contemplate ['kɒntəmpleɪt] vt contempler;
(consider) envisager

contemporary [kən'tɛmpərəri] *adj* contemporain(e); *(design, wallpaper)* moderne ▷ *n* contemporain(e)

contempt [kən'tɛmpt] *n* mépris *m*, dédain *m*; **~ of court** *(Law)* outrage *m* à l'autorité de la justice

contend [kən'tɛnd] *vt*: **to ~ that** soutenir *or* prétendre que ▷ *vi*: **to ~ with** *(compete)* rivaliser avec; *(struggle)* lutter avec

content [kən'tɛnt] *adj* content(e), satisfait(e) ▷ *vt* contenter, satisfaire ▷ *n* ['kɔntɛnt] contenu *m*; *(of fat, moisture)* teneur *f*; **contents** *npl (of container etc)* contenu *m*; **(table of) ~s** table *f* des matières; **contented** *adj* content(e), satisfait(e)

contest *n* ['kɔntɛst] combat *m*, lutte *f*; *(competition)* concours *m* ▷ *vt* [kən'tɛst] contester, discuter; *(compete for)* disputer; *(Law)* attaquer; **contestant** [kən'tɛstənt] *n* concurrent(e); *(in fight)* adversaire *m/f*

context ['kɔntɛkst] *n* contexte *m*

continent ['kɔntɪnənt] *n* continent *m*; **the C~** *(BRIT)* l'Europe continentale; **continental** [kɔntɪ'nɛntl] *adj* continental(e); **continental breakfast** *n* café *(or* thé*)* complet; **continental quilt** *n (BRIT)* couette *f*

continual [kən'tɪnjuəl] *adj* continuel(le); **continually** *adv* continuellement, sans cesse

continue [kən'tɪnju:] *vi* continuer ▷ *vt* continuer; *(start again)* reprendre

continuity [kɔntɪ'nju:ɪtɪ] *n* continuité *f*; *(TV etc)* enchaînement *m*

continuous [kən'tɪnjuəs] *adj* continu(e), permanent(e); *(Ling)* progressif(-ive); **continuous assessment** *(BRIT)* *n* contrôle continu; **continuously** *adv (repeatedly)* continuellement; *(uninterruptedly)* sans interruption

contour ['kɔntuə'] *n* contour *m*, profil *m*; *(also:* **~ line)** courbe *f* de niveau

contraception [kɔntrə'sɛpʃən] *n* contraception *f*

contraceptive [kɔntrə'sɛptɪv] *adj* contraceptif(-ive), anticonceptionnel(le) ▷ *n* contraceptif *m*

contract *n* ['kɔntrækt] contrat *m* ▷ *vb* [kən'trækt] ▷ *vi (become smaller)* se contracter, se resserrer ▷ *vt* contracter; *(Comm)*: **to ~ to do sth** s'engager *(par contrat)* à faire qch; **contractor** *n* entrepreneur *m*

contradict [kɔntrə'dɪkt] *vt* contredire; **contradiction** [kɔntrə'dɪkʃən] *n* contradiction *f*

contrary[1] ['kɔntrərɪ] *adj* contraire, opposé(e) ▷ *n* contraire *m*; **on the ~** au contraire; **unless you hear to the ~** sauf avis contraire

contrary[2] [kən'trɛərɪ] *adj (perverse)* contrariant(e), entêté(e)

contrast *n* ['kɔntrɑːst] contraste *m* ▷ *vt* [kən'trɑːst] mettre en contraste, contraster; **in ~ to** *or* **with** contrairement à, par opposition à

contribute [kən'trɪbjuːt] *vi* contribuer ▷ *vt*: **to ~ £10/an article to** donner 10 livres/un article à; **to ~ to** *(gen)* contribuer à; *(newspaper)* collaborer à; *(discussion)* prendre part à; **contribution** [kɔntrɪ'bjuːʃən] *n* contribution *f*; *(BRIT: for social security)* cotisation *f*; *(to publication)* article *m*; **contributor** *n (to newspaper)* collaborateur(-trice); *(of money, goods)* donateur(-trice)

control [kən'trəul] *vt (process, machinery)* commander; *(temper)* maîtriser; *(disease)* enrayer ▷ *n* maîtrise *f*; *(power)* autorité *f*; **controls** *npl (of machine etc)* commandes *fpl*; *(on radio)* boutons *mpl* de réglage; **to be in ~ of** être maître de, maîtriser; *(in charge of)* être responsable de; **everything is under ~** j'ai *(or* il a *etc)* la situation en main; **the car went out of ~** j'ai *(or* il a *etc)* perdu le contrôle du véhicule; **control tower** *n (Aviat)* tour *f* de contrôle

controversial [kɔntrə'vəːʃl] *adj* discutable, controversé(e)

controversy ['kɔntrəvəːsɪ] *n* controverse *f*, polémique *f*

convenience [kən'viːnɪəns] *n* commodité *f*; **at your ~** quand *or* comme cela vous convient; **all modern ~s**, **all mod cons** *(BRIT)* avec tout le confort moderne, tout confort

convenient [kən'viːnɪənt] *adj* commode

convent ['kɔnvənt] *n* couvent *m*

convention [kən'vɛnʃən] *n* convention *f*; *(custom)* usage *m*; **conventional** *adj* conventionnel(le)

conversation [kɔnvə'seɪʃən] *n* conversation *f*

conversely [kɔn'vəːslɪ] *adv* inversement, réciproquement

conversion [kən'vəːʃən] *n* conversion *f*; *(BRIT: of house)* transformation *f*, aménagement *m*; *(Rugby)* transformation *f*

convert *vt* [kən'vəːt] *(Rel, Comm)* convertir; *(alter)* transformer; *(house)* aménager ▷ *n* ['kɔnvəːt] converti(e); **convertible** *adj* convertible ▷ *n (voiture f)* décapotable *f*

convey [kən'veɪ] *vt* transporter; *(thanks)* transmettre; *(idea)* communiquer; **conveyor belt** *n* convoyeur *m* tapis roulant

convict *vt* [kən'vɪkt] déclarer *(or* reconnaître*)* coupable ▷ *n* ['kɔnvɪkt] forçat *m*, convict *m*; **conviction** [kən'vɪkʃən] *n (Law)* condamnation *f*; *(belief)* conviction *f*

convince [kən'vɪns] *vt* convaincre, persuader; **convinced** *adj*: **convinced of/that** convaincu(e) de/que; **convincing** *adj* persuasif(-ive), convaincant(e)

convoy ['kɔnvɔɪ] *n* convoi *m*

cook [kuk] *vt (faire)* cuire ▷ *vi* cuire; *(person)*

faire la cuisine ▷ n cuisinier(-ière); **cookbook** n livre m de cuisine; **cooker** n cuisinière f; **cookery** n cuisine f; **cookery book** n (BRIT) = **cookbook**; **cookie** n (US) biscuit m, petit gâteau sec; **cooking** n cuisine f

cool [ku:l] adj frais (fraîche); (not afraid) calme; (unfriendly) froid(e); (inf: trendy) cool inv (inf); (: great) super inv (inf) ▷ vt, vi rafraîchir, refroidir; **cool down** vi refroidir; (fig: person, situation) se calmer; **cool off** vi (become calmer) se calmer; (lose enthusiasm) perdre son enthousiasme

cop [kɔp] n (inf) flic m

cope [kəup] vi s'en sortir, tenir le coup; **to ~ with** (problem) faire face à

copper ['kɔpə'] n cuivre m; (BRIT: inf: policeman) flic m

copy ['kɔpɪ] n copie f; (book etc) exemplaire m ▷ vt copier; (imitate) imiter; **copyright** n droit m d'auteur, copyright m

coral ['kɔrəl] n corail m

cord [kɔ:d] n corde f; (fabric) velours côtelé; (Elec) cordon m (d'alimentation), fil m (électrique); **cords** npl (trousers) pantalon m de velours côtelé; **cordless** adj sans fil

corduroy ['kɔ:dərɔɪ] n velours côtelé

core [kɔ:'] n (of fruit) trognon m, cœur m; (fig: of problem etc) cœur m ▷ vt enlever le trognon or le cœur de

coriander [kɔrɪ'ændə'] n coriandre f

cork [kɔ:k] n (material) liège m; (of bottle) bouchon m; **corkscrew** n tire-bouchon m

corn [kɔ:n] n (BRIT: wheat) blé m; (US: maize) maïs m; (on foot) cor m; **~ on the cob** (Culin) épi m de maïs au naturel

corned beef ['kɔ:nd-] n corned-beef m

corner ['kɔ:nə'] n coin m; (in road) tournant m, virage m; (Football) corner m ▷ vt (trap: prey) acculer; (fig) coincer; (Comm: market) accaparer ▷ vi prendre un virage; **corner shop** n (BRIT) magasin m du coin

cornflakes ['kɔ:nfleɪks] npl cornflakes mpl

cornflour ['kɔ:nflauə'] n (BRIT) farine f de maïs, maïzena® f

cornstarch ['kɔ:nstɑ:tʃ] n (US) farine f de maïs, maïzena® f

Cornwall ['kɔ:nwəl] n Cornouailles f

coronary ['kɔrənərɪ] n: **~ (thrombosis)** infarctus m (du myocarde), thrombose f coronaire

coronation [kɔrə'neɪʃən] n couronnement m

coroner ['kɔrənə'] n coroner m, officier de police judiciaire chargé de déterminer les causes d'un décès

corporal ['kɔ:pərl] n caporal m, brigadier m ▷ adj: **~ punishment** châtiment corporel

corporate ['kɔ:pərɪt] adj (action, ownership) en commun; (Comm) de la société

corporation [kɔ:pə'reɪʃən] n (of town) municipalité f, conseil municipal; (Comm) société f

corps [kɔ:', pl kɔ:z] n corps m; **the diplomatic ~** le corps diplomatique; **the press ~** la presse

corpse [kɔ:ps] n cadavre m

correct [kə'rɛkt] adj (accurate) correct(e), exact(e); (proper) correct, convenable ▷ vt corriger; **correction** [kə'rɛkʃən] n correction f

correspond [kɔrɪs'pɔnd] vi correspondre; **to ~ to sth** (be equivalent to) correspondre à qch; **correspondence** n correspondance f; **correspondent** n correspondant(e); **corresponding** adj correspondant(e)

corridor ['kɔrɪdɔ:'] n couloir m, corridor m

corrode [kə'rəud] vt corroder, ronger ▷ vi se corroder

corrupt [kə'rʌpt] adj corrompu(e); (Comput) altéré(e) ▷ vt corrompre; (Comput) altérer; **corruption** n corruption f; (Comput) altération f (de données)

Corsica ['kɔ:sɪkə] n Corse f

cosmetic [kɔz'mɛtɪk] n produit m de beauté, cosmétique m ▷ adj (fig: reforms) symbolique, superficiel(le); **cosmetic surgery** n chirurgie f esthétique

cosmopolitan [kɔzmə'pɔlɪtn] adj cosmopolite

cost [kɔst] n coût m ▷ vb (pt, pp ~) ▷ vi coûter ▷ vt établir or calculer le prix de revient de; **costs** npl (Comm) frais mpl; (Law) dépens mpl; **how much does it ~?** combien ça coûte?; **to ~ sb time/effort** demander du temps/un effort à qn; **it ~ him his life/job** ça lui a coûté la vie/son emploi; **at all ~s** coûte que coûte, à tout prix

co-star ['kəustɑ:'] n partenaire m/f

costly ['kɔstlɪ] adj coûteux(-euse)

cost of living n coût m de la vie

costume ['kɔstju:m] n costume m; (BRIT: also: **swimming ~**) maillot m (de bain)

cosy (US **cozy**) ['kəuzɪ] adj (room, bed) douillet(te); **to be ~** (person) être bien (au chaud)

cot [kɔt] n (BRIT: child's) lit m d'enfant, petit lit; (US: campbed) lit de camp

cottage ['kɔtɪdʒ] n petite maison (à la campagne), cottage m; **cottage cheese** n fromage blanc (maigre)

cotton ['kɔtn] n coton m; (thread) fil m (de coton); **cotton on** vi (inf): **to ~ on (to sth)** piger (qch); **cotton bud** (BRIT) n coton-tige ® m; **cotton candy** (US) n barbe f à papa; **cotton wool** n (BRIT) ouate f, coton m hydrophile

couch [kautʃ] n canapé m; divan m

cough [kɔf] vi tousser ▷ n toux f; **I've got a ~** j'ai la toux; **cough mixture, cough syrup** n sirop m pour la toux

could [kud] pt of **can²**; **couldn't** = **could not**

council ['kaunsl] n conseil m; **city** or **town ~** conseil municipal; **council**

estate n (BRIT) (quartier m or zone f de) logements loués à/par la municipalité; **council house** n (BRIT) maison f (à loyer modéré) louée par la municipalité; **councillor** (US **councilor**) n conseiller(-ère); **council tax** n (BRIT) impôts locaux

counsel [ˈkaunsl] n conseil m; (lawyer) avocat(e) ▷ vt: **to ~ (sb to do sth)** conseiller (à qn de faire qch); **counselling** (US **counseling**) n (Psych) aide psychosociale; **counsellor** (US **counselor**) n conseiller(-ère); (US Law) avocat m

count [kaunt] vt, vi compter ▷ n compte m; (nobleman) comte m; **count in** vt (inf): **to ~ sb in on sth** inclure qn dans qch; **count on** vt fus compter sur; **countdown** n compte m à rebours

counter [ˈkauntər] n comptoir m; (in post office, bank) guichet m; (in game) jeton m ▷ vt aller à l'encontre de, opposer ▷ adv: **~ to** à l'encontre de; contrairement à; **counterclockwise** (US) adv en sens inverse des aiguilles d'une montre

counterfeit [ˈkauntəfɪt] n faux m, contrefaçon f ▷ vt contrefaire ▷ adj faux (fausse)

counterpart [ˈkauntəpɑːt] n (of person) homologue m/f

countess [ˈkauntɪs] n comtesse f

countless [ˈkauntlɪs] adj innombrable

country [ˈkʌntrɪ] n pays m; (native land) patrie f; (as opposed to town) campagne f; (region) région f, pays; **country and western (music)** n musique f country; **country house** n manoir m, (petit) château; **countryside** n campagne f

county [ˈkauntɪ] n comté m

coup [kuː, pl kuːz] n (achievement) beau coup; (also: **~ d'état**) coup d'État

couple [ˈkʌpl] n couple m; **a ~ of** (two) deux; (a few) deux ou trois

coupon [ˈkuːpɔn] n (voucher) bon m de réduction; (detachable form) coupon m détachable, coupon-réponse m

courage [ˈkʌrɪdʒ] n courage m; **courageous** [kəˈreɪdʒəs] adj courageux(-euse)

courgette [kuəˈʒɛt] n (BRIT) courgette f

courier [ˈkurɪər] n messager m, courrier m; (for tourists) accompagnateur(-trice)

course [kɔːs] n cours m; (of ship) route f; (for golf) terrain m; (part of meal) plat m; **of ~** adv bien sûr; **(no,) of ~ not!** bien sûr que non!, évidemment que non!; **~ of treatment** (Med) traitement m

court [kɔːt] n cour f; (Law) cour, tribunal m; (Tennis) court m ▷ vt (woman) courtiser, faire la cour à; **to take to ~** actionner or poursuivre en justice

courtesy [ˈkəːtəsɪ] n courtoisie f, politesse f; **(by) ~ of** avec l'aimable autorisation de;

courtesy bus, courtesy coach n navette gratuite

court: **court-house** [ˈkɔːthaus] n (US) palais m de justice; **courtroom** [ˈkɔːtrum] n salle f de tribunal; **courtyard** [ˈkɔːtjɑːd] n cour f

cousin [ˈkʌzn] n cousin(e); **first ~** cousin(e) germain(e)

cover [ˈkʌvər] vt couvrir; (Press: report on) faire un reportage sur; (feelings, mistake) cacher; (include) englober; (discuss) traiter ▷ n (of book, Comm) couverture f; (of pan) couvercle m; (over furniture) housse f; (shelter) abri m; **covers** npl (on bed) couvertures; **to take ~** se mettre à l'abri; **under ~** à l'abri; **under ~ of darkness** à la faveur de la nuit; **under separate ~** (Comm) sous pli séparé; **cover up** vi: **to ~ up for sb** (fig) couvrir qn; **coverage** n (in media) reportage m; **cover charge** n couvert m (supplément à payer); **cover-up** n tentative f pour étouffer une affaire

cow [kau] n vache f ▷ vt effrayer, intimider

coward [ˈkauəd] n lâche m/f; **cowardly** adj lâche

cowboy [ˈkaubɔɪ] n cow-boy m

cozy [ˈkəuzɪ] adj (US) = **cosy**

crab [kræb] n crabe m

crack [kræk] n (split) fente f, fissure f; (in cup, bone) fêlure f; (in wall) lézarde f; (noise) craquement m, coup (sec); (Drugs) crack m ▷ vt fendre, fissurer; fêler; lézarder; (whip) faire claquer; (nut) casser; (problem) résoudre; (code) déchiffrer ▷ cpd (athlete) de première classe, d'élite; **crack down on** vt fus (crime) sévir contre, réprimer; **cracked** adj (cup, bone) fêlé(e); (broken) cassé(e); (wall) lézardé(e); (surface) craquelé(e); (inf) toqué(e), timbré(e); **cracker** n (also: **Christmas cracker**) pétard m; (biscuit) biscuit (salé), craquelin m

crackle [ˈkrækl] vi crépiter, grésiller

cradle [ˈkreɪdl] n berceau m

craft [krɑːft] n métier (artisanal); (cunning) ruse f, astuce f; (boat: pl inv) embarcation f, barque f; (plane: pl inv) appareil m; **craftsman** (irreg) n artisan m ouvrier (qualifié); **craftsmanship** n métier m, habileté f

cram [kræm] vt (fill): **to ~ sth with** bourrer qch de; (put): **to ~ sth into** fourrer qch dans ▷ vi (for exams) bachoter

cramp [kræmp] n crampe f; **I've got ~ in my leg** j'ai une crampe à la jambe; **cramped** adj à l'étroit, très serré(e)

cranberry [ˈkrænbərɪ] n canneberge f

crane [kreɪn] n grue f

crap [kræp] n (inf!: nonsense) conneries fpl (!); (!: excrement) merde f (!)

crash [kræʃ] n fracas m; (of car, plane) collision f; (of business) faillite f ▷ vt (plane) écraser ▷ vi (plane) s'écraser; (two cars) se percuter, s'emboutir; (business) s'effondrer;

to ~ into se jeter or se fracasser contre; **crash course** n cours intensif; **crash helmet** n casque (protecteur)

crate [kreɪt] n cageot m; (for bottles) caisse f

crave [kreɪv] vt, vi: **to ~ (for)** avoir une envie irrésistible de

crawl [krɔːl] vi ramper; (vehicle) avancer au pas ▷ n (Swimming) crawl m

crayfish ['kreɪfɪʃ] n (pl inv: freshwater) écrevisse f; (saltwater) langoustine f

crayon ['kreɪən] n crayon m (de couleur)

craze [kreɪz] n engouement m

crazy ['kreɪzɪ] adj fou (folle); **to be ~ about sb/sth** (inf) être fou de qn/qch

creak [kriːk] vi (hinge) grincer; (floor, shoes) craquer

cream [kriːm] n crème f ▷ adj (colour) crème inv; **cream cheese** n fromage m à la crème, fromage blanc; **creamy** adj crémeux(-euse)

crease [kriːs] n pli m ▷ vt froisser, chiffonner ▷ vi se froisser, se chiffonner

create [kriːˈeɪt] vt créer; **creation** [kriːˈeɪʃən] n création f; **creative** adj créatif(-ive); **creator** n créateur(-trice)

creature ['kriːtʃəʳ] n créature f

crèche [krɛʃ] n garderie f, crèche f

credentials [krɪˈdɛnʃlz] npl (references) références fpl; (identity papers) pièce f d'identité

credibility [krɛdɪˈbɪlɪtɪ] n crédibilité f

credible ['krɛdɪbl] adj digne de foi, crédible

credit ['krɛdɪt] n crédit m; (recognition) honneur m; (Scol) unité f de valeur ▷ vt (Comm) créditer; (believe: also: **give ~ to**) ajouter foi à, croire; **credits** npl (Cine) générique m; **to be in ~** (person, bank account) être créditeur(-trice); **to ~ sb with** (fig) prêter or attribuer à qn; **credit card** n carte f de crédit; **do you take credit cards?** acceptez-vous les cartes de crédit?

creek [kriːk] n (inlet) crique f, anse f; (us: stream) ruisseau m, petit cours d'eau

creep (pt, pp **crept**) [kriːp, krɛpt] vi ramper

cremate [krɪˈmeɪt] vt incinérer

crematorium (pl **crematoria**) [krɛməˈtɔːrɪəm, -ˈtɔːrɪə] n four m crématoire

crept [krɛpt] pt, pp of **creep**

crescent ['krɛsnt] n croissant m; (street) rue f (en arc de cercle)

cress [krɛs] n cresson m

crest [krɛst] n crête f; (of coat of arms) timbre m

crew [kruː] n équipage m; (Cine) équipe f (de tournage); **crew-neck** n col ras

crib [krɪb] n lit m d'enfant; (for baby) berceau m ▷ vt (inf) copier

cricket ['krɪkɪt] n (insect) grillon m, cri-cri m inv; (game) cricket m; **cricketer** n joueur m de cricket

crime [kraɪm] n crime m; **criminal** ['krɪmɪnl] adj, n criminel(le)

crimson ['krɪmzn] adj cramoisi(e)

cringe [krɪndʒ] vi avoir un mouvement de recul

cripple ['krɪpl] n boiteux(-euse), infirme m/f ▷ vt (person) estropier, paralyser; (ship, plane) immobiliser; (production, exports) paralyser

crisis (pl **crises**) ['kraɪsɪs, -siːz] n crise f

crisp [krɪsp] adj croquant(e); (weather) vif (vive); (manner etc) brusque; **crisps** (BRIT) npl (pommes fpl) chips fpl; **crispy** adj croustillant(e)

criterion (pl **criteria**) [kraɪˈtɪərɪən, -ˈtɪərɪə] n critère m

critic ['krɪtɪk] n critique m/f; **critical** adj critique; **criticism** ['krɪtɪsɪzəm] n critique f; **criticize** ['krɪtɪsaɪz] vt critiquer

Croat ['krəuæt] adj, n = **Croatian**

Croatia [krəuˈeɪʃə] n Croatie f; **Croatian** adj croate ▷ n Croate m/f; (Ling) croate m

crockery ['krɔkərɪ] n vaisselle f

crocodile ['krɔkədaɪl] n crocodile m

crocus ['krəukəs] n crocus m

croissant ['krwasɑ̃] n croissant m

crook [kruk] n escroc m; (of shepherd) houlette f; **crooked** ['krukɪd] adj courbé(e), tordu(e); (action) malhonnête

crop [krɔp] n (produce) culture f; (amount produced) récolte f; (riding crop) cravache f ▷ vt (hair) tondre; **crop up** vi surgir, se présenter, survenir

cross [krɔs] n croix f; (Biol) croisement m ▷ vt (street etc) traverser; (arms, legs, Biol) croiser; (cheque) barrer ▷ adj en colère, fâché(e); **cross off** or **out** vt barrer, rayer; **cross over** vi traverser; **cross-Channel ferry** ['krɔsˈtʃænl-] n ferry m qui fait la traversée de la Manche; **crosscountry (race)** n cross-(country) m; **crossing** n (sea passage) traversée f; (also: **pedestrian crossing**) passage clouté; **how long does the crossing take?** combien de temps dure la traversée?; **crossing guard** (us) n contractuel qui fait traverser la rue aux enfants; **crossroads** n carrefour m; **crosswalk** n (us) passage clouté; **crossword** n mots mpl croisés

crotch [krɔtʃ] n (of garment) entrejambe m; (Anat) entrecuisse m

crouch [krautʃ] vi s'accroupir; (hide) se tapir; (before springing) se ramasser

crouton ['kruːtɔn] n croûton m

crow [krəu] n (bird) corneille f; (of cock) chant m du coq, cocorico m ▷ vi (cock) chanter

crowd [kraud] n foule f ▷ vt bourrer, remplir ▷ vi affluer, s'attrouper, s'entasser; **crowded** adj bondé(e), plein(e)

crown [kraun] n couronne f; (of head) sommet m de la tête; (of hill) sommet m ▷ vt (also tooth) couronner; **crown jewels** npl joyaux mpl de la Couronne

crucial ['kruːʃl] adj crucial(e), décisif(-ive)

crucifix ['kru:sɪfɪks] n crucifix m
crude [kru:d] adj (materials) brut(e); non raffiné(e); (basic) rudimentaire, sommaire; (vulgar) cru(e), grossier(-ière); **crude (oil)** n (pétrole) brut m
cruel ['kruəl] adj cruel(le); **cruelty** n cruauté f
cruise [kru:z] n croisière f ▷ vi (ship) croiser; (car) rouler; (aircraft) voler
crumb [krʌm] n miette f
crumble ['krʌmbl] vt émietter ▷ vi (plaster etc) s'effriter; (land, earth) s'ébouler; (building) s'écrouler, crouler; (fig) s'effondrer
crumpet ['krʌmpɪt] n petite crêpe (épaisse)
crumple ['krʌmpl] vt froisser, friper
crunch [krʌntʃ] vt croquer; (underfoot) faire craquer, écraser; faire crisser ▷ n (fig) instant m or moment m critique, moment de vérité; **crunchy** adj croquant(e), croustillant(e)
crush [krʌʃ] n (crowd) foule f, cohue f; (love): **to have a ~ on sb** avoir le béguin pour qn; (drink): **lemon ~** citron pressé ▷ vt écraser; (crumple) froisser; (grind, break up: garlic, ice) piler; (: grapes) presser; (hopes) anéantir
crust [krʌst] n croûte f; **crusty** adj (bread) croustillant(e); (inf: person) revêche, bourru(e)
crutch [krʌtʃ] n béquille f; (also: **crotch**) entrejambe m
cry [kraɪ] vi pleurer; (shout: also: ~ **out**) crier ▷ n cri m; **cry out** vi (call out, shout) pousser un cri ▷ vt crier
crystal ['krɪstl] n cristal m
cub [kʌb] n petit m (d'un animal); (also: ~ **scout**) louveteau m
Cuba ['kju:bə] n Cuba m
cube [kju:b] n cube m ▷ vt (Math) élever au cube
cubicle ['kju:bɪkl] n (in hospital) box m; (at pool) cabine f
cuckoo ['kuku:] n coucou m
cucumber ['kju:kʌmbəʳ] n concombre m
cuddle ['kʌdl] vt câliner, caresser ▷ vi se blottir l'un contre l'autre
cue [kju:] n queue f de billard; (Theat etc) signal m
cuff [kʌf] n (BRIT: of shirt, coat etc) poignet m, manchette f; (US: on trousers) revers m; (blow) gifle f; **off the ~** adv à l'improviste; **cufflinks** n boutons m de manchette
cuisine [kwɪ'zi:n] n cuisine f
cul-de-sac ['kʌldəsæk] n cul-de-sac m, impasse f
cull [kʌl] vt sélectionner ▷ n (of animals) abattage sélectif
culminate ['kʌlmɪneɪt] vi: **to ~ in** finir or se terminer par; (lead to) mener à
culprit ['kʌlprɪt] n coupable m/f
cult [kʌlt] n culte m
cultivate ['kʌltɪveɪt] vt cultiver
cultural ['kʌltʃərəl] adj culturel(le)

culture ['kʌltʃəʳ] n culture f
cumin ['kʌmɪn] n (spice) cumin m
cunning ['kʌnɪŋ] n ruse f, astuce f ▷ adj rusé(e), malin(-igne); (clever: device, idea) astucieux(-euse)
cup [kʌp] n tasse f; (prize, event) coupe f; (of bra) bonnet m
cupboard ['kʌbəd] n placard m
cup final n (BRIT Football) finale f de la coupe
curator [kjuə'reɪtəʳ] n conservateur m (d'un musée etc)
curb [kə:b] vt refréner, mettre un frein à ▷ n (fig) frein m; (US) bord m du trottoir
curdle ['kə:dl] vi (se) cailler
cure [kjuəʳ] vt guérir; (Culin: salt) saler; (: smoke) fumer; (: dry) sécher ▷ n remède m
curfew ['kə:fju:] n couvre-feu m
curiosity [kjuərɪ'ɔsɪtɪ] n curiosité f
curious ['kjuərɪəs] adj curieux(-euse); **I'm ~ about him** il m'intrigue
curl [kə:l] n boucle f (de cheveux) ▷ vt, vi boucler; (tightly) friser; **curl up** vi s'enrouler; (person) se pelotonner; **curler** n bigoudi m, rouleau m; **curly** adj bouclé(e); (tightly curled) frisé(e)
currant ['kʌrnt] n raisin m de Corinthe, raisin sec; (fruit) groseille f
currency ['kʌrnsɪ] n monnaie f; **to gain ~** (fig) s'accréditer
current ['kʌrnt] n courant m ▷ adj (common) courant(e); (tendency, price, event) actuel(le); **current account** n (BRIT) compte courant; **current affairs** npl (questions fpl d')actualité f; **currently** adv actuellement
curriculum (pl ~**s** or **curricula**) [kə'rɪkjuləm, -lə] n programme m d'études; **curriculum vitae** [-'vi:taɪ] n curriculum vitae (CV) m
curry ['kʌrɪ] n curry m ▷ vt: **to ~ favour with** chercher à gagner la faveur or à s'attirer les bonnes grâces de; **curry powder** n poudre f de curry
curse [kə:s] vi jurer, blasphémer ▷ vt maudire ▷ n (spell) malédiction f; (problem, scourge) fléau m; (swearword) juron m
cursor ['kə:səʳ] n (Comput) curseur m
curt [kə:t] adj brusque, sec(-sèche)
curtain ['kə:tn] n rideau m
curve [kə:v] n courbe f; (in the road) tournant m, virage m ▷ vi se courber; (road) faire une courbe; **curved** adj courbe
cushion ['kuʃən] n coussin m ▷ vt (fall, shock) amortir
custard ['kʌstəd] n (for pouring) crème anglaise
custody ['kʌstədɪ] n (of child) garde f; (for offenders): **to take sb into ~** placer qn en détention préventive
custom ['kʌstəm] n coutume f, usage m; (Comm) clientèle f

customer ['kʌstəmər] n client(e)
customized ['kʌstəmaɪzd] adj
personnalisé(e); (car etc) construit(e) sur
commande
customs ['kʌstəmz] npl douane f; **customs
officer** n douanier m
cut [kʌt] vb (pt, pp ~) ▷ vt couper; (meat)
découper; (reduce) réduire ▷ vi couper ▷ n
(gen) coupure f; (of clothes) coupe f; (in salary
etc) réduction f; (of meat) morceau m; **to ~ a
tooth** percer une dent; **to ~ one's finger** se
couper le doigt; **to get one's hair ~** se faire
couper les cheveux; **I've ~ myself** je me suis
coupé; **cut back** vt (plants) tailler; (production,
expenditure) réduire; **cut down** vt (tree)
abattre; (reduce) réduire; **cut off** vt couper;
(fig) isoler; **cut out** vt (picture etc) découper;
(remove) supprimer; **cut up** vt découper;
cutback n réduction f
cute [kjuːt] adj mignon(ne), adorable
cutlery ['kʌtlərɪ] n couverts mpl
cutlet ['kʌtlɪt] n côtelette f
cut-price ['kʌt'praɪs] (us **cut-rate** ['kʌt'reɪt])
adj au rabais, à prix réduit
cutting ['kʌtɪŋ] adj (fig) cinglant(e) ▷ n (BRIT:
from newspaper) coupure f (de journal); (from
plant) bouture f
CV n abbr = **curriculum vitae**
cwt abbr = **hundredweight(s)**
cyberspace ['saɪbəspeɪs] n cyberespace m
cycle ['saɪkl] n cycle m; (bicycle) bicyclette f,
vélo m ▷ vi faire de la bicyclette; **cycle hire** n
location f de vélos; **cycle lane, cycle path** n
piste f cyclable; **cycling** n cyclisme m; **cyclist**
n cycliste m/f
cyclone ['saɪkləun] n cyclone m
cylinder ['sɪlɪndə'] n cylindre m
cymbals ['sɪmblz] npl cymbales fpl
cynical ['sɪnɪkl] adj cynique
Cypriot ['sɪprɪət] adj cypriote, chypriote ▷ n
Cypriote m/f, Chypriote m/f
Cyprus ['saɪprəs] n Chypre f
cyst [sɪst] n kyste m; **cystitis** [sɪs'taɪtɪs] n
cystite f
czar [zɑː'] n tsar m
Czech [tʃɛk] adj tchèque ▷ n Tchèque m/f;
(Ling) tchèque m; **Czech Republic** n: **the
Czech Republic** la République tchèque

D [diː] n (Mus): **D** ré m
dab [dæb] vt (eyes, wound) tamponner; (paint,
cream) appliquer (par petites touches or
rapidement)
dad, daddy [dæd, 'dædɪ] n papa m
daffodil ['dæfədɪl] n jonquille f
daft [dɑːft] adj (inf) idiot(e), stupide
dagger ['dægə'] n poignard m
daily ['deɪlɪ] adj quotidien(ne), journalier(-ière)
▷ adv tous les jours
dairy ['dɛərɪ] n (shop) crémerie f, laiterie f;
(on farm) laiterie; **dairy produce** n produits
laitiers
daisy ['deɪzɪ] n pâquerette f
dam [dæm] n (wall) barrage m; (water)
réservoir m, lac m de retenue ▷ vt endiguer
damage ['dæmɪdʒ] n dégâts mpl, dommages
mpl; (fig) tort m ▷ vt endommager, abîmer;
(fig) faire du tort à; **damages** npl (Law)
dommages-intérêts mpl
damn [dæm] vt condamner; (curse) maudire
▷ n (inf): **I don't give a ~** je m'en fous ▷ adj
(inf: also: **~ed**): **this ~ ...** ce sacré or foutu ...; **~
(it)!** zut!
damp [dæmp] adj humide ▷ n humidité f ▷ vt
(also: **~en**: cloth, rag) humecter; (: enthusiasm
etc) refroidir
dance [dɑːns] n danse f; (ball) bal m ▷ vi
danser; **dance floor** n piste f de danse;
dancer n danseur(-euse); **dancing** n danse f

dandelion ['dændɪlaɪən] n pissenlit m

dandruff ['dændrəf] n pellicules fpl

D & T n abbr (BRIT: Scol) = **design and technology**

Dane [deɪn] n Danois(e)

danger ['deɪndʒəʳ] n danger m; ~! (on sign) danger!; **in ~** en danger; **he was in ~ of falling** il risquait de tomber; **dangerous** adj dangereux(-euse)

dangle ['dæŋgl] vt balancer ▷ vi pendre, se balancer

Danish ['deɪnɪʃ] adj danois(e) ▷ n (Ling) danois m

dare [dɛəʳ] vt: **to ~ sb to do** défier qn or mettre qn au défi de faire ▷ vi: **to ~ (to) do sth** oser faire qch; **I ~ say he'll turn up** il est probable qu'il viendra; **daring** adj hardi(e), audacieux(-euse) ▷ n audace f, hardiesse f

dark [dɑːk] adj (night, room) obscur(e), sombre; (colour, complexion) foncé(e), sombre ▷ n: **in the ~** dans le noir; **to be in the ~ about** (fig) ignorer tout de; **after ~** après la tombée de la nuit; **darken** vt obscurcir, assombrir ▷ vi s'obscurcir, s'assombrir; **darkness** n obscurité f; **darkroom** n chambre noire

darling ['dɑːlɪŋ] adj, n chéri(e)

dart [dɑːt] n fléchette f; (in sewing) pince f ▷ vi: **to ~ towards** se précipiter or s'élancer vers; **dartboard** n cible f (de jeu de fléchettes); **darts** n jeu m de fléchettes

dash [dæʃ] n (sign) tiret m; (small quantity) goutte f, larme f ▷ vt (throw) jeter or lancer violemment; (hopes) anéantir ▷ vi: **to ~ towards** se précipiter or se ruer vers

dashboard ['dæʃbɔːd] n (Aut) tableau m de bord

data ['deɪtə] npl données fpl; **database** n base f de données; **data processing** n traitement m (électronique) de l'information

date [deɪt] n date f; (with sb) rendez-vous m; (fruit) datte f ▷ vt dater; (person) sortir avec; ~ **of birth** date de naissance; **to ~** adv à ce jour; **out of ~** périmé(e); **up to ~** à la page, mis(e) à jour, moderne; **dated** adj démodé(e)

daughter ['dɔːtəʳ] n fille f; **daughter-in-law** n belle-fille f, bru f

daunting ['dɔːntɪŋ] adj décourageant(e), intimidant(e)

dawn [dɔːn] n aube f, aurore f ▷ vi (day) se lever, poindre; **it ~ed on him that ...** il lui vint à l'esprit que ...

day [deɪ] n jour m; (as duration) journée f; (period of time, age) époque f, temps m; **the ~ before** la veille, le jour précédent; **the ~ after, the following ~** le lendemain, le jour suivant; **the ~ before yesterday** avant-hier; **the ~ after tomorrow** après-demain; **by ~** de jour; **day-care centre** ['deɪkɛə-] n (for elderly etc) centre m d'accueil de jour; (for children) garderie f;

daydream vi rêver (tout éveillé); **daylight** n (lumière f du) jour m; **day return** n (BRIT) billet m d'aller-retour (valable pour la journée); **daytime** n jour m, journée f; **day-to-day** adj (routine, expenses) journalier(-ière); **day trip** n excursion f (d'une journée)

dazed [deɪzd] adj abruti(e)

dazzle ['dæzl] vt éblouir, aveugler; **dazzling** adj (light) aveuglant(e), éblouissant(e); (fig) éblouissant(e)

DC abbr (Elec) = **direct current**

dead [dɛd] adj mort(e); (numb) engourdi(e), insensible; (battery) à plat ▷ adv (completely) absolument, complètement; (exactly) juste; **he was shot ~** il a été tué d'un coup de revolver; ~ **tired** éreinté(e), complètement fourbu(e); **to stop ~** s'arrêter pile or net; **the line is ~** (Tel) la ligne est coupée; **dead end** n impasse f; **deadline** n date f or heure f limite; **deadly** adj mortel(le); (weapon) meurtrier(-ière); **Dead Sea** n: **the Dead Sea** la mer Morte

deaf [dɛf] adj sourd(e); **deafen** vt rendre sourd(e); **deafening** adj assourdissant(e)

deal [diːl] n affaire f, marché m ▷ vt (pt, pp ~**t**) (blow) porter; (cards) donner, distribuer; **a great ~ of** beaucoup de; **deal with** vt fus (handle) s'occuper or se charger de; (be about: book etc) traiter de; **dealer** n (Comm) marchand m; (Cards) donneur m; **dealings** npl (in goods, shares) opérations fpl, transactions fpl; (relations) relations fpl, rapports mpl

dealt [dɛlt] pt, pp of **deal**

dean [diːn] n (Rel, BRIT Scol) doyen m; (US Scol) conseiller principal (conseillère principale) d'éducation

dear [dɪəʳ] adj cher (chère); (expensive) cher, coûteux(-euse) ▷ n: **my ~** mon cher (ma chère) ▷ excl: ~ **me!** mon Dieu!; **D~ Sir/Madam** (in letter) Monsieur/Madame; **D~ Mr/Mrs X** Cher Monsieur X (Chère Madame X); **dearly** adv (love) tendrement; (pay) cher

death [dɛθ] n mort f; (Admin) décès m; **death penalty** n peine f de mort; **death sentence** n condamnation f à mort

debate [dɪ'beɪt] n discussion f, débat m ▷ vt discuter, débattre

debit ['dɛbɪt] n débit m ▷ vt: **to ~ a sum to sb** or **to sb's account** porter une somme au débit de qn, débiter qn d'une somme; **debit card** n carte f de paiement

debris ['dɛbriː] n débris mpl, décombres mpl

debt [dɛt] n dette f; **to be in ~** avoir des dettes, être endetté(e)

debut ['deɪbjuː] n début(s) m(pl)

Dec. abbr (= December) déc

decade ['dɛkeɪd] n décennie f, décade f

decaffeinated [dɪ'kæfɪneɪtɪd] adj décaféiné(e)

decay [dɪ'keɪ] n (of building) délabrement m;

(also: **tooth ~**) carie f (dentaire) ▷ vi (rot) se décomposer, pourrir; (: teeth) se carier

deceased [dɪ'siːst] n: **the ~** le (la) défunt(e)

deceit [dɪ'siːt] n tromperie f, supercherie f; **deceive** [dɪ'siːv] vt tromper

December [dɪ'sɛmbəʳ] n décembre m

decency [ˈdiːsənsɪ] n décence f

decent [ˈdiːsənt] adj (proper) décent(e), convenable

deception [dɪ'sɛpʃən] n tromperie f

deceptive [dɪ'sɛptɪv] adj trompeur(-euse)

decide [dɪ'saɪd] vt (subj: person) décider; (question, argument) trancher, régler ▷ vi décider, décider; **to ~ to do/that** décider de faire/que; **to ~ on** décider, se décider pour

decimal [ˈdɛsɪməl] adj décimal(e) ▷ n décimale f

decision [dɪ'sɪʒən] n décision f

decisive [dɪ'saɪsɪv] adj décisif(-ive); (manner, person) décidé(e), catégorique

deck [dɛk] n (Naut) pont m; (of cards) jeu m; (record deck) platine f; (of bus): **top ~** impériale f; **deckchair** n chaise longue

declaration [dɛklə'reɪʃən] n déclaration f

declare [dɪ'klɛəʳ] vt déclarer

decline [dɪ'klaɪn] n (decay) déclin m; (lessening) baisse f ▷ vt refuser, décliner ▷ vi décliner; (business) baisser

decrease n [ˈdiːkriːs] diminution f ▷ vt, vi [diː'kriːs] diminuer

decree [dɪ'kriː] n (Pol, Rel) décret m; (Law) arrêt m, jugement m

dedicate [ˈdɛdɪkeɪt] vt consacrer; (book etc) dédier; **dedicated** adj (person) dévoué(e); (Comput) spécialisé(e), dédié(e); **dedicated word processor** station f de traitement de texte; **dedication** [dɛdɪ'keɪʃən] n (devotion) dévouement m; (in book) dédicace f

deduce [dɪ'djuːs] vt déduire, conclure

deduct [dɪ'dʌkt] vt: **to ~ sth (from)** déduire qch (de), retrancher qch (de); **deduction** [dɪ'dʌkʃən] n (deducting, deducing) déduction f; (from wage etc) prélèvement m, retenue f

deed [diːd] n action f, acte m; (Law) acte notarié, contrat m

deem [diːm] vt (formal) juger, estimer

deep [diːp] adj profond(e); (voice) grave ▷ adv: **spectators stood 20 ~** il y avait 20 rangs de spectateurs; **4 metres ~** de 4 mètres de profondeur; **how ~ is the water?** l'eau a quelle profondeur?; **deep-fry** vt faire frire (dans une friteuse); **deeply** adv profondément; (regret, interested) vivement

deer [dɪəʳ] n (pl inv): **(red) ~** cerf m; **(fallow) ~**

daim m; **(roe) ~** chevreuil m

default [dɪ'fɔːlt] n (Comput: also: **~ value**) valeur f par défaut; **by ~** (Law) par défaut, par contumace; (Sport) par forfait

defeat [dɪ'fiːt] n défaite f ▷ vt (team, opponents) battre

defect n [ˈdiːfɛkt] défaut m ▷ vi [dɪ'fɛkt]: **to ~ to the enemy/the West** passer à l'ennemi/l'Ouest; **defective** [dɪ'fɛktɪv] adj défectueux(-euse)

defence (us **defense**) [dɪ'fɛns] n défense f

defend [dɪ'fɛnd] vt défendre; **defendant** n défendeur(-deresse); (in criminal case) accusé(e), prévenu(e); **defender** n défenseur m

defense [dɪ'fɛns] (us) = **defence**

defensive [dɪ'fɛnsɪv] adj défensif(-ive) ▷ n: **on the ~** sur la défensive

defer [dɪ'fəːʳ] vt (postpone) différer, ajourner

defiance [dɪ'faɪəns] n défi m; **in ~ of** au mépris de; **defiant** [dɪ'faɪənt] adj provocant(e), de défi; (person) rebelle, intraitable

deficiency [dɪ'fɪʃənsɪ] n (lack) insuffisance f; (: Med) carence f; (flaw) faiblesse f; **deficient** [dɪ'fɪʃənt] adj (inadequate) insuffisant(e); **to be deficient in** manquer de

deficit [ˈdɛfɪsɪt] n déficit m

define [dɪ'faɪn] vt définir

definite [ˈdɛfɪnɪt] adj (fixed) défini(e), (bien) déterminé(e); (clear, obvious) net(te), manifeste; (certain) sûr(e); **he was ~ about it** il a été catégorique; **definitely** adv sans aucun doute

definition [dɛfɪ'nɪʃən] n définition f; (clearness) netteté f

deflate [diː'fleɪt] vt dégonfler

deflect [dɪ'flɛkt] vt détourner, faire dévier

defraud [dɪ'frɔːd] vt: **to ~ sb of sth** escroquer qch à qn

defrost [diː'frɔst] vt (fridge) dégivrer; (frozen food) décongeler

defuse [diː'fjuːz] vt désamorcer

defy [dɪ'faɪ] vt défier; (efforts etc) résister à; **it defies description** cela défie toute description

degree [dɪ'griː] n degré m; (Scol) diplôme m (universitaire); **a (first) ~ in maths** (BRIT) une licence en maths; **by ~s** (gradually) par degrés; **to some ~** jusqu'à un certain point, dans une certaine mesure

dehydrated [diːhaɪ'dreɪtɪd] adj déshydraté(e); (milk, eggs) en poudre

de-icer [ˈdiː'aɪsəʳ] n dégivreur m

delay [dɪ'leɪ] vt retarder; (payment) différer ▷ vi s'attarder ▷ n délai m, retard m; **to be ~ed** être en retard

delegate n [ˈdɛlɪgɪt] délégué(e) ▷ vt [ˈdɛlɪgeɪt] déléguer

delete [dɪ'liːt] vt rayer, supprimer; (Comput)

effacer

deli ['dɛlɪ] n épicerie fine

deliberate adj [dɪ'lɪbərɪt] (intentional) délibéré(e); (slow) mesuré(e) ▷ vi [dɪ'lɪbəreɪt] délibérer, réfléchir; **deliberately** adv (on purpose) exprès, délibérément

delicacy ['dɛlɪkəsɪ] n délicatesse f; (choice food) mets fin or délicat, friandise f

delicate ['dɛlɪkɪt] adj délicat(e)

delicatessen [dɛlɪkə'tɛsn] n épicerie fine

delicious [dɪ'lɪʃəs] adj délicieux(-euse)

delight [dɪ'laɪt] n (grande) joie, grand plaisir ▷ vt enchanter; **she's a ~ to work with** c'est un plaisir de travailler avec elle; **to take ~ in** prendre grand plaisir à; **delighted** adj: **delighted (at or with sth)** ravi(e) (de qch); **to be delighted to do sth/that** être enchanté(e) or ravi(e) de faire qch/que; **delightful** adj (person) adorable; (meal, evening) merveilleux(-euse)

delinquent [dɪ'lɪŋkwənt] adj, n délinquant(e)

deliver [dɪ'lɪvər] vt (mail) distribuer; (goods) livrer; (message) remettre; (speech) prononcer; (Med: baby) mettre au monde; **delivery** n (of mail) distribution f; (of goods) livraison f; (of speaker) élocution f; (Med) accouchement m; **to take delivery of** prendre livraison de

delusion [dɪ'luːʒən] n illusion f

de luxe [də'lʌks] adj de luxe

delve [dɛlv] vi: **to ~ into** fouiller dans

demand [dɪ'mɑːnd] vt réclamer, exiger ▷ n exigence f; (claim) revendication f; (Econ) demande f; **in ~** demandé(e), recherché(e); **on ~** sur demande; **demanding** adj (person) exigeant(e); (work) astreignant(e)

> Be careful not to translate **to demand** by the French word **demander**.

demise [dɪ'maɪz] n décès m

demo ['dɛməu] n abbr (inf) = **demonstration** (protest) manif f; (Comput) démonstration f

democracy [dɪ'mɔkrəsɪ] n démocratie f; **democrat** ['dɛməkræt] n démocrate m/f; **democratic** [dɛmə'krætɪk] adj démocratique

demolish [dɪ'mɔlɪʃ] vt démolir

demolition [dɛmə'lɪʃən] n démolition f

demon ['diːmən] n démon m

demonstrate ['dɛmənstreɪt] vt démontrer, prouver; (show) faire une démonstration de ▷ vi: **to ~ (for/against)** manifester (en faveur de/contre); **demonstration** [dɛmən'streɪʃən] n démonstration f; (Pol etc) manifestation f; **demonstrator** n (Pol etc) manifestant(e)

demote [dɪ'məut] vt rétrograder

den [dɛn] n (of lion) tanière f; (room) repaire m

denial [dɪ'naɪəl] n (of accusation) démenti m; (of rights, guilt, truth) dénégation f

denim ['dɛnɪm] n jean m; **denims** npl (blue-)jeans mpl

Denmark ['dɛnmɑːk] n Danemark m

denomination [dɪnɔmɪ'neɪʃən] n (money) valeur f; (Rel) confession f

denounce [dɪ'nauns] vt dénoncer

dense [dɛns] adj dense; (inf: stupid) obtus(e)

density ['dɛnsɪtɪ] n densité f; **single-/double-~ disk** (Comput) disquette f (à) simple/double densité

dent [dɛnt] n bosse f ▷ vt (also: **make a ~ in**) cabosser

dental ['dɛntl] adj dentaire; **dental floss** [-flɔs] n fil m dentaire; **dental surgery** n cabinet m de dentiste

dentist ['dɛntɪst] n dentiste m/f

dentures ['dɛntʃəz] npl dentier msg

deny [dɪ'naɪ] vt nier; (refuse) refuser

deodorant [diː'əudərənt] n déodorant m

depart [dɪ'pɑːt] vi partir; **to ~ from** (fig: differ from) s'écarter de

department [dɪ'pɑːtmənt] n (Comm) rayon m; (Scol) section f; (Pol) ministère m, département m; **department store** n grand magasin

departure [dɪ'pɑːtʃər] n départ m; (fig): **a new ~** une nouvelle voie; **departure lounge** n salle f de départ

depend [dɪ'pɛnd] vi: **to ~ (up)on** dépendre de; (rely on) compter sur; **it ~s** cela dépend; **~ing on the result ...** selon le résultat ...; **dependant** n personne f à charge; **dependent** adj: **to be dependent (on)** dépendre (de) ▷ n = **dependant**

depict [dɪ'pɪkt] vt (in picture) représenter; (in words) (dé)peindre, décrire

deport [dɪ'pɔːt] vt déporter, expulser

deposit [dɪ'pɔzɪt] n (Chem, Comm, Geo) dépôt m; (of ore, oil) gisement m; (part payment) arrhes fpl, acompte m; (on bottle etc) consigne f; (for hired goods etc) cautionnement m, garantie f ▷ vt déposer; **deposit account** n compte m sur livret

depot ['dɛpəu] n dépôt m; (US: Rail) gare f

depreciate [dɪ'priːʃɪeɪt] vi se déprécier, se dévaloriser

depress [dɪ'prɛs] vt déprimer; (press down) appuyer sur, abaisser; (wages etc) faire baisser; **depressed** adj (person) déprimé(e); (area) en déclin, touché(e) par le sous-emploi; **depressing** adj déprimant(e); **depression** [dɪ'prɛʃən] n dépression f

deprive [dɪ'praɪv] vt: **to ~ sb of** priver qn de; **deprived** adj déshérité(e)

dept. abbr (= department) dép, dépt

depth [dɛpθ] n profondeur f; **to be in the ~s of despair** être au plus profond du désespoir; **to be out of one's ~** (BRIT: swimmer) ne plus avoir pied; (fig) être dépassé(e), nager

deputy ['dɛpjutɪ] n (second in command) adjoint(e); (Pol) député m; (US: also: ~ sheriff) shérif adjoint ▷ adj: **~ head**

(Scol) directeur(-trice) adjoint(e), sous-directeur(-trice)

derail [dɪˈreɪl] vt: **to be ~ed** dérailler

derelict [ˈderɪlɪkt] adj abandonné(e), à l'abandon

derive [dɪˈraɪv] vt: **to ~ sth from** tirer qch de; trouver qch dans ▷ vi: **to ~ from** provenir de, dériver de

descend [dɪˈsɛnd] vt, vi descendre; **to ~ from** descendre de, être issu(e) de; **to ~ to** s'abaisser à; **descendant** n descendant(e); **descent** n descente f; (origin) origine f

describe [dɪsˈkraɪb] vt décrire; **description** [dɪsˈkrɪpʃən] n description f; (sort) sorte f, espèce f

desert n [ˈdezət] désert m ▷ vb [dɪˈzɜːt] ▷ vt déserter, abandonner ▷ vi (Mil) déserter; **deserted** [dɪˈzɜːtɪd] adj désert(e)

deserve [dɪˈzɜːv] vt mériter

design [dɪˈzaɪn] n (sketch) plan m, dessin m; (layout, shape) conception f, ligne f; (pattern) dessin, motif(s) m(pl); (of dress, car) modèle m; (art) design m, stylisme m; (intention) dessein m ▷ vt dessiner; (plan) concevoir; **design and technology** n (BRIT: Scol) technologie f

designate vt [ˈdezɪgneɪt] désigner ▷ adj [ˈdezɪgnɪt] désigné(e)

designer [dɪˈzaɪnəʳ] n (Archit, Art) dessinateur(-trice); (Industry) concepteur m, designer m; (Fashion) styliste m/f

desirable [dɪˈzaɪərəbl] adj (property, location, purchase) attrayant(e)

desire [dɪˈzaɪəʳ] n désir m ▷ vt désirer, vouloir

desk [desk] n (in office) bureau m; (for pupil) pupitre m; (BRIT: in shop, restaurant) caisse f; (in hotel, at airport) réception f; **desk-top publishing** [ˈdesktɒp-] n publication assistée par ordinateur, PAO f

despair [dɪsˈpeəʳ] n désespoir m ▷ vi: **to ~ of** désespérer de

despatch [dɪsˈpætʃ] n, vt = **dispatch**

desperate [ˈdespərɪt] adj désespéré(e); (fugitive) prêt(e) à tout; **to be ~ for sth/to do sth** avoir désespérément besoin de qch/de faire qch; **desperately** adv désespérément; (very) terriblement, extrêmement; **desperation** [despəˈreɪʃən] n désespoir m; **in (sheer) desperation** en désespoir de cause

despise [dɪsˈpaɪz] vt mépriser

despite [dɪsˈpaɪt] prep malgré, en dépit de

dessert [dɪˈzɜːt] n dessert m; **dessertspoon** n cuiller f à dessert

destination [destɪˈneɪʃən] n destination f

destined [ˈdestɪnd] adj: **~ for London** à destination de Londres

destiny [ˈdestɪnɪ] n destinée f, destin m

destroy [dɪsˈtrɔɪ] vt détruire; (injured horse) abattre; (dog) faire piquer

destruction [dɪsˈtrʌkʃən] n destruction f

destructive [dɪsˈtrʌktɪv] adj destructeur(-trice)

detach [dɪˈtætʃ] vt détacher; **detached** adj (attitude) détaché(e); **detached house** n pavillon m maison(nette) (individuelle)

detail [ˈdiːteɪl] n détail m ▷ vt raconter en détail, énumérer; **in ~** en détail; **detailed** adj détaillé(e)

detain [dɪˈteɪn] vt retenir; (in captivity) détenir

detect [dɪˈtɛkt] vt déceler, percevoir; (Med, Police) dépister; (Mil, Radar, Tech) détecter; **detection** [dɪˈtɛkʃən] n découverte f; **detective** n policier m; **private detective** détective privé; **detective story** n roman policier

detention [dɪˈtɛnʃən] n détention f; (Scol) retenue f, consigne f

deter [dɪˈtɜːʳ] vt dissuader

detergent [dɪˈtɜːdʒənt] n détersif m, détergent m

deteriorate [dɪˈtɪərɪəreɪt] vi se détériorer, se dégrader

determination [dɪtəˌmɪˈneɪʃən] n détermination f

determine [dɪˈtɜːmɪn] vt déterminer; **to ~ to do** résoudre de faire, se déterminer à faire; **determined** adj (person) déterminé(e), décidé(e); **determined to do** bien décidé à faire

deterrent [dɪˈtɛrənt] n effet m de dissuasion; force f de dissuasion

detest [dɪˈtɛst] vt détester, avoir horreur de

detour [ˈdiːtuəʳ] n détour m; (US Aut: diversion) déviation f

detract [dɪˈtrækt] vt: **to ~ from** (quality, pleasure) diminuer; (reputation) porter atteinte à

detrimental [detrɪˈmentl] adj: **~ to** préjudiciable or nuisible à

devastating [ˈdevəsteɪtɪŋ] adj dévastateur(-trice); (news) accablant(e)

develop [dɪˈveləp] vt (gen) développer; (disease) commencer à souffrir de; (resources) mettre en valeur, exploiter; (land) aménager ▷ vi se développer; (situation, disease: evolve) évoluer; (facts, symptoms: appear) se manifester, se produire; **can you ~ this film?** pouvez-vous développer cette pellicule?; **developing country** n pays m en voie de développement; **development** n développement m; (of land) exploitation f; (new fact, event) rebondissement m, fait(s) nouveau(x)

device [dɪˈvaɪs] n (apparatus) appareil m, dispositif m

devil [ˈdevl] n diable m; démon m

devious [ˈdiːvɪəs] adj (person) sournois(e), dissimulé(e)

devise [dɪˈvaɪz] vt imaginer, concevoir

devote [dɪˈvəut] vt: **to ~ sth to** consacrer qch

à; **devoted** adj dévoué(e); **to be devoted to** être dévoué(e) or très attaché(e) à; (book etc) être consacré(e) à; **devotion** n dévouement m, attachement m; (Rel) dévotion f, piété f

devour [dɪ'vauə^r] vt dévorer

devout [dɪ'vaut] adj pieux(-euse), dévot(e)

dew [dju:] n rosée f

diabetes [daɪə'bi:ti:z] n diabète m

diabetic [daɪə'bɛtɪk] n diabétique m/f ▷ adj (person) diabétique

diagnose [daɪəg'nəuz] vt diagnostiquer

diagnosis (pl **diagnoses**) [daɪəg'nəusɪs, -si:z] n diagnostic m

diagonal [daɪ'ægənl] adj diagonal(e) ▷ n diagonale f

diagram ['daɪəgræm] n diagramme m, schéma m

dial ['daɪəl] n cadran m ▷ vt (number) faire, composer

dialect ['daɪəlɛkt] n dialecte m

dialling code ['daɪəlɪŋ-] (us **dial code**) n indicatif m (téléphonique); **what's the ~ for Paris?** quel est l'indicatif de Paris?

dialling tone ['daɪəlɪŋ-] (us **dial tone**) n tonalité f

dialogue (us **dialog**) ['daɪəlɔg] n dialogue m

diameter [daɪ'æmɪtə^r] n diamètre m

diamond ['daɪəmənd] n diamant m; (shape) losange m; **diamonds** npl (Cards) carreau m

diaper ['daɪəpə^r] n (us) couche f

diarrhoea (us **diarrhea**) [daɪə'ri:ə] n diarrhée f

diary ['daɪərɪ] n (daily account) journal m; (book) agenda m

dice [daɪs] n (pl inv) dé m ▷ vt (Culin) couper en dés or en cubes

dictate [dɪk'teɪt] vt dicter; **dictation** [dɪk'teɪʃən] n dictée f

dictator [dɪk'teɪtə^r] n dictateur m

dictionary ['dɪkʃənrɪ] n dictionnaire m

did [dɪd] pt of **do**

didn't [dɪdnt] = **did not**

die [daɪ] vi mourir; **to be dying for sth** avoir une envie folle de qch; **to be dying to do sth** mourir d'envie de faire qch; **die down** vi se calmer, s'apaiser; **die out** vi disparaître, s'éteindre

diesel ['di:zl] n (vehicle) diesel m; (also: **~ oil**) carburant m diesel, gas-oil m

diet ['daɪət] n alimentation f; (restricted food) régime m ▷ vi (also: **be on a ~**) suivre un régime

differ ['dɪfə^r] vi: **to ~ from sth** (be different) être différent(e) de qch, différer de qch; **to ~ from sb over sth** ne pas être d'accord avec qn au sujet de qch; **difference** n différence f; (quarrel) différend m, désaccord m; **different** adj différent(e); **differentiate** [dɪfə'rɛnʃɪeɪt] vi: **to differentiate between**

faire une différence entre; **differently** adv différemment

difficult ['dɪfɪkəlt] adj difficile; **difficulty** n difficulté f

dig [dɪg] vt (pt, pp **dug**) (hole) creuser; (garden) bêcher ▷ n (prod) coup m de coude; (fig: remark) coup de griffe or de patte; (Archaeology) fouille f; **to ~ one's nails into** enfoncer ses ongles dans; **dig up** vt déterrer

digest vt [daɪ'dʒɛst] digérer ▷ n ['daɪdʒɛst] sommaire m, résumé m; **digestion** [dɪ'dʒɛstʃən] n digestion f

digit ['dɪdʒɪt] n (number) chiffre m (de o à 9); (finger) doigt m; **digital** adj (system, recording, radio) numérique, digital(e); (watch) à affichage numérique or digital; **digital camera** n appareil m photo numérique; **digital TV** n télévision f numérique

dignified ['dɪgnɪfaɪd] adj digne

dignity ['dɪgnɪtɪ] n dignité f

digs [dɪgz] npl (BRIT inf) piaule f, chambre meublée

dilemma [daɪ'lɛmə] n dilemme m

dill [dɪl] n aneth m

dilute [daɪ'lu:t] vt diluer

dim [dɪm] adj (light, eyesight) faible; (memory, outline) vague, indécis(e); (room) sombre; (inf: stupid) borné(e), obtus(e) ▷ vt (light) réduire, baisser; (us Aut) mettre en code, baisser

dime [daɪm] n (us) pièce f de 10 cents

dimension [daɪ'mɛnʃən] n dimension f

diminish [dɪ'mɪnɪʃ] vt, vi diminuer

din [dɪn] n vacarme m

dine [daɪn] vi dîner; **diner** n (person) dîneur(-euse); (us: eating place) petit restaurant

dinghy ['dɪŋgɪ] n youyou m; (inflatable) canot m pneumatique; (also: **sailing ~**) voilier m, dériveur m

dingy ['dɪndʒɪ] adj miteux(-euse), minable

dining car ['daɪnɪŋ-] n (BRIT) voiture-restaurant f, wagon-restaurant m

dining room ['daɪnɪŋ-] n salle f à manger

dining table [daɪnɪŋ-] n table f de (la) salle à manger

dinner ['dɪnə^r] n (evening meal) dîner m; (lunch) déjeuner m; (public) banquet m; **dinner jacket** n smoking m; **dinner party** n dîner m; **dinner time** n (evening) heure f du dîner; (midday) heure du déjeuner

dinosaur ['daɪnəsɔ:^r] n dinosaure m

dip [dɪp] n (slope) déclivité f; (in sea) baignade f, bain m; (Culin) ≈ sauce f ▷ vt tremper, plonger; (BRIT Aut: lights) mettre en code, baisser ▷ vi plonger

diploma [dɪ'pləumə] n diplôme m

diplomacy [dɪ'pləuməsɪ] n diplomatie f

diplomat ['dɪpləmæt] n diplomate m; **diplomatic** [dɪplə'mætɪk] adj diplomatique

dipstick ['dɪpstɪk] n (BRIT Aut) jauge f de niveau d'huile

dire [daɪə'] adj (poverty) extrême; (awful) affreux(-euse)

direct [daɪ'rɛkt] adj direct(e) ▷ vt (tell way) diriger, orienter; (letter, remark) adresser; (Cine, TV) réaliser; (Theat) mettre en scène; (order): **to ~ sb to do sth** ordonner à qn de faire qch ▷ adv directement; **can you ~ me to ...?** pouvez-vous m'indiquer le chemin de ...?; **direct debit** n (BRIT Banking) prélèvement m automatique

direction [dɪ'rɛkʃən] n direction f; **directions** npl (to a place) indications fpl; **~s for use** mode m d'emploi; **sense of ~** sens m de l'orientation

directly [dɪ'rɛktlɪ] adv (in straight line) directement, tout droit; (at once) tout de suite, immédiatement

director [dɪ'rɛktə'] n directeur m; (Theat) metteur en scène; (Cine, TV) réalisateur(-trice)

directory [dɪ'rɛktərɪ] n annuaire m; (Comput) répertoire m; **directory enquiries** (US **directory assistance**) n (Tel: service) renseignements mpl

dirt [də:t] n saleté f; (mud) boue f; **dirty** adj sale; (joke) cochon(ne) ▷ vt salir

disability [dɪsə'bɪlɪtɪ] n invalidité f, infirmité f

disabled [dɪs'eɪbld] adj handicapé(e); (maimed) mutilé(e)

disadvantage [dɪsəd'vɑ:ntɪdʒ] n désavantage m, inconvénient m

disagree [dɪsə'gri:] vi (differ) ne pas concorder; (be against, think otherwise): **to ~ (with)** ne pas être d'accord (avec); **disagreeable** adj désagréable; **disagreement** n désaccord m, différend m

disappear [dɪsə'pɪə'] vi disparaître; **disappearance** n disparition f

disappoint [dɪsə'pɔɪnt] vt décevoir; **disappointed** adj déçu(e); **disappointing** adj décevant(e); **disappointment** n déception f

disapproval [dɪsə'pru:vəl] n désapprobation f

disapprove [dɪsə'pru:v] vi: **to ~ of** désapprouver

disarm [dɪs'ɑ:m] vt désarmer; **disarmament** [dɪs'ɑ:məmənt] n désarmement m

disaster [dɪ'zɑ:stə'] n catastrophe f, désastre m; **disastrous** adj désastreux(-euse)

disbelief ['dɪsbə'li:f] n incrédulité f

disc [dɪsk] n disque m; (Comput) = **disk**

discard [dɪs'kɑ:d] vt (old things) se débarrasser de; (fig) écarter, renoncer à

discharge vt [dɪs'tʃɑ:dʒ] (duties) s'acquitter de; (waste etc) déverser; décharger; (patient) renvoyer (chez lui); (employee, soldier) congédier, licencier ▷ n ['dɪstʃɑ:dʒ] (Elec, Med) émission f; (dismissal) renvoi m; licenciement m

discipline ['dɪsɪplɪn] n discipline f ▷ vt

discipliner; (punish) punir

disc jockey n disque-jockey m (DJ)

disclose [dɪs'kləuz] vt révéler, divulguer

disco ['dɪskəu] n abbr discothèque f

discoloured [dɪs'kʌləd] (US **discolored**) adj décoloré(e), jauni(e)

discomfort [dɪs'kʌmfət] n malaise m, gêne f; (lack of comfort) manque m de confort

disconnect [dɪskə'nɛkt] vt (Elec, Radio) débrancher; (gas, water) couper

discontent [dɪskən'tɛnt] n mécontentement m

discontinue [dɪskən'tɪnju:] vt cesser, interrompre; **"~d"** (Comm) "fin de série"

discount n ['dɪskaunt] remise f, rabais m ▷ vt [dɪs'kaunt] (report etc) ne pas tenir compte de

discourage [dɪs'kʌrɪdʒ] vt décourager

discover [dɪs'kʌvə'] vt découvrir; **discovery** n découverte f

discredit [dɪs'krɛdɪt] vt (idea) mettre en doute; (person) discréditer

discreet [dɪ'skri:t] adj discret(-ète)

discrepancy [dɪ'skrɛpənsɪ] n divergence f, contradiction f

discretion [dɪ'skrɛʃən] n discrétion f; **at the ~ of** à la discrétion de

discriminate [dɪ'skrɪmɪneɪt] vi: **to ~ between** établir une distinction entre, faire la différence entre; **to ~ against** pratiquer une discrimination contre; **discrimination** [dɪskrɪmɪ'neɪʃən] n discrimination f; (judgment) discernement m

discuss [dɪ'skʌs] vt discuter de; (debate) discuter; **discussion** [dɪ'skʌʃən] n discussion f

disease [dɪ'zi:z] n maladie f

disembark [dɪsɪm'bɑ:k] vt, vi débarquer

disgrace [dɪs'greɪs] n honte f; (disfavour) disgrâce f ▷ vt déshonorer, couvrir de honte; **disgraceful** adj scandaleux(-euse), honteux(-euse)

disgruntled [dɪs'grʌntld] adj mécontent(e)

disguise [dɪs'gaɪz] n déguisement m ▷ vt déguiser; **in ~** déguisé(e)

disgust [dɪs'gʌst] n dégoût m, aversion f ▷ vt dégoûter, écœurer

disgusted [dɪs'gʌstɪd] adj dégoûté(e), écœuré(e)

disgusting [dɪs'gʌstɪŋ] adj dégoûtant(e)

dish [dɪʃ] n plat m; **to do or wash the ~es** faire la vaisselle; **dishcloth** n (for drying) torchon m; (for washing) lavette f

dishonest [dɪs'ɔnɪst] adj malhonnête

dishtowel ['dɪʃtauəl] n (US) torchon m (à vaisselle)

dishwasher ['dɪʃwɔʃə'] n lave-vaisselle m

disillusion [dɪsɪ'lu:ʒən] vt désabuser, désenchanter

disinfectant [dɪsɪn'fɛktənt] n désinfectant m

disintegrate [dɪs'ɪntɪgreɪt] vi se désintégrer

disk [dɪsk] n (Comput) disquette f; **single-/double-sided ~** disquette une face/double face; **disk drive** n lecteur m de disquette; **diskette** n (Comput) disquette f

dislike [dɪs'laɪk] n aversion f, antipathie f ▷ vt ne pas aimer

dislocate ['dɪsləkeɪt] vt disloquer, déboîter

disloyal [dɪs'lɔɪəl] adj déloyal(e)

dismal ['dɪzml] adj (gloomy) lugubre, maussade; (very bad) lamentable

dismantle [dɪs'mæntl] vt démonter

dismay [dɪs'meɪ] n consternation f ▷ vt consterner

dismiss [dɪs'mɪs] vt congédier, renvoyer; (idea) écarter; (Law) rejeter; **dismissal** n renvoi m

disobedient [dɪsə'biːdɪənt] adj désobéissant(e), indiscipliné(e)

disobey [dɪsə'beɪ] vt désobéir à

disorder [dɪs'ɔːdəʳ] n désordre m; (rioting) désordres mpl; (Med) troubles mpl

disorganized [dɪs'ɔːgənaɪzd] adj désorganisé(e)

disown [dɪs'əun] vt renier

dispatch [dɪs'pætʃ] vt expédier, envoyer ▷ n envoi m, expédition f; (Mil, Press) dépêche f

dispel [dɪs'pel] vt dissiper, chasser

dispense [dɪs'pens] vt (medicine) préparer (et vendre); **dispense with** vt fus se passer de; **dispenser** n (device) distributeur m

disperse [dɪs'pəːs] n disperser ▷ vi se disperser

display [dɪs'pleɪ] n (of goods) étalage m; affichage m; (Comput: information) visualisation f; (: device) visuel m; (of feeling) manifestation f ▷ vt montrer; (goods) mettre à l'étalage, exposer; (results, departure times) afficher; (pej) faire étalage de

displease [dɪs'pliːz] vt mécontenter, contrarier

disposable [dɪs'pəuzəbl] adj (pack etc) jetable; (income) disponible

disposal [dɪs'pəuzl] n (of rubbish) évacuation f, destruction f; (of property etc: by selling) vente f; (: by giving away) cession f; **at one's ~** à sa disposition

dispose [dɪs'pəuz] vi: **to ~ of** (unwanted goods) se débarrasser de, se défaire de; (problem) expédier; **disposition** [dɪspə'zɪʃən] n disposition f; (temperament) naturel m

disproportionate [dɪsprə'pɔːʃənət] adj disproportionné(e)

dispute [dɪs'pjuːt] n discussion f; (also: **industrial ~**) conflit m ▷ vt (question) contester; (matter) discuter

disqualify [dɪs'kwɔlɪfaɪ] vt (Sport) disqualifier; **to ~ sb for sth/from doing** rendre qn inapte à qch/à faire

disregard [dɪsrɪ'gɑːd] vt ne pas tenir compte de

disrupt [dɪs'rʌpt] vt (plans, meeting, lesson) perturber, déranger; **disruption** [dɪs'rʌpʃən] n perturbation f, dérangement m

dissatisfaction [dɪssætɪs'fækʃən] n mécontentement m, insatisfaction f

dissatisfied [dɪs'sætɪsfaɪd] adj: **~ (with)** insatisfait(e) (de)

dissect [dɪ'sɛkt] vt disséquer

dissent [dɪ'sɛnt] n dissentiment m, différence f d'opinion

dissertation [dɪsə'teɪʃən] n (Scol) mémoire m

dissolve [dɪ'zɔlv] vt dissoudre ▷ vi se dissoudre, fondre; **to ~ in(to) tears** fondre en larmes

distance ['dɪstns] n distance f; **in the ~** au loin

distant ['dɪstnt] adj lointain(e), éloigné(e); (manner) distant(e), froid(e)

distil (us **distill**) [dɪs'tɪl] vt distiller; **distillery** n distillerie f

distinct [dɪs'tɪŋkt] adj distinct(e); (clear) marqué(e); **as ~ from** par opposition à; **distinction** [dɪs'tɪŋkʃən] n distinction f; (in exam) mention f très bien; **distinctive** adj distinctif(-ive)

distinguish [dɪs'tɪŋgwɪʃ] vt distinguer; **to ~ o.s.** se distinguer; **distinguished** adj (eminent, refined) distingué(e)

distort [dɪs'tɔːt] vt déformer

distract [dɪs'trækt] vt distraire, déranger; **distracted** adj (not concentrating) distrait(e); (worried) affolé(e); **distraction** [dɪs'trækʃən] n distraction f

distraught [dɪs'trɔːt] adj éperdu(e)

distress [dɪs'trɛs] n détresse f ▷ vt affliger; **distressing** adj douloureux(-euse), pénible

distribute [dɪs'trɪbjuːt] vt distribuer; **distribution** [dɪstrɪ'bjuːʃən] n distribution f; **distributor** n (gen: Tech) distributeur m; (Comm) concessionnaire m/f

district ['dɪstrɪkt] n (of country) région f; (of town) quartier m; (Admin) district m; **district attorney** n (us) ≈ procureur m de la République

distrust [dɪs'trʌst] n méfiance f, doute m ▷ vt se méfier de

disturb [dɪs'təːb] vt troubler; (inconvenience) déranger; **disturbance** n dérangement m; (political etc) troubles mpl; **disturbed** adj (worried, upset) agité(e), troublé(e); **to be emotionally disturbed** avoir des problèmes affectifs; **disturbing** adj troublant(e), inquiétant(e)

ditch [dɪtʃ] n fossé m; (for irrigation) rigole f ▷ vt (inf) abandonner; (person) plaquer

ditto ['dɪtəu] adv idem

dive [daɪv] n plongeon m; (of submarine) plongée f ▷ vi plonger; **to ~ into** (bag etc) plonger la main dans; (place) se précipiter dans; **diver** n plongeur m

diverse[daɪˈvəːs] *adj* divers(e)
diversion[daɪˈvəːʃən] *n* (BRIT Aut) déviation *f*; (*distraction, Mil*) diversion *f*
diversity[daɪˈvəːsɪtɪ] *n* diversité *f*, variété *f*
divert[daɪˈvəːt] *vt* (BRIT: *traffic*) dévier; (*plane*) dérouter; (*train, river*) détourner
divide[dɪˈvaɪd] *vt* diviser; (*separate*) séparer ▷ *vi* se diviser; **divided highway**(US) *n* route *f* à quatre voies
divine[dɪˈvaɪn] *adj* divin(e)
diving[ˈdaɪvɪŋ] *n* plongée (sous-marine); **diving board** *n* plongeoir *m*
division[dɪˈvɪʒən] *n* division *f*; (*separation*) séparation *f*; (Comm) service *m*
divorce[dɪˈvɔːs] *n* divorce *m* ▷ *vt* divorcer d'avec; (*fig*) **divorced** *adj* divorcé(e); **divorcee** [dɪvɔːˈsiː] *n* divorcé(e)
D.I.Y. *adj, n abbr* (BRIT) = **do-it-yourself**
dizzy[ˈdɪzɪ] *adj*: **I feel ~** la tête me tourne, j'ai la tête qui tourne
DJ *n abbr* = **disc jockey**
DNA *n abbr* (= deoxyribonucleic acid) ADN *m*

 KEYWORD

do[duː] (*pt* **did**, *pp* **done**) *n* (inf: party etc) soirée *f*, fête *f*
▷ *vb* **1** (in negative constructions) non traduit; **I don't understand** je ne comprends pas
2 (to form questions) non traduit; **didn't you know?** vous ne le saviez pas?; **what do you think?** qu'en pensez-vous?
3 (for emphasis, in polite expressions): **people do make mistakes sometimes** on peut toujours se tromper; **she does seem rather late** je trouve qu'elle est bien en retard; **do sit down/help yourself** asseyez-vous/servez-vous je vous en prie; **do take care!** faites bien attention à vous!
4 (used to avoid repeating vb): **she swims better than I do** elle nage mieux que moi; **do you agree? - yes, I do/no, I don't** vous êtes d'accord? - oui/non; **she lives in Glasgow - so do I** elle habite Glasgow - moi aussi; **he didn't like it and neither did we** il n'a pas aimé ça, et nous non plus; **who broke it? - I did** qui l'a cassé? - c'est moi; **he asked me to help him and I did** il m'a demandé de l'aider, et c'est ce que j'ai fait
5 (in question tags): **you like him, don't you?** vous l'aimez bien, n'est-ce pas?; **I don't know him, do I?** je ne crois pas le connaître
▷ *vt* **1** (gen: carry out, perform etc) faire; (visit: city, museum) faire, visiter; **what are you doing tonight?** qu'est-ce que vous faites ce soir?; **what do you do?** (job) que faites-vous dans la vie?; **what can I do for you?** que puis-je faire pour vous?; **to do the cooking/washing-up** faire la cuisine/la vaisselle; **to do one's teeth/**hair/nails se brosser les dents/se coiffer/se faire les ongles
2 (Aut etc: distance) faire; (: speed) faire du; **we've done 200 km already** nous avons déjà fait 200 km; **the car was doing 100** la voiture faisait du 100 (à l'heure); **he can do 100 in that car** il peut faire du 100 (à l'heure) dans cette voiture-là
▷ *vi* **1** (act, behave) faire; **do as I do** faites comme moi
2 (get on, fare) marcher; **the firm is doing well** l'entreprise marche bien; **he's doing well/badly at school** ça marche bien/mal pour lui à l'école; **how do you do?** comment allez-vous?; (on being introduced) enchanté(e)!
3 (suit) aller; **will it do?** est-ce que ça ira?
4 (be sufficient) suffire, aller; **will £10 do?** est-ce que 10 livres suffiront?; **that'll do** ça suffit, ça ira; **that'll do!** (in annoyance) ça va or suffit comme ça!; **to make do (with)** se contenter (de)

do up *vt* (laces, dress) attacher; (buttons) boutonner; (zip) fermer; (renovate: room) refaire; (: house) remettre à neuf
do with *vt fus* (need): **I could do with a drink/some help** quelque chose à boire/un peu d'aide ne serait pas de refus; **it could do with a wash** ça ne lui ferait pas de mal d'être lavé; (be connected with): **that has nothing to do with you** cela ne vous concerne pas; **I won't have anything to do with it** je ne veux pas m'en mêler
do without *vi* s'en passer; **if you're late for tea then you'll do without** si vous êtes en retard pour le dîner il faudra vous en passer
▷ *vt fus* se passer de; **I can do without a car** je peux me passer de voiture

dock[dɔk] *n* dock *m*; (wharf) quai *m*; (Law) banc *m* des accusés ▷ *vi* se mettre à quai; (Space) s'arrimer; **docks** *npl* (Naut) docks
doctor[ˈdɔktəʳ] *n* médecin *m*, docteur *m*; (PhD etc) docteur ▷ *vt* (drink) frelater; **call a ~!** appelez un docteur or un médecin!; **Doctor of Philosophy (PhD)** *n* (degree) doctorat *m*; (person) titulaire *m/f* d'un doctorat
document[ˈdɔkjumənt] *n* document *m*; **documentary**[dɔkjuˈmɛntərɪ] *adj, n* documentaire (*m*); **documentation** [dɔkjumənˈteɪʃən] *n* documentation *f*
dodge[dɔdʒ] *n* truc *m*; combine *f* ▷ *vt* esquiver, éviter
dodgy[ˈdɔdʒɪ] *adj* (inf: uncertain) douteux(-euse); (: shady) louche
does[dʌz] *vb see* **do**
doesn't[ˈdʌznt] = **does not**
dog[dɔg] *n* chien(ne) ▷ *vt* (follow closely) suivre de près; (fig: memory etc) poursuivre, harceler; **doggy bag**[ˈdɔgɪ-] *n* petit sac pour emporter

les restes

do-it-yourself ['du:ɪtjɔ:'sɛlf] n bricolage m

dole [dəul] n (BRIT: payment) allocation f de chômage; **on the ~** au chômage

doll [dɔl] n poupée f

dollar ['dɔlə'] n dollar m

dolphin ['dɔlfɪn] n dauphin m

dome [dəum] n dôme m

domestic [də'mɛstɪk] adj (duty, happiness) familial(e); (policy, affairs, flight) intérieur(e); (animal) domestique; **domestic appliance** n appareil ménager

dominant ['dɔmɪnənt] adj dominant(e)

dominate ['dɔmɪneɪt] vt dominer

domino ['dɔmɪnəu] (pl **~es**) n domino m; **dominoes** n (game) dominos mpl

donate [də'neɪt] vt faire don de, donner; **donation** [də'neɪʃən] n donation f, don m

done [dʌn] pp of **do**

donkey ['dɔŋkɪ] n âne m

donor ['dəunə'] n (of blood etc) donneur(-euse); (to charity) donateur(-trice); **donor card** n carte f de don d'organes

don't [dəunt] = **do not**

donut ['dəunʌt] (US) n = **doughnut**

doodle ['du:dl] vi griffonner, gribouiller

doom [du:m] n (fate) destin m ▷ vt: **to be ~ed to failure** être voué(e) à l'échec

door [dɔ:'] n porte f; (Rail, car) portière f; **doorbell** n sonnette f; **door handle** n poignée f de porte; (of car) poignée f de portière; **doorknob** n poignée f or bouton m de porte; **doorstep** n pas m de (la) porte, seuil m; **doorway** n (embrasure f de) porte f

dope [dəup] n (inf: drug) drogue f; (: person) andouille f ▷ vt (horse etc) doper

dormitory ['dɔ:mɪtrɪ] n (BRIT) dortoir m; (US: hall of residence) résidence f universitaire

DOS [dɔs] n abbr (= disk operating system) DOS m

dosage ['dəusɪdʒ] n dose f; dosage m; (on label) posologie f

dose [dəus] n dose f

dot [dɔt] n point m; (on material) pois m ▷ vt: **~ted with** parsemé(e) de; **on the ~** à l'heure tapante; **dotcom** [dɔt'kɔm] n point com m, pointcom m; **dotted line** ['dɔtɪd-] n ligne pointillée; **to sign on the dotted line** signer à l'endroit indiqué or sur la ligne pointillée

double ['dʌbl] adj double ▷ adv (twice): **to cost ~ (sth)** coûter le double (de qch) or deux fois plus (que qch) ▷ n double m; (Cine) doublure f ▷ vt doubler; (fold) plier en deux ▷ vi doubler; **on the ~, at the ~** au pas de course; **double back** vi (person) revenir sur ses pas; **double bass** n contrebasse f; **double bed** n grand lit; **double-check** vt, vi revérifier; **double-click** vi (Comput) double-cliquer; **double-cross** vt doubler, trahir; **doubledecker** n autobus m à impériale; **double glazing** n (BRIT) double

vitrage m; **double room** n chambre f pour deux; **doubles** n (Tennis) double m; **double yellow lines** npl (BRIT: Aut) double bande jaune marquant l'interdiction de stationner

doubt [daut] n doute m ▷ vt douter de; **no ~** sans doute; **to ~ that** douter que + sub; **doubtful** adj douteux(-euse); (person) incertain(e); **doubtless** adv sans doute, sûrement

dough [dəu] n pâte f; **doughnut** (US **donut**) n beignet m

dove [dʌv] n colombe f

Dover ['dəuvə'] n Douvres

down [daun] n (fluff) duvet m ▷ adv en bas, vers le bas; (on the ground) par terre ▷ prep en bas de; (along) le long de ▷ vt (inf: drink) siffler; **to walk ~ a hill** descendre une colline; **to run ~ the street** descendre la rue en courant; **~ with X!** à bas X!; **down-and-out** n (tramp) clochard(e); **downfall** n chute f; ruine f; **downhill** adv: **to go downhill** descendre; (business) péricliter

Downing Street ['daunɪŋ-] n (BRIT): **10 ~** résidence du Premier ministre

⬤ **DOWNING STREET**

⬤
⬤ **Downing Street** est une rue de
⬤ Westminster (à Londres) où se trouvent
⬤ la résidence officielle du Premier ministre
⬤ et celle du ministre des Finances. Le nom
⬤ **Downing Street** est souvent utilisé pour
⬤ désigner le gouvernement britannique.

down: **download** vt (Comput) télécharger; **downright** adj (lie etc) effronté(e); (refusal) catégorique

Down's syndrome [daunz-] n trisomie f

down: **downstairs** adv (on or to ground floor) au rez-de-chaussée; (on or to floor below) à l'étage inférieur; **down-to-earth** adj terre à terre inv; **downtown** adv en ville; **under** adv en Australie or Nouvelle Zélande; **downward** ['daunwəd] adj, adv vers le bas; **downwards** ['daunwədz] adv vers le bas

doz. abbr = **dozen**

doze [dəuz] vi sommeiller

dozen ['dʌzn] n douzaine f; **a ~ books** une douzaine de livres; **~s of** des centaines de

Dr. abbr (= doctor) Dr; (in street names) = **drive**

drab [dræb] adj terne, morne

draft [drɑ:ft] n (of letter, school work) brouillon m; (of literary work) ébauche f; (Comm) traite f; (US: call-up) conscription f ▷ vt faire le brouillon de; (Mil: send) détacher; see also **draught**

drag [dræg] vt traîner; (river) draguer ▷ vi traîner ▷ n (inf) casse-pieds m/f; (women's clothing): **in ~** (en) travesti; **to ~ and drop**

(Comput) glisser-poser
dragon ['drægn] n dragon m
dragonfly ['drægənflaɪ] n libellule f
drain [dreɪn] n égout m; (on resources) saignée f ▷ vt (land, marshes) drainer, assécher; (vegetables) égoutter; (reservoir etc) vider ▷ vi (water) s'écouler; **drainage** n (system) système m d'égouts; (act) drainage m; **drainpipe** n tuyau m d'écoulement
drama ['drɑːmə] n (art) théâtre m, art m dramatique; (play) pièce f; (event) drame m; **dramatic** [drə'mætɪk] adj (Theat) dramatique; (impressive) spectaculaire
drank [dræŋk] pt of **drink**
drape [dreɪp] vt draper; **drapes** npl (US) rideaux mpl
drastic ['dræstɪk] adj (measures) d'urgence, énergique; (change) radical(e)
draught (US **draft**) [drɑːft] n courant m d'air; **on ~** (beer) à la pression; **draught beer** n bière f (à la) pression; **draughts** n (BRIT: game) (jeu m de) dames fpl
draw [drɔː] (vb: pt **drew**, pp **~n**) vt tirer; (picture) dessiner; (attract) attirer; (line, circle) tracer; (money) retirer; (wages) toucher ▷ vi (Sport) faire match nul ▷ n match nul; (lottery) loterie f; (: picking of ticket) tirage m au sort; **draw out** vi (lengthen) s'allonger ▷ vt (money) retirer; **draw up** vi (stop) s'arrêter ▷ vt (document) établir, dresser; (plan) formuler, dessiner; (chair) approcher; **drawback** n inconvénient m, désavantage m
drawer [drɔːʳ] n tiroir m
drawing ['drɔːɪŋ] n dessin m; **drawing pin** n (BRIT) punaise f; **drawing room** n salon m
drawn [drɔːn] pp of **draw**
dread [drɛd] n épouvante f, effroi m ▷ vt redouter, appréhender; **dreadful** adj épouvantable, affreux(-euse)
dream [driːm] n rêve m ▷ vt, vi (pt, pp **~ed** or **~t**) rêver; **dreamer** n rêveur(-euse)
dreamt [drɛmt] pt, pp of **dream**
dreary ['drɪərɪ] adj triste; monotone
drench [drɛntʃ] vt tremper
dress [drɛs] n robe f; (clothing) habillement m, tenue f ▷ vt habiller; (wound) panser ▷ vi: **to get ~ed** s'habiller; **dress up** vi s'habiller; (in fancy dress) se déguiser; **dress circle** n (BRIT) premier balcon; **dresser** n (furniture) vaisselier m; (: us) coiffeuse f, commode f; **dressing** n (Med) pansement m; (Culin) sauce f, assaisonnement m; **dressing gown** n (BRIT) robe f de chambre; **dressing room** n (Theat) loge f; (Sport) vestiaire m; **dressing table** n coiffeuse f; **dressmaker** n couturière f
drew [druː] pt of **draw**
dribble ['drɪbl] vi (baby) baver ▷ vt (ball) dribbler
dried [draɪd] adj (fruit, beans) sec (sèche); (eggs, milk) en poudre

drier ['draɪəʳ] n = **dryer**
drift [drɪft] n (of current etc) force f; direction f; (of snow) rafale f; coulée f; (: on ground) congère f; (general meaning) sens général ▷ vi (boat) aller à la dérive, dériver; (sand, snow) s'amonceler, s'entasser
drill [drɪl] n perceuse f; (bit) foret m; (of dentist) roulette f, fraise f; (Mil) exercice m ▷ vt percer; (troops) entraîner ▷ vi (for oil) faire un or des forage(s)
drink [drɪŋk] n boisson f; (alcoholic) verre m ▷ vt, vi (pt **drank**, pp **drunk**) boire; **to have a ~** boire quelque chose, boire un verre; **a ~ of water** un verre d'eau; **would you like a ~?** tu veux boire quelque chose?; **drink-driving** n conduite f en état d'ivresse; **drinker** n buveur(-euse); **drinking water** n eau f potable
drip [drɪp] n (drop) goutte f; (Med: device) goutte-à-goutte m inv; (: liquid) perfusion f ▷ vi tomber goutte à goutte; (tap) goutter
drive [draɪv] n promenade f or trajet m en voiture; (also: **~way**) allée f; (energy) dynamisme m, énergie f; (push) effort (concerté); campagne f; (Comput: also: **disk ~**) lecteur m de disquette ▷ vb (pt **drove**, pp **~n**) ▷ vt conduire; (nail) enfoncer; (push) chasser, pousser; (Tech: motor) actionner; entraîner ▷ vi (be at the wheel) conduire; (travel by car) aller en voiture; **left-/right-hand ~** (Aut) conduite f à gauche/droite; **to ~ sb mad** rendre qn fou (folle); **drive out** vt (force out) chasser; **drive-in** adj, n (esp us) drive-in m
driven ['drɪvn] pp of **drive**
driver ['draɪvəʳ] n conducteur(-trice); (of taxi, bus) chauffeur m; **driver's license** n (US) permis m de conduire
driveway ['draɪvweɪ] n allée f
driving ['draɪvɪŋ] n conduite f; **driving instructor** n moniteur m d'auto-école; **driving lesson** n leçon f de conduite; **driving licence** n (BRIT) permis m de conduire; **driving test** n examen m du permis de conduire
drizzle ['drɪzl] n bruine f, crachin m
droop [druːp] vi (flower) commencer à se faner; (shoulders, head) tomber
drop [drɔp] n (of liquid) goutte f; (fall) baisse f; (also: **parachute ~**) saut m ▷ vt laisser tomber; (voice, eyes, price) baisser; (passenger) déposer ▷ vi tomber; **drop in** vi (inf: visit): **to ~ in (on)** faire un saut (chez), passer (chez); **drop off** vi (sleep) s'assoupir ▷ vt (passenger) déposer; **drop out** vi (withdraw) se retirer; (student etc) abandonner, décrocher
drought [draut] n sécheresse f
drove [drəuv] pt of **drive**
drown [draun] vt noyer ▷ vi se noyer
drowsy ['drauzɪ] adj somnolent(e)

drug [drʌg] n médicament m; (narcotic) drogue f ▷ vt droguer; **to be on ~s** se droguer; **drug addict** n toxicomane m/f; **drug dealer** n revendeur(-euse) de drogue; **druggist** n (US) pharmacien(ne)-droguiste; **drugstore** n (US) pharmacie-droguerie f, drugstore m

drum [drʌm] n tambour m; (for oil, petrol) bidon m; **drums** npl (Mus) batterie f; **drummer** n (joueur m de) tambour m

drunk [drʌŋk] pp of **drink** ▷ adj ivre, soûl(e) ▷ n (also: **~ard**) ivrogne m/f; **to get ~** se soûler; **drunken** adj ivre, soûl(e); (rage, stupor) ivrogne, d'ivrogne

dry [draɪ] adj sec (sèche); (day) sans pluie ▷ vt sécher; (clothes) faire sécher ▷ vi sécher; **dry off** vi, vt sécher; **dry up** vi sécher; (river, supplies) se tarir; **dry-cleaner's** n teinturerie f; **dry-cleaning** n (process) nettoyage m à sec; **dryer** n (tumble-dryer) sèche-linge m inv; (for hair) sèche-cheveux m inv

DSS n abbr (BRIT) = **Department of Social Security**

DTP n abbr (= desktop publishing) PAO f

dual ['djuəl] adj double; **dual carriageway** n (BRIT) route f à quatre voies

dubious ['djuːbɪəs] adj hésitant(e), incertain(e); (reputation, company) douteux(-euse)

duck [dʌk] n canard m ▷ vi se baisser vivement, baisser subitement la tête

due [djuː] adj (money, payment) dû (due); (expected) attendu(e); (fitting) qui convient ▷ adv: ~ **north** droit vers le nord; ~ **to** (because of) en raison de; (caused by) dû à; **the train is ~ at 8 a.m.** le train est attendu à 8 h; **she is ~ back tomorrow** elle doit rentrer demain; **he is ~ £10 on** lui doit 10 livres; **to give sb his or her ~** être juste envers qn

duel ['djuəl] n duel m

duet [djuː'ɛt] n duo m

dug [dʌg] pt, pp of **dig**

duke [djuːk] n duc m

dull [dʌl] adj (boring) ennuyeux(-euse); (not bright) morne, terne; (sound, pain) sourd(e); (weather, day) gris(e), maussade ▷ vt (pain, grief) atténuer; (mind, senses) engourdir

dumb [dʌm] adj muet(te); (stupid) bête

dummy ['dʌmɪ] n (tailor's model) mannequin m; (mock-up) factice m, maquette f; (BRIT: for baby) tétine f ▷ adj faux (fausse), factice

dump [dʌmp] n (also: **rubbish ~**) décharge (publique); (inf: place) trou m ▷ vt (put down) déposer; déverser; (get rid of) se débarrasser de; (Comput) lister

dumpling ['dʌmplɪŋ] n boulette f (de pâte)

dune [djuːn] n dune f

dungarees [dʌŋgə'riːz] npl bleu(s) m(pl); (for child, woman) salopette f

dungeon ['dʌndʒən] n cachot m

duplex ['djuːplɛks] n (US: also: **~ apartment**) duplex m

duplicate n ['djuːplɪkət] double m ▷ vt ['djuːplɪkeɪt] faire un double de; (on machine) polycopier; **in ~** en deux exemplaires, en double

durable ['djuərəbl] adj durable; (clothes, metal) résistant(e), solide

duration [djuə'reɪʃən] n durée f

during ['djuərɪŋ] prep pendant, au cours de

dusk [dʌsk] n crépuscule m

dust [dʌst] n poussière f ▷ vt (furniture) essuyer, épousseter; (cake etc): **to ~ with** saupoudrer de; **dustbin** n (BRIT) poubelle f; **duster** n chiffon m; **dustman** n (BRIT: irreg) boueux m, éboueur m; **dustpan** n pelle f à poussière; **dusty** adj poussiéreux(-euse)

Dutch [dʌtʃ] adj hollandais(e), néerlandais(e) ▷ n (Ling) hollandais m, néerlandais m ▷ adv: **to go ~** or **dutch** (inf) partager les frais; **the Dutch** npl les Hollandais, les Néerlandais; **Dutchman** (irreg) n Hollandais m; **Dutchwoman** (irreg) n Hollandaise f

duty ['djuːtɪ] n devoir m; (tax) droit m, taxe f; **on ~** de service; (at night etc) de garde; **off ~** libre, pas de service or de garde; **duty-free** adj exempté(e) de douane, hors-taxe

duvet ['duːveɪ] n (BRIT) couette f

DVD n abbr (= digital versatile or video disc) DVD m; **DVD burner** n graveur m de DVD; **DVD player** n lecteur m de DVD; **DVD writer** n graveur m de DVD

dwarf (pl **dwarves**) [dwɔːf, dwɔːvz] n nain(e) ▷ vt écraser

dwell (pt, pp **dwelt**) [dwɛl, dwɛlt] vi demeurer; **dwell on** vt fus s'étendre sur

dwelt [dwɛlt] pt, pp of **dwell**

dwindle ['dwɪndl] vi diminuer, décroître

dye [daɪ] n teinture f ▷ vt teindre

dying ['daɪɪŋ] adj mourant(e), agonisant(e)

dynamic [daɪ'næmɪk] adj dynamique

dynamite ['daɪnəmaɪt] n dynamite f

dyslexia [dɪs'lɛksɪə] n dyslexie f

dyslexic [dɪs'lɛksɪk] adj, n dyslexique m/f

E [iː] n (Mus): **E** mi m

E111 n abbr (= form E111) formulaire m E111

each [iːtʃ] adj chaque ▷ pron chacun(e); **~ other** l'un l'autre; **they hate ~ other** ils se détestent (mutuellement); **they have 2 books ~** ils ont 2 livres chacun; **they cost £5 ~** ils coûtent 5 livres (la) pièce

eager ['iːgəʳ] adj (person, buyer) empressé(e); (keen: pupil, worker) enthousiaste; **to be ~ to do sth** (impatient) brûler de faire qch; (keen) désirer vivement faire qch; **to be ~ for** (event) désirer vivement; (vengeance, affection, information) être avide de

eagle ['iːgl] n aigle m

ear [ɪəʳ] n oreille f; (of corn) épi m; **earache** n mal m aux oreilles; **eardrum** n tympan m

earl [əːl] n comte m

earlier ['əːlɪəʳ] adj (date etc) plus rapproché(e); (edition etc) plus ancien(ne), antérieur(e) ▷ adv plus tôt

early ['əːlɪ] adv tôt, de bonne heure; (ahead of time) en avance; (near the beginning) au début ▷ adj précoce, qui se manifeste (or se fait) tôt or de bonne heure; (Christians, settlers) premier(-ière); (reply) rapide; (death) prématuré(e); (work) de jeunesse; **to have an ~ night/start** se coucher/partir tôt or de bonne heure; **in the ~ or ~ in the spring/19th century** au début or commencement du printemps/19ème siècle; **early retirement** n retraite anticipée

earmark ['ɪəmɑːk] vt: **to ~ sth for** réserver or destiner qch à

earn [əːn] vt gagner; (Comm: yield) rapporter; **to ~ one's living** gagner sa vie

earnest ['əːnɪst] adj sérieux(-euse) ▷ n: **in ~** adv sérieusement, pour de bon

earnings ['əːnɪŋz] npl salaire m; gains mpl; (of company etc) profits mpl, bénéfices mpl

ear: earphones npl écouteurs mpl; **earplugs** npl boules fpl Quiès®; (to keep out water) protège-tympans mpl; **earring** n boucle f d'oreille

earth [əːθ] n (gen, also BRIT Elec) terre f ▷ vt (BRIT Elec) relier à la terre; **earthquake** n tremblement m de terre, séisme m

ease [iːz] n facilité f, aisance f; (comfort) bien-être m ▷ vt (soothe: mind) tranquilliser; (reduce: pain, problem) atténuer; (: tension) réduire; (loosen) relâcher, détendre; (help pass): **to ~ sth in/out** faire pénétrer/sortir qch délicatement or avec douceur, faciliter la pénétration/la sortie de qch; **at ~** à l'aise; (Mil) au repos

easily ['iːzɪlɪ] adv facilement; (by far) de loin

east [iːst] n est m ▷ adj (wind) d'est; (side) est inv ▷ adv à l'est, vers l'est; **the E~** l'Orient m; (Pol) les pays mpl de l'Est; **eastbound** adj en direction de l'est; (carriageway) est inv

Easter ['iːstəʳ] n Pâques fpl; **Easter egg** n œuf m de Pâques

eastern ['iːstən] adj de l'est, oriental(e)

Easter Sunday n le dimanche de Pâques

easy ['iːzɪ] adj facile; (manner) aisé(e) ▷ adv: **to take it** or **things ~** (rest) ne pas se fatiguer; (not worry) ne pas (trop) s'en faire; **easy-going** adj accommodant(e), facile à vivre

eat (pt **ate**, pp **~en**) [iːt, eɪt, 'iːtn] vt, vi manger; **can we have something to ~?** est-ce qu'on peut manger quelque chose?; **eat out** vi manger au restaurant

eavesdrop ['iːvzdrɔp] vi: **to ~ (on)** écouter de façon indiscrète

e-book ['iːbuk] n livre m électronique

e-business ['iːbɪznɪs] n (company) entreprise f électronique; (commerce) commerce m électronique

EC n abbr (= European Community) CE f

eccentric [ɪk'sɛntrɪk] adj, n excentrique m/f

echo, echoes ['ɛkəu] n écho m ▷ vt répéter ▷ vi résonner; faire écho

eclipse [ɪ'klɪps] n éclipse f

eco-friendly [iːkəu'frɛndlɪ] adj non nuisible à or qui ne nuit pas à l'environnement

ecological [iːkə'lɔdʒɪkəl] adj écologique

ecology [ɪ'kɔlədʒɪ] n écologie f

e-commerce [iːkɔmə:s] n commerce m électronique

economic [iːkə'nɔmɪk] adj économique; (profitable) rentable; **economical** adj

économique; (*person*) économe; **economics** *n*
(*Scol*) économie *f* politique ▷ *npl* (*of project etc*)
côté *m* or aspect *m* économique
economist [ɪˈkɒnəmɪst] *n* économiste *m/f*
economize [ɪˈkɒnəmaɪz] *vi* économiser, faire
des économies
economy [ɪˈkɒnəmɪ] *n* économie *f*; **economy
class** *n* (*Aviat*) classe *f* touriste; **economy
class syndrome** *n* syndrome *m* de la classe
économique
ecstasy [ˈɛkstəsɪ] *n* extase *f*; (*Drugs*) ecstasy *m*;
ecstatic [ɛksˈtætɪk] *adj* extatique, en extase
eczema [ˈɛksɪmə] *n* eczéma *m*
edge [ɛdʒ] *n* bord *m*; (*of knife etc*) tranchant *m*,
fil *m* ▷ *vt* border; **on ~** (*fig*) crispé(e), tendu(e)
edgy [ˈɛdʒɪ] *adj* crispé(e), tendu(e)
edible [ˈɛdɪbl] *adj* comestible; (*meal*)
mangeable
Edinburgh [ˈɛdɪnbərə] *n* Édimbourg

edit [ˈɛdɪt] *vt* (*text, book*) éditer; (*report*)
préparer; (*film*) monter; (*magazine*) diriger;
(*newspaper*) être le rédacteur or la rédactrice
en chef de; **edition** [ɪˈdɪʃən] *n* édition *f*;
editor *n* (*of newspaper*) rédacteur(-trice),
rédacteur(-trice) en chef; (*of sb's work*)
éditeur(-trice); (*also:* **film editor**)
monteur(-euse); **political/ foreign editor**
rédacteur politique/au service étranger;
editorial [ɛdɪˈtɔːrɪəl] *adj* de la rédaction,
éditorial(e) ▷ *n* éditorial *m*
educate [ˈɛdjukeɪt] *vt* (*teach*) instruire; (*bring
up*) éduquer; **educated** [ˈɛdjukeɪtɪd] *adj*
(*person*) cultivé(e)
education [ɛdjuˈkeɪʃən] *n* éducation *f*;
(*studies*) études *fpl*; (*teaching*) enseignement *m*,
instruction *f*; **educational** *adj* pédagogique;
(*institution*) scolaire; (*game, toy*) éducatif(-ive)
eel [iːl] *n* anguille *f*
eerie [ˈɪərɪ] *adj* inquiétant(e), spectral(e),
surnaturel(le)
effect [ɪˈfɛkt] *n* effet *m* ▷ *vt* effectuer; **effects**
npl (*property*) effets, affaires *fpl*; **to take ~**
(*Law*) entrer en vigueur, prendre effet; (*drug*)
agir, faire son effet; **in ~** en fait; **effective**
adj

efficace; (*actual*) véritable; **effectively** *adv*
efficacement; (*in reality*) effectivement, en fait
efficiency [ɪˈfɪʃənsɪ] *n* efficacité *f*; (*of machine,
car*) rendement *m*
efficient [ɪˈfɪʃənt] *adj* efficace; (*machine,
car*) d'un bon rendement; **efficiently** *adv*
efficacement
effort [ˈɛfət] *n* effort *m*; **effortless** *adj* sans
effort, aisé(e); (*achievement*) facile
e.g. *adv abbr* (= *exempli gratia*) par exemple,
p. ex.
egg [ɛg] *n* œuf *m*; **hard-boiled/soft-boiled
~** œuf dur/à la coque; **eggcup** *n* coquetier *m*;
egg plant (*us*) *n* aubergine *f*; **eggshell** *n*
coquille *f* d'œuf; **egg white** *n* blanc *m* d'œuf;
egg yolk *n* jaune *m* d'œuf
ego [ˈiːgəu] *n* (*self-esteem*) amour-propre *m*;
(*Psych*) moi *m*
Egypt [ˈiːdʒɪpt] *n* Égypte *f*; **Egyptian**
[ɪˈdʒɪpʃən] *adj* égyptien(ne) ▷ *n* Égyptien(ne)
Eiffel Tower [ˈaɪfəl-] *n* tour *f* Eiffel
eight [eɪt] *num* huit; **eighteen** *num* dix-huit;
eighteenth *num* dix-huitième; **eighth** *num*
huitième; **eightieth** [ˈeɪtɪɪθ] *num* quatre-
vingtième
eighty [ˈeɪtɪ] *num* quatre-vingt(s)
Eire [ˈɛərə] *n* République *f* d'Irlande
either [ˈaɪðə*] *adj* l'un ou l'autre; (*both, each*)
chaque ▷ *pron*: **~ (of them)** l'un ou l'autre
▷ *adv* non plus ▷ *conj*: **~ good or bad** soit
bon soit mauvais; **on ~ side** de chaque côté;
I don't like ~ je n'aime ni l'un ni l'autre; **no, I
don't ~** moi non plus; **which bike do you
want? - ~ will do** quel vélo voulez-vous?
- n'importe lequel; **answer with ~ yes or no**
répondez par oui ou par non
eject [ɪˈdʒɛkt] *vt* (*tenant etc*) expulser; (*object*)
éjecter
elaborate *adj* [ɪˈlæbərɪt] compliqué(e),
recherché(e), minutieux(-euse) ▷ *vb*
[ɪˈlæbəreɪt] ▷ *vt* élaborer ▷ *vi* entrer dans les
détails
elastic [ɪˈlæstɪk] *adj*, *n* élastique (*m*); **elastic
band** *n* (*BRIT*) élastique *m*
elbow [ˈɛlbəu] *n* coude *m*
elder [ˈɛldə*] *adj* aîné(e) ▷ *n* (*tree*) sureau *m*;
one's ~s ses aînés; **elderly** *adj* âgé(e) ▷ *npl*:
the elderly les personnes âgées
eldest [ˈɛldɪst] *adj*, *n*: **the ~ (child)** l'aîné(e)
(des enfants)
elect [ɪˈlɛkt] *vt* élire; (*choose*): **to ~ to do** choisir
de faire ▷ *adj*: **the president ~** le président
désigné; **election** *n* élection *f*; **electoral** *adj*
électoral(e); **electorate** *n* électorat *m*
electric [ɪˈlɛktrɪk] *adj* électrique; **electrical**
adj électrique; **electric blanket** *n* couverture
chauffante; **electric fire** *n* (*BRIT*) radiateur
m électrique; **electrician** [ɪlɛkˈtrɪʃən] *n*
électricien *m*; **electricity** [ɪlɛkˈtrɪsɪtɪ] *n*

électricité f; **electric shock** n choc m or décharge f électrique; **electrify** [ɪ'lɛktrɪfaɪ] vt (Rail) électrifier; (audience) électriser

electronic [ɪlɛk'trɒnɪk] adj électronique; **electronic mail** n courrier m électronique; **electronics** n électronique f

elegance ['ɛlɪɡəns] n élégance f

elegant ['ɛlɪɡənt] adj élégant(e)

element ['ɛlɪmənt] n (gen) élément m; (of heater, kettle etc) résistance f

elementary [ɛlɪ'mɛntərɪ] adj élémentaire; (school, education) primaire; **elementary school** n (us) école f primaire

elephant ['ɛlɪfənt] n éléphant m

elevate ['ɛlɪveɪt] vt élever

elevator ['ɛlɪveɪtə'] n (in warehouse etc) élévateur m, monte-charge m inv; (us: lift) ascenseur m

eleven [ɪ'lɛvn] num onze; **eleventh** num onzième

eligible ['ɛlɪdʒəbl] adj éligible; (for membership) admissible; **an ~ young man** un beau parti; **to be ~ for sth** remplir les conditions requises pour qch

eliminate [ɪ'lɪmɪneɪt] vt éliminer

elm [ɛlm] n orme m

eloquent ['ɛləkwənt] adj éloquent(e)

else [ɛls] adv: **something ~** quelque chose d'autre, autre chose; **somewhere ~** ailleurs, autre part; **everywhere ~** partout ailleurs; **everyone ~** tous les autres; **nothing ~** rien d'autre; **where ~?** à quel autre endroit?; **little ~** pas grand-chose d'autre; **elsewhere** adv ailleurs, autre part

elusive [ɪ'luːsɪv] adj insaisissable

e-mail ['iːmeɪl] n abbr (= electronic mail) e-mail m, courriel m ▷ vt: **to ~ sb** envoyer un e-mail or un courriel à qn; **e-mail address** n adresse f e-mail

embankment [ɪm'bæŋkmənt] n (of road, railway) remblai m, talus m; (of river) berge f, quai m; (dyke) digue f

embargo, embargoes [ɪm'bɑːgəu] n (Comm, Naut) embargo m; (prohibition) interdiction f

embark [ɪm'bɑːk] vi embarquer ▷ vt embarquer; **to ~ on** (journey etc) commencer, entreprendre; (fig) se lancer or s'embarquer dans

embarrass [ɪm'bærəs] vt embarrasser, gêner; **embarrassed** adj gêné(e); **embarrassing** adj gênant(e), embarrassant(e); **embarrassment** n embarras m, gêne f; (embarrassing thing, person) source f d'embarras

embassy ['ɛmbəsɪ] n ambassade f

embrace [ɪm'breɪs] vt embrasser, étreindre; (include) embrasser ▷ vi s'embrasser, s'étreindre ▷ n étreinte f

embroider [ɪm'brɔɪdə'] vt broder;

embroidery n broderie f

embryo ['ɛmbrɪəu] n (also fig) embryon m

emerald ['ɛmərəld] n émeraude f

emerge [ɪ'məːdʒ] vi apparaître; (from room, car) surgir; (from sleep, imprisonment) sortir

emergency [ɪ'məːdʒənsɪ] n (crisis) cas m d'urgence; (Med) urgence f; **in an ~** en cas d'urgence; **state of ~** état m d'urgence; **emergency brake** (us) n frein m à main; **emergency exit** n sortie f de secours; **emergency landing** n atterrissage forcé; **emergency room** n (us: Med) urgences fpl; **emergency services** npl: **the emergency services** (fire, police, ambulance) les services mpl d'urgence

emigrate ['ɛmɪgreɪt] vi émigrer; **emigration** [ɛmɪ'greɪʃən] n émigration f

eminent ['ɛmɪnənt] adj éminent(e)

emissions [ɪ'mɪʃənz] npl émissions fpl

emit [ɪ'mɪt] vt émettre

emotion [ɪ'məuʃən] n sentiment m; **emotional** adj (person) émotif(-ive), très sensible; (needs) affectif(-ive); (scene) émouvant(e); (tone, speech) qui fait appel aux sentiments

emperor ['ɛmpərə'] n empereur m

emphasis (pl **-ases**) ['ɛmfəsɪs, -siːz] n accent m; **to lay** or **place ~ on sth** (fig) mettre l'accent sur, insister sur

emphasize ['ɛmfəsaɪz] vt (syllable, word, point) appuyer or insister sur; (feature) souligner, accentuer

empire ['ɛmpaɪə'] n empire m

employ [ɪm'plɔɪ] vt employer; **employee** [ɪmplɔɪ'iː] n employé(e); **employer** n employeur(-euse); **employment** n emploi m; **employment agency** n agence f or bureau m de placement

empower [ɪm'pauə'] vt: **to ~ sb to do** autoriser or habiliter qn à faire

empress ['ɛmprɪs] n impératrice f

emptiness ['ɛmptɪnɪs] n vide m; (of area) aspect m désertique

empty ['ɛmptɪ] adj vide; (street, area) désert(e); (threat, promise) en l'air, vain(e) ▷ vt vider ▷ vi se vider; (liquid) s'écouler; **empty-handed** adj les mains vides

EMU n abbr (= European Monetary Union) UME f

emulsion [ɪ'mʌlʃən] n émulsion f; (also: ~ **paint**) peinture mate

enable [ɪ'neɪbl] vt: **to ~ sb to do** permettre à qn de faire

enamel [ɪ'næməl] n émail m; (also: ~ **paint**) (peinture f) laque f

enchanting [ɪn'tʃɑːntɪŋ] adj ravissant(e), enchanteur(-eresse)

encl. abbr (on letters etc: = enclosed) ci-joint(e); (= enclosure) PJ f

enclose [ɪn'kləʊz] vt (land) clôturer; (space, object) entourer; (letter etc) **to ~ (with)** joindre (à); **please find ~d** veuillez trouver ci-joint

enclosure [ɪn'kləʊʒəʳ] n enceinte f

encore [ɔŋ'kɔːʳ] excl, n bis (m)

encounter [ɪn'kaʊntəʳ] n rencontre f ▷ vt rencontrer

encourage [ɪn'kʌrɪdʒ] vt encourager; **encouragement** n encouragement m

encouraging [ɪn'kʌrɪdʒɪŋ] adj encourageant(e)

encyclop(a)edia [ɛnsaɪkləʊ'piːdɪə] n encyclopédie f

end [ɛnd] n fin f; (of table, street, rope etc) bout m, extrémité f ▷ vt terminer; (also: **bring to an ~, put an ~ to**) mettre fin à ▷ vi se terminer, finir; **in the ~** finalement; **on ~** (object) debout, dressé(e); **to stand on ~** (hair) se dresser sur la tête; **for hours on ~** pendant des heures (et des heures); **end up** vi: **to ~ up in** (condition) finir or se terminer par; (place) finir or aboutir à

endanger [ɪn'deɪndʒəʳ] vt mettre en danger; **an ~ed species** une espèce en voie de disparition

endearing [ɪn'dɪərɪŋ] adj attachant(e)

endeavour (US **endeavor**) [ɪn'dɛvəʳ] n effort m; (attempt) tentative f ▷ vt: **to ~ to do** tenter or s'efforcer de faire

ending ['ɛndɪŋ] n dénouement m, conclusion f; (Ling) terminaison f

endless ['ɛndlɪs] adj sans fin, interminable

endorse [ɪn'dɔːs] vt (cheque) endosser; (approve) appuyer, approuver, sanctionner; **endorsement** n (approval) appui m, aval m; (BRIT: on driving licence) contravention f (portée au permis de conduire)

endurance [ɪn'djʊərəns] n endurance f

endure [ɪn'djʊəʳ] vt (bear) supporter, endurer ▷ vi (last) durer

enemy ['ɛnəmɪ] adj, n ennemi(e)

energetic [ɛnə'dʒɛtɪk] adj énergique; (activity) très actif(-ive), qui fait se dépenser (physiquement)

energy ['ɛnədʒɪ] n énergie f

enforce [ɪn'fɔːs] vt (law) appliquer, faire respecter

engaged [ɪn'geɪdʒd] adj (BRIT: busy, in use) occupé(e); (betrothed) fiancé(e); **to get ~** se fiancer; **the line's ~** la ligne est occupée; **engaged tone** n (BRIT Tel) tonalité f occupé inv

engagement [ɪn'geɪdʒmənt] n (undertaking) obligation f, engagement m; (appointment) rendez-vous m inv; (to marry) fiançailles fpl; **engagement ring** n bague f de fiançailles

engaging [ɪn'geɪdʒɪŋ] adj engageant(e), attirant(e)

engine ['ɛndʒɪn] n (Aut) moteur m; (Rail) locomotive f

> Be careful not to translate **engine** by the French word **engin**.

engineer [ɛndʒɪ'nɪəʳ] n ingénieur m; (BRIT: repairer) dépanneur m; (Navy, US Rail) mécanicien m; **engineering** n engineering m, ingénierie f; (of bridges, ships) génie m; (of machine) mécanique f

England ['ɪŋglənd] n Angleterre f

English ['ɪŋglɪʃ] adj anglais(e) ▷ n (Ling) anglais m; **the ~** npl les Anglais; **English Channel** n: **the English Channel** la Manche; **Englishman** (irreg) n Anglais m; **Englishwoman** (irreg) n Anglaise f

engrave [ɪn'greɪv] vt graver

engraving [ɪn'greɪvɪŋ] n gravure f

enhance [ɪn'hɑːns] vt rehausser, mettre en valeur

enjoy [ɪn'dʒɔɪ] vt aimer, prendre plaisir à; (have benefit of: health, fortune) jouir de; (: success) connaître; **to ~ o.s.** s'amuser; **enjoyable** adj agréable; **enjoyment** n plaisir m

enlarge [ɪn'lɑːdʒ] vt accroître; (Phot) agrandir ▷ vi: **to ~ on** (subject) s'étendre sur; **enlargement** n (Phot) agrandissement m

enlist [ɪn'lɪst] vt recruter; (support) s'assurer ▷ vi s'engager

enormous [ɪ'nɔːməs] adj énorme

enough [ɪ'nʌf] adj: **~ time/books** assez or suffisamment de temps/livres ▷ adv: **big ~** assez or suffisamment grand ▷ pron: **have you got ~?** (en) avez-vous assez?; **~ to eat** assez à manger; **that's ~, thanks** cela suffit or c'est assez, merci; **I've had ~ of him** j'en ai assez de lui; **he has not worked ~** il n'a pas assez or suffisamment travaillé, il n'a pas travaillé assez or suffisamment; **... which, funnily** or **oddly ~ ...** qui, chose curieuse

enquire [ɪn'kwaɪəʳ] vt, vi = **inquire**

enquiry [ɪn'kwaɪərɪ] n = **inquiry**

enrage [ɪn'reɪdʒ] vt mettre en fureur or en rage, rendre furieux(-euse)

enrich [ɪn'rɪtʃ] vt enrichir

enrol (US **enroll**) [ɪn'rəʊl] vt inscrire ▷ vi s'inscrire; **enrolment** (US **enrollment**) n inscription f

en route [ɔn'ruːt] adv en route, en chemin

en suite ['ɔnswiːt] adj: **with ~ bathroom** avec salle de bains en attenante

ensure [ɪn'ʃʊəʳ] vt assurer, garantir

entail [ɪn'teɪl] vt entraîner, nécessiter

enter ['ɛntəʳ] vt (room) entrer dans, pénétrer dans; (club, army) entrer à; (competition) s'inscrire à or pour; (sb for a competition) (faire) inscrire; (write down) inscrire, noter; (Comput) entrer, introduire ▷ vi entrer

enterprise ['ɛntəpraɪz] n (company, undertaking) entreprise f; (initiative) (esprit *m* d')initiative *f*; **free ~** libre entreprise; **private ~** entreprise privée; **enterprising** *adj* entreprenant(e), dynamique; (*scheme*) audacieux(-euse)

entertain [ɛntə'teɪn] *vt* amuser, distraire; (*invite*) recevoir (à dîner); (*idea, plan*) envisager; **entertainer** *n* artiste *m/f* de variétés; **entertaining** *adj* amusant(e), distrayant(e); **entertainment** *n* (*amusement*) distraction *f*, divertissement *m*, amusement *m*; (*show*) spectacle *m*

enthusiasm [ɪn'θuːzɪæzəm] *n* enthousiasme *m*

enthusiast [ɪn'θuːzɪæst] *n* enthousiaste *m/f*; **enthusiastic** [ɪnθuːzɪ'æstɪk] *adj* enthousiaste; **to be enthusiastic about** être enthousiasmé(e) par

entire [ɪn'taɪə'] *adj* (tout) entier(-ère); **entirely** *adv* entièrement, complètement

entitle [ɪn'taɪtl] *vt*: **to ~ sb to sth** donner droit à qch à qn; **entitled** *adj* (*book*) intitulé(e); **to be entitled to do** avoir le droit de faire

entrance *n* ['ɛntrns] entrée *f* ▷ *vt* [ɪn'trɑːns] enchanter, ravir; **where's the ~?** où est l'entrée?; **to gain ~ to** (*university etc*) être admis à; **entrance examination** *n* examen *m* d'entrée *or* d'admission; **entrance fee** *n* (*to museum etc*) prix *m* d'entrée; (*to join club etc*) droit *m* d'inscription; **entrance ramp** *n* (*us Aut*) bretelle *f* d'accès; **entrant** *n* (*in race etc*) participant(e), concurrent(e); (*BRIT: in exam*) candidat(e)

entrepreneur ['ɔntrəprə'nəː'] *n* entrepreneur *m*

entrust [ɪn'trʌst] *vt*: **to ~ sth to** confier qch à

entry ['ɛntrɪ] *n* entrée *f*; (*in register, diary*) inscription *f*; **"no ~"** "défense d'entrer", "entrée interdite"; (*Aut*) "sens interdit"; **entry phone** *n* (*BRIT*) interphone *m* (à l'entrée d'un immeuble)

envelope ['ɛnvələup] *n* enveloppe *f*

envious ['ɛnvɪəs] *adj* envieux(-euse)

environment [ɪn'vaɪrnmənt] *n* (*social, moral*) milieu *m*; (*natural world*): **the ~** l'environnement *m*; **environmental** [ɪnvaɪərn'mɛntl] *adj* (*of surroundings*) du milieu; (*issue, disaster*) écologique; **environmentally** [ɪnvaɪərn'mɛntlɪ] *adv*: **environmentally sound/friendly** qui ne nuit pas à l'environnement

envisage [ɪn'vɪzɪdʒ] *vt* (*foresee*) prévoir

envoy ['ɛnvɔɪ] *n* envoyé(e); (*diplomat*) ministre *m* plénipotentiaire

envy ['ɛnvɪ] *n* envie *f* ▷ *vt* envier; **to ~ sb sth** envier qch à qn

epic ['ɛpɪk] *n* épopée *f* ▷ *adj* épique

epidemic [ɛpɪ'dɛmɪk] *n* épidémie *f*

epilepsy ['ɛpɪlɛpsɪ] *n* épilepsie *f*; **epileptic** *adj, n* épileptique *m/f*; **epileptic fit** *n* crise *f*

d'épilepsie

episode ['ɛpɪsəud] *n* épisode *m*

equal ['iːkwl] *adj* égal(e) ▷ *vt* égaler; **~ to** (*task*) à la hauteur de; **equality** [iː'kwɔlɪtɪ] *n* égalité *f*; **equalize** *vt, vi* (*Sport*) égaliser; **equally** *adv* également; (*share*) en parts égales; (*treat*) de la même façon; (*pay*) autant; (*just as*) tout aussi

equation [ɪ'kweɪʃən] *n* (*Math*) équation *f*

equator [ɪ'kweɪtə'] *n* équateur *m*

equip [ɪ'kwɪp] *vt* équiper; **to ~ sb/sth with** équiper *or* munir qn/qch de; **equipment** *n* équipement *m*; (*electrical etc*) appareillage *m*, installation *f*

equivalent [ɪ'kwɪvəlnt] *adj* équivalent(e) ▷ *n* équivalent *m*; **to be ~ to** équivaloir à, être équivalent(e) à

ER *abbr* (*BRIT*: = Elizabeth Regina) la reine Élisabeth; (*US: Med*: = emergency room) urgences *fpl*

era ['ɪərə] *n* ère *f*, époque *f*

erase [ɪ'reɪz] *vt* effacer; **eraser** *n* gomme *f*

erect [ɪ'rɛkt] *adj* droit(e) ▷ *vt* construire; (*monument*) ériger, élever; (*tent etc*) dresser; **erection** [ɪ'rɛkʃən] *n* (*Physiol*) érection *f*; (*of building*) construction *f*

ERM *n abbr* (= Exchange Rate Mechanism) mécanisme *m* des taux de change

erode [ɪ'rəud] *vt* éroder; (*metal*) ronger

erosion [ɪ'rəuʒən] *n* érosion *f*

erotic [ɪ'rɔtɪk] *adj* érotique

errand ['ɛrnd] *n* course *f*, commission *f*

erratic [ɪ'rætɪk] *adj* irrégulier(-ière), inconstant(e)

error ['ɛrə'] *n* erreur *f*

erupt [ɪ'rʌpt] *vi* entrer en éruption; (*fig*) éclater; **eruption** [ɪ'rʌpʃən] *n* éruption *f*; (*of anger, violence*) explosion *f*

escalate ['ɛskəleɪt] *vi* s'intensifier; (*costs*) monter en flèche

escalator ['ɛskəleɪtə'] *n* escalier roulant

escape [ɪ'skeɪp] *n* évasion *f*, fuite *f*; (*of gas etc*) fuite ▷ *vi* s'échapper, fuir; (*from jail*) s'évader; (*fig*) s'en tirer; (*leak*) s'échapper ▷ *vt* échapper à; **to ~ from** (*person*) échapper à; (*place*) s'échapper de; (*fig*) fuir; **his name ~s me** son nom m'échappe

escort *vt* [ɪ'skɔːt] escorter ▷ *n* ['ɛskɔːt] (*Mil*) escorte *f*

especially [ɪ'spɛʃlɪ] *adv* (*particularly*) particulièrement; (*above all*) surtout

espionage ['ɛspɪənɑːʒ] *n* espionnage *m*

essay ['ɛseɪ] *n* (*Scol*) dissertation *f*; (*Literature*) essai *m*

essence ['ɛsns] *n* essence *f*; (*Culin*) extrait *m*

essential [ɪ'sɛnʃl] *adj* essentiel(le); (*basic*) fondamental(e); **essentials** *npl* éléments essentiels; **essentially** *adv* essentiellement

establish [ɪ'stæblɪʃ] *vt* établir; (*business*)

fonder, créer; (one's power etc) asseoir, affirmir; **establishment** n établissement m; (founding) création f; (institution) établissement; **the Establishment** les pouvoirs établis; l'ordre établi

estate [ɪˈsteɪt] n (land) domaine m, propriété f; (Law) biens mpl, succession f; (BRIT: also: **housing ~**) lotissement m; **estate agent** n (BRIT) agent immobilier; **estate car** n (BRIT) break m

estimate n [ˈɛstɪmət] estimation f; (Comm) devis m ▷ vb [ˈɛstɪmeɪt] ▷ vt estimer

etc abbr (= et cetera) etc

eternal [ɪˈtəːnl] adj éternel(le)

eternity [ɪˈtəːnɪtɪ] n éternité f

ethical [ˈɛθɪkl] adj moral(e); **ethics** [ˈɛθɪks] n éthique f ▷ npl moralité f

Ethiopia [iːθɪˈəʊpɪə] n Éthiopie f

ethnic [ˈɛθnɪk] adj ethnique; (clothes, food) folklorique, exotique, propre aux minorités ethniques non-occidentales; **ethnic minority** n minorité f ethnique

e-ticket [ˈiːtɪkɪt] n billet m électronique

etiquette [ˈɛtɪkɛt] n convenances fpl, étiquette f

EU n abbr (= European Union) UE f

euro [ˈjuərəu] n (currency) euro m

Europe [ˈjuərəp] n Europe f; **European** [juərəˈpiːən] adj européen(ne) ▷ n Européen(ne); **European Community** n Communauté européenne; **European Union** n Union européenne

Eurostar® [ˈjuərəustɑːʳ] n Eurostar® m

evacuate [ɪˈvækjueɪt] vt évacuer

evade [ɪˈveɪd] vt échapper à; (question etc) éluder; (duties) se dérober à

evaluate [ɪˈvæljueɪt] vt évaluer

evaporate [ɪˈvæpəreɪt] vi s'évaporer; (fig: hopes, fear) s'envoler; (anger) se dissiper

eve [iːv] n: **on the ~ of** à la veille de

even [ˈiːvn] adj (level, smooth) régulier(-ière); (equal) égal(e); (number) pair(e) ▷ adv même; **~ if** même si + indic; **~ though** alors même que + cond; **~ more** encore plus; **~ faster** encore plus vite; **~ so** quand même; **not ~** pas même; **~ he was there** même lui était là; **~ on Sundays** même le dimanche; **to get ~ with sb** prendre sa revanche sur qn

evening [ˈiːvnɪŋ] n soir m; (as duration, event) soirée f; **in the ~** le soir; **evening class** n cours m du soir; **evening dress** n (man's) tenue f de soirée, smoking m; (woman's) robe f de soirée

event [ɪˈvɛnt] n événement m; (Sport) épreuve f; **in the ~ of** en cas de; **eventful** adj mouvementé(e)

eventual [ɪˈvɛntʃuəl] adj final(e)

> Be careful not to translate **eventual** by the French word **éventuel**.

eventually [ɪˈvɛntʃuəlɪ] adv finalement

> Be careful not to translate **eventually** by the French word **éventuellement**.

ever [ˈɛvəʳ] adv jamais; (at all times) toujours; (in questions): **why ~ not?** mais enfin, pourquoi pas?; **the best ~** le meilleur qu'on ait jamais vu; **have you ~ seen it?** l'as-tu déjà vu?, as-tu eu l'occasion or t'est-il arrivé de le voir?; **~ since** (as adv) depuis; (as conj) depuis que; **~ so pretty** si joli; **evergreen** n arbre m à feuilles persistantes

 KEYWORD

every [ˈɛvrɪ] adj **1** (each) chaque; **every one of them** (sans exception) tous; **every shop in town was closed** tous les magasins en ville étaient fermés

2 (all possible) tous (toutes) les; **I gave you every assistance** j'ai fait tout mon possible pour vous aider; **I have every confidence in him** j'ai entièrement or pleinement confiance en lui; **we wish you every success** nous vous souhaitons beaucoup de succès

3 (showing recurrence) tous les; **every day** tous les jours, chaque jour; **every other car** une voiture sur deux; **every other/third day** tous les deux/trois jours; **every now and then** de temps en temps; **everybody = everyone**; **everyday** adj (expression) courant(e), d'usage courant; (use) courant; (clothes, life) de tous les jours; (occurrence, problem) quotidien(ne); **everyone** pron tout le monde, tous pl; **everything** pron tout; **everywhere** adv partout; **everywhere you go you meet ...** où qu'on aille, on rencontre ...

evict [ɪˈvɪkt] vt expulser

evidence [ˈɛvɪdns] n (proof) preuve(s) f(pl); (of witness) témoignage m; (sign): **to show ~ of** donner des signes de; **to give ~** témoigner, déposer

evident [ˈɛvɪdnt] adj évident(e); **evidently** adv de toute évidence; (apparently) apparemment

evil [ˈiːvl] adj mauvais(e) ▷ n mal m

evoke [ɪˈvəuk] vt évoquer

evolution [iːvəˈluːʃən] n évolution f

evolve [ɪˈvɔlv] vt élaborer ▷ vi évoluer, se transformer

ewe [juː] n brebis f

ex [ɛks] n (inf): **my ex** mon ex

ex- [ɛks] prefix ex-

exact [ɪgˈzækt] adj exact(e) ▷ vt: **to ~ sth (from)** (signature, confession) extorquer qch (à); (apology) exiger qch (de); **exactly** adv exactement

exaggerate [ɪgˈzædʒəreɪt] vt, vi exagérer; **exaggeration** [ɪgzædʒəˈreɪʃən] n exagération f

exam [ɪgˈzæm] n abbr (Scol) = **examination**

examination [ɪgzæmɪˈneɪʃən] n (Scol, Med) examen m; **to take** or **sit an ~** (BRIT) passer un examen

examine [ɪgˈzæmɪn] vt (gen) examiner; (Scol, Law: person) interroger; **examiner** n examinateur(-trice)

example [ɪgˈzɑːmpl] n exemple m; **for ~** par exemple

exasperated [ɪgˈzɑːspəreɪtɪd] adj exaspéré(e)

excavate [ˈɛkskəveɪt] vt (site) fouiller, excaver; (object) mettre au jour

exceed [ɪkˈsiːd] vt dépasser; (one's powers) outrepasser; **exceedingly** adv extrêmement

excel [ɪkˈsɛl] vi exceller ▷ vt surpasser; **to ~ o.s.** se surpasser

excellence [ˈɛksələns] n excellence f

excellent [ˈɛksələnt] adj excellent(e)

except [ɪkˈsɛpt] prep (also: **~ for, ~ing**) sauf, excepté, à l'exception de ▷ vt excepter; **~ if/when** sauf si/quand; **~ that** excepté que, si ce n'est que; **exception** [ɪkˈsɛpʃən] n exception f; **to take exception to** s'offusquer de; **exceptional** [ɪkˈsɛpʃənl] adj exceptionnel(le); **exceptionally** [ɪkˈsɛpʃənəlɪ] adv exceptionnellement

excerpt [ˈɛksəːpt] n extrait m

excess [ɪkˈsɛs] n excès m; **excess baggage** n excédent m de bagages; **excessive** adj excessif(-ive)

exchange [ɪksˈtʃeɪndʒ] n échange m; (also: **telephone ~**) central m ▷ vt: **to ~ (for)** échanger (contre); **could I ~ this, please?** est-ce que je peux échanger ceci, s'il vous plaît?; **exchange rate** n taux m de change

excite [ɪkˈsaɪt] vt exciter; **excited** adj (tout) (toute) excité(e); **to get excited** s'exciter; **excitement** n excitation f; **exciting** adj passionnant(e)

exclaim [ɪkˈskleɪm] vi s'exclamer; **exclamation** [ɛkskləˈmeɪʃən] n exclamation f; **exclamation mark** (us **exclamation point**) n point m d'exclamation

exclude [ɪkˈskluːd] vt exclure

excluding [ɪkˈskluːdɪŋ] prep: **~ VAT** la TVA non comprise

exclusion [ɪkˈskluːʒən] n exclusion f

exclusive [ɪkˈskluːsɪv] adj exclusif(-ive); (club, district) sélect(e); (item of news) en exclusivité; **~ of VAT** TVA non comprise; **exclusively** adv exclusivement

excruciating [ɪkˈskruːʃɪeɪtɪŋ] adj (pain) atroce, déchirant(e); (embarrassing) pénible

excursion [ɪkˈskəːʃən] n excursion f

excuse n [ɪkˈskjuːs] excuse f ▷ vt [ɪkˈskjuːz] (forgive) excuser; **to ~ sb from** (activity) dispenser qn de; **~ me!** excusez-moi!, pardon!;

now if you will ~ me, ... maintenant, si vous (le) permettez ...

ex-directory [ˈɛksdɪˈrɛktərɪ] adj (BRIT) sur la liste rouge

execute [ˈɛksɪkjuːt] vt exécuter; **execution** [ɛksɪˈkjuːʃən] n exécution f

executive [ɪgˈzɛkjutɪv] n (person) cadre m; (managing group) bureau m; (Pol) exécutif m ▷ adj exécutif(-ive); (position, job) de cadre

exempt [ɪgˈzɛmpt] adj: **~ from** exempté(e) or dispensé(e) de ▷ vt: **to ~ sb from** exempter or dispenser qn de

exercise [ˈɛksəsaɪz] n exercice m ▷ vt exercer; (patience etc) faire preuve de; (dog) promener ▷ vi (also: **to take ~**) prendre de l'exercice; **exercise book** n cahier m

exert [ɪgˈzəːt] vt exercer, employer; **to ~ o.s.** se dépenser; **exertion** [ɪgˈzəːʃən] n effort m

exhale [ɛksˈheɪl] vt exhaler ▷ vi expirer

exhaust [ɪgˈzɔːst] n (also: **~ fumes**) gaz mpl d'échappement; (also: **~ pipe**) tuyau m d'échappement ▷ vt épuiser; **exhausted** adj épuisé(e); **exhaustion** [ɪgˈzɔːstʃən] n épuisement m; **nervous exhaustion** fatigue nerveuse

exhibit [ɪgˈzɪbɪt] n (Art) pièce f or objet m exposé(e); (Law) pièce à conviction ▷ vt (Art) exposer; (courage, skill) faire preuve de; **exhibition** [ɛksɪˈbɪʃən] n exposition f

exhilarating [ɪgˈzɪləreɪtɪŋ] adj grisant(e), stimulant(e)

exile [ˈɛksaɪl] n exil m; (person) exilé(e) ▷ vt exiler

exist [ɪgˈzɪst] vi exister; **existence** n existence f; **existing** adj actuel(le)

exit [ˈɛksɪt] n sortie f ▷ vi (Comput, Theat) sortir; **where's the ~?** où est la sortie?; **exit ramp** n (us Aut) bretelle f d'accès

exotic [ɪgˈzɔtɪk] adj exotique

expand [ɪkˈspænd] vt (area) agrandir; (quantity) accroître ▷ vi (trade, etc) se développer, s'accroître; (gas, metal) se dilater

expansion [ɪkˈspænʃən] n (territorial, economic) expansion f; (of trade, influence etc) développement m; (of production) accroissement m; (of population) croissance f; (of gas, metal) expansion, dilatation f

expect [ɪkˈspɛkt] vt (anticipate) s'attendre à, s'attendre à ce que + sub; (count on) compter sur, escompter; (require) demander, exiger; (suppose) supposer; (await: also baby) attendre ▷ vi: **to be ~ing** (pregnant woman) être enceinte; **expectation** [ɛkspɛkˈteɪʃən] n (hope) attente f, espérance(s) f(pl); (belief) attente

expedition [ɛkspəˈdɪʃən] n expédition f

expel [ɪkˈspɛl] vt chasser, expulser; (Scol) renvoyer, exclure

expenditure [ɪkˈspɛndɪtʃəʳ] n (act of spending)

dépense f; (money spent) dépenses fpl
expense [ɪk'spɛns] n (high cost) coût m;
(spending) dépense f, frais mpl; **expenses**
npl frais mpl; dépenses; **at the ~ of** (fig) aux
dépens de; **expense account** n (note f de)
frais mpl
expensive [ɪk'spɛnsɪv] adj cher (chère),
coûteux(-euse); **it's too ~** ça coûte trop cher
experience [ɪk'spɪərɪəns] n expérience f ▷ vt
connaître; (feeling) éprouver; **experienced** adj
expérimenté(e)
experiment [ɪk'spɛrɪmənt] n expérience
f ▷ vi faire une expérience; **experimental**
[ɪkspɛrɪ'mɛntl] adj expérimental(e)
expert ['ɛkspə:t] adj expert(e) ▷ n expert m;
expertise [ɛkspə:'ti:z] n (grande)
compétence
expire [ɪk'spaɪəʳ] vi expirer; **expiry** n
expiration f; **expiry date** n date f d'expiration;
(on label) à utiliser avant ...
explain [ɪk'spleɪn] vt expliquer; **explanation**
[ɛksplə'neɪʃən] n explication f
explicit [ɪk'splɪsɪt] adj explicite; (definite)
formel(le)
explode [ɪk'spləud] vi exploser
exploit n ['ɛksplɔɪt] exploit m ▷ vt [ɪk'splɔɪt]
exploiter; **exploitation** [ɛksplɔɪ'teɪʃən] n
exploitation f
explore [ɪk'splɔ:ʳ] vt explorer; (possibilities)
étudier, examiner; **explorer** n
explorateur(-trice)
explosion [ɪk'spləuʒən] n explosion f;
explosive [ɪk'spləusɪv] adj explosif(-ive) ▷ n
explosif m
export vt [ɛk'spɔ:t] exporter ▷ n ['ɛkspɔ:t]
exportation f ▷ cpd d'exportation; **exporter** n
exportateur m
expose [ɪk'spəuz] vt exposer; (unmask)
démasquer, dévoiler; **exposed** adj (land,
house) exposé(e); **exposure** [ɪk'spəuʒəʳ] n
exposition f; (publicity) couverture f; (Phot:
speed) (temps m de) pose f; (: shot) pose; **to die
of exposure** (Med) mourir de froid
express [ɪk'sprɛs] adj (definite) formel(le),
exprès(-esse); (BRIT: letter etc) exprès inv ▷ n
(train) rapide m ▷ vt exprimer; **expression**
[ɪk'sprɛʃən] n expression f; **expressway** n
(US) voie f express (à plusieurs files)
exquisite [ɛk'skwɪzɪt] adj exquis(e)
extend [ɪk'stɛnd] vt (visit, street) prolonger,
remettre; (building) agrandir; (offer) présenter,
offrir; (hand, arm) tendre ▷ vi (land) s'étendre;
extension n (of visit, street) prolongation
f; (building) annexe f; (telephone: in offices)
poste m; (: in private house) téléphone m
supplémentaire; **extension cable, extension
lead** n (Elec) rallonge f; **extensive** adj
étendu(e), vaste; (damage, alterations)
considérable; (inquiries) approfondi(e)

extent [ɪk'stɛnt] n étendue f; **to some ~** dans
une certaine mesure; **to the ~ of ...** au point
de ...; **to what ~?** dans quelle mesure?, jusqu'à
quel point?; **to such an ~ that ...** à tel point
que ...
exterior [ɛk'stɪərɪəʳ] adj extérieur(e) ▷ n
extérieur m
external [ɛk'stə:nl] adj externe
extinct [ɪk'stɪŋkt] adj (volcano) éteint(e);
(species) disparu(e); **extinction** n extinction f
extinguish [ɪk'stɪŋgwɪʃ] vt éteindre
extra ['ɛkstrə] adj supplémentaire, de plus
▷ adv (in addition) en plus ▷ n supplément m;
(perk) à-coté m; (Cine, Theat) figurant(e)
extract vt [ɪk'strækt] extraire; (tooth)
arracher; (money, promise) soutirer ▷ n
['ɛkstrækt] extrait m
extradite ['ɛkstrədaɪt] vt extrader
extraordinary [ɪk'strɔ:dnrɪ] adj
extraordinaire
extravagance [ɪk'strævəgəns] n (excessive
spending) prodigalités fpl; (thing bought)
folie f, dépense excessive; **extravagant** adj
extravagant(e); (in spending: person) prodigue,
dépensier(-ière); (: tastes) dispendieux(-euse)
extreme [ɪk'stri:m] adj, n extrême (m);
extremely adv extrêmement
extremist [ɪk'stri:mɪst] adj, n extrémiste m/f
extrovert ['ɛkstrəvə:t] n extraverti(e)
eye [aɪ] n œil m ((yeux) pl); (of needle) trou
m, chas m ▷ vt examiner; **to keep an ~ on**
surveiller; **eyeball** n globe m oculaire;
eyebrow n sourcil m; **eyedrops** npl
gouttes fpl pour les yeux; **eyelash** n cil m;
eyelid n paupière f; **eyeliner** n eye-liner m;
eyeshadow n ombre f à paupières; **eyesight**
n vue f; **eye witness** n témoin m oculaire

F [ɛf] n (Mus): **F** fa m
fabric ['fæbrɪk] n tissu m
fabulous ['fæbjʊləs] adj fabuleux(-euse); (inf: super) formidable, sensationnel(le)
face [feɪs] n visage m, figure f; (expression) air m; (of clock) cadran m; (of cliff) paroi f; (of mountain) face f; (of building) façade f ▷ vt faire face à; (facts etc) accepter; **~ down** (person) à plat ventre; (card) face en dessous; **to lose/save ~** perdre/sauver la face; **to pull a ~** faire une grimace; **in the ~ of** (difficulties etc) face à, devant; **on the ~ of it** à première vue; **~ to ~** face à face; **face up to** vt fus faire face à, affronter; **face cloth** n (BRIT) gant m de toilette; **face pack** n (BRIT) masque m (de beauté)
facial ['feɪʃl] adj facial(e) ▷ n soin complet du visage
facilitate [fə'sɪlɪteɪt] vt faciliter
facilities [fə'sɪlɪtɪz] npl installations fpl, équipement m; **credit ~** facilités de paiement
fact [fækt] n fait m; **in ~** en fait
faction ['fækʃən] n faction f
factor ['fæktər] n facteur m; (of sun cream) indice m (de protection); **I'd like a ~ 15 suntan lotion** je voudrais une crème solaire d'indice 15
factory ['fæktərɪ] n usine f, fabrique f
factual ['fæktjʊəl] adj basé(e) sur les faits
faculty ['fækəltɪ] n faculté f; (US: teaching staff) corps enseignant

fad [fæd] n (personal) manie f; (craze) engouement m
fade [feɪd] vi se décolorer, passer; (light, sound) s'affaiblir; (flower) se faner; (sound) s'affaiblir; **fade away** vi (sound) s'affaiblir
fag [fæg] n (BRIT inf: cigarette) clope f
Fahrenheit ['fɑːrənhaɪt] n Fahrenheit m inv
fail [feɪl] vt (exam) échouer à; (candidate) recaler; (subj: courage, memory) faire défaut à ▷ vi échouer; (eyesight, health, light: also: **be ~ing**) baisser, s'affaiblir; (brakes) lâcher; **to ~ to do sth** (neglect) négliger de or ne pas faire qch; (be unable) ne pas arriver or parvenir à faire qch; **without ~** à coup sûr; sans faute; **failing** n défaut m ▷ prep faute de; **failing that** à défaut, sinon; **failure** ['feɪljər] n échec m; (person) raté(e); (mechanical) défaillance f
faint [feɪnt] adj faible; (recollection) vague; (mark) à peine visible ▷ n évanouissement m ▷ vi s'évanouir; **to feel ~** défaillir; **faintest** adj: **I haven't the faintest idea** je n'en ai pas la moindre idée; **faintly** adv faiblement; (vaguely) vaguement
fair [feər] adj équitable, juste; (hair) blond(e); (skin, complexion) pâle, blanc (blanche); (weather) beau (belle); (good enough) assez bon(ne); (sizeable) considérable ▷ adv: **to play ~** jouer franc jeu ▷ n foire f; (BRIT: funfair) fête (foraine); **fairground** n champ m de foire; **fair-haired** adj (person) aux cheveux clairs, blond(e); **fairly** adv (justly) équitablement; (quite) assez; **fair trade** n commerce m équitable; **fairway** n (Golf) fairway m
fairy ['fɛərɪ] n fée f; **fairy tale** n conte m de fées
faith [feɪθ] n foi f; (trust) confiance f; (sect) culte m, religion f; **faithful** adj fidèle; **faithfully** adv fidèlement; **yours faithfully** (BRIT: in letters) veuillez agréer l'expression de mes salutations les plus distinguées
fake [feɪk] n (painting etc) faux m; (person) imposteur m ▷ adj faux (fausse) ▷ vt (emotions) simuler; (painting) faire un faux de
falcon ['fɔːlkən] n faucon m
fall [fɔːl] n chute f; (decrease) baisse f; (US: autumn) automne m ▷ vi (pt **fell**, pp **~en**) tomber; (price, temperature, dollar) baisser; **falls** npl (waterfall) chute f d'eau, cascade f; **to ~ flat** vi (on one's face) tomber de tout son long, s'étaler; (joke) tomber à plat; (plan) échouer; **fall apart** vi (object) tomber en morceaux; **fall down** vi (person) tomber; (building) s'effondrer, s'écrouler; **fall for** vt fus (trick) se laisser prendre à; (person) tomber amoureux(-euse) de; **fall off** vi tomber; (diminish) baisser, diminuer; **fall out** vi (friends etc) se brouiller; (hair, teeth) tomber; **fall over** vi tomber (par terre); **fall through** vi (plan, project) tomber à l'eau

fallen ['fɔːlən] pp of **fall**

fallout ['fɔːlaut] n retombées (radioactives)

false [fɔːls] adj faux (fausse); **under ~ pretences** sous un faux prétexte; **false alarm** n fausse alerte; **false teeth** npl (BRIT) fausses dents, dentier m

fame [feim] n renommée f, renom m

familiar [fə'miliə'] adj familier(-ière); **to be ~ with sth** connaître qch; **familiarize** [fə'miliəraiz] vt: **to familiarize o.s. with** se familiariser avec

family ['fæmili] n famille f; **family doctor** n médecin m de famille; **family planning** n planning familial

famine ['fæmin] n famine f

famous ['feiməs] adj célèbre

fan [fæn] n (folding) éventail m; (Elec) ventilateur m; (person) fan m, admirateur(-trice); (Sport) supporter m/f ▷ vt éventer; (fire, quarrel) attiser

fanatic [fə'nætik] n fanatique m/f

fan belt n courroie f de ventilateur

fan club n fan-club m

fancy ['fænsi] n (whim) fantaisie f, envie f; (imagination) imagination f ▷ adj (luxury) de luxe; (elaborate: jewellery, packaging) fantaisie inv ▷ vt (feel like, want) avoir envie de; (imagine) imaginer; **to take a ~ to** se prendre d'affection pour; s'enticher de; **he fancies her** elle lui plaît; **fancy dress** n déguisement m, travesti m

fan heater n (BRIT) radiateur soufflant

fantasize ['fæntəsaiz] vi fantasmer

fantastic [fæn'tæstik] adj fantastique

fantasy ['fæntəsi] n imagination f, fantaisie f; (unreality) fantasme m

fanzine ['fænziːn] n fanzine m

FAQ n abbr (= frequently asked question) FAQ f inv, faq f inv

far [fɑː'] adj (distant) lointain(e), éloigné(e) ▷ adv loin; **the ~ side/end** l'autre côté/bout; **it's not ~ (from here)** ce n'est pas loin (d'ici); **~ away, ~ off** au loin, dans le lointain; **~ better** beaucoup mieux; **~ from** loin de; **by ~** de loin, de beaucoup; **go as ~ as the bridge** allez jusqu'au pont; **as ~ as I know** pour autant que je sache; **how ~ is it to ...?** combien y a-t-il jusqu'à ...?; **how ~ have you got with your work?** où en êtes-vous dans votre travail?

farce [fɑːs] n farce f

fare [feə'] n (on trains, buses) prix m du billet; (in taxi) prix de la course; (food) table f, chère f; **half ~** demi-tarif; **full ~** plein tarif

Far East n: **the ~** l'Extrême-Orient m

farewell [feə'wel] excl, n adieu m

farm [fɑːm] n ferme f ▷ vt cultiver; **farmer** n fermier(-ière); **farmhouse** n (maison f de) ferme f; **farming** n agriculture f; (of animals) élevage m; **farmyard** n cour f de ferme

far-reaching ['fɑː'riːtʃiŋ] adj d'une grande portée

fart [fɑːt] (inf!) vi péter

farther ['fɑːðə'] adv plus loin ▷ adj plus eloigné(e), plus lointain(e)

farthest ['fɑːðist] superlative of **far**

fascinate ['fæsineit] vt fasciner, captiver; **fascinated** adj fasciné(e)

fascinating ['fæsineitiŋ] adj fascinant(e)

fascination [fæsi'neiʃən] n fascination f

fascist ['fæʃist] adj, n fasciste m/f

fashion ['fæʃən] n mode f; (manner) façon f, manière f ▷ vt façonner; **in ~** à la mode; **out of ~** démodé(e); **fashionable** adj à la mode; **fashion show** n défilé m de mannequins or de mode

fast [fɑːst] adj rapide; (clock): **to be ~** avancer; (dye, colour) grand or bon teint inv ▷ adv vite, rapidement; (stuck, held) solidement ▷ n jeûne m ▷ vi jeûner; **~ asleep** profondément endormi

fasten ['fɑːsn] vt attacher, fixer; (coat) attacher, fermer ▷ vi se fermer, s'attacher

fast food n fast food m, restauration f rapide

fat [fæt] adj gros(se) ▷ n graisse f; (on meat) gras m; (for cooking) matière grasse

fatal ['feitl] adj (mistake) fatal(e); (injury) mortel(le); **fatality** [fə'tæliti] n (road death etc) victime f, décès m; **fatally** adv fatalement; (injured) mortellement

fate [feit] n destin m; (of person) sort m

father ['fɑːðə'] n père m; **Father Christmas** n le Père Noël; **father-in-law** n beau-père m

fatigue [fə'tiːg] n fatigue f

fattening ['fætniŋ] adj (food) qui fait grossir

fatty ['fæti] adj (food) gras(se) ▷ n (inf) gros (grosse)

faucet ['fɔːsit] n (US) robinet m

fault [fɔːlt] n faute f; (defect) défaut m; (Geo) faille f ▷ vt trouver des défauts à, prendre en défaut; **it's my ~** c'est de ma faute; **to find ~ with** trouver à redire or à critiquer à; **at ~** fautif(-ive), coupable; **faulty** adj défectueux(-euse)

fauna ['fɔːnə] n faune f

favour etc (US **favor** etc) ['feivə'] n faveur f; (help) service m ▷ vt (proposition) être en faveur de; (pupil etc) favoriser; (team, horse) donner gagnant; **to do sb a ~** rendre un service à qn; **in ~ of** en faveur de; **to find ~ with sb** trouver grâce aux yeux de qn; **favourable** adj favorable; **favourite** ['feivrit] adj, n favori(te)

fawn [fɔːn] n (deer) faon m ▷ adj (also: **~-coloured**) fauve ▷ vi: **to ~ (up)on** flatter servilement

fax [fæks] n (document) télécopie f; (machine) télécopieur m ▷ vt envoyer par télécopie

FBI n abbr (US: = Federal Bureau of Investigation) FBI m

fear [fɪə^r] *n* crainte *f*, peur *f* ▷ *vt* craindre; **for ~ of** de peur que + *sub* or de + *infinitive*; **fearful** *adj* craintif(-ive); (*sight, noise*) affreux(-euse), épouvantable; **fearless** *adj* intrépide

feasible ['fi:zəbl] *adj* faisable, réalisable

feast [fi:st] *n* festin *m*, banquet *m*; (*Rel: also: ~ day*) fête *f* ▷ *vi* festoyer

feat [fi:t] *n* exploit *m*, prouesse *f*

feather ['fɛðə^r] *n* plume *f*

feature ['fi:tʃə^r] *n* caractéristique *f*; (*article*) chronique *f*, rubrique *f* ▷ *vt* (*film*) avoir pour vedette(s) ▷ *vi* figurer (en bonne place); **features** *npl* (*of face*) traits *mpl*; **a (special) ~ on sth/sb** un reportage sur qch/qn; **feature film** *n* long métrage

Feb. *abbr* (= *February*) fév

February ['fɛbruərɪ] *n* février *m*

fed [fɛd] *pt, pp of* **feed**

federal ['fɛdərəl] *adj* fédéral(e)

federation [fɛdə'reɪʃən] *n* fédération *f*

fed up *adj*: **to be ~ (with)** en avoir marre *or* plein le dos (de)

fee [fi:] *n* rémunération *f*; (*of doctor, lawyer*) honoraires *mpl*; (*of school, college etc*) frais *mpl* de scolarité; (*for examination*) droits *mpl*

feeble ['fi:bl] *adj* faible; (*attempt, excuse*) pauvre; (*joke*) piteux(-euse)

feed [fi:d] *n* (*of animal*) nourriture *f*, pâture *f*; (*on printer*) mécanisme *m* d'alimentation ▷ *vt* (*pt, pp* **fed**) (*person*) nourrir; (*BRIT: baby: breastfeed*) allaiter; (: *with bottle*) donner le biberon à; (*horse etc*) donner à manger à; (*machine*) alimenter; (*data etc*) **to ~ sth into** enregistrer qch dans; **feedback** *n* (*Elec*) effet *m* Larsen; (*from person*) réactions *fpl*

feel [fi:l] *n* (*sensation*) sensation *f*; (*impression*) impression *f* ▷ *vt* (*pt, pp* **felt**) (*touch*) toucher; (*explore*) tâter, palper; (*cold, pain*) sentir; (*grief, anger*) ressentir, éprouver; (*think, believe*): **to ~ (that)** trouver que; **to ~ hungry/cold** avoir faim/froid; **to ~ lonely/better** se sentir seul/ mieux; **I don't ~ well** je ne me sens pas bien; **it ~s soft** c'est doux au toucher; **to ~ like** (*want*) avoir envie de; **feeling** *n* (*physical*) sensation *f*; (*emotion, impression*) sentiment *m*; **to hurt sb's feelings** froisser qn

feet [fi:t] *npl of* **foot**

fell [fɛl] *pt of* **fall** ▷ *vt* (*tree*) abattre

fellow ['fɛləu] *n* type *m*; (*comrade*) compagnon *m*; (*of learned society*) membre *m* ▷ *cpd*: **their ~ prisoners/students** leurs camarades prisonniers/étudiants; **fellow citizen** *n* concitoyen(ne); **fellow countryman** *n* (*irreg*) compatriote *m*; **fellow men** *npl* semblables *mpl*; **fellowship** *n* (*society*) association *f*; (*comradeship*) amitié *f*, camaraderie *f*; (*Scol*) sorte de bourse universitaire

felony ['fɛlənɪ] *n* crime *m*, forfait *m*

felt [fɛlt] *pt, pp of* **feel** ▷ *n* feutre *m*; **felt-tip** *n*

(*also*: **felt-tip pen**) stylo-feutre *m*

female ['fi:meɪl] *n* (*Zool*) femelle *f*; (*pej: woman*) bonne femme ▷ *adj* (*Biol*) femelle; (*sex, character*) féminin(e); (*vote etc*) des femmes

feminine ['fɛmɪnɪn] *adj* féminin(e)

feminist ['fɛmɪnɪst] *n* féministe *m/f*

fence [fɛns] *n* barrière *f* ▷ *vi* faire de l'escrime; **fencing** *n* (*sport*) escrime *m*

fend [fɛnd] *vi*: **to ~ for o.s.** se débrouiller (tout seul); **fend off** *vt* (*attack etc*) parer; (*questions*) éluder

fender ['fɛndə^r] *n* garde-feu *m inv*; (*on boat*) défense *f*; (*US: of car*) aile *f*

fennel ['fɛnl] *n* fenouil *m*

ferment *vi* [fə'mɛnt] fermenter ▷ *n* ['fə:mɛnt] (*fig*) agitation *f*, effervescence *f*

fern [fə:n] *n* fougère *f*

ferocious [fə'rəuʃəs] *adj* féroce

ferret ['fɛrɪt] *n* furet *m*

ferry ['fɛrɪ] *n* (*small*) bac *m*; (*large: also:* **~boat**) ferry(-boat *m*) *m* ▷ *vt* transporter

fertile ['fə:taɪl] *adj* fertile; (*Biol*) fécond(e); **fertilize** ['fə:tɪlaɪz] *vt* fertiliser; (*Biol*) féconder; **fertilizer** *n* engrais *m*

festival ['fɛstɪvəl] *n* (*Rel*) fête *f*; (*Art, Mus*) festival *m*

festive ['fɛstɪv] *adj* de fête; **the ~ season** (*BRIT: Christmas*) la période des fêtes

fetch [fɛtʃ] *vt* aller chercher; (*BRIT: sell for*) rapporter

fête [feɪt] *n* fête *f*, kermesse *f*

fetus ['fi:təs] *n* (*US*) = **foetus**

feud [fju:d] *n* querelle *f*, dispute *f*

fever ['fi:və^r] *n* fièvre *f*; **feverish** *adj* fiévreux(-euse), fébrile

few [fju:] *adj* (*not many*) peu de ▷ *pron* peu; **a ~** (*as adj*) quelques; (*as pron*) quelques-uns(-unes); **quite a ~ ...** *adj* un certain nombre de ..., pas mal de ...; **in the past ~ days** ces derniers jours; **fewer** *adj* moins de; **fewest** *adj* le moins nombreux

fiancé [fɪ'ɑ̃:ŋseɪ] *n* fiancé *m*; **fiancée** *n* fiancée *f*

fiasco [fɪ'æskəu] *n* fiasco *m*

fib [fɪb] *n* bobard *m*

fibre (*US* **fiber**) ['faɪbə^r] *n* fibre *f*; **fibreglass** (*US* **Fiberglass®**) *n* fibre *f* de verre

fickle ['fɪkl] *adj* inconstant(e), volage, capricieux(-euse)

fiction ['fɪkʃən] *n* romans *mpl*, littérature *f* romanesque; (*invention*) fiction *f*; **fictional** *adj* fictif(-ive)

fiddle ['fɪdl] *n* (*Mus*) violon *m*; (*cheating*) combine *f*; escroquerie *f* ▷ *vt* (*BRIT: accounts*) falsifier, maquiller; **fiddle with** *vt fus* tripoter

fidelity [fɪ'dɛlɪtɪ] *n* fidélité *f*

fidget ['fɪdʒɪt] *vi* se trémousser, remuer

field [fi:ld] *n* champ *m*; (*fig*) domaine *m*, champ *m*; (*Sport: ground*) terrain *m*; **field**

marshal *n* maréchal *m*

fierce [fɪəs] *adj* (*look, animal*) féroce, sauvage; (*wind, attack, person*) (très) violent(e); (*fighting, enemy*) acharné(e)

fifteen [fɪf'tiːn] *num* quinze; **fifteenth** *num* quinzième

fifth [fɪfθ] *num* cinquième

fiftieth ['fɪftɪɪθ] *num* cinquantième

fifty ['fɪftɪ] *num* cinquante; **fifty-fifty** *adv* moitié-moitié ▷ *adj*: **to have a fifty-fifty chance (of success)** avoir une chance sur deux (de réussir)

fig [fɪg] *n* figue *f*

fight [faɪt] *n* (*between persons*) bagarre *f*; (*argument*) dispute *f*; (*Mil*) combat *m*; (*against cancer etc*) lutte *f* ▷ *vb* (*pt, pp* **fought**) ▷ *vt* se battre contre; (*cancer, alcoholism, emotion*) combattre, lutter contre; (*election*) se présenter à ▷ *vi* se battre; (*argue*) se disputer; (*fig*): **to ~ (for/against)** lutter (pour/contre); **fight back** *vi* rendre les coups; (*after illness*) reprendre le dessus ▷ *vt* (*tears*) réprimer; **fight off** *vt* repousser; (*disease, sleep, urge*) lutter contre; **fighting** *n* combats *mpl*; (*brawls*) bagarres *fpl*

figure ['fɪgə^r] *n* (*Drawing, Geom*) figure *f*; (*number*) chiffre *m*; (*body, outline*) silhouette *f*; (*person's shape*) ligne *f*, formes *fpl*; (*person*) personnage *m* ▷ *vt* (*us: make think*) supposer ▷ *vi* (*appear*) figurer; (*us: make sense*) s'expliquer; **figure out** *vt* (*understand*) arriver à comprendre; (*plan*) calculer

file [faɪl] *n* (*tool*) lime *f*; (*dossier*) dossier *m*; (*folder*) dossier, chemise *f*; (: *binder*) classeur *m*; (*Comput*) fichier *m*; (*row*) file *f* ▷ *vt* (*nails, wood*) limer; (*papers*) classer; (*Law: claim*) faire enregistrer; déposer; **filing cabinet** *n* classeur *m* (*meuble*)

Filipino [fɪlɪ'piːnəu] *adj* philippin(e) ▷ *n* (*person*) Philippin(e)

fill [fɪl] *vt* remplir; (*vacancy*) pourvoir à ▷ *n*: **to eat one's ~** manger à sa faim; **to ~ with** remplir de; **fill in** *vt* (*hole*) boucher; (*form*) remplir; **fill out** *vt* (*form, receipt*) remplir; **fill up** *vt* remplir ▷ *vi* (*Aut*) faire le plein

fillet ['fɪlɪt] *n* filet *m*; **fillet steak** *n* filet *m* de bœuf, tournedos *m*

filling ['fɪlɪŋ] *n* (*Culin*) garniture *f*, farce *f*; (*for tooth*) plombage *m*; **filling station** *n* station-service *f*, station *f* d'essence

film [fɪlm] *n* film *m*; (*Phot*) pellicule *f*, film; (*of powder, liquid*) couche *f*, pellicule *f* ▷ *vt* (*scene*) filmer ▷ *vi* tourner; **I'd like a 36-exposure ~** je voudrais une pellicule de 36 poses; **film star** *n* vedette *f* de cinéma

filter ['fɪltə^r] *n* filtre *m* ▷ *vt* filtrer; **filter lane** *n* (*BRIT Aut: at traffic lights*) voie *f* de dégagement; (: *on motorway*) voie *f* de sortie

filth [fɪlθ] *n* saleté *f*; **filthy** *adj* sale,

dégoûtant(e); (*language*) ordurier(-ière), grossier(-ière)

fin [fɪn] *n* (*of fish*) nageoire *f*; (*of shark*) aileron *m*; (*of diver*) palme *f*

final ['faɪnl] *adj* final(e), dernier(-ière); (*decision, answer*) définitif(-ive) ▷ *n* (*BRIT Sport*) finale *f*; **finals** *npl* (*Scol*) examens *mpl* de dernière année; (*US Sport*) finale *f*; **finale** [fɪ'nɑːlɪ] *n* finale *m*; **finalist** *n* (*Sport*) finaliste *m/f*; **finalize** *vt* mettre au point; **finally** *adv* (*eventually*) enfin, finalement; (*lastly*) en dernier lieu

finance [faɪ'næns] *n* finance *f* ▷ *vt* financer; **finances** *npl* finances *fpl*; **financial** [faɪ'nænʃəl] *adj* financier(-ière); **financial year** *n* année *f* budgétaire

find [faɪnd] *vt* (*pt, pp* **found**) trouver; (*lost object*) retrouver ▷ *n* trouvaille *f*, découverte *f*; **to ~ sb guilty** (*Law*) déclarer qn coupable; **find out** *vt* se renseigner sur; (*truth, secret*) découvrir; (*person*) démasquer ▷ *vi*: **to ~ out about** (*make enquiries*) se renseigner sur; (*by chance*) apprendre; **findings** *npl* (*Law*) conclusions *fpl*, verdict *m*; (*of report*) constatations *fpl*

fine [faɪn] *adj* (*weather*) beau (belle); (*excellent*) excellent(e); (*thin, subtle, not coarse*) fin(e); (*acceptable*) bien *inv* ▷ *adv* (*well*) très bien; (*small*) fin, finement ▷ *n* (*Law*) amende *f*; contravention *f* ▷ *vt* (*Law*) condamner à une amende; donner une contravention à; **he's ~** il va bien; **the weather is ~** il fait beau; **fine arts** *npl* beaux-arts *mpl*

finger ['fɪŋgə^r] *n* doigt *m* ▷ *vt* palper, toucher; **index ~** index *m*; **fingernail** *n* ongle *m* (de la main); **fingerprint** *n* empreinte digitale; **fingertip** *n* bout *m* du doigt

finish ['fɪnɪʃ] *n* fin *f*; (*Sport*) arrivée *f*; (*polish etc*) finition *f* ▷ *vt* finir, terminer ▷ *vi* finir, se terminer; **to ~ doing sth** finir de faire qch; **to ~ third** arriver *or* terminer troisième; **when does the show ~?** quand est-ce que le spectacle se termine?; **finish off** *vt* finir, terminer; (*kill*) achever; **finish up** *vi, vt* finir

Finland ['fɪnlənd] *n* Finlande *f*; **Finn** *n* Finnois(e), Finlandais(e); **Finnish** *adj* finnois(e), finlandais(e) ▷ *n* (*Ling*) finnois *m*

fir [fəː^r] *n* sapin *m*

fire ['faɪə^r] *n* feu *m*; (*accidental*) incendie *m*; (*heater*) radiateur *m* ▷ *vt* (*discharge*): **to ~ a gun** tirer un coup de feu; (*fig: interest*) enflammer, animer; (*inf: dismiss*) mettre à la porte, renvoyer ▷ *vi* (*shoot*) tirer, faire feu; **~! au feu!; on ~** en feu; **to set ~ to sth, set sth on ~** mettre le feu à qch; **fire alarm** *n* avertisseur *m* d'incendie; **firearm** *n* arme *f* à feu; **fire brigade** *n* (*US* **fire department**) (régiment *m* de sapeurs-)pompiers *mpl*; **fire engine** *n* (*BRIT*) pompe *f* à incendie; **fire**

escape *n* escalier *m* de secours; **fire exit** *n* issue *f* or sortie *f* de secours; **fire extinguisher** *n* extincteur *m*; **fireman** (*irreg*) *n* pompier *m*; **fireplace** *n* cheminée *f*; **fire station** *n* caserne *f* de pompiers; **fire truck** (*US*) *n* = **fire engine**; **firewall** *n* (*Internet*) pare-feu *m*; **firewood** *n* bois *m* de chauffage; **fireworks** *npl* (*display*) feu(x) *m(pl)* d'artifice

firm [fəːm] *adj* ferme ▷ *n* compagnie *f*, firme *f*; **firmly** *adv* fermement

first [fəːst] *adj* premier(-ière) ▷ *adv* (*before other people*) le premier, la première; (*before other things*) en premier, d'abord; (*when listing reasons etc*) en premier lieu, premièrement; (*in the beginning*) au début ▷ *n* (*person: in race*) premier(-ière); (*BRIT Scol*) mention *f* très bien; (*Aut*) première *f*; **the ~ of January** le premier janvier; **at ~** au commencement, au début; **~ of all** tout d'abord, pour commencer; **first aid** *n* premiers secours *or* soins; **first-aid kit** *n* trousse *f* à pharmacie; **first-class** *adj* (*ticket etc*) de première classe; (*excellent*) excellent(e), exceptionnel(le); (*post*) en tarif prioritaire; **first-hand** *adj* de première main; **first lady** *n* (*US*) femme *f* du président; **firstly** *adv* premièrement, en premier lieu; **first name** *n* prénom *m*; **first-rate** *adj* excellent(e)

fiscal ['fɪskl] *adj* fiscal(e); **fiscal year** *n* exercice financier

fish [fɪʃ] *n* (*pl inv*) poisson *m* ▷ *vt, vi* pêcher; **~ and chips** poisson frit et frites; **fisherman** (*irreg*) *n* pêcheur *m*; **fish fingers** *npl* (*BRIT*) bâtonnets de poisson (congelés); **fishing** *n* pêche *f*; **to go fishing** aller à la pêche; **fishing boat** *n* barque *f* de pêche; **fishing line** *n* ligne *f* (de pêche); **fishmonger** *n* (*BRIT*) marchand *m* de poisson; **fishmonger's (shop)** *n* (*BRIT*) poissonnerie *f*; **fish sticks** *npl* (*US*) = **fish fingers**; **fishy** *adj* (*inf*) suspect(e), louche

fist [fɪst] *n* poing *m*

fit [fɪt] *adj* (*Med, Sport*) en (bonne) forme; (*proper*) convenable; approprié(e) ▷ *vt* (*subj: clothes*) aller à; (*put in, attach*) installer, poser; (*equip*) équiper, garnir, munir; (*suit*) convenir à ▷ *vi* (*clothes*) aller; (*parts*) s'adapter; (*in space, gap*) s'adapter ▷ *n* (*Med*) accès *m*, crise *f*; (*of anger*) accès; (*of hysterics, jealousy*) crise; **~ to** (*ready to*) en état de; **~ for** (*worthy*) digne de; (*capable*) apte à; **to keep ~** se maintenir en forme; **this dress is a tight/good ~** cette robe est un peu juste/(me) va très bien; **a ~ of coughing** une quinte de toux; **by ~s and starts** par à-coups; **fit in** *vi* (*add up*) cadrer; (*integrate*) s'intégrer; (*to new situation*) s'adapter; **fitness** *n* (*Med*) forme *f* physique; **fitted** *adj* (*jacket, shirt*) ajusté(e); **fitted carpet** *n* moquette *f*; **fitted kitchen** *n* (*BRIT*) cuisine équipée; **fitted sheet** *n* drap-housse *m*; **fitting** *adj* approprié(e) ▷ *n* (*of dress*) essayage *m*; (*of piece of equipment*) pose *f*, installation *f*; **fitting room** *n* (*in shop*) cabine *f* d'essayage; **fittings** *npl* installations *fpl*

five [faɪv] *num* cinq; **fiver** *n* (*inf*: *BRIT*) billet *m* de cinq livres; (: *US*) billet de cinq dollars

fix [fɪks] *vt* (*date, amount etc*) fixer; (*sort out*) arranger; (*mend*) réparer; (*make ready: meal, drink*) préparer ▷ *n*: **to be in a ~** être dans le pétrin; **fix up** *vt* (*meeting*) arranger; **to ~ sb up with sth** faire avoir qch à qn; **fixed** *adj* (*prices etc*) fixe; **fixture** *n* installation *f* (fixe); (*Sport*) rencontre *f* (au programme)

fizzy ['fɪzɪ] *adj* pétillant(e), gazeux(-euse)

flag [flæg] *n* drapeau *m*; (*also*: **~stone**) dalle *f* ▷ *vi* faiblir; fléchir; **flag down** *vt* héler, faire signe (de s'arrêter) à; **flagpole** *n* mât *m*

flair [flɛəʳ] *n* flair *m*

flak [flæk] *n* (*Mil*) tir antiaérien; (*inf*: *criticism*) critiques *fpl*

flake [fleɪk] *n* (*of rust, paint*) écaille *f*; (*of snow, soap powder*) flocon *m* ▷ *vi* (*also*: **~ off**) s'écailler

flamboyant [flæm'bɔɪənt] *adj* flamboyant(e), éclatant(e); (*person*) haut(e) en couleur

flame [fleɪm] *n* flamme *f*

flamingo [flə'mɪŋgəʊ] *n* flamant *m* (rose)

flammable ['flæməbl] *adj* inflammable

flan [flæn] *n* (*BRIT*) tarte *f*

flank [flæŋk] *n* flanc *m* ▷ *vt* flanquer

flannel ['flænl] *n* (*BRIT: also*: **face ~**) gant *m* de toilette; (*fabric*) flanelle *f*

flap [flæp] *n* (*of pocket, envelope*) rabat *m* ▷ *vt* (*wings*) battre (de) ▷ *vi* (*sail, flag*) claquer

flare [flɛəʳ] *n* (*signal*) signal lumineux; (*Mil*) fusée éclairante; (*in skirt etc*) évasement *m*; **flares** *npl* (*trousers*) pantalon *m* à pattes d'éléphant; **flare up** *vi* s'embraser; (*fig: person*) se mettre en colère, s'emporter; (: *revolt*) éclater

flash [flæʃ] *n* éclair *m*; (*also*: **news ~**) flash *m* (d'information); (*Phot*) flash ▷ *vt* (*switch on*) allumer (brièvement); (*direct*): **to ~ sth at** braquer qch sur; (*send: message*) câbler; (*smile*) lancer ▷ *vi* briller; jeter des éclairs; (*light on ambulance etc*) clignoter; **a ~ of lightning** un éclair; **in a ~** en un clin d'œil; **to ~ one's headlights** faire un appel de phares; **he ~ed by** *or* **past** il passa (devant nous) comme un éclair; **flashback** *n* flashback *m*, retour *m* en arrière; **flashbulb** *n* ampoule *f* de flash; **flashlight** *n* lampe *f* de poche

flask [flɑːsk] *n* flacon *m*, bouteille *f*; (*also*: **vacuum ~**) bouteille *f* thermos®

flat [flæt] *adj* plat(e); (*tyre*) dégonflé(e), à plat; (*beer*) éventé(e); (*battery*) à plat; (*denial*) catégorique; (*Mus*) bémol *inv*; (: *voice*) faux (fausse) ▷ *n* (*BRIT: apartment*) appartement *m*; (*Aut*) crevaison *f*, pneu crevé; (*Mus*) bémol *m*; **~ out** (*work*) sans relâche; (*race*) à fond; **flatten**

vt (also: **flatten out**) aplatir; (crop) coucher; (house, city) raser

flatter ['flætə^r] vt flatter; **flattering** adj flatteur(-euse); (clothes etc) seyant(e)

flaunt [flɔːnt] vt faire étalage de

flavour etc (us **flavor** etc) ['fleɪvə^r] n goût m, saveur f; (of ice cream etc) parfum m ▷ vt parfumer, aromatiser; **vanilla-~ed** à l'arôme de vanille, vanillé(e); **what ~s do you have?** quels parfums avez-vous?; **flavouring** n arôme m (synthétique)

flaw [flɔː] n défaut m; **flawless** adj sans défaut

flea [fliː] n puce f; **flea market** n marché m aux puces

flee (pt, pp **fled**) [fliː, flɛd] vt fuir, s'enfuir de ▷ vi fuir, s'enfuir

fleece [fliːs] n (of sheep) toison f; (top) (laine f) polaire f ▷ vt (inf) voler, filouter

fleet [fliːt] n flotte f; (of lorries, cars etc) parc m; convoi m

fleeting ['fliːtɪŋ] adj fugace, fugitif(-ive); (visit) très bref (brève)

Flemish ['flɛmɪʃ] adj flamand(e) ▷ n (Ling) flamand m; **the ~** npl les Flamands

flesh [flɛʃ] n chair f

flew [fluː] pt of **fly**

flex [flɛks] n fil m or câble m électrique (souple) ▷ vt (knee) fléchir; (muscles) tendre; **flexibility** n flexibilité f; **flexible** adj flexible; (person, schedule) souple; **flexitime** (us **flextime**) n horaire m variable or à la carte

flick [flɪk] n petit coup m; (with finger) chiquenaude f ▷ vt donner un petit coup à; (switch) appuyer sur; **flick through** vt fus feuilleter

flicker ['flɪkə^r] vi (light, flame) vaciller

flies [flaɪz] npl of **fly**

flight [flaɪt] n vol m; (escape) fuite f; (also: ~ **of steps**) escalier m; **flight attendant** n steward m, hôtesse f de l'air

flimsy ['flɪmzɪ] adj peu solide; (clothes) trop léger(-ère); (excuse) pauvre, mince

flinch [flɪntʃ] vi tressaillir; **to ~ from** se dérober à, reculer devant

fling [flɪŋ] vt (pt, pp **flung**) jeter, lancer

flint [flɪnt] n silex m; (in lighter) pierre f (à briquet)

flip [flɪp] vt (throw) donner une chiquenaude à; (switch) appuyer sur; (us: pancake) faire sauter; **to ~ sth over** retourner qch

flip-flops ['flɪpflɔps] npl (esp BRIT) tongs fpl

flipper ['flɪpə^r] n (of animal) nageoire f; (for swimmer) palme f

flirt [flɜːt] vi flirter ▷ n flirteur(-euse)

float [fləut] n flotteur m; (in procession) char m; (sum of money) réserve f ▷ vi flotter

flock [flɔk] n (of sheep) troupeau m; (of birds) vol m; (of people) foule f

flood [flʌd] n inondation f; (of letters, refugees etc) flot m ▷ vt inonder ▷ vi (place) être inondé; (people): **to ~ into** envahir; **flooding** n inondation f; **floodlight** n projecteur m

floor [flɔː^r] n sol m; (storey) étage m; (of sea, valley) fond m ▷ vt (knock down) terrasser; (baffle) désorienter; **ground ~**, (us) **first ~** rez-de-chaussée m; **first ~**, (us) **second ~** premier étage; **what ~ is it on?** c'est à quel étage?; **floorboard** n planche f (du plancher); **flooring** n sol m; (wooden) plancher m; (covering) revêtement m de sol; **floor show** n spectacle m de variétés

flop [flɔp] n fiasco m ▷ vi (fail) faire fiasco; (fall) s'affaler, s'effondrer; **floppy** adj lâche, flottant(e) ▷ n (Comput: also: **floppy disk**) disquette f

flora ['flɔːrə] n flore f

floral ['flɔːrl] adj floral(e); (dress) à fleurs

florist ['flɔrɪst] n fleuriste m/f; **florist's (shop)** n magasin m or boutique f de fleuriste

flotation [fləu'teɪʃən] n (of shares) émission f; (of company) lancement m (en Bourse)

flour ['flauə^r] n farine f

flourish ['flʌrɪʃ] vi prospérer ▷ n (gesture) moulinet m

flow [fləu] n (of water, traffic etc) écoulement m; (tide, influx) flux m; (of blood, Elec) circulation f; (of river) courant m ▷ vi couler; (traffic) s'écouler; (robes, hair) flotter

flower ['flauə^r] n fleur f ▷ vi fleurir; **flower bed** n plate-bande f; **flowerpot** n pot m (à fleurs)

flown [fləun] pp of **fly**

fl. oz. abbr = **fluid ounce**

flu [fluː] n grippe f

fluctuate ['flʌktjueɪt] vi varier, fluctuer

fluent ['fluːənt] adj (speech, style) coulant(e), aisé(e); **he speaks ~ French, he's ~ in French** il parle le français couramment

fluff [flʌf] n duvet m; (on jacket, carpet) peluche f; **fluffy** adj duveteux(-euse); (toy) en peluche

fluid ['fluːɪd] n fluide m; (in diet) liquide m ▷ adj fluide; **fluid ounce** n (BRIT) = 0.028 l; 0.05 pints

fluke [fluːk] n coup m de veine

flung [flʌŋ] pt, pp of **fling**

fluorescent [fluə'rɛsnt] adj fluorescent(e)

fluoride ['fluəraɪd] n fluor m

flush [flʌʃ] n (on face) rougeur f; (fig: of youth etc) éclat m ▷ vt nettoyer à grande eau ▷ vi rougir ▷ adj (level): **~ with** au ras de, de niveau avec; **to ~ the toilet** tirer la chasse (d'eau)

flute [fluːt] n flûte f

flutter ['flʌtə^r] n (of panic, excitement) agitation f; (of wings) battement m ▷ vi (bird) battre des ailes, voleter

fly [flaɪ] n (insect) mouche f; (on trousers: also:

flies) braguette f ▷ vb (pt **flew**, pp **flown**) ▷ vt (*plane*) piloter; (*passengers, cargo*) transporter (par avion); (*distance*) parcourir ▷ vi voler; (*passengers*) aller en avion; (*escape*) s'enfuir, fuir; (*flag*) se déployer; **fly away, fly off** vi s'envoler; **fly-drive** n formule f avion plus voiture; **flying** n (*activity*) aviation f; (*action*) vol m ▷ adj: **flying visit** visite f éclair inv; **with flying colours** haut la main; **flying saucer** n soucoupe volante; **flyover** n (BRIT: *overpass*) pont routier

FM abbr (*Radio: = frequency modulation*) FM

foal [fəul] n poulain m

foam [fəum] n écume f; (*on beer*) mousse f; (*also: ~ rubber*) caoutchouc m mousse ▷ vi (*liquid*) écumer; (*soapy water*) mousser

focus ['fəukəs] n (pl **-es**) foyer m; (*of interest*) centre m ▷ vt (*field glasses etc*) mettre au point ▷ vi: **to ~ (on)** (*with camera*) régler la mise au point (sur); (*with eyes*) fixer son regard (sur); (*fig: concentrate*) se concentrer; **out of/in ~** (*picture*) flou(e)/net(te); (*camera*) pas au point/au point

foetus (US **fetus**) ['fiːtəs] n fœtus m

fog [fɔg] n brouillard m; **foggy** adj: **it's foggy** il y a du brouillard; **fog lamp** (US **fog light**) n (Aut) phare m anti-brouillard

foil [fɔil] vt déjouer, contrecarrer ▷ n feuille f de métal; (*kitchen foil*) papier m d'alu(minium); **to act as a ~ to** (*fig*) servir de repoussoir or de faire-valoir à

fold [fəuld] n (*bend, crease*) pli m; (Agr) parc m à moutons; (*fig*) bercail m ▷ vt plier; **to ~ one's arms** croiser les bras; **fold up** vi (*map etc*) se plier, se replier; (*business*) fermer boutique ▷ vt (*map etc*) plier; **folder** n (*for papers*) chemise f; (: *binder*) classeur m; (Comput) dossier m; **folding** adj (*chair, bed*) pliant(e)

foliage ['fəuliidʒ] n feuillage m

folk [fəuk] npl gens mpl ▷ cpd folklorique; **folks** npl (inf: *parents*) famille f, parents mpl; **folklore** ['fəuklɔːʳ] n folklore m; **folk music** n musique f folklorique; (*contemporary*) musique folk, folk m; **folk song** n chanson f folklorique; (*contemporary*) chanson folk inv

follow ['fɔləu] vt suivre ▷ vi suivre; (*result*) s'ensuivre; **to ~ suit** (*fig*) faire de même; **follow up** vt (*letter, offer*) donner suite à; (*case*) suivre; **follower** n disciple m/f, partisan(e); **following** adj suivant(e) ▷ n partisans mpl, disciples mpl; **follow-up** n suite f; (*on file, case*) suivi m

fond [fɔnd] adj (*memory, look*) tendre, affectueux(-euse); (*hopes, dreams*) un peu fou (folle); **to be ~ of** aimer beaucoup

food [fuːd] n nourriture f; **food mixer** n mixeur m; **food poisoning** n intoxication f alimentaire; **food processor** n robot m de cuisine; **food stamp** n (US) bon m de

nourriture (*pour indigents*)

fool [fuːl] n idiot(e); (Culin) mousse f de fruits f ▷ vt berner, duper; **fool about, fool around** vi (*pej: waste time*) traînailler, glandouiller; (: *behave foolishly*) faire l'idiot or l'imbécile; **foolish** adj idiot(e), stupide; (*rash*) imprudent(e); **foolproof** adj (*plan etc*) infaillible

foot [fut] (pl **feet**) [fiːt] n pied m; (*of animal*) patte f; (*measure*) pied m (= 30.48 cm; 12 inches) ▷ vt (*bill*) payer; **on ~** à pied; **footage** n (Cine: *length*) ≈ métrage m; (: *material*) séquences fpl; **foot-and-mouth (disease)** [futənd'mauθ-] n fièvre aphteuse; **football** n (*ball*) ballon m (de football); (*sport*: BRIT) football m; (: US) football américain; **footballer** n (BRIT) = **football player**; **football match** n (BRIT) match m de foot(ball); **football player** n footballeur(-euse), joueur(-euse) de football; (US) joueur(-euse) de football américain; **footbridge** n passerelle f; **foothills** npl contreforts mpl; **foothold** n prise f (de pied); **footing** n (*fig*) position f; **to lose one's footing** perdre pied; **footnote** n note f (en bas de page); **footpath** n sentier m; **footprint** n trace f (de pied); **footstep** n pas m; **footwear** n chaussures fpl

KEYWORD

for [fɔːʳ] prep **1** (*indicating destination, intention, purpose*) pour; **the train for London** le train pour (or à destination de) Londres; **he left for Rome** il est parti pour Rome; **he went for the paper** il est allé chercher le journal; **is this for me?** c'est pour moi?; **it's time for lunch** c'est l'heure du déjeuner; **what's it for?** ça sert à quoi?; **what for?** (*why*) pourquoi?; (*to what end*) pour quoi faire?, à quoi bon?; **for sale** à vendre; **to pray for peace** prier pour la paix

2 (*on behalf of, representing*) pour; **the MP for Hove** le député de Hove; **to work for sb/sth** travailler pour qn/qch; **I'll ask him for you** je vais lui demander pour toi; **G for George** G comme Georges

3 (*because of*) pour; **for this reason** pour cette raison; **for fear of being criticized** de peur d'être critiqué

4 (*with regard to*) pour; **it's cold for July** il fait froid pour juillet; **a gift for languages** un don pour les langues

5 (*in exchange for*): **I sold it for £5** je l'ai vendu 5 livres; **to pay 50 pence for a ticket** payer un billet 50 pence

6 (*in favour of*) pour; **are you for or against us?** êtes-vous pour ou contre nous?; **I'm all for it** je suis tout à fait pour; **vote for X** votez pour X

7 (*referring to distance*) pendant, sur; **there**

are roadworks for **5** km il y a des travaux sur
or pendant 5 km; **we walked for miles** nous
avons marché pendant des kilomètres
8 (*referring to time*) pendant; depuis; pour; **he
was away for 2 years** il a été absent pendant
2 ans; **she will be away for a month** elle sera
absente (pendant) un mois; **it hasn't rained
for 3 weeks** ça fait 3 semaines qu'il ne pleut
pas, il ne pleut pas depuis 3 semaines; **I have
known her for years** je la connais depuis des
années; **can you do it for tomorrow?** est-ce
que tu peux le faire pour demain?
9 (*with infinitive clauses*): **it is not for me to
decide** ce n'est pas à moi de décider; **it would
be best for you to leave** le mieux serait que
vous partiez; **there is still time for you to
do it** vous avez encore le temps de le faire;
for this to be possible ... pour que cela soit
possible ...
10 (*in spite of*): **for all that** malgré cela,
néanmoins; **for all his work/efforts** malgré
tout son travail/tous ses efforts; **for all his
complaints, he's very fond of her** il a beau
se plaindre, il l'aime beaucoup
▷ *conj* (*since, as: rather formal*) car

forbid (*pt* **forbad(e)**, *pp* **~den**) [fə'bɪd, -'bæd,
-'bɪdn] *vt* défendre, interdire; **to ~ sb to do**
défendre or interdire à qn de faire; **forbidden**
adj défendu(e)
force [fɔːs] *n* force *f* ▷ *vt* forcer; (*push*) pousser
(de force); **to ~ o.s. to do** se forcer à faire; **in
~** (*being used: rule, law, prices*) en vigueur; (*in
large numbers*) en force; **forced** *adj* forcé(e);
forceful *adj* énergique
ford [fɔːd] *n* gué *m*
fore [fɔːʳ] *n*: **to the ~** en évidence; **forearm**
n avant-bras *m inv*; **forecast** *n* prévision
f; (*also*: **weather forecast**) prévisions *fpl*
météorologiques, météo *f* ▷ *vt* (*irreg: like* **cast**)
prévoir; **forecourt** *n* (*of garage*) devant *m*;
forefinger *n* index *m*; **forefront** *n*: **in the
forefront of** au premier rang or plan de;
foreground *n* premier plan; **forehead** ['fɔrɪd]
n front *m*
foreign ['fɔrɪn] *adj* étranger(-ère); (*trade*)
extérieur(e); (*travel*) à l'étranger; **foreign
currency** *n* devises étrangères; **foreigner** *n*
étranger(-ère); **foreign exchange** *n* (*system*)
change *m*; (*money*) devises *fpl*; **Foreign Office**
n (*BRIT*) ministère *m* des Affaires étrangères;
Foreign Secretary *n* (*BRIT*) ministre *m* des
Affaires étrangères
fore: **foreman** (*irreg*) *n* (*in construction*)
contremaître *m*; **foremost** *adj* le (la) plus en
vue, premier(-ière) ▷ *adv*: **first and foremost**
avant tout, tout d'abord; **forename** *n*
prénom *m*
forensic [fə'rɛnsɪk] *adj*: **~ medicine** médecine

légale
foresee (*pt* **foresaw**, *pp* **~n**) [fɔː'siː, -'sɔː, -'siːn]
vt prévoir; **foreseeable** *adj* prévisible
forest ['fɔrɪst] *n* forêt *f*; **forestry** *n*
sylviculture *f*
forever [fə'rɛvəʳ] *adv* pour toujours; (*fig:
endlessly*) continuellement
foreword ['fɔːwəːd] *n* avant-propos *m inv*
forfeit ['fɔːfɪt] *vt* perdre
forgave [fə'geɪv] *pt of* **forgive**
forge [fɔːdʒ] *n* forge *f* ▷ *vt* (*signature*)
contrefaire; (*wrought iron*) forger; **to ~ money**
(*BRIT*) fabriquer de la fausse monnaie; **forger** *n*
faussaire *m*; **forgery** *n* faux *m*, contrefaçon *f*
forget (*pt* **forgot**, *pp* **forgotten**) [fə'gɛt, -'gɔt,
-'gɔtn] *vt*, *vi* oublier; **I've forgotten my key/
passport** j'ai oublié ma clé/mon passeport;
forgetful *adj* distrait(e), étourdi(e)
forgive (*pt* **forgave**, *pp* **~n**) [fə'gɪv, -'geɪv, -
'gɪvn] *vt* pardonner; **to ~ sb for sth/for doing
sth** pardonner qch à qn/à qn de faire qch
forgot [fə'gɔt] *pt of* **forget**
forgotten [fə'gɔtn] *pp of* **forget**
fork [fɔːk] *n* (*for eating*) fourchette *f*; (*for
gardening*) fourche *f*; (*of roads*) bifurcation *f* ▷ *vi*
(*road*) bifurquer
forlorn [fə'lɔːn] *adj* (*deserted*) abandonné(e);
(*hope, attempt*) désespéré(e)
form [fɔːm] *n* forme *f*; (*Scol*) classe *f*;
(*questionnaire*) formulaire *m* ▷ *vt* former;
(*habit*) contracter; **to ~ part of sth** faire partie
de qch; **on top ~** en pleine forme
formal ['fɔːməl] *adj* (*offer, receipt*) en bonne
et due forme; (*person*) cérémonieux(-euse);
(*occasion, dinner*) officiel(le); (*garden*) à la
française; (*clothes*) de soirée; **formality**
[fɔː'mælɪtɪ] *n* formalité *f*
format ['fɔːmæt] *n* format *m* ▷ *vt* (*Comput*)
formater
formation [fɔː'meɪʃən] *n* formation *f*
former ['fɔːməʳ] *adj* ancien(ne); (*before n*)
précédent(e); **the ~ ... the latter** le premier ...
le second, celui-là ... celui-ci; **formerly** *adv*
autrefois
formidable ['fɔːmɪdəbl] *adj* redoutable
formula ['fɔːmjulə] *n* formule *f*
fort [fɔːt] *n* fort *m*
forthcoming [fɔːθ'kʌmɪŋ] *adj* qui va paraître
or avoir lieu prochainement; (*character*)
ouvert(e), communicatif(-ive); (*available*)
disponible
fortieth ['fɔːtɪɪθ] *num* quarantième
fortify ['fɔːtɪfaɪ] *vt* (*city*) fortifier; (*person*)
remonter
fortnight ['fɔːtnaɪt] *n* (*BRIT*) quinzaine
f, quinze jours *mpl*; **fortnightly** *adj*
bimensuel(le) ▷ *adv* tous les quinze jours
fortress ['fɔːtrɪs] *n* forteresse *f*
fortunate ['fɔːtʃənɪt] *adj* heureux(-euse);

(*person*) chanceux(-euse); **it is ~ that** c'est une chance que, il est heureux que; **fortunately** *adv* heureusement, par bonheur
fortune ['fɔːtʃən] *n* chance *f*; (*wealth*) fortune *f*; **fortune-teller** *n* diseuse *f* de bonne aventure
forty ['fɔːtɪ] *num* quarante
forum ['fɔːrəm] *n* forum *m*, tribune *f*
forward ['fɔːwəd] *adj* (*movement, position*) en avant, vers l'avant; (*not shy*) effronté(e); (*in time*) en avance ▷ *adv* (*also:* **~s**) en avant ▷ *n* (*Sport*) avant *m* ▷ *vt* (*letter*) faire suivre; (*parcel, goods*) expédier; (*fig*) promouvoir, favoriser; **to move ~** avancer; **forwarding address** *n* adresse *f* de réexpédition
forward slash *n* barre *f* oblique
fossil ['fɒsl] *adj, n* fossile *m*
foster ['fɒstə^r] *vt* (*encourage*) encourager, favoriser; (*child*) élever (*sans adopter*); **foster child** *n* enfant élevé dans une famille d'accueil
foster parent *n* parent qui élève un enfant sans l'adopter
fought [fɔːt] *pt, pp of* **fight**
foul [faul] *adj* (*weather, smell, food*) infect(e); (*language*) ordurier(-ière) ▷ *n* (*Football*) faute *f* ▷ *vt* (*dirty*) salir, encrasser; **he's got a ~ temper** il a un caractère de chien; **foul play** *n* (*Law*) acte criminel
found [faund] *pt, pp of* **find** ▷ *vt* (*establish*) fonder; **foundation** [faun'deɪʃən] *n* (*act*) fondation *f*; (*base*) fondement *m*; (*also:* **foundation cream**) fond *m* de teint; **foundations** *npl* (*of building*) fondations *fpl*
founder ['faundə^r] *n* fondateur *m* ▷ *vi* couler, sombrer
fountain ['fauntɪn] *n* fontaine *f*; **fountain pen** *n* stylo *m* (à encre)
four [fɔː^r] *num* quatre; **on all ~s** à quatre pattes; **four-letter word** *n* obscénité *f*, gros mot; **four-poster** *n* (*also:* **four-poster bed**) lit *m* à baldaquin; **fourteen** *num* quatorze; **fourteenth** *num* quatorzième; **fourth** *num* quatrième ▷ *n* (*Aut: also:* **fourth gear**) quatrième *f*; **four-wheel drive** *n* (*Aut: car*) voiture *f* à quatre roues motrices
fowl [faul] *n* volaille *f*
fox [fɒks] *n* renard *m* ▷ *vt* mystifier
foyer ['fɔɪeɪ] *n* (*in hotel*) vestibule *m*; (*Theat*) foyer *m*
fraction ['frækʃən] *n* fraction *f*
fracture ['fræktʃə^r] *n* fracture *f* ▷ *vt* fracturer
fragile ['frædʒaɪl] *adj* fragile
fragment ['frægmənt] *n* fragment *m*
fragrance ['freɪgrəns] *n* parfum *m*
frail [freɪl] *adj* fragile, délicat(e); (*person*) frêle
frame [freɪm] *n* (*of building*) charpente *f*; (*of human, animal*) charpente *f*, ossature *f*; (*of picture*) cadre *m*; (*of door, window*) encadrement *m*, chambranle *m*; (*of spectacles: also:* **~s**) monture *f* ▷ *vt* (*picture*) encadrer; **~ of mind**

disposition *f* d'esprit; **framework** *n* structure *f*
France [frɑːns] *n* la France
franchise ['fræntʃaɪz] *n* (*Pol*) droit *m* de vote; (*Comm*) franchise *f*
frank [fræŋk] *adj* franc (franche) ▷ *vt* (*letter*) affranchir; **frankly** *adv* franchement
frantic ['fræntɪk] *adj* (*hectic*) frénétique; (*distraught*) hors de soi
fraud [frɔːd] *n* supercherie *f*, fraude *f*, tromperie *f*; (*person*) imposteur *m*
fraught [frɔːt] *adj* (*tense: person*) très tendu(e); (*: situation*) pénible; **~ with** (*difficulties etc*) chargé(e) de, plein(e) de
fray [freɪ] *vt* effilocher ▷ *vi* s'effilocher
freak [friːk] *n* (*eccentric person*) phénomène *m*; (*unusual event*) hasard *m* extraordinaire; (*pej: fanatic*): **health food ~** fana *m/f* or obsédé(e) de l'alimentation saine ▷ *adj* (*storm*) exceptionnel(le); (*accident*) bizarre
freckle ['frekl] *n* tache *f* de rousseur
free [friː] *adj* libre; (*gratis*) gratuit(e) ▷ *vt* (*prisoner etc*) libérer; (*jammed object or person*) dégager; **is this seat ~?** la place est libre?; **~ (of charge)** gratuitement; **freedom** *n* liberté *f*; **Freefone®** *n* numéro vert; **free gift** *n* prime *f*; **free kick** *n* (*Sport*) coup franc; **freelance** *adj* (*journalist etc*) indépendant(e), free-lance *inv* ▷ *adv* en free-lance; **freely** *adv* librement; (*liberally*) libéralement; **Freepost®** *n* (*BRIT*) port payé; **free-range** *adj* (*egg*) de ferme; (*chicken*) fermier; **freeway** *n* (*US*) autoroute *f*; **free will** *n* libre arbitre *m*; **of one's own free will** de son plein gré
freeze [friːz] *vb* (*pt* **froze**, *pp* **frozen**) ▷ *vi* geler ▷ *vt* geler; (*food*) congeler; (*prices, salaries*) bloquer, geler ▷ *n* gel *m*; (*of prices, salaries*) blocage *m*; **freezer** *n* congélateur *m*; **freezing** *adj*: **freezing (cold)** (*room etc*) glacial(e); (*person, hands*) gelé(e), glacé(e) ▷ *n*: **3 degrees below freezing** 3 degrés au-dessous de zéro; **it's freezing** il fait un froid glacial; **freezing point** *n* point *m* de congélation
freight [freɪt] *n* (*goods*) fret *m*, cargaison *f*; (*money charged*) fret, prix *m* du transport; **freight train** *n* (*US*) train *m* de marchandises
French [frentʃ] *adj* français(e) ▷ *n* (*Ling*) français *m*; **the ~** *npl* les Français; **what's the ~ (word) for ...?** comment dit-on ... en français?; **French bean** *n* (*BRIT*) haricot vert; **French bread** *n* pain *m* français; **French dressing** *n* (*Culin*) vinaigrette *f*; **French fried potatoes** (*US* **French fries**) *npl* (pommes de terre *fpl*) frites *fpl*; **Frenchman** (*irreg*) *n* Français *m*; **French stick** *n* ≈ baguette *f*; **French window** *n* porte-fenêtre *f*; **Frenchwoman** (*irreg*) *n* Française *f*
frenzy ['frenzi] *n* frénésie *f*
frequency ['friːkwənsi] *n* fréquence *f*
frequent *adj* ['friːkwənt] fréquent(e) ▷ *vt*

[frɪ'kwɛnt] fréquenter; **frequently**
['fri:kwəntlɪ] adv fréquemment

fresh [frɛʃ] adj frais (fraîche); (new) nouveau
(nouvelle); (cheeky) familier(-ière), culotté(e);
freshen vi (wind, air) fraîchir; **freshen up**
vi faire un brin de toilette; **fresher** n (BRIT
University: inf) bizuth m, étudiant(e) de
première année; **freshly** adv nouvellement,
récemment; **freshman** (US: irreg) n = **fresher**;
freshwater adj (fish) d'eau douce

fret [frɛt] vi s'agiter, se tracasser

Fri abbr (= Friday) ve

friction ['frɪkʃən] n friction f, frottement m

Friday ['fraɪdɪ] n vendredi m

fridge [frɪdʒ] n (BRIT) frigo m, frigidaire® m

fried [fraɪd] adj frit(e); **~ egg** œuf m sur le plat

friend [frɛnd] n ami(e) f; **friendly** adj amical(e);
(kind) sympathique, gentil(le); (place)
accueillant(e); (Pol: country) ami(e) ▷ n (also:
friendly match) match amical; **friendship**
n amitié f

fries [fraɪz] (esp US) npl = **French fried
potatoes**

frigate ['frɪgɪt] n frégate f

fright [fraɪt] n peur f, effroi m; **to give sb
a ~** faire peur à qn; **to take ~** prendre peur,
s'effrayer; **frighten** vt effrayer, faire peur
à; **frightened** adj: **to be frightened (of)**
avoir peur (de); **frightening** adj effrayant(e);
frightful adj affreux(-euse)

frill [frɪl] n (of dress) volant m; (of shirt) jabot m

fringe [frɪndʒ] n (BRIT: of hair) frange f; (edge:
of forest etc) bordure f

Frisbee® ['frɪzbɪ] n Frisbee® m

fritter ['frɪtə^r] n beignet m

frivolous ['frɪvələs] adj frivole

fro [frəʊ] see **to**

frock [frɒk] n robe f

frog [frɒg] n grenouille f; **frogman** (irreg) n
homme-grenouille m

 KEYWORD

from [frɒm] prep **1** (indicating starting place,
origin etc) de; **where do you come from?,
where are you from?** d'où venez-vous?;
where has he come from? d'où arrive-t-il?;
from London to Paris de Londres à Paris; **to
escape from sb/sth** échapper à qn/qch; **a
letter/telephone call from my sister** une
lettre/un appel de ma sœur; **to drink from
the bottle** boire à (même) la bouteille; **tell
him from me that ...** dites-lui de ma part
que ...

2 (indicating time) (à partir) de; **from one
o'clock to** or **until** or **till two** d'une heure à
deux heures; **from January (on)** à partir de
janvier

3 (indicating distance) de; **the hotel is one**

kilometre from the beach l'hôtel est à un
kilomètre de la plage

4 (indicating price, number etc) de; **prices range
from £10 to £50** les prix varient entre 10 livres
et 50 livres; **the interest rate was increased
from 9% to 10%** le taux d'intérêt est passé de
9% à 10%

5 (indicating difference) de; **he can't tell red
from green** il ne peut pas distinguer le rouge
du vert; **to be different from sb/sth** être
différent de qn/qch

6 (because of, on the basis of): **from what he
says** d'après ce qu'il dit; **weak from hunger**
affaibli par la faim

front [frʌnt] n (of house, dress) devant m; (of
coach, train) avant m; (promenade: also: **sea ~**)
bord m de mer; (Mil, Pol, Meteorology) front
m; (fig: appearances) contenance f, façade f
▷ adj de devant; (seat, wheel) avant inv ▷ vi: **in
~ (of)** devant; **front door** n porte f d'entrée;
(of car) portière f avant; **frontier** ['frʌntɪə^r] n
frontière f; **front page** n première page; **front-
wheel drive** n traction f avant

frost [frɒst] n gel m, gelée f; (also: **hoar~**)
givre m; **frostbite** n gelures fpl; **frosting** n
(esp US: on cake) glaçage m; **frosty** adj (window)
couvert(e) de givre; (weather, welcome)
glacial(e)

froth [frɒθ] n mousse f, écume f

frown [fraʊn] n froncement m de sourcils ▷ vi
froncer les sourcils

froze [frəʊz] pt of **freeze**

frozen ['frəʊzn] pp of **freeze** ▷ adj (food)
congelé(e); (very cold: person; Comm: assets)
gelé(e)

fruit [fruːt] n (pl inv) fruit m; **fruit juice** n jus
m de fruit; **fruit machine** n (BRIT) machine f à
sous; **fruit salad** n salade f de fruits

frustrate [frʌs'treɪt] vt frustrer; **frustrated**
adj frustré(e)

fry (pt, pp **fried**) [fraɪ, -d] vt (faire) frire; **small ~**
le menu fretin; **frying pan** n poêle f (à frire)

ft. abbr = **foot; feet**

fudge [fʌdʒ] n (Culin) sorte de confiserie à base de
sucre, de beurre et de lait

fuel [fjuəl] n (for heating) combustible m; (for
engine) carburant m; **fuel tank** n (in vehicle)
réservoir m or à carburant

fulfil (US **fulfill**) [ful'fɪl] vt (function, condition)
remplir; (order) exécuter; (wish, desire)
satisfaire, réaliser

full [ful] adj plein(e); (details, hotel, bus)
complet(-ète); (busy: day) chargé(e); (skirt)
ample, large ▷ adv: **to know ~ well that** savoir
fort bien que; **I'm ~ (up)** j'ai bien mangé; **~
employment/fare** plein emploi/tarif; **a ~
two hours** deux bonnes heures; **at ~ speed**
à toute vitesse; **in ~** (reproduce, quote, pay)

intégralement; (*write name etc*) en toutes lettres; **full-length** *adj* (*portrait*) en pied; (*coat*) long(ue); **full-length film** long métrage; **full moon** *n* pleine lune; **full-scale** *adj* (*model*) grandeur nature *inv*; (*search, retreat*) complet(-ète), total(e); **full stop** *n* point *m*; **full-time** *adj, adv* (*work*) à plein temps; **fully** *adv* entièrement, complètement; (*at least*)

fumble ['fʌmbl] *vi* fouiller, tâtonner; **fumble with** *vt fus* tripoter

fume [fju:m] *vi* (*rage*) rager; **fumes** *npl* vapeurs *fpl*, émanations *fpl*, gaz *mpl*

fun [fʌn] *n* amusement *m*, divertissement *m*; **to have ~** s'amuser; **for ~** pour rire; **to make ~ of** se moquer de

function ['fʌŋkʃən] *n* fonction *f*; (*reception, dinner*) cérémonie *f*, soirée officielle ▷ *vi* fonctionner

fund [fʌnd] *n* caisse *f*, fonds *m*; (*source, store*) source *f*, mine *f*; **funds** *npl* (*money*) fonds *mpl*

fundamental [fʌndə'mɛntl] *adj* fondamental(e)

funeral ['fju:nərəl] *n* enterrement *m*, obsèques *fpl* (*more formal occasion*); **funeral director** *n* entrepreneur *m* des pompes funèbres; **funeral parlour** [-'pɑ:lə*] *n* (BRIT) dépôt *m* mortuaire

funfair ['fʌnfɛə*] *n* (BRIT) fête (foraine)

fungus (*pl* **fungi**) ['fʌŋgəs, -gaɪ] *n* champignon *m*; (*mould*) moisissure *f*

funnel ['fʌnl] *n* entonnoir *m*; (*of ship*) cheminée *f*

funny ['fʌnɪ] *adj* amusant(e), drôle; (*strange*) curieux(-euse), bizarre

fur [fə:*] *n* fourrure *f*; (BRIT: *in kettle etc*) (dépôt *m* de) tartre *m*; **fur coat** *n* manteau *m* de fourrure

furious ['fjuərɪəs] *adj* furieux(-euse); (*effort*) acharné(e)

furnish ['fə:nɪʃ] *vt* meubler; (*supply*) fournir; **furnishings** *npl* mobilier *m*, articles *mpl* d'ameublement

furniture ['fə:nɪtʃə*] *n* meubles *mpl*, mobilier *m*; **piece of ~** meuble *m*

furry ['fə:rɪ] *adj* (*animal*) à fourrure; (*toy*) en peluche

further ['fə:ðə*] *adj* supplémentaire, autre; nouveau (nouvelle) ▷ *adv* plus loin; (*more*) davantage; (*moreover*) de plus ▷ *vt* faire avancer *or* progresser, promouvoir; **further education** *n* enseignement *m* postscolaire (*recyclage, formation professionnelle*); **furthermore** *adv* de plus, en outre

furthest ['fə:ðɪst] *superlative of* **far**

fury ['fjuərɪ] *n* fureur *f*

fuse (*US* **fuze**) [fju:z] *n* fusible *m*; (*for bomb etc*) amorce *f*, détonateur *m* ▷ *vt, vi* (*metal*) fondre; (BRIT: *Elec*): **to ~ the lights** faire sauter les fusibles *or* les plombs; **fuse box** *n* boîte *f* à fusibles

fusion ['fju:ʒən] *n* fusion *f*

fuss [fʌs] *n* (*anxiety, excitement*) chichis *mpl*, façons *fpl*; (*commotion*) tapage *m*; (*complaining, trouble*) histoire(s) *f(pl)*; **to make a ~** faire des façons (*or* des histoires); **to make a ~ of sb** dorloter qn; **fussy** *adj* (*person*) tatillon(ne), difficile, chichiteux(-euse); (*dress, style*) tarabiscoté(e)

future ['fju:tʃə*] *adj* futur(e) ▷ *n* avenir *m*; (*Ling*) futur *m*; **futures** *npl* (*Comm*) opérations *fpl* à terme; **in (the) ~** à l'avenir

fuze [fju:z] *n, vt, vi* (*US*) = **fuse**

fuzzy ['fʌzɪ] *adj* (*Phot*) flou(e); (*hair*) crépu(e)

G [dʒiː] n (Mus): **G** sol m

g. abbr (= gram) g

gadget ['gædʒɪt] n gadget m

Gaelic ['geɪlɪk] adj, n (Ling) gaélique (m)

gag [gæg] n (on mouth) bâillon m; (joke) gag m ▷ vt (prisoner etc) bâillonner

gain [geɪn] n (improvement) gain m; (profit) gain, profit m ▷ vt gagner ▷ vi (watch) avancer; **to ~ from/by** gagner de/à; **to ~ on sb** (catch up) rattraper qn; **to ~ 3lbs (in weight)** prendre 3 livres; **to ~ ground** gagner du terrain

gal. abbr = **gallon**

gala ['gɑːlə] n gala m

galaxy ['gæləksɪ] n galaxie f

gale [geɪl] n coup m de vent

gall bladder ['gɔːl-] n vésicule f biliaire

gallery ['gælərɪ] n (also: **art ~**) musée m; (: private) galerie f; (: in theatre) dernier balcon

gallon ['gæln] n gallon m (BRIT = 4.543 l; US = 3.785 l)

gallop ['gæləp] n galop m ▷ vi galoper

gallstone ['gɔːlstəun] n calcul m (biliaire)

gamble ['gæmbl] n pari m, risque calculé ▷ vt, vi jouer; **to ~ on** (fig) miser sur; **gambler** n joueur m; **gambling** n jeu m

game [geɪm] n jeu m; (event) match m; (of tennis, chess, cards) partie f; (Hunting) gibier m ▷ adj (willing): **to be ~ (for)** être prêt(e) (à or pour); **big ~** gros gibier; **games** npl (Scol) sport m; (sport event) jeux; **games console** ['geɪmz-]

n console f de jeux vidéo; **game show** n jeu télévisé

gammon ['gæmən] n (bacon) quartier m de lard fumé; (ham) jambon fumé or salé

gang [gæŋ] n bande f; (of workmen) équipe f

gangster ['gæŋstəʳ] n gangster m, bandit m

gap [gæp] n trou m; (in time) intervalle m; (difference): **~ (between)** écart m (entre)

gape [geɪp] vi (person) être or rester bouche bée; (hole, shirt) être ouvert(e)

gap year n année que certains étudiants prennent pour voyager ou pour travailler avant d'entrer à l'université

garage ['gærɑːʒ] n garage m; **garage sale** n vide-grenier m

garbage ['gɑːbɪdʒ] n (US: rubbish) ordures fpl, détritus mpl; (inf: nonsense) âneries fpl; **garbage can** n (US) poubelle f, boîte f à ordures; **garbage collector** n (US) éboueur m

garden ['gɑːdn] n jardin m; **gardens** npl (public) jardin public; (private) parc m; **garden centre** (BRIT) n pépinière f, jardinerie f; **gardener** n jardinier m; **gardening** n jardinage m

garlic ['gɑːlɪk] n ail m

garment ['gɑːmənt] n vêtement m

garnish ['gɑːnɪʃ] (Culin) vt garnir ▷ n décoration f

garrison ['gærɪsn] n garnison f

gas [gæs] n gaz m; (US: gasoline) essence f ▷ vt asphyxier; **I can smell ~** ça sent le gaz; **gas cooker** n (BRIT) cuisinière f à gaz; **gas cylinder** n bouteille f de gaz; **gas fire** n (BRIT) radiateur m à gaz

gasket ['gæskɪt] n (Aut) joint m de culasse

gasoline ['gæsəliːn] n (US) essence f

gasp [gɑːsp] n halètement m; (of shock etc): **she gave a small ~ of pain** la douleur lui coupa le souffle ▷ vi haleter; (fig) avoir le souffle coupé

gas: **gas pedal** n (US) accélérateur m; **gas station** n (US) station-service f; **gas tank** n (US Aut) réservoir m d'essence

gate [geɪt] n (of garden) portail m; (of field, at level crossing) barrière f; (of building, town, at airport) porte f

gateau (pl **~x**) ['gætəu, -z] n gros gâteau à la crème

gatecrash ['geɪtkræʃ] vt s'introduire sans invitation dans

gateway ['geɪtweɪ] n porte f

gather ['gæðəʳ] vt (flowers, fruit) cueillir; (pick up) ramasser; (assemble: objects) rassembler; (: people) réunir; (: information) recueillir; (understand) comprendre; (Sewing) froncer ▷ vi (assemble) se rassembler; **to ~ speed** prendre de la vitesse; **gathering** n rassemblement m

gauge [geɪdʒ] n (instrument) jauge f ▷ vt jauger; (fig) juger de

gave [geɪv] pt of **give**

gay [geɪ] *adj* (*homosexual*) homosexuel(le); (*colour*) gai, vif (vive)

gaze [geɪz] *n* regard *m* fixe ▷ *vi*: **to ~ at** vt fixer du regard

GB *abbr* = **Great Britain**

GCSE *n abbr* (BRIT: = *General Certificate of Secondary Education*) *examen passé à l'âge de 16 ans sanctionnant les connaissances de l'élève*

gear [gɪə^r] *n* matériel *m*, équipement *m*; (Tech) engrenage *m*; (Aut) vitesse *f* ▷ *vt* (fig: *adapt*) adapter; **top** *or* (US) **high/low ~** quatrième (*or* cinquième)/première vitesse; **in ~** en prise; **gear up** *vi*: **to ~ up (to do)** se préparer (à faire); **gear box** *n* boîte *f* de vitesse; **gear lever** *n* levier *m* de vitesse; **gear shift** (US) *n* = **gear lever**; **gear stick** (BRIT) *n* = **gear lever**

geese [giːs] *npl of* **goose**

gel [dʒɛl] *n* gelée *f*

gem [dʒɛm] *n* pierre précieuse

Gemini [ˈdʒɛmɪnaɪ] *n* les Gémeaux *mpl*

gender [ˈdʒɛndə^r] *n* genre *m*; (*person's sex*) sexe *m*

gene [dʒiːn] *n* (Biol) gène *m*

general [ˈdʒɛnərl] *n* général *m* ▷ *adj* général(e); **in ~** en général; **general anaesthetic** (US **general anesthetic**) *n* anesthésie générale; **general election** *n* élection(s) législative(s); **generalize** *vi* généraliser; **generally** *adv* généralement; **general practitioner** *n* généraliste *m/f*; **general store** *n* épicerie *f*

generate [ˈdʒɛnəreɪt] *vt* engendrer; (*electricity*) produire

generation [dʒɛnəˈreɪʃən] *n* génération *f*; (*of electricity etc*) production *f*

generator [ˈdʒɛnəreɪtə^r] *n* générateur *m*

generosity [dʒɛnəˈrɒsɪtɪ] *n* générosité *f*

generous [ˈdʒɛnərəs] *adj* généreux(-euse); (*copious*) copieux(-euse)

genetic [dʒɪˈnɛtɪk] *adj* génétique; **~ engineering** ingénierie *m* génétique; **~ fingerprinting** système *m* d'empreinte génétique; **genetically modified** *adj* (*food etc*) génétiquement modifié(e); **genetics** *n* génétique *f*

Geneva [dʒɪˈniːvə] *n* Genève

genitals [ˈdʒɛnɪtlz] *npl* organes génitaux

genius [ˈdʒiːnɪəs] *n* génie *m*

gent [dʒɛnt] *n abbr* (BRIT *inf*) = **gentleman**

gentle [ˈdʒɛntl] *adj* doux (douce); (*breeze, touch*) léger(-ère)

gentleman (*irreg*) [ˈdʒɛntlmən] *n* monsieur *m*; (*well-bred man*) gentleman *m*

gently [ˈdʒɛntlɪ] *adv* doucement

gents [dʒɛnts] *n* W.-C. *mpl* (pour hommes)

genuine [ˈdʒɛnjuɪn] *adj* véritable, authentique; (*person, emotion*) sincère; **genuinely** *adv* sincèrement, vraiment

geographic(al) [dʒɪəˈɡræfɪk(l)] *adj* géographique

geography [dʒɪˈɒɡrəfɪ] *n* géographie *f*

geology [dʒɪˈɒlədʒɪ] *n* géologie *f*

geometry [dʒɪˈɒmətrɪ] *n* géométrie *f*

geranium [dʒɪˈreɪnɪəm] *n* géranium *m*

geriatric [dʒɛrɪˈætrɪk] *adj* gériatrique ▷ *n* patient(e) gériatrique

germ [dʒə:m] *n* (Med) microbe *m*

German [ˈdʒə:mən] *adj* allemand(e) ▷ *n* Allemand(e); (Ling) allemand *m*; **German measles** *n* rubéole *f*

Germany [ˈdʒə:mənɪ] *n* Allemagne *f*

gesture [ˈdʒɛstjə^r] *n* geste *m*

 KEYWORD

get [gɛt] (*pt, pp* **got**, *pp* **gotten** (US)) *vi*
1 (*become, be*) devenir; **to get old/tired** devenir vieux/fatigué, vieillir/se fatiguer; **to get drunk** s'enivrer; **to get dirty** se salir; **to get married** se marier; **when do I get paid?** quand est-ce que je serai payé?; **it's getting late** il se fait tard

2 (*go*): **to get to/from** aller à/de; **to get home** rentrer chez soi; **how did you get here?** comment es-tu arrivé ici?

3 (*begin*) commencer *or* se mettre à; **to get to know sb** apprendre à connaître qn; **I'm getting to like him** je commence à l'apprécier; **let's get going** *or* **started** allons-y

4 (*modal aux vb*): **you've got to do it** il faut que vous le fassiez; **I've got to tell the police** je dois le dire à la police

▷ *vt* **1**: **to get sth done** (*do*) faire qch; (*have done*) faire faire qch; **to get sth/sb ready** préparer qch/qn; **to get one's hair cut** se faire couper les cheveux; **to get the car going** *or* **to go** (faire) démarrer la voiture; **to get sb to do sth** faire faire qch à qn

2 (*obtain: money, permission, results*) obtenir, avoir; (*buy*) acheter; (*find: job, flat*) trouver; (*fetch: person, doctor, object*) aller chercher; **to get sth for sb** procurer qch à qn; **get me Mr Jones, please** (*on phone*) passez-moi Mr Jones, s'il vous plaît; **can I get you a drink?** est-ce que je peux vous servir à boire?

3 (*receive: present, letter*) recevoir, avoir; (*acquire: reputation*) avoir; (*prize*) obtenir; **what did you get for your birthday?** qu'est-ce que tu as eu pour ton anniversaire?; **how much did you get for the painting?** combien avez-vous vendu le tableau?

4 (*catch*) prendre, saisir, attraper; (*hit: target etc*) atteindre; **to get sb by the arm/throat** prendre *or* saisir *or* attraper qn par le bras/à la gorge; **get him!** arrête-le!; **the bullet got him in the leg** il a pris la balle dans la jambe

5 (*take, move*): **to get sth to sb** faire parvenir qch à qn; **do you think we'll get it through**

the door? on arrivera à le faire passer par la porte?
6 (*catch, take: plane, bus etc*) prendre; **where do I get the train for Birmingham?** où prend-on le train pour Birmingham?
7 (*understand*) comprendre, saisir; (*hear*) entendre; **I've got it!** j'ai compris!; **I don't get your meaning** je ne vois or comprends pas ce que vous voulez dire; **I didn't get your name** je n'ai pas entendu votre nom
8 (*have, possess*): **to have got** avoir; **how many have you got?** vous en avez combien?
9 (*illness*) avoir; **I've got a cold** j'ai le rhume; **she got pneumonia and died** elle a fait une pneumonie et elle en est morte
get away *vi* partir, s'en aller; (*escape*) s'échapper
get away with *vt fus* (*punishment*) en être quitte pour; (*crime etc*) se faire pardonner
get back *vi* (*return*) rentrer
▷ *vt* récupérer, recouvrer; **when do we get back?** quand serons-nous de retour?
get in *vi* entrer; (*arrive home*) rentrer; (*train*) arriver
get into *vt fus* entrer dans; (*car, train etc*) monter dans; (*clothes*) mettre, enfiler, endosser; **to get into bed/a rage** se mettre au lit/en colère
get off *vi* (*from train etc*) descendre; (*depart: person, car*) s'en aller
▷ *vt* (*remove: clothes, stain*) enlever
▷ *vt fus* (*train, bus*) descendre de; **where do I get off?** où est-ce que je dois descendre?
get on *vi* (*at exam etc*) se débrouiller; (*agree*): **to get on (with)** s'entendre (avec); **how are you getting on?** comment ça va?
▷ *vt fus* monter dans; (*horse*) monter sur
get out *vi* sortir; (*of vehicle*) descendre
▷ *vt* sortir
get out of *vt fus* sortir de; (*duty etc*) échapper à, se soustraire à
get over *vt fus* (*illness*) se remettre de
get through *vi* (*Tel*) avoir la communication; **to get through to sb** atteindre qn
get up *vi* (*rise*) se lever
▷ *vt fus* monter

getaway ['gɛtəweɪ] *n* fuite *f*
Ghana ['gɑ:nə] *n* Ghana *m*
ghastly ['gɑ:stlɪ] *adj* atroce, horrible
ghetto ['gɛtəu] *n* ghetto *m*
ghost [gəust] *n* fantôme *m*, revenant *m*
giant ['dʒaɪənt] *n* géant(e) ▷ *adj* géant(e), énorme
gift [gɪft] *n* cadeau *m*; (*donation, talent*) don *m*; **gifted** *adj* doué(e); **gift shop** (*US* **gift store**) *n* boutique *f* de cadeaux; **gift token, gift voucher** *n* chèque-cadeau *m*
gig [gɪg] *n* (*inf: concert*) concert *m*

gigabyte ['dʒɪgəbaɪt] *n* gigaoctet *m*
gigantic [dʒaɪ'gæntɪk] *adj* gigantesque
giggle ['gɪgl] *vi* pouffer, ricaner sottement
gills [gɪlz] *npl* (*of fish*) ouïes *fpl*, branchies *fpl*
gilt [gɪlt] *n* dorure *f* ▷ *adj* doré(e)
gimmick ['gɪmɪk] *n* truc *m*
gin [dʒɪn] *n* gin *m*
ginger ['dʒɪndʒə'] *n* gingembre *m*
gipsy ['dʒɪpsɪ] *n* = **gypsy**
giraffe [dʒɪ'rɑ:f] *n* girafe *f*
girl [gə:l] *n* fille *f*, fillette *f*; (*young unmarried woman*) jeune fille; (*daughter*) fille; **an English ~** une jeune Anglaise; **girl band** *n* girls band *m*; **girlfriend** *n* (*of girl*) amie *f*; (*of boy*) petite amie; **Girl Guide** *n* (*BRIT*) éclaireuse *f*; (*Roman Catholic*) guide *f*; **Girl Scout** *n* (*US*) = **Girl Guide**
gist [dʒɪst] *n* essentiel *m*
give [gɪv] *vb* (*pt* **gave**, *pp* **~n**) ▷ *vt* donner ▷ *vi* (*break*) céder; (*stretch: fabric*) se prêter; **to ~ sb sth, ~ sth to sb** donner qch à qn; (*gift*) offrir qch à qn; (*message*) transmettre qch à qn; **to ~ sb a call/kiss** appeler/embrasser qn; **to ~ a cry/sigh** pousser un cri/un soupir; **give away** *vt* donner; (*give free*) faire cadeau de; (*betray*) donner, trahir; (*disclose*) révéler; **give back** *vt* rendre; **give in** *vi* céder ▷ *vt* donner; **give out** *vt* (*food etc*) distribuer; **give up** *vi* renoncer ▷ *vt* renoncer à; **to ~ up smoking** arrêter de fumer; **to ~ o.s. up** se rendre
given ['gɪvn] *pp* of **give** ▷ *adj* (*fixed: time, amount*) donné(e), déterminé(e) ▷ *conj*: **~ the circumstances ...** étant donné les circonstances ..., vu les circonstances ...; **~ that ...** étant donné que ...
glacier ['glæsɪə'] *n* glacier *m*
glad [glæd] *adj* content(e); **gladly** ['glædlɪ] *adv* volontiers
glamorous ['glæmərəs] *adj* (*person*) séduisant(e); (*job*) prestigieux(-euse)
glamour (*US* **glamor**) ['glæmə'] *n* éclat *m*, prestige *m*
glance [glɑ:ns] *n* coup *m* d'œil ▷ *vi*: **to ~ at** jeter un coup d'œil à
gland [glænd] *n* glande *f*
glare [glɛə'] *n* (*of anger*) regard furieux; (*of light*) lumière éblouissante; (*of publicity*) feux *mpl* ▷ *vi* briller d'un éclat aveuglant; **to ~ at** lancer un regard or des regards furieux à; **glaring** *adj* (*mistake*) criant(e), qui saute aux yeux
glass [glɑ:s] *n* verre *m*; **glasses** *npl* (*spectacles*) lunettes *fpl*
glaze [gleɪz] *vt* (*door*) vitrer; (*pottery*) vernir ▷ *n* vernis *m*
gleam [gli:m] *vi* luire, briller
glen [glɛn] *n* vallée *f*
glide [glaɪd] *vi* glisser; (*Aviat, bird*) planer; **glider** *n* (*Aviat*) planeur *m*
glimmer ['glɪmə'] *n* lueur *f*
glimpse [glɪmps] *n* vision passagère, aperçu

m ▷ *vt* entrevoir, apercevoir

glint [glɪnt] *vi* étinceler

glisten ['glɪsn] *vi* briller, luire

glitter ['glɪtə*] *vi* scintiller, briller

global ['gləʊbl] *adj* (*world-wide*) mondial(e); (*overall*) global(e); **globalization** *n* mondialisation *f*; **global warming** *n* réchauffement *m* de la planète

globe [gləʊb] *n* globe *m*

gloom [glu:m] *n* obscurité *f*; (*sadness*) tristesse *f*, mélancolie *f*; **gloomy** *adj* (*person*) morose; (*place, outlook*) sombre

glorious ['glɔːrɪəs] *adj* glorieux(-euse); (*beautiful*) splendide

glory ['glɔːrɪ] *n* gloire *f*; splendeur *f*

gloss [glɔs] *n* (*shine*) brillant *m*, vernis *m*; (*also:* ~ **paint**) peinture brillante *or* laquée

glossary ['glɔsərɪ] *n* glossaire *m*, lexique *m*

glossy ['glɔsɪ] *adj* brillant(e), luisant(e) ▷ *n* (*also:* ~ **magazine**) revue *f* de luxe

glove [glʌv] *n* gant *m*; **glove compartment** *n* (*Aut*) boîte *f* à gants, vide-poches *m inv*

glow [gləʊ] *vi* rougeoyer; (*face*) rayonner; (*eyes*) briller

glucose ['glu:kəʊs] *n* glucose *m*

glue [glu:] *n* colle *f* ▷ *vt* coller

GM *abbr* (= *genetically modified*) génétiquement modifié(e)

gm *abbr* (= *gram*) g

GMO *n abbr* (= *genetically modified organism*) OGM *m*

GMT *abbr* (= *Greenwich Mean Time*) GMT

gnaw [nɔː] *vt* ronger

go [gəʊ] *vb* (*pt* **went**, *pp* **gone**) ▷ *vi* aller; (*depart*) partir, s'en aller; (*work*) marcher; (*break*) céder; (*time*) passer; (*be sold*): **to go for £10** se vendre 10 livres; (*become*): **to go pale/mouldy** pâlir/moisir ▷ *n* (*pl* **goes**): **to have a go (at)** essayer (de faire); **to be on the go** être en mouvement; **whose go is it?** à qui est-ce de jouer?; **he's going to do it** il va le faire, il est sur le point de le faire; **to go for a walk** aller se promener; **to go dancing/ shopping** aller danser/faire les courses; **to go and see sb, go to see sb** aller voir qn; **how did it go?** comment cela s'est passé?; **to go round the back/by the shop** passer par derrière/devant le magasin; **... to go** (*us: food*) ... à emporter; **go ahead** *vi* (*take place*) avoir lieu; (*get going*) y aller; **go away** *vi* partir, s'en aller; **go back** *vi* rentrer; revenir; (*go again*) retourner; **go by** *vi* (*years, time*) passer, s'écouler ▷ *vt fus* s'en tenir à; (*believe*) en croire; **go down** *vi* descendre; (*number, price, amount*) baisser; (*ship*) couler; (*sun*) se coucher ▷ *vt fus* descendre; **go for** *vt fus* (*fetch*) aller chercher; (*like*) aimer; (*attack*) s'en prendre à; attaquer; **go in** *vi* entrer; **go into** *vt fus* entrer dans; (*investigate*) étudier, examiner; (*embark on*) se

lancer dans; **go off** *vi* partir, s'en aller; (*food*) se gâter; (*milk*) tourner; (*bomb*) sauter; (*alarm clock*) sonner; (*alarm*) se déclencher; (*lights etc*) s'éteindre; (*event*) se dérouler ▷ *vt fus* ne plus aimer; **the gun went off** le coup est parti; **go on** *vi* continuer; (*happen*) se passer; (*lights*) s'allumer ▷ *vt fus*: **to go on doing** continuer à faire; **go out** *vi* sortir; (*fire, light*) s'éteindre; (*tide*) descendre; **to go out with sb** sortir avec qn; **go over** *vi, vt fus* (*check*) revoir, vérifier; **go past** *vt fus*: **to go past sth** passer devant qch; **go round** *vi* (*circulate: news, rumour*) circuler; (*revolve*) tourner; (*suffice*) suffire (pour tout le monde); (*visit*): **to go round to sb's** passer chez qn; aller chez qn; (*make a detour*): **to go round (by)** faire un détour (par); **go through** *vt fus* (*town etc*) traverser; (*search through*) fouiller; (*suffer*) subir; **go up** *vi* monter; (*price*) augmenter ▷ *vt fus* gravir; **go with** *vt fus* aller avec; **go without** *vt fus* se passer de

go-ahead ['gəʊəhɛd] *adj* dynamique, entreprenant(e) ▷ *n* feu vert

goal [gəʊl] *n* but *m*; **goalkeeper** *n* gardien *m* de but; **goal-post** *n* poteau *m* de but

goat [gəʊt] *n* chèvre *f*

gobble ['gɔbl] *vt* (*also:* ~ **down**, ~ **up**) engloutir

god [gɔd] *n* dieu *m*; **G~** Dieu; **godchild** *n* filleul(e); **goddaughter** *n* filleule *f*; **goddess** *n* déesse *f*; **godfather** *n* parrain *m*; **godmother** *n* marraine *f*; **godson** *n* filleul *m*

goggles ['gɔglz] *npl* (*for skiing etc*) lunettes (protectrices); (*for swimming*) lunettes de piscine

going ['gəʊɪŋ] *n* (*conditions*) état *m* du terrain ▷ *adj*: **the ~ rate** le tarif (en vigueur)

gold [gəʊld] *n* or *m* ▷ *adj* en or; (*reserves*) d'or; **golden** *adj* (*made of gold*) en or; (*gold in colour*) doré(e); **goldfish** *n* poisson *m* rouge; **goldmine** *n* mine *f* d'or; **gold-plated** *adj* plaqué(e) or *inv*

golf [gɔlf] *n* golf *m*; **golf ball** *n* balle *f* de golf; (*on typewriter*) boule *f*; **golf club** *n* club *m* de golf; (*stick*) club *m*, crosse *f* de golf; **golf course** *n* terrain *m* de golf; **golfer** *n* joueur(-euse) de golf

gone [gɔn] *pp of* **go**

gong [gɔŋ] *n* gong *m*

good [gʊd] *adj* bon(ne); (*kind*) gentil(le); (*child*) sage; (*weather*) beau (belle) ▷ *n* bien *m*; **goods** *npl* marchandise *f*, articles *mpl*; **~! bon!**, très bien!; **to be ~ at** être bon en; **to be ~ for** être bon pour; **it's no ~ complaining** cela ne sert à rien de se plaindre; **to make ~** (*deficit*) combler; (*losses*) compenser; **for ~** (*for ever*) pour de bon, une fois pour toutes; **would you be ~ enough to ...?** auriez-vous la bonté *or* l'amabilité de ...?; **is this any ~?** (*will it do?*) est-ce que ceci fera l'affaire?, est-ce que cela peut vous rendre service?; (*what's it like?*)

qu'est-ce que ça vaut?; **a ~ deal (of)** beaucoup (de); **a ~ many** beaucoup (de); **~ morning/ afternoon!** bonjour!; **~ evening!** bonsoir!; **~ night!** bonsoir!; *(on going to bed)* bonne nuit!; **goodbye** *excl* au revoir!; **to say goodbye to sb** dire au revoir à qn; **Good Friday** n Vendredi saint; **good-looking** *adj* beau (belle), bien *inv*; **good-natured** *adj* (person) qui a un bon naturel; **goodness** n (of person) bonté f; **for goodness sake!** je vous en prie!; **goodness gracious!** mon Dieu!; **goods train** n (BRIT) train m de marchandises; **goodwill** n bonne volonté

goose (pl **geese**) [guːs, giːs] n oie f

gooseberry ['guzbərɪ] n groseille f à maquereau; **to play ~** (BRIT) tenir la chandelle

goose bumps, goose pimples npl chair f de poule

gorge [gɔːdʒ] n gorge f ▷ vt: **to ~ o.s. (on)** se gorger (de)

gorgeous ['gɔːdʒəs] *adj* splendide, superbe

gorilla [gə'rɪlə] n gorille m

gosh (inf) [gɔʃ] *excl* mince alors!

gospel ['gɔspl] n évangile m

gossip ['gɔsɪp] n (chat) bavardages mpl; (malicious) commérage m, cancans mpl; (person) commère f ▷ vi bavarder; cancaner, faire des commérages; **gossip column** n (Press) échos mpl

got [gɔt] pt, pp of **get**

gotten ['gɔtn] (US) pp of **get**

gourmet ['guəmeɪ] n gourmet m, gastronome m/f

govern ['gʌvən] vt gouverner; (influence) déterminer; **government** n gouvernement m; (BRIT: ministers) ministère m; **governor** n (of colony, state, bank) gouverneur m; (of school, hospital etc) administrateur(-trice); (BRIT: of prison) directeur(-trice)

gown [gaun] n robe f; (of teacher, BRIT: of judge) toge f

G.P. n abbr (Med) = **general practitioner**

grab [græb] vt saisir, empoigner ▷ vi: **to ~ at** essayer de saisir

grace [greɪs] n grâce f ▷ vt (honour) honorer; (adorn) orner; **5 days' ~** un répit de 5 jours; **graceful** *adj* gracieux(-euse), élégant(e); **gracious** ['greɪʃəs] *adj* bienveillant(e)

grade [greɪd] n (Comm: quality) qualité f; (size) calibre m; (type) catégorie f; (in hierarchy) grade m, échelon m; (Scol) note f; (US: school class) classe f; (: gradient) pente f ▷ vt classer; (by size) calibrer; **grade crossing** n (US) passage m à niveau; **grade school** n (US) école f primaire

gradient ['greɪdɪənt] n inclinaison f, pente f

gradual ['grædjuəl] *adj* graduel(le), progressif(-ive); **gradually** *adv* peu à peu, graduellement

graduate n ['grædjuɪt] diplômé(e)

d'université; (US: of high school) diplômé(e) de fin d'études ▷ vi ['grædjueɪt] obtenir un diplôme d'université (or de fin d'études); **graduation** [grædju'eɪʃən] n cérémonie f de remise des diplômes

graffiti [grə'fiːtɪ] npl graffiti mpl

graft [grɑːft] n (Agr, Med) greffe f; (bribery) corruption f ▷ vt greffer; **hard ~** (BRIT: inf) boulot acharné

grain [greɪn] n (single piece) grain m; (no pl: cereals) céréales fpl; (US: corn) blé m

gram [græm] n gramme m

grammar ['græməʳ] n grammaire f; **grammar school** n (BRIT) = lycée m

gramme [græm] n = **gram**

gran (inf) [græn] n (BRIT) mamie f (inf), mémé f (inf)

grand [grænd] *adj* magnifique, splendide; (gesture etc) noble; **grandad** (inf) n = **granddad**; **grandchild** (pl ~ren) n petit-fils m, petite-fille f; **grandchildren** npl petits-enfants; **granddad** n (inf) papy m (inf), papi m (inf), pépé m (inf); **granddaughter** n petite-fille f; **grandfather** n grand-père m; **grandma** n (inf) = **gran**; **grandmother** n grand-mère f; **grandpa** n (inf) = **granddad**; **grandparents** npl grands-parents mpl; **grand piano** n piano m à queue; **Grand Prix** ['grɑ̃ː'priː] n (Aut) grand prix automobile; **grandson** n petit-fils m

granite ['grænɪt] n granit m

granny ['grænɪ] n (inf) = **gran**

grant [grɑːnt] vt accorder; (a request) accéder à; (admit) concéder ▷ n (Scol) bourse f; (Admin) subside m, subvention f; **to take sth for ~ed** considérer qch comme acquis; **to take sb for ~ed** considérer qn comme faisant partie du décor

grape [greɪp] n raisin m

grapefruit ['greɪpfruːt] n pamplemousse m

graph [grɑːf] n graphique m, courbe f; **graphic** ['græfɪk] *adj* graphique; (vivid) vivant(e); **graphics** n (art) arts mpl graphiques; (process) graphisme m ▷ npl (drawings) illustrations fpl

grasp [grɑːsp] vt saisir ▷ n (grip) prise f; (fig) compréhension f, connaissance f

grass [grɑːs] n herbe f; (lawn) gazon m; **grasshopper** n sauterelle f

grate [greɪt] n grille f de cheminée ▷ vi grincer ▷ vt (Culin) râper

grateful ['greɪtful] *adj* reconnaissant(e)

grater ['greɪtəʳ] n râpe f

gratitude ['grætɪtjuːd] n gratitude f

grave [greɪv] n tombe f ▷ *adj* grave, sérieux(-euse)

gravel ['grævl] n gravier m

gravestone ['greɪvstəun] n pierre tombale

graveyard ['greɪvjɑːd] n cimetière m

gravity ['grævɪtɪ] n (Physics) gravité f;

pesanteur f; (seriousness) gravité

gravy ['greɪvɪ] n jus m (de viande), sauce f (au jus de viande)

gray [greɪ] adj (us) = **grey**

graze [greɪz] vi paître, brouter ▷ vt (touch lightly) frôler, effleurer; (scrape) écorcher ▷ n écorchure f

grease [gri:s] n (fat) graisse f; (lubricant) lubrifiant m ▷ vt graisser; lubrifier; **greasy** adj gras(se), graisseux(-euse); (hands, clothes) graisseux

great [greɪt] adj grand(e); (heat, pain etc) très fort(e), intense; (inf) formidable; **Great Britain** n Grande-Bretagne f; **great-grandfather** n arrière-grand-père m; **great-grandmother** n arrière-grand-mère f; **greatly** adv très, grandement; (with verbs) beaucoup

Greece [gri:s] n Grèce f

greed [gri:d] n (also: **~iness**) avidité f; (for food) gourmandise f; **greedy** adj avide; (for food) gourmand(e)

Greek [gri:k] adj grec (grecque) ▷ n Grec (Grecque); (Ling) grec m

green [gri:n] adj vert(e); (inexperienced) (bien) jeune, naïf (-ive); (ecological: product etc) écologique ▷ n (colour) vert m; (on golf course) green m; (stretch of grass) pelouse f; **greens** npl (vegetables) légumes verts; **green card** n (Aut) carte verte; (us: work permit) permis m de travail; **greengage** n reine-claude f; **greengrocer** n (BRIT) marchand m de fruits et légumes; **greengrocer's (shop)** n magasin m de fruits et légumes; **greenhouse** n serre f; **greenhouse effect** n: **the greenhouse effect** l'effet m de serre

Greenland ['gri:nlənd] n Groenland m

green salad n salade verte

greet [gri:t] vt accueillir; **greeting** n salutation f; **Christmas/birthday greetings** souhaits mpl de Noël/de bon anniversaire; **greeting(s) card** n carte f de vœux

grew [gru:] pt of **grow**

grey (us **gray**) [greɪ] adj gris(e); (dismal) sombre; **grey-haired** adj aux cheveux gris; **greyhound** n lévrier m

grid [grɪd] n grille f; (Elec) réseau m; **gridlock** n (traffic jam) embouteillage m

grief [gri:f] n chagrin m, douleur f

grievance ['gri:vəns] n doléance f, grief m; (cause for complaint) grief

grieve [gri:v] vi avoir du chagrin; se désoler ▷ vt faire de la peine à, affliger; **to ~ for sb** pleurer qn

grill [grɪl] n (on cooker) gril m; (also: **mixed ~**) grillade(s) f(pl) ▷ vt (BRIT) griller; (inf: question) cuisiner

grille [grɪl] n grillage m; (Aut) calandre f

grim [grɪm] adj sinistre, lugubre; (serious, stern) sévère

grime [graɪm] n crasse f

grin [grɪn] n large sourire m ▷ vi sourire

grind [graɪnd] vb (pt, pp **ground**) ▷ vt écraser; (coffee, pepper etc) moudre; (us: meat) hacher ▷ n (work) corvée f

grip [grɪp] n (handclasp) poigne f; (control) prise f; (handle) poignée f; (holdall) sac m de voyage ▷ vt saisir, empoigner; (viewer, reader) captiver; **to come to ~s with** se colleter avec, en venir aux prises avec; **to ~ the road** (Aut) adhérer à la route; **gripping** adj prenant(e), palpitant(e)

grit [grɪt] n gravillon m; (courage) cran m ▷ vt (road) sabler; **to ~ one's teeth** serrer les dents

grits [grɪts] npl (us) gruau m de maïs

groan [grəun] n (of pain) gémissement m ▷ vi gémir

grocer ['grəusə^r] n épicier m; **groceries** npl provisions fpl; **grocer's (shop)**, **grocery** n épicerie f

groin [grɔɪn] n aine f

groom [gru:m] n (for horses) palefrenier m; (also: **bride~**) marié m ▷ vt (horse) panser; (fig): **to ~ sb for** former qn pour

groove [gru:v] n sillon m, rainure f

grope [grəup] vi tâtonner; **to ~ for** chercher à tâtons

gross [grəus] adj grossier(-ière); (Comm) brut(e); **grossly** adv (greatly) très, grandement

grotesque [grə'tɛsk] adj grotesque

ground [graund] pt, pp of **grind** ▷ n sol m, terre f; (land) terrain m, terres fpl; (Sport) terrain; (reason: gen pl) raison f; (us: also: **~ wire**) terre f ▷ vt (plane) empêcher de décoller, retenir au sol; (us Elec) équiper d'une prise de terre; **grounds** npl (gardens etc) parc m, domaine m; (of coffee) marc m; **on the ~, to the ~** par terre; **to gain/lose ~** gagner/perdre du terrain; **ground floor** n rez-de-chaussée m; **groundsheet** n (BRIT) tapis m de sol; **groundwork** n préparation f

group [gru:p] n groupe m ▷ vt (also: **~ together**) grouper ▷ vi (also: **~ together**) se grouper

grouse [graus] n (pl inv: bird) grouse f (sorte de coq de bruyère) ▷ vi (complain) rouspéter, râler

grovel ['grɔvl] vi (fig): **to ~ (before)** ramper (devant)

grow (pt **grew**, pp **~n**) [grəu, gru:, grəun] vi (plant) pousser, croître; (person) grandir; (increase) augmenter, se développer; (become) devenir; **to ~ rich/weak** s'enrichir/s'affaiblir ▷ vt cultiver, faire pousser; (hair, beard) laisser pousser; **grow on** vt fus: **that painting is ~ing on me** je finirai par aimer ce tableau; **grow up** vi grandir

growl [graul] vi grogner

grown [grəun] pp of **grow**; **grown-up** n adulte m/f, grande personne

growth [grəuθ] n croissance f, développement m; (what has grown) pousse f; poussée f; (Med) grosseur f, tumeur f

grub [grʌb] n larve f; (inf: food) bouffe f

grubby ['grʌbɪ] adj crasseux(-euse)

grudge [grʌdʒ] n rancune f ▷ vt: **to ~ sb sth** (in giving) donner qch à qn à contre-cœur; (resent) reprocher qch à qn; **to bear sb a ~ (for)** garder rancune or en vouloir à qn (de)

gruelling (us **grueling**) ['gruəlɪŋ] adj exténuant(e)

gruesome ['gru:səm] adj horrible

grumble ['grʌmbl] vi rouspéter, ronchonner

grumpy ['grʌmpɪ] adj grincheux(-euse)

grunt [grʌnt] vi grogner

guarantee [gærən'ti:] n garantie f ▷ vt garantir

guard [gɑ:d] n garde f; (one man) garde m; (BRIT Rail) chef m de train; (safety device: on machine) dispositif m de sûreté; (also: **fire~**) garde-feu m inv ▷ vt garder, surveiller; (protect): **to ~ sb/sth (against** or **from)** protéger qn/qch (contre); **to be on one's ~** (fig) être sur ses gardes; **guardian** n gardien(ne); (of minor) tuteur(-trice)

guerrilla [gə'rɪlə] n guérillero m

guess [ges] vi deviner ▷ vt deviner; (estimate) évaluer; (us) croire, penser ▷ n supposition f, hypothèse f; **to take** or **have a ~** essayer de deviner

guest [gest] n invité(e); (in hotel) client(e); **guest house** n pension f; **guest room** n chambre f d'amis

guidance ['gaɪdəns] n (advice) conseils mpl

guide [gaɪd] n (person) guide m/f; (book) guide m; (also: **Girl G~**) éclaireuse f; (Roman Catholic) guide f ▷ vt guider; **is there an English-speaking ~?** est-ce que l'un des guides parle anglais?; **guidebook** n guide m; **guide dog** n chien m d'aveugle; **guided tour** n visite guidée; **what time does the guided tour start?** la visite guidée commence à quelle heure?; **guidelines** npl (advice) instructions générales, conseils mpl

guild [gɪld] n (History) corporation f, (sharing interests) cercle m, association f

guilt [gɪlt] n culpabilité f; **guilty** adj coupable

guinea pig ['gɪnɪ-] n cobaye m

guitar [gɪ'tɑ:'] n guitare f; **guitarist** n guitariste m/f

gulf [gʌlf] n golfe m; (abyss) gouffre m

gull [gʌl] n mouette f

gulp [gʌlp] vi avaler sa salive; (from emotion) avoir la gorge serrée, s'étrangler ▷ vt (also: **~ down**) avaler

gum [gʌm] n (Anat) gencive f; (glue) colle f; (also: **chewing-~**) chewing-gum m ▷ vt coller

gun [gʌn] n (small) revolver m, pistolet m; (rifle) fusil m, carabine f; (cannon) canon m; **gunfire** n fusillade f; **gunman** (irreg) n bandit armé; **gunpoint** n: **at gunpoint** sous la menace du pistolet (or fusil); **gunpowder** n poudre f à canon; **gunshot** n coup m de feu

gush [gʌʃ] vi jaillir; (fig) se répandre en effusions

gust [gʌst] n (of wind) rafale f

gut [gʌt] n intestin m, boyau m; **guts** npl (Anat) boyaux mpl; (inf: courage) cran m

gutter ['gʌtə'] n (of roof) gouttière f; (in street) caniveau m

guy [gaɪ] n (inf: man) type m; (also: **~rope**) corde f; (figure) effigie de Guy Fawkes

Guy Fawkes' Night [gaɪ'fɔːks-] n voir encadré

● GUY FAWKES' NIGHT
●
●
● **Guy Fawkes' Night**, que l'on appelle
● également "bonfire night", commémore
● l'échec du complot (le "Gunpowder Plot")
● contre James Ist et son parlement le 5
● novembre 1605. L'un des conspirateurs,
● Guy Fawkes, avait été surpris dans les
● caves du parlement alors qu'il s'apprêtait
● à y mettre le feu. Chaque année pour le 5
● novembre, les enfants préparent à l'avance
● une effigie de Guy Fawkes et ils demandent
● aux passants "un penny pour le guy" avec
● lequel ils pourront s'acheter des fusées de
● feu d'artifice. Beaucoup de gens font encore
● un feu dans leur jardin sur lequel ils brûlent
● le "guy".

gym [dʒɪm] n (also: **~nasium**) gymnase m; (also: **~nastics**) gym f; **gymnasium** n gymnase m; **gymnast** n gymnaste m/f; **gymnastics** n, npl gymnastique f; **gym shoes** npl chaussures fpl de gym(nastique)

gynaecologist (us **gynecologist**) [gaɪnɪ'kɔlədʒɪst] n gynécologue m/f

gypsy ['dʒɪpsɪ] n gitan(e), bohémien(ne)

haberdashery [ˈhæbəˈdæʃərɪ] n (BRIT) mercerie f

habit [ˈhæbɪt] n habitude f; (costume: Rel) habit m

habitat [ˈhæbɪtæt] n habitat m

hack [hæk] vt hacher, tailler ▷ n (pej: writer) nègre m; **hacker** n (Comput) pirate m (informatique)

had [hæd] pt, pp of **have**

haddock (pl ~ or ~s) [ˈhædək] n églefin m; **smoked ~** haddock m

hadn't [ˈhædnt] = **had not**

haemorrhage (US **hemorrhage**) [ˈhɛmərɪdʒ] n hémorragie f

haemorrhoids (US **hemorrhoids**) [ˈhɛmərɔɪdz] npl hémorroïdes fpl

haggle [ˈhægl] vi marchander

Hague [heɪg] n: **The ~** La Haye

hail [heɪl] n grêle f ▷ vt (call) héler; (greet) acclamer ▷ vi grêler; **hailstone** n grêlon m

hair [hɛər] n cheveux mpl; (on body) poils mpl; (of animal) pelage m; (single hair: on head) cheveu m; (: on body, of animal) poil m; **to do one's ~** se coiffer; **hairband** n (elasticated) bandeau m; (plastic) serre-tête m; **hairbrush** n brosse f à cheveux; **haircut** n coupe f (de cheveux); **hairdo** n coiffure f; **hairdresser** n coiffeur(-euse); **hairdresser's** n salon m de coiffure, coiffeur m; **hair dryer** n sèche-cheveux m, séchoir m; **hair gel** n gel m pour cheveux; **hair spray** n laque f (pour les cheveux); **hairstyle** n coiffure f; **hairy** adj poilu(e), chevelu(e); (inf: frightening) effrayant(e)

hake (pl ~ or ~s) [heɪk] n colin m, merlu m

half [hɑːf] n (pl **halves**) moitié f; (of beer: also: ~ **pint**) ≈ demi m; (Rail, bus: also: ~ **fare**) demi-tarif m; (Sport: of match) mi-temps f ▷ adj demi(e) ▷ adv (à) moitié, à demi; ~ **an hour** une demi-heure; ~ **a dozen** une demi-douzaine; ~ **a pound** une demi-livre, ≈ 250 g; **two and a ~** deux et demi; **to cut sth in ~** couper qch en deux; **half board** n (BRIT: in hotel) demi-pension f; **half-brother** n demi-frère m; **half day** n demi-journée f; **half fare** n demi-tarif m; **half-hearted** adj tiède, sans enthousiasme; **half-hour** n demi-heure f; **half-price** adj à moitié prix ▷ adv (also: **at half-price**) à moitié prix; **half term** n (BRIT Scol) vacances fpl (de demi-trimestre); **half-time** n mi-temps f; **halfway** adv à mi-chemin; **halfway through sth** au milieu de qch

hall [hɔːl] n salle f; (entrance way: big) hall m; (small) entrée f; (US: corridor) couloir m; (mansion) château m, manoir m

hallmark [ˈhɔːlmɑːk] n poinçon m; (fig) marque f

hallo [həˈləu] excl = **hello**

hall of residence n (BRIT) pavillon m or résidence f universitaire

Halloween, Hallowe'en [ˈhæləuˈiːn] n veille f de la Toussaint; voir encadré

● **HALLOWEEN**

Selon la tradition, **Halloween** est la nuit des fantômes et des sorcières. En Écosse et aux États-Unis surtout (et de plus en plus en Angleterre) les enfants, pour fêter **Halloween**, se déguisent ce soir-là et ils vont ainsi de porte en porte en demandant de petits cadeaux (du chocolat, une pomme etc).

hallucination [həluːsɪˈneɪʃən] n hallucination f

hallway [ˈhɔːlweɪ] n (entrance) vestibule m; (corridor) couloir m

halo [ˈheɪləu] n (of saint etc) auréole f

halt [hɔːlt] n halte f, arrêt m ▷ vt faire arrêter; (progress etc) interrompre ▷ vi faire halte, s'arrêter

halve [hɑːv] vt (apple etc) partager or diviser en deux; (reduce by half) réduire de moitié

halves [hɑːvz] npl of **half**

ham [hæm] n jambon m

hamburger [ˈhæmbəːgər] n hamburger m

hamlet [ˈhæmlɪt] n hameau m

hammer [ˈhæmər] n marteau m ▷ vt (nail)

enfoncer; (*fig*) éreinter, démolir ▷ *vi* (*at door*)
frapper à coups redoublés; **to ~ a point home
to sb** faire rentrer qch dans la tête de qn
hammock ['hæmək] *n* hamac *m*
hamper ['hæmpə^r] *vt* gêner ▷ *n* panier *m*
(d'osier)
hamster ['hæmstə^r] *n* hamster *m*
hamstring ['hæmstrɪŋ] *n* (*Anat*) tendon *m*
du jarret
hand [hænd] *n* main *f*; (*of clock*) aiguille
f; (*handwriting*) écriture *f*; (*at cards*) jeu *m*;
(*worker*) ouvrier(-ière) ▷ *vt* passer, donner;
to give sb a ~ donner un coup de main à qn;
at ~ à portée de la main; **in ~** (*situation*) en
main; (*work*) en cours; **to be on ~** (*person*)
être disponible; (*emergency services*) se tenir
prêt(e) (à intervenir); **to ~** (*information etc*)
sous la main, à portée de la main; **on the
one ~ ..., on the other ~** d'une part ...,
d'autre part; **hand down** *vt* passer; (*tradition,
heirloom*) transmettre; (*us: sentence, verdict*)
prononcer; **hand in** *vt* remettre; **hand
out** *vt* distribuer; **hand over** *vt* remettre;
(*powers etc*) transmettre; **handbag** *n* sac *m*
à main; **hand baggage** *n* = **hand luggage**;
handbook *n* manuel *m*; **handbrake** *n* frein *m*
à main; **handcuffs** *npl* menottes *fpl*; **handful**
n poignée *f*
handicap ['hændɪkæp] *n* handicap *m* ▷ *vt*
handicaper; **mentally/physically ~ped**
handicapé(e) mentalement/physiquement
handkerchief ['hæŋkətʃɪf] *n* mouchoir *m*
handle ['hændl] *n* (*of door etc*) poignée *f*; (*of cup
etc*) anse *f*; (*of knife etc*) manche *m*; (*of saucepan*)
queue *f*; (*for winding*) manivelle *f* ▷ *vt* toucher,
manier; (*deal with*) s'occuper de; (*treat: people*)
prendre; **"~ with care"** "fragile"; **to fly off the
~** s'énerver; **handlebar(s)** *n(pl)* guidon *m*
hand: **hand luggage** *n* bagages *mpl* à main;
handmade *adj* fait(e) à la main; **handout** *n*
(*money*) aide *f*, don *m*; (*leaflet*) prospectus *m*; (*at
lecture*) polycopié *m*; **hands-free** *adj* (*phone*)
mains libres *inv* ▷ *n* (*also*: **hands-free kit**) kit *m*
mains libres *inv*
handsome ['hænsəm] *adj* beau (belle);
(*profit*) considérable
handwriting ['hændraɪtɪŋ] *n* écriture *f*
handy ['hændɪ] *adj* (*person*) adroit(e); (*close at
hand*) sous la main; (*convenient*) pratique
hang (*pt, pp* **hung**) [hæŋ, hʌŋ] *vt* accrocher;
(*criminal: pt, pp* **~ed**) pendre ▷ *vi* pendre; (*hair,
drapery*) tomber ▷ *n*: **to get the ~ of (doing)
sth** (*inf*) attraper le coup pour faire qch; **hang
about, hang around** *vi* traîner; **hang down**
vi pendre; **hang on** *vi* (*wait*) attendre; **hang
out** *vt* (*washing*) étendre (dehors) ▷ *vi* (*inf: live*)
habiter, percher; (: *spend time*) traîner; **hang
round** *vi* = **hang around**; **hang up** *vi* (*Tel*)
raccrocher ▷ *vt* (*coat, painting etc*) accrocher,

suspendre
hanger ['hæŋə^r] *n* cintre *m*, portemanteau *m*
hang-gliding ['hæŋglaɪdɪŋ] *n* vol *m* libre *or*
sur aile delta
hangover ['hæŋəuvə^r] *n* (*after drinking*)
gueule *f* de bois
hankie, hanky ['hæŋkɪ] *n abbr*
= **handkerchief**
happen ['hæpən] *vi* arriver, se passer, se
produire; **what's ~ing?** que se passe-t-il?; **she
~ed to be free** il s'est trouvé (*or* se trouvait)
qu'elle était libre; **as it ~s** justement
happily ['hæpɪlɪ] *adv* heureusement;
(*cheerfully*) joyeusement
happiness ['hæpɪnɪs] *n* bonheur *m*
happy ['hæpɪ] *adj* heureux(-euse); **~ with**
(*arrangements etc*) satisfait(e) de; **to be ~ to do**
faire volontiers; **~ birthday!** bon anniversaire!
harass ['hærəs] *vt* accabler, tourmenter;
harassment *n* tracasseries *fpl*
harbour (*us* **harbor**) ['hɑːbə^r] *n* port *m* ▷ *vt*
héberger, abriter; (*hopes, suspicions*) entretenir
hard [hɑːd] *adj* dur(e); (*question, problem*)
difficile; (*facts, evidence*) concret(-ète) ▷ *adv*
(*work*) dur; (*think, try*) sérieusement; **to look
~ at** regarder fixement; (*fig*) regarder de
près; **no ~ feelings!** sans rancune!; **to be ~ of
hearing** être dur(e) d'oreille; **to be ~ done by**
être traité(e) injustement; **hardback** *n* livre
relié *m*; **hardboard** *n* Isorel® *m*; **hard disk** *n*
(*Comput*) disque dur; **harden** *vt* durcir; (*fig*)
endurcir ▷ *vi* (*substance*) durcir
hardly ['hɑːdlɪ] *adv* (*scarcely*) à peine; (*harshly*)
durement; **~ anywhere/ever** presque nulle
part/jamais
hard: **hardship** *n* (*difficulties*) épreuves *fpl*;
(*deprivation*) privations *fpl*; **hard shoulder**
n (*BRIT Aut*) accotement stabilisé; **hard-up**
adj (*inf*) fauché(e); **hardware** *n* quincaillerie
f; (*Comput, Mil*) matériel *m*; **hardware shop**
(*us* **hardware store**) *n* quincaillerie *f*;
hard-working *adj* travailleur(-euse),
consciencieux(-euse)
hardy ['hɑːdɪ] *adj* robuste; (*plant*) résistant(e)
au gel
hare [hɛə^r] *n* lièvre *m*
harm [hɑːm] *n* mal *m*; (*wrong*) tort *m* ▷ *vt*
(*person*) faire du mal *or* du tort à; (*thing*)
endommager; **out of ~'s way** à l'abri du
danger, en lieu sûr; **harmful** *adj* nuisible;
harmless *adj* inoffensif(-ive)
harmony ['hɑːmənɪ] *n* harmonie *f*
harness ['hɑːnɪs] *n* harnais *m* ▷ *vt* (*horse*)
harnacher; (*resources*) exploiter
harp [hɑːp] *n* harpe *f* ▷ *vi*: **to ~ on about**
revenir toujours sur
harsh [hɑːʃ] *adj* (*hard*) dur(e); (*severe*) sévère;
(*unpleasant: sound*) discordant(e); (: *light*) cru(e)
harvest ['hɑːvɪst] *n* (*of corn*) moisson *f*; (*of*

fruit) récolte *f*; (*of grapes*) vendange *f* ▷ *vt*
moissonner; récolter; vendanger

has [hæz] *vb see* **have**

hasn't ['hæznt] = **has not**

hassle ['hæsl] *n* (*inf: fuss*) histoire(s) *f(pl)*

haste [heɪst] *n* hâte *f*, précipitation *f*; **hasten**
['heɪsn] *vt* hâter, accélérer ▷ *vi* se hâter,
s'empresser; **hastily** *adv* à la hâte, (*leave*)
précipitamment; **hasty** *adj* (*decision, action*)
hâtif(-ive); (*departure, escape*) précipité(e)

hat [hæt] *n* chapeau *m*

hatch [hætʃ] *n* (*Naut: also:* **~way**) écoutille *f*;
(*BRIT: also:* **service ~**) passe-plats *m inv* ▷ *vi*
éclore

hatchback ['hætʃbæk] *n* (*Aut*) modèle *m* avec
hayon arrière

hate [heɪt] *vt* haïr, détester ▷ *n* haine *f*;
hatred ['heɪtrɪd] *n* haine *f*

haul [hɔːl] *vt* traîner, tirer ▷ *n* (*of fish*) prise *f*; (*of
stolen goods etc*) butin *m*

haunt [hɔːnt] *vt* (*subj: ghost, fear*) hanter; (:
person) fréquenter ▷ *n* repaire *m*; **haunted** *adj*
(*castle etc*) hanté(e); (*look*) égaré(e), hagard(e)

 KEYWORD

have [hæv] (*pt, pp* **had**) *aux vb* **1** (*gen*) avoir;
être; **to have eaten/slept** avoir mangé/
dormi; **to have arrived/gone** être arrivé(e)/
allé(e); **having finished** *or* **when he had
finished, he left** quand il a eu fini, il est parti;
we'd already eaten nous avions déjà mangé
2 (*in tag questions*) **you've done it, haven't
you?** vous l'avez fait, n'est-ce pas?
3 (*in short answers and questions*): **no I
haven't!/yes we have!** mais non!/mais si!;
so I have! ah oui!, oui c'est vrai!; **I've been
there before, have you?** j'y suis déjà allé, et
vous?
▷ *modal aux vb* (*be obliged*): **to have (got) to do
sth** devoir faire qch, être obligé(e) de faire qch;
she has (got) to do it elle doit le faire, il faut
qu'elle le fasse; **you haven't to tell her** vous
n'êtes pas obligé de le lui dire; (*must not*) ne le
lui dites surtout pas; **do you have to book?** il
faut réserver?
▷ *vt* **1** (*possess*) avoir; **he has (got) blue eyes/
dark hair** il a les yeux bleus/les cheveux bruns
2 (*referring to meals etc*): **to have breakfast**
prendre le petit déjeuner; **to have dinner/
lunch** dîner/déjeuner; **to have a drink**
prendre un verre; **to have a cigarette** fumer
une cigarette
3 (*receive*) avoir, recevoir; (*obtain*) avoir;
may I have your address? puis-je avoir
votre adresse?; **you can have it for £5** vous
pouvez l'avoir pour 5 livres; **I must have it for
tomorrow** il me le faut pour demain; **to have
a baby** avoir un bébé

4 (*maintain, allow*): **I won't have it!** ça ne se
passera pas comme ça!; **we can't have that**
nous ne tolérerons pas ça
5 (*by sb else*): **to have sth done** faire faire qch;
to have one's hair cut se faire couper les
cheveux; **to have sb do sth** faire faire qch à qn
6 (*experience, suffer*): **to have a cold/flu**
avoir un rhume/la grippe; **to have an
operation** se faire opérer; **she had her bag
stolen** elle s'est fait voler son sac
7 (*+noun*): **to have a swim/walk** nager/se
promener; **to have a bath/shower** prendre
un bain/une douche; **let's have a look**
regardons; **to have a meeting** se réunir; **to
have a party** organiser une fête; **let me have
a try** laissez-moi essayer

haven ['heɪvn] *n* port *m*; (*fig*) havre *m*

haven't ['hævnt] = **have not**

havoc ['hævək] *n* ravages *mpl*

Hawaii [hə'waɪ:] *n* (*îles fpl*) Hawaï *m*

hawk [hɔːk] *n* faucon *m*

hawthorn ['hɔːθɔːn] *n* aubépine *f*

hay [heɪ] *n* foin *m*; **hay fever** *n* rhume *m* des
foins; **haystack** *n* meule *f* de foin

hazard ['hæzəd] *n* (*risk*) danger *m*, risque
m ▷ *vt* risquer, hasarder; **hazardous** *adj*
hasardeux(-euse), risqué(e); **hazard warning
lights** *npl* (*Aut*) feux *mpl* de détresse

haze [heɪz] *n* brume *f*

hazel ['heɪzl] *n* (*tree*) noisetier *m* ▷ *adj* (*eyes*)
noisette *inv*; **hazelnut** *n* noisette *f*

hazy ['heɪzɪ] *adj* brumeux(-euse); (*idea*) vague

he [hiː] *pron* il; **it is he who ...** c'est lui qui ...;
here he is le voici

head [hɛd] *n* tête *f*; (*leader*) chef *m*; (*of school*)
directeur(-trice); (*of secondary school*) proviseur
m ▷ *vt* (*list*) être en tête de; (*group, company*)
être à la tête de; (*ball*) faire une tête; **~s or tails**
pile ou face; **~ first** la tête la première; **~ over
heels in love** follement *or* éperdument amoureux(-euse);
to ~ the ball faire une tête; **head for** *vt fus*
se diriger vers; (*disaster*) aller à; **head off** *vt*
(*threat, danger*) détourner; **headache** *n* mal
m de tête; **to have a headache** avoir mal
à la tête; **heading** *n* titre *m*; (*subject title*)
rubrique *f*; **headlamp** (*BRIT*) *n* = **headlight**;
headlight *n* phare *m*; **headline** *n* titre *m*;
head office *n* siège *m*, bureau *m* central;
headphones *npl* casque *m* (à écouteurs);
headquarters *npl* (*of business*) bureau *or* siège
central; (*Mil*) quartier général; **headroom**
n (*in car*) hauteur *f* de plafond; (*under bridge*)
hauteur limite; **headscarf** *n* foulard *m*;
headset *n* = **headphones**; **headteacher**
n directeur(-trice); (*of secondary school*)
proviseur *m*; **head waiter** *n* maître *m* d'hôtel

heal [hiːl] *vt, vi* guérir

health [hɛlθ] *n* santé *f*; **health care** *n* services médicaux; **health centre** n (BRIT) centre m de santé; **health food** n aliment(s) naturel(s); **Health Service** n: **the Health Service** (BRIT) ≈ la Sécurité Sociale; **healthy** adj (person) en bonne santé; (climate, food, attitude etc) sain(e)

heap [hi:p] n tas m ▷ vt (also: **~ up**) entasser, amonceler; **she ~ed her plate with cakes** elle a chargé son assiette de gâteaux; **~s (of)** (inf: lots) des tas (de)

hear (pt, pp **~d**) [hɪər, hɜːd] vt entendre; (news) apprendre ▷ vi entendre; **to ~ about** entendre parler de; (have news of) avoir des nouvelles de; **to ~ from sb** recevoir des nouvelles de qn

heard [hɜːd] pt, pp of **hear**

hearing ['hɪərɪŋ] n (sense) ouïe f; (of witnesses) audition f; (of a case) audience f; **hearing aid** n appareil m acoustique

hearse [hɜːs] n corbillard m

heart [hɑːt] n cœur m; **hearts** npl (Cards) cœur m; **at ~** au fond; **by ~** (learn, know) par cœur; **to lose/take ~** perdre/prendre courage; **heart attack** n crise f cardiaque; **heartbeat** n battement m de cœur; **heartbroken** adj: **to be heartbroken** avoir beaucoup de chagrin; **heartburn** n brûlures fpl d'estomac; **heart disease** n maladie f cardiaque

hearth [hɑːθ] n foyer m, cheminée f

heartless ['hɑːtlɪs] adj (person) sans cœur, insensible; (treatment) cruel(le)

hearty ['hɑːtɪ] adj chaleureux(-euse), (appetite) solide; (dislike) cordial(e); (meal) copieux(-euse)

heat [hi:t] n chaleur f; (Sport: also: **qualifying ~**) éliminatoire f ▷ vt chauffer; **heat up** vi (liquid) chauffer; (room) se réchauffer ▷ vt réchauffer; **heated** adj chauffé(e); (fig) passionné(e), échauffé(e), excité(e); **heater** n appareil m de chauffage; radiateur m; (in car) chauffage m; (water heater) chauffe-eau m

heather ['hɛðər] n bruyère f

heating ['hi:tɪŋ] n chauffage m

heatwave ['hi:tweɪv] n vague f de chaleur

heaven ['hɛvn] n ciel m, paradis m; (fig) paradis; **heavenly** adj céleste, divin(e)

heavily ['hɛvɪlɪ] adv lourdement; (drink, smoke) beaucoup; (sleep, sigh) profondément

heavy ['hɛvɪ] adj lourd(e); (work, rain, user, eater) gros(se); (drinker, smoker) grand(e); (schedule, week) chargé(e)

Hebrew ['hi:bru:] adj hébraïque ▷ n (Ling) hébreu m

Hebrides ['hɛbrɪdi:z] npl: **the ~** les Hébrides fpl

hectare ['hɛktɑː] n (BRIT) hectare m

hectic ['hɛktɪk] adj (schedule) très chargé(e); (day) mouvementé(e); (lifestyle) trépidant(e)

he'd [hi:d] = **he would**; **he had**

hedge [hɛdʒ] n haie f ▷ vi se dérober ▷ vt: **to ~ one's bets** (fig) se couvrir

hedgehog ['hɛdʒhɒg] n hérisson m

heed [hi:d] vt (also: **take ~ of**) tenir compte de, prendre garde à

heel [hi:l] n talon m ▷ vt retalonner

hefty ['hɛftɪ] adj (person) costaud(e); (parcel) lourd(e); (piece, price) gros(se)

height [haɪt] n (of person) taille f, grandeur f; (of object) hauteur f; (of plane, mountain) altitude f; (high ground) hauteur f, éminence f; (fig: of glory, fame, power) sommet m; (: of luxury, stupidity) comble m; **at the ~ of summer** au cœur de l'été; **heighten** vt hausser, surélever; (fig) augmenter

heir [ɛər] n héritier m; **heiress** n héritière f

held [hɛld] pt, pp of **hold**

helicopter ['hɛlɪkɒptər] n hélicoptère m

hell [hɛl] n enfer m; **oh ~!** (inf) merde!

he'll [hi:l] = **he will**; **he shall**

hello [hə'ləu] excl bonjour!; (to attract attention) hé!; (surprise) tiens!

helmet ['hɛlmɪt] n casque m

help [hɛlp] n aide f; (cleaner etc) femme f de ménage ▷ vt, vi aider; **~!** au secours!; **~ yourself** servez-vous; **can you ~ me?** pouvez-vous m'aider?; **can I ~ you?** (in shop) vous désirez??; **he can't ~ it** il n'y peut rien; **help out** vi aider ▷ vt: **to ~ sb out** aider qn; **helper** n aide m/f, assistant(e); **helpful** adj serviable, obligeant(e); (useful) utile; **helping** n portion f; **helpless** adj impuissant(e); (baby) sans défense; **helpline** n service m d'assistance téléphonique; (free) ≈ numéro vert

hem [hɛm] n ourlet m ▷ vt ourler

hemisphere ['hɛmɪsfɪər] n hémisphère m

hemorrhage ['hɛmərɪdʒ] n (US) = **haemorrhage**

hemorrhoids ['hɛmərɔɪdz] npl (US) = **haemorrhoids**

hen [hɛn] n poule f; (female bird) femelle f

hence [hɛns] adv (therefore) d'où, de là; **2 years ~** d'ici 2 ans

hen night, hen party n soirée f entre filles (avant le mariage de l'une d'elles)

hepatitis [hɛpə'taɪtɪs] n hépatite f

her [hɜːr] pron (direct) la, l' + vowel or h mute; (indirect) lui; (stressed, after prep) elle ▷ adj son (sa), ses pl; see also **me**; **my**

herb [hɜːb] n herbe f; **herbal** adj à base de plantes; **herbal tea** n tisane f

herd [hɜːd] n troupeau m

here [hɪər] adv ici; (time) alors ▷ excl tiens!, tenez!; **~!** (present) présent!; **~ is**, **~ are** voici; **~ he/she is** le (la) voici

hereditary [hɪ'rɛdɪtrɪ] adj héréditaire

heritage ['hɛrɪtɪdʒ] n héritage m, patrimoine m

hernia ['hɜːnɪə] n hernie f

hero (pl **~es**) ['hɪərəu] n héros m; **heroic** [hɪ'rəuɪk] adj héroïque

heroin ['hɛrəʊɪn] n héroïne f (drogue)
heroine ['hɛrəʊɪn] n héroïne f (femme)
heron ['hɛrən] n héron m
herring ['hɛrɪŋ] n hareng m
hers [hə:z] pron le (la) sien(ne), les siens (siennes); see also **mine¹**
herself [hə:'sɛlf] pron (reflexive) se; (emphatic) elle-même; (after prep) elle; see also **oneself**
he's [hi:z] = **he is**; **he has**
hesitant ['hɛzɪtənt] adj hésitant(e), indécis(e)
hesitate ['hɛzɪteɪt] vi: **to ~ (about/to do)** hésiter (sur/à faire); **hesitation** [hɛzɪ'teɪʃən] n hésitation f
heterosexual ['hɛtərəʊ'sɛksjuəl] adj, n hétérosexuel(le)
hexagon ['hɛksəgən] n hexagone m
hey [heɪ] excl hé!
heyday ['heɪdeɪ] n: **the ~ of** l'âge m d'or de, les beaux jours de
HGV n abbr = **heavy goods vehicle**
hi [haɪ] excl salut!; (to attract attention) hé!
hibernate ['haɪbəneɪt] vi hiberner
hiccough, hiccup ['hɪkʌp] vi hoqueter ▷ n: **to have (the) ~s** avoir le hoquet
hid [hɪd] pt of **hide**
hidden ['hɪdn] pp of **hide** ▷ adj: **~ agenda** intentions non déclarées
hide [haɪd] n (skin) peau f ▷ vb (pt **hid**, pp **hidden**) ▷ vt cacher ▷ vi: **to ~ (from sb)** se cacher (de qn)
hideous ['hɪdɪəs] adj hideux(-euse), atroce
hiding ['haɪdɪŋ] n (beating) correction f, volée f de coups; **to be in ~** (concealed) se tenir caché(e)
hi-fi ['haɪfaɪ] adj, n abbr (= high fidelity) hi-fi f inv
high [haɪ] adj haut(e); (speed, respect, number) grand(e); (price) élevé(e); (wind) fort(e), violent(e); (voice) aigu(ë) ▷ adv haut, en haut; **20 m ~** haut(e) de 20 m; **~ in the air** haut dans le ciel; **highchair** n (child's) chaise haute; **high-class** adj (neighbourhood, hotel) chic inv, de grand standing; **higher education** n études supérieures; **high heels** npl talons hauts, hauts talons; **high jump** n (Sport) saut m en hauteur; **highlands** ['haɪləndz] npl région montagneuse; **the Highlands** (in Scotland) les Highlands mpl; **highlight** n (fig: of event) point culminant ▷ vt (emphasize) faire ressortir, souligner; **highlights** npl (in hair) reflets mpl; **highlighter** n (pen) surligneur (lumineux); **highly** adv extrêmement, très; (unlikely) fort; (recommended, skilled, qualified) hautement; **to speak highly of** dire beaucoup de bien de; **highness** n: **His/Her Highness** son Altesse f; **high-rise** n (also: **high-rise block, high-rise building**) tour f (d'habitation); **high school** n lycée m; (us) établissement m d'enseignement supérieur; **high season** n (BRIT) haute saison; **high street** n (BRIT) grand-rue f; **high-tech** (inf) adj de pointe; **highway** n (BRIT) route f; (us) route nationale; **Highway Code** n (BRIT) code m de la route

hijack ['haɪdʒæk] vt détourner (par la force); **hijacker** n auteur m d'un détournement d'avion, pirate m de l'air
hike [haɪk] vi faire des excursions à pied ▷ n excursion f à pied, randonnée f; **hiker** n promeneur(-euse), excursionniste m/f; **hiking** n excursions fpl à pied, randonnée f
hilarious [hɪ'lɛərɪəs] adj (behaviour, event) désopilant(e)
hill [hɪl] n colline f; (fairly high) montagne f; (on road) côte f; **hillside** n (flanc m de) coteau m; **hill walking** n randonnée f de basse montagne; **hilly** adj vallonné(e), montagneux(-euse)
him [hɪm] pron (direct) le, l' + vowel or h mute; (stressed, indirect, after prep) lui; see also **me**; **himself** pron (reflexive) se; (emphatic) lui-même; (after prep) lui; see also **oneself**
hind [haɪnd] adj de derrière
hinder ['hɪndə*] vt gêner; (delay) retarder
hindsight ['haɪndsaɪt] n: **with (the benefit of) ~** avec du recul, rétrospectivement
Hindu ['hɪndu:] n Hindou(e); **Hinduism** n (Rel) hindouisme m
hinge [hɪndʒ] n charnière f ▷ vi (fig): **to ~ on** dépendre de
hint [hɪnt] n allusion f; (advice) conseil m; (clue) indication f ▷ vt: **to ~ that** insinuer que ▷ vi: **to ~ at** faire une allusion à
hip [hɪp] n hanche f
hippie, hippy ['hɪpɪ] n hippie m/f
hippo ['hɪpəʊ] (pl **~s**) n hippopotame m
hippopotamus [hɪpə'pɔtəməs] (pl **~es** or **hippopotami**) n hippopotame m
hippy ['hɪpɪ] n = **hippie**
hire ['haɪə*] vt (BRIT: car, equipment) louer; (worker) embaucher, engager ▷ n location f; **for ~** à louer; (taxi) libre; **I'd like to ~ a car** je voudrais louer une voiture; **hire(d) car** n (BRIT) voiture f de location; **hire purchase** n (BRIT) achat m (or vente f) à tempérament or crédit
his [hɪz] pron le (la) sien(ne), les siens (siennes) ▷ adj son (sa), ses pl; see also **mine¹**; **my**
Hispanic [hɪs'pænɪk] adj (in US) hispano-américain(e) ▷ n Hispano-Américain(e)
hiss [hɪs] vi siffler
historian [hɪ'stɔ:rɪən] n historien(ne)
historic(al) [hɪ'stɔrɪk(l)] adj historique
history ['hɪstərɪ] n histoire f
hit [hɪt] vt (pt, pp **~**) frapper; (reach: target) atteindre, toucher; (collide with: car) entrer en collision avec, heurter; (fig: affect) toucher ▷ n coup m; (success) succès m; (song) tube m; (to website) visite f; (on search engine) résultat m de recherche; **to ~ it off with sb** bien s'entendre

avec qn; **hit back** vi: **to ~ back at sb** prendre sa revanche sur qn

hitch [hɪtʃ] vt (*fasten*) accrocher, attacher; (*also: ~ up*) remonter d'une saccade ▷ vi faire de l'autostop ▷ n (*difficulty*) anicroche f, contretemps m; **to ~ a lift** faire du stop; **hitch-hike** vi faire de l'auto-stop; **hitch-hiker** n auto-stoppeur(-euse); **hitch-hiking** n auto-stop m, stop m (*inf*)

hi-tech ['haɪ'tɛk] adj de pointe

hitman ['hɪtmæn] (*irreg*) n (*inf*) tueur m à gages

HIV n abbr (= *human immunodeficiency virus*) HIV m, VIH m; **~-negative/positive** séronégatif(-ive)/positif(-ive)

hive [haɪv] n ruche f

hoard [hɔːd] n (*of food*) provisions fpl, réserves fpl; (*of money*) trésor m ▷ vt amasser

hoarse [hɔːs] adj enroué(e)

hoax [həʊks] n canular m

hob [hɔb] n plaque chauffante

hobble ['hɔbl] vi boitiller

hobby ['hɔbɪ] n passe-temps favori

hobo ['həʊbəʊ] n (*us*) vagabond m

hockey ['hɔkɪ] n hockey m; **hockey stick** n crosse f de hockey

hog [hɔg] n porc (châtré) ▷ vt (*fig*) accaparer; **to go the whole ~** aller jusqu'au bout

Hogmanay [hɔgmə'neɪ] n réveillon m du jour de l'An, Saint-Sylvestre f; *voir encadré*

● HOGMANAY
●
● La Saint-Sylvestre ou "New Year's Eve" se
● nomme **Hogmanay** en Écosse. En cette
● occasion, la famille et les amis se réunissent
● pour entendre sonner les douze coups de
● minuit et pour fêter le "first-footing", une
● coutume qui veut qu'on se rende chez
● ses amis et voisins en apportant quelque
● chose à boire (du whisky en général) et un
● morceau de charbon en gage de prospérité
● pour la nouvelle année.

hoist [hɔɪst] n palan m ▷ vt hisser

hold [həʊld] (*pt, pp* **held**) vt tenir; (*contain*) contenir; (*meeting*) tenir; (*keep back*) retenir; (*believe*) considérer; (*possess*) avoir ▷ vi (*withstand pressure*) tenir (bon); (*be valid*) valoir; (*on telephone*) attendre ▷ n prise f; (*find*) influence f; (*Naut*) cale f; **to catch** or **get (a) ~ of** saisir; **to get ~ of** (*find*) trouver; **~ the line!** (*Tel*) ne quittez pas!; **to ~ one's own** (*fig*) (bien) se défendre; **hold back** vt retenir; (*secret*) cacher; **hold on** vi tenir bon; (*wait*) attendre; **~ on!** (*Tel*) ne quittez pas!; **to ~ on to sth** (*grasp*) se cramponner à qch; (*keep*) conserver or garder qch; **hold out** vt offrir ▷ vi (*resist*): **to ~ out (against)** résister (devant), tenir bon

(*devant*); **hold up** vt (*raise*) lever; (*support*) soutenir; (*delay*) retarder; (: *traffic*) ralentir; (*rob*) braquer; **holdall** n (*BRIT*) fourre-tout m inv; **holder** n (*container*) support m; (*of ticket, record*) détenteur(-trice); (*of office, title, passport etc*) titulaire m/f

hole [həʊl] n trou m

holiday ['hɔlədɪ] n (*BRIT: vacation*) vacances fpl; (*day off*) jour m de congé; (*public*) jour férié; **to be on ~** être en vacances; **I'm here on ~** je suis ici en vacances; **holiday camp** n (*also:* **holiday centre**) camp m de vacances; **holiday job** n (*BRIT*) boulot m (*inf*) de vacances; **holiday-maker** n (*BRIT*) vacancier(-ière); **holiday resort** n centre m de villégiature or de vacances

Holland ['hɔlənd] n Hollande f

hollow ['hɔləʊ] adj creux(-euse); (*fig*) faux (fausse) ▷ n creux m; (*in land*) dépression f (de terrain), cuvette f ▷ vt: **to ~ out** creuser, évider

holly ['hɔlɪ] n houx m

Hollywood ['hɔlɪwʊd] n Hollywood m

holocaust ['hɔləkɔːst] n holocauste m

holy ['həʊlɪ] adj saint(e); (*bread, water*) bénit(e); (*ground*) sacré(e)

home [həʊm] n foyer m, maison f; (*country*) pays natal, patrie f; (*institution*) maison ▷ adj de famille; (*Econ, Pol*) national(e), intérieur(e); (*Sport: team*) qui reçoit; (: *match, win*) sur leur (*or* notre) terrain ▷ adv chez soi, à la maison; au pays natal; (*right in: nail etc*) à fond; **at ~** chez soi, à la maison; **to go** (*or* **come**) **~** rentrer (chez soi), rentrer à la maison (*or* au pays); **make yourself at ~** faites comme chez vous; **home address** n domicile permanent; **homeland** n patrie f; **homeless** adj sans foyer, sans abri; **homely** adj (*plain*) simple, sans prétention; (*welcoming*) accueillant(e); **home-made** adj fait(e) à la maison; **home match** n match m à domicile; **Home Office** n (*BRIT*) ministère m de l'Intérieur; **home owner** n propriétaire occupant; **home page** n (*Comput*) page f d'accueil; **Home Secretary** n (*BRIT*) ministre m de l'Intérieur; **homesick** adj: **to be homesick** avoir le mal du pays; (*missing one's family*) s'ennuyer de sa famille; **home town** n ville natale; **homework** n devoirs mpl

homicide ['hɔmɪsaɪd] n (*us*) homicide m

homoeopathic (*us* **homeopathic**) [həʊmɪə'pæθɪk] adj (*medicine*) homéopathique; (*doctor*) homéopathe

homoeopathy (*us* **homeopathy**) [həʊmɪ'ɔpəθɪ] n homéopathie f

homosexual [hɔməʊ'sɛksjuəl] adj, n homosexuel(le)

honest ['ɔnɪst] adj honnête; (*sincere*) franc (franche); **honestly** adv honnêtement; franchement; **honesty** n honnêteté f

honey ['hʌnɪ] n miel m; **honeymoon** n

lune f de miel, voyage m de noces; **we're on honeymoon** nous sommes en voyage de noces; **honeysuckle** n chèvrefeuille m

Hong Kong ['hɔŋ'kɔŋ] n Hong Kong

honorary ['ɔnərərɪ] adj honoraire; (duty, title) honorifique; **~ degree** diplôme m honoris causa

honour (us **honor**) ['ɔnəʳ] vt honorer ▷ n honneur m; **to graduate with ~s** obtenir sa licence avec mention; **honourable** (us **honorable**) adj honorable; **honours degree** n (Scol) ≈ licence f avec mention

hood [hud] n capuchon m; (of cooker) hotte f; (brit Aut) capote f; (us Aut) capot m; **hoodie** ['hudɪ] n (top) sweat m à capuche

hoof (pl **~s** or **hooves**) [hu:f, hu:vz] n sabot m

hook [huk] n crochet m; (on dress) agrafe f; (for fishing) hameçon m ▷ vt accrocher; **off the ~** (Tel) décroché

hooligan ['hu:lɪgən] n voyou m

hoop [hu:p] n cerceau m

hooray [hu:'reɪ] excl = **hurray**

hoot [hu:t] vi (brit Aut) klaxonner; (siren) mugir; (owl) hululer

Hoover® ['hu:vəʳ] n (brit) aspirateur m ▷ vt: **to hoover** (room) passer l'aspirateur dans; (carpet) passer l'aspirateur sur

hooves [hu:vz] npl of **hoof**

hop [hɔp] vi sauter; (on one foot) sauter à cloche-pied; (bird) sautiller

hope [həup] vt, vi espérer ▷ n espoir m; **I ~ so** je l'espère; **I ~ not** j'espère que non; **hopeful** adj (person) plein(e) d'espoir; (situation) prometteur(-euse), encourageant(e); **hopefully** adv (expectantly) avec espoir, avec optimisme; (one hopes) avec un peu de chance; **hopeless** adj désespéré(e); (useless) nul(le)

hops [hɔps] npl houblon m

horizon [hə'raɪzn] n horizon m; **horizontal** [hɔrɪ'zɔntl] adj horizontal(e)

hormone ['hɔːməun] n hormone f

horn [hɔːn] n corne f; (Mus) cor m; (Aut) klaxon m

horoscope ['hɔrəskəup] n horoscope m

horrendous [hə'rɛndəs] adj horrible, affreux(-euse)

horrible ['hɔrɪbl] adj horrible, affreux(-euse)

horrid ['hɔrɪd] adj (person) détestable; (weather, place, smell) épouvantable

horrific [hɔ'rɪfɪk] adj horrible

horrifying ['hɔrɪfaɪɪŋ] adj horrifiant(e)

horror ['hɔrəʳ] n horreur f; **horror film** n film m d'épouvante

hors d'œuvre [ɔː'dəːvrə] n hors d'œuvre m

horse [hɔːs] n cheval m; **horseback: on horseback** adj, adv à cheval; **horse chestnut** n (nut) marron m (d'Inde); (tree) marronnier m (d'Inde); **horsepower** n puissance f (en chevaux); (unit) cheval-vapeur m (CV); **horse-**

racing n courses fpl de chevaux; **horseradish** n raifort m; **horse riding** n (brit) équitation f

hose [həuz] n (also: **~pipe**) tuyau m; (also: **garden ~**) tuyau d'arrosage; **hosepipe** n tuyau m; (in garden) tuyau d'arrosage

hospital ['hɔspɪtl] n hôpital m; **in ~** à l'hôpital; **where's the nearest ~?** où est l'hôpital le plus proche?

hospitality [hɔspɪ'tælɪtɪ] n hospitalité f

host [həust] n hôte m; (TV, Radio) présentateur(-trice), animateur(-trice); (large number): **a ~ of** une foule de; (Rel) hostie f

hostage ['hɔstɪdʒ] n otage m

hostel ['hɔstl] n foyer m; (also: **youth ~**) auberge f de jeunesse

hostess ['həustɪs] n hôtesse f; (brit: also: **air ~**) hôtesse de l'air; (TV, Radio) animatrice f

hostile ['hɔstaɪl] adj hostile

hostility [hɔ'stɪlɪtɪ] n hostilité f

hot [hɔt] adj chaud(e); (as opposed to only warm) très chaud; (spicy) fort(e); (fig: contest) acharné(e); (topic) brûlant(e); (temper) violent(e), passionné(e); **to be ~** (person) avoir chaud; (thing) être (très) chaud; (weather) faire chaud; **hot dog** n hot-dog m

hotel [həu'tɛl] n hôtel m

hot-water bottle [hɔt'wɔːtə-] n bouillotte f

hound [haund] vt poursuivre avec acharnement ▷ n chien courant

hour ['auəʳ] n heure f; **hourly** adj toutes les heures; (rate) horaire

house n [haus] maison f; (Pol) chambre f; (Theat) salle f, auditoire m ▷ vt [hauz] (person) loger, héberger; **on the ~** (fig) aux frais de la maison; **household** n (Admin etc) ménage m; (people) famille f, maisonnée f; **householder** n propriétaire m/f; (head of house) chef m de famille; **housekeeper** n gouvernante f; **housekeeping** n (work) ménage m; **housewife** (irreg) n ménagère f; femme f au foyer; **house wine** n cuvée f maison or du patron; **housework** n (travaux mpl du) ménage m

housing ['hauzɪŋ] n logement m; **housing development** (brit **housing estate**) n (blocks of flats) cité f; (houses) lotissement m

hover ['hɔvəʳ] vi planer; **hovercraft** n aéroglisseur m, hovercraft m

how [hau] adv comment; **~ are you?** comment allez-vous?; **~ do you do?** bonjour; (on being introduced) enchanté(e); **~ long have you been here?** depuis combien de temps êtes-vous là?; **~ lovely/awful!** que or comme c'est joli/affreux!; **~ much time/many people?** combien de temps/gens?; **~ much does it cost?** ça coûte combien?; **~ old are you?** quel âge avez-vous?; **~ tall is he?** combien mesure-t-il?; **~ is school?** ça va à l'école?; **~ was the film?** comment était le film?

however [hau'evə^r] *conj* pourtant, cependant ▷ *adv*: **~ I do it** de quelque manière que je m'y prenne; **~ cold it is** même s'il fait très froid; **~ did you do it?** comment y êtes-vous donc arrivé?

howl [haul] *n* hurlement *m* ▷ *vi* hurler; *(wind)* mugir

H.P. *n abbr* (BRIT) = **hire purchase**

h.p. *abbr* (Aut) = **horsepower**

HQ *n abbr* (= *headquarters*) QG *m*

hr(s) *abbr* (= *hour(s)*) h

HTML *n abbr* (= *hypertext markup language*) HTML *m*

hubcap ['hʌbkæp] *n* (Aut) enjoliveur *m*

huddle ['hʌdl] *vi*: **to ~ together** se blottir les uns contre les autres

huff [hʌf] *n*: **in a ~** fâché(e)

hug [hʌɡ] *vt* serrer dans ses bras; *(shore, kerb)* serrer ▷ *n*: **to give sb a ~** serrer qn dans ses bras

huge [hjuːdʒ] *adj* énorme, immense

hull [hʌl] *n* (of ship) coque *f*

hum [hʌm] *vt* (tune) fredonner ▷ *vi* fredonner; (insect) bourdonner; (plane, tool) vrombir

human ['hjuːmən] *adj* humain(e) ▷ *n* (also: **~ being**) être humain

humane [hjuː'meɪn] *adj* humain(e), humanitaire

humanitarian [hjuːmænɪ'teəriən] *adj* humanitaire

humanity [hjuː'mænɪtɪ] *n* humanité *f*

human rights *npl* droits *mpl* de l'homme

humble ['hʌmbl] *adj* humble, modeste

humid ['hjuːmɪd] *adj* humide; **humidity** [hjuː'mɪdɪtɪ] *n* humidité *f*

humiliate [hjuː'mɪlɪeɪt] *vt* humilier

humiliating [hjuː'mɪlɪeɪtɪŋ] *adj* humiliant(e)

humiliation [hjuːmɪlɪ'eɪʃən] *n* humiliation *f*

hummus ['huməs] *n* houm(m)ous *m*

humorous ['hjuːmərəs] *adj* humoristique

humour (US **humor**) ['hjuːmə^r] *n* humour *m*; (mood) humeur *f* ▷ *vt* (person) faire plaisir à; se prêter aux caprices de

hump [hʌmp] *n* bosse *f*

hunch [hʌntʃ] *n* (premonition) intuition *f*

hundred ['hʌndrəd] *num* cent; **~s of** des centaines de; **hundredth** [-ɪdθ] *num* centième

hung [hʌŋ] *pt, pp of* **hang**

Hungarian [hʌŋ'ɡeəriən] *adj* hongrois(e) ▷ *n* Hongrois(e); (Ling) hongrois *m*

Hungary ['hʌŋɡərɪ] *n* Hongrie *f*

hunger ['hʌŋɡə^r] *n* faim *f* ▷ *vi*: **to ~ for** avoir faim de, désirer ardemment

hungry ['hʌŋɡrɪ] *adj* affamé(e); **to be ~** avoir faim; **~ for** (fig) avide de

hunt [hʌnt] *vt* (seek) chercher; (Sport) chasser ▷ *vi* (search): **to ~ for** chercher (partout); (Sport) chasser ▷ *n* (Sport) chasse *f*; **hunter** *n* chasseur *m*; **hunting** *n* chasse *f*

hurdle ['hə:dl] *n* (Sport) haie *f*; (fig) obstacle *m*

hurl [hə:l] *vt* lancer (avec violence); (abuse, insults) lancer

hurrah, hurray [hu'rɑː, hu'reɪ] *excl* hourra!

hurricane ['hʌrɪkən] *n* ouragan *m*

hurry ['hʌrɪ] *n* hâte *f*, précipitation *f* ▷ *vi* se presser, se dépêcher ▷ *vt* (person) faire presser, faire se dépêcher; (work) presser; **to be in a ~** être pressé(e); **to do sth in a ~** faire qch en vitesse; **hurry up** *vi* se dépêcher

hurt [hə:t] (*pt, pp* **~**) *vt* (cause pain to) faire mal à; (injure, fig) blesser ▷ *vi* faire mal ▷ *adj* blessé(e); **my arm ~s** j'ai mal au bras; **to ~ o.s.** se faire mal

husband ['hʌzbənd] *n* mari *m*

hush [hʌʃ] *n* calme *m*, silence *m* ▷ *vt* faire taire; **~!** chut!

husky ['hʌskɪ] *adj* (voice) rauque ▷ *n* chien *m* esquimau *or* de traîneau

hut [hʌt] *n* hutte *f*; (shed) cabane *f*

hyacinth ['haɪəsɪnθ] *n* jacinthe *f*

hydrangea [haɪ'dreɪndʒə] *n* hortensia *m*

hydrofoil ['haɪdrəfɔɪl] *n* hydrofoil *m*

hydrogen ['haɪdrədʒən] *n* hydrogène *m*

hygiene ['haɪdʒiːn] *n* hygiène *f*; **hygienic** [haɪ'dʒiːnɪk] *adj* hygiénique

hymn [hɪm] *n* hymne *m*; cantique *m*

hype [haɪp] *n* (inf) matraquage *m* publicitaire *or* médiatique

hypermarket ['haɪpəmɑːkɪt] (BRIT) *n* hypermarché *m*

hyphen ['haɪfn] *n* trait *m* d'union

hypnotize ['hɪpnətaɪz] *vt* hypnotiser

hypocrite ['hɪpəkrɪt] *n* hypocrite *m/f*

hypocritical [hɪpə'krɪtɪkl] *adj* hypocrite

hypothesis (*pl* **hypotheses**) [haɪ'pɔθɪsɪs, -siːz] *n* hypothèse *f*

hysterical [hɪ'sterɪkl] *adj* hystérique; (funny) hilarant(e)

hysterics [hɪ'sterɪks] *npl*: **to be in/have ~** (anger, panic) avoir une crise de nerfs; (laughter) attraper un fou rire

I [aɪ] *pron* je; (*before vowel*) j'; (*stressed*) moi

ice [aɪs] *n* glace *f*; (*on road*) verglas *m* ▷ *vt* (*cake*) glacer ▷ *vi* (*also:* **~ over**) geler; (*also:* **~ up**) se givrer; **iceberg** *n* iceberg *m*; **ice cream** *n* glace *f*; **ice cube** *n* glaçon *m*; **ice hockey** *n* hockey *m* sur glace

Iceland ['aɪslənd] *n* Islande *f*; **Icelander** *n* Islandais(e); **Icelandic** [aɪs'lændɪk] *adj* islandais(e) ▷ *n* (*Ling*) islandais *m*

ice: ice lolly *n* (*BRIT*) esquimau *m*; **ice rink** *n* patinoire *f*; **ice skating** *n* patinage *m* (sur glace)

icing ['aɪsɪŋ] *n* (*Culin*) glaçage *m*; **icing sugar** *n* (*BRIT*) sucre *m* glace

icon ['aɪkɔn] *n* icône *f*

ICT *n abbr* (*BRIT: Scol: = information and communications technology*) TIC *fpl*

icy ['aɪsɪ] *adj* glacé(e); (*road*) verglacé(e); (*weather, temperature*) glacial(e)

I'd [aɪd] = **I would**; **I had**

ID card *n* carte *f* d'identité

idea [aɪ'dɪə] *n* idée *f*

ideal [aɪ'dɪəl] *n* idéal *m* ▷ *adj* idéal(e); **ideally** [aɪ'dɪəlɪ] *adv* (*preferably*) dans l'idéal; (*perfectly*): **he is ideally suited to the job** il est parfait pour ce poste

identical [aɪ'dɛntɪkl] *adj* identique

identification [aɪdɛntɪfɪ'keɪʃən] *n* identification *f*; **means of ~** pièce *f* d'identité

identify [aɪ'dɛntɪfaɪ] *vt* identifier

identity [aɪ'dɛntɪtɪ] *n* identité *f*; **identity card** *n* carte *f* d'identité; **identity theft** *n* usurpation *f* d'identité

ideology [aɪdɪ'ɔlədʒɪ] *n* idéologie *f*

idiom ['ɪdɪəm] *n* (*phrase*) expression *f* idiomatique; (*style*) style *m*

idiot ['ɪdɪət] *n* idiot(e), imbécile *m/f*

idle ['aɪdl] *adj* (*doing nothing*) sans occupation, désœuvré(e); (*lazy*) oisif(-ive), paresseux(-euse); (*unemployed*) au chômage; (*machinery*) au repos; (*question, pleasures*) vain(e), futile ▷ *vi* (*engine*) tourner au ralenti

idol ['aɪdl] *n* idole *f*

idyllic [ɪ'dɪlɪk] *adj* idyllique

i.e. *abbr* (= *id est: that is*) c. à d., c'est-à-dire

if [ɪf] *conj* si; **if necessary** si nécessaire, le cas échéant; **if so** si c'est le cas; **if not** sinon; **if only I could!** si seulement je pouvais!; *see also* **as**; **even**

ignite [ɪg'naɪt] *vt* mettre le feu à, enflammer ▷ *vi* s'enflammer

ignition [ɪg'nɪʃən] *n* (*Aut*) allumage *m*; **to switch on/off the ~** mettre/couper le contact

ignorance ['ɪgnərəns] *n* ignorance *f*

ignorant ['ɪgnərənt] *adj* ignorant(e); **to be ~ of** (*subject*) ne rien connaître en; (*events*) ne pas être au courant de

ignore [ɪg'nɔːʳ] *vt* ne tenir aucun compte de; (*mistake*) ne pas relever; (*person: pretend to not see*) faire semblant de ne pas reconnaître; (: *pay no attention to*) ignorer

ill [ɪl] *adj* (*sick*) malade; (*bad*) mauvais(e) ▷ *n* mal *m* ▷ *adv*: **to speak/think ~ of sb** dire/penser du mal de qn; **to be taken ~** tomber malade

I'll [aɪl] = **I will**; **I shall**

illegal [ɪ'liːgl] *adj* illégal(e)

illegible [ɪ'lɛdʒɪbl] *adj* illisible

illegitimate [ɪlɪ'dʒɪtɪmət] *adj* illégitime

ill health *n* mauvaise santé

illiterate [ɪ'lɪtərət] *adj* illettré(e)

illness ['ɪlnɪs] *n* maladie *f*

illuminate [ɪ'luːmɪneɪt] *vt* (*room, street*) éclairer; (*for special effect*) illuminer

illusion [ɪ'luːʒən] *n* illusion *f*

illustrate ['ɪləstreɪt] *vt* illustrer

illustration [ɪlə'streɪʃən] *n* illustration *f*

I'm [aɪm] = **I am**

image ['ɪmɪdʒ] *n* image *f*; (*public face*) image de marque

imaginary [ɪ'mædʒɪnərɪ] *adj* imaginaire

imagination [ɪmædʒɪ'neɪʃən] *n* imagination *f*

imaginative [ɪ'mædʒɪnətɪv] *adj* imaginatif(-ive); (*person*) plein(e) d'imagination

imagine [ɪ'mædʒɪn] *vt* s'imaginer; (*suppose*) imaginer, supposer

imbalance [ɪmˈbæləns] *n* déséquilibre *m*
imitate [ˈɪmɪteɪt] *vt* imiter; **imitation**
[ɪmɪˈteɪʃən] *n* imitation *f*
immaculate [ɪˈmækjʊlət] *adj* impeccable;
(*Rel*) immaculé(e)
immature [ɪməˈtjʊəʳ] *adj* (*fruit*) qui n'est pas
mûr(e); (*person*) qui manque de maturité
immediate [ɪˈmiːdɪət] *adj* immédiat(e);
immediately *adv* (*at once*) immédiatement;
immediately next to juste à côté de
immense [ɪˈmɛns] *adj* immense, énorme;
immensely *adv* (*+adj*) extrêmement; (*+vb*)
énormément
immerse [ɪˈməːs] *vt* immerger, plonger; **to be
~d in** (*fig*) être plongé dans
immigrant [ˈɪmɪɡrənt] *n* immigrant(e);
(*already established*) immigré(e); **immigration**
[ɪmɪˈɡreɪʃən] *n* immigration *f*
imminent [ˈɪmɪnənt] *adj* imminent(e)
immoral [ɪˈmɔrl] *adj* immoral(e)
immortal [ɪˈmɔːtl] *adj*, *n* immortel(le)
immune [ɪˈmjuːn] *adj*: **~ (to)** immunisé(e)
(contre); **immune system** *n* système *m*
immunitaire
immunize [ˈɪmjunaɪz] *vt* immuniser
impact [ˈɪmpækt] *n* choc *m*, impact *m*; (*fig*)
impact
impair [ɪmˈpɛəʳ] *vt* détériorer, diminuer
impartial [ɪmˈpɑːʃl] *adj* impartial(e)
impatience [ɪmˈpeɪʃəns] *n* impatience *f*
impatient [ɪmˈpeɪʃənt] *adj* impatient(e); **to
get** *or* **grow ~** s'impatienter
impeccable [ɪmˈpɛkəbl] *adj* impeccable,
parfait(e)
impending [ɪmˈpɛndɪŋ] *adj* imminent(e)
imperative [ɪmˈpɛrətɪv] *adj* (*need*) urgent(e),
pressant(e); (*tone*) impérieux(-euse) ▷ *n* (*Ling*)
impératif *m*
imperfect [ɪmˈpəːfɪkt] *adj* imparfait(e);
(*goods etc*) défectueux(-euse) ▷ *n* (*Ling: also: ~
tense*) imparfait *m*
imperial [ɪmˈpɪərɪəl] *adj* impérial(e); (*BRIT:
measure*) légal(e)
impersonal [ɪmˈpəːsənl] *adj* impersonnel(le)
impersonate [ɪmˈpəːsəneɪt] *vt* se faire passer
pour; (*Theat*) imiter
impetus [ˈɪmpətəs] *n* impulsion *f*; (*of runner*)
élan *m*
implant [ɪmˈplɑːnt] *vt* (*Med*) implanter; (*fig:
idea, principle*) inculquer
implement *n* [ˈɪmplɪmənt] outil *m*,
instrument *m*; (*for cooking*) ustensile *m* ▷ *vt*
[ˈɪmplɪment] exécuter
implicate [ˈɪmplɪkeɪt] *vt* impliquer,
compromettre
implication [ɪmplɪˈkeɪʃən] *n* implication *f*; **by
~** indirectement
implicit [ɪmˈplɪsɪt] *adj* implicite; (*complete*)
absolu(e), sans réserve

imply [ɪmˈplaɪ] *vt* (*hint*) suggérer, laisser
entendre; (*mean*) indiquer, supposer
impolite [ɪmpəˈlaɪt] *adj* impoli(e)
import *vt* [ɪmˈpɔːt] importer ▷ *n* [ˈɪmpɔː
t] (*Comm*) importation *f*; (*meaning*) portée *f*,
signification *f*
importance [ɪmˈpɔːtns] *n* importance *f*
important [ɪmˈpɔːtnt] *adj* important(e);
it's not ~ c'est sans importance, ce n'est pas
important
importer [ɪmˈpɔːtəʳ] *n* importateur(-trice)
impose [ɪmˈpəuz] *vt* imposer ▷ *vi*: **to ~ on sb**
abuser de la gentillesse de qn; **imposing** *adj*
imposant(e), impressionnant(e)
impossible [ɪmˈpɔsɪbl] *adj* impossible
impotent [ˈɪmpətnt] *adj* impuissant(e)
impoverished [ɪmˈpɔvərɪʃt] *adj* pauvre,
appauvri(e)
impractical [ɪmˈpræktɪkl] *adj* pas pratique;
(*person*) qui manque d'esprit pratique
impress [ɪmˈprɛs] *vt* impressionner, faire
impression sur; (*mark*) imprimer, marquer; **to ~
sth on sb** faire bien comprendre qch à qn
impression [ɪmˈprɛʃən] *n* impression *f*; (*of
stamp, seal*) empreinte *f*; (*imitation*) imitation *f*;
to be under the ~ that avoir l'impression que
impressive [ɪmˈprɛsɪv] *adj* impressionnant(e)
imprison [ɪmˈprɪzn] *vt* emprisonner, mettre
en prison; **imprisonment** *n* emprisonnement
m; (*period*): **to sentence sb to 10 years'
imprisonment** condamner qn à 10 ans de
prison
improbable [ɪmˈprɔbəbl] *adj* improbable;
(*excuse*) peu plausible
improper [ɪmˈprɔpəʳ] *adj* (*unsuitable*)
déplacé(e), de mauvais goût; (*indecent*)
indécent(e); (*dishonest*) malhonnête
improve [ɪmˈpruːv] *vt* améliorer ▷ *vi*
s'améliorer; (*pupil etc*) faire des progrès;
improvement *n* amélioration *f*; (*of pupil etc*)
progrès *m*
improvise [ˈɪmprəvaɪz] *vt*, *vi* improviser
impulse [ˈɪmpʌls] *n* impulsion *f*; **on ~**
impulsivement, sur un coup de tête;
impulsive [ɪmˈpʌlsɪv] *adj* impulsif(-ive)

 KEYWORD

in [ɪn] *prep* **1** (*indicating place, position*) dans;
in the house/the fridge dans la maison/le
frigo; **in the garden** dans le *or* au jardin; **in
town** en ville; **in the country** à la campagne;
in school à l'école; **in here/there** ici/là
2 (*with place names: of town, region, country*): **in
London** à Londres; **in England** en Angleterre;
in Japan au Japon; **in the United States** aux
États-Unis
3 (*indicating time: during*): **in spring** au
printemps; **in summer** en été; **in May/2005**

en mai/2005; **in the afternoon** (dans) l'après-midi; **at 4 o'clock in the afternoon** à 4 heures de l'après-midi
4 (indicating time: in the space of) en; (: future) dans; **I did it in 3 hours/days** je l'ai fait en 3 heures/jours; **I'll see you in 2 weeks** or **in 2 weeks' time** je te verrai dans 2 semaines
5 (indicating manner etc) à; **in a loud/soft voice** à voix haute/basse; **in pencil** au crayon; **in writing** par écrit; **in French** en français; **the boy in the blue shirt** le garçon à or avec la chemise bleue
6 (indicating circumstances): **in the sun** au soleil; **in the shade** à l'ombre; **in the rain** sous la pluie; **a change in policy** un changement de politique
7 (indicating mood, state): **in tears** en larmes; **in anger** sous le coup de la colère; **in despair** au désespoir; **in good condition** en bon état; **to live in luxury** vivre dans le luxe
8 (with ratios, numbers): **1 in 10 households, 1 household in 10** 1 ménage sur 10; **20 pence in the pound** 20 pence par livre sterling; **they lined up in twos** ils se mirent en rangs (deux) par deux; **in hundreds** par centaines
9 (referring to people, works) chez; **the disease is common in children** c'est une maladie courante chez les enfants; **in (the works of) Dickens** chez Dickens, dans (l'œuvre de) Dickens
10 (indicating profession etc) dans; **to be in teaching** être dans l'enseignement
11 (after superlative) de; **the best pupil in the class** le meilleur élève de la classe
12 (with present participle): **in saying this** en disant ceci
▷ adv: **to be in** (person: at home, work) être là; (train, ship, plane) être arrivé(e); (in fashion) être à la mode; **to ask sb in** inviter qn à entrer; **to run/limp** etc **in** entrer en courant/boitant etc
▷ n: **the ins and outs (of)** (of proposal, situation etc) les tenants et aboutissants (de)

inability [ɪnə'bɪlɪtɪ] n incapacité f; **~ to pay** incapacité de payer
inaccurate [ɪn'ækjurət] adj inexact(e); (person) qui manque de précision
inadequate [ɪn'ædɪkwət] adj insuffisant(e), inadéquat(e)
inadvertently [ɪnəd'və:tntlɪ] adv par mégarde
inappropriate [ɪnə'prəuprɪət] adj inopportun(e), mal à propos; (word, expression) impropre
inaugurate [ɪ'nɔ:gjureɪt] vt inaugurer; (president, official) investir de ses fonctions
Inc. abbr = **incorporated**
incapable [ɪn'keɪpəbl] adj: **~ (of)** incapable (de)

incense n ['ɪnsɛns] encens m ▷ vt [ɪn'sɛns] (anger) mettre en colère
incentive [ɪn'sɛntɪv] n encouragement m, raison f de se donner de la peine
inch [ɪntʃ] n pouce m (=25 mm; 12 in a foot); **within an ~ of** à deux doigts de; **he wouldn't give an ~** (fig) il n'a pas voulu céder d'un pouce
incidence ['ɪnsɪdns] n (of crime, disease) fréquence f
incident ['ɪnsɪdnt] n incident m
incidentally [ɪnsɪ'dɛntəlɪ] adv (by the way) à propos
inclination [ɪnklɪ'neɪʃən] n inclination f; (desire) envie f
incline n ['ɪnklaɪn] pente f, plan incliné ▷ vb [ɪn'klaɪn] ▷ vt (surface) s'incliner; **to be ~d to do** (have a tendency to do) avoir tendance à faire
include [ɪn'klu:d] vt inclure, comprendre; **service is/is not ~d** le service est compris/ n'est pas compris; **including** prep y compris; **inclusion** n inclusion f; **inclusive** adj inclus(e), compris(e); **inclusive of tax** taxes comprises
income ['ɪnkʌm] n revenu m; (from property etc) rentes fpl; **income support** n (BRIT) ≈ revenu m minimum d'insertion, RMI m; **income tax** n impôt m sur le revenu
incoming ['ɪnkʌmɪŋ] adj (passengers, mail) à l'arrivée; (government, tenant) nouveau (nouvelle)
incompatible [ɪnkəm'pætɪbl] adj incompatible
incompetence [ɪn'kɔmpɪtns] n incompétence f, incapacité f
incompetent [ɪn'kɔmpɪtnt] adj incompétent(e), incapable
incomplete [ɪnkəm'pli:t] adj incomplet(-ète)
inconsistent [ɪnkən'sɪstnt] adj qui manque de constance; (work) irrégulier(-ière); (statement) peu cohérent(e); **~ with** en contradiction avec
inconvenience [ɪnkən'vi:njəns] n inconvénient m; (trouble) dérangement m ▷ vt déranger
inconvenient [ɪnkən'vi:njənt] adj malcommode; (time, place) mal choisi(e), qui ne convient pas; (visitor) importun(e)
incorporate [ɪn'kɔ:pəreɪt] vt incorporer; (contain) contenir
incorrect [ɪnkə'rɛkt] adj incorrect(e); (opinion, statement) inexact(e)
increase n ['ɪnkri:s] augmentation f ▷ vi, vt [ɪn'kri:s] augmenter; **increasingly** adv de plus en plus
incredible [ɪn'krɛdɪbl] adj incroyable; **incredibly** adv incroyablement
incur [ɪn'kə:r] vt (expenses) encourir; (anger, risk) s'exposer à; (debt) contracter; (loss) subir

indecent [ɪn'diːsnt] adj indécent(e), inconvenant(e)

indeed [ɪn'diːd] adv (confirming, agreeing) en effet, effectivement; (for emphasis) vraiment; (furthermore) d'ailleurs; **yes ~!** certainement!

indefinitely [ɪn'dɛfɪnɪtlɪ] adv (wait) indéfiniment

independence [ɪndɪ'pɛndns] n indépendance f; **Independence Day** n (US) fête de l'Indépendance américaine; voir encadré

○ **INDEPENDENCE DAY**
○
○ L'**Independence Day** est la fête nationale
○ aux États-Unis, le 4 juillet. Il commémore
○ l'adoption de la déclaration d'Indépendance,
○ en 1776, écrite par Thomas Jefferson et
○ proclamant la séparation des 13 colonies
○ américaines de la Grande-Bretagne.

independent [ɪndɪ'pɛndnt] adj indépendant(e); (radio) libre; **independent school** n (BRIT) école privée

index ['ɪndɛks] n (pl **-es**) (in book) index m; (: in library etc) catalogue m (pl **indices**) (ratio, sign) indice m

India ['ɪndɪə] n Inde f; **Indian** adj indien(ne) ▷ n Indien(ne); **(American) Indian** Indien(ne) (d'Amérique)

indicate ['ɪndɪkeɪt] vt indiquer ▷ vi (BRIT Aut): **to ~ left/right** mettre son clignotant à gauche/à droite; **indication** [ɪndɪ'keɪʃən] n indication f, signe m; **indicative** [ɪn'dɪkətɪv] adj: **to be indicative of sth** être symptomatique de qch ▷ n (Ling) indicatif m; **indicator** n (sign) indicateur m; (Aut) clignotant m

indices ['ɪndɪsiːz] npl of **index**

indict [ɪn'daɪt] vt accuser; **indictment** n accusation f

indifference [ɪn'dɪfrəns] n indifférence f

indifferent [ɪn'dɪfrənt] adj indifférent(e); (poor) médiocre, quelconque

indigenous [ɪn'dɪdʒɪnəs] adj indigène

indigestion [ɪndɪ'dʒɛstʃən] n indigestion f, mauvaise digestion

indignant [ɪn'dɪgnənt] adj: **~ (at sth/with sb)** indigné(e) (de qch/contre qn)

indirect [ɪndɪ'rɛkt] adj indirect(e)

indispensable [ɪndɪ'spɛnsəbl] adj indispensable

individual [ɪndɪ'vɪdjuəl] n individu m ▷ adj individuel(le); (characteristic) particulier(-ière), original(e); **individually** adv individuellement

Indonesia [ɪndəʊ'niːzɪə] n Indonésie f

indoor ['ɪndɔːʳ] adj d'intérieur; (plant) d'appartement; (swimming pool) couvert(e); (sport, games) pratiqué(e) en salle; **indoors** [ɪn'dɔːz] adv à l'intérieur

induce [ɪn'djuːs] vt (persuade) persuader; (bring about) provoquer; (labour) déclencher

indulge [ɪn'dʌldʒ] vt (whim) céder à, satisfaire; (child) gâter ▷ vi: **to ~ in sth** (luxury) s'offrir qch, se permettre qch; (fantasies etc) se livrer à qch; **indulgent** adj indulgent(e)

industrial [ɪn'dʌstrɪəl] adj industriel(le); (injury) du travail; (dispute) ouvrier(-ière); **industrial estate** n (BRIT) zone industrielle; **industrialist** n industriel m; **industrial park** n (US) zone industrielle

industry ['ɪndəstrɪ] n industrie f; (diligence) zèle m, application f

inefficient [ɪnɪ'fɪʃənt] adj inefficace

inequality [ɪnɪ'kwɔlɪtɪ] n inégalité f

inevitable [ɪn'ɛvɪtəbl] adj inévitable; **inevitably** adv inévitablement, fatalement

inexpensive [ɪnɪk'spɛnsɪv] adj bon marché inv

inexperienced [ɪnɪk'spɪərɪənst] adj inexpérimenté(e)

inexplicable [ɪnɪk'splɪkəbl] adj inexplicable

infamous ['ɪnfəməs] adj infâme, abominable

infant ['ɪnfənt] n (baby) nourrisson m; (young child) petit(e) enfant

infantry ['ɪnfəntrɪ] n infanterie f

infant school n (BRIT) classes fpl préparatoires (entre 5 et 7 ans)

infect [ɪn'fɛkt] vt (wound) infecter; (person, blood) contaminer; **infection** [ɪn'fɛkʃən] n infection f; (contagion) contagion f; **infectious** [ɪn'fɛkʃəs] adj infectieux(-euse); (also fig) contagieux(-euse)

infer [ɪn'fəːʳ] vt: **to ~ (from)** conclure (de), déduire (de)

inferior [ɪn'fɪərɪəʳ] adj inférieur(e); (goods) de qualité inférieure ▷ n inférieur(e); (in rank) subalterne m/f

infertile [ɪn'fəːtaɪl] adj stérile

infertility [ɪnfəˈtɪlɪtɪ] n infertilité f, stérilité f

infested [ɪn'fɛstɪd] adj: **~ (with)** infesté(e) (de)

infinite ['ɪnfɪnɪt] adj infini(e); (time, money) illimité(e); **infinitely** adv infiniment

infirmary [ɪn'fəːmərɪ] n hôpital m; (in school, factory) infirmerie f

inflamed [ɪn'fleɪmd] adj enflammé(e)

inflammation [ɪnflə'meɪʃən] n inflammation f

inflatable [ɪn'fleɪtəbl] adj gonflable

inflate [ɪn'fleɪt] vt (tyre, balloon) gonfler; (fig: exaggerate) grossir; (: increase) gonfler; **inflation** [ɪn'fleɪʃən] n (Econ) inflation f

inflexible [ɪn'flɛksɪbl] adj inflexible, rigide

inflict [ɪn'flɪkt] vt: **to ~ on** infliger à

influence ['ɪnfluəns] n influence f ▷ vt influencer; **under the ~ of alcohol** en état d'ébriété; **influential** [ɪnflu'ɛnʃl] adj influent(e)

influenza [ɪnflu'ɛnzə] n grippe f

influx ['ɪnflʌks] n afflux m

info (inf) ['ɪnfəu] n (= information) renseignements mpl

inform [ɪn'fɔːm] vt: **to ~ sb (of)** informer or avertir qn (de) ▷ vi: **to ~ on sb** dénoncer qn, informer contre qn

informal [ɪn'fɔːml] adj (person, manner, party) simple; (visit, discussion) dénué(e) de formalités; (announcement, invitation) non officiel(le); (colloquial) familier(-ère)

information [ɪnfə'meɪʃən] n information(s) f(pl); renseignements mpl; (knowledge) connaissances fpl; **a piece of ~** un renseignement; **information office** n bureau m de renseignements; **information technology** n informatique f

informative [ɪn'fɔːmətɪv] adj instructif(-ive)

infra-red [ɪnfrə'rɛd] adj infrarouge

infrastructure ['ɪnfrəstrʌktʃəʳ] n infrastructure f

infrequent [ɪn'friːkwənt] adj peu fréquent(e), rare

infuriate [ɪn'fjuərɪeɪt] vt mettre en fureur

infuriating [ɪn'fjuərɪeɪtɪŋ] adj exaspérant(e)

ingenious [ɪn'dʒiːnjəs] adj ingénieux(-euse)

ingredient [ɪn'griːdɪənt] n ingrédient m; (fig) élément m

inhabit [ɪn'hæbɪt] vt habiter; **inhabitant** n habitant(e)

inhale [ɪn'heɪl] vt inhaler; (perfume) respirer; (smoke) avaler ▷ vi (breathe in) aspirer; (in smoking) avaler la fumée; **inhaler** n inhalateur m

inherent [ɪn'hɪərənt] adj: **~ (in or to)** inhérent(e) (à)

inherit [ɪn'hɛrɪt] vt hériter (de); **inheritance** n héritage m

inhibit [ɪn'hɪbɪt] vt (Psych) inhiber; (growth) freiner; **inhibition** [ɪnhɪ'bɪʃən] n inhibition f

initial [ɪ'nɪʃl] adj initial(e) ▷ n initiale f ▷ vt parafer; **initials** npl initiales fpl; (as signature) parafe m; **initially** adv initialement, au début

initiate [ɪ'nɪʃɪeɪt] vt (start) entreprendre; amorcer; (enterprise) lancer; (person) initier; **to ~ proceedings against sb** (Law) intenter une action à qn, engager des poursuites contre qn

initiative [ɪ'nɪʃətɪv] n initiative f

inject [ɪn'dʒɛkt] vt injecter; (person): **to ~ sb with sth** faire une piqûre de qch à qn; **injection** [ɪn'dʒɛkʃən] n injection f, piqûre f

injure ['ɪndʒəʳ] vt blesser; (damage: reputation etc) compromettre; **to ~ o.s.** se blesser; **injured** adj (person, leg etc) blessé(e); **injury** n blessure f; (wrong) tort m

injustice [ɪn'dʒʌstɪs] n injustice f

ink [ɪŋk] n encre f; **ink-jet printer** ['ɪŋkdʒɛt-] n imprimante f à jet d'encre

inland adj ['ɪnlənd] intérieur(e) ▷ adv [ɪn'lænd] à l'intérieur, dans les terres; **Inland**

Revenue n (BRIT) fisc m

in-laws ['ɪnlɔːz] npl beaux-parents mpl; belle famille

inmate ['ɪnmeɪt] n (in prison) détenu(e); (in asylum) interné(e)

inn [ɪn] n auberge f

inner ['ɪnəʳ] adj intérieur(e); **inner-city** adj (schools, problems) de quartiers déshérités

inning ['ɪnɪŋ] n (us: Baseball) tour m de batte; **innings** npl (Cricket) tour de batte

innocence ['ɪnəsns] n innocence f

innocent ['ɪnəsnt] adj innocent(e)

innovation [ɪnəu'veɪʃən] n innovation f

innovative ['ɪnəu'veɪtɪv] adj novateur(-trice); (product) innovant(e)

in-patient ['ɪnpeɪʃənt] n malade hospitalisé(e)

input ['ɪnput] n (contribution) contribution f; (resources) ressources fpl; (Comput) entrée f (de données); (: data) données fpl ▷ vt (Comput) introduire, entrer

inquest ['ɪnkwɛst] n enquête (criminelle); (coroner's) enquête judiciaire

inquire [ɪn'kwaɪəʳ] vi demander ▷ vt demander; **to ~ about** s'informer de, se renseigner sur; **to ~ when/where/whether** demander quand/où/si; **inquiry** n demande f de renseignements; (Law) enquête f, investigation f; **"inquiries"** "renseignements"

ins. abbr = **inches**

insane [ɪn'seɪn] adj fou (folle); (Med) aliéné(e)

insanity [ɪn'sænɪtɪ] n folie f; (Med) aliénation (mentale)

insect ['ɪnsɛkt] n insecte m; **insect repellent** n crème f anti-insectes

insecure [ɪnsɪ'kjuəʳ] adj (person) anxieux(-euse); (job) précaire; (building etc) peu sûr(e)

insecurity [ɪnsɪ'kjuərɪtɪ] n insécurité f

insensitive [ɪn'sɛnsɪtɪv] adj insensible

insert vt [ɪn'səːt] insérer ▷ n ['ɪnsəːt] insertion f

inside ['ɪn'saɪd] n intérieur m ▷ adj intérieur(e) ▷ adv à l'intérieur, dedans ▷ prep à l'intérieur de; (of time): **~ 10 minutes** en moins de 10 minutes; **to go ~** rentrer; **inside lane** n (Aut: in Britain) voie f de gauche; (: in US, Europe) voie f de droite; **inside out** adv à l'envers; (know) à fond; **to turn sth inside out** retourner qch

insight ['ɪnsaɪt] n perspicacité f; (glimpse, idea) aperçu m

insignificant [ɪnsɪg'nɪfɪknt] adj insignifiant(e)

insincere [ɪnsɪn'sɪəʳ] adj hypocrite

insist [ɪn'sɪst] vi insister; **to ~ on doing** insister pour faire; **to ~ on sth** exiger qch; **to ~ that** insister pour que + sub; (claim) maintenir or soutenir que; **insistent** adj insistant(e), pressant(e); (noise, action) ininterrompu(e)

insomnia [ɪnˈsɒmnɪə] n insomnie f
inspect [ɪnˈspɛkt] vt inspecter; (BRIT:
ticket) contrôler; **inspection** [ɪnˈspɛkʃən]
n inspection f; (BRIT: of tickets) contrôle m;
inspector n inspecteur(-trice); (BRIT: on buses,
trains) contrôleur(-euse)
inspiration [ɪnspəˈreɪʃən] n inspiration f;
inspire [ɪnˈspaɪəʳ] vt inspirer; **inspiring** adj
inspirant(e)
instability [ɪnstəˈbɪlɪtɪ] n instabilité f
install (US **instal**) [ɪnˈstɔːl] vt installer;
installation [ɪnstəˈleɪʃən] n installation f
instalment (US **installment**) [ɪnˈstɔːlmənt]
n (payment) acompte m, versement partiel;
(of TV serial etc) épisode m; **in ~s** (pay) à
tempérament; (receive) en plusieurs fois
instance [ˈɪnstəns] n exemple m; **for ~** par
exemple; **in the first ~** tout d'abord, en
premier lieu
instant [ˈɪnstənt] n instant m ▷ adj
immédiat(e), urgent(e); (coffee, food)
instantané(e), en poudre; **instantly** adv
immédiatement, tout de suite; **instant
messaging** n messagerie f instantanée
instead [ɪnˈstɛd] adv au lieu de cela; **~ of** au
lieu de; **~ of sb** à la place de qn
instinct [ˈɪnstɪŋkt] n instinct m; **instinctive**
adj instinctif(-ive)
institute [ˈɪnstɪtjuːt] n institut m ▷ vt
instituer, établir; (inquiry) ouvrir; (proceedings)
entamer
institution [ɪnstɪˈtjuːʃən] n institution f;
(school) établissement m (scolaire); (for care)
établissement (psychiatrique etc)
instruct [ɪnˈstrʌkt] vt: **to ~ sb in sth** enseigner
qch à qn; **to ~ sb to do** charger qn or ordonner
à qn de faire; **instruction** [ɪnˈstrʌkʃən]
n instruction f; **instructions** npl (orders)
directives fpl; **instructions for use** mode m
d'emploi; **instructor** n professeur m; (for skiing,
driving) moniteur m
instrument [ˈɪnstrumənt] n instrument m;
instrumental [ɪnstruˈmɛntl] adj (Mus)
instrumental(e); **to be instrumental in sth/
in doing sth** contribuer à qch/à faire qch
insufficient [ɪnsəˈfɪʃənt] adj insuffisant(e)
insulate [ˈɪnsjuleɪt] vt isoler; (against sound)
insonoriser; **insulation** [ɪnsjuˈleɪʃən] n
isolation f; (against sound) insonorisation f
insulin [ˈɪnsjulɪn] n insuline f
insult n [ˈɪnsʌlt] insulte f, affront m ▷ vt
[ɪnˈsʌlt] insulter, faire un affront à; **insulting**
adj insultant(e), injurieux(-euse)
insurance [ɪnˈʃuərəns] n assurance
f; **fire/life ~** assurance-incendie/-vie;
insurance company n compagnie for société
f d'assurances; **insurance policy** n police f
d'assurance
insure [ɪnˈʃuəʳ] vt assurer; **to ~ (o.s.) against**

(fig) parer à
intact [ɪnˈtækt] adj intact(e)
intake [ˈɪnteɪk] n (Tech) admission f;
(consumption) consommation f; (BRIT Scol): **an ~
of 200 a year** 200 admissions par an
integral [ˈɪntɪɡrəl] adj (whole) intégral(e);
(part) intégrant(e)
integrate [ˈɪntɪɡreɪt] vt intégrer ▷ vi
s'intégrer
integrity [ɪnˈtɛɡrɪtɪ] n intégrité f
intellect [ˈɪntəlɛkt] n intelligence f;
intellectual [ɪntəˈlɛktjuəl] adj, n
intellectuel(le)
intelligence [ɪnˈtɛlɪdʒəns] n intelligence f;
(Mil etc) informations fpl, renseignements mpl
intelligent [ɪnˈtɛlɪdʒənt] adj intelligent(e)
intend [ɪnˈtɛnd] vt (gift etc): **to ~ sth for**
destiner qch à; **to ~ to do** avoir l'intention
de faire
intense [ɪnˈtɛns] adj intense; (person)
véhément(e)
intensify [ɪnˈtɛnsɪfaɪ] vt intensifier
intensity [ɪnˈtɛnsɪtɪ] n intensité f
intensive [ɪnˈtɛnsɪv] adj intensif(-ive);
intensive care n: **to be in intensive care**
être en réanimation; **intensive care unit** n
service m de réanimation
intent [ɪnˈtɛnt] n intention f ▷ adj
attentif(-ive), absorbé(e); **to all ~s and
purposes** en fait, pratiquement; **to be ~ on
doing sth** être (bien) décidé à faire qch
intention [ɪnˈtɛnʃən] n intention f;
intentional adj intentionnel(le), délibéré(e)
interact [ɪntərˈækt] vi avoir une action
réciproque; (people) communiquer;
interaction [ɪntərˈækʃən] n interaction f;
interactive adj (Comput) interactif,
conversationnel(le)
intercept [ɪntəˈsɛpt] vt intercepter; (person)
arrêter au passage
interchange n [ˈɪntətʃeɪndʒ] (exchange)
échange m; (on motorway) échangeur m
intercourse [ˈɪntəkɔːs] n: **sexual ~** rapports
sexuels
interest [ˈɪntrɪst] n intérêt m; (Comm:
stake, share) participation f, intérêts mpl ▷ vt
intéresser; **interested** adj intéressé(e); **to
be interested in sth** s'intéresser à qch; **I'm
interested in going** ça m'intéresse d'y aller;
interesting adj intéressant(e); **interest rate**
n taux m d'intérêt
interface [ˈɪntəfeɪs] n (Comput) interface f
interfere [ɪntəˈfɪəʳ] vi: **to ~ in** (quarrel)
s'immiscer dans; (other people's business) se
mêler de; **to ~ with** (object) tripoter, toucher à;
(plans) contrecarrer; (duty) être en conflit avec;
interference n (gen) ingérence f; (Radio, TV)
parasites mpl
interim [ˈɪntərɪm] adj provisoire; (post)

intérimaire ▷ *n*: **in the ~** dans l'intérim
interior [ɪnˈtɪərɪə*] *n* intérieur *m* ▷ *adj*
intérieur(e); (*minister, department*) de
l'intérieur; **interior design** *n* architecture *f*
d'intérieur
intermediate [ɪntəˈmiːdɪət] *adj*
intermédiaire; (*Scol: course, level*) moyen(ne)
intermission [ɪntəˈmɪʃən] *n* pause *f*; (*Theat,
Cine*) entracte *m*
intern *vt* [ɪnˈtəːn] interner ▷ *n* [ˈɪntəːn] (*US*)
interne *m/f*
internal [ɪnˈtəːnl] *adj* interne; (*dispute, reform
etc*) intérieur(e); **Internal Revenue Service**
n (*US*) fisc *m*
international [ɪntəˈnæʃənl] *adj*
international(e) ▷ *n* (*BRIT Sport*)
international *m*
Internet [ɪntəˈnet] *n*: **the ~** l'Internet *m*;
Internet café *n* cybercafé *m*; **Internet
Service Provider** *n* fournisseur *m* d'accès à
Internet; **Internet user** *n* internaute *m/f*
interpret [ɪnˈtəːprɪt] *vt* interpréter ▷ *vi* servir
d'interprète; **interpretation** [ɪntəːprɪˈteɪʃən]
n interprétation *f*; **interpreter** *n* interprète
m/f; **could you act as an interpreter for us?**
pourriez-vous nous servir d'interprète?
interrogate [ɪnˈtɛrəugeɪt] *vt* interroger;
(*suspect etc*) soumettre à un interrogatoire;
interrogation [ɪntɛrəuˈgeɪʃən] *n*
interrogation *f*; (*by police*) interrogatoire *m*
interrogative [ɪntəˈrɔgətɪv] *adj*
interrogateur(-trice) ▷ *n* (*Ling*) interrogatif *m*
interrupt [ɪntəˈrʌpt] *vt, vi* interrompre;
interruption [ɪntəˈrʌpʃən] *n* interruption *f*
intersection [ɪntəˈsɛkʃən] *n* (*of roads*)
croisement *m*
interstate [ˈɪntəsteɪt] (*US*) *n* autoroute *f* (qui
relie plusieurs États)
interval [ˈɪntəvl] *n* intervalle *m*; (*BRIT Theat*)
entracte *m*; (: *Sport*) mi-temps *f*; **at ~s** par
intervalles
intervene [ɪntəˈviːn] *vi* (*time*) s'écouler (entre-
temps); (*event*) survenir; (*person*) intervenir
interview [ˈɪntəvjuː] *n* (*Radio, TV etc*)
interview *f*; (*for job*) entrevue *f* ▷ *vt*
interviewer; avoir une entrevue avec;
interviewer *n* (*Radio, TV etc*) interviewer *m*
intimate *adj* [ˈɪntɪmət] intime; (*friendship*)
profond(e); (*knowledge*) approfondi(e)
▷ *vt* [ˈɪntɪmeɪt] suggérer, laisser entendre;
(*announce*) faire savoir
intimidate [ɪnˈtɪmɪdeɪt] *vt* intimider
intimidating [ɪnˈtɪmɪdeɪtɪŋ] *adj*
intimidant(e)
into [ˈɪntu] *prep* dans; **~ pieces/French** en
morceaux/français
intolerant [ɪnˈtɔlərnt] *adj*: **~ (of)**
intolérant(e) (de)
intranet [ɪnˈtrænet] *n* intranet *m*

intransitive [ɪnˈtrænsɪtɪv] *adj*
intransitif(-ive)
intricate [ˈɪntrɪkət] *adj* complexe,
compliqué(e)
intrigue [ɪnˈtriːg] *n* intrigue *f* ▷ *vt* intriguer;
intriguing *adj* fascinant(e)
introduce [ɪntrəˈdjuːs] *vt* introduire; (*TV show
etc*) présenter; **to ~ sb (to sb)** présenter qn (à
qn); **to ~ sb to** (*pastime, technique*) initier qn à;
introduction [ɪntrəˈdʌkʃən] *n* introduction
f, (*of person*) présentation *f*; (*to new experience*)
initiation *f*; **introductory** [ɪntrəˈdʌktərɪ] *adj*
préliminaire, introductif(-ive)
intrude [ɪnˈtruːd] *vi* (*person*) être importun(e);
to ~ on *or* **into** (*conversation etc*) s'immiscer
dans; **intruder** *n* intrus(e)
intuition [ɪntjuːˈɪʃən] *n* intuition *f*
inundate [ˈɪnʌndeɪt] *vt*: **to ~ with** inonder de
invade [ɪnˈveɪd] *vt* envahir
invalid *n* [ˈɪnvəlɪd] malade *m/f*; (*with
disability*) invalide *m/f* ▷ *adj* [ɪnˈvælɪd] (*not
valid*) invalide, non valide
invaluable [ɪnˈvæljuəbl] *adj* inestimable,
inappréciable
invariably [ɪnˈvɛərɪəblɪ] *adv* invariablement;
she is ~ late elle est toujours en retard
invasion [ɪnˈveɪʒən] *n* invasion *f*
invent [ɪnˈvɛnt] *vt* inventer; **invention**
[ɪnˈvɛnʃən] *n* invention *f*; **inventor** *n*
inventeur(-trice)
inventory [ˈɪnvəntrɪ] *n* inventaire *m*
inverted commas [ɪnˈvəːtɪd-] *npl* (*BRIT*)
guillemets *mpl*
invest [ɪnˈvɛst] *vt* investir ▷ *vi*: **to ~ in** placer
de l'argent *or* investir dans; (*fig: acquire*) s'offrir,
faire l'acquisition de
investigate [ɪnˈvɛstɪgeɪt] *vt* étudier,
examiner; (*crime*) faire une enquête sur;
investigation [ɪnvɛstɪˈgeɪʃən] *n* (*of crime*)
enquête *f*, investigation *f*
investigator [ɪnˈvɛstɪgeɪtə*] *n*
investigateur(-trice); **private ~** détective privé
investment [ɪnˈvɛstmənt] *n* investissement
m, placement *m*
investor [ɪnˈvɛstə*] *n* épargnant(e);
(*shareholder*) actionnaire *m/f*
invisible [ɪnˈvɪzɪbl] *adj* invisible
invitation [ɪnvɪˈteɪʃən] *n* invitation *f*
invite [ɪnˈvaɪt] *vt* inviter; (*opinions etc*)
demander; **inviting** *adj* engageant(e),
attrayant(e)
invoice [ˈɪnvɔɪs] *n* facture *f* ▷ *vt* facturer
involve [ɪnˈvɔlv] *vt* (*entail*) impliquer; (*concern*)
concerner; (*require*) nécessiter; **to ~ sb in** (*theft
etc*) impliquer qn dans; (*activity, meeting*) faire
participer qn à; **involved** *adj* (*complicated*)
complexe; **to be involved in** (*take part*)
participer à; **involvement** *n* (*personal role*) rôle
m; (*participation*) participation *f*; (*enthusiasm*)

enthousiasme *m*

inward ['ɪnwəd] *adj* (*movement*) vers l'intérieur; (*thought, feeling*) profond(e), intime ▷ *adv* = **inwards**; **inwards** *adv* vers l'intérieur

IQ *n abbr* (= *intelligence quotient*) Q.I. *m*

IRA *n abbr* (= *Irish Republican Army*) IRA *f*

Iran [ɪˈrɑːn] *n* Iran *m*; **Iranian** [ɪˈreɪnɪən] *adj* iranien(ne) ▷ *n* Iranien(ne)

Iraq [ɪˈrɑːk] *n* Irak *m*; **Iraqi** *adj* irakien(ne) ▷ *n* Irakien(ne)

Ireland ['aɪələnd] *n* Irlande *f*

iris, irises ['aɪrɪs, -ɪz] *n* iris *m*

Irish ['aɪrɪʃ] *adj* irlandais(e) ▷ *npl*: **the ~** les Irlandais; **Irishman** (*irreg*) *n* Irlandais *m*; **Irishwoman** (*irreg*) *n* Irlandaise *f*

iron ['aɪən] *n* fer *m*; (*for clothes*) fer m à repasser ▷ *adj* de or en fer ▷ *vt* (*clothes*) repasser

ironic(al) [aɪˈrɒnɪk(l)] *adj* ironique; **ironically** *adv* ironiquement

ironing ['aɪənɪŋ] *n* (*activity*) repassage *m*; (*clothes: ironed*) linge repassé; (: *to be ironed*) linge à repasser; **ironing board** *n* planche *f* à repasser

irony ['aɪrənɪ] *n* ironie *f*

irrational [ɪˈræʃənl] *adj* irrationnel(le); (*person*) qui n'est pas rationnel

irregular [ɪˈrɛɡjulə] *adj* irrégulier(-ière); (*surface*) inégal(e); (*action, event*) peu orthodoxe

irrelevant [ɪˈrɛləvənt] *adj* sans rapport, hors de propos

irresistible [ɪrɪˈzɪstɪbl] *adj* irrésistible

irresponsible [ɪrɪˈspɒnsɪbl] *adj* (*act*) irréfléchi(e); (*person*) qui n'a pas le sens des responsabilités

irrigation [ɪrɪˈɡeɪʃən] *n* irrigation *f*

irritable ['ɪrɪtəbl] *adj* irritable

irritate ['ɪrɪteɪt] *vt* irriter; **irritating** *adj* irritant(e); **irritation** [ɪrɪˈteɪʃən] *n* irritation *f*

IRS *n abbr* (*us*) = **Internal Revenue Service**

is [ɪz] *vb see* **be**

ISDN *n abbr* (= *Integrated Services Digital Network*) RNIS *m*

Islam ['ɪzlɑːm] *n* Islam *m*; **Islamic** [ɪzˈlɑːmɪk] *adj* islamique

island ['aɪlənd] *n* île *f*; (*also*: **traffic ~**) refuge *m* (pour piétons); **islander** *n* habitant(e) d'une île, insulaire *m/f*

isle [aɪl] *n* île *f*

isn't ['ɪznt] = **is not**

isolated ['aɪsəleɪtɪd] *adj* isolé(e)

isolation [aɪsəˈleɪʃən] *n* isolement *m*

ISP *n abbr* = **Internet Service Provider**

Israel ['ɪzreɪl] *n* Israël *m*; **Israeli** [ɪzˈreɪlɪ] *adj* israélien(ne) ▷ *n* Israélien(ne)

issue ['ɪʃuː] *n* question *f*, problème *m*; (*of banknotes*) émission *f*; (*of newspaper*) numéro *m*; (*of book*) publication *f*, parution *f* ▷ *vt* (*rations, equipment*) distribuer; (*orders*) donner; (*statement*) publier, faire; (*certificate, passport*) délivrer; (*banknotes, cheques, stamps*) émettre, mettre en circulation; **at ~** en jeu, en cause; **to take ~ with sb (over sth)** exprimer son désaccord avec qn (sur qch)

IT *n abbr* = **information technology**

 KEYWORD

it [ɪt] *pron* **1** (*specific: subject*) il (elle); (: *direct object*) le (la, l'); (: *indirect object*) lui; **it's on the table** c'est or il (or elle) est sur la table; **I can't find it** je n'arrive pas à le trouver; **give it to me** donne-le-moi

2 (*after prep*): **about/from/of it** en; **I spoke to him about it** je lui en ai parlé; **what did you learn from it?** qu'est-ce que vous en avez retiré?; **I'm proud of it** j'en suis fier; **in/to it** y; **put the book in it** mettez-y le livre; **he agreed to it** il y a consenti; **did you go to it?** (*party, concert etc*) est-ce que vous y êtes allé(s)?

3 (*impersonal*) il; ce, cela, ça; **it's raining** il pleut; **it's Friday tomorrow** demain, c'est vendredi *or* nous sommes, vendredi; **it's 6 o'clock** il est 6 heures; **how far is it? — it's 10 miles** c'est loin? — c'est à 10 miles; **who is it? — it's me** qui est-ce? — c'est moi

Italian [ɪˈtæljən] *adj* italien(ne) ▷ *n* Italien(ne); (*Ling*) italien *m*

italics [ɪˈtælɪks] *npl* italique *m*

Italy ['ɪtəlɪ] *n* Italie *f*

itch [ɪtʃ] *n* démangeaison *f* ▷ *vi* (*person*) éprouver des démangeaisons; (*part of body*) démanger; **I'm ~ing to do** l'envie me démange de faire; **itchy** *adj*: **my back is itchy** j'ai le dos qui me démange

it'd ['ɪtd] = **it would**; **it had**

item ['aɪtəm] *n* (*gen*) article *m*; (*on agenda*) question *f*, point *m*; (*also*: **news ~**) nouvelle *f*

itinerary [aɪˈtɪnərərɪ] *n* itinéraire *m*

it'll ['ɪtl] = **it will**; **it shall**

its [ɪts] *adj* son (sa), ses *pl*

it's [ɪts] = **it is**; **it has**

itself [ɪtˈsɛlf] *pron* (*reflexive*) se; (*emphatic*) lui-même (elle-même)

ITV *n abbr* (*BRIT* = *Independent Television*) chaîne de télévision commerciale

I've [aɪv] = **I have**

ivory ['aɪvərɪ] *n* ivoire *m*

ivy ['aɪvɪ] *n* lierre *m*

j

jab [dʒæb] *vt*: **to ~ sth into** enfoncer *or* planter qch dans ▷ *n* (*Med: inf*) piqûre *f*

jack [dʒæk] *n* (*Aut*) cric *m*; (*Cards*) valet *m*

jacket ['dʒækɪt] *n* veste *f*, veston *m*; (*of book*) couverture *f*, jaquette *f*; **jacket potato** *n* pomme *f* de terre en robe des champs

jackpot ['dʒækpɔt] *n* gros lot

Jacuzzi® [dʒə'ku:zɪ] *n* jacuzzi® *m*

jagged ['dʒægɪd] *adj* dentelé(e)

jail [dʒeɪl] *n* prison *f* ▷ *vt* emprisonner, mettre en prison; **jail sentence** *n* peine *f* de prison

jam [dʒæm] *n* confiture *f*; (*also*: **traffic ~**) embouteillage *m* ▷ *vt* (*passage etc*) encombrer, obstruer; (*mechanism, drawer etc*) bloquer, coincer; (*Radio*) brouiller ▷ *vi* (*mechanism, sliding part*) se coincer, se bloquer; (*gun*) s'enrayer; **to be in a ~** (*inf*) être dans le pétrin; **to ~ sth into** (*stuff*) entasser *or* comprimer qch dans; (*thrust*) enfoncer qch dans

Jamaica [dʒə'meɪkə] *n* Jamaïque *f*

jammed [dʒæmd] *adj* (*window etc*) coincé(e)

Jan *abbr* (= *January*) janv

janitor ['dʒænɪtə'] *n* (*caretaker*) concierge *m*

January ['dʒænjuərɪ] *n* janvier *m*

Japan [dʒə'pæn] *n* Japon *m*; **Japanese** [dʒæpə'ni:z] *adj* japonais(e) ▷ *n* (*pl inv*) Japonais(e); (*Ling*) japonais *m*

jar [dʒɑ:'] *n* (*stone, earthenware*) pot *m*; (*glass*) bocal *m* ▷ *vi* (*sound*) produire un son grinçant *or* discordant; (*colours etc*) détonner, jurer

jargon ['dʒɑ:gən] *n* jargon *m*

javelin ['dʒævlɪn] *n* javelot *m*

jaw [dʒɔ:] *n* mâchoire *f*

jazz [dʒæz] *n* jazz *m*

jealous ['dʒɛləs] *adj* jaloux(-ouse); **jealousy** *n* jalousie *f*

jeans [dʒi:nz] *npl* jean *m*

Jello® ['dʒɛləu] (*us*) *n* gelée *f*

jelly ['dʒɛlɪ] *n* (*dessert*) gelée *f*; (*us: jam*) confiture *f*; **jellyfish** *n* méduse *f*

jeopardize ['dʒɛpədaɪz] *vt* mettre en danger *or* péril

jerk [dʒə:k] *n* secousse *f*, saccade *f*; (*of muscle*) spasme *m*; (*inf*) pauvre type *m* ▷ *vt* (*shake*) donner une secousse à; (*pull*) tirer brusquement ▷ *vi* (*vehicles*) cahoter

jersey ['dʒə:zɪ] *n* tricot *m*; (*fabric*) jersey *m*

Jesus ['dʒi:zəs] *n* Jésus

jet [dʒɛt] *n* (*of gas, liquid*) jet *m*; (*Aviat*) avion *m* à réaction, jet *m*; **jet lag** *n* décalage *m* horaire; **jet-ski** *vi* faire du jet-ski *or* scooter des mers

jetty ['dʒɛtɪ] *n* jetée *f*, digue *f*

Jew [dʒu:] *n* Juif *m*

jewel ['dʒu:əl] *n* bijou *m*, joyau *m*; (*in watch*) rubis *m*; **jeweller** (*us* **jeweler**) *n* bijoutier(-ière), joaillier *m*; **jeweller's (shop)** (*us* **jewelry store**) *n* bijouterie *f*, joaillerie *f*; **jewellery** (*us* **jewelry**) *n* bijoux *mpl*

Jewish ['dʒu:ɪʃ] *adj* juif (juive)

jigsaw ['dʒɪgsɔ:] *n* (*also*: **~ puzzle**) puzzle *m*

job [dʒɔb] *n* (*chore, task*) travail *m*, tâche *f*; (*employment*) emploi *m*, poste *m*, place *f*; **it's a good ~ that …** c'est heureux *or* c'est une chance que … + *sub*; **just the ~!** (*c'est*) juste *or* exactement ce qu'il faut!; **job centre** (*BRIT*) *n* ≈ ANPE *f*, ≈ Agence nationale pour l'emploi; **jobless** *adj* sans travail, au chômage

jockey ['dʒɔkɪ] *n* jockey *m* ▷ *vi*: **to ~ for position** manœuvrer pour être bien placé

jog [dʒɔg] *vt* secouer ▷ *vi* (*Sport*) faire du jogging; **to ~ sb's memory** rafraîchir la mémoire de qn; **jogging** *n* jogging *m*

join [dʒɔɪn] *vt* (*put together*) unir, assembler; (*become member of*) s'inscrire à; (*meet*) rejoindre, retrouver; (*queue*) se joindre à ▷ *vi* (*roads, rivers*) se rejoindre, se rencontrer ▷ *n* raccord *m*; **join in** *vi* se mettre de la partie ▷ *vt fus* se mêler à; **join up** *vi* (*meet*) se rejoindre; (*Mil*) s'engager

joiner ['dʒɔɪnə'] (*BRIT*) *n* menuisier *m*

joint [dʒɔɪnt] *n* (*Tech*) jointure *f*; joint *m*; (*Anat*) articulation *f*, jointure; (*BRIT Culin*) rôti *m*; (*inf: place*) boîte *f*; (*of cannabis*) joint *m* ▷ *adj* commun(e); (*committee*) mixte, paritaire; (*winner*) ex aequo; **joint account** *n* compte joint; **jointly** *adv* ensemble, en commun

joke [dʒəuk] *n* plaisanterie *f*; (*also*: **practical ~**) farce *f* ▷ *vi* plaisanter; **to play a ~ on** jouer un tour à, faire une farce à; **joker** *n* (*Cards*) joker *m*

jolly ['dʒɔlɪ] *adj* gai(e), enjoué(e); (*enjoyable*)

amusant(e), plaisant(e) ▷ *adv* (BRIT *inf*) rudement, drôlement

jolt [dʒəult] *n* cahot *m*, secousse *f*; (*shock*) choc *m* ▷ *vt* cahoter, secouer

Jordan [dʒɔːdən] *n* (*country*) Jordanie *f*

journal ['dʒəːnl] *n* journal *m*; **journalism** *n* journalisme *m*; **journalist** *n* journaliste *m/f*

journey ['dʒəːnɪ] *n* voyage *m*; (*distance covered*) trajet *m*; **the ~ takes two hours** le trajet dure deux heures; **how was your ~?** votre voyage s'est bien passé?

joy [dʒɔɪ] *n* joie *f*; **joyrider** *n* voleur(-euse) de voiture (*qui fait une virée dans le véhicule volé*); **joy stick** *n* (*Aviat*) manche *m* à balai; (*Comput*) manche à balai, manette *f* (de jeu)

Jr *abbr* = **junior**

judge [dʒʌdʒ] *n* juge *m* ▷ *vt* juger; (*estimate: weight, size etc*) apprécier; (*consider*) estimer

judo ['dʒuːdəu] *n* judo *m*

jug [dʒʌg] *n* pot *m*, cruche *f*

juggle ['dʒʌgl] *vi* jongler; **juggler** *n* jongleur *m*

juice [dʒuːs] *n* jus *m*; **juicy** *adj* juteux(-euse)

Jul *abbr* (= *July*) juil

July [dʒuːˈlaɪ] *n* juillet *m*

jumble ['dʒʌmbl] *n* fouillis *m* ▷ *vt* (*also*: **~ up, ~ together**) mélanger, brouiller; **jumble sale** *n* (BRIT) vente *f* de charité

● **JUMBLE SALE**
●
● Les **jumble sales** ont lieu dans les églises,
● salles des fêtes ou halls d'écoles, et l'on
● y vend des articles de toutes sortes, en
● général bon marché et surtout d'occasion,
● pour collecter des fonds pour une œuvre
● de charité, une école (par exemple, pour
● acheter un ordinateur), ou encore une
● église (pour réparer un toit etc).

jumbo ['dʒʌmbəu] *adj* (*also*: **~ jet**) (avion) gros porteur (à réaction)

jump [dʒʌmp] *vi* sauter, bondir; (*with fear etc*) sursauter; (*increase*) monter en flèche ▷ *vt* sauter, franchir ▷ *n* saut *m*, bond *m*; (*with fear etc*) sursaut *m*; (*fence*) obstacle *m*; **to ~ the queue** (BRIT) passer avant son tour

jumper ['dʒʌmpəʳ] *n* (BRIT: *pullover*) pull-over *m*; (US: *pinafore dress*) robe-chasuble *f*

jump leads (US **jumper cables**) *npl* câbles *mpl* de démarrage

Jun. *abbr* = **June**; **junior**

junction ['dʒʌŋkʃən] *n* (BRIT: *of roads*) carrefour *m*; (*of rails*) embranchement *m*

June [dʒuːn] *n* juin *m*

jungle ['dʒʌŋgl] *n* jungle *f*

junior ['dʒuːnɪəʳ] *adj, n*: **he's ~ to me (by 2 years), he's my ~ (by 2 years)** il est mon cadet (de 2 ans), il est plus jeune que moi (de 2 ans); **he's ~ to me** (*seniority*) il est en

dessous de moi (dans la hiérarchie), j'ai plus d'ancienneté que lui; **junior high school** *n* (US) ≈ collège *m* d'enseignement secondaire; *see also* **high school**; **junior school** *n* (BRIT) école *f* primaire, cours moyen

junk [dʒʌŋk] *n* (*rubbish*) camelote *f*; (*cheap goods*) bric-à-brac *m inv*; **junk food** *n* snacks vite prêts (*sans valeur nutritive*)

junkie ['dʒʌŋkɪ] *n* (*inf*) junkie *m*, drogué(e)

junk mail *n* prospectus *mpl*; (*Comput*) messages *mpl* publicitaires

Jupiter ['dʒuːpɪtəʳ] *n* (*planet*) Jupiter *f*

jurisdiction [dʒuərɪsˈdɪkʃən] *n* juridiction *f*; **it falls** *or* **comes within/outside our ~** cela est/n'est pas de notre compétence *or* ressort

jury ['dʒuərɪ] *n* jury *m*

just [dʒʌst] *adj* juste ▷ *adv*: **he's ~ done it/left** il vient de le faire/partir; **~ right/two o'clock** exactement *or* juste ce qu'il faut/deux heures; **we were ~ going** nous partions; **I was ~ about to phone** j'allais téléphoner; **~ as he was leaving** au moment *or* à l'instant précis où il partait; **~ before/enough/here** juste avant/assez/là; **it's ~ me/a mistake** ce n'est que moi/(rien) qu'une erreur; **~ missed/ caught** manqué/attrapé de justesse; **~ listen to this!** écoutez un peu ça!; **she's ~ as clever as you** elle est tout aussi intelligente que vous; **it's ~ as well that you ...** heureusement que vous ...; **~ a minute!, ~ one moment!** un instant (s'il vous plaît)!

justice ['dʒʌstɪs] *n* justice *f*; (US: *judge*) juge *m* de la Cour suprême

justification [dʒʌstɪfɪˈkeɪʃən] *n* justification *f*

justify ['dʒʌstɪfaɪ] *vt* justifier

jut [dʒʌt] *vi* (*also*: **~ out**) dépasser, faire saillie

juvenile ['dʒuːvənaɪl] *adj* juvénile; (*court, books*) pour enfants ▷ *n* adolescent(e)

K, k [keɪ] *abbr* (= *one thousand*) K; (= *kilobyte*) Ko
kangaroo [kæŋgəˈruː] *n* kangourou *m*
karaoke [kɑːrəˈəʊkɪ] *n* karaoké *m*
karate [kəˈrɑːtɪ] *n* karaté *m*
kebab [kəˈbæb] *n* kébab *m*
keel [kiːl] *n* quille *f*; **on an even ~** (*fig*) à flot
keen [kiːn] *adj* (*eager*) plein(e) d'enthousiasme; (*interest, desire, competition*) vif (vive); (*eye, intelligence*) pénétrant(e); (*edge*) effilé(e); **to be ~ to do** *or* **on doing sth** désirer vivement faire qch, tenir beaucoup à faire qch; **to be ~ on sth/sb** aimer beaucoup qch/qn
keep [kiːp] (*pt, pp* **kept**) *vt* (*retain, preserve*) garder; (*hold back*) retenir; (*shop, accounts, promise, diary*) tenir; (*support*) entretenir; (*chickens, bees, pigs etc*) élever ▷ *vi* (*food*) se conserver; (*remain: in a certain state or place*) rester ▷ *n* (*of castle*) donjon *m*; (*food etc*): **enough for his ~** assez pour (assurer) sa subsistance; **to ~ doing sth** (*continue*) continuer à faire qch; (*repeatedly*) ne pas arrêter de faire qch; **to ~ sb from doing/sth from happening** empêcher qn de faire *or* que qch (ne) fasse/que qch (n')arrive; **to ~ sb happy/a place tidy** faire que qn soit content/qu'un endroit reste propre; **to ~ sth to o.s.** garder qch pour soi, tenir qch secret; **to ~ sth from sb** cacher qch à qn; **to ~ time** (*clock*) être à l'heure, ne pas retarder; **for ~s** (*inf*) pour de bon, pour toujours; **keep away** *vt*: **to ~ sth/sb away**
from sb tenir qch/qn éloigné de qn ▷ *vi*: **to ~ away (from)** ne pas s'approcher (de); **keep back** *vt* (*crowds, tears, money*) retenir; (*conceal: information*): **to ~ sth back from sb** cacher qch à qn ▷ *vi* rester en arrière; **keep off** *vt* (*dog, person*) éloigner ▷ *vi*: **if the rain ~s off** s'il ne pleut pas; **~ your hands off!** pas touché! (*inf*); **"~ off the grass"** "pelouse interdite"; **keep on** *vi* continuer; **to ~ on doing** continuer à faire; **don't ~ on about it!** arrête (d'en parler)!; **keep out** *vt* empêcher d'entrer ▷ *vi* (*stay out*) rester en dehors; **"~ out"** "défense d'entrer"; **keep up** *vi* (*fig: in comprehension*) suivre ▷ *vt* continuer, maintenir; **to ~ up with sb** (*in work etc*) se maintenir au même niveau que qn; (*in race etc*) aller aussi vite que qn; **keeper** *n* gardien(ne); **keep-fit** *n* gymnastique *f* (d'entretien); **keeping** *n* (*care*) garde *f*; **in keeping with** en harmonie avec
kennel [ˈkɛnl] *n* niche *f*; **kennels** *npl* (*for boarding*) chenil *m*
Kenya [ˈkɛnjə] *n* Kenya *m*
kept [kɛpt] *pt, pp of* **keep**
kerb [kəːb] *n* (BRIT) bordure *f* du trottoir
kerosene [ˈkɛrəsiːn] *n* kérosène *m*
ketchup [ˈkɛtʃəp] *n* ketchup *m*
kettle [ˈkɛtl] *n* bouilloire *f*
key [kiː] *n* (*gen, Mus*) clé *f*; (*of piano, typewriter*) touche *f*; (*on map*) légende *f* ▷ *adj* (*factor, role, area*) clé *inv* ▷ *vt* (*also*: **~ in**: *text*) saisir; **can I have my ~?** je peux avoir ma clé?; **a ~ issue** un problème fondamental; **keyboard** *n* clavier *m*; **keyhole** *n* trou *m* de la serrure; **keyring** *n* porte-clés *m*
kg *abbr* (= *kilogram*) K
khaki [ˈkɑːkɪ] *adj, n* kaki *m*
kick [kɪk] *vt* donner un coup de pied à ▷ *vi* (*horse*) ruer ▷ *n* coup *m* de pied; (*inf: thrill*): **he does it for ~s** il le fait parce que ça l'excite, il le fait pour le plaisir; **to ~ the habit** (*inf*) arrêter; **kick off** *vi* (*Sport*) donner le coup d'envoi; **kick-off** *n* (*Sport*) coup *m* d'envoi
kid [kɪd] *n* (*inf: child*) gamin(e), gosse *m/f*; (*animal, leather*) chevreau *m* ▷ *vi* (*inf*) plaisanter, blaguer
kidnap [ˈkɪdnæp] *vt* enlever, kidnapper; **kidnapping** *n* enlèvement *m*
kidney [ˈkɪdnɪ] *n* (*Anat*) rein *m*; (*Culin*) rognon *m*; **kidney bean** *n* haricot *m* rouge
kill [kɪl] *vt* tuer ▷ *n* mise *f* à mort; **to ~ time** tuer le temps; **killer** *n* tueur(-euse); (*murderer*) meurtrier(-ière); **killing** *n* meurtre *m*; (*of group of people*) tuerie *f*, massacre *m*; (*inf*): **to make a killing** se remplir les poches, réussir un beau coup
kiln [kɪln] *n* four *m*
kilo [ˈkiːləʊ] *n* kilo *m*; **kilobyte** *n* (*Comput*) kilo-octet *m*; **kilogram(me)** *n* kilogramme *m*; **kilometre** (US **kilometer**) [ˈkɪləmiːtər] *n*

kilomètre *m*; **kilowatt** *n* kilowatt *m*
kilt [kɪlt] *n* kilt *m*
kin [kɪn] *n see* **next-of-kin**
kind [kaɪnd] *adj* gentil(le), aimable ▷ *n* sorte
f, espèce *f*; (*species*) genre *m*; **to be two of a
~** se ressembler; **in ~** (*Comm*) en nature; **~ of**
(*inf: rather*) plutôt; **a ~ of** une sorte de; **what ~
of ...?** quelle sorte de ...?
kindergarten ['kɪndəgɑːtn] *n* jardin *m*
d'enfants
kindly ['kaɪndlɪ] *adj* bienveillant(e), plein(e)
de gentillesse ▷ *adv* avec bonté; **will you ~ ...**
auriez-vous la bonté *or* l'obligeance de ...
kindness ['kaɪndnɪs] *n* (*quality*) bonté *f*,
gentillesse *f*
king [kɪŋ] *n* roi *m*; **kingdom** *n* royaume *m*;
kingfisher *n* martin-pêcheur *m*; **king-size(d)
bed** *n* grand lit (*de 1,95 m de large*)
kiosk ['kiːɔsk] *n* kiosque *m*; (*BRIT: also:*
telephone ~) cabine *f* (téléphonique)
kipper ['kɪpə^r] *n* hareng fumé et salé
kiss [kɪs] *n* baiser *m* ▷ *vt* embrasser; **to ~ (each
other)** s'embrasser; **kiss of life** *n* (*BRIT*)
bouche à bouche *m*
kit [kɪt] *n* équipement *m*, matériel *m*; (*set of
tools etc*) trousse *f*; (*for assembly*) kit *m*
kitchen ['kɪtʃɪn] *n* cuisine *f*
kite [kaɪt] *n* (*toy*) cerf-volant *m*
kitten ['kɪtn] *n* petit chat, chaton *m*
kitty ['kɪtɪ] *n* (*money*) cagnotte *f*
kiwi ['kiːwiː] *n* (*also:* **~ fruit**) kiwi *m*
km *abbr* (= *kilometre*) km
km/h *abbr* (= *kilometres per hour*) km/h
knack [næk] *n*: **to have the ~ (of doing)** avoir
le coup (pour faire)
knee [niː] *n* genou *m*; **kneecap** *n* rotule *f*
kneel (*pt, pp* **knelt**) [niːl, nɛlt] *vi* (*also:* **~ down**)
s'agenouiller
knelt [nɛlt] *pt, pp of* **kneel**
knew [njuː] *pt of* **know**
knickers ['nɪkəz] *npl* (*BRIT*) culotte *f* (de
femme)
knife [naɪf] *n* (*pl* **knives**) couteau *m* ▷ *vt*
poignarder, frapper d'un coup de couteau
knight [naɪt] *n* chevalier *m*; (*Chess*) cavalier *m*
knit [nɪt] *vt* tricoter ▷ *vi* tricoter; (*broken bones*)
se ressouder; **to ~ one's brows** froncer les
sourcils; **knitting** *n* tricot *m*; **knitting needle**
n aiguille *f* à tricoter; **knitwear** *n* tricots *mpl*,
lainages *mpl*
knives [naɪvz] *npl of* **knife**
knob [nɔb] *n* bouton *m*; (*BRIT*): **a ~ of butter**
une noix de beurre
knock [nɔk] *vt* frapper; (*bump into*) heurter;
(*fig: col*) dénigrer ▷ *vi* (*at door etc*): **to ~ at/on**
frapper à/sur ▷ *n* coup *m*; **knock down** *vt*
renverser; (*price*) réduire; **knock off** *vi* (*inf:
finish*) s'arrêter (de travailler) ▷ *vt* (*vase, object*)
faire tomber; (*inf: steal*) piquer; (*fig: from price*

etc): **to ~ off £10** faire une remise de 10 livres;
knock out *vt* assommer; (*Boxing*) mettre
k.-o.; (*in competition*) éliminer; **knock over** *vt*
(*object*) faire tomber; (*pedestrian*) renverser;
knockout *n* (*Boxing*) knock-out *m*, K.-O. *m*;
knockout competition (*BRIT*) compétition *f*
avec épreuves éliminatoires
knot [nɔt] *n* (*gen*) nœud *m* ▷ *vt* nouer
know [nəu] *vt* (*pt* **knew**, *pp* **~n**) savoir; (*person,
place*) connaître; **to ~ that** savoir que; **to ~
how to do** savoir faire; **to ~ how to swim**
savoir nager; **to ~ about/of sth** (*event*) être au
courant de qch; (*subject*) connaître qch; **I don't
~** je ne sais pas; **do you ~ where I can ...?**
savez-vous où je peux ...?; **know-all** *n* (*BRIT pej*)
je-sais-tout *m/f*; **know-how** *n* savoir-faire *m*,
technique *f*, compétence *f*; **knowing** *adj* (*look
etc*) entendu(e); **knowingly** *adv* (*on purpose*)
sciemment; (*smile, look*) d'un air entendu;
know-it-all *n* (*US*) = **know-all**
knowledge ['nɔlɪdʒ] *n* connaissance *f*;
(*learning*) connaissances, savoir *m*; **without
my ~** à mon insu; **knowledgeable** *adj* bien
informé(e)
known [nəun] *pp of* **know** ▷ *adj* (*thief, facts*)
notoire; (*expert*) célèbre
knuckle ['nʌkl] *n* articulation *f* (des
phalanges), jointure *f*
koala [kəuˈɑːlə] *n* (*also:* **~ bear**) koala *m*
Koran [kɔˈrɑːn] *n* Coran *m*
Korea [kəˈrɪə] *n* Corée *f*; **Korean** *adj*
coréen(ne) ▷ *n* Coréen(ne)
kosher ['kəuʃə^r] *adj* kascher *inv*
Kosovar, Kosovan ['kɔsəvɑː^r, 'kɔsəvən] *adj*
kosovar(e)
Kosovo ['kɔsəvəu] *n* Kosovo *m*
Kuwait [kuˈweɪt] *n* Koweït *m*

L abbr (BRIT Aut: = learner) signale un conducteur débutant

l. abbr (= litre) l

lab [læb] n abbr (= laboratory) labo m

label ['leɪbl] n étiquette f; (brand: of record) marque f ▷ vt étiqueter

labor etc ['leɪbə'] (US) = **labour** etc

laboratory [lə'bɔrətəri] n laboratoire m

Labor Day n (US, CANADA) fête f du travail (le premier lundi de septembre)

labor union n (US) syndicat m

Labour ['leɪbə'] n (BRIT Pol: also: **the ~ Party**) le parti travailliste, les travaillistes mpl

labour (US **labor**) ['leɪbə'] n (work) travail m; (workforce) main-d'œuvre f ▷ vi: **to ~ (at)** travailler dur (à), peiner (sur) ▷ vt: **to ~ a point** insister sur un point; **in ~** (Med) en travail; **labourer** n manœuvre m; **farm labourer** ouvrier m agricole

lace [leɪs] n dentelle f; (of shoe etc) lacet m ▷ vt (shoe: also: **~ up**) lacer

lack [læk] n manque m ▷ vt manquer de; **through** or **for ~ of** faute de, par manque de; **to be ~ing** manquer, faire défaut; **to be ~ing in** manquer de

lacquer ['lækə'] n laque f

lacy ['leɪsɪ] adj (of lace) en dentelle; (like lace) comme de la dentelle

lad [læd] n garçon m, gars m

ladder ['lædə'] n échelle f; (BRIT: in tights) maille filée f ▷ vt, vi (BRIT: tights) filer

ladle ['leɪdl] n louche f

lady ['leɪdɪ] n dame f; **"ladies and gentlemen ..."** "Mesdames (et) Messieurs ..."; **young ~** jeune fille f; (married) jeune femme f; **the ladies' (room)** les toilettes fpl des dames; **ladybird** (US **ladybug**) n coccinelle f

lag [læg] n retard m ▷ vi (also: **~ behind**) rester en arrière, traîner; (fig) rester à la traîne ▷ vt (pipes) calorifuger

lager ['lɑːgə'] n bière blonde

lagoon [lə'guːn] n lagune f

laid [leɪd] pt, pp of **lay**; **laid back** adj (inf) relaxe, décontracté(e)

lain [leɪn] pp of **lie**

lake [leɪk] n lac m

lamb [læm] n agneau m

lame [leɪm] adj (also fig) boiteux(-euse)

lament [lə'mɛnt] n lamentation f ▷ vt pleurer, se lamenter sur

lamp [læmp] n lampe f; **lamppost** n (BRIT) réverbère m; **lampshade** n abat-jour m inv

land [lænd] n (as opposed to sea) terre f (ferme); (country) pays m; (soil) terre; (piece of land) terrain m; (estate) terre(s), domaine(s) m(pl) ▷ vi (from ship) débarquer; (Aviat) atterrir; (fig: fall) (re)tomber ▷ vt (passengers, goods) débarquer; (obtain) décrocher; **to ~ sb with sth** (inf) coller qch à qn; **landing** n (from ship) débarquement m; (Aviat) atterrissage m; (of staircase) palier m; **landing card** n carte f de débarquement; **landlady** n propriétaire f, logeuse f; (of pub) patronne f; **landlord** n propriétaire m, logeur m; (of pub etc) patron m; **landmark** n (point m de) repère m; **to be a landmark** (fig) faire date or époque; **landowner** n propriétaire foncier or terrien; **landscape** n paysage m; **landslide** n (Geo) glissement m (de terrain); (fig: Pol) raz-de-marée (électoral)

lane [leɪn] n (in country) chemin m; (Aut: of road) voie f; (: line of traffic) file f; (in race) couloir m

language ['læŋgwɪdʒ] n langue f; (way one speaks) langage m; **what ~s do you speak?** quelles langues parlez-vous?; **bad ~**

grossièretés *fpl*, langage grossier; **language laboratory** *n* laboratoire *m* de langues; **language school** *n* école *f* de langue
lantern ['læntn] *n* lanterne *f*
lap [læp] *n* (*of track*) tour *m* (de piste); (*of body*): **in** or **on one's ~** sur les genoux ▷ *vt* (*also:* **~ up**) laper ▷ *vi* (*waves*) clapoter
lapel [lə'pɛl] *n* revers *m*
lapse [læps] *n* défaillance *f*; (*in behaviour*) écart *m* (de conduite) ▷ *vi* (*Law*) cesser d'être en vigueur; (*contract*) expirer; **to ~ into bad habits** prendre de mauvaises habitudes; **~ of time** laps *m* de temps, intervalle *m*
laptop (computer) ['læptɔp-] *n* portable *m*
lard [lɑːd] *n* saindoux *m*
larder ['lɑːdə'] *n* garde-manger *m* inv
large [lɑːdʒ] *adj* grand(e); (*person, animal*) gros (grosse); **at ~** (*free*) en liberté; (*generally*) en général; pour la plupart; **largely** *adv* en grande partie; (*principally*) surtout; **large-scale** *adj* (*map, drawing etc*) à grande échelle; (*fig*) important(e)
lark [lɑːk] *n* (*bird*) alouette *f*; (*joke*) blague *f*, farce *f*
laryngitis [lærɪn'dʒaɪtɪs] *n* laryngite *f*
lasagne [lə'zænjə] *n* lasagne *f*
laser ['leɪzə'] *n* laser *m*; **laser printer** *n* imprimante *f* laser
lash [læʃ] *n* coup *m* de fouet; (*also:* **eye~**) cil *m* ▷ *vt* fouetter; (*tie*) attacher; **lash out** *vi*: **to ~ out (at** or **against sb/sth)** attaquer violemment (qn/qch)
lass [læs] (*BRIT*) *n* (jeune) fille *f*
last [lɑːst] *adj* dernier(-ière) ▷ *adv* en dernier; (*most recently*) la dernière fois; (*finally*) finalement ▷ *vi* durer; **~ week** la semaine dernière; **~ night** (*evening*) hier soir; (*night*) la nuit dernière; **at ~** enfin; **~ but one** avant-dernier(-ière); **lastly** *adv* en dernier lieu, pour finir; **last-minute** *adj* de dernière minute
latch [lætʃ] *n* loquet *m*; **latch onto** *vt fus* (*cling to: person, group*) s'accrocher à; (*idea*) se mettre en tête
late [leɪt] *adj* (*not on time*) en retard; (*far on in day etc*) tardif(-ive); (*: edition, delivery*) dernier(-ière); (*dead*) défunt(e) ▷ *adv* tard; (*behind time, schedule*) en retard; **to be 10 minutes ~** avoir 10 minutes de retard; **sorry I'm ~** désolé d'être en retard; **it's too ~** il est trop tard; **of ~** dernièrement; **in ~ May** vers la fin (du mois) de mai, fin mai; **the ~ Mr X** feu M. X; **latecomer** *n* retardataire *m/f*; **lately** *adv* récemment; **later** *adj* (*date etc*) ultérieur(e); (*version etc*) plus récent(e) ▷ *adv* plus tard; **latest** ['leɪtɪst] *adj* tout(e) dernier(-ière); **at the latest** au plus tard
lather ['lɑːðə'] *n* mousse *f* (de savon) ▷ *vt* savonner
Latin ['lætɪn] *n* latin *m* ▷ *adj* latin(e); **Latin**

America *n* Amérique latine; **Latin American** *adj* latino-américain(e), d'Amérique latine ▷ *n* Latino-Américain(e)
latitude ['lætɪtjuːd] *n* (*also fig*) latitude *f*
latter ['lætə'] *adj* deuxième, dernier(-ière) ▷ *n*: **the ~** ce dernier, celui-ci
laugh [lɑːf] *n* rire *m* ▷ *vi* rire; **(to do sth) for a ~** (faire qch) pour rire; **laugh at** *vt fus* se moquer de; (*joke*) rire de; **laughter** *n* rire *m*; (*of several people*) rires *mpl*
launch [lɔːntʃ] *n* lancement *m*; (*also:* **motor ~**) vedette *f* ▷ *vt* (*ship, rocket, plan*) lancer; **launch into** *vt fus* se lancer dans
launder ['lɔːndə'] *vt* laver; (*fig: money*) blanchir
Launderette® [lɔːn'drɛt] (*BRIT*) (*US* **Laundromat®** ['lɔːndrəmæt]) *n* laverie *f* (automatique)
laundry ['lɔːndrɪ] *n* (*clothes*) linge *m*; (*business*) blanchisserie *f*; (*room*) buanderie *f*; **to do the ~** faire la lessive
lava ['lɑːvə] *n* lave *f*
lavatory ['lævətərɪ] *n* toilettes *fpl*
lavender ['lævəndə'] *n* lavande *f*
lavish ['lævɪʃ] *adj* (*amount*) copieux(-euse); (*person: giving freely*): **~ with** prodigue de ▷ *vt*: **to ~ sth on sb** prodiguer qch à qn; (*money*) dépenser qch sans compter pour qn
law [lɔː] *n* loi *f*; (*science*) droit *m*; **lawful** *adj* légal(e), permis(e); **lawless** *adj* (*action*) illégal(e); (*place*) sans loi
lawn [lɔːn] *n* pelouse *f*; **lawnmower** *n* tondeuse *f* à gazon
lawsuit ['lɔːsuːt] *n* procès *m*
lawyer ['lɔːjə'] *n* (*consultant, with company*) juriste *m*; (*for sales, wills etc*) ≈ notaire *m*; (*partner, in court*) ≈ avocat *m*
lax [læks] *adj* relâché(e)
laxative ['læksətɪv] *n* laxatif *m*
lay [leɪ] *pt of* **lie** ▷ *adj* laïque; (*not expert*) profane ▷ *vt* (*pt, pp* **laid**) poser, mettre; (*eggs*) pondre; (*trap*) tendre; (*plans*) élaborer; **to ~ the table** mettre la table; **lay down** *vt* poser; (*rules etc*) établir; **to ~ down the law** (*fig*) faire la loi; **lay off** *vt* (*workers*) licencier; (*provide: meal etc*) fournir; **lay out** *vt* (*design*) dessiner, concevoir; (*display*) disposer; (*spend*) dépenser; **lay-by** *n* (*BRIT*) aire *f* de stationnement (sur le bas-côté)
layer ['leɪə'] *n* couche *f*
layman ['leɪmən] (*irreg*) *n* (*Rel*) laïque *m*; (*non-expert*) profane *m*
layout ['leɪaut] *n* disposition *f*, plan *m*, agencement *m*; (*Press*) mise *f* en page
lazy ['leɪzɪ] *adj* paresseux(-euse)
lb. *abbr* (*weight*) = **pound**
lead¹ [liːd] *n* (*front position*) tête *f*; (*distance, time ahead*) avance *f*; (*clue*) piste *f*; (*Elec*) fil *m*; (*for dog*) laisse *f*; (*Theat*) rôle principal ▷ *vb* (*pt, pp* **led**) ▷ *vt* (*guide*) mener, conduire; (*be leader of*)

être à la tête de ▷ vi (Sport) mener, être en tête;
to ~ to (road, pipe) mener à, conduire à; (result
in) conduire à; aboutir à; **to be in the ~** (Sport:
in race) mener, être en tête; (: in match) mener
(à la marque); **to ~ sb to do sth** amener qn
à faire qch; **to ~ the way** montrer le chemin;
lead up to vt conduire à; (in conversation) en
venir à
lead² [lɛd] n (metal) plomb m; (in pencil) mine f
leader ['liːdə'] n (of team) chef m; (of party etc)
dirigeant(e), leader m; (Sport: in league) leader;
(: in race) coureur m de tête; **leadership** n
(position) direction f; **under the leadership
of ...** sous la direction de ...; **qualities of
leadership** qualités fpl de chef or de meneur
lead-free ['lɛdfriː] adj sans plomb
leading ['liːdɪŋ] adj de premier plan; (main)
principal(e); (in race) de tête
lead singer [liːd-] n (in pop group) (chanteur
m) vedette f
leaf (pl **leaves**) [liːf, liːvz] n feuille f; (of table)
rallonge f; **to turn over a new ~** (fig) changer
de conduite or d'existence; **leaf through** vt
(book) feuilleter
leaflet ['liːflɪt] n prospectus m, brochure f; (Pol,
Rel) tract m
league [liːg] n ligue f; (Football) championnat
m; **to be in ~ with** avoir partie liée avec, être
de mèche avec
leak [liːk] n (out: also fig) fuite f ▷ vi (pipe, liquid
etc) fuir; (shoes) prendre l'eau; (ship) faire eau
▷ vt (liquid) répandre; (information) divulguer
lean [liːn] adj maigre ▷ vb (pt, pp ~ed or ~t)
▷ vt: **to ~ sth on** appuyer qch sur ▷ vi (slope)
pencher; (rest): **to ~ against** s'appuyer contre;
être appuyé(e) contre; **to ~ on** s'appuyer sur;
lean forward vi se pencher en avant; **lean
over** vi se pencher; **leaning** n: **leaning
(towards)** penchant m (pour)
leant [lɛnt] pt, pp of **lean**
leap [liːp] n bond m, saut m ▷ vi (pt, pp ~ed or
~t) bondir, sauter
leapt [lɛpt] pt, pp of **leap**
leap year n année f bissextile
learn (pt, pp ~ed or ~t) [ləːn, -t] vt, vi
apprendre; **to ~ (how) to do sth** apprendre
à faire qch; **to ~ about sth** (Scol) étudier
qch; (hear, read) apprendre qch; **learner** n
débutant(e); (BRIT: also: **learner driver**)
(conducteur -trice) débutant(e); **learning**
n savoir m
learnt [ləːnt] pp of **learn**
lease [liːs] n bail m ▷ vt louer à bail
leash [liːʃ] n laisse f
least [liːst] adj: **the ~** (+ noun) le (la) plus
petit(e), le (la) moindre; (smallest amount of)
le moins de ▷ pron: **(the) ~** le moins ▷ adv (+
verb) le moins; (+ adj): **the ~** le (la) moins; **the ~
money** le moins d'argent; **the ~ expensive** le

(la) moins cher (chère); **the ~ possible effort**
le moins d'effort possible; **at ~** au moins;
(or rather) du moins; **you could at ~ have
written** tu aurais au moins pu écrire; **not in
the ~** pas le moins du monde
leather ['lɛðə'] n cuir m
leave [liːv] (vb: pt, pp **left**) vt laisser; (go away
from) quitter; (forget) oublier ▷ vi partir, s'en
aller ▷ n (time off) congé m; (Mil, also: consent)
permission f; **what time does the train/bus
~?** le train/le bus part à quelle heure?; **to ~ sth
to sb** (money etc) laisser qch à qn; **to be left**
rester; **there's some milk left over** il reste
du lait; **~ it to me!** laissez-moi faire!, je m'en
occupe!; **on ~** en permission; **leave behind** vt
(also fig) laisser; (forget) laisser, oublier; **leave
out** vt oublier, omettre
leaves [liːvz] npl of **leaf**
Lebanon ['lɛbənən] n Liban m
lecture ['lɛktʃə'] n conférence f; (Scol) cours
(magistral) ▷ vi donner des cours; enseigner
▷ vt (scold) sermonner, réprimander; **to give
a ~ (on)** faire une conférence (sur), faire un
cours (sur); **lecture hall** n amphithéâtre m;
lecturer n (speaker) conférencier(-ière); (BRIT:
at university) professeur m (d'université), prof
m/f de fac (inf); **lecture theatre** n = **lecture
hall**

> Be careful not to translate **lecture** by the
> French word **lecture**.

led [lɛd] pt, pp of **lead¹**
ledge [lɛdʒ] n (of window, on wall) rebord m; (of
mountain) saillie f, corniche f
leek [liːk] n poireau m
left [lɛft] pt, pp of **leave** ▷ adj gauche ▷ adv à
gauche ▷ n gauche f; **there are two ~** il en
reste deux; **on the ~, to the ~** à gauche; **the L~**
(Pol) la gauche; **left-hand** adj: **the left-hand
side** la gauche; **left-hand drive** n (BRIT:
vehicle) véhicule m avec la conduite à gauche;
left-handed adj gaucher(-ère); (scissors
etc) pour gauchers; **left-luggage locker** n
(BRIT) casier m à) consigne f automatique;
left-luggage (office) n (BRIT) consigne f;
left-overs npl restes mpl; **left-wing** adj (Pol)
de gauche
leg [lɛg] n jambe f; (of animal) patte f; (of
furniture) pied m; (Culin: of chicken) cuisse f;
(of journey) étape f; **1st/2nd ~** (Sport) match
m aller/retour; **~ of lamb** (Culin) gigot m
d'agneau
legacy ['lɛgəsɪ] n (also fig) héritage m, legs m
legal ['liːgl] adj (permitted by law) légal(e);
(relating to law) juridique; **legal holiday** (us)
n jour férié; **legalize** vt légaliser; **legally** adv
légalement
legend ['lɛdʒənd] n légende f; **legendary**
['lɛdʒəndərɪ] adj légendaire
leggings ['lɛgɪŋz] npl caleçon m

legible [ˈlɛdʒəbl] *adj* lisible
legislation [lɛdʒɪsˈleɪʃən] *n* législation *f*
legislative [ˈlɛdʒɪslətɪv] *adj* législatif(-ive)
legitimate [lɪˈdʒɪtɪmət] *adj* légitime
leisure [ˈlɛʒə*r*] *n* (*free time*) temps libre, loisirs *mpl*; **at ~** (tout) à loisir; **at your ~** (*later*) à tête reposée; **leisure centre** *n* (BRIT) centre *m* de loisirs; **leisurely** *adj* tranquille, fait(e) sans se presser
lemon [ˈlɛmən] *n* citron *m*; **lemonade** *n* (*fizzy*) limonade *f*; **lemon tea** *n* thé *m* au citron
lend (*pt, pp* **lent**) [lɛnd, lɛnt] *vt*: **to ~ sth (to sb)** prêter qch (à qn); **could you ~ me some money?** pourriez-vous me prêter de l'argent?
length [lɛŋθ] *n* longueur *f*; (*section: of road, pipe etc*) morceau *m*, bout *m*; **~ of time** durée *f*; **it is 2 metres in ~** cela fait 2 mètres de long; **at ~** (*at last*) enfin, à la fin; (*lengthily*) longuement; **lengthen** *vt* allonger, prolonger ▷ *vi* s'allonger; **lengthways** *adv* dans le sens de la longueur, en long; **lengthy** *adj* (très) long (longue)
lens [lɛnz] *n* lentille *f*; (*of spectacles*) verre *m*; (*of camera*) objectif *m*
Lent [lɛnt] *n* carême *m*
lent [lɛnt] *pt, pp of* **lend**
lentil [ˈlɛntl] *n* lentille *f*
Leo [ˈliːəu] *n* le Lion
leopard [ˈlɛpəd] *n* léopard *m*
leotard [ˈliːətɑːd] *n* justaucorps *m*
leprosy [ˈlɛprəsɪ] *n* lèpre *f*
lesbian [ˈlɛzbɪən] *n* lesbienne *f* ▷ *adj* lesbien(ne)
less [lɛs] *adj* moins de ▷ *pron, adv* moins ▷ *prep*: **~ tax/10% discount** avant impôt/moins 10% de remise; **~ than that/you** moins que cela/vous; **~ than half** moins de la moitié; **~ than ever** moins que jamais; **~ and ~** de moins en moins; **the ~ he works …** moins il travaille …; **lessen** *vi* diminuer, s'amoindrir, s'atténuer ▷ *vt* diminuer, réduire, atténuer; **lesser** [ˈlɛsə*r*] *adj* moindre; **to a lesser extent** *or* **degree** à un degré moindre
lesson [ˈlɛsn] *n* leçon *f*; **to teach sb a ~** (*fig*) donner une bonne leçon à qn
let (*pt, pp* **~**) [lɛt] *vt* laisser; (BRIT: *lease*) louer; **to ~ sb do sth** laisser qn faire qch; **to ~ sb know sth** faire savoir qch à qn, prévenir qn de qch; **to ~ go** lâcher prise; **to ~ go of sth, to ~ sth go** lâcher qch; **~'s go** allons-y; **~ him come** qu'il vienne; **"to ~"** (BRIT) "à louer"; **let down** *vt* (*lower*) baisser; (BRIT: *tyre*) dégonfler; (*disappoint*) décevoir; **let in** *vt* laisser entrer; (*visitor etc*) faire entrer; **let off** *vt* (*allow to leave*) laisser partir; (*not punish*) ne pas punir; (*firework etc*) faire partir; (*bomb*) faire exploser; **let out** *vt* laisser sortir; (*scream*) laisser échapper; (BRIT: *rent out*) louer
lethal [ˈliːθl] *adj* mortel(le), fatal(e); (*weapon*)

meurtrier(-ère)
letter [ˈlɛtə*r*] *n* lettre *f*; **letterbox** *n* (BRIT) boîte *f* aux or à lettres
lettuce [ˈlɛtɪs] *n* laitue *f*, salade *f*
leukaemia (US **leukemia**) [luːˈkiːmɪə] *n* leucémie *f*
level [ˈlɛvl] *adj* (*flat*) plat(e), plan(e), uni(e); (*horizontal*) horizontal(e) ▷ *n* niveau *m* ▷ *vt* niveler, aplanir; **"A" ~s** *npl* (BRIT) ≈ baccalauréat *m*; **to be ~ with** être au même niveau que; **to draw ~ with** (*runner, car*) arriver à la hauteur de, rattraper; **on the ~** (*fig: honest*) régulier(-ière); **level crossing** *n* (BRIT) passage *m* à niveau
lever [ˈliːvə*r*] *n* levier *m*; **leverage** *n* (*influence*): **leverage (on** *or* **with)** prise *f* (sur)
levy [ˈlɛvɪ] *n* taxe *f*, impôt *m* ▷ *vt* (*tax*) lever; (*fine*) infliger
liability [laɪəˈbɪlətɪ] *n* responsabilité *f*; (*handicap*) handicap *m*
liable [ˈlaɪəbl] *adj* (*subject*): **~ to** sujet(te) à, passible de; (*responsible*): **~ (for)** responsable (de); (*likely*): **~ to do** susceptible de faire
liaise [liːˈeɪz] *vi*: **to ~ with** assurer la liaison avec
liar [ˈlaɪə*r*] *n* menteur(-euse)
libel [ˈlaɪbl] *n* diffamation *f*; (*document*) écrit *m* diffamatoire ▷ *vt* diffamer
liberal [ˈlɪbərl] *adj* libéral(e); (*generous*): **~ with** prodigue de, généreux(-euse) avec ▷ *n*: **L~** (*Pol*) libéral(e); **Liberal Democrat** *n* (BRIT) libéral(e)-démocrate *m/f*
liberate [ˈlɪbəreɪt] *vt* libérer
liberation [lɪbəˈreɪʃən] *n* libération *f*
liberty [ˈlɪbətɪ] *n* liberté *f*; **to be at ~** (*criminal*) être en liberté; **at ~ to do** libre de faire; **to take the ~ of** prendre la liberté de, se permettre de
Libra [ˈliːbrə] *n* la Balance
librarian [laɪˈbrɛərɪən] *n* bibliothécaire *m/f*
library [ˈlaɪbrərɪ] *n* bibliothèque *f*

> Be careful not to translate *library* by the French word *librairie*.

Libya [ˈlɪbɪə] *n* Libye *f*
lice [laɪs] *npl of* **louse**
licence (US **license**) [ˈlaɪsns] *n* autorisation *f*, permis *m*; (*Comm*) licence *f*; (*Radio, TV*) redevance *f*; (*also*: **driving ~**, US: *also*: **driver's license**) permis *m* (de conduire)
license [ˈlaɪsns] *n* (US) = **licence** ▷ *vt* autoriser, donner une patente à; **licensed** *adj* (*for alcohol*) patenté(e) pour la vente des spiritueux, qui a une patente de débit de boissons; (*car*) muni(e) de la vignette; **license plate** *n* (US Aut) plaque *f* minéralogique; **licensing hours** (BRIT) *npl* heures *fpl* d'ouvertures (*des pubs*)
lick [lɪk] *vt* lécher; (*inf: defeat*) écraser, flanquer une piquette *or* raclée à; **to ~ one's lips** (*fig*) se frotter les mains
lid [lɪd] *n* couvercle *m*; (*eyelid*) paupière *f*

lie [laɪ] n mensonge m ▷ vi (pt, pp **~d**) (tell lies) mentir; (pt **lay**, pp **lain**) (rest) être étendu(e) or allongé(e) or couché(e); (object: be situated) se trouver, être; **to ~ low** (fig) se cacher, rester caché(e); **to tell ~s** mentir; **lie about, lie around** vi (things) traîner; (BRIT: person) traînasser, flemmarder; **lie down** vi se coucher, s'étendre

Liechtenstein ['lɪktənstaɪn] n Liechtenstein m

lie-in ['laɪɪn] n (BRIT): **to have a ~** faire la grasse matinée

lieutenant [lɛf'tɛnənt, US luː'tɛnənt] n lieutenant m

life (pl **lives**) [laɪf, laɪvz] n vie f; **to come to ~** (fig) s'animer; **life assurance** n (BRIT) = **life insurance**; **lifeboat** n canot m or chaloupe f de sauvetage; **lifeguard** n surveillant m de baignade; **life insurance** n assurance-vie f; **life jacket** n gilet m or ceinture f de sauvetage; **lifelike** adj qui semble vrai(e) or vivant(e), ressemblant(e); (painting) réaliste; **life preserver** n (US) gilet m or ceinture f de sauvetage; **life sentence** n condamnation f à vie or à perpétuité; **lifestyle** n style m de vie; **lifetime** n: **in his lifetime** de son vivant

lift [lɪft] vt soulever, lever; (end) supprimer, lever ▷ vi (fog) se lever ▷ n (BRIT: elevator) ascenseur m; **to give sb a ~** (BRIT) emmener or prendre qn en voiture; **can you give me a ~ to the station?** pouvez-vous m'emmener à la gare?; **lift up** vt soulever; **lift-off** n décollage m

light [laɪt] n lumière f; (lamp) lampe f; (Aut: rear light) feu m; (: headlamp) phare m; (for cigarette etc): **have you got a ~?** avez-vous du feu? ▷ vt (pt, pp **~ed** or **lit**) (candle, cigarette, fire) allumer; (room) éclairer ▷ adj (room, colour) clair(e); (not heavy, also fig) léger(-ère); (not strenuous) peu fatigant(e); **lights** npl (traffic lights) feux mpl; **to come to ~** être dévoilé(e) or découvert(e); **in the ~ of** à la lumière de; étant donné; **light up** vi s'allumer; (face) s'éclairer; (smoke) allumer une cigarette or une pipe etc ▷ vt (illuminate) éclairer, illuminer; **light bulb** n ampoule f; **lighten** vt (light up) éclairer; (make lighter) éclaircir; (make less heavy) alléger; **lighter** n (also: **cigarette lighter**) briquet m; **light-hearted** adj gai(e), joyeux(-euse), enjoué(e); **lighthouse** n phare m; **lighting** n éclairage m; (in theatre) éclairages; **lightly** adv légèrement; **to get off lightly** s'en tirer à bon compte

lightning ['laɪtnɪŋ] n foudre f; (flash) éclair m

lightweight ['laɪtweɪt] adj (suit) léger(-ère) ▷ n (Boxing) poids léger

like [laɪk] vt aimer (bien) ▷ prep comme ▷ adj semblable, pareil(le) ▷ n: **the ~** (pej) (d')autres du même genre or acabit; **his ~s and dislikes** ses goûts mpl or préférences fpl; **I would ~**, **I'd ~** je voudrais, j'aimerais; **would you ~ a coffee?** voulez-vous du café?; **to be/look ~ sb/sth** ressembler à qn/qch; **what's he ~?** comment est-il?; **what does it look ~?** de quoi est-ce que ça a l'air?; **what does it taste ~?** quel goût est-ce que ça a?; **that's just ~ him** c'est bien de lui, ça lui ressemble; **do it ~ this** fais-le comme ceci; **it's nothing ~ ...** ce n'est pas du tout comme ...; **likeable** adj sympathique, agréable

likelihood ['laɪklɪhud] n probabilité f

likely ['laɪklɪ] adj (result, outcome) probable; (excuse) plausible; **he's ~ to leave** il va sûrement partir, il risque fort de partir; **not ~!** (inf) pas de danger!

likewise ['laɪkwaɪz] adv de même, pareillement

liking ['laɪkɪŋ] n (for person) affection f; (for thing) penchant m, goût m; **to be to sb's ~** être au goût de qn, plaire à qn

lilac ['laɪlək] n lilas m

Lilo® ['laɪləu] n (for person) matelas m pneumatique

lily ['lɪlɪ] n lis m; **~ of the valley** muguet m

limb [lɪm] n membre m

limbo ['lɪmbəu] n: **to be in ~** (fig) être tombé(e) dans l'oubli

lime [laɪm] n (tree) tilleul m; (fruit) citron vert, lime f; (Geo) chaux f

limelight ['laɪmlaɪt] n: **in the ~** (fig) en vedette, au premier plan

limestone ['laɪmstəun] n pierre f à chaux; (Geo) calcaire m

limit ['lɪmɪt] n limite f ▷ vt limiter; **limited** adj limité(e), restreint(e); **to be limited to** se limiter à, ne concerner que

limousine ['lɪməziːn] n limousine f

limp [lɪmp] n: **to have a ~** boiter ▷ vi boiter ▷ adj mou (molle)

line [laɪn] n (gen) ligne f; (stroke) trait m; (wrinkle) ride f; (rope) corde f; (wire) fil m; (of poem) vers m; (row, series) rangée f; (of people) file f, queue f; (railway track) voie f; (Comm: series of goods) article(s) m(pl), ligne de produits; (work) métier m ▷ vt: **to ~ (with)** (clothes) doubler (de); (box) garnir or tapisser (de); (subj: trees, crowd) border; **to stand in ~** (US) faire la queue; **in his ~ of business** dans sa partie, dans son rayon; **to be in ~ for sth** (fig) être en lice pour qch; **in ~ with** en accord avec, en conformité avec; **in a ~** aligné(e); **line up** vi s'aligner, se mettre en rang(s); (in queue) faire la queue ▷ vt aligner; (event) prévoir; (find) trouver; **to have sb/sth ~d up** avoir qn/qch en vue or de prévu(e)

linear ['lɪnɪəʳ] adj linéaire

linen ['lɪnɪn] n linge m (de corps or de maison); (cloth) lin m

liner ['laɪnəʳ] n (ship) paquebot m de ligne; (for

bin) sac-poubelle m

line-up ['laɪnʌp] n (US: queue) file f; (also: **police ~**) parade f d'identification; (Sport) (composition f de l')équipe f

linger ['lɪŋgə'] vi s'attarder, traîner; (smell, tradition) persister

lingerie ['lænʒəri:] n lingerie f

linguist ['lɪŋgwɪst] n linguiste m/f; **to be a good ~** être doué(e) pour les langues; **linguistic** adj linguistique

lining ['laɪnɪŋ] n doublure f; (of brakes) garniture f

link [lɪŋk] n (connection) lien m, rapport m; (Internet) lien; (of a chain) maillon m ▷ vt relier, lier, unir; **links** npl (Golf) (terrain m de) golf m; **link up** vt relier ▷ vi (people) se rejoindre; (companies etc) s'associer

lion ['laɪən] n lion m; **lioness** n lionne f

lip [lɪp] n lèvre f; (of cup etc) rebord m; **lipread** vi lire sur les lèvres; **lip salve** [-sælv] n pommade f pour les lèvres, pommade rosat; **lipstick** n rouge m à lèvres

liqueur [lɪ'kjuə'] n liqueur f

liquid ['lɪkwɪd] n liquide m ▷ adj liquide; **liquidizer** ['lɪkwɪdaɪzə'] n (BRIT Culin) mixer m

liquor ['lɪkə'] n spiritueux m, alcool m; **liquor store** (US) n magasin m de vins et spiritueux

Lisbon ['lɪzbən] n Lisbonne f

lisp [lɪsp] n zézaiement m ▷ vi zézayer

list [lɪst] n liste f ▷ vt (write down) inscrire; (make list of) faire la liste de; (enumerate) énumérer

listen ['lɪsn] vi écouter; **to ~ to** écouter; **listener** n auditeur(-trice)

lit [lɪt] pt, pp of **light**

liter ['li:tə'] n (US) = **litre**

literacy ['lɪtərəsɪ] n degré m d'alphabétisation, fait m de savoir lire et écrire

literal ['lɪtərl] adj littéral(e); **literally** adv littéralement; (really) réellement

literary ['lɪtərərɪ] adj littéraire

literate ['lɪtərət] adj qui sait lire et écrire; (educated) instruit(e)

literature ['lɪtrɪtʃə'] n littérature f; (brochures etc) copie f publicitaire, prospectus mpl

litre (US **liter**) ['li:tə'] n litre m

litter ['lɪtə'] n (rubbish) détritus mpl; (dirtier) ordures fpl; (young animals) portée f; **litter bin** n (BRIT) poubelle f; **littered** adj: **littered with** (scattered) jonché(e) de

little ['lɪtl] adj (small) petit(e); (not much): **~ milk** peu de lait ▷ adv peu; **a ~** un peu (de); **a ~ milk** un peu de lait; **a ~ bit** un peu; **as ~ as possible** le moins possible; **~ by ~** petit à petit, peu à peu; **little finger** n auriculaire m, petit doigt

live¹ [laɪv] adj (animal) vivant(e), en vie; (wire) sous tension; (broadcast) (transmis(e)) en direct; (unexploded) non explosé(e)

live² [lɪv] vi vivre; (reside) vivre, habiter; **to ~ in London** habiter (à) Londres; **where do you ~?** où habitez-vous?; **live together** vivre ensemble, cohabiter; **live up to** vt fus se montrer à la hauteur de

livelihood ['laɪvlɪhud] n moyens mpl d'existence

lively ['laɪvlɪ] adj vif (vive), plein(e) d'entrain; (place, book) vivant(e)

liven up ['laɪvn-] vt (room etc) égayer; (discussion, evening) animer ▷ vi s'animer

liver ['lɪvə'] n foie m

lives [laɪvz] npl of **life**

livestock ['laɪvstɔk] n cheptel m, bétail m

living ['lɪvɪŋ] adj vivant(e), en vie ▷ n: **to earn** or **make a ~** gagner sa vie; **living room** n salle f de séjour

lizard ['lɪzəd] n lézard m

load [ləud] n (weight) poids m; (thing carried) chargement m, charge f; (Elec, Tech) charge ▷ vt (also: **~ up**): **to ~ (with)** (lorry, ship) charger (de); (gun, camera) charger (avec); (Comput) charger; **a ~ of, ~s of** (fig) un or des tas de, des masses de; **to talk a ~ of rubbish** (inf) dire des bêtises; **loaded** adj (dice) pipé(e); (question) insidieux(-euse); (inf: rich) bourré(e) de fric

loaf (pl **loaves**) [ləuf, ləuvz] n pain m, miche f ▷ vi (also: **~ about, ~ around**) fainéanter, traîner

loan [ləun] n prêt m ▷ vt prêter; **on ~** prêté(e), en prêt

loathe [ləuð] vt détester, avoir en horreur

loaves [ləuvz] npl of **loaf**

lobby ['lɔbɪ] n hall m, entrée f; (Pol) groupe m de pression, lobby m ▷ vt faire pression sur

lobster ['lɔbstə'] n homard m

local ['ləukl] adj local(e) ▷ n (BRIT: pub) pub m or café m du coin; **the locals** npl les gens mpl du pays or du coin; **local anaesthetic** n anesthésie locale; **local authority** n collectivité locale, municipalité f; **local government** n administration locale or municipale; **locally** ['ləukəlɪ] adv localement; dans les environs or la région

locate [ləu'keɪt] vt (find) trouver, repérer; (situate) situer; **to be ~d in** être situé e or en

location [ləu'keɪʃən] n emplacement m; **on ~** (Cine) en extérieur

▮ Be careful not to translate location by the French word **location**.

loch [lɔx] n lac m, loch m

lock [lɔk] n (of door, box) serrure f; (of canal) écluse f; (of hair) mèche f, boucle f ▷ vt (with key) fermer à clé ▷ vi (door etc) fermer à clé; (wheels) se bloquer; **lock in** vt enfermer; **lock out** vt enfermer dehors; (on purpose) mettre à la porte; **lock up** vt (person) enfermer; (house) fermer à clé ▷ vi tout fermer (à clé)

locker ['lɔkə'] n casier m; (in station) consigne

f automatique; **locker-room** (US) n (Sport) vestiaire m

locksmith ['lɔksmɪθ] n serrurier m

locomotive [ləukə'məutɪv] n locomotive f

locum ['ləukəm] n (Med) suppléant(e) de médecin etc

lodge [lɔdʒ] n pavillon m (de gardien); (also: **hunting ~**) pavillon de chasse ▷ vi (person): **to ~ with** être logé(e) chez, être en pension chez; (bullet) se loger ▷ vt (appeal etc) présenter; déposer; **to ~ a complaint** porter plainte; **lodger** n locataire m/f; (with room and meals) pensionnaire m/f

lodging ['lɔdʒɪŋ] n logement m

loft [lɔft] n grenier m; (apartment) grenier aménagé en appartement (gén dans ancien entrepôt ou fabrique)

log [lɔg] n (of wood) bûche f; (Naut) livre m or journal m de bord; (of car) ≈ carte grise ▷ vt enregistrer; **log in, log on** vi (Comput) ouvrir une session, entrer dans le système; **log off, log out** vi (Comput) clore une session, sortir du système

logic ['lɔdʒɪk] n logique f; **logical** adj logique

logo ['ləugəu] n logo m

Loire [lwa:] n: **the (River) ~** la Loire

lollipop ['lɔlɪpɔp] n sucette f; **lollipop man/ lady** (BRIT: irreg) n contractuel qui fait traverser la rue aux enfants

lolly ['lɔlɪ] n (inf: ice) esquimau m; (: lollipop) sucette f

London ['lʌndən] n Londres; **Londoner** n Londonien(ne)

lone [ləun] adj solitaire

loneliness ['ləunlɪnɪs] n solitude f, isolement m

lonely ['ləunlɪ] adj seul(e); (childhood etc) solitaire; (place) solitaire, isolé(e)

long [lɔŋ] adj long (longue) ▷ adv longtemps ▷ vi: **to ~ for sth/to do sth** avoir très envie de qch/de faire qch, attendre qch avec impatience/attendre avec impatience de faire qch; **how ~ is this river/course?** quelle est la longueur de ce fleuve/la durée de ce cours?; **6 metres ~** (long) de 6 mètres; **6 months ~** qui dure 6 mois, de 6 mois; **all night ~** toute la nuit; **he no ~er comes** il ne vient plus; **I can't stand it any ~er** je ne peux plus le supporter; **~ before** longtemps avant; **before ~** (+ future) avant peu, dans peu de temps; (+ past) peu de temps après; **don't be ~!** fais vite!, dépêche-toi!; **I shan't be ~** je n'en ai pas pour longtemps; **at ~ last** enfin; **so** or **as ~ as** à condition que + sub; **long-distance** adj (race) de fond; (call) interurbain(e); **long-haul** adj (flight) long-courrier; **longing** n désir m, envie f; (nostalgia) nostalgie f ▷ adj plein(e) d'envie or de nostalgie

longitude ['lɔŋgɪtju:d] n longitude f

long: **long jump** n saut m en longueur; **long-life** adj (batteries etc) longue durée inv; (milk) longue conservation; **long-sighted** adj (BRIT) presbyte; (fig) prévoyant(e); **long-standing** adj de longue date; **long-term** adj à long terme

loo [lu:] n (BRIT inf) w.-c mpl, petit coin

look [luk] vi regarder; (seem) sembler, paraître, avoir l'air; (building etc): **to ~ south/on to the sea** donner au sud/sur la mer ▷ n regard m; (appearance) air m, allure f, aspect m; **looks** npl (good looks) physique m, beauté f; **to ~ like** ressembler à; **to have a ~** regarder; **to have a ~ at sth** jeter un coup d'œil à qch; **~ (here)!** (annoyance) écoutez!; **look after** vt fus s'occuper de; (luggage etc: watch over) garder, surveiller; **look around** vi regarder autour de soi; **look at** vt fus regarder; (problem etc) examiner; **look back** vi: **to ~ back to** sth/sb se retourner pour regarder qch/qn; **to ~ back on** (event, period) évoquer, repenser à; **look down on** vt fus (fig) regarder de haut, dédaigner; **look for** vt fus chercher; **we're ~ing for a hotel/restaurant** nous cherchons un hôtel/restaurant; **look forward to** vt fus attendre avec impatience; **~ing forward to hearing from you** (in letter) dans l'attente de vous lire; **look into** vt fus (matter, possibility) examiner, étudier; **look out** vi (beware): **to ~ out (for)** prendre garde (à), faire attention (à); **~ out!** attention!; **look out for** vt fus (seek) être à la recherche de; (try to spot) guetter; **look round** vt fus (house, shop) faire le tour de ▷ vi (turn) regarder derrière soi, se retourner; **look through** vt fus (papers, book) examiner; (: briefly) parcourir; **look up** vi lever les yeux; (improve) s'améliorer ▷ vt (word) chercher; **look up to** vt fus avoir du respect pour; **lookout** n (tower etc) poste m de guet; (person) guetteur m; **to be on the lookout (for)** guetter

loom [lu:m] vi (also: **~ up**) surgir; (event) paraître imminent(e); (threaten) menacer

loony ['lu:nɪ] adj, n (inf) timbré(e), cinglé(e) m/f

loop [lu:p] n boucle f ▷ vt: **to ~ sth round sth** passer qch autour de qch; **loophole** n (fig) porte f de sortie; échappatoire f

loose [lu:s] adj (knot, screw) desserré(e); (clothes) vague, ample, lâche; (hair) dénoué(e), épars(e); (not firmly fixed) pas solide; (morals, discipline) relâché(e); (translation) approximatif(-ive) ▷ n: **to be on the ~** être en liberté; **~ connection** (Elec) mauvais contact; **to be at a ~ end** or (US) **at ~ ends** (fig) ne pas trop savoir quoi faire; **loosely** adv sans serrer; (imprecisely) approximativement; **loosen** vt desserrer, relâcher, défaire

loot [lu:t] n butin m ▷ vt piller

lop-sided ['lɒp'saɪdɪd] *adj* de travers, asymétrique

lord [lɔːd] *n* seigneur *m*; **L~ Smith** lord Smith; **the L~** (*Rel*) le Seigneur; **my L~** (*to noble*) Monsieur le comte/le baron; (*to judge*) Monsieur le juge; (*to bishop*) Monseigneur; **good L~!** mon Dieu!; **Lords** *npl* (BRIT: *Pol*): **the (House of) Lords** (BRIT) la Chambre des Lords

lorry ['lɒrɪ] *n* (BRIT) camion *m*; **lorry driver** *n* (BRIT) camionneur *m*, routier *m*

lose (*pt, pp* **lost**) [luːz, lɒst] *vt* perdre ▷ *vi* perdre; **I've lost my wallet/passport** j'ai perdu mon portefeuille/passeport; **to ~ (time)** (*clock*) retarder; **lose out** *vi* être perdant(e); **loser** *n* perdant(e)

loss [lɒs] *n* perte *f*; **to make a ~** enregistrer une perte; **to be at a ~** être perplexe *or* embarrassé(e)

lost [lɒst] *pt, pp of* **lose** ▷ *adj* perdu(e); **to get ~** *vi* se perdre; **I'm ~** je me suis perdu; **~ and found property** *n* (US) objets trouvés; **~ and found** *n* (US) (bureau *m* des) objets trouvés; **lost property** *n* (BRIT) objets trouvés; **lost property office** *or* **department** (bureau *m* des) objets trouvés

lot [lɒt] *n* (*at auctions, set*) lot *m*; (*destiny*) sort *m*, destinée *f*; **the ~** (*everything*) le tout; (*everyone*) tous *mpl*, toutes *fpl*; **a ~** beaucoup; **a ~ of** beaucoup de; **~s of** des tas de; **to draw ~s (for sth)** tirer (qch) au sort

lotion ['ləʊʃən] *n* lotion *f*

lottery ['lɒtərɪ] *n* loterie *f*

loud [laud] *adj* bruyant(e), sonore; (*voice*) fort(e); (*condemnation etc*) vigoureux(-euse); (*gaudy*) voyant(e), tapageur(-euse) ▷ *adv* (*speak etc*) fort; **out ~** tout haut; **loudly** *adv* fort, bruyamment; **loudspeaker** *n* haut-parleur *m*

lounge [laundʒ] *n* salon *m*; (*of airport*) salle *f*; (BRIT: *also*: **~ bar**) (salle de) café *or* bar *m* ▷ *vi* (*also*: **~ about** *or* **around**) se prélasser, paresser

louse (*pl* **lice**) [laus, laɪs] *n* pou *m*

lousy ['lauzɪ] (*inf*) *adj* (*bad quality*) infect(e), moche; **I feel ~** je suis mal fichu(e)

love [lʌv] *n* amour *m* ▷ *vt* aimer; (*caringly, kindly*) aimer beaucoup; **I ~ chocolate** j'adore le chocolat; **to ~ to do** aimer beaucoup *or* adorer faire; **"15 ~"** (*Tennis*) "15 à rien *or* zéro"; **to be/fall in ~ with** être/tomber amoureux(-euse) de; **to make ~** faire l'amour; **~ from Anne, ~, Anne** affectueusement, Anne; **I ~ you** je t'aime; **love affair** *n* liaison (amoureuse); **love life** *n* vie sentimentale

lovely ['lʌvlɪ] *adj* (*pretty*) ravissant(e); (*friend, wife*) charmant(e); (*holiday, surprise*) très agréable, merveilleux(-euse)

lover ['lʌvə^r] *n* amant *m*; (*person in love*) amoureux(-euse); (*amateur*): **a ~ of** un(e) ami(e) de, un(e) amoureux(-euse) de

loving ['lʌvɪŋ] *adj* affectueux(-euse), tendre, aimant(e)

low [ləu] *adj* bas (basse); (*quality*) mauvais(e), inférieur(e) ▷ *adv* bas ▷ *n* (*Meteorology*) dépression *f*; **to feel ~** se sentir déprimé(e); **he's very ~** (*ill*) il est bien bas *or* très affaibli; **to turn (down) ~** *vt* baisser; **to be ~ on** (*supplies etc*) être à court de; **to reach a new** *or* **an all-time ~** tomber au niveau le plus bas; **low-alcohol** *adj* à faible teneur en alcool, peu alcoolisé(e); **low-calorie** *adj* hypocalorique

lower ['ləuə^r] *adj* inférieur(e) ▷ *vt* baisser; (*resistance*) diminuer; **to ~ o.s. to** s'abaisser à

low-fat ['ləu'fæt] *adj* maigre

loyal ['lɔɪəl] *adj* loyal(e), fidèle; **loyalty** *n* loyauté *f*, fidélité *f*; **loyalty card** *n* carte *f* de fidélité

L.P. *n abbr* = **long-playing record**

L-plates ['ɛlpleɪts] *npl* (BRIT) plaques *fpl* (obligatoires) d'apprenti conducteur

Lt *abbr* (= *lieutenant*) Lt.

Ltd *abbr* (*Comm: company*: = *limited*) ≈ S.A.

luck [lʌk] *n* chance *f*; **bad ~** malchance *f*, malheur *m*; **good ~!** bonne chance!; **bad** *or* **hard** *or* **tough ~!** pas de chance!; **luckily** *adv* heureusement, par bonheur; **lucky** *adj* (*person*) qui a de la chance; (*coincidence*) heureux(-euse); (*number etc*) qui porte bonheur

lucrative ['luːkrətɪv] *adj* lucratif(-ive), rentable, qui rapporte

ludicrous ['luːdɪkrəs] *adj* ridicule, absurde

luggage ['lʌgɪdʒ] *n* bagages *mpl*; **our ~ hasn't arrived** nos bagages ne sont pas arrivés; **could you send someone to collect our ~?** pourriez-vous envoyer quelqu'un chercher nos bagages?; **luggage rack** *n* (*in train*) porte-bagages *m inv*; (: *on car*) galerie *f*

lukewarm ['luːkwɔːm] *adj* tiède

lull [lʌl] *n* accalmie *f*; (*in conversation*) pause *f* ▷ *vt*: **to ~ sb to sleep** bercer qn pour qu'il s'endorme; **to be ~ed into a false sense of security** s'endormir dans une fausse sécurité

lullaby ['lʌləbaɪ] *n* berceuse *f*

lumber ['lʌmbə^r] *n* (*wood*) bois *m* de charpente; (*junk*) bric-à-brac *m inv* ▷ *vt* (BRIT *inf*): **to ~ sb with sth/sb** coller *or* refiler qch/qn à qn

luminous ['luːmɪnəs] *adj* lumineux(-euse)

lump [lʌmp] *n* morceau *m*; (*in sauce*) grumeau *m*; (*swelling*) grosseur *f* ▷ *vt* (*also*: **~ together**) réunir, mettre en tas; **lump sum** *n* somme globale *or* forfaitaire; **lumpy** *adj* (*sauce*) qui a des grumeaux; (*bed*) défoncé(e), peu confortable

lunatic ['luːnətɪk] *n* fou (folle), dément(e) ▷ *adj* fou (folle), dément(e)

lunch [lʌntʃ] *n* déjeuner *m* ▷ *vi* déjeuner; **lunch break, lunch hour** *n* pause *f* de midi, heure *f* du déjeuner; **lunchtime** *n*: **it's**

lunchtime c'est l'heure du déjeuner
lung [lʌŋ] *n* poumon *m*
lure [luə^r] *n* (*attraction*) attrait *m*, charme *m*; (*in hunting*) appât *m*, leurre *m* ▷ *vt* attirer *or* persuader par la ruse
lurk [lə:k] *vi* se tapir, se cacher
lush [lʌʃ] *adj* luxuriant(e)
lust [lʌst] *n* (*sexual*) désir (sexuel); (*Rel*) luxure *f*; (*fig*): **~ for** soif *f* de
Luxembourg ['lʌksəmbə:g] *n* Luxembourg *m*
luxurious [lʌg'zjuəriəs] *adj* luxueux(-euse)
luxury ['lʌkʃəri] *n* luxe *m* ▷ *cpd* de luxe
Lycra® ['laɪkrə] *n* Lycra® *m*
lying ['laɪɪŋ] *n* mensonge(s) *m(pl)* ▷ *adj* (*statement, story*) mensonger(-ère), faux (fausse); (*person*) menteur(-euse)
Lyons ['ljɔ̃] *n* Lyon
lyrics ['lɪrɪks] *npl* (*of song*) paroles *fpl*

m. *abbr* (= metre) m; (= million) M; (= mile) mi
M.A. *n abbr* (*Scol*) = **Master of Arts**
ma [mɑ:] (*inf*) *n* maman *f*
mac [mæk] *n* (*BRIT*) imper(méable *m*) *m*
macaroni [mækə'rəunɪ] *n* macaronis *mpl*
Macedonia [mæsɪ'dəunɪə] *n* Macédoine *f*;
Macedonian [mæsɪ'dəunɪən] *adj* macédonien(ne) ▷ *n* Macédonien(ne); (*Ling*) macédonien *m*
machine [mə'ʃi:n] *n* machine *f* ▷ *vt* (*dress etc*) coudre à la machine; (*Tech*) usiner;
machine gun *n* mitrailleuse *f*; **machinery** *n* machinerie *f*, machines *fpl*; (*fig*) mécanisme(s) *m(pl)*; **machine washable** *adj* (*garment*) lavable en machine
macho ['mætʃəu] *adj* macho *inv*
mackerel ['mækrɪl] *n* (*pl inv*) maquereau *m*
mackintosh ['mækɪntəʃ] *n* (*BRIT*) imperméable *m*
mad [mæd] *adj* fou (folle); (*foolish*) insensé(e); (*angry*) furieux(-euse); **to be ~ (keen) about** *or* **on sth** (*inf*) être follement passionné de qch, être fou de qch
Madagascar [mædə'gæskə^r] *n* Madagascar *m*
madam ['mædəm] *n* madame *f*
mad cow disease *n* maladie *f* des vaches folles
made [meɪd] *pt, pp of* **make**; **made-to-measure** *adj* (*BRIT*) fait(e) sur mesure;

made-up ['meɪdʌp] *adj* (*story*) inventé(e), fabriqué(e)

madly ['mædlɪ] *adv* follement; **~ in love** éperdument amoureux(-euse)

madman ['mædmən] (*irreg*) *n* fou *m*, aliéné *m*

madness ['mædnɪs] *n* folie *f*

Madrid [mə'drɪd] *n* Madrid

Mafia ['mæfɪə] *n* maf(f)ia *f*

mag [mæg] *n abbr* (BRIT *inf*: = *magazine*) magazine *m*

magazine [mægə'ziːn] *n* (*Press*) magazine *m*, revue *f*; (*Radio, TV*) magazine

maggot ['mægət] *n* ver *m*, asticot *m*

magic ['mædʒɪk] *n* magie *f* ▷ *adj* magique; **magical** *adj* magique; (*experience, evening*) merveilleux(-euse); **magician** [mə'dʒɪʃən] *n* magicien(ne)

magistrate ['mædʒɪstreɪt] *n* magistrat *m*; juge *m*

magnet ['mægnɪt] *n* aimant *m*; **magnetic** [mæg'nɛtɪk] *adj* magnétique

magnificent [mæg'nɪfɪsnt] *adj* superbe, magnifique; (*splendid: robe, building*) somptueux(-euse), magnifique

magnify ['mægnɪfaɪ] *vt* grossir; (*sound*) amplifier; **magnifying glass** *n* loupe *f*

magpie ['mægpaɪ] *n* pie *f*

mahogany [mə'hɔgənɪ] *n* acajou *m*

maid [meɪd] *n* bonne *f*; (*in hotel*) femme *f* de chambre; **old ~** (*pej*) vieille fille

maiden name *n* nom *m* de jeune fille

mail [meɪl] *n* poste *f*; (*letters*) courrier *m* ▷ *vt* envoyer (par la poste); **by ~** par la poste; **mailbox** *n* (US: *also Comput*) boîte *f* aux lettres; **mailing list** *n* liste *f* d'adresses; **mailman** (*irreg*) *n* (US) facteur *m*; **mail-order** *n* vente *f* or achat *m* par correspondance

main [meɪn] *adj* principal(e) ▷ *n* (*pipe*) conduite principale, canalisation *f*; **the ~s** (*Elec*) le secteur; **the ~ thing** l'essentiel *m*; **in the ~** dans l'ensemble; **main course** *n* (*Culin*) plat *m* de résistance; **mainland** *n* continent *m*; **mainly** *adv* principalement, surtout; **main road** *n* grand axe, route nationale; **mainstream** *n* (*fig*) courant principal; **main street** *n* rue *f* principale

maintain [meɪn'teɪn] *vt* entretenir; (*continue*) maintenir, préserver; (*affirm*) soutenir; **maintenance** ['meɪntənəns] *n* entretien *m*; (*Law: alimony*) pension *f* alimentaire

maisonette [meɪzə'nɛt] *n* (BRIT) appartement *m* en duplex

maize [meɪz] *n* (BRIT) maïs *m*

majesty ['mædʒɪstɪ] *n* majesté *f*; (*title*): **Your M~** Votre Majesté

major ['meɪdʒəʳ] *n* (*Mil*) commandant *m* ▷ *adj* (*important*) important(e); (*most important*) principal(e); (*Mus*) majeur(e) ▷ *vi* (US *Scol*): **to ~ (in)** se spécialiser (en)

Majorca [mə'jɔːkə] *n* Majorque *f*

majority [mə'dʒɔrɪtɪ] *n* majorité *f*

make [meɪk] *vt* (*pt, pp* **made**) faire; (*manufacture*) faire, fabriquer; (*earn*) gagner; (*decision*) prendre; (*friend*) se faire; (*speech*) faire, prononcer; (*cause to be*): **to ~ sb sad** *etc* rendre qn triste *etc*; (*force*): **to ~ sb do sth** obliger qn à faire qch, faire faire qch à qn; (*equal*): **2 and 2 ~ 4** 2 et 2 font 4 ▷ *n* (*manufacture*) fabrication *f*; (*brand*) marque *f*; **to ~ the bed** faire le lit; **to ~ a fool of sb** (*ridicule*) ridiculiser qn; (*trick*) avoir *or* duper qn; **to ~ a profit** faire un *or* des bénéfice(s); **to ~ a loss** essuyer une perte; **to ~ it** (*in time etc*) y arriver; (*succeed*) réussir; **what time do you ~ it?** quelle heure avez-vous?; **I ~ it £249** d'après mes calculs ça fait 249 livres; **to be made of** être en; **to ~ do with** se contenter de; se débrouiller avec; **make off** *vi* filer; **make out** *vt* (*write out: cheque*) faire; (*decipher*) déchiffrer; (*understand*) comprendre; (*see*) distinguer; (*claim, imply*) prétendre, vouloir faire croire; **make up** *vt* (*invent*) inventer, imaginer; (*constitute*) constituer; (*parcel, bed*) faire ▷ *vi* se réconcilier; (*with cosmetics*) se maquiller, se farder; **to be made up of** se composer de; **make up for** *vt fus* compenser; (*lost time*) rattraper; **makeover** ['meɪkəuvəʳ] *n* (*by beautician*) soins *mpl* de maquillage; (*change of image*) changement *m* d'image; **maker** *n* fabricant *m*; (*of film, programme*) réalisateur(-trice); **makeshift** *adj* provisoire, improvisé(e); **make-up** *n* maquillage *m*

making ['meɪkɪŋ] *n* (*fig*): **in the ~** en formation *or* gestation; **to have the ~s of** (*actor, athlete*) avoir l'étoffe de

malaria [mə'lɛərɪə] *n* malaria *f*, paludisme *m*

Malaysia [mə'leɪzɪə] *n* Malaisie *f*

male [meɪl] *n* (*Biol, Elec*) mâle *m* ▷ *adj* (*sex, attitude*) masculin(e); (*animal*) mâle; (*child etc*) du sexe masculin

malicious [mə'lɪʃəs] *adj* méchant(e), malveillant(e)

> Be careful not to translate *malicious* by the French word *malicieux*.

malignant [mə'lɪgnənt] *adj* (*Med*) malin(-igne)

mall [mɔːl] *n* (*also:* **shopping ~**) centre commercial

mallet ['mælɪt] *n* maillet *m*

malnutrition [mælnjuːˈtrɪʃən] *n* malnutrition *f*

malpractice [mælˈpræktɪs] *n* faute professionnelle; négligence *f*

malt [mɔːlt] *n* malt *m* ▷ *cpd* (*whisky*) pur malt

Malta ['mɔːltə] *n* Malte *f*; **Maltese** [mɔːl'tiːz] *adj* maltais(e) ▷ *n* (*pl inv*) Maltais(e)

mammal ['mæml] *n* mammifère *m*

mammoth ['mæməθ] *n* mammouth *m* ▷ *adj* géant(e), monstre

man (pl **men**) [mæn, mɛn] n homme m;
(Sport) joueur m; (Chess) pièce f ▷ vt (Naut:
ship) garnir d'hommes; (machine) assurer le
fonctionnement de; (Mil: gun) servir; (: post)
être de service à; **an old ~** un vieillard; **~ and
wife** mari et femme

manage ['mænɪdʒ] vi se débrouiller; (succeed)
y arriver, réussir ▷ vt (business) gérer; (team,
operation) diriger; (control: ship) manier,
manœuvrer; (: person) savoir s'y prendre avec;
to ~ to do se débrouiller pour faire; (succeed)
réussir à faire; **manageable** adj maniable;
(task etc) faisable; (number) raisonnable;
management n (running) administration f,
direction f; (people in charge: of business, firm)
dirigeants mpl, cadres mpl; (: of hotel, shop,
theatre) direction f; **manager** n (of business)
directeur m; (of institution etc) administrateur
m; (of department, unit) responsable m/f, chef
m; (of hotel etc) gérant m; (Sport) manager
m; (of artist) impresario m; **manageress** n
directrice f; (of hotel etc) gérante f; **managerial**
[mænɪ'dʒɪərɪəl] adj directorial(e); (skills)
de cadre, de gestion; **managing director** n
directeur général

mandarin ['mændərɪn] n (also: **~ orange**)
mandarine f

mandate ['mændeɪt] n mandat m

mandatory ['mændətərɪ] adj obligatoire

mane [meɪn] n crinière f

maneuver [mə'nu:və'] (US) = **manoeuvre**

mangetout ['mɔnʒ'tu:] n mange-tout m inv

mango (pl **~es**) ['mæŋɡəu] n mangue f

man: manhole n trou m d'homme; **manhood**
n (age) âge m d'homme; (manliness) virilité f

mania ['meɪnɪə] n manie f; **maniac**
['meɪnɪæk] n maniaque m/f; (fig) fou (folle)

manic ['mænɪk] adj maniaque

manicure ['mænɪkjuə'] n manucure f

manifest ['mænɪfɛst] vt manifester ▷ adj
manifeste, évident(e)

manifesto [mænɪ'fɛstəu] n (Pol) manifeste m

manipulate [mə'nɪpjuleɪt] vt manipuler;
(system, situation) exploiter

man: mankind [mæn'kaɪnd] n humanité f,
genre humain; **manly** adj viril(e); **man-made**
adj artificiel(le); (fibre) synthétique

manner ['mænə'] n manière f, façon f;
(behaviour) attitude f, comportement m;
manners npl: (**good**) **~s** (bonnes) manières f;
bad ~s mauvaises manières; **all ~ of** toutes
sortes de

manoeuvre (US **maneuver**) [mə'nu:və'']
vt (move) manœuvrer; (manipulate: person)
manipuler; (: situation) exploiter ▷ n
manœuvre f

manpower ['mænpauə'] n main-d'œuvre f

mansion ['mænʃən] n château m, manoir m

manslaughter ['mænslɔːtə'] n homicide m

involontaire

mantelpiece ['mæntlpi:s] n cheminée f

manual ['mænjuəl] adj manuel(le) ▷ n
manuel m

manufacture [mænju'fæktʃə'] vt fabriquer
▷ n fabrication f; **manufacturer** n fabricant m

manure [mə'njuə'] n fumier m; (artificial)
engrais m

manuscript ['mænjuskrɪpt] n manuscrit m

many ['mɛnɪ] adj beaucoup de, de
nombreux(-euses) ▷ pron beaucoup, un grand
nombre; **a great ~** un grand nombre (de); **~ a ...**
bien des ..., plus d'un(e) ...

map [mæp] n carte f; (of town) plan m; **can
you show it to me on the ~?** pouvez-vous me
l'indiquer sur la carte?; **map out** vt tracer; (fig:
task) planifier

maple ['meɪpl] n érable m

Mar abbr = **March**

mar [mɑː'] vt gâcher, gâter

marathon ['mærəθən] n marathon m

marble ['mɑːbl] n marbre m; (toy) bille f

March [mɑːtʃ] n mars m

march [mɑːtʃ] vi marcher au pas;
(demonstrators) défiler ▷ n marche f;
(demonstration) manifestation f

mare [mɛə'] n jument f

margarine [mɑːdʒə'ri:n] n margarine f

margin ['mɑːdʒɪn] n marge f; **marginal**
adj marginal(e); **marginal seat** (Pol) siège
disputé; **marginally** adv très légèrement,
sensiblement

marigold ['mærɪɡəuld] n souci m

marijuana [mærɪ'wɑːnə] n marijuana f

marina [mə'ri:nə] n marina f

marinade n [mærɪ'neɪd] marinade f

marinate ['mærɪneɪt] vt (faire) mariner

marine [mə'ri:n] adj marin(e) ▷ n fusilier
marin; (US) marine m

marital ['mærɪtl] adj matrimonial(e); **marital
status** n situation f de famille

maritime ['mærɪtaɪm] adj maritime

marjoram ['mɑːdʒərəm] n marjolaine f

mark [mɑːk] n marque f; (of skid etc) trace
f; (BRIT Scol) note f; (oven temperature): (**gas**)
~ 4 thermostat m 4 ▷ vt (also Sport: player)
marquer; (stain) tacher; (BRIT Scol) corriger,
noter; **to ~ time** marquer le pas; **marked** adj
(obvious) marqué(e), net(te); **marker** n (sign)
jalon m; (bookmark) signet m

market ['mɑːkɪt] n marché m ▷ vt (Comm)
commercialiser; **marketing** n marketing m;
marketplace n place f du marché; (Comm)
marché m; **market research** n étude f de
marché

marmalade ['mɑːməleɪd] n confiture f
d'oranges

maroon [mə'ru:n] vt: **to be ~ed** être
abandonné(e); (fig) être bloqué(e) ▷ adj

(*colour*) bordeaux *inv*

marquee [mɑːˈkiː] *n* chapiteau *m*

marriage [ˈmærɪdʒ] *n* mariage *m*; **marriage certificate** *n* extrait *m* d'acte de mariage

married [ˈmærɪd] *adj* marié(e); (*life, love*) conjugal(e)

marrow [ˈmærəʊ] *n* (*of bone*) moelle *f*; (*vegetable*) courge *f*

marry [ˈmærɪ] *vt* épouser, se marier avec; (*subj: father, priest etc*) marier ▷ *vi* (*also*: **get married**) se marier

Mars [mɑːz] *n* (*planet*) Mars *f*

Marseilles [mɑːˈseɪ] *n* Marseille

marsh [mɑːʃ] *n* marais *m*, marécage *m*

marshal [ˈmɑːʃl] *n* maréchal *m*; (*us: fire, police*) ≈ capitaine *m*; (*for demonstration, meeting*) membre *m* du service d'ordre ▷ *vt* rassembler

martyr [ˈmɑːtəʳ] *n* martyr(e)

marvel [ˈmɑːvl] *n* merveille *f* ▷ *vi*: **to ~ (at)** s'émerveiller (de); **marvellous** (*us* **marvelous**) *adj* merveilleux(-euse)

Marxism [ˈmɑːksɪzəm] *n* marxisme *m*

Marxist [ˈmɑːksɪst] *adj*, *n* marxiste (*m/f*)

marzipan [ˈmɑːzɪpæn] *n* pâte *f* d'amandes

mascara [mæsˈkɑːrə] *n* mascara *m*

mascot [ˈmæskət] *n* mascotte *f*

masculine [ˈmæskjʊlɪn] *adj* masculin(e) ▷ *n* masculin *m*

mash [mæʃ] *vt* (*Culin*) faire une purée de; **mashed potato(es)** *n(pl)* purée *f* de pommes de terre

mask [mɑːsk] *n* masque *m* ▷ *vt* masquer

mason [ˈmeɪsn] *n* (*also*: **stone~**) maçon *m*; (*also*: **free~**) franc-maçon *m*; **masonry** *n* maçonnerie *f*

mass [mæs] *n* multitude *f*, masse *f*; (*Physics*) masse; (*Rel*) messe *f* ▷ *cpd* (*communication*) de masse; (*unemployment*) massif(-ive) ▷ *vi* se masser; **masses** *npl*: **the ~es** les masses; **~es of** (*inf*) des tas de

massacre [ˈmæsəkəʳ] *n* massacre *m*

massage [ˈmæsɑːʒ] *n* massage *m* ▷ *vt* masser

massive [ˈmæsɪv] *adj* énorme, massif(-ive)

mass media *npl* mass-media *mpl*

mass-produce [ˈmæsprəˈdjuːs] *vt* fabriquer en série

mast [mɑːst] *n* mât *m*; (*Radio, TV*) pylône *m*

master [ˈmɑːstəʳ] *n* maître *m*; (*in secondary school*) professeur *m*; (*in primary school*) instituteur *m*; (*title for boys*): **M~ X** Monsieur X ▷ *vt* maîtriser; (*learn*) apprendre à fond; **M~ of Arts/Science (MA/MSc)** *n* ≈ titulaire *m/f* d'une maîtrise (en lettres/science); **M~ of Arts/Science degree (MA/MSc)** *n* ≈ maîtrise *f*; **mastermind** *n* esprit supérieur ▷ *vt* diriger, être le cerveau de; **masterpiece** *n* chef-d'œuvre *m*

masturbate [ˈmæstəbeɪt] *vi* se masturber

mat [mæt] *n* petit tapis; (*also*: **door~**)

paillasson *m*; (*also*: **table~**) set *m* de table ▷ *adj* = **matt**

match [mætʃ] *n* allumette *f*; (*game*) match *m*, partie *f*; (*fig*) égal(e) ▷ *vt* (*also*: **~ up**) assortir; (*go well with*) aller bien avec, s'assortir à; (*equal*) égaler, valoir ▷ *vi* être assorti(e); **to be a good ~** être bien assorti(e); **matchbox** *n* boîte *f* d'allumettes; **matching** *adj* assorti(e)

mate [meɪt] *n* (*inf*) copain (copine); (*animal*) partenaire *m/f*, mâle (femelle); (*in merchant navy*) second *m* ▷ *vi* s'accoupler

material [məˈtɪərɪəl] *n* (*substance*) matière *f*, matériau *m*; (*cloth*) tissu *m*, étoffe *f*; (*information, data*) données *fpl* ▷ *adj* matériel(le); (*relevant: evidence*) pertinent(e); **materials** *npl* matériaux *mpl*

materialize [məˈtɪərɪəlaɪz] *vi* se matérialiser, se réaliser

maternal [məˈtəːnl] *adj* maternel(le)

maternity [məˈtəːnɪtɪ] *n* maternité *f*; **maternity hospital** *n* maternité *f*; **maternity leave** *n* congé *m* de maternité

math [mæθ] *n* (*us*: = *mathematics*) maths *fpl*

mathematical [mæθəˈmætɪkl] *adj* mathématique

mathematician [mæθəməˈtɪʃən] *n* mathématicien(ne)

mathematics [mæθəˈmætɪks] *n* mathématiques *fpl*

maths [mæθs] *n abbr* (*BRIT*: = *mathematics*) maths *fpl*

matinée [ˈmætɪneɪ] *n* matinée *f*

matron [ˈmeɪtrən] *n* (*in hospital*) infirmière-chef *f*; (*in school*) infirmière *f*

matt [mæt] *adj* mat(e)

matter [ˈmætəʳ] *n* question *f*; (*Physics*) matière *f*, substance *f*; (*Med: pus*) pus *m* ▷ *vi* importer; **matters** *npl* (*affairs, situation*) la situation; **it doesn't ~** cela n'a pas d'importance; (*I don't mind*) cela ne fait rien; **what's the ~?** qu'est-ce qu'il y a?, qu'est-ce qui ne va pas?; **no ~ what** quoi qu'il arrive; **as a ~ of course** tout naturellement; **as a ~ of fact** en fait; **reading ~** (*BRIT*) de quoi lire, de la lecture

mattress [ˈmætrɪs] *n* matelas *m*

mature [məˈtjʊəʳ] *adj* mûr(e); (*cheese*) fait(e); (*wine*) arrivé(e) à maturité ▷ *vi* mûrir; (*cheese, wine*) se faire; **mature student** *n* étudiant(e) plus âgé(e) que la moyenne; **maturity** *n* maturité *f*

maul [mɔːl] *vt* lacérer

mauve [məʊv] *adj* mauve

max *abbr* = **maximum**

maximize [ˈmæksɪmaɪz] *vt* (*profits etc, chances*) maximiser

maximum [ˈmæksɪməm] (*pl* **maxima**) *adj* maximum ▷ *n* maximum *m*

May [meɪ] *n* mai *m*

may [meɪ] (*conditional* **might**) *vi* (*indicating*

possibility): **he ~ come** il se peut qu'il vienne;
(*be allowed to*): **~ I smoke?** puis-je fumer?;
(*wishes*): **~ God bless you!** (que) Dieu vous
bénisse!; **you ~ as well go** vous feriez aussi
bien d'y aller

maybe ['meɪbiː] *adv* peut-être; **~ he'll ...** peut-
être qu'il ...

May Day *n* le Premier mai

mayhem ['meɪhɛm] *n* grabuge *m*

mayonnaise [meɪəˈneɪz] *n* mayonnaise *f*

mayor [mɛəʳ] *n* maire *m*; **mayoress** *n* (*female
mayor*) maire *m*; (*wife of mayor*) épouse *f* du
maire

maze [meɪz] *n* labyrinthe *m*, dédale *m*

MD *n abbr* (*Comm*) = **managing director**

me [miː] *pron* me, m' + *vowel or h mute*; (*stressed,
after prep*) moi; **it's me** c'est moi; **he heard me**
il m'a entendu; **give me a book** donnez-moi
un livre; **it's for me** c'est pour moi

meadow ['mɛdəʊ] *n* prairie *f*, pré *m*

meagre (*us* **meager**) ['miːgəʳ] *adj* maigre

meal [miːl] *n* repas *m*; (*flour*) farine *f*;
mealtime *n* heure *f* du repas

mean [miːn] *adj* (*with money*) avare, radin(e);
(*unkind*) mesquin(e), méchant(e); (*shabby*)
misérable; (*average*) moyen(ne) ▷ *vt* (*pt, pp* **~t**)
(*signify*) signifier, vouloir dire; (*refer to*) faire
allusion à, parler de; (*intend*): **to ~ to do** avoir
l'intention de faire ▷ *n* moyenne *f*; **means** *npl*
(*way, money*) moyens *mpl*; **by ~s of** (*instrument*)
au moyen de; **by all ~s** je vous en prie; **to be
~t for** être destiné(e) à; **do you ~ it?** vous êtes
sérieux?; **what do you ~?** que voulez-vous
dire?

meaning ['miːnɪŋ] *n* signification *f*, sens *m*;
meaningful *adj* significatif(-ive); (*relationship*)
valable; **meaningless** *adj* dénué(e) de sens

meant [mɛnt] *pt, pp of* **mean**

meantime ['miːntaɪm] *adv* (*also*: **in the ~**)
pendant ce temps

meanwhile ['miːnwaɪl] *adv* = **meantime**

measles ['miːzlz] *n* rougeole *f*

measure ['mɛʒəʳ] *vt, vi* mesurer ▷ *n* mesure *f*;
(*ruler*) règle (graduée)

measurements ['mɛʒəməntz] *npl* mesures
fpl; **chest/hip ~** tour *m* de poitrine/hanches

meat [miːt] *n* viande *f*; **I don't eat ~** je ne
mange pas de viande; **cold ~s** (*BRIT*) viandes
froides; **meatball** *n* boulette *f* de viande

Mecca ['mɛkə] *n* la Mecque

mechanic [mɪˈkænɪk] *n* mécanicien *m*; **can
you send a ~?** pouvez-vous nous envoyer un
mécanicien?; **mechanical** *adj* mécanique

mechanism ['mɛkənɪzəm] *n* mécanisme *m*

medal ['mɛdl] *n* médaille *f*; **medallist** (*us*
medalist) *n* (*Sport*) médaillé(e)

meddle ['mɛdl] *vi*: **to ~ in** se mêler de,
s'occuper de; **to ~ with** toucher à

media ['miːdɪə] *npl* media *mpl* ▷ *npl of*
medium

mediaeval [mɛdɪˈiːvl] *adj* = **medieval**

mediate ['miːdɪeɪt] *vi* servir d'intermédiaire

medical ['mɛdɪkl] *adj* médical(e) ▷ *n* (*also*:
~ examination) visite médicale; (*private*)
examen médical; **medical certificate** *n*
certificat médical

medicated ['mɛdɪkeɪtɪd] *adj* traitant(e),
médicamenteux(-euse)

medication [mɛdɪˈkeɪʃən] *n* (*drugs etc*)
médication *f*

medicine ['mɛdsɪn] *n* médecine *f*; (*drug*)
médicament *m*

medieval [mɛdɪˈiːvl] *adj* médiéval(e)

mediocre [miːdɪˈəʊkəʳ] *adj* médiocre

meditate ['mɛdɪteɪt] *vi*: **to ~ (on)** méditer
(sur)

meditation [mɛdɪˈteɪʃən] *n* méditation *f*

Mediterranean [mɛdɪtəˈreɪnɪən] *adj*
méditerranéen(ne); **the ~ (Sea)** la (mer)
Méditerranée

medium ['miːdɪəm] *adj* moyen(ne) ▷ *n*
(*pl* **media**: *means*) moyen *m*; (*pl* **~s**: *person*)
médium *m*; **the happy ~** le juste milieu;
medium-sized *adj* de taille moyenne;
medium wave *n* (*Radio*) ondes moyennes,
petites ondes

meek [miːk] *adj* doux (douce), humble

meet (*pt, pp* **met**) [miːt, mɛt] *vt* rencontrer;
(*by arrangement*) retrouver, rejoindre; (*for
the first time*) faire la connaissance de; (*go
and fetch*): **I'll ~ you at the station** j'irai
te chercher à la gare; (*opponent, danger,
problem*) faire face à; (*requirements*) satisfaire
à, répondre à ▷ *vi* (*friends*) se rencontrer; se
retrouver; (*in session*) se réunir; (*join: lines,
roads*) se joindre; **nice ~ing you** ravi d'avoir
fait votre connaissance; **meet up** *vi*: **to ~ up
with sb** rencontrer qn; **meet with** *vt fus*
(*difficulty*) rencontrer; **to ~ with success** être
couronné(e) de succès; **meeting** *n* (*of group of
people*) réunion *f*; (*between individuals*) rendez-
vous *m*; **she's at or in a meeting** (*Comm*) elle
est en réunion; **meeting place** *n* lieu *m* de (la)
réunion; (*for appointment*) lieu de rendez-vous

megabyte ['mɛgəbaɪt] *n* (*Comput*) mégaoctet *m*

megaphone ['mɛgəfəʊn] *n* porte-voix *m inv*

megapixel ['mɛgəpɪksl] *n* mégapixel *m*

melancholy ['mɛlənkəlɪ] *n* mélancolie *f* ▷ *adj*
mélancolique

melody ['mɛlədɪ] *n* mélodie *f*

melon ['mɛlən] *n* melon *m*

melt [mɛlt] *vi* fondre ▷ *vt* faire fondre

member ['mɛmbəʳ] *n* membre *m*; **Member
of Congress** (*us*) *n* membre *m* du Congrès,
≈ député *m*; **Member of Parliament (MP)** *n*
(*BRIT*) député *m*; **Member of the European
Parliament (MEP)** *n* Eurodéputé *m*;

Member of the House of Representatives (MHR) n (US) membre m de la Chambre des représentants; **Member of the Scottish Parliament (MSP)** n (BRIT) député m au Parlement écossais; **membership** n (becoming a member) adhésion f; admission f; (the members) membres mpl, adhérents mpl; **membership card** n carte f de membre

memento [mə'mɛntəu] n souvenir m

memo ['mɛməu] n note f (de service)

memorable ['mɛmərəbl] adj mémorable

memorandum (pl **memoranda**) [mɛmə'rændəm, -də] n note f (de service)

memorial [mɪ'mɔːrɪəl] n mémorial m ▷ adj commémoratif(-ive)

memorize ['mɛməraɪz] vt apprendre or retenir par cœur

memory ['mɛmərɪ] n (also Comput) mémoire f; (recollection) souvenir m; **in ~ of** à la mémoire de; **memory card** n (for digital camera) carte f mémoire

men [mɛn] npl of **man**

menace ['mɛnɪs] n menace f; (inf: nuisance) peste f, plaie f ▷ vt menacer

mend [mɛnd] vt réparer; (darn) raccommoder, repriser ▷ n: **on the ~** en voie de guérison; **to ~ one's ways** s'amender

meningitis [mɛnɪn'dʒaɪtɪs] n méningite f

menopause ['mɛnəupɔːz] n ménopause f

men's room n (US): **the men's room** les toilettes fpl pour hommes

menstruation [mɛnstru'eɪʃən] n menstruation f

menswear ['mɛnzwɛəʳ] n vêtements mpl d'hommes

mental ['mɛntl] adj mental(e); **mental hospital** n hôpital m psychiatrique; **mentality** [mɛn'tælɪtɪ] n mentalité f; **mentally** adv: **to be mentally handicapped** être handicapé(e) mental(e); **the mentally ill** les malades mentaux

menthol ['mɛnθɒl] n menthol m

mention ['mɛnʃən] n mention f ▷ vt mentionner, faire mention de; **don't ~ it!** je vous en prie, il n'y a pas de quoi!

menu ['mɛnjuː] n (set menu, Comput) menu m; (list of dishes) carte f; **could we see the ~?** est-ce qu'on peut voir la carte?

MEP n abbr = **Member of the European Parliament**

mercenary ['mɜːsɪnərɪ] adj (person) intéressé(e), mercenaire ▷ n mercenaire m

merchandise ['mɜːtʃəndaɪz] n marchandises fpl

merchant ['mɜːtʃənt] n négociant m, marchand m; **merchant bank** n (BRIT) banque f d'affaires; **merchant navy** (US **merchant marine**) n marine marchande

merciless ['mɜːsɪlɪs] adj impitoyable, sans pitié

mercury ['mɜːkjurɪ] n mercure m

mercy ['mɜːsɪ] n pitié f, merci f; (Rel) miséricorde f; **at the ~ of** à la merci de

mere [mɪəʳ] adj simple; (chance) pur(e); **a ~ two hours** seulement deux heures; **merely** adv simplement, purement

merge [mɜːdʒ] vt unir; (Comput) fusionner, interclasser ▷ vi (colours, shapes, sounds) se mêler; (roads) se joindre; (Comm) fusionner; **merger** n (Comm) fusion f

meringue [mə'ræŋ] n meringue f

merit ['mɛrɪt] n mérite m, valeur f ▷ vt mériter

mermaid ['mɜːmeɪd] n sirène f

merry ['mɛrɪ] adj gai(e); **M~ Christmas!** joyeux Noël!; **merry-go-round** n manège m

mesh [mɛʃ] n mailles fpl

mess [mɛs] n désordre m, fouillis m, pagaille f; (muddle: of life) gâchis m; (: of economy) pagaille f; (dirt) saleté f; (Mil) mess m, cantine f; **to be (in) a ~** être en désordre; **to be/get o.s. in a ~** (fig) être/se mettre dans le pétrin; **mess about** or **around** (inf) vi perdre son temps; **mess up** vt (dirty) salir; (spoil) gâcher; **mess with** (inf) vt fus (challenge, confront) se frotter à; (interfere with) toucher à

message ['mɛsɪdʒ] n message m; **can I leave a ~?** est-ce que je peux laisser un message?; **are there any ~s for me?** est-ce que j'ai des messages?

messenger ['mɛsɪndʒəʳ] n messager m

Messrs, Messrs. ['mɛsəz] abbr (on letters: = messieurs) MM

messy ['mɛsɪ] adj (dirty) sale; (untidy) en désordre

met [mɛt] pt, pp of **meet**

metabolism [mɛ'tæbəlɪzəm] n métabolisme m

metal ['mɛtl] n métal m ▷ cpd en métal; **metallic** [mɛ'tælɪk] adj métallique

metaphor ['mɛtəfəʳ] n métaphore f

meteor ['miːtɪəʳ] n météore m; **meteorite** ['miːtɪəraɪt] n météorite m or f

meteorology [miːtɪə'rɒlədʒɪ] n météorologie f

meter ['miːtəʳ] n (instrument) compteur m; (also: **parking ~**) parc(o)mètre m; (US: unit) = **metre** ▷ vt (US Post) affranchir à la machine

method ['mɛθəd] n méthode f; **methodical** [mɪ'θɒdɪkl] adj méthodique

methylated spirit ['mɛθɪleɪtɪd-] n (BRIT: also: **meths**) alcool m à brûler

meticulous [mɛ'tɪkjuləs] adj méticuleux(-euse)

metre (US **meter**) ['miːtəʳ] n mètre m

metric ['mɛtrɪk] adj métrique

metro ['mɛtrəu] n métro m

metropolitan [mɛtrə'pɒlɪtən] adj métropolitain(e); **the M~ Police** (BRIT) la police londonienne

Mexican ['mɛksɪkən] adj mexicain(e) ▷ n Mexicain(e)

Mexico ['mɛksɪkəʊ] n Mexique m

mg abbr (= milligram) mg

mice [maɪs] npl of **mouse**

micro... [maɪkrəʊ] prefix: **microchip** n (Elec) puce f; **microphone** n microphone m; **microscope** n microscope m; **microwave** n (also: **microwave oven**) four m à micro-ondes

mid [mɪd] adj: **~ May** la mi-mai; **~ afternoon** le milieu de l'après-midi; **in ~ air** en plein ciel; **he's in his ~ thirties** il a dans les trente-cinq ans; **midday** n midi m

middle ['mɪdl] n milieu m; (waist) ceinture f, taille f ▷ adj du milieu; (average) moyen(ne); **in the ~ of the night** au milieu de la nuit; **middle-aged** adj d'un certain âge, ni vieux ni jeune; **Middle Ages** npl: **the Middle Ages** le moyen âge; **middle-class** adj bourgeois(e); **middle class(es)** n(pl): **the middle class(es)** ≈ les classes moyennes; **Middle East** n: **the Middle East** le Proche-Orient, le Moyen-Orient; **middle name** n second prénom; **middle school** n (us) école pour les enfants de 12 à 14 ans, ≈ collège m; (BRIT) école pour les enfants de 8 à 14 ans

midge [mɪdʒ] n moucheron m

midget ['mɪdʒɪt] n nain(e)

midnight ['mɪdnaɪt] n minuit m

midst [mɪdst] n: **in the ~ of** au milieu de

midsummer [mɪd'sʌmər] n milieu m de l'été

midway [mɪd'weɪ] adj, adv: **~ (between)** à mi-chemin (entre); **~ through ...** au milieu de ..., en plein(e) ...

midweek [mɪd'wiːk] adv au milieu de la semaine, en pleine semaine

midwife (pl **midwives**) ['mɪdwaɪf, -vz] n sage-femme f

midwinter [mɪd'wɪntər] n milieu m de l'hiver

might [maɪt] vb see **may** ▷ n puissance f, force f; **mighty** adj puissant(e)

migraine ['miːɡreɪn] n migraine f

migrant ['maɪɡrənt] n (bird, animal) migrateur m; (person) migrant(e) ▷ adj migrateur(-trice); migrant(e); (worker) saisonnier(-ière)

migrate [maɪ'ɡreɪt] vi migrer

migration [maɪ'ɡreɪʃən] n migration f

mike [maɪk] n abbr (= microphone) micro m

mild [maɪld] adj doux (douce), (reproach, infection) léger(-ère); (illness) bénin(-igne); (interest) modéré(e); (taste) peu relevé(e); **mildly** ['maɪldlɪ] adv doucement; légèrement; **to put it mildly** (inf) c'est le moins qu'on puisse dire

mile [maɪl] n mil(l)e m (=1609 m); **mileage** n distance f en milles, ≈ kilométrage m; **mileometer** [maɪ'lɒmɪtər] n compteur m kilométrique; **milestone** n borne f; (fig)

jalon m

military ['mɪlɪtərɪ] adj militaire

militia [mɪ'lɪʃə] n milice f

milk [mɪlk] n lait m ▷ vt (cow) traire; (fig: person) dépouiller, plumer; (: situation) exploiter à fond; **milk chocolate** n chocolat m au lait; **milkman** (irreg) n laitier m; **milky** adj (drink) au lait; (colour) laiteux(-euse)

mill [mɪl] n moulin m; (factory) usine f, fabrique f; (spinning mill) filature f; (flour mill) minoterie f ▷ vt moudre, broyer ▷ vi (also: **~ about**) grouiller

millennium (pl **~s** or **millennia**) [mɪ'lɛnɪəm, -'lɛnɪə] n millénaire m

milli... ['mɪlɪ] prefix milli...; **milligram(me)** n milligramme m; **millilitre** (us **milliliter**) ['mɪlɪliːtər] n millilitre m; **millimetre** (us **millimeter**) n millimètre m

million ['mɪljən] n million m; **a ~ pounds** un million de livres sterling; **millionaire** [mɪljə'nɛər] n millionnaire m; **millionth** [-θ] num millionième

milometer [maɪ'lɒmɪtər] n = **mileometer**

mime [maɪm] n mime m ▷ vt, vi mimer

mimic ['mɪmɪk] n imitateur(-trice) ▷ vt, vi imiter, contrefaire

min. abbr (= minute(s)) mn.; (= minimum) min.

mince [mɪns] vt hacher ▷ n (BRIT Culin) viande hachée, hachis m; **mincemeat** n hachis de fruits secs utilisés en pâtisserie; (us) viande hachée, hachis m; **mince pie** n sorte de tarte aux fruits secs

mind [maɪnd] n esprit m ▷ vt (attend to, look after) s'occuper de; (be careful) faire attention à; (object to): **I don't ~ the noise** je ne crains pas le bruit, le bruit ne me dérange pas; **it is on my ~** cela me préoccupe; **to change one's ~** changer d'avis; **to my ~** à mon avis, selon moi; **to bear sth in ~** tenir compte de qch; **to have sb/sth in ~** avoir qn/qch en tête; **to make up one's ~** se décider; **do you ~ if ...?** est-ce que cela vous gêne si ...?; **I don't ~** cela ne me dérange pas; (don't care) ça m'est égal; **~ you, ...** remarquez, ...; **never ~** peu importe, ça ne fait rien; (don't worry) ne vous en faîtes pas; "**~ the step**" "attention à la marche"; **mindless** adj irréfléchi(e); (violence, crime) insensé(e); (boring: job) idiot(e)

mine[1] [maɪn] pron le (la) mien(ne), les miens (miennes); **a friend of ~** un de mes amis, un ami à moi; **this book is ~** ce livre est à moi

mine[2] [maɪn] n mine f ▷ vt (coal) extraire; (ship, beach) miner; **minefield** n champ m de mines; **miner** n mineur m

mineral ['mɪnərəl] adj minéral(e) ▷ n minéral m; **mineral water** n eau minérale

mingle ['mɪŋɡl] vi: **to ~ with** se mêler à

miniature ['mɪnətʃər] adj (en) miniature ▷ n miniature f

minibar ['mɪnɪbɑːʳ] n minibar m
minibus ['mɪnɪbʌs] n minibus m
minicab ['mɪnɪkæb] n (BRIT) taxi m
indépendant
minimal ['mɪnɪml] adj minimal(e)
minimize ['mɪnɪmaɪz] vt (reduce) réduire au
minimum; (play down) minimiser
minimum ['mɪnɪməm] n (pl **minima**)
minimum m ▷ adj minimum
mining ['maɪnɪŋ] n exploitation minière
miniskirt ['mɪnɪskəːt] n mini-jupe f
minister ['mɪnɪstəʳ] n (BRIT Pol) ministre m;
(Rel) pasteur m
ministry ['mɪnɪstrɪ] n (BRIT Pol) ministère m;
(Rel): **to go into the ~** devenir pasteur
minor ['maɪnəʳ] adj petit(e), de peu
d'importance; (Mus, poet, problem) mineur(e)
▷ n (Law) mineur(e)
minority [maɪ'nɔrɪtɪ] n minorité f
mint [mɪnt] n (plant) menthe f; (sweet) bonbon
m à la menthe ▷ vt (coins) battre; **the (Royal)
M~**, **the (US) M~** = l'hôtel m de la Monnaie; **in ~
condition** à l'état de neuf
minus ['maɪnəs] n (also: **~ sign**) signe m moins
▷ prep moins; **12 – 6 equals 6** 12 moins 6 égal 6;
~ 24 °C moins 24 °C
minute¹ n ['mɪnɪt] minute f; **minutes** npl (of
meeting) procès-verbal m, compte rendu; **wait
a ~!** (attendez) un instant!; **at the last ~** à la
dernière minute
minute² adj [maɪ'njuːt] minuscule; (detailed)
minutieux(-euse); **in ~ detail** par le menu
miracle ['mɪrəkl] n miracle m
miraculous [mɪ'rækjuləs] adj
miraculeux(-euse)
mirage ['mɪrɑːʒ] n mirage m
mirror ['mɪrəʳ] n miroir m, glace f; (in car)
rétroviseur m
misbehave [mɪsbɪ'heɪv] vi mal se conduire
misc. abbr = **miscellaneous**
miscarriage ['mɪskærɪdʒ] n (Med) fausse
couche; **~ of justice** erreur f judiciaire
miscellaneous [mɪsɪ'leɪnɪəs] adj (items,
expenses) divers(es); (selection) varié(e)
mischief ['mɪstʃɪf] n (naughtiness) sottises
fpl; (playfulness) espièglerie f; (harm) mal m,
dommage m; (maliciousness) méchanceté f;
mischievous ['mɪstʃɪvəs] adj (playful,
naughty) coquin(e), espiègle
misconception ['mɪskən'sɛpʃən] n idée
fausse
misconduct [mɪs'kɔndʌkt] n inconduite f;
professional ~ faute professionnelle
miser ['maɪzəʳ] n avare m/f
miserable ['mɪzərəbl] adj (person, expression)
malheureux(-euse); (conditions) misérable;
(weather) maussade; (offer, donation) minable;
(failure) pitoyable
misery ['mɪzərɪ] n (unhappiness) tristesse f;

(pain) souffrances fpl; (wretchedness) misère f
misfortune [mɪs'fɔːtʃən] n malchance f,
malheur m
misgiving [mɪs'gɪvɪŋ] n (apprehension)
craintes fpl; **to have ~s about sth** avoir des
doutes quant à qch
misguided [mɪs'gaɪdɪd] adj malavisé(e)
mishap ['mɪshæp] n mésaventure f
misinterpret [mɪsɪn'təːprɪt] vt mal
interpréter
misjudge [mɪs'dʒʌdʒ] vt méjuger, se
méprendre sur le compte de
mislay [mɪs'leɪ] vt (irreg: like **lay**) égarer
mislead [mɪs'liːd] vt (irreg: like **lead**) induire
en erreur; **misleading** adj trompeur(-euse)
misplace [mɪs'pleɪs] vt égarer; **to be ~d** (trust
etc) être mal placé(e)
misprint ['mɪsprɪnt] n faute f d'impression
misrepresent [mɪsreprɪ'zɛnt] vt présenter
sous un faux jour
Miss [mɪs] n Mademoiselle
miss [mɪs] vt (fail to get, attend, see) manquer,
rater; (regret the absence of): **I ~ him/it** il/cela
me manque ▷ vi manquer ▷ n (shot) coup
manqué; **we ~ed our train** nous avons raté
notre train; **you can't ~ it** vous ne pouvez
pas vous tromper; **miss out** vt (BRIT) oublier;
miss out on vt fus (fun, party) rater, manquer;
(chance, bargain) laisser passer
missile ['mɪsaɪl] n (Aviat) missile m; (object
thrown) projectile m
missing ['mɪsɪŋ] adj manquant(e); (after
escape, disaster: person) disparu(e); **to go
~** disparaître; **~ in action** (Mil) porté(e)
disparu(e)
mission ['mɪʃən] n mission f; **on a ~ to sb**
en mission auprès de qn; **missionary** n
missionnaire m/f
misspell ['mɪs'spɛl] vt (irreg: like **spell**) mal
orthographier
mist [mɪst] n brume f ▷ vi (also: **~ over**, **~ up**)
devenir brumeux(-euse); (BRIT: windows)
s'embuer
mistake [mɪs'teɪk] n erreur f, faute f ▷ vt
(irreg: like **take**) (meaning) mal comprendre;
(intentions) se méprendre sur; **to ~ for** prendre
pour; **by ~** par erreur, par inadvertance;
to make a ~ (in writing) faire une faute; (in
calculating etc) faire une erreur; **there must be
some ~** il doit y avoir une erreur, se tromper;
mistaken pp of **mistake** ▷ adj (idea etc)
erroné(e); **to be mistaken** faire erreur, se
tromper
mister ['mɪstəʳ] n (inf) Monsieur m; see **Mr**
mistletoe ['mɪsltəu] n gui m
mistook [mɪs'tuk] pt of **mistake**
mistress ['mɪstrɪs] n maîtresse f; (BRIT: in
primary school) institutrice f; (: in secondary
school) professeur m

mistrust [mɪs'trʌst] vt se méfier de

misty ['mɪstɪ] adj brumeux(-euse); (glasses, window) embué(e)

misunderstand [mɪsʌndə'stænd] vt, vi (irreg: like **stand**) mal comprendre; **misunderstanding** n méprise f, malentendu m; **there's been a misunderstanding** il y a eu un malentendu

misunderstood [mɪsʌndə'stud] pt, pp of **misunderstand** ▷ adj (person) incompris(e)

misuse n [mɪs'juːs] mauvais emploi; (of power) abus m ▷ vt [mɪs'juːz] mal employer; abuser de

mitt(en) ['mɪt(n)] n moufle f; (fingerless) mitaine f

mix [mɪks] vt mélanger; (sauce, drink etc) préparer ▷ vi se mélanger; (socialize): **he doesn't ~ well** il est peu sociable ▷ n mélange m; **to ~ sth with sth** mélanger qch à qch; **cake ~** préparation f pour gâteau; **mix up** vt mélanger; (confuse) confondre; **to be ~ed up in sth** être mêlé(e) à qch ou impliqué(e) dans qch; **mixed** adj (feelings, reactions) contradictoire; (school, marriage) mixte; **mixed grill** n (BRIT) assortiment m de grillades; **mixed salad** n salade f de crudités; **mixed-up** adj (person) désorienté(e), embrouillé(e); **mixer** n (for food) batteur m, mixeur m; (drink) boisson gazeuse (servant à couper un alcool); (person): **he is a good mixer** il est très sociable; **mixture** n assortiment m, mélange m; (Med) préparation f; **mix-up** n: **there was a mix-up** il y a eu confusion

ml abbr (= millilitre(s)) ml

mm abbr (= millimetre) mm

moan [məun] n gémissement m ▷ vi gémir; (inf: complain): **to ~ (about)** se plaindre (de)

moat [məut] n fossé m, douves fpl

mob [mɔb] n foule f; (disorderly) cohue f ▷ vt assaillir

mobile ['məubaɪl] adj mobile ▷ n (Art) mobile m; **mobile home** n caravane f; **mobile phone** n téléphone portatif

mobility [məu'bɪlɪtɪ] n mobilité f

mobilize ['məubɪlaɪz] vt, vi mobiliser

mock [mɔk] vt ridiculiser; (laugh at) se moquer de ▷ adj faux (fausse); **mocks** npl (BRIT: Scol) examens blancs; **mockery** n moquerie f, raillerie f

mod cons ['mɔd'kɔnz] npl abbr (BRIT) = **modern conveniences**; see **convenience**

mode [məud] n mode m; (of transport) moyen m

model ['mɔdl] n modèle m; (person: for fashion) mannequin m; (: for artist) modèle ▷ vt (with clay etc) modeler ▷ vi travailler comme mannequin ▷ adj (railway: toy) modèle réduit inv; (child, factory) modèle; **to ~ clothes** présenter des vêtements; **to ~ o.s. on** imiter

modem ['məudɛm] n modem m

moderate adj ['mɔdərət] modéré(e); (amount, change) peu important(e) ▷ vb ['mɔdəreɪt] ▷ vi se modérer, se calmer ▷ vt modérer; **moderation** [mɔdə'reɪʃən] n modération f, mesure f; **in ~** à dose raisonnable, pris(e) or pratiqué(e) modérément

modern ['mɔdən] adj moderne; **modernize** vt moderniser; **modern languages** npl langues vivantes

modest ['mɔdɪst] adj modeste; **modesty** n modestie f

modification [mɔdɪfɪ'keɪʃən] n modification f

modify ['mɔdɪfaɪ] vt modifier

module ['mɔdjuːl] n module m

mohair ['məuhɛər] n mohair m

Mohammed [mə'hæmɛd] n Mahomet m

moist [mɔɪst] adj humide, moite; **moisture** ['mɔɪstʃər] n humidité f; (on glass) buée f; **moisturizer** ['mɔɪstʃəraɪzər] n crème hydratante

mold etc [məuld] (US) = **mould** etc

mole [məul] n (animal, spy) taupe f; (spot) grain m de beauté

molecule ['mɔlɪkjuːl] n molécule f

molest [məu'lɛst] vt (assault sexually) attenter à la pudeur de

molten ['məultən] adj fondu(e); (rock) en fusion

mom [mɔm] n (US) = **mum**

moment ['məumənt] n moment m, instant m; **at the ~** en ce moment; **momentarily** ['məuməntrɪlɪ] adv momentanément; (US: soon) bientôt; **momentary** adj momentané(e), passager(-ère); **momentous** [məu'mɛntəs] adj important(e), capital(e)

momentum [məu'mɛntəm] n élan m, vitesse acquise; (fig) dynamique f; **to gather ~** prendre de la vitesse; (fig) gagner du terrain

mommy ['mɔmɪ] n (US: mother) maman f

Mon abbr (= Monday) l.

Monaco ['mɔnəkəu] n Monaco f

monarch ['mɔnək] n monarque m; **monarchy** n monarchie f

monastery ['mɔnəstərɪ] n monastère m

Monday ['mʌndɪ] n lundi m

monetary ['mʌnɪtərɪ] adj monétaire

money ['mʌnɪ] n argent m; **to make ~** (person) gagner de l'argent; (business) rapporter; **money belt** n ceinture-portefeuille f; **money order** n mandat m

mongrel ['mʌŋgrəl] n (dog) bâtard m

monitor ['mɔnɪtər] n (TV, Comput) écran m, moniteur m ▷ vt contrôler; (foreign station) être à l'écoute de; (progress) suivre de près

monk [mʌŋk] n moine m

monkey ['mʌŋkɪ] n singe m

monologue ['mɔnəlɔg] n monologue m

monopoly [mə'nɔpəlɪ] n monopole m

monosodium glutamate [mɔnə'səudɪəm 'glu:təmeɪt] n glutamate m de sodium

monotonous [mə'nɔtənəs] adj monotone

monsoon [mɔn'su:n] n mousson f

monster ['mɔnstər] n monstre m

month [mʌnθ] n mois m; **monthly** adj mensuel(le) ▷ adv mensuellement

Montreal [mɔntrɪ'ɔ:l] n Montréal

monument ['mɔnjumənt] n monument m

mood [mu:d] n humeur f, disposition f; **to be in a good/bad ~** être de bonne/mauvaise humeur; **moody** adj (variable) d'humeur changeante, lunatique; (sullen) morose, maussade

moon [mu:n] n lune f; **moonlight** n clair m de lune

moor [muər] n lande f ▷ vt (ship) amarrer ▷ vi mouiller

moose [mu:s] n (pl inv) élan m

mop [mɔp] n balai m à laver; (for dishes) lavette f à vaisselle ▷ vt éponger, essuyer; **~ of hair** tignasse f; **mop up** vt éponger

mope [məup] vi avoir le cafard, se morfondre

moped ['məuped] n cyclomoteur m

moral ['mɔrl] adj moral(e) ▷ n morale f; **morals** npl moralité f

morale [mɔ'rɑ:l] n moral m

morality [mə'rælɪtɪ] n moralité f

morbid ['mɔ:bɪd] adj morbide

 KEYWORD

more [mɔ:ʳ] adj **1** (greater in number etc) plus (de), davantage (de); **more people/work (than)** plus de gens/de travail (que) **2** (additional) encore (de); **do you want (some) more tea?** voulez-vous encore du thé?; **is there any more wine?** reste-t-il du vin?; **I have no** or **I don't have any more money** je n'ai plus d'argent; **it'll take a few more weeks** ça prendra encore quelques semaines ▷ pron plus, davantage; **more than 10** plus de 10; **it cost more than we expected** cela a coûté plus cher que prévu; **I want more** j'en veux plus or davantage; **is there any more?** est-ce qu'il en reste?; **there's no more** il n'y en a plus; **a little more** un peu plus; **many/much more** beaucoup plus, bien davantage ▷ adv plus; **more dangerous/easily (than)** plus dangereux/facilement (que); **more and more expensive** de plus en plus cher; **more or less** plus ou moins; **more than ever** plus que jamais; **once more** encore une fois, une fois de plus

moreover [mɔ:'rəuvəʳ] adv de plus

morgue [mɔ:g] n morgue f

morning ['mɔ:nɪŋ] n matin m; (as duration) matinée f ▷ cpd matinal(e); (paper) du matin; **in the ~** le matin; **7 o'clock in the ~** 7 heures du matin; **morning sickness** n nausées matinales

Moroccan [mə'rɔkən] adj marocain(e) ▷ n Marocain(e)

Morocco [mə'rɔkəu] n Maroc m

moron ['mɔ:rɔn] n idiot(e), minus m/f

morphine ['mɔ:fi:n] n morphine f

morris dancing ['mɔrɪs-] n (BRIT) danses folkloriques anglaises

● **MORRIS DANCING**
●
● Le **Morris dancing** est une danse
● folklorique anglaise traditionnellement
● réservée aux hommes. Habillés tout
● en blanc et portant des clochettes, ils
● exécutent différentes figures avec des
● mouchoirs et de longs bâtons. Cette danse
● est très populaire dans les fêtes de village.

Morse [mɔ:s] n (also: **~ code**) morse m

mortal ['mɔ:tl] adj, n mortel(le)

mortar ['mɔ:təʳ] n mortier m

mortgage ['mɔ:gɪdʒ] n hypothèque f; (loan) prêt m (or crédit m) hypothécaire ▷ vt hypothéquer

mortician [mɔ:'tɪʃən] n (US) entrepreneur m de pompes funèbres

mortified ['mɔ:tɪfaɪd] adj mort(e) de honte

mortuary ['mɔ:tjuərɪ] n morgue f

mosaic [məu'zeɪɪk] n mosaïque f

Moscow ['mɔskəu] n Moscou

Moslem ['mɔzləm] adj, n = **Muslim**

mosque [mɔsk] n mosquée f

mosquito (pl **~es**) [mɔs'ki:təu] n moustique m

moss [mɔs] n mousse f

most [məust] adj (majority of) la plupart de; (greatest amount of) le plus de ▷ pron la plupart ▷ adv le plus; (very) très, extrêmement; **the ~** le plus; **~ fish** la plupart des poissons; **the ~ beautiful woman in the world** la plus belle femme du monde; **~ of** (with plural) la plupart de; (with singular) la plus grande partie de; **~ of them** la plupart d'entre eux; **~ of the time** la plupart du temps; **I saw ~** (a lot but not all) j'en ai vu la plupart; (more than anyone else) c'est moi qui en ai vu le plus; **at the (very) ~** au plus; **to make the ~ of** profiter au maximum de; **mostly** adv (chiefly) surtout, principalement; (usually) généralement

MOT n abbr (BRIT) = **Ministry of Transport**; **the ~ (test)** visite technique (annuelle) obligatoire des véhicules à moteur

motel [məu'tɛl] n motel m

moth [mɔθ] n papillon m de nuit; (in clothes)

mite f

mother ['mʌðə'] n mère f ▷ vt (pamper, protect) dorloter; **motherhood** n maternité f; **mother-in-law** n belle-mère f; **mother-of-pearl** n nacre f, **Mother's Day** n fête f des Mères; **mother-to-be** n future maman; **mother tongue** n langue maternelle

motif [məu'ti:f] n motif m

motion ['məuʃən] n mouvement m; (gesture) geste m; (at meeting) motion f ▷ vt, vi: **to ~ (to) sb to do** faire signe à qn de faire; **motionless** adj immobile, sans mouvement; **motion picture** n film m

motivate ['məutiveit] vt motiver

motivation [məuti'veiʃən] n motivation f

motive ['məutiv] n motif m, mobile m

motor ['məutə'] n moteur m; (BRIT inf: vehicle) auto f; **motorbike** n moto f; **motorboat** n bateau m à moteur; **motorcar** n (BRIT) automobile f; **motorcycle** n moto f; **motorcyclist** n motocycliste m/f; **motoring** (BRIT) n tourisme m automobile; **motorist** n automobiliste m/f; **motor racing** n (BRIT) course f automobile; **motorway** n (BRIT) autoroute f

motto (pl **~es**) ['mɔtəu] n devise f

mould (US **mold**) [məuld] n moule m; (mildew) moisissure f ▷ vt mouler, modeler; (fig) façonner; **mouldy** adj moisi(e); (smell) de moisi

mound [maund] n monticule m, tertre m

mount [maunt] n (hill) mont m, montagne f; (horse) monture f; (for picture) carton m de montage ▷ vt monter; (horse) monter à; (bike) monter sur; (picture) monter sur carton ▷ vi (inflation, tension) augmenter; **mount up** vi s'élever, monter; (bills, problems, savings) s'accumuler

mountain ['mauntin] n montagne f ▷ cpd de (la) montagne; **mountain bike** n VTT m, vélo m tout terrain; **mountaineer** n alpiniste m/f; **mountaineering** n alpinisme m; **mountainous** adj montagneux(-euse); **mountain range** n chaîne f de montagnes

mourn [mɔ:n] vt pleurer ▷ vi: **to ~ for sb** pleurer qn; **to ~ for sth** se lamenter sur qch; **mourner** n parent(e) or ami(e) du défunt; personne f en deuil or venue rendre hommage au défunt; **mourning** n deuil m; **in mourning** en deuil

mouse (pl **mice**) [maus, mais] n (also Comput) souris f; **mouse mat** n (Comput) tapis m de souris

moussaka [mu'sɑːkə] n moussaka f

mousse [mu:s] n mousse f

moustache (US **mustache**) [məs'tɑːʃ] n moustache(s) f(pl)

mouth [mauθ, pl -ðz] n bouche f; (of dog, cat) gueule f; (of river) embouchure f; (of hole,

cave) ouverture f; **mouthful** n bouchée f; **mouth organ** n harmonica m; **mouthpiece** n (of musical instrument) bec m, embouchure f; (spokesperson) porte-parole m inv; **mouthwash** n eau f dentifrice

move [mu:v] n (movement) mouvement m; (in game) coup m; (: turn to play) tour m; (change of house) déménagement m; (change of job) changement m d'emploi ▷ vt déplacer, bouger; (emotionally) émouvoir; (Pol: resolution etc) proposer ▷ vi (gen) bouger, remuer; (traffic) circuler; (also: **~ house**) déménager; (in game) jouer; **can you ~ your car, please?** pouvez-vous déplacer votre voiture, s'il vous plaît?; **to ~ sb to do sth** pousser or inciter qn à faire qch; **to get a ~ on** se dépêcher, se remuer; **move back** vi revenir, retourner; **move in** vi (to a house) emménager; (police, soldiers) intervenir; **move off** vi s'éloigner, s'en aller; **move on** vi se remettre en route; **move out** vi (of house) déménager; **move over** vi se pousser, se déplacer; **move up** vi avancer; (employee) avoir de l'avancement; (pupil) passer dans la classe supérieure; **movement** n mouvement m

movie ['mu:vi] n film m; **movies** npl: **the ~s** le cinéma; **movie theater** (US) n cinéma m

moving ['mu:viŋ] adj en mouvement; (touching) émouvant(e)

mow (pt **~ed**, pp **~ed** or **~n**) [məu, -d, -n] vt faucher; (lawn) tondre; **mower** n (also: **lawnmower**) tondeuse f à gazon

Mozambique [məuzəm'bi:k] n Mozambique m

MP n abbr (BRIT) = **Member of Parliament**

MP3 n mp3 m; **MP3 player** n lecteur m mp3

mpg n abbr = miles per gallon (30 mpg = 9,4 l. aux 100 km)

m.p.h. abbr = miles per hour (60 mph = 96 km/h)

Mr (US **Mr.**) ['mistə'] n: **Mr X** Monsieur X, M. X

Mrs (US **Mrs.**) ['misiz] n: **~ X** Madame X, Mme X

Ms (US **Ms.**) [miz] n (Miss or Mrs): **Ms X** Madame X, Mme X

MSP n abbr (= Member of the Scottish Parliament) député m au Parlement écossais

Mt abbr (Geo: = mount) Mt

much [mʌtʃ] adj beaucoup de ▷ adv, n or pron beaucoup; **we don't have ~ time** nous n'avons pas beaucoup de temps; **how ~ is it?** combien est-ce que ça coûte?; **it's not ~** ce n'est pas beaucoup; **too ~** trop (de); **so ~** tant (de); **I like it very/so ~** j'aime beaucoup/ tellement ça; **as ~ as** autant que; **that's ~ better** c'est beaucoup mieux

muck [mʌk] n (mud) boue f; (dirt) ordures fpl; **muck up** vt (inf: ruin) gâcher, esquinter; (: dirty) salir; (: exam, interview) se planter à; **mucky** adj (dirty) boueux(-euse), sale

mucus ['mju:kəs] n mucus m

mud [mʌd] n boue f

muddle ['mʌdl] *n* (*mess*) pagaille *f*, fouillis *m*; (*mix-up*) confusion *f* ▷ *vt* (*also*: **~ up**) brouiller, embrouiller; **to get in a ~** (*while explaining etc*) s'embrouiller

muddy ['mʌdɪ] *adj* boueux(-euse)

mudguard ['mʌdɡɑːd] *n* garde-boue *m inv*

muesli ['mjuːzlɪ] *n* muesli *m*

muffin ['mʌfɪn] *n* (*roll*) petit pain rond et plat; (*cake*) petit gâteau au chocolat ou aux fruits

muffled ['mʌfld] *adj* étouffé(e), voilé(e)

muffler ['mʌfləʳ] *n* (*scarf*) cache-nez *m inv*; (*us Aut*) silencieux *m*

mug [mʌɡ] *n* (*cup*) tasse *f* (*sans soucoupe*); (*: for beer*) chope *f*; (*inf: face*) bouille *f*; (*: fool*) poire *f* ▷ *vt* (*assault*) agresser; **mugger** ['mʌɡəʳ] *n* agresseur *m*; **mugging** *n* agression *f*

muggy ['mʌɡɪ] *adj* lourd(e), moite

mule [mjuːl] *n* mule *f*

multicoloured (*us* **multicolored**) ['mʌltɪkʌləd] *adj* multicolore

multimedia ['mʌltɪ'miːdɪə] *adj* multimédia *inv*

multinational [mʌltɪ'næʃənl] *n* multinationale *f* ▷ *adj* multinational(e)

multiple ['mʌltɪpl] *adj* multiple ▷ *n* multiple *m*; **multiple choice (test)** *n* QCM *m*, questionnaire *m* à choix multiple; **multiple sclerosis** [-sklɪ'rəʊsɪs] *n* sclérose *f* en plaques

multiplex (cinema) ['mʌltɪpleks-] *n* (*cinéma m*) multisalles *m*

multiplication [mʌltɪplɪ'keɪʃən] *n* multiplication *f*

multiply ['mʌltɪplaɪ] *vt* multiplier ▷ *vi* se multiplier

multistorey ['mʌltɪ'stɔːrɪ] *adj* (*brit: building*) à étages, à étages; (*: car park*) à étages *or* niveaux multiples

mum [mʌm] *n* (*brit*) maman *f* ▷ *adj*: **to keep ~** ne pas souffler mot

mumble ['mʌmbl] *vt*, *vi* marmotter, marmonner

mummy ['mʌmɪ] *n* (*brit: mother*) maman *f*; (*embalmed*) momie *f*

mumps [mʌmps] *n* oreillons *mpl*

munch [mʌntʃ] *vt*, *vi* mâcher

municipal [mjuː'nɪsɪpl] *adj* municipal(e)

mural ['mjʊərl] *n* peinture murale

murder ['məːdəʳ] *n* meurtre *m*, assassinat *m* ▷ *vt* assassiner; **murderer** *n* meurtrier *m*, assassin *m*

murky ['məːkɪ] *adj* sombre, ténébreux(-euse); (*water*) trouble

murmur ['məːməʳ] *n* murmure *m* ▷ *vt*, *vi* murmurer

muscle ['mʌsl] *n* muscle *m*; (*fig*) force *f*; **muscular** ['mʌskjʊləʳ] *adj* musculaire; (*person, arm*) musclé(e)

museum [mjuː'zɪəm] *n* musée *m*

mushroom ['mʌʃrum] *n* champignon *m* ▷ *vi*

(*fig*) pousser comme un (*or des*) champignon(s)

music ['mjuːzɪk] *n* musique *f*; **musical** *adj* musical(e); (*person*) musicien(ne) ▷ *n* (*show*) comédie musicale; **musical instrument** *n* instrument *m* de musique; **musician** [mjuː'zɪʃən] *n* musicien(ne)

Muslim ['mʌzlɪm] *adj*, *n* musulman(e)

muslin ['mʌzlɪn] *n* mousseline *f*

mussel ['mʌsl] *n* moule *f*

must [mʌst] *aux vb* (*obligation*): **I ~ do it** je dois le faire, il faut que je le fasse; (*probability*): **he ~ be there by now** il doit y être maintenant, il y est probablement maintenant; (*suggestion, invitation*): **you ~ come and see me** il faut que vous veniez me voir ▷ *n* nécessité *f*, impératif *m*; **it's a ~** c'est indispensable; **I ~ have made a mistake** j'ai dû me tromper

mustache ['mʌstæʃ] *n* (*us*) = **moustache**

mustard ['mʌstəd] *n* moutarde *f*

mustn't ['mʌsnt] = **must not**

mute [mjuːt] *adj*, *n* muet(te)

mutilate ['mjuːtɪleɪt] *vt* mutiler

mutiny ['mjuːtɪnɪ] *n* mutinerie *f* ▷ *vi* se mutiner

mutter ['mʌtəʳ] *vt*, *vi* marmonner, marmotter

mutton ['mʌtn] *n* mouton *m*

mutual ['mjuːtʃʊəl] *adj* mutuel(le), réciproque; (*benefit, interest*) commun(e)

muzzle ['mʌzl] *n* museau *m*; (*protective device*) muselière *f*; (*of gun*) gueule *f* ▷ *vt* museler

my [maɪ] *adj* mon (ma), mes *pl*; **my house/ car/gloves** ma maison/ma voiture/mes gants; **I've washed my hair/cut my finger** je me suis lavé les cheveux/coupé le doigt; **is this my pen or yours?** c'est mon stylo ou c'est le vôtre?

myself [maɪ'self] *pron* (*reflexive*) me; (*emphatic*) moi-même; (*after prep*) moi; *see also* **oneself**

mysterious [mɪs'tɪərɪəs] *adj* mystérieux(-euse)

mystery ['mɪstərɪ] *n* mystère *m*

mystical ['mɪstɪkl] *adj* mystique

mystify ['mɪstɪfaɪ] *vt* (*deliberately*) mystifier; (*puzzle*) ébahir

myth [mɪθ] *n* mythe *m*; **mythology** [mɪ'θɒlədʒɪ] *n* mythologie *f*

n

n/a *abbr* (= *not applicable*) n.a.

nag [næg] *vt* (*scold*) être toujours après, reprendre sans arrêt

nail [neɪl] *n* (*human*) ongle *m*; (*metal*) clou *m* ▷ *vt* clouer; **to ~ sth to sth** clouer qch à qch; **to ~ sb down to a date/price** contraindre qn à accepter *or* donner une date/un prix; **nailbrush** *n* brosse *f* à ongles; **nailfile** *n* lime *f* à ongles; **nail polish** *n* vernis *m* à ongles; **nail polish remover** *n* dissolvant *m*; **nail scissors** *npl* ciseaux *mpl* à ongles; **nail varnish** *n* (*BRIT*) = **nail polish**

naïve [naɪˈiːv] *adj* naïf(-ive)

naked [ˈneɪkɪd] *adj* nu(e)

name [neɪm] *n* nom *m*; (*reputation*) réputation *f* ▷ *vt* nommer; (*identify: accomplice etc*) citer; (*price, date*) fixer, donner; **by ~** par son nom; de nom; **in the ~ of** au nom de; **what's your ~?** comment vous appelez-vous?, quel est votre nom?; **namely** *adv* à savoir

nanny [ˈnænɪ] *n* bonne *f* d'enfants

nap [næp] *n* (*sleep*) (petit) somme

napkin [ˈnæpkɪn] *n* serviette *f* (de table)

nappy [ˈnæpɪ] *n* (*BRIT*) couche *f*

narcotics [nɑːˈkɔtɪkz] *npl* (*illegal drugs*) stupéfiants *mpl*

narrative [ˈnærətɪv] *n* récit *m* ▷ *adj* narratif(-ive)

narrator [nəˈreɪtəʳ] *n* narrateur(-trice)

narrow [ˈnærəʊ] *adj* étroit(e); (*fig*) restreint(e), limité(e) ▷ *vi* (*road*) devenir plus étroit, se rétrécir; (*gap, difference*) se réduire; **to have a ~ escape** l'échapper belle; **narrow down** *vt* restreindre; **narrowly** *adv*: **he narrowly missed injury/the tree** il a failli se blesser/rentrer dans l'arbre; **he only narrowly missed the target** il a manqué la cible de peu *or* de justesse; **narrow-minded** *adj* à l'esprit étroit, borné(e); (*attitude*) borné(e)

nasal [ˈneɪzl] *adj* nasal(e)

nasty [ˈnɑːstɪ] *adj* (*person: malicious*) méchant(e); (: *rude*) très désagréable; (*smell*) dégoûtant(e); (*wound, situation*) mauvais(e), vilain(e)

nation [ˈneɪʃən] *n* nation *f*

national [ˈnæʃənl] *adj* national(e) ▷ *n* (*abroad*) ressortissant(e); (*when home*) national(e); **national anthem** *n* hymne national; **national dress** *n* costume national; **National Health Service** *n* (*BRIT*) *service national de santé*, ≈ Sécurité Sociale; **National Insurance** *n* (*BRIT*) ≈ Sécurité Sociale; **nationalist** *adj, n* nationaliste *m/f*; **nationality** [næʃəˈnælɪtɪ] *n* nationalité *f*; **nationalize** *vt* nationaliser; **national park** *n* parc national; **National Trust** *n* (*BRIT*) ≈ Caisse *f* nationale des monuments historiques et des sites

⊙ **NATIONAL TRUST**

⊙ Le **National Trust** est un organisme
⊙ indépendant, à but non lucratif, dont
⊙ la mission est de protéger et de mettre
⊙ en valeur les monuments et les sites
⊙ britanniques en raison de leur intérêt
⊙ historique ou de leur beauté naturelle.

nationwide [ˈneɪʃənwaɪd] *adj* s'étendant à l'ensemble du pays; (*problem*) à l'échelle du pays entier

native [ˈneɪtɪv] *n* habitant(e) du pays, autochtone *m/f* ▷ *adj* du pays, indigène; (*country*) natal(e); (*language*) maternel(le); (*ability*) inné(e); **Native American** *n* Indien(ne) d'Amérique ▷ *adj* amérindien(ne); **native speaker** *n* locuteur natif

NATO [ˈneɪtəʊ] *n abbr* (= *North Atlantic Treaty Organization*) OTAN *f*

natural [ˈnætʃrəl] *adj* naturel(le); **natural gas** *n* gaz naturel; **natural history** *n* histoire naturelle; **naturally** *adv* naturellement; **natural resources** *npl* ressources naturelles

nature [ˈneɪtʃəʳ] *n* nature *f*; **by ~** par tempérament, de nature; **nature reserve** *n* (*BRIT*) réserve naturelle

naughty [ˈnɔːtɪ] *adj* (*child*) vilain(e), pas sage

nausea [ˈnɔːsɪə] *n* nausée *f*

naval [ˈneɪvl] *adj* naval(e)

navel ['neɪvl] n nombril m

navigate ['nævɪgeɪt] vt (steer) diriger, piloter ▷ vi naviguer; (Aut) indiquer la route à suivre; **navigation** [nævɪ'geɪʃən] n navigation f

navy ['neɪvɪ] n marine f

navy-blue ['neɪvɪ'bluː] adj bleu marine inv

Nazi ['nɑːtsɪ] n Nazi(e)

NB abbr (= nota bene) NB

near [nɪəʳ] adj proche ▷ adv près ▷ prep (also: ~ to) près de ▷ vt approcher de; **in the ~ future** dans un proche avenir; **nearby** [nɪə'baɪ] adj proche ▷ adv tout près, à proximité; **nearly** adv presque; **I nearly fell** j'ai failli tomber; **it's not nearly big enough** ce n'est vraiment pas assez grand, c'est loin d'être assez grand; **near-sighted** adj myope

neat [niːt] adj (person, work) soigné(e); (room etc) bien tenu(e) or rangé(e); (solution, plan) habile; (spirits) pur(e); **neatly** adv avec soin or ordre; (skilfully) habilement

necessarily ['nɛsɪsrɪlɪ] adv nécessairement; **not ~** pas nécessairement or forcément

necessary ['nɛsɪsrɪ] adj nécessaire; **if ~** si besoin est, le cas échéant

necessity [nɪ'sɛsɪtɪ] n nécessité f; chose nécessaire or essentielle

neck [nɛk] n cou m; (of horse, garment) encolure f; (of bottle) goulot m; **~ and ~** à égalité; **necklace** ['nɛklɪs] n collier m; **necktie** ['nɛktaɪ] n (esp US) cravate f

nectarine ['nɛktərɪn] n brugnon m, nectarine f

need [niːd] n besoin m ▷ vt avoir besoin de; **to ~ to do** devoir faire; avoir besoin de faire; **you don't ~ to go** vous n'avez pas besoin or vous n'êtes pas obligé de partir; **a signature is ~ed** il faut une signature; **there's no ~ to do ....** il n'y a pas lieu de faire ..., il n'est pas nécessaire de faire ...

needle ['niːdl] n aiguille f ▷ vt (inf) asticoter, tourmenter

needless ['niːdlɪs] adj inutile; **~ to say, ...** inutile de dire que ...

needlework ['niːdlwəːk] n (activity) travaux mpl d'aiguille; (object) ouvrage m

needn't ['niːdnt] = **need not**

needy ['niːdɪ] adj nécessiteux(-euse)

negative ['nɛgətɪv] n (Phot, Elec) négatif m; (Ling) terme m de négation ▷ adj négatif(-ive)

neglect [nɪ'glɛkt] vt négliger; (garden) ne pas entretenir; (duty) manquer à ▷ n (of person, duty, garden) le fait de négliger; (state of) ~ abandon m; **to ~ to do sth** négliger or omettre de faire qch; **to ~ one's appearance** se négliger

negotiate [nɪ'gəuʃɪeɪt] vi négocier ▷ vt négocier; (obstacle) franchir, négocier; **to ~ with sb for sth** négocier avec qn en vue d'obtenir qch

negotiation [nɪgəuʃɪ'eɪʃən] n négociation f, pourparlers mpl

negotiator [nɪ'gəuʃɪeɪtəʳ] n négociateur(-trice)

neighbour (US **neighbor** etc) ['neɪbəʳ] n voisin(e); **neighbourhood** n (place) quartier m; (people) voisinage m; **neighbouring** adj voisin(e), avoisinant(e)

neither ['naɪðəʳ] adj, pron aucun(e) (des deux), ni l'un(e) ni l'autre ▷ conj: **I don't like him ~ do I nor do I** moi non plus ▷ adv: **~ good nor bad** ni bon ni mauvais; **~ of them** ni l'un ni l'autre

neon ['niːɔn] n néon m

Nepal [nɪ'pɔːl] n Népal m

nephew ['nɛvjuː] n neveu m

nerve [nəːv] n nerf m; (bravery) sang-froid m, courage m; (cheek) aplomb m, toupet m; **nerves** npl (nervousness) nervosité f; **he gets on my ~s** il m'énerve

nervous ['nəːvəs] adj nerveux(-euse); (anxious) inquiet(-ète), plein(e) d'appréhension; (timid) intimidé(e); **nervous breakdown** n dépression nerveuse

nest [nɛst] n nid m ▷ vi (se) nicher, faire son nid

Net [nɛt] n (Comput): **the ~** (Internet) le Net

net [nɛt] n filet m; (fabric) tulle f ▷ adj net(te) ▷ vt (fish etc) prendre au filet; **netball** n netball m

Netherlands ['nɛðələndz] npl: **the ~** les Pays-Bas mpl

nett [nɛt] adj = **net**

nettle ['nɛtl] n ortie f

network ['nɛtwəːk] n réseau m

neurotic [njuə'rɔtɪk] adj névrosé(e)

neuter ['njuːtəʳ] adj neutre ▷ vt (cat etc) châtrer, couper

neutral ['njuːtrəl] adj neutre ▷ n (Aut) point mort

never ['nɛvəʳ] adv (ne ...) jamais; **I ~ went** je n'y suis pas allé; **I've ~ been to Spain** je ne suis jamais allé en Espagne; **~ again** plus jamais; **~ in my life** jamais de ma vie; see also **mind**; **never-ending** adj interminable; **nevertheless** [nɛvəðə'lɛs] adv néanmoins, malgré tout

new [njuː] adj nouveau (nouvelle); (brand new) neuf (neuve); **New Age** n New Age m; **newborn** adj nouveau-né(e); **newcomer** ['njuːkʌməʳ] n nouveau venu (nouvelle venue); **newly** adv nouvellement, récemment

news [njuːz] n nouvelle(s) f(pl); (Radio, TV) informations fpl, actualités fpl; **a piece of ~** une nouvelle; **news agency** n agence f de presse; **newsagent** n (BRIT) marchand m de journaux; **newscaster** n (Radio, TV) présentateur(-trice); **news dealer** n (US) marchand m de journaux; **newsletter** n bulletin m; **newspaper** n journal m;

newsreader n = **newscaster**

newt [njuːt] n triton m

New Year n Nouvel An; **Happy ~!** Bonne
Année!; **New Year's Day** n le jour de l'An; **New
Year's Eve** n la Saint-Sylvestre

New York [-ʹjɔːk] n New York

New Zealand [-ʹziːlənd] n Nouvelle-
Zélande f; **New Zealander** n Néo-
Zélandais(e)

next [nɛkst] adj (in time) prochain(e); (seat,
room) voisin(e), d'à côté; (meeting, bus stop)
suivant(e) ▷ adv la fois suivante; la prochaine
fois; (afterwards) ensuite; **~ to** prep à côté
de; **~ to nothing** presque rien; **~ time** adv la
prochaine fois; **the ~ day** le lendemain, le jour
suivant or d'après; **~ year** l'année prochaine; **~
please!** (at doctor's etc) au suivant!; **the week
after ~** dans deux semaines; **next door** adv à
côté ▷ adj (neighbour) d'à côté; **next-of-kin** n
parent m le plus proche

NHS n abbr (BRIT) = **National Health Service**

nibble [ʹnɪbl] vt grignoter

nice [naɪs] adj (holiday, trip, taste) agréable; (flat,
picture) joli(e); (person) gentil(le); (distinction,
point) subtil(e); **nicely** adv agréablement;
joliment; gentiment; subtilement

niche [niːʃ] n (Archit) niche f

nick [nɪk] n (indentation) encoche f; (wound)
entaille f; **in good ~** en bon état ▷ vt
(cut): **to ~ o.s.** se couper; (inf: steal) faucher,
piquer; **in the ~ of time** juste à temps

nickel [ʹnɪkl] n nickel m; (US) pièce f de 5 cents

nickname [ʹnɪkneɪm] n surnom m ▷ vt
surnommer

nicotine [ʹnɪkətiːn] n nicotine f

niece [niːs] n nièce f

Nigeria [naɪʹdʒɪərɪə] n Nigéria m or f

night [naɪt] n nuit f; (evening) soir m; **at ~** la
nuit; **by ~** de nuit; **last ~** (evening) hier soir;
(night-time) la nuit dernière; **night club** n
boîte f de nuit; **nightdress** n chemise f de nuit;
nightie [ʹnaɪtɪ] n chemise f de nuit; **nightlife**
n vie f nocturne; **nightly** adj (news) du soir; (by
night) nocturne ▷ adv (every evening) tous les
soirs; (every night) toutes les nuits; **nightmare**
n cauchemar m; **night school** n cours mpl
du soir; **night shift** n équipe f de nuit; **night-
time** n nuit f

nil [nɪl] n (BRIT Sport) zéro m

nine [naɪn] num neuf; **nineteen** num dix-neuf;
nineteenth [naɪnʹtiːnθ] num dix-neuvième;
ninetieth [ʹnaɪntɪɪθ] num quatre-vingt-
dixième; **ninety** num quatre-vingt-dix

ninth [naɪnθ] num neuvième

nip [nɪp] vt pincer ▷ vi (BRIT inf): **to ~
out/down/up** sortir/descendre/monter
en vitesse

nipple [ʹnɪpl] n (Anat) mamelon m, bout m
du sein

nitrogen [ʹnaɪtrədʒən] n azote m

 KEYWORD

no [nəu] (pl **noes**) adv (opposite of "yes") non;
are you coming? — no (I'm not) est-ce que
vous venez? — non; **would you like some
more? — no thank you** vous en voulez
encore? — non merci
▷ adj (not any) (ne …) pas de, (ne …) aucun(e);
I have no money/books je n'ai pas d'argent/
de livres; **no student would have done it**
aucun étudiant ne l'aurait fait; **"no smoking"**
"défense de fumer"; **"no dogs"** "les chiens ne
sont pas admis"
▷ n non m

nobility [nəuʹbɪlɪtɪ] n noblesse f

noble [ʹnəubl] adj noble

nobody [ʹnəubədɪ] pron (ne …) personne

nod [nɔd] vi faire un signe de (la) tête (affirmatif
ou amical); (sleep) somnoler ▷ vt: **to ~ one's
head** faire un signe de (la) tête; (in agreement)
faire signe que oui ▷ n signe m de (la) tête; **nod
off** vi s'assoupir

noise [nɔɪz] n bruit m; **I can't sleep for the ~**
je n'arrive pas à dormir à cause du bruit; **noisy**
adj bruyant(e)

nominal [ʹnɔmɪnl] adj (rent, fee) symbolique;
(value) nominal(e)

nominate [ʹnɔmɪneɪt] vt (propose) proposer;
(appoint) nommer; **nomination** [nɔmɪʹneɪʃən]
n nomination f; **nominee** [nɔmɪʹniː] n
candidat agréé; personne nommée

none [nʌn] pron aucun(e); **~ of you** aucun
d'entre vous, personne parmi vous; **I have ~
left** je n'en ai plus; **he's ~ the worse for it** il ne
s'en porte pas plus mal

nonetheless [ʹnʌnðəʹlɛs] adv néanmoins

non-fiction [nɔnʹfɪkʃən] n littérature f non-
romanesque

nonsense [ʹnɔnsəns] n absurdités fpl, idioties
fpl; **~!** ne dites pas d'idioties!

non: **non-smoker** n non-fumeur m; **non-
smoking** adj non-fumeur; **non-stick** adj qui
n'attache pas

noodles [ʹnuːdlz] npl nouilles fpl

noon [nuːn] n midi m

no-one [ʹnəuwʌn] pron = **nobody**

nor [nɔːʳ] conj = **neither** ▷ adv see **neither**

norm [nɔːm] n norme f

normal [ʹnɔːml] adj normal(e); **normally** adv
normalement

Normandy [ʹnɔːməndɪ] n Normandie f

north [nɔːθ] n nord m ▷ adj nord inv; (wind)
du nord ▷ adv au or vers le nord; **North
Africa** n Afrique f du Nord; **North African** adj
nord-africain(e), d'Afrique du Nord ▷ n Nord-
Africain(e); **North America** n Amérique f du

Nord; **North American** n Nord-Américain(e) ▷ adj nord-américain(e), d'Amérique du Nord; **northbound** ['nɔːθbaund] adj (traffic) en direction du nord; (carriageway) nord inv; **north-east** n nord-est m; **northeastern** adj (du) nord-est inv; **northern** ['nɔːðən] adj du nord, septentrional(e); **Northern Ireland** n Irlande f du Nord; **North Korea** n Corée f du Nord; **North Pole** n: **the North Pole** le pôle Nord; **North Sea** n: **the North Sea** la mer du Nord; **north-west** n nord-ouest m; **northwestern** ['nɔːθ'westən] adj (du) nord-ouest inv

Norway ['nɔːweɪ] n Norvège f; **Norwegian** [nɔː'wiːdʒən] adj norvégien(ne) ▷ n Norvégien(ne); (Ling) norvégien m

nose [nəuz] n nez m; (of dog, cat) museau m; (fig) flair m; **nose about, nose around** vi fouiner or fureter (partout); **nosebleed** n saignement m de nez; **nosey** adj (inf) curieux(-euse)

nostalgia [nɔs'tældʒɪə] n nostalgie f

nostalgic [nɔs'tældʒɪk] adj nostalgique

nostril ['nɔstrɪl] n narine f; (of horse) naseau m

nosy ['nəuzɪ] (inf) adj = **nosey**

not [nɔt] adv (ne ...) pas; **he is ~** or **isn't here** il n'est pas ici; **you must ~** or **mustn't do that** tu ne dois pas faire ça; **I hope ~** j'espère que non; **~ at all** pas du tout; (after thanks) de rien; **it's too late, isn't it?** c'est trop tard, n'est-ce pas?; **~ yet/now** pas encore/maintenant; see also **only**

notable ['nəutəbl] adj notable; **notably** adv (particularly) en particulier; (markedly) spécialement

notch [nɔtʃ] n encoche f

note [nəut] n note f; (letter) mot m; (banknote) billet m ▷ vt (also: **~ down**) noter; (notice) constater; **notebook** n carnet m; (for shorthand etc) bloc-notes m; **noted** ['nəutɪd] adj réputé(e); **notepad** n bloc-notes m; **notepaper** n papier m à lettres

nothing ['nʌθɪŋ] n rien m; **he does ~** il ne fait rien; **~ new** rien de nouveau; **for ~** (free) pour rien, gratuitement; (in vain) pour rien; **~ at all** rien du tout; **~ much** pas grand-chose

notice ['nəutɪs] n (announcement, warning) avis m ▷ vt remarquer, s'apercevoir de; **advance ~** préavis m; **at short ~** dans un délai très court; **until further ~** jusqu'à nouvel ordre; **to give ~, hand in one's ~** (employee) donner sa démission, démissionner; **to take ~ of** prêter attention à; **to bring sth to sb's ~** porter qch à la connaissance de qn; **noticeable** adj visible

notice board n (BRIT) panneau m d'affichage

notify ['nəutɪfaɪ] vt: **to ~ sb of sth** avertir qn de qch

notion ['nəuʃən] n idée f; (concept) notion f; **notions** npl (US: haberdashery) mercerie f

notorious [nəu'tɔːrɪəs] adj notoire (souvent en mal)

notwithstanding [nɔtwɪθ'stændɪŋ] adv néanmoins ▷ prep en dépit de

nought [nɔːt] n zéro m

noun [naun] n nom m

nourish ['nʌrɪʃ] vt nourrir; **nourishment** n nourriture f

Nov. abbr (= November) nov

novel ['nɔvl] n roman m ▷ adj nouveau (nouvelle), original(e); **novelist** n romancier m; **novelty** n nouveauté f

November [nəu'vɛmbə*] n novembre m

novice ['nɔvɪs] n novice m/f

now [nau] adv maintenant ▷ conj: **~ (that)** maintenant (que); **right ~** tout de suite; **by ~** à l'heure qu'il est; **just ~: that's the fashion just ~** c'est la mode en ce moment or maintenant; **~ and then, ~ and again** de temps en temps; **from ~ on** dorénavant; **nowadays** ['nauədeɪz] adv de nos jours

nowhere ['nəuwɛə*] adv (ne ...) nulle part

nozzle ['nɔzl] n (of hose) jet m, lance f; (of vacuum cleaner) suceur m

nr abbr (BRIT) = **near**

nuclear ['njuːklɪə*] adj nucléaire

nucleus (pl **nuclei**) ['njuːklɪəs, 'njuːklɪaɪ] n noyau m

nude [njuːd] adj nu(e) ▷ n (Art) nu m; **in the ~** (tout) nu(e)

nudge [nʌdʒ] vt donner un (petit) coup de coude à

nudist ['njuːdɪst] n nudiste m/f

nudity ['njuːdɪtɪ] n nudité f

nuisance ['njuːsns] n: **it's a ~** c'est (très) ennuyeux or gênant; **he's a ~** il est assommant or casse-pieds; **what a ~!** quelle barbe!

numb [nʌm] adj engourdi(e); (with fear) paralysé(e)

number ['nʌmbə*] n nombre m; (numeral) chiffre m; (of house, car, telephone, newspaper) numéro m ▷ vt numéroter; (amount to) compter; **a ~ of** un certain nombre de; **they were seven in ~** ils étaient (au nombre de) sept; **to be ~ed among** compter parmi; **number plate** n (BRIT Aut) plaque f minéralogique or d'immatriculation; **Number Ten** n (BRIT: 10 Downing Street) résidence du Premier ministre

numerical [njuː'mɛrɪkl] adj numérique

numerous ['njuːmərəs] adj nombreux(-euse)

nun [nʌn] n religieuse f, sœur f

nurse [nəːs] n infirmière f; (also: **~maid**) bonne f d'enfants ▷ vt (patient, cold) soigner

nursery ['nəːsərɪ] n (room) nursery f; (institution) crèche f, garderie f; (for plants) pépinière f; **nursery rhyme** n comptine f, chansonnette f pour enfants; **nursery school** n école maternelle; **nursery slope** n (BRIT Ski)

piste f pour débutants

nursing ['nə:sɪŋ] n (profession) profession f
d'infirmière; (care) soins mpl; **nursing home**
n clinique f; (for convalescence) maison f de
convalescence or de repos; (for old people)
maison de retraite

nurture ['nə:tʃə'] vt élever

nut [nʌt] n (of metal) écrou m; (fruit: walnut)
noix f; (: hazelnut) noisette f; (: peanut)
cacahuète f (terme générique en anglais)

nutmeg ['nʌtmɛg] n (noix f) muscade f

nutrient ['nju:trɪənt] n substance nutritive

nutrition [nju:'trɪʃən] n nutrition f,
alimentation f

nutritious [nju:'trɪʃəs] adj nutritif(-ive),
nourrissant(e)

nuts [nʌts] (inf) adj dingue

NVQ n abbr (BRIT) = **National Vocational
Qualification**

nylon ['naɪlɔn] n nylon m ▷ adj de or en nylon

oak [əuk] n chêne m ▷ cpd de or en (bois de)
chêne

O.A.P. n abbr (BRIT) = **old age pensioner**

oar [ɔ:'] n aviron m, rame f

oasis (pl **oases**) [əu'eɪsɪs, əu'eɪsi:z] n oasis f

oath [əuθ] n serment m; (swear word) juron
m; **on** (BRIT) or **under ~** sous serment;
assermenté(e)

oatmeal ['əutmi:l] n flocons mpl d'avoine

oats [əuts] n avoine f

obedience [ə'bi:dɪəns] n obéissance f

obedient [ə'bi:dɪənt] adj obéissant(e)

obese [əu'bi:s] adj obèse

obesity [əu'bi:sɪtɪ] n obésité f

obey [ə'beɪ] vt obéir à; (instructions, regulations)
se conformer à ▷ vi obéir

obituary [ə'bɪtjuərɪ] n nécrologie f

object n ['ɔbdʒɪkt] objet m; (purpose) but
m, objet; (Ling) complément m d'objet ▷ vi
[əb'dʒɛkt]: **to ~ to** (attitude) désapprouver;
(proposal) protester contre, élever une
objection contre; **I ~!** je proteste!; **he ~ed
that ...** il a fait valoir or a objecté que ...;
money is no ~ l'argent n'est pas un problème;
objection [əb'dʒɛkʃən] n objection f; **if you
have no objection** si vous n'y voyez pas
d'inconvénient; **objective** n objectif m ▷ adj
objectif(-ive)

obligation [ɔblɪ'geɪʃən] n obligation f, devoir
m; (debt) dette f (de reconnaissance)

obligatory [əˈblɪɡətərɪ] *adj* obligatoire
oblige [əˈblaɪdʒ] *vt* (*force*): **to ~ sb to do** obliger *or* forcer qn à faire; (*do a favour*) rendre service à, obliger; **to be ~d to sb for sth** être obligé(e) à qn de qch
oblique [əˈbliːk] *adj* oblique; (*allusion*) indirect(e)
obliterate [əˈblɪtəreɪt] *vt* effacer
oblivious [əˈblɪvɪəs] *adj*: **~ of** oublieux(-euse) de
oblong [ˈɒblɒŋ] *adj* oblong(ue) ▷ *n* rectangle *m*
obnoxious [əbˈnɒkʃəs] *adj* odieux(-euse); (*smell*) nauséabond(e)
oboe [ˈəubəu] *n* hautbois *m*
obscene [əbˈsiːn] *adj* obscène
obscure [əbˈskjuəʳ] *adj* obscur(e) ▷ *vt* obscurcir; (*hide: sun*) cacher
observant [əbˈzəːvnt] *adj* observateur(-trice)
observation [ɔbzəˈveɪʃən] *n* observation *f*; (*by police etc*) surveillance *f*
observatory [əbˈzəːvətrɪ] *n* observatoire *m*
observe [əbˈzəːv] *vt* observer; (*remark*) faire observer *or* remarquer; **observer** *n* observateur(-trice)
obsess [əbˈsɛs] *vt* obséder; **obsession** [əbˈsɛʃən] *n* obsession *f*; **obsessive** *adj* obsédant(e)
obsolete [ˈɔbsəliːt] *adj* dépassé(e), périmé(e)
obstacle [ˈɔbstəkl] *n* obstacle *m*
obstinate [ˈɔbstɪnɪt] *adj* obstiné(e); (*pain, cold*) persistant(e)
obstruct [əbˈstrʌkt] *vt* (*block*) boucher, obstruer; (*hinder*) entraver; **obstruction** [əbˈstrʌkʃən] *n* obstruction *f*; (*to plan, progress*) obstacle *m*
obtain [əbˈteɪn] *vt* obtenir
obvious [ˈɔbvɪəs] *adj* évident(e), manifeste; **obviously** *adv* manifestement; (*of course*): **obviously!** bien sûr!; **obviously not!** évidemment pas!, bien sûr que non!
occasion [əˈkeɪʒən] *n* occasion *f*; (*event*) événement *m*; **occasional** *adj* pris(e) (or fait(e) etc) de temps en temps; (*worker, spending*) occasionnel(le); **occasionally** *adv* de temps en temps, quelquefois
occult [ɔˈkʌlt] *adj* occulte ▷ *n*: **the ~** le surnaturel
occupant [ˈɔkjupənt] *n* occupant *m*
occupation [ɔkjuˈpeɪʃən] *n* occupation *f*; (*job*) métier *m*, profession *f*
occupy [ˈɔkjupaɪ] *vt* occuper; **to ~ o.s. with** *or* **by doing** s'occuper à faire
occur [əˈkəːʳ] *vi* se produire; (*difficulty, opportunity*) se présenter; (*phenomenon, error*) se rencontrer; **to ~ to sb** venir à l'esprit de qn; **occurrence** [əˈkʌrəns] *n* (*existence*) présence *f*, existence *f*; (*event*) cas *m*, fait *m*
ocean [ˈəuʃən] *n* océan *m*

o'clock [əˈklɔk] *adv*: **it is 5 o'clock** il est 5 heures
Oct. *abbr* (= *October*) oct
October [ɔkˈtəubəʳ] *n* octobre *m*
octopus [ˈɔktəpəs] *n* pieuvre *f*
odd [ɔd] *adj* (*strange*) bizarre, curieux(-euse); (*number*) impair(e); (*not of a set*) dépareillé(e); **60-~** 60 et quelques; **at ~ times** de temps en temps; **the ~ one out** l'exception *f*; **oddly** *adv* bizarrement, curieusement; **odds** *npl* (*in betting*) cote *f*; **it makes no odds** cela n'a pas d'importance; **odds and ends** de petites choses; **at odds** en désaccord
odometer [ɔˈdɔmɪtəʳ] *n* (*us*) odomètre *m*
odour (*us* **odor**) [ˈəudəʳ] *n* odeur *f*

 KEYWORD

of [ɔv, əv] *prep* **1** (*gen*) de; **a friend of ours** un de nos amis; **a boy of 10** un garçon de 10 ans; **that was kind of you** c'était gentil de votre part
2 (*expressing quantity, amount, dates etc*) de; **a kilo of flour** un kilo de farine; **how much of this do you need?** combien vous en faut-il?; **there were three of them** (*people*) ils étaient 3; (*objects*) il y en avait 3; **three of us went** 3 d'entre nous y sont allé(e)s; **the 5th of July** le 5 juillet; **a quarter of 4** (*us*) 4 heures moins le quart
3 (*from, out of*) en, de; **a statue of marble** une statue de *or* en marbre; **made of wood** (fait) en bois

off [ɔf] *adj, adv* (*engine*) coupé(e); (*light, TV*) éteint(e); (*tap*) fermé(e); (: *food*) mauvais(e), avancé(e); (: *milk*) tourné(e); (*absent*) absent(e); (*cancelled*) annulé(e); (*removed*): **the lid was ~** le couvercle était retiré *or* n'était pas mis; (*away*): **to run/drive ~** partir en courant/en voiture ▷ *prep* de; **to be ~** (*to leave*) partir, s'en aller; **to be ~ sick** être absent pour cause de maladie; **a day ~** un jour de congé; **to have an ~ day** n'être pas en forme; **he had his coat ~** il avait enlevé son manteau; **10% ~** (*Comm*) 10% de rabais; **5 km ~ (the road)** à 5 km (de la route); **~ the coast** au large de la côte; **it's a long way ~** c'est loin (d'ici); **I'm ~ meat** je ne mange plus de viande; je n'aime plus la viande; **on the ~ chance** à tout hasard; **~ and on, on and ~** de temps à autre
offence (*us* **offense**) [əˈfɛns] *n* (*crime*) délit *m*, infraction *f*; **to take ~ at** se vexer de, s'offenser de
offend [əˈfɛnd] *vt* (*person*) offenser, blesser; **offender** *n* délinquant(e); (*against regulations*) contrevenant(e)
offense [əˈfɛns] *n* (*us*) = **offence**

offensive [əˈfɛnsɪv] adj offensant(e), choquant(e); (smell etc) très déplaisant(e); (weapon) offensif(-ive) ▷ n (Mil) offensive f

offer [ˈɔfəʳ] n offre f, proposition f ▷ vt offrir, proposer; **"on ~"** (Comm) "en promotion"

offhand [ɔfˈhænd] adj désinvolte ▷ adv spontanément

office [ˈɔfɪs] n (place) bureau m; (position) charge f, fonction f; **doctor's ~** (us) cabinet (médical); **to take ~** entrer en fonctions; **office block** (us **office building**) n immeuble m de bureaux; **office hours** npl heures fpl de bureau; (us Med) heures de consultation

officer [ˈɔfɪsəʳ] n (Mil etc) officier m; (also: **police ~**) agent m (de police); (of organization) membre m du bureau directeur

office worker n employé(e) de bureau

official [əˈfɪʃl] adj (authorized) officiel(le) ▷ n officiel m; (civil servant) fonctionnaire m/f; (of railways, post office, town hall) employé(e)

off: **off-licence** n (BRIT: shop) débit m de vins et de spiritueux; **off-line** adj, adv (Comput) (en mode) autonome; (: switched off) non connecté(e); **off-peak** adj aux heures creuses; (electricity, ticket) au tarif heures creuses; **off-putting** adj (BRIT: remark) rébarbatif(-ive); (person) rebutant(e), peu engageant(e); **off-season** adj, adv hors-saison inv

offset [ˈɔfsɛt] vt (irreg: like **set**) (counteract) contrebalancer, compenser

offshore [ɔfˈʃɔːʳ] adj (breeze) de terre; (island) proche du littoral; (fishing) côtier(-ière)

offside [ˈɔfˈsaɪd] adj (Sport) hors jeu; (Aut: in Britain) de droite; (: in US, Europe) de gauche

offspring [ˈɔfsprɪŋ] n progéniture f

often [ˈɔfn] adv souvent; **how ~ do you go?** vous y allez tous les combien?; **every so ~** de temps en temps, de temps à autre

oh [əu] excl ô!, oh!, ah!

oil [ɔɪl] n huile f; (petroleum) pétrole m; (for central heating) mazout m ▷ vt (machine) graisser; **oil filter** n (Aut) filtre m à huile; **oil painting** n peinture f à l'huile; **oil refinery** n raffinerie f de pétrole; **oil rig** n derrick m; (at sea) plate-forme pétrolière; **oil slick** n nappe f de mazout; **oil tanker** n (ship) pétrolier m; (truck) camion-citerne m; **oil well** n puits m de pétrole; **oily** adj huileux(-euse); (food) gras(se)

ointment [ˈɔɪntmənt] n onguent m

O.K., okay [ˈəuˈkeɪ] (inf) excl d'accord! ▷ vt approuver, donner son accord à ▷ adj (not bad) pas mal; **is it O.K.?**, **are you O.K.?** ça va?

old [əuld] adj vieux (vieille); (person) vieux, âgé(e); (former) ancien(ne), vieux; **how ~ are you?** quel âge avez-vous?; **he's 10 years ~** il a 10 ans, il est âgé de 10 ans; **~er brother/sister** frère/sœur aîné(e); **old age** n vieillesse f; **old-age pension** n (BRIT) (pension f de) retraite f (de la sécurité sociale); **old-age pensioner**

n (BRIT) retraité(e); **old-fashioned** adj démodé(e); (person) vieux jeu inv; **old people's home** n (esp BRIT) maison f de retraite

olive [ˈɔlɪv] n (fruit) olive f; (tree) olivier m ▷ adj (also: **~-green**) (vert) olive inv; **olive oil** n huile f d'olive

Olympic [əuˈlɪmpɪk] adj olympique; **the ~ Games**, **the ~s** les Jeux mpl olympiques

omelet(te) [ˈɔmlɪt] n omelette f

omen [ˈəumən] n présage m

ominous [ˈɔmɪnəs] adj menaçant(e), inquiétant(e); (event) de mauvais augure

omit [əuˈmɪt] vt omettre

 KEYWORD

on [ɔn] prep 1 (indicating position) sur; **on the table** sur la table; **on the wall** sur le or au mur; **on the left** à gauche

2 (indicating means, method, condition etc): **on foot** à pied; **on the train/plane** (be) dans le train/l'avion; (go) en train/avion; **on the telephone/radio/television** au téléphone/à la radio/à la télévision; **to be on drugs** se droguer; **on holiday** (BRIT), **on vacation** (US) en vacances

3 (referring to time): **on Friday** vendredi; **on Fridays** le vendredi; **on June 20th** le 20 juin; **a week on Friday** vendredi en huit; **on arrival** à l'arrivée; **on seeing this** en voyant cela

4 (about, concerning) sur, de; **a book on Balzac/physics** un livre sur Balzac/de physique

▷ adv 1 (referring to dress): **to have one's coat on** avoir (mis) son manteau; **to put one's coat on** mettre son manteau; **what's she got on?** qu'est-ce qu'elle porte?

2 (referring to covering): **screw the lid on tightly** vissez bien le couvercle

3 (further, continuously): **to walk** etc **on** continuer à marcher etc; **from that day on** depuis ce jour

▷ adj 1 (in operation: machine) en marche; (: radio, TV, light) allumé(e); (: tap, gas) ouvert(e); (: brakes) mis(e); **is the meeting still on?** (not cancelled) est-ce que la réunion a bien lieu?; (in progress) la réunion dure-t-elle encore?; **when is this film on?** quand passe ce film?

2 (inf): **that's not on!** (not acceptable) cela ne se fait pas!; (not possible) pas question!

once [wʌns] adv une fois; (formerly) autrefois ▷ conj une fois que + sub; **~ he had left/it was done** une fois qu'il fut parti/ que ce fut terminé; **at ~** tout de suite, immédiatement; (simultaneously) à la fois; **all at ~** adv tout d'un coup; **~ a week** une fois par semaine; **~ more** encore une fois; **~ and for all** une fois pour

toutes; **~ upon a time there was ...** il y avait
une fois ..., il était une fois ...
oncoming ['ɒnkʌmɪŋ] *adj* (*traffic*) venant en
sens inverse

 KEYWORD

one [wʌn] *num* un(e); **one hundred and fifty**
cent cinquante; **one by one** un(e) à *or* par
un(e); **one day** un jour
▷ *adj* 1 (*sole*) seul(e), unique; **the one book
which** l'unique *or* le seul livre qui; **the one
man who** le seul (homme) qui
2 (*same*) même; **they came in the one car** ils
sont venus dans la même voiture
▷ *pron* 1 : **this one** celui-ci (celle-ci); **that one**
celui-là (celle-là); **I've already got one/a red
one** j'en ai déjà un(e)/un(e) rouge; **which one
do you want?** lequel voulez-vous?
2 : **one another** l'un(e) l'autre; **to look at one
another** se regarder
3 (*impersonal*) on; **one never knows** on ne sait
jamais; **to cut one's finger** se couper le doigt;
one needs to eat il faut manger

one-off [wʌn'ɒf] (*BRIT inf*) *n* exemplaire *m*
unique
oneself [wʌn'sɛlf] *pron* se; (*after prep, also
emphatic*) soi-même; **to hurt ~** se faire mal; **to
keep sth for ~** garder qch pour soi; **to talk to ~**
se parler à soi-même; **by ~** tout seul
one : **one-shot** [wʌn'ʃɒt] (*US*) *n* = **one-off**; **one-
sided** *adj* (*argument, decision*) unilatéral(e);
one-to-one *adj* (*relationship*) univoque; **one-
way** *adj* (*street, traffic*) à sens unique
ongoing ['ɒngəʊɪŋ] *adj* en cours; (*relationship*)
suivi(e)
onion ['ʌnjən] *n* oignon *m*
on-line ['ɒnlaɪn] *adj* (*Comput*) en ligne; (:
switched on) connecté(e)
onlooker ['ɒnlʊkər] *n* spectateur(-trice)
only ['əʊnlɪ] *adv* seulement ▷ *adj* seul(e),
unique ▷ *conj* seulement, mais; **an ~ child**
un enfant unique; **not ~ ... but also** non
seulement ... mais aussi; **I ~ took one** j'en ai
seulement pris un, je n'en ai pris qu'un
on-screen [ɒn'skri:n] *adj* à l'écran
onset ['ɒnsɛt] *n* début *m*; (*of winter, old age*)
approche *f*
onto ['ɒntu] *prep* = **on to**
onward(s) ['ɒnwəd(z)] *adv* (*move*) en avant;
from that time ~ à partir de ce moment
oops [ʊps] *excl* houp!
ooze [u:z] *vi* suinter
opaque [əʊ'peɪk] *adj* opaque
open ['əʊpn] *adj* ouvert(e); (*car*) découvert(e);
(*road, view*) dégagé(e); (*meeting*) public(-ique);
(*admiration*) manifeste ▷ *vt* ouvrir ▷ *vi* (*flower,
eyes, door, debate*) s'ouvrir; (*shop, bank, museum*)

ouvrir; (*book etc: commence*) commencer,
débuter; **is it ~ to public?** est-ce ouvert au
public?; **what time do you ~?** à quelle heure
ouvrez-vous?; **in the ~ (air)** en plein air;
open up *vt* ouvrir; (*blocked road*) dégager ▷ *vi*
s'ouvrir; **open-air** *adj* en plein air; **opening**
n ouverture *f*; (*opportunity*) occasion *f*; (*work*)
débouché *m*; (*job*) poste vacant; **opening
hours** *npl* heures *fpl* d'ouverture; **open
learning** *n* enseignement universitaire à la
carte, notamment par correspondance; (*distance
learning*) télé-enseignement *m*; **openly** *adv*
ouvertement; **open-minded** *adj* à l'esprit
ouvert; **open-necked** *adj* à col ouvert; **open-
plan** *adj* sans cloisons; **Open University** *n*
(*BRIT*) *cours universitaires par correspondance*

opera ['ɒpərə] *n* opéra *m*; **opera house** *n*
opéra *m*; **opera singer** *n* chanteur(-euse)
d'opéra
operate ['ɒpəreɪt] *vt* (*machine*) faire marcher,
faire fonctionner ▷ *vi* fonctionner; **to ~ on sb
(for)** (*Med*) opérer qn (de)
operating room *n* (*US: Med*) salle *f*
d'opération
operating theatre *n* (*BRIT: Med*) salle *f*
d'opération
operation [ɒpə'reɪʃən] *n* opération *f*; (*of
machine*) fonctionnement *m*; **to have an ~
(for)** se faire opérer (de); **to be in ~** (*machine*)
être en service; (*system*) être en vigueur;
operational *adj* opérationnel(le); (*ready for
use*) en état de marche
operative ['ɒpərətɪv] *adj* (*measure*) en vigueur
▷ *n* (*in factory*) ouvrier(-ière)
operator ['ɒpəreɪtər] *n* (*of machine*)
opérateur(-trice); (*Tel*) téléphoniste *m/f*
opinion [ə'pɪnjən] *n* opinion *f*, avis *m*; **in
my ~** à mon avis; **opinion poll** *n* sondage *m*
d'opinion
opponent [ə'pəʊnənt] *n* adversaire *m/f*
opportunity [ɒpə'tju:nɪtɪ] *n* occasion *f*;
to take the ~ to do *or* **of doing** profiter de
l'occasion pour faire

oppose [ə'pəuz] vt s'opposer à; **to be ~d to sth** être opposé(e) à qch; **as ~d to** par opposition à

opposite ['ɔpəzɪt] adj opposé(e); (house etc) d'en face ▷ adv en face ▷ prep en face de ▷ n opposé m, contraire m; (of word) contraire f

opposition [ɔpə'zɪʃən] n opposition f

oppress [ə'prɛs] vt opprimer

opt [ɔpt] vi: **to ~ for** opter pour; **to ~ to do** choisir de faire; **opt out** vi: **to ~ out of** choisir de ne pas participer à or de ne pas faire

optician [ɔp'tɪʃən] n opticien(ne)

optimism ['ɔptɪmɪzəm] n optimisme m

optimist ['ɔptɪmɪst] n optimiste m/f; **optimistic** [ɔptɪ'mɪstɪk] adj optimiste

optimum ['ɔptɪməm] adj optimum

option ['ɔpʃən] n choix m, option f; (Scol) matière f à option; **optional** adj facultatif(-ive)

or [ɔːʳ] conj ou; (with negative): **he hasn't seen or heard anything** il n'a rien vu ni entendu; **or else** sinon; ou bien

oral ['ɔːrəl] adj oral(e) ▷ n oral m

orange ['ɔrɪndʒ] n (fruit) orange f ▷ adj orange inv; **orange juice** n jus m d'orange; **orange squash** n orangeade f

orbit ['ɔːbɪt] n orbite f ▷ vt graviter autour de

orchard ['ɔːtʃəd] n verger m

orchestra ['ɔːkɪstrə] n orchestre m; (us: seating) (fauteuils mpl d')orchestre

orchid ['ɔːkɪd] n orchidée f

ordeal [ɔː'diːl] n épreuve f

order ['ɔːdəʳ] n ordre m; (Comm) commande f ▷ vt ordonner; (Comm) commander; **in ~** en ordre; (of document) en règle; **out of ~** (not in correct order) en désordre; (machine) hors service; (telephone) en dérangement; **a machine in working ~** une machine en état de marche; **in ~ to do/that** pour faire/que + sub; **could I ~ now, please?** je peux commander, s'il vous plaît?; **to be on ~** être en commande; **to ~ sb to do** ordonner à qn de faire; **order form** n bon m de commande; **orderly** n (Mil) ordonnance f; (Med) garçon m de salle ▷ adj (room) en ordre; (mind) méthodique; (person) qui a de l'ordre

ordinary ['ɔːdnrɪ] adj ordinaire, normal(e); (pej) ordinaire, quelconque; **out of the ~** exceptionnel(le)

ore [ɔːʳ] n minerai m

oregano [ɔrɪ'gɑːnəu] n origan m

organ ['ɔːgən] n organe m; (Mus) orgue m, orgues fpl; **organic** [ɔː'gænɪk] adj organique; (crops etc) biologique, naturel(le); **organism** n organisme m

organization [ɔːgənaɪ'zeɪʃən] n organisation f

organize ['ɔːgənaɪz] vt organiser; **organized** ['ɔːgənaɪzd] adj (planned) organisé(e);

(efficient) bien organisé; **organizer** n organisateur(-trice)

orgasm ['ɔːgæzəm] n orgasme m

orgy ['ɔːdʒɪ] n orgie f

oriental [ɔːrɪ'ɛntl] adj oriental(e)

orientation [ɔːrɪɛn'teɪʃən] n (attitudes) tendance f; (in job) orientation f; (of building) orientation, exposition f

origin ['ɔrɪdʒɪn] n origine f

original [ə'rɪdʒɪnl] adj original(e); (earliest) originel(le) ▷ n original m; **originally** adv (at first) à l'origine

originate [ə'rɪdʒɪneɪt] vi: **to ~ from** être originaire de; (suggestion) provenir de; **to ~ in** (custom) prendre naissance dans, avoir son origine dans

Orkney ['ɔːknɪ] n (also: **the ~s, the ~ Islands**) les Orcades fpl

ornament ['ɔːnəmənt] n ornement m; (trinket) bibelot m; **ornamental** [ɔːnə'mɛntl] adj décoratif(-ive); (garden) d'agrément

ornate [ɔː'neɪt] adj très orné(e)

orphan ['ɔːfn] n orphelin(e)

orthodox ['ɔːθədɔks] adj orthodoxe

orthopaedic (us **orthopedic**) [ɔːθə'piːdɪk] adj orthopédique

osteopath ['ɔstɪəpæθ] n ostéopathe m/f

ostrich ['ɔstrɪtʃ] n autruche f

other ['ʌðəʳ] adj autre ▷ pron: **the ~ (one)** l'autre; **~s** (other people) d'autres ▷ adv: **~ than** autrement que; à part; **the ~ day** l'autre jour; **otherwise** adv, conj autrement

Ottawa ['ɔtəwə] n Ottawa

otter ['ɔtəʳ] n loutre f

ouch [autʃ] excl aïe!

ought (pt **~**) [ɔːt] aux vb: **I ~ to do it** je devrais le faire, il faudrait que je le fasse; **this ~ to have been corrected** cela aurait dû être corrigé; **he ~ to win** (probability) il devrait gagner

ounce [auns] n once f (28.35g; 16 in a pound)

our ['auəʳ] adj notre, nos pl; see also **my**; **ours** pron le (la) nôtre, les nôtres; see also **mine¹**; **ourselves** pron pl (reflexive, after preposition) nous; (emphatic) nous-mêmes; see also **oneself**

oust [aust] vt évincer

out [aut] adv dehors; (published, not at home etc) sorti(e); (light, fire) éteint(e); **~ there** là-bas; **he's ~** (absent) il est sorti; **to be ~ in one's calculations** s'être trompé dans ses calculs; **to run/back** etc **~** sortir en courant/en reculant etc; **~ loud** adv à haute voix; **~ of** prep (outside) en dehors de; (because of: anger etc) par; (from among): **10 ~ of 10** 10 sur 10; (without): **~ of petrol** sans essence, à court d'essence; **~ of order** (machine) en panne; (Tel: line) en dérangement; **outback** n (in Australia) intérieur m; **outbound** adj: **outbound (from/for)** en partance (de/pour); **outbreak** n (of violence) éruption f, explosion f; (of disease) de nombreux cas; **the outbreak of war south of the border** la guerre qui s'est déclarée au sud de la frontière; **outburst** n explosion f, accès m; **outcast** n exilé(e); (socially) paria m; **outcome** n issue f, résultat m; **outcry** n tollé (général); **outdated** adj démodé(e); **outdoor** adj de or en plein air; **outdoors** adv dehors; au grand air

outer ['autə'] adj extérieur(e); **outer space** n espace m cosmique

outfit ['autfıt] n (clothes) tenue f

out: **outgoing** adj (president, tenant) sortant(e); (character) ouvert(e), extraverti(e); **outgoings** npl (BRIT: expenses) dépenses fpl; **outhouse** n appentis m, remise f

outing ['autıŋ] n sortie f; excursion f

out: **outlaw** n hors-la-loi m inv ▷ vt (person) mettre hors la loi; (practice) proscrire; **outlay** n dépenses fpl; (investment) mise f de fonds; **outlet** n (for liquid etc) issue f, sortie f; (for emotion) exutoire m; (also: **retail outlet**) point m de vente; (us: Elec) prise f de courant; **outline** n (shape) contour m; (summary) esquisse f, grandes lignes ▷ vt (fig: theory, plan) exposer à grands traits; **outlook** n perspective f; (point of view) attitude f; **outnumber** vt surpasser en nombre; **out-of-date** adj (passport, ticket) périmé(e); (theory, idea) dépassé(e); (custom) désuet(-ète); (clothes) démodé(e); **out-of-doors** adv = **outdoors**; **out-of-the-way** adj loin de tout; **out-of-town** adj (shopping centre etc) en périphérie; **outpatient** n malade m/f en consultation externe; **outpost** n avant-poste m; **output** n rendement m, production f; (Comput) sortie f ▷ vt (Comput) sortir

outrage ['autreıdʒ] n (anger) indignation f; (violent act) atrocité f, acte m de violence; (scandal) scandale m ▷ vt outrager; **outrageous** [aut'reıdʒəs] adj atroce; (scandalous) scandaleux(-euse)

outright adv [aut'raıt] complètement; (deny, refuse) catégoriquement; (ask) carrément; (kill) sur le coup ▷ adj ['autraıt] complet(-ète); catégorique

outset ['autsɛt] n début m

outside [aut'saıd] n extérieur m ▷ adj extérieur(e) ▷ adv (au) dehors, à l'extérieur ▷ prep hors de, à l'extérieur de; (in front of) devant; **at the ~** (fig) au plus or maximum; **outside lane** n (Aut: in Britain) voie f de droite; (: in US, Europe) voie de gauche; **outside line** n (Tel) ligne extérieure; **outsider** n (stranger) étranger(-ère)

out: **outsize** adj énorme; (clothes) grande taille inv; **outskirts** npl faubourgs mpl; **outspoken** adj très franc (franche); **outstanding** adj remarquable, exceptionnel(le); (unfinished: work, business)

en suspens, en souffrance; (debt) impayé(e); (problem) non réglé(e)

outward ['autwəd] adj (sign, appearances) extérieur(e); (journey) (d')aller; **outwards** adv (esp BRIT) = **outward**

outweigh [aut'weı] vt l'emporter sur

oval ['əuvl] adj, n ovale m

ovary ['əuvərı] n ovaire m

oven ['ʌvn] n four m; **oven glove** n gant m de cuisine; **ovenproof** adj allant au four; **oven-ready** adj prêt(e) à cuire

over ['əuvə'] adv (par-)dessus ▷ adj (or adv) (finished) fini(e), terminé(e); (too much) en plus ▷ prep sur; par-dessus; (above) au-dessus de; (on the other side of) de l'autre côté de; (more than) plus de; (during) pendant; (about, concerning): **they fell out ~ money/her** ils se sont brouillés pour des questions d'argent/à cause d'elle; **~ here** ici; **~ there** là-bas; **all ~ (everywhere)** partout; **~ and ~ (again)** à plusieurs reprises; **~ and above** en plus de; **to ask sb ~** inviter qn (à passer); **to fall ~** tomber; **to turn sth ~** retourner qch

overall ['əuvərɔːl] adj (length) total(e); (study, impression) d'ensemble ▷ n (BRIT) blouse f ▷ adv [əuvər'ɔːl] dans l'ensemble, en général; **overalls** npl (boiler suit) bleus mpl (de travail)

overboard ['əuvəbɔːd] adv (Naut) par-dessus bord

overcame [əuvə'keım] pt of **overcome**

overcast ['əuvəkɑːst] adj couvert(e)

overcharge [əuvə'tʃɑːdʒ] vt: **to ~ sb for sth** faire payer qch trop cher à qn

overcoat ['əuvəkəut] n pardessus m

overcome [əuvə'kʌm] vt (irreg: like **come**) (defeat) triompher de; (difficulty) surmonter ▷ adj (emotionally) bouleversé(e); **~ with grief** accablé(e) de douleur

over: **overcrowded** adj bondé(e); (city, country) surpeuplé(e); **overdo** vt (irreg: like **do**) exagérer; (overcook) trop cuire; **to overdo it, to overdo things** (work too hard) en faire trop, se surmener; **overdone** [əuvə'dʌn] adj (vegetables, steak) trop cuit(e); **overdose** n dose excessive; **overdraft** n découvert m; **overdrawn** adj (account) à découvert; **overdue** adj en retard; (bill) impayé(e); (change) qui tarde; **overestimate** vt surestimer

overflow vi [əuvə'fləu] déborder ▷ n ['əuvəfləu] (also: **~ pipe**) tuyau m d'écoulement, trop-plein m

overgrown [əuvə'grəun] adj (garden) envahi(e) par la végétation

overhaul vt [əuvə'hɔːl] réviser ▷ n ['əuvəhɔːl] révision f

overhead adv [əuvə'hɛd] au-dessus ▷ adj, n ['əuvəhɛd] ▷ adj aérien(ne); (lighting) vertical(e) ▷ n (us) = **overheads**; **overhead**

projector n rétroprojecteur m; **overheads** npl (BRIT) frais généraux

over: **overhear** vt (irreg: like **hear**) entendre (par hasard); **overheat** vi (engine) chauffer; **overland** adj, adv par voie de terre; **overlap** vi se chevaucher; **overleaf** adv au verso; **overload** vt surcharger; **overlook** vt (have view of) donner sur; (miss) oublier, négliger; (forgive) fermer les yeux sur

overnight adv [əuvə'naɪt] (happen) durant la nuit; (fig) soudain ▷ adj ['əuvənaɪt] d'une (or de) nuit; soudain(e); **to stay ~ (with sb)** passer la nuit (chez qn); **overnight bag** n nécessaire m de voyage

overpass ['əuvəpɑːs] n (US: for cars) pont autoroutier; (: for pedestrians) passerelle f, pont m

overpower [əuvə'pauəʳ] vt vaincre; (fig) accabler; **overpowering** adj irrésistible; (heat, stench) suffocant(e)

over: **overreact** [əuvəriː'ækt] vi réagir de façon excessive; **overrule** vt (decision) annuler; (claim) rejeter; (person) rejeter l'avis de; **overrun** vt (irreg: like **run**) (Mil: country etc) occuper; (time limit etc) dépasser ▷ vi dépasser le temps imparti

overseas [əuvə'siːz] adv outre-mer; (abroad) à l'étranger ▷ adj (trade) extérieur(e); (visitor) étranger(-ère)

oversee [əuvə'siː] vt (irreg: like **see**) surveiller

overshadow [əuvə'ʃædəu] vt (fig) éclipser

oversight ['əuvəsaɪt] n omission f, oubli m

oversleep [əuvə'sliːp] vi (irreg: like **sleep**) se réveiller (trop) tard

overspend [əuvə'spɛnd] vi (irreg: like **spend**) dépenser de trop

overt [əu'vəːt] adj non dissimulé(e)

overtake [əuvə'teɪk] vt (irreg: like **take**) dépasser; (BRIT: Aut) dépasser, doubler

over: **overthrow** vt (irreg: like **throw**) (government) renverser; **overtime** n heures fpl supplémentaires

overtook [əuvə'tuk] pt of **overtake**

over: **overturn** vt renverser; (decision, plan) annuler ▷ vi se retourner; **overweight** adj (person) trop gros(se); **overwhelm** vt (subj: emotion) accabler, submerger; (enemy, opponent) écraser; **overwhelming** adj (victory, defeat) écrasant(e); (desire) irrésistible

ow [au] excl aïe!

owe [əu] vt devoir; **to ~ sb sth, to ~ sth to sb** devoir qch à qn; **how much do I ~ you?** combien est-ce que je vous dois?; **owing to** prep à cause de, en raison de

owl [aul] n hibou m

own [əun] vt posséder ▷ adj propre; **a room of my ~** une chambre à moi, ma propre chambre; **to get one's ~ back** prendre sa revanche; **on one's ~** tout(e) seul(e); **own up** vi avouer;

owner n propriétaire m/f; **ownership** n possession f

ox (pl **oxen**) [ɔks, 'ɔksn] n bœuf m

Oxbridge ['ɔksbrɪdʒ] n (BRIT) les universités d'Oxford et de Cambridge

oxen ['ɔksən] npl of **ox**

oxygen ['ɔksɪdʒən] n oxygène m

oyster ['ɔɪstəʳ] n huître f

oz. abbr = **ounce(s)**

ozone ['əuzəun] n ozone m; **ozone friendly** adj qui n'attaque pas or qui préserve la couche d'ozone; **ozone layer** n couche f d'ozone

P

p *abbr* (BRIT) = **penny**; **pence**

P.A. *n abbr* = **personal assistant**; **public address system**

p.a. *abbr* = **per annum**

pace [peɪs] *n* pas *m*; (*speed*) allure *f*, vitesse *f* ▷ *vi*: **to ~ up and down** faire les cent pas; **to keep ~ with** aller à la même vitesse que; (*events*) se tenir au courant de; **pacemaker** *n* (*Med*) stimulateur *m* cardiaque; (*Sport: also*: **pacesetter**) meneur(-euse) de train

Pacific [pə'sɪfɪk] *n*: **the ~ (Ocean)** le Pacifique, l'océan *m* Pacifique

pacifier ['pæsɪfaɪə'] *n* (US: *dummy*) tétine *f*

pack [pæk] *n* paquet *m*; (*of hounds*) meute *f*; (*of thieves, wolves etc*) bande *f*; (*of cards*) jeu *m*; (US: *of cigarettes*) paquet; (*back pack*) sac *m* à dos ▷ *vt* (*goods*) empaqueter, emballer; (*in suitcase etc*) emballer; (*box*) remplir; (*cram*) entasser ▷ *vi* **to ~ (one's bags)** faire ses bagages; **pack in** (BRIT *inf*) ▷ *vi* (*machine*) tomber en panne ▷ *vt* (*boyfriend*) plaquer; **~ it in!** laisse tomber!; **pack off** *vt*: **to ~ sb off to** expédier qn à; **pack up** *vi* (BRIT *inf*: *machine*) tomber en panne; (: *person*) se tirer ▷ *vt* (*belongings*) ranger; (*goods, presents*) empaqueter, emballer

package ['pækɪdʒ] *n* paquet *m*; (*also*: **~ deal**: *agreement*) marché global; (: *purchase*) forfait *m*; (*Comput*) progiciel *m* ▷ *vt* (*goods*) conditionner; **package holiday** *n* (BRIT) vacances organisées; **package tour** *n* voyage organisé

packaging ['pækɪdʒɪŋ] *n* (*wrapping materials*) emballage *m*

packed [pækt] *adj* (*crowded*) bondé(e); **packed lunch** (BRIT) *n* repas froid

packet ['pækɪt] *n* paquet *m*

packing ['pækɪŋ] *n* emballage *m*

pact [pækt] *n* pacte *m*, traité *m*

pad [pæd] *n* bloc(-notes *m*) *m*; (*to prevent friction*) tampon *m* ▷ *vt* rembourrer; **padded** *adj* (*jacket*) matelassé(e); (*bra*) rembourré(e)

paddle ['pædl] *n* (*oar*) pagaie *f*; (US: *for table tennis*) raquette *f* de ping-pong ▷ *vi* (*with feet*) barboter, faire trempette ▷ *vt*: **to ~ a canoe** *etc* pagayer; **paddling pool** *n* petit bassin

paddock ['pædək] *n* enclos *m*; (*Racing*) paddock *m*

padlock ['pædlɔk] *n* cadenas *m*

paedophile (US **pedophile**) ['piːdəufaɪl] *n* pédophile *m*

page [peɪdʒ] *n* (*of book*) page *f*; (*also*: **~ boy**) groom *m*, chasseur *m*; (*at wedding*) garçon *m* d'honneur ▷ *vt* (*in hotel etc*) (faire) appeler

pager ['peɪdʒə'] *n* bip *m* (*inf*), Alphapage® *m*

paid [peɪd] *pt, pp of* **pay** ▷ *adj* (*work, official*) rémunéré(e); (*holiday*) payé(e); **to put ~ to** (BRIT) mettre fin à, mettre par terre

pain [peɪn] *n* douleur *f*; (*inf: nuisance*) plaie *f*; **to be in ~** souffrir, avoir mal; **to take ~s to do** se donner du mal pour faire; **painful** *adj* douloureux(-euse); (*difficult*) difficile, pénible; **painkiller** *n* calmant *m*, analgésique *m*; **painstaking** ['peɪnzteɪkɪŋ] *adj* (*person*) soigneux(-euse); (*work*) soigné(e)

paint [peɪnt] *n* peinture *f* ▷ *vt* peindre; **to ~ the door blue** peindre la porte en bleu; **paintbrush** *n* pinceau *m*; **painter** *n* peintre *m*; **painting** *n* peinture *f*; (*picture*) tableau *m*

pair [pɛə'] *n* (*of shoes, gloves etc*) paire *f*; (*of people*) couple *m*; **~ of scissors** (paire de) ciseaux *mpl*; **~ of trousers** pantalon *m*

pajamas [pə'dʒɑːməz] *npl* (US) pyjama(s) *m(pl)*

Pakistan [pɑːkɪ'stɑːn] *n* Pakistan *m*; **Pakistani** *adj* pakistanais(e) ▷ *n* Pakistanais(e)

pal [pæl] *n* (*inf*) copain (copine)

palace ['pæləs] *n* palais *m*

pale [peɪl] *adj* pâle; **~ blue** *adj* bleu pâle *inv*

Palestine ['pælɪstaɪn] *n* Palestine *f*; **Palestinian** [pælɪs'tɪnɪən] *adj* palestinien(ne) ▷ *n* Palestinien(ne)

palm [pɑːm] *n* (*Anat*) paume *f*; (*also*: **~ tree**) palmier *m* ▷ *vt*: **to ~ sth off on sb** (*inf*) refiler qch à qn

pamper ['pæmpə'] *vt* gâter, dorloter

pamphlet ['pæmflət] *n* brochure *f*

pan [pæn] *n* (*also*: **sauce~**) casserole *f*; (*also*:

frying ~) poêle f
pancake ['pænkeɪk] n crêpe f
panda ['pændə] n panda m
pane [peɪn] n carreau m (de fenêtre), vitre f
panel ['pænl] n (of wood, cloth etc) panneau m; (Radio, TV) panel m, invités mpl; (for interview, exams) jury m
panhandler ['pænhændlə⁰] n (US inf) mendiant(e)
panic ['pænɪk] n panique f, affolement m ▷ vi s'affoler, paniquer
panorama [pænə'rɑ:mə] n panorama m
pansy ['pænzɪ] n (Bot) pensée f
pant [pænt] vi haleter
panther ['pænθə⁰] n panthère f
panties ['pæntɪz] npl slip m, culotte f
pantomime ['pæntəmaɪm] n (BRIT) spectacle m de Noël; voir encadré

◉ **PANTOMIME**

◉ Une **pantomime** (à ne pas confondre
◉ avec le mot tel qu'on l'utilise en français,
◉ que l'on appelle également de façon
◉ familière "panto", est un genre de farce où
◉ le personnage principal est souvent un
◉ jeune garçon et où il y a toujours une "dame",
◉ c'est-à-dire une vieille femme jouée par
◉ un homme, et un méchant. La plupart du
◉ temps, l'histoire est basée sur un conte de
◉ fées comme Cendrillon ou Le Chat botté,
◉ et le public est encouragé à participer en
◉ prévenant le héros d'un danger imminent.
◉ Ce genre de spectacle, qui s'adresse
◉ surtout aux enfants, vise également un
◉ public d'adultes au travers des nombreuses
◉ plaisanteries faisant allusion à des faits
◉ d'actualité.

pants [pænts] n (BRIT: woman's) culotte f, slip m; (: man's) slip m, caleçon m; (US: trousers) pantalon m
pantyhose ['pæntɪhəʊz] (US) npl collant m
paper ['peɪpə⁰] n papier m; (also: **wall~**) papier peint; (also: **news~**) journal m; (academic essay) article m; (exam) épreuve écrite ▷ adj en or de papier ▷ vt tapisser (de papier peint); **papers** npl (also: **identity ~s**) papiers mpl (d'identité); **paperback** n livre broché or non relié; (small) livre m de poche; **paper bag** n sac m en papier; **paper clip** n trombone m; **paper shop** n (BRIT) marchand m de journaux; **paperwork** n papiers mpl; (pej) paperasserie f
paprika ['pæprɪkə] n paprika m
par [pɑ:⁰] n pair m; (Golf) normale f du parcours; **on a ~ with** à égalité avec, au même niveau que
paracetamol [pærə'si:təmɔl] (BRIT) n paracétamol m

parachute ['pærəʃu:t] n parachute m
parade [pə'reɪd] n défilé m ▷ vt (fig) faire étalage de ▷ vi défiler
paradise ['pærədaɪs] n paradis m
paradox ['pærədɔks] n paradoxe m
paraffin ['pærəfɪn] n (BRIT): **~ (oil)** pétrole (lampant)
paragraph ['pærəgrɑ:f] n paragraphe m
parallel ['pærəlɛl] adj: **~ (with or to)** parallèle (à); (fig) analogue (à) ▷ n (line) parallèle f; (fig, Geo) parallèle m
paralysed ['pærəlaɪzd] adj paralysé(e)
paralysis (pl **paralyses**) [pə'rælɪsɪs, -si:z] n paralysie f
paramedic [pærə'mɛdɪk] n auxiliaire m/f médical(e)
paranoid ['pærənɔɪd] adj (Psych) paranoïaque; (neurotic) paranoïde
parasite ['pærəsaɪt] n parasite m
parcel ['pɑ:sl] n paquet m, colis m ▷ vt (also: **~ up**) empaqueter
pardon ['pɑ:dn] n pardon m; (Law) grâce f ▷ vt pardonner à; (Law) gracier; **~!** pardon!; **~ me!** (after burping etc) excusez-moi!; **I beg your ~!** (I'm sorry) pardon!, je suis désolé!; **(I beg your) ~?**, (US) **~ me?** (what did you say?) pardon?
parent ['pɛərənt] n (father) père m; (mother) mère f; **parents** npl parents mpl; **parental** [pə'rɛntl] adj parental(e), des parents
Paris ['pærɪs] n Paris
parish ['pærɪʃ] n paroisse f; (BRIT: civil) ≈ commune f
Parisian [pə'rɪzɪən] adj parisien(ne), de Paris ▷ n Parisien(ne)
park [pɑ:k] n parc m, jardin public ▷ vt garer ▷ vi se garer; **can I ~ here?** est-ce que je peux me garer ici?
parking ['pɑ:kɪŋ] n stationnement m; **"no ~"** "stationnement interdit"; **parking lot** n (US) parking m, parc m de stationnement; **parking meter** n parc(o)mètre m; **parking ticket** n P.-V. m

▌ Be careful not to translate **parking** by the
▌ French word **parking**.

parkway ['pɑ:kweɪ] n (US) route f express (en site vert ou aménagé)
parliament ['pɑ:ləmənt] n parlement m; **parliamentary** [pɑ:lə'mɛntərɪ] adj parlementaire
Parmesan [pɑ:mɪ'zæn] n (also: **~ cheese**) Parmesan m
parole [pə'rəʊl] n: **on ~** en liberté conditionnelle
parrot ['pærət] n perroquet m
parsley ['pɑ:slɪ] n persil m
parsnip ['pɑ:snɪp] n panais m
parson ['pɑ:sn] n ecclésiastique m; (Church of England) pasteur m
part [pɑ:t] n partie f; (of machine) pièce f; (Theat

etc) rôle m; (of serial) épisode m; (us: in hair) raie f ▷ adv = **partly** ▷ vt séparer ▷ vi (people) se séparer; (crowd) s'ouvrir; **to take ~ in** participer à, prendre part à; **to take sb's ~** prendre le parti de qn, prendre parti pour qn; **for my ~** en ce qui me concerne; **for the most ~** en grande partie; dans la plupart des cas; **in ~** en partie; **to take sth in good/bad ~** prendre qch du bon/mauvais côté; **part with** vt fus (person) se séparer de; (possessions) se défaire de

partial ['pɑːʃl] adj (incomplete) partiel(le); **to be ~ to** aimer, avoir un faible pour

participant [pɑː'tɪsɪpənt] n (in competition, campaign) participant(e)

participate [pɑː'tɪsɪpeɪt] vi: **to ~ (in)** participer (à), prendre part (à)

particle ['pɑːtɪkl] n particule f; (of dust) grain m

particular [pə'tɪkjʊlə'] adj (specific) particulier(-ière); (special) particulier, spécial(e); (fussy) difficile, exigeant(e); (careful) méticuleux(-euse); **in ~** en particulier, surtout; **particularly** adv particulièrement; (in particular) en particulier; **particulars** npl détails mpl; (information) renseignements mpl

parting ['pɑːtɪŋ] n séparation f; (BRIT: in hair) raie f

partition [pɑː'tɪʃən] n (Pol) partition f, division f; (wall) cloison f

partly ['pɑːtlɪ] adv en partie, partiellement

partner ['pɑːtnə'] n (Comm) associé(e); (Sport) partenaire m/f; (spouse) conjoint(e); (lover) ami(e); (at dance) cavalier(-ière); **partnership** n association f

part of speech n (Ling) partie f du discours

partridge ['pɑːtrɪdʒ] n perdrix f

part-time ['pɑːt'taɪm] adj, adv à mi-temps, à temps partiel

party ['pɑːtɪ] n (Pol) parti m; (celebration) fête f; (: formal) réception f; (: in evening) soirée f; (group) groupe m; (Law) partie f

pass [pɑːs] vt (time, object) passer; (place) passer devant; (friend) croiser; (exam) être reçu(e) à, réussir; (overtake) dépasser; (approve) approuver, accepter ▷ vi passer; (Scol) être reçu(e) or admis(e), réussir ▷ n (permit) laissez-passer m inv; (membership card) carte f d'accès or d'abonnement; (in mountains) col m; (Sport) passe f; (Scol: also: ~ mark): **to get a ~** être reçu(e) (sans mention); **to ~ sb sth** passer qch à qn; **could you ~ the salt/oil, please?** pouvez-vous me passer le sel/l'huile, s'il vous plaît?; **to make a ~ at sb** (inf) faire des avances à qn; **pass away** vi mourir; **pass by** vi passer ▷ vt (ignore) négliger; **pass on** vt (hand on): **to ~ on (to)** transmettre (à); **pass out** vi s'évanouir; **pass over** vt (ignore) passer sous silence; **pass up** vt (opportunity) laisser passer; **passable** adj

(road) praticable; (work) acceptable

> Be careful not to translate **to pass an exam** by the French expression **passer un examen**.

passage ['pæsɪdʒ] n (also: **~way**) couloir m; (gen, in book) passage m; (by boat) traversée f

passenger ['pæsɪndʒə'] n passager(-ère)

passer-by [pɑːsə'baɪ] n passant(e)

passing place n (Aut) aire f de croisement

passion ['pæʃən] n passion f; **passionate** adj passionné(e); **passion fruit** n fruit m de la passion

passive ['pæsɪv] adj (also Ling) passif(-ive)

passport ['pɑːspɔːt] n passeport m; **passport control** n contrôle m des passeports; **passport office** n bureau m de délivrance des passeports

password ['pɑːswɜːd] n mot m de passe

past [pɑːst] prep (in front of) devant; (further than) au delà de, plus loin que; après; (later than) après ▷ adv: **to run ~** passer en courant ▷ adj passé(e); (president etc) ancien(ne) ▷ n passé m; **he's ~ forty** il a dépassé la quarantaine, il a plus de or passé quarante ans; **ten/quarter ~ eight** huit heures dix/un or et quart; **for the ~ few/3 days** depuis or ces derniers/3 derniers jours

pasta ['pæstə] n pâtes fpl

paste [peɪst] n pâte f; (Culin: meat) pâté m (à tartiner; (: tomato) purée f, concentré m; (glue) colle f (de pâte) ▷ vt coller

pastel ['pæstl] adj n inv ▷ n (Art: pencil) (crayon m) pastel m; (: drawing) (dessin m au) pastel; (colour) ton m pastel inv

pasteurized ['pæstəraɪzd] adj pasteurisé(e)

pastime ['pɑːstaɪm] n passe-temps m inv, distraction f

pastor ['pɑːstə'] n pasteur m

past participle [-'pɑːtɪsɪpl] adj (Ling) participe passé

pastry ['peɪstrɪ] n pâte f; (cake) pâtisserie f

pasture ['pɑːstʃə'] n pâturage m

pasty¹ n ['pæstɪ] petit pâté (en croûte)

pasty² ['peɪstɪ] adj (complexion) terreux(-euse)

pat [pæt] vt donner une petite tape à; (dog) caresser

patch [pætʃ] n (of material) pièce f; (eye patch) cache m; (spot) tache f; (of land) parcelle f; (on tyre) rustine f ▷ vt (clothes) rapiécer; **a bad ~** (BRIT) une période difficile; **patchy** adj inégal(e); (incomplete) fragmentaire

pâté ['pæteɪ] n pâté m, terrine f

patent ['peɪtnt, us 'pætnt] n brevet m (d'invention) ▷ vt faire breveter ▷ adj patent(e), manifeste

paternal [pə'tɜːnl] adj paternel(le)

paternity leave [pə'tɜːnɪtɪ-] n congé m de paternité

path [pɑːθ] n chemin m, sentier m; (in garden)

allée f; (of missile) trajectoire f
pathetic [pə'θεtɪk] adj (pitiful) pitoyable; (very bad) lamentable, minable
pathway ['pɑːθweɪ] n chemin m, sentier m; (in garden) allée f
patience ['peɪʃns] n patience f; (BRIT: Cards) réussite f
patient ['peɪʃnt] n malade m/f; (of dentist etc) patient(e) ▷ adj patient(e)
patio ['pætɪəʊ] n patio m
patriotic [pætrɪ'ɒtɪk] adj patriotique; (person) patriote
patrol [pə'trəʊl] n patrouille f ▷ vt patrouiller dans; **patrol car** n voiture f de police
patron ['peɪtrən] n (in shop) client(e); (of charity) patron(ne); **~ of the arts** mécène m
patronizing ['pætrənaɪzɪŋ] adj condescendant(e)
pattern ['pætən] n (Sewing) patron m; (design) motif m; **patterned** adj à motifs
pause [pɔːz] n pause f, arrêt m ▷ vi faire une pause, s'arrêter
pave [peɪv] vt paver, daller; **to ~ the way for** ouvrir la voie à
pavement ['peɪvmənt] n (BRIT) trottoir m; (US) chaussée f
pavilion [pə'vɪlɪən] n pavillon m; (Sport) stand m
paving ['peɪvɪŋ] n (material) pavé m, dalle f
paw [pɔː] n patte f
pawn [pɔːn] n (Chess, also fig) pion m ▷ vt mettre en gage; **pawnbroker** n prêteur m sur gages
pay [peɪ] n salaire m; (of manual worker) paie f ▷ vb (pt, pp **paid**) ▷ vt payer ▷ vi payer; (be profitable) être rentable; **can I ~ by credit card?** est-ce que je peux payer par carte de crédit?; **to ~ attention (to)** prêter attention (à); **to ~ sb a visit** rendre visite à qn; **to ~ one's respects to sb** présenter ses respects à qn; **pay back** vt rembourser; **pay for** vt fus payer; **pay in** vt verser; **pay off** vt (debts) régler, acquitter; (person) rembourser ▷ vi (scheme, decision) se révéler payant(e); **pay out** vt (money) payer, sortir de sa poche; **pay up** vt (amount) payer; **payable** adj payable; **to make a cheque payable to sb** établir un chèque à l'ordre de qn; **pay day** n jour m de paie; **pay envelope** n (US) paie f; **payment** n paiement m; (of bill) règlement m; (of deposit, cheque) versement m; **monthly payment** mensualité f; **payout** n (from insurance) dédommagement m; (in competition) prix m; **pay packet** n (BRIT) paie f; **pay phone** n cabine f téléphonique, téléphone public; **pay raise** n (US) = **pay rise**; **pay rise** n (BRIT) augmentation f (de salaire); **payroll** n registre m du personnel; **pay slip** n (BRIT) bulletin m de paie, feuille f de paie; **pay television** n

chaînes fpl payantes
PC n abbr = **personal computer**; (BRIT) = **police constable** ▷ adj abbr = **politically correct**
p.c. abbr = **per cent**
PDA n abbr (= personal digital assistant) agenda m électronique
PE n abbr (= physical education) EPS f
pea [piː] n (petit) pois
peace [piːs] n paix f; (calm) calme m, tranquillité f; **peaceful** adj paisible, calme
peach [piːtʃ] n pêche f
peacock ['piːkɒk] n paon m
peak [piːk] n (mountain) pic m, cime f; (of cap) visière f; (fig: highest level) maximum m; (: of career, fame) apogée m; **peak hours** npl heures fpl d'affluence or de pointe
peanut ['piːnʌt] n arachide f, cacahuète f; **peanut butter** n beurre m de cacahuète
pear [pɛəʳ] n poire f
pearl [pəːl] n perle f
peasant ['pɛznt] n paysan(ne)
peat [piːt] n tourbe f
pebble ['pɛbl] n galet m, caillou m
peck [pɛk] vt (also: **~ at**) donner un coup de bec à; (food) picorer ▷ n coup m de bec; (kiss) bécot m; **peckish** adj (BRIT inf): **I feel peckish** je mangerais bien quelque chose, j'ai la dent
peculiar [pɪ'kjuːlɪəʳ] adj (odd) étrange, bizarre, curieux(-euse); (particular) particulier(-ière); **~ to** particulier à
pedal ['pɛdl] n pédale f ▷ vi pédaler
pedalo ['pɛdələʊ] n pédalo m
pedestal ['pɛdəstl] n piédestal m
pedestrian [pɪ'dɛstrɪən] n piéton m; **pedestrian crossing** n (BRIT) passage clouté; **pedestrianized** adj: **a pedestrianized street** une rue piétonne; **pedestrian precinct** (US **pedestrian zone**) n (BRIT) zone piétonne
pedigree ['pɛdɪgriː] n ascendance f; (of animal) pedigree m ▷ cpd (animal) de race
pedophile ['piːdəʊfaɪl] (US) n = **paedophile**
pee [piː] vi (inf) faire pipi, pisser
peek [piːk] vi jeter un coup d'œil (furtif)
peel [piːl] n pelure f, épluchure f; (of orange, lemon) écorce f ▷ vt peler, éplucher ▷ vi (paint etc) s'écailler; (wallpaper) se décoller; (skin) peler
peep [piːp] n (BRIT: look) coup d'œil furtif; (sound) pépiement m ▷ vi (BRIT) jeter un coup d'œil (furtif)
peer [pɪəʳ] vi: **to ~ at** regarder attentivement, scruter ▷ n (noble) pair m; (equal) pair, égal(e)
peg [pɛg] n (for coat etc) patère f; (BRIT: also: **clothes ~**) pince f à linge
pelican ['pɛlɪkən] n pélican m; **pelican crossing** n (BRIT Aut) feu m à commande manuelle
pelt [pɛlt] vt: **to ~ sb (with)** bombarder qn (de)

▷ vi (rain) tomber à seaux; (inf: run) courir à toutes jambes ▷ n peau f

pelvis ['pɛlvɪs] n bassin m

pen [pɛn] n (for writing) stylo m; (for sheep) parc m

penalty ['pɛnltɪ] n pénalité f; sanction f; (fine) amende f; (Sport) pénalisation f; (Football) penalty m; (Rugby) pénalité f

pence [pɛns] npl of **penny**

pencil ['pɛnsl] n crayon m; **pencil in** vt noter provisoirement; **pencil case** n trousse f (d'écolier); **pencil sharpener** n taille-crayon(s) m inv

pendant ['pɛndnt] n pendentif m

pending ['pɛndɪŋ] prep en attendant ▷ adj en suspens

penetrate ['pɛnɪtreɪt] vt pénétrer dans; (enemy territory) entrer en

penfriend ['pɛnfrɛnd] n (BRIT) correspondant(e)

penguin ['pɛŋgwɪn] n pingouin m

penicillin [pɛnɪ'sɪlɪn] n pénicilline f

peninsula [pə'nɪnsjulə] n péninsule f

penis ['piːnɪs] n pénis m, verge f

penitentiary [pɛnɪ'tɛnʃərɪ] n (US) prison f

penknife ['pɛnnaɪf] n canif m

penniless ['pɛnɪlɪs] adj sans le sou

penny (pl **pennies** or **pence**) ['pɛnɪ, 'pɛnɪz, pɛns] n (BRIT) penny m; (US) cent m

penpal ['pɛnpæl] n correspondant(e)

pension ['pɛnʃən] n (from company) retraite f; **pensioner** n (BRIT) retraité(e)

pentagon ['pɛntəgən] n: **the P~** (US Pol) le Pentagone

penthouse ['pɛnthaus] n appartement m (de luxe) en attique

penultimate [pɪ'nʌltɪmət] adj pénultième, avant-dernier(-ière)

people ['piːpl] npl gens mpl; personnes fpl; (inhabitants) population f; (Pol) peuple m ▷ n (nation, race) peuple m; **several ~ came** plusieurs personnes sont venues; **~ say that ...** on dit or les gens disent que ...

pepper ['pɛpər] n poivre m; (vegetable) poivron m ▷ vt (Culin) poivrer; **peppermint** n (sweet) pastille f de menthe

per [pəːr] prep par; **~ hour** (miles etc) à l'heure; (fee) (de) l'heure; **~ kilo** etc le kilo etc; **~ day/person** par jour/personne; **~ annum** par an

perceive [pə'siːv] vt percevoir; (notice) remarquer, s'apercevoir de

per cent adv pour cent

percentage [pə'sɛntɪdʒ] n pourcentage m

perception [pə'sɛpʃən] n perception f; (insight) sensibilité f

perch [pəːtʃ] n (fish) perche f; (for bird) perchoir m ▷ vi (se) percher

percussion [pə'kʌʃən] n percussion f

perennial [pə'rɛnɪəl] n (Bot) plante f vivace f, plante pluriannuelle

perfect ['pəːfɪkt] adj parfait(e) ▷ n (also: ~ **tense**) parfait m ▷ vt [pə'fɛkt] (technique, skill, work of art) parfaire; (method, plan) mettre au point; **perfection** [pə'fɛkʃən] n perfection f; **perfectly** ['pəːfɪktlɪ] adv parfaitement

perform [pə'fɔːm] vt (carry out) exécuter; (concert etc) jouer, donner ▷ vi (actor, musician) jouer; **performance** n représentation f, spectacle m; (of an artist) interprétation f; (Sport: of car, engine) performance f; (of company, economy) résultats mpl; **performer** n artiste m/f

perfume ['pəːfjuːm] n parfum m

perhaps [pə'hæps] adv peut-être

perimeter [pə'rɪmɪtər] n périmètre m

period ['pɪərɪəd] n période f; (History) époque f; (Scol) cours m; (full stop) point m; (Med) règles fpl ▷ adj (costume, furniture) d'époque; **periodical** [pɪərɪ'ɔdɪkl] n périodique m; **periodically** adv périodiquement

perish ['pɛrɪʃ] vi périr, mourir; (decay) se détériorer

perjury ['pəːdʒərɪ] n (Law: in court) faux témoignage; (breach of oath) parjure m

perk [pəːk] n (inf) avantage m, à-côté m

perm [pəːm] n (for hair) permanente f

permanent ['pəːmənənt] adj permanent(e); **permanently** adv de façon permanente; (move abroad) définitivement; (open, closed) en permanence; (tired, unhappy) constamment

permission [pə'mɪʃən] n permission f, autorisation f

permit n ['pəːmɪt] permis m

perplex [pə'plɛks] vt (person) rendre perplexe

persecute ['pəːsɪkjuːt] vt persécuter

persecution [pəːsɪ'kjuːʃən] n persécution f

persevere [pəːsɪ'vɪər] vi persévérer

Persian ['pəːʃən] adj persan(e); **the ~ Gulf** le golfe Persique

persist [pə'sɪst] vi: **to ~ (in doing)** persister (à faire), s'obstiner (à faire); **persistent** adj persistant(e), tenace

person ['pəːsn] n personne f; **in ~** en personne; **personal** adj personnel(le); **personal assistant** n secrétaire personnel(le); **personal computer** n ordinateur individuel, PC m; (to take abroad) [pə'sænɪtɪ] n personnalité f; **personally** adv personnellement; **to take sth personally** se sentir visé(e) par qch; **personal organizer** n agenda (personnel); (style Filofax®); (electronic) agenda électronique; **personal stereo** n Walkman® m, baladeur m

personnel [pəːsə'nɛl] n personnel m

perspective [pə'spɛktɪv] n perspective f

perspiration [pəːspɪ'reɪʃən] n transpiration f

persuade [pə'sweɪd] vt: **to ~ sb to do sth** persuader qn de faire qch, amener or décider qn à faire qch

persuasion [pə'sweɪʒən] n persuasion f; (creed) conviction f

persuasive [pə'sweɪsɪv] adj persuasif(-ive)

perverse [pə'vəːs] adj pervers(e); (contrary) entêté(e), contrariant(e)

pervert n ['pəːvəːt] perverti(e) ▷ vt [pə'vəːt] pervertir; (words) déformer

pessimism ['pɛsɪmɪzəm] n pessimisme m

pessimist ['pɛsɪmɪst] n pessimiste m/f; **pessimistic** [pɛsɪ'mɪstɪk] adj pessimiste

pest [pɛst] n animal m (or insecte m) nuisible; (fig) fléau m

pester ['pɛstəʳ] vt importuner, harceler

pesticide ['pɛstɪsaɪd] n pesticide m

pet [pɛt] n animal familier ▷ cpd (favourite) favori(e) ▷ vt (stroke) caresser, câliner; **teacher's ~** chouchou m du professeur; **~ hate** bête noire

petal ['pɛtl] n pétale m

petite [pə'tiːt] adj menu(e)

petition [pə'tɪʃən] n pétition f

petrified ['pɛtrɪfaɪd] adj (fig) mort(e) de peur

petrol ['pɛtrəl] n (BRIT) essence f; **I've run out of ~** je suis en panne d'essence

> Be careful not to translate *petrol* by the French word *pétrole*.

petroleum [pə'trəulɪəm] n pétrole m

petrol: **petrol pump** n (BRIT: in car, at garage) pompe f à essence; **petrol station** n (BRIT) station-service f; **petrol tank** n (BRIT) réservoir m d'essence

petticoat ['pɛtɪkəut] n jupon m

petty ['pɛtɪ] adj (mean) mesquin(e); (unimportant) insignifiant(e), sans importance

pew [pjuː] n banc m (d'église)

pewter ['pjuːtəʳ] n étain m

phantom ['fæntəm] n fantôme m

pharmacist ['fɑːməsɪst] n pharmacien(ne)

pharmacy ['fɑːməsɪ] n pharmacie f

phase [feɪz] n phase f, période f; **phase in** vt introduire progressivement; **phase out** vt supprimer progressivement

Ph.D. abbr = **Doctor of Philosophy**

pheasant ['fɛznt] n faisan m

phenomena [fə'nɔmɪnə] npl of **phenomenon**

phenomenal [fɪ'nɔmɪnl] adj phénoménal(e)

phenomenon (pl **phenomena**) [fə'nɔmɪnən, -nə] n phénomène m

Philippines ['fɪlɪpiːnz] npl (also: **Philippine Islands**): **the ~** les Philippines fpl

philosopher [fɪ'lɔsəfəʳ] n philosophe m

philosophical [fɪlə'sɔfɪkl] adj philosophique

philosophy [fɪ'lɔsəfɪ] n philosophie f

phlegm [flɛm] n flegme m

phobia ['fəubjə] n phobie f

phone [fəun] n téléphone m ▷ vt téléphoner à ▷ vi téléphoner; **to be on the ~** avoir le téléphone; (be calling) être au téléphone; **phone back** vt, vi rappeler; **phone up** vt téléphoner à ▷ vi téléphoner; **phone book** n annuaire m; **phone box** (US **phone booth**) n cabine f téléphonique; **phone call** n coup m de fil or de téléphone; **phonecard** n télécarte f; **phone number** n numéro m de téléphone

phonetics [fə'nɛtɪks] n phonétique f

phoney ['fəunɪ] adj faux (fausse), factice; (person) pas franc (franche)

photo ['fəutəu] n photo f; **photo album** n album m de photos; **photocopier** n copieur m; **photocopy** n photocopie f ▷ vt photocopier

photograph ['fəutəgræf] n photographie f ▷ vt photographier; **photographer** [fə'tɔgrəfəʳ] n photographe m/f; **photography** [fə'tɔgrəfɪ] n photographie f

phrase [freɪz] n expression f; (Ling) locution f ▷ vt exprimer; **phrase book** n recueil m d'expressions (pour touristes)

physical ['fɪzɪkl] adj physique; **physical education** n éducation f physique; **physically** adv physiquement

physician [fɪ'zɪʃən] n médecin m

physicist ['fɪzɪsɪst] n physicien(ne)

physics ['fɪzɪks] n physique f

physiotherapist [fɪzɪəu'θɛrəpɪst] n kinésithérapeute m/f

physiotherapy [fɪzɪəu'θɛrəpɪ] n kinésithérapie f

physique [fɪ'ziːk] n (appearance) physique m; (health etc) constitution f

pianist ['piːənɪst] n pianiste m/f

piano [pɪ'ænəu] n piano m

pick [pɪk] n (tool: also: **-axe**) pic m, pioche f ▷ vt choisir; (gather) cueillir; (remove) prendre; (lock) forcer; **take your ~** faites votre choix; **the ~ of** le (la) meilleur(e) de; **to ~ one's nose** se mettre les doigts dans le nez; **to ~ one's teeth** se curer les dents; **to ~ a quarrel with sb** chercher noise à qn; **pick on** vt fus (person) harceler; **pick out** vt choisir; (distinguish) distinguer; **pick up** vi (improve) remonter, s'améliorer ▷ vt ramasser; (collect) passer prendre; (Aut: give lift to) prendre; (learn) apprendre; (Radio) capter; **to ~ up speed** prendre de la vitesse; **to ~ o.s. up** se relever

pickle ['pɪkl] n (also: **-s**: as condiment) pickles mpl ▷ vt conserver dans du vinaigre or dans de la saumure; **in a ~** (fig) dans le pétrin

pickpocket ['pɪkpɔkɪt] n pickpocket m

pick-up ['pɪkʌp] n (also: **- truck**) pick-up m inv

picnic ['pɪknɪk] n pique-nique m ▷ vi pique-niquer; **picnic area** n aire f de pique-nique

picture ['pɪktʃəʳ] n (also TV) image f; (painting) peinture f, tableau m; (photograph) photo(graphie) f; (drawing) dessin m; (film) film m; (fig: description) description f ▷ vt (imagine) se représenter; **pictures** npl: **the ~s** (BRIT) le cinéma; **to take a ~ of sb/sth** prendre qn/qch en photo; **would you take a ~ of us, please?** pourriez-vous nous prendre en photo, s'il vous plaît?; **picture frame** n cadre m; **picture messaging** n picture messaging m, messagerie f d'images

picturesque [pɪktʃə'rɛsk] adj pittoresque

pie [paɪ] n tourte f; (of fruit) tarte f; (of meat) pâté m en croûte

piece [piːs] n morceau m; (item): **a ~ of furniture/advice** un meuble/conseil ▷ vt: **to ~ together** rassembler; **to take to ~s** démonter

pie chart n graphique m à secteurs, camembert m

pier [pɪəʳ] n jetée f

pierce [pɪəs] vt percer, transpercer; **pierced** adj (ears) percé(e)

pig [pɪg] n cochon m, porc m; (pej: unkind person) mufle m; (: greedy person) goinfre m

pigeon ['pɪdʒən] n pigeon m

piggy bank ['pɪgɪ-] n tirelire f

pigsty ['pɪgstaɪ] n porcherie f

pigtail ['pɪgteɪl] n natte f, tresse f

pike [paɪk] n (fish) brochet m

pilchard ['pɪltʃəd] n pilchard m (sorte de sardine)

pile [paɪl] n (pillar, of books) pile f; (heap) tas m; (of carpet) épaisseur f; **pile up** vi (accumulate) s'entasser, s'accumuler ▷ vt (put in heap) empiler, entasser; (accumulate) accumuler; **piles** npl hémorroïdes fpl; **pile-up** n (Aut) télescopage m, collision f en série

pilgrim ['pɪlgrɪm] n pèlerin m

pilgrimage ['pɪlgrɪmɪdʒ] n pèlerinage m

pill [pɪl] n pilule f; **the ~** la pilule

pillar ['pɪləʳ] n pilier m

pillow ['pɪləu] n oreiller m; **pillowcase, pillowslip** n taie f d'oreiller

pilot ['paɪlət] n pilote m ▷ cpd (scheme etc) pilote, expérimental(e) ▷ vt piloter; **pilot light** n veilleuse f

pimple ['pɪmpl] n bouton m

PIN n abbr (= personal identification number) code m confidentiel

pin [pɪn] n épingle f; (Tech) cheville f ▷ vt épingler; **~s and needles** fourmis fpl; **to ~ sb down** (fig) coincer qn; **to ~ sth on sb** (fig) mettre qch sur le dos de qn

pinafore ['pɪnəfɔːʳ] n tablier m

pinch [pɪntʃ] n pincement m; (of salt etc) pincée f ▷ vt pincer; (inf: steal) piquer, chiper ▷ vi (shoe) serrer; **at a ~** à la rigueur

pine [paɪn] n (also: ~ tree) pin m ▷ vi: **to ~ for** aspirer à, désirer ardemment

pineapple ['paɪnæpl] n ananas m

ping [pɪŋ] n (noise) tintement m; **ping-pong®** n ping-pong® m

pink [pɪŋk] adj rose ▷ n (colour) rose m

pinpoint ['pɪnpɔɪnt] vt indiquer (avec précision)

pint [paɪnt] n pinte f (BRIT = 0.57 l; US = 0.47 l); (BRIT inf) ≈ demi m, ≈ pot m

pioneer [paɪə'nɪəʳ] n pionnier m

pious ['paɪəs] adj pieux(-euse)

pip [pɪp] n (seed) pépin m; **pips** npl: **the ~s** (BRIT: time signal on radio) le top

pipe [paɪp] n tuyau m, conduite f; (for smoking) pipe f ▷ vt amener par tuyau; **pipeline** n (for gas) gazoduc m, pipeline m; (for oil) oléoduc m, pipeline; **piper** n (flautist) joueur(-euse) de pipeau; (of bagpipes) joueur(-euse) de cornemuse

pirate ['paɪərət] n pirate m ▷ vt (CD, video, book) pirater

Pisces ['paɪsiːz] n les Poissons mpl

piss [pɪs] vi (inf!) pisser (!); **pissed** (inf!) adj (BRIT: drunk) bourré(e); (US: angry) furieux(-euse)

pistol ['pɪstl] n pistolet m

piston ['pɪstən] n piston m

pit [pɪt] n trou m, fosse f; (also: **coal ~**) puits m de mine; (also: **orchestra ~**) fosse d'orchestre; (US: fruit stone) noyau m ▷ vt: **to ~ o.s. or one's wits against** se mesurer à

pitch [pɪtʃ] n (BRIT Sport) terrain m; (Mus) ton m; (fig: degree) degré m; (tar) poix f ▷ vt (throw) lancer; (tent) dresser ▷ vi (fall): **to ~ into/off** tomber dans/de; **pitch-black** adj noir(e) comme poix

pitfall ['pɪtfɔːl] n piège m

pith [pɪθ] n (of orange etc) intérieur m de l'écorce

pitiful ['pɪtɪful] adj (touching) pitoyable; (contemptible) lamentable

pity ['pɪtɪ] n pitié f ▷ vt plaindre; **what a ~!** quel dommage!

pizza ['piːtsə] n pizza f

placard ['plækɑːd] n affiche f; (in march) pancarte f

place [pleɪs] n endroit m, lieu m; (proper position, job, rank, seat) place f; (home): **at/to his ~** chez lui ▷ vt (position) placer, mettre; (identify) situer; reconnaître; **to take ~** avoir lieu; **to change ~s with sb** changer de place avec qn; **out of ~** (*not suitable*) déplacé(e), inopportun(e); **in the first ~** d'abord, en premier; **place mat** n set m de table; (*in linen etc*) napperon m; **placement** n (*during studies*) stage m

placid ['plæsɪd] adj placide

plague [pleɪg] n (*Med*) peste f ▷ vt (*fig*) tourmenter

plaice [pleɪs] n (pl inv) carrelet m

plain [pleɪn] adj (*in one colour*) uni(e); (*clear*) clair(e), évident(e); (*simple*) simple; (*not handsome*) quelconque, ordinaire ▷ adv franchement, carrément ▷ n plaine f; **plain chocolate** n chocolat m à croquer; **plainly** adv clairement; (*frankly*) carrément, sans détours

plaintiff ['pleɪntɪf] n plaignant(e)

plait [plæt] n tresse f, natte f

plan [plæn] n plan m; (*scheme*) projet m ▷ vt (*think in advance*) projeter; (*prepare*) organiser ▷ vi faire des projets; **to ~ to do** projeter de faire

plane [pleɪn] n (*Aviat*) avion m; (*also: ~ tree*) platane m; (*tool*) rabot m; (*Art, Math etc*) plan m; (*fig*) niveau m, plan ▷ vt (*with tool*) raboter

planet ['plænɪt] n planète f

plank [plæŋk] n planche f

planning ['plænɪŋ] n planification f; **family ~** planning familial

plant [plɑːnt] n plante f; (*machinery*) matériel m; (*factory*) usine f ▷ vt planter; (*bomb*) déposer, poser; (*microphone, evidence*) cacher

plantation [plæn'teɪʃən] n plantation f

plaque [plæk] n plaque f

plaster ['plɑːstəʳ] n plâtre m; (*also: ~ of Paris*) plâtre à mouler; (*BRIT: also: sticking ~*) pansement adhésif ▷ vt plâtrer; (*cover*): **to ~ with** couvrir de; **plaster cast** n (*Med*) plâtre m; (*model, statue*) moule m

plastic ['plæstɪk] n plastique m ▷ adj (*made of plastic*) en plastique; **plastic bag** n sac m en plastique; **plastic surgery** n chirurgie f esthétique

plate [pleɪt] n (*dish*) assiette f; (*sheet of metal, on door; Phot*) plaque f; (*in book*) gravure f; (*dental*) dentier m

plateau (*pl ~s or ~x*) ['plætəʊ, -z] n plateau m

platform ['plætfɔːm] n (*at meeting*) tribune f; (*stage*) estrade f; (*Rail*) quai m; (*Pol*) plateforme f

platinum ['plætɪnəm] n platine m

platoon [plə'tuːn] n peloton m

platter ['plætəʳ] n plat m

plausible ['plɔːzɪbl] adj plausible; (*person*) convaincant(e)

play [pleɪ] n jeu m; (*Theat*) pièce f (de théâtre) ▷ vt (*game*) jouer à; (*team, opponent*) jouer contre; (*instrument*) jouer de; (*part, piece of music, note*) jouer; (*CD etc*) passer ▷ vi jouer; **to ~ safe** ne prendre aucun risque; **play back** vt repasser, réécouter; **play up** vi (*cause trouble*) faire des siennes; **player** n joueur(-euse); (*Mus*) musicien(ne); **playful** adj enjoué(e); **playground** n cour f de récréation; (*in park*) aire f de jeux; **playgroup** n garderie f; **playing card** n carte f à jouer; **playing field** n terrain m de sport; **playschool** n = **playgroup**; **playtime** n (*Scol*) récréation f; **playwright** n dramaturge m

plc abbr (*BRIT: = public limited company*) ≈ SARL f

plea [pliː] n (*request*) appel m; (*Law*) défense f

plead [pliːd] vt plaider; (*give as excuse*) invoquer ▷ vi (*Law*) plaider; (*beg*): **to ~ with sb (for sth)** implorer qn (d'accorder qch); **to ~ guilty/not guilty** plaider coupable/non coupable

pleasant ['plɛznt] adj agréable

please [pliːz] excl s'il te (*or* vous) plaît ▷ vt plaire à ▷ vi (*think fit*): **do as you ~** faites comme il vous plaira; **~ yourself!** (*inf*) (faites) comme vous voulez!; **pleased** adj: **pleased (with)** content(e) (de); **pleased to meet you** enchanté (de faire votre connaissance)

pleasure ['plɛʒəʳ] n plaisir m; **"it's a ~"** "je vous en prie"

pleat [pliːt] n pli m

pledge [plɛdʒ] n (*promise*) promesse f ▷ vt promettre

plentiful ['plɛntɪfʊl] adj abondant(e), copieux(-euse)

plenty ['plɛntɪ] n: **~ of** beaucoup de; (*sufficient*) (bien) assez de

pliers ['plaɪəz] npl pinces fpl

plight [plaɪt] n situation f critique

plod [plɒd] vi avancer péniblement; (*fig*) peiner

plonk [plɒŋk] (*inf*) n (*BRIT: wine*) pinard m, piquette f ▷ vt: **to ~ sth down** poser brusquement qch

plot [plɒt] n complot m, conspiration f; (*of story, play*) intrigue f; (*of land*) lot m de terrain, lopin m ▷ vt (*mark out*) tracer point par point; (*Naut*) pointer; (*make graph of*) faire le graphique de; (*conspire*) comploter ▷ vi comploter

plough (*US* **plow**) [plaʊ] n charrue f ▷ vt (*earth*) labourer; **to ~ money into** investir dans; **ploughman's lunch** n (*BRIT*) assiette froide avec du pain, du fromage et des pickles

plow [plaʊ] (*US*) = **plough**

ploy [plɔɪ] n stratagème m

pluck [plʌk] vt (*fruit*) cueillir; (*musical instrument*) pincer; (*bird*) plumer; **to ~ one's eyebrows** s'épiler les sourcils; **to ~ up courage** prendre son courage à deux mains

plug [plʌg] n (*stopper*) bouchon m, bonde f; (*Elec*) prise f de courant; (*Aut: also: spark(ing) ~*) bougie f ▷ vt (*hole*) boucher; (*inf: advertise*) faire du battage pour, matraquer; **plug in** vt (*Elec*) brancher; **plughole** n (*BRIT*) trou m

(d'écoulement)

plum [plʌm] *n* (*fruit*) prune *f*

plumber [ˈplʌmə^r] *n* plombier *m*

plumbing [ˈplʌmɪŋ] *n* (*trade*) plomberie *f*; (*piping*) tuyauterie *f*

plummet [ˈplʌmɪt] *vi* (*person, object*) plonger; (*sales, prices*) dégringoler

plump [plʌmp] *adj* rondelet(te), dodu(e), bien en chair; **plump for** *vt fus* (*inf: choose*) se décider pour

plunge [plʌndʒ] *n* plongeon *m*; (*fig*) chute *f* ▷ *vt* plonger ▷ *vi* (*fall*) tomber, dégringoler; (*dive*) plonger; **to take the ~** se jeter à l'eau

pluperfect [pluːˈpəːfɪkt] *n* (*Ling*) plus-que-parfait *m*

plural [ˈpluərl] *adj* pluriel(le) ▷ *n* pluriel *m*

plus [plʌs] *n* (*also:* **~ sign**) signe *m* plus; (*advantage*) atout *m* ▷ *prep* plus; **ten/twenty ~** plus de dix/vingt

ply [plaɪ] *n* (*of wool*) fil *m* ▷ *vt* (*a trade*) exercer ▷ *vi* (*ship*) faire la navette; **to ~ sb with drink** donner continuellement à boire à qn; **plywood** *n* contreplaqué *m*

P.M. *n abbr* (BRIT) = **prime minister**

p.m. *adv abbr* (= *post meridiem*) de l'après-midi

PMS *n abbr* (= *premenstrual syndrome*) syndrome prémenstruel

PMT *n abbr* (= *premenstrual tension*) syndrome prémenstruel

pneumatic drill [njuːˈmætɪk-] *n* marteau-piqueur *m*

pneumonia [njuːˈməunɪə] *n* pneumonie *f*

poach [pəutʃ] *vt* (*cook*) pocher; (*steal*) pêcher (*or chasser*) sans permis ▷ *vi* braconner; **poached** *adj* (*egg*) poché(e)

P.O. Box *n abbr* = **post office box**

pocket [ˈpɔkɪt] *n* poche *f* ▷ *vt* empocher; **to be (£5) out of ~** (BRIT) en être de sa poche (pour 5 livres); **pocketbook** *n* (US: *wallet*) portefeuille *m*; **pocket money** *n* argent *m* de poche

pod [pɔd] *n* cosse *f*

podcast *n* podcast *m*

podiatrist [pɔˈdiːətrɪst] *n* (US) pédicure *m/f*

podium [ˈpəudɪəm] *n* podium *m*

poem [ˈpəuɪm] *n* poème *m*

poet [ˈpəuɪt] *n* poète *m*; **poetic** [pəuˈɛtɪk] *adj* poétique; **poetry** *n* poésie *f*

poignant [ˈpɔɪnjənt] *adj* poignant(e)

point [pɔɪnt] *n* point *m*; (*tip*) pointe *f*; (*in time*) moment *m*; (*in space*) endroit *m*; (*subject, idea*) point, sujet *m*; (*purpose*) but *m*; (*also:* **decimal ~**): **2 ~ 3 (2.3)** 2 virgule 3 (2,3); (BRIT *Elec: also:* **power ~**) prise *f* (de courant) ▷ *vt* (*show*) indiquer; (*gun etc*): **to ~ sth at** braquer *or* diriger qch sur ▷ *vi*: **to ~ at** montrer du doigt; **points** *npl* (*Rail*) aiguillage *m*; **to make a ~ of doing sth** ne pas manquer de faire qch; **to get/miss the ~** comprendre/ne pas

comprendre; **to come to the ~** en venir au fait; **there's no ~ (in doing)** cela ne sert à rien (de faire), à quoi ça sert?; **to be on the ~ of doing sth** être sur le point de faire qch; **point out** *vt* (*mention*) faire remarquer, souligner; **point-blank** *adv* (*fig*) catégoriquement; (*also:* **at point-blank range**) à bout portant; **pointed** *adj* (*shape*) pointu(e); (*remark*) plein(e) de sous-entendus; **pointer** *n* (*needle*) aiguille *f*; (*clue*) indication *f*; (*advice*) tuyau *m*; **pointless** *adj* inutile, vain(e); **point of view** *n* point *m* de vue

poison [ˈpɔɪzn] *n* poison *m* ▷ *vt* empoisonner; **poisonous** *adj* (*snake*) venimeux(-euse); (*substance, plant*) vénéneux(-euse); (*fumes*) toxique

poke [pəuk] *vt* (*jab with finger, stick etc*) piquer; pousser du doigt; (*put*): **to ~ sth in(to)** fourrer *or* enfoncer qch dans; **poke about** *vi* fureter; **poke out** *vi* (*stick out*) sortir

poker [ˈpəukə^r] *n* tisonnier *m*; (*Cards*) poker *m*

Poland [ˈpəulənd] *n* Pologne *f*

polar [ˈpəulə^r] *adj* polaire; **polar bear** *n* ours blanc

Pole [pəul] *n* Polonais(e)

pole [pəul] *n* (*of wood*) mât *m*, perche *f*; (*Elec*) poteau *m*; (*Geo*) pôle *m*; **pole bean** *n* (US) haricot *m* (à rames); **pole vault** *n* saut *m* à la perche

police [pəˈliːs] *npl* police *f* ▷ *vt* maintenir l'ordre dans; **police car** *n* voiture *f* de police; **police constable** *n* (BRIT) agent *m* de police; **police force** *n* police *f*, forces *fpl* de l'ordre; **policeman** (*irreg*) *n* agent *m* de police, policier *m*; **police officer** *n* agent *m* de police; **police station** *n* commissariat *m* de police; **policewoman** (*irreg*) *n* femme-agent *f*

policy [ˈpɔlɪsɪ] *n* politique *f*; (*also:* **insurance ~**) police *f* (d'assurance)

polio [ˈpəulɪəu] *n* polio *f*

Polish [ˈpəulɪʃ] *adj* polonais(e) ▷ *n* (*Ling*) polonais *m*

polish [ˈpɔlɪʃ] *n* (*for shoes*) cirage *m*; (*for floor*) cire *f*, encaustique *f*; (*for nails*) vernis *m*; (*shine*) éclat *m*, poli *m*; (*fig: refinement*) raffinement *m* ▷ *vt* (*put polish on: shoes, wood*) cirer; (*make shiny*) astiquer, faire briller; **polish off** *vt* (*food*) liquider; **polished** *adj* (*fig*) raffiné(e)

polite [pəˈlaɪt] *adj* poli(e); **politeness** *n* politesse *f*

political [pəˈlɪtɪkl] *adj* politique; **politically** *adv* politiquement; **politically correct** politiquement correct(e)

politician [pɔlɪˈtɪʃən] *n* homme/femme politique, politicien(ne)

politics [ˈpɔlɪtɪks] *n* politique *f*

poll [pəul] *n* scrutin *m*, vote *m*; (*also:* **opinion ~**) sondage *m* (d'opinion) ▷ *vt* (*votes*) obtenir

pollen [ˈpɔlən] *n* pollen *m*

polling station n (BRIT) bureau m de vote

pollute [pə'lu:t] vt polluer

pollution [pə'lu:ʃən] n pollution f

polo ['pəuləu] n polo m; **polo-neck** adj à col roulé ▷ n (sweater) pull m à col roulé; **polo shirt** n polo m

polyester [pɔlɪ'estəʳ] n polyester m

polystyrene [pɔlɪ'staɪri:n] n polystyrène m

polythene ['pɔlɪθi:n] n (BRIT) polyéthylène m; **polythene bag** n sac m en plastique

pomegranate ['pɔmɪgrænɪt] n grenade f

pompous ['pɔmpəs] adj pompeux(-euse)

pond [pɔnd] n étang m; (stagnant) mare f

ponder ['pɔndəʳ] vt considérer, peser

pony ['pəunɪ] n poney m; **ponytail** n queue f de cheval; **pony trekking** n (BRIT) randonnée f équestre or à cheval

poodle ['pu:dl] n caniche m

pool [pu:l] n (of rain) flaque f; (pond) mare f; (artificial) bassin m; (also: **swimming ~**) piscine f; (sth shared) fonds commun; (billiards) poule f ▷ vt mettre en commun; **pools** npl (football) ≈ loto sportif

poor [puəʳ] adj pauvre; (mediocre) médiocre, faible, mauvais(e) ▷ npl: **the ~** les pauvres mpl; **poorly** adv (badly) mal, médiocrement ▷ adj souffrant(e), malade

pop [pɔp] n (noise) bruit sec; (Mus) musique f pop; (inf: drink) soda m; (US inf: father) papa m ▷ vt (put) fourrer, mettre (rapidement) ▷ vi éclater; (cork) sauter; **pop in** vi entrer en passant; **pop out** vi sortir; **popcorn** n pop-corn m

pope [pəup] n pape m

poplar ['pɔpləʳ] n peuplier m

popper ['pɔpəʳ] n (BRIT) bouton-pression m

poppy ['pɔpɪ] n (wild) coquelicot m; (cultivated) pavot m

Popsicle® ['pɔpsɪkl] n (US) esquimau m (glace)

pop star n pop star f

popular ['pɔpjuləʳ] adj populaire; (fashionable) à la mode; **popularity** [pɔpju'lærɪtɪ] n popularité f

population [pɔpju'leɪʃən] n population f

pop-up adj (Comput: menu, window) pop up inv ▷ n pop up m inv, fenêtre f pop up

porcelain ['pɔ:slɪn] n porcelaine f

porch [pɔ:tʃ] n porche m; (US) véranda f

pore [pɔ:ʳ] n pore m ▷ vi: **to ~ over** s'absorber dans, être plongé(e) dans

pork [pɔ:k] n porc m; **pork chop** n côte f de porc; **pork pie** n pâté m de porc en croûte

porn [pɔ:n] adj (inf) porno ▷ n (inf) porno m; **pornographic** [pɔ:nə'græfɪk] adj pornographique; **pornography** [pɔ:'nɔgrəfɪ] n pornographie f

porridge ['pɔrɪdʒ] n porridge m

port [pɔ:t] n (harbour) port m; (Naut: left side) bâbord m; (wine) porto m; (Comput) port m,

accès m; **~ of call** (port d')escale f

portable ['pɔ:təbl] adj portatif(-ive)

porter ['pɔ:təʳ] n (for luggage) porteur m; (doorkeeper) gardien(ne); portier m

portfolio [pɔ:t'fəulɪəu] n portefeuille m; (of artist) portfolio m

portion ['pɔ:ʃən] n portion f, part f

portrait ['pɔ:treɪt] n portrait m

portray [pɔ:'treɪ] vt faire le portrait de; (in writing) dépeindre, représenter; (subj: actor) jouer

Portugal ['pɔ:tjugl] n Portugal m

Portuguese [pɔ:tju'gi:z] adj portugais(e) ▷ n (pl inv) Portugais(e); (Ling) portugais m

pose [pəuz] n pose f ▷ vi poser; (pretend): **to ~ as** se faire passer pour ▷ vt poser; (problem) créer

posh [pɔʃ] adj (inf) chic inv

position [pə'zɪʃən] n position f; (job, situation) situation f ▷ vt mettre en place or en position

positive ['pɔzɪtɪv] adj positif(-ive); (certain) sûr(e), certain(e); (definite) formel(le), catégorique; **positively** adv (affirmatively, enthusiastically) de façon positive; (inf: really) carrément

possess [pə'zɛs] vt posséder; **possession** [pə'zɛʃən] n possession f; **possessions** npl (belongings) affaires fpl; **possessive** adj possessif(-ive)

possibility [pɔsɪ'bɪlɪtɪ] n possibilité f; (event) éventualité f

possible ['pɔsɪbl] adj possible; **as big as ~** aussi gros que possible; **possibly** adv (perhaps) peut-être; **I cannot possibly come** il m'est impossible de venir

post [pəust] n (BRIT: mail) poste f; (: letters, delivery) courrier m; (job, situation) poste m; (pole) poteau m ▷ vt (BRIT: send by post) poster; (: appoint): **to ~ to** affecter à; **where can I ~ these cards?** où est-ce que je peux poster ces cartes postales?; **postage** n tarifs mpl d'affranchissement; **postal** adj postal(e); **postal order** n mandat-(poste m) m; **postbox** n (BRIT) boîte f aux lettres (publique); **postcard** n carte postale; **postcode** n (BRIT) code postal

poster ['pəustəʳ] n affiche f

postgraduate ['pəust'grædjuət] n ≈ étudiant(e) de troisième cycle

postman ['pəustmən] (BRIT: irreg) n facteur m

postmark ['pəustmɑ:k] n cachet m (de la poste)

post-mortem [pəust'mɔ:təm] n autopsie f

post office n (building) poste f; (organization): **the Post Office** les postes fpl

postpone [pəs'pəun] vt remettre (à plus tard), reculer

posture ['pɔstʃəʳ] n posture f; (fig) attitude f

postwoman ['pəust'wumən] (BRIT: irreg) n factrice f

pot [pɒt] n (for cooking) marmite f; casserole f; (teapot) théière f; (for coffee) cafetière f; (for plants, jam) pot m; (inf: marijuana) herbe f ▷ vt (plant) mettre en pot; **to go to ~** (inf) aller à vau-l'eau

potato (pl **~es**) [pə'teɪtəu] n pomme f de terre; **potato peeler** n épluche-légumes m

potent ['pəutnt] adj puissant(e); (drink) fort(e), très alcoolisé(e); (man) viril

potential [pə'tɛnʃl] adj potentiel(le) ▷ n potentiel m

pothole ['pɔthəul] n (in road) nid m de poule; (BRIT: underground) gouffre m, caverne f

pot plant n plante f d'appartement

potter ['pɔtə'] n potier m ▷ vi (BRIT): **to ~ around** or **about** bricoler; **pottery** n poterie f

potty ['pɔtɪ] n (child's) pot m

pouch [pautʃ] n (Zool) poche f; (for tobacco) blague f; (for money) bourse f

poultry ['pəultrɪ] n volaille f

pounce [pauns] vi: **to ~ (on)** bondir (sur), fondre (sur)

pound [paund] n livre f (weight = 453g, 16 ounces; money = 100 pence); (for dogs, cars) fourrière f ▷ vt (beat) bourrer de coups, marteler; (crush) piler, pulvériser ▷ vi (heart) battre violemment, taper; **pound sterling** n livre f sterling

pour [pɔː'] vt verser ▷ vi couler à flots; (rain) pleuvoir à verse; **to ~ sb a drink** verser or servir à boire à qn; **pour in** vi (people) affluer, se précipiter; (news, letters) arriver en masse; **pour out** vi (people) sortir en masse ▷ vt vider; (fig) déverser; (serve: a drink) verser; **pouring** adj: **pouring rain** pluie torrentielle

pout [paut] vi faire la moue

poverty ['pɔvətɪ] n pauvreté f, misère f

powder ['paudə'] n poudre f ▷ vt poudrer; **powdered milk** n lait m en poudre

power ['pauə'] n (strength, nation) puissance f, force f; (ability, Pol: of party, leader) pouvoir m; (of speech, thought) faculté f; (Elec) courant m; **to be in ~** être au pouvoir; **power cut** n (BRIT) coupure f de courant; **power failure** n panne f de courant; **powerful** adj puissant(e); (performance etc) très fort(e); **powerless** adj impuissant(e); **power point** n (BRIT) prise f de courant; **power station** n centrale f électrique

p.p. abbr (= per procurationem: by proxy) p.p.

PR n abbr = **public relations**

practical ['præktɪkl] adj pratique; **practical joke** n farce f; **practically** adv (almost) pratiquement

practice ['præktɪs] n pratique f; (of profession) exercice m; (at football etc) entraînement m; (business) cabinet m ▷ vt, vi (US) = **practise**; **in ~** (in reality) en pratique; **out of ~** rouillé(e)

practise (US **practice**) ['præktɪs] vt (work

at: piano, backhand etc) s'exercer à, travailler; (train for: sport) s'entraîner à; (a sport, religion, method) pratiquer; (profession) exercer ▷ vi s'exercer, travailler; (train) s'entraîner; (lawyer, doctor) exercer; **practising** (US **practicing**) adj (Christian etc) pratiquant(e); (lawyer) en exercice

practitioner [præk'tɪʃənə'] n praticien(ne)

pragmatic [præg'mætɪk] adj pragmatique

prairie ['prɛərɪ] n savane f

praise [preɪz] n éloge(s) m(pl), louange(s) f(pl) ▷ vt louer, faire l'éloge de

pram [præm] n (BRIT) landau m, voiture f d'enfant

prank [præŋk] n farce f

prawn [prɔːn] n crevette f (rose); **prawn cocktail** n cocktail m de crevettes

pray [preɪ] vi prier; **prayer** [prɛə'] n prière f

preach [priːtʃ] vi prêcher; **preacher** n prédicateur m; (US: clergyman) pasteur m

precarious [prɪ'kɛərɪəs] adj précaire

precaution [prɪ'kɔːʃən] n précaution f

precede [prɪ'siːd] vt, vi précéder; **precedent** ['prɛsɪdənt] n précédent m; **preceding** [prɪ'siːdɪŋ] adj qui précède (or précédait)

precinct ['priːsɪŋkt] n (US: district) circonscription f, arrondissement m; **pedestrian ~** (BRIT) zone piétonnière; **shopping ~** (BRIT) centre commercial

precious ['prɛʃəs] adj précieux(-euse)

precise [prɪ'saɪs] adj précis(e); **precisely** adv précisément

precision [prɪ'sɪʒən] n précision f

predator ['prɛdətə'] n prédateur m, rapace m

predecessor ['priːdɪsɛsə'] n prédécesseur m

predicament [prɪ'dɪkəmənt] n situation f difficile

predict [prɪ'dɪkt] vt prédire; **predictable** adj prévisible; **prediction** [prɪ'dɪkʃən] n prédiction f

predominantly [prɪ'dɔmɪnəntlɪ] adv en majeure partie; (especially) surtout

preface ['prɛfəs] n préface f

prefect ['priːfɛkt] n (BRIT: in school) élève chargé de certaines fonctions de discipline

prefer [prɪ'fəː'] vt préférer; **preferable** ['prɛfrəbl] adj préférable; **preferably** ['prɛfrəblɪ] adv de préférence; **preference** ['prɛfrəns] n préférence f

prefix ['priːfɪks] n préfixe m

pregnancy ['prɛgnənsɪ] n grossesse f

pregnant ['prɛgnənt] adj enceinte adj f; (animal) pleine

prehistoric ['priːhɪs'tɔrɪk] adj préhistorique

prejudice ['prɛdʒudɪs] n préjugé m; **prejudiced** adj (person) plein(e) de préjugés; (in a matter) partial(e)

preliminary [prɪ'lɪmɪnərɪ] adj préliminaire

prelude ['prɛljuːd] n prélude m

premature ['prɛmətʃuəʳ] *adj* prématuré(e)
premier ['prɛmɪəʳ] *adj* premier(-ière),
principal(e) ▷ *n* (*Pol*: *Prime Minister*) premier
ministre; (*Pol*: *President*) chef *m* de l'État
premiere ['prɛmɪɛəʳ] *n* première *f*
Premier League *n* première division
premises ['prɛmɪsɪz] *npl* locaux *mpl*; **on the ~**
sur les lieux; sur place
premium ['pri:mɪəm] *n* prime *f*; **to be at a
~** (*fig*: *housing etc*) être très demandé(e), être
rarissime
premonition [prɛmə'nɪʃən] *n* prémonition *f*
preoccupied [pri:'ɔkjupaɪd] *adj*
préoccupé(e)
prepaid [pri:'peɪd] *adj* payé(e) d'avance
preparation [prɛpə'reɪʃən] *n* préparation *f*;
preparations *npl* (*for trip, war*) préparatifs *mpl*
preparatory school *n* école primaire privée;
(*us*) lycée privé
prepare [prɪ'pɛəʳ] *vt* préparer ▷ *vi*: **to ~ for** se
préparer à
prepared [prɪ'pɛəd] *adj*: **~ for** préparé(e) à; **~
to** prêt(e) à
preposition [prɛpə'zɪʃən] *n* préposition *f*
prep school *n* = **preparatory school**
prerequisite [pri:'rɛkwɪzɪt] *n* condition *f*
préalable
preschool ['pri:'sku:l] *adj* préscolaire; (*child*)
d'âge préscolaire
prescribe [prɪ'skraɪb] *vt* prescrire
prescription [prɪ'skrɪpʃən] *n* (*Med*)
ordonnance *f*; (*: medicine*) médicament
m (obtenu sur ordonnance); **could you
write me a ~?** pouvez-vous me faire une
ordonnance?
presence ['prɛzns] *n* présence *f*; **in sb's ~** en
présence de qn; **~ of mind** présence d'esprit
present ['prɛznt] *adj* présent(e); (*current*)
présent, actuel(le) ▷ *n* cadeau *m*; (*actuality*)
présent *m* ▷ *vt* [prɪ'zɛnt] présenter; (*prize,
medal*) remettre; (*give*): **to ~ sb with sth**
offrir qch à qn; **at ~** en ce moment; **to give
sb a ~** offrir un cadeau à qn; **presentable**
[prɪ'zɛntəbl] *adj* présentable; **presentation**
[prɛznteɪʃən] *n* présentation *f*; (*ceremony*)
remise *f* du cadeau (or de la médaille *etc*);
present-day *adj* contemporain(e), actuel(le);
presenter [prɪ'zɛntəʳ] *n* (*BRIT Radio, TV*)
présentateur(-trice); **presently** *adv* (*soon*)
tout à l'heure, bientôt; (*with verb in past*) peu
après; (*at present*) en ce moment; **present
participle** [-'pɑ:tɪsɪpl] *n* participe *m* présent
preservation [prɛzə'veɪʃən] *n* préservation
f, conservation *f*
preservative [prɪ'zə:vətɪv] *n* agent *m* de
conservation
preserve [prɪ'zə:v] *vt* (*keep safe*) préserver,
protéger; (*maintain*) conserver, garder; (*food*)
mettre en conserve ▷ *n* (*for game, fish*) réserve

f; (*often pl*: *jam*) confiture *f*
preside [prɪ'zaɪd] *vi* présider
president ['prɛzɪdənt] *n* président(e);
presidential [prɛzɪ'dɛnʃl] *adj* présidentiel(le)
press [prɛs] *n* (*tool, machine, newspapers*)
presse *f*; (*for wine*) pressoir *m* ▷ *vt* (*push*)
appuyer sur; (*squeeze*) presser, serrer; (*clothes:
iron*) repasser; (*insist*): **to ~ sth on sb** presser
qn d'accepter qch; (*urge, entreat*): **to ~ sb to
do** *or* **into doing sth** pousser qn à faire qch
▷ *vi* appuyer; **we are ~ed for time** le temps
nous manque; **to ~ for sth** faire pression pour
obtenir qch; **press conference** *n* conférence *f*
de presse; **pressing** *adj* urgent(e), pressant(e);
press stud *n* (*BRIT*) bouton-pression *m*; **press-
up** *n* (*BRIT*) traction *f*
pressure ['prɛʃəʳ] *n* pression *f*; (*stress*) tension
f; **to put ~ on sb (to do sth)** faire pression sur
qn (pour qu'il fasse qch); **pressure cooker** *n*
cocotte-minute *f*; **pressure group** *n* groupe
m de pression
prestige [prɛs'ti:ʒ] *n* prestige *m*
prestigious [prɛs'tɪdʒəs] *adj*
prestigieux(-euse)
presumably [prɪ'zju:məblɪ] *adv*
vraisemblablement
presume [prɪ'zju:m] *vt* présumer, supposer
pretence (*us* **pretense**) [prɪ'tɛns] *n* (*claim*)
prétention *f*; **under false ~s** sous des
prétextes fallacieux
pretend [prɪ'tɛnd] *vt* (*feign*) feindre, simuler
▷ *vi* (*feign*) faire semblant
pretense [prɪ'tɛns] *n* (*us*) = **pretence**
pretentious [prɪ'tɛnʃəs] *adj*
prétentieux(-euse)
pretext ['pri:tɛkst] *n* prétexte *m*
pretty ['prɪtɪ] *adj* joli(e) ▷ *adv* assez
prevail [prɪ'veɪl] *vi* (*win*) l'emporter, prévaloir;
(*be usual*) avoir cours; **prevailing** *adj*
(*widespread*) courant(e), répandu(e); (*wind*)
dominant(e)
prevalent ['prɛvələnt] *adj* répandu(e),
courant(e)
prevent [prɪ'vɛnt] *vt*: **to ~ (from doing)**
empêcher (de faire); **prevention** [prɪ'vɛnʃən]
n prévention *f*; **preventive** *adj* préventif(-ive)
preview ['pri:vju:] *n* (*of film*) avant-première *f*
previous ['pri:vɪəs] *adj* (*last*) précédent(e);
(*earlier*) antérieur(e); **previously** *adv*
précédemment, auparavant
prey [preɪ] *n* proie *f* ▷ *vi*: **to ~ on** s'attaquer à; **it
was ~ing on his mind** ça le rongeait *or* minait
price [praɪs] *n* prix *m* ▷ *vt* (*goods*) fixer le prix
de; **priceless** *adj* sans prix, inestimable; **price
list** *n* tarif *m*
prick [prɪk] *n* (*sting*) piqûre *f* ▷ *vt* piquer; **to ~
up one's ears** dresser *or* tendre l'oreille
prickly ['prɪklɪ] *adj* piquant(e), épineux(-euse);
(*fig*: *person*) irritable

pride [praɪd] n fierté f; (pej) orgueil m ▷ vt: **to ~ o.s. on** se flatter de; s'enorgueillir de
priest [priːst] n prêtre m
primarily ['praɪmərɪlɪ] adv principalement, essentiellement
primary ['praɪmərɪ] adj primaire; (first in importance) premier(-ière), primordial(e) ▷ n (us: election) (élection f) primaire f; **primary school** n (BRIT) école f primaire
prime [praɪm] adj primordial(e), fondamental(e); (excellent) excellent(e) ▷ vt (fig) mettre au courant ▷ n: **in the ~ of life** dans la fleur de l'âge; **Prime Minister** n Premier ministre
primitive ['prɪmɪtɪv] adj primitif(-ive)
primrose ['prɪmrəuz] n primevère f
prince [prɪns] n prince m
princess [prɪn'ses] n princesse f
principal ['prɪnsɪpl] adj principal(e) ▷ n (head teacher) directeur m, principal m; **principally** adv principalement
principle ['prɪnsɪpl] n principe m; **in ~** en principe; **on ~** par principe
print [prɪnt] n (mark) empreinte f; (letters) caractères mpl; (fabric) imprimé m; (Art) gravure f, estampe f; (Phot) épreuve f ▷ vt imprimer; (publish) publier; (write in capitals) écrire en majuscules; **out of ~** épuisé(e); **print out** vt (Comput) imprimer; **printer** n (machine) imprimante f; (person) imprimeur m; **printout** n (Comput) sortie f imprimante
prior ['praɪər] adj antérieur(e), précédent(e); (more important) prioritaire ▷ adv: **~ to doing** avant de faire
priority [praɪ'ɔrɪtɪ] n priorité f; **to have** or **take ~ over sth/sb** avoir la priorité sur qch/qn
prison [prɪzn] n prison f ▷ cpd pénitentiaire; **prisoner** n prisonnier(-ière); **prisoner of war** n prisonnier(-ière) de guerre
pristine ['prɪstiːn] adj virginal(e)
privacy ['prɪvəsɪ] n intimité f, solitude f
private ['praɪvɪt] adj (not public) privé(e); (personal) personnel(le); (house, café, lesson) particulier(-ière); (quiet: place) tranquille ▷ n soldat m de deuxième classe; **"~"** (on envelope) "personnelle"; (on door) "privé"; **in ~** en privé; **privately** adv en privé; (within oneself) intérieurement; **private property** n propriété privée; **private school** n école privée
privatize ['praɪvɪtaɪz] vt privatiser
privilege ['prɪvɪlɪdʒ] n privilège m
prize [praɪz] n prix m ▷ adj (example, idiot) parfait(e); (bull, novel) primé(e) ▷ vt priser, faire grand cas de; **prize-giving** n distribution f des prix; **prizewinner** n gagnant(e)
pro [prəu] n (inf: Sport) professionnel(le) ▷ prep pro ...; **pros** npl: **the ~s and cons** le pour et le contre

probability [prɔbə'bɪlɪtɪ] n probabilité f; **in all ~** très probablement
probable ['prɔbəbl] adj probable
probably ['prɔbəblɪ] adv probablement
probation [prə'beɪʃən] n: **on ~** (employee) à l'essai; (Law) en liberté surveillée
probe [prəub] n (Med, Space) sonde f; (enquiry) enquête f, investigation f ▷ vt sonder, explorer
problem ['prɔbləm] n problème m
procedure [prə'siːdʒər] n (Admin, Law) procédure f; (method) marche f à suivre, façon f de procéder
proceed [prə'siːd] vi (go forward) avancer; (act) procéder; (continue): **to ~ (with)** continuer, poursuivre; **to ~ to do** se mettre à faire; **proceedings** npl (measures) mesures fpl; (Law: against sb) poursuites fpl; (meeting) réunion f, séance f; (records) compte rendu; actes mpl; **proceeds** ['prəusiːdz] npl produit m, recette f
process ['prəuses] n processus m; (method) procédé m ▷ vt traiter
procession [prə'seʃən] n défilé m, cortège m; **funeral ~** (on foot) cortège funèbre; (in cars) convoi m mortuaire
proclaim [prə'kleɪm] vt déclarer, proclamer
prod [prɔd] vt pousser
produce n ['prɔdjuːs] (Agr) produits mpl ▷ vt [prə'djuːs] produire; (show) présenter; (cause) provoquer, causer; (Theat) monter, mettre en scène; (TV: programme) réaliser; (: play, film) mettre en scène; (Radio: programme) réaliser; (: play) mettre en ondes; **producer** n (Theat) metteur m en scène; (Agr, Comm, Cine) producteur m; (TV: of programme) réalisateur m; (: of play, film) metteur en scène; (Radio: of programme) réalisateur m; (: of play) metteur en ondes
product ['prɔdʌkt] n produit m; **production** [prə'dʌkʃən] n production f; (Theat) mise f en scène; **productive** [prə'dʌktɪv] adj productif(-ive); **productivity** [prɔdʌk'tɪvɪtɪ] n productivité f
Prof. [prɔf] abbr (= professor) Prof
profession [prə'feʃən] n profession f; **professional** n professionnel(le) ▷ adj professionnel(le); (work) de professionnel
professor [prə'fesər] n professeur m (titulaire d'une chaire); (us: teacher) professeur m
profile ['prəufaɪl] n profil m
profit ['prɔfɪt] n (from trading) bénéfice m; (advantage) profit m ▷ vi: **to ~ (by** or **from)** profiter (de); **profitable** adj lucratif(-ive), rentable
profound [prə'faund] adj profond(e)
programme (us **program**) ['prəugræm] n (Comput: also BRIT: **program**) programme m; (Radio, TV) émission f ▷ vt programmer; **programmer** (us **programer**) n

programmeur(-euse); **programming** (*us* **programing**) *n* programmation *f*

progress *n* ['prəʊgrɛs] progrès *m(pl)* ▷ *vi* [prə'grɛs] progresser, avancer; **in ~** en cours; **progressive** [prə'grɛsɪv] *adj* progressif(-ive); (*person*) progressiste

prohibit [prə'hɪbɪt] *vt* interdire, défendre

project *n* ['prɒdʒɛkt] (*plan*) projet *m*, plan *m*; (*venture*) opération *f*, entreprise *f*; (*Scol: research*) étude *f*, dossier *m* ▷ *vb* [prə'dʒɛkt] ▷ *vt* projeter ▷ *vi* (*stick out*) faire saillie, s'avancer; **projection** [prə'dʒɛkʃən] *n* projection *f*; (*overhang*) saillie *f*; **projector** [prə'dʒɛktə'] *n* projecteur *m*

prolific [prə'lɪfɪk] *adj* prolifique

prolong [prə'lɒŋ] *vt* prolonger

prom [prɒm] *n abbr* = **promenade** (*us: ball*) bal *m* d'étudiants; **the P~s** *série de concerts de musique classique; voir encadré*

● **PROM**

● En Grande-Bretagne, un **promenade**
● **concert** ou **prom** est un concert de
● musique classique, ainsi appelé car, à
● l'origine, le public restait debout et se
● promenait au lieu de rester assis. De nos
● jours, une partie du public reste debout,
● mais il y a également des places assises
● (plus chères). Les **Proms** les plus connus
● sont les Proms londoniens. La dernière
● séance (the "Last Night of the Proms") est
● un grand événement médiatique où se
● jouent des airs traditionnels et patriotiques.
● Aux États-Unis et au Canada, le **prom** ou
● **promenade** est un bal organisé par le lycée.

promenade [prɒmə'nɑːd] *n* (*by sea*) esplanade *f*, promenade *f*

prominent ['prɒmɪnənt] *adj* (*standing out*) proéminent(e); (*important*) important(e)

promiscuous [prə'mɪskjuəs] *adj* (*sexually*) de mœurs légères

promise ['prɒmɪs] *n* promesse *f* ▷ *vt*, *vi* promettre; **promising** *adj* prometteur(-euse)

promote [prə'məut] *vt* promouvoir; (*new product*) lancer; **promotion** [prə'məuʃən] *n* promotion *f*

prompt [prɒmpt] *adj* rapide ▷ *n* (*Comput*) message *m* (de guidage) ▷ *vt* (*cause*) entraîner, provoquer; (*Theat*) souffler (son rôle *or* ses répliques) à; **at 8 o'clock ~** à 8 heures précises; **to ~ sb to do** inciter *or* pousser qn à faire; **promptly** *adv* (*quickly*) rapidement, sans délai; (*on time*) ponctuellement

prone [prəun] *adj* (*lying*) couché(e) (face contre terre); (*liable*): **~ to** enclin(e) à

prong [prɒŋ] *n* (*of fork*) dent *f*

pronoun ['prəunaun] *n* pronom *m*

pronounce [prə'nauns] *vt* prononcer; **how do you ~ it?** comment est-ce que ça se prononce?

pronunciation [prənʌnsɪ'eɪʃən] *n* prononciation *f*

proof [pruːf] *n* preuve *f* ▷ *adj*: **~ against** à l'épreuve de

prop [prɒp] *n* support *m*, étai *m*; (*fig*) soutien *m* ▷ *vt* (*also*: **~ up**) étayer, soutenir; **props** *npl* accessoires *mpl*

propaganda [prɒpə'gændə] *n* propagande *f*

propeller [prə'pɛlə'] *n* hélice *f*

proper ['prɒpə'] *adj* (*suited, right*) approprié(e), bon (bonne); (*seemly*) correct(e), convenable; (*authentic*) vrai(e), véritable; (*referring to place*): **the village ~** le village proprement dit; **properly** *adv* correctement, convenablement; **proper noun** *n* nom *m* propre

property ['prɒpətɪ] *n* (*possessions*) biens *mpl*; (*house etc*) propriété *f*; (*land*) terres *fpl*, domaine *m*

prophecy ['prɒfɪsɪ] *n* prophétie *f*

prophet ['prɒfɪt] *n* prophète *m*

proportion [prə'pɔːʃən] *n* proportion *f*; (*share*) part *f*; partie *f*; **proportions** *npl* (*size*) dimensions *fpl*; **proportional, proportionate** *adj* proportionnel(le)

proposal [prə'pəuzl] *n* proposition *f*, offre *f*; (*plan*) projet *m*; (*of marriage*) demande *f* en mariage

propose [prə'pəuz] *vt* proposer, suggérer ▷ *vi* faire sa demande en mariage; **to ~ to do** avoir l'intention de faire

proposition [prɒpə'zɪʃən] *n* proposition *f*

proprietor [prə'praɪətə'] *n* propriétaire *m/f*

prose [prəuz] *n* prose *f*; (*Scol: translation*) thème *m*

prosecute ['prɒsɪkjuːt] *vt* poursuivre; **prosecution** [prɒsɪ'kjuːʃən] *n* poursuites *fpl* judiciaires; (*accusing side: in criminal case*) accusation *f*; (: *in civil case*) la partie plaignante; **prosecutor** *n* (*lawyer*) procureur *m*; (*also*: **public prosecutor**) ministère public; (*us: plaintiff*) plaignant(e)

prospect *n* ['prɒspɛkt] perspective *f*; (*hope*) espoir *m*, chances *fpl* ▷ *vt*, *vi* [prə'spɛkt] prospecter; **prospects** *npl* (*for work etc*) possibilités *fpl* d'avenir, débouchés *mpl*; **prospective** [prə'spɛktɪv] *adj* (*possible*) éventuel(le); (*future*) futur(e)

prospectus [prə'spɛktəs] *n* prospectus *m*

prosper ['prɒspə'] *vi* prospérer; **prosperity** [prɔ'spɛrɪtɪ] *n* prospérité *f*; **prosperous** *adj* prospère

prostitute ['prɒstɪtjuːt] *n* prostituée *f*; **male ~** prostitué *m*

protect [prə'tɛkt] *vt* protéger; **protection** [prə'tɛkʃən] *n* protection *f*; **protective** *adj* protecteur(-trice); (*clothing*) de protection

protein ['prəʊtiːn] n protéine f

protest n ['prəʊtɛst] protestation f ▷ vb [prə'tɛst] ▷ vi: **to ~ against/about** protester contre/à propos de; **to ~ (that)** protester que

Protestant ['prɒtɪstənt] adj, n protestant(e)

protester, protestor [prə'tɛstəʳ] n (in demonstration) manifestant(e)

protractor [prə'træktəʳ] n (Geom) rapporteur m

proud [praʊd] adj fier(-ère); (pej) orgueilleux(-euse)

prove [pruːv] vt prouver, démontrer ▷ vi: **to ~ correct** etc s'avérer juste etc; **to ~ o.s.** montrer ce dont on est capable

proverb ['prɒvəːb] n proverbe m

provide [prə'vaɪd] vt fournir; **to ~ sb with sth** fournir qch à qn; **provide for** vt fus (person) subvenir aux besoins de; (future event) prévoir; **provided** conj: **provided (that)** à condition que + sub; **providing** [prə'vaɪdɪŋ] conj à condition que + sub

province ['prɒvɪns] n province f; (fig) domaine m; **provincial** [prə'vɪnʃəl] adj provincial(e)

provision [prə'vɪʒən] n (supplying) fourniture f; approvisionnement m; (stipulation) disposition f; **provisions** npl (food) provisions fpl; **provisional** adj provisoire

provocative [prə'vɒkətɪv] adj provocateur(-trice), provocant(e)

provoke [prə'vəʊk] vt provoquer

prowl [praʊl] vi (also: **~ about, ~ around**) rôder

proximity [prɒk'sɪmɪtɪ] n proximité f

proxy ['prɒksɪ] n: **by ~** par procuration

prudent ['pruːdnt] adj prudent(e)

prune [pruːn] n pruneau m ▷ vt élaguer

pry [praɪ] vi: **to ~ into** fourrer son nez dans

PS n abbr (= postscript) PS m

pseudonym ['sjuːdənɪm] n pseudonyme m

PSHE n abbr (BRIT: Scol: = personal, social and health education) cours d'éducation personnelle, sanitaire et sociale préparant à la vie adulte

psychiatric [saɪkɪ'ætrɪk] adj psychiatrique

psychiatrist [saɪ'kaɪətrɪst] n psychiatre m/f

psychic ['saɪkɪk] adj (also: **~al**) (méta)psychique; (person) doué(e) de télépathie or d'un sixième sens

psychoanalysis (pl **-ses**) [saɪkəʊə'nælɪsɪs, -siːz] n psychanalyse f

psychological [saɪkə'lɒdʒɪkl] adj psychologique

psychologist [saɪ'kɒlədʒɪst] n psychologue m/f

psychology [saɪ'kɒlədʒɪ] n psychologie f

psychotherapy [saɪkəʊ'θɛrəpɪ] n psychothérapie f

pt abbr = **pint(s)**; **point(s)**

PTO abbr (= please turn over) TSVP

pub [pʌb] n abbr (= public house) pub m

puberty ['pjuːbətɪ] n puberté f

public ['pʌblɪk] adj public(-ique) ▷ n public m; **in ~** en public; **to make ~** rendre public

publication [pʌblɪ'keɪʃən] n publication f

public: **public company** n société f anonyme; **public convenience** n (BRIT) toilettes fpl; **public holiday** n (BRIT) jour férié; **public house** n (BRIT) pub m

publicity [pʌb'lɪsɪtɪ] n publicité f

publicize ['pʌblɪsaɪz] vt (make known) faire connaître, rendre public; (advertise) faire de la publicité pour

public: **public limited company** n ≈ société f anonyme (SA) (cotée en Bourse); **publicly** adv publiquement, en public; **public opinion** n opinion publique; **public relations** n or npl relations publiques (RP); **public school** n (BRIT) école privée; (US) école publique; **public transport** (US **public transportation**) n transports mpl en commun

publish ['pʌblɪʃ] vt publier; **publisher** n éditeur m; **publishing** n (industry) édition f

pub lunch n repas m de bistrot

pudding ['pʊdɪŋ] n (BRIT: dessert) dessert m, entremets m; (sweet dish) pudding m, gâteau m

puddle ['pʌdl] n flaque f d'eau

puff [pʌf] n bouffée f ▷ vt (also: **~ out**: sails, cheeks) gonfler ▷ vi (pant) haleter; **puff pastry** (US **puff paste**) n pâte feuilletée

pull [pʊl] n (tug): **to give sth a ~** tirer sur qch ▷ vt tirer; (trigger) presser; (strain: muscle, tendon) se claquer ▷ vi tirer; **to ~ to pieces** mettre en morceaux; **to ~ one's punches** (also fig) ménager son adversaire; **to ~ one's weight** y mettre du sien; **to ~ o.s. together** se ressaisir; **to ~ sb's leg** (fig) faire marcher qn; **pull apart** vt (break) mettre en pièces, démantibuler; **pull away** vi (vehicle: move off) partir; (draw back) s'éloigner; **pull back** vt (lever etc) tirer sur; (curtains) ouvrir ▷ vi (refrain) s'abstenir; (Mil: withdraw) se retirer; **pull down** vt baisser, abaisser; (house) démolir; **pull in** vi (Aut) se ranger; (Rail) entrer en gare; **pull off** vt enlever, ôter; (deal etc) conclure; **pull out** vi démarrer, partir; (Aut: come out of line) déboîter ▷ vt (from bag, pocket) sortir; (remove) arracher; **pull over** vi (Aut) se ranger; **pull up** vi (stop) s'arrêter ▷ vt remonter; (uproot) déraciner, arracher

pulley ['pʊlɪ] n poulie f

pullover ['pʊləʊvəʳ] n pull-over m, tricot m

pulp [pʌlp] n (of fruit) pulpe f; (for paper) pâte f à papier

pulpit ['pʊlpɪt] n chaire f

pulse [pʌls] n (of blood) pouls m; (of heart) battement m; **pulses** npl (Culin) légumineuses fpl

puma ['pjuːmə] n puma m

pump [pʌmp] n pompe f; (shoe) escarpin m
▷ vt pomper; **pump up** vt gonfler
pumpkin ['pʌmpkɪn] n potiron m, citrouille f
pun [pʌn] n jeu m de mots, calembour m
punch [pʌntʃ] n (blow) coup m de poing; (tool)
poinçon m; (drink) punch m ▷ vt (make a hole in)
poinçonner, perforer; (hit): **to ~ sb/sth** donner
un coup de poing à qn/sur qch; **punch-up** n
(BRIT inf) bagarre f
punctual ['pʌŋktjuəl] adj ponctuel(le)
punctuation [pʌŋktju'eɪʃən] n ponctuation f
puncture ['pʌŋktʃəʳ] n (BRIT) crevaison f ▷ vt
crever
punish ['pʌnɪʃ] vt punir; **punishment** n
punition f, châtiment m
punk [pʌŋk] n (person: also: **~ rocker**) punk
m/f; (music: also: **~ rock**) le punk; (US inf:
hoodlum) voyou m
pup [pʌp] n chiot m
pupil ['pjuːpl] n élève m/f; (of eye) pupille f
puppet ['pʌpɪt] n marionnette f, pantin m
puppy ['pʌpɪ] n chiot m, petit chien
purchase ['pəːtʃɪs] n achat m ▷ vt acheter
pure [pjuəʳ] adj pur(e); **purely** adv purement
purify ['pjuərɪfaɪ] vt purifier, épurer
purity ['pjuərɪtɪ] n pureté f
purple ['pəːpl] adj violet(te); (face) cramoisi(e)
purpose ['pəːpəs] n intention f, but m; **on ~**
exprès
purr [pəːʳ] vi ronronner
purse [pəːs] n (BRIT: for money) porte-monnaie
m inv; (US: handbag) sac m (à main) ▷ vt serrer,
pincer
pursue [pə'sjuː] vt poursuivre
pursuit [pə'sjuːt] n poursuite f; (occupation)
occupation f, activité f
pus [pʌs] n pus m
push [puʃ] n poussée f ▷ vt pousser; (button)
appuyer sur; (fig: product) mettre en avant,
faire de la publicité pour ▷ vi pousser; **to ~
for** (better pay, conditions) réclamer; **push
in** vi s'introduire de force; **push off** vi (inf)
filer, ficher le camp; **push on** vi (continue)
continuer; **push over** vt renverser; **push
through** vi (in crowd) se frayer un chemin;
pushchair n (BRIT) poussette f; **pusher** n
(also: **drug pusher**) revendeur(-euse) (de
drogue), ravitailleur(-euse) (en drogue); **push-
up** n (US) traction f
pussy(-cat) ['pusɪ-] n (inf) minet m
put (pt, pp **~**) [put] vt mettre; (place) poser,
placer; (say) dire, exprimer; (a question) poser;
(case, view) exposer, présenter; (estimate)
estimer; **put aside** vt mettre de côté; **put
away** vt (store) ranger; **put back** vt (replace)
remettre, replacer; (postpone) remettre; **put
by** vt (money) mettre de côté, économiser; **put
down** vt (parcel etc) poser, déposer; (in writing)
mettre par écrit, inscrire; (suppress: revolt etc)
réprimer, écraser; (attribute) attribuer; (animal)
abattre; (cat, dog) faire piquer; **put forward** vt
(ideas) avancer, proposer; **put in** vt (complaint)
soumettre; (time, effort) consacrer; **put off**
vt (postpone) remettre à plus tard, ajourner;
(discourage) dissuader; **put on** vt (clothes,
lipstick, CD) mettre; (light etc) allumer; (play
etc) monter; (weight) prendre; (assume: accent,
manner) prendre; **put out** vt (take outside)
mettre dehors; (one's hand) tendre; (light etc)
éteindre; (person: inconvenience) déranger,
gêner; **put through** vt (Tel: caller) mettre en
communication; (: call) passer; (plan) faire
accepter; **put together** vt mettre ensemble;
(assemble: furniture) monter, assembler; (meal)
préparer; **put up** vt (raise) lever, relever,
remonter; (hang) accrocher; (build) construire,
ériger; (increase) augmenter; (accommodate)
loger; **put up with** vt fus supporter
putt [pʌt] n putt m; **putting green** n green m
puzzle ['pʌzl] n énigme f, mystère m; (game)
jeu m, casse-tête m; (jigsaw) puzzle m; (also:
crossword ~) mots croisés ▷ vt intriguer,
rendre perplexe ▷ vi: **to ~ over** chercher à
comprendre; **puzzled** adj perplexe; **puzzling**
adj déconcertant(e), inexplicable
pyjamas [pɪ'dʒɑːməz] npl (BRIT) pyjama m
pylon ['paɪlən] n pylône m
pyramid ['pɪrəmɪd] n pyramide f
Pyrenees [pɪrə'niːz] npl Pyrénées fpl

quack [kwæk] n (of duck) coin-coin m inv; (pej: doctor) charlatan m

quadruple [kwɔ'druːpl] vt, vi quadrupler

quail [kweɪl] n (Zool) caille f ▷ vi: **to ~ at** or **before** reculer devant

quaint [kweɪnt] adj bizarre; (old-fashioned) désuet(-ète); (picturesque) au charme vieillot, pittoresque

quake [kweɪk] vi trembler ▷ n abbr = **earthquake**

qualification [kwɔlɪfɪ'keɪʃən] n (often pl: degree etc) diplôme m; (training) qualification(s) f(pl); (ability) compétence(s) f(pl); (limitation) réserve f, restriction f

qualified ['kwɔlɪfaɪd] adj (trained) qualifié(e); (professionally) diplômé(e); (fit, competent) compétent(e), qualifié(e); (limited) conditionnel(le)

qualify ['kwɔlɪfaɪ] vt qualifier; (modify) atténuer, nuancer ▷ vi: **to ~ (as)** obtenir son diplôme (de); **to ~ (for)** remplir les conditions requises (pour); (Sport) se qualifier (pour)

quality ['kwɔlɪtɪ] n qualité f

qualm [kwɑːm] n doute m; scrupule m

quantify ['kwɔntɪfaɪ] vt quantifier

quantity ['kwɔntɪtɪ] n quantité f

quarantine ['kwɔrntiːn] n quarantaine f

quarrel ['kwɔrl] n querelle f, dispute f ▷ vi se disputer, se quereller

quarry ['kwɔrɪ] n (for stone) carrière f; (animal) proie f, gibier m

quart [kwɔːt] n ≈ litre m

quarter ['kwɔːtəʳ] n quart m; (of year) trimestre m; (district) quartier m; (US, CANADA: 25 cents) (pièce f de) vingt-cinq cents mpl ▷ vt partager en quartiers or en quatre; (Mil) caserner, cantonner; **quarters** npl logement m; (Mil) quartiers mpl, cantonnement m; **a ~ of an hour** un quart d'heure; **quarter final** n quart m de finale; **quarterly** adj trimestriel(le) ▷ adv tous les trois mois

quartet(te) [kwɔː'tɛt] n quatuor m; (jazz players) quartette m

quartz [kwɔːts] n quartz m

quay [kiː] n (also: **~side**) quai m

queasy ['kwiːzɪ] adj: **to feel ~** avoir mal au cœur

Quebec [kwɪ'bɛk] n (city) Québec; (province) Québec m

queen [kwiːn] n (gen) reine f; (Cards etc) dame f

queer [kwɪəʳ] adj étrange, curieux(-euse); (suspicious) louche ▷ n (inf: highly offensive) homosexuel m

quench [kwɛntʃ] vt: **to ~ one's thirst** se désaltérer

query ['kwɪərɪ] n question f ▷ vt (disagree with, dispute) mettre en doute, questionner

quest [kwɛst] n recherche f, quête f

question ['kwɛstʃən] n question f ▷ vt (person) interroger; (plan, idea) mettre en question or en doute; **beyond ~** sans aucun doute; **out of the ~** hors de question; **questionable** adj discutable; **question mark** n point m d'interrogation; **questionnaire** [kwɛstʃə'nɛəʳ] n questionnaire m

queue [kjuː] n (BRIT) queue f, file f ▷ vi (also: **~ up**) faire la queue

quiche [kiːʃ] n quiche f

quick [kwɪk] adj rapide; (mind) vif (vive); (agile) agile, vif (vive) ▷ n: **cut to the ~** (fig) touché(e) au vif; **be ~!** dépêche-toi!; **quickly** adv (fast) vite, rapidement; (immediately) tout de suite

quid [kwɪd] n (pl inv: BRIT inf) livre f

quiet ['kwaɪət] adj tranquille, calme; (voice) bas(se); (ceremony, colour) discret(-ète) ▷ n tranquillité f, calme m; (silence) silence m; **quietly** adv tranquillement; (silently) silencieusement; (discreetly) discrètement

quilt [kwɪlt] n édredon m; (continental quilt) couette f

quirky ['kwɜːkɪ] adj singulier(-ère)

quit [kwɪt] (pt, pp **~** or **~ted**) vt quitter ▷ vi (give up) abandonner, renoncer; (resign) démissionner

quite [kwaɪt] adv (rather) assez, plutôt; (entirely) complètement, tout à fait; **~ a few of them** un assez grand nombre d'entre eux; **that's not ~ right** ce n'est pas tout à fait juste; **~ (so)!** exactement!

quits [kwɪts] *adj*: **~ (with)** quitte (envers); **let's call it ~** restons-en là

quiver ['kwɪvə'] *vi* trembler, frémir

quiz [kwɪz] *n* (*on TV*) jeu-concours *m* (télévisé); (*in magazine etc*) test *m* de connaissances ▷ *vt* interroger

quota ['kwəutə] *n* quota *m*

quotation [kwəu'teɪʃən] *n* citation *f*; (*estimate*) devis *m*; **quotation marks** *npl* guillemets *mpl*

quote [kwəut] *n* citation *f*; (*estimate*) devis *m* ▷ *vt* (*sentence, author*) citer; (*price*) donner, soumettre ▷ *vi*: **to ~ from** citer; **quotes** *npl* (*inverted commas*) guillemets *mpl*

Rabat [rə'bɑːt] *n* Rabat

rabbi ['ræbaɪ] *n* rabbin *m*

rabbit ['ræbɪt] *n* lapin *m*

rabies ['reɪbiːz] *n* rage *f*

RAC *n abbr* (BRIT: = *Royal Automobile Club*) ≈ ACF *m*

rac(c)oon [rə'kuːn] *n* raton *m* laveur

race [reɪs] *n* (*species*) race *f*; (*competition, rush*) course *f* ▷ *vt* (*person*) faire la course avec ▷ *vi* (*compete*) faire la course, courir; (*pulse*) battre très vite; **race car** *n* (US) = **racing car**; **racecourse** *n* champ *m* de courses; **racehorse** *n* cheval *m* de course; **racetrack** *n* piste *f*

racial ['reɪʃl] *adj* racial(e)

racing ['reɪsɪŋ] *n* courses *fpl*; **racing car** *n* (BRIT) voiture *f* de course; **racing driver** *n* (BRIT) pilote *m* de course

racism ['reɪsɪzəm] *n* racisme *m*; **racist** ['reɪsɪst] *adj, n* raciste *m/f*

rack [ræk] *n* (*for guns, tools*) râtelier *m*; (*for clothes*) portant *m*; (*for bottles*) casier *m*; (*also*: **luggage ~**) filet *m* à bagages; (*also*: **roof ~**) galerie *f*; (*also*: **dish ~**) égouttoir *m* ▷ *vt* tourmenter; **to ~ one's brains** se creuser la cervelle

racket ['rækɪt] *n* (*for tennis*) raquette *f*; (*noise*) tapage *m*, vacarme *m*; (*swindle*) escroquerie *f*

racquet ['rækɪt] *n* raquette *f*

radar ['reɪdɑː'] *n* radar *m*

radiation [reɪdɪ'eɪʃən] n rayonnement m;
(radioactive) radiation f

radiator ['reɪdɪeɪtəʳ] n radiateur m

radical ['rædɪkl] adj radical(e)

radio ['reɪdɪəu] n radio f ▷ vt (person) appeler
par radio; **on the ~** à la radio; **radioactive**
adj radioactif(-ive); **radio station** n station
f de radio

radish ['rædɪʃ] n radis m

RAF n abbr (BRIT) = **Royal Air Force**

raffle ['ræfl] n tombola f

raft [rɑːft] n (craft: also: **life ~**) radeau m; (logs)
train m de flottage

rag [ræg] n chiffon m; (pej: newspaper) feuille f,
torchon m; (for charity) attractions organisées par
les étudiants au profit d'œuvres de charité; **rags**
npl haillons mpl

rage [reɪdʒ] n (fury) rage f, fureur f ▷ vi (person)
être fou (folle) de rage; (storm) faire rage, être
déchaîné(e); **it's all the ~** cela fait fureur

ragged ['rægɪd] adj (edge) inégal(e), qui
accroche; (clothes) en loques; (appearance)
déguenillé(e)

raid [reɪd] n (Mil) raid m; (criminal) hold-up m
inv; (by police) descente f, rafle f ▷ vt faire un
raid sur ou un hold-up dans ou une descente
dans

rail [reɪl] n (on stair) rampe f; (on bridge, balcony)
balustrade f; (of ship) bastingage m; (for train)
rail m; **railcard** n (BRIT) carte f de chemin
de fer; **railing(s)** n(pl) grille f; **railway** (US
railroad) n chemin m de fer; (track) voie f
ferrée; **railway line** n (BRIT) ligne f de chemin
de fer; (track) voie ferrée; **railway station** n
(BRIT) gare f

rain [reɪn] n pluie f ▷ vi pleuvoir; **in the ~** sous
la pluie; **it's ~ing** il pleut; **rainbow** n arc-en-
ciel m; **raincoat** n imperméable m; **raindrop**
n goutte f de pluie; **rainfall** n chute f de pluie;
(measurement) hauteur f des précipitations;
rainforest n forêt tropicale; **rainy** adj
pluvieux(-euse)

raise [reɪz] n augmentation f ▷ vt (lift) lever;
hausser; (increase) augmenter; (morale)
remonter; (standards) améliorer; (a protest,
doubt) provoquer, causer; (a question) soulever;
(cattle, family) élever; (crop) faire pousser; (army,
funds) rassembler; (loan) obtenir; **to ~ one's
voice** élever la voix

raisin ['reɪzn] n raisin sec

rake [reɪk] n (tool) râteau m; (person) débauché
m ▷ vt (garden) ratisser

rally ['rælɪ] n (Pol etc) meeting m,
rassemblement m; (Aut) rallye m; (Tennis)
échange m ▷ vt rassembler, rallier; (support)
gagner ▷ vi (sick person) aller mieux; (Stock
Exchange) reprendre

RAM [ræm] n abbr (Comput: = random access
memory) mémoire vive

ram [ræm] n bélier m ▷ vt (push) enfoncer;
(crash into: vehicle) emboutir; (: lamppost etc)
percuter

Ramadan [ræmə'dæn] n Ramadan m

ramble ['ræmbl] n randonnée f ▷ vi (walk)
se promener, faire une randonnée; (pej:
also: **~ on**) discourir, pérorer; **rambler** n
promeneur(-euse), randonneur(-euse);
rambling adj (speech) décousu(e); (house)
plein(e) de coins et de recoins; (Bot)
grimpant(e)

ramp [ræmp] n (incline) rampe f; (Aut)
dénivellation f; (in garage) pont m; **on/off ~** (US
Aut) bretelle f d'accès

rampage [ræm'peɪdʒ] n: **to be on the ~** se
déchaîner

ran [ræn] pt of **run**

ranch [rɑːntʃ] n ranch m

random ['rændəm] adj fait(e) or établi(e) au
hasard; (Comput, Math) aléatoire ▷ n: **at ~** au
hasard

rang [ræŋ] pt of **ring**

range [reɪndʒ] n (of mountains) chaîne f; (of
missile, voice) portée f; (of products) choix m,
gamme f; (also: **shooting ~**) champ m de tir;
(also: **kitchen ~**) fourneau m (de cuisine) ▷ vt
(place) mettre en rang, placer ▷ vi: **to ~ over**
couvrir; **to ~ from ... to** aller de ... à

ranger ['reɪndʒəʳ] n garde m forestier

rank [ræŋk] n rang m; (Mil) grade m; (BRIT:
also: **taxi ~**) station f de taxis ▷ vi: **to ~ among**
compter or se classer parmi ▷ adj (smell)
nauséabond(e); **the ~ and file** (fig) la masse,
la base

ransom ['rænsəm] n rançon f; **to hold sb to ~**
(fig) exercer un chantage sur qn

rant [rænt] vi fulminer

rap [ræp] n (music) rap m ▷ vt (door) frapper sur
or à; (table etc) taper sur

rape [reɪp] n viol m; (Bot) colza m ▷ vt violer

rapid ['ræpɪd] adj rapide; **rapidly** adv
rapidement; **rapids** npl (Geo) rapides mpl

rapist ['reɪpɪst] n auteur m d'un viol

rapport [ræ'pɔːʳ] n entente f

rare [rɛəʳ] adj rare; (Culin: steak) saignant(e);
rarely adv rarement

rash [ræʃ] adj imprudent(e), irréfléchi(e) ▷ n
(Med) rougeur f, éruption f; (of events) série f
(noire)

rasher ['ræʃəʳ] n fine tranche (de lard)

raspberry ['rɑːzbərɪ] n framboise f

rat [ræt] n rat m

rate [reɪt] n (ratio) taux m, pourcentage m;
(speed) vitesse f, rythme m; (price) tarif m ▷ vt
(price) évaluer, estimer; (people) classer; **rates**
npl (BRIT: property tax) impôts locaux; **to ~
sb/sth as** considérer qn/qch comme

rather ['rɑːðəʳ] adv (somewhat) assez, plutôt;
(to some extent) un peu; **it's ~ expensive**

c'est assez cher; (*too much*) c'est un peu cher; **there's ~ a lot** il y en a beaucoup; **I would** or **I'd ~ go** j'aimerais mieux or je préférerais partir; **or ~** (*more accurately*) ou plutôt

rating ['reɪtɪŋ] *n* (*assessment*) évaluation *f*; (*score*) classement *m*; (*Finance*) cote *f*; **ratings** *npl* (*Radio*) indice(s) *m(pl)* d'écoute; (*TV*) Audimat®

ratio ['reɪʃɪəu] *n* proportion *f*; **in the ~ of 100 to 1** dans la proportion de 100 contre 1

ration ['ræʃən] *n* ration *f* ▷ *vt* rationner; **rations** *npl* (*food*) vivres *mpl*

rational ['ræʃənl] *adj* raisonnable, sensé(e); (*solution, reasoning*) logique; (*Med: person*) lucide

rat race *n* foire *f* d'empoigne

rattle ['rætl] *n* (*of door, window*) battement *m*; (*of coins, chain*) cliquetis *m*; (*of train, engine*) bruit *m* de ferraille; (*for baby*) hochet *m* ▷ *vi* cliqueter; (*car, bus*): **to ~ along** rouler en faisant un bruit de ferraille ▷ *vt* agiter (bruyamment); (*inf: disconcert*) déconcenancer

rave [reɪv] *vi* (*in anger*) s'emporter; (*with enthusiasm*) s'extasier; (*Med*) délirer ▷ *n* (*inf: party*) rave *f*, soirée *f* techno

raven ['reɪvən] *n* grand corbeau

ravine [rə'viːn] *n* ravin *m*

raw [rɔː] *adj* (*uncooked*) cru(e); (*not processed*) brut(e); (*sore*) à vif, irrité(e); (*inexperienced*) inexpérimenté(e); **~ materials** matières premières

ray [reɪ] *n* rayon *m*; **~ of hope** lueur *f* d'espoir

razor ['reɪzə'] *n* rasoir *m*; **razor blade** *n* lame *f* de rasoir

Rd *abbr* = **road**

RE *n abbr* (*BRIT*) = **religious education**

re [riː] *prep* concernant

reach [riːtʃ] *n* portée *f*, atteinte *f*; (*of river etc*) étendue *f* ▷ *vt* atteindre, arriver à; (*conclusion, decision*) parvenir à ▷ *vi* s'étendre; **out of/ within ~** (*object*) hors de/à portée; **reach out** *vt* tendre ▷ *vi*: **to ~ out (for)** allonger le bras (pour prendre)

react [riː'ækt] *vi* réagir; **reaction** [riː'ækʃən] *n* réaction *f*; **reactor** [riː'æktə'] *n* réacteur *m*

read (*pt, pp* ~) [riːd, rɛd] *vi* lire ▷ *vt* lire; (*understand*) comprendre, interpréter; (*study*) étudier; (*meter*) relever; (*subj: instrument etc*) indiquer, marquer; **read out** *vt* lire à haute voix; **reader** *n* lecteur(-trice)

readily ['rɛdɪlɪ] *adv* volontiers, avec empressement; (*easily*) facilement

reading ['riːdɪŋ] *n* lecture *f*; (*understanding*) interprétation *f*; (*on instrument*) indications *fpl*

ready ['rɛdɪ] *adj* prêt(e); (*willing*) prêt, disposé(e); (*available*) disponible ▷ *n*: **at the ~** (*Mil*) prêt à faire feu; **when will my photos be ~?** quand est-ce que mes photos seront prêtes?; **to get ~** (*as vi*) se préparer; (*as vt*) préparer;

ready-cooked *adj* précuit(e); **ready-made** *adj* tout(e) faite(e)

real [rɪəl] *adj* (*world, life*) réel(le); (*genuine*) véritable; (*proper*) vrai(e) ▷ *adv* (*US inf: very*) vraiment; **real ale** *n* bière traditionnelle; **real estate** *n* biens fonciers or immobiliers; **realistic** [rɪə'lɪstɪk] *adj* réaliste; **reality** [riː'ælɪtɪ] *n* réalité *f*

reality TV *n* télé-réalité *f*

realization [rɪəlaɪ'zeɪʃən] *n* (*awareness*) prise *f* de conscience; (*fulfilment: also: of asset*) réalisation *f*

realize ['rɪəlaɪz] *vt* (*understand*) se rendre compte de, prendre conscience de; (*a project, Comm: asset*) réaliser

really ['rɪəlɪ] *adv* vraiment; **~?** vraiment?, c'est vrai?

realm [rɛlm] *n* royaume *m*; (*fig*) domaine *m*

realtor ['rɪəltɔːʳ] *n* (*US*) agent immobilier

reappear [riːə'pɪəʳ] *vi* réapparaître, reparaître

rear [rɪəʳ] *adj* de derrière, arrière *inv*; (*Aut: wheel etc*) arrière ▷ *n* arrière *m* ▷ *vt* (*cattle, family*) élever ▷ *vi* (*also*: **~ up**: *animal*) se cabrer

rearrange [riːə'reɪndʒ] *vt* réarranger

rear: **rear-view mirror** *n* (*Aut*) rétroviseur *m*; **rear-wheel drive** *n* (*Aut*) traction *f* arrière

reason ['riːzn] *n* raison *f* ▷ *vi*: **to ~ with sb** raisonner qn, faire entendre raison à qn; **it stands to ~ that** il va sans dire que; **reasonable** *adj* raisonnable; (*not bad*) acceptable; **reasonably** *adv* (*behave*) raisonnablement; (*fairly*) assez; **reasoning** *n* raisonnement *m*

reassurance [riːə'ʃuərəns] *n* (*factual*) assurance *f*, garantie *f*; (*emotional*) réconfort *m*

reassure [riːə'ʃuəʳ] *vt* rassurer

rebate ['riːbeɪt] *n* (*on tax etc*) dégrèvement *m*

rebel *n* ['rɛbl] rebelle *m/f* ▷ *vi* [rɪ'bɛl] se rebeller, se révolter; **rebellion** [rɪ'bɛljən] *n* rébellion *f*, révolte *f*; **rebellious** [rɪ'bɛljəs] *adj* rebelle

rebuild [riː'bɪld] *vt* (*irreg: like* **build**) reconstruire

recall *vt* [rɪ'kɔːl] rappeler; (*remember*) se rappeler, se souvenir de ▷ *n* ['riːkɔl] rappel *m*; (*ability to remember*) mémoire *f*

rec'd *abbr of* **received**

receipt [rɪ'siːt] *n* (*document*) reçu *m*; (*for parcel etc*) accusé *m* de réception; (*act of receiving*) réception *f*; **receipts** *npl* (*Comm*) recettes *fpl*; **can I have a ~, please?** je peux avoir un reçu, s'il vous plaît?

receive [rɪ'siːv] *vt* recevoir; (*guest*) recevoir, accueillir; **receiver** *n* (*Tel*) récepteur *m*, combiné *m*; (*Radio*) récepteur; (*of stolen goods*) receleur *m*; (*for bankruptcies*) administrateur *m* judiciaire

recent ['riːsnt] *adj* récent(e); **recently** *adv* récemment

reception [rɪ'sɛpʃən] n réception f; (welcome) accueil m, réception; **reception desk** n réception f; **receptionist** n réceptionniste m/f

recession [rɪ'sɛʃən] n (Econ) récession f

recharge [riː'tʃɑːdʒ] vt (battery) recharger

recipe ['rɛsɪpɪ] n recette f

recipient [rɪ'sɪpɪənt] n (of payment) bénéficiaire m/f; (of letter) destinataire m/f

recital [rɪ'saɪtl] n récital m

recite [rɪ'saɪt] vt (poem) réciter

reckless ['rɛkləs] adj (driver etc) imprudent(e); (spender etc) insouciant(e)

reckon ['rɛkən] vt (count) calculer, compter; (consider) considérer, estimer; (think): **I ~ (that)** ... je pense (que) ..., j'estime (que) ...

reclaim [rɪ'kleɪm] vt (land: from sea) assécher; (demand back) réclamer (le remboursement or la restitution de); (waste materials) récupérer

recline [rɪ'klaɪn] vi être allongé(e) or étendu(e)

recognition [rɛkəg'nɪʃən] n reconnaissance f; **transformed beyond ~** méconnaissable

recognize ['rɛkəgnaɪz] vt: **to ~ (by/as)** reconnaître (à/comme étant)

recollection [rɛkə'lɛkʃən] n souvenir m

recommend [rɛkə'mɛnd] vt recommander; **can you ~ a good restaurant?** pouvez-vous me conseiller un bon restaurant?; **recommendation** [rɛkəmɛn'deɪʃən] n recommandation f

reconcile ['rɛkənsaɪl] vt (two people) réconcilier; (two facts) concilier, accorder; **to ~ o.s.** se résigner à

reconsider [riːkən'sɪdəʳ] vt reconsidérer

reconstruct [riːkən'strʌkt] vt (building) reconstruire; (crime, system) reconstituer

record n ['rɛkɔːd] rapport m, récit m; (of meeting etc) procès-verbal m; (register) registre m; (file) dossier m; (Comput) article m; (also: **police ~**) casier m judiciaire; (Mus: disc) disque m; (Sport) record m ▷ adj record inv ▷ vt ['rɪ'kɔːd] (set down) noter; (Mus: song etc) enregistrer; **public ~s** archives fpl; **in ~ time** dans un temps record; **recorded delivery** n (BRIT Post): **to send sth recorded delivery** ≈ envoyer qch en recommandé; **recorder** n (Mus) flûte f à bec; **recording** n (Mus) enregistrement m; **record player** n tourne-disque m

recount [rɪ'kaunt] vt raconter

recover [rɪ'kʌvəʳ] vt récupérer ▷ vi (from illness) se rétablir; (from shock) se remettre; **recovery** n récupération f; rétablissement m; (Econ) redressement m

recreate [riːkrɪ'eɪt] vt recréer

recreation [rɛkrɪ'eɪʃən] n (leisure) récréation f, détente f; **recreational drug** n drogue récréative; **recreational vehicle** n (US) camping-car m

recruit [rɪ'kruːt] n recrue f ▷ vt recruter; **recruitment** n recrutement m

rectangle ['rɛktæŋgl] n rectangle m; **rectangular** [rɛk'tæŋgjuləʳ] adj rectangulaire

rectify ['rɛktɪfaɪ] vt (error) rectifier, corriger

rector ['rɛktəʳ] n (Rel) pasteur m

recur [rɪ'kəːʳ] vi se reproduire; (idea, opportunity) se retrouver; (symptoms) réapparaître; **recurring** adj (problem) périodique, fréquent(e); (Math) périodique

recyclable [riː'saɪkləbl] adj recyclable

recycle [riː'saɪkl] vt, vi recycler

recycling [riː'saɪklɪŋ] n recyclage m

red [rɛd] n rouge m; (Pol: pej) rouge m/f ▷ adj rouge; (hair) roux (rousse); **in the ~** (account) à découvert; (business) en déficit; **Red Cross** n Croix-Rouge f; **redcurrant** n groseille f (rouge)

redeem [rɪ'diːm] vt (debt) rembourser; (sth in pawn) dégager; (fig, also Rel) racheter

red: red-haired adj roux (rousse); **redhead** n roux (rousse); **red-hot** adj chauffé(e) au rouge, brûlant(e); **red light** n: **to go through a red light** (Aut) brûler un feu rouge; **red-light district** n quartier mal famé

red meat n viande f rouge

reduce [rɪ'djuːs] vt réduire; (lower) abaisser; **"~ speed now"** (Aut) "ralentir"; **to ~ sb to tears** faire pleurer qn; **reduced** adj réduit(e); **"greatly reduced prices"** "gros rabais", **at a reduced price** (goods) au rabais; (ticket etc) à prix réduit; **reduction** [rɪ'dʌkʃən] n réduction f; (of price) baisse f; (discount) rabais m; réduction; **is there a reduction for children/students?** y a-t-il une réduction pour les enfants/les étudiants?

redundancy [rɪ'dʌndənsɪ] n (BRIT) licenciement m, mise f au chômage

redundant [rɪ'dʌndnt] adj (BRIT: worker) licencié(e), mis(e) au chômage; (detail, object) superflu(e); **to be made ~** (worker) être licencié, être mis au chômage

reed [riːd] n (Bot) roseau m

reef [riːf] n (at sea) récif m, écueil m

reel [riːl] n bobine f; (Fishing) moulinet m; (Cine) bande f; (dance) quadrille écossais ▷ vi (sway) chanceler

ref [rɛf] n abbr (inf: = referee) arbitre m

refectory [rɪ'fɛktərɪ] n réfectoire m

refer [rɪ'fəːʳ] vt: **to ~ sb to** (inquirer, patient) adresser qn à; (reader: to text) renvoyer qn à ▷ vi: **to ~ to** (allude to) parler de, faire allusion à; (consult) se reporter à; (apply to) s'adresser à

referee [rɛfə'riː] n arbitre m; (BRIT: for job application) répondant(e) ▷ vt arbitrer

reference ['rɛfrəns] n référence f, renvoi m; (mention) allusion f, mention f; (for job application: letter) références; lettre f de recommandation; **with ~ to** en ce qui concerne; (Comm: in letter) me référant à; **reference number** n (Comm) numéro m de référence

refill vt [ri:'fɪl] remplir à nouveau; (pen, lighter etc) recharger ▷ n ['ri:fɪl] (for pen etc) recharge f

refine [rɪ'faɪn] vt (sugar, oil) raffiner; (taste) affiner; (idea, theory) peaufiner; **refined** adj (person, taste) raffiné(e); **refinery** n raffinerie f

reflect [rɪ'flɛkt] vt (light, image) réfléchir, refléter ▷ vi (think) réfléchir, méditer; **it ~s badly on him** cela le discrédite; **it ~s well on him** c'est tout à son honneur; **reflection** [rɪ'flɛkʃən] n réflexion f; (image) reflet m; **on reflection** réflexion faite

reflex ['ri:flɛks] adj, n réflexe (m)

reform [rɪ'fɔːm] n réforme f ▷ vt réformer

refrain [rɪ'freɪn] vi: **to ~ from doing** s'abstenir de faire ▷ n refrain m

refresh [rɪ'frɛʃ] vt rafraîchir; (subj: food, sleep etc) redonner des forces à; **refreshing** adj (drink) rafraîchissant(e); (sleep) réparateur(-trice); **refreshments** npl rafraîchissements mpl

refrigerator [rɪ'frɪdʒəreɪtə'] n réfrigérateur m, frigidaire m

refuel [ri:'fjʊəl] vi se ravitailler en carburant

refuge ['rɛfjuːdʒ] n refuge m; **to take ~ in** se réfugier dans; **refugee** [rɛfju'dʒiː] n réfugié(e)

refund n ['ri:fʌnd] remboursement m ▷ vt [rɪ'fʌnd] rembourser

refurbish [ri:'fɜːbɪʃ] vt remettre à neuf

refusal [rɪ'fjuːzəl] n refus m; **to have first ~ on sth** avoir droit de préemption sur qch

refuse¹ ['rɛfjuːs] n ordures fpl, détritus mpl

refuse² [rɪ'fjuːz] vt, vi refuser; **to ~ to do sth** refuser de faire qch

regain [rɪ'geɪn] vt (lost ground) regagner; (strength) retrouver

regard [rɪ'gɑːd] n respect m, estime f, considération f ▷ vt considérer; **to give one's ~s to** faire ses amitiés à; **"with kindest ~s"** "bien amicalement"; **as ~s, with ~ to** en ce qui concerne; **regarding** prep en ce qui concerne; **regardless** adv quand même; **regardless of** sans se soucier de

regenerate [rɪ'dʒɛnəreɪt] vt régénérer ▷ vi se régénérer

reggae ['rɛgeɪ] n reggae m

regiment ['rɛdʒɪmənt] n régiment m

region ['ri:dʒən] n région f; **in the ~ of** (fig) aux alentours de; **regional** adj régional(e)

register ['rɛdʒɪstə'] n registre m; (also: **electoral ~**) liste électorale ▷ vt enregistrer, inscrire; (birth) déclarer; (vehicle) immatriculer; (letter) envoyer en recommandé; (subj: instrument) marquer ▷ vi s'inscrire; (at hotel) signer le registre; (make impression) être (bien) compris(e); **registered** adj (BRIT: letter) recommandé(e)

registered trademark n marque déposée

registrar ['rɛdʒɪstrɑː'] n officier m de l'état civil

registration [rɛdʒɪs'treɪʃən] n (act) enregistrement m; (of student) inscription f; (BRIT Aut: also: **~ number**) numéro m d'immatriculation

registry office ['rɛdʒɪstrɪ-] n (BRIT) bureau m de l'état civil; **to get married in a ~** ≈ se marier à la mairie

regret [rɪ'grɛt] n regret m ▷ vt regretter; **regrettable** adj regrettable, fâcheux(-euse)

regular ['rɛgjulə'] adj régulier(-ière); (usual) habituel(le), normal(e); (soldier) de métier; (Comm: size) ordinaire ▷ n (client etc) habitué(e); **regularly** adv régulièrement

regulate ['rɛgjuleɪt] vt régler; **regulation** [rɛgju'leɪʃən] n (rule) règlement m; (adjustment) réglage m

rehabilitation ['ri:əbɪlɪ'teɪʃən] n (of offender) réhabilitation f; (of addict) réadaptation f

rehearsal [rɪ'hɜːsəl] n répétition f

rehearse [rɪ'hɜːs] vt répéter

reign [reɪn] n règne m ▷ vi régner

reimburse [ri:ɪm'bɜːs] vt rembourser

rein [reɪn] n (for horse) rêne f

reincarnation [ri:ɪnkɑː'neɪʃən] n réincarnation f

reindeer ['reɪndɪə'] n (pl inv) renne m

reinforce [ri:ɪn'fɔːs] vt renforcer; **reinforcements** npl (Mil) renfort(s) m(pl)

reinstate [ri:ɪn'steɪt] vt rétablir, réintégrer

reject n ['ri:dʒɛkt] (Comm) article m de rebut ▷ vt [rɪ'dʒɛkt] refuser; (idea) rejeter; **rejection** [rɪ'dʒɛkʃən] n rejet m, refus m

rejoice [rɪ'dʒɔɪs] vi: **to ~ (at or over)** se réjouir (de)

relate [rɪ'leɪt] vt (tell) raconter; (connect) établir un rapport entre ▷ vi: **to ~ to** (connect) se rapporter à; **to ~ to sb** (interact) entretenir des rapports avec qn; **related** adj apparenté(e); **related to** (subject) lié(e) à; **relating to** prep concernant

relation [rɪ'leɪʃən] n (person) parent(e); (link) rapport m, lien m; **relations** npl (relatives) famille f; **relationship** n rapport m, lien m; (personal ties) relations fpl, rapports; (also: **family relationship**) lien de parenté; (affair) liaison f

relative ['rɛlətɪv] n parent(e) ▷ adj relatif(-ive); (respective) respectif(-ive); **relatively** adv relativement

relax [rɪ'læks] vi (muscle) se relâcher; (person: unwind) se détendre ▷ vt relâcher; (mind, person) détendre; **relaxation** [ri:læk'seɪʃən] n relâchement m; (of mind) détente f; (recreation) détente, délassement m; **relaxed** adj relâché(e); détendu(e); **relaxing** adj délassant(e)

relay ['ri:leɪ] n (Sport) course f de relais ▷ vt

(*message*) retransmettre, relayer

release [rɪ'liːs] *n* (*from prison, obligation*)
libération *f*; (*of gas etc*) émission *f*; (*of film etc*)
sortie *f*; (*new recording*) disque *m* ▷ *vt* (*prisoner*)
libérer; (*book, film*) sortir; (*report, news*) rendre
public, publier; (*gas etc*) émettre, dégager;
(*free: from wreckage etc*) dégager; (*Tech: catch,
spring etc*) déclencher; (*let go: person, animal*)
relâcher; (: *hand, object*) lâcher; (: *grip, brake*)
desserrer

relegate ['rɛləgeɪt] *vt* reléguer; (*BRIT Sport*): **to
be ~d** descendre dans une division inférieure

relent [rɪ'lɛnt] *vi* se laisser fléchir; **relentless**
adj implacable; (*non-stop*) continuel(le)

relevant ['rɛləvənt] *adj* (*question*)
pertinent(e); (*corresponding*) approprié(e);
(*fact*) significatif(-ive); (*information*) utile

reliable [rɪ'laɪəbl] *adj* (*person, firm*)
sérieux(-euse), fiable; (*method, machine*) fiable;
(*news, information*) sûr(e)

relic ['rɛlɪk] *n* (*Rel*) relique *f*; (*of the past*)
vestige *m*

relief [rɪ'liːf] *n* (*from pain, anxiety*) soulagement
m; (*help, supplies*) secours *m(pl)*; (*Art, Geo*)
relief *m*

relieve [rɪ'liːv] *vt* (*pain, patient*) soulager;
(*fear, worry*) dissiper; (*bring help*) secourir;
(*take over from: gen*) relayer; (: *guard*) relever;
to ~ sb of sth débarrasser qn de qch; **to ~ o.s.**
(*euphemism*) se soulager, faire ses besoins;
relieved *adj* soulagé(e)

religion [rɪ'lɪdʒən] *n* religion *f*

religious [rɪ'lɪdʒəs] *adj* religieux(-euse); (*book*)
de piété; **religious education** *n* instruction
religieuse

relish ['rɛlɪʃ] *n* (*Culin*) condiment *m*; (*enjoyment*)
délectation *f* ▷ *vt* (*food etc*) savourer; **to ~
doing** se délecter à faire

relocate [riːləu'keɪt] *vt* (*business*) transférer
▷ *vi* se transférer, s'installer or s'établir ailleurs

reluctance [rɪ'lʌktəns] *n* répugnance *f*

reluctant [rɪ'lʌktənt] *adj* peu disposé(e), qui
hésite; **reluctantly** *adv* à contrecœur, sans
enthousiasme

rely on [rɪ'laɪ-] *vt fus* (*be dependent on*)
dépendre de; (*trust*) compter sur

remain [rɪ'meɪn] *vi* rester; **remainder** *n* reste
m; (*Comm*) fin *f* de série; **remaining** *adj* qui
reste; **remains** *npl* restes *mpl*

remand [rɪ'mɑːnd] *n*: **on ~** en détention
préventive ▷ *vt*: **to be ~ed in custody** être
placé(e) en détention préventive

remark [rɪ'mɑːk] *n* remarque *f*, observation
f ▷ *vt* (*faire*) remarquer, dire; **remarkable** *adj*
remarquable

remarry [riː'mærɪ] *vi* se remarier

remedy ['rɛmədɪ] *n*: **~ (for)** remède *m* (contre
or à) ▷ *vt* remédier à

remember [rɪ'mɛmbəʳ] *vt* se rappeler, se

souvenir de; (*send greetings*): **~ me to him**
saluez-le de ma part; **Remembrance
Day** [rɪ'mɛmbrəns-] *n* (*BRIT*) ≈ (le jour de)
l'Armistice *m*, ≈ le 11 novembre

● **REMEMBRANCE DAY**
●
●
● **Remembrance Day** ou **Remembrance
● Sunday** est le dimanche le plus proche du
● 11 novembre, jour où la Première Guerre
● mondiale a officiellement pris fin. Il rend
● hommage aux victimes des deux guerres
● mondiales. À cette occasion, on observe
● deux minutes de silence à 11h, heure de la
● signature de l'armistice avec l'Allemagne
● en 1918; certaines membres de la famille
● royale et du gouvernement déposent des
● gerbes de coquelicots au cénotaphe de
● Whitehall, et des couronnes sont placées
● sur les monuments aux morts dans toute
● la Grande-Bretagne; par ailleurs, les gens
● portent des coquelicots artificiels fabriqués
● et vendus par des membres de la légion
● britannique blessés au combat, au profit
● des blessés de guerre et de leur famille.

remind [rɪ'maɪnd] *vt*: **to ~ sb of sth** rappeler
qch à qn; **to ~ sb to do** faire penser à qn à
faire, rappeler à qn qu'il doit faire; **reminder** *n*
(*Comm: letter*) rappel *m*; (*note etc*) pense-bête
m; (*souvenir*) souvenir *m*

reminiscent [rɛmɪ'nɪsnt] *adj*: **~ of** qui
rappelle, qui fait penser à

remnant ['rɛmnənt] *n* reste *m*, restant *m*; (*of
cloth*) coupon *m*

remorse [rɪ'mɔːs] *n* remords *m*

remote [rɪ'məut] *adj* éloigné(e), lointain(e);
(*person*) distant(e); (*possibility*) vague; **remote
control** *n* télécommande *f*; **remotely** *adv* au
loin; (*slightly*) très vaguement

removal [rɪ'muːvəl] *n* (*taking away*)
enlèvement *m*; suppression *f*; (*BRIT: from
house*) déménagement *m*; (*from office:
dismissal*) renvoi *m*; (*of stain*) nettoyage *m*;
(*Med*) ablation *f*; **removal man** (*irreg*) *n* (*BRIT*)
déménageur *m*; **removal van** *n* (*BRIT*) camion
m de déménagement

remove [rɪ'muːv] *vt* enlever, retirer; (*employee*)
renvoyer; (*stain*) faire partir; (*abuse*) supprimer;
(*doubt*) chasser

Renaissance [rɪ'neɪsɑ̃s] *n*: **the ~** la
Renaissance

rename [riː'neɪm] *vt* rebaptiser

render ['rɛndəʳ] *vt* rendre

rendezvous ['rɔndɪvuː] *n* rendez-vous *m inv*

renew [rɪ'njuː] *vt* renouveler; (*negotiations*)
reprendre; (*acquaintance*) renouer

renovate ['rɛnəveɪt] *vt* rénover; (*work of art*)
restaurer

renowned [rɪ'naʊnd] *adj* renommé(e)
rent [rɛnt] *pt, pp of* **rend** ▷ *n* loyer *m* ▷ *vt*
louer; **rental** *n* (*for television, car*) (prix *m* de)
location *f*
reorganize [riːˈɔːgənaɪz] *vt* réorganiser
rep [rɛp] *n abbr* (Comm) = **representative**
repair [rɪ'pɛəʳ] *n* réparation *f* ▷ *vt* réparer; **in
good/bad ~** en bon/mauvais état; **where
can I get this ~ed?** où est-ce que je peux
faire réparer ceci?; **repair kit** *n* trousse *f* de
réparations
repay [riːˈpeɪ] *vt* (*irreg: like* **pay**) (*money,
creditor*) rembourser; (*sb's efforts*) récompenser;
repayment *n* remboursement *m*
repeat [rɪ'piːt] *n* (Radio, TV) reprise *f* ▷ *vt*
répéter; (*promise, attack, also Comm: order*)
renouveler; (*Scol: a class*) redoubler ▷ *vi*
répéter; **can you ~ that, please?** pouvez-
vous répéter, s'il vous plaît?; **repeatedly**
adv souvent, à plusieurs reprises; **repeat
prescription** *n* (BRIT): **I'd like a repeat
prescription** je voudrais renouveler mon
ordonnance
repellent [rɪ'pɛlənt] *adj* repoussant(e) ▷ *n*:
insect ~ insectifuge *m*
repercussions [riːpə'kʌʃənz] *npl*
répercussions *fpl*
repetition [rɛpɪ'tɪʃən] *n* répétition *f*
repetitive [rɪ'pɛtɪtɪv] *adj* (*movement, work*)
répétitif(-ive); (*speech*) plein(e) de redites
replace [rɪ'pleɪs] *vt* (*put back*) remettre,
replacer; (*take the place of*) remplacer;
replacement *n* (*substitution*) remplacement
m; (*person*) remplaçant(e)
replay ['riːpleɪ] *n* (*of match*) match rejoué; (*of
tape, film*) répétition *f*
replica ['rɛplɪkə] *n* réplique *f*, copie exacte
reply [rɪ'plaɪ] *n* réponse *f* ▷ *vi* répondre
report [rɪ'pɔːt] *n* rapport *m*; (*Press etc*)
reportage *m*; (BRIT: *also*: **school ~**) bulletin *m*
(scolaire); (*of gun*) détonation *f* ▷ *vt* rapporter,
faire un compte rendu de; (*Press etc*) faire
un reportage sur; (*notify: accident*) signaler;
(: *culprit*) dénoncer ▷ *vi* (*make a report*) faire
un rapport; **I'd like to ~ a theft** je voudrais
signaler un vol; (*present o.s.*): **to ~ (to sb)**
se présenter (chez qn); **report card** *n* (US,
SCOTTISH) bulletin *m* (scolaire); **reportedly**
adv: **she is reportedly living in Spain** elle
habiterait en Espagne; **he reportedly told
them to ...** il leur aurait dit de ...; **reporter** *n*
reporter *m*
represent [rɛprɪ'zɛnt] *vt* représenter;
(*view, belief*) présenter, expliquer; (*describe*):
to ~ sth as présenter or décrire qch
comme; **representation** [rɛprɪzɛn'teɪʃən]
n représentation *f*; **representative** *n*
représentant(e); (*US Pol*) député *m* ▷ *adj*
représentatif(-ive), caractéristique

repress [rɪ'prɛs] *vt* réprimer; **repression**
[rɪ'prɛʃən] *n* répression *f*
reprimand ['rɛprɪmɑːnd] *n* réprimande *f* ▷ *vt*
réprimander
reproduce [riːprə'djuːs] *vt* reproduire ▷ *vi* se
reproduire; **reproduction** [riːprə'dʌkʃən] *n*
reproduction *f*
reptile ['rɛptaɪl] *n* reptile *m*
republic [rɪ'pʌblɪk] *n* république *f*; **republican**
adj, n républicain(e)
reputable ['rɛpjutəbl] *adj* de bonne
réputation; (*occupation*) honorable
reputation [rɛpju'teɪʃən] *n* réputation *f*
request [rɪ'kwɛst] *n* demande *f*; (*formal*)
requête *f* ▷ *vt*: **to ~ (of or from sb)** demander
(à qn); **request stop** *n* (BRIT: *for bus*) arrêt
facultatif
require [rɪ'kwaɪəʳ] *vt* (*need: subj: person*)
avoir besoin de; (: *thing, situation*) nécessiter,
demander; (*want*) exiger; (*order*): **to ~ sb to do
sth/sth of sb** exiger que qn fasse qch/qch de
qn; **requirement** *n* (*need*) exigence *f*; besoin
m; (*condition*) condition *f* (requise)
resat [riː'sæt] *pt, pp of* **resit**
rescue ['rɛskjuː] *n* (*from accident*) sauvetage *m*;
(*help*) secours *mpl* ▷ *vt* sauver
research [rɪ'sɜːtʃ] *n* recherche(s) *f(pl)* ▷ *vt*
faire des recherches sur
resemblance [rɪ'zɛmbləns] *n* ressemblance *f*
resemble [rɪ'zɛmbl] *vt* ressembler à
resent [rɪ'zɛnt] *vt* être contrarié(e)
par; **resentful** *adj* irrité(e), plein(e) de
ressentiment; **resentment** *n* ressentiment *m*
reservation [rɛzə'veɪʃən] *n* (*booking*)
réservation *f*; **to make a ~ (in an hotel/a
restaurant/on a plane)** réserver or
retenir une chambre/une table/une place;
reservation desk *n* (US: *in hotel*) réception *f*
reserve [rɪ'zəːv] *n* réserve *f*; (*Sport*)
remplaçant(e) ▷ *vt* (*seats etc*) réserver, retenir;
reserved *adj* réservé(e)
reservoir ['rɛzəvwɑːʳ] *n* réservoir *m*
reshuffle [riːˈʃʌfl] *n*: **Cabinet ~** (Pol)
remaniement ministériel
residence ['rɛzɪdəns] *n* résidence *f*; **residence
permit** *n* (BRIT) permis *m* de séjour
resident ['rɛzɪdənt] *n* (*of country*) résident(e);
(*of area, house*) habitant(e); (*in hotel*)
pensionnaire ▷ *adj* résidant(e); **residential**
[rɛzɪ'dɛnʃəl] *adj* de résidence; (*area*)
résidentiel(le); (*course*) avec hébergement
sur place
residue ['rɛzɪdjuː] *n* reste *m*; (Chem, Physics)
résidu *m*
resign [rɪ'zaɪn] *vt* (*one's post*) se démettre
de ▷ *vi* démissionner; **to ~ o.s. to** (*endure*) se
résigner à; **resignation** [rɛzɪg'neɪʃən] *n* (*from
post*) démission *f*; (*state of mind*) résignation *f*
resin ['rɛzɪn] *n* résine *f*

resist [rɪ'zɪst] *vt* résister à; **resistance** *n* résistance *f*

resit (*BRIT*) *vt* [ri:'sɪt] (*pt, pp* **resat**) (*exam*) repasser ▷ *n* ['ri:sɪt] deuxième session *f* (*d'un examen*)

resolution [rɛzə'lu:ʃən] *n* résolution *f*

resolve [rɪ'zɔlv] *n* résolution *f* ▷ *vt* (*decide*): **to ~ to do** résoudre *or* décider de faire; (*problem*) résoudre

resort [rɪ'zɔ:t] *n* (*seaside town*) station *f* balnéaire; (*for skiing*) station de ski; (*recourse*) recours *m* ▷ *vi*: **to ~ to** avoir recours à; **in the last ~** en dernier ressort

resource [rɪ'sɔ:s] *n* ressource *f*; **resourceful** *adj* ingénieux(-euse), débrouillard(e)

respect [rɪs'pɛkt] *n* respect *m* ▷ *vt* respecter; **respectable** *adj* respectable; (*quite good: result etc*) honorable; **respectful** *adj* respectueux(-euse); **respective** *adj* respectif(-ive); **respectively** *adv* respectivement

respite ['rɛspaɪt] *n* répit *m*

respond [rɪs'pɔnd] *vi* répondre; (*react*) réagir; **response** [rɪs'pɔns] *n* réponse *f*; (*reaction*) réaction *f*

responsibility [rɪspɔnsɪ'bɪlɪtɪ] *n* responsabilité *f*

responsible [rɪs'pɔnsɪbl] *adj* (*liable*): **~ (for)** responsable (de); (*person*) digne de confiance; (*job*) qui comporte des responsabilités; **responsibly** *adv* avec sérieux

responsive [rɪs'pɔnsɪv] *adj* (*student, audience*) réceptif(-ive); (*brakes, steering*) sensible

rest [rɛst] *n* repos *m*; (*stop*) arrêt *m*, pause *f*; (*Mus*) silence *m*; (*support*) support *m*, appui *m*; (*remainder*) reste *m*, restant *m* ▷ *vi* se reposer; (*be supported*): **to ~ on** appuyer *or* reposer sur ▷ *vt* (*lean*): **to ~ sth on/against** appuyer qch sur/contre; **the ~ of them** les autres

restaurant ['rɛstərɔŋ] *n* restaurant *m*; **restaurant car** *n* (*BRIT Rail*) wagon-restaurant *m*

restless ['rɛstlɪs] *adj* agité(e)

restoration [rɛstə'reɪʃən] *n* (*of building*) restauration *f*; (*of stolen goods*) restitution *f*

restore [rɪ'stɔ:'] *vt* (*building*) restaurer; (*sth stolen*) restituer; (*peace, health*) rétablir; **to ~ to** (*former state*) ramener à

restrain [rɪs'treɪn] *vt* (*feeling*) contenir; (*person*): **to ~ (from doing)** retenir (de faire); **restraint** *n* (*restriction*) contrainte *f*; (*moderation*) retenue *f*; (*of style*) sobriété *f*

restrict [rɪs'trɪkt] *vt* restreindre, limiter; **restriction** [rɪs'trɪkʃən] *n* restriction *f*, limitation *f*

rest room *n* (*US*) toilettes *fpl*

restructure [ri:'strʌktʃə'] *vt* restructurer

result [rɪ'zʌlt] *n* résultat *m* ▷ *vi*: **to ~ in** aboutir à, se terminer par; **as a ~ of** à la suite de

resume [rɪ'zju:m] *vt* (*work, journey*) reprendre ▷ *vi* (*work etc*) reprendre

résumé ['reɪzju:meɪ] *n* (*summary*) résumé *m*; (*US: curriculum vitae*) curriculum vitae *m inv*

resuscitate [rɪ'sʌsɪteɪt] *vt* (*Med*) réanimer

retail ['ri:teɪl] *adj* de *or* au détail ▷ *adv* au détail; **retailer** *n* détaillant(e)

retain [rɪ'teɪn] *vt* (*keep*) garder, conserver

retaliation [rɪtælɪ'eɪʃən] *n* représailles *fpl*, vengeance *f*

retarded [rɪ'tɑ:dɪd] *adj* retardé(e)

retire [rɪ'taɪə'] *vi* (*give up work*) prendre sa retraite; (*withdraw*) se retirer, partir; (*go to bed*) (aller) se coucher; **retired** *adj* (*person*) retraité(e); **retirement** *n* retraite *f*

retort [rɪ'tɔ:t] *vi* riposter

retreat [rɪ'tri:t] *n* retraite *f* ▷ *vi* battre en retraite

retrieve [rɪ'tri:v] *vt* (*sth lost*) récupérer; (*situation, honour*) sauver; (*error, loss*) réparer; (*Comput*) rechercher

retrospect ['rɛtrəspɛkt] *n*: **in ~** rétrospectivement, après coup; **retrospective** [rɛtrə'spɛktɪv] *adj* rétrospectif(-ive); (*law*) rétroactif(-ive) ▷ *n* (*Art*) rétrospective *f*

return [rɪ'tə:n] *n* (*going or coming back*) retour *m*; (*of sth stolen etc*) restitution *f*; (*Finance: from land, shares*) rapport *m* ▷ *cpd* (*journey*) de retour; (*BRIT: ticket*) aller et retour; (*match*) retour ▷ *vi* (*person etc: come back*) revenir; (*: go back*) retourner ▷ *vt* rendre; (*bring back*) rapporter; (*send back*) renvoyer; (*put back*) remettre; (*Pol: candidate*) élire; **returns** *npl* (*Comm*) recettes *fpl*; (*Finance*) bénéfices *mpl*; **many happy ~s (of the day)!** bon anniversaire!; **by ~ (of post)** par retour (du courrier); **in ~ (for)** en échange (de); **a ~ (ticket) for …** un billet aller et retour pour …; **return ticket** *n* (*esp BRIT*) billet *m* aller-retour

reunion [ri:'ju:nɪən] *n* réunion *f*

reunite [ri:ju:'naɪt] *vt* réunir

revamp [ri:'væmp] *vt* (*house*) retaper; (*firm*) réorganiser

reveal [rɪ'vi:l] *vt* (*make known*) révéler; (*display*) laisser voir; **revealing** *adj* révélateur(-trice); (*dress*) au décolleté généreux *or* suggestif

revel ['rɛvl] *vi*: **to ~ in sth/in doing** se délecter de qch/à faire

revelation [rɛvə'leɪʃən] *n* révélation *f*

revenge [rɪ'vɛndʒ] *n* vengeance *f*; (*in game etc*) revanche *f* ▷ *vt* venger; **to take ~ (on)** se venger (sur)

revenue ['rɛvənju:] *n* revenu *m*

Reverend ['rɛvərənd] *adj* (*in titles*): **the ~ John Smith** (*Anglican*) le révérend John Smith; (*Catholic*) l'abbé (John) Smith; (*Protestant*) le pasteur (John) Smith

reversal [rɪ'və:sl] *n* (*of opinion*) revirement

m; *(of order)* renversement *m*; *(of direction)* changement *m*

reverse [rɪ'vɜːs] *n* contraire *m*, opposé *m*; *(back)* dos *m*, envers *m*; *(of paper)* verso *m*; *(of coin)* revers *m*; *(Aut: also:* ~ **gear)** marche f arrière ▷ *adj (order, direction)* opposé(e), inverse ▷ *vt (order, position)* changer, inverser; *(direction, policy)* changer complètement de; *(decision)* annuler; *(roles)* renverser ▷ *vi (BRIT Aut)* faire marche arrière; **reverse-charge call** *n (BRIT Tel)* communication f en PCV; **reversing lights** *npl (BRIT Aut)* feux *mpl* de marche arrière *or* de recul

revert [rɪ'vɜːt] *vi:* **to** ~ **to** revenir à, retourner à

review [rɪ'vjuː] *n* revue f; *(of book, film)* critique f; *(of situation, policy)* examen *m*, bilan *m*; *(US: examination)* examen ▷ *vt* passer en revue; faire la critique de; examiner

revise [rɪ'vaɪz] *vt* réviser, modifier; *(manuscript)* revoir, corriger ▷ *vi (study)* réviser; **revision** [rɪ'vɪʒən] *n* révision f

revival [rɪ'vaɪvəl] *n* reprise f; *(recovery)* rétablissement *m*; *(of faith)* renouveau *m*

revive [rɪ'vaɪv] *vt (person)* ranimer; *(custom)* rétablir; *(economy)* relancer; *(hope, courage)* raviver, faire renaître; *(play, fashion)* reprendre ▷ *vi (person)* reprendre connaissance; *(: from ill health)* se rétablir; *(hope etc)* renaître; *(activity)* reprendre

revolt [rɪ'vəʊlt] *n* révolte f ▷ *vi* se révolter, se rebeller ▷ *vt* révolter, dégoûter; **revolting** *adj* dégoûtant(e)

revolution [rɛvə'luːʃən] *n* révolution f; *(of wheel etc)* tour *m*, révolution; **revolutionary** *adj*, *n* révolutionnaire *(m/f)*

revolve [rɪ'vɒlv] *vi* tourner

revolver [rɪ'vɒlvə*] *n* revolver *m*

reward [rɪ'wɔːd] *n* récompense f ▷ *vt:* **to** ~ **(for)** récompenser (de); **rewarding** *adj (fig)* qui (en) vaut la peine, gratifiant(e)

rewind [riː'waɪnd] *vt (irreg: like* **wind)** *(tape)* réembobiner

rewritable [riː'raɪtəbl] *adj (CD, DVD)* réinscriptible

rewrite [riː'raɪt] *(pt* **rewrote,** *pp* **rewritten)** *vt* récrire

rheumatism ['ruːmətɪzəm] *n* rhumatisme *m*

Rhine [raɪn] *n:* **the (River)** ~ le Rhin

rhinoceros [raɪ'nɒsərəs] *n* rhinocéros *m*

Rhône [rəʊn] *n:* **the (River)** ~ le Rhône

rhubarb ['ruːbɑːb] *n* rhubarbe f

rhyme [raɪm] *n* rime f; *(verse)* vers *mpl*

rhythm ['rɪðm] *n* rythme *m*

rib [rɪb] *n (Anat)* côte f

ribbon ['rɪbən] *n* ruban *m*; **in ~s** *(torn)* en lambeaux

rice [raɪs] *n* riz *m*; **rice pudding** *n* riz *m* au lait

rich [rɪtʃ] *adj* riche; *(gift, clothes)* somptueux(-euse); **to be ~ in sth** être riche en qch

rid [rɪd] *(pt, pp* ~**)** *vt:* **to** ~ **sb of** débarrasser qn de; **to get** ~ **of** se débarrasser de

riddle ['rɪdl] *n (puzzle)* énigme f ▷ *vt:* **to be ~d with** être criblé(e) de; *(fig)* être en proie à

ride [raɪd] *n* promenade f, tour *m*; *(distance covered)* trajet *m* ▷ *vb (pt* **rode,** *pp* **ridden)** ▷ *vi (as sport)* monter (à cheval), faire du cheval; *(go somewhere: on horse, bicycle)* aller (à cheval or bicyclette etc); *(travel: on bicycle, motor cycle, bus)* rouler ▷ *vt (a horse)* monter; *(distance)* parcourir, faire; **to** ~ **a horse/bicycle** monter à cheval/à bicyclette; **to take sb for a** ~ *(fig)* faire marcher qn; *(cheat)* rouler qn; **rider** *n* cavalier(-ière); *(in race)* jockey *m*; *(on bicycle)* cycliste *m/f*; *(on motorcycle)* motocycliste *m/f*

ridge [rɪdʒ] *n (of hill)* faîte *m*; *(of roof, mountain)* arête f; *(on object)* strie f

ridicule ['rɪdɪkjuːl] *n* ridicule *m*; dérision f ▷ *vt* ridiculiser, tourner en dérision; **ridiculous** [rɪ'dɪkjʊləs] *adj* ridicule

riding ['raɪdɪŋ] *n* équitation f; **riding school** *n* manège *m*, école f d'équitation

rife [raɪf] *adj* répandu(e); ~ **with** abondant(e) en

rifle ['raɪfl] *n* fusil *m* (à canon rayé) ▷ *vt* vider, dévaliser

rift [rɪft] *n* fente f, fissure f; *(fig: disagreement)* désaccord *m*

rig [rɪg] *n (also:* **oil** ~**:** *on land)* derrick *m*; *(: at sea)* plate-forme pétrolière ▷ *vt (election etc)* truquer

right [raɪt] *adj (true)* juste, exact(e); *(correct)* bon (bonne); *(suitable)* approprié(e), convenable; *(just)* juste, équitable; *(morally good)* bien *inv*; *(not left)* droit(e) ▷ *n (moral good)* bien *m*; *(title, claim)* droit *m*; *(not left)* droite f ▷ *adv (answer)* correctement; *(treat)* bien, comme il faut; *(not on the left)* à droite ▷ *vt* redresser ▷ *excl* bon!; **do you have the** ~ **time?** avez-vous l'heure juste or exacte?; **to be** ~ *(person)* avoir raison; *(answer)* être juste or correct(e); **by ~s** en toute justice; **on the** ~ à droite; **to be in the** ~ avoir raison; ~ **in the middle** en plein milieu; ~ **away** immédiatement; **right angle** *n (Math)* angle droit; **rightful** *adj (heir)* légitime; **right-hand** *adj:* **the right-hand side** la droite; **right-hand drive** *n (BRIT)* conduite f à droite; *(vehicle)* véhicule *m* avec la conduite à droite; **right-handed** *adj (person)* droitier(-ère); **rightly** *adv* bien, correctement; *(with reason)* à juste titre; **right of way** *n (on path etc)* droit *m* de passage; *(Aut)* priorité f; **right-wing** *adj (Pol)* de droite

rigid ['rɪdʒɪd] *adj* rigide; *(principle, control)* strict(e)

rigorous ['rɪgərəs] *adj* rigoureux(-euse)

rim [rɪm] *n* bord *m*; *(of spectacles)* monture f; *(of* *wheel*) jante *f*

rind [raɪnd] *n* (*of bacon*) couenne *f*; (*of lemon etc*) écorce *f*, zeste *m*; (*of cheese*) croûte *f*

ring [rɪŋ] *n* anneau *m*; (*on finger*) bague *f*; (*also:* **wedding ~**) alliance *f*; (*of people, objects*) cercle *m*; (*of spies*) réseau *m*; (*of smoke etc*) rond *m*; (*arena*) piste *f*, arène *f*; (*for boxing*) ring *m*; (*sound of bell*) sonnerie *f* ▷ *vb* (*pt* **rang**, *pp* **rung**) ▷ *vi* (*telephone, bell*) sonner; (*person: by telephone*) téléphoner; (*ears*) bourdonner; (*also:* **~ out**: *voice, words*) retentir ▷ *vt* (*BRIT Tel: also:* **~ up**) téléphoner à, appeler; **to ~ the bell** sonner; **to give sb a ~** (*Tel*) passer un coup de téléphone or de fil à qn; **ring back** *vt, vi* (*BRIT Tel*) rappeler; **ring off** *vi* (*BRIT Tel*) raccrocher; **ring up** (*BRIT*) ▷ *vt* (*Tel*) téléphoner à, appeler; **ringing tone** *n* (*BRIT Tel*) tonalité *f* d'appel; **ringleader** *n* (*of gang*) chef *m*, meneur *m*; **ring road** *n* (*BRIT*) rocade *f*; (*motorway*) périphérique *m*; **ringtone** *n* (*on mobile*) sonnerie *f* (*de téléphone portable*)

rink [rɪŋk] *n* (*also:* **ice ~**) patinoire *f*

rinse [rɪns] *n* rinçage *m* ▷ *vt* rincer

riot ['raɪət] *n* émeute *f*, bagarres *fpl* ▷ *vi* (*demonstrators*) manifester avec violence; (*population*) se soulever, se révolter; **to run ~** se déchaîner

rip [rɪp] *n* déchirure *f* ▷ *vt* déchirer ▷ *vi* se déchirer; **rip off** *vt* (*inf: cheat*) arnaquer; **rip up** *vt* déchirer

ripe [raɪp] *adj* (*fruit*) mûr(e); (*cheese*) fait(e)

rip-off ['rɪpɔf] *n* (*inf*): **it's a ~!** c'est du vol manifeste!, c'est de l'arnaque!

ripple ['rɪpl] *n* ride *f*, ondulation *f*; (*of applause, laughter*) cascade *f* ▷ *vi* se rider, onduler

rise [raɪz] *n* (*slope*) côte *f*, pente *f*; (*hill*) élévation *f*; (*increase: in wages: BRIT*) augmentation *f*; (: *in prices, temperature*) hausse *f*, augmentation; (*fig: to power etc*) ascension *f* ▷ *vi* (*pt* **rose**, *pp* **~n**) s'élever, monter; (*prices, numbers*) augmenter, monter; (*waters, river*) monter; (*sun, wind, person: from chair, bed*) se lever; (*also:* **~ up**: *tower, building*) s'élever; (: *rebel*) se révolter; se rebeller; (*in rank*) s'élever; **to give ~ to** donner lieu à; **to ~ to the occasion** se montrer à la hauteur; **risen** ['rɪzn] *pp of* **rise**; **rising** *adj* (*increasing: number, prices*) en hausse; (*tide*) montant(e); (*sun, moon*) levant(e)

risk [rɪsk] *n* risque *m* ▷ *vt* risquer; **to take** *or* **run the ~ of doing** courir le risque de faire; **at ~** en danger; **at one's own ~** à ses risques et périls; **risky** *adj* risqué(e)

rite [raɪt] *n* rite *m*; **the last ~s** les derniers sacrements

ritual ['rɪtjuəl] *adj* rituel(le) ▷ *n* rituel *m*

rival ['raɪvl] *n* rival(e); (*in business*) concurrent(e) ▷ *adj* rival(e); qui fait concurrence ▷ *vt* (*match*) égaler; **rivalry** *n* rivalité *f*; (*in business*) concurrence *f*

river ['rɪvə'] *n* rivière *f*; (*major: also fig*) fleuve *m* ▷ *cpd* (*port, traffic*) fluvial(e); **up/down ~** en amont/aval; **riverbank** *n* rive *f*, berge *f*

rivet ['rɪvɪt] *n* rivet *m* ▷ *vt* (*fig*) river, fixer

Riviera [rɪvɪ'ɛərə] *n*: **the (French) ~** la Côte d'Azur

road [rəud] *n* route *f*; (*in town*) rue *f*; (*fig*) chemin, voie *f* ▷ *cpd* (*accident*) de la route; **major/minor ~** route principale *or* à priorité/voie secondaire; **which ~ do I take for …?** quelle route dois-je prendre pour aller à…?; **roadblock** *n* barrage routier; **road map** *n* carte routière; **road rage** *n* comportement très agressif de certains usagers de la route; **road safety** *n* sécurité routière; **roadside** *n* bord *m* de la route, bas-côté *m*; **roadsign** *n* panneau *m* de signalisation; **road tax** *n* (*BRIT Aut*) taxe *f* sur les automobiles; **roadworks** *npl* travaux *mpl* (de réfection des routes)

roam [rəum] *vi* errer, vagabonder

roar [rɔː'] *n* rugissement *m*; (*of crowd*) hurlements *mpl*; (*of vehicle, thunder, storm*) grondement *m* ▷ *vi* rugir; hurler; gronder; **to ~ with laughter** rire à gorge déployée; **to do a ~ing trade** faire des affaires en or

roast [rəust] *n* rôti *m* ▷ *vt* (*meat*) (faire) rôtir; (*coffee*) griller, torréfier; **roast beef** *n* rôti *m* de bœuf, rosbif *m*

rob [rɔb] *vt* (*person*) voler; (*bank*) dévaliser; **to ~ sb of sth** voler *or* dérober qch à qn; (*fig: deprive*) priver qn de qch; **robber** *n* bandit *m*, voleur *m*; **robbery** *n* vol *m*

robe [rəub] *n* (*for ceremony etc*) robe *f*; (*also:* **bath~**) peignoir *m*; (*us: rug*) couverture *f* ▷ *vt* revêtir (d'une robe)

robin ['rɔbɪn] *n* rouge-gorge *m*

robot ['rəubɔt] *n* robot *m*

robust [rəu'bʌst] *adj* robuste; (*material, appetite*) solide

rock [rɔk] *n* (*substance*) roche *f*, roc *m*; (*boulder*) rocher *m*, roche; (*us: small stone*) caillou *m*; (*BRIT: sweet*) ≈ sucre *m* d'orge ▷ *vt* (*swing gently: cradle*) balancer; (: *child*) bercer; (*shake*) ébranler, secouer ▷ *vi* se balancer, être ébranlé(e) *or* secoué(e); **on the ~s** (*drink*) avec des glaçons; (*marriage etc*) en train de craquer; **rock and roll** *n* rock (and roll) *m*, rock'n'roll *m*; **rock climbing** *n* varappe *f*

rocket ['rɔkɪt] *n* fusée *f*; (*Mil*) fusée, roquette *f*; (*Culin*) roquette

rocking chair ['rɔkɪŋ-] *n* fauteuil *m* à bascule

rocky ['rɔkɪ] *adj* (*hill*) rocheux(-euse); (*path*) rocailleux(-euse)

rod [rɔd] *n* (*metallic*) tringle *f*; (*Tech*) tige *f*; (*wooden*) baguette *f*; (*also:* **fishing ~**) canne *f* à pêche

rode [rəud] *pt of* **ride**

rodent ['rəudnt] *n* rongeur *m*

rogue [rəug] *n* coquin(e)

role [rəʊl] n rôle m; **role-model** n modèle m
à émuler

roll [rəʊl] n rouleau m; (of banknotes) liasse
f; (also: **bread ~**) petit pain; (register) liste f;
(sound: of drums etc) roulement m ▷ vt rouler;
(also: **~ up**: string) enrouler; (also: **~ out**:
pastry) étendre au rouleau, abaisser ▷ vi
rouler; **roll over** vi se retourner; **roll up**
vi (inf: arrive) arriver, s'amener ▷ vt (carpet,
cloth, map) rouler; (sleeves) retrousser; **roller**
n rouleau m; (wheel) roulette f; (for road)
rouleau compresseur; (for hair) bigoudi m;
roller coaster n montagnes fpl russes; **roller
skates** npl patins mpl à roulettes; **roller-
skating** n patin m à roulettes; **to go roller-
skating** faire du patin à roulettes; **rolling pin**
n rouleau m à pâtisserie

ROM [rɒm] n abbr (Comput: = read-only memory)
mémoire morte, ROM f

Roman ['rəʊmən] adj romain(e) ▷ n
Romain(e); **Roman Catholic** adj, n
catholique (m/f)

romance [rə'mæns] n (love affair) idylle f;
(charm) poésie f; (novel) roman m à l'eau de rose

Romania etc [rəʊ'meɪnɪə] = **Rumania** etc

Roman numeral n chiffre romain

romantic [rə'mæntɪk] adj romantique; (novel,
attachment) sentimental(e)

Rome [rəʊm] n Rome

roof [ruːf] n toit m; (of tunnel, cave) plafond m
▷ vt couvrir (d'un toit); **the ~ of the mouth** la
voûte du palais; **roof rack** n (Aut) galerie f

rook [rʊk] n (bird) freux m; (Chess) tour f

room [ruːm] n (in house) pièce f; (also: **bed~**)
chambre f (à coucher); (in school etc) salle
f; (space) place f; **roommate** n camarade
m/f de chambre; **room service** n service
m des chambres (dans un hôtel); **roomy** adj
spacieux(-euse); (garment) ample

rooster ['ruːstəʳ] n coq m

root [ruːt] n (Bot, Math) racine f; (fig: of problem)
origine f, fond m ▷ vi (plant) s'enraciner

rope [rəʊp] n corde f; (Naut) cordage m ▷ vt
(tie up or together) attacher; (climbers: also: **~
together**) encorder; (area: also: **~ off**) interdire
l'accès de; (: divide off) séparer; **to know the ~s**
(fig) être au courant, connaître les ficelles

rose [rəʊz] pt of **rise** ▷ n rose f; (also: **~bush**)
rosier m

rosé ['rəʊzeɪ] n rosé m

rosemary ['rəʊzmərɪ] n romarin m

rosy ['rəʊzɪ] adj rose; **a ~ future** un bel avenir

rot [rɒt] n (decay) pourriture f; (fig: pej: nonsense)
idioties fpl, balivernes fpl ▷ vt, vi pourrir

rota ['rəʊtə] n liste f, tableau m de service

rotate [rəʊ'teɪt] vt (revolve) faire tourner;
(change round: crops) alterner; (: jobs) faire à
tour de rôle ▷ vi (revolve) tourner

rotten ['rɒtn] adj (decayed) pourri(e);

(dishonest) corrompu(e); (inf: bad) mauvais(e),
moche; **to feel ~** (ill) être mal fichu(e)

rough [rʌf] adj (cloth, skin) rêche,
rugueux(-euse); (terrain) accidenté(e); (path)
rocailleux(-euse); (voice) rauque, rude;
(person, manner: coarse) rude, fruste; (: violent)
brutal(e); (district, weather) mauvais(e); (sea)
houleux(-euse); (plan) ébauché(e); (guess)
approximatif(-ive) ▷ n (Golf) rough m ▷ vt: **to
~ it** vivre à la dure; **to sleep ~** (BRIT) coucher
à la dure; **roughly** adv (handle) rudement,
brutalement; (speak) avec brusquerie; (make)
grossièrement; (approximately) à peu près, en
gros

roulette [ruː'lɛt] n roulette f

round [raʊnd] adj rond(e) ▷ n rond m, cercle
m; (BRIT: of toast) tranche f; (duty: of policeman,
milkman etc) tournée f; (: of doctor) visites fpl;
(game: of cards, in competition) partie f; (Boxing)
round m; (of talks) série f ▷ vt (corner) tourner
▷ prep autour de ▷ adv: **right ~, all ~** tout
autour; **~ of ammunition** cartouche f; **~ of
applause** applaudissements mpl; **~ of drinks**
tournée f; **~ of sandwiches** (BRIT) sandwich
m; **the long way ~** (par) le chemin le plus long;
all (the) year ~ toute l'année; **it's just ~ the
corner** (fig) c'est tout près; **to go ~ to sb's
(house)** aller chez qn; **go ~ the back** passez
par derrière; **enough to go ~** assez pour tout
le monde; **she arrived ~ (about) noon** (BRIT)
elle est arrivée vers midi; **~ the clock** 24 heures
sur 24; **round off** vt (speech etc) terminer;
round up vt rassembler; (criminals) effectuer
une rafle de; (prices) arrondir (au chiffre
supérieur); **roundabout** n (BRIT Aut) rond-
point m (à sens giratoire); (at fair) manège
m (de chevaux de bois) ▷ adj (route, means)
détourné(e); **round trip** n (voyage m) aller et
retour m; **roundup** n rassemblement m; (of
criminals) rafle f

rouse [raʊz] vt (wake up) réveiller; (stir
up) susciter, provoquer; (interest) éveiller;
(suspicions) susciter, éveiller

route [ruːt] n itinéraire m; (of bus) parcours m;
(of trade, shipping) route f

routine [ruː'tiːn] adj (work) ordinaire,
courant(e); (procedure) d'usage ▷ n (habits)
habitudes fpl; (pej) train-train m; (Theat)
numéro m

row[1] [rəʊ] n (line) rangée f; (of people, seats,
Knitting) rang m; (behind one another: of cars,
people) file f ▷ vi (in boat) ramer; (as sport) faire
de l'aviron ▷ vt (boat) faire aller à la rame or à
l'aviron; **in a ~** (fig) d'affilée

row[2] [raʊ] n (noise) vacarme m; (dispute)
dispute f, querelle f; (scolding) réprimande f,
savon m ▷ vi (also: **to have a ~**) se disputer, se
quereller

rowboat ['rəʊbəʊt] n (US) canot m (à rames)

rowing ['rəʊɪŋ] n canotage m; (as sport) aviron m; **rowing boat** n (BRIT) canot m (à rames)

royal ['rɔɪəl] adj royal(e); **royalty** n (royal persons) (membres mpl de la) famille royale; (payment: to author) droits mpl d'auteur; (: to inventor) royalties fpl

rpm abbr (= revolutions per minute) t/mn (= tours/minute)

R.S.V.P. abbr (= répondez s'il vous plaît) RSVP

Rt. Hon. abbr (BRIT: = Right Honourable) titre donné aux députés de la Chambre des communes

rub [rʌb] n: **to give sth a ~** donner un coup de chiffon or de torchon à qch ▷ vt frotter; (person) frictionner; (hands) se frotter; **to ~ sb up** (BRIT) or **to ~ sb** (US) **the wrong way** prendre qn à rebrousse-poil; **rub in** vt (ointment) faire pénétrer; **rub off** vi partir; **rub out** vt effacer

rubber ['rʌbəʳ] n caoutchouc m; (BRIT: eraser) gomme f (à effacer); **rubber band** n élastique m; **rubber gloves** npl gants mpl en caoutchouc

rubbish ['rʌbɪʃ] n (from household) ordures fpl; (fig: pej) choses fpl sans valeur; camelote f; (nonsense) bêtises fpl, idioties fpl; **rubbish bin** n (BRIT) boîte f à ordures, poubelle f; **rubbish dump** n (BRIT: in town) décharge publique, dépotoir m

rubble ['rʌbl] n décombres mpl; (smaller) gravats mpl; (Constr) blocage m

ruby ['ruːbɪ] n rubis m

rucksack ['rʌksæk] n sac m à dos

rudder ['rʌdəʳ] n gouvernail m

rude [ruːd] adj (impolite: person) impoli(e); (: word, manners) grossier(-ière); (shocking) indécent(e), inconvenant(e)

ruffle ['rʌfl] vt (hair) ébouriffer; (clothes) chiffonner; (fig: person): **to get ~d** s'énerver

rug [rʌɡ] n petit tapis; (BRIT: blanket) couverture f

rugby ['rʌɡbɪ] n (also: ~ **football**) rugby m

rugged ['rʌɡɪd] adj (landscape) accidenté(e); (features, character) rude

ruin ['ruːɪn] n ruine f ▷ vt ruiner; (spoil: clothes) abîmer; (: event) gâcher; **ruins** npl (of building) ruine(s)

rule [ruːl] n règle f; (regulation) règlement m; (government) autorité f, gouvernement m ▷ vt (country) gouverner; (person) dominer; (decide) décider ▷ vi commander; (Law): **as a ~** normalement, en règle générale; **rule out** vt exclure; **ruler** n (sovereign) souverain(e); (leader) chef m (d'État); (for measuring) règle f; **ruling** adj (party) au pouvoir; (class) dirigeant(e) ▷ n (Law) décision f

rum [rʌm] n rhum m

Rumania [ruːˈmeɪnɪə] n Roumanie f; **Rumanian** adj roumain(e) ▷ n Roumain(e);

(Ling) roumain m

rumble ['rʌmbl] n grondement m; (of stomach, pipe) gargouillement m ▷ vi gronder; (stomach, pipe) gargouiller

rumour (US **rumor**) ['ruːməʳ] n rumeur f, bruit m (qui court) ▷ vt: **it is ~ed that** le bruit court que

rump steak n romsteck m

run [rʌn] n (race) course f; (outing) tour m or promenade f (en voiture); (distance travelled) parcours m, trajet m; (series) suite f, série f; (Theat) série de représentations; (Ski) piste f; (Cricket, Baseball) point m; (in tights, stockings) maille filée, échelle f ▷ vb (pt **ran**, pp **~**) ▷ vt (business) diriger; (competition, course) organiser; (hotel, house) tenir; (race) participer à; (Comput: program) exécuter; (to pass: hand, finger): **to ~ sth over** promener or passer qch sur; (water, bath) faire couler; (Press: feature) publier ▷ vi courir; (pass: road etc) passer; (work: machine, factory) marcher; (bus, train) circuler; (continue: play) se jouer, être à l'affiche; (: contract) être valide or en vigueur; (flow: river, bath, nose) couler; (colours, washing) déteindre; (in election) être candidat, se présenter; **at a ~** au pas de course; **to go for a ~** aller courir or faire un peu de course à pied; (in car) faire un tour or une promenade (en voiture); **there was a ~ on** (meat, tickets) les gens se sont rués sur; **in the long ~** à la longue; **on the ~** en fuite; **I'll ~ you to the station** je vais vous emmener or conduire à la gare; **to ~ a risk** courir un risque; **run after** vt fus (to catch up) courir après; (chase) poursuivre; **run away** vi s'enfuir; **run down** vt (Aut: knock over) renverser; (BRIT: reduce: production) réduire progressivement; (: factory/shop) réduire progressivement la production/l'activité de; (criticize) critiquer, dénigrer; **to be ~ down** (tired) être fatigué(e) or à plat; **run into** vt fus (meet: person) rencontrer par hasard; (: trouble) se heurter à; (collide with) heurter; **run off** vi s'enfuir ▷ vt (water) laisser s'écouler; (copies) tirer; **run out** vi (person) sortir en courant; (liquid) couler; (lease) expirer; (money) être épuisé(e); **run out of** vt fus se trouver à court de; **run over** vt (Aut) écraser ▷ vt fus (revise) revoir, reprendre; **run through** vt fus (recap) reprendre, revoir; (play) répéter; **run up** vi: **to ~ up against** (difficulties) se heurter à; **runaway** adj (horse) emballé(e); (truck) fou (folle); (person) fugitif(-ive); (child) fugueur(-euse)

rung [rʌŋ] pp of **ring** ▷ n (of ladder) barreau m

runner ['rʌnəʳ] n (in race: person) coureur(-euse); (: horse) partant m; (on sledge) patin m; (for drawer etc) coulisseau m; **runner bean** n (BRIT) haricot m (à rames); **runner-up** n second(e)

running ['rʌnɪŋ] n (in race etc) course f; (of

business, organization) direction *f*, gestion *f*
▷ *adj* (*water*) courant(e); (*commentary*) suivi(e);
6 days ~ 6 jours de suite; **to be in/out of the ~
for sth** être/ne pas être sur les rangs pour qch
runny ['rʌnɪ] *adj* qui coule
run-up ['rʌnʌp] *n* (*BRIT*) **~ to sth** période *f*
précédant qch
runway ['rʌnweɪ] *n* (*Aviat*) piste *f* (d'envol *or*
d'atterrissage)
rupture ['rʌptʃər] *n* (*Med*) hernie *f*
rural ['ruərl] *adj* rural(e)
rush [rʌʃ] *n* (*of crowd, Comm: sudden demand*)
ruée *f*; (*hurry*) hâte *f*; (*of anger, joy*) accès
m; (*current*) flot *m*; (*Bot*) jonc *m* ▷ *vt* (*hurry*)
transporter *or* envoyer d'urgence ▷ *vi* se
précipiter; **to ~ sth off** (*do quickly*) faire qch à
la hâte; **rush hour** *n* heures *fpl* de pointe *or*
d'affluence
Russia ['rʌʃə] *n* Russie *f*; **Russian** *adj* russe ▷ *n*
Russe *m/f*; (*Ling*) russe *m*
rust [rʌst] *n* rouille *f* ▷ *vi* rouiller
rusty ['rʌstɪ] *adj* rouillé(e)
ruthless ['ruːθlɪs] *adj* sans pitié, impitoyable
RV *n abbr* (*US*) = **recreational vehicle**
rye [raɪ] *n* seigle *m*

S

Sabbath ['sæbəθ] *n* (*Jewish*) sabbat *m*;
(*Christian*) dimanche *m*
sabotage ['sæbətɑːʒ] *n* sabotage *m* ▷ *vt*
saboter
saccharin(e) ['sækərɪn] *n* saccharine *f*
sachet ['sæʃeɪ] *n* sachet *m*
sack [sæk] *n* (*bag*) sac *m* ▷ *vt* (*dismiss*) renvoyer,
mettre à la porte; (*plunder*) piller, mettre à sac;
to get the ~ être renvoyé(e) *or* mis(e) à la porte
sacred ['seɪkrɪd] *adj* sacré(e)
sacrifice ['sækrɪfaɪs] *n* sacrifice *m* ▷ *vt*
sacrifier
sad [sæd] *adj* (*unhappy*) triste; (*deplorable*)
triste, fâcheux(-euse); (*inf: pathetic: thing*)
triste, lamentable; (*: person*) minable
saddle ['sædl] *n* selle *f* ▷ *vt* (*horse*) seller; **to be
~d with sth** (*inf*) avoir qch sur les bras
sadistic [sə'dɪstɪk] *adj* sadique
sadly ['sædlɪ] *adv* tristement; (*unfortunately*)
malheureusement; (*seriously*) fort
sadness ['sædnɪs] *n* tristesse *f*
s.a.e. *n abbr* (*BRIT*: = stamped addressed envelope)
enveloppe affranchie pour la réponse
safari [sə'fɑːrɪ] *n* safari *m*
safe [seɪf] *adj* (*out of danger*) hors de danger,
en sécurité; (*not dangerous*) sans danger;
(*cautious*) prudent(e); (*sure: bet etc*) assuré(e)
▷ *n* coffre-fort *m*; **could you put this in
the ~, please?** pourriez-vous mettre ceci
dans le coffre-fort?; **~ and sound** sain(e) et

sauf (sauve); **(just) to be on the ~ side** pour plus de sûreté, par précaution; **safely** adv (assume, say) sans risque d'erreur; (drive, arrive) sans accident; **safe sex** n rapports sexuels protégés

safety ['seɪftɪ] n sécurité f; **safety belt** n ceinture f de sécurité; **safety pin** n épingle f de sûreté or de nourrice

saffron ['sæfrən] n safran m

sag [sæg] vi s'affaisser, fléchir; (hem, breasts) pendre

sage [seɪdʒ] n (herb) sauge f; (person) sage m

Sagittarius [sædʒɪˈtɛərɪəs] n le Sagittaire

Sahara [səˈhɑːrə] n: **the ~ (Desert)** le (désert du) Sahara m

said [sɛd] pt, pp of **say**

sail [seɪl] n (on boat) voile f; (trip): **to go for a ~** faire un tour en bateau ▷ vt (boat) manœuvrer, piloter ▷ vi (travel: ship) avancer, naviguer; (set off) partir, prendre la mer; (Sport) faire de la voile; **they ~ed into Le Havre** ils sont entrés dans le port du Havre; **sailboat** n (us) bateau m à voiles, voilier m; **sailing** n (Sport) voile f; **to go sailing** faire de la voile; **sailing boat** n bateau m à voiles, voilier m; **sailor** n marin m, matelot m

saint [seɪnt] n saint(e)

sake [seɪk] n: **for the ~ of** (out of concern for) pour (l'amour de), dans l'intérêt de; (out of consideration for) par égard pour

salad ['sæləd] n salade f; **salad cream** n (BRIT) (sorte f de) mayonnaise f; **salad dressing** n vinaigrette f

salami [səˈlɑːmɪ] n salami m

salary ['sælərɪ] n salaire m, traitement m

sale [seɪl] n vente f; (at reduced prices) soldes mpl; **sales** npl (total amount sold) chiffre m de ventes; **"for ~"** "à vendre"; **on ~** en vente; **sales assistant** (us **sales clerk**) n vendeur(-euse); **salesman** (irreg) n (in shop) vendeur m; **salesperson** (irreg) n (in shop) vendeur(-euse); **sales rep** n (Comm) représentant(e) m/f; **saleswoman** (irreg) n (in shop) vendeuse f

saline ['seɪlaɪn] adj salin(e)

saliva [səˈlaɪvə] n salive f

salmon ['sæmən] n (pl inv) saumon m

salon ['sælɔn] n salon m

saloon [səˈluːn] n (us) bar m; (BRIT Aut) berline f; (ship's lounge) salon m

salt [sɔːlt] n sel m ▷ vt saler; **saltwater** adj (fish etc) d'eau; (de mer) salt; **salty** adj salé(e)

salute [səˈluːt] n salut m; (of guns) salve f ▷ vt saluer

salvage ['sælvɪdʒ] n (saving) sauvetage m; (things saved) biens sauvés or récupérés ▷ vt sauver, récupérer

Salvation Army [sælˈveɪʃən-] n Armée f du Salut

same [seɪm] adj même ▷ pron: **the ~** le (la) même, les mêmes; **the ~ book as** le même livre que; **at the ~ time** en même temps; (yet) néanmoins; **all** or **just the ~** tout de même, quand même; **to do the ~** faire de même, en faire autant; **to do the ~ as sb** faire comme qn; **and the ~ to you!** et à vous de même!; (after insult) toi-même!

sample ['sɑːmpl] n échantillon m; (Med) prélèvement m ▷ vt (food, wine) goûter

sanction ['sæŋkʃən] n approbation f, sanction f ▷ vt cautionner, sanctionner; **sanctions** npl (Pol) sanctions

sanctuary ['sæŋktjʊərɪ] n (holy place) sanctuaire m; (refuge) asile m; (for wildlife) réserve f

sand [sænd] n sable m ▷ vt (also: ~ **down**: wood etc) poncer

sandal ['sændl] n sandale f

sand: sandbox n (us: for children) tas m de sable; **sandcastle** n château m de sable; **sand dune** n dune f de sable; **sandpaper** n papier m de verre; **sandpit** n (BRIT: for children) tas m de sable; **sands** npl plage f (de sable); **sandstone** ['sændstəʊn] n grès m

sandwich ['sændwɪtʃ] n sandwich m ▷ vt (also: ~ **in**) intercaler; **~ed between** pris en sandwich entre; **cheese/ham ~** sandwich au fromage/jambon

sandy ['sændɪ] adj sablonneux(-euse); (colour) sable inv, blond roux inv

sane [seɪn] adj (person) sain(e) d'esprit; (outlook) sensé(e), sain(e)

sang [sæŋ] pt of **sing**

sanitary towel (us **sanitary napkin**) ['sænɪtərɪ-] n serviette f hygiénique

sanity ['sænɪtɪ] n santé mentale; (common sense) bon sens

sank [sæŋk] pt of **sink**

Santa Claus [sæntəˈklɔːz] n le Père Noël

sap [sæp] n (of plants) sève f ▷ vt (strength) saper, miner

sapphire ['sæfaɪər] n saphir m

sarcasm ['sɑːkæzm] n sarcasme m, raillerie f

sarcastic [sɑːˈkæstɪk] adj sarcastique

sardine [sɑːˈdiːn] n sardine f

SASE n abbr (us: = self-addressed stamped envelope) enveloppe affranchie pour la réponse

sat [sæt] pt, pp of **sit**

Sat. abbr (= Saturday) sa

satchel ['sætʃl] n cartable m

satellite ['sætəlaɪt] n satellite m; **satellite dish** n antenne f parabolique; **satellite television** n télévision f par satellite

satin ['sætɪn] n satin m ▷ adj en or de satin, satiné(e)

satire ['sætaɪər] n satire f

satisfaction [sætɪsˈfækʃən] n satisfaction f

satisfactory [sætɪsˈfæktərɪ] adj satisfaisant(e)

satisfied ['sætɪsfaɪd] *adj* satisfait(e); **to be ~ with sth** être satisfait de qch

satisfy ['sætɪsfaɪ] *vt* satisfaire, contenter; (*convince*) convaincre, persuader

Saturday ['sætədɪ] *n* samedi *m*

sauce [sɔːs] *n* sauce *f*; **saucepan** *n* casserole *f*

saucer ['sɔːsə'] *n* soucoupe *f*

Saudi Arabia ['saudɪ-] *n* Arabie *f* Saoudite

sauna ['sɔːnə] *n* sauna *m*

sausage ['sɔsɪdʒ] *n* saucisse *f*; (*salami etc*) saucisson *m*; **sausage roll** *n* friand *m*

sautéed ['səuteɪd] *adj* sauté(e)

savage ['sævɪdʒ] *adj* (*cruel, fierce*) brutal(e), féroce; (*primitive*) primitif(-ive), sauvage ▷ *n* sauvage *m/f* ▷ *vt* attaquer férocement

save [seɪv] *vt* (*person, belongings*) sauver; (*money*) mettre de côté, économiser; (*time*) (faire) gagner; (*keep*) garder; (*Comput*) sauvegarder; (*Sport: stop*) arrêter; (*avoid: trouble*) éviter ▷ *vi* (*also: ~ up*) mettre de l'argent de côté ▷ *n* (*Sport*) arrêt *m* (du ballon) ▷ *prep* sauf, à l'exception de

savings ['seɪvɪŋz] *npl* économies *fpl*; **savings account** *n* compte *m* d'épargne; **savings and loan association** (*us*) *n* ≈ société *f* de crédit immobilier

savoury (*us* **savory**) ['seɪvərɪ] *adj* savoureux(-euse); (*dish: not sweet*) salé(e)

saw [sɔː] *pt of* **see** ▷ *n* (*tool*) scie *f* ▷ *vt* (*pt* **~ed**, *pp* **~ed** *or* **~n**) scier; **sawdust** *n* sciure *f*

sawn [sɔːn] *pp of* **saw**

saxophone ['sæksəfəun] *n* saxophone *m*

say [seɪ] *n*: **to have one's ~** dire ce qu'on a à dire ▷ *vt* (*pt, pp* **said**) dire; **to have a ~** avoir voix au chapitre; **could you ~ that again?** pourriez-vous répéter ce que vous venez de dire?; **to ~ yes/no** dire oui/non; **my watch ~s 3 o'clock** ma montre indique 3 heures, il est 3 heures à ma montre; **that is to ~** c'est-à-dire, cela va sans dire, cela va de soi; **saying** *n* dicton *m*, proverbe *m*

scab [skæb] *n* croûte *f*; (*pej*) jaune *m*

scaffolding ['skæfəldɪŋ] *n* échafaudage *m*

scald [skɔːld] *n* brûlure *f* ▷ *vt* ébouillanter

scale [skeɪl] *n* (*of fish*) écaille *f*; (*Mus*) gamme *f*; (*of ruler, thermometer etc*) graduation *f*, échelle (graduée); (*of salaries, fees etc*) barème *m*; (*of map, also size, extent*) échelle ▷ *vt* (*mountain*) escalader; **scales** *npl* balance *f*; (*larger*) bascule *f*; (*also: **bathroom ~s**) pèse-personne *m inv*; **~ of charges** tableau *m* des tarifs; **on a large ~** sur une grande échelle, en grand

scallion ['skæljən] *n* (*us: salad onion*) ciboule *f*

scallop ['skɔləp] *n* coquille *f* Saint-Jacques; (*Sewing*) feston *m*

scalp [skælp] *n* cuir chevelu ▷ *vt* scalper

scalpel ['skælpl] *n* scalpel *m*

scam [skæm] *n* (*inf*) arnaque *f*

scampi ['skæmpɪ] *npl* langoustines (frites),

scampi *mpl*

scan [skæn] *vt* (*examine*) scruter, examiner; (*glance at quickly*) parcourir; (*TV, Radar*) balayer ▷ *n* (*Med*) scanographie *f*

scandal ['skændl] *n* scandale *m*; (*gossip*) ragots *mpl*

Scandinavia [skændɪ'neɪvɪə] *n* Scandinavie *f*; **Scandinavian** *adj* scandinave ▷ *n* Scandinave *m/f*

scanner ['skænə'] *n* (*Radar, Med*) scanner *m*, scanographe *m*; (*Comput*) scanner, numériseur *m*

scapegoat ['skeɪpgəut] *n* bouc *m* émissaire

scar [skɑː'] *n* cicatrice *f* ▷ *vt* laisser une cicatrice *or* une marque à

scarce [skɛəs] *adj* rare, peu abondant(e); **to make o.s. ~** (*inf*) se sauver; **scarcely** *adv* à peine, presque pas

scare [skɛə'] *n* peur *f*, panique *f* ▷ *vt* effrayer, faire peur à; **to ~ sb stiff** faire une peur bleue à qn; **bomb ~** alerte *f* à la bombe; **scarecrow** *n* épouvantail *m*; **scared** *adj*: **to be scared** avoir peur

scarf (*pl* **scarves**) [skɑːf, skɑːvz] *n* (*long*) écharpe *f*; (*square*) foulard *m*

scarlet ['skɑːlɪt] *adj* écarlate

scarves [skɑːvz] *npl of* **scarf**

scary ['skɛərɪ] *adj* (*inf*) effrayant(e); (*film*) qui fait peur

scatter ['skætə'] *vt* éparpiller, répandre; (*crowd*) disperser ▷ *vi* se disperser

scenario [sɪ'nɑːrɪəu] *n* scénario *m*

scene [siːn] *n* (*Theat, fig etc*) scène *f*; (*of crime, accident*) lieu(x) *m(pl)*, endroit *m*; (*sight, view*) spectacle *m*, vue *f*; **scenery** *n* (*Theat*) décor(s) *m(pl)*; (*landscape*) paysage *m*; **scenic** *adj* offrant de beaux paysages *or* panoramas

scent [sɛnt] *n* parfum *m*, odeur *f*; (*fig: track*) piste *f*

sceptical (*us* **skeptical**) ['skɛptɪkl] *adj* sceptique

schedule ['ʃɛdjuːl, *us* 'skɛdjuːl] *n* programme *m*, plan *m*; (*of trains*) horaire *m*; (*of prices etc*) barème *m*, tarif *m* ▷ *vt* prévoir; **on ~** à l'heure (prévue); **to be ahead of/behind ~** avoir de l'avance/du retard; **scheduled flight** *n* vol régulier

scheme [skiːm] *n* plan *m*, projet *m*; (*plot*) complot *m*, combine *f*; (*arrangement*) arrangement *m*, classification *f*; (*pension scheme etc*) régime *m* ▷ *vt, vi* comploter, manigancer

schizophrenic [skɪtsə'frɛnɪk] *adj* schizophrène

scholar ['skɔlə'] *n* érudit(e); (*pupil*) boursier(-ère); **scholarship** *n* érudition *f*; (*grant*) bourse *f* (d'études)

school [skuːl] *n* (*gen*) école *f*; (*secondary school*) collège *m*, lycée *m*; (*in university*) faculté *f*;

(us: university) université f ▷ cpd scolaire; **schoolbook** n livre m scolaire or de classe; **schoolboy** n écolier m; (at secondary school) collégien m, lycéen m; **schoolchildren** npl écoliers mpl; (at secondary school) collégiens mpl, lycéens mpl; **schoolgirl** n écolière f; (at secondary school) collégienne f, lycéenne f; **schooling** n instruction f, études fpl; **schoolteacher** n (primary) instituteur(-trice), (secondary) professeur m

science ['saɪəns] n science f; **science fiction** n science-fiction f; **scientific** [saɪən'tɪfɪk] adj scientifique; **scientist** n scientifique m/f; (eminent) savant m

sci-fi ['saɪfaɪ] n abbr (inf: = science fiction) SF f

scissors ['sɪzəz] npl ciseaux mpl; **a pair of ~** une paire de ciseaux

scold [skəuld] vt gronder

scone [skɒn] n sorte de petit pain rond au lait

scoop [sku:p] n pelle f (à main); (for ice cream) boule f à glace; (Press) reportage exclusif or à sensation

scooter ['sku:tər] n (motor cycle) scooter m; (toy) trottinette f

scope [skəup] n (capacity: of plan, undertaking) portée f, envergure f; (: of person) compétence f, capacités fpl; (opportunity) possibilités fpl

scorching ['skɔ:tʃɪŋ] adj torride, brûlant(e)

score [skɔ:ʳ] n score m, décompte m des points; (Mus) partition f ▷ vt (goal, point) marquer; (success) remporter; (cut: leather, wood, card) entailler, inciser ▷ vi marquer des points; (Football) marquer un but; (keep score) compter les points; **on that ~** sur ce chapitre, à cet égard; **a ~ of** (twenty) vingt; **~s of** (fig) des tas de; **to ~ 6 out of 10** obtenir 6 sur 10; **score out** vt rayer, barrer, biffer; **scoreboard** n tableau m; **scorer** n (Football) auteur m du but; buteur m; (keeping score) marqueur m

scorn [skɔ:n] n mépris m, dédain m

Scorpio ['skɔ:pɪəu] n le Scorpion

scorpion ['skɔ:pɪən] n scorpion m

Scot [skɒt] n Écossais(e)

Scotch [skɒtʃ] n whisky m, scotch m

Scotch tape® (us) n scotch® m, ruban adhésif

Scotland ['skɒtlənd] n Écosse f

Scots [skɒts] adj écossais(e); **Scotsman** (irreg) n Écossais m; **Scotswoman** (irreg) n Écossaise f; **Scottish** ['skɒtɪʃ] adj écossais(e); **Scottish Parliament** n Parlement écossais

scout [skaut] n (Mil) éclaireur m; (also: **boy ~**) scout m; **girl ~** (us) guide f

scowl [skaul] vi se renfrogner, avoir l'air maussade; **to ~ at** regarder de travers

scramble ['skræmbl] n (rush) bousculade f, ruée f ▷ vi grimper/descendre tant bien que mal; **to ~ for** se bousculer or se disputer pour (avoir); **to go scrambling** (Sport) faire du trial;

scrambled eggs npl œufs brouillés

scrap [skræp] n bout m, morceau m; (fight) bagarre f; (also: **~ iron**) ferraille f ▷ vt jeter, mettre au rebut; (fig) abandonner, laisser tomber ▷ vi se bagarrer; **scraps** npl (waste) déchets mpl; **scrapbook** n album m

scrape [skreɪp] vt, vi gratter, racler ▷ n: **to get into a ~** s'attirer des ennuis; **scrape through** vi (exam etc) réussir de justesse

scrap paper n papier m brouillon

scratch [skrætʃ] n égratignure f, rayure f; (on paint) éraflure f; (from claw) coup m de griffe ▷ vt (rub) (se) gratter; (paint etc) érafler; (with claw, nail) griffer ▷ vi (se) gratter; **to start from ~** partir de zéro; **to be up to ~** être à la hauteur; **scratch card** n carte f à gratter

scream [skri:m] n cri perçant, hurlement m ▷ vi crier, hurler

screen [skri:n] n écran m; (in room) paravent m; (fig) écran, rideau m ▷ vt masquer, cacher; (from the wind etc) abriter, protéger; (film) projeter; (candidates etc) filtrer; **screening** n (of film) projection f; (Med) test m (or tests) de dépistage; **screenplay** n scénario m; **screen saver** n (Comput) économiseur m d'écran

screw [skru:] n vis f ▷ vt (also: **~ in**) visser; **screw up** vt (paper etc) froisser; **to ~ up one's eyes** se plisser les yeux; **screwdriver** n tournevis m

scribble ['skrɪbl] n gribouillage m ▷ vt gribouiller, griffonner

script [skrɪpt] n (Cine etc) scénario m, texte m; (writing) (écriture f) script m

scroll [skrəul] n rouleau m ▷ vt (Comput) faire défiler (sur l'écran)

scrub [skrʌb] n (land) broussailles fpl ▷ vt (floor) nettoyer à la brosse; (pan) récurer; (washing) frotter

scruffy ['skrʌfɪ] adj débraillé(e)

scrum(mage) ['skrʌm(ɪdʒ)] n mêlée f

scrutiny ['skru:tɪnɪ] n examen minutieux

scuba diving ['sku:bə-] n plongée sous-marine (autonome)

sculptor ['skʌlptər] n sculpteur m

sculpture ['skʌlptʃər] n sculpture f

scum [skʌm] n écume f, mousse f; (pej: people) rebut m, lie f

scurry ['skʌrɪ] vi filer à toute allure; **to ~ off** détaler, se sauver

sea [si:] n mer f ▷ cpd marin(e), de (la) mer, maritime; **by** or **beside the ~** (holiday, town) au bord de la mer; **by ~** par mer, en bateau; **out to ~** au large; **(out) at ~** en mer; **to be all at ~** (fig) nager complètement; **seafood** n fruits mpl de mer; **sea front** n bord m de mer; **seagull** n mouette f

seal [si:l] n (animal) phoque m; (stamp) sceau m, cachet m ▷ vt sceller; (envelope) coller; (: with seal) cacheter; **seal off** vt (forbid entry to) interdire l'accès de

sea level n niveau m de la mer

seam [siːm] n couture f; (of coal) veine f, filon m

search [sɜːtʃ] n (for person, thing, Comput) recherche(s) f(pl); (of drawer, pockets) fouille f; (Law: at sb's home) perquisition f ▷ vt fouiller; (examine) examiner minutieusement; scruter ▷ vi: **to ~ for** chercher; **in ~ of** à la recherche de; **search engine** n (Comput) moteur m de recherche; **search party** n expédition f de secours

sea: **seashore** n rivage m, plage f, bord m de (la) mer; **seasick** adj: **to be seasick** avoir le mal de mer; **seaside** n bord m de mer; **seaside resort** n station f balnéaire

season ['siːzn] n saison f ▷ vt assaisonner, relever; **to be in/out of ~** être/ne pas être de saison; **seasonal** adj saisonnier(-ière); **seasoning** n assaisonnement m; **season ticket** n carte f d'abonnement

seat [siːt] n siège m; (in bus, train: place) place f; (buttocks) postérieur m; (of trousers) fond m ▷ vt faire asseoir, placer; (have room for) avoir des places assises pour, pouvoir accueillir; **I'd like to book two ~s** je voudrais réserver deux places; **to be ~ed** être assis; **seat belt** n ceinture f de sécurité; **seating** n sièges fpl, places assises

sea: **sea water** n eau f de mer; **seaweed** n algues fpl

sec. abbr (= second) sec

secluded [sɪ'kluːdɪd] adj retiré(e), à l'écart

second ['sɛkənd] num deuxième, second(e) ▷ adv (in race etc) en seconde position ▷ n (unit of time) seconde f; (Aut: also: **~ gear**) seconde; (Comm: imperfect) article m de second choix; (BRIT Scol) ≈ licence f avec mention ▷ vt (motion) appuyer; **seconds** npl (inf: food) rab m (inf); **secondary** adj secondaire; **secondary school** n collège m; lycée m; **second-class** adj de deuxième classe; (Rail) de seconde (classe); (Post) au tarif réduit; (pej) de qualité inférieure ▷ adv (Rail) en seconde; (Post) au tarif réduit; **secondhand** adj d'occasion; (information) de seconde main; **secondly** adv deuxièmement; **second-rate** adj de deuxième ordre, de qualité inférieure; **second thoughts** npl: **to have second thoughts** changer d'avis; **on second thoughts** or **thought** (US) à la réflexion

secrecy ['siːkrəsɪ] n secret m

secret ['siːkrɪt] adj secret(-ète) ▷ n secret m; **in ~** adv en secret, secrètement, en cachette

secretary ['sɛkrətrɪ] n secrétaire m/f; **S~ of State (for)** (Brit Pol) ministre m (de)

secretive ['siːkrətɪv] adj réservé(e); (pej) cachottier(-ière), dissimulé(e)

secret service n services secrets

sect [sɛkt] n secte f

section ['sɛkʃən] n section f; (Comm) rayon m; (of document) section, article m, paragraphe m; (cut) coupe f

sector ['sɛktər] n secteur m

secular ['sɛkjʊlər] adj laïque

secure [sɪ'kjʊər] adj (free from anxiety) sans inquiétude, sécurisé(e); (firmly fixed) solide, bien attaché(e) (or fermé(e) etc); (in safe place) en lieu sûr, en sûreté f ▷ vt (fix) fixer, attacher; (get) obtenir, se procurer

security [sɪ'kjʊərɪtɪ] n sécurité f, mesures fpl de sécurité; (for loan) caution f, garantie f; **securities** npl (Stock Exchange) valeurs fpl, titres mpl; **security guard** n garde chargé de la sécurité; (transporting money) convoyeur m de fonds

sedan [sə'dæn] n (US Aut) berline f

sedate [sɪ'deɪt] adj calme; posé(e) ▷ vt donner des sédatifs à

sedative ['sɛdɪtɪv] n calmant m, sédatif m

seduce [sɪ'djuːs] vt séduire; **seductive** [sɪ'dʌktɪv] adj séduisant(e); (smile) séducteur(-trice); (fig: offer) alléchant(e)

see [siː] vb (pt **saw**, pp **~n**) ▷ vt (gen) voir; (accompany): **to ~ sb to the door** reconduire or raccompagner qn jusqu'à la porte ▷ vi voir; **to ~ that** (ensure) veiller à ce que + sub, faire en sorte que + sub, s'assurer que; **~ you soon/later/tomorrow!** à bientôt/plus tard/demain!; **see off** vt accompagner (à la gare or à l'aéroport etc); **see out** vt (take to door) raccompagner à la porte; **see through** vt mener à bonne fin ▷ vt fus voir clair dans; **see to** vt fus s'occuper de, se charger de

seed [siːd] n graine f; (fig) germe m; (Tennis etc) tête f de série; **to go to ~** (plant) monter en graine; (fig) se laisser aller

seeing ['siːɪŋ] conj: **~ (that)** vu que, étant donné que

seek (pt, pp **sought**) [siːk, sɔːt] vt chercher, rechercher

seem [siːm] vi sembler, paraître; **there ~s to be ...** il semble qu'il y a ..., on dirait qu'il y a ...; **seemingly** adv apparemment

seen [siːn] pp of **see**

seesaw ['siːsɔː] n (jeu m de) bascule f

segment ['sɛgmənt] n segment m; (of orange) quartier m

segregate ['sɛgrɪgeɪt] vt séparer, isoler

Seine [seɪn] n: **the (River) ~** la Seine

seize [siːz] vt (grasp) saisir, attraper; (take possession of) s'emparer de; (opportunity) saisir

seizure ['siːʒər] n (Med) crise f, attaque f; (of power) prise f

seldom ['sɛldəm] adv rarement

select [sɪ'lɛkt] adj choisi(e), d'élite; (hotel, restaurant, club) chic inv, sélect inv ▷ vt sélectionner, choisir; **selection** n sélection f, choix m; **selective** adj sélectif(-ive); (school) à recrutement sélectif

self [sɛlf] n (pl **selves**): **the ~** le moi inv ▷ prefix auto-; **self-assured** adj sûr(e) de soi, plein(e) d'assurance; **self-catering** adj (BRIT: flat) avec cuisine, où l'on peut faire sa cuisine; (: holiday) en appartement (ou chalet etc) loué; **self-centred** (US **self-centered**) adj égocentrique; **self-confidence** n confiance f en soi; **self-confident** adj sûr(e) de soi, plein(e) d'assurance; **self-conscious** adj timide, qui manque d'assurance; **self-contained** adj (BRIT: flat) avec entrée particulière, indépendant(e); **self-control** n maîtrise f de soi; **self-defence** (US **self-defense**) n autodéfense f; (Law) légitime défense f; **self-drive** adj (BRIT): **self-drive car** voiture f de location; **self-employed** adj qui travaille à son compte; **self-esteem** n amour-propre m; **self-indulgent** adj qui ne se refuse rien; **self-interest** n intérêt personnel; **selfish** adj égoïste; **self-pity** n apitoiement m sur soi-même; **self-raising** [sɛlfˈreɪzɪŋ] (US **self-rising** [sɛlfˈraɪzɪŋ]) adj: **self-raising flour** farine f pour gâteaux (avec levure incorporée); **self-respect** n respect m de soi, amour-propre m; **self-service** adj, n libre-service (m), self-service (m)

sell (pt, pp **sold**) [sɛl, səʊld] vt vendre ▷ vi se vendre; **to ~ at or for 10 euros** se vendre 10 euros; **sell off** vt liquider; **sell out** vi: **to ~ out (of sth)** (use up stock) vendre tout son stock (de qch); **sell-by date** n date f limite de vente; **seller** n vendeur(-euse), marchand(e)

Sellotape® [ˈsɛləʊteɪp] n (BRIT) scotch® m

selves [sɛlvz] npl of **self**

semester [sɪˈmɛstəʳ] n (esp US) semestre m

semi... [ˈsɛmɪ] prefix semi-, demi-; à demi, à moitié; **semicircle** n demi-cercle m; **semidetached (house)** n (BRIT) maison jumelée or jumelle; **semi-final** n demi-finale f

seminar [ˈsɛmɪnɑːʳ] n séminaire m

semi-skimmed [ˈsɛmɪˈskɪmd] adj demi-écrémé(e)

senate [ˈsɛnɪt] n sénat m; (US): **the S~** le Sénat; **senator** n sénateur m

send (pt, pp **sent**) [sɛnd, sɛnt] vt envoyer; **send back** vt renvoyer; **send for** vt fus (by post) se faire envoyer, commander par correspondance; **send in** vt (report, application, resignation) remettre; **send off** vt (goods) envoyer, expédier; (BRIT Sport: player) expulser or renvoyer du terrain; **send on** vt (BRIT: letter) faire suivre; (luggage etc: in advance) (faire) expédier à l'avance; **send out** vt (invitation) envoyer (par la poste); (emit: light, heat, signal) émettre; **send up** vt (person, price) faire monter; (BRIT: parody) mettre en boîte, parodier; **sender** n expéditeur(-trice); **send-off** n: **a good send-off** des adieux chaleureux

senile [ˈsiːnaɪl] adj sénile

senior [ˈsiːnɪəʳ] adj (high-ranking) de haut niveau; (of higher rank): **to be ~ to sb** être le supérieur de qn; **senior citizen** n personne f du troisième âge; **senior high school** n (US) ≈ lycée m

sensation [sɛnˈseɪʃən] n sensation f; **sensational** adj qui fait sensation; (marvellous) sensationnel(le)

sense [sɛns] n sens m; (feeling) sentiment m; (meaning) sens, signification f; (wisdom) bon sens ▷ vt sentir, pressentir; **it makes ~** c'est logique; **senseless** adj insensé(e), stupide; (unconscious) sans connaissance; **sense of humour** (US **sense of humor**) n sens m de l'humour

sensible [ˈsɛnsɪbl] adj sensé(e), raisonnable; (shoes etc) pratique

> Be careful not to translate **sensible** by the French word **sensible**.

sensitive [ˈsɛnsɪtɪv] adj: **~ (to)** sensible (à)

sensual [ˈsɛnsjʊəl] adj sensuel(le)

sensuous [ˈsɛnsjʊəs] adj voluptueux(-euse), sensuel(le)

sent [sɛnt] pt, pp of **send**

sentence [ˈsɛntns] n (Ling) phrase f; (Law: judgment) condamnation f, sentence f; (: punishment) peine f ▷ vt: **to ~ sb to death/to 5 years** condamner qn à mort/à 5 ans

sentiment [ˈsɛntɪmənt] n sentiment m; (opinion) opinion f, avis m; **sentimental** [sɛntɪˈmɛntl] adj sentimental(e)

Sep. abbr (= September) septembre

separate adj [ˈsɛprɪt] séparé(e); (organization) indépendant(e); (day, occasion, issue) différent(e) ▷ vb [ˈsɛpəreɪt] ▷ vt séparer; (distinguish) distinguer ▷ vi se séparer; **separately** adv séparément; **separates** npl (clothes) coordonnés mpl; **separation** [sɛpəˈreɪʃən] n séparation f

September [sɛpˈtɛmbəʳ] n septembre m

septic [ˈsɛptɪk] adj (wound) infecté(e); **septic tank** n fosse f septique

sequel [ˈsiːkwl] n conséquence f; séquelles fpl; (of story) suite f

sequence [ˈsiːkwəns] n ordre m, suite f; (in film) séquence f; (dance) numéro m

sequin [ˈsiːkwɪn] n paillette f

Serb [sɜːb] adj, n = **Serbian**

Serbia [ˈsɜːbɪə] n Serbie f

Serbian [ˈsɜːbɪən] adj serbe ▷ n Serbe m/f; (Ling) serbe m

sergeant [ˈsɑːdʒənt] n sergent m; (Police) brigadier m

serial [ˈsɪərɪəl] n feuilleton m; **serial killer** n meurtrier m tuant en série; **serial number** n numéro m de série

series [ˈsɪəriz] n série f; (Publishing) collection f

serious [ˈsɪərɪəs] adj sérieux(-euse); (accident

etc) grave; **seriously** *adv* sérieusement; (*hurt*) gravement

sermon ['sɜːmən] *n* sermon *m*

servant ['sɜːvənt] *n* domestique *m/f*; (*fig*) serviteur (servante)

serve [sɜːv] *vt* (*employer etc*) servir, être au service de; (*purpose*) servir à; (*customer, food, meal*) servir; (*subj: train*) desservir; (*apprenticeship*) faire, accomplir; (*prison term*) faire; purger ▷ *vi* (*Tennis*) servir; (*be useful*): **to ~ as/for/to do** servir de/à/à faire ▷ *n* (*Tennis*) service *m*; **it ~s him right** c'est bien fait pour lui; **server** *n* (*Comput*) serveur *m*

service ['sɜːvɪs] *n* (*gen*) service *m*; (*Aut*) révision *f*; (*Rel*) office *m* ▷ *vt* (*car etc*) réviser; **services** *npl* (*Econ: tertiary sector*) (secteur *m*) tertiaire *m*, secteur des services; (*BRIT: on motorway*) station-service *f*; (*Mil*): **the S~s** *npl* les forces armées; **to be of ~ to sb, to do sb a ~** rendre service à qn; **~ included/not included** service compris/non compris; **service area** *n* (*on motorway*) aire *f* de services; **service charge** *n* (*BRIT*) service *m*; **serviceman** (*irreg*) *n* militaire *m*; **service station** *n* station-service *f*

serviette [sɜːvɪˈɛt] *n* (*BRIT*) serviette *f* (de table)

session ['sɛʃən] *n* (*sitting*) séance *f*; **to be in ~** siéger, être en session or en séance

set [sɛt] *n* série *f*, assortiment *m*; (*of tools etc*) jeu *m*; (*Radio, TV*) poste *m*; (*Tennis*) set *m*; (*group of people*) cercle *m*, milieu *m*; (*Cine*) plateau *m*; (*Theat: stage*) scène *f*; (*: scenery*) décor *m*; (*Math*) ensemble *m*; (*Hairdressing*) mise *f* en plis ▷ *adj* (*fixed*) fixe, déterminé(e); (*ready*) prêt(e) ▷ *vb* (*pt, pp* **~**) ▷ *vt* (*place*) mettre, poser, placer; (*fix, establish*) fixer; (*: record*) établir; (*assign: task, homework*) donner; (*exam*) composer; (*adjust*) régler; (*decide: rules etc*) fixer, choisir ▷ *vi* (*sun*) se coucher; (*jam, jelly, concrete*) prendre; (*bone*) se ressouder; **to be ~ on doing** être résolu(e) à faire; **to ~ to music** mettre en musique; **to ~ on fire** mettre le feu à; **to ~ free** libérer; **to ~ sth going** déclencher qch; **to ~ sail** partir, prendre la mer; **set aside** *vt* mettre de côté; (*time*) garder; **set down** *vt* (*subj: bus, train*) déposer; **set in** *vi* (*infection, bad weather*) s'installer; (*complications*) survenir, surgir; **set off** *vi* se mettre en route, partir ▷ *vt* (*bomb*) faire exploser; (*cause to start*) déclencher; (*show up well*) mettre en valeur, faire valoir; **set out** *vi*: **to ~ out (from)** partir (de) ▷ *vt* (*arrange*) disposer; (*state*) présenter, exposer; **to ~ out to do** entreprendre de faire; avoir pour but or intention de faire; **set up** *vt* (*organization*) fonder, créer; **setback** *n* (*hitch*) revers *m*, contretemps *m*; **set menu** *n* menu *m*

settee [sɛˈtiː] *n* canapé *m*

setting ['sɛtɪŋ] *n* cadre *m*; (*of jewel*) monture *f*;

(*position: of controls*) réglage *m*

settle ['sɛtl] *vt* (*argument, matter, account*) régler; (*problem*) résoudre; (*Med: calm*) calmer ▷ *vi* (*bird, dust etc*) se poser; **to ~ for sth** accepter qch, se contenter de qch; **to ~ on sth** opter or se décider pour qch; **settle down** *vi* (*get comfortable*) s'installer; (*become calmer*) se calmer; se ranger; (*live quietly*) se fixer; **settle in** *vi* s'installer; **settle up** *vi*: **to ~ up with sb** régler (ce que l'on doit à) qn; **settlement** *n* (*payment*) règlement *m*; (*agreement*) accord *m*; (*village etc*) village *m*, hameau *m*

setup ['sɛtʌp] *n* (*arrangement*) manière *f* dont les choses sont organisées; (*situation*) situation *f*, allure *f* des choses

seven ['sɛvn] *num* sept; **seventeen** *num* dix-sept; **seventeenth** [sɛvnˈtiːnθ] *num* dix-septième; **seventh** *num* septième; **seventieth** ['sɛvntɪɪθ] *num* soixante-dixième; **seventy** *num* soixante-dix

sever ['sɛvəʳ] *vt* couper, trancher; (*relations*) rompre

several ['sɛvərl] *adj, pron* plusieurs *pl*; **~ of us** plusieurs d'entre nous

severe [sɪˈvɪəʳ] *adj* (*stern*) sévère, strict(e); (*serious*) grave, sérieux(-euse); (*plain*) sévère, austère

sew (*pt* **~ed**, *pp* **~n**) [səu, səud, səun] *vt, vi* coudre

sewage ['suːɪdʒ] *n* vidange(s) *f(pl)*

sewer ['suːəʳ] *n* égout *m*

sewing ['səuɪŋ] *n* couture *f*; (*item(s)*) ouvrage *m*; **sewing machine** *n* machine *f* à coudre

sewn [səun] *pp of* **sew**

sex [sɛks] *n* sexe *m*; **to have ~ with** avoir des rapports (sexuels) avec; **sexism** ['sɛksɪzəm] *n* sexisme *m*; **sexist** *adj* sexiste; **sexual** ['sɛksjuəl] *adj* sexuel(le); **sexual intercourse** *n* rapports sexuels; **sexuality** [sɛksjuˈælɪtɪ] *n* sexualité *f*; **sexy** *adj* sexy *inv*

shabby ['ʃæbɪ] *adj* miteux(-euse); (*behaviour*) mesquin(e), méprisable

shack [ʃæk] *n* cabane *f*, hutte *f*

shade [ʃeɪd] *n* ombre *f*; (*for lamp*) abat-jour *m inv*; (*of colour*) nuance *f*, ton *m*; (*US: window shade*) store *m*; (*small quantity*): **a ~ of** un soupçon de ▷ *vt* abriter du soleil, ombrager; **shades** *npl* (*US: sunglasses*) lunettes *fpl* de soleil; **in the ~** à l'ombre; **a ~ smaller** un tout petit peu plus petit

shadow ['ʃædəu] *n* ombre *f* ▷ *vt* (*follow*) filer; **shadow cabinet** *n* (*BRIT Pol*) cabinet parallèle formé par le parti qui n'est pas au pouvoir

shady ['ʃeɪdɪ] *adj* ombragé(e); (*fig: dishonest*) louche, véreux(-euse)

shaft [ʃɑːft] *n* (*of arrow, spear*) hampe *f*; (*Aut, Tech*) arbre *m*; (*of mine*) puits *m*; (*of lift*) cage *f*; (*of light*) rayon *m*, trait *m*

shake [ʃeɪk] *vb* (*pt* **shook**, *pp* **~n**) ▷ *vt* secouer; (*bottle, cocktail*) agiter; (*house, confidence*) ébranler ▷ *vi* trembler; **to ~ one's head** (*in refusal etc*) dire or faire non de la tête; (*in dismay*) secouer la tête; **to ~ hands with sb** serrer la main à qn; **shake off** *vt* secouer; (*pursuer*) se débarrasser de; **shake up** *vt* secouer; **shaky** *adj* (*hand, voice*) tremblant(e); (*building*) branlant(e), peu solide

shall [ʃæl] *aux vb*: **I ~ go** j'irai; **~ I open the door?** j'ouvre la porte?; **I'll get the coffee, ~ I?** je vais chercher le café, d'accord?

shallow [ˈʃæləʊ] *adj* peu profond(e); (*fig*) superficiel(le), qui manque de profondeur

sham [ʃæm] *n* frime *f*

shambles [ˈʃæmblz] *n* confusion *f*, pagaïe *f*, fouillis *m*

shame [ʃeɪm] *n* honte *f* ▷ *vt* faire honte à; **it is a ~ (that/to do)** c'est dommage (que + *sub*/de faire); **what a ~!** quel dommage!; **shameful** *adj* honteux(-euse), scandaleux(-euse); **shameless** *adj* éhonté(e), effronté(e)

shampoo [ʃæmˈpuː] *n* shampooing *m* ▷ *vt* faire un shampooing à

shandy [ˈʃændɪ] *n* bière panachée

shan't [ʃɑːnt] = **shall not**

shape [ʃeɪp] *n* forme *f* ▷ *vt* façonner, modeler; (*sb's ideas, character*) former; (*sb's life*) déterminer ▷ *vi* (*also*: **~ up**: *events*) prendre tournure; (: *person*) faire des progrès, s'en sortir; **to take ~** prendre forme or tournure

share [ʃɛər] *n* part *f*; (*Comm*) action *f* ▷ *vt* partager; (*have in common*) avoir en commun; **to ~ out (among** or **between)** partager (entre); **shareholder** *n* (BRIT) actionnaire *m/f*

shark [ʃɑːk] *n* requin *m*

sharp [ʃɑːp] *adj* (*razor, knife*) tranchant(e), bien aiguisé(e); (*point, voice*) aigu(ë); (*nose, chin*) pointu(e); (*outline, increase*) net(te); (*cold, pain*) vif (vive); (*taste*) piquant(e), âcre; (*Mus*) dièse; (*person: quick-witted*) vif (vive), éveillé(e); (: *unscrupulous*) malhonnête ▷ *n* (*Mus*) dièse *m* ▷ *adv*: **at 2 o'clock ~** à 2 heures pile or tapantes; **sharpen** *vt* aiguiser; (*pencil*) tailler; (*fig*) aviver; **sharpener** *n* (*also*: **pencil sharpener**) taille-crayon(s) *m inv*; **sharply** *adv* (*turn, stop*) brusquement; (*stand out*) nettement; (*criticize, retort*) sèchement, vertement

shatter [ˈʃætər] *vt* briser; (*fig: upset*) bouleverser; (: *ruin*) briser, ruiner ▷ *vi* voler en éclats, se briser; **shattered** *adj* (*overwhelmed, grief-stricken*) bouleversé(e); (*inf: exhausted*) éreinté(e)

shave [ʃeɪv] *vt* raser ▷ *vi* se raser ▷ *n*: **to have a ~** se raser; **shaver** *n* (*also*: **electric shaver**) rasoir *m* électrique

shaving cream *n* crème *f* à raser

shaving foam *n* mousse *f* à raser

shavings [ˈʃeɪvɪŋz] *npl* (*of wood etc*) copeaux *mpl*

shawl [ʃɔːl] *n* châle *m*

she [ʃiː] *pron* elle

sheath [ʃiːθ] *n* gaine *f*, fourreau *m*, étui *m*; (*contraceptive*) préservatif *m*

shed [ʃɛd] *n* remise *f*, resserre *f* ▷ *vt* (*pt, pp* **~**) (*leaves, fur etc*) perdre; (*tears*) verser, répandre; (*workers*) congédier

she'd [ʃiːd] = **she had**; **she would**

sheep [ʃiːp] *n* (*pl inv*) mouton *m*; **sheepdog** *n* chien *m* de berger; **sheepskin** *n* peau *f* de mouton

sheer [ʃɪər] *adj* (*utter*) pur(e), pur et simple; (*steep*) à pic, abrupt(e); (*almost transparent*) extrêmement fin(e) ▷ *adv* à pic, abruptement

sheet [ʃiːt] *n* (*on bed*) drap *m*; (*of glass, metal etc*) feuille *f*; (*of paper*) feuille *f*; plaque *f*

sheik(h) [ʃeɪk] *n* cheik *m*

shelf (*pl* **shelves**) [ʃɛlf, ʃɛlvz] *n* étagère *f*, rayon *m*

shell [ʃɛl] *n* (*on beach*) coquillage *m*; (*of egg, nut etc*) coquille *f*; (*explosive*) obus *m*; (*of building*) carcasse *f* ▷ *vt* (*peas*) écosser; (*Mil*) bombarder (d'obus)

she'll [ʃiːl] = **she will**; **she shall**

shellfish [ˈʃɛlfɪʃ] *n* (*pl inv*: *crab etc*) crustacé *m*; (: *scallop etc*) coquillage *m* ▷ *npl* (*as food*) fruits *mpl* de mer

shelter [ˈʃɛltər] *n* abri *m*, refuge *m* ▷ *vt* abriter, protéger; (*give lodging to*) donner asile à ▷ *vi* s'abriter, se mettre à l'abri; **sheltered** *adj* (*life*) retiré(e), à l'abri des soucis; (*spot*) abrité(e)

shelves [ʃɛlvz] *npl* of **shelf**

shelving [ˈʃɛlvɪŋ] *n* (*shelves*) rayonnage(s) *m(pl)*

shepherd [ˈʃɛpəd] *n* berger *m* ▷ *vt* (*guide*) guider, escorter; **shepherd's pie** *n* ≈ hachis *m* Parmentier

sheriff [ˈʃɛrɪf] (US) *n* shérif *m*

sherry [ˈʃɛrɪ] *n* xérès *m*, sherry *m*

she's [ʃiːz] = **she is**; **she has**

Shetland [ˈʃɛtlənd] *n* (*also*: **the ~s, the ~ Isles** or **Islands**) les îles *fpl* Shetland

shield [ʃiːld] *n* bouclier *m*; (*protection*) écran *m* de protection ▷ *vt*: **to ~ (from)** protéger (de or contre)

shift [ʃɪft] *n* (*change*) changement *m*; (*work period*) période *f* de travail; (*of workers*) équipe *f*, poste *m* ▷ *vt* déplacer, changer de place; (*remove*) enlever ▷ *vi* changer de place, bouger

shin [ʃɪn] *n* tibia *m*

shine [ʃaɪn] *n* éclat *m*, brillant *m* ▷ *vb* (*pt, pp* **shone**) ▷ *vi* briller ▷ *vt* (*torch*): **to ~ on** braquer sur; (*polish*: *pt, pp* **~d**) faire briller or reluire

shingles [ˈʃɪŋglz] *n* (*Med*) zona *m*

shiny [ˈʃaɪnɪ] *adj* brillant(e)

ship [ʃɪp] *n* bateau *m*; (*large*) navire *m* ▷ *vt* transporter (par mer); (*send*) expédier (par mer); **shipment** *n* cargaison *f*; **shipping**

n (*ships*) navires *mpl*; (*traffic*) navigation *f*; (*the industry*) industrie navale; (*transport*) transport *m*; **shipwreck** *n* épave *f*; (*event*) naufrage *m* ▷ *vt*: **to be shipwrecked** faire naufrage; **shipyard** *n* chantier naval

shirt [ʃəːt] *n* chemise *f*; (*woman's*) chemisier *m*; **in ~ sleeves** en bras de chemise

shit [ʃɪt] *excl* (*inf!*) merde (*!*)

shiver ['ʃɪvəʳ] *n* frisson *m* ▷ *vi* frissonner

shock [ʃɔk] *n* choc *m*; (*Elec*) secousse *f*, décharge *f*; (*Med*) commotion *f*, choc ▷ *vt* (*scandalize*) choquer, scandaliser; (*upset*) bouleverser; **shocking** *adj* (*outrageous*) choquant(e), scandaleux(-euse); (*awful*) épouvantable

shoe [ʃuː] *n* chaussure *f*, soulier *m*; (*also*: **horse~**) fer *m* à cheval ▷ *vt* (*pt, pp* **shod**) (*horse*) ferrer; **shoelace** *n* lacet *m* (de soulier); **shoe polish** *n* cirage *m*; **shoeshop** *n* magasin *m* de chaussures

shone [ʃɔn] *pt, pp of* **shine**

shook [ʃuk] *pt, pp of* **shake**

shoot [ʃuːt] *n* (*on branch, seedling*) pousse *f* ▷ *vb* (*pt, pp* **shot**) ▷ *vt* (*game: hunt*) chasser; (*: aim at*) tirer; (*: kill*) abattre; (*person*) blesser/tuer d'un coup de fusil (*or de revolver*); (*execute*) fusiller; (*arrow*) tirer; (*gun*) tirer un coup de; (*Cine*) tourner ▷ *vi* (*with gun, bow*): **to ~ (at)** tirer (sur); (*Football*) shooter, tirer; **shoot down** *vt* (*plane*) abattre; **shoot up** *vi* (*fig: prices etc*) monter en flèche; **shooting** *n* (*shots*) coups *mpl* de feu; (*attack*) fusillade *f*; (*murder*) homicide *m* (*à l'aide d'une arme à feu*); (*Hunting*) chasse *f*

shop [ʃɔp] *n* magasin *m*; (*workshop*) atelier *m* ▷ *vi* (*also*: **go ~ping**) faire ses courses *or* ses achats; **shop assistant** *n* (*BRIT*) vendeur(-euse); **shopkeeper** *n* marchand(e), commerçant(e); **shoplifting** *n* vol *m* à l'étalage; **shopping** *n* (*goods*) achats *mpl*, provisions *fpl*; **shopping bag** *n* sac *m* (à provisions); **shopping centre** (*US* **shopping center**) *n* centre commercial; **shopping mall** *n* centre commercial; **shopping trolley** *n* (*BRIT*) Caddie®*m*; **shop window** *n* vitrine *f*

shore [ʃɔːʳ] *n* (*of sea, lake*) rivage *m*, rive *f* ▷ *vt*: **to ~ (up)** étayer; **on ~** à terre

short [ʃɔːt] *adj* (*not long*) court(e); (*soon finished*) court, bref (brève); (*person, step*) petit(e); (*curt*) brusque, sec (sèche); (*insufficient*) insuffisant(e) ▷ *n* (*also*: **~ film**) court métrage; (*Elec*) court-circuit *m*; **to be ~ of sth** être à court de *or* manquer de qch; **in ~** bref; en bref; **~ of doing** à moins de faire; **everything ~ of** tout sauf; **it is ~ for** c'est l'abréviation *or* le diminutif de; **to cut ~** (*speech, visit*) abréger, écourter; **to fall ~ of** ne pas être à la hauteur de; **to run ~ of** arriver à court de, venir à manquer de; **to stop ~** s'arrêter net;

to stop ~ of ne pas aller jusqu'à; **shortage** *n* manque *m*, pénurie *f*; **shortbread** *n* ≈ sablé *m*; **shortcoming** *n* défaut *m*; **short(crust) pastry** *n* (*BRIT*) pâte brisée; **shortcut** *n* raccourci *m*; **shorten** *vt* raccourcir; (*text, visit*) abréger; **shortfall** *n* déficit *m*; **shorthand** *n* (*BRIT*) sténo(graphie) *f*; **shortlist** *n* (*BRIT*: *for job*) liste *f* des candidats sélectionnés; **short-lived** *adj* de courte durée; **shortly** *adv* bientôt, sous peu; **shorts** *npl*: (**a pair of**) **shorts** un short; **short-sighted** *adj* (*BRIT*) myope; (*fig*) qui manque de clairvoyance; **short-sleeved** *adj* à manches courtes; **short story** *n* nouvelle *f*; **short-tempered** *adj* qui s'emporte facilement; **short-term** *adj* (*effect*) à court terme

shot [ʃɔt] *pt, pp of* **shoot** ▷ *n* coup *m* (de feu); (*try*) coup, essai *m*; (*injection*) piqûre *f*; (*Phot*) photo *f*; **to be a good/poor ~** (*person*) tirer bien/mal; **like a ~** comme une flèche; (*very readily*) sans hésiter; **shotgun** *n* fusil *m* de chasse

should [ʃud] *aux vb*: **I ~ go now** je devrais partir maintenant; **he ~ be there now** il devrait être arrivé maintenant; **I ~ go if I were you** si j'étais vous j'irais; **I ~ like to** j'aimerais bien, volontiers

shoulder ['ʃəuldəʳ] *n* épaule *f* ▷ *vt* (*fig*) endosser, se charger de; **shoulder blade** *n* omoplate *f*

shouldn't ['ʃudnt] = **should not**

shout [ʃaut] *n* cri *m* ▷ *vt* crier ▷ *vi* crier, pousser des cris

shove [ʃʌv] *vt* pousser; (*inf: put*): **to ~ sth in** fourrer *or* ficher qch dans ▷ *n* poussée *f*

shovel ['ʃʌvl] *n* pelle *f* ▷ *vt* pelleter, enlever (*or* enfourner) à la pelle

show [ʃəu] *n* (*of emotion*) manifestation *f*, démonstration *f*; (*semblance*) semblant *m*, apparence *f*; (*exhibition*) exposition *f*, salon *m*; (*Theat, TV*) spectacle *m*; (*Cine*) séance *f* ▷ *vb* (*pt* **~ed**, *pp* **~n**) ▷ *vt* montrer; (*film*) passer; (*courage etc*) faire preuve de, manifester; (*exhibit*) exposer ▷ *vi* se voir, être visible; **can you ~ me where it is, please?** pouvez-vous me montrer où c'est?; **to be on ~** être exposé(e); **it's just for ~** c'est juste pour l'effet; **show in** *vt* faire entrer; **show off** *vi* (*pej*) crâner ▷ *vt* (*display*) faire valoir; (*pej*) faire étalage de; **show out** *vt* reconduire à la porte; **show up** *vi* (*stand out*) ressortir; (*inf: turn up*) se montrer ▷ *vt* (*unmask*) démasquer, dénoncer; (*flaw*) faire ressortir; **show business** *n* le monde du spectacle

shower ['ʃauəʳ] *n* (*for washing*) douche *f*; (*rain*) averse *f*; (*of stones etc*) pluie *f*, grêle *f*; (*US: party*) *réunion organisée pour la remise de cadeaux* ▷ *vi* prendre une douche, se doucher ▷ *vt*: **to ~ sb with** (*gifts etc*) combler qn de; **to have** *or* **take a ~** prendre une douche, se doucher; **shower**

cap n bonnet m de douche; **shower gel** n gel m douche

showing [ˈʃəʊɪŋ] n (of film) projection f

show jumping [-dʒʌmpɪŋ] n concours m hippique

shown [ʃəʊn] pp of **show**

show: **show-off** n (inf: person) crâneur(-euse), m'as-tu-vu(e); **showroom** n magasin m or salle f d'exposition

shrank [ʃræŋk] pt of **shrink**

shred [ʃrɛd] n (gen pl) lambeau m, petit morceau; (fig: of truth, evidence) parcelle f ▷ vt mettre en lambeaux, déchirer; (documents) détruire; (Culin: grate) râper; (: lettuce etc) couper en lanières

shrewd [ʃruːd] adj astucieux(-euse), perspicace; (business person) habile

shriek [ʃriːk] n cri perçant or aigu, hurlement m ▷ vt, vi hurler, crier

shrimp [ʃrɪmp] n crevette grise

shrine [ʃraɪn] n (place) lieu m de pèlerinage

shrink (pt **shrank**, pp **shrunk**) [ʃrɪŋk, ʃræŋk, ʃrʌŋk] vi rétrécir; (fig) diminuer; (also: ~ away) reculer ▷ vt (wool) (faire) rétrécir ▷ n (inf: pej) psychanalyste m/f; **to ~ from (doing) sth** reculer devant (la pensée de faire) qch

shrivel [ˈʃrɪvl] (also: ~ up) vt ratatiner, flétrir ▷ vi se ratatiner, se flétrir

shroud [ʃraud] n linceul m ▷ vt: **~ed in mystery** enveloppé(e) de mystère

Shrove Tuesday [ˈʃrəʊv-] n (le) Mardi gras

shrub [ʃrʌb] n arbuste m

shrug [ʃrʌg] n haussement m d'épaules ▷ vt, vi: **to ~ (one's shoulders)** hausser les épaules; **shrug off** vt faire fi de

shrunk [ʃrʌŋk] pp of **shrink**

shudder [ˈʃʌdəʳ] n frisson m, frémissement m ▷ vi frissonner, frémir

shuffle [ˈʃʌfl] vt (cards) battre; **to ~ (one's feet)** traîner les pieds

shun [ʃʌn] vt éviter, fuir

shut (pt, pp ~) [ʃʌt] vt fermer ▷ vi (se) fermer; **shut down** vt fermer définitivement ▷ vi fermer définitivement; **shut up** vi (inf: keep quiet) se taire ▷ vt (close) fermer; (silence) faire taire; **shutter** n volet m; (Phot) obturateur m

shuttle [ˈʃʌtl] n navette f; (also: ~ service) (service m de) navette f; **shuttlecock** n volant m (de badminton)

shy [ʃaɪ] adj timide

siblings [ˈsɪblɪŋz] npl (formal) frères et sœurs mpl (de mêmes parents)

Sicily [ˈsɪsɪlɪ] n Sicile f

sick [sɪk] adj (ill) malade; (BRIT: vomiting): **to be ~** vomir; (humour) noir(e), macabre; **to feel ~** avoir envie de vomir, avoir mal au cœur; **to be ~ of** (fig) en avoir assez de; **sickening** adj (fig) écœurant(e), révoltant(e), répugnant(e); **sick leave** n congé m de maladie; **sickly** adj

maladif(-ive), souffreteux(-euse); (causing nausea) écœurant(e); **sickness** n maladie f; (vomiting) vomissement(s) m(pl)

side [saɪd] n côté m; (of lake, road) bord m; (of mountain) versant m; (fig: aspect) côté, aspect m; (team: Sport) équipe f; (TV: channel) chaîne f ▷ adj (door, entrance) latéral(e) ▷ vi: **to ~ with sb** prendre le parti de qn, se ranger du côté de qn; **by the ~ of** au bord de; **~ by ~** côte à côte; **to rock from ~ to ~** se balancer; **to take ~s (with)** prendre parti (pour); **sideboard** n buffet m; **sideboards** (BRIT), **sideburns** npl (whiskers) pattes fpl; **side effect** n effet m secondaire; **sidelight** n (Aut) veilleuse f; **sideline** n (Sport) (ligne f de) touche f; (fig) activité f secondaire; **side order** n garniture f; **side road** n petite route, route transversale; **side street** n rue transversale; **sidetrack** vt (fig) faire dévier de son sujet; **sidewalk** n (US) trottoir m; **sideways** adv de côté

siege [siːdʒ] n siège m

sieve [sɪv] n tamis m, passoire f ▷ vt tamiser, passer (au tamis)

sift [sɪft] vt passer au tamis or au crible; (fig) passer au crible

sigh [saɪ] n soupir m ▷ vi soupirer, pousser un soupir

sight [saɪt] n (faculty) vue f; (spectacle) spectacle m; (on gun) mire f ▷ vt apercevoir; **in ~** visible; (fig) en vue; **out of ~** hors de vue; **sightseeing** n tourisme m; **to go sightseeing** faire du tourisme

sign [saɪn] n (gen) signe m; (with hand etc) signe, geste m; (notice) panneau m, écriteau m; (also: **road ~**) panneau de signalisation ▷ vt signer; **where do I ~?** où dois-je signer?; **sign for** vt fus (item) signer le reçu pour; **sign in** vi signer le registre (en arrivant); **sign on** vi (BRIT: as unemployed) s'inscrire au chômage; (enrol) s'inscrire ▷ vt (employee) embaucher; **sign over** vt: **to ~ sth over to sb** céder qch par écrit à qn; **sign up** vi (Mil) s'engager; (for course) s'inscrire

signal [ˈsɪgnl] n signal m ▷ vi (Aut) mettre son clignotant ▷ vt (person) faire signe à; (message) communiquer par signaux

signature [ˈsɪgnətʃəʳ] n signature f

significance [sɪgˈnɪfɪkəns] n signification f; importance f

significant [sɪgˈnɪfɪkənt] adj significatif(-ive); (important) important(e), considérable

signify [ˈsɪgnɪfaɪ] vt signifier

sign language n langage m par signes

signpost [ˈsaɪnpəʊst] n poteau indicateur

Sikh [siːk] adj, n Sikh m/f

silence [ˈsaɪlns] n silence m ▷ vt faire taire, réduire au silence

silent [ˈsaɪlnt] adj silencieux(-euse); (film) muet(te); **to keep** or **remain ~** garder le silence, ne rien dire

silhouette [sɪluː'ɛt] n silhouette f

silicon chip ['sɪlɪkən-] n puce f électronique

silk [sɪlk] n soie f ▷ cpd de or en soie

silly ['sɪlɪ] adj stupide, sot(te), bête

silver ['sɪlvəʳ] n argent m; (money) monnaie f (en pièces d'argent); (also: **~ware**) argenterie f ▷ adj (made of silver) d'argent, en argent; (in colour) argenté(e); **silver-plated** adj plaqué(e) argent

similar ['sɪmɪləʳ] adj: **~ (to)** semblable (à); **similarity** [sɪmɪ'lærɪtɪ] n ressemblance f, similarité f; **similarly** adv de la même façon, de même

simmer ['sɪməʳ] vi cuire à feu doux, mijoter

simple ['sɪmpl] adj simple; **simplicity** [sɪm'plɪsɪtɪ] n simplicité f; **simplify** ['sɪmplɪfaɪ] vt simplifier; **simply** adv simplement; (without fuss) avec simplicité; (absolutely) absolument

simulate ['sɪmjuleɪt] vt simuler, feindre

simultaneous [sɪməl'teɪnɪəs] adj simultané(e); **simultaneously** adv simultanément

sin [sɪn] n péché m ▷ vi pécher

since [sɪns] adv, prep depuis ▷ conj (time) depuis que; (because) puisque, étant donné que, comme; **~ then**, **ever ~** depuis ce moment-là

sincere [sɪn'sɪəʳ] adj sincère; **sincerely** adv sincèrement; **Yours sincerely** (at end of letter) veuillez agréer, Monsieur (or Madame) l'expression de mes sentiments distingués or les meilleurs

sing (pt **sang**, pp **sung**) [sɪŋ, sæŋ, sʌŋ] vt, vi chanter

Singapore [sɪŋgə'pɔːʳ] n Singapour m

singer ['sɪŋəʳ] n chanteur(-euse)

singing ['sɪŋɪŋ] n (of person, bird) chant m

single ['sɪŋgl] adj seul(e), unique; (unmarried) célibataire; (not double) simple ▷ n (BRIT: also: **~ ticket**) aller m simple; (record) 45 tours m; **singles** npl (Tennis) simple m; **every ~ day** chaque jour sans exception; **single out** vt choisir; (distinguish) distinguer; **single bed** n lit m d'une personne or à une place; **single file** n: **in single file** en file indienne; **single-handed** adv tout(e) seul(e), sans (aucune) aide; **single-minded** adj résolu(e), tenace; **single parent** n parent unique (or célibataire); **single-parent family** famille monoparentale; **single room** n chambre f à un lit or pour une personne

singular ['sɪŋgjuləʳ] adj singulier(-ière); (odd) singulier, étrange; (outstanding) remarquable; (Ling) (au) singulier, du singulier ▷ n (Ling) singulier m

sinister ['sɪnɪstəʳ] adj sinistre

sink [sɪŋk] n évier m; (washbasin) lavabo

m ▷ vb (pt **sank**, pp **sunk**) ▷ vt (ship) (faire) couler, faire sombrer; (foundations) creuser ▷ vi couler, sombrer; (ground etc) s'affaisser; **to ~ into sth** (chair) s'enfoncer dans qch; **sink in** vi (explanation) rentrer (inf), être compris

sinus ['saɪnəs] n (Anat) sinus m inv

sip [sɪp] n petite gorgée ▷ vt boire à petites gorgées

sir [səʳ] n monsieur m; **S~ John Smith** sir John Smith; **yes ~** oui Monsieur

siren ['saɪərn] n sirène f

sirloin ['səːlɔɪn] n (also: **~ steak**) aloyau m

sister ['sɪstəʳ] n sœur f; (nun) religieuse f, (bonne) sœur; (BRIT: nurse) infirmière f en chef; **sister-in-law** n belle-sœur f

sit (pt, pp **sat**) [sɪt, sæt] vi s'asseoir; (be sitting) être assis(e); (assembly) être en séance, siéger; (for painter) poser ▷ vt (exam) passer, se présenter à; **sit back** vi (in seat) bien s'installer, se carrer; **sit down** vi s'asseoir; **sit on** vt fus (jury, committee) faire partie de; **sit up** vi s'asseoir; (straight) se redresser; (not go to bed) rester debout, ne pas se coucher

sitcom ['sɪtkɔm] n abbr (TV: = situation comedy) sitcom f, comédie f de situation

site [saɪt] n emplacement m, site m; (also: **building ~**) chantier m ▷ vt placer

sitting ['sɪtɪŋ] n (of assembly etc) séance f; (in canteen) service m; **sitting room** n salon m

situated ['sɪtjueɪtɪd] adj situé(e)

situation [sɪtju'eɪʃən] n situation f; **"~s vacant/wanted"** (BRIT) "offres/demandes d'emploi"

six [sɪks] num six; **sixteen** num seize; **sixteenth** [sɪks'tiːnθ] num seizième; **sixth** ['sɪksθ] num sixième; **sixth form** n (BRIT) ≈ classes fpl de première et de terminale; **sixth-form college** n lycée n'ayant que des classes de première et de terminale; **sixtieth** ['sɪkstɪɪθ] num soixantième; **sixty** num soixante

size [saɪz] n dimensions fpl; (of person) taille f, (of clothing) taille; (of shoes) pointure f; (of problem) ampleur f; (glue) colle f; **sizeable** adj assez grand(e); (amount, problem, majority) assez important(e)

sizzle ['sɪzl] vi grésiller

skate [skeɪt] n patin m; (fish: pl inv) raie f ▷ vi patiner; **skateboard** n skateboard m, planche f à roulettes; **skateboarding** n skateboard m; **skater** n patineur(-euse); **skating** n patinage m; **skating rink** n patinoire f

skeleton ['skɛlɪtn] n squelette m; (outline) schéma m

skeptical ['skɛptɪkl] (US) = **sceptical**

sketch [skɛtʃ] n (drawing) croquis m, esquisse f; (outline plan) aperçu m; (Theat) sketch m, saynète f ▷ vt esquisser, faire un croquis or une esquisse de; (plan etc) esquisser

skewer ['skjuːəʳ] n brochette f

ski [skiː] *n* ski *m* ▷ *vi* skier, faire du ski; **ski boot** *n* chaussure *f* de ski

skid [skɪd] *n* dérapage *m* ▷ *vi* déraper

ski: skier *n* skieur(-euse); **skiing** *n* ski *m*; **to go skiing** (aller) faire du ski

skilful (*US* **skillful**) ['skɪlful] *adj* habile, adroit(e)

ski lift *n* remonte-pente *m inv*

skill [skɪl] *n* (*ability*) habileté *f*, adresse *f*, talent *m*; (*requiring training*) compétences *fpl*; **skilled** *adj* habile, adroit(e); (*worker*) qualifié(e)

skim [skɪm] *vt* (*soup*) écumer; (*glide over*) raser, effleurer ▷ *vi*: **to ~ through** (*fig*) parcourir; **skimmed milk** (*US* **skim milk**) *n* lait écrémé

skin [skɪn] *n* peau *f* ▷ *vt* (*fruit etc*) éplucher; (*animal*) écorcher; **skinhead** *n* skinhead *m*; **skinny** *adj* maigre, maigrichon(ne)

skip [skɪp] *n* petit bond *or* saut *m*; (*BRIT: container*) benne *f* ▷ *vi* gambader, sautiller; (*with rope*) sauter à la corde ▷ *vt* (*pass over*) sauter

ski: ski pass *n* forfait-skieur(s) *m*; **ski pole** *n* bâton *m* de ski

skipper ['skɪpə^r] *n* (*Naut, Sport*) capitaine *m*; (*in race*) skipper *m*

skipping rope ['skɪpɪŋ-] (*US* **skip rope**) *n* (*BRIT*) corde *f* à sauter

skirt [skə:t] *n* jupe *f* ▷ *vt* longer, contourner

skirting board ['skə:tɪŋ-] *n* (*BRIT*) plinthe *f*

ski slope *n* piste *f* de ski

ski suit *n* combinaison *f* de ski

skull [skʌl] *n* crâne *m*

skunk [skʌŋk] *n* mouffette *f*

sky [skaɪ] *n* ciel *m*; **skyscraper** *n* gratte-ciel *m inv*

slab [slæb] *n* (*of stone*) dalle *f*; (*of meat, cheese*) tranche épaisse

slack [slæk] *adj* (*loose*) lâche, desserré(e); (*slow*) stagnant(e); (*careless*) négligent(e), peu sérieux(-euse) *or* consciencieux(-euse); **slacks** *npl* pantalon *m*

slain [sleɪn] *pp of* **slay**

slam [slæm] *vt* (*door*) (faire) claquer; (*throw*) jeter violemment, flanquer; (*inf: criticize*) éreinter, démolir ▷ *vi* claquer

slander ['slɑ:ndə^r] *n* calomnie *f*; (*Law*) diffamation *f*

slang [slæŋ] *n* argot *m*

slant [slɑ:nt] *n* inclinaison *f*; (*fig*) angle *m*, point *m* de vue

slap [slæp] *n* claque *f*, gifle *f*; (*on the back*) tape *f* ▷ *vt* donner une claque *or* une gifle (*or* une tape) à; **to ~ on** (*paint*) appliquer rapidement ▷ *adv* (*directly*) tout droit, en plein

slash [slæʃ] *vt* entailler, taillader; (*fig: prices*) casser

slate [sleɪt] *n* ardoise *f* ▷ *vt* (*fig: criticize*) éreinter, démolir

slaughter ['slɔ:tə^r] *n* carnage *m*, massacre *m*; (*of animals*) abattage *m* ▷ *vt* (*animal*) abattre; (*people*) massacrer; **slaughterhouse** *n* abattoir *m*

Slav [slɑ:v] *adj* slave

slave [sleɪv] *n* esclave *m/f* ▷ *vi* (*also*: **~ away**) trimer, travailler comme un forçat; **slavery** *n* esclavage *m*

slay (*pt* **slew**, *pp* **slain**) [sleɪ, sluː, sleɪn] *vt* (*literary*) tuer

sleazy ['sli:zɪ] *adj* miteux(-euse), minable

sled [slɛd] (*US*) = **sledge**

sledge [slɛdʒ] *n* luge *f*

sleek [sli:k] *adj* (*hair, fur*) brillant(e), luisant(e); (*car, boat*) aux lignes pures *or* élégantes

sleep [sli:p] *n* sommeil *m* ▷ *vi* (*pt, pp* **slept**) dormir; **to go to ~** s'endormir; **sleep in** *vi* (*oversleep*) se réveiller trop tard; (*on purpose*) faire la grasse matinée; **sleep together** *vi* (*have sex*) coucher ensemble; **sleeper** *n* (*person*) dormeur(-euse); (*BRIT Rail: on track*) traverse *f*; (*: train*) train-couchettes *m*; (*: berth*) couchette *f*; **sleeping bag** *n* sac *m* de couchage; **sleeping car** *n* wagon-lits *m*, voiture-lits *f*; **sleeping pill** *n* somnifère *m*; **sleepover** *n* nuit *f* chez un copain *or* une copine; **we're having a sleepover at Jo's** nous allons passer la nuit chez Jo; **sleepwalk** *vi* marcher en dormant; **sleepy** *adj* (*fig*) endormi(e)

sleet [sli:t] *n* neige fondue

sleeve [sli:v] *n* manche *f*; (*of record*) pochette *f*; **sleeveless** *adj* (*garment*) sans manches

sleigh [sleɪ] *n* traîneau *m*

slender ['slɛndə^r] *adj* svelte, mince; (*fig*) faible, ténu(e)

slept [slɛpt] *pt, pp of* **sleep**

slew [sluː] *pt of* **slay**

slice [slaɪs] *n* tranche *f*; (*round*) rondelle *f*; (*utensil*) spatule *f*; (*also*: **fish ~**) pelle *f* à poisson ▷ *vt* couper en tranches (*or* en rondelles)

slick [slɪk] *adj* (*skilful*) bien ficelé(e); (*salesperson*) qui a du bagout ▷ *n* (*also*: **oil ~**) nappe *f* de pétrole, marée noire

slide [slaɪd] *n* (*in playground*) toboggan *m*; (*Phot*) diapositive *f*; (*BRIT: also*: **hair ~**) barrette *f*; (*in prices*) chute *f*, baisse *f* ▷ *vb* (*pt, pp* **slid**) ▷ *vt* (*faire*) glisser ▷ *vi* glisser; **sliding** *adj* (*door*) coulissant(e)

slight [slaɪt] *adj* (*slim*) mince, menu(e); (*frail*) frêle; (*trivial*) faible, insignifiant(e); (*small*) petit(e), léger(-ère) *before n* ▷ *n* offense *f*, affront *m* ▷ *vt* (*offend*) blesser, offenser; **not in the ~est** pas le moins du monde, pas du tout; **slightly** *adv* légèrement, un peu

slim [slɪm] *adj* mince ▷ *vi* maigrir; (*diet*) suivre un régime amaigrissant; **slimming** *n* amaigrissement *m* ▷ *adj* (*diet, pills*) amaigrissant(e), pour maigrir; (*food*) qui ne fait pas grossir

slimy ['slaɪmɪ] *adj* visqueux(-euse), gluant(e)

sling [slɪŋ] n (Med) écharpe f; (for baby) porte-bébé m; (weapon) fronde f, lance-pierre m ▷ vt (pt, pp **slung**) lancer, jeter

slip [slɪp] n faux pas; (mistake) erreur f, bévue f; (underskirt) combinaison f; (of paper) petite feuille, fiche f ▷ vt (slide) glisser ▷ vi (slide) glisser; (move smoothly): **to ~ into/out of** se glisser or se faufiler dans/hors de; (decline) baisser; **to ~ sth on/off** enfiler/enlever qch; **to give sb the ~** fausser compagnie à qn; **a ~ of the tongue** un lapsus; **slip up** vi faire une erreur, gaffer

slipped disc [slɪpt-] n déplacement m de vertèbre

slipper ['slɪpəʳ] n pantoufle f

slippery ['slɪpərɪ] adj glissant(e)

slip road n (BRIT: to motorway) bretelle f d'accès

slit [slɪt] n fente f; (cut) incision f ▷ vt (pt, pp ~) fendre; couper, inciser

slog [slɔg] n (BRIT: effort) gros effort; (: work) tâche fastidieuse ▷ vi travailler très dur

slogan ['sləugən] n slogan m

slope [sləup] n pente f, côte f; (side of mountain) versant m; (slant) inclinaison f ▷ vi: **to ~ down** être or descendre en pente; **to ~ up** monter; **sloping** adj en pente, incliné(e); (handwriting) penché(e)

sloppy ['slɔpɪ] adj (work) peu soigné(e), bâclé(e); (appearance) négligé(e), débraillé(e)

slot [slɔt] n fente f ▷ vt: **to ~ sth into** encastrer or insérer qch dans; **slot machine** n (BRIT: vending machine) distributeur m (automatique), machine f à sous; (for gambling) appareil m or machine à sous

Slovakia [sləu'vækɪə] n Slovaquie f

Slovene [sləu'vi:n] adj slovène ▷ n Slovène m/f; (Ling) slovène m

Slovenia [sləu'vi:nɪə] n Slovénie f; **Slovenian** adj, n = **Slovene**

slow [sləu] adj lent(e); (watch): **to be ~** retarder ▷ adv lentement ▷ vt, vi ralentir; **"~"** (road sign) "ralentir"; **slow down** vi ralentir; **slowly** adv lentement; **slow motion** n: **in slow motion** au ralenti

slug [slʌg] n limace f; (bullet) balle f; **sluggish** adj (person) mou (molle), lent(e); (stream, engine, trading) lent(e)

slum [slʌm] n (house) taudis m; **slums** npl (area) quartiers mpl pauvres

slump [slʌmp] n baisse soudaine, effondrement m; (Econ) crise f ▷ vi s'effondrer, s'affaisser

slung [slʌŋ] pt, pp of **sling**

slur [slə:ʳ] n (smear): **~ (on)** atteinte f (à); insinuation f (contre) ▷ vt mal articuler

slush [slʌʃ] n neige fondue

sly [slaɪ] adj (person) rusé(e); (smile, expression, remark) sournois(e)

smack [smæk] n (slap) tape f; (on face) gifle f ▷ vt donner une tape à; (on face) gifler; (on bottom) donner la fessée à ▷ vi: **to ~ of** avoir des relents de, sentir

small [smɔ:l] adj petit(e); **small ads** npl (BRIT) petites annonces; **small change** n petite or menue monnaie

smart [smɑ:t] adj élégant(e), chic inv; (clever) intelligent(e); (quick) vif (vive), prompt(e) ▷ vi faire mal, brûler; **smartcard** n carte f à puce

smash [smæʃ] n (also: **~-up**) collision f, accident m; (Mus) succès foudroyant ▷ vt casser, briser, fracasser; (opponent) écraser; (Sport: record) pulvériser ▷ vi se briser, se fracasser; s'écraser; **smashing** adj (inf) formidable

smear [smɪəʳ] n (stain) tache f; (mark) trace f; (Med) frottis m ▷ vt enduire; (make dirty) salir; **smear test** n (BRIT Med) frottis m

smell [smɛl] n odeur f; (sense) odorat m ▷ vb (pt, pp **smelt** or **~ed**) ▷ vt sentir ▷ vi (pej) sentir mauvais; **smelly** adj qui sent mauvais, malodorant(e)

smelt [smɛlt] pt, pp of **smell**

smile [smaɪl] n sourire m ▷ vi sourire

smirk [smə:k] n petit sourire suffisant or affecté

smog [smɔg] n brouillard mêlé de fumée

smoke [sməuk] n fumée f ▷ vt, vi fumer; **do you mind if I ~?** ça ne vous dérange pas que je fume?; **smoke alarm** n détecteur m de fumée; **smoked** adj (bacon, glass) fumé(e); **smoker** n (person) fumeur(-euse); (Rail) wagon m fumeurs; **smoking** n: **"no smoking"** (sign) "défense de fumer"; **smoky** adj enfumé(e); (taste) fumé(e)

smooth [smu:ð] adj lisse; (sauce) onctueux(-euse); (flavour, whisky) moelleux(-euse); (movement) régulier(-ière), sans à-coups or heurts; (flight) sans secousses; (pej: person) doucereux(-euse), mielleux(-euse) ▷ vt (also: **~ out**) lisser, défroisser; (creases, difficulties) faire disparaître

smother ['smʌðəʳ] vt étouffer

SMS n abbr (= short message service) SMS m; **SMS message** n message m SMS

smudge [smʌdʒ] n tache f, bavure f ▷ vt salir, maculer

smug [smʌg] adj suffisant(e), content(e) de soi

smuggle ['smʌgl] vt passer en contrebande or en fraude; **smuggling** n contrebande f

snack [snæk] n casse-croûte m inv; **snack bar** n snack(-bar) m

snag [snæg] n inconvénient m, difficulté f

snail [sneɪl] n escargot m

snake [sneɪk] n serpent m

snap [snæp] n (sound) claquement m, bruit sec; (photograph) photo f, instantané m ▷ adj subit(e), fait(e) sans réfléchir ▷ vt (*fingers*) faire claquer; (*break*) casser net ▷ vi se casser net *or* avec un bruit sec; (*speak sharply*) parler d'un ton brusque; **to ~ open/shut** s'ouvrir/se refermer brusquement; **snap at** vt fus (*subj: dog*) essayer de mordre; **snap up** vt sauter sur, saisir; **snapshot** n photo f, instantané m

snarl [snɑːl] vi gronder

snatch [snætʃ] n (*small amount*) ▷ vt saisir (*d'un geste vif*); (*steal*) voler; **to ~ some sleep** arriver à dormir un peu

sneak [sniːk] (*us: pt* **snuck**) vi: **to ~ in/out** entrer/sortir furtivement *or* à la dérobée ▷ n (*inf: pej: informer*) faux jeton; **to ~ up on sb** s'approcher de qn sans faire de bruit; **sneakers** npl tennis mpl, baskets fpl

sneer [snɪəʳ] vi ricaner; **to ~ at sb/sth** se moquer de qn/qch avec mépris

sneeze [sniːz] vi éternuer

sniff [snɪf] vi renifler ▷ vt renifler, flairer; (*glue, drug*) sniffer, respirer

snigger ['snɪɡəʳ] vi ricaner

snip [snɪp] n (*cut*) entaille f; (ʙʀɪᴛ: *inf: bargain*) (bonne) occasion *or* affaire ▷ vt couper

sniper ['snaɪpəʳ] n (*marksman*) tireur embusqué

snob [snɔb] n snob m/f

snooker ['snuːkəʳ] n sorte de jeu de billard

snoop [snuːp] vi: **to ~ about** fureter

snooze [snuːz] n petit somme ▷ vi faire un petit somme

snore [snɔːʳ] vi ronfler ▷ n ronflement m

snorkel ['snɔːkl] n (*of swimmer*) tuba m

snort [snɔːt] n grognement m ▷ vi grogner; (*horse*) renâcler

snow [snəu] n neige f ▷ vi neiger; **snowball** n boule f de neige; **snowdrift** n congère f; **snowman** (*irreg*) n bonhomme m de neige; **snowplough** (us **snowplow**) n chasse-neige m inv; **snowstorm** n tempête f de neige

snub [snʌb] vt repousser, snober ▷ n rebuffade f

snug [snʌɡ] adj douillet(te), confortable; (*person*) bien au chaud

⬤ **KEYWORD**

so [səu] adv 1 (*thus, likewise*) ainsi, de cette façon; **if so** si oui; **so do** *or* **have I** moi aussi; **it's 5 o'clock - so it is!** il est 5 heures - en effet! *or* c'est vrai!; **I hope/think so** je l'espère/le crois; **so far** jusqu'ici, jusqu'à maintenant; (*in past*) jusque-là

2 (*in comparisons etc: to such a degree*) si, tellement; **so big (that)** si *or* tellement grand (que); **she's not so clever as her brother** elle n'est pas aussi intelligente que son frère

3: **so much** adj, adv tant (de); **I've got so much work** j'ai tant de travail; **I love you so much** je vous aime tant; **so many** tant (de)

4 (*phrases*): **10 or so** à peu près *or* environ 10; **so long!** (*inf: goodbye*) au revoir!, à un de ces jours!; **so (what)?** (*inf*) (bon) et alors?, et après? ▷ conj 1 (*expressing purpose*): **so as to do** pour faire, afin de faire; **so (that)** pour que *or* afin que + sub

2 (*expressing result*) donc, par conséquent; **so that** si bien que, de (telle) sorte que; **so that's the reason!** c'est donc (pour) ça!; **so you see, I could have gone** alors tu vois, j'aurais pu y aller

soak [səuk] vt faire *or* laisser tremper; (*drench*) tremper ▷ vi tremper; **soak up** vt absorber; **soaking** adj (*also*: **soaking wet**) trempé(e)

so-and-so ['səuənsəu] n (*somebody*) un(e) tel(le)

soap [səup] n savon m; **soap opera** n feuilleton télévisé (*quotidienneté réaliste ou embellie*); **soap powder** n lessive f, détergent m

soar [sɔːʳ] vi monter (en flèche), s'élancer; (*building*) s'élancer

sob [sɔb] n sanglot m ▷ vi sangloter

sober ['səubəʳ] adj qui n'est pas (*or* plus) ivre; (*serious*) sérieux(-euse), sensé(e); (*colour, style*) sobre, discret(-ète); **sober up** vi se dégriser

so-called ['səu'kɔːld] adj soi-disant inv

soccer ['sɔkəʳ] n football m

sociable ['səuʃəbl] adj sociable

social ['səuʃl] adj social(e); (*sociable*) sociable ▷ n (petite) fête; **socialism** n socialisme m; **socialist** adj, n socialiste (m/f); **socialize** vi: **to socialize with** (*meet often*) fréquenter; (*get to know*) lier connaissance *or* parler avec; **social life** n vie sociale; **socially** adv socialement, en société; **social security** n aide sociale; **social services** npl services sociaux; **social work** n assistance sociale; **social worker** n assistant(e) sociale(e)

society [sə'saɪətɪ] n société f; (*club*) société, association f; (*also*: **high ~**) (haute) société, grand monde

sociology [səusɪ'ɔlədʒɪ] n sociologie f

sock [sɔk] n chaussette f

socket ['sɔkɪt] n cavité f; (Elec: *also*: **wall ~**) prise f de courant

soda ['səudə] n (Chem) soude f; (*also*: **~ water**) eau f de Seltz; (us: *also*: **~ pop**) soda m

sodium ['səudɪəm] n sodium m

sofa ['səufə] n sofa m, canapé m; **sofa bed** n canapé-lit m

soft [sɔft] adj (*not rough*) doux (douce); (*not hard*) doux, mou (molle); (*not loud*) doux, léger(-ère); (*kind*) doux, gentil(le); **soft drink** n boisson non alcoolisée; **soft drugs** npl drogues douces; **soften** ['sɔfn] vt (r)amollir; (*fig*) adoucir ▷ vi se ramollir; (*fig*) s'adoucir;

softly adv doucement; (touch) légèrement; (kiss) tendrement; **software** n (Comput) logiciel m, software m

soggy ['sɔgɪ] adj (clothes) trempé(e); (ground) détrempé(e)

soil [sɔɪl] n (earth) sol m, terre f ▷ vt salir; (fig) souiller

solar ['səʊlər] adj solaire; **solar power** n énergie f solaire; **solar system** n système m solaire

sold [səʊld] pt, pp of **sell**

soldier ['səʊldʒər] n soldat m, militaire m

sold out adj (Comm) épuisé(e)

sole [səʊl] n (of foot) plante f; (of shoe) semelle f; (fish: pl inv) sole f ▷ adj seul(e), unique; **solely** adv seulement, uniquement

solemn ['sɔləm] adj solennel(le); (person) sérieux(-euse), grave

solicitor [sə'lɪsɪtər] n (BRIT: for wills etc) ≈ notaire m; (: in court) ≈ avocat m

solid ['sɔlɪd] adj (not liquid) solide; (not hollow: mass) compact(e); (: metal, rock, wood) massif(-ive) ▷ n solide m

solitary ['sɔlɪtərɪ] adj solitaire

solitude ['sɔlɪtjuːd] n solitude f

solo ['səʊləʊ] n solo m ▷ adv (fly) en solitaire; **soloist** n soliste m/f

soluble ['sɔljʊbl] adj soluble

solution [sə'luːʃən] n solution f

solve [sɔlv] vt résoudre

solvent ['sɔlvənt] adj (Comm) solvable ▷ n (Chem) (dis)solvant m

sombre (us **somber**) ['sɔmbər] adj sombre, morne

 KEYWORD

some [sʌm] adj 1 (a certain amount or number of): **some tea/water/ice cream** du thé/de l'eau/de la glace; **some children/apples** des enfants/pommes; **I've got some money but not much** j'ai de l'argent mais pas beaucoup 2 (certain: in contrasts): **some people say that ...** il y a des gens qui disent que ...; **some films were excellent, but most were mediocre** certains films étaient excellents, mais la plupart étaient médiocres 3 (unspecified): **some woman was asking for you** il y avait une dame qui vous demandait; **he was asking for some book (or other)** il demandait un livre quelconque; **some day** un de ces jours; **some day next week** un jour la semaine prochaine ▷ pron 1 (a certain number) quelques-un(e)s, certain(e)s; **I've got some** (books etc) j'en ai (quelques-uns); **some (of them) have been sold** certains ont été vendus 2 (a certain amount) un peu; **I've got some** (money, milk) j'en ai (un peu); **would you like**

some? est-ce que vous en voulez?, en voulez-vous?; **could I have some of that cheese?** pourrais-je avoir un peu de ce fromage?; **I've read some of the book** j'ai lu une partie du livre ▷ adv: **some 10 people** quelque 10 personnes, 10 personnes environ; **somebody** ['sʌmbədɪ] pron = **someone**; **somehow** adv d'une façon ou d'une autre; (for some reason) pour une raison ou une autre; **someone** pron quelqu'un; **someplace** adv (us) = **somewhere**; **something** pron quelque chose m; **something interesting** quelque chose d'intéressant; **something to do** quelque chose à faire; **sometime** adv (in future) un de ces jours, un jour ou l'autre; (in past): **sometime last month** au cours du mois dernier; **sometimes** adv quelquefois, parfois; **somewhat** adv quelque peu, un peu; **somewhere** adv quelque part; **somewhere else** ailleurs, autre part

son [sʌn] n fils m

song [sɔŋ] n chanson f; (of bird) chant m

son-in-law ['sʌnɪnlɔː] n gendre m, beau-fils m

soon [suːn] adv bientôt; (early) tôt; **~ afterwards** peu après; see also **as**; **sooner** adv (time) plus tôt; (preference): **I would sooner do that** j'aimerais autant or je préférerais faire ça; **sooner or later** tôt ou tard

soothe [suːð] vt calmer, apaiser

sophisticated [sə'fɪstɪkeɪtɪd] adj raffiné(e), sophistiqué(e); (machinery) hautement perfectionné(e), très complexe

sophomore ['sɔfəmɔːr] n (us) étudiant(e) de seconde année

soprano [sə'prɑːnəʊ] n (singer) soprano m/f

sorbet ['sɔːbeɪ] n sorbet m

sordid ['sɔːdɪd] adj sordide

sore [sɔːr] adj (painful) douloureux(-euse), sensible ▷ n plaie f

sorrow ['sɔrəʊ] n peine f, chagrin m

sorry ['sɔrɪ] adj désolé(e); (condition, excuse, tale) triste, déplorable; **~!** pardon!, excusez-moi!; **~?** pardon? **to feel ~ for sb** plaindre qn

sort [sɔːt] n genre m, espèce f, sorte f; (make: of coffee, car etc) marque f ▷ vt (also: **~ out**: select which to keep) trier; (classify) classer; (tidy) ranger; **sort out** vt (problem) résoudre, régler

SOS n SOS m

so-so ['səʊsəʊ] adv comme ci comme ça

sought [sɔːt] pt, pp of **seek**

soul [səʊl] n âme f

sound [saʊnd] adj (healthy) en bonne santé, sain(e); (safe, not damaged) solide, en bon état; (reliable, not superficial) sérieux(-euse), solide; (sensible) sensé(e) ▷ adv: **~ asleep** profondément endormi(e) ▷ n (noise, volume) son m; (louder) bruit m; (Geo) détroit m, bras *m* de mer ▷ *vt* (*alarm*) sonner, retentir; (*fig: seem*) sembler (être); **to ~ like** ressembler à; **sound bite** *n* phrase toute faite (*pour être citée dans les médias*); **soundtrack** *n* (*of film*) bande *f* sonore

soup [suːp] *n* soupe *f*, potage *m*

sour ['saʊəʳ] *adj* aigre; **it's ~ grapes** c'est du dépit

source [sɔːs] *n* source *f*

south [saʊθ] *n* sud *m* ▷ *adj* sud *inv*; (*wind*) du sud ▷ *adv* au sud, vers le sud; **South Africa** *n* Afrique *f* du Sud; **South African** *adj* sud-africain(e) ▷ *n* Sud-Africain(e); **South America** *n* Amérique *f* du Sud; **South American** *adj* sud-américain(e) ▷ *n* Sud-Américain(e); **southbound** *adj* en direction du sud; (*carriageway*) sud *inv*; **south-east** *n* sud-est *m*; **southeastern** [saʊθ'iːstən] *adj* du *ou* au sud-est; **southern** ['sʌðən] *adj* (du) sud; méridional(e); **South Korea** *n* Corée *f* du Sud; **South of France** *n*: **the South of France** le Sud de la France, le Midi; **South Pole** *n* Pôle *m* Sud; **southward(s)** *adv* vers le sud; **south-west** *n* sud-ouest *m*; **southwestern** [saʊθ'westən] *adj* du *ou* au sud-ouest

souvenir [suːvə'nɪəʳ] *n* souvenir *m* (*objet*)

sovereign ['sɔvrɪn] *adj*, *n* souverain(e)

sow[1] [səʊ] (*pt* **~ed**, *pp* **~n**) *vt* semer

sow[2] *n* [saʊ] truie *f*

soya ['sɔɪə] (*us* **soy** [sɔɪ]) *n*: **~ bean** graine *f* de soja; **~ sauce** sauce *f* au soja

spa [spɑː] *n* (*town*) station thermale; (*us: also*: **health ~**) établissement *m* de cure de rajeunissement

space [speɪs] *n* (*gen*) espace *m*; (*room*) place *f*, espace; (*length of time*) laps *m* de temps ▷ *cpd* spatial(e) ▷ *vt* (*also*: **~ out**) espacer; **spacecraft** *n* engin *ou* vaisseau spatial; **spaceship** *n* = **spacecraft**

spacious ['speɪʃəs] *adj* spacieux(-euse), grand(e)

spade [speɪd] *n* (*tool*) bêche *f*, pelle *f*; (*child's*) pelle; **spades** *npl* (*Cards*) pique *m*

spaghetti [spə'gɛtɪ] *n* spaghetti *mpl*

Spain [speɪn] *n* Espagne *f*

spam [spæm] *n* (*Comput*) spam *m*

span [spæn] *n* (*of bird, plane*) envergure *f*; (*of arch*) portée *f*; (*in time*) espace *m* de temps, durée *f* ▷ *vt* enjamber, franchir; (*fig*) couvrir, embrasser

Spaniard ['spænjəd] *n* Espagnol(e)

Spanish ['spænɪʃ] *adj* espagnol(e), d'Espagne ▷ *n* (*Ling*) espagnol *m*; **the Spanish** *npl* les Espagnols

spank [spæŋk] *vt* donner une fessée à

spanner ['spænəʳ] *n* (*BRIT*) clé *f* (de mécanicien)

spare [spɛəʳ] *adj* de réserve, de rechange; (*surplus*) de *ou* en trop, de reste ▷ *n* (*part*) pièce *f* de rechange, pièce détachée ▷ *vt* (*do without*) se passer de; (*afford to give*) accorder, donner, passer; (*not hurt*) épargner; **to ~** (*surplus*) en surplus, de trop; **spare part** *n* pièce *f* de rechange, pièce détachée; **spare room** *n* chambre *f* d'ami; **spare time** *n* moments *mpl* de loisir; **spare tyre** (*us* **spare tire**) *n* (*Aut*) pneu *m* de rechange; **spare wheel** *n* (*Aut*) roue *f* de secours

spark [spɑːk] *n* étincelle *f*; **spark(ing) plug** *n* bougie *f*

sparkle ['spɑːkl] *n* scintillement *m*, étincellement *m*, éclat *m* ▷ *vi* étinceler, scintiller

sparkling ['spɑːklɪŋ] *adj* (*wine*) mousseux(-euse), pétillant(e); (*water*) pétillant(e), gazeux(-euse)

sparrow ['spærəʊ] *n* moineau *m*

sparse [spɑːs] *adj* clairsemé(e)

spasm ['spæzəm] *n* (*Med*) spasme *m*

spat [spæt] *pt*, *pp* of **spit**

spate [speɪt] *n* (*fig*): **~ of** avalanche *f* or torrent *m* de

spatula ['spætjulə] *n* spatule *f*

speak (*pt* **spoke**, *pp* **spoken**) [spiːk, spəʊk, 'spəʊkn] *vt* (*language*) parler; (*truth*) dire ▷ *vi* parler; (*make a speech*) prendre la parole; **to ~ to sb/of** *or* **about sth** parler à qn/de qch; **I don't ~ French** je ne parle pas français; **do you ~ English?** parlez-vous anglais?; **can I ~ to ...?** est-ce que je peux parler à ...?; **speaker** *n* (*in public*) orateur *m*; (*also*: **loudspeaker**) haut-parleur *m*; (*for stereo etc*) baffle *m*, enceinte *f*; (*Pol*): **the Speaker** (*BRIT*) le président de la Chambre des communes *or* des représentants; (*us*) le président de la Chambre

spear [spɪəʳ] *n* lance *f* ▷ *vt* transpercer

special ['spɛʃl] *adj* spécial(e); **special delivery** *n* (*Post*): **by special delivery** en express; **special effects** *npl* (*Cine*) effets spéciaux; **specialist** *n* spécialiste *m/f*; **speciality** [spɛʃɪ'ælɪtɪ] *n* (*BRIT*) spécialité *f*; **specialize** *vi*: **to specialize (in)** se spécialiser (dans); **specially** *adv* spécialement, particulièrement; **special needs** *npl* (*BRIT*) difficultés *fpl* d'apprentissage scolaire; **special offer** *n* (*Comm*) réclame *f*; **special school** *n* (*BRIT*) établissement *m* d'enseignement spécialisé; **specialty** *n* (*us*) = **speciality**

species ['spiːʃiːz] *n* (*pl inv*) espèce *f*

specific [spə'sɪfɪk] *adj* (*not vague*) précis(e), explicite; (*particular*) particulier(-ière); **specifically** *adv* explicitement, précisément; (*intend, ask, design*) expressément, spécialement

specify ['spɛsɪfaɪ] *vt* spécifier, préciser

specimen ['spɛsɪmən] *n* spécimen *m*, échantillon *m*; (*Med: of blood*) prélèvement *m*; (: *of urine*) échantillon *m*

speck [spɛk] n petite tache, petit point; (*particle*) grain m

spectacle ['spɛktəkl] n spectacle m; **spectacles** npl (BRIT) lunettes fpl; **spectacular** [spɛk'tækjuləʳ] adj spectaculaire

spectator [spɛk'teɪtəʳ] n spectateur(-trice)

spectrum (pl **spectra**) ['spɛktrəm, -rə] n spectre m; (fig) gamme f

speculate ['spɛkjuleɪt] vi spéculer; (*try to guess*): **to ~ about** s'interroger sur

sped [spɛd] pt, pp of **speed**

speech [spi:tʃ] n (*faculty*) parole f; (*talk*) discours m, allocution f; (*manner of speaking*) façon f de parler, langage m; (*enunciation*) élocution f; **speechless** adj muet(te)

speed [spi:d] n vitesse f; (*promptness*) rapidité f ▷ vi (pt, pp **sped** Aut: *exceed speed limit*) faire un excès de vitesse; **at full** or **top ~** à toute vitesse or allure; **speed up** (pt, pp **~ed up**) vi aller plus vite, accélérer vt accélérer; **speedboat** n vedette f, hors-bord m inv; **speeding** n (Aut) excès m de vitesse; **speed limit** n limitation f de vitesse, vitesse maximale permise; **speedometer** [spɪ'dɔmɪtəʳ] n compteur m (de vitesse); **speedy** adj rapide, prompt(e)

spell [spɛl] n (*also*: **magic ~**) sortilège m, charme m; (*period of time*) (courte) période ▷ vt (pt, pp **spelt** or **~ed**) (*in writing*) écrire, orthographier; (*aloud*) épeler; (fig) signifier; **to cast a ~ on sb** jeter un sort à qn; **he can't ~** il fait des fautes d'orthographe; **spell out** vt (*explain*): **to ~ sth out for sb** expliquer qch clairement à qn; **spellchecker** ['spɛltʃekəʳ] n (Comput) correcteur m or vérificateur m orthographique; **spelling** n orthographe f

spelt [spɛlt] pt, pp of **spell**

spend (pt, pp **spent**) [spɛnd, spɛnt] vt (*money*) dépenser; (*time, life*) passer; (*devote*) consacrer; **spending** n: **government spending** les dépenses publiques

spent [spɛnt] pt, pp of **spend** ▷ adj (*cartridge, bullets*) vide

sperm [spə:m] n spermatozoïde m; (*semen*) sperme m

sphere [sfɪəʳ] n sphère f; (fig) sphère, domaine m

spice [spaɪs] n épice f ▷ vt épicer

spicy ['spaɪsɪ] adj épicé(e), relevé(e); (fig) piquant(e)

spider ['spaɪdəʳ] n araignée f

spike [spaɪk] n pointe f; (Bot) épi m

spill (pt, pp **spilt** or **~ed**) [spɪl, -t, -d] vt renverser; répandre ▷ vi se répandre; **spill over** vi déborder

spin [spɪn] n (*revolution of wheel*) tour m; (Aviat) (chute f en) vrille f; (*trip in car*) petit tour, balade f; (*on ball*) effet m ▷ vb (pt, pp **spun**) ▷ vt (*wool etc*) filer; (*wheel*) faire tourner ▷ vi (*turn*) tourner, tournoyer

spinach ['spɪnɪtʃ] n épinards mpl

spinal ['spaɪnl] adj vertébral(e), spinal(e)

spinal cord n moelle épinière

spin doctor n (inf) personne employée pour présenter un parti politique sous un jour favorable

spin-dryer [spɪn'draɪəʳ] n (BRIT) essoreuse f

spine [spaɪn] n colonne vertébrale; (*thorn*) épine f, piquant m

spiral ['spaɪərl] n spirale f ▷ vi (fig: *prices etc*) monter en flèche

spire ['spaɪəʳ] n flèche f, aiguille f

spirit ['spɪrɪt] n (*soul*) esprit m, âme f; (*ghost*) esprit, revenant m; (*mood*) esprit, état m d'esprit; (*courage*) courage m, énergie f; **spirits** npl (*drink*) spiritueux mpl, alcool m; **in good ~s** de bonne humeur

spiritual ['spɪrɪtjuəl] adj spirituel(le); (*religious*) religieux(-euse)

spit [spɪt] n (*for roasting*) broche f; (*spittle*) crachat m; (*saliva*) salive f ▷ vi (pt, pp **spat**) cracher; (*sound*) crépiter; (*rain*) crachiner

spite [spaɪt] n rancune f, dépit m ▷ vt contrarier, vexer; **in ~ of** en dépit de, malgré; **spiteful** adj malveillant(e), rancunier(-ière)

splash [splæʃ] n (*sound*) plouf m; (*of colour*) tache f ▷ vt éclabousser ▷ vi (*also*: **~ about**) barboter, patauger; **splash out** vi (BRIT) faire une folie

splendid ['splɛndɪd] adj splendide, superbe, magnifique

splinter ['splɪntəʳ] n (*wood*) écharde f; (*metal*) éclat m ▷ vi (*wood*) se fendre; (*glass*) se briser

split [splɪt] n fente f, déchirure f; (fig: Pol) scission f ▷ vb (pt, pp **~**) ▷ vt fendre, déchirer; (*party*) diviser; (*work, profits*) partager, répartir ▷ vi (*break*) se fendre, se briser; (*divide*) se diviser; **split up** vi (*couple*) se séparer, rompre; (*meeting*) se disperser

spoil (pt, pp **~ed** or **~t**) [spɔɪl, -d, -t] vt (*damage*) abîmer; (*mar*) gâcher; (*child*) gâter

spoilt [spɔɪlt] pt, pp of **spoil** ▷ adj (*child*) gâté(e); (*ballot paper*) nul(le)

spoke [spəʊk] pt of **speak** ▷ n rayon m

spoken ['spəʊkn] pp of **speak**

spokesman ['spəʊksmən] (*irreg*) n porte-parole m inv

spokesperson ['spəʊkspə:sn] n porte-parole m inv

spokeswoman ['spəʊkswʊmən] (*irreg*) n porte-parole m inv

sponge [spʌndʒ] n éponge f; (Culin: *also*: **~ cake**) ≈ biscuit m de Savoie ▷ vt éponger ▷ vi: **to ~ off** or **on** vivre aux crochets de; **sponge bag** n (BRIT) trousse f de toilette

sponsor ['spɔnsəʳ] n (Radio, TV, Sport) sponsor m; (*for application*) parrain m, marraine f; (BRIT: *for fund-raising event*) donateur(-trice) ▷ vt sponsoriser, parrainer, faire un don à;

sponsorship n sponsoring m, parrainage m; dons mpl

spontaneous [spɔn'teɪnɪəs] adj spontané(e)

spooky ['spu:kɪ] adj (inf) qui donne la chair de poule

spoon [spu:n] n cuiller f; **spoonful** n cuillerée f

sport [spɔ:t] n sport m; (person) chic type m/chic fille f ▷ vt (wear) arborer; **sport jacket** n (US) = **sports jacket**; **sports car** n voiture f de sport; **sports centre** (BRIT) n centre sportif; **sports jacket** n (BRIT) veste f de sport; **sportsman** (irreg) n sportif m; **sports utility vehicle** n véhicule m de loisirs (de type SUV); **sportswear** n vêtements mpl de sport; **sportswoman** (irreg) n sportive f; **sporty** adj sportif(-ive)

spot [spɔt] n tache f; (dot: on pattern) pois m; (pimple) bouton m; (place) endroit m, coin m; (small amount): **a ~ of** un peu de ▷ vt (notice) apercevoir, repérer; **on the ~** sur place, sur les lieux; (immediately) sur le champ; **spotless** adj immaculé(e); **spotlight** n projecteur m; (Aut) phare m auxiliaire

spouse [spauz] n époux (épouse)

sprain [spreɪn] n entorse f, foulure f ▷ vt: **to ~ one's ankle** se fouler or se tordre la cheville

sprang [spræŋ] pt of **spring**

sprawl [sprɔ:l] vi s'étaler

spray [spreɪ] n jet m (en fines gouttelettes); (from sea) embruns mpl; (aerosol) vaporisateur m, bombe f; (for garden) pulvérisateur m; (of flowers) petit bouquet ▷ vt vaporiser, pulvériser; (crops) traiter

spread [sprɛd] n (distribution) répartition f; (Culin) pâte f à tartiner; (inf: meal) festin m ▷ vb (pt, pp ~) ▷ vt (paste, contents) étendre, étaler; (rumour, disease) répandre, propager; (wealth) répartir ▷ vi s'étendre; se répandre; se propager; (stain) s'étaler; **spread out** vi (people) se disperser; **spreadsheet** n (Comput) tableur m

spree [spri:] n: **to go on a ~** faire la fête

spring [sprɪŋ] n (season) printemps m; (leap) bond m, saut m; (coiled metal) ressort m; (of water) source f ▷ vb (pt **sprang**, pp **sprung**) ▷ vi bondir, sauter; **spring up** vi (problem) se présenter, surgir; (plant, buildings) surgir de terre; **spring onion** n (BRIT) ciboule f, cive f

sprinkle ['sprɪŋkl] vt: **to ~ water** etc **on**, **~ with water** etc asperger d'eau etc; **to ~ sugar** etc **on**, **~ with sugar** etc saupoudrer de sucre etc

sprint [sprɪnt] n sprint m ▷ vi courir à toute vitesse; (Sport) sprinter

sprung [sprʌŋ] pp of **spring**

spun [spʌn] pt, pp of **spin**

spur [spə:ʳ] n éperon m; (fig) aiguillon m ▷ vt (also: **~ on**) éperonner; aiguillonner; **on the ~ of the moment** sous l'impulsion du moment

spurt [spə:t] n jet m; (of blood) jaillissement m; (of energy) regain m, sursaut m ▷ vi jaillir, gicler

spy [spaɪ] n espion(ne) f ▷ vi: **to ~ on** espionner, épier ▷ vt (see) apercevoir

sq. abbr = **square**

squabble ['skwɔbl] vi se chamailler

squad [skwɔd] n (Mil, Police) escouade f, groupe m; (Football) contingent m

squadron ['skwɔdrn] n (Mil) escadron m; (Aviat, Naut) escadrille f

squander ['skwɔndəʳ] vt gaspiller, dilapider

square [skwɛəʳ] n carré m; (in town) place f ▷ adj carré(e) ▷ vt (arrange) régler; arranger; (Math) élever au carré; (reconcile) concilier; **all ~** quitte; à égalité; **a ~ meal** un repas convenable; **2 metres ~** (de) 2 mètres sur 2; **1 ~ metre** 1 mètre carré; **square root** n racine carrée

squash [skwɔʃ] n (BRIT: drink): **lemon/orange ~** citronnade f/orangeade f; (Sport) squash m; (US: vegetable) courge f ▷ vt écraser

squat [skwɔt] adj petit(e) et épais(se), ramassé(e) ▷ vi (also: **~ down**) s'accroupir; **squatter** n squatter m

squeak [skwi:k] vi (hinge, wheel) grincer; (mouse) pousser un petit cri

squeal [skwi:l] vi pousser un or des cri(s) aigu(s) or perçant(s); (brakes) grincer

squeeze [skwi:z] n pression f ▷ vt presser; (hand, arm) serrer

squid [skwɪd] n calmar m

squint [skwɪnt] vi loucher

squirm [skwə:m] vi se tortiller

squirrel ['skwɪrəl] n écureuil m

squirt [skwə:t] vi jaillir, gicler ▷ vt faire gicler

Sr abbr = **senior**

Sri Lanka [srɪ'læŋkə] n Sri Lanka m

St abbr = **saint**; **street**

stab [stæb] n (with knife etc) coup m (de couteau etc); (of pain) lancée f; (inf: try): **to have a ~ at (doing) sth** s'essayer à (faire) qch ▷ vt poignarder

stability [stə'bɪlɪtɪ] n stabilité f

stable ['steɪbl] n écurie f ▷ adj stable

stack [stæk] n tas m, pile f ▷ vt empiler, entasser

stadium ['steɪdɪəm] n stade m

staff [sta:f] n (work force) personnel m; (BRIT Scol: also: **teaching ~**) professeurs mpl, enseignants mpl, personnel enseignant ▷ vt pourvoir en personnel

stag [stæg] n cerf m

stage [steɪdʒ] n scène f; (platform) estrade f; (point) étape f, stade m; (profession): **the ~** le théâtre ▷ vt (play) monter, mettre en scène; (demonstration) organiser; **in ~s** par étapes, par degrés

> Be careful not to translate **stage** by the French word **stage**.

stagger['stægə'] vi chanceler, tituber ▷ vt (person: amaze) stupéfier; (hours, holidays) étaler, échelonner; **staggering** adj (amazing) stupéfiant(e), renversant(e)

stagnant['stægnənt] adj stagnant(e)

stag night, stag party n enterrement m de vie de garçon

stain[steɪn] n tache f; (colouring) colorant m ▷ vt tacher; (wood) teindre; **stained glass** n (decorative) verre coloré; (in church) vitraux mpl; **stainless steel** n inox m, acier m inoxydable

staircase['stɛəkeɪs] n = **stairway**

stairs[stɛəz] npl escalier m

stairway['stɛəweɪ] n escalier m

stake[steɪk] n pieu m, poteau m; (Comm: interest) intérêts mpl; (Betting) enjeu m ▷ vt risquer, jouer; (also: **~ out**: area) marquer, délimiter; **to be at ~** être en jeu

stale[steɪl] adj (bread) rassis(e); (food) pas frais (fraîche); (beer) éventé(e); (smell) de renfermé; (air) confiné(e)

stalk[stɔ:k] n tige f ▷ vt traquer

stall[stɔ:l] n (BRIT: in street, market etc) éventaire m, étal m; (in stable) stalle f ▷ vt (Aut) caler; (fig: delay) retarder ▷ vi (Aut) caler; (fig) essayer de gagner du temps; **stalls** npl (BRIT: in cinema, theatre) orchestre m

stamina['stæmɪnə] n vigueur f, endurance f

stammer['stæmə'] n bégaiement m ▷ vi bégayer

stamp[stæmp] n timbre m; (also: **rubber ~**) tampon m; (mark, also fig) empreinte f; (on document) cachet m ▷ vi (also: **~ one's foot**) taper du pied ▷ vt (letter) timbrer; (with rubber stamp) tamponner; **stamp out** vt (fire) piétiner; (crime) éradiquer; (opposition) éliminer; **stamped addressed envelope** n (BRIT) enveloppe affranchie pour la réponse

stampede[stæm'pi:d] n ruée f; (of cattle) débandade f

stance[stæns] n position f

stand[stænd] n (position) position f; (for taxis) station f (de taxis); (Comm) étalage m, stand m; (Sport: also: **~s**) tribune f; (also: **music ~**) pupitre m ▷ vb (pt, pp **stood**) ▷ vi être or se tenir (debout); (rise) se lever, se mettre debout; (be placed) se trouver; (remain: offer etc) rester valable ▷ vt (place) mettre, poser; (tolerate, withstand) supporter; (treat, invite) offrir, payer; **to make a ~** prendre position; **to ~ for parliament** (BRIT) se présenter aux élections (comme candidat à la députation); **I can't ~ him** je ne peux pas le voir; **stand back** vi (move back) reculer, s'écarter; **stand by** vi (be ready) se tenir prêt(e) ▷ vt fus (opinion) s'en tenir à; (person) ne pas abandonner, soutenir; **stand down** vi (withdraw) se retirer; **stand for** vt fus (signify) représenter, signifier; (tolerate) supporter, tolérer; **stand in for** vt

fus remplacer; **stand out** vi (be prominent) ressortir; **stand up** vi (rise) se lever, se mettre debout; **stand up for** vt fus défendre; **stand up to** vt fus tenir tête à, résister à

standard['stændəd] n (norm) norme f, étalon m; (level) niveau m (voulu); (criterion) critère m; (flag) étendard m ▷ adj (size etc) ordinaire, normal(e); (model, feature) standard inv; (practice) courant(e); (text) de base; **standards** npl (morals) morale f, principes mpl; **standard of living** n niveau m de vie

stand-by ticket n (Aviat) billet m stand-by

standing['stændɪŋ] adj debout inv; (permanent) permanent(e) ▷ n réputation f, rang m, standing m; **of many years' ~** qui dure or existe depuis longtemps; **standing order** n (BRIT: at bank) virement m automatique, prélèvement m bancaire

stand: **standpoint** n point m de vue; **standstill** n: **at a standstill** à l'arrêt; (fig) au point mort; **to come to a standstill** s'immobiliser, s'arrêter

stank[stæŋk] pt of **stink**

staple['steɪpl] n (for papers) agrafe f ▷ adj (food, crop, industry etc) de base principal(e) ▷ vt agrafer

star[stɑ:'] n étoile f; (celebrity) vedette f ▷ vt (Cine) avoir pour vedette; **stars** npl: **the ~s** (Astrology) l'horoscope m

starboard['stɑ:bəd] n tribord m

starch[stɑ:tʃ] n amidon m; (in food) fécule f

stardom['stɑ:dəm] n célébrité f

stare[stɛə'] n regard m fixe ▷ vi: **to ~ at** regarder fixement

stark[stɑ:k] adj (bleak) désolé(e), morne ▷ adv: **~ naked** complètement nu(e)

start[stɑ:t] n commencement m, début m; (of race) départ m; (sudden movement) sursaut m; (advantage) avance f, avantage m ▷ vt commencer; (cause: fight) déclencher; (rumour) donner naissance à; (fashion) lancer; (found: business, newspaper) lancer, créer; (engine) mettre en marche ▷ vi (begin) commencer; (begin journey) partir, se mettre en route; (jump) sursauter; **when does the film ~?** à quelle heure est-ce que le film commence?; **to ~ doing** or **to do sth** se mettre à faire qch; **start off** vi commencer; (leave) partir; **start out** vi (begin) commencer; (set out) partir; **start up** vi commencer; (car) démarrer ▷ vt (fight) déclencher; (business) créer; (car) mettre en marche; **starter** n (Aut) démarreur m; (Sport: official) starter m; (BRIT Culin) entrée f; **starting point** n point m de départ

startle['stɑ:tl] vt faire sursauter; donner un choc à; **startling** adj surprenant(e), saisissant(e)

starvation[stɑ:'veɪʃən] n faim f, famine f

starve[stɑ:v] vi mourir de faim ▷ vt laisser

mourir de faim

state [steɪt] n état m; (Pol) État m ⊳ vt (declare) déclarer, affirmer; (specify) indiquer, spécifier; **States** npl: **the S~s** les États-Unis; **to be in a ~** être dans tous ses états; **stately home** n manoir m or château m (ouvert au public); **statement** n déclaration f; (Law) déposition f; **state school** n école publique; **statesman** (irreg) n homme m d'État

static ['stætɪk] n (Radio) parasites mpl; (also: **~ electricity**) électricité f statique ⊳ adj statique

station ['steɪʃən] n gare f; (also: **police ~**) poste m or commissariat m (de police) ⊳ vt placer, poster

stationary ['steɪʃnərɪ] adj à l'arrêt, immobile

stationer's (shop) n (BRIT) papeterie f

stationery ['steɪʃnərɪ] n papier m à lettres, petit matériel de bureau

station wagon n (US) break m

statistic [stə'tɪstɪk] n statistique f; **statistics** n (science) statistique f

statue ['stætju:] n statue f

stature ['stætʃər] n stature f; (fig) envergure f

status ['steɪtəs] n position f, situation f; (prestige) prestige m; (Admin, official position) statut m; **status quo** [-'kwəu] n: **the status quo** le statu quo

statutory ['stætjutrɪ] adj statutaire, prévu(e) par un article de loi

staunch [stɔ:ntʃ] adj sûr(e), loyal(e)

stay [steɪ] n (period of time) séjour m ⊳ vi rester; (reside) loger; (spend some time) séjourner; **to ~ put** ne pas bouger; **to ~ the night** passer la nuit; **stay away** vi (from person, building) ne pas s'approcher; (from event) ne pas venir; **stay behind** vi rester en arrière; **stay in** vi (at home) rester à la maison; **stay on** vi rester; **stay out** vi (of house) ne pas rentrer; (strikers) rester en grève; **stay up** vi (at night) ne pas se coucher

steadily ['stɛdɪlɪ] adv (regularly) progressivement; (firmly) fermement; (walk) d'un pas ferme; (fixedly: look) sans détourner les yeux

steady ['stɛdɪ] adj stable, solide, ferme; (regular) constant(e), régulier(-ière); (person) calme, pondéré(e) ⊳ vt assurer, stabiliser; (nerves) calmer; **a ~ boyfriend** un petit ami

steak [steɪk] n (meat) bifteck m, steak m; (fish, pork) tranche f

steal (pt **stole**, pp **stolen**) [sti:l, stəul, 'stəuln] vt, vi voler; (move) se faufiler, se déplacer furtivement; **my wallet has been stolen** on m'a volé mon portefeuille

steam [sti:m] n vapeur f ⊳ vt (Culin) cuire à la vapeur ⊳ vi fumer; **steam up** vi (window) se couvrir de buée; **to get ~ed up about sth** (fig: inf) s'exciter à propos de qch; **steamy** adj

humide; (window) embué(e); (sexy) torride

steel [sti:l] n acier m ⊳ cpd d'acier

steep [sti:p] adj raide, escarpé(e); (price) très élevé(e), excessif(-ive) ⊳ vt (faire) tremper

steeple ['sti:pl] n clocher m

steer [stɪər] vt diriger; (boat) gouverner; (lead: person) guider, conduire ⊳ vi tenir le gouvernail; **steering** n (Aut) conduite f; **steering wheel** n volant m

stem [stɛm] n (of plant) tige f; (of glass) pied m ⊳ vt contenir, endiguer; (attack, spread of disease) juguler

step [stɛp] n pas m; (stair) marche f; (action) mesure f, disposition f ⊳ vi: **to ~ forward/ back** faire un pas en avant/arrière, avancer/ reculer; **steps** npl (BRIT) = **stepladder**; **to be in/out of ~ (with)** (fig) aller dans le sens (de)/être déphasé(e) (par rapport à); **step down** vi (fig) se retirer, se désister; **step in** vi (fig) intervenir; **step up** vt (production, sales) augmenter; (campaign, efforts) intensifier; **stepbrother** n demi-frère m; **stepchild** (pl **~ren**) n beau-fils m, belle-fille f; **stepdaughter** n belle-fille f; **stepfather** n beau-père m; **stepladder** n (BRIT) escabeau m; **stepmother** n belle-mère f; **stepsister** n demi-sœur f; **stepson** n beau-fils m

stereo ['stɛrɪəu] n (sound) stéréo f; (hi-fi) chaîne f stéréo ⊳ adj (also: **~phonic**) stéréo(phonique)

stereotype ['stɪərɪətaɪp] n stéréotype m ⊳ vt stéréotyper

sterile ['stɛraɪl] adj stérile; **sterilize** ['stɛrɪlaɪz] vt stériliser

sterling ['stə:lɪŋ] adj (silver) de bon aloi, fin(e) ⊳ n (currency) livre f sterling inv

stern [stə:n] adj sévère ⊳ n (Naut) arrière m, poupe f

steroid ['stɪərɔɪd] n stéroïde m

stew [stju:] n ragoût m ⊳ vt, vi cuire à la casserole

steward ['stju:əd] n (Aviat, Naut, Rail) steward m; **stewardess** n hôtesse f

stick [stɪk] n bâton m; (for walking) canne f; (of chalk etc) morceau m ⊳ vb (pt, pp **stuck**) ⊳ vt (glue) coller; (thrust): **to ~ sth into** piquer or planter or enfoncer qch dans; (inf: put) mettre, fourrer; (: tolerate) supporter ⊳ vi (adhere) tenir, coller; (remain) rester; (get jammed: door, lift) se bloquer; **stick out** vi dépasser, sortir; **stick up** vi dépasser, sortir; **stick up for** vt fus défendre; **sticker** n auto-collant m; **sticking plaster** n sparadrap m, pansement adhésif; **stick insect** n phasme m; **stick shift** n (US Aut) levier m de vitesses

sticky ['stɪkɪ] adj poisseux(-euse); (label) adhésif(-ive); (fig: situation) délicat(e)

stiff [stɪf] adj (gen) raide, rigide; (door, brush) dur(e); (difficult) difficile, ardu(e); (cold) froid(e),

distant(e); (*strong, high*) fort(e), élevé(e) ▷ *adv*:
to be bored/scared/frozen ~ s'ennuyer à
mourir/être mort(e) de peur/froid
stifling ['staɪflɪŋ] *adj* (*heat*) suffocant(e)
stigma ['stɪɡmə] *n* stigmate *m*
stiletto [stɪ'letəʊ] *n* (BRIT: *also:* **~ heel**) talon
m aiguille
still [stɪl] *adj* immobile ▷ *adv* (*up to this time*)
encore, toujours; (*even*) encore; (*nonetheless*)
quand même, tout de même
stimulate ['stɪmjʊleɪt] *vt* stimuler
stimulus (*pl* **stimuli**) ['stɪmjʊləs, 'stɪmjʊlaɪ]
n stimulant *m*; (*Biol, Psych*) stimulus *m*
sting [stɪŋ] *n* piqûre *f*; (*organ*) dard *m* ▷ *vt, vi* (*pt,
pp* **stung**) piquer
stink [stɪŋk] *n* puanteur *f* ▷ *vi* (*pt* **stank**, *pp*
stunk) puer, empester
stir [stəːʳ] *n* agitation *f*, sensation *f* ▷ *vt* remuer
▷ *vi* remuer, bouger; **stir up** *vt* (*trouble*)
fomenter, provoquer; **stir-fry** *vt* faire sauter
▷ *n*: **vegetable stir-fry** légumes sautés à la
poêle
stitch [stɪtʃ] *n* (*Sewing*) point *m*; (*Knitting*)
maille *f*; (*Med*) point de suture; (*pain*) point de
côté ▷ *vt* coudre, piquer; (*Med*) suturer
stock [stɔk] *n* réserve *f*, provision *f*; (*Comm*)
stock *m*; (*Agr*) cheptel *m*, bétail *m*; (*Culin*)
bouillon *m*; (*Finance*) valeurs *fpl*, titres *mpl*;
(*descent, origin*) souche *f* ▷ *adj* (*fig: reply
etc*) classique ▷ *vt* (*have in stock*) avoir,
vendre; **in ~** en stock, en magasin; **out of ~**
épuisé(e); **to take ~** (*fig*) faire le point; **~s
and shares** valeurs (mobilières), titres;
stockbroker ['stɔkbrəʊkəʳ] *n* agent *m* de
change; **stock cube** *n* (BRIT *Culin*) bouillon-
cube *m*; **stock exchange** *n* Bourse *f* (des
valeurs); **stockholder** ['stɔkhəʊldəʳ] *n* (US)
actionnaire *m/f*
stocking ['stɔkɪŋ] *n* bas *m*
stock market *n* Bourse *f*, marché financier
stole [stəʊl] *pt of* **steal** ▷ *n* étole *f*
stolen ['stəʊln] *pp of* **steal**
stomach ['stʌmək] *n* estomac *m*;
(*abdomen*) ventre *m* ▷ *vt* supporter, digérer;
stomachache *n* mal *m* à l'estomac *or* au
ventre
stone [stəʊn] *n* pierre *f*; (*pebble*) caillou *m*,
galet *m*; (*in fruit*) noyau *m*; (*Med*) calcul *m*;
(BRIT: *weight*) = 6.348 *kg*; 14 *pounds* ▷ *cpd* de *or*
en pierre ▷ *vt* (*person*) lancer des pierres sur,
lapider; (*fruit*) dénoyauter
stood [stʊd] *pt, pp of* **stand**
stool [stuːl] *n* tabouret *m*
stoop [stuːp] *vi* (*also:* **have a ~**) être voûté(e);
(*also:* **~ down**: *bend*) se baisser, se courber
stop [stɔp] *n* arrêt *m*; (*in punctuation*) point *m*
▷ *vt* arrêter; (*break off*) interrompre; (*also:* **put
a ~ to**) mettre fin à; (*prevent*) empêcher ▷ *vi*
s'arrêter; (*rain, noise etc*) cesser, s'arrêter; **to ~**

doing sth cesser *or* arrêter de faire qch; **to ~ sb
(from) doing sth** empêcher qn de faire qch; **~
it!** arrête!; **stop by** *vi* s'arrêter (au passage);
stop off *vi* faire une courte halte; **stopover**
n halte *f*; (*Aviat*) escale *f*; **stoppage** *n* (*strike*)
arrêt *m* de travail; (*obstruction*) obstruction *f*
storage ['stɔːrɪdʒ] *n* emmagasinage *m*
store [stɔːʳ] *n* (*stock*) provision *f*, réserve
f; (*depot*) entrepôt *m*; (BRIT: *large shop*)
grand magasin; (US: *shop*) magasin *m* ▷ *vt*
emmagasiner; (*information*) enregistrer;
stores *npl* (*food*) provisions *f*; **who knows
what is in ~ for us?** qui sait ce que l'avenir
nous réserve *or* ce qui nous attend?;
storekeeper *n* (US) commerçant(e)
storey (US **story**) ['stɔːrɪ] *n* étage *m*
storm [stɔːm] *n* tempête *f*; (*thunderstorm*)
orage *m* ▷ *vi* (*fig*) fulminer ▷ *vt* prendre
d'assaut; **stormy** *adj* orageux(-euse)
story ['stɔːrɪ] *n* histoire *f*; (*Press: article*) article
m; (US) = **storey**
stout [staʊt] *adj* (*strong*) solide; (*fat*) gros(se),
corpulent(e) ▷ *n* bière brune
stove [stəʊv] *n* (*for cooking*) fourneau *m*; (:
small) réchaud *m*; (*for heating*) poêle *m*
straight [streɪt] *adj* droit(e); (*hair*) raide;
(*frank*) honnête, franc (franche); (*simple*)
simple ▷ *adv* (tout) droit; (*drink*) sec, sans
eau; **to put** *or* **get ~** = mettre en ordre, mettre
de l'ordre dans; (*fig*) mettre au clair; **~ away**,
~ off (*at once*) tout de suite; **straighten** *vt*
ajuster; (*bed*) arranger; **straighten out** *vt* (*fig*)
débrouiller; **straighten up** *vi* (*stand up*) se
redresser; **straightforward** *adj* simple; (*frank*)
honnête, direct(e)
strain [streɪn] *n* (*Tech*) tension *f*; pression *f*;
(*physical*) effort *m*; (*mental*) tension (nerveuse);
(*Med*) entorse *f*; (*breed: of plants*) variété *f*; (: *of
animals*) race *f* ▷ *vt* (*fig: resources etc*) mettre
à rude épreuve, grever; (*hurt: back etc*) se
faire mal à; (*vegetables*) égoutter; **strains**
npl (*Mus*) accords *mpl*, accents *mpl*; **strained**
adj (*muscle*) froissé(e); (*laugh etc*) forcé(e),
contraint(e); (*relations*) tendu(e); **strainer** *n*
passoire *f*
strait [streɪt] *n* (*Geo*) détroit *m*; **straits** *npl*: **to
be in dire ~s** (*fig*) avoir de sérieux ennuis
strand [strænd] *n* (*of thread*) fil *m*, brin *m*;
(*of rope*) toron *m*; (*of hair*) mèche *f* ▷ *vt* (*boat*)
échouer; **stranded** *adj* en rade, en plan
strange [streɪndʒ] *adj* (*not known*) inconnu(e);
(*odd*) étrange, bizarre; **strangely** *adv*
étrangement, bizarrement; *see also* **enough**;
stranger *n* (*unknown*) inconnu(e); (*from
somewhere else*) étranger(-ère)
strangle ['stræŋgl] *vt* étrangler
strap [stræp] *n* lanière *f*, courroie *f*, sangle *f*; (*of
slip, dress*) bretelle *f*
strategic [strə'tiːdʒɪk] *adj* stratégique

strategy ['strætɪdʒɪ] n stratégie f
straw [strɔ:] n paille f; **that's the last ~!** ça c'est le comble!
strawberry ['strɔ:bərɪ] n fraise f
stray [streɪ] adj (animal) perdu(e), errant(e); (scattered) isolé(e) ▷ vi s'égarer; **~ bullet** balle perdue
streak [stri:k] n bande f, filet m; (in hair) raie f ▷ vt zébrer, strier
stream [stri:m] n (brook) ruisseau m; (current) courant m, flot m; (of people) défilé ininterrompu, flot ▷ vt (Scol) répartir par niveau ▷ vi ruisseler; **to ~ in/out** entrer/sortir à flots
street [stri:t] n rue f; **streetcar** n (us) tramway m; **street light** n réverbère m; **street map, street plan** n plan m des rues
strength [strɛŋθ] n force f; (of girder, knot etc) solidité f; **strengthen** vt renforcer; (muscle) fortifier; (building, Econ) consolider
strenuous ['strɛnjuəs] adj vigoureux(-euse), énergique; (tiring) ardu(e), fatigant(e)
stress [strɛs] n (force, pressure) pression f; (mental strain) tension (nerveuse), stress m; (accent) accent m; (emphasis) insistance f ▷ vt insister sur, souligner; (syllable) accentuer; **stressed** adj (tense) stressé(e); (syllable) accentué(e); **stressful** adj (job) stressant(e)
stretch [strɛtʃ] n (of sand etc) étendue f ▷ vi s'étirer; (extend): **to ~ to or as far as** s'étendre jusqu'à ▷ vt tendre, étirer; (fig) pousser (au maximum); **at a ~** d'affilée; **stretch out** vi s'étendre ▷ vt (arm etc) allonger, tendre; (to spread) étendre
stretcher ['strɛtʃə'] n brancard m, civière f
strict [strɪkt] adj strict(e); **strictly** adv strictement
stride [straɪd] n grand pas, enjambée f ▷ vi (pt **strode**, pp **stridden**) marcher à grands pas
strike [straɪk] n grève f; (of oil etc) découverte f; (attack) raid m ▷ vb (pt, pp **struck**) ▷ vt frapper; (oil etc) trouver, découvrir; (make: agreement, deal) conclure ▷ vi faire grève; (attack) attaquer; (clock) sonner; **to go on** or **come out on ~** se mettre en grève, faire grève; **to ~ a match** frotter une allumette; **striker** n gréviste m/f; (Sport) buteur m; **striking** adj frappant(e), saisissant(e); (attractive) éblouissant(e)
string [strɪŋ] n ficelle f, fil m; (row: of beads) rang m; (Mus) corde f ▷ vt (pt, pp **strung**); **to ~ out** échelonner; **to ~ together** enchaîner; **the strings** npl (Mus) les instruments mpl à cordes; **to pull ~s** (fig) faire jouer le piston
strip [strɪp] n bande f; (Sport) tenue f ▷ vt (undress) déshabiller; (paint) décaper; (fig) dégarnir, dépouiller; (also: **~ down**: machine) démonter ▷ vi se déshabiller; **strip off** vt (paint etc) décaper ▷ vi (person) se déshabiller

stripe [straɪp] n raie f, rayure f; (Mil) galon m; **striped** adj rayé(e), à rayures
stripper ['strɪpə'] n strip-teaseuse f
strip-search ['strɪpsə:tʃ] vt: **to ~ sb** fouiller qn (en le faisant se déshabiller)
strive (pt **strove**, pp **~n**) [straɪv, strəʊv, 'strɪvn] vi: **to ~ to do/for sth** s'efforcer de faire/d'obtenir qch
strode [strəʊd] pt of **stride**
stroke [strəʊk] n coup m; (Med) attaque f; (Swimming: style) (sorte f de) nage f ▷ vt caresser; **at a ~** d'un (seul) coup
stroll [strəʊl] n petite promenade ▷ vi flâner, se promener nonchalamment; **stroller** n (us: for child) poussette f
strong [strɔŋ] adj (gen) fort(e); (healthy) vigoureux(-euse); (heart, nerves) solide; **they are 50 ~** ils sont au nombre de 50; **stronghold** n forteresse f, fort m; (fig) bastion m; **strongly** adv fortement, avec force; vigoureusement; solidement
strove [strəʊv] pt of **strive**
struck [strʌk] pt, pp of **strike**
structure ['strʌktʃə'] n structure f; (building) construction f
struggle ['strʌgl] n lutte f ▷ vi lutter, se battre
strung [strʌŋ] pt, pp of **string**
stub [stʌb] n (of cigarette) bout m, mégot m; (of ticket etc) talon m ▷ vt: **to ~ one's toe (on sth)** se heurter le doigt de pied (contre qch); **stub out** vt écraser
stubble ['stʌbl] n chaume m; (on chin) barbe f de plusieurs jours
stubborn ['stʌbən] adj têtu(e), obstiné(e), opiniâtre
stuck [stʌk] pt, pp of **stick** ▷ adj (jammed) bloqué(e), coincé(e)
stud [stʌd] n (on boots etc) clou m; (collar stud) bouton m de col; (earring) petite boucle d'oreille; (of horses: also: **~ farm**) écurie f, haras m; (also: **~ horse**) étalon m ▷ vt (fig): **~ded with** parsemé(e) or criblé(e) de
student ['stju:dənt] n étudiant(e) ▷ adj (life) estudiantin(e), étudiant(e), d'étudiant; (residence, restaurant) universitaire; (loan, movement) étudiant; **student driver** n (us) (conducteur(-trice)) débutant(e); **students' union** n (BRIT: association) ≈ union f des étudiants; (: building) ≈ foyer m des étudiants
studio ['stju:dɪəʊ] n studio m, atelier m; (TV etc) studio; **studio flat** (us **studio apartment**) n studio m
study ['stʌdɪ] n étude f; (room) bureau m ▷ vt étudier; (examine) examiner ▷ vi étudier, faire ses études
stuff [stʌf] n (gen) chose(s) f(pl), truc m; (belongings) affaires fpl, trucs; (substance) substance f ▷ vt rembourrer; (Culin) farcir; (inf: push) fourrer; **stuffing** n bourre f,

rembourrage m; (Culin) farce f; **stuffy** adj
(room) mal ventilé(e) or aéré(e); (ideas) vieux
jeu inv
stumble ['stʌmbl] vi trébucher; **to ~ across** or
on (fig) tomber sur
stump [stʌmp] n souche f; (of limb) moignon
m ▷ vt: **to be ~ed** sécher, ne pas savoir que
répondre
stun [stʌn] vt (blow) étourdir; (news)
abasourdir, stupéfier
stung [stʌŋ] pt, pp of **sting**
stunk [stʌŋk] pp of **stink**
stunned [stʌnd] adj assommé(e); (fig)
sidéré(e)
stunning ['stʌnɪŋ] adj (beautiful)
étourdissant(e); (news etc) stupéfiant(e)
stunt [stʌnt] n (in film) cascade f, acrobatie
f; (publicity) truc m publicitaire ▷ vt retarder,
arrêter
stupid ['stjuːpɪd] adj stupide, bête; **stupidity**
[stjuːˈpɪdɪtɪ] n stupidité f, bêtise f
sturdy ['stɜːdɪ] adj (person, plant) robuste,
vigoureux(-euse); (object) solide
stutter ['stʌtə*] n bégaiement m ▷ vi bégayer
style [staɪl] n style m; (distinction) allure f,
cachet m, style; (design) modèle m; **stylish**
adj élégant(e), chic inv; **stylist** n (hair stylist)
coiffeur(-euse)
sub... [sʌb] prefix sub..., sous-; **subconscious**
adj subconscient(e)
subdued [səbˈdjuːd] adj (light) tamisé(e);
(person) qui a perdu de son entrain
subject n ['sʌbdʒɪkt] sujet m; (Scol) matière
f ▷ vt [səbˈdʒɛkt]: **to ~ to** soumettre à; **to
be ~ to** (law) être soumis(e) à; **subjective**
[səbˈdʒɛktɪv] adj subjectif(-ive); **subject
matter** n (content) contenu m
subjunctive [səbˈdʒʌŋktɪv] n subjonctif m
submarine [sʌbməˈriːn] n sous-marin m
submission [səbˈmɪʃən] n soumission f
submit [səbˈmɪt] vt soumettre ▷ vi se
soumettre
subordinate [səˈbɔːdɪnət] adj (junior)
subalterne; (Grammar) subordonné(e) ▷ n
subordonné(e)
subscribe [səbˈskraɪb] vi cotiser; **to ~ to**
(opinion, fund) souscrire à; (newspaper)
s'abonner à; être abonné(e) à
subscription [səbˈskrɪpʃən] n (to magazine
etc) abonnement m
subsequent ['sʌbsɪkwənt] adj ultérieur(e),
suivant(e); **subsequently** adv par la suite
subside [səbˈsaɪd] vi (land) s'affaisser; (flood)
baisser; (wind, feelings) tomber
subsidiary [səbˈsɪdɪərɪ] adj subsidiaire;
accessoire; (BRIT Scol: subject) complémentaire
▷ n filiale f
subsidize ['sʌbsɪdaɪz] vt subventionner
subsidy ['sʌbsɪdɪ] n subvention f

substance ['sʌbstəns] n substance f
substantial [səbˈstænʃl] adj substantiel(le);
(fig) important(e)
substitute ['sʌbstɪtjuːt] n (person)
remplaçant(e); (thing) succédané m ▷ vt: **to ~
sth/sb for** substituer qch/qn à, remplacer par
qch/qn; **substitution** n substitution f
subtitles ['sʌbtaɪtlz] npl (Cine) sous-titres mpl
subtle ['sʌtl] adj subtil(e)
subtract [səbˈtrækt] vt soustraire, retrancher
suburb ['sʌbəːb] n faubourg m; **the ~s** la
banlieue; **suburban** [səˈbəːbən] adj de
banlieue, suburbain(e)
subway ['sʌbweɪ] n (BRIT: underpass) passage
souterrain; (US: railway) métro m
succeed [səkˈsiːd] vi réussir ▷ vt succéder à;
to ~ in doing réussir à faire
success [səkˈsɛs] n succès m; réussite f;
successful adj (business) prospère, qui
réussit; (attempt) couronné(e) de succès; **to
be successful (in doing)** réussir (à faire);
successfully adv avec succès
succession [səkˈsɛʃən] n succession f
successive [səkˈsɛsɪv] adj successif(-ive)
successor [səkˈsɛsə*] n successeur m
succumb [səˈkʌm] vi succomber
such [sʌtʃ] adj tel (telle); (of that kind): **~ a
book** un livre de ce genre or pareil, un tel livre;
(so much): **~ courage** un tel courage ▷ adv
si; **~ a long trip** un si long voyage; **~ a lot of**
tellement or tant de; **~ as** (like) tel (telle) que,
comme; **as ~** adv en tant que tel (telle), à
proprement parler; **such-and-such** adj tel ou
tel (telle ou telle)
suck [sʌk] vt sucer; (breast, bottle) téter
Sudan [suˈdɑːn] n Soudan m
sudden ['sʌdn] adj soudain(e), subit(e); **all
of a ~** soudain, tout à coup; **suddenly** adv
brusquement, tout à coup, soudain
sue [suː] vt poursuivre en justice, intenter un
procès à
suede [sweɪd] n daim m, cuir suédé m
suffer ['sʌfə*] vt souffrir, subir; (bear) tolérer,
supporter, subir ▷ vi souffrir; **to ~ from**
(illness) souffrir de, avoir; **suffering** n
souffrance(s) f(pl)
suffice [səˈfaɪs] vi suffire
sufficient [səˈfɪʃənt] adj suffisant(e)
suffocate ['sʌfəkeɪt] vi suffoquer; étouffer
sugar ['ʃugə*] n sucre m ▷ vt sucrer
suggest [səˈdʒɛst] vt suggérer, proposer;
(indicate) sembler indiquer; **suggestion**
[səˈdʒɛstʃən] n suggestion f
suicide ['suɪsaɪd] n suicide m; **~ bombing**
attentat m suicide; see also **commit**; **suicide
bomber** n kamikaze m/f
suit [suːt] n (man's) costume m, complet m;
(woman's) tailleur m, ensemble m; (Cards)
couleur f; (lawsuit) procès m ▷ vt (subj: clothes,

hairstyle) aller à; (*be convenient for*) convenir à; (*adapt*): **to ~ sth to** adapter ou approprier qch à; **well ~ed** (*couple*) faits l'un pour l'autre, très bien assortis; **suitable** *adj* qui convient; approprié(e), adéquat(e); **suitcase** *n* valise *f*

suite [swi:t] *n* (*of rooms, also Mus*) suite *f*; (*furniture*): **bedroom/dining room ~** (ensemble *m* de) chambre *f* à coucher/salle *f* à manger; **a three-piece ~** un salon (canapé et deux fauteuils)

sulfur ['sʌlfə^r] (*us*) *n* = **sulphur**

sulk [sʌlk] *vi* bouder

sulphur (*us* **sulfur**) ['sʌlfə^r] *n* soufre *m*

sultana [sʌl'tɑ:nə] *n* (*fruit*) raisin (sec) de Smyrne

sum [sʌm] *n* somme *f*; (*Scol etc*) calcul *m*; **sum up** *vt* résumer ▷ *vi* résumer

summarize ['sʌməraɪz] *vt* résumer

summary ['sʌmərɪ] *n* résumé *m*

summer ['sʌmə^r] *n* été *m* ▷ *cpd* d'été, estival(e); **in (the) ~** en été, pendant l'été; **summer holidays** *npl* grandes vacances; **summertime** *n* (*season*) été *m*

summit ['sʌmɪt] *n* sommet *m*; (*also*: **~ conference**) (conférence *f* au) sommet *m*

summon ['sʌmən] *vt* appeler, convoquer; **to ~ a witness** citer *or* assigner un témoin

Sun. *abbr* (= *Sunday*) dim

sun [sʌn] *n* soleil *m*; **sunbathe** *vi* prendre un bain de soleil; **sunbed** *n* lit pliant; (*with sun lamp*) lit à ultra-violets; **sunblock** *n* écran *m* total; **sunburn** *n* coup *m* de soleil; **sunburned**, **sunburnt** *adj* bronzé(e), hâlé(e); (*painfully*) brûlé(e) par le soleil

Sunday ['sʌndɪ] *n* dimanche *m*

sunflower ['sʌnflauə^r] *n* tournesol *m*

sung [sʌŋ] *pp of* **sing**

sunglasses ['sʌnglɑ:sɪz] *npl* lunettes *fpl* de soleil

sunk [sʌŋk] *pp of* **sink**

sun: **sunlight** *n* (lumière *f* du) soleil *m*; **sun lounger** *n* chaise longue; **sunny** *adj* ensoleillé(e); **it is sunny** il fait (du) soleil, il y a du soleil; **sunrise** *n* lever *m* du soleil; **sun roof** *n* (*Aut*) toit ouvrant; **sunscreen** *n* crème *f* solaire; **sunset** *n* coucher *m* du soleil; **sunshade** *n* (*over table*) parasol *m*; **sunshine** *n* (lumière *f* du) soleil *m*; **sunstroke** *n* insolation *f*, coup *m* de soleil; **suntan** *n* bronzage *m*; **suntan lotion** *n* lotion *f* or lait *m* solaire; **suntan oil** *n* huile *f* solaire

super ['su:pə^r] *adj* (*inf*) formidable

superb [su:'pə:b] *adj* superbe, magnifique

superficial [su:pə'fɪʃəl] *adj* superficiel(le)

superintendent [su:pərɪn'tɛndənt] *n* directeur(-trice); (*Police*) ≈ commissaire *m*

superior [su:'pɪərɪə^r] *adj* supérieur(e); (*smug*) condescendant(e), méprisant(e) ▷ *n* supérieur(e)

superlative [su:'pə:lətɪv] *n* (*Ling*) superlatif *m*

supermarket ['su:pəmɑ:kɪt] *n* supermarché *m*

supernatural [su:pə'nætʃərəl] *adj* surnaturel(le) ▷ *n*: **the ~** le surnaturel

superpower ['su:pəpauə^r] *n* (*Pol*) superpuissance *f*

superstition [su:pə'stɪʃən] *n* superstition *f*

superstitious [su:pə'stɪʃəs] *adj* superstitieux(-euse)

superstore ['su:pəstɔ:^r] *n* (*brit*) hypermarché *m*, grande surface

supervise ['su:pəvaɪz] *vt* (*children etc*) surveiller; (*organization, work*) diriger; **supervision** [su:pə'vɪʒən] *n* surveillance *f*; (*monitoring*) contrôle *m*; (*management*) direction *f*; **supervisor** *n* surveillant(e); (*in shop*) chef *m* de rayon

supper ['sʌpə^r] *n* dîner *m*; (*late*) souper *m*

supple ['sʌpl] *adj* souple

supplement *n* ['sʌplɪmənt] supplément *m* ▷ *vt* [sʌplɪ'mɛnt] ajouter à, compléter

supplier [sə'plaɪə^r] *n* fournisseur *m*

supply [sə'plaɪ] *vt* (*provide*) fournir; (*equip*): **to ~ (with)** approvisionner *or* ravitailler (en); fournir (en) ▷ *n* provision *f*, réserve *f*; (*supplying*) approvisionnement *m*; **supplies** *npl* (*food*) vivres *mpl*; (*Mil*) subsistances *fpl*

support [sə'pɔ:t] *n* (*moral, financial etc*) soutien *m*, appui *m*; (*Tech*) support *m*, soutien ▷ *vt* soutenir, supporter; (*financially*) subvenir aux besoins de; (*uphold*) être pour, être partisan de, appuyer; (*Sport: team*) être pour; **supporter** *n* (*Pol etc*) partisan(e); (*Sport*) supporter *m*

suppose [sə'pəuz] *vt, vi* supposer; imaginer; **to be ~d to do/be** être censé(e) faire/être; **supposedly** [sə'pəuzɪdlɪ] *adv* soi-disant; **supposing** *conj* si, à supposer que + *sub*

suppress [sə'prɛs] *vt* (*revolt, feeling*) réprimer; (*information*) faire disparaître; (*scandal, yawn*) étouffer

supreme [su:'pri:m] *adj* suprême

surcharge ['sə:tʃɑ:dʒ] *n* surcharge *f*

sure [ʃuə^r] *adj* (*gen*) sûr(e); (*definite, convinced*) sûr, certain(e); **~!** (*of course*) bien sûr!; **~ enough** effectivement; **to make ~ of sth/ that** s'assurer de qch/que, vérifier qch/que; **surely** *adv* sûrement; certainement

surf [sə:f] *n* (*waves*) ressac *m* ▷ *vt*: **to ~ the Net** surfer sur Internet, surfer sur le net

surface ['sə:fɪs] *n* surface *f* ▷ *vt* (*road*) poser un revêtement sur ▷ *vi* remonter à la surface; (*fig*) faire surface; **by ~ mail** par voie de terre; (*by sea*) par voie maritime

surfboard ['sə:fbɔ:d] *n* planche *f* de surf

surfer ['sə:fə^r] *n* (*in sea*) surfeur(-euse); **web** *or* **net ~** internaute *m/f*

surfing ['sə:fɪŋ] *n* surf *m*

surge [sə:dʒ] *n* (*of emotion*) vague *f* ▷ *vi* déferler

surgeon ['sə:dʒən] *n* chirurgien *m*

surgery ['sə:dʒərɪ] *n* chirurgie *f*; (BRIT: *room*) cabinet *m* (de consultation); (*also*: **~ hours**) heures *fpl* de consultation

surname ['sə:neɪm] *n* nom *m* de famille

surpass [sə:'pɑ:s] *vt* surpasser, dépasser

surplus ['sə:pləs] *n* surplus *m*, excédent *m* ▷ *adj* en surplus, de trop; (*Comm*) excédentaire

surprise [sə'praɪz] *n* (*gen*) surprise *f*; (*astonishment*) étonnement *m* ▷ *vt* surprendre, étonner; **surprised** *adj* (*look, smile*) surpris(e), étonné(e); **to be surprised** être surpris; **surprising** *adj* surprenant(e), étonnant(e); **surprisingly** *adv* (*easy, helpful*) étonnamment, étrangement; **(somewhat) surprisingly, he agreed** curieusement, il a accepté

surrender [sə'rɛndə'] *n* reddition *f*, capitulation *f* ▷ *vi* se rendre, capituler

surround [sə'raund] *vt* entourer; (*Mil etc*) encercler; **surrounding** *adj* environnant(e); **surroundings** *npl* environs *mpl*, alentours *mpl*

surveillance [sə:'veɪləns] *n* surveillance *f*

survey *n* ['sə:veɪ] enquête *f*, étude *f*; (*in house buying etc*) inspection *f*, (*rapport m d*)expertise *f*; (*of land*) levé *m* ▷ *vt* [sə:'veɪ] (*situation*) passer en revue; (*examine carefully*) inspecter; (*building*) expertiser; (*land*) faire le levé de; (*look at*) embrasser du regard; **surveyor** *n* (*of building*) expert *m*; (*of land*) (arpenteur *m*) géomètre *m*

survival [sə'vaɪvl] *n* survie *f*

survive [sə'vaɪv] *vi* survivre; (*custom etc*) subsister ▷ *vt* (*accident etc*) survivre à, réchapper de; (*person*) survivre à; **survivor** *n* survivant(e)

suspect *adj, n* ['sʌspɛkt] suspect(e) ▷ *vt* [səs'pɛkt] soupçonner, suspecter

suspend [səs'pɛnd] *vt* suspendre; **suspended sentence** *n* (*Law*) condamnation *f* avec sursis; **suspenders** *npl* (BRIT) jarretelles *fpl*; (US) bretelles *fpl*

suspense [səs'pɛns] *n* attente *f*, incertitude *f*; (*in film etc*) suspense *m*; **to keep sb in ~** tenir qn dans l'incertitude, laisser qn dans l'incertitude

suspension [səs'pɛnʃən] *n* (*gen, Aut*) suspension *f*; (*of driving licence*) retrait *m* provisoire; **suspension bridge** *n* pont suspendu

suspicion [səs'pɪʃən] *n* soupçon(s) *m(pl)*; **suspicious** *adj* (*suspecting*) soupçonneux(-euse), méfiant(e); (*causing suspicion*) suspect(e)

sustain [səs'teɪn] *vt* soutenir; (*subj: food*) nourrir, donner des forces à; (*damage*) subir; (*injury*) recevoir

SUV *n abbr* (*esp US*: = *sports utility vehicle*) SUV *m*, véhicule *m* de loisirs

swallow ['swɔləu] *n* (*bird*) hirondelle *f* ▷ *vt* avaler; (*fig: story*) gober

swam [swæm] *pt of* **swim**

swamp [swɔmp] *n* marais *m*, marécage *m* ▷ *vt* submerger

swan [swɔn] *n* cygne *m*

swap [swɔp] *n* échange *m*, troc *m* ▷ *vt*: **to ~ (for)** échanger (contre), troquer (contre)

swarm [swɔ:m] *n* essaim *m* ▷ *vi* (*bees*) essaimer; (*people*) grouiller; **to be ~ing with** grouiller de

sway [sweɪ] *vi* se balancer, osciller ▷ *vt* (*influence*) influencer

swear [swɛə'] (*pt* **swore**, *pp* **sworn**) *vt, vi* jurer; **swear in** *vt* assermenter; **swearword** *n* gros mot, juron *m*

sweat [swɛt] *n* sueur *f*, transpiration *f* ▷ *vi* suer

sweater ['swɛtə'] *n* tricot *m*, pull *m*

sweatshirt ['swɛtʃə:t] *n* sweat-shirt *m*

sweaty ['swɛtɪ] *adj* en sueur, moite *or* mouillé(e) de sueur

Swede [swi:d] *n* Suédois(e)

swede [swi:d] *n* (BRIT) rutabaga *m*

Sweden ['swi:dn] *n* Suède *f*; **Swedish** ['swi:dɪʃ] *adj* suédois(e) ▷ *n* (*Ling*) suédois *m*

sweep [swi:p] *n* (*curve*) grande courbe; (*also*: **chimney ~**) ramoneur *m* ▷ *vb* (*pt, pp* **swept**) ▷ *vt* balayer; (*subj: current*) emporter

sweet [swi:t] *n* (BRIT: *pudding*) dessert *m*; (*candy*) bonbon *m* ▷ *adj* doux (douce); (*not savoury*) sucré(e); (*kind*) gentil(le); (*baby*) mignon(ne); **sweetcorn** *n* maïs doux; **sweetener** ['swi:tnə'] *n* (*Culin*) édulcorant *m*; **sweetheart** *n* amoureux(-euse); **sweetshop** *n* (BRIT) confiserie *f*

swell [swɛl] *n* (*of sea*) houle *f* ▷ *adj* (US: *inf: excellent*) chouette ▷ *vb* (*pt* **~ed**, *pp* **swollen** *or* **~ed**) ▷ *vt* (*increase*) grossir, augmenter ▷ *vi* (*increase*) grossir, augmenter; (*sound*) s'enfler; (*Med: also*: **~ up**) enfler; **swelling** *n* (*Med*) enflure *f*; (: *lump*) grosseur *f*

swept [swɛpt] *pt, pp of* **sweep**

swerve [swə:v] *vi* (*to avoid obstacle*) faire une embardée *or* un écart; (*off the road*) dévier

swift [swɪft] *n* (*bird*) martinet *m* ▷ *adj* rapide, prompt(e)

swim [swɪm] *n*: **to go for a ~** aller nager *or* se baigner ▷ *vb* (*pt* **swam**, *pp* **swum**) ▷ *vi* nager; (*Sport*) faire de la natation; (*fig: head, room*) tourner ▷ *vt* traverser (à la nage); **to ~ a length** nager une longueur; **swimmer** *n* nageur(-euse); **swimming** *n* nage *f*, natation *f*; **swimming costume** *n* (BRIT) maillot *m* (de bain); **swimming pool** *n* piscine *f*; **swimming trunks** *npl* maillot *m* de bain; **swimsuit** *n* maillot *m* (de bain)

swing [swɪŋ] *n* (*in playground*) balançoire *f*;

(*movement*) balancement *m*, oscillations *fpl*; (*change in opinion etc*) revirement *m* ▷ vb (*pt, pp* **swung**) ▷ vt balancer, faire osciller; (*also*: **~ round**) tourner, faire virer ▷ vi se balancer, osciller; (*also*: **~ round**) virer, tourner; **to be in full ~** battre son plein

swipe card [swaɪp-] *n* carte *f* magnétique

swirl [swəːl] *vi* tourbillonner, tournoyer

Swiss [swɪs] *adj* suisse ▷ *n* (*pl inv*) Suisse(-esse)

switch [swɪtʃ] *n* (*for light, radio etc*) bouton *m*; (*change*) changement *m*, revirement *m* ▷ vt (*change*) changer; **switch off** vt éteindre; (*engine, machine*) arrêter; **could you ~ off the light?** pouvez-vous éteindre la lumière?; **switch on** vt allumer; (*engine, machine*) mettre en marche; **switchboard** *n* (*Tel*) standard *m*

Switzerland ['swɪtsələnd] *n* Suisse *f*

swivel ['swɪvl] *vi* (*also*: **~ round**) pivoter, tourner

swollen ['swəʊlən] *pp of* **swell**

swoop [swuːp] *n* (*by police etc*) rafle *f*, descente *f* ▷ vi (*bird: also*: **~ down**) descendre en piqué, piquer

swop [swɒp] *n, vt* = **swap**

sword [sɔːd] *n* épée *f*; **swordfish** *n* espadon *m*

swore [swɔːʳ] *pt of* **swear**

sworn [swɔːn] *pp of* **swear** ▷ *adj* (*statement, evidence*) donné(e) sous serment; (*enemy*) juré(e)

swum [swʌm] *pp of* **swim**

swung [swʌŋ] *pt, pp of* **swing**

syllable ['sɪləbl] *n* syllabe *f*

syllabus ['sɪləbəs] *n* programme *m*

symbol ['sɪmbl] *n* symbole *m*; **symbolic(al)** [sɪm'bɒlɪk(l)] *adj* symbolique

symmetrical [sɪ'metrɪkl] *adj* symétrique

symmetry ['sɪmɪtrɪ] *n* symétrie *f*

sympathetic [sɪmpə'θetɪk] *adj* (*showing pity*) compatissant(e); (*understanding*) bienveillant(e), compréhensif(-ive); **~ towards** bien disposé(e) envers

Be careful not to translate *sympathetic* by the French word *sympathique*.

sympathize ['sɪmpəθaɪz] *vi*: **to ~ with sb** plaindre qn; (*in grief*) s'associer à la douleur de qn; **to ~ with sth** comprendre qch

sympathy ['sɪmpəθɪ] *n* (*pity*) compassion *f*

symphony ['sɪmfənɪ] *n* symphonie *f*

symptom ['sɪmptəm] *n* symptôme *m*; indice *m*

synagogue ['sɪnəgɒg] *n* synagogue *f*

syndicate ['sɪndɪkɪt] *n* syndicat *m*, coopérative *f*; (*Press*) agence *f* de presse

syndrome ['sɪndrəʊm] *n* syndrome *m*

synonym ['sɪnənɪm] *n* synonyme *m*

synthetic [sɪn'θetɪk] *adj* synthétique

Syria ['sɪrɪə] *n* Syrie *f*

syringe [sɪ'rɪndʒ] *n* seringue *f*

syrup ['sɪrəp] *n* sirop *m*; (BRIT: *also*: **golden ~**) mélasse raffinée

system ['sɪstəm] *n* système *m*; (*Anat*) organisme *m*; **systematic** [sɪstə'mætɪk] *adj* systématique; méthodique; **systems analyst** *n* analyste-programmeur *m/f*

ta [tɑ:] *excl* (BRIT inf) merci!

tab [tæb] *n* (*label*) étiquette *f*; (*on drinks can etc*) languette *f*; **to keep ~s on** (*fig*) surveiller

table ['teɪbl] *n* table *f* ▷ *vt* (BRIT: *motion etc*) présenter; **a ~ for 4, please** une table pour 4, s'il vous plaît; **to lay** *or* **set the ~** mettre le couvert *or* la table; **tablecloth** *n* nappe *f*; **table d'hôte** [tɑ:bl'dəut] *adj* (*meal*) à prix fixe; **table lamp** *n* lampe décorative *or* de table; **tablemat** *n* (*for plate*) napperon *m*, set *m*; (*for hot dish*) dessous-de-plat *m inv*; **tablespoon** *n* cuiller *f* de service; (*also:* **tablespoonful**: *as measurement*) cuillerée *f* à soupe

tablet ['tæblɪt] *n* (Med) comprimé *m*; (*of stone*) plaque *f*

table tennis *n* ping-pong *m*, tennis *m* de table

tabloid ['tæblɔɪd] *n* (*newspaper*) quotidien *m* populaire

taboo [tə'bu:] *adj*, *n* tabou (*m*)

tack [tæk] *n* (*nail*) petit clou *m*; (*fig*) direction *f* ▷ *vt* (*nail*) clouer; (*sew*) bâtir ▷ *vi* (Naut) tirer un *or* des bord(s); **to ~ sth on to (the end of) sth** (*of letter, book*) rajouter qch à la fin de qch

tackle ['tækl] *n* matériel *m*, équipement *m*; (*for lifting*) appareil *m* de levage; (Football, Rugby) plaquage *m* ▷ *vt* (*difficulty, animal, burglar*) s'attaquer à; (*person: challenge*) s'expliquer avec; (Football, Rugby) plaquer

tacky ['tækɪ] *adj* collant(e); (*paint*) pas sec (sèche); (*pej: poor-quality*) minable; (: *showing bad taste*) ringard(e)

tact [tækt] *n* tact *m*; **tactful** *adj* plein(e) de tact

tactics ['tæktɪks] *npl* tactique *f*

tactless ['tæktlɪs] *adj* qui manque de tact

tadpole ['tædpəul] *n* têtard *m*

taffy ['tæfɪ] *n* (US) (bonbon *m* au) caramel *m*

tag [tæg] *n* étiquette *f*

tail [teɪl] *n* queue *f*; (*of shirt*) pan *m* ▷ *vt* (*follow*) suivre, filer; **tails** *npl* (*suit*) habit *m*; *see also* **head**

tailor ['teɪləʳ] *n* tailleur *m* (*artisan*)

Taiwan ['taɪ'wɑ:n] *n* Taïwan (*no article*); **Taiwanese** [taɪwə'ni:z] *adj* taïwanais(e) ▷ *n inv* Taïwanais(e)

take [teɪk] *vb* (*pt* **took**, *pp* **~n**) ▷ *vt* prendre; (*gain: prize*) remporter; (*require: effort, courage*) demander; (*tolerate*) accepter, supporter; (*hold: passengers etc*) contenir; (*accompany*) emmener, accompagner; (*bring, carry*) apporter, emporter; (*exam*) passer, se présenter à; **to ~ sth from** (*drawer etc*) prendre qch dans; (*person*) prendre qch à; **I ~ it that** je suppose que; **to be ~n ill** tomber malade; **it won't ~ long** ça ne prendra pas longtemps; **I was quite ~n with her/it** elle/cela m'a beaucoup plu; **take after** *vt fus* ressembler à; **take apart** *vt* démonter; **take away** *vt* (*carry off*) emporter; (*remove*) enlever; (*subtract*) soustraire; **take back** *vt* (*return*) rendre, rapporter; (*one's words*) retirer; **take down** *vt* (*building*) démolir; (*letter etc*) prendre, écrire; **take in** *vt* (*deceive*) tromper, rouler; (*understand*) comprendre, saisir; (*include*) couvrir, inclure; (*lodger*) prendre; (*dress, waistband*) reprendre; **take off** *vi* (Aviat) décoller ▷ *vt* (*remove*) enlever; **take on** *vt* (*work*) accepter, se charger de; (*employee*) prendre, embaucher; (*opponent*) accepter de se battre contre; **take out** *vt* sortir; (*remove*) enlever; (*invite*) sortir avec; **to ~ sth out of** (*out of drawer etc*) prendre qch dans; **to ~ sb out to a restaurant** emmener qn au restaurant; **take over** *vt* (*business*) reprendre ▷ *vi*: **to ~ over from sb** prendre la relève de qn; **take up** *vt* (*one's story*) reprendre; (*dress*) raccourcir; (*occupy: time, space*) prendre, occuper; (*engage in: hobby etc*) se mettre à; (*accept: offer, challenge*) accepter; **takeaway** (BRIT) *adj* (*food*) à emporter ▷ *n* (*shop, restaurant*) ≈ magasin *m* qui vend des plats à emporter; **taken** *pp of* **take**; **is this seat taken?** la place est prise?; **takeoff** *n* (Aviat) décollage *m*; **takeout** *adj*, *n* (US) = **takeaway**; **takeover** *n* (Comm) rachat *m*; **takings** *npl* (Comm) recette *f*

talc [tælk] *n* (*also:* **~um powder**) talc *m*

tale [teɪl] *n* (*story*) conte *m*, histoire *f*; (*account*) récit *m*; **to tell ~s** (*fig*) rapporter

talent ['tælnt] *n* talent *m*, don *m*; **talented** *adj* doué(e), plein(e) de talent

talk [tɔ:k] n (a speech) causerie f, exposé m; (conversation) discussion f; (interview) entretien m; (gossip) racontars mpl (pej) ▷ vi parler; (chatter) bavarder; **talks** npl (Pol etc) pourparlers mpl; **to ~ about** parler de; **to ~ sb out of/into doing** persuader qn de ne pas faire/de faire; **to ~ shop** parler métier or affaires; **talk over** vt discuter (de); **talk show** n (TV, Radio) émission-débat f

tall [tɔ:l] adj (person) grand(e); (building, tree) haut(e); **to be 6 feet ~** ≈ mesurer 1 mètre 80

tambourine [tæmbə'ri:n] n tambourin m

tame [teɪm] adj apprivoisé(e); (fig: story, style) insipide

tamper ['tæmpəʳ] vi: **to ~ with** toucher à (en cachette ou sans permission)

tampon ['tæmpɒn] n tampon m hygiénique or périodique

tan [tæn] n (also: **sun~**) bronzage m ▷ vt, vi bronzer, brunir ▷ adj (colour) marron clair inv

tandem ['tændəm] n tandem m

tangerine [tændʒə'ri:n] n mandarine f

tangle ['tæŋgl] n enchevêtrement m; **to get in(to) a ~** s'emmêler

tank [tæŋk] n réservoir m; (for fish) aquarium m; (Mil) char m d'assaut, tank m

tanker ['tæŋkəʳ] n (ship) pétrolier m, tanker m; (truck) camion-citerne m

tanned [tænd] adj bronzé(e)

tantrum ['tæntrəm] n accès m de colère

Tanzania [tænzə'nɪə] n Tanzanie f

tap [tæp] n (on sink etc) robinet m; (gentle blow) petite tape f ▷ vt frapper or taper légèrement; (resources) exploiter, utiliser; (telephone) mettre sur écoute; **on ~** (fig: resources) disponible; **tap dancing** n claquettes fpl

tape [teɪp] n (for tying) ruban m; (also: **magnetic ~**) bande f (magnétique); (cassette) cassette f; (sticky) Scotch® m ▷ vt (record) enregistrer (au magnétoscope or sur cassette); (stick) coller avec du Scotch®; **tape measure** n mètre m à ruban; **tape recorder** n magnétophone m

tapestry ['tæpɪstrɪ] n tapisserie f

tar [tɑ:] n goudron m

target ['tɑ:gɪt] n cible f; (fig: objective) objectif m

tariff ['tærɪf] n (Comm) tarif m; (taxes) tarif douanier

tarmac ['tɑ:mæk] n (BRIT: on road) macadam m; (Aviat) aire f d'envol

tarpaulin [tɑ:'pɔ:lɪn] n bâche goudronnée

tarragon ['tærəgən] n estragon m

tart [tɑ:t] n (Culin) tarte f; (BRIT inf: pej: prostitute) poule f ▷ adj (flavour) âpre, aigrelet(te)

tartan ['tɑ:tn] n tartan m ▷ adj écossais(e)

tartar(e) sauce n sauce f tartare

task [tɑ:sk] n tâche f; **to take to ~** prendre à partie

taste [teɪst] n goût m; (fig: glimpse, idea) idée f, aperçu m ▷ vt goûter ▷ vi: **to ~ of** (fish etc) avoir le or un goût de; **you can ~ the garlic (in it)** on sent bien l'ail; **to have a ~ of sth** goûter (à) qch; **can I have a ~?** je peux goûter?; **to be in good/bad** or **poor ~** être de bon/mauvais goût; **tasteful** adj de bon goût; **tasteless** adj (food) insipide; (remark) de mauvais goût; **tasty** adj savoureux(-euse), délicieux(-euse)

tatters ['tætəz] npl: **in ~** (also: **tattered**) en lambeaux

tattoo [tə'tu:] n tatouage m; (spectacle) parade f militaire ▷ vt tatouer

taught [tɔ:t] pt, pp of **teach**

taunt [tɔ:nt] n raillerie f ▷ vt railler

Taurus ['tɔ:rəs] n le Taureau

taut [tɔ:t] adj tendu(e)

tax [tæks] n (on goods etc) taxe f; (on income) impôts mpl, contributions fpl ▷ vt taxer; imposer; (fig: patience etc) mettre à l'épreuve; **tax disc** n (BRIT Aut) vignette f (automobile); **tax-free** adj exempt(e) d'impôts

taxi ['tæksɪ] n taxi m ▷ vi (Aviat) rouler (lentement) au sol; **can you call me a ~, please?** pouvez-vous m'appeler un taxi, s'il vous plaît?; **taxi driver** n chauffeur m de taxi; **taxi rank** (BRIT), **taxi stand** n station f de taxis

tax payer [-peɪəʳ] n contribuable m/f

tax return n déclaration f d'impôts or de revenus

TB n abbr = **tuberculosis**

tea [ti:] n thé m; (BRIT: snack: for children) goûter m; **high ~** (BRIT) collation combinant goûter et dîner; **tea bag** n sachet m de thé; **tea break** n (BRIT) pause-thé f

teach (pt, pp **taught**) [ti:tʃ, tɔ:t] vt: **to ~ sb sth, to ~ sth to sb** apprendre qch à qn; (in school etc) enseigner qch à qn ▷ vi enseigner; **teacher** n (in secondary school) professeur m; (in primary school) instituteur(-trice); **teaching** n enseignement m

tea : tea cloth n (BRIT) torchon m; **teacup** n tasse f à thé

tea leaves npl feuilles fpl de thé

team [ti:m] n équipe f; (of animals) attelage m; **team up** vi: **to ~ up (with)** faire équipe (avec)

teapot ['ti:pɒt] n théière f

tear¹ [tɪəʳ] n larme f; **in ~s** en larmes

tear² n [tɛəʳ] déchirure f ▷ vb (pt **tore**, pp **torn**) ▷ vt déchirer ▷ vi se déchirer; **tear apart** vt (also fig) déchirer; **tear down** vt (building, statue) démolir; (poster, flag) arracher; **tear off** vt (sheet of paper etc) arracher; (one's clothes) enlever à toute vitesse; **tear up** vt (sheet of paper etc) déchirer, mettre en morceaux or pièces

tearful ['tɪəful] *adj* larmoyant(e)

tear gas ['tɪə-] *n* gaz *m* lacrymogène

tearoom ['tiːruːm] *n* salon *m* de thé

tease [tiːz] *vt* taquiner; (*unkindly*) tourmenter

tea: **teaspoon** *n* petite cuiller; (*also*: **teaspoonful**: *as measurement*) ≈ cuillerée *f* à café; **teatime** *n* l'heure *f* du thé; **tea towel** *n* (BRIT) torchon *m* (à vaisselle)

technical ['tɛknɪkl] *adj* technique

technician [tɛk'nɪʃən] *n* technicien(ne)

technique [tɛk'niːk] *n* technique *f*

technology [tɛk'nɔlədʒɪ] *n* technologie *f*

teddy (bear) ['tɛdɪ-] *n* ours *m* (en peluche)

tedious ['tiːdɪəs] *adj* fastidieux(-euse)

tee [tiː] *n* (*Golf*) tee *m*

teen [tiːn] *adj* = **teenage** ▷ *n* (US) = **teenager**

teenage ['tiːneɪdʒ] *adj* (*fashions etc*) pour jeunes, pour adolescents; (*child*) qui est adolescent(e); **teenager** *n* adolescent(e)

teens [tiːnz] *npl*: **to be in one's ~** être adolescent(e)

teeth [tiːθ] *npl of* **tooth**

teetotal ['tiː'təutl] *adj* (*person*) qui ne boit jamais d'alcool

telecommunications ['tɛlɪkəmjuːnɪ'keɪʃənz] *n* télécommunications *fpl*

telegram ['tɛlɪɡræm] *n* télégramme *m*

telegraph pole ['tɛlɪɡrɑːf-] *n* poteau *m* télégraphique

telephone ['tɛlɪfəun] *n* téléphone *m* ▷ *vt* (*person*) téléphoner à; (*message*) téléphoner; **to be on the ~** (*be speaking*) être au téléphone; **telephone book** *n* = **telephone directory**; **telephone box** (BRIT), **telephone box** *n* cabine *f* téléphonique; **telephone call** *n* appel *m* téléphonique; **telephone directory** *n* annuaire *m* (du téléphone); **telephone number** *n* numéro *m* de téléphone

telesales ['tɛlɪseɪlz] *npl* télévente *f*

telescope ['tɛlɪskəup] *n* télescope *m*

televise ['tɛlɪvaɪz] *vt* téléviser

television ['tɛlɪvɪʒən] *n* télévision *f*; **on ~** à la télévision; **television programme** *n* émission *f* de télévision

tell (*pt, pp* **told**) [tɛl, təuld] *vt* dire; (*relate: story*) raconter; (*distinguish*): **to ~ sth from** distinguer qch de ▷ *vi* (*talk*): **to ~ of** parler de; (*have effect*) se faire sentir, se voir; **to ~ sb to do** dire à qn de faire; **to ~ the time** (*know how to*) savoir lire l'heure; **tell off** *vt* réprimander, gronder; **teller** *n* (*in bank*) caissier(-ière)

telly ['tɛlɪ] *n abbr* (BRIT *inf*: = *television*) télé *f*

temp [tɛmp] *n abbr* (BRIT = *temporary worker*) intérimaire *m/f* ▷ *vi* travailler comme intérimaire

temper ['tɛmpəʳ] *n* (*nature*) caractère *m*; (*mood*) humeur *f*; (*fit of anger*) colère *f* ▷ *vt* (*moderate*) tempérer, adoucir; **to be in a ~** être

en colère; **to lose one's ~** se mettre en colère

temperament ['tɛmprəmənt] *n* (*nature*) tempérament *m*; **temperamental** [tɛmprə'mɛntl] *adj* capricieux(-euse)

temperature ['tɛmprətʃəʳ] *n* température *f*; **to have** *or* **run a ~** avoir de la fièvre

temple ['tɛmpl] *n* (*building*) temple *m*; (*Anat*) tempe *f*

temporary ['tɛmpərərɪ] *adj* temporaire, provisoire; (*job, worker*) temporaire

tempt [tɛmpt] *vt* tenter; **to ~ sb into doing** induire qn à faire; **temptation** *n* tentation *f*; **tempting** *adj* tentant(e); (*food*) appétissant(e)

ten [tɛn] *num* dix

tenant ['tɛnənt] *n* locataire *m/f*

tend [tɛnd] *vt* s'occuper de ▷ *vi*: **to ~ to do** avoir tendance à faire; **tendency** ['tɛndənsɪ] *n* tendance *f*

tender ['tɛndəʳ] *adj* tendre; (*delicate*) délicat(e); (*sore*) sensible ▷ *n* (*Comm: offer*) soumission *f*; (*money*): **legal ~** cours légal ▷ *vt* offrir

tendon ['tɛndən] *n* tendon *m*

tenner ['tɛnəʳ] *n* (BRIT *inf*) billet *m* de dix livres

tennis ['tɛnɪs] *n* tennis *m*; **tennis ball** *n* balle *f* de tennis; **tennis court** *n* (court *m* de) tennis *m*; **tennis match** *n* match *m* de tennis; **tennis player** *n* joueur(-euse) de tennis; **tennis racket** *n* raquette *f* de tennis

tenor ['tɛnəʳ] *n* (*Mus*) ténor *m*

tenpin bowling ['tɛnpɪn-] *n* (BRIT) bowling *m* (à 10 quilles)

tense [tɛns] *adj* tendu(e) ▷ *n* (*Ling*) temps *m*

tension ['tɛnʃən] *n* tension *f*

tent [tɛnt] *n* tente *f*

tentative ['tɛntətɪv] *adj* timide, hésitant(e); (*conclusion*) provisoire

tenth [tɛnθ] *num* dixième

tent: **tent peg** *n* piquet *m* de tente; **tent pole** *n* montant *m* de tente

tepid ['tɛpɪd] *adj* tiède

term [təːm] *n* terme *m*; (*Scol*) trimestre *m* ▷ *vt* appeler; **terms** *npl* (*conditions*) conditions *fpl*; (*Comm*) tarif *m*; **in the short/long ~** à court/ long terme; **to come to ~s with** (*problem*) faire face à; **to be on good ~s with** bien s'entendre avec, être en bons termes avec

terminal ['təːmɪnl] *adj* (*disease*) dans sa phase terminale; (*patient*) incurable ▷ *n* (*Elec*) borne *f*; (*for oil, ore etc, also Comput*) terminal *m*; (*also*: **air ~**) aérogare *f*; (BRIT: *also*: **coach ~**) gare routière

terminate ['təːmɪneɪt] *vt* mettre fin à; (*pregnancy*) interrompre

termini ['təːmɪnaɪ] *npl of* **terminus**

terminology [təːmɪ'nɔlədʒɪ] *n* terminologie *f*

terminus (*pl* **termini**) ['təːmɪnəs, 'təːmɪnaɪ] *n* terminus *m inv*

terrace ['tɛrəs] n terrasse f; (BRIT: row of
houses) rangée f de maisons (attenantes les unes
aux autres); **the ~s** (BRIT Sport) les gradins mpl;
terraced adj (garden) en terrasses; (in a row:
house, cottage etc) attenant(e) aux maisons
voisines

terrain [tɛ'reɪn] n terrain m (sol)

terrestrial [tɪ'rɛstrɪəl] adj terrestre

terrible ['tɛrɪbl] adj terrible, atroce; (weather,
work) affreux(-euse), épouvantable; **terribly**
adv terriblement; (very badly) affreusement
mal

terrier ['tɛrɪəʳ] n terrier m (chien)

terrific [tə'rɪfɪk] adj (very great) fantastique,
incroyable, terrible; (wonderful) formidable,
sensationnel(le)

terrified ['tɛrɪfaɪd] adj terrifié(e); **to be ~ of
sth** avoir très peur de qch

terrify ['tɛrɪfaɪ] vt terrifier; **terrifying** adj
terrifiant(e)

territorial [tɛrɪ'tɔːrɪəl] adj territorial(e)

territory ['tɛrɪtərɪ] n territoire m

terror ['tɛrəʳ] n terreur f; **terrorism** n
terrorisme m; **terrorist** n terroriste m/f;
terrorist attack n attentat m terroriste

test [tɛst] n (trial, check) essai m; (: of courage
etc) épreuve f; (Med) examen m; (Chem) analyse
f; (Scol) interrogation f de contrôle; (also:
driving ~) (examen du) permis m de conduire
▷ vt essayer; mettre à l'épreuve; examiner;
analyser; faire subir une interrogation (de
contrôle) à

testicle ['tɛstɪkl] n testicule m

testify ['tɛstɪfaɪ] vi (Law) témoigner, déposer;
to ~ to sth (Law) attester qch

testimony ['tɛstɪmənɪ] n (Law) témoignage
m, déposition f

test: **test match** n (Cricket, Rugby) match
international; **test tube** n éprouvette f

tetanus ['tɛtənəs] n tétanos m

text [tɛkst] n texte m; (on mobile phone) texto m,
SMS m inv ▷ vt (inf) envoyer un texto or SMS à;
textbook n manuel m

textile ['tɛkstaɪl] n textile m

text message n texto m, SMS m inv

text messaging [-'mɛsɪdʒɪŋ] n messagerie
textuelle

texture ['tɛkstʃəʳ] n texture f; (of skin, paper
etc) grain m

Thai [taɪ] adj thaïlandais(e) ▷ n
Thaïlandais(e)

Thailand ['taɪlænd] n Thaïlande f

Thames [tɛmz] n: **the (River) ~** la Tamise

than [ðæn, ðən] conj que; (with numerals):
more ~ 10/once plus de
10/d'une fois; **I have more/less ~ you** j'en ai
plus/moins que toi; **she has more apples ~
pears** elle a plus de pommes que de poires; **it
is better to phone ~ to write** il vaut mieux

téléphoner (plutôt) qu'écrire; **she is older ~
you think** elle est plus âgée que tu le crois

thank [θæŋk] vt remercier, dire merci à;
thanks npl remerciements mpl ▷ excl merci!;
~ you (very much) merci (beaucoup);
~ God Dieu merci; **~s to** prep grâce à;
thankfully adv (fortunately) heureusement;
Thanksgiving (Day) n jour m d'action de
grâce; voir encadré

⬤ **THANKSGIVING (DAY)**
⬤
⬤ **Thanksgiving (Day)** est un jour de
⬤ congé aux États-Unis, le quatrième jeudi
⬤ du mois de novembre, commémorant
⬤ la bonne récolte que les Pèlerins venus
⬤ de Grande-Bretagne ont eue en 1621;
⬤ traditionnellement, c'était un jour où l'on
⬤ remerciait Dieu et où l'on organisait un
⬤ grand festin. Une fête semblable, mais qui
⬤ n'a aucun rapport avec les Pères Pèlerins, a
⬤ lieu au Canada le deuxième lundi d'octobre.

⬤ **KEYWORD**

that [ðæt] adj (demonstrative: pl **those**) ce, cet
+ vowel or h mute, cette f; **that man/woman/
book** cet homme/cette femme/ce livre; (not
this) cet homme-là/cette femme-là/ce livre-
là; **that one** celui-là (celle-là)
▷ pron **1** (demonstrative: pl **those**) ce; (not this
one) cela, ça; (that one) celui (celle); **who's
that?** qui est-ce?; **what's that?** qu'est-ce que
c'est?; **is that you?** c'est toi?; **I prefer this to
that** je préfère ceci à cela or ça; **that's what
he said** c'est or voilà ce qu'il a dit; **will you eat
all that?** est-ce que tu vas manger tout ça?;
that is (to say) c'est-à-dire, à savoir
2 (relative: subject) qui; (: object) que;
(: after prep) lequel (laquelle), lesquels
(lesquelles) pl; **the book that I read** le livre
que j'ai lu; **the books that are in the library**
les livres qui sont dans la bibliothèque; **all
that I have** tout ce que j'ai; **the box that I
put it in** la boîte dans laquelle je l'ai mis; **the
people that I spoke to** les gens auxquels or à
qui j'ai parlé
3 (relative: of time) où; **the day that he came**
le jour où il est venu
▷ conj que; **he thought that I was ill** il pensait
que j'étais malade
▷ adv (demonstrative): **I don't like it that
much** ça ne me plaît pas tant que ça; **I didn't
know it was that bad** je ne savais pas que
c'était si or aussi mauvais; **it's about that
high** c'est à peu près de cette hauteur

thatched [θætʃt] adj (roof) de chaume; **~
cottage** chaumière f

thaw [θɔː] *n* dégel *m* ▷ *vi* (ice) fondre; (food) dégeler ▷ *vt* (food) (faire) dégeler

 KEYWORD

the [ðiː, ðə] *def art* **1** (gen) le, la *f*, l' + *vowel or h mute*, les *pl* (NB: *à + le(s)* = **au(x)**; *de + le* = **du**; *de + les* = **des**); **the boy/girl/ink** le garçon/la fille/l'encre; **the children** les enfants; **the history of the world** l'histoire du monde; **give it to the postman** donne-le au facteur; **to play the piano/flute** jouer du piano/de la flûte **2** (+ *adj to form n*) le, la *f*, l' + *vowel or h mute*, les *pl*; **the rich and the poor** les riches et les pauvres; **to attempt the impossible** tenter l'impossible

3 (in titles): **Elizabeth the First** Elisabeth première; **Peter the Great** Pierre le Grand **4** (in comparisons): **the more he works, the more he earns** plus il travaille, plus il gagne de l'argent

theatre (*us* **theater**) ['θɪətər] *n* théâtre *m*; (Med: also: **operating ~**) salle *f* d'opération
theft [θɛft] *n* vol *m* (larcin)
their [ðɛər] *adj* leur, leurs *pl*; see also **my**; **theirs** *pron* le (la) leur, les leurs; see also **mine¹**
them [ðɛm, ðəm] *pron* (direct) les; (indirect) leur; (stressed, after prep) eux (elles); **give me a few of ~** donnez m'en quelques uns (or quelques unes); see also **me**
theme [θiːm] *n* thème *m*; **theme park** *n* parc *m* à thème
themselves [ðəm'sɛlvz] *pl pron* (reflexive) se; (emphatic, after prep) eux-mêmes (elles-mêmes); **between ~** entre eux (elles); see also **oneself**
then [ðɛn] *adv* (at that time) alors, à ce moment-là; (next) puis, ensuite; (and also) et puis ▷ *conj* (therefore) alors, dans ce cas ▷ *adj*: **the ~ president** le président d'alors or de l'époque; **by ~** (past) à ce moment-là; (future) d'ici là; **from ~ on** dès lors; **until ~** jusqu'à ce moment-là, jusque-là
theology [θɪ'ɔlədʒɪ] *n* théologie *f*
theory ['θɪərɪ] *n* théorie *f*
therapist ['θɛrəpɪst] *n* thérapeute *m/f*
therapy ['θɛrəpɪ] *n* thérapie *f*

 KEYWORD

there [ðɛər] *adv* **1**: **there is**, **there are** il y a; **there are 3 of them** (people, things) il y en a 3; **there is no-one here/no bread left** il n'y a personne/il n'y a plus de pain; **there has been an accident** il y a eu un accident

2 (referring to place) là, là-bas; **it's there** c'est là(-bas); **in/on/up/down there** là-dedans/là-dessus/là-haut/en bas; **he went there on**

Friday il y est allé vendredi; **I want that book there** je veux ce livre-là; **there he is!** le voilà! **3**: **there, there** (esp to child) allons, allons!

there: **thereabouts** *adv* (place) par là, près de là; (amount) environ, à peu près; **thereafter** *adv* par la suite; **thereby** *adv* ainsi; **therefore** *adv* donc, par conséquent
there's ['ðɛəz] = **there is**; **there has**
thermal ['θəːml] *adj* thermique; **~ underwear** sous-vêtements *mpl* en Thermolactyl®
thermometer [θə'mɔmɪtər] *n* thermomètre *m*
thermostat ['θəːməustæt] *n* thermostat *m*
these [ðiːz] *pl pron* ceux-ci (celles-ci) ▷ *pl adj* ces; (not those): **~ books** ces livres-ci
thesis (*pl* **theses**) ['θiːsɪs, 'θiːsiːz] *n* thèse *f*
they [ðeɪ] *pl pron* ils (elles); (stressed) eux (elles); **~ say that ...** (it is said that) on dit que ...; **they'd = they had**; **they would**; **they'll = they shall**; **they will**; **they're = they are**; **they've = they have**
thick [θɪk] *adj* épais(se); (stupid) bête, borné(e) ▷ *n*: **in the ~ of** au beau milieu de, en plein cœur de; **it's 20 cm ~** ça a 20 cm d'épaisseur; **thicken** *vi* s'épaissir ▷ *vt* (sauce etc) épaissir; **thickness** *n* épaisseur *f*
thief (*pl* **thieves**) [θiːf, θiːvz] *n* voleur(-euse)
thigh [θaɪ] *n* cuisse *f*
thin [θɪn] *adj* mince; (skinny) maigre; (soup) peu épais(se); (hair, crowd) clairsemé(e) ▷ *vt* (also: **~ down**: sauce, paint) délayer
thing [θɪŋ] *n* chose *f*; (object) objet *m*; (contraption) truc *m*; **things** *npl* (belongings) affaires *fpl*; **the ~ is ...** c'est que ...; **the best ~ would be to** le mieux serait de; **how are ~s?** comment ça va?; **to have a ~ about** (be obsessed by) être obsédé(e) par; (hate) détester; **poor ~!** le (or la) pauvre!
think (*pt, pp* **thought**) [θɪŋk, θɔːt] *vi* penser, réfléchir ▷ *vt* penser, croire; (imagine) s'imaginer; **what did you ~ of them?** qu'avez-vous pensé d'eux?; **to ~ about sth/sb** penser à qch/qn; **I'll ~ about it** je vais y réfléchir; **to ~ of doing** avoir l'idée de faire; **I ~ so/not** je crois que oui/non; **to ~ well of** avoir une haute opinion de; **think over** *vt* bien réfléchir à; **think up** *vt* inventer, trouver
third [θəːd] *num* troisième ▷ *n* (fraction) tiers *m*; (Aut) troisième (vitesse) *f*; (BRIT Scol: degree) ≈ licence *f* avec mention passable; **thirdly** *adv* troisièmement; **third party insurance** *n* (BRIT) assurance *f* au tiers; **Third World** *n*: **the Third World** le Tiers-Monde
thirst [θəːst] *n* soif *f*; **thirsty** *adj* qui a soif, assoiffé(e); (work) qui donne soif; **to be thirsty** avoir soif
thirteen [θəː'tiːn] *num* treize; **thirteenth** [-'tiːnθ] *num* treizième

thirtieth ['θɜːtɪɪθ] *num* trentième
thirty ['θɜːtɪ] *num* trente

KEYWORD

this [ðɪs] *adj* (*demonstrative: pl* **these**) ce, cet
+ *vowel or h mute*, cette *f*; **this man/woman/
book** cet homme/cette femme/ce livre; (*not
that*) cet homme-ci/cette femme-ci/ce livre-
ci; **this one** celui-ci (celle-ci)
▷ *pron* (*demonstrative: pl* **these**) ce; (*not that
one*) celui-ci (celle-ci), ceci; **who's this?** qui
est-ce?; **what's this?** qu'est-ce que c'est?; **I
prefer this to that** je préfère ceci à cela; **this
is where I live** c'est ici que j'habite; **this is
what he said** voici ce qu'il a dit; **this is Mr
Brown** (*in introductions*) je vous présente Mr
Brown; (*in photo*) c'est Mr Brown; (*on telephone*)
ici Mr Brown
▷ *adv* (*demonstrative*): **it was about this big**
c'était à peu près de cette grandeur *or* grand
comme ça; **I didn't know it was this bad** je
ne savais pas que c'était si *or* aussi mauvais

thistle ['θɪsl] *n* chardon *m*
thorn [θɔːn] *n* épine *f*
thorough ['θʌrə] *adj* (*search*)
minutieux(-euse); (*knowledge,
research*) approfondi(e); (*work, person*)
consciencieux(-euse); (*cleaning*) à fond;
thoroughly *adv* (*search*) minutieusement;
(*study*) en profondeur; (*clean*) à fond; (*very*)
tout à fait
those [ðəʊz] *pl pron* ceux-là (celles-là) ▷ *pl adj*
ces; (*not these*): **~ books** ces livres-là
though [ðəʊ] *conj* bien que + *sub*, quoique +
sub ▷ *adv* pourtant
thought [θɔːt] *pt, pp of* **think** ▷ *n* pensée
f; (*idea*) idée *f*; (*opinion*) avis *m*; **thoughtful**
adj (*deep in thought*) pensif(-ive); (*serious*)
réfléchi(e); (*considerate*) prévenant(e);
thoughtless *adj* qui manque de
considération
thousand ['θaʊzənd] *num* mille; **one ~**
mille; **two ~** deux mille; **~s of** des milliers de;
thousandth *num* millième
thrash [θræʃ] *vt* rouer de coups; (*as
punishment*) donner une correction à; (*inf:
defeat*) battre à plate(s) couture(s)
thread [θrɛd] *n* fil *m*; (*of screw*) pas *m*, filetage
m ▷ *vt* (*needle*) enfiler
threat [θrɛt] *n* menace *f*; **threaten** *vi* (*storm*)
menacer ▷ *vt*: **to threaten sb with sth/to do**
menacer qn de qch/de faire; **threatening** *adj*
menaçant(e)
three [θriː] *num* trois; **three-dimensional** *adj*
à trois dimensions; **three-piece suite** *n* salon
m (canapé et deux fauteuils); **three-quarters**
npl trois-quarts *mpl*; **three-quarters full** aux
trois-quarts plein
threshold ['θrɛʃhəʊld] *n* seuil *m*
threw [θruː] *pt of* **throw**
thrill [θrɪl] *n* (*excitement*) émotion *f*, sensation
forte; (*shudder*) frisson *m* ▷ *vt* (*audience*)
électriser; **thrilled** *adj*: **thrilled (with)** ravi(e)
de; **thriller** *n* film *m* (*or roman m or pièce
f*) à suspense; **thrilling** *adj* (*book, play etc*)
saisissant(e); (*news, discovery*) excitant(e)
thriving ['θraɪvɪŋ] *adj* (*business, community*)
prospère
throat [θrəʊt] *n* gorge *f*; **to have a sore ~**
avoir mal à la gorge
throb [θrɒb] *vi* (*heart*) palpiter; (*engine*) vibrer;
my head is ~bing j'ai des élancements dans
la tête
throne [θrəʊn] *n* trône *m*
through [θruː] *prep* à travers; (*time*) pendant,
durant; (*by means of*) par, par l'intermédiaire
de; (*owing to*) à cause de ▷ *adj* (*ticket, train,
passage*) direct(e) ▷ *adv* à travers; **(from)
Monday ~ Friday** (*us*) de lundi à vendredi;
to put sb ~ to sb (*Tel*) passer qn à qn; **to
be ~** (*Brit: Tel*) avoir la communication; (*esp
us: have finished*) avoir fini; **"no ~ traffic"**
(*us*) "passage interdit"; **"no ~ road"** (*Brit*)
"impasse"; **throughout** *prep* (*place*) partout
dans; (*time*) durant tout(e) le (la) ▷ *adv* partout
throw [θrəʊ] *n* jet *m*; (*Sport*) lancer *m* ▷ *vt* (*pt
threw, pp **~n***) lancer, jeter; (*Sport*) lancer;
(*rider*) désarçonner; (*fig*) déconcerter; **to ~
a party** donner une réception; **throw away**
vt jeter; (*money*) gaspiller; **throw in** *vt* (*Sport:
ball*) remettre en jeu; (*include*) ajouter; **throw
off** *vt* se débarrasser de; **throw out** *vt* jeter;
(*reject*) rejeter; (*person*) mettre à la porte;
throw up *vi* vomir
thru [θruː] (*us*) (= **through**
thrush [θrʌʃ] *n* (*Zool*) grive *f*
thrust [θrʌst] *vt* (*pt, pp ~*) pousser
brusquement; (*push in*) enfoncer
thud [θʌd] *n* bruit sourd
thug [θʌg] *n* voyou *m*
thumb [θʌm] *n* (*Anat*) pouce *m* ▷ *vt*: **to ~ a
lift** faire de l'auto-stop, arrêter une voiture;
thumbtack *n* (*us*) punaise *f* (*clou*)
thump [θʌmp] *n* grand coup; (*sound*) bruit
sourd ▷ *vt* cogner sur ▷ *vi* cogner, frapper
thunder ['θʌndər] *n* tonnerre *m* ▷ *vi*
tonner; (*train etc*): **to ~ past** passer dans
un grondement *or* un bruit de tonnerre;
thunderstorm *n* orage *m*
Thur(s) *abbr* (= Thursday) jeu
Thursday ['θɜːzdɪ] *n* jeudi *m*
thus [ðʌs] *adv* ainsi
thwart [θwɔːt] *vt* contrecarrer
thyme [taɪm] *n* thym *m*
Tibet [tɪˈbɛt] *n* Tibet *m*
tick [tɪk] *n* (*sound: of clock*) tic-tac *m*; (*mark*)

coche f; (Zool) tique f; (BRIT inf): **in a ~** dans un instant ▷ vi faire tic-tac ▷ vt (item on list) cocher; **tick off** vt (item on list) cocher; (person) réprimander, attraper

ticket ['tɪkɪt] n billet m; (for bus, tube) ticket m; (in shop: on goods) étiquette f; (for library) carte f; (also: **parking ~**) contravention f, p.-v. m; **ticket barrier** n (BRIT: Rail) portillon m automatique; **ticket collector** n contrôleur(-euse); **ticket inspector** n contrôleur(-euse); **ticket machine** n billetterie f automatique; **ticket office** n guichet m, bureau m de vente des billets

tickle ['tɪkl] vi chatouiller ▷ vt chatouiller; **ticklish** adj (person) chatouilleux(-euse); (problem) épineux(-euse)

tide [taɪd] n marée f; (fig: of events) cours m

tidy ['taɪdɪ] adj (room) bien rangé(e); (dress, work) net (nette), soigné(e); (person) ordonné(e), qui a de l'ordre ▷ vt (also: **~ up**) ranger

tie [taɪ] n (string etc) cordon m; (BRIT: also: **neck~**) cravate f; (fig: link) lien m; (Sport: draw) égalité f de points; match nul ▷ vt (parcel) attacher; (ribbon) nouer ▷ vi (Sport) faire match nul; finir à égalité de points; **to ~ sth in a bow** faire un nœud à or avec qch; **to ~ a knot in sth** faire un nœud à qch; **tie down** vt (fig): **to ~ sb down to** contraindre qn à accepter; **to feel ~d down** (by relationship) se sentir coincé(e); **tie up** vt (parcel) ficeler; (dog, boat) attacher; (prisoner) ligoter; (arrangements) conclure; **to be ~d up** (busy) être pris(e) or occupé(e)

tier [tɪər] n gradin m; (of cake) étage m

tiger ['taɪɡər] n tigre m

tight [taɪt] adj (rope) tendu(e), raide; (clothes) étroit(e), très juste; (budget, programme, bend) serré(e); (control) strict(e), sévère; (inf: drunk) ivre, rond(e) ▷ adv (squeeze) très fort; (shut) à bloc, hermétiquement; **hold ~!** accrochez-vous bien!; **tighten** vt (rope) tendre; (screw) resserrer; (control) renforcer ▷ vi se tendre; se resserrer; **tightly** adv (grasp) bien, très fort; **tights** npl (BRIT) collant m

tile [taɪl] n (on roof) tuile f; (on wall or floor) carreau m

till [tɪl] n caisse (enregistreuse) ▷ prep, conj = **until**

tilt [tɪlt] vt pencher, incliner ▷ vi pencher, être incliné(e)

timber ['tɪmbər] n (material) bois m de construction

time [taɪm] n temps m; (epoch: often pl) époque f, temps; (by clock) heure f; (moment) moment m; (occasion, also Math) fois f; (Mus) mesure f ▷ vt (race) chronométrer; (programme) minuter; (visit) fixer; (remark etc) choisir le moment de; **a long ~** un long moment, longtemps;

four at a ~ quatre à la fois; **for the ~ being** pour le moment; **from ~ to ~** de temps en temps; **at ~s** parfois; **in ~** (soon enough) à temps; (after some time) avec le temps, à la longue; (Mus) en mesure; **in a week's ~** dans une semaine; **in no ~** en un rien de temps; **any ~** n'importe quand; **on ~** à l'heure; **5 ~s 5** 5 fois 5; **what ~ is it?** quelle heure est-il?; **what ~ is the museum/shop open?** à quelle heure ouvre le musée/magasin?; **to have a good ~** bien s'amuser; **time limit** n limite f de temps, délai m; **timely** adj opportun(e); **timer** (in kitchen) compte-minutes m inv; (Tech) minuteur m; **time-share** n maison f/ appartement m en multipropriété; **timetable** n (Rail) (indicateur m) horaire m; (Scol) emploi m du temps; **time zone** n fuseau m horaire

timid ['tɪmɪd] adj timide; (easily scared) peureux(-euse)

timing ['taɪmɪŋ] n (Sport) chronométrage m; **the ~ of his resignation** le moment choisi pour sa démission

tin [tɪn] n étain m; (also: **~ plate**) fer-blanc m; (BRIT: can) boîte f (de conserve); (: for baking) moule m (à gâteau); (for storage) boîte f; **tinfoil** n papier m d'étain or d'aluminium

tingle ['tɪŋɡl] vi picoter; (person) avoir des picotements

tinker ['tɪŋkər]; **tinker with** vt fus bricoler, rafistoler

tinned [tɪnd] adj (BRIT: food) en boîte, en conserve

tin opener [-'əʊpnər] n (BRIT) ouvre-boîte(s) m

tinsel ['tɪnsl] n guirlandes fpl de Noël (argentées)

tint [tɪnt] n teinte f; (for hair) shampooing colorant; **tinted** adj (hair) teint(e); (spectacles, glass) teinté(e)

tiny ['taɪnɪ] adj minuscule

tip [tɪp] n (end) bout m; (gratuity) pourboire m; (BRIT: for rubbish) décharge f; (advice) tuyau m ▷ vt (waiter) donner un pourboire à; (tilt) incliner; (overturn: also: **~ over**) renverser; (empty: also: **~ out**) déverser; **how much should I ~?** combien de pourboire est-ce qu'il faut laisser?; **tip off** vt prévenir, avertir

tiptoe ['tɪptəʊ] n: **on ~** sur la pointe des pieds

tire ['taɪər] n (US) = **tyre** ▷ vt fatiguer ▷ vi se fatiguer; **tired** adj fatigué(e); **to be tired of** en avoir assez de, être las (lasse) de; **tire pressure** (US) = **tyre pressure**; **tiring** adj fatigant(e)

tissue ['tɪʃuː] n tissu m; (paper handkerchief) mouchoir m en papier, kleenex® m; **tissue paper** n papier m de soie

tit [tɪt] n (bird) mésange f; **to give ~ for tat** rendre coup pour coup

title ['taɪtl] n titre m

T-junction ['tiː'dʒʌŋkʃən] n croisement m en T

TM *n abbr* = trademark

 KEYWORD

to [tuː, tə] *prep* 1 (*direction*) à; (*towards*) vers; envers; (*to go to France/Portugal/London/school*) aller en France/au Portugal/à Londres/à l'école; **to go to Claude's/the doctor's** aller chez Claude/le docteur; **the road to Edinburgh** la route d'Édimbourg
2 (*as far as*) (jusqu')à; **to count to 10** compter jusqu'à 10; **from 40 to 50 people** de 40 à 50 personnes
3 (*with expressions of time*): **a quarter to 5** 5 heures moins le quart; **it's twenty to 3** il est 3 heures moins vingt
4 (*for, of*) de; **the key to the front door** la clé de la porte d'entrée; **a letter to his wife** une lettre (adressée) à sa femme
5 (*expressing indirect object*) à; **to give sth to sb** donner qch à qn; **to talk to sb** parler à qn; **to be a danger to sb** être dangereux(-euse) pour qn
6 (*in relation to*) à; **3 goals to 2** 3 (buts) à 2; **30 miles to the gallon** ≈ 9,4 litres aux cent (km)
7 (*purpose, result*): **to come to sb's aid** venir au secours de qn, porter secours à qn; **to sentence sb to death** condamner qn à mort; **to my surprise** à ma grande surprise
▷ *with vb* 1 (*simple infinitive*): **to go/eat** aller/manger
2 (*following another vb*): **to want/try/start to do** vouloir/essayer de/commencer à faire
3 (*with vb omitted*): **I don't want to** je ne veux pas
4 (*purpose, result*) pour; **I did it to help you** je l'ai fait pour vous aider
5 (*equivalent to relative clause*): **I have things to do** j'ai des choses à faire; **the main thing is to try** l'important est d'essayer
6 (*after adjective etc*): **ready to go** prêt(e) à partir; **too old/young to ...** trop vieux/jeune pour ...
▷ *adv*: **push/pull the door to** tirez/poussez la porte

toad [təud] *n* crapaud *m*; **toadstool** *n* champignon (vénéneux)
toast [təust] *n* (*Culin*) pain grillé, toast *m*; (*drink, speech*) toast ▷ *vt* (*Culin*) faire griller; (*drink to*) porter un toast à; **toaster** *n* grille-pain *m inv*
tobacco [tə'bækəu] *n* tabac *m*
toboggan [tə'bɔgən] *n* toboggan *m*; (*child's*) luge *f*
today [tə'deɪ] *adv, n* (*also fig*) aujourd'hui (*m*)
toddler ['tɔdlə'] *n* enfant *m/f* qui commence à marcher, bambin *m*
toe [təu] *n* doigt *m* de pied, orteil *m*; (*of shoe*)

bout *m* ▷ *vt*: **to ~ the line** (*fig*) obéir, se conformer; **toenail** *n* ongle *m* de l'orteil
toffee ['tɔfɪ] *n* caramel *m*
together [tə'geðə'] *adv* ensemble; (*at same time*) en même temps; **~ with** *prep* avec
toilet ['tɔɪlət] *n* (*BRIT: lavatory*) toilettes *fpl*, cabinets *mpl*; **to go to the ~** aller aux toilettes; **where's the ~?** où sont les toilettes?; **toilet bag** *n* (*BRIT*) nécessaire *m* de toilette; **toilet paper** *n* papier *m* hygiénique; **toiletries** *npl* articles *mpl* de toilette; **toilet roll** *n* rouleau *m* de papier hygiénique
token ['təukən] *n* (*sign*) marque *f*, témoignage *m*; (*metal disc*) jeton *m* ▷ *adj* (*fee, strike*) symbolique; **book/record ~** (*BRIT*) chèque-livre/-disque *m*
Tokyo ['təukjəu] *n* Tokyo
told [təuld] *pt, pp of* **tell**
tolerant ['tɔlərnt] *adj*: **~ (of)** tolérant(e) (à l'égard de)
tolerate ['tɔləreɪt] *vt* supporter
toll [təul] *n* (*tax, charge*) péage *m* ▷ *vi* (*bell*) sonner; **the accident ~ on the roads** le nombre des victimes de la route; **toll call** *n* (*US Tel*) appel *m* (à) longue distance; **toll-free** *adj* (*US*) gratuit(e) ▷ *adv* gratuitement
tomato [tə'mɑːtəu] (*pl* **~es**) *n* tomate *f*; **tomato sauce** *n* sauce *f* tomate
tomb [tuːm] *n* tombe *f*; **tombstone** *n* pierre tombale
tomorrow [tə'mɔrəu] *adv, n* (*also fig*) demain (*m*); **the day after ~** après-demain; **a week ~** demain en huit; **~ morning** demain matin
ton [tʌn] *n* tonne *f* (*BRIT: = 1016 kg; US = 907 kg; metric: = 1000 kg*); **~s of** (*inf*) des tas de
tone [təun] *n* ton *m*; (*of radio, BRIT Tel*) tonalité *f* ▷ *vi* (*also:* **~ in**) s'harmoniser; **tone down** *vt* (*colour, criticism*) adoucir
tongs [tɔŋz] *npl* pinces *fpl*; (*for coal*) pincettes *fpl*; (*for hair*) fer *m* à friser
tongue [tʌŋ] *n* langue *f*; **~ in cheek** *adv* ironiquement
tonic ['tɔnɪk] *n* (*Med*) tonique *m*; (*also:* **~ water**) Schweppes® *m*
tonight [tə'naɪt] *adv, n* cette nuit; (*this evening*) ce soir
tonne [tʌn] *n* (*BRIT: metric ton*) tonne *f*
tonsil ['tɔnsl] *n* amygdale *f*; **tonsillitis** [tɔnsɪ'laɪtɪs] *n*: **to have tonsillitis** avoir une angine *or* une amygdalite
too [tuː] *adv* (*excessively*) trop; (*also*) aussi; **~ much** (*as adv*) trop; (*as adj*) trop de; **~ many** *adj* trop de
took [tuk] *pt of* **take**
tool [tuːl] *n* outil *m*; **tool box** *n* boîte *f* à outils; **tool kit** *n* trousse *f* à outils
tooth [tuːθ] (*pl* **teeth**) [tiːθ] *n* (*Anat, Tech*) dent *f*; **to brush one's teeth** se laver les dents; **toothache** *n* mal *m* de dents; **to have**

toothache avoir mal aux dents; **toothbrush** n brosse f à dents; **toothpaste** n (pâte f) dentifrice m; **toothpick** n cure-dent m

top [tɔp] n (of mountain, head) sommet m; (of page, ladder) haut m; (of box, cupboard, table) dessus m; (lid: of box, jar) couvercle m; (: of bottle) bouchon m; (toy) toupie f; (Dress: blouse etc) haut; (: of pyjamas) veste f ▷ adj du haut; (in rank) premier(-ière); (best) meilleur(e) ▷ vt (exceed) dépasser; (be first in) être en tête de; **from ~ to bottom** de fond en comble; **on ~ of** sur; (in addition to) en plus de; **over the ~** (inf: behaviour etc) qui dépasse les limites; **top up** (US **top off**) vt (bottle) remplir; (salary) compléter; **to ~ up one's mobile (phone)** recharger son compte; **top floor** n dernier étage; **top hat** n haut-de-forme m

topic ['tɔpɪk] n sujet m, thème m; **topical** adj d'actualité

topless ['tɔplɪs] adj (bather etc) aux seins nus

topping ['tɔpɪŋ] n (Culin) couche de crème, fromage etc qui recouvre un plat

topple ['tɔpl] vt renverser, faire tomber ▷ vi basculer; tomber

top-up ['tɔpʌp] n (for mobile phone) recharge f, minutes fpl; **top-up card** n (for mobile phone) recharge f

torch [tɔːtʃ] n torche f; (BRIT: electric) lampe f de poche

tore [tɔːʳ] pt of **tear²**

torment n ['tɔːmɛnt] tourment m ▷ vt [tɔː'mɛnt] tourmenter; (fig: annoy) agacer

torn [tɔːn] pp of **tear²**

tornado [tɔː'neɪdəu] (pl **-es**) n tornade f

torpedo [tɔː'piːdəu] (pl **-es**) n torpille f

torrent ['tɔrnt] n torrent m; **torrential** [tɔ'rɛnʃl] adj torrentiel(le)

tortoise ['tɔːtəs] n tortue f

torture ['tɔːtʃəʳ] n torture f ▷ vt torturer

Tory ['tɔːrɪ] adj, n (BRIT Pol) tory m/f, conservateur(-trice)

toss [tɔs] vt lancer, jeter; (BRIT: pancake) faire sauter; (head) rejeter en arrière ▷ vi: **to ~ up for sth** (BRIT) jouer qch à pile ou face; **to ~ a coin** jouer à pile ou face; **to ~ and turn** (in bed) se tourner et se retourner

total ['təutl] adj total(e) ▷ n total m ▷ vt (add up) faire le total de, additionner; (amount to) s'élever à

totalitarian [təutælɪ'tɛərɪən] adj totalitaire

totally ['təutəlɪ] adv totalement

touch [tʌtʃ] n contact m, toucher m; (sense, skill: of pianist etc) toucher ▷ vt (gen) toucher; (tamper with) toucher à; **a ~ of** (fig) un petit peu de; une touche de; **to get in ~ with** prendre contact avec; **to lose ~** (friends) se perdre de vue; **touch down** vi (Aviat) atterrir; (on sea) amerrir; **touchdown** n (Aviat) atterrissage m; (on sea) amerrissage m; (US Football) essai m;

touched adj (moved) touché(e); **touching** adj touchant(e), attendrissant(e); **touchline** n (Sport) (ligne f de) touche f; **touch-sensitive** adj (keypad) à effleurement; (screen) tactile

tough [tʌf] adj dur(e); (resistant) résistant(e), solide; (meat) dur, coriace; (firm) inflexible; (task, problem, situation) difficile

tour ['tuəʳ] n voyage m; (also: **package ~**) voyage organisé; (of town, museum) tour m, visite f; (by band) tournée f ▷ vt visiter; **tour guide** n (person) guide m/f

tourism ['tuərɪzm] n tourisme m

tourist ['tuərɪst] n touriste m/f ▷ cpd touristique; **tourist office** n syndicat m d'initiative

tournament ['tuənəmənt] n tournoi m

tour operator n (BRIT) organisateur m de voyages, tour-opérateur m

tow [təu] vt remorquer; (caravan, trailer) tracter; **"on ~"**, (US) **"in ~"** (Aut) "véhicule en remorque"; **tow away** vt (subj: police) emmener à la fourrière; (: breakdown service) remorquer

toward(s) [tə'wɔːd(z)] prep vers; (of attitude) envers, à l'égard de; (of purpose) pour

towel ['tauəl] n serviette f (de toilette); **towelling** n (fabric) tissu-éponge m

tower ['tauəʳ] n tour f; **tower block** n (BRIT) tour f (d'habitation)

town [taun] n ville f; **to go to ~** aller en ville; (fig) y mettre le paquet; **town centre** n (BRIT) centre m de la ville, centre-ville m; **town hall** n ≈ mairie f

tow truck n (US) dépanneuse f

toxic ['tɔksɪk] adj toxique

toy [tɔɪ] n jouet m; **toy with** vt fus jouer avec; (idea) caresser; **toyshop** n magasin m de jouets

trace [treɪs] n trace f ▷ vt (draw) tracer, dessiner; (follow) suivre la trace de; (locate) retrouver

tracing paper ['treɪsɪŋ-] n papier-calque m

track [træk] n (mark) trace f; (path: gen) chemin m, piste f; (: of bullet etc) trajectoire f; (: of suspect, animal) piste f; (Rail) voie ferrée, rails mpl; (on tape, Comput, Sport) piste; (on CD) piste f; (on record) plage f ▷ vt suivre la trace or la piste de; **to keep ~ of** suivre; **track down** vt (prey) trouver et capturer; (sth lost) finir par retrouver; **tracksuit** n survêtement m

tractor ['træktəʳ] n tracteur m

trade [treɪd] n commerce m; (skill, job) métier m ▷ vi faire du commerce ▷ vt (exchange): **to ~ sth (for sth)** échanger qch (contre qch); **to ~ with/in** faire du commerce avec/le commerce de; **trade in** vt (old car etc) faire reprendre; **trademark** n marque f de fabrique; **trader** n commerçant(e), négociant(e); **tradesman** (irreg) n (shopkeeper) commerçant m; **trade**

union n syndicat m

trading ['treɪdɪŋ] n affaires fpl, commerce m

tradition [trə'dɪʃən] n tradition f; **traditional** adj traditionnel(le)

traffic ['træfɪk] n trafic m; (cars) circulation f ▷ vi: **to ~ in** (pej: liquor, drugs) faire le trafic de; **traffic circle** n (US) rond-point m; **traffic island** n refuge m (pour piétons); **traffic jam** n embouteillage m; **traffic lights** npl feux mpl (de signalisation); **traffic warden** n contractuel(le)

tragedy ['trædʒədɪ] n tragédie f

tragic ['trædʒɪk] adj tragique

trail [treɪl] n (tracks) trace f, piste f; (path) chemin m, piste; (of smoke etc) traînée f ▷ vt (drag) traîner, tirer; (follow) suivre ▷ vi traîner; (in game, contest) être en retard; **trailer** n (Aut) remorque f; (US) caravane f; (Cine) bande-annonce f

train [treɪn] n train m; (in underground) rame f; (of dress) traîne f; (BRIT: series): **~ of events** série f d'événements ▷ vt (apprentice, doctor etc) former; (Sport) entraîner; (dog) dresser; (memory) exercer; (point: gun etc): **to ~ sth on** braquer qch sur ▷ vi recevoir sa formation; (Sport) s'entraîner; **one's ~ of thought** le fil de sa pensée; **what time does the ~ from Paris get in?** à quelle heure arrive le train de Paris?; **is this the ~ for ...?** c'est bien le train pour...?; **trainee** [treɪ'niː] n stagiaire m/f; (in trade) apprenti(e); **trainer** n (Sport) entraîneur(-euse); (of dogs etc) dresseur(-euse); **trainers** npl (shoes) chaussures fpl de sport; **training** n formation f; (Sport) entraînement m; (of dog etc) dressage m; **in training** (Sport) à l'entraînement; (fit) en forme; **training course** n cours m de formation professionnelle; **training shoes** npl chaussures fpl de sport

trait [treɪt] n trait m (de caractère)

traitor ['treɪtər] n traître m

tram [træm] n (BRIT: also: **~car**) tram(way) m

tramp [træmp] n (person) vagabond(e), clochard(e); (inf: pej: woman): **to be a ~** être coureuse

trample ['træmpl] vt: **to ~ (underfoot)** piétiner

trampoline ['træmpəliːn] n trampoline m

tranquil ['træŋkwɪl] adj tranquille; **tranquillizer** (US **tranquilizer**) n (Med) tranquillisant m

transaction [træn'zækʃən] n transaction f

transatlantic ['trænzət'læntɪk] adj transatlantique

transcript ['trænskrɪpt] n transcription f (texte)

transfer n ['trænsfər] (gen, also Sport) transfert m; (Pol: of power) passation f; (of money) virement m; (picture, design) décalcomanie f; (: stick-on) autocollant m ▷ vt [træns'fəː] transférer; passer; virer; **to ~ the charges** (BRIT Tel) téléphoner en P.C.V.

transform [træns'fɔːm] vt transformer; **transformation** n transformation f

transfusion [træns'fjuːʒən] n transfusion f

transit ['trænzɪt] n: **in ~** en transit

transition [træn'zɪʃən] n transition f

transitive ['trænzɪtɪv] adj (Ling) transitif(-ive)

translate [trænz'leɪt] vt: **to ~ (from/into)** traduire (du/en); **can you ~ this for me?** pouvez-vous me traduire ceci?; **translation** [trænz'leɪʃən] n traduction f; (Scol: as opposed to prose) version f; **translator** n traducteur(-trice)

transmission [trænz'mɪʃən] n transmission f

transmit [trænz'mɪt] vt transmettre; (Radio, TV) émettre; **transmitter** n émetteur m

transparent [træns'pærnt] adj transparent(e)

transplant n ['trænsplɑːnt] (Med) transplantation f

transport n ['trænspɔːt] transport m ▷ vt [træns'pɔːt] transporter; **transportation** [trænspɔː'teɪʃən] n (moyen m de) transport m

transvestite [trænz'vestaɪt] n travesti m

trap [træp] n (snare, trick) piège m; (carriage) cabriolet m ▷ vt prendre au piège; (confine) coincer

trash [træʃ] n (pej: goods) camelote f; (: nonsense) sottises fpl; (US: rubbish) ordures fpl; **trash can** n (US) poubelle f

trauma ['trɔːmə] n traumatisme m; **traumatic** [trɔː'mætɪk] adj traumatisant(e)

travel ['trævl] n voyage(s) m(pl) ▷ vi voyager; (news, sound) se propager ▷ vt (distance) parcourir; **travel agency** n agence f de voyages; **travel agent** n agent m de voyages; **travel insurance** n assurance-voyage f; **traveller** (US **traveler**) n voyageur(-euse); **traveller's cheque** (US **traveler's check**) n chèque m de voyage; **travelling** (US **traveling**) n voyage(s) m(pl); **travel-sick** adj: **to get travel-sick** avoir le mal de la route (or de mer or de l'air); **travel sickness** n mal m de la route (or de mer or de l'air)

tray [treɪ] n (for carrying) plateau m; (on desk) corbeille f

treacherous ['tretʃərəs] adj traître(sse); (ground, tide) dont il faut se méfier

treacle ['triːkl] n mélasse f

tread [tred] n (step) pas m; (sound) bruit m de pas; (of tyre) chape f, bande f de roulement ▷ vi (pt **trod**, pp **trodden**) marcher; **tread on** vt fus marcher sur

treasure ['treʒər] n trésor m ▷ vt (value) tenir beaucoup à; **treasurer** n trésorier(-ière)

treasury ['treʒərɪ] n: **the T~**, (US) **the T~ Department** ≈ le ministère des Finances

treat [tri:t] n petit cadeau, petite surprise
▷ vt traiter; **to ~ sb to sth** offrir qch à qn;
treatment n traitement m

treaty ['tri:tɪ] n traité m

treble ['trɛbl] adj triple ▷ vt, vi tripler

tree [tri:] n arbre m

trek [trɛk] n (long walk) randonnée f; (tiring
walk) longue marche, trotte f

tremble ['trɛmbl] vi trembler

tremendous [trɪ'mɛndəs] adj (enormous)
énorme; (excellent) formidable, fantastique

trench [trɛntʃ] n tranchée f

trend [trɛnd] n (tendency) tendance f; (of
events) cours m; (fashion) mode f; **trendy** adj
(idea, person) dans le vent; (clothes) dernier
cri inv

trespass ['trɛspəs] vi: **to ~ on** s'introduire sans
permission dans; **"no ~ing"** "propriété privée",
"défense d'entrer"

trial ['traɪəl] n (Law) procès m, jugement
m; (test: of machine etc) essai m; **trials** npl
(unpleasant experiences) épreuves fpl; **trial
period** n période f d'essai

triangle ['traɪæŋgl] n (Math, Mus) triangle m

triangular [traɪ'æŋgjulər] adj triangulaire

tribe [traɪb] n tribu f

tribunal [traɪ'bju:nl] n tribunal m

tribute ['trɪbju:t] n tribut m, hommage m; **to
pay ~ to** rendre hommage à

trick [trɪk] n (magic) tour m; (joke, prank) tour,
farce f; (skill, knack) astuce f; (Cards) levée f
▷ vt attraper, rouler; **to play a ~ on sb** jouer
un tour à qn; **that should do the ~** (fam) ça
devrait faire l'affaire

trickle ['trɪkl] n (of water etc) filet m ▷ vi couler
en un filet or goutte à goutte

tricky ['trɪkɪ] adj difficile, délicat(e)

tricycle ['traɪsɪkl] n tricycle m

trifle ['traɪfl] n bagatelle f; (Culin) ≈ diplomate
m ▷ adv: **a ~ long** un peu long

trigger ['trɪgər] n (of gun) gâchette f

trim [trɪm] adj (house, garden) bien tenu(e);
(figure) svelte ▷ n (haircut etc) légère coupe;
(on car) garnitures fpl ▷ vt (cut) couper
légèrement; (decorate): **to ~ (with)** décorer
(de); (Naut: a sail) gréer

trio ['tri:əu] n trio m

trip [trɪp] n voyage m; (excursion) excursion
f; (stumble) faux pas ▷ vi faire un faux pas,
trébucher; **trip up** vi trébucher ▷ vt faire un
croc-en-jambe à

triple ['trɪpl] adj triple

triplets ['trɪplɪts] npl triplés(-ées)

tripod ['traɪpɔd] n trépied m

triumph ['traɪʌmf] n triomphe m ▷ vi:
to ~ (over) triompher (de); **triumphant**
[traɪ'ʌmfənt] adj triomphant(e)

trivial ['trɪvɪəl] adj insignifiant(e);
(commonplace) banal(e)

trod [trɔd] pt of **tread**

trodden ['trɔdn] pp of **tread**

trolley ['trɔlɪ] n chariot m

trombone [trɔm'bəun] n trombone m

troop [tru:p] n bande f, groupe m; **troops**
npl (Mil) troupes fpl; (: men) hommes mpl,
soldats mpl

trophy ['trəufɪ] n trophée m

tropical ['trɔpɪkl] adj tropical(e)

trot [trɔt] n trot m ▷ vi trotter; **on the ~** (BRIT:
fig) d'affilée

trouble ['trʌbl] n difficulté(s) f(pl), problème(s)
m(pl); (worry) ennuis mpl, soucis mpl; (bother,
effort) peine f; (Pol) conflit(s) m(pl), troubles
mpl; (Med): **stomach** etc **~** troubles gastriques
etc ▷ vt (disturb) déranger, gêner; (worry)
inquiéter ▷ vi: **to ~ to do** prendre la peine de
faire; **troubles** npl (Pol etc) troubles; (personal)
ennuis, soucis; **to be in ~** avoir des ennuis;
(ship, climber etc) être en difficulté; **to have ~
doing sth** avoir du mal à faire qch; **it's no ~!**
je vous en prie!; **the ~ is ...** le problème, c'est
que ...; **what's the ~?** qu'est-ce qui ne va
pas?; **troubled** adj (person) inquiet(-ète);
(times, life) agité(e); **troublemaker** n
élément perturbateur, fauteur m de troubles;
troublesome adj (child) fatigant(e), difficile;
(cough) gênant(e)

trough [trɔf] n (also: **drinking ~**) abreuvoir m;
(also: **feeding ~**) auge f; (depression) creux m

trousers ['trauzəz] npl pantalon m; **short ~**
(BRIT) culottes courtes

trout [traut] n (pl inv) truite f

trowel ['trauəl] n truelle f; (garden tool)
déplantoir m

truant ['truənt] n: **to play ~** (BRIT) faire l'école
buissonnière

truce [tru:s] n trêve f

truck [trʌk] n camion m; (Rail) wagon m à
plate-forme; **truck driver** n camionneur m

true [tru:] adj vrai(e); (accurate) exact(e);
(genuine) vrai, véritable; (faithful) fidèle; **to
come ~** se réaliser

truly ['tru:lɪ] adv vraiment, réellement;
(truthfully) sans mentir; **yours ~** (in letter) je
vous prie d'agréer, Monsieur (or Madame etc),
l'expression de mes sentiments respectueux

trumpet ['trʌmpɪt] n trompette f

trunk [trʌŋk] n (of tree, person) tronc m; (of
elephant) trompe f; (case) malle f; (us Aut) coffre
m; **trunks** npl (also: **swimming ~s**) maillot m
or slip m de bain

trust [trʌst] n confiance f; (responsibility): **to
place sth in sb's ~** confier la responsabilité
de qch à qn; (Law) fidéicommis m ▷ vt (rely on)
avoir confiance en; (entrust): **to ~ sth to sb**
confier qch à qn; (hope): **to ~ (that)** espérer
(que); **to take sth on ~** accepter qch les yeux
fermés; **trusted** adj en qui l'on a confiance;

trustworthy adj digne de confiance
truth [truːθ, (pl) truːðz] n vérité f; **truthful** adj (person) qui dit la vérité; (answer) sincère
try [traɪ] n essai m, tentative f; (Rugby) essai ▷ vt (attempt) essayer, tenter; (test: sth new: also: ~ **out**) essayer, tester; (Law: person) juger; (strain) éprouver ▷ vi essayer; **to ~ to do** essayer de faire; (seek) chercher à faire; **try on** vt (clothes) essayer; **trying** adj pénible
T-shirt ['tiːʃəːt] n tee-shirt m
tub [tʌb] n cuve f; (for washing clothes) baquet m; (bath) baignoire f
tube [tjuːb] n tube m; (BRIT: underground) métro m; (for tyre) chambre f à air
tuberculosis [tjubəːkjuˈləusɪs] n tuberculose f
tube station n (BRIT) station f de métro
tuck [tʌk] vt (put) mettre; **tuck away** vt cacher, ranger; (money) mettre de côté; (building): **to be ~ed away** être caché(e); **tuck in** vt rentrer; (child) border ▷ vi (eat) manger de bon appétit; attaquer le repas; **tuck shop** n (BRIT Scol) boutique f à provisions
Tue(s) abbr (= Tuesday)
Tuesday ['tjuːzdɪ] n mardi m
tug [tʌg] n (ship) remorqueur m ▷ vt tirer (sur)
tuition [tjuːˈɪʃən] n (BRIT: lessons) leçons fpl; (: private) cours particuliers; (US: fees) frais mpl de scolarité
tulip ['tjuːlɪp] n tulipe f
tumble ['tʌmbl] n (fall) chute f, culbute f ▷ vi tomber, dégringoler; **to ~ to sth** (inf) réaliser qch; **tumble dryer** n (BRIT) séchoir m (à linge) à air chaud
tumbler ['tʌmblə'] n verre (droit), gobelet m
tummy ['tʌmɪ] n (inf) ventre m
tumour (US **tumor**) ['tjuːmə'] n tumeur f
tuna ['tjuːnə] n (pl inv: also: ~ **fish**) thon m
tune [tjuːn] n (melody) air m ▷ vt (Mus) accorder; (Radio, TV, Aut) régler, mettre au point; **to be in/out of ~** (instrument) être accordé/désaccordé; (singer) chanter juste/faux; **to ~ in (to)** vi (Radio, TV) se mettre à l'écoute (de); **tune up** vi (musician) accorder son instrument
tunic ['tjuːnɪk] n tunique f
Tunis ['tjuːnɪs] n Tunis
Tunisia [tjuːˈnɪzɪə] n Tunisie f
Tunisian [tjuːˈnɪzɪən] adj tunisien(ne) ▷ n Tunisien(ne)
tunnel ['tʌnl] n tunnel m; (in mine) galerie f ▷ vi creuser un tunnel (or une galerie)
turbulence ['təːbjuləns] n (Aviat) turbulence f
turf [təːf] n gazon m; (clod) motte f (de gazon) ▷ vt gazonner
Turk [təːk] n Turc (Turque)
Turkey ['təːkɪ] n Turquie f
turkey ['təːkɪ] n dindon m, dinde f
Turkish ['təːkɪʃ] adj turc (turque) ▷ n (Ling)

turc m
turmoil ['təːmɔɪl] n trouble m, bouleversement m
turn [təːn] n tour m; (in road) tournant m; (tendency: of mind, events) tournure f; (performance) numéro m; (Med) crise f, attaque f ▷ vt tourner; (collar, steak) retourner; (change): **to ~ sth into** changer qch en; (age) atteindre ▷ vi (object, wind, milk) tourner; (person: look back) se (re)tourner; (reverse direction) faire demi-tour; (become) devenir; **to ~ into** se changer en, se transformer en; **a good ~** un service; **it gave me quite a ~** ça m'a fait un coup; **"no left ~"** (Aut) "défense de tourner à gauche"; **~ left/right at the next junction** tournez à gauche/droite au prochain carrefour; **it's your ~** c'est (à) votre tour; **in ~** à son tour; **to take ~s** se relayer; **turn around** vi (person) se retourner ▷ vt (object) tourner; **turn away** vi se détourner, tourner la tête ▷ vt (reject: person) renvoyer; (: business) refuser; **turn back** vi revenir, faire demi-tour; **turn down** vt (refuse) rejeter, refuser; (reduce) baisser; (fold) rabattre; **turn in** vi (inf: go to bed) aller se coucher ▷ vt (fold) rentrer; **turn off** vi (from road) tourner ▷ vt (light, radio etc) éteindre; (tap) fermer; (engine) arrêter; **I can't ~ the heating off** je n'arrive pas à éteindre le chauffage; **turn on** vt (light, radio etc) allumer; (tap) ouvrir; (engine) mettre en marche; **I can't ~ the heating on** je n'arrive pas à allumer le chauffage; **turn out** vt (light, gas) éteindre; (produce) produire ▷ vi (voters, troops) se présenter; **to ~ out to be ...** s'avérer ..., se révéler ...; **turn over** vi (person) se retourner ▷ vt (object) retourner; (page) tourner; **turn round** vi faire demi-tour; (rotate) tourner; **turn to** vt fus: **to ~ to sb** s'adresser à qn; **turn up** vi (person) arriver, pointer (inf); (lost object) être retrouvé(e) ▷ vt (collar) remonter; (radio, heater) mettre plus fort; **turning** n (in road) tournant m; **turning point** n (fig) tournant m, moment décisif
turnip ['təːnɪp] n navet m
turn: **turnout** n (of voters) taux m de participation; **turnover** n (Comm: amount of money) chiffre m d'affaires; (: of goods) roulement m; (of staff) renouvellement m, changement m; **turnstile** n tourniquet m (d'entrée); **turn-ups** npl (BRIT: on trousers) revers m
turquoise ['təːkwɔɪz] n (stone) turquoise f ▷ adj turquoise inv
turtle ['təːtl] n tortue marine; **turtleneck (sweater)** n pullover m à col montant
tusk [tʌsk] n défense f (d'éléphant)
tutor ['tjuːtə'] n (BRIT Scol: in college) directeur(-trice) d'études; (private teacher) précepteur(-trice); **tutorial** [tjuːˈtɔːrɪəl] n (Scol) (séance f de) travaux mpl pratiques

tuxedo [tʌk'siːdəu] n (US) smoking m

TV [tiː'viː] n abbr (= television) télé f, TV f

tweed [twiːd] n tweed m

tweezers [ˈtwiːzəz] npl pince f à épiler

twelfth [twɛlfθ] num douzième

twelve [twɛlv] num douze; **at ~ (o'clock)** à midi; (midnight) à minuit

twentieth [ˈtwɛntɪɪθ] num vingtième

twenty [ˈtwɛntɪ] num vingt

twice [twaɪs] adv deux fois; **~ as much** deux fois plus

twig [twɪg] n brindille f ▷ vt, vi (inf) piger

twilight [ˈtwaɪlaɪt] n crépuscule m

twin [twɪn] adj, n jumeau(-elle) ▷ vt jumeler; **twin(-bedded) room** n chambre f à deux lits; **twin beds** npl lits mpl jumeaux

twinkle [ˈtwɪŋkl] vi scintiller; (eyes) pétiller

twist [twɪst] n torsion f, tour m; (in wire, flex) tortillon m; (bend: in road) tournant m; (in story) coup m de théâtre ▷ vt tordre; (weave) entortiller; (roll around) enrouler; (fig) déformer ▷ vi (road, river) serpenter; **to ~ one's ankle/wrist** (Med) se tordre la cheville/le poignet

twit [twɪt] n (inf) crétin(e)

twitch [twɪtʃ] n (pull) coup sec, saccade f; (nervous) tic m ▷ vi se convulser; avoir un tic

two [tuː] num deux; **to put ~ and ~ together** (fig) faire le rapprochement

type [taɪp] n (category) genre m, espèce f; (model) modèle m; (example) type m; (Typ) type, caractère m ▷ vt (letter etc) taper (à la machine); **typewriter** n machine f à écrire

typhoid [ˈtaɪfɔɪd] n typhoïde f

typhoon [taɪˈfuːn] n typhon m

typical [ˈtɪpɪkl] adj typique, caractéristique; **typically** adv (as usual) comme d'habitude; (characteristically) typiquement

typing [ˈtaɪpɪŋ] n dactylo(graphie) f

typist [ˈtaɪpɪst] n dactylo m/f

tyre (US **tire**) [ˈtaɪər] n pneu m; **I've got a flat ~** j'ai un pneu crevé; **tyre pressure** n (BRIT) pression f (de gonflage)

UFO [ˈjuːfəu] n abbr (= unidentified flying object) ovni m

Uganda [juːˈgændə] n Ouganda m

ugly [ˈʌglɪ] adj laid(e), vilain(e); (fig) répugnant(e)

UHT adj abbr = **ultra-heat treated**; **~ milk** lait m UHT or longue conservation

UK n abbr = **United Kingdom**

ulcer [ˈʌlsər] n ulcère m; **mouth ~** aphte f

ultimate [ˈʌltɪmət] adj ultime, final(e); (authority) suprême; **ultimately** adv (at last) en fin de compte; (fundamentally) finalement; (eventually) par la suite

ultimatum (pl **~s** or **ultimata**) [ʌltɪˈmeɪtəm, -tə] n ultimatum m

ultrasound [ˈʌltrəsaund] n (Med) ultrason m

ultraviolet [ˈʌltrəˈvaɪəlɪt] adj ultraviolet(te)

umbrella [ʌmˈbrɛlə] n parapluie m; (for sun) parasol m

umpire [ˈʌmpaɪər] n arbitre m; (Tennis) juge m de chaise

UN n abbr = **United Nations**

unable [ʌnˈeɪbl] adj: **to be ~ to** ne (pas) pouvoir, être dans l'impossibilité de; (not capable) être incapable de

unacceptable [ʌnəkˈsɛptəbl] adj (behaviour) inadmissible; (price, proposal) inacceptable

unanimous [juːˈnænɪməs] adj unanime

unarmed [ʌnˈɑːmd] adj (person) non armé(e); (combat) sans armes

unattended [ʌnəˈtɛndɪd] adj (car, child, luggage) sans surveillance

unattractive [ʌnəˈtræktɪv] adj peu attrayant(e); (character) peu sympathique

unavailable [ʌnəˈveɪləbl] adj (article, room, book) (qui n'est) pas disponible; (person) (qui n'est) pas libre

unavoidable [ʌnəˈvɔɪdəbl] adj inévitable

unaware [ʌnəˈwɛər] adj: **to be ~ of** ignorer, ne pas savoir, être inconscient(e) de; **unawares** adv à l'improviste, au dépourvu

unbearable [ʌnˈbɛərəbl] adj insupportable

unbeatable [ʌnˈbiːtəbl] adj imbattable

unbelievable [ʌnbɪˈliːvəbl] adj incroyable

unborn [ʌnˈbɔːn] adj à naître

unbutton [ʌnˈbʌtn] vt déboutonner

uncalled-for [ʌnˈkɔːldfɔːr] adj déplacé(e), injustifié(e)

uncanny [ʌnˈkænɪ] adj étrange, troublant(e)

uncertain [ʌnˈsəːtn] adj incertain(e); (hesitant) hésitant(e); **uncertainty** n incertitude f, doutes mpl

unchanged [ʌnˈtʃeɪndʒd] adj inchangé(e)

uncle [ˈʌŋkl] n oncle m

unclear [ʌnˈklɪər] adj (qui n'est) pas clair(e) or évident(e); **I'm still ~ about what I'm supposed to do** je ne sais pas encore exactement ce que je dois faire

uncomfortable [ʌnˈkʌmfətəbl] adj inconfortable, peu confortable; (uneasy) mal à l'aise, gêné(e); (situation) désagréable

uncommon [ʌnˈkɔmən] adj rare, singulier(-ière), peu commun(e)

unconditional [ʌnkənˈdɪʃənl] adj sans conditions

unconscious [ʌnˈkɔnʃəs] adj sans connaissance, évanoui(e); (unaware): **~ (of)** inconscient(e) (de) ▷ n: **the ~** l'inconscient m

uncontrollable [ʌnkənˈtrəʊləbl] adj (child, dog) indiscipliné(e); (temper, laughter) irrépressible

unconventional [ʌnkənˈvɛnʃənl] adj peu conventionnel(le)

uncover [ʌnˈkʌvər] vt découvrir

undecided [ʌndɪˈsaɪdɪd] adj indécis(e), irrésolu(e)

undeniable [ʌndɪˈnaɪəbl] adj indéniable, incontestable

under [ˈʌndər] prep sous; (less than) (de) moins de; au-dessous de; (according to) selon, en vertu de ▷ adv au-dessous; en dessous; **~ there** là-dessous; **~ the circumstances** étant donné les circonstances; **~ repair** en (cours de) réparation; **undercover** adj secret(-ète), clandestin(e); **underdone** adj (Culin) saignant(e); (: pej) pas assez cuit(e); **underestimate** vt sous-estimer, mésestimer; **undergo** vt (irreg: like **go**) subir; (treatment) suivre; **undergraduate** n étudiant(e)

(qui prépare la licence); **underground** adj souterrain(e); (fig) clandestin(e) ▷ n (BRIT: railway) métro m; (Pol) clandestinité f; **undergrowth** n broussailles fpl, sous-bois m; **underline** vt souligner; **undermine** vt saper, miner; **underneath** [ʌndəˈniːθ] adv (en) dessous ▷ prep sous, au-dessous de; **underpants** npl caleçon m, slip m; **underpass** n (BRIT: for pedestrians) passage souterrain; (: for cars) passage inférieur; **underprivileged** adj défavorisé(e); **underscore** vt souligner; **undershirt** n (US) tricot m de corps; **underskirt** n (BRIT) jupon m

understand [ʌndəˈstænd] vt, vi (irreg: like **stand**) comprendre; **I don't ~** je ne comprends pas; **understandable** adj compréhensible; **understanding** adj compréhensif(-ive) ▷ n compréhension f; (agreement) accord m

understatement [ˈʌndəsteɪtmənt] n: **that's an ~** c'est (bien) peu dire, le terme est faible

understood [ʌndəˈstʊd] pt, pp of **understand** ▷ adj entendu(e); (implied) sous-entendu(e)

undertake [ʌndəˈteɪk] vt (irreg: like **take**) (job, task) entreprendre; (duty) se charger de; **to ~ to do sth** s'engager à faire qch

undertaker [ˈʌndəteɪkər] n (BRIT) entrepreneur m des pompes funèbres, croque-mort m

undertaking [ˈʌndəteɪkɪŋ] n entreprise f; (promise) promesse f

under: **underwater** adv sous l'eau ▷ adj sous-marin(e); **underway** adj: **to be underway** (meeting, investigation) être en cours; **underwear** n sous-vêtements mpl; (women's only) dessous mpl; **underwent** pt of **undergo**; **underworld** n (of crime) milieu m, pègre f

undesirable [ʌndɪˈzaɪərəbl] adj peu souhaitable; (person, effect) indésirable

undisputed [ʌndɪsˈpjuːtɪd] adj incontesté(e)

undo [ʌnˈduː] vt (irreg: like **do**) défaire

undone [ʌnˈdʌn] pp of **undo** ▷ adj: **to come ~** se défaire

undoubtedly [ʌnˈdautɪdlɪ] adv sans aucun doute

undress [ʌnˈdrɛs] vi se déshabiller

unearth [ʌnˈəːθ] vt déterrer; (fig) dénicher

uneasy [ʌnˈiːzɪ] adj mal à l'aise, gêné(e); (worried) inquiet(-ète); (feeling) désagréable; (peace, truce) fragile

unemployed [ʌnɪmˈplɔɪd] adj sans travail, au chômage ▷ n: **the ~** les chômeurs mpl

unemployment [ʌnɪmˈplɔɪmənt] n chômage m; **unemployment benefit** (US **unemployment compensation**) n allocation f de chômage

unequal [ʌnˈiːkwəl] adj inégal(e)

uneven [ʌnˈiːvn] adj inégal(e); (quality, work)

irrégulier(-ière)

unexpected [ʌnɪkˈspɛktɪd] adj inattendu(e), imprévu(e); **unexpectedly** adv (succeed) contre toute attente; (arrive) à l'improviste

unfair [ʌnˈfɛəʳ] adj: **~ (to)** injuste (envers)

unfaithful [ʌnˈfeɪθful] adj infidèle

unfamiliar [ʌnfəˈmɪlɪəʳ] adj étrange, inconnu(e); **to be ~ with sth** mal connaître qch

unfashionable [ʌnˈfæʃnəbl] adj (clothes) démodé(e); (place) peu chic inv

unfasten [ʌnˈfɑːsn] vt défaire; (belt, necklace) détacher; (open) ouvrir

unfavourable (US **unfavorable**) [ʌnˈfeɪvrəbl] adj défavorable

unfinished [ʌnˈfɪnɪʃt] adj inachevé(e)

unfit [ʌnˈfɪt] adj (physically: ill) en mauvaise santé; (: out of condition) pas en forme; (incompetent): **~ (for)** impropre (à); (work, service) inapte (à)

unfold [ʌnˈfəuld] vt déplier ▷ vi se dérouler

unforgettable [ʌnfəˈgɛtəbl] adj inoubliable

unfortunate [ʌnˈfɔːtʃnət] adj malheureux(-euse); (event, remark) malencontreux(-euse); **unfortunately** adv malheureusement

unfriendly [ʌnˈfrɛndlɪ] adj peu aimable, froid(e)

unfurnished [ʌnˈfəːnɪʃt] adj non meublé(e)

unhappiness [ʌnˈhæpɪnɪs] n tristesse f, peine f

unhappy [ʌnˈhæpɪ] adj triste, malheureux(-euse); (unfortunate: remark etc) malheureux(-euse); (not pleased): **~ with** mécontent(e) de, peu satisfait(e) de

unhealthy [ʌnˈhɛlθɪ] adj (gen) malsain(e); (person) maladif(-ive)

unheard-of [ʌnˈhəːdɔv] adj inouï(e), sans précédent

unhelpful [ʌnˈhɛlpful] adj (person) peu serviable; (advice) peu utile

unhurt [ʌnˈhəːt] adj indemne, sain(e) et sauf (sauve)

unidentified [ʌnaɪˈdɛntɪfaɪd] adj non identifié(e); see also **UFO**

uniform [ˈjuːnɪfɔːm] n uniforme m ▷ adj uniforme

unify [ˈjuːnɪfaɪ] vt unifier

unimportant [ʌnɪmˈpɔːtənt] adj sans importance

uninhabited [ʌnɪnˈhæbɪtɪd] adj inhabité(e)

unintentional [ʌnɪnˈtɛnʃənəl] adj involontaire

union [ˈjuːnjən] n union f; (also: **trade ~**) syndicat m ▷ cpd du syndicat, syndical(e); **Union Jack** n drapeau du Royaume-Uni

unique [juːˈniːk] adj unique

unisex [ˈjuːnɪsɛks] adj unisexe

unit [ˈjuːnɪt] n unité f; (section: of furniture etc) élément m, bloc m; (team, squad) groupe m, service m; **kitchen ~** élément de cuisine

unite [juːˈnaɪt] vt unir ▷ vi s'unir; **united** adj uni(e); (country, party) unifié(e); (efforts) conjugué(e); **United Kingdom** n Royaume-Uni m (R.U.); **United Nations (Organization)** n (Organisation f des) Nations unies (ONU); **United States (of America)** n États-Unis mpl

unity [ˈjuːnɪtɪ] n unité f

universal [juːnɪˈvəːsl] adj universel(le)

universe [ˈjuːnɪvəːs] n univers m

university [juːnɪˈvəːsɪtɪ] n université f ▷ cpd (student, professor) d'université; (education, year, degree) universitaire

unjust [ʌnˈdʒʌst] adj injuste

unkind [ʌnˈkaɪnd] adj peu gentil(le), méchant(e)

unknown [ʌnˈnəun] adj inconnu(e)

unlawful [ʌnˈlɔːful] adj illégal(e)

unleaded [ʌnˈlɛdɪd] n (also: **~ petrol**) essence f sans plomb

unleash [ʌnˈliːʃ] vt (fig) déchaîner, déclencher

unless [ʌnˈlɛs] conj: **~ he leaves** à moins qu'il (ne) parte; **~ otherwise stated** sauf indication contraire

unlike [ʌnˈlaɪk] adj dissemblable, différent(e) ▷ prep à la différence de, contrairement à

unlikely [ʌnˈlaɪklɪ] adj (result, event) improbable; (explanation) invraisemblable

unlimited [ʌnˈlɪmɪtɪd] adj illimité(e)

unlisted [ˈʌnˈlɪstɪd] adj (US Tel) sur la liste rouge

unload [ʌnˈləud] vt décharger

unlock [ʌnˈlɔk] vt ouvrir

unlucky [ʌnˈlʌkɪ] adj (person) malchanceux(-euse); (object, number) qui porte malheur; **to be ~** (person) ne pas avoir de chance

unmarried [ʌnˈmærɪd] adj célibataire

unmistak(e)able [ʌnmɪsˈteɪkəbl] adj indubitable; qu'on ne peut pas ne pas reconnaître

unnatural [ʌnˈnætʃrəl] adj non naturel(le); (perversion) contre nature

unnecessary [ʌnˈnɛsəsərɪ] adj inutile, superflu(e)

UNO [ˈjuːnəu] n abbr = **United Nations Organization**

unofficial [ʌnəˈfɪʃl] adj (news) officieux(-euse), non officiel(le); (strike) ≈ sauvage

unpack [ʌnˈpæk] vi défaire sa valise ▷ vt (suitcase) défaire; (belongings) déballer

unpaid [ʌnˈpeɪd] adj (bill) impayé(e); (holiday) non-payé(e), sans salaire; (work) non rétribué(e)

unpleasant [ʌnˈplɛznt] adj déplaisant(e), désagréable

unplug [ʌnˈplʌg] vt débrancher

unpopular [ʌnˈpɔpjuləʳ] adj impopulaire

unprecedented [ʌn'prɛsɪdɛntɪd] *adj* sans précédent

unpredictable [ʌnprɪ'dɪktəbl] *adj* imprévisible

unprotected ['ʌnprə'tɛktɪd] *adj* (*sex*) non protégé(e)

unqualified [ʌn'kwɔlɪfaɪd] *adj* (*teacher*) non diplômé(e), sans titres; (*success*) sans réserve, total(e); (*disaster*) total(e)

unravel [ʌn'rævl] *vt* démêler

unreal [ʌn'rɪəl] *adj* irréel(le); (*extraordinary*) incroyable

unrealistic ['ʌnrɪə'lɪstɪk] *adj* (*idea*) irréaliste; (*estimate*) peu réaliste

unreasonable [ʌn'ri:znəbl] *adj* qui n'est pas raisonnable

unrelated [ʌnrɪ'leɪtɪd] *adj* sans rapport; (*people*) sans lien de parenté

unreliable [ʌnrɪ'laɪəbl] *adj* sur qui (*or* quoi) on ne peut pas compter, peu fiable

unrest [ʌn'rɛst] *n* agitation *f*, troubles *mpl*

unroll [ʌn'rəul] *vt* dérouler

unruly [ʌn'ru:lɪ] *adj* indiscipliné(e)

unsafe [ʌn'seɪf] *adj* (*in danger*) en danger; (*journey, car*) dangereux(-euse)

unsatisfactory ['ʌnsætɪs'fæktərɪ] *adj* peu satisfaisant(e)

unscrew [ʌn'skru:] *vt* dévisser

unsettled [ʌn'sɛtld] *adj* (*restless*) perturbé(e); (*unpredictable*) instable; incertain(e); (*not finalized*) non résolu(e)

unsettling [ʌn'sɛtlɪŋ] *adj* qui a un effet perturbateur

unsightly [ʌn'saɪtlɪ] *adj* disgracieux(-euse), laid(e)

unskilled [ʌn'skɪld] *adj*: ~ **worker** manœuvre *m*

unspoiled [ʌn'spɔɪld], **unspoilt** ['ʌn'spɔɪlt] *adj* (*place*) non dégradé(e)

unstable [ʌn'steɪbl] *adj* instable

unsteady [ʌn'stɛdɪ] *adj* mal assuré(e), chancelant(e), instable

unsuccessful [ʌnsək'sɛsful] *adj* (*attempt*) infructueux(-euse); (*writer, proposal*) qui n'a pas de succès; **to be ~** (*in attempting sth*) ne pas réussir; ne pas avoir de succès; (*application*) ne pas être retenu(e)

unsuitable [ʌn'su:təbl] *adj* qui ne convient pas, peu approprié(e); (*time*) inopportun(e)

unsure [ʌn'fuə'] *adj* pas sûr(e); **to be ~ of o.s.** ne pas être sûr de soi, manquer de confiance en soi

untidy [ʌn'taɪdɪ] *adj* (*room*) en désordre; (*appearance, person*) débraillé(e); (*person: in character*) sans ordre, désordonné(e); (*work*) peu soigné(e)

untie [ʌn'taɪ] *vt* (*knot, parcel*) défaire; (*prisoner, dog*) détacher

until [ən'tɪl] *prep* jusqu'à; (*after negative*)

avant ▷ *conj* jusqu'à ce que + *sub*; (*in past, after negative*) avant que + *sub*; **~ he comes** jusqu'à ce qu'il vienne, jusqu'à son arrivée; **~ now** jusqu'à présent, jusqu'ici; **~ then** jusque-là

untrue [ʌn'tru:] *adj* (*statement*) faux (fausse)

unused¹ [ʌn'ju:zd] *adj* (*new*) neuf (neuve)

unused² [ʌn'ju:st] *adj*: **to be ~ to sth/to doing sth** ne pas avoir l'habitude de qch/de faire qch

unusual [ʌn'ju:ʒuəl] *adj* insolite, exceptionnel(le), rare; **unusually** *adv* exceptionnellement, particulièrement

unveil [ʌn'veɪl] *vt* dévoiler

unwanted [ʌn'wɔntɪd] *adj* (*child, pregnancy*) non désiré(e); (*clothes etc*) à donner

unwell [ʌn'wɛl] *adj* souffrant(e); **to feel ~** ne pas se sentir bien

unwilling [ʌn'wɪlɪŋ] *adj*: **to be ~ to do** ne pas vouloir faire

unwind [ʌn'waɪnd] *vb* (*irreg: like* **wind**) ▷ *vt* dérouler ▷ *vi* (*relax*) se détendre

unwise [ʌn'waɪz] *adj* imprudent(e), peu judicieux(-euse)

unwittingly [ʌn'wɪtɪŋlɪ] *adv* involontairement

unwrap [ʌn'ræp] *vt* défaire; ouvrir

unzip [ʌn'zɪp] *vt* ouvrir (la fermeture éclair de); (*Comput*) dézipper

 KEYWORD

up [ʌp] *prep*: **he went up the stairs/the hill** il a monté l'escalier/la colline; **the cat was up a tree** le chat était dans un arbre; **they live further up the street** ils habitent plus haut dans la rue; **go up that road and turn left** remontez la rue et tournez à gauche
▷ *adv* **1** en haut; en l'air; (*upwards, higher*): **up in the sky/the mountains** (là-haut) dans le ciel/les montagnes; **put it a bit higher up** mettez-le un peu plus haut; **to stand up** (*get up*) se lever, se mettre debout; (*be standing*) être debout; **up there** là-haut; **up above** au-dessus

2: **to be up** (*out of bed*) être levé(e); (*prices*) avoir augmenté *or* monté; (*finished*): **when the year was up** à la fin de l'année

3: **up to** (*as far as*) jusqu'à; **up to now** jusqu'à présent

4: **to be up to** (*depending on*): **it's up to you** c'est à vous de décider; (*equal to*): **he's not up to it** (*job, task etc*) il n'en est pas capable; (*inf: be doing*): **what is he up to?** qu'est-ce qu'il peut bien faire?
▷ *n*: **ups and downs** hauts et bas *mpl*

up-and-coming [ʌpənd'kʌmɪŋ] *adj* plein(e) d'avenir *or* de promesses

upbringing ['ʌpbrɪŋɪŋ] *n* éducation *f*

update [ʌp'deɪt] *vt* mettre à jour
upfront [ʌp'frʌnt] *adj* (*open*) franc (franche)
▷ *adv* (*pay*) d'avance; **to be ~ about sth** ne rien
cacher de qch
upgrade [ʌp'greɪd] *vt* (*person*) promouvoir;
(*job*) revaloriser; (*property, equipment*)
moderniser
upheaval [ʌp'hi:vl] *n* bouleversement *m*; (*in
room*) branle-bas *m*; (*event*) crise *f*
uphill [ʌp'hɪl] *adj* qui monte; (*fig: task*) difficile,
pénible ▷ *adv* (*face, look*) en amont, vers
l'amont; **to go ~** monter
upholstery [ʌp'həulstəri] *n* rembourrage
m; (*cover*) tissu *m* d'ameublement; (*of car*)
garniture *f*
upmarket [ʌp'mɑ:kɪt] *adj* (*product*) haut de
gamme *inv*; (*area*) chic *inv*
upon [ə'pɔn] *prep* sur
upper [ʌpə^r] *adj* supérieur(e); du dessus ▷ *n* (*of
shoe*) empeigne *f*; **upper-class** *adj* de la haute
société, aristocratique; (*district*) élégant(e),
huppé(e); (*accent, attitude*) caractéristique des
classes supérieures
upright [ʌpraɪt] *adj* droit(e); (*fig*) droit,
honnête
uprising [ʌpraɪzɪŋ] *n* soulèvement *m*,
insurrection *f*
uproar [ʌprɔ:^r] *n* tumulte *m*, vacarme *m*;
(*protests*) protestations *fpl*
upset *n* [ʌpset] dérangement *m* ▷ *vt* (*irreg:
like set* [ʌp'set]) (*glass etc*) renverser; (*plan*)
déranger; (*person: offend*) contrarier; (: *grieve*)
faire de la peine à; bouleverser ▷ *adj* [ʌp'set]
contrarié(e); peiné(e); **to have a stomach ~**
(*BRIT*) avoir une indigestion
upside down [ʌpsaɪd-] *adv* à l'envers; **to
turn sth ~** (*fig: place*) mettre sens dessus
dessous
upstairs [ʌp'stɛəz] *adv* en haut ▷ *adj* (*room*) du
dessus, d'en haut ▷ *n*: **the ~** l'étage *m*
up-to-date [ʌptə'deɪt] *adj* moderne;
(*information*) très récent(e)
uptown [ʌptaun] (*US*) *adv* (*live*) dans les
quartiers chics; (*go*) vers les quartiers chics
▷ *adj* des quartiers chics
upward [ʌpwəd] *adj* ascendant(e); vers le
haut; **upward(s)** *adv* vers le haut; (*more than*):
upward(s) of plus de
uranium [juə'reɪnɪəm] *n* uranium *m*
Uranus [juə'reɪnəs] *n* Uranus *f*
urban [ʌ:bən] *adj* urbain(e)
urge [ə:dʒ] *n* besoin (impératif), envie
(pressante) ▷ *vt* (*person*): **to ~ sb to do**
exhorter qn à faire, pousser qn à faire,
recommander vivement à qn de faire
urgency [ʌ:dʒənsɪ] *n* urgence *f*; (*of tone*)
insistance *f*
urgent [ʌ:dʒənt] *adj* urgent(e); (*plea, tone*)
pressant(e)

urinal [ˈjuərɪnl] *n* (*BRIT: place*) urinoir *m*
urinate [ˈjuərɪneɪt] *vi* uriner
urine [ˈjuərɪn] *n* urine *f*
URL *abbr* (= *uniform resource locator*) URL *f*
US *n abbr* = **United States**
us [ʌs] *pron* nous; *see also* **me**
USA *n abbr* = **United States of America**
use *n* [ju:s] emploi *m*, utilisation *f*; (*usefulness*)
utilité *f* ▷ *vt* [ju:z] se servir de, utiliser,
employer; **in ~** en usage; **out of ~** hors d'usage;
to be of ~ servir, être utile; **it's no ~** ça ne
sert à rien; **to have the ~ of** avoir l'usage de;
she ~d to do it elle le faisait (autrefois), elle
avait coutume de le faire; **to be ~d to** avoir
l'habitude de, être habitué(e) à; **use up** *vt*
finir, épuiser; (*food*) consommer; **used** [ju:
zd] *adj* (*car*) d'occasion; **useful** *adj* utile;
useless *adj* inutile; (*inf: person*) nul(le); **user** *n*
utilisateur(-trice), usager *m*; **user-friendly** *adj*
convivial(e), facile d'emploi
usual [ˈju:ʒuəl] *adj* habituel(le); **as ~** comme
d'habitude; **usually** *adv* d'habitude,
d'ordinaire
utensil [ju:'tɛnsl] *n* ustensile *m*; **kitchen ~s**
batterie *f* de cuisine
utility [ju:'tɪlɪtɪ] *n* utilité *f*; (*also: public ~*)
service public
utilize [ˈju:tɪlaɪz] *vt* utiliser; (*make good use of*)
exploiter
utmost [ˈʌtməust] *adj* extrême, le (la) plus
grand(e) ▷ *n*: **to do one's ~** faire tout son
possible
utter [ˈʌtə^r] *adj* total(e), complet(-ète) ▷ *vt*
prononcer, proférer; (*sounds*) émettre; **utterly**
adv complètement, totalement
U-turn [ˈju:'tə:n] *n* demi-tour *m*; (*fig*) volte-
face *f inv*

v. *abbr* = **verse** (= *vide*) v.; (= *versus*) c.; (= *volt*) V

vacancy ['veɪkənsɪ] *n* (BRIT: *job*) poste vacant; (*room*) chambre *f* disponible; **"no vacancies"** "complet"

vacant ['veɪkənt] *adj* (*post*) vacant(e); (*seat etc*) libre, disponible; (*expression*) distrait(e)

vacate [və'keɪt] *vt* quitter

vacation [və'keɪʃən] *n* (*esp US*) vacances *fpl*; **on ~** en vacances; **vacationer**(*US* **vacationist**) *n* vacancier(-ière)

vaccination [væksɪ'neɪʃən] *n* vaccination *f*

vaccine ['væksiːn] *n* vaccin *m*

vacuum ['vækjum] *n* vide *m*; **vacuum cleaner** *n* aspirateur *m*

vagina [və'dʒaɪnə] *n* vagin *m*

vague [veɪg] *adj* vague, imprécis(e); (*blurred: photo, memory*) flou(e)

vain [veɪn] *adj* (*useless*) vain(e); (*conceited*) vaniteux(-euse); **in ~** en vain

Valentine's Day ['væləntaɪnz-] *n* Saint-Valentin *f*

valid ['vælɪd] *adj* (*document*) valide, valable; (*excuse*) valable

valley ['vælɪ] *n* vallée *f*

valuable ['væljuəbl] *adj* (*jewel*) de grande valeur; (*time, help*) précieux(-euse); **valuables** *npl* objets *mpl* de valeur

value ['væljuː] *n* valeur *f* ▷ *vt* (*fix price*) évaluer, expertiser; (*appreciate*) apprécier; **values** *npl* (*principles*) valeurs *fpl*

valve [vælv] *n* (*in machine*) soupape *f*; (*on tyre*) valve *f*; (*Med*) valve, valvule *f*

vampire ['væmpaɪər] *n* vampire *m*

van [væn] *n* (*Aut*) camionnette *f*

vandal ['vændl] *n* vandale *m/f*; **vandalism** *n* vandalisme *m*; **vandalize** *vt* saccager

vanilla [və'nɪlə] *n* vanille *f*

vanish ['vænɪʃ] *vi* disparaître

vanity ['vænɪtɪ] *n* vanité *f*

vapour (*US* **vapor**) ['veɪpər] *n* vapeur *f*; (*on window*) buée *f*

variable ['vɛərɪəbl] *adj* variable; (*mood*) changeant(e)

variant ['vɛərɪənt] *n* variante *f*

variation [vɛərɪ'eɪʃən] *n* variation *f*; (*in opinion*) changement *m*

varied ['vɛərɪd] *adj* varié(e), divers(e)

variety [və'raɪətɪ] *n* variété *f*; (*quantity*) nombre *m*, quantité *f*

various ['vɛərɪəs] *adj* divers(e), différent(e); (*several*) divers, plusieurs

varnish ['vɑːnɪʃ] *n* vernis *m* ▷ *vt* vernir

vary ['vɛərɪ] *vt, vi* varier, changer

vase [vɑːz] *n* vase *m*

Vaseline® ['væsɪliːn] *n* vaseline *f*

vast [vɑːst] *adj* vaste, immense; (*amount, success*) énorme

VAT [væt] *n abbr* (BRIT: = *value added tax*) TVA *f*

vault [vɔːlt] *n* (*of roof*) voûte *f*; (*tomb*) caveau *m*; (*in bank*) salle *f* des coffres; chambre forte ▷ *vt* (*also*: **~ over**) sauter (d'un bond)

VCR *n abbr* = **video cassette recorder**

VDU *n abbr* = **visual display unit**

veal [viːl] *n* veau *m*

veer [vɪər] *vi* tourner; (*car, ship*) virer

vegan ['viːgən] *n* végétalien(ne)

vegetable ['vɛdʒtəbl] *n* légume *m* ▷ *adj* végétal(e)

vegetarian [vɛdʒɪ'tɛərɪən] *adj, n* végétarien(ne); **do you have any ~ dishes?** avez-vous des plats végétariens?

vegetation [vɛdʒɪ'teɪʃən] *n* végétation *f*

vehicle ['viːɪkl] *n* véhicule *m*

veil [veɪl] *n* voile *m*

vein [veɪn] *n* veine *f*; (*on leaf*) nervure *f*

Velcro® ['vɛlkrəu] *n* velcro® *m*

velvet ['vɛlvɪt] *n* velours *m*

vending machine ['vɛndɪŋ-] *n* distributeur *m* automatique

vendor ['vɛndər] *n* vendeur(-euse); **street ~** marchand ambulant

Venetian blind [vɪ'niːʃən-] *n* store vénitien

vengeance ['vɛndʒəns] *n* vengeance *f*; **with a ~** (*fig*) vraiment, pour de bon

venison ['vɛnɪsn] *n* venaison *f*

venom ['vɛnəm] *n* venin *m*

vent [vɛnt] *n* conduit *m* d'aération; (*in dress, jacket*) fente *f* ▷ *vt* (*fig: one's feelings*) donner libre cours à

ventilation [vɛntɪ'leɪʃən] n ventilation f, aération f

venture ['vɛntʃə^r] n entreprise f ▷ vt risquer, hasarder ▷ vi s'aventurer, se risquer; **a business ~** une entreprise commerciale

venue ['vɛnjuː] n lieu m

Venus ['viːnəs] n (planet) Vénus f

verb [vəːb] n verbe m; **verbal** adj verbal(e)

verdict ['vəːdɪkt] n verdict m

verge [vəːdʒ] n bord m; **"soft ~s"** (BRIT) "accotements non stabilisés"; **on the ~ of doing** sur le point de faire

verify ['vɛrɪfaɪ] vt vérifier

versatile ['vəːsətaɪl] adj polyvalent(e)

verse [vəːs] n vers mpl; (stanza) strophe f; (in Bible) verset m

version ['vəːʃən] n version f

versus ['vəːsəs] prep contre

vertical ['vəːtɪkl] adj vertical(e)

very ['vɛrɪ] adv très ▷ adj: **the ~ book which** le livre même que; **the ~ last** le tout dernier; **at the ~ least** au moins; **~ much** beaucoup

vessel ['vɛsl] n (Anat, Naut) vaisseau m; (container) récipient m; see also **blood**

vest [vɛst] n (BRIT: underwear) tricot m de corps; (US: waistcoat) gilet m

vet [vɛt] n abbr (BRIT: = veterinary surgeon) vétérinaire m/f; (US: = veteran) ancien(ne) combattant(e) ▷ vt examiner minutieusement

veteran ['vɛtərn] n vétéran m; (also: **war ~**) ancien combattant

veterinary surgeon ['vɛtrɪnərɪ-] (BRIT) (US **veterinarian** [vɛtrɪ'nɛərɪən]) n vétérinaire m/f

veto ['viːtəu] n (pl **~es**) veto m ▷ vt opposer son veto à

via ['vaɪə] prep par, via

viable ['vaɪəbl] adj viable

vibrate [vaɪ'breɪt] vi: **to ~ (with)** vibrer (de)

vibration [vaɪ'breɪʃən] n vibration f

vicar ['vɪkə^r] n pasteur m (de l'Église anglicane)

vice [vaɪs] n (evil) vice m; (Tech) étau m; **vice-chairman** n vice-président m

vice versa ['vaɪsɪ'vəːsə] adv vice versa

vicinity [vɪ'sɪnɪtɪ] n environs mpl, alentours mpl

vicious ['vɪʃəs] adj (remark) cruel(le), méchant(e); (blow) brutal(e); (dog) méchant(e), dangereux(-euse); **a ~ circle** un cercle vicieux

victim ['vɪktɪm] n victime f

victor ['vɪktə^r] n vainqueur m

Victorian [vɪk'tɔːrɪən] adj victorien(ne)

victorious [vɪk'tɔːrɪəs] adj victorieux(-euse)

victory ['vɪktərɪ] n victoire f

video ['vɪdɪəu] n (video film) vidéo f; (also: **~ cassette**) vidéocassette f; (also: **~ cassette recorder**) magnétoscope m ▷ vt (with recorder) enregistrer; (with camera) filmer;

video camera n caméra f vidéo inv; **video (cassette) recorder** n magnétoscope m; **video game** n jeu m vidéo inv; **video shop** n vidéoclub m; **video tape** n bande f vidéo inv; (cassette) vidéocassette f

vie [vaɪ] vi: **to ~ with** lutter avec, rivaliser avec

Vienna [vɪ'ɛnə] n Vienne

Vietnam, Viet Nam ['vjɛt'næm] n Viêt-nam or Vietnam m; **Vietnamese** [vjɛtnə'miːz] adj vietnamien(ne) ▷ n (pl inv) Vietnamien(ne)

view [vjuː] n vue f; (opinion) avis m, vue f ▷ vt voir, regarder; (situation) considérer; (house) visiter; **on ~** (in museum etc) exposé(e); **in full ~ of sb** sous les yeux de qn; **in my ~** à mon avis; **in ~ of the fact that** étant donné que; **viewer** n (TV) téléspectateur(-trice); **viewpoint** n point m de vue

vigilant ['vɪdʒɪlənt] adj vigilant(e)

vigorous ['vɪgərəs] adj vigoureux(-euse)

vile [vaɪl] adj (action) vil(e); (smell, food) abominable; (temper) massacrant(e)

villa ['vɪlə] n villa f

village ['vɪlɪdʒ] n village m; **villager** n villageois(e)

villain ['vɪlən] n (scoundrel) scélérat m; (BRIT: criminal) bandit m; (in novel etc) traître m

vinaigrette [vɪneɪ'grɛt] n vinaigrette f

vine [vaɪn] n vigne f

vinegar ['vɪnɪgə^r] n vinaigre m

vineyard ['vɪnjɑːd] n vignoble m

vintage ['vɪntɪdʒ] n (year) année f, millésime m ▷ cpd (car) d'époque; (wine) de grand cru

vinyl ['vaɪnl] n vinyle m

viola [vɪ'əulə] n alto m

violate ['vaɪəleɪt] vt violer

violation [vaɪə'leɪʃən] n violation f; **in ~ of** (rule, law) en infraction à, en violation de

violence ['vaɪələns] n violence f

violent ['vaɪələnt] adj violent(e)

violet ['vaɪələt] adj (colour) violet(te) ▷ n (plant) violette f

violin [vaɪə'lɪn] n violon m

VIP n abbr (= very important person) VIP m

virgin ['vəːdʒɪn] n vierge f

Virgo ['vəːgəu] n la Vierge

virtual ['vəːtjuəl] adj (Comput, Physics) virtuel(le); (in effect): **it's a ~ impossibility** c'est quasiment impossible; **virtually** adv (almost) pratiquement; **virtual reality** n (Comput) réalité virtuelle

virtue ['vəːtjuː] n vertu f; (advantage) mérite m, avantage m; **by ~ of** en vertu or raison de

virus ['vaɪərəs] n (Med, Comput) virus m

visa ['viːzə] n visa m

vise [vaɪs] n (US Tech) = **vice**

visibility [vɪzɪ'bɪlɪtɪ] n visibilité f

visible ['vɪzəbl] adj visible

vision ['vɪʒən] n (sight) vue f, vision f; (foresight, in dream) vision

visit ['vɪzɪt] n visite f; (stay) séjour m ▷ vt (person: us: also: **~ with**) rendre visite à; (place) visiter; **visiting hours** npl heures fpl de visite; **visitor** n visiteur(-euse); (to one's house) invité(e); **visitor centre** (us **visitor center**) n hall m or centre m d'accueil

visual ['vɪʒjuəl] adj visuel(le); **visualize** vt se représenter

vital ['vaɪtl] adj vital(e); **of ~ importance (to sb/sth)** d'une importance capitale (pour qn/qch)

vitality [vaɪ'tælɪtɪ] n vitalité f

vitamin ['vɪtəmɪn] n vitamine f

vivid ['vɪvɪd] adj (account) frappant(e), vivant(e); (light, imagination) vif (vive)

V-neck ['viːnɛk] n décolleté m en V

vocabulary [vəu'kæbjʊlərɪ] n vocabulaire m

vocal ['vəukl] adj vocal(e); (articulate) qui n'hésite pas à s'exprimer, qui sait faire entendre ses opinions

vocational [vəu'keɪʃənl] adj professionnel(le)

vodka ['vɔdkə] n vodka f

vogue [vəug] n: **to be in ~** être en vogue or à la mode

voice [vɔɪs] n voix f ▷ vt (opinion) exprimer, formuler; **voice mail** n (system) messagerie f vocale; (device) boîte f vocale

void [vɔɪd] n vide m ▷ adj (invalid) nul(le); (empty): **~ of** vide de, dépourvu(e) de

volatile ['vɔlətaɪl] adj volatil(e); (fig: person) versatile; (: situation) explosif(-ive)

volcano (pl **-es**) [vɔl'keɪnəu] n volcan m

volleyball ['vɔlɪbɔːl] n volley(-ball) m

volt [vəult] n volt m; **voltage** n tension f, voltage m

volume ['vɔljuːm] n volume m; (of tank) capacité f

voluntarily ['vɔləntrɪlɪ] adv volontairement

voluntary ['vɔləntərɪ] adj volontaire; (unpaid) bénévole

volunteer [vɔlən'tɪəʳ] n volontaire m/f ▷ vt (information) donner spontanément ▷ vi (Mil) s'engager comme volontaire; **to ~ to do** se proposer pour faire

vomit ['vɔmɪt] n vomissure f ▷ vt, vi vomir

vote [vəut] n vote m, suffrage m; (votes cast) voix f, vote; (franchise) droit m de vote ▷ vt (chairman) élire; (propose): **to ~ that** proposer que + sub ▷ vi voter; **~ of thanks** discours m de remerciement; **voter** n électeur(-trice); **voting** n scrutin m, vote m

voucher ['vautʃəʳ] n (for meal, petrol, gift) bon m

vow [vau] n vœu m, serment m ▷ vi jurer

vowel ['vauəl] n voyelle f

voyage ['vɔɪɪdʒ] n voyage m par mer, traversée f

vulgar ['vʌlgəʳ] adj vulgaire

vulnerable ['vʌlnərəbl] adj vulnérable

vulture ['vʌltʃəʳ] n vautour m

waddle ['wɔdl] vi se dandiner

wade [weɪd] vi: **to ~ through** marcher dans, patauger dans; (fig: book) venir à bout de

wafer ['weɪfəʳ] n (Culin) gaufrette f

waffle ['wɔfl] n (Culin) gaufre f ▷ vi parler pour ne rien dire; faire du remplissage

wag [wæg] vt agiter, remuer ▷ vi remuer

wage [weɪdʒ] n (also: **~s**) salaire m, paye f ▷ vt: **to ~ war** faire la guerre

wag(g)on ['wægən] n (horse-drawn) chariot m; (BRIT Rail) wagon m (de marchandises)

wail [weɪl] n gémissement m; (of siren) hurlement m ▷ vi gémir; (siren) hurler

waist [weɪst] n taille f, ceinture f; **waistcoat** n (BRIT) gilet m

wait [weɪt] n attente f ▷ vi attendre; **to ~ for sb/sth** attendre qn/qch; **to keep sb ~ing** faire attendre qn; **~ for me, please** attendez-moi, s'il vous plaît; **I can't ~ to ...** (fig) je meurs d'envie de ...; **to lie in ~ for** guetter; **wait on** vt fus servir; **waiter** n garçon m (de café), serveur m; **waiting list** n liste f d'attente; **waiting room** n salle f d'attente; **waitress** ['weɪtrɪs] n serveuse f

waive [weɪv] vt renoncer à, abandonner

wake [weɪk] vb (pt **woke** or **~d**, pp **woken** or **~d**) ▷ vt (also: **~ up**) réveiller ▷ vi (also: **~ up**) se réveiller ▷ n (for dead person) veillée f mortuaire; (Naut) sillage m

Wales [weɪlz] n pays m de Galles; **the Prince**

of ~ le prince de Galles

walk [wɔːk] n promenade f; (short) petit tour; (gait) démarche f; (path) chemin m; (in park etc) allée f ▷ vi marcher; (for pleasure, exercise) se promener ▷ vt (distance) faire à pied; (dog) promener; **10 minutes' ~ from** à 10 minutes de marche de; **to go for a ~** se promener; faire un tour; **from all ~s of life** de toutes conditions sociales; **walk out** vi (go out) sortir; (as protest) partir (en signe de protestation); (strike) se mettre en grève; **to ~ out on sb** quitter qn; **walker** n (person) marcheur(-euse); **walkie-talkie** ['wɔːkɪ'tɔː kɪ] n talkie-walkie m; **walking** n marche f à pied; **walking shoes** npl chaussures fpl de marche; **walking stick** n canne f; **Walkman®** n Walkman® m; **walkway** n promenade f, cheminement piéton

wall [wɔːl] n mur m; (of tunnel, cave) paroi f

wallet ['wɔlɪt] n portefeuille m; **I can't find my ~** je ne retrouve plus mon portefeuille

wallpaper ['wɔːlpeɪpəʳ] n papier peint ▷ vt tapisser

walnut ['wɔːlnʌt] n noix f; (tree, wood) noyer m

walrus (pl ~ or ~es) ['wɔːlrəs] n morse m

waltz [wɔːlts] n valse f ▷ vi valser

wand [wɔnd] n (also: **magic ~**) baguette f (magique)

wander ['wɔndəʳ] vi (person) errer, aller sans but; (thoughts) vagabonder ▷ vt errer dans

want [wɔnt] vt vouloir; (need) avoir besoin de ▷ n: **for ~ of** par manque de, faute de; **to ~ to do** vouloir faire; **to ~ sb to do** vouloir que qn fasse; **wanted** adj (criminal) recherché(e) par la police; **"cook wanted"** "on recherche un cuisinier"

war [wɔːʳ] n guerre f; **to make ~ (on)** faire la guerre (à)

ward [wɔːd] n (in hospital) salle f; (Pol) section électorale; (Law: child: also: **~ of court**) pupille m/f

warden ['wɔːdn] n (BRIT: of institution) directeur(-trice); (of park, game reserve) gardien(ne); (BRIT: also: **traffic ~**) contractuel(le)

wardrobe ['wɔːdrəub] n (cupboard) armoire f; (clothes) garde-robe f

warehouse ['wɛəhaus] n entrepôt m

warfare ['wɔːfɛəʳ] n guerre f

warhead ['wɔːhɛd] n (Mil) ogive f

warm [wɔːm] adj chaud(e); (person, thanks, welcome, applause) chaleureux(-euse); **it's ~** il fait chaud; **I'm ~** j'ai chaud; **warm up** vi (person, room) se réchauffer; (athlete, discussion) s'échauffer ▷ vt (food) (faire) réchauffer; (water) (faire) chauffer; (engine) faire chauffer; **warmly** adv (dress) chaudement; (thank, welcome) chaleureusement; **warmth** n chaleur f

warn [wɔːn] vt avertir, prévenir; **to ~ sb (not) to do** conseiller à qn de (ne pas) faire; **warning** n avertissement m; (notice) avis m; **warning light** n avertisseur lumineux

warrant ['wɔrnt] n (guarantee) garantie f; (Law: to arrest) mandat m d'arrêt; (: to search) mandat de perquisition ▷ vt (justify, merit) justifier

warranty ['wɔrəntɪ] n garantie f

warrior ['wɔrɪəʳ] n guerrier(-ière)

Warsaw ['wɔːsɔː] n Varsovie

warship ['wɔːʃɪp] n navire m de guerre

wart [wɔːt] n verrue f

wartime ['wɔːtaɪm] n: **in ~** en temps de guerre

wary ['wɛərɪ] adj prudent(e)

was [wɔz] pt of **be**

wash [wɔʃ] vt laver ▷ vi se laver; (sea): **to ~ over/against sth** inonder/baigner qch ▷ n (clothes) lessive f; (washing programme) lavage m; (of ship) sillage m; **to have a ~** se laver, faire sa toilette; **wash up** vi (BRIT) faire la vaisselle; (US: have a wash) se débarbouiller; **washbasin** n lavabo m; **wash cloth** n (US) gant m de toilette; **washer** n (Tech) rondelle f, joint m; **washing** n (BRIT: linen etc: dirty) linge m; (: clean) lessive f; **washing line** n (BRIT) corde f à linge; **washing machine** n machine f à laver; **washing powder** n (BRIT) lessive f (en poudre)

Washington ['wɔʃɪŋtən] n Washington m

wash: **washing-up** n (BRIT) vaisselle f; **washing-up liquid** n (BRIT) produit m pour la vaisselle; **washroom** n (US) toilettes fpl

wasn't ['wɔznt] = **was not**

wasp [wɔsp] n guêpe f

waste [weɪst] n gaspillage m; (of time) perte f; (rubbish) déchets mpl; (also: **household ~**) ordures fpl ▷ adj (land, ground: in city) à l'abandon; (leftover): **~ material** déchets ▷ vt gaspiller; (time, opportunity) perdre; **waste ground** n (BRIT) terrain m vague; **wastepaper basket** n corbeille f à papier

watch [wɔtʃ] n montre f; (act of watching) surveillance f; (guard: Mil) sentinelle f; (: Naut) homme m de quart; (Naut: spell of duty) quart m ▷ vt (look at) observer; (: match, programme) regarder; (spy on, guard) surveiller; (be careful of) faire attention à ▷ vi regarder; (keep guard) monter la garde; **to keep ~** faire le guet; **watch out** vi faire attention; **watchdog** n chien m de garde; (fig) gardien(ne); **watch strap** n bracelet m de montre

water ['wɔːtəʳ] n eau f ▷ vt (plant, garden) arroser ▷ vi (eyes) larmoyer; **in British ~s** dans les eaux territoriales Britanniques; **to make sb's mouth ~** mettre l'eau à la bouche de qn; **water down** vt (milk etc) couper avec de l'eau; (fig: story) édulcorer; **watercolour** (US **watercolor**) n aquarelle f; **watercress** n cresson m (de fontaine); **waterfall** n chute f d'eau; **watering can** n arrosoir m; **watermelon** n pastèque f; **waterproof** adj imperméable; **water-skiing** n ski m nautique

watt [wɔt] n watt m

wave [weɪv] n vague f; (of hand) geste m, signe m; (Radio) onde f; (in hair) ondulation f; (fig: of enthusiasm, strikes etc) vague ▷ vi faire signe de la main; (flag) flotter au vent; (grass) ondoyer ▷ vt (handkerchief) agiter; (stick) brandir; **wavelength** n longueur f d'ondes

waver ['weɪvə'] vi vaciller; (voice) trembler; (person) hésiter

wavy ['weɪvɪ] adj (hair, surface) ondulé(e); (line) onduleux(-euse)

wax [wæks] n cire f; (for skis) fart m ▷ vt cirer; (car) lustrer; (skis) farter ▷ vi (moon) croître

way [weɪ] n chemin m, voie f; (distance) distance f; (direction) chemin, direction f; (manner) façon f, manière f; (habit) habitude f, façon; **which ~? — this ~/that ~** par où or de quel côté? — par ici/par là; **to lose one's ~** perdre son chemin; **on the ~ (to)** en route (pour); **to be on one's ~** être en route; **to be in the ~** bloquer le passage; (fig) gêner; **it's a long ~ a~** c'est loin d'ici; **to go out of one's ~ to do** (fig) se donner beaucoup de mal pour faire; **to be under ~** (work, project) être en cours; **in a ~** dans un sens; **by the ~** à propos; **"~ in"** (BRIT) "entrée"; **"~ out"** (BRIT) "sortie"; **the ~ back** le chemin du retour; **"give ~"** (BRIT Aut) "cédez la priorité"; **no ~!** (inf) pas question!

W.C. n abbr (BRIT: = water closet) w.-c. mpl, waters mpl

we [wiː] pl pron nous

weak [wiːk] adj faible; (health) fragile; (beam etc) peu solide; (tea, coffee) léger(-ère); **weaken** vi faiblir ▷ vt affaiblir; **weakness** n faiblesse f; (fault) point m faible

wealth [wɛlθ] n (money, resources) richesse(s) f(pl); (of details) profusion f; **wealthy** adj riche

weapon ['wɛpən] n arme f; **~s of mass destruction** armes fpl de destruction massive

wear [wɛə'] n (use) usage m; (deterioration through use) usure f ▷ vb (pt **wore**, pp **worn**) ▷ vt (clothes) porter; (put on) mettre; (damage: through use) user ▷ vi (last) faire de l'usage; (rub etc through) s'user; **sports/baby~** vêtements mpl de sport/pour bébés; **evening ~** tenue f de soirée; **wear off** vi disparaître; **wear out** vt user; (person, strength) épuiser

weary ['wɪərɪ] adj (tired) épuisé(e); (dispirited) las(lasse), abattu(e) ▷ vi: **to ~ of** se lasser de

weasel ['wiːzl] n (Zool) belette f

weather ['wɛðə'] n temps m ▷ vt (storm: lit, fig) survivre à; (crisis) survivre à; **under the ~** (fig: ill) mal fichu(e); **weather forecast** n prévisions fpl météorologiques, météo f

weave (pt **wove**, pp **woven**) [wiːv, wəuv, 'wəuvn] vt (cloth) tisser; (basket) tresser

web [wɛb] n (of spider) toile f; (on duck's foot) palmure f; (fig) tissu m; (Comput): **the (World-Wide) W~** le Web; **web page** n (Comput) page f Web; **website** n (Comput) site m web

wed [wɛd] (pt, pp **~ded**) vt épouser ▷ vi se marier

Wed abbr (= Wednesday) me

we'd [wiːd] = **we had**; **we would**

wedding ['wɛdɪŋ] n mariage m; **wedding anniversary** n anniversaire m de mariage; **silver/golden wedding anniversary** noces fpl d'argent/d'or; **wedding day** n jour m du mariage; **wedding dress** n robe f de mariée; **wedding ring** n alliance f

wedge [wɛdʒ] n (of wood etc) coin m; (under door etc) cale f; (of cake) part f ▷ vt (fix) caler; (push) enfoncer, coincer

Wednesday ['wɛnzdɪ] n mercredi m

wee [wiː] adj (SCOTTISH) petit(e); tout(e) petit(e)

weed [wiːd] n mauvaise herbe f ▷ vt désherber; **weedkiller** n désherbant m

week [wiːk] n semaine f; **a ~ today/on Tuesday** aujourd'hui/mardi en huit; **weekday** n jour m de semaine; (Comm) jour ouvrable; **weekend** n week-end m; **weekly** adv une fois par semaine, chaque semaine ▷ adj, n hebdomadaire (m)

weep [wiːp] (pt, pp **wept**) vi (person) pleurer

weigh [weɪ] vt, vi peser; **to ~ anchor** lever l'ancre; **weigh up** vt examiner

weight [weɪt] n poids m; **to put on/lose ~** grossir/maigrir; **weightlifting** n haltérophilie f

weir [wɪə'] n barrage m

weird [wɪəd] adj bizarre; (eerie) surnaturel(le)

welcome ['wɛlkəm] adj bienvenu(e) ▷ n accueil m ▷ vt accueillir; (also: **bid ~**) souhaiter la bienvenue à; (be glad of) se réjouir de; **you're ~!** (after thanks) de rien, il n'y a pas de quoi

weld [wɛld] vt souder

welfare ['wɛlfɛə'] n (wellbeing) bien-être m; (social aid) assistance sociale; **welfare state** n État-providence m

well [wɛl] n puits m ▷ adv bien ▷ adj: **to be ~** aller bien ▷ excl eh bien!; (relief also) bon!; (resignation) enfin!; **~ done!** bravo!; **get ~ soon!** remets-toi vite!; **to do ~** bien réussir; (business) prospérer; **as ~** (in addition) aussi, également; **as ~ as** aussi bien que or de; en plus de

we'll [wiːl] = **we will**; **we shall**

well: **well-behaved** adj sage, obéissant(e); **well-built** adj (person) bien bâti(e); **well-dressed** adj bien habillé(e), bien vêtu(e)

well-groomed ['-gruːmd] adj très soigné(e)

wellies ['wɛlɪz] (inf) npl (BRIT) = **wellingtons**

wellingtons ['wɛlɪŋtənz] npl (also: **wellington boots**) bottes fpl en caoutchouc

well: **well-known** adj (person) bien connu(e); **well-off** adj aisé(e), assez riche; **well-paid** [wɛl'peɪd] adj bien payé(e)

Welsh [wɛlʃ] adj gallois(e) ▷ n (Ling) gallois m; **the Welsh** npl (people) les Gallois; **Welshman** (irreg) n Gallois m; **Welshwoman** (irreg) n Galloise f

went [wɛnt] pt of **go**

wept [wɛpt] pt, pp of **weep**

were [wəːʳ] pt of **be**

we're [wɪəʳ] = **we are**

weren't [wəːnt] = **were not**

west [wɛst] n ouest m ▷ adj (wind) d'ouest; (side) ouest inv ▷ adv à or vers l'ouest; **the W~** l'Occident m, l'Ouest; **westbound** ['wɛstbaund] adj en direction de l'ouest; (carriageway) ouest inv; **western** adj occidental(e), de or à l'ouest ▷ n (Cine) western m; **West Indian** adj antillais(e) ▷ n Antillais(e)

West Indies [-'ɪndɪz] npl Antilles fpl

wet [wɛt] adj mouillé(e); (damp) humide; (soaked: also: **~ through**) trempé(e); (rainy) pluvieux(-euse); **to get ~** se mouiller; "**~ paint**" "attention peinture fraîche"; **wetsuit** n combinaison f de plongée

we've [wiːv] = **we have**

whack [wæk] vt donner un grand coup à

whale [weɪl] n (Zool) baleine f

wharf (pl **wharves**) [wɔːf, wɔːvz] n quai m

 KEYWORD

what [wɔt] adj **1** (in questions) quel(le); **what size is he?** quelle taille fait-il?; **what colour is it?** de quelle couleur est-ce?; **what books do you need?** quels livres vous faut-il?
2 (in exclamations): **what a mess!** quel désordre!; **what a fool I am!** que je suis bête!
▷ pron **1** (interrogative) que; de/à/en etc quoi; **what are you doing?** que faites-vous?, qu'est-ce que vous faites?; **what is happening?** qu'est-ce qui se passe?, que se passe-t-il?; **what are you talking about?** de quoi parlez-vous?; **what are you thinking about?** à quoi pensez-vous?; **what is it called?** comment est-ce que ça s'appelle?; **what about me?** et moi?; **what about doing ...?** et si on faisait ...?
2 (relative: subject) ce qui; (: direct object) ce que; (: indirect object) ce à quoi, ce dont; **I saw what you did/was on the table** j'ai vu ce que vous avez fait/ce qui était sur la table; **tell me what you remember** dites-moi ce dont vous vous souvenez; **what I want is a cup of tea** ce que je veux, c'est une tasse de thé
▷ excl (disbelieving) quoi!, comment!

whatever [wɔt'ɛvəʳ] adj: **take ~ book you prefer** prenez le livre que vous préférez, peu

importe lequel; **~ book you take** quel que soit le livre que vous preniez ▷ pron: **do ~ is necessary** faites (tout) ce qui est nécessaire; **~ happens** quoi qu'il arrive; **no reason ~** or **whatsoever** pas la moindre raison; **nothing ~** or **whatsoever** rien du tout

whatsoever [wɔtsəu'ɛvəʳ] adj see **whatever**

wheat [wiːt] n blé m, froment m

wheel [wiːl] n roue f; (Aut: also: **steering ~**) volant m; (Naut) gouvernail m ▷ vt (pram etc) pousser, rouler ▷ vi (birds) tournoyer; (also: **~ round**: person) se retourner, faire volte-face; **wheelbarrow** n brouette f; **wheelchair** n fauteuil roulant; **wheel clamp** n (Aut) sabot m (de Denver)

wheeze [wiːz] vi respirer bruyamment

 KEYWORD

when [wɛn] adv quand; **when did he go?** quand est-ce qu'il est parti?
▷ conj **1** (at, during, after the time that) quand, lorsque; **she was reading when I came in** elle lisait quand or lorsque je suis entré
2 (on, at which): **on the day when I met him** le jour où je l'ai rencontré
3 (whereas) alors que; **I thought I was wrong when in fact I was right** j'ai cru que j'avais tort alors qu'en fait j'avais raison

whenever [wɛn'ɛvəʳ] adv quand donc ▷ conj quand; (every time that) chaque fois que

where [wɛəʳ] adv, conj où; **this is ~** c'est là que; **whereabouts** adv où donc ▷ n: **nobody knows his whereabouts** personne ne sait où il se trouve; **whereas** conj alors que; **whereby** adv (formal) par lequel (or laquelle etc); **wherever** adv où donc ? où que + sub; **sit wherever you like** asseyez-vous (là) où vous voulez

whether ['wɛðəʳ] conj si; **I don't know ~ to accept or not** je ne sais pas si je dois accepter ou non; **it's doubtful ~** il est peu probable que + sub; **~ you go or not** que vous y alliez ou non

 KEYWORD

which [wɪtʃ] adj **1** (interrogative: direct, indirect) quel(le); **which picture do you want?** quel tableau voulez-vous?; **which one?** lequel (laquelle)
2: **in which case** auquel cas; **we got there at 8pm, by which time the cinema was full** quand nous sommes arrivés à 20h, le cinéma était complet
▷ pron **1** (interrogative) lequel (laquelle), lesquels (lesquelles) pl; **I don't mind which** peu importe lequel; **which (of these) are yours?** lesquels sont à vous?; **tell me which**

you want dites-moi lesquels *or* ceux que vous voulez
2 (*relative: subject*) qui; (*: object*) que; sur/vers *etc* lequel (laquelle) (NB: *à* + *lequel* = **auquel**; *de* + *lequel* = **duquel**); **the apple which you ate/which is on the table** la pomme que vous avez mangée/qui est sur la table; **the chair on which you are sitting** la chaise sur laquelle vous êtes assis; **the book of which you spoke** le livre dont vous avez parlé; **he said he knew, which is true/I was afraid of** il a dit qu'il le savait, ce qui est vrai/ce que je craignais; **after which** après quoi

whichever [wɪtʃˈɛvəʳ] *adj*: **take ~ book you prefer** prenez le livre que vous préférez, peu importe lequel; **~ book you take** quel que soit le livre que vous preniez

while [waɪl] *n* moment *m* ▷ *conj* pendant que; (*as long as*) tant que; (*as, whereas*) alors que; (*though*) bien que + *sub*, quoique + *sub*; **for a ~** pendant quelque temps; **in a ~** dans un moment

whilst [waɪlst] *conj* = **while**

whim [wɪm] *n* caprice *m*

whine [waɪn] *n* gémissement *m*; (*of engine, siren*) plainte stridente ▷ *vi* gémir, geindre, pleurnicher; (*dog, engine, siren*) gémir

whip [wɪp] *n* fouet *m*; (*for riding*) cravache *f*; (*Pol: person*) chef *m* de file (*assurant la discipline dans son groupe parlementaire*) ▷ *vt* fouetter; (*snatch*) enlever (*or sortir*) brusquement; **whipped cream** *n* crème fouettée

whirl [wəːl] *vi* tourbillonner; (*dancers*) tournoyer ▷ *vt* faire tourbillonner; faire tournoyer

whisk [wɪsk] *n* (*Culin*) fouet *m* ▷ *vt* (*eggs*) fouetter, battre; **to ~ sb away** *or* **off** emmener qn rapidement

whiskers [ˈwɪskəz] *npl* (*of animal*) moustaches *fpl*; (*of man*) favoris *mpl*

whisky (*IRISH, US* **whiskey**) [ˈwɪskɪ] *n* whisky *m*

whisper [ˈwɪspəʳ] *n* chuchotement *m* ▷ *vt, vi* chuchoter

whistle [ˈwɪsl] *n* (*sound*) sifflement *m*; (*object*) sifflet *m* ▷ *vi* siffler ▷ *vt* siffler, siffloter

white [waɪt] *adj* blanc (blanche); (*with fear*) blême ▷ *n* blanc *m*; (*person*) blanc (blanche); **White House** *n* (*us*): **the White House** la Maison-Blanche; **whitewash** *n* (*paint*) lait *m* de chaux ▷ *vt* blanchir à la chaux; (*fig*) blanchir

whiting [ˈwaɪtɪŋ] *n* (*pl inv: fish*) merlan *m*

Whitsun [ˈwɪtsn] *n* la Pentecôte

whittle [ˈwɪtl] *vt*: **to ~ away**, **to ~ down** (*costs*) réduire, rogner

whizz [wɪz] *vi* aller (*or* passer) à toute vitesse

who [huː] *pron* qui

whoever [huːˈɛvəʳ] *pron*: **~ finds it** celui (celle) qui le trouve (, qui que ce soit), quiconque le trouve; **ask ~ you like** demandez à qui vous voulez; **~ he marries** qui que ce soit *or* quelle que soit la personne qu'il épouse; **~ told you that?** qui a bien pu vous dire ça?, qui donc vous a dit ça?

whole [həul] *adj* (*complete*) entier(-ière), tout(e); (*not broken*) intact(e), complet(-ète) ▷ *n* (*all*): **the ~ of** la totalité de, tout(e) le (la); (*entire unit*) tout *m*; **the ~ of the town** la ville tout entière; **on the ~, as a ~** dans l'ensemble; **wholefood(s)** *n(pl)* aliments complets; **wholeheartedly** [həulˈhɑːtɪdlɪ] *adv* sans réserve; **to agree wholeheartedly** être entièrement d'accord; **wholemeal** *adj* (*BRIT: flour, bread*) complet(-ète); **wholesale** *n* (*vente f en*) gros *m* ▷ *adj* (*price*) de gros; (*destruction*) systématique; **wholewheat** *adj* = **wholemeal**; **wholly** *adv* entièrement, tout à fait

 KEYWORD

whom [huːm] *pron* **1** (*interrogative*) qui; **whom did you see?** qui avez-vous vu?; **to whom did you give it?** à qui l'avez-vous donné?
2 (*relative*) que; à/de *etc* qui; **the man whom I saw/to whom I spoke** l'homme que j'ai vu/à qui j'ai parlé

whore [hɔːʳ] *n* (*inf: pej*) putain *f*

 KEYWORD

whose [huːz] *adj* **1** (*possessive: interrogative*): **whose book is this?**, **whose is this book?** à qui est ce livre?; **whose pencil have you taken?** à qui est le crayon que vous avez pris?, c'est le crayon de qui que vous avez pris?; **whose daughter are you?** de qui êtes-vous la fille?
2 (*possessive: relative*): **the man whose son you rescued** l'homme dont *or* de qui vous avez sauvé le fils; **the girl whose sister you were speaking to** la fille à la sœur de qui *or* de laquelle vous parliez; **the woman whose car was stolen** la femme dont la voiture a été volée
▷ *pron* à qui; **whose is this?** à qui est ceci?; **I know whose it is** je sais à qui c'est

 KEYWORD

why [waɪ] *adv* pourquoi; **why not?** pourquoi pas?
▷ *conj*: **I wonder why he said that** je me demande pourquoi il a dit ça; **that's not why**

I'm here ce n'est pas pour ça que je suis là; **the reason why** la raison pour laquelle
▷ *excl* eh bien!, tiens!; **why, it's you!** tiens, c'est vous!; **why, that's impossible!** voyons, c'est impossible!

wicked ['wɪkɪd] *adj* méchant(e); (*mischievous: grin, look*) espiègle, malicieux(-euse); (*crime*) pervers(e); (*inf: very good*) génial(e) (*inf*)
wicket ['wɪkɪt] *n* (*Cricket: stumps*) guichet *m*; (*: grass area*) espace compris entre les deux guichets
wide [waɪd] *adj* large; (*area, knowledge*) vaste, très étendu(e); (*choice*) grand(e) ▷ *adv*: **to open ~** ouvrir tout grand; **to shoot ~** tirer à côté; **it is 3 metres ~** cela fait 3 mètres de large; **widely** *adv* (*different*) radicalement; (*spaced*) sur une grande étendue; (*believed*) généralement; (*travel*) beaucoup; **widen** *vt* élargir ▷ *vi* s'élargir; **wide open** *adj* grand(e) ouvert(e); **widespread** *adj* (*belief etc*) très répandu(e)
widow ['wɪdəu] *n* veuve *f*; **widower** *n* veuf *m*
width [wɪdθ] *n* largeur *f*
wield [wiːld] *vt* (*sword*) manier; (*power*) exercer
wife (*pl* **wives**) [waɪf, waɪvz] *n* femme *f*, épouse *f*
wig [wɪg] *n* perruque *f*
wild [waɪld] *adj* sauvage; (*sea*) déchaîné(e); (*idea, life*) fou (folle); (*behaviour*) déchaîné(e), extravagant(e); (*inf: angry*) hors de soi, furieux(-euse) ▷ *n*: **the ~** la nature; **wilderness** ['wɪldənɪs] *n* désert *m*, région *f* sauvage; **wildlife** *n* faune *f* (et flore *f*); **wildly** *adv* (*behave*) de manière déchaînée; (*applaud*) frénétiquement; (*hit, guess*) au hasard; (*happy*) follement

 KEYWORD

will [wɪl] *aux vb* **1** (*forming future tense*): **I will finish it tomorrow** je le finirai demain; **I will have finished it by tomorrow** je l'aurai fini d'ici demain; **will you do it? - yes I will/no I won't** le ferez-vous? - oui/non
2 (*in conjectures, predictions*): **he will** or **he'll be there by now** il doit être arrivé à l'heure qu'il est; **that will be the postman** ça doit être le facteur
3 (*in commands, requests, offers*): **will you be quiet!** voulez-vous bien vous taire!; **will you help me?** est-ce que vous pouvez m'aider?; **will you have a cup of tea?** voulez-vous une tasse de thé?; **I won't put up with it!** je ne le tolérerai pas!
▷ *vt* (*pt, pp* **willed**): **to will sb to do** souhaiter ardemment que qn fasse; **he willed himself to go on** par un suprême effort de volonté, il

continua
▷ *n* volonté *f*; (*document*) testament *m*; **against one's will** à contre-cœur

willing ['wɪlɪŋ] *adj* de bonne volonté, serviable; **he's ~ to do it** il est disposé à le faire, il veut bien le faire; **willingly** *adv* volontiers
willow ['wɪləu] *n* saule *m*
willpower ['wɪl'pauəʳ] *n* volonté *f*
wilt [wɪlt] *vi* dépérir
win [wɪn] *n* (*in sports etc*) victoire *f* ▷ *vb* (*pt, pp* **won**) ▷ *vt* (*battle, money*) gagner; (*prize, contract*) remporter; (*popularity*) acquérir ▷ *vi* gagner; **win over** *vt* convaincre
wince [wɪns] *vi* tressaillir
wind¹ [wɪnd] *n* (*also Med*) vent *m*; (*breath*) souffle *m* ▷ *vt* (*take breath away*) couper le souffle à; **the ~(s)** (*Mus*) les instruments *mpl* à vent
wind² (*pt, pp* **wound**) [waɪnd, waund] *vt* enrouler; (*wrap*) envelopper; (*clock, toy*) remonter ▷ *vi* (*road, river*) serpenter; **wind down** *vt* (*car window*) baisser; (*fig: production, business*) réduire progressivement; **wind up** *vt* (*clock*) remonter; (*debate*) terminer, clôturer
windfall ['wɪndfɔːl] *n* coup *m* de chance
winding ['waɪndɪŋ] *adj* (*road*) sinueux(-euse); (*staircase*) tournant(e)
windmill ['wɪndmɪl] *n* moulin *m* à vent
window ['wɪndəu] *n* fenêtre *f*; (*in car, train: also*: **~pane**) vitre *f*; (*in shop etc*) vitrine *f*; **window box** *n* jardinière *f*; **window cleaner** *n* (*person*) laveur(-euse) de vitres; **window pane** *n* vitre *f*, carreau *m*; **window seat** *n* (*in vehicle*) place *f* côté fenêtre; **windowsill** *n* (*inside*) appui *m* de la fenêtre; (*outside*) rebord *m* de la fenêtre
windscreen ['wɪndskriːn] *n* pare-brise *m inv*; **windscreen wiper** *n* essuie-glace *m inv*
windshield ['wɪndʃiːld] (*us*) *n* = **windscreen**
windsurfing ['wɪndsəːfɪŋ] *n* planche *f* à voile
windy ['wɪndɪ] *adj* (*day*) de vent, venteux(-euse); (*place, weather*) venteux; **it's ~** il y a du vent
wine [waɪn] *n* vin *m*; **wine bar** *n* bar *m* à vin; **wine glass** *n* verre *m* à vin; **wine list** *n* carte *f* des vins; **wine tasting** *n* dégustation *f* (de vins)
wing [wɪŋ] *n* aile *f*; **wings** *npl* (*Theat*) coulisses *fpl*; **wing mirror** *n* (BRIT) rétroviseur latéral
wink [wɪŋk] *n* clin *m* d'œil ▷ *vi* faire un clin d'œil; (*blink*) cligner des yeux
winner ['wɪnəʳ] *n* gagnant(e)
winning ['wɪnɪŋ] *adj* (*team*) gagnant(e); (*goal*) décisif(-ive); (*charming*) charmeur(-euse)
winter ['wɪntəʳ] *n* hiver *m* ▷ *vi* hiverner; **in ~** en hiver; **winter sports** *npl* sports *mpl* d'hiver; **wintertime** *n* hiver *m*

wipe [waɪp] n: **to give sth a ~** donner un coup de torchon/de chiffon/d'éponge à qch ▷ vt essuyer; (*erase: tape*) effacer; **to ~ one's nose** se moucher; **wipe out** vt (*debt*) éteindre, amortir; (*memory*) effacer; (*destroy*) anéantir; **wipe up** vt essuyer

wire ['waɪəʳ] n fil m (de fer); (*Elec*) fil électrique; (*Tel*) télégramme m ▷ vt (*house*) faire l'installation électrique de; (*also: ~ up*) brancher; (*person: send telegram to*) télégraphier à

wiring ['waɪərɪŋ] n (*Elec*) installation f électrique

wisdom ['wɪzdəm] n sagesse f; (*of action*) prudence f; **wisdom tooth** n dent f de sagesse

wise [waɪz] adj sage, prudent(e); (*remark*) judicieux(-euse)

wish [wɪʃ] n (*desire*) désir m; (*specific desire*) souhait m, vœu m ▷ vt souhaiter, désirer, vouloir; **best ~es** (*on birthday etc*) meilleurs vœux; **with best ~es** (*in letter*) bien amicalement; **to ~ sb goodbye** dire au revoir à qn; **he ~ed me well** il m'a souhaité bonne chance; **to ~ to do/sb to do** désirer or vouloir faire/que qn fasse; **to ~ for** souhaiter

wistful ['wɪstful] adj mélancolique

wit [wɪt] n (*also: ~s: intelligence*) intelligence f, esprit m; (*presence of mind*) présence f d'esprit; (*wittiness*) esprit; (*person*) homme/femme d'esprit

witch [wɪtʃ] n sorcière f

 KEYWORD

with [wɪð, wɪθ] prep 1 (*in the company of*) avec; (*at the home of*) chez; **we stayed with friends** nous avons logé chez des amis; **I'll be with you in a minute** je suis à vous dans un instant
2 (*descriptive*): **a room with a view** une chambre avec vue; **the man with the grey hat/blue eyes** l'homme au chapeau gris/aux yeux bleus
3 (*indicating manner, means, cause*): **with tears in her eyes** les larmes aux yeux; **to walk with a stick** marcher avec une canne; **red with anger** rouge de colère; **to shake with fear** trembler de peur; **to fill sth with water** remplir qch d'eau
4 (*in phrases*): **I'm with you** (*I understand*) je vous suis; **to be with it** (*inf: up-to-date*) être dans le vent

withdraw [wɪθ'drɔː] vt (*irreg: like* **draw**) retirer ▷ vi se retirer; **withdrawal** n retrait m; (*Med*) état m de manque; **withdrawn** pp of **withdraw** ▷ adj (*person*) renfermé(e)

withdrew [wɪθ'druː] pt of **withdraw**

wither ['wɪðəʳ] vi se faner

withhold [wɪθ'həuld] vt (*irreg: like* **hold**) (*money*) retenir; (*decision*) remettre; (*permission*): **to ~ (from)** (*permission*) refuser (à); (*information*): **to ~ (from)** cacher (à)

within [wɪð'ɪn] prep à l'intérieur de ▷ adv à l'intérieur; **~ his reach** à sa portée; **~ sight of** en vue de; **~ a mile of** à moins d'un mille de; **~ the week** avant la fin de la semaine

without [wɪð'aut] prep sans; **~ a coat** sans manteau; **~ speaking** sans parler; **to go or do ~ sth** se passer de qch

withstand [wɪθ'stænd] vt (*irreg: like* **stand**) résister à

witness ['wɪtnɪs] n (*person*) témoin m ▷ vt (*event*) être témoin de; (*document*) attester l'authenticité de; **to bear ~ to sth** témoigner de qch

witty ['wɪtɪ] adj spirituel(le), plein(e) d'esprit

wives [waɪvz] npl of **wife**

wizard ['wɪzəd] n magicien m

wk abbr = **week**

wobble ['wɔbl] vi trembler; (*chair*) branler

woe [wəu] n malheur m

woke [wəuk] pt of **wake**

woken ['wəukn] pp of **wake**

wolf (*pl* **wolves**) [wulf, wulvz] n loup m

woman (*pl* **women**) ['wumən, 'wɪmɪn] n femme f ▷ cpd: **~ doctor** femme f médecin; **~ teacher** professeur m femme

womb [wuːm] n (*Anat*) utérus m

women ['wɪmɪn] npl of **woman**

won [wʌn] pt, pp of **win**

wonder ['wʌndəʳ] n merveille f, miracle m; (*feeling*) émerveillement m ▷ vi: **to ~ whether/why** se demander si/pourquoi; **to ~ at** (*surprise*) s'étonner de; (*admiration*) s'émerveiller de; **to ~ about** songer à; **it's no ~ that** il n'est pas étonnant que + sub; **wonderful** adj merveilleux(-euse)

won't [wəunt] = **will not**

wood [wud] n (*timber, forest*) bois m; **wooden** adj en bois; (*fig: actor*) raide; (: *performance*) qui manque de naturel; **woodwind** n: **the woodwind** (*Mus*) les bois mpl; **woodwork** n menuiserie f

wool [wul] n laine f; **to pull the ~ over sb's eyes** (*fig*) en faire accroire à qn; **woollen** (*us* **woolen**) adj de or en laine; **woolly** (*us* **wooly**) adj laineux(-euse); (*fig: ideas*) confus(e)

word [wəːd] n mot m; (*spoken*) mot m, parole f; (*promise*) parole; (*news*) nouvelles fpl ▷ vt rédiger, formuler; **in other ~s** en d'autres termes; **to have a ~ with sb** toucher un mot à qn; **to break/keep one's ~** manquer à sa parole/tenir (sa) parole; **wording** n termes mpl, langage m; (*of document*) libellé m; **word processing** n traitement m de texte; **word processor** n machine f de traitement de texte

wore [wɔː] pt of **wear**

work [wəːk] n travail m; (*Art, Literature*)

œuvre f ▷ vi travailler; (*mechanism*) marcher, fonctionner; (*plan etc*) marcher; (*medicine*) agir ▷ vt (*clay, wood etc*) travailler; (*mine etc*) exploiter; (*machine*) faire marcher or fonctionner; (*miracles etc*) faire; **works** n (BRIT: *factory*) usine f; **how does this ~?** comment est-ce que ça marche?; **the TV isn't ~ing** la télévision est en panne or ne marche pas; **to be out of ~** être au chômage or sans emploi; **to ~ loose** se défaire, se desserrer; **work out** vi (*plans etc*) marcher; (*Sport*) s'entraîner ▷ vt (*problem*) résoudre; (*plan*) élaborer; **it ~s out at £100** ça fait 100 livres; **worker** n travailleur(-euse), ouvrier(-ière); **work experience** n stage m; **workforce** n main-d'œuvre f; **working class** n classe ouvrière ▷ adj: **working-class** ouvrier(-ière), de la classe ouvrière; **working week** n semaine f de travail; **workman** (*irreg*) n ouvrier m; **work of art** n œuvre f d'art; **workout** n (*Sport*) séance f d'entraînement; **work permit** n permis m de travail; **workplace** n lieu m de travail; **worksheet** n (*Scol*) feuille f d'exercices; **workshop** n atelier m; **work station** n poste m de travail; **work surface** n plan m de travail; **worktop** n plan m de travail
world [wəːld] n monde m ▷ cpd (*champion*) du monde; (*power, war*) mondial(e); **to think the ~ of sb** (*fig*) ne jurer que par qn; **World Cup** n: **the World Cup** (*Football*) la Coupe du monde; **world-wide** adj universel(le); **World-Wide Web** n: **the World-Wide Web** le Web
worm [wəːm] n (*also*: **earth~**) ver m
worn [wɔːn] pp of **wear** ▷ adj usé(e); **worn-out** adj (*object*) complètement usé(e); (*person*) épuisé(e)
worried ['wʌrɪd] adj inquiet(-ète); **to be ~ about sth** être inquiet au sujet de qch
worry ['wʌrɪ] n souci m ▷ vt inquiéter ▷ vi s'inquiéter, se faire du souci; **worrying** adj inquiétant(e)
worse [wəːs] adj pire, plus mauvais(e) ▷ adv plus mal ▷ n pire m; **to get ~** (*condition, situation*) empirer, se dégrader; **a change for the ~** une détérioration; **worsen** vt, vi empirer; **worse off** adj moins à l'aise financièrement; (*fig*): **you'll be worse off this way** ça ira moins bien de cette façon
worship ['wəːʃɪp] n culte m ▷ vt (*God*) rendre un culte à; (*person*) adorer
worst [wəːst] adj le (la) pire, le (la) plus mauvais(e) ▷ adv le plus mal ▷ n pire m; **at ~** au pis aller
worth [wəːθ] n valeur f ▷ adj: **to be ~** valoir; **it's ~ it** cela en vaut la peine, ça vaut la peine; **it is ~ one's while (to do)** ça vaut le coup (*inf*) (de faire); **worthless** adj qui ne vaut rien; **worthwhile** adj (*activity*) qui en vaut la peine; (*cause*) louable

worthy ['wəːðɪ] adj (*person*) digne de; (*motive*) louable; **~ of** digne de

 KEYWORD

would [wʊd] aux vb **1** (*conditional tense*): **if you asked him he would do it** si vous le lui demandiez, il le ferait; **if you had asked him he would have done it** si vous le lui aviez demandé, il l'aurait fait
2 (*in offers, invitations, requests*): **would you like a biscuit?** voulez-vous un biscuit?; **would you close the door please?** voulez-vous fermer la porte, s'il vous plaît?
3 (*in indirect speech*): **I said I would do it** j'ai dit que je le ferais
4 (*emphatic*): **it WOULD have to snow today!** naturellement il neige aujourd'hui! or il fallait qu'il neige aujourd'hui!
5 (*insistence*): **she wouldn't do it** elle n'a pas voulu or elle a refusé de le faire
6 (*conjecture*): **it would have been midnight** il devait être minuit; **it would seem so** on dirait bien
7 (*indicating habit*): **he would go there on Mondays** il y allait le lundi

wouldn't ['wʊdnt] = **would not**
wound¹ [wuːnd] n blessure f ▷ vt blesser
wound² [waʊnd] pt, pp of **wind**
wove [wəʊv] pt of **weave**
woven ['wəʊvn] pp of **weave**
wrap [ræp] vt (*also*: **~ up**) envelopper; (*parcel*) emballer; (*wind*) enrouler; **wrapper** n (*on chocolate etc*) papier m; (BRIT: *of book*) couverture f; **wrapping** n (*of sweet, chocolate*) papier m; (*of parcel*) emballage m; **wrapping paper** n papier m d'emballage; (*for gift*) papier cadeau
wreath [riːθ, pl riːðz] n couronne f
wreck [rɛk] n (*sea disaster*) naufrage m; (*ship*) épave f; (*vehicle*) véhicule accidenté; (*pej: person*) loque (humaine) ▷ vt démolir; (*fig*) briser, ruiner; **wreckage** n débris mpl; (*of building*) décombres mpl; (*of ship*) naufrage m
wren [rɛn] n (*Zool*) troglodyte m
wrench [rɛntʃ] n (*Tech*) clé f (à écrous); (*tug*) violent mouvement de torsion; (*fig*) déchirement m ▷ vt tirer violemment sur, tordre; **to ~ sth from** arracher qch (violemment) à or de
wrestle ['rɛsl] vi: **to ~ (with sb)** lutter (avec qn); **wrestler** n lutteur(-euse); **wrestling** n lutte f; (*also*: **all-in wrestling** BRIT) catch m
wretched ['rɛtʃɪd] adj misérable
wriggle ['rɪgl] vi (*also*: **~ about**) se tortiller
wring (*pt, pp* **wrung**) [rɪŋ, rʌŋ] vt tordre; (*wet clothes*) essorer; (*fig*): **to ~ sth out of** arracher qch à

wrinkle ['rɪŋkl] n (on skin) ride f; (on paper etc) pli m ▷ vt rider, plisser ▷ vi se plisser

wrist [rɪst] n poignet m

write (pt **wrote**, pp **written**) [raɪt, rəut, 'rɪtn] vt, vi écrire; (prescription) rédiger; **write down** vt noter; (put in writing) mettre par écrit; **write off** vt (debt) passer aux profits et pertes; (project) mettre une croix sur; (smash up: car etc) démolir complètement; **write out** vt écrire; (copy) recopier; **write-off** n perte totale; **the car is a write-off** la voiture est bonne pour la casse; **writer** n auteur m, écrivain m

writing ['raɪtɪŋ] n écriture f; (of author) œuvres fpl; **in ~** par écrit; **writing paper** n papier m à lettres

written ['rɪtn] pp of **write**

wrong [rɒŋ] adj (incorrect) faux (fausse); (incorrectly chosen: number, road etc) mauvais(e); (not suitable) qui ne convient pas; (wicked) mal; (unfair) injuste ▷ adv mal ▷ n tort m ▷ vt faire du tort à, léser; **you are ~ to do it** tu as tort de le faire; **you are ~ about that, you've got it ~** tu te trompes; **what's ~?** qu'est-ce qui ne va pas?; **what's ~ with the car?** qu'est-ce qu'elle a, la voiture?; **to go ~** (person) se tromper; (plan) mal tourner; (machine) se détraquer; **I took a ~ turning** je me suis trompé de route; **wrongly** adv à tort; (answer, do, count) mal, incorrectement; **wrong number** n (Tel): **you have the wrong number** vous vous êtes trompé de numéro

wrote [rəut] pt of **write**

wrung [rʌŋ] pt, pp of **wring**

WWW n abbr = **World-Wide Web**; **the ~** le Web

XL abbr (= extra large) XL

Xmas ['ɛksməs] n abbr = **Christmas**

X-ray ['ɛksreɪ] n (ray) rayon m X; (photograph) radio(graphie) f ▷ vt radiographier

xylophone ['zaɪləfəun] n xylophone m

Y

yacht [jɔt] n voilier m; (motor, luxury yacht) yacht m; **yachting** n yachting m, navigation f de plaisance

yard [jɑːd] n (of house etc) cour f; (US: garden) jardin m; (measure) yard m (= 914 mm; 3 feet); **yard sale** n (US) brocante f (dans son propre jardin)

yarn [jɑːn] n fil m; (tale) longue histoire

yawn [jɔːn] n bâillement m ⊳ vi bâiller

yd. abbr = **yard(s)**

yeah [jɛə] adv (inf) ouais

year [jɪəʳ] n an m, année f; (Scol etc) année; **to be 8 ~s old** avoir 8 ans; **an eight-~-old child** un enfant de huit ans; **yearly** adj annuel(le) ⊳ adv annuellement; **twice yearly** deux fois par an

yearn [jəːn] vi: **to ~ for sth/to do** aspirer à qch/à faire

yeast [jiːst] n levure f

yell [jɛl] n hurlement m, cri m ⊳ vi hurler

yellow ['jɛləu] adj, n jaune (m); **Yellow Pages®** npl (Tel) pages fpl jaunes

yes [jɛs] adv oui; (answering negative question) si ⊳ n oui m; **to say ~ (to)** dire oui (à)

yesterday ['jɛstədɪ] adv, n hier (m); **~ morning/evening** hier matin/soir; **all day ~** toute la journée d'hier

yet [jɛt] adv encore; (in questions) déjà ⊳ conj pourtant, néanmoins; **it is not finished ~** ce n'est pas encore fini or toujours pas fini; **have**

you eaten ~? vous avez déjà mangé?; **the best ~** le meilleur jusqu'ici or jusque-là; **as ~** jusqu'ici, encore

yew [juː] n if m

Yiddish ['jɪdɪʃ] n yiddish m

yield [jiːld] n production f, rendement m; (Finance) rapport m ⊳ vt produire, rendre, rapporter; (surrender) céder ⊳ vi céder; (US Aut) céder la priorité

yob(bo) ['jɔb(əu)] n (BRIT inf) loubar(d) m

yoga ['jəugə] n yoga m

yog(h)ourt n = **yog(h)urt**

yog(h)urt ['jɔgət] n yaourt m

yolk [jəuk] n jaune m (d'œuf)

 KEYWORD

you [juː] pron **1** (subject) tu; (polite form) vous; (plural) vous; **you are very kind** vous êtes très gentil; **you French enjoy your food** vous autres Français, vous aimez bien manger; **you and I will go** toi et moi or vous et moi, nous irons; **there you are!** vous voilà!

2 (object: direct, indirect) te, t' + vowel; vous; **I know you** je te or vous connais; **I gave it to you** je te l'ai donné, je vous l'ai donné

3 (stressed) toi; vous; **I told YOU to do it** c'est à toi or vous que j'ai dit de le faire

4 (after prep, in comparisons) toi; vous; **it's for you** c'est pour toi or vous; **she's younger than you** elle est plus jeune que toi or vous

5 (impersonal: one) on; **fresh air does you good** l'air frais fait du bien; **you never know** on ne sait jamais; **you can't do that!** ça ne se fait pas!

you'd [juːd] = **you had**; **you would**

you'll [juːl] = **you will**; **you shall**

young [jʌŋ] adj jeune ⊳ npl (of animal) petits mpl; (people): **the ~** les jeunes, la jeunesse; **my ~er brother** mon frère cadet; **youngster** n jeune m/f; (child) enfant m/f

your [jɔːʳ] adj ton (ta), tes pl; (polite form, pl) votre, vos pl; see also **my**

you're [juəʳ] = **you are**

yours [jɔːz] pron le (la) tien(ne), les tiens (tiennes); (polite form, pl) le (la) vôtre, les vôtres; **is it ~?** c'est à toi (or à vous)?; **a friend of ~** un(e) de tes (or de vos) amis; see also **faithfully**; **mine¹**; **sincerely**

yourself [jɔːˈsɛlf] pron (reflexive) te; (: polite form) vous; (after prep) toi; vous; (emphatic) toi-même; vous-même; see also **oneself**; **yourselves** pl pron vous; (: emphatic) vous-mêmes; see also **oneself**

youth [juːθ] n jeunesse f; (young man) (pl ~s) jeune homme m; **youth club** n centre m de jeunes; **youthful** adj jeune; (enthusiasm etc) juvénile; **youth hostel** n auberge f de jeunesse

you've [juːv] = **you have**

Yugoslav ['juːgəuslɑːv] *adj* yougoslave ▷ *n* Yougoslave *m/f*

Yugoslavia [juːgəu'slɑːvɪə] *n* (Hist) Yougoslavie *f*

Z

zeal [ziːl] *n* (revolutionary etc) ferveur *f*; (keenness) ardeur *f*, zèle *m*

zebra ['ziːbrə] *n* zèbre *m*; **zebra crossing** *n* (BRIT) passage clouté or pour piétons

zero ['zɪərəu] *n* zéro *m*

zest [zɛst] *n* entrain *m*, élan *m*; (of lemon etc) zeste *m*

zigzag ['zɪgzæg] *n* zigzag *m* ▷ *vi* zigzaguer, faire des zigzags

Zimbabwe [zɪm'bɑːbwɪ] *n* Zimbabwe *m*

zinc [zɪŋk] *n* zinc *m*

zip [zɪp] *n* (also: **~ fastener**) fermeture *f* éclair® or à glissière ▷ *vt* (file) zipper; (also: **~ up**) fermer (avec une fermeture éclair®); **zip code** *n* (US) code postal; **zip file** *n* (Comput) fichier *m* zip inv; **zipper** *n* (US) = **zip**

zit [zɪt] (inf) *n* bouton *m*

zodiac ['zəudɪæk] *n* zodiaque *m*

zone [zəun] *n* zone *f*

zoo [zuː] *n* zoo *m*

zoology [zuːˈɔlədʒɪ] *n* zoologie *f*

zoom [zuːm] *vi*: **to ~ past** passer en trombe; **zoom lens** *n* zoom *m*

zucchini [zuːˈkiːnɪ] *n(pl)* (US) courgette(s) *f(pl)*